BLACK LITERATURE

C R I T I C I S M

BLACK LITERATURE
C R I T I C I S M

Excerpts from Criticism of the Most Significant Works
of Black Authors over the Past 200 Years

VOLUME 2: Emecheta-Malcolm X

James P. Draper, Editor

 **Gale Research Inc.** · DETROIT · LONDON

STAFF

James P. Draper, *Editor*

Andrea M. Gacki, Kyung-Sun Lim, *Assistant Editors, Black Literature Criticism*

The paper used in this publication meets the minimum requirements
of American National Standard for Information Sciences—Permanence Paper for Printed Library Materials, ANSI Z39.48-1984. ∞™

Copyright © 1992
Gale Research Inc.
835 Penobscot Building
Detroit, MI 48226-4094

ISBN 0-8103-7929-5 (3-volume set)
ISBN 0-8103-7931-7 (Volume 2)
A CIP catalogue record for this book is available from the British Library

Printed in the United States of America

Published simultaneously in the United Kingdom
by Gale Research International Limited
(An affiliated company of Gale Research Inc.)

Contents of Volume 2

Buchi Emecheta 1944-
As Nigeria's best-known female writer, Emecheta typically writes of female
heroines who challenge their restricted lives and aspire to economic and social
Olaudah Equiano 1745?-1797
Widely regarded as the most influential English-speaking black writer of the
eighteenth century, Equiano was a catalyst for the abolitionist movement in
England with his autobiography *The Interesting Narrative of the Life of Olaudah*
Frantz Fanon 1925-1961
Fanon denounced colonialism and racism in his famous *The Wretched of the*
Earth, a collection of essays considered the manifesto of Third World revolution
Nuruddin Farah 1945-
Somali novelist Farah—often called the first male feminist author to come out of
Africa—wrote of the plight of women in African society in such works as *From a*
Jessie Redmon Fauset 1882-1961
As literary editor of the *Crisis*—the magazine of the NAACP founded by W. E. B.
Du Bois—Fauset discovered and published works by Langston Hughes, Jean
Rudolph Fisher 1897-1934
The Conjure Man Dies, a novel by this Harlem Renaissance writer and physician,
Charlotte L. Forten 1837?-1914
Forten is best known as the author of *The Journal of Charlotte L. Forten: A Free*
Charles Fuller 1939-
American dramatist Fuller is widely known for his Pulitzer Prize-winning *A*
Soldier's Play, a drama in which he explored military racism through a murder
Ernest Gaines 1933-
Highly esteemed for *The Autobiography of Miss Jane Pittman*, Gaines draws on
Marcus Garvey 1887-1940
Founder of the "back to Africa" movement, Garvey was a charismatic and
flamboyant twentieth-century black activist who is considered both a pioneer of

Introduction

A Comprehensive Information Source
on Black Literature

*B*lack Literature Criticism (*BLC*) presents a broad selection of the best criticism of works by major black writers of the past two hundred years. Among the authors included in *BLC* are eighteenth-century memoirist Olaudah Equiano, poet Jupiter Hammon, and poet Phillis Wheatley; nineteenth-century autobiographer Frederick Douglass, poet Paul Laurence Dunbar, diarist Charlotte Forten, and essayist Booker T. Washington; such twentieth-century masters as novelist Chinua Achebe, novelist James Baldwin, poet Gwendolyn Brooks, poet Countee Cullen, novelist Ralph Ellison, dramatist Lorraine Hansberry, poet Langston Hughes, fiction writer Zora Neale Hurston, novelist Toni Morrison, novelist Ngugi wa Thiong'o, dramatist Wole Soyinka, and novelist Richard Wright; and emerging writers Andrea Lee, Charles Johnson, Lewis Nkosi, and August Wilson. The scope of *BLC* is wide: one hundred twenty-five writers representing the United States, Nigeria, South Africa, Jamaica, and over a dozen other nations are covered in comprehensive author entries.

Coverage

This three-volume set is designed for high school, college, and university students, as well as for the general reader who wants to learn more about black literature. *BLC* was developed in response to strong demand by students, librarians, and other readers for a one-stop, authoritative guide to the whole spectrum of black literature. No other compendium like it exists in the marketplace. About half of the entries in *BLC* were selected from Gale's acclaimed Literary Criticism Series and completely updated for publication here. Typically, the revisions are extensive, ranging from completely rewritten author introductions to wide changes in the selection of criticism. Other entries were prepared especially for *BLC* in order to furnish the most comprehensive coverage possible. Authors were selected for inclusion based on the range and amount of critical material available as well as on the advice of leading experts on black literature. A special effort was made to identify important new writers and to give the greatest coverage to the most studied authors.

Each author entry in *BLC* attempts to present a historical survey of critical response to the author's works. Typically, early criticism is offered to indicate initial responses, later selections document any rise or decline in literary reputations, and retrospective analyses provide modern views. Every endeavor has been made to include the seminal essays on each author's work along with recent commentary providing current perspectives. Interviews and author statements are also included in many entries. Thus, *BLC* is both timely and comprehensive.

Organization of Author Entries

Information about authors and their works is presented through eight key access points:

■ The **Author Heading** cites the name under which the author most commonly wrote, followed by birth and death dates. Uncertain birth or death dates are indicated by question marks. Name variations, including full birth names when available, are given in parentheses on the first line of the **Biographical and Critical Introduction**.

■ The **Biographical and Critical Introduction** contains background information about the life and works of the author. Emphasis is given to four main areas: 1) biographical details that help reveal the life, character, and personality of the author; 2) overviews of the major literary interests of the author—for example, novel writing, autobiography, social reform, documentary, etc.; 3) descriptions and summaries of the author's best-known works; and 4) critical commentary about the author's achievement, stature, and importance. The concluding paragraph of the **Biographical and Critical Introduction** directs readers to other Gale series containing information about the author.

■ Most *BLC* entries include an **Author Portrait**. Most also contain **Illustrations** documenting the author's career, including holographs, title pages of works, letters, or pictures of important people, places, and events in the author's life.

■ The **List of Principal Works** is chronological by date of first book publication and identifies the genre of each work. For non-English-language authors whose works have been translated into English, the title and date of the first English-language edition are given in brackets beneath the foreign-language listing. Unless otherwise indicated, dramas are dated by first performance rather than first publication.

■ **Criticism** is arranged chronologically in each author entry to provide a useful perspective on changes in critical evaluation over the years. Most entries contain a detailed, comprehensive study of the author's career as well as book reviews, studies of individual works, and comparative examinations. To ensure timeliness, current views are most often presented, but never to the exclusion of important early pieces. For the purpose of easy identification, the critic's name and the date of the critical work are given at the beginning of each piece of criticism. Unsigned criticism is preceded by the title of the source in which it appeared. Within the criticism, titles of works by the author are printed in boldface type. Publication information (such as publisher names and book prices) and certain numerical references (such as footnotes or page and line references to specific editions of works) have been deleted at the editor's discretion to provide smoother reading of the text.

■ Critical essays are prefaced by **Explanatory Notes** as an additional aid to readers of *BLC*. These notes may provide several types of valuable information, including: 1) the reputation of the critic; 2) the perceived importance of the work of criticism; 3) the commentator's approach to the author's work; 4) the apparent purpose of the criticism; and 5) changes in critical trends regarding the author. In some cases, **Explanatory Notes** cross-reference the work of critics within the entry who agree or disagree with each other.

■ A complete **Bibliographical Citation** of the original essay or book follows each piece of criticism.

■ An annotated **Further Reading List** appears at the end of each entry and suggests resources for additional study.

Other Features

BLC contains three distinct indexes to help readers find information quickly and easily:

■ The **Author Index** lists all the authors appearing in *BLC*. To ensure easy access, name variations and name changes are fully cross-indexed.

■ The **Nationality Index** lists all authors featured in *BLC* by nationality. For expatriate authors and authors identified with more than one nation, multiple listings are offered.

■ The **Title Index** lists in alphabetical order all individual works by the authors appearing in *BLC*. English-language translations of original foreign-language titles are cross-referenced to the foreign titles so that all references to a work are combined in one listing.

Citing *Black Literature Criticism*

When writing papers, students who quote directly from *BLC* may use the following general forms to footnote reprinted criticism. The first example is for material drawn from periodicals, the second for material reprinted from books.

Robert B. Stepto, "Storytelling in Early Afro-American Fiction: Frederick Douglass' 'The Heroic Slave'," *The Georgia Review*, XXXVI (Summer 1982), 355-68; excerpted and reprinted in *Black Literature Criticism*, ed. James P. Draper (Detroit: Gale Research, 1992), pp. 585-88.

Edward Margolies, *Native Sons: A Critical Study of Twentieth-Century Negro American Authors* (J. B. Lippincott, 1968); excerpted and reprinted in *Black Literature Criticism*, ed. James P. Draper (Detroit: Gale Research, 1992), pp. 59-64.

Acknowledgments

The editor wishes to acknowledge the valuable contributions of the many librarians, authors, and scholars who assisted in the compilation of *BLC* with their responses to telephone and mail inquiries. Special thanks are offered to *BLC*'s two chief advisors: Clarence Chisholm, Chairman of the Afro-American Studies Section of the Association of College and Research Libraries, and Arnold Rampersad, Woodrow Wilson Professor of English and Director of American Studies at Princeton University.

Comments Are Welcome

The editor hopes that readers will find *BLC* to be a useful reference tool and welcomes comments about the work. Send comments and suggestions to: Editor, *Black Literature Criticism*, Gale Research Inc., Penobscot Building, Detroit, MI 48226-4094.

Authors Included
in *Black Literature Criticism*

Chinua Achebe 1930-

Jamil Abdullah Al-Amin (H. Rap
  Brown) 1943-

Maya Angelou 1928-

Ayi Kwei Armah 1939-

William Attaway 1911?-1986

James Baldwin 1924-1987

Toni Cade Bambara 1939-

Amiri Baraka (LeRoi
  Jones) 1934-

Barry Beckham 1944-

James Madison Bell 1826-1902

Louise Bennett 1919-

Mongo Beti (Alexandre
  Biyidi) 1932-

Arna Bontemps 1902-1973

David Bradley 1950-

William Stanley
  Braithwaite 1878-1962

Gwendolyn Brooks 1917-

Claude Brown 1937-

Sterling Brown 1901-1989

William Wells Brown 1816?-1884

Dennis Brutus 1924-

Ed Bullins 1935-

J. E. Casely-Hayford 1866-1930

Aimé Césaire 1913-

Charles W. Chesnutt 1858-1932

Alice Childress 1920-

John Pepper Clark 1935-

Austin Clarke 1934-

Eldridge Cleaver 1935-

Lucille Clifton 1936-

Joseph Seamon Cotter, Sr. 1861-
  1949

Countee Cullen 1903-1946

Frank Marshall Davis 1905-1987

Samuel R. Delany 1942-

William Demby 1922-

Owen Dodson 1914-1983

Frederick Douglass 1817?-1895

W. E. B. Du Bois 1868-1963

Paul Laurence Dunbar 1872-1906

Cyprian Ekwensi 1921-

Lonne Elder III 1931-

Ralph Ellison 1914-

Buchi Emecheta 1944-

Olaudah Equiano 1745?-1797

Frantz Fanon 1925-1961

Nuruddin Farah 1945-

Jessie Redmon Fauset 1882-1961

Rudolph Fisher   1897-1934

Charlotte L. Forten   1837?-1914

Charles Fuller   1939-

Ernest Gaines   1933-

Marcus Garvey   1887-1940

Nikki Giovanni   1943-

Donald Goines   1937?-1974

Nicolás Guillén   1902-1989

Alex Haley   1921-

Jupiter Hammon   1711?-1800?

Lorraine Hansberry   1930-1965

Frances Ellen Watkins Harper   1825-1911

Robert Hayden   1913-1980

Bessie Head   1937-1986

Chester Himes   1909-1984

Pauline Elizabeth Hopkins   1859-1930

Langston Hughes   1902-1967

Zora Neale Hurston   1901?-1960

Charles Johnson   1948-

Fenton Johnson   1888-1958

James Weldon Johnson   1871-1938

Gayl Jones   1949-

Adrienne Kennedy   1931-

Jamaica Kincaid   1949-

Martin Luther King, Jr.   1929-1968

Etheridge Knight   1931-1991

George Lamming   1927-

Nella Larsen   1891-1964

Camara Laye   1928-1980

Andrea Lee   1953-

George Washington Lee   1894-1976

Audre Lorde   1934-

Joaquim Maria Machado de Assis   1839-1908

Haki R. Madhubuti (Don L. Lee)   1942-

Clarence Major   1936-

Malcolm X (Malcolm Little; El-Hajj Malik El-Shabazz)   1925-1965

Paule Marshall   1929-

Claude McKay   1889-1948

Ron Milner   1938-

Thomas Mofolo   1876-1948

Toni Morrison   1931-

Ezekiel Mphahlele   1919-

S. E. K. Mqhayi   1875-1945

Walter Dean Myers   1937-

Gloria Naylor   1950-

Ngugi wa Thiong'o   1938-

Lewis Nkosi   1936-

Christopher Okigbo   1932-1967

Sembène Ousmane   1923-

Gordon Parks   1912-

Okot p'Bitek   1931-1982

Adam Clayton Powell, Jr.   1908-1972

Dudley Randall   1914-

Ishmael Reed 1938-

Jacques Roumain 1907-1944

Sonia Sanchez 1934-

Léopold Sédar Senghor 1906-

Ntozake Shange 1948-

Wole Soyinka 1934-

Wallace Thurman 1902-1934

Melvin B. Tolson 1898?-1966

Jean Toomer 1894-1967

Desmond Tutu 1931-

Amos Tutuola 1920-

Derek Walcott 1930-

Alice Walker 1944-

Margaret Walker 1915-

Booker T. Washington 1856-1915

Phillis Wheatley 1753?-1784

Walter White 1893-1955

John Edgar Wideman 1941-

John A. Williams 1925-

Sherley Anne Williams 1944-

August Wilson 1945-

Harriet Wilson 1827?-?

Charles Wright 1932-

Richard Wright 1908-1960

Frank Yerby 1916-

Al Young 1939-

ACKNOWLEDGMENTS

The editor wishes to thank the copyright holders of the excerpted criticism included in this volume, the permissions managers of many book and magazine publishing companies for assisting in securing reprint rights, and Anthony Bogucki for assistance with copyright research. The editor is also grateful to the staffs of the Detroit Public Library, Wayne State University Purdy/Kresge Library Complex, and the University of Michigan Libraries for making their resources available. Following is a list of the copyright holders who have granted permission to reprint material in this volume of *BLC*. Every effort has been made to trace copyright, but if omissions have been made, please let the editor know.

COPYRIGHTED EXCERPTS IN *BLC*, VOLUME 2, WERE REPRINTED FROM THE FOLLOWING PERIODICALS:

African Literature Today, n. 5, 1971. Copyright (c) 1971 by Heinemann Educational Books Ltd. All rights reserved. Reprinted by permission of Africana Publishing Company, New York, NY.—*Afro-American Studies,* v. 2, March, 1972 for "The Didactic Achievement of Malcolm X's Autobiography" by Barrett John Mandel. Copyright (c) 1972 Gordon and Breach Science Publishers Ltd. Reprinted by permission of the publisher and the author.—*Afro-Americans in New York Life and History,* v. 5, July, 1981. (c) 1981 Afro-American History Association of the Niagara Frontier, Inc. Reprinted by permission of the publisher.—*America,* v. 126, February 19, 1972. (c) 1972. All rights reserved. Reprinted with permission of America Press, Inc., 106 West 56th Street, New York, NY 10019.—*American Literature,* v. 43, March, 1971. Copyright (c) 1971 Duke University Press, Durham, NC. Reprinted with permission of the publisher.—*American Poetry,* v. 4, Winter, 1987. (c) 1987 by Lee Bartlett and Peter White. All rights reserved. Reprinted by permission of the publisher.—*Amistad,* v. I, February, 1970. Copyright (c) 1970 by John A. Williams. Reprinted by permission of Random House, Inc.—*Ariel: A Review of International English Literature,* v. 12, July, 1981 for "The Personal and the Political: The Case of Nuruddin Farah" by Kirsten Holst Petersen. Copyright (c) 1981 The Board of Governors, The University of Calgary. Reprinted by permission of the publisher and the author.—*Black Academy Review,* v. 1, Winter, 1970. Reprinted by permission of the publisher.— *Black American Literature Forum,* v. 23, Summer, 1989 for "Necessary Distance: Afterthoughts on Becoming a Writer" by Clarence Major. Copyright (c) 1989 by the author. Reprinted by permission of the author./ v. 17, Summer, 1983 for "The Descent of Charlie Fuller into Pulitzerland and the Need for African-American Institutions" by Amiri Baraka. Copyright (c) 1983 Indiana State University. Copyright (c) 1983 by Amiri Baraka. Reprinted by permission of Indiana State University and Sterling Lord Literistic, Inc./ v. 11, Spring, 1977 for "To Make These Bones Live: History and Community in Ernest Gaines' Fiction" by Jack Hicks; v. 13, Summer, 1979 for "A Reading of Clarence Major's Fiction" by Doug Bolling; v. 13, Summer, 1979 for "Clarence Major: Poet & Language Man" by Fanny Howe; v. 14, Winter, 1980 for "Nella Larsen's 'Passing': A Problem of Interpretation" by Claudia Tate; v. 14, Fall, 1980 for " 'The Violent Space': The Function of the New Black Aesthetic in Etheridge Knight's Prison Poetry" by Patricia Liggins Hill; v. 15, Summer, 1981 for " 'Let Me Make the Songs for the People': A Study of Frances Watkins Harper's Poetry" by Patricia Liggins Hill; v. 19, Winter, 1985 for "James Weldon Johnson's Portrait of the Artist as Invisible Man" by Howard Faulkner; v. 19, Summer, 1985 for "Disguised Voice in 'The Interesting Narrative of Olaudah Equiano, or Gustavus Vassa, the African' " by Wilfred D. Samuels. Copyright (c) 1977, 1979, 1980, 1981, 1985 Indiana State University. All reprinted by permission of Indiana State University and the respective authors.—*Book Week—New York Herald Tribune,* November 14, 1965. (c) 1965, *The Washington Post.* Reprinted by permission of the publisher.—*Book World—The Washington Post,* October 25, 1981; September 25, 1983; February 14, 1988. (c) 1981, 1983, 1988, *The Washington Post.* All reprinted with permission of the publisher.—*Boston Review,* v. X, February, 1985 for a review of "Sarah Phillips" by Patricia Vigderman. Copyright (c) 1985 by the Boston Critic, Inc. Reprinted by permission of the author.—*Callaloo,* v. 7, Winter, 1984 for "In-Between" by Steven Weisenburger. Copyright (c) 1984 by Charles H. Rowell. All rights reserved. Reprinted by permission of the author./ v. 9, Winter, 1986; v. 10, Spring, 1987; v. 12, Spring, 1989. Copyright (c) 1986, 1987, 1989 by Charles H. Rowell. All rights reserved. All reprinted with permission of the publisher.—*The Carleton Miscellany,* v. XVIII, March 2, 1981 for "Remembering Robert E. Hayden" by Michael S. Harper. Copyright 1981 by Carleton College. Reprinted by permission of the publisher and the author.—*Chicago Tribune—Books,* July 8, 1990. (c) copyrighted 1990, Chicago Tribune Company. All rights reserved. Used with permission.—*CLA Journal,* v. XVI, December, 1972; v. XX, December, 1976; v. XXII, December, 1978; v. XXII, June, 1979. Copyright (c) 1972, 1976, 1978, 1979 by The College Language Association. All used by permission of The College Language Association.—*Commentary,* v. 91, March, 1991 for "Literature by Quota" by Carol Iannone. Copyright (c) 1991 by the American Jewish Committee. All rights reserved. Reprinted by permission of the publisher and the author./ v. 27, June 27, 1959 for "Thoughts on 'A Raisin in the Sun' " by Gerald Weales. Copyright (c) 1959 by

COPYRIGHTED EXCERPTS IN *BLC*, VOLUME 2, WERE REPRINTED FROM THE FOLLOWING BOOKS:

PHOTOGRAPHS AND ILLUSTRATIONS APPEARING IN *BLC,* VOLUME 2, WERE RECEIVED FROM THE FOLLOWING SOURCES:

BLACK LITERATURE

C R I T I C I S M

Buchi Emecheta

1944-

(Full name Florence Onye Buchi Emecheta) Nigerian-born novelist, autobiographer, scriptwriter, and author of children's books.

Although Emecheta has lived in London since 1962, she is "Nigeria's best-known female writer," according to John Updike in the *New Yorker.* "Indeed, few writers of her sex . . . have arisen in any part of tropical Africa." Emecheta has written numerous children's books and teleplays, but she is best known for her historical novels set in Nigeria, both before and after independence. These works, which treat the clash of cultures and the impact of Western values upon agrarian traditions and customs, typically present female heroines who challenge their restrictive lives and aspire to economic and social independence. Emecheta's work is strongly autobiographical; and, as Updike has observed, much of it is especially concerned with "the situation of women in a society where their role, though crucial, was firmly subordinate and where the forces of potential liberation have arrived with bewildering speed."

Emecheta was born in Yaba, a small village near Lagos, Nigeria. She was orphaned as a young child and taken in by foster parents who mistreated her. She attended a missionary high school until she was sixteen, when she married a man to whom she had been betrothed since the age of eleven. A mother at seventeen, she had two sons and three daughters by the time she was twenty-two. After the birth of her second child, Emecheta followed her husband to London. There she endured poor living conditions, including one-room apartments without heat or hot water, to help finance his education. According to Mary Bray in the *Voice Literary Supplement,* "The culture shock of London was great" for Emecheta, "but even more distressing was her husband's physical abuse and his constant resistance to her attempts at independence." The marriage ended when Emecheta's husband read and then burned the manuscript of her first book. Supporting herself and five children on public assistance and by scrubbing floors, Emecheta wrote in the mornings before her children arose. She also managed to earn an honors degree in sociology.

Emecheta's first two novels, *In the Ditch* (1972) and *Second-Class Citizen* (1975), are loosely based on her own experiences as a single parent and are regarded as among her most accomplished works. Both books revolve around Adah, a young Nigerian woman who is searching for a better life. In the first work, which originally appeared as a series of columns in the *New Statesman,* Emecheta depicted Adah's struggle to raise five small children while living on welfare payments, attending college, and attempting to complete her first novel. The second work recounts Adah's emigration to

England and her marriage to a domineering man who attempts to thwart her educational and professional aspirations. Their marriage dissolves as Adah, influenced by the women's liberation movement, begins to assert her individuality. Critics praised Emecheta for her straightforward prose and amusing yet poignant evocation of her heroine's tribulations. Bray commented: "Both books are simply told, bearing the mark of painful authenticity even before you know they're autobiographical. [Emecheta] wrote them to rid herself of rage at a society and a man who could not accept her independent spirit."

Emecheta's next three novels dramatize the problems African women encounter in a traditional, male-oriented society. *The Bride Price* (1976) centers on a young woman who defies tribal custom by marrying a man outside her social class. After her husband fails to pay her dowry, or bride price, she dies in childbirth, as prophesied by tribal myth. *The Slave Girl* (1977), which accuses the patriarchal social system of treating females as commodities, focuses on the coming-of-age of an orphan girl whose older brother sells her to a distant relative. In *The Joys of Motherhood* (1979) Emecheta condemned the practice of polygamy, the stigma associated with barrenness, and the pressures placed on African women to produce male children. The central characters are two women who are married to the same man and compete to bear the most children for him. Both women are ultimately doomed in this relationship: one is discovered to be sterile, and the other is reduced to servitude after bearing several children in rapid succession. Katherine Frank stated that these three novels, along with *In the Ditch* and *Second-Class Citizen,* "compose the most exhaustive and moving portrayal extant of the African woman, an unparalleled portrayal in African fiction and with few equals in other literatures as well."

Although praised for its versatility, Emecheta's later fiction has met with less enthusiasm from reviewers. *Destination Biafra* (1982) is a dense historical novel set during the Nigerian civil war. *Double Yoke* (1982), a lighthearted tale of sexual politics at a Nigerian university, examines the conflict between tradition and modernity. In the futuristic fantasy *The Rape of Shavi* (1983), Emecheta commented on the impact of westernization on the inhabitants of a mythical African kingdom. *Head above Water* (1984) is a nonfiction work detailing Emecheta's childhood in a small Nigerian village, her career as a social worker in London, and the problems she encountered in finding a publisher for her writings.

"Emecheta has reaffirmed her dedication to be a full-time writer," stated Charlotte and David Bruner in *World Literature Today.* "Her culture and her education at first were obstacles to her literary inclination. She had to struggle against precedent, against reluctant publishers, and later against male-dominated audiences and readership." Her fiction is intensely autobiographical, drawing on the difficulties she has witnessed and experienced as a woman, most especially as a Nigerian woman. Indicating that in Nigeria, however, "Emecheta is a prophet without honor," Bray added that "she is frustrated at not being able to reach women—the audience she desires most. She feels a sense of isolation as she attempts to stake out the middle ground between the old and the new." "What I am trying to do is get our profession back," Emecheta told Bray. "Women are born storytellers. We keep the history. We are the true conservatives—we conserve things and we never forget. What I do is not clever or unusual. It is what my aunt and my grandmother did, and their mothers before them."

(For further information about Emecheta's life and works, see *Black Writers; Contemporary Authors,* Vols. 81-84; *Contemporary Authors New Revision Series,* Vol. 27; and *Contemporary Literary Criticism,* Vols. 14, 48. For related criticism, see the entry on Nigerian Literature in *Twentieth-Century Literary Criticism,* Vol. 30.)

PRINCIPAL WORKS

In the Ditch (novel) 1972
Second-Class Citizen (novel) 1975
The Bride Price (novel) 1976
The Slave Girl (novel) 1977
The Joys of Motherhood (novel) 1979
Titch the Cat (juvenile fiction) 1979
Nowhere to Play (juvenile fiction) 1980
The Moonlight Bride (juvenile fiction) 1981
The Wrestling Match (juvenile fiction) 1981
Destination Biafra (novel) 1982
Double Yoke (novel) 1982
Naira Power (novelette) 1982
Adah's Story (novel) 1983
The Rape of Shavi (novel) 1983
Head above Water (autobiography) 1984
A Kind of Marriage (novelette) 1987

Katherine Frank (essay date 1982)

[*In the following excerpt, Frank examines Emecheta's portrayal of African womanhood in five of her novels:* In the Ditch, Second-Class Citizen, The Bride Price, The Slave Girl, *and* The Joys of Motherhood.]

For the most part, the world of African fiction has been a masculine domain in which women are conspicuous mainly by their absence. A glance through Heinemann's African Writers Series yields only five women writers, two of them white South Africans. And such standard critical works as Gerald Moore's, Charles Larson's, and Eustace Palmer's studies of the African novel also focus on its dominant male tradition. But despite this tradition and its basis in the fact that until recently the overwhelming majority of African literary works in all genres have been produced by men, there is a growing body of African literature written by women—an alternate, female tradition with its own peculiar vision of contemporary African experience. Writers such as Flora Nwapa, Bessie Head, Mariama Bâ, Rebeka Njau, and Grace Ogot are no longer solo voices crying in the wilderness. In a recent interview, in fact, Ogot explained that the dearth of women writers in Africa is quickly disappearing, and went on to predict that "in another five years the market will be flooded by women writers, writing serious literature on all aspects of life." As their educational opportunities have improved over the past several decades and as they have begun to penetrate the social and political spheres that constitute the main arena of African fiction, women writers have begun to record and interpret the cataclysmic changes they and their world are undergoing in contemporary Africa.

The profound upheaval effected in women's lives by these changes is the particular territory of one of the most gifted and prolific of the African women novelists, the Nigerian writer Buchi Emecheta. In less than seven years Emecheta has produced five novels: *In the Ditch* (1972), *Second Class Citizen* (1974), *The Bride Price* (1976), *The Slave Girl* (1977), and *The Joys of Motherhood* (1979). The first two autobiographical books recount the near heroism of Emecheta's performance. Through the struggles of their central character, Adah Obi, we learn how Emecheta began writing in a tiny council flat in North London, somehow carving out enough time to write from her hectic life as a university student, British Museum librarian, and single parent of five small children. An awareness of the hardships surrounding their genesis, however, is not necessary for an appreciation of Emecheta's novels and the totality of their achievement. For though they are not inter-related installments of one encompassing work, it is revealing to look at the five novels as parts of "chapters" of a larger whole—a single, continuous narrative which amounts to a kind of epic of female experience in twentieth-century Africa. Taken together, in fact, Emecheta's novels compose the most exhaustive and moving portrayal extant of the African woman, an unparalleled portrayal in African fiction and with few equals in other literatures as well. The entire realm of African female experience can be found in these books, from birth to death, with all the intermediate steps of childhood, adolescence, marriage, and motherhood. And Emecheta's historical and social breadth in the novels is equally impressive: covering a period from 1910 to the present and moving from the small Nigerian village of Ibuza which figures in all the books to westernized, urban Lagos, and finally to London, the promised land of Emecheta's Adah.

Apart from the largeness in scope, Emecheta's account of African womanhood is an unapologetically feminist one. She exposes and repudiates the feminine stereotypes of male writers such as Achebe, Amadi and others, and reveals the dark underside of their fictional celebrations of the African woman. She explores the psychological and physical toll on women of such things as arranged marriages, polygamy, perpetual pregnancy and childbirth, and widowhood. The female figures hovering in the wings and background or burdened with symbolic cargo in male-authored African fiction are brought centre stage by Emecheta, and an entirely new drama emerges as a result of this radical change in sexual perspective.

Taken on its most stark terms, this drama involves three inter-related but also conflicting issues or problems: the oppression—sometimes tantamount to slavery—of African women; their education; and the effect upon their lives of westernization or "development" (the familiar traditional or rural versus Western or urban conflict from a new, female point of view). It is the clash among these three forces and a faltering but persistent desire for female autonomy and fulfillment that gives rise to the central dilemma posed by Emecheta's fiction. A tragic because seemingly irresolvable dilemma: the African woman, far more than the Western woman or African man, is caught in a terrible bind. In order to be free and fulfilled as a woman she must renounce her

African identity because of the inherent sexism of traditional African culture. Or, if she wishes to cherish and affirm her "Africanness," she must renounce her claims to feminine independence and self-determination. Either way she stands to lose; either way she will find herself diminished, impoverished. It is Emecheta's growing awareness of the futility of attempting to resolve this dilemma that accounts for the growing bitterness we can trace in the development of her novels. Indeed, there is an almost retrogressive movement in the fiction, moving from the qualified optimism of her first book, *In the Ditch,* to the unrelieved despair of her last, the ironically entitled *Joys of Motherhood.*

The feminist narrative that we can discern in Emecheta's five novels would seem to conclude with the liberated, self-sufficient heroine of her first and second books whom we leave on the brink of successful authorship in England. With each succeeding novel Emecheta moves progressively backward, and this retreat proceeds on several levels. In *Joys of Motherhood, The Bride Price,* and *The Slave Girl* we move backward historically from the 1960s of the first two books through the fifties, forties, thirties and finally to the early decades of the century. We also retreat to the beginning of the African woman's life cycle, to her infancy and childhood in *The Slave Girl* and her adolescence, marriage, and motherhood in *The Bride Price* and *Joys of Motherhood.* And finally, we backtrack culturally from England to Lagos to Ibuza, the traditional village that despite the incursions of white missionaries remains relatively immune to colonial invasion. Not only, then, does Emecheta explore the plight of the contemporary woman torn between her African culture and her feminist aspiration, she also searches the past, the traditional worlds of her mother and grandmother, in order to fathom the origin of her current entrapment between two visions, two worlds, two destinies.

But the best place to approach Emecheta's fiction is with neither her first nor her last book, but instead with one of the middle novels, *The Slave Girl.* For as its title discloses, it is in this book that Emecheta most fully explores her central vision of female bondage, her underlying metaphor of African womanhood as a condition of victimization and servitude. The tyrants and oppressors who reduce women to slaves vary from novel to novel: from husbands and racist whites in *Second Class Citizen* to traditional mores and taboos in *The Bride Price,* to men (brothers, masters, husbands) in *The Slave Girl,* and finally to children in *Joys of Motherhood.* But whoever or whatever the enslaving power may be, Emecheta shows that the oppression of women is an invariable constant. The most a woman can hope for is to be able to choose the least cruel available master.

About a third of the way through *The Slave Girl* Emecheta presents an appalling dramatic episode that she repeats almost verbatim in her last novel, *The Joys of Motherhood.* The scene provides a kind of objective correlative of her vision of African womanhood, a haunting incident that reverberates backwards and forwards to the novels which precede and come after *The Slave Girl.* One of the secondary characters, a young girl named Chiago, tells the heroine, Ogbanje Ojebeta, how she witnessed the live burial of a slave girl not unlike themselves:

> The chief wife of the master of the house had died, and it was necessary for her husband to send her to the land of the dead accompanied by a female slave. The one chosen was a particularly beautiful slave, with smooth skin and black closely cropped hair. . . . On the eve of the burial she was brought and ordered to lie down in the shallow grave. As might be expected, she resisted but there was no pity on the faces of the men who stood by watching amused by her cries. She made appeals to the gods of her people to save her, she begged some of the mourners to spare her life . . . but to no avail. One of the sons of the dead woman lost his patience and . . . took a club and struck the defenceless woman hard at the back of her shaved head. . . . She did not drop into the grave. . . . Instead, she turned to look at the chief, who was calling on his son to cease his brutality, and she said to him, "For showing me this little mercy, chief, I shall come again, I shall come again" . . . She was not allowed to finish her valedictory statement, for the stubborn young man, disregarding his father's appeal, gave the woman a final blow so that she fell by the side of the grave. But she was still struggling even when the body of her dead mistress was placed on her. She still fought and cried out, so alive. Soon her voice was completely silenced by the damp earth that was piled on both her and the dead woman.

The live burial of the beautiful and futilely defiant slave girl symbolically expresses the plight of all Emecheta's heroines.

With Ogbanje Ojebeta, the heroine of *The Slave Girl,* we go back in time—all the way back to 1910, the year of Ojebeta's birth—and back to the beginning of woman's life cycle in order to understand the roots or origin of women's slavery. In fact, Emecheta is casting an entire generation behind her own birth. While *In the Ditch* and *Second Class Citizen* are thinly disguised autobiographies, *The Slave Girl* seems to be a fictionalized biography of Emecheta's mother. Towards the end of the novel Ogbanje Ojebeta acquires the English name of Alice; *The Bride Price,* the novel which directly precedes *The Slave Girl,* is dedicated to Emecheta's mother, Alice Ogbanje Emecheta.

At the outset, Ojebeta's life seems to be highly atypical because she is eagerly anticipated and cherished as the only female child of her mother to survive infancy. As Emecheta remarks, such joy in a daughter's birth is extremely rare: "Girl children were not normally particularly prized creatures, but her father had lost so many that they now assumed a quality of preciousness." Both Ojebeta's parents, in fact, lavish love and attention on their precious daughter. Her father makes a long and dangerous journey to Idu to purchase charms to protect Ojebeta from the spirits who want to lure her away to the next world, and her mother has elaborate, beautiful tatoos stenciled on her daughter's face. But such indulgences abruptly end when Ojebeta is orphaned at the age

of seven and her brother sells her to a distant relative, a wealthy trader named Ma Palagada who lives far away from Ibuza in Onitsha. Just at the age when she is passing from dependent infancy (her mother had allowed her to nurse until she was six) to young girl-hood—the age when the young child begins to grope towards autonomy and the creation of a distinct identity—Ojebeta is sold off by her brother for eight pounds so that he can purchase scarves, anklets, and beads for his coming-of-age dance costume.

The young Ojebeta in many ways seems the prototypical Emecheta heroine. She is beautiful, intelligent, and headstrong, restively unhappy and yearning in her constrained existence. Perhaps the most dangerous aspect of her servitude at the Palagadas' is that it is not an entirely abhorrent life. She forms close bonds with a number of the other slave girls and even Ma Palagada seems a kind of foster mother to her at times. Indeed, there is much to lull Ojebeta into acceptance of her slavery: she lives in a palatial house, has plenty to eat, nice clothes (Ma Palagada is a cloth trader and dress-maker), and above all, she receives the rudiments of education.

Education, as Wilhelmina Lamb has shown, is the crucial liberating force in the lives of Emecheta's heroines, and in fact their degree of servitude is inversely proportional to the amount of education they receive. Emecheta has no faith in social change or in the prospect that the environment will ever grant African women freedom. Instead they must wrest it from the environment themselves, and the only thing that will give them the power to do it is education. Hence Emecheta's most autonomous and fulfilled heroine is the university-educated Adah in *In the Ditch* and *Second Class Citizen* , while her most powerless and oppressed is the illiterate Nnu Ego in *Joys of Motherhood.* In *The Slave Girl* we see the very rudiments of education and the profound effect that even such scanty learning can have on women's lives. Ojebeta is allowed to attend a Sunday school run by an Englishwoman and here she learns to read Ibo, an accomplishment which not only gives her and the other slave girls a modicum of power and prestige as "elite slaves," but also "endless amusement; they read and re-read the stories [from an Ibo storybook] . . . until they knew most of the little book by heart." The power of education for women is a double power: it is the first step towards social and sexual freedom, but less pragmatically, it also frees their hearts and minds. Books can transport Emecheta's heroines from their own cramped, miserable worlds to far-off places and exciting experiences they could never know in their real lives. Hence Ojebeta's absorption in the Ibo story book. And in *Second Class Citizen* education becomes the route to self-knowledge, as we can see in Adah's eager reading of Flora Nwapa and James Baldwin.

Ojebeta's later education, however, takes on the lineaments of traditional female learning. She leaves the Sunday school and is enrolled in an "academy," also run by the Englishwoman, where she learns such domestic skills as how to bake cakes, crochet, and embroider. And this training, of course, has the opposite effect of her earlier education. It serves to confine her to the appointed feminine sphere of domestic labour.

For Emecheta makes it abundantly clear that for Ojebeta coming of age in the twenties and thirties there is no possible escape from this sphere. During her early days at the Palagadas', Ojebeta reflects, "All her life a woman always belonged to some male. At birth you were owned by your people, and when you were sold you belonged to a new master, when you grew up your new master who had paid something for you would control you." Even when she is released from her servitude and returns to Ibuza after Ma Palagada's death, Ojebeta is still not free, because "no woman or girl in Ibuza was free, except those who committed the abominable sin of prostitution or those who had been completely cast off or rejected by their people for offending one custom or another. A girl was owned, in particular, by her father or someone in place of her father or her older brother, and then, in general, by her group or homestead."

The slave masters, the tyrannical oppressors, in *The Slave Girl* are all men, and it is this vision of male oppression along with the literal condition of slavery in the novel which makes *The Slave Girl* the most overtly feminist of Emecheta's books and the best one with which to approach her other writing. At the end of the book Ojebeta marries a westernized, Christian man and moves with him to Lagos. He is, as she says, "a master of her own choice," but Emecheta tells us that it is pointless to speculate whether they loved and cared for each other forever after:

> Those words make no sense in a situation like this. There was certainly a kind of eternal bond between husband and wife, a bond produced maybe by centuries of traditions, taboos, and latterly, Christian dogma. Slave, obey your master. Wife, honour your husband, who is your father, your head, your heart, your soul. So there was little room for Ojebeta to exercise her own individuality, her own feelings, for these were entwined in Jacob's. She was lucky, however, that although Jacob proved to be quite a jealous man, he was above all a Christian. In her own way, Ojebeta was content and did not want more of life; she was happy in her husband, happy to be submissive, even to accept an occasional beating because that was what she had been brought up to believe a wife should expect.

Despite the compensations of her life with the Palagadas, Ojebeta never acquiesces in her slavery with them, but the great irony of her story is that when she voluntarily chooses her own master, her husband Jacob, she seals her doom. There is no denying that by the end of the novel, the once beautiful, restive, hungry-spirited Ojebeta is a broken woman. Ma Palagada's son Clifford turns up some years after Ojebeta's marriage to collect the eight pounds which Jacob owes him for Ojebeta, and Clifford is astonished at the drastic change in her: "The old Ojebeta—the energetic, laughing one" has been replaced by a thin, nervous, prematurely middle-aged and worn matron.

With her paltry education, not even the defiant and clever Ojebeta can hope to escape her fate of slavery. The most she can do, as she realizes, is to select her own master. Hence the novel concludes with Jacob's formal purchase of his wife from Clifford, the son of her previous owner. Ojebeta herself is too defeated, too cowed to be fully aware of, much less rail against, her abasement. She kneels before Jacob and confesses, "I could not wish for a better master." But Emecheta herself has the last word. Ojebeta may capitulate, but her creator does not endorse her capitulation. The time is 1945, the year after Emecheta was born, and she concludes the novel with the bitterly ironic statement that "as Britain was emerging from war once more victorious, and claiming to have stopped the slavery which she had helped to spread in all her black colonies, Ojebeta, now a woman of thirty-five, was changing masters."

If *The Slave Girl* is a study of the oppression of women by men, *The Bride Price* explores the enslavement of women by traditional society and its rules and taboos. As such, *The Bride Price* provides a striking contrast to the celebration of traditional life among male African writers. While Emecheta's portrayal of traditional society is not entirely untinged by nostalgia for a simpler and in some ways purer rural existence, she is not blind to the injustices and suffering inflicted upon women by traditional customs and mores. Such customs and mores, in fact, are actually institutionalized forms of male oppression. The inheritance of widows by their brothers-in-law, the custom that a man may make an unwilling woman his wife by kidnapping her and cutting off a lock of her hair, the prohibition against woman marrying descendents of slaves, and numerous other inhibiting manifestations of traditional culture in *The Bride Price* are all determined and enforced by men. The major difference, then, between *The Bride Price* and *The Slave Girl* is not seen in the oppressive power so much as in women's response to it. In time Ojebeta is crushed by her environment and in the end she willingly submits to it. Aku-nna, the heroine of *The Bride Price,* in contrast bravely flouts tradition, though in return she too is crushed, even more completely than Ojebeta. For Aku-nna dies at the end of *The Bride Price,* giving birth to a daughter who seems to represent the new, free female self that Aku-nna has aspired to be. (pp. 476-83)

The Joys of Motherhood, Emecheta's most recent novel, in some ways seems a prologue and in other ways a sequel to *The Slave Girl* and *The Bride Price.* Its illiterate heroine, Nnu Ego, is certainly the most oppressed and powerless of all Emecheta's women characters, largely because she is denied the education Ojebeta and Aku-nna enjoy. Thus when we look at Emecheta's five novels as a tale of the African woman's evolution from enslavement to qualified liberation, Nnu Ego's life is the point at which we must begin. At the same time, though, her story seems a continuation of Ojebeta's and Aku-nna's because it focuses on a later period of woman's life cycle—the years of relentless pregnancy, childbirth, and motherhood that the other two novels stop short of. In addition, though Nnu Ego is the most traditional of Emecheta's heroines, she lives in modern Lagos and much of the hardship she endures results from her attempt to live by values that her environment has outgrown. Thus the conflict between traditional and Western ways of life that is peripheral to *The Slave Girl* and *The Bride Price* becomes a major concern here.

Foremost among these traditional practices and values that govern Nnu Ego's life are polygamy and the stigma of barrenness. Both derive from the traditional vision of womanhood that perceives women only in relation to their husbands and children. The traditional woman's primary function is to bear male children who will perpetuate her husband's name, and Nnu Ego is remarkable among Emecheta's heroines for never questioning—much less defying—the justice of this pre-determined female destiny. This is due in part to the fact that in *Joys of Motherhood* Emecheta seems to have divided up the traits that characterize her previous heroines among three important female figures. Nnu Ego herself is by far the least complex of them, though her stoical strength and fidelity to a way of life no longer relevant to her world make her a sympathetic, even compelling figure. She resembles the striking mother figures of the earlier books, Ma Blackie in *The Bride Price* and Akunna's mother Umeadi in *The Slave Girl*. The pity of Nnu Ego's story is that she has been taken from the traditional environment that bestows a kind of dignity, even grandeur, on these other women. She is caught in the middle between two worlds, unable to go back to that of her own mother, Ona, and unable to adapt to modern Lagos as does her self-sufficient co-wife, Adaku. (pp. 486-87)

Instead of the traditional vision of children as a source of joy and wealth who more than amply repay the trouble of their upbringing, in *Joys of Motherhood* children and the man who fathers them are portrayed as millstones around the mother's neck, or as greedy insects who suck out and drain her life's blood. By the time her second set of twins is born, Nnu Ego has been bled dry by her long years of motherhood:

> "God, when will you create a woman who will be fulfilled in herself, a full human being, not anybody's appendage?" she prayed desperately. "After all, I was born alone, and I shall die alone. What have I gained from all this? Yes, I have many children, but what do I have to feed them on? On my life. I have to work myself to the bone to look after them, I have to give them my all. And if I am lucky enough to die in peace, I even have to give them my soul. . . . When will I be free?"

When indeed? Of course, Nnu Ego never is free, and she has very little to show for her protracted years of maternal servitude. She is particularly disappointed by her male children. After receiving good educations in Lagos, the two older boys go abroad to study and never bother to write their mother. It is only by word of

mouth, in fact, that Nnu Ego learns that her eldest son has married a white woman in America. Her daughters, in contrast, give her a small measure of comfort, though it is the elopement of one of them with a Yoruba boy that brings about the disintegration of Nnu Ego's marriage to Naife.

The complete futility of motherhood that we find in *Joys of Motherhood* is the most heretical and radical aspect of Emecheta's vision of the African woman. The backbreaking grind of childbearing and child rearing is a common theme among contemporary Western women writers, but it is unusual among their African counterparts because of the sanctity of the mother-child relationship in African society. The primary commitment or bond in Western women's lives is to their lovers or husbands; a man rather than children confers status on women. Among educated women, at least, children are clearly of secondary importance so that raising a family is often deferred for years or rejected altogether because children are seen as interfering with women's autonomy and also with their primary love relationship with a man. Such is rarely the case with African women, and hence the daring of Emecheta's harsh and embittered portrayal of motherhood. Nnu Ego's children, at least her sons, first exploit and then betray her, finally denying her the most basic of African children's responsibilities, the care of their parents in old age. Instead, Nnu Ego dies one night alone in the roadside, "with no child to hold her hand and no friend to talk to her. She had never really made many friends, so busy had she been building up her joys as a mother." Not surprisingly, when the people of her natal village build a shrine to Nnu Ego's memory, she fails to answer their prayers for children. (pp. 490-91)

Because of her loyalty to her traditional role and identity Nnu Ego's fate is inevitable. But though Lagos crushes anachronisms like Nnu Ego, it is certainly not ready for liberated women such as Adaku. And herein lies the crisis that Emecheta shows faces the African woman. Adaku's fate demonstrates that the very notion of a liberated African woman is a contradiction in terms. There is an irremediable antagonism between the African woman's identity as an African and as a woman. She must choose one over the other, and if she decides on female independence and self-sufficiency she will almost certainly have to turn her back on her homeland and go, as the heroine of Emecheta's first two novels does, to England or some other Western country. Like Adah Obi, she will have to sacrifice her African consciousness to her feminist aspiration. And though it may appear that once abroad she merely exchanges sexual for racial oppression, the real second class citizenship that informs Emecheta's first two books derives far more from Adah's anatomy than from the colour of her skin.

In the Ditch and *Second Class Citizen* were written within two years of each other and because of their shared setting and cast of characters they seem to constitute a single novel. Though it was written first, *In the Ditch* is actually the sequel to *Second Class Citizen* and indeed is virtually incomprehensible if read before the later novel. For it is in *Second Class Citizen* that we first encounter Adah as a young eager school girl with her great dream of becoming a been-to. In Adah's eyes, England is the promised land. Even as a small girl she thinks that "going to the United Kingdom must surely be like paying God a visit. The United Kingdom, then, must be like heaven." England is the necessary stage for the enactment of Adah's liberation, a goal towards which she falteringly progresses in the course of the two novels.

There are essentially two phases involved in Adah's progress towards independence, the first of which dominates *Second Class Citizen* and the second *In the Ditch.* In *Second Class Citizen* she is primarily reacting against and escaping from all that constrains and inhibits her. First and foremost this means fleeing Africa for England, though it is significant that Adah is able to go abroad only because her worthless and repulsive husband, Francis, goes there to study. It is inconceivable that she could have gone alone to pursue her own education. Francis, indeed, throughout *Second Class Citizen* tries to maintain the African male's power and authority over Adah, but as he himself realizes fairly early on, "the greatest mistake an African could make was to bring an educated girl to London and let her mix with middle class English women. They soon knew their rights."

Nevertheless, Adah remains under Francis' sadistic thumb until the very end of the novel. While he lounges about their one-room flat all day making only the most desultory gestures of studying, Adah goes out and works as a librarian and does all the domestic chores as well as caring for their rapidly growing family. Thus arrival on English soil is only the first step towards Adah's freedom. The main action of *Second Class Citizen* involves the next necessary step of escaping from Francis.

Despite the fact that Adah is the family's breadwinner and thus is financially self-sufficient, getting Francis out of her life is more easily said than done. She may be learning her "rights" in England, but it does not follow that she can shrug off years of conditioning that have inculcated wifely subservience to one's husband. It is only Francis' rather melodramatic villainy that enables Adah to vow she will not be his victim. Her initial move to escape his grasp is to get some means of contraception and gain the most fundamental kind of female control over her own body, and thus protect herself from Francis' voracious sexual appetite. But when Francis discovers that Adah has been fitted with a diaphragm, he beats her, and soon after she is pregnant again.

Defensive maneuvers such as birth control are inadequate, and so Adah must enter the second phase of her move towards freedom and create some sort of future for herself to which she can turn when she is finally rid of Francis. As might be expected from the other novels, this future is intimately involved with Adah's education. She resolves to study sociology at a London university and even more importantly, she determines to bring to fruition her long standing dream of becoming a writer.

The career of authorship which Adah pursues in the last pages of *Second Class Citizen* (where she, in effect, writes Emecheta's next novel, *The Bride Price*), and then more fully in *In the Ditch* is dictated by the narrowly autobiographical nature of the two novels. Emecheta is telling her own story in these books, and as she has confessed in an article in *West Africa,* her life in London in the late sixties was a carbon copy of her heroine's. Like Adah she would finish up long days of work as a librarian and university student by writing far into the night. She tells how "having tucked my kids to bed, I banged away at an old Godforsaken typewriter which I picked from the market where I then lived in North London for five pounds. . . . I spent almost every week of 1968, 1969, and 1970 trying to persuade publishers just to read my work . . . my only wish was that someone should share my dreams. . . . I soon got used to the sound of returned manuscripts on the lino-covered floor of my council flat."

Quite apart from this autobiographical explanation for Adah's desire to be a writer, there is another reason why it seems such an appropriate career for her. As nearly all women writers have come to realize, to write about their experience is to gain some sort of power or control over it. Women writers may not be able to work great revolutions in their daily lives as such, but by re-creating their lives in literary works they may nevertheless radically transform them. And this literary impulse towards imaginatively restructuring and gaining control over one's life has always been particularly strong among those women writers most liable to repressive social constraints. Such was clearly the case, for example, with the Brontes in nineteenth-century England and with their contemporary Emily Dickinson in America. The very same process seems to be going on with Adah in *Second Class Citizen* and *In the Ditch.* She must rewrite her life before she can actually change it, just as Emecheta herself had to write out her eventual liberation via writing before she actually became a published author. (pp. 492-94)

As Emecheta's gifts as a novelist developed from the awkward, diffuse autobiography of her first two books to the lyricism of *The Bride Price* and finally to the tragic dignity of *The Joys of Motherhood,* her vision of African womanhood steadily darkened. In her first novel she exhausted her imaginative vision of the African woman's struggle for freedom—an unfinished and only vaguely adumbrated struggle as it turns out. In all her subsequent novels she explored not her own success or the possibility and forms of female fulfillment, but rather the social, cultural, and historical reasons why such fulfillment should seem so tenuous and problematical.

Thus Emecheta now seems to be at a crossroads in her career. She has exhaustively and definitively recorded the reality of life for African women at every stage of their lives and in all possible social and cultural contexts. Her five novels are no less than an epic account of African womanhood. The question is now whether, having explored the present and cast a search-light back on the past, Emecheta will be able to look ahead and imagine a future for African women—a future which will embrace and integrate their African and female identities and bestow a measure of whole-ness on lives that have been so fragmented and incomplete. (pp. 495-96)

> Katherine Frank, "The Death of the Slave Girl: African Womanhood in the Novels of Buchi Emecheta," in World Literature Written in English, Vol. 21, No. 3, Autumn, 1982, pp. 476-97.

Linda Barrett Osborne (essay date 1983)

[*In the following excerpt, Osborne comments on the structure and style of* Double Yoke.]

In an earlier book by Nigerian novelist Buchi Emecheta, the protagonist, confronted with her husband's disapproval, "prayed that the two of them would be strong enough to accept civilisation into their relationship." Now in Emecheta's eighth novel, **Double Yoke,** Ete Kamba and Nko, two students at the University of Calabar in Nigeria, wrestle with the same conflict created by the tension between tradition and modernity and its effects on identity, love, and marriage.

Emecheta, the most prolific and probably the best known woman writer from tropical Africa, has been living in England since 1962. Her first documentary novels, **In the Ditch** (1972) and **Second Class Citizen** (1974), were autobiographical, describing her struggle against poor living conditions and a failing marriage in London, and her experiences with the British welfare system as she raised her five children alone and studied for a degree in sociology. **Double Yoke** embodies the same energetic, candid, and ubiquitous voice of these earlier works, but it lacks their touching immediacy. Like the themes it considers, it is a mixture, the simple narrative laced with ethnographic and sociological details as well as comment on the foibles and potentials of a rapidly changing society. Even as it is propelled by the natural vitality of Emecheta's writing, it is limited by structural problems.

The story follows the quarrel-filled courtship of Ete and Nko as they try to come to terms with their different perceptions of love and marriage. They are both from small villages and both ambitious, but he is the more traditional of the two. When he first meets Nko as a teenager, he thinks,

> he would like her to be younger than he was and to be in a lower grade at school . . . ; after seeing the way his parents lived, he would like to live like that. Not

as poor, perhaps, but with a woman who would be like his mother, but with this difference; she must be well educated. A very quiet and submissive woman, a good cook, a good listener, a good worker, a good mother with a good education to match. But her education must be a little less than his own, otherwise they would start talking on the same level.

Nko, however, will not accept this inequality. She wants an education and a husband as well, but not one who will govern her behavior. She refuses to reassure him that she was a virgin when they first made love, a question which drives him to seek advice from the Reverend Professor Ikot, a spiritual and educational leader. Ikot in turn appoints himself Nko's advisor and offers her the choice of sleeping with him or losing her degree. Nko, feeling men have forced her into this position, decides to use "bottom power" to get what she wants. The results are mixed and painful, but in the end Miss Buleweo, Ete's creative writing teacher, helps him to understand his feelings and accept his responsibility as a modern African man who is able to love his woman regardless of her ability to fit traditional molds.

The novel's perspective is strongly feminist, a mature feminism sensitive to the struggle of both men and women to free themselves from double standards and hypocrisy. An older woman student pinpoints the dilemma of Nko and her friends:

> Here feminism means everything the society says is bad in women. Independence, outspokenness, immo-rality, all the ills you can think of. So even the educated ones who are classically feminist and liberated in their attitudes and behavior, will come round and say to you, "but I am gentle and not the pushful type."

While such problems are true for most women, the world Emecheta describes is specifically Nigerian and considerably different from the pre-independence Afri-ca of earlier novelists such as Chinua Achebe. Elements of village life remain, but here the local celebration depicted is a thanksgiving service and party for a young woman who has passed her hair-dressing exams. Lengthy passages discuss the unreliability of electrical power, the difficulty of crossing auto-clogged roads through a major market, or the educated Nigerian's penchant for titles. . . . Not only are the details different, but in a more basic sense so are the values. Characters like Ete and Nko don't question modernity so much as wonder how to incorporate it into their own lives.

Although **Double Yoke** gives us a view of this new Nigeria, it seems to be a view of the surface. One feels the pain of Ete and Nko, but not the underlying complexity of their experience or its deep connections to the communal experience of their country. The sociolog-ical passages too often intrude on the narrative, rather than make these connections. Emecheta can write with grace, insight, and humor, but she also uses stock descriptions and awkward language, and the ending is abrupt, leaving several incidents of consequence unde-veloped or unresolved. In the end, **Double Yoke** is engaging but uneven, its simplicity of language, structure and characterization not always a mark of clarity but a mark of a turning unexplored. (pp. 4, 14)

Linda Barrett Osborne, "Growing Pains in the New Nigeria," in Book World—The Washington Post, *September 25, 1983, pp. 4, 14.*

Abioseh Michael Porter (essay date 1988)

[*In the following essay, Porter explores* Second-Class Citizen *as a novel of personal development.*]

[It has been said by Lloyd Wellesley Brown in *Women Writers in Black Africa* (1981)] that "of all the women writers in contemporary African literature Buchi Emecheta of Nigeria has been the most sustained and vigorous voice of direct feminist protest." While there is no doubt about the validity of this statement, one thing that is questionable is the persistent attempt by some scholars (Katherine Frank [see excerpt dated 1982] and Eustace Palmer, for example) to read Emecheta's *Second Class Citizen* only within the feminist protest tradition. It would not make sense, of course, to suggest that in evaluating the works of a writer such as Emecheta (who in all of her novels deals quite seriously with the role of women in various societies), one can avoid the feminist question. It is something else, however, to imply that this is the only aspect worth examining in her oeuvre. In fact, Frank, in her essay, "The Death of the Slave Girl: African Womanhood in the Novels of Buchi Emecheta," demonstrates the danger of focusing almost exclusively on Emecheta's feminist theme by making all kinds of sweeping and erroneous generalizations about the African woman's "bondage" and the Western woman's "freedom" in Emecheta's works. We can also say that because *Second Class Citizen* has often been seen as a somewhat flawed feminist novel, critics such as Lloyd W. Brown have failed to notice the novel's full generic potential. Brown comments that "the emphasis on individual growth and self-reliance is more fully developed in *Second Class Citizen*" than in Emecheta's first novel, *In the Ditch;* however, he also consistently deplores the heroine, Adah, in those sections where she is obviously displaying naivete, immaturity, and ignorance—qualities commonly found among protagonists of the novel of personal development. One other critic does not even mention Emecheta in an essay dealing with the female bildungsroman in the Commonwealth.

It is my view, however, that if *Second Class Citizen* were read as a novel of personal development (bildungsroman), some of the seeming inconsistencies within the text would be more fully understood. Also, a look at this work as a novel dealing with a young African woman's gradual acquisition of knowledge about herself as a potential artist and about the themes of love, marriage, and the subject of student life overseas (especially in a hostile environment) will add more weight to the already popular feminist theme in the book. Finally, Emecheta's (albeit lukewarm) acceptance of Dickens—that master creator of apprenticeship novels—as a possible source of influence and the structure of *Second Class Citizen* can be seen as further reasons for reading the work as a novel of personal development.

Adah, the protagonist of *Second Class Citizen,* is portrayed as an intelligent, ambitious young girl who has to fight against considerable odds to gain an education in Lagos. As a child, she has to inject herself into the classroom of a friendly neighboring teacher before she is finally enrolled in school. This is so because her parents (especially her mother) have doubts about the wisdom of sending girls to school. Tragedy soon strikes for Adah when her relatively liberal father dies not too long after her registration at school. She then moves into a relative's home where she is kept as a ward-cum-slave. After a life of abject misery and exploitation and also by dint of hard work and proper self-motivation, Adah is able to win a scholarship in the highly competitive secondary school entrance examinations.

As a result of a first-rate performance at the school-leaving examinations, the heroine is able to procure a job as a librarian at the American consulate in Lagos—a job which easily brings her the comforts of middle-class life. During this same period, she meets Francis Obi, a young student of accounting whom she agrees to marry because she thinks he will provide some necessary protection, support and, above all, love for her in Lagos. Looking at Adah's salary as a convenient means of financial support, Francis (with his parents' approval) decides to go and continue his studies in Britain. The idea is accepted by Adah because, in part, it provides an avenue for her to fulfill her own childhood dreams of going to study in England.

Francis goes to England and is soon followed by Adah and their three children. But, from the time she arrives in Britain, Adah (like some other protagonists in African novels dealing with student life overseas) begins to notice that that country is far different from the fairyland she had been brought up to conjure. Worse, she realizes that Francis, who had always been dependent on her, has become even more so and more manipulative in England. His life-style is now characterized by gross antisocial behavior, a feeling of inferiority, laziness, and utter irresponsibility. Adah tries at first to support the family and take care of the home but it also becomes clear to her that Francis's irresponsibility is in direct proportion to his desire to create more children. When Adah confronts him with this obvious domestic problem, Francis becomes defensive and starts brutalizing her. The final clash occurs when, after the birth of their fifth child (at a time when Adah is barely twenty-two), Francis spitefully burns the manuscript of Adah's first novel. *Second Class Citizen* ends with the heroine seizing independence for herself and her children and with preparations to start a fresh life at last.

As with all works belonging to the apprenticeship novel tradition, Adah's innocence and naivete serve as generic markers in the initial sections of the story. Significantly, *Second Class Citizen* starts with a reference to Adah's "dream" of going to England. Using rhetoric that clearly emphasizes her innocence, Adah mentions how, with the help of her father, she goes through adolescence with an exaggerated and false conception of Britain. Like her father, she grows up believing that the United Kingdom is synonymous with heaven. She makes a "secret vow" quite early to herself that "she would go to this United Kingdom one day," and she wrongly assumes that her arrival in the United Kingdom "would be the pinnacle of her ambition." If there were any doubts about the differences in point of view between the novelist and her young alter ego, statements such as these should erase such doubts.

Adah's problems, however, go deeper than merely being ignorant of the culture of a foreign country. As descriptions of life with her husband show, she enters into a hastily arranged and ill-conceived marriage without the least idea about the real nature of love, marriage, and the related notions of individual liberty and mutual support. This situation is so because Adah has grown up in environments where she has been deprived of learning about or experiencing such concepts that are so vital for successful marital relationships. In fact, it is shown that up to the time Adah and Francis get married she has neither experienced any serious love relationship nor has she ever thought deeply about the implications of marriage. She sincerely believes that all it takes to have a successful marriage is to be married to a young spouse of modest means.

It is important to consider the true nature of Adah's naivete and her juvenile interpretations of love, marriage, and "life outside school" (as the narrator calls it), because without such consideration it becomes quite inviting to blame Emecheta for what looks like her endorsement of the young Adah's seemingly amoral manipulation of Francis, especially with regard to their marriage. Brown, for example, suggests that "the casualness with which Adah enters and describes her loveless marriage is the more striking when we remember her own invectives against parents who sell their daughters into loveless matches for the profit of the bride price, and even more disconcertingly, neither Adah nor Emecheta seems aware of or concerned about the apparent inconsistency." One suspects, however, that in a scene such as this one Brown is asking Emecheta to impose a point of view that would have been totally incongruous with Adah's immaturity at the time of Adah's wedding. It is only if we assume that the novelist is using the narrator to describe events as they should have been, instead of as they happened to Adah, that we will agree with the view that Adah should have been presented at the outset as being less dependent, less manipulative, and less manipulable.

At the time of their wedding, Adah is shown as a young woman who, with no home to live in, imagines that a seemingly ambitious and modest young man like Francis will ultimately provide protection, shelter and, maybe, love for her. It is also implied that it is Adah's artlessness that makes her equate happiness in marriage with youth and unhappiness in marriage with old spouses. Indeed, it is only when we consider Adah's lack of experience at the beginning that most of her subsequent shocks, disappointments, and eventual independence make sense. Adah's initial naivete explains why this otherwise bright woman has to depend upon her less astute husband and in-laws—people who rely so much on her for financial sustenance—for intellectual and other forms of guidance.

But, although this type of situation continues for the greater part of *Second Class Citizen,* it becomes obvious that by the end of the novel Adah demonstrates that in order to become both the good writer and independent human being that she hopes to become, she has to free herself from the exploitative relationship between herself and Francis, create her own identity and, in general, try to understand human relationships better. Thus, in the end, Adah asserts her independence in a way which shows that she is now ready to be in complete control of her own and her children's lives. The scene is in the family court in London and Francis, who has been charged with assaulting Adah, resorts to all kinds of mean tricks (including denying paternity of their children) in order to avoid payment of alimony. Here is how the narrator describes Adah's reaction: "Francis said they had never been married. He then asked Adah if she could produce the marriage certificate. Adah could not. She could not even produce her passport and the children's birth certificates. Francis had burnt them all. To him Adah and the children ceased to exist. Francis told her this in court in low tones and in their language. . . . Something happened to Adah then. It was like a big hope and a kind of energy charging into her, giving her so much strength even though she was physically ill with her fifth child. Then she said very loud and very clear, "*Don't worry sir. The children are mine and that is enough. I shall never let them down as long as I am alive*" (my emphasis). The finality in the tone of voice and the determined manner in which Adah decides to formally accept responsibility for the children (which had always been hers anyway) are decidedly different from her behavior in most of the earlier scenes, situations in which she was invariably portrayed as a compliant character. She obviously understands now that she was totally wrong in looking up to Francis as a source of support; she also realizes that if she wants to succeed in both her creative endeavors and in the rearing of her children she has to take full control of her life. From this moment henceforth, one cannot imagine either the narrator saying of Adah (as on previous occasions) that "she simply accepted her role as defined for her by her husband" or Adah herself relying on the unworthy Francis (or any man for that matter) as she had previously done.

As a novel of personal development, *Second Class Citizen* is quite successful in the depiction of Adah's growth from the initial stage of naivete and ignorance to her final stage of self-realization and independence. She starts confronting the well-known tests usually set for all protagonists of apprenticeship novels when upon her arrival in England which, as we know, she had always equated with heaven, she is given only a "cold welcome." But Adah's initial introduction to the British weather, landscape, and people is nothing compared to the other forms of initiation she goes through as she continues her stay in England. She has hardly overcome her first real shock over the legendary lack of warmth in England when she is faced with an even greater shock, i.e., learning to live in the hovel which Francis (now referred to as the "new Francis" by the narrator) shows her as their new home in London.

The protagonist gradually learns that coming to England is not and should not necessarily be the pinnacle of one's dream. She gets to know, through her experiences with the children's· nanny Trudy, that some British people can be just as dishonest and irresponsible as people anywhere else. Adah becomes aware of the true nature of racism when, together with Francis, she goes house hunting in London. She is also exposed to petty jealousy and envy from some of her fellow Nigerians living in London. These characters (who include the landlord and landlady of the Ashdown Street house), out of spite and malice, do all they can to bring Adah down to the inferior level they have partly allowed society to relegate them to. It is thus evident that, because of their hateful attitude toward Adah, these characters (who should otherwise have been helping the young woman) qualify for the roles of "faux-destinateurs" or detractors of the main character. As Susan Suleiman points out in an essay on the structure of the apprenticeship novel, in almost all novels of this type, there is always at least one character who, instead of helping the protagonist, will serve as an impediment to the latter's progress. In addition, there also are other structural categories— "destinateurs" and "adjuvants" on the one hand and "opposants" and "faux-destinateurs" on the other— who, as their names suggest, will also either serve as positive guides or hindrances to the protagonist.

It is also clear that Francis, Adah's husband, is her leading "opposant" or opponent. But before discussing Francis's role as Adah's chief opponent, I must refer to a basic weakness in Emecheta's writing style—a weakness which, I suspect, makes it difficult for some critics to recognize the artistic distance Emecheta creates between herself and Adah. Again, as Lloyd Brown asserts, Emecheta's criticisms of African men "are often marred by generalizations that are too shrill and transparently overstated to be altogether convincing." I will refer to two examples to back up this assertion: when Francis endorses his father's disapproval of Adah going to study in Britain, the narrator comments that "Francis was an African through and through. A much more civilized man would probably have found a better way of saying this to his wife. But to him, he was the male, and he was right to tell her what she was going to do." The narrative voice here certainly seems to be that of the adult (and presumably more mature) Adah; we therefore cannot understand why she makes such a stupid remark. In another episode, the narrator tries to convey Francis's unwillingness to support his wife but, as in the first

example, Emecheta succeeds only in conveying the impression that she endorses racial stereotypes about black men by suggesting that if only Francis were an Englishman, he would know how to treat his wife with love and respect. Surely, Emecheta knows that selfishness and inconsideration are not innate traits of African men, nor are supportive behavior and common decency toward one's spouse peculiar to English men. But, despite these and other obvious fallacies of hasty and inaccurate generalizations, it is true that Francis is Adah's leading opponent in *Second Class Citizen.*

Using descriptions that inevitably allow Francis to degenerate into a caricature, Emecheta depicts him (with good reason) as being one of the most unredeemable villains in African literature. In scenes that are too numerous to elaborate upon here, Francis is shown to be self-centered, cruel, narrow-minded, and in fact downright venal. Instead of helping Adah to develop the creative potential which she obviously has (and part of which she uses to support him), Francis only proves himself to be an obstacle on her route toward self-improvement. Because he is so selfish and greedy, Francis readily agrees with his parents' decision that Adah should remain working in Lagos to support him and his parents while he is "studying" in London. When (after outmaneuvering Francis's mother) Adah finally joins Francis in England, she quickly realizes that if Francis had been dependent, lazy, and manipulative in Lagos, he becomes even worse overseas. He is correctly shown as an irresponsible parent, spouse, and student. As was mentioned earlier, he brutalizes Adah, deliberately tries to inject a feeling of inferiority into her and, when all that fails, he tries to deprive her of what she values most—her children and her potential to become a writer.

It is also true, however, that toward the end of the story Adah fully recognizes Francis's absolute lack of love for her as well as the need for her own freedom. She is greatly assisted in this regard by another cast of characters who, in different ways, help her on the path toward the knowledge of her self-worth. Several of these characters (such as her boss at the Finchley Road library, Mrs. Konrad, and Mr. Okpara, the Nigerian who repeatedly urges Francis to smarten up) belong to the structural category often referred to as "adjuvants," i.e., those characters who guide the protagonist of a novel of personal development on the right path. But one "adjuvant" who is of particular note is Bill, the bibliophile from Canada. He is the character who not only encourages Adah to read several African and other literary works, but who also literally guides her on the path of becoming a writer. Nor surprisingly, the narrator remarks that "Bill was the first real friend [Adah] had had outside her family."

The success of *Second Class Citizen* as a literary work rests largely on Emecheta's evocation of childhood and its concomitant problems. The work is also very good in its depiction of a young woman who not only tries to survive in rather hostile environments (both domestic and elsewhere), but who does in the end acquire her personal independence. But, on balance, this Emecheta novel loses some of its strength because of the way it is inadequately structured. Emecheta demonstrates a pitfall common among writers of the bildungsroman by blatantly intruding to pour what looks like personal venom in the text. Because the narrator is nearly always prepared to explain ways in which Francis brings disappointment to Adah, we are never made to see most of the other characters in full perspective. Some characters who play very important roles (such as Bill and Mr. Okpara) are not developed as they otherwise should have been.

Notwithstanding these minor aesthetic blemishes, *Second Class Citizen* can and should be seen as a powerful example of the bildungsroman in Africa. This novel does not match Emecheta's later, more sophisticated, and more overtly feminist works such as *The Bride Price* (1976), *The Slave Girl* (1977) and especially *The Joys of Motherhood* (1982). It is also true, however, that the novelist's sustained attention to the themes of individual growth, progress, development, and the coherence of selfhood—all of which have pervaded her later writings and for which she received genuine and well-deserved critical acclaim—have their roots in this early piece. Thus, even just this reason would have been enough for me to agree at least partly with Katherine Frank's assertion that "the best place to approach Emecheta's fiction is with neither her first nor her last book, but with *Second Class Citizen.* (pp. 123-29)

> *Abioseh Michael Porter, "'Second Class Citizen': The Point of Departure for Understanding Buchi Emecheta's Major Fiction," in* The International Fiction Review, *Vol. 15, No. 2, Summer, 1988, pp. 123-29.*

FURTHER READING

Barthelemy, Anthony. "Western Time, African Lives: Time in the Novels of Buchi Emecheta." *Callaloo* 12, No. 3 (Summer 1989): 559-74.
Studies time and modes of existence in Emecheta's major works. Barthelemy states: "Torn between loyalties of race, culture, and sex, Emecheta writes about a world lost and a world becoming, a world destroyed and a world indestructible. The Africa of Emecheta's novels is a continent reeling in two times: Western diachronicity and traditional African synchronicity. And in these novels, Emecheta chronicles the personal dilemma of the African confronted and lured by Western time and Western culture."

Emenyonu, Ernest N. "Technique and Language in Buchi Emecheta's *The Bride Price, The Slave Girl,* and *The Joys of Motherhood." The Journal of Commonwealth Literature* XXIII, No. 1 (1988): 130-41.
Stylistic study of Emecheta's use of language in three novels: *The Bride Price, The Slave Girl,* and *The Joys of Motherhood.*

Katrak, Ketu H. "Womanhood/Motherhood: Variations on a Theme in Selected Novels of Buchi Emecheta." *The Journal of Commonwealth Literature* XXII, No. 1 (1987): 159-70.
Discusses Emecheta's treatment of womanhood and motherhood in her major works.

Kemp, Yakini. "Romantic Love and the Individual in Novels by Mariama Bâ, Buchi Emecheta and Bessie Head." *Obsidian II* 3, No. 3 (Winter 1988): 1-16.
Explores the novels of Emecheta, Mariama Bâ, and Bessie Head as documents of social criticism. The critic focuses on such romantic elements in the works as "the preponderance of sentiment, the inclusion of a gallant or mesmerizing male, and the melodramatic conclusion."

Nwankwo, Chimalum. "Emecheta's Social Vision: Fantasy or Reality." *Ufahamu* 17, No. 1 (1988): 35-43.
Examines feminist issues in Emecheta's writings. According to the critic, "For Emecheta the panacea for all Igbo woes arising from the battle of the sexes is love and understanding predicated on a rejection of the seamy aspects of the past. That prescription is right but eventually what counts is what individuals work out for themselves according to the peculiar demands of their private circumstances."

Updike, John. "Three Tales from Nigeria." *The New Yorker* LX, No. 10 (23 April 1984): 119-26, 129.
Favorable review of *Double Yoke.*

Olaudah Equiano

1745?-1797

(Also known as Gustavus Vassa) Beninese-born Anglo-African autobiographer and poet.

Equiano is widely regarded as the most influential English-speaking black writer of the eighteenth century. His autobiography, *The Interesting Narrative of the Life of Olaudah Equiano, or Gustavus Vassa, the African* (1789), figured prominently as a catalyst of the abolitionist movement in England during the 1790s. Today, it remains a seminal document of black history—particularly in the development of slave narrative literature—admired both for its candid portrayal of the vicissitudes of its author's life and as a lively and observant travel narrative. Sidney Kaplan wrote of Equiano's narrative: "a classic of its genre,... recounting the evolution of a bewildered, exiled slave into a statesman of his people, it surely ranks with the autobiographies of Benjamin Franklin and Frederick Douglass."

Though scholars frequently dispute the exactness of Equiano's childhood memories in his narrative, most agree that he was born around 1745 in the village of Esseka, somewhere in the interior of modern-day eastern Nigeria. It is believed that his father held tribal positions of power and prestige—positions Equiano had been destined to inherit. Kidnapped by local tribesmen when he was about eleven years old, Equiano was sold into slavery along with his sister and traded among African natives for nearly six months. When he was finally delivered to white slavers on the coast, he was loaded onto a slave ship bound for Barbados. Once there, he was purchased by a Virginia planter, who later sold him to Michael Henry Pascal, the captain of a slave-trader ship and a lieutenant in the Royal Navy. Pascal transported Equiano to England and renamed him Gustavus Vassa after the sixteenth-century Swedish king Gustavus Vasa.

During the first half of 1757 Equiano sailed in and out of various ports around the British Isles, visited Holland twice, and witnessed naval engagements off the coast of France—all the while acclimating himself to European manners and customs and learning the English language. Within a year he had served Pascal aboard a number of ships, eventually accompanying the captain to North America. Returning to England in 1759, Equiano was placed by Pascal under the tutelage of the latter's relations in London, the Misses Guerin, who taught him to read and write and educated him in Christian dogma; they eventually persuaded Pascal to have Equiano baptized. A few months later, however, Pascal set sail for the Mediterranean. Equiano was made ship steward on this voyage and gained the friendship of Pascal's personal attendant, Daniel Queen, a sailor in his forties. He taught Equiano how to read the Bible and how to dress hair; perhaps more importantly, he instilled in

young Equiano a sense of human dignity and personal freedom. Equiano later wrote of Queen: "He was like a father to me.... Indeed I almost loved him with the affection of a son." Equiano returned to England in early 1761 for a brief stay and then accompanied Pascal on an expedition that included naval engagements off the Breton coast. This was Equiano's last voyage with Pascal. Upon their return to London in late 1762, Pascal falsely accused Equiano of planning to escape and immediately sold him to Captain Doran, who, upon their arrival in Montserrat in early 1763, sold Equiano to Robert King, a Philadelphia Quaker and merchant. Equiano further improved his seamanship and education and learned the commercial arts while in service aboard King's ships, which plied the American coast to the Caribbean. A devoted Quaker, King insisted that Equiano purchase his freedom through earned money and permitted him to conduct his own trading. Finally, in 1766, Equiano, at age twenty-one, received his manumission papers for 40 pounds, but he continued to work aboard King's ships as a freeman. Equiano observed that he had been more fortunate than most American and West Indian slaves, who often suffered brutal cruelty at the hands of savage masters. Thus his dream of abolition was ignited, and, in early 1767, he left King to sail for England.

When he arrived in London, Equiano called upon the Guerin sisters, who found him employment as a hairdresser to a gentleman, Captain O'Hara. Equiano worked for O'Hara until early 1768, then hired himself out as hairdresser to Dr. Charles Irving, a scientist noted for his desalination experiments. During this period Equiano converted to Methodism, while his wanderlust for seafaring adventure grew stronger. In 1773 he accompanied explorer Constantine Phipps on a scientific expedition to the Arctic in search of the North Pole. In 1775 he rejoined Irving, this time as his partner in a short-lived venture to establish a plantation on the Mosquito Shore of Central America. Some years later, Equiano attempted to direct English philanthropist Granville Sharp's attention to the massacre of over 130 slaves aboard the HMS *Zong* off the West African coast in 1783. This disclosure prompted a storm of parliamentary debates over the slave trade. In the meantime Equiano returned to the seas and briefly stopped at Philadelphia, his "favorite old town." In 1787 he was appointed Commissary for Stores for a British expedition of freed slaves who were settling in Sierra Leone. In 1788, undaunted by the abrupt dismissal from his appointment, Equiano petitioned the Queen of England "that . . . a period may now be put to [the slaves'] misery." This event marks the conclusion of Equiano's autobiography, and relatively little is known about the rest of his life. Upon completion of *The Interesting Narrative* in 1789, he traveled throughout the British Isles, selling copies of his book and speaking out against the slave trade. In 1792 he married an Englishwoman, Susanna Cullen. He may have had children, but no conclusive evidence survives. Equiano died on 31 March 1797.

Equiano concluded his narrative by asking his readers to bear in mind that the work "was written by one who was as unwilling as unable to adorn the plainness of truth by the colouring of imagination." Yet the *Interesting Narrative* became immediately popular upon publication in 1789; within three years it ran through eight English editions, one of which included the poetry of the black American poet Phillis Wheatley, and one American edition. Early reviews were generally favorable, though some critics questioned whether Equiano himself actually wrote the whole book. *The Monthly Review* of June 1789 posited that "it is not improbable that some English writer has assisted him in the compilement, or at least the correction of his book, for it is sufficiently well written." Nonetheless, critics generally acknowledge the presence of Equiano's hand throughout his autobiography; one eighteenth-century reviewer reasoned in *The General Magazine and Impartial Review* that only Equiano could have written the *Interesting Narrative*, since it is "a round unvarnished tale . . . written with much truth and simplicity." However, some recent critics have strongly questioned the truthfulness and authenticity of Equiano's recollections of his native Africa, noting striking similarities between descriptive passages in the *Interesting Narrative* and those of contemporary European travel narratives. According to S. E. Ogude, the first chapter of Equiano's *Interesting Narrative* is "the work of a very competent collector of tales. . . . The most interesting part of his story is the least reliable as a historical document." One of the most debated issues concerning the *Interesting Narrative* involves the matters of genre and canon. Most scholars tend to view slave narrative as an almost exclusively American literary phenomenon; hence, Equiano perhaps may not deserve recognition in the "American canon." According to some commentators, since Equiano spent only a negligible amount of his life in America and identified himself with the abolitionist movement in England, he more correctly "belongs" to Anglo-African letters. Still others accord his work a place in the development of the literature of spiritual conversion. Wilfred D. Samuels noted that "the crux of his narrative is related more to his spiritual freedom than his physical freedom. . . . An eighteenth-century reader would have realized at once that Equiano's focus was his effort to make straight 'the crooked paths' of a 'sinful' life."

Equiano's *Interesting Narrative* is recognized as a classic by merit of its lasting popularity and its shaping role in the development of slave narrative literature. Critics on both sides of the Atlantic continue to consider Equiano's *Interesting Narrative* an extremely valuable account of eighteenth-century black life. Ogude noted that Equiano initiated "for the African the image of the achiever. For *Interesting Narrative,* in spite of its occasional display of spiritual humility, is perhaps the first deliberate attempt to celebrate black achievement in print."

(For further information about Equiano's life and work, see *Dictionary of Literary Biography,* Vols. 37, 50.)

PRINCIPAL WORK

The Interesting Narrative of the Life of Olaudah Equiano, or Gustavas Vassa, the African. 2 vols. (autobiography and poetry) 1789; also published as *The Life and Adventures of Olaudah Equiano; or Gustavus, the African. From an Account Written By Himself* [abridged edition], 1829; also published as *Equiano's Travels* [abridged edition], 1967; also published as *The Life of Olaudah Equiano or Gustavus Vassa, the African, 1789.* 2 vols., 1969

---

*The first edition of this work contains an appendix entitled "Miscellaneous Verses, or Reflections on the State of My Mind during My First Convictions; of the Necessity of Believing Truth, and Experiencing the Inestimable Benefits of Christianity."

The Monthly Review, London (essay date 1789)

[In the following excerpt, the anonymous critic favorably appraises "the sable author"—Equiano—and his Interesting Narrative.*]*

We entertain no doubt of the general authenticity of this very intelligent African's interesting story [***The Interesting Narrative of the Life of Olaudah Equiano, or Gustavas Vassa, the African***]; though it is not improbable that some English writer has assisted him in the compilement, or, at least, the correction of his book: for it is sufficiently well written. The narrative wears an honest face: and we have conceived a good opinion of the man, from the artless manner in which he has detailed the variety of adventures and vicissitudes which have fallen to his lot. His publication appears very seasonably, at a time when negroe-slavery is the subject of public investigation; and it seems calculated to increase the odium that hath been excited against the West-India planters, on account of the cruelties that some of them are said to have exercised on their slaves; many instances of which are here detailed.

The sable author of these volumes appears to be a very sensible man; and he is, surely, not the less worthy of credit from being a convert to Christianity. He is a Methodist; and has filled many pages, toward the end of his work, with accounts of his dreams, visions, and divine impulses; but all this, supposing him to have been under any delusive influence, only serves to convince us that he is guided by principle; and that he is not one of those poor converts who, having undergone the ceremony of baptism, have remained content with that portion, only, of the Christian Religion: instances of which are said to be almost innumerable in America, and the West-Indies; Gustavus Vassa appears to possess a very different character; and, therefore, we heartily wish success to his publication, which we are glad to see has been encouraged by a very respectable subscription. (pp. 551-52)

> *A review of "The Interesting Narrative of the Life of Olaudah Equiano, or Gustavus Vassa, the African," in* The Monthly Review, London, *Vol. LXXX, 1789, pp. 551-52.*

Paul Edwards (essay date 1971)

[Edwards is an English educator, essayist, and author. He has translated Icelandic romances and legends into English and has written on West African literature. In the following excerpt, he perceives conscious artistic efforts in Equiano's Interesting Narrative, *a work usually admired, Edwards notes, for its simple "unvarnished" style.]*

A contemporary review of Equiano's ***Interesting Narrative*** speaks of it as a 'round unvarnished tale . . . with much truth and simplicity' and indeed it is this very quality which is likely to convince the reader of the book's authenticity. Equiano's friend, Ottobah Cugoano, a Fante who worked as manservant to the court painter Cosway in London, had published in 1787 his book 'Thoughts and Sentiments on the Evil of Slavery'; this was so rhetorical in style that many readers have expressed doubts about whether it could have been written by Cugoano at all. A comparison of the surviving manuscript letters of Cugoano with the text of his book leaves no doubt that it must have been extensively revised and in many places entirely rewritten—there is some evidence pointing to Equiano himself as reviser. In the case of Equiano's ***Narrative,*** the one existing manuscript letter indicates that Equiano would have been perfectly capable of writing his book, which is less elaborate than Cugoano's both in style and argument. But a question I want to raise here is whether Equiano's style is quite as simple and 'unvarnished' as it might at first appear.

Equiano made no claim to be a literary artist, only a man telling the story of his life; and so it would be unreasonable to make close comparisons between his book and the works of the major writers of fiction and biography at that time. All the same, the situation of Equiano has a touch of both Robinson Crusoe and Gulliver: from one point of view, his is a story of economic and moral survival on the bleak rock of slavery, a study in initiative and adaptability not entirely unlike Robinson Crusoe's; and from another, it is a tale, like Gulliver's, of new perspectives gained by physical alienation, in this case of the black man in a white world. An important difference, of course, is that Crusoe, Gulliver, and their adventures, emerge largely from their creators' imaginations and have the distinctive marks of conscious creative artistry about them, whereas Equiano is apparently doing no more than trying to tell the direct truth about his own experience. At the same time, he has many of the qualities of the more interesting eighteenth century literary heroes, particularly those of Defoe, revealing himself in the narrative in a wholly convincing way and never resorting to affectation or self-display merely in an effort to sentimentalise and to conceal his true nature. At times he presents himself as entirely ignorant, confused and vulnerable, at others as boastful or self-seeking, and is always prepared to mock his own weaknesses . . . . (pp. 12-13)

[While] the author deliberately reveals himself in these instances in a comical or grotesque light, this is balanced by our recognition that self-mockery implies self-knowledge; tensions are set up in our response to the narrator, so that even his devotion to writing his journal gives to the comic a touch of the heroic. Self-revelation through self-mockery is a persistent feature of the ***Narrative***—see for instance the episode of the grampuses or the wild ride on horseback. The comic possibilities are never avoided in an effort to adopt heroic or pathetic postures, and in consequence the author's character as narrator of his own tale is seen in deeper perspective.

Still more interesting are the ambivalent feelings which Equiano displays from time to time for those who help him, particularly in chapters nine and ten, where there is considerable tension between the affection he feels for Captain Farmer, and the nagging irritation of his subordinate place in life: what becomes apparent is Equiano's need to release himself not only from his enemies, but also from his friends. This whole section offers a remarkable example of the psychology of subordination, as regret for Farmer's death mingles inextricably with the pleasure Equiano feels (and is prepared to reveal as having its boastful and complacent side) about the opportunity which Farmer's death has given him to display his own skills as a navigator and leader of men . . . .

There are a number of reversal situations like this in the narrative. For instance, the former slave who has been saved by the paternalistic attentions of others, dreams that his master's ship was 'wrecked amidst the surfs and rocks, and that I was the means of saving every one on board.' The dream comes true. As in the previous chapter, Equiano again takes over from the ship's captain, and remarks with some satisfaction on the superior conduct of the 'three black men and a Dutch creole sailor' to that of the white men. Significantly, when the Captain orders the hatches to be nailed down on the slaves in the hold, Equiano the former slave takes over from him and the hatches are not nailed down. Of course, this is not to say that the racial attitudes taken up by Equiano are simple ones for the white men of his experience form a very mixed company, and for this reason his responses to the world into which he has been thrown at the age of eleven are bound to be complex, as the episode of the death of Captain Farmer shows. But the emancipation of the slave Equiano is brought about by more than the mere payment of forty pounds sterling: he also has to act out roles of dominance through which he can shed his past.

It might be unwise to make much of the rhetorical passages in the *Narrative* in view of the doubts that have been expressed about whether these might not have been added by another hand, but there is really no good reason why Equiano, an avid reader of eighteenth-century religious tracts as well as the Bible and (bearing in mind his frequent quotations) at least the first two books of *Paradise Lost,* should not have written with some degree of expansive eloquence. But these passages are in a way less interesting than the plainer ones. One reason for thinking them to be additions by another author might be their occurrence alongside episodes described in a very much plainer language, and nowhere is this more marked than in Chapter 2, which begins in the plain style and ends with a fine rhetorical flourish. But if we look closely at this chapter it becomes clear that these two manners of writing are being used deliberately and appropriately, and that the plain style is in a sense the subtler of the two. This style occurs in its most naïve form when Equiano is describing his initial fear and perplexity at the ways of the white men:

> One white man in particular I saw, when we were permitted to be on deck, flogged so unmercifully with a large rope near the foremast, that he died in consequence of it; and they tossed him over the side

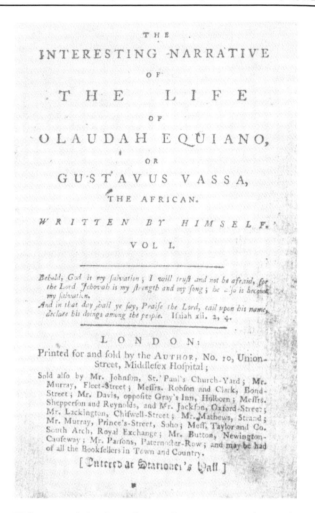

Title page of the first edition of Equiano's autobiography.

as they would have done a brute. This made me fear these people the more; and I expected nothing less than to be treated in the same manner. I could not help expressing my fears and apprehensions to some of my countrymen; I asked them if these people had no country, but lived in this hollow place? (the ship): they told me they did not, but came from a distant one. 'Then,' said I, 'how comes it in all our country we never heard of them?' They told me because they lived so very far off. I then asked where were their women? had they any like themselves? I was told they had. 'And why,' said I, 'do we not see them?' They answered, because they were left behind. I asked how the vessel could go? they told me they could not tell; but that there was cloth put upon the masts by the help of the ropes I saw, and then the vessel went on; and the white men had some spell or magic they put in the water when they liked, in order to stop the vessel. I was exceedingly amazed at this account, and really thought they were spirits. I therefore wished much to be from amongst them for I expected they would sacrifice me; but my wishes were vain—for we were so quartered that it was impossible for any of us to make our escape.

What is distinctive here is Equiano's skill in creating a dramatic language, not merely to describe in literal terms, but to recreate the very sense of the speakers' childhood simplicity and incomprehension and to distinguish this from an articulate and informed 'present'. Thus objects are described in naïve terms—the ship is 'this hollow place', the sails 'cloth put upon the mast' and the anchor becomes 'some spell or magic they put upon the water, when they liked, to stop the vessel.' Equiano does not merely write about his perplexity; his language becomes, dramatically, that of the perplexed boy he once was. This is true of the whole dialogue, in the naïve assumption behind 'how comes it in all our country we never heard of them?', the implied ignorance of the more 'knowledgeable' people who are replying to the boy's questions, and the very simplicity of the sentences in which question and response are formed, itself suggesting an innocent, untutored view of life.

Many of the best effects of the *Narrative,* in fact, are gained by this kind of dramatic or ironic simplicity— the episode of the dying man on board the ship already referred to, the account of Equiano's petty trading and the theft of the bags of fruit or of yet another reversal situation, where the Indians are the perplexed innocents and Equiano is now in the position of authority and wisdom. Notice in particular how a complex sentence structure and a literary vocabulary are suddenly and dramatically discarded for particular effect. Equiano is describing the conduct of the drunken Indian Governor who,

> getting quite drunk, grew very unruly and struck one of our most friendly chiefs, who was our nearest neighbour, and also took his gold-laced hat from him. At this a great commotion took place, and the Doctor interfered to make peace as we could all understand one another, but to no purpose; and at last they became so outrageous that the Doctor, fearing he might get into trouble, left the house and made the best of his way to the nearest wood, leaving me to do as well as I could among them. I was so enraged with the Governor that I could have wished to have seen him tied fast to a tree and flogged for his behaviour, but I had not people enough to cope with his party. I therefore thought of a strategem to appease the riot. Recollecting a passage I had read in the life of Columbus when he was amongst the Indians in Mexico or Peru, where on some occasion he frightened them by telling them of certain events in the heavens, I had recourse to the same expedient, and it succeeded beyond my most sanguine expectations. When I had formed my determination I went in the midst of them, and, taking hold of the Governor, I pointed up to the heavens. I menaced him and the rest: I told them God lived there, and that he was angry with them, and they must not quarrel so; that they were all brothers, and if they did not leave off and go away quietly, I would take the book (pointing to the Bible), read, and *tell* God to make them dead. This was something like magic. The clamour immediately ceased and I gave them some rum and a few other things, after which they went away peaceably, and the Governor afterwards gave our neighbour, who was Called Captain Plasmyah, his hat again. When the Doctor returned he was exceedingly glad at my success in thus getting rid of our troublesome guests.

It is worth noting that up to this point, the Indians have been established as at least moderately noble savages, with many of the virtues of Equiano's 'Eboes' of the opening chapters, and capable of being compared advantageously to the Europeans. But it is at this moment that the drunken Indian Governor appears to disrupt the happy proceedings, the situation being saved by the trickery of the original white adventurer Columbus, the doctrines of European Christianity, and the sharp wit of an African ex-slave, who adds, characteristically, a note on Dr. Irving's reliance on him to settle the situation. The effects gained by Equiano in his narrative are often, it seems to me, conscious artistic effects; they may at times be unconscious; but one thing must be clear, that his simplicities are really not quite so simple. (pp. 15-19)

> *Paul Edwards, "Equiano's Round Unvar-nished Tale," in* African Literature Today, *No. 5, 1971, pp. 12-20.*

Houston A. Baker, Jr. (essay date 1980)

[*Baker is an American educator, editor, critic, and poet. His works, which focus on black culture and the aesthetics of the black literary tradition, include* Long Black Song: Essays in Black American Literature and Culture *(1972),* Singers at Daybreak: Studies in Black American Literature *(1974), and* Modernism and the Harlem Renaissance *(1987). In the following excerpt, he argues that Equiano's narrative not only promotes humanitarian values but also provides "an enthralling narration of terms for order that subsequent African writers in America have adopted."*]

The Africanness, the Christian import, and the creative self-consciousness that combine to form a discernible pattern in Wheatley's canon are more than matched in the work of Gustavus Vassa. To judge by the time span between Hammon's "An Evening Thought" and *The Life of Olaudah Equiano,* early black American literature developed with amazing rapidity, leaving behind the devout otherworldliness of its first published author and in just thirty years bringing forth an assured, at times brilliant, treatment of the secular problems of Africans in an alien world. Gustavus Vassa's narrative begins with a description of Essaka, a village in Benin (now Nigeria), where the author was born in 1745. Life in the village, where all men and women are chaste and free, serves as a referent for the author throughout his account. Against Essaka's seemly backdrop are set the brutality of the European slave trade, the horrors of West Indian slavery, the changing fortunes of the Seven Years' War between England and France, the cunning mechanics of the eighteenth-century industrial revolution, and the various competing theologies of a world in transition. As one might gather from the foregoing, the narrator sets forth myriad experiences, but he always remains the "African" specified by the work's title, one upon whom "all the adversity and variety of fortune... served only to rivet and record" the manner and customs of his homeland.

It is not Vassa's love of country alone that provided a unifying cast for the work. There is a subtlety in the *Life* that defies the single view. For it contains certain collocations of words, or "foregroundings," that do not easily yield their meanings to the casual reader. The Russian formalists were the first to introduce the concept of "foregrounding" to describe an instance in literary works where an unusual grouping of words calls attention to itself. In more recent years, Geoffrey Leech has employed the concept in interpreting Dylan Thomas and has also used the phrase, "cohesion of foregrounding," to describe the repetition of certain foregroundings within a single text. What I am suggesting in the case of Vassa is that foregroundings and their cohesion provide a certain force of meaning in the narrative.

The deeper semantic aspects of the book are seen in the narrator's progressive ease in the company of his "new" countrymen (the British), his omnipresent urge to enjoy the rights and privileges of a free man, his growing comprehension of the industrial revolution, and his expanding awareness of the true path to Christian salvation. What one has is a sophisticated developmental autobiography. The only way to take it as the episodic rambling of an exotic primitive is to fail to provide an adequate code to contain the work's elusive possibilities. For only at a very primitive level of literary understanding could one interpret Vassa's assertions of the "unbounded credulity and superstition" of his fellow Essakans and his descriptions of the indigenous purity of Africa's interior as testimony from the school of noble savagery.

A consideration of one of the *Life's* more striking foregroundings lends support to a claim for the work as a carefully crafted aesthetic text. Vassa says of his long journey with his kidnapers to the west coast of Africa: "I saw no mechanics whatever in all the way . . . . The chief employment in all these countries was agriculture, and both the males and females, as with us, were brought up to it, and trained in the arts of war." His first encounter with machine culture is aboard the *African Snow,* the slave ship that carried him to the West Indies. On board, he is amazed by the quadrant and by all other aspects of navigation. But in one of those vivid verbal structures so prevalent in the *Life,* Vassa—who is almost the only black on a Virginia plantation—captures one of the most significant implications of the European industrial revolution:

> I was one day sent for to his [the master's] dwelling house to fan him; when I came into the room where he was I was very much affrighted at some things I saw, and the more so as I had seen a black woman slave as I came through the house, who was cooking the dinner, and the poor creature was cruelly loaded with various kinds of iron machines; she had one particularly on her head, which locked her mouth so fast that she could scarcely speak and could not eat or drink. I was astonished and shocked at this contrivance, which I afterwards learned was called the iron muzzle.

Not only has he arrived in a land moving toward a new mechanical order (one in which the African is muzzled and cut off from nourishment), but also he has come face to face with a culture where objects of manufacture are put to cruel and inhumane use.

These conclusions are hinted in the first chapter of the *Life* when the author notes that the Africans' desire for products of industry (e.g., firearms) often occasioned intertribal wars designed to procure slaves as objects of barter in the transatlantic slave trade. The narrator's final response, however, is not to advocate casting out technology. Instead, he urges the conversion of technology to a more salutary end. Near the conclusion of his narrative, he asserts that various articles of "usefulness" are the "pleasing substitutes for the *torturing thumbscrew,* and the *galling chain."* Those who will welcome such a shift are none other than British industrialists. It is they who recognize the desirability of ending the slave trade and engaging Africa as a source of raw materials and a market for commerce.

From a bemused, frightened child overwhelmed by machines, the narrator moves to a stance as a prophet for a new commercial-industrial utopia in which England and Africa play complementary roles. Of course, such a projection and the way in which it is reached in the *Life* do not simply manifest Vassa's skill at foregrounding. They also reveal a stunning awareness of eighteenth-century economic and political currents. British industrialists did, finally, exert a large influence in the abolition of the slave trade, and they certainly had very fixed notions about the "civilizing" effects of commerce on the peoples of the world.

There are other unusual groupings of words and episodes that illustrate the depth and complexity of the *Life.* They surround the narrator's experiences with the sea, mercantilism, and religion as ordering constructs in a variegated existence. By careful juxtapositions (e.g., Christian baptism and a nearly fatal plunge into the Thames), seemingly naive disclaimers, and an artful blend of simple narration and forceful exposition, Vassa shows that it is possible for an African to become a complete, gentle Christian and a learned abolitionist. For if there is a public voice in the *Life,* it is one that ceaselessly condemns the abuses of slavery and seeks to justify the equality of Africans, while revealing, at the same instant, the author's own personal sense of salvation and freedom in a manifold world. In sum, the work amply satisfies the expectations set forth by its demurring author: "If, then, the following narrative does not appear sufficiently interesting to engage general attention, let my motive be some excuse for its publication . . . . If it affords any satisfaction to my numerous friends, at whose request it has been written, or in the smallest degree promotes the interest of humanity, the ends for which it was undertaken will be fully attained, and every wish of my heart gratified." Not only did Vassa promote the interests of humanity, but he also provided an enthralling narration of terms for order that subsequent African writers in America have adopted.

His adamant call for black liberation and his repeated speculations that Africans are the chosen people of the Lord combine to give the *Life* a peculiarly modern tenor. It stands well in a line of accomplished successors. (pp. 15-18)

> Houston A. Baker, Jr., "Terms for Order: Acculturation, Meaning, and the Early Record of the Journey," in his The Journey Back: Issues in Black Literature and Criticism, *The University of Chicago Press, 1980, pp. 1-26.*

S. E. Ogude (essay date 1982)

[*In the following excerpt, Ogude posits that Equiano's* Interesting Narrative *is largely fictional, claiming that Equiano borrowed heavily from European travel literature and African legend.*]

There is a strong tendency to ignore the literary quality of Olaudah Equiano's *Interesting Narrative,* but as I shall demonstrate, the book has definite literary pretensions. For one thing Equiano's *Interesting Narrative* is presented in a popular eighteenth century literary form: the voyage. In the second place, Equiano's narrative is to a large extent fictional. Let us observe here that Equiano the narrator and Equiano the commentator are two different characters who perform different roles in the overall conception of the book. The narrator tends to be fictional in his accounts, while the commentator shows evidence of the historical man. The fictional content of Equiano's narrative may be illustrated from the early part of the *Interesting Narrative.*

The first chapter of Equiano's *Narrative* is the work of a very competent collector of tales. It fuses together two disparate sets of experience: the wide range of tales about Africa that were generally retailed in travel literature and the body of legends about Africa that naturally developed among the African slaves. It is also natural that these legends should romanticize Africa and, for his immediate purposes, Equiano definitely had cause to paint a brighter picture of what was to be called the Dark Continent.

Equiano's account of his early life cannot bear close scrutiny and it is to his credit that genuine and serious attempts have been made to locate his exact home in the Ibo country. If he were kidnapped at a little over ten in 1755, it is unlikely that he would remember so much about his home at the age of 45. If we accept his surname as an anglicized version of some Ibo name, his first name, however, is not immediately recognizably Ibo. I am not myself clear why Equiano's people refer to some mahogany-colored people as "Oye Eboe," an expression that Equiano interprets as "red men living at a distance." It is possible, of course, that Essaka and Timnah, the only two African towns specifically mentioned in the *Interesting Narrative,* may have disappeared from the face of the earth. The sort of analysis in which G. I. Jones indulges in his "Olaudah Equiano of

the Niger Ibo" [see Further Reading] is based on the assumption that Equiano's account is historically and ethnographically reliable. Equiano's achievement, however, lies in his talent as a compelling narrator rather than in the authenticity of his narrative. The most interesting part of his story is the least reliable as a historical document.

For Equiano's story of his early life in Africa is an imaginative reorganization of a wide variety of tales about Africa from an equally wide range of sources. We should always bear in mind that Equiano was only ten or so when he was captured and that he was recollecting his early experience some thirty years later. Even with the best of memory there were bound to be real problems. The tenderness of his age would naturally limit the range of his experience, but Equiano's narrative suggests that he was well acquainted with every aspect of his society. The only obvious conclusion is that in his narrative, Equiano relied less on the memory of his experience and more on other sources. I would further suggest that these sources include various published accounts of travels on the Guinea Coast, accounts of fellow slaves, and, not least, Equiano's considerable narrative power that successfully blended these divergent sources into one imaginative reconstruction of what his African society might have been in the middle of the eighteenth century.

There is evidence to show that Equiano was conversant with a wide range of travel literature and that he drew heavily on these often lopsided views of Africa. A classic case is Equiano's attempt to define Guinea. He must have drawn his information from a number of sources. One obvious source is William Snelgrave's *A New Account of Some Parts of Guinea and the Slave Trade* (1734): "Guinea extends from Cape de Verde to Angola, the River Kongo being the farthest place where the English carry-on their trade." Another example from Snelgrave occurs in a general definition that combines a number of other definitions: "Guinea or Ghinney is a large extent of coast, reaching from River Sanaga to Cape Lope Gonsalvo." Equiano's definition:

> That part of Africa known by the name of Guinea to which the trade for slaves is carried on extends along the coast above 3,400 miles, from the Senegal to Angola, and includes a variety of kingdoms.

In spite of his attempt to be precise, Equiano's definition definitely derives from the same source as the two already given. Indeed, as the passage piles on information, we discover that Equiano had telescoped a number of "facts" that were available in the travel literature of the eighteenth century. For instance, when he characterized the kingdom of Benin as "The most considerable... both as to extent and wealth, the richness and cultivation of the soil, the power of its king and the number and warlike disposition of the inhabitants," he was obviously using non-African sources. He continues:

> It is situated nearly under the Line and extends along the coast about 170 miles, but runs back into the interior part of Africa to a distance hitherto I believe,

unexplored by any traveller; and seems only terminated at length by the Empire of Abyssinia, near 1500 miles from its beginning.

First, let us compare the above vaguely worded (in spite of the deceptive attempt to play with figures) description of the limits of Benin with Thomas Astley's abstract from the literature of early eighteenth century: "The kingdom of Benin, Binnin, Binni or Benni (for so it is variously written by authors) is a country whose bounds are not well-known travellers, or defined by geographers."

After examining various configurations of the exact position of Benin in relation to other kingdoms, including "the countries of Awerri [Warri] and Kalbari or Kallabar," Astley concludes: "We cannot pretend to vouch, much less can we ascertain its due dimension" and then adds significantly, "further than that it may extend along the coast, from Cape Lagoa, or Lagos, to Rio Forcados about an hundred or sixty, or an hundred and seventy miles." The point is not that Equiano copied Astley who was himself a mere collector of other people's accounts; the point is that Equiano's geography is directly derived from eighteenth century geography of Africa as it was then conceived by European writers. As a rule, Astley either used his sources directly or used material that occurs in several authors and, therefore, commands a degree of relative accuracy. Indeed, Equiano's assertions about the military strength of the king of Benin appear to derive originally from Dapper whom Astley credits with the story that "the king of Benin is reported able to raise in one day, twenty thousand men, and in time of need, eighty or an hundred thousand: so that he is formidable to all his neighbours...."

Even in those areas where we expect Equiano's account to have an authentic stamp of originality, we discover, much to our disappointment, that his reliance on European sources is extensive. So much so that we begin to suspect that Equiano's life in his beautiful village named Essaka is quintessentially inspired by travel literature. As I shall demonstrate, much of what is authentic in *Interesting Narrative* has behind it the authority of travel literature. Whenever he departs from this primary source, Equiano's attempt to reconstruct his early experience from memory almost ends in disaster. We realize of course that he was considerably hampered in his effort by the necessity to adapt Ibo sounds to English sound pattern and then represent them in English orthography. The result of Equiano's experience has been nearly disastrous to his claim to a reliable memory, producing such minor riddles as *Olaudah, Timnah,* and *Essaka.* I am aware that Chinua Achebe has argued that Equiano was from "Isieke in Ihiala division" and has explained in a footnote:

> There is more than a mere hunch in my choice of Isieke (pronounced Iseke) for Equiano's Essaka. If one puts together the evidence of Igbo words in Equiano's book (including Equiano's name itself); the dialect suggested by the words; the house-building technique etc. described by Equiano, one would be led inevitably, I think, to Isieke.

The matter, however, is not as simple as that. In spite of his appeal to his memory, or his slender recollection, Equiano was conscious of his sources of information. His extraordinary personality has misled many to accept his narrative at its face value. Yet it is clear from his comment on the Igbo community of Essaka that he knew a lot more than was credibly probably, knowing fully well that traditional African societies were organized on a system of age groups with their respective taboos. His comments on the organization of his village society, on such taboo subjects as adultery and what Astley referred to as "the monthly disorder of women" are incompatible with his tender age. Few European travellers and writers of travel books failed to comment on the severity with which adultery was punished in African societies. It is part of the myth of the libidinous nature of the African character and his destructive jealousy so cruelly dramatized in Shakespeare's *Othello.* Thus we learn that even among the Hottentots, adultery "is always punished with death." Astley, citing both Jobson and Barbot, writes:

> In case of adultery, both the offenders ... are sold out of the country without redemption; ... the Negroes are very jealous; and if they can surprise their wives in any act of infidelity, the husband will kill the adulterer, and repudiate the wife....

We may profitably compare the above quotations with Equiano's version:

> Adultery, however, was sometimes punished with slavery or death, a punishment which I believe is inflicted on it throughout most of the nations of Africa, so sacred among them is the honour of the marriage bed and so jealous are they of the fidelity of their wives....

Almost all the information in the above passage is derived from the accounts of the travellers. Indeed, Equiano's extension of his comments "to most of the nations of Africa" is a veiled acknowledgement of his debt to these Europeans who delighted in retailing salacious information about Africa.

It comes as a shock to discover that Equiano's proud assertions about the industry of his people, their cleanliness, their humanity, and their religious institutions were probably derived from these foreign sources. His observations on certain African traditional beliefs and practice and their similarity to Jewish tradition would, at first, appear original. Again, much of the observation may have been derived from contemporary accounts of travellers. Take the following passage from Equiano, for instance:

> I have before remarked that the natives of this part of Africa are extremely cleanly. This necessary habit of decency was with us a part of religion, and therefore we had many purifications and washings; indeed almost as many and used on the same occasions, if my recollection does not fail me, as the Jews. Those that touched the dead at any time were obliged to wash and purify themselves before they could enter a dwelling house. Every woman too, at certain times,

was forbidden to come into a dwelling-house or touch any person or anything we ate.

Now compare with the above passage, the following from Astley, taking note of the context of both passages:

the Whidah Negroes seem to have borrowed from the Jews the law of separation from their wives at certain seasons. On these occasions the women are obliged, on pain of death, to quit the husbands or parents' house as soon as they find themselves ill, and to forsake all correspondence with any person as long as their disorder continues. According to the number of women in a family, there is one or several houses at the end of the inclosure, where they remain under the care of some old women who tend them, and take care to wash and purify them before they return to their families.

Thus where it is verifiable, the evidence presented by Equiano almost always leads to a European source. The conclusive evidence of nearly total dependence on other sources for what he claimed to be his personal experience strengthens, in a curious way, the personality of Equiano. It also gives *Interesting Narrative* a literary quality that it shares with the fiction of Defoe and Swift.

Equiano's talent as a narrator and his ability to impose his personality on a whole range of experiences and dominate every bit of them with confidence and conviction is evident throughout *Interesting Narrative.* In Equiano, credibility becomes an aspect of character rather than of the tale. He tells every story from his standpoint and always with considerable advantage to himself. If Constantine Phipps (Lord Mulgrave) had not published the account of his voyage to the North Pole, we would have had to conclude from Equiano's account of that nearly disastrous voyage that Equiano played a much more important part than that of the personal servant of a scientist. Indeed, from the way Equiano introduced the subject of the voyage in his *Interesting Narrative,* one would think that he was one of the principal actors in the undertaking:

Thus I went on [purifying the briny element and making it fresh] till May 1773, when I was roused by the sound of fame to seek new adventures, and find, towards the North Pole what our Creator never intended we should, a passage to India.

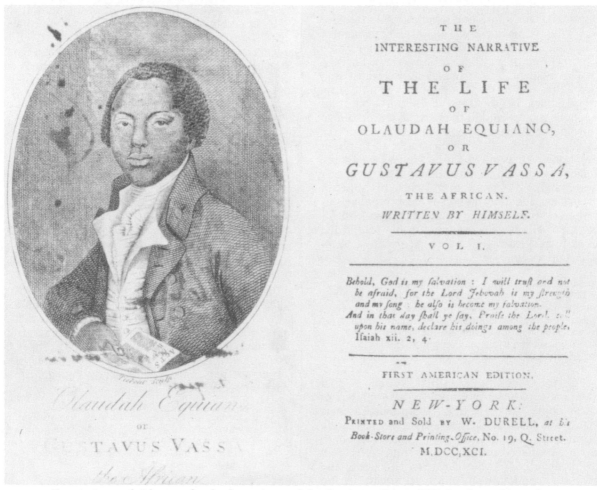

Frontispiece and title page for the first volume of the American edition of Equiano's autobiography.

It is easy to demonstrate that the ensuing narrative could have been different if Lord Mulgrave never published his *Voyage Towards the North Pole.* Similarly, much of the last section of the *Interesting Narrative* was not particularly original and, although suggestions for alternative commodities to slaves in the trade between England and Africa were common, Equiano's ideas appear closest to those of Clarkson in *The Impolicy of the African Slave Trade.*

Yet in spite of these apparently alarming revelations, the integrity of Equiano's primary purpose remains unimpaired. We might almost say that it was essential for the realization of his purpose, that Equiano did what he did: create for the African the image of the achiever. For *Interesting Narrative,* in spite of its occasional display of spiritual humility, is perhaps the first deliberate attempt to celebrate black achievement in print. Equiano must have had at the back of his mind the ideas of Hume, later eminently reechoed by Thomas Jefferson, about the inferiority of the black race. He refutes these ideas, first by creating the fiction of beautiful Essaka and second by realizing in himself the portrait of the supreme black achiever. He elevates his meanest act to the highest level of heroism. He definitely was not a prince, but he was high born and was destined to receive the highest title in his society. He was a born man of action and was, if we believe him, definitely acquainted with all the horrors of war before he was ten. Equiano expects us to suspend our disbelief as we watch him watching a battle at the village common from a tree top. He has a charmed life. Nothing really hurts him, not even poisonous snakes, and at the battle front in foreign lands and in naval engagements far away from the beautiful plains of Essaka, the bullets were to fly about him without as much as grazing him. He was even more successful as a sailor who in moments of extreme danger always took charge of the situation when his superior white officers had lost their nerve. What is more he saw his achievement as a divine gift that he held in trust for his fellow men. His own comments on his role in the Bahamas shipwreck sufficiently underscore his sense of his own importance:

> I could not help thinking, that if any of these people had been lost God would charge me with their lives, which perhaps was one cause of my labouring so hard for their preservation, and indeed every one of them afterwards seemed so sensible of the service I had rendered them, and while we were on the key I was a kind of chieftain amongst them.

Always, Equiano sees and presents himself as first among men, be they black or white. Even in matters of religion he occupied the pride of place among all comers and so great was his zeal for the Christian life that an Indian prince on board the ship bound for South America was compelled to ask: "How comes it that all the white men on board who can read and write, and observe the sun, and know all things, yet swear, lie, and get drunk, only excepting yourself?" It is true that the Indian, wisely or foolishly, chose to go to hell with the white men, but Equiano has made his point; that is what

really matters. Above all, Equiano is the great achiever who bought his own liberty and, in spite of all odds, maintained a respectable position in a hostile world.

Because of the insistent note of self-dramatization and self-approval in the characterization of the central actor-character of the *Interesting Narrative* we tend to forget that the book is built on a solid fictional base. Indeed, it follows the traditions of the travelogue and the adventure tale that were popular throughout the eighteenth century. In many respects Equiano emerges as a typical Defoe character whose strength lies in his wide experience as a traveller and his survival instincts even in the most hopeless situation. Equiano was, by any standard, a well-traveled man. His experience spans the continents of Africa, America, Europe, and part of Asia. *Interesting Narrative* belongs in some respects to the tradition of the *voyage imaginaire* and shares some of the characteristic traits of the tradition. Equiano has and shows all the weaknesses of great travellers—a love of exaggeration, a respect for lies about distant places, and an open display of prejudice in order to conceal ignorance. The voyage form was therefore a splendid vehicle for the propagation of the new ideas about Africa. Always Equiano was aware of his self-imposed duty of giving Africa a new image among Europeans and thus constantly opposed black values to European ideals. He seems to have seen himself as a typical Ibo man and the Ibo people as typical Africans. His record of achievement is thus the record of black achievement. According to Equiano the Ibo people combine hardiness, intelligence, zeal, and integrity with perfection of form and physical fitness. In his naive idealization of his people, and in utter disregard for the European idea of the Ibo, Equiano proudly declares: "Deformity is indeed unknown amongst us.... Numbers of the natives of Eboe now in London might be brought in support of this assertion, for in regard to complexion, ideas of beauty are wholly relative." This history is worse than false, for Equiano definitely knew that only physically healthy blacks were ever allowed to cross the Atlantic. Besides, the idea that blacks were generally physically perfect was fairly commonplace. It was part of the noble savage cult that endowed the Indian, the African, and later the Polynesian with remarkable physical vitality and perfection of parts; hence black characters in English and French fiction were generally "well proportioned," for it was believed that physical and moral degeneration was a concomitant of civilization. James Grainger, in his *Essay on the More Common West India Diseases,* observed that black women rarely had deformed children and offered his medical opinion:

> Deformity in children would seem to be owing to swathing the infants too tight, and by the preposterous use of stays and straight clothing—Negro children are not thus encombered; and never deformed except by accidents....

Grainger's explanation has all the marks of primitivistic adoration of the natural man with his dark heroic frame. It is a different matter when ethnic groups are described.

Bryan Edwards, whose account of the various ethnic groups of Africa in British West Indies is generally accurate, describes the Ibos as cowardly. When James Grainger, in *The Sugar Cane* describes the various ethnic groups of African slaves in the West Indies, the portrait of the Ibos that emerges is far from heroic. The Ibos are not like the Kormantyns who formed the cream of the Maroons and the dread of every West Indian Planter. These must not be bought, because they are "of breed too generous for the servile field," the slaves from the Guinea coast were chronic suicides, and those from Cape Coast were stubborn. Then he comments on the ravages leashed on the plantations by cane rats and advises the planter to cherish the cat and spare the snake for obvious reasons. Then he adds: "Thy foes, the teeth-filled Ibbos also love/Nor thou their wayward appetite restrain." His explanatory note on the above lines adds an entirely new angle to the Ibo image:

> Teethfil'd Ibbos or Ebbos, as they are more common-ly called are a numerous nation. Many of them have their teeth filed and are blackened in an extra-ordinary manner. They make good slaves when bought young, but are in general foul feeders.

Dr. James Grainger had varied medical experience, having served as an army surgeon before establishing a private practice in London. He then went to St. Kitts in 1759 as a physician. He had links with the literary circle of London and was well known to Samuel Johnson, Dr. Thomas Percy, and the landscape enthusiast and poet William Shenstone. Grainger's ode on solitude had appeared in 1755, and, according to Boswell, Johnson had characterized the first stanza of the poem as "very noble." Grainger showed evidence of great learning in *The Sugar Cane*, which combines considerable literary quality with fairly reliable information not only on sugar cane culture and the white planter, but also on the ethnography of the slave population in the West Indies. Indeed, his *Essay on the More Common West India Diseases* contained "hints on the management of ne-groes." His note on the Ibos here is also far from flattering and, although it was obviously erroneous, it would appear to have been the general opinion about the Ibos in the West Indies and to a large extent agrees with his explanatory note:

> In Ibbo country, the women chiefly work; they therefore are to be preferred to the men of the same country at a Negro sale; And yet there is a great risk in buying women; for from their scantiness of clothing in their country, not to mention other reasons, they often labour under incurable obstruc-tions of the menses, whence proceed barrenness and many disorders.

Grainger's pseudomedical explanation is sheer fiction, but it is hardly worse than Equiano's romanticized recollections of his early childhood. To judge by his own account, Equiano's Africa is a veritable paradise where man is at one with man and nature rewards with prodigious yield the labor of man. Indeed the slave raider merely underscores the essential goodness of this natural society where the harshest words of reproach are "may you rot" or "may you swell" or "may a beast take you." That was part of Equiano's deliberate purpose, though unstated, of reversing the contemporary Europe-an image of Africa as a land of barbarous hordes of savages, the type of image which slave traders and plantation owners paraded in the popular press. In the process, Equiano had to romanticize a past that he never knew, and it is to the credit of his creative commonsense that not only his contemporaries, but even modern commentators have willingly accepted his portrait of his "Igbo heritage" as faithfully if somewhat nostalgically presented. The fact, of course, is that the first chapter of Equiano's book is a synthesis of aspects of a wide range of African societies as represented in travel literature as well as in romantic tales about Africa that sustained the spirit of the slaves in their forced and unbearably harsh exile. (pp. 31-40)

> *S. E. Ogude, "Facts into Fiction: Equiano's Narrative Reconsidered," in* Research in African Literatures, *Vol. 13, No. 1, Spring, 1982, pp. 31-43.*

Wilfred D. Samuels (essay date 1983)

[*Samuels is a Costa Rican-born American educator, literary critic, and editor whose work includes* Five Afro-Carribean Voices in American Culture, 1917-1929 *(1979). In the following excerpt, he examines Equiano's creation of a "prototypical Black hero" in the* Interesting Narrative.]

For the most part, the recent literature concerning Black Slave narrative/autobiographical texts continues to overlook the significant role that Olaudah Equiano and his narrative, *The Interesting Narrative of the Life of Olaudah Equiano, or Gustavus Vassa, The African, Writ-ten by Himself* (1789), play in the development of the Black literary tradition. Although several historians have identified his seminal role as an eighteenth century abolitionist, and although a few literary scholars have suggested the central place his narrative should occupy among the works published by the cadre of Black writers who were in the vanguard, most omit this luminary writer of Black life or fail to explore the relation of his work to modern Black fiction. Yet, it is impossible not to agree with Arna Bontemps that Equiano's narrative is perhaps "the first truly notable book in the genre." In fact, it is not in any way farfetched to perceive it as the mold from which successive narratives were cast, and even more importantly to see it as an important prototype of the Black novel. This is particularly true when one takes into consideration the fact that Olaudah Equiano was one of the first Black writers to record the African *and* the diaspora experiences of slavery, which he knew first-hand while a slave in Africa, the Carib-bean, the North American Colonies, and England. It becomes even more convincing when one takes careful assessment of the thematics and characterizations of the narrative, for like the modern hero in Black fictions, Equiano remains, above all in his narrative, an exile in a manner that differs very little from Bigger Thomas in

Wright's *Native Son* (1940), Ellison's protagonist in *Invisible Man* (1952), Milkman Dead in Morrison's *Song of Solomon* (1978), or Okonkwo in Chinua Achebe's *Things Fall Apart* (1959). Suffering for the most part from a sense of socio-cultural liminality and ontological void, he is engulfed throughout his work with a sense of nothingness which results, to a degree, either from circumstances over which he has no control, or from the conscious decisions which he makes. In his response to life, Equiano epitomizes the Black fictional character whose research is for wholeness and meaning in a world that often does not offer incorporation or fulfillment.

An Igbo born in what is perhaps now eastern Nigeria, Equiano was kidnapped, along with his sister, into slavery at the age of eleven. In his narrative, he recapitulates his severance from his African homeland, the horror of the journey through the "Middle Passages," and his multifarious experiences as a slave in Barbados, Virginia, Philadelphia, and England, his adopted home. Equiano begins his twelve-chapter, two-volume work with an introduction to the manners and customs of his Essakan community, which includes descriptions of the social, political, and economic systems of eighteenth century traditional Igboan life. He seems careful to emphasize his belief that though his culture was built on simple manners and few luxuries, and though it was one in which slavery was practiced and polygamy was a way of life, it was judicious. Adultery was condemned, and slaves were often considered members of the community.

Because Equiano's announced purpose is to promote the abolitionist's cause, he uses both volumes to call the attention of his audience to the real nature of slavery. After carefully delineating, with the most vivid images possible, the perilous path traveled by the slave vessels, the decadent behavior of the slavers, the effort of those taken to commit suicide by jumping overboard, the galling of chains, and excruciating cries of the women and the dying, Equiano turns his attention to what to him was the most unpardonable aspect of the experience: the separation of family members. He declares:

> O ye nominal Christans! might not an African ask you—Learned you this from your God, who says unto you, Do unto all men as you would men should do unto you? Must every tender feeling be likewise sacrificed to your avarice? . . . Why are parents to lose their children, brother their sisters, or husbands their wives? Surely, this is a new refinement in cruelty, which, while it has no advantage to atone for it, thus aggravate distress and adds fresh horrors even to the wretchedness of slavery.

Although the frightening experiences that he either witnessed or experienced directly during ten years of enslavement led him to wish for his death on several occasions, Equiano succeeded, through his own business ventures, shrewdness, and perseverance, to amass the necessary amount to purchase his freedom. Never returning to Africa, although he traveled as commissary of provisions in the first party of emigrants who set out

to settle Sierra Leone, Equiano spent the remainder of his life in England working to abolish slavery.

The polemical nature of his narrative obscures the fact that the then forty-four-year-old Igboan wanted to do more than graphically describe the horrors and atrocities of slavery. In the spirit of his high maritime adventures which took him half way around the world and on an expedition to the Arctic, Equiano seems to venture beyond the limits of the extant slave narratives into the unchartered waters of the developmental stages of this genre. Consequently, in the process of recreating his historical self, Equiano succeeds in creating a narrative voice and a fictional self that emerge at the end of the second volume to form a prototypical Black hero and introduce themes and styles that continue to dominate the Black literary tradition. His practice of combining and ordering words (a form of masking) to pull out of them a wide variety of meaning allows us to see in the introduction to Chapter Two yet another and perhaps more important reason for writing his narrative, for here Equiano confesses that he still looks "back with pleasure on the first scenes of (his) life, though that pleasure has been for the most part mingled with sorrows."

Equiano, who had explained earlier that art in his community focused on "some interesting scene of life," carefully designs episodic chapters for his narrative, and he uses them as vehicles to transport him retrospectively to the earliest stages of his life, the formative years which were spent in Africa, to better understand the development, discovery, and creation of an identity which for him remained salient and which is to be found in his identification of himself as THE AFRICAN. The narrative, then, allows him to vicariously travel the labyrinthian path that had led him from his *axis mundi* and had left him, the son of a village elder, a slave—an identity which stood in direct contrast to his perception of himself. Incorporated into his pronouncements, then, is the crux of the conflicts which result from his idealized African self, which Equiano accepts as his legacy, and the harsh reality that, having served as a slave in a foreign culture, he had not been able to fully realize this self. Thus, Equiano is not merely concerned with historical truth or abolitionist propaganda: him he is fundamentally interested in his private experiences which he presents through his creation of a single self. This results more in autobiography than in history, and it allows us to look at "the self as the container of meaning."

What can be perceived as Equiano's interest in presenting a single self is firmly embedded in the frontispiece with which he begins the narrative. An engraved portrait, the frontispiece features an individual who, precisionly adorned in both frock and waist coats, ruffled shirt, and cravat, bears the appearance of eighteenth century gentility: he presents an image of an individual of excellent character, sincerity, humility, integrity, and confidence. Although this dress might cause one to associate him with the elegantly dressed and indulgently treated Black slave-servant of the likes of Dr. Johnson's Francis, Equiano's self-portraiture throughout the narrative reveals that the self which he attempts to depict in the frontispiece must not be divorced from the name that appears beneath it: OLAUDAH EQUIANO, THE AFRICAN. Although he dons for his portrait, then, the most conventional clothing of British aristocracy, he does not do so solely to reflect the social order of his Georgian world or the formulaic role which is his. His clothing serves in fact to disguise and introduce from the outset the fundamental metaphor of self which he will amplify throughout the narrative: Africa(n), a metaphor for rebirth and rejuvenation, also signifies dignity, honor and perhaps the wholeness which he seeks. Its name, like his image, must be associated with the highest values, morals, and qualities one might seek.

Without a doubt, then, Equiano's portrait, an iconic signifier, projects the idea that he is a paragon of African virtues. His dark oval face frames a luminously dignified smile, and his high, intelligent forehead gives way to noble eyes that sparkle with honesty and integrity, a broad, African nose and heavy but sturdy lips. Crowned by a crop of carefully manicured hair that cascades naturally like a pharoah's khat down the back of his unwigged head, his elliptical visage resembles a ritual mask that is imperviously pedestaled to his broad shoulders. Instead of a former slave or a pampered servant, Equiano, in dress and aire, bears a *mark of grandeur and distinction*—one which might be considered commensurate with British aristocracy, but also one which, when we are mindful of the fact that he was born into the Essakan aristocracy and that he believed himself *destined* to be titled like his father and brother, must not only bear ties to his African self but fundamentally to the metaphor of self that Equiano wished to develop. When one further considers that Equiano published his own narrative without the introductory authenticating documents that later became important instruments of verification in the slave narrative, the significance of this powerful portrait and the meaning he intends it to convey reveal his complexity as a creative writer and his effort to use symbols competently in his narrative. He is, from the outset, a master masker.

To be sure, the unique and powerful aspects of Equiano's narrative are to be found in the narrator's voice and eyes, which present the gamut of the Black experience in Africa, the Caribbean, North American Colonies, and England during the late eighteenth century. Equally important, however, is the masterful manner in which Equiano successfully masks his intention of developing and maintaining a metaphor of self from the frontispiece to the very last page of his narrative, suggesting in the process the intricate foundation of the Black literary tradition. (pp. 99-100)

Wilfred D. Samuels, "Retrospective Glance: The Interesting Narrative of the Life of Olaudah Equiano Reconsidered," in Negro

History Bulletin, *Vol. 46, No. 4, October-December, 1983, pp. 99-100.*

Wilfred D. Samuels (essay date 1985)

[In the following excerpt, Samuels examines metaphors of self in Equiano's Interesting Narrative.*]*

The author of the slave narrative confronted the difficult task of reporting his lived experiences during slavery to an audience which did not recognize him as a member of its society and, in fact, viewed him "as an alien whose assertion of common humanity and civil rights conflicted with some of its basic beliefs," including the institutionalization of theories of the racial superiority of whites and the inferiority of African slaves. This difficulty was further compounded in certain cases by the former slave, who addressed the question of abolishing slavery, an institution to which members of his audience were often inextricably bound, because, economically speaking, their prosperity was ensured by the slave trade. Consequently, although the narrator often sought, on the one hand, to garner support and sympathy for the abolition of slavery, he recognized, on the other hand, that the very act of writing his narrative or the simplest error on his part could not only be viewed as insolence, but could alienate the very audience that he needed if he were to accomplish his goal.

The already difficult task of not alienating the audience became especially complex for Olaudah Equiano, an Ibo who, after being kidnapped at age eleven and experiencing ten years of slavery, published his two-volume narrative **The Interesting Narrative of the Life of Olaudah Equiano, or Gustavus Vassa, the African, Written by Himself** in 1789. To be sure, the condescending tone of the review which appeared in *The Gentleman's Magazine* reveals the dilemma of the slave narrator in general and specifically of Equiano. According to the reviewer, "These memoirs, written in very unequal style, place the writer on a par with the general mass of men in the *subordinate stations of civilized society,* and so prove that there is no general rule without an exception."

That Equiano had in the foreground of his interest the objective of attracting an audience whose power and voice could, if it decided to act, strike a meaningful blow against the slave trade and slavery is, I believe, suggested in the overtly stated purpose which Equiano couches in the humblest language and tone at the beginning of Chapter I:

> I am not so foolishly vain as to expect from it [his narrative] either immortality or literary reputation. If it affords any satisfaction to my numerous friends, at whose request it has been written, or in the smallest degree promotes the interest of humanity, the ends for which it was undertaken will be fully attained, and every wish of my heart gratified.

Equiano further reveals his anticipation of some negative response as well as his awareness of the importance of audience when he declares that, in order to avoid censure, he has chosen not to "aspire to praise." In fact, Equiano, one might argue, purposely designs a narrative that is as much about travel in the Mediterranean as it is about slavery in the New World to assure his audience that his purpose throughout is not to offend or alienate.

Yet a common error is made by the critic who, taking Equiano's announced purpose at face value, fails to see his creation of a self whose muted voice veils covert intentions that lie hidden behind the facade—the mask, with which he disguises himself from the very opening lines of the work. For example, Frances Foster Smith incorrectly concludes that "Equiano rarely alters the dispassionate and modest tone of his prefatory remarks.... His denial of personal involvement beyond the desire to please friends and to make a small contribution to 'the interest of humanity' is in accordance with accepted standards of gentlemanly humanitarianism."

Although it is indeed correct that Equiano was interested in "gentlemanly humanitarianism," it can be argued that Equiano's posture here allows us to see the control that he seeks to establish over his narrative from the beginning, for as Robert Stepto tells us, the letters, introductions, prefaces, appendices, and other such documents that formed authenticating auxiliary voices in the slave narratives dictated who, in the final analysis, had control: the former slave or his white guarantor.

Thus, more important than Equiano's announced purpose in Chapter I, one might argue, is the significance of an introductory document, in the form of a letter written by him, which begins the narrative. In it, Equiano's voice emerges, cogently though humbly, to address "the Lords Spiritual and Temporal, the Commons of the Parliament of Great Britain":

My Lords and Gentlemen,

Permit me, with the greatest deference and respect to lay at your feet the following genuine Narrative; the chief design of which is to excite in your august assemblies a sense of compassion for the miseries which the Slave-Trade has entailed on my unfortunate countrymen. By the horrors of that trade was I first torn away from all the tender connexions that were naturally dear to my heart; but these, through the mysterious ways of Providence, I ought regard as infinitely more than compensated by the introduction I have thence obtained to the knowledge of the Christian religion, and of a nation which, by its liberal sentiments, its humanity, the glorious freedom of its government, and its proficiency in arts and sciences, has exalted the dignity of human nature.

I am sensible I ought to entreat your pardon for addressing to you a work so wholly devoid of literary merit; but, as the production of an unlettered African, who is actuated by the hope of becoming an instrument toward the relief of his suffering countrymen, I trust that *such a man,* pleading in *such a cause,* will be acquitted of boldness and presumption.

May the God of heaven inspire your heart with peculiar benevolence on that important day when the question of Abolition is to be discussed, when thousands in consequence of your Determination, are to look for Happiness or Misery!

I am,
My Lords and Gentlemen,
Your most obedient,
And devoted humble Servant,
OLAUDAH EQUIANO
or
GUSTAVUS VASSA

Clearly, Equiano, in his introductory letter, takes an overt posture that someone interested in operating from a basic logic of humility would assume. He accomplishes this with such carefully chosen phrases as "greatest deference," "respect," and "august assemblies"; and by his flattering description of Great Britain as "liberal" and humane and as a nation whose government knew "glorious freedom." Although the "chief design" of his narrative might not be obvious, the result is; for with this stance, Equiano—a Black and a former slave, by definition a pariah to some of his eighteenth-century readers—captures the attention of his white audience. He succeeds in establishing what Mary Louis Pratt calls an "affective relation" with his audience, one that reduces hostility and gets attention without being offensive. Simultaneously, he gains the upper hand, and from the beginning he succeeds in establishing a power relation in which he takes control. Like a champion chess player who, after making certain instrumental moves, castles his king for safeguarding while he uses his queen to wreak havoc on his opponent, Equiano, by assuming this position, is able to race across the pages of his narrative like a powerful monarch in a "game" that sees him overtly genuflecting and groveling but covertly, and primarily through language, slashing away at his oppressors. Indeed, his use of irony in his opening letter reveals this, for how can a nation known for its liberal sentiments, humanity, and the glorious freedom of its government directly or indirectly justify its involvement in a slave trade that, in its horror, would tear an individual, especially a child, "from all the tender connexions that were naturally dear to [his] heart"?

Equiano's letter, coupled with a frontispiece that features him poised with Bible in hand, pages of errata, and a table of contents, listing exciting chapter-by-chapter captions of the author's adventures, served to present the author's point of view as that of an inoffensive African who wishes to describe his "interesting" experiences to his reading audience. Moreover, his inclusion of an impressive list of subscribers—headed by the Prince of Wales and the Duke of York, but also including the names of England's top dignitaries, Members of Parliament, esquires, barristers, and clergymen, from the Duke of Bedford and the Bishop of Banghor to the Duke of Northumberland and Lord Mulgrave, Granville Sharp, Esq., and the Reverend Mr. John Wesley—serve only to crystallize this idea for his audience. Also, by publishing his narrative on August first, the "Queen's Birthday," Equiano enhances this

BAHAMA BANKS. 1767.

The wreck of the slave ship Nancy *on the Bahama Banks in 1767. This engraving was used as the frontispiece for the second volume of the American edition of Equiano's* Narrative.

perception, for the sacred manner with which her subjects view the Queen would have led them to see the **Narrative's** appearance as an activity in her honor. Finally, that Equiano's portrait was engraved by Daniel Orme, who, as Historical Engraver to the Prince of Wales, was responsible for engraving the chief heroes of the time, only served to further reduce any possibly negative perception by his audience.

Thus, from the beginning, Equiano's intentions are enhanced by his disguises. With his posture, Equiano catches the interest and imagination of the populace; and with an impressive list of subscribers, which not only suggested that these individuals contributed financially by purchasing copies (some as many as six), but also that they supported and approved of the work, he is able to ensure himself of an audience. Equiano's success in this regard is suggested in the review his narrative received in the prestigious *Monthly Review; or, Literary Journal,* in which, ironically, the reviewer claims that "the narrative wears an honest face."

In presenting these images of himself, Equiano reminds us of the African folk trickster hero Anansi. For like

Anansi, who, though small, is able to outwit and overpower the larger animals, often leading to their destruction, Equiano, the powerless former slave, outsmarts, with his tricks, his British audience. By donning the mask of the docile slave, he outwits his audience and simultaneously reveals that its members are unscrupulous and uncaring.

What remains important, however, is that each factor comes together to solidify the control which Equiano maintains from the beginning over his two-volume work. There are no auxiliary voices, no mitigating voices stealing the thrust of his words. Equiano organizes, coordinates, lays out, writes, and publishes his narrative, regardless of who else might assist. What we are left with, then, is what for Pierre Macherey is a "literary production," for we can see that Equiano is conscious of his purpose and the power of the written word.

Because we are able to find in the narrative's structure the author's strong association with Africa, both suggested and stated, it is possible to argue that Equiano's muted voice camouflages what one might deem the single most important purpose of his narrative: the recreation of a "single self" which is related to an idealized African identity that Equiano wishes to claim as his legacy.

In the light of my contention, Equiano's narrative can be best understood if we make a distinction between the actual sequence of events of the test (*l'histoire*) and the presentation of these events (*recit*). I don't mean to suggest here, of course, that Equiano, at forty-five years of age, was not interested in historicity, in the events that identified his outer self. His interest in the dynamics of his early life in Africa, ten years of slavery in the New World, maritime experiences which included participation in the Seven Years' War and travel to the Arctic, involvement in British culture during the eighteenth century, in the Abolitionist Movement and the colonization of Sierra Leone—historical events in which he participated actively or inactively—is clear. However, it becomes equally clear that what concerns him more than *what* he has done is who he has or has not become as a result of these events. In short, his feelings and thoughts, the "inner man," remain salient to him. In what must be viewed as his careful self-study, Equiano in his ***Interesting Narrative of the Life*** seems anxious to know, in the words of Carlyle: "In God's name, what *art* thou?" Consequently, what ultimately concerns us here is related to a question of intentionality: What, in the final analysis, did Equiano intend?

It is in the interpretation or "the construction of textual meaning, "to borrow a phrase from E. D. Hirsch, that one might find deeper insights into the meaning of Equiano's text. For Hirsch the critic's first task is the construction of textual meaning: One must interpret the text correctly. This is to be done, he further argues, by identifying the "Intentional Object" of the narrator's awareness as well as the "Intentional Act," the mode by which the narrator becomes aware of the object. Through these, the critic can ascertain the verbal meaning of the text and gain insight into its explicit meaning, which is shared by all. Furthermore, to distinguish what a text implies from what it does not imply, Hirsch argues, the critic must posit, insofar as it is possible, the "horizon" of the text, or "a system of typical expectations and probabilities," to unravel its total meaning. And to specify horizon, the interpreter must familiarize him- or herself with the "typical meaning of the author's mental and experiential world." In spite of what must be clearly designated the inaccessibility of the author's intention, Hirsch's argument is particularly useful.

From what I have suggested thus far, it is possible to conclude that Equiano's narrative is the "intentional act" through which he becomes aware of his intentional object: slavery. However, in the prefatory remarks of Chapter II, Equiano lists an implied and perhaps more important intentional object, one that—because he wishes to avoid censure, as he tells us at the beginning of Chapter I—he subverts with the question of slavery. Apologizing for what some might have considered

boldness on his part in sharing with his readers in Chapter I an account of the manners and customs of his African community, Equiano declares that " . . . whether the love of one[']s country be real or imaginary, or a lesson or reason, or an instinct of nature, *I still look back with pleasure on the first scenes of my life, though that pleasure has been for the most part mingled with sorrow*" (my emphasis). Equiano's use of the present tense here is important, for it connotes a contemporaneous act; there is, in other words, a sense of "now-ness" to his act of "looking back with pleasure" over his earlier life; and there are further implications that the desire to do so is continuous. In the present tense verb *look* is found Equiano's point of view, which embodies implications and irony, for his discourse conceals his simultaneous activity: He will not only be relating his experiences in slavery, whose abolition would enhance, as he says, "the interest of humanity," but concurrently recalling a past life which remains, without a doubt, more meaningful to him with each passing day.

We can better understand the development, discovery, and creation of identity, which for Equiano remains salient, as well as come to grips with his experiences as a slave, which came in direct conflict with this identity, by adopting Hirsch's hermeneutics, which would lead us to unravel the meaning of the text in what we might call the "horizon" of Equiano's experiences. Interestingly enough, the very images that lead us to perceive Equiano as a subservient and passive former slave also embody the very complex characterization of him that we find in the narrative. Perhaps no other image offers a clearer example than the one that emerges from his treatment of his participation in the Seven Years' War. (pp. 64-6)

Ironically, in this very war that was fought to gain dominance over a part of West Africa that was not very far from his own homeland, and to control such "commodities" as sugar, tobacco, indigo, and Black African slaves, Equiano found an avenue for rising above the "blood-stained gates of slavery," to find meaning, dignity, and honor while still enslaved. Equiano wants his readers to believe that he was able to find in the Seven Years' War an avenue for regaining the power, valor, honor, and respect—in short, the humanity—of which he had been robbed by his abduction into slavery.

In the same manner that his documentations throughout the narrative are more than random inclusions of unrelated voices, the lengthy descriptions of Equiano's experiences at sea contain more than scattered and isolated incidents for the sake of rambling. They, too, reveal an Equiano who in his own tale successfully fashions himself as a protagonist who, in his traditional African experiences, could easily have risen to heroic stature. If, as he seems to suggest throughout his narrative, traditional African communal life must be associated with that which is heroic and ideal, then the Equiano we see in his implied characterization epitomizes the traditional African man, who would manifestly have been the great traditional warrior and title bearer. Consequently, the enigma that characterizes his narrative must be carefully examined when found in his tales about his experiences at sea with his master, Captain Pascal of the Royal Navy, especially those involving Pascal's service under Admiral Boscawen during the Seven Years' War.

On the surface, in his narration of the war Equiano serves as an eyewitness—as an on-the-scene correspondent, reporting with precision the land and sea engagements between the British and the French. But he seems especially aware of those battles in which Boscawen's gallant feats were accomplished when the *Namur*, the vessel on which Equiano along with his master-captain is sailing, is Boscawen's flagship. Perhaps no battle was more important to Boscawen (and, indeed, to Equiano) than the one at Gibraltar in August 1759. A firsthand eyewitness and participant, Equiano carefully details the events of the encounter. He dramatically and suspensefully reports the August battle:

> The engagement now commenced with great fury on both sides. The *Ocean* immediately returned our fire, and we continued engaged with each other for some time; during which I was frequently stunned with the thundering of the great guns, whose dreadful contents hurried many of my companions into awful eternity. At last the French line was entirely broken, and we obtained the victory, which was immediately pro-

claimed with loud huzzas and acclamations. We took three prizes, *La Modeste,* of sixty-four guns, and *Le Temeraire* and *Centair,* of seventy-four guns each. The rest of the French ships took to flight with all the sail they could crowd.

To be sure, Equiano, by creating an image of the war, is able to catch the unique moment in history and to reproduce it for his British audience, who must have been dazzled by the former slave's careful and detailed reporting, his enviable knowledge of naval vessels, and his apparent sense of nationalism.

Although his tale of the engagement ends, Equiano continues by explaining to the reader his assigned role during the battle, making it clear that his role as active participant cannot be gainsaid. Indeed, unlike Robinson Crusoe's Friday or the servant in the plantation literature of Thomas Page, who goes to war with his master to polish his boots and care for his horse, Equiano reveals that he functioned as more than a personal servant during the engagement. He was a fighter:

> My station during the engagement was on the middle deck, where I was quartered with another boy, to bring powder to the aftermost gun; and here I was witness of the dreadful fate of many of my companions, who, in the twinkling of an eye, were dashed in pieces, and launched into eternity. Happily I escaped unhurt, though the shot and splinters flew thick about me during the whole fight. Towards the latter

The Racehorse *and the* Carcass *in the Arctic, 1773. Equiano sailed on these ships as part of Constantine Phipps's Arctic expedition.*

part of it, my master was wounded, and I saw him carried down to the surgeon; but though I was much alarmed for him, and wished to assist him, I dared not leave my post. At this station, my gun-mate (a partner in bringing powder for the same gun) and I ran a very risk, for more than half an hour, of blowing up the ship. For, when we had taken the cartridges out of the boxes, the bottoms of many of them proving rotten, the powder ran all about the deck, near the match tub; we scarcely had water enough at the last to throw on it. We were also, from our employment, very much exposed to the enemy's shots, for we had to go through nearly the whole length of the ship to bring the powder. I expected, therefore, every minute to be my last especially when I saw our men fall so thick about me; but, wishing to guard as much against the dangers as possible, at first I thought would be safest not to go for the powder till the Frenchmen had fired their broadside . . . . But immediately afterwards I thought this caution was fruitless; and cheering myself with the reflection that there was time alloted for me to die, as well as to be born, I instantly cast off all fear or thought whatever of death, and went through the whole of my duty with alacrity.

Here Equiano again resembles the African folk trickster Anansi, who is sometimes caught in the traps that he sets for others, for although he undoubtedly is aware of the possibly indignant reaction of his audience to his work were they to conclude that he had overstepped the bounds of his assured social role, Equiano can be found unmasked for a brief moment when we peer behind the facade. We find in the above passage not the subservient or passive slave, but instead an Equiano who has covertly assumed the role of the chivalrous warrior from the very beginning. And, again, we are made aware the Equiano is saying more in his discourse than what immediately stands before us.

Unlike Admiral Byng, whose retreat jeopardized Great Britain's safety and cost him his life, Equiano, a man of action, "casts off all fear" and rises to the occasion. Though his human instincts cause him to be slow in reacting at first, he, responding with bravery, answers the call of duty nevertheless. Indeed, by telling us that he fearlessly carried the gun powder that was used to send the solid cannonballs splitting over the vast ocean, in spite of the immediate danger, Equiano, one might even be led to conclude, wants his reader to believe that this historical battle could not have been won without the brave Ibo's role and the chivalrous manner in which he met his duties during these pre-armoured-warship days when Britain's wooden naval vessels gained control of the ocean.

One cannot help but notice that the humility with which Equiano generally garbs himself seems to have been completely stripped away here, as he calls attention to his heroic performance, and the shift from the observing eye in the "I" of the narration to the "I" of the action becomes important because it moves the focus inward, taking Equiano beyond the explicit meaning that his activities may have conveyed to his British audience. Equiano is in fact saying, I believe: This is not only a world that I objectively experienced, but one that I, through my intrepid acts, helped to create.

To be sure, through his exciting narration and careful choice of words of action and through his functional use of the first-person plural "we," he allows his British readers to participate in the battle, and he gives them a reason for celebration. Here in his narrative they could find yet another record of their undaunting strength and power; here they could find yet another testimony to the masterful skills of their beloved Admiral Boscawen; and here they had evidence of their ability to overcome the enemy, France. Thus, at the explicit level of his narrative, he succeeds in giving his audience both the romance and the drama that it might have associated with naval battle and encounter, a fact that was undoubtedly heightened by the knowledge that this was "Pitt's War," and he boosted their pride in their maritime war for maritime empire, providing rejuvenation after the universal disgrace they had suffered with Byng's defeat.

Equally important, however, is what might be perceived as Equiano's effort to guide his readers' response towards his abolitionist concerns, for with his description and powerful rhetoric he indirectly forces his audience to confront the question of the injustice of slavery and, indeed, to find validation in his argument against this inhuman system that had enslaved an individual of his caliber, one whose personal qualities, dignity, and values represented the highest ideals of British culture. His audience, one might even believe, might somehow have become infuriated by their own participation, direct or indirect, in this heinous system, and with Equiano, they might have concluded that slavery "depresses the mind and extinguishes all its fire and every noble sentiment." Equiano's success in capturing and controlling his audience, and his personal account of one of England's finest hours, undoubtedly contributed to the popularity of his narrative, which was to undergo more than fifteen editions.

What remains of paramount importance, however, are the implications of Equiano's text, because throughout his reported acts he places himself firmly in the middle of this "world wide struggle in which the main lines of the British Empire were finally laid down." Rather than hide, escape, or skirt responsibilities, although armorless, Equiano, the African, girds his loins and resolves to meet head on his task, no matter what the required sacrifice, danger, or outcome. A mere lad of fourteen at the time of the battle, he here assumes, he wants us to believe, the role of leader. Overcoming his initial fears and showing tremendous discipline, Equiano in the final analysis emerges as one who had risen to the status that would have been his in Essaka, where the male youth's self-understanding was firmly grounded in the conceptual metaphor "man is warrior" and "warrior is a person of honour, action, and bravery." Consequently, the horizon of Equiano's experience, the conscious and unconscious meanings that are present in his discourse, must be unraveled before the full meaning of his text can be ascertained. The horizon would inevitably include his African past.

The son of a village elder, Equiano retrospectively views his childhood in Africa as his "former happy state," during which he basked in the warmth of his mother's love, was cradled in an awareness of his aristocratic father's wealth and prestige, and was nourished by the knowledge that his parents were committed to securing for him a place within their community through which he, too, would gain the mark of grandeur and distinction that was borne by his father and brother. In preparing him for his *destined* role as a communal leader, Equiano's mother, unaware, of course, of the tragic future that awaited her favorite child, dressed him "with the emblems, after the manner of our greatest warrior." He tells us that, before being kidnapped, he was "trained up in the earliest years in the art of war: my daily exercise was shooting and throwing javelins."

Implied in Equiano's text here is the suggestion that the personal history of a pariah, which had been carved out in the wasteland of Western slavery and culture, is not his sole interest. Present also is the notion that the Ibo wants to confront questions related to the loss of personal legacy that this history has wrought. He tells us that slavery did not divert him from the course on which he had been set by a mother who dressed him after the manner of the great Ibo warriors. In fact, in his own traditional world, he would have crossed the threshold into manhood after such dauntless actions, and indeed, he could have danced to the drum beat reserved for the great warriors.

Finding no warrior's circle in which to dance proudly, finding no marketplace in which to display his war trophies, although he had brought home the "enemies'" head in the form of the ships taken as prizes, Equiano finds, in his narrative-autobiography, not only an avenue for celebrating his valorous act, but also a means of claiming the achievement of his identity and thereby assuming the social role that was rightfully his as an Ibo, Essakan, and African. Equiano thus weaves into his narrative an important "metaphor of self," which, as James Olney tells us, is used by the autobiographer to grasp and understand the unique self that he is—"to grasp the unknown for the known." Equiano's "metaphor of self" is one that makes him the African traditional warrior-man.

Given Hume's contention that the mind is a theater which "parades a variety of posture and situation," one finds it difficult not to agree with Sir Victor Pritchett, who claimed that what the autobiographer is faced with in the final analysis is a decision of "what play [he is] putting on, what its theme is and what postures fit into it." Pritchett tells us: "The play is not '*the* truth' but '*a* truth' of '*our* truth.'" In other words, it is possible to argue that the historicity and veracity of Equiano's tale about his role in the Seven Years' War is, in a sense, unimportant. What ultimately *is* important is the metaphor of self that he has chosen in relating the events.

Thus, although the explicit "posture" he assumes for his audience, that of the abolitionist, is one that we continuously see, it is the implicit posture, grounded in the signification of warriorhood to his traditional African community, that eventually presents the represented self that he has chosen to amplify in the hidden purpose of his narrative.

Consequently, although he succeeds through narration and description in recreating for his readers a sense of the slave trade during the eighteenth century, Equiano ends up recreating what Roy Pascal, in a related context, terms "a part of [his] life in the actual circumstance in which it was lived." In the final analysis, what we get is closer to autobiography, in which, as Pascal tells us, "The centre of interest is the self, not the outside world, though necessarily the outside world must appear so that the personality can find its particular shape."

What we learn from Equiano's autobiographical acts, I believe, is that he can only find in his retrospective assessment of slavery an excruciating severance and senseless extirpation: As he came to realize, slavery meant physical separation from the community and culture which offered reciprocity during the first eleven years of his life. Whereas Essaka meant bonding, security, and aggregation, slavery meant separation, alienation, and liminality. It was for him a void to be transcended, an overpowering force that threatened to dash him into a world of eternal meaninglessness, an experience from which, through the narrative, he would seek a sense of wholeness and being.

Deeply embedded in Equiano's discourse, specifically in its ironies and implications, is the conflict which resulted from conflict between the idealized African self, which he as a member of his Essakan community and as an Ibo accepts as his legacy, and the harsh reality that, having served as a slave in a foreign land, away from family and culture, he had not been able fully to realize this self. The act of writing the narrative becomes not only a process, then, of taking a retrospective glance over the primary experiences that served to form Equiano's historical self, but perhaps more importantly, it functions as praxis, for it allows him to explore his life and at the same time create, develop, and extract from it the meaning which to him remains important. Equiano's self-portraiture contains ironic and metaphoric values which upon examination reveal the dual nature of the thematics and characterization of his narrative. Fundamentally, it reveals that in his efforts to build subjectivity in a world of reification, Equiano reclaims his voice by masking and disguising it. Indirectly, he teaches us to not only listen to the explicit voice of Gustavus Vassa, the person created by the Western enslavers who gave him this name, but also to the voice of Olaudah Equiano, the would-be warrior, whose name means 'fortunate' and 'favored.' (pp. 67-9)

Wilfred D. Samuels, "Disguised Voice in 'The Interesting Narrative of Olaudah Equiano, or Gustavus Vassa, the African'," in

Black American Literature Forum, *Vol. 19,*
No. 2, Summer, *1985, pp. 64-9.*

FURTHER READING

Acholonu, Catherine Obianju. "The Home of Olaudah
Equiano—A Linguistic and Anthropological Search." *The*
Journal of Commonwealth Literature XXII, No. 1 (1987):
5-16.
Cultural and anthropological study of Equiano's use of
English orthography for transcribing sounds and ideas
in Igbo, his native language.

Baker, Houston A., Jr. "Figurations for a New American
Literary History." In his *Blues, Ideology, and Afro-Ameri-*
can Literature: A Vernacular Theory, pp. 15-63. Chicago:
University of Chicago Press, 1984.
Examines the relationship between the *Narrative* and
the economics of slavery, attempting to identify a
historical subtext that distinguishes the work from
"traditional, historical, and literary historical discourse."

Bontemps, Arna. Introduction to *Great Slave Narratives,*
edited by Arna Bontemps, pp. vii-xix. Boston: Beacon
Press, 1969.
Claims that Equiano's *Narrative* achieves its strength
on the basis of "the book's naturalness, its wealth of
fascinating detail and narrative events."

Costanzo, Angelo. *Suprizing Narrative: Olaudah Equiano*
and the Beginnings of Black Autobiography. Contributions
in Afro-American and African Studies, No. 104. New York:
Greenwood Press, 1987, 149 p.
Detailed study of early black biography, focusing on
Equiano's *Narrative.*

Edwards, Paul. Introduction to *Equiano's Travels: The*
Interesting Narrative of the Life of Olaudah Equiano or
Gustavus Vassa the African, by Olaudah Equiano, abridged
and edited by Paul Edwards, pp. ix-xviii. New York:
Frederick A. Praeger, 1967.
Discusses critical problems surrounding Equiano and
his work, particularly the veracity, authenticity, and
literary significance of his *Narrative.*

————. "Olaudah Equiano." *History Today* 31 (Septem-
ber 1981): 44.
Brief biography, emphasizing the origins of written
Nigerian literature.

————. "Three West African Writers of the 1780s." In
The Slave's Narrative, edited by Charles T. Davis and
Henry Louis Gates, Jr., pp. 175-98. Oxford: Oxford
University Press, 1985.
Discusses how Equiano, Ignatius Sancho, and Ottobah
Cugoano attempted to come to terms with contrary
aspects of white European society in their writings.

Francis, Elman V. "Olaudah Equiano: A Profile." *Negro*
History Bulletin 44, No. 2 (August-June 1981): 31, 43-4.

General biography, concluding that Equiano "is one of
the unsung heroes of the unexplored and unnoticed
black people who helped to build the European civilization."

Gates, Henry Louis, Jr. "The Trope of the Talking Book."
In his *The Signifying Monkey: A Theory of Afro-American*
Literary Criticism, pp. 127-69. New York: Oxford University Press, 1988.
Probes the ultimate meaning of Equiano's *Narrative* in
terms of the author's "strategies of self-presentation
and rhetorical presentation."

Review of *The Interesting Narrative of the Life of Olaudah*
Equiano, by Olaudah Equiano. *The Gentleman's Magazine*
and Historical Chronicle 59, No. 6 (June 1789): 539.
Brief review of Equiano's *Narrative.* The anonymous
critic points out that the work is "written in a very
unequal style."

Jones, G. I. "Olaudah Equiano of the Niger Ibo." In *Africa*
Remembered, edited by P. D. Curtin, pp. 60-69. Madison:
University of Wisconsin Press, 1967.
Locates and describes Equiano's ancestral home in the
Ibo country of Nigeria.

Kaplan, Sidney. "Olaudah Equiano: The Image of Africa."
In his *The Black Presence in the Era of the American*
Revolution, pp. 193-206. Greenwich, Conn.: New York
Graphic Society, 1973.
Detailed biography, offering a "sketch of his rich life
with a few scattered passages, in his own good words,
from *The Interesting Narrative.*"

Koike, Sekio. "Olaudah Equiano: The Prototypal Christian
Abolitionist Transfigured from an African Heathen." *Kyu-*
shu American Literature 20 (June 1979): 3-13.
Determines that Equiano integrated "supplementary"
elements of abolitionism and religion in his *Narrative.*

Loggins, Vernon. "The Beginnings of Negro Authorship,
1760-1790." In his *The Negro Author: His Development in*
America to 1900, pp. 1-47.
Comments on the literary significance of works by late
eighteenth-century black authors, including Equiano's
autobiography, Phillis Wheatley's poetry, and Benjamin Banneker's almanacs.

Mtubani, Victor C. D. "The Black Voice in Eighteenth-
Century Britain: African Writers Against Slavery and the
Slave Trade." *Phylon* 45, No. 2 (June 1984): 85-97.
Examines contemporary black participation in and
reaction to late eighteenth-century abolitionist efforts,
particularly the impact and influence of Equiano's
autobiography.

Porter, Dorothy B. "Early American Negro Writings: A
Bibliographical Study." *The Papers of the Bibliographical*
Society of America 39 (1945): 192-268.
Primary bibliography of writings by eighteenth-century
black American authors, with a discussion of the
related problems of identification and location.

Sandiford, Keith A. "Olaudah Equiano: The Appeal to
Humanity and the Political Self." In his *Measuring the*
Moment: Strategies of Protest in Eighteenth-Century Afro-

English Writing, pp. 118-48. Cranbury, N.J.: Associated University Presses, 1988.

Explores Equiano's apparent political motives in the *Interesting Narrative,* noting how the work bolstered the abolitionist cause in eighteenth-century England.

Walvin, James. "The Free Black Voice." In his *Black and White: The Negro and English Society, 1555-1945,* pp. 80-104. London: Allen Lane, 1973.

General biography, highlighting Equiano's religious conversion and abolitionist activities.

Frantz Fanon

1925-1961

West Indian essayist.

A Caribbean political essayist, Fanon is chiefly remembered for *Les damnés de la terre* (1961; *The Wretched of the Earth*), a collection of prose denouncing colonialism and racism in the Third World. Although his proposal of using violence to obtain political liberation met with heavy criticism, Fanon is nonetheless praised as a great humanist and hero among black people.

Fanon was a man of contradictions. He was born to a middle-class family in 1925 and spent his early life on Martinique. One of eight children, he was labeled a "troublemaker" by his mother and was often told by her to "stop acting like a nigger." According to his older brother Joby, with whom he maintained a close relationship, Fanon was a sensitive but difficult child who often got into fights with his peers. At school he learned to speak French, sing patriotic French songs, and read French literature and history. Like other Martinicans, he regarded himself as a Frenchman and grew up hearing that the "negroes" in Africa were "savages." In 1943, inspired by General de Gaulle's call to defend France, Fanon eagerly joined the French army. There he encountered blatant racism and came to realize that France, and subsequently the world, saw him as a black man. Disillusioned by this growing awareness of what it means to be black in a white world, Fanon returned to Martinique in 1946. According to Emmanuel Hansen: "The picture we have of Fanon at this time was that of an introspective, withdrawn, and serious student. It is possible to surmise that he was brooding and turning over in his mind his experience in the French army." About this time, Fanon came into contact with fellow West Indian writer Aimé Césaire, and he quickly embraced Césaire's philosophy of negritude. For the next year, Fanon campaigned to get Césaire elected a member of the French National Assembly. In 1947 Fanon left for France to begin his studies in psychiatry. While enrolled as a medical student, he briefly considered a career as a dramatist and wrote three plays: *Les mains parallèls, L'oeil se noie,* and *La conspiration.* These plays, written between 1949 and 1950, remain unpublished at Fanon's request.

Having successfully completed his medical examinations, Fanon left for French-controlled Algeria in 1953 to serve as the psychiatric director of Blida-Joinville Hospital. A year after his arrival, the Algerian War erupted, and Fanon quickly aligned with the Algerian Front de Libération Nationale (FLN). In 1956 Fanon resigned his position at the hospital, stating that it was useless to cure individuals only to send them back into a "sick" society. Psychiatric disorders were the direct result of societal oppression, Fanon believed, and therefore society must change before one can help individu-

als. After participating in a work stoppage with other doctors sympathetic to FLN, Fanon was expelled from Algeria in 1957. Now in Tunisia, he continued to speak out against white colonialism. Writing in *El Moudjahid* and *Resistance algérienne,* the underground newspapers for revolutionary forces, Fanon attracted numerous supporters. As his political influence grew, so did the number of assassination attempts on his life. After surviving several car bombings and machine-gun attacks, Fanon was afflicted with leukemia in the late 1950s. Seeking treatment, he went first to the Soviet Union and then reluctantly to the United States, calling the latter a "nation of lynchers." Just prior to his death in Washington, D. C., in 1961, Fanon completed *The Wretched of the Earth.* In accordance with his wishes, his body was returned to Algeria for burial.

Fanon wrote four books in his lifetime, each dealing with the effects of colonialism and racism and his solutions for societal change. Fanon's first book, *Peau noire, masques blancs* (1952; *Black Skins, White*

Masks)—an essay collection heavily influenced by the works of Friedrich Nietzsche, Karl Marx, and Jean-Paul Sartre—examines black life in a white-dominated world. Criticizing attempts by blacks to hide their blackness under a "white mask," Fanon sought to expose blacks to what he viewed as the delusionary tactics of whites. According to critic Robert Coles, Fanon made no attempt in this work to be "systematic, comprehensive, or even orderly. Quite the contrary, one feels a brilliant, vivid and hurt mind, walking the thin line that separates effective outrage from despair." Fanon's lesser-known books, *L'an V de la révolution algérienne* (1959; *A Dying Colonialism*) and *Pour la révolution africaine: Écrits politiques* (1964; *Toward the African Revolution: Political Essays*), also denounce racism and colonialism. Fanon's reputation as a literary and political figure rests, however, on his third book, *The Wretched of the Earth.*

The Wretched of the Earth has been praised as the manifesto of Third World revolution and heralded as the "bible" of black movement groups in the United States. According to Barbara Abrash, "*The Wretched of the Earth* is an analysis of racism and colonialism, and a prescription for revolutionary action by which colonized men may redeem their humanity." In this work Fanon argued that political independence is the essential precursor to genuine economic and social change. Convinced that Western countries had infiltrated the Third World to exploit its resources and its people, Fanon deemed revolution the only feasible path to liberation. He therefore proposed that the "wretched of the earth," the poorest of the poor, lead others in political liberation, and he advocated using violence to achieve this end. His much-publicized and controversial solution alarmed many people. Fanon maintained, however, that for the black man whose "back is to the wall, the knife . . . at his throat, or more precisely, the electrode at his genitals," violence was the only option. Furthermore, violence for the "wretched" was a "cleansing" force: "Violence frees the native from his inferiority complex and from his despair and inaction; it makes him fearless and restores his self-respect." Far from being the "glorifier of violence" or the "prisoner of hate," as some critics have called him, Fanon found violence personally abhorrent. "In a war of liberation," Fanon argued, "the colonized people must win, but they must do so cleanly, without barbarity." Peter Geismar, writing in his 1977 biography of Fanon, stated: "Though Fanon lived amidst violence, and wrote about the prime necessity of political violence, bloodletting traumatized him . . . ." Nevertheless, Fanon firmly believed that violence was the only way to bring down an intolerable, oppressive society.

Criticism of *The Wretched of the Earth* has dealt chiefly with Fanon's depictions of colonialism and his solution for its demise. Albert Memmi, for example, argued that Fanon overestimated the leadership role of the Third World poor. Furthermore, he found Fanon's theory of violence "disturbing and surprising for a psychiatrist." Similarly, Lewis Coser regarded Fanon as an "apostle of violence" with an "evil and destructive" vision. In contrast, Dennis Forsythe proclaimed Fanon a "great symbolic hero" whose vision energized civil rights movements across the world. Emile Capouya also reminded Fanon's detractors that "violence is the essential feature of colonialism at all times; Fanon did not invent it." Instead, he proposed violence, according to Césaire, in order to create a non-violent world: "[Fanon's] violence, and this is not paradoxical, was that of the non-violent. By this I mean the violence of justice, of purity and intransigence . . . his revolt was ethical, and his endeavour generous."

Today, *The Wretched of the Earth* continues to provoke and inspire readers. Although Fanon's call for a violent action against colonialism has been criticized, the author himself remains a "saint" among black militants. "We are nothing on earth," Fanon wrote shortly before his death, "if we are not, first of all, slaves of a cause, the cause of the people, the cause of justice, the cause of liberty." *The Wretched of the Earth,* commentators maintain, is Fanon's legacy to the cause of humanity.

(For further information about Fanon's life and works, see *Black Writers* and *Contemporary Authors,* Vol. 116.)

PRINCIPAL WORKS

Peau noire, masques blancs (essays) 1952
  [*Black Skins and White Masks,* 1965; also published as *Black Skins, White Masks,* 1967]
L'an V de la révolution algérienne (essays) 1959; also published as *Sociologie d'une révolution (L'an V de la révolution algérienne),* 1966
  [*Studies in a Dying Colonialism,* 1965; also published as *A Dying Colonialism,* 1967]
Les damnés de la terre (essays) 1961
  [*The Damned,* 1963; also published as *The Wretched of the Earth,* 1965]
* *Pour la révolution africaine: Écrits politiques* (essays) 1964
  [*Toward the African Revolution: Political Essays,* 1967]

*This work was published posthumously.

Emile Capouya (essay date 1965)

[*In the following review, Capouya, characterizing* The Wretched of the Earth *as an "explosion," examines Fanon's assertion that violence and freedom are inseparable in colonial revolution.*]

The Publisher describes **The Wretched of the Earth** in these terms: "A Negro psychoanalysts's study of the problems of racism and colonialism in the world today." That is accurate as far as it goes, but it is rather like describing the Declaration of Independence as "A Virginia planter's criticisms of the colonial policies of

Great Britain." Thomas Jefferson's document was not a position paper but an explosion. *The Wretched of the Earth* is an explosion.

Frantz Fanon was born in Martinique and educated in France. During the Algerian revolution he was attached to a hospital as a psychiatrist, and largely as a result of his experiences in treating the mental illnesses of French torturers and Algerian victims, he decided to join the rebels. (He died of cancer in 1961, when he was thirty-six, so he did not live to see the establishment of torture centers for Algerians in a free Algeria, such as were reported by the *Canard enchaîné* a month or so ago; however, his largely unheeded prophecies and counsels allow the reader to make his own diagnosis of this new outbreak of an old disease.) Fanon quickly established himself as one of the most significant theoreticians of colonial revolution. Together with the essays on guerrilla warfare of Mao Tse-tung and Major Ernesto Guevara, *The Wretched of the Earth* supplies whatever technical and ideological inspiration may be needed for current and future revolutions of that kind.

It is not addressed to the French, the white South Africans, or the Americans, but to their antagonists in Africa, Latin America, and Vietnam. Nevertheless, it concerns us, for it gives the ground plan of that new world coming into being, in which we shall no longer be the leaders—let alone the masters—since we have shown ourselves to be too stupid and too immoral to provide leadership in the terms demanded by the age. When Malcolm, trying Macduff's temper, loads himself with supposititious crimes, and says, "If such a one be fit to govern, speak," Macduff returns, "Fit to govern! No, not to live!" In our case it may come to that, since our trespasses are real and not imaginary.

Fanon's book is divided into four sections that deal with the connection between violence and freedom in the context of colonial revolution, the difficulty of maintaining the purity of the revolutionary impulse after liberation, the significance of nationalism in newly independent states, and the question of culture in the nations born of revolution. A fifth section presents a series of clinical reports of mental disorder in the setting of colonial war. The first of these discussions is the most immediately striking, and is, indeed, the particular concern of Jean-Paul Sartre's preface.

The relations that Western countries have had with the so-called backward regions, and the effects of those relations, are hard for us to grasp. In the first place, most of our dealings with colonials are carried on by specialized groups—soldiers, technicians, merchants, government officials, and lay or religious welfare workers. Such persons, as a result of long sojourns in the colonized countries, most often come to accept the conditions obtaining there as normal, or at least unavoidable, particularly since they themselves always enjoy privileged economic and social status with regard to the native population. Intercourse with that population is governed by assumptions of superiority on the part of the Westerners, expressed now in terms of a patronizing condescension, now in rudeness that turns easily to violence. Those attitudes represent the underlying reality of the colonial situation—that the Westerners are in the country in order to exploit its natural resources and its human population, and where indirect and gentle means fail, direct and brutal ones are resorted to. In any case, the gentle means are unfailingly backed up by garrisons and gunboats.

All this goes on far from our own shores and far from our thoughts. Here at home, colonial conditions for the most part are reflected in abstract summaries only: the manifests of cargo vessels bringing in ore, palm-nut oil, industrial gums, or the cargo lists of the outwardbound ships loaded with machinery, bales of secondhand clothing, old newspapers, and small quantities of luxury goods; official surveys of balance-of-trade figures, investment figures, earnings reports, and so on. In the very best case, the process of colonial exploitation is carried on so smoothly and invisibly that Americans—to take the outstanding example—are generally unaware that their country is the most successful colonial power in the world, that all the territory between the Rio Grande and the Tierra del Fuego belongs to them and supports their enviable standard of living. Luckily for the success of the system, the American government is better informed. When a small island nation attempts to break out of the system and expropriate its American owners, our government institutes a blockade designed to starve the population. In other cases it makes and unmakes governments by offering or withholding loans, by subsidizing and arming rebels, by raising or lowering tariffs and import quotas, and in extreme cases by sending in the marines.

So what? Well, it turns out that per capita caloric intake in the underdeveloped countries has been decreasing rather than rising—and not because their populations have no appetite. On the contrary, they are sincerely hungry. From their point of view, the intention of our loans and tariffs and subsidies and soldiery is to make them hungrier, *to underdevelop them.* That is why Latin Americans do not like North Americans and call us by an unpleasant name. And at that our intervention in their lives has been on the whole abstract and gentlemanly. We have not usually dealt with them as with conquered nations, in the manner of the French in North Africa, the Portuguese in Angola, the Belgians in the Congo, or the British in India. We haven't had to. Only in Korea and Vietnam has the United States resorted to the ultimate argument in dealing with restive colonials. And as we know from reports in *Life* magazine and the *New York Times,* the ultimate argument includes petroleum jelly for incinerating native villages, torture of prisoners, and a gas that the State Department calls harmless but that other nations call poisonous.

All this has been going on, *mutatis mutandis,* for 500 years. The spread of modern technology is bringing it to a halt. The colonized peoples feel a hatred for us that knots them into one universal cramp. As a psychiatrist,

Frantz Fanon recommends that they get us out of their system by killing as many of us as they can. Especially since nothing short of death seems likely to make us let go.

To us, the intended victims, the treatment sounds rather drastic. Why should the colonial populations want to burden their souls with our murder? As individuals, we feel no bad conscience for their misery. We did not, as individuals, take the decisions that converted their subsistence-economies into one-crop export economies tied to our needs. Right here at home, those of us who are white do not feel personally responsible for the misery and frustration suffered by our black fellow-citizens. When Mr. LeRoi Jones expresses to audiences of white liberals his complete disaffection and lack of interest in their doings, to the point that their deaths would leave him unmoved, those of us at least who are white find his remarks scarcely comprehensible. What can he possibly have against good-natured us? How much more unseemly, then, the diatribe of the black psychiatrist and arch-rebel, and his suggestion that killing colonists is mental hygiene for the colonized.

Whence this exaltation of violence on the part of a man whose words on every other subject proclaim him a passionate humanitarian? To begin with, violence is the essential feature of colonialism at all times; Fanon did not invent it. It is directed against the colonized population by the foreign overlords or by those native élites that keep the bank business looking good in Switzerland. The armed forces of such states have only one function, to keep the populace from revolting. And that populace, reduced for the most part to a brutalized proletariat, is violent to its own members—but that is familiar enough to us from our experience of the class-ghettos and race-ghettos of great American cities. Further, the colonial overlords will not go without a fight. Nor after their departure will they leave off arming opportunist elements among the natives with whom they think they can do business, the Tschombes of this world.

Violence characterizes the colonial situation from first to last, and Fanon tells the colonial peoples, if you wish to be free you must fight, that is, reverse the current of violence. You will find your manhood in doing so. And in this period of history, colonial rebellion makes good sense, since it can be stated categorically that the great powers cannot deal effectively with struggles for liberation conducted in the form of guerrilla war.

I have dealt with the rationale of only one section of Fanon's book because it is the one that administers the most salutary shock. But I believe that readers owe it to their education to study the whole of it. They will see how it was possible for Fanon to draw in advance the physiognomy of the newly-created states, and point out what triumphs and what dreadful disillusionments await the makers of revolution. They may catch, in particular, a hint of the humanism and egalitarian aspiration that has all but abandoned our own societies

to take refuge among the wretched of the earth. (pp. 33-4)

Emile Capouya, "Time to Turn a Tide of Violence?" in Saturday Review, *Vol. 48, No. 17, April 24, 1965, pp. 33-4.*

Conor Cruise O'Brien (essay date 1965)

[*A former chancellor of the University of Ghana, O'Brien is also a political writer, dramatist, and literary critic. In the following essay, he offers a favorable review of* The Wretched of the Earth, *focusing on Fanon's depictions of "le colonisé" and the Algerian revolution.*]

Frantz Fanon was an exceptionally brave and honest man; he was also exceptional in his love and respect for the oppressed. He demonstrated these qualities by his professional work as a psychiatrist in Blida, Algeria, by throwing in his lot with the F.L.N. and by his writing. As a writer, he is distinguished by his passionate seriousness and his frequent, penetrating insights. He is neither an easy nor a systematic writer; one feels that his writing is wrung from him by his experience. *The Wretched of the Earth* is not so much a tract or essay as a series of intellectual explosions. Experience detonates an idea; hardly has the dust settled before another idea, equally unsettling, goes up. There are almost no transitions; he writes in the implicit belief that history itself provides the element of continuity in his book, as he moves from reflections on violence in the anti-colonial struggles to the deceptions of decolonization, from that to national consciousness and culture, and finally to the mental hospital in Blida: "The truth is that colonialism in its essence, was already beginning to show itself as a great recruiter for the psychiatric hospitals."

Yet Fanon's book has an unchanging central figure: that of "the colonized": *le colonisé*. (The present translator, in an understandable anxiety to avoid a clumsy word in English has rendered *le colonisé* as "the native," but Fanon did not write *indigène*; the native is not the same as the colonized, because the native was there before the colony.)

Who is *le colonisé?* He is any man who has been brought up in one of the poor regions of the world, under the domination, covert or overt, of people from the rich regions. Most of *les colonisés* are non-white—like Frantz Fanon himself, who was a Negro from Martinique—and *les colonisés* form the majority of the population of the globe. The colonized is a product of the colonial system: "The settler (*colon*) and the colonized are old acquaintances. As a matter of fact the settler is right when he makes the claim that he knows 'them.' It is the settler who *made* and *continues to make* the colonized." (Fanon's italics.)

This idea—which is true in certain regions, times and situations—became almost an obsession with Fanon. There are times when he writes as if the colonial experience brought into being an entirely new kind of being, all of whose characteristics derive from colonialism. Even tribal warfare is a product of colonialism: "Collective self-destruction in tribal warfare is one of the means by which the muscular tension of the colonized releases itself." There is an element of truth in this: under colonialism and especially under settler rule—Fanon never adequately distinguishes between these two phenomena—the black man, say, will often want to hit a white man, but finds if much safer to hit another black man, and derives some relief from doing so. Nor is it necessarily a question of blacks and whites: witness the shillelagh fights of 18th-century Ireland, which gave the word *donnybrook* to the English language for "a scene of uproar, disorder and free fighting" (O.E.D.). This was before the Irish got down to the more notable achievement of adding the word *boycott* to the English language. It is a reasonable hypothesis that donnybrook was in part a *spontaneous* response to settler rule, just as boycott was the beginning of successful *organized* response to the same rule. But this is not the whole truth; for the Irish and the Africans were fighting each other before the foreigners came.

Violence is not, as Fanon often seems to suggest, a creation of colonialism. On the contrary, colonialism is a form of violence: a form developed by the most tightly organized and most effectively violent human societies. The British and the Ashanti, the Belgians and the Bayeke, were alike in that they all wanted power and loot, and used force to get them; the British and the Belgians, disposing of more force, got more power and loot, and the Ashanti and Bayeke became *les colonisés* along with their former subjects, the pre-colonial *colonisés*. As far as violence and power are concerned, colonialism introduced no new principles into Africa, merely the more effective application of existing principles.

In this respect, it seems to me that Fanon overrates the originality of colonialism. He is also inclined, I think, to exaggerate its effects and underrate the degree of continuity which exists between pre-colonial and post-colonial Africa. All African phenomena—even dancing—are to him functions of colonialism: "The relaxation of the colonized is just this muscular orgy, during which the keenest aggression, the most immediate violence, are canalized, transformed, conjured away.... These disintegrations of personality, these doublings and dissolutions discharge a basic economic function in the stability of the colonized world." It is curious to find Fanon, of all people, falling into the kind of wild anthropological generalization characteristic of an earlier generation of European observers. In order to establish the correctness of his diagnosis of the dance, it would be necessary to show that orgiastic dancing of the kind described did not exist before the coming of the colonizers—that the Australian Corroboree, for example, sprang into existence only after the First Fleet sailed into Botany Bay in 1788. I wonder whether any anthropologist would subscribe to this thesis. (It is attested, however, that the Australian aborigines did use the Corroboree to express their feelings about the settlers; to that extent Fanon's theory is justified.) It would also be necessary to account for the survival, through the colonial period, of so much dancing of a quite different character from that described—gay and flirtatious dances of the Fanti, grave and ceremonious dances of the Dagomba.

The truth is that *le colonisé* is far less uniform a person than Fanon's French-instilled taste for generalization leads him to suggest. There are people whose colonial experience has been such that they have become culturally part of the metropolis—though a rather special part. Fanon's own Antillais belong to this group, as do almost all the intellectuals of the French tropical colonies. In extreme cases—like those of the Antillais and the Creoles of Sierra Leone—this has been accompanied for years by a sense of actually being French or British and a nearly complete divorce from pre-colonial culture and traditions. In other cases—as in Africa between the forest belt and the Sahara—large populations continued their traditional way of life, hardly touched by the colonial experience. Others have been more deeply affected, but without at all losing their sense of national identity or feeling the slightest temptation to "be" French or British. Colonial rule was often too brief to penetrate the psyche as thoroughly as Fanon assumes. Thus in Ashanti the present Asantehene, Prempeh II, born in Kumasi when it was the capital of the independent Ashanti kingdom, now keeps state in Kumasi, which is the second city of independent Ghana. And young Ashantis have been brought up to believe that Ashanti was never conquered at all—and behave with the assurance of men who so believe. Yet they too are among *les colonisés.*

The value of **The Wretched of the Earth** does not lie in its often fanciful generalizations but in its relation to direct experience, in the perspective of the Algerian revolution. We are only too liable to look at the poor world through rich-world spectacles, and to be unconscious that there can be other ways of looking at it. Fanon forces his readers to see the Algerian revolution—and by analogy other contemporary revolutions—from the viewpoint of the rebels. This is not the viewpoint of the European liberal, sympathetic to the aims of the revolution, but deploring its excesses and seeking a nonviolent way out. It is not even the viewpoint of a French sympathizer with the revolution like Sartre, whose introduction to this volume is mainly preoccupied with France's guilt. Fanon preaches violence, including violence against civilians, as a legitimate resource of the oppressed.

The French established and maintained their rule in Algeria by violence, including violence against civilians; the conquered have the right to use equivalent violence to end that rule; they will rightly refuse to allow their conquerors to instruct them on what forms of violence are to be considered legitimate. Fanon here touches a raw nerve in his Western readers. One of the forms of violence frequently practiced by Algerian rebels was the murder and mutilation of settlers, including women and children. Fanon shows that, as regards the women and children, A.L.N. commanders tried to discourage such acts; they did not always succeed; Fanon neither condones, nor explicitly condemns, the murder and mutilation of women and children: many will regard him as implicitly condoning such acts, and if silence is condonation they are right. Before we cry out in horror at this, we might do well to consider what we ourselves implicitly condone or have condoned, by our silence. The peasants who did these things acted in accordance with a certain logic: the logic of war. They believed that the more atrocities could be perpetrated against settler families and the more horrible these atrocities were, the sooner the settlers would begin to leave the country and the sooner the war would be over—bringing safety to the women and children of the peasants. This peasant logic is in all essentials the same as that applied by the very civilized James B. Conant when he advised that the best target for the first atomic bomb would be a war plant "employing a large number of workers and closely surrounded by workers' houses." Those who can permit themselves the luxury of being advised by people like James B. Conant have murdered and mutilated, and are continuing to murder and mutilate, in Vietnam and elsewhere, far more children than the Algerian peasants ever did. But we do not call it murder when it is done from the air. And we do not feel so bad about it when the children are not white.

Fanon's position essentially is that all crimes committed by both sides in the Algerian War derive from the basic crime of a rule imposed and maintained by violence, and inaccessible to any appeal save that of violence. On the plane of generalities, I think Fanon is right. Yet personal responsibility, on both sides, inescapably remained, as the astonishing Algerian psychiatric case histories which conclude the book show. A young A.L.N. soldier who killed a settler's wife, becomes obsessed by a double image combining his own mother with the disembowled European woman. A French policeman, whose daily work is the torturing of Algerian suspects, takes to torturing his own wife and children, and asks Fanon to cure him of this—that is to say, of torturing his wife and children. "This man was well aware that all his troubles were caused by the sort of work he did in the interrogation rooms, although he tried to throw the whole responsibility for this work on to 'the situation.' As he had no intention—it would make no sense—of stopping torturing (he would have had to resign if he did) he asked me straight out to help him to torture Algerian patriots without remorse, without behavioral disturbances, in all serenity."

Feeling unable to supply such services, Fanon left the French-run mental hospital in 1956 and devoted the brief remainder of his life to the cause of Algerian freedom. He did not live long enough to see an independent Algeria. He did see other independent African states and writes about postindependence problems without illusions. He is skeptical about African unity, one-party states, the cult of the leader. He

noted—no later than in 1961—that despite "the sonorous affirmations about the unity of the continent," African unity "was sinking into evanescence." As for the one-party state, it was "the modern form of bourgeois dictatorship, without mask, make-up or scruples, cynical." Here again we may note the excessive tendency to generalize; the one-party states are not all alike, or all averse from masks and make-up; bourgeois dictatorships can be assured without a one-party state as every Nigerian knows.

About leaders also he does not fear to generalize, and he hits hard: "Before independence the leader generally incarnated the aspirations of the people; independence, political liberty, national dignity. But after independence, far from incarnating in a concrete way the needs of the people, far from promoting the real dignity of the people . . . the leader will reveal his inner function: that of being the chairman of that great company composed of greedy profiteers which is the national bourgeoisie."

After independence, as before it, Frantz Fanon remained a champion of the people and a harsh and fearless critic of their rulers. (pp. 674-76)

> *Conor Cruise O'Brien, "The Neurosis of Colonialism," in* The Nation, *New York, Vol. 200, No. 25, June 21, 1965, pp. 674-6.*

Robert Coles (essay date 1965)

[*In the following essay, Coles examines* The Wretched of the Earth, *praising it as a "subtle work of art" with a "healing" message.*]

Is it possible to get a comfortable people like ours to examine—and do it with feeling—the terrible underpinnings of their own comfort? I am not only speaking of the historical sources of the present wealth owned by Europe and the United States, a subject less touchy to review, but the present day actualities: the tin and bauxite, the rubber, the sugar, the coffee and bananas, the oil—all supplied us by foreign lands and foreign labor, at sacrifices to those nations and their people we do not usually wish to contemplate. How many of us care to find out about the role of American corporations in the politics of Central America and South America? Who has the time and energy to anguish over what the farflung "informants" of our Central Intelligence Agency are doing toward keeping harsh and dishonest governments in power, or preventing their overthrow at the hands of enraged, too long denied mobs?

Then there is the matter of the individuals in those mobs, those whose faces sometimes confront us, their resentful, hungry, suddenly awakened expressions spread over our newspapers and television screens on a particularly bad day in Bolivia or the Congo, in Iran or the nearby Dominican Republic. If there is one bit of redemption we of the West claim it is our dedication to the dignity of each person, to his rights and overall worth, his simply for being human. We look in horror at the totalitarian regimes elsewhere—a horror, we constantly remind ourselves, that has its origins in our regard for the private citizen. (The millions in this country who still live hard-up lives, some of them under the meanest of "local" political and social systems are the unhappy exception that proves the rule.)

That being the case, how many of us see the people in those foreign mobs as the "individuals" they are, or were born to be? Such mobs confuse us. They get too insistent. They become illogical and wild. They seem thoroughly unappeased by our attention and our diplomacy. They scorn our suddenly aroused offers of money and advice. Only reluctantly do they take our parcels of food and our emissaries, fresh and eager with their bureaucratic training or engineering skills. Ingratitude is foolish, we remind them; pride a sin. The problems of power are "complicated," we tell ourselves. These things cannot be settled all at once (though it is interesting how fast many of them are settled by the sudden uprisings of the thoughtless poor and their conspiratorial, anti-colonialist leaders). Anyway, let the past be forgotten; today we are sensitive as well as what we always were, sensible. All the natives need to do is cooperate. Not only do we want progress for ourselves, we want it for everyone.

Yet, the masses continue to doubt our protestations, even our basic goodwill. Perhaps they are collectively irrational, or perhaps it is their leaders who are crazed. Often they do seem a sick lot: Castro shouting at inordinate length, Sukarno exhibiting extreme capriciousness if not chronically unstable nerves; and those fellows like vain Nkrumah, or wily Tshombe, or Kenyatta, so long associated with the eerily murderous Mau-Mau. What can you do with a shaky collection like that?

Well, we are lucky; a psychiatrist has come along, willing and able to tell us what ails such far away people and their leaders. Frantz Fanon was born in Martinique and educated in France to be a physician and specialize in treating mental disorders. At 27 he tried to describe the feelings of a Negro living in a predominately white world *(Black Skin, White Masks).* Soon thereafter he was summoned to Africa, there serving with the French during the "internal" war, the rebellion of the Algerians against the mother country. Instead he deserted to the foe, convinced that colonialism must die. He worked as a doctor for the rebels, and wrote passionately for them, publishing *Year Five of the Algerian Revolution* and this present volume, which is a study of the political and economic nature of racism and colonialism as well as an analysis of what they both do to the minds of their victims. In 1961, at 36, Fanon was dead of a cancer he knowingly ignored in order to work as a revolutionary. As he so often observed, the oppressed live short lives.

This book tells what is happening to those lives now (as colonialism relinquishes its grasp on them) and it does so in a singular way, mixing the doctor's and psychiatrist's concern for the health of the individual with the political rebel's interest in institutional change and the street fighter's canny sense of tactics and power.

Before we can hear Fanon, we have to contend with Sartre, whose preface shows all too clearly how little of the book's spirit he has absorbed. The Parisian intellectual tries to outdo Fanon's anger, and at the same time wants to give it direction. Where Fanon cries his specific outrage at European sins, then goes on to abstain hating Europe as such, or Europeans in general (he took on French patients in Algeria) Sartre forecasts the doom of Europe with uninhibited enthusiasm and wrath, showing not the slightest effort—and he is a philosopher—to differentiate between the West's past behavior, its present struggles, or the honest future it just might have. He writes "to bring the argument to a conclusion," then follows that remark with what is the least charitable assault on Europe ever written, one that fairly quickly focuses—of all places—on Paris and its "narcissism." (It is the philosopher, not the psychiatrist, who gets tied up with language like that.)

Just as Fanon cannot escape the purposes of Sartre, the colonial peoples in general have found themselves caught in the blunt competition of the Cold War. Fanon desperately wants a way out for Africans, calling it a "Third World" that will hopefully avoid commitment either to Washington, Moscow or Peking. For him, a Stalin would be merely another imperialist.

In the major portion of the book Fanon talks mainly to—though sometimes about—this beloved Third World. I suppose, sitting at my comfortable desk, I can dismiss many of the pages as repetitious and tiring. Again and again the poor are exhorted to rise up, to break away from their jailers. (Again and again the jailers have hunted them down; and so the repetition I find in the book has been experienced by others.) The violence, the brute force that once enslaved people and still holds them at sword's point is relentlessly exposed. The violence in the violated, potential vengeance run amok, is not neglected either.

Fanon's "wretched" have yet to find true freedom, and he knew it when he died, in spite of the so-called "sovereignty" granted one nation after another in Africa. Are those countries, or the many "republics" of Central and South America, free when they are at the various mercies of foreign stock exchanges, industrial complexes, and a nondescript assortment of mercenaries, spies, agents, and what have you—in the clutch, troops—whose activities probably match the most lurid fantasies any of us can make up?

What distinguishes this book, turns it from a blazing manifesto to an authentic and subtle work of art, is the author's extraordinary capacity to join his sharp social and political sense with the doctor's loyalty to the individual, whatever his particular worth or folly. As a result, fierce hatred—to hell with the merciless exploiters, still bleeding their victims—is qualified by an alarmed recognition that native tyranny can replace its foreign predecessor. Indeed, the author systematically exposes such dangers as ultranationalism in the newly liberated countries; the cult of the leader; the kind of excessive regard for the "spontaneity" of the people that results in disorder all around; the mystification that ideas like "negritude" can produce; and the extreme betrayal threatening millions in the countryside of Africa at the hands of the colonial-trained native civil servants—to Fanon they are a rigid, arrogant crew—who try to take over the new governments when the Europeans make their reluctant or relieved departure.

It is in the book's last section that Dr. Fanon reveals his skills as narrator and artist. Shunning any temptation to avoid confusion and ambiguity, the gray in life, he gives us instead a terrifying glimpse into the mental disorders associated with both colonialism and the revolutions that aim to end it. The crushed people are brought to life as only the novelist or clinician can do it, by detailed descriptions of their private lives, their fears and terrors. One price of rebellion, the mental pain, is revealed, as are the tortures rebellion evokes from the desperate colonial authorities, many of whom eventually collapse, prey to their own bestiality.

Fanon at a Front de Libération Nationale (FLN) press conference in Tunis, 1957.

Fanon is impressively and painstakingly willing to see hurt and suffering on all sides, guilt everywhere, the entire population saturated with anxiety and night-mares. Children cringe; natives lunge, then collapse in panic; some of the oppressors, at last unnerved and petulant, are seized with remorse. People are tortured, pressed for information, left cowering, not for hours or days, but for the long months they, their families and their doctors must confront.

It is an awful spectacle; and in many ways the justice Fanon does to the mind of the native African under such circumstances resembles what Conrad did to the white man's in *Heart of Darkness*. Western man shares "the horror, the horror" of his nature with millions of others in all corners of the globe. Terror and madness will unite ruler and sufferer if it must come to chaos before brazen tyranny is ended. Insofar as we realize that fact, and act on what we realize, we will live safer and less corrupt lives. For all the resentment and hurt in him, Dr. Fanon had that message for us when he wrote this book, and it is a healing one. (pp. 20, 22-3)

> *Robert Coles, "What Colonialism Does," in* The New Republic, *Vol. 153, No. 12, September 18, 1965, pp. 20, 22-3.*

Frances Foster (essay date 1970)

[*In the following excerpt, Foster discusses Fanon's concept of black identity. In an unexcerpted portion of the article, Foster also compares the black man in* Black Skin, White Masks *with the anonymous protagonist in Ralph Ellison's* Invisible Man.]

In his book ***Black Skin, White Masks,*** Frantz Fanon uses psychoanalysis with a sociodiagnostic perspective to examine "the experiences of a black man in a white world." Basing his theories upon personal observation, case studies, and the writings of several philosophers, he analyzes the psychology of the phenomenon known as the Negro in terms of environmental influences. Fanon's conclusion is that the black man is not a man and that he can become a man only through a process of disalienation which includes liberation from himself. (p. 46)

Fanon makes it very clear that he is not speaking of all blacks. He limits his remarks to the black who fits within the cultural, class, and psychological boundaries which he delineates. He says his conclusions, especially those concerning the black man at home, are valid only for the Negro of the Antilles. His concern in this work is limited to the intellectual alienation of the middle class, an alienation that is different from the alienation of the worker or the "jungle savage." Though these limitations seem to narrow his subject considerably, he, neverthe-less, acknowledges that most of his observations and conclusions can be applied to a more universal group of blacks. In reality, Fanon is speaking of any Negro in contact with white civilization who is "the slave of the spontaneous and cosmic Negro myth" and who in a struggle to discover the meaning of his black identity directly confronts his race. Within this context, Fanon does three things. He states that the black is not a man. He shows the process by which this loss of humanity has occurred. He concludes that only through a process of disalienation can the black regain his humanity and, thus, to be a man.

Then Fanon defines his concept of humanity, indicating that manhood requires two essential conditions: self-consciousness which leads to confrontation, and mutual recognition by two men. One must first recognize his own humanity. One must then risk this recognition by asserting himself upon another whom he recognizes as man and be recognized as man in return. Fanon says, "Man is human only to the extent to which he tries to impose his existence upon another man in order to be recognized by him . . . human reality in-itself-for-itself can be achieved only through conflict and through the risk that conflict implies." This concept is seen also in the writings of Eldridge Cleaver, who in his chapter, "On Becoming," [in *Soul on Ice* (1968)], says that his emergence into a realization of his humanity began when he discovered that he had to act and take the initiative, instead of merely reacting. He had to discover his manhood, then force others to acknowledge it. In his "Prelude to Love—Three Letters" he declares also the importance of mutual recognition in the achievement of any valid humanity.

The same concept is shared by Malcolm X who writes [in *The Autobiography of Malcolm X* (1966)] that "One thing the white man can never give the black man is self-respect," and that the black man can be "recognized as a human being who is truly equal with other human beings" when he becomes an actional person and acts in his own best interests.

Fanon declares that a man is one who is all his actions shows respect for the basic values of the human world, and accepts the universality which is inherent in the human condition as a valid objective truth. Fanon says, "Man is a *Yes* that vibrates to cosmic harmonies." Man affirms life, love, and generosity. Man is also a *No* to scorn, degradation, exploitation, and butchery of "what is most human in man: freedom." Since in Fanon's estimation, the white man has not displayed the *Yes* and *No* of being a man, he is not a man. In *The Fire Next Time,* James Baldwin speaks of the same idea: "White people cannot, in the generality, be taken as models of how to live. Rather, the white man is himself in sore need of new standards which will release him from his confusion and place him once again in fruitful communication with the depths of his own being." The alienated black man, according to Fanon, is not a man because he makes two basic mistakes by seeing the white as a man and by petitioning the white to recognize him as a man. The bestowal of manhood upon a person is impossible.

Fanon says that what is known as the black man is a peculiar creation of white civilization, and even what is called the black soul is actually a white artifact. In order to perpetrate and perpetuate the expansion of the white civilization and Western culture, the white had to eradicate the black civilization and African culture. The black man's humanity could not be recognized as containing the universality of all man, but had to be deviated. Thus, the whites found dehumanization necessary in order to justify their colonialization of blacks, for even they could not deliberately exploit, degrade, and scorn those considered their equals. In other words, the racists created their inferiors in order to prove their superiority and thus justify their domination.

This concept is quite evident in the writings of many American blacks. Malcolm X says the American blacks are a "homemade, handmade, brainwashed race" created by whites. Cleaver says, "Let us recall that the white man, in order to justify slavery and, later on, to justify segregation, elaborated a complex, all pervasive myth which at one time classified the black man as a subhuman beast of burden" and "the white devils killed the black man—killed him mentally, culturally, spiritually, economically, politically, and morally—transforming him into a 'Negro'." John Oliver Killens takes the concept even further when he states in *Black Man's Burden* that "Having invented the Negro to justify slavery, the Negro invention was used as an apologia for the colonialization of three-quarters of the world's people, in Asia, Africa, and the Islands."

Many blacks are in agreement with Frantz Fanon when he states that the white created an "*imago* of the Negro which is responsible for all the conflicts that may arise." They agree that "In the collective unconscious of *homo occidentalis,* the Negro—or if one prefers, the color black—symbolizes evil, sin, wretchedness, death, war, famine. All birds of prey are black," To the white, the Negro is not a fellow man, he is a phobogenic object. Fanon agrees with James Baldwin who says, "The white man's unadmitted . . . private fears and longings are projected onto the Negro."

This concept is precisely that which Richard Wright exposes in *Native Son*. Throughout the novel, the whites are able to see Bigger and his actions only in terms of their *imago*. At first they overlook Bigger as a suspect in Mary Dalton's murder because their concept of the black denied his capability of appearing innocent when guilty. Later, they can only account for his actions in terms of an animalistic, sex impassioned act. Even Max, Bigger's lawyer, cannot see past his liberal Communist sociological stereotypes and comprehend Bigger as a man.

Fanon further states that not only is the black so surrounded by myth, fantasy and projection that he accepts the European evaluation of his blackness but that to the extent that he agrees with this *imago,* he realizes an inferiority complex. Fanon explains this by the clinical explanation that "The neurotic structure of an individual is simply the elaboration, the formation, the eruption within the ego, of conflictual clusters arising in part out of the environment and in part out of the purely personal way in which an individual reacts to these influences." The white man had defined the black. Because of the white man's power, which is primarily economic, the white causes the black to question the reality of his own manhood. One result is the loss of that self consciousness which is the basis of humanity. Thus, Fanon, speaking as the black man, "I begin to suffer from not being a white man to the degree that the white man imposes discrimination on me, makes me a colonized native, robs me of all worth, all individuality, tells me I am a parasite on the world, that I must bring myself as quickly as possible into step with the white world."

The black man wants to be accepted as a man; therefore, he must make himself white in order to compel the white's acknowledgment that he is human. This means he has accepted the idea that the white is more than equal, that the white is in a position to demand proof of humanity rather than simply to recognize it, a condition that Cleaver describes as pathological. The black has accepted the defensive, reactional role rather than the offensive, actional. He becomes a comparison. He is preoccupied always with self-evaluation and his closeness to the ideal. Fanon says "The Antilleans have no inherent values of their own, they are always contingent on the presence of The Other. The question is always whether he is less intelligent than I, blacker than I, less respectable than I. Every position of one's own, every effort—at security, is based on relations of dependence, with the diminution of the other." The black needs The Other to corroborate him in his search for self validation. The governing force is no longer personal—man confronting man, but it is black compared to black against the pattern of white.

In a further effort to support his declaration that the black is not a man, but is, in fact, an aberration created by whites, Fanon explains the process by which this dehumanization is achieved. He begins with the obvious fact that Western culture is white and any man raised in this culture having no knowledge of any other culture will use this white world as his reference point. He says, "There is a constellation of postulates, a series of propositions that slowly and subtly—with the help of books, newspapers, schools and their texts, advertisements, films, radio—work their way into one's mind and shape one's view of the world of the group to which one belongs. In the Antilles that view of the world is white because no black voice exists." Through this process, which can be called the collective unconscious, it is normal for the black man to perceive black as the symbol of evil. It is normal for the Antillean to be anti-Negro.

This concept is also supported by those American blacks previously quoted as well as by Leopold Senghor who says, "... our secret enemies, in defending their values, have made us despise our own. And so we now go around shouting slogans from their ideologies which we are naive enough to believe in."

It is only when the rejection, that comes from contact with the white world, is applied to him does the black realize he, too, is considered black. This realization results in a sense of shame. This shame fills him with a rage that hinders human communication and thus causes a great sense of isolation. Condemned by those with whom he identifies as one of those whom he himself condemns, he realizes an involuntary insularity which is intolerable. Curiously, however, the black believes he is black only to the extent that he portrays those qualities attributed to blackness, that is, only to the extent that he is sinful, sloppy, malicious, and emotional. Thus, he tries to be the opposite of black— he tries to be white. Fanon says, "When the Negro makes contact with the white world, a certain sensitizing action takes place. If his psychic structure is weak, one observes a collapse of the ego." In his frantic attempt to become white, language becomes of basic importance. Through mastery of its language, a person can assume a culture, for he can be privy to its history, philosophies, and aspirations. In the case of colonized peoples, such as blacks in Western society, one's status is escalated in proportion to his comprehension and assimilation of the colonizer's cultural standards. Thus, for the black, comprehension of the white man's language is basic to his becoming white and thereby, human. Therefore, the black man is partially responsible for his alienation from humanity. He abandons his self-consciousness in the effort to receive from the dominating culture what he believes is manhood. Using language as his basic tool, he insists upon being recognized for his intellect and his academic achievement.

This appeal to Reason for deliverance from blackness is effective only to a limited extent. Often a black is accepted—tentatively—by a group of whites. For him, the barriers are lowered and he is considered a special kind of black man who is accorded some degree of individuality. Usually his acceptance is a temporary thing. He is accepted theoretically as an equal member of the human race in spite of his color. However, since his physical appearance is a constant reminder of his difference, acceptance is never total. For this reason, a common reaction is to become very black, to embrace the *imago* of blackness and to assert oneself as a Black Man whose blackness is not evil, but is good. The obstacles here are almost insurmountable for the battle is at once internal and external. It becomes a vicious circle. The only solution is to break out.

The black man's situation and alternatives are summed up thus: Living in a culture wherein the black symbolizes sin, he begins to hate the black. Upon recognition that he is black, he must either deny his color or assert it. Having conceded that the black man is the color of evil, he must try to find value for what is bad. In order to terminate this neurotic situation, the only solution is "to rise above this absurd drama that others have staged... to reject the two terms that are equally unacceptable, and, through one human being, to reach out for the universal." Thus, from his analysis of the black man's predicament, Fanon concludes that the only possibility for him to achieve humanity is to rise above the "absurd drama" through disalienation.

The disalienation which Fanon espouses is intellectual and individual. The first step for the black is to become conscious of his unconscious self-destruction and to cease his attempts to become white. Instead, he must recognize those forces which are perpetrating his aberration and challenge them. The black man must refuse to be trapped by his past and must refuse to accept the present social structure as definitive. He must recognize that a black skin does not inherently surround specific characteristics. He must realize that what is called the Negro is nothing more than a manifestation of desires and fears, a creation of society. He must become actional. Fanon suggests that the black turn to Aime Cesaire for inspiration and repeat: "And more than anything my body, as well as my soul, do not allow yourself to cross your arms like a sterile spectator, for life is not a spectacle, for a sea of sorrows is not a stage, for a man who cries out is not a dancing bear...."

Although many black intellectuals concur with Fanon on his basic principles, they do not all agree upon the application of these ideas, for in the final analysis, Fanon says, a man has no right to be a Negro and no duty to be this or that. A man has one right: that of demanding human behavior from the other, and one duty: that of not renouncing freedom through his choices. However, Richard Wright arrived at this conclusion when he said in a 1960 interview for *L'Express,* "Color is not my country. I am a human being before being a Negro." Another person who admits the ultimate goal in this is one of the proponents of Negritude, Leopold Senghor, who says the ultimate goal of Negritude is "the building of the *Civilization of the Universal.*" (pp. 46-51)

> Frances Foster, "The Black and White Masks of Frantz Fanon and Ralph Ellison," in Black Academy Review, *Vol. 1, No. 4, Winter, 1970, pp. 46-58.*

Edmund Burke III (essay date 1976)

[*In the following review essay, Burke favorably appraises* The Wretched of the Earth, *describing it as a "spiritual guide for an unspiritual age on how to achieve revolutionary beatitude."*]

Frantz Fanon's **The Wretched of the Earth,** first published in 1961, is probably the most widely read of the books to emerge from the Third World upheaval of the post-war period; it has been translated into sixteen languages and has reached an international audience. Initially, it was widely hailed as the most passionate and brilliant analysis of the process of decolonization. Rereading the book today, one realizes how much the world has changed in the interval: we now see the extent to which Fanon was a man of his times and the extent to which he was a throwback to the Romantic nationalists of the nineteenth century. Far from having been the

Marx of the African revolution (and there were some who mistook him for that), Fanon now emerges more clearly as having been its Mazzini. For the strength of **The Wretched of the Earth** rests less on the incisiveness of its analysis than on the violence and inspiration of its rhetoric. It is a call to arms, not a scholarly autopsy. In the end, it seems more appropriate to apply to it the methods of literary criticism than those of political science. Despite its many contradictions and excesses, **The Wretched of the Earth** remains a remarkable achievement. The universalism of Fanon's imagination and the forcefulness of his language have given the work an appeal that has already made it a modern classic.

In some ways, what one makes of the book depends on what one makes of Fanon himself. By the details of his biography, Frantz Fanon was a kind of black Everyman, a marginal man who was nonetheless able to transcend his marginality. He was born in 1925 into a middle-class black family in Martinique in the French West Indies. Intensely conscious of his race, but also irrevocably within the orbit of French society by virtue of his education and class position, he found himself unable unambiguously to throw in his lot with either. Like others of his background, Fanon fell under the influence of Aimé Césaire, the Martiniquean poet and politician, and of the movement of *négritude* of which Césaire was a leader. He was to remain deeply marked by this early encounter, although *négritude* came increasingly to seem shallow and parochial to him as time went on. His first book, **Black Skin, White Masks,** published in 1952, publicly revealed this ambiguous break with Césaire. It also shows something else—the manner in which Fanon was able to use this ambivalent position among cultures and races to develop a series of penetrating insights into the psychology of racism and colonial domination. His continual preoccupation with these themes was later to give rise to some of the most incandescent passages in **The Wretched of the Earth.**

The life of Frantz Fanon contains a number of additional paradoxes for our reflection. Outwardly, he was the very model of the successful young professional, a psychiatrist of undoubted talents and ambition. He completed his medical degree in 1953 and soon thereafter was posted to the mental hospital at Blida, a small city near Algiers, with the position of *chef de service.* When the revolution broke out at the end of 1954, he was initially slow to take sides. But by 1956 his growing involvement with the rebels led him to resign his position and openly to join the revolution. Even after he became an editor of *El Moudjahid,* the F.L.N. newspaper in Tunis in 1957, however, he continued to practice medicine.

The fact that Fanon was a psychiatrist was to have a major impact on his analysis of the Third World revolution. On the one hand, it was to make him more sensitive than most to the sufferings of individuals in the grip of the colonial system and of the ambivalences of colonizers and colonized. On the other hand, it was to lead him to underestimate the importance of social and economic structures and, consequently, to overrate the possibilities of change. Fanon remained a deeply committed partisan of the cause of Algerian independence until his death. His duties for the F.L.N. brought him into continual contact with the leaders of the independence movements in black Africa, and he was thus able to renew his commitment to the Pan-African dream and to black liberation. In 1960, he served for a time as F.L.N. representative to the All-African People's Conference in Accra, Ghana. In the end, of course, Frantz Fanon was neither an Algerian nor an African. This fact gave his treatment of both movements a curious ambivalence, at once the sympathetic supporter and the clear-sighted critic. Like Albert Memmi, whose *Colonizer and Colonized* presents an analysis of French colonialism which in important ways parallels his own, Fanon was the perpetual outsider. Unlike Memmi, he was able to transcend his marginality to take part in the struggle. *The Wretched of the Earth* can be seen as a kind of synthesis of his life's experience.

The favorable reception of *The Wretched of the Earth* needs to be understood in terms of the movements of decolonization in the postwar world. The steady, ineluctable retreat of European colonialism evoked a feeling of excitement and expectancy throughout Asia and Africa. For a time all things were believed possible; it was the dawn of a new age, of a new chance for humanity. It was at the apogee of this wave of enthusiasm that *The Wretched of the Earth* was published. The forcefulness of its language, its condemnation of colonialism and justification of armed resistance elicited an immediate response throughout the Third World. The book echoed the hopes and fears of its times, and it did so with an idealism that is hard to imagine being expressed today.

The Wretched of the Earth needs also to be situated within the political and intellectual context of postwar France. French intellectuals, already bitterly divided over the Cold War and Stalinism, found themselves in the early nineteen-fifties at odds over decolonization as well. The Algerian war further intensified this conflict. On the Left, the battle was joined between the supporters of the F.L.N. and the French Communist Party. As a leading F.L.N. publicist, Fanon wanted to widen the base of support in French left-wing circles for the insurgents, and *The Wretched of the Earth* was the political manifesto by which he sought to accomplish this task.

The book is the product of an intellectual milieu, as well as a political debate—the cafés of Saint-Germain-des-Prés and postwar Marxism and Existentialism are never far from its pages. The influence of Jean-Paul Sartre, one of the few leading French intellectuals to display an active sympathy for the aspirations of Third World peoples, is especially to be noted. Fanon frequented Sartre's circle in the early nineteen-fifties, and, as has been shown by Irene Gendzier, Sartre's essay *Anti-Semite and Jew* exercised a considerable influence upon Fanon's approach to racism and colonial domination. It

was therefore especially fitting that the first edition of *The Wretched of the Earth* should contain a preface by Sartre.

Tracing intellectual influences on Fanon is a frustrating game, for he freely appropriated concepts which appealed to him, frequently without fully understanding them. His Sartreanism is of this sort, and so is his Marxism. Fanon cannot be described as an orthodox Marxist, although he utilizes Marxist categories and his thought tends to be dialectical. His analysis is indeed impregnated with a kind of folk Marxism which appears to have struck an immediate chord with many of his readers. One suspects that it was less the originality of *The Wretched of the Earth* which assured its success than the way in which it stated what was already widely believed by those for whom it was written.

Another reason for the book's appeal is that, like other classics, it permits a wide range of interpretation. The list of those who claim to have been influenced by it includes (among others) African nationalists, Palestinian commandos, and the Bangladesh guerrillas of 1971-72. It enjoyed particular success among black militants in the United States. For a time it was regarded by the Black Panthers as their "Bible." Third World groups found in it a sympathy for their sufferings, justification for their struggles, and encouragement to persist in overcoming all obstacles. In a sense, the book is a kind of mirror; one sees in it who one is. The quasi-literate militant is carried along by the flow of the language and never led to take the analysis very seriously. Others, with more education and experience, are encouraged to meditate on the pitfalls of bourgeois nationalism, but miss the section on national culture. The liberal critic is horrified by the passages on violence, which he takes as confirmation of his fears of Third World nationalism. Armchair theorists of revolution disparage the book as pre-political. Its heart is in the right place, but its analysis is hopelessly soft-headed, if not dangerously voluntarist. In this way, everyone can have the Fanon he chooses. Somewhere, presumably, Fanon himself is smiling.

It is important to realize that *The Wretched of the Earth* was written by a man who knew that he had but a few short months to live. The greater part of the book was written over a ten-week period in the spring of 1961. Previously, Fanon had planned to write a book that would show the relevance of the Algerian revolution to black Africa. Stricken with leukemia toward the end of 1960, he abandoned that earlier project to address himself to a far more ambitious task, a general study of the Third World upheaval. *The Wretched of the Earth* is thus, in effect, Fanon's revolutionary will and testament, a final personal exorcism of the demons which haunted his life. The first chapter, "On Violence," already contains in embryo the main themes that would be developed subsequently. It is almost as if, fearing that he would never be able to complete the manuscript, Fanon sought to disgorge it all in these first few pages. The argument is extremely difficult to follow, as it is presented in an abrupt, violent, and convulsive fashion that eludes all but the most careful of readings. The writing is here at its most searing, an extraordinary outpouring of white-hot emotion—sarcasm, anger, and contempt.

It is clear that Fanon had a very personal sense of language, and this has a great deal to do with the impact the book has had on its readers. Fanon had little patience with most of what passes for intellectual discourse. As he wrote to the French editor of his first book, **Black Skin, White Masks,** in response to a request for clarification on a point in the text, "I cannot explain that phrase more fully. I try, when I write such things, to touch the nerves of my reader.... That's to say irrationally, almost sensually." It seems to me that his style had its roots in the popular culture of Martinique. It is as if **The Wretched of the Earth** were written more to be declaimed like some enormous and terrifying prose poem than it was to be read. No one who has ever encountered the book has come away unmoved.

One key to what the book is about is contained in the final chapter. Here, we are given a vision of the future of mankind, of a new golden age. The chapter begins with some corrosive remarks on the decadence of Western civilization:

> When I search for Man in the technique and the style of Europe, I see only a succession of negations of man, and an avalanche of murders.

> The human condition, plans for mankind, and collaboration between men in those tasks which increase the sum total of humanity are new problems, which demand true inventions.

Then there follows a series of exhortations:

> Let us decide not to imitate Europe; let us combine our muscles and our brains in a new direction. Let us try to create the whole man, whom Europe has been incapable of bringing to triumphant birth.

> Two centuries ago, a former European colony decided to catch up with Europe. It succeeded so well that the United States of America became a monster, in which the taints, the sickness, and the inhumanity of Europe have grown to appalling dimensions.

> Comrades, have we not other work to do than to create a third Europe? The West saw itself as a spiritual adventure. It is in the name of the spirit, in the name of the spirit of Europe, that Europe has made her encroachments, that she has justified her crimes and legitimized the slavery in which she holds the four-fifths of humanity.

Finally, there come the visions of the future:

> It is a question of the Third World starting a new history of Man, a history which will have regard to the sometimes prodigious theses which Europe has put forward, but which will also not forget Europe's crimes, of which the most horrible was committed in the heart of man, and consisted of the pathological tearing apart of his functions and the crumbling away of his unity.

> ... For Europe, for ourselves, and for humanity, comrades, we must turn over a new leaf, we must work out new concepts, and try to set afoot a new man.

The notions that the confrontation between European civilization and the societies of the Third World would produce a new man and a new chance for humanity were commonplaces of African writings in French at the time. In Fanon, they become part of a new golden age which would be attained through the success of the Third World revolution. In this sense, **The Wretched of the Earth** is a utopian work, a mighty hymn to the advent of the new man, freed from colonialism, racism, national chauvinism, and class oppression. If we view the work as a whole, rather than taking individual sections out of context (the better to criticize them), it is here that we must start.

The Black Panthers were more correct than they knew when they regarded Fanon's book as their "Bible." I would insist on the biblical metaphor. Even though Fanon was not a Christian, the work is permeated with salvationism, albeit of a secular kind. Indeed, I would go even further and suggest that to read the book in its entirety is, in a sense, to undergo a conversion. The argument is not always easy to follow; each succeeding chapter negates and supplants the main points in the one that comes before. By this method, one progresses from the crippling Manicheism of the colonial experience to the pitfalls of national consciousness and finally to the vision of the new man. The individual who conscientiously follows this path achieves a kind of secular salvation or, in Fanon's terms, he becomes politically educated. The book is thus a spiritual guide for an unspiritual age on how to achieve revolutionary beatitude. Like a sermon in a Southern Baptist church, **The Wretched of the Earth** shows us the fires of hell and the glories of the world to come, warns us of the dangers along the way, and encourages us to lend our energies to the work of the Lord. We emerge from the experience transformed, no longer the same men and women.

Like most such experiences, however, there is the letdown of the morning after—the realization that our faults and those of society are not so easily corrected. Given Fanon's suspicions of fancy words and high-flown phrases (by which the bourgeois nationalist leaders deceive the people), there is a chilling irony here. How to warn the people of the intoxication brought by words, when one is intoxicated by them oneself? In the end, one begins to doubt that Fanon has managed to escape from his own rhetorical trap.

The Wretched of the Earth is filled with ideas which flow in many different, often contradictory, directions. Despite the rhetoric, there is an orderly progression to the argument, although it is difficult to perceive at first, so dazzling are its individual passages. If the purpose of the book is didactic—what Fanon calls (following Césaire) the inventing of souls—its structure rests on four interwoven levels of analysis, which are successively introduced in the first four chapters. The levels progress

The Fanon brothers—Joby, Felix, and Frantz—posing before a soccer game in 1946.

from the psychological (the analysis of colonialism), to the societal (the study of spontaneity), to the political (the unreliability of the national bourgeoisie), to the cultural (the call for a national culture). Allied to this is a parallel temporal progression, in which we are led from the colonial system, to armed struggle, to independence (with its disappointments), to an authentically national culture (which can only arise from the revolution). The fifth chapter documents (using Fanon's case notes) the violence of the colonizer, thereby reinforcing the original diagnosis. Finally the conclusion, with its visions of the new man, provides an inspiring *envoi*.

There is little doubt that *The Wretched of the Earth* will in the end prove far more important for the myths it has helped generate than for the quality of its analysis. Chief among these myths is the liberating force of violence in the anti-colonial struggle, which, taken out of context, has been used by a variety of groups to justify programs based solely on killing. Is violence psychologically liberating to the native? The question is never directly posed, but the answer Fanon gives seems to be affirmative. But is it? To deal with what Fanon in fact says requires confronting the structure of his argument as well as his own personal ambivalences.

The section on violence comes toward the end of the first chapter and follows the discussion of the colonial system. The colonial world, we learn, is a Manichean world, a dualistic world, in which the settler stands for all that is good and the native for all that is evil. It is also a world built on violence—first on the bayonets of the conquering armies, then on the psychological violence inflicted on the native to keep him in his place by convincing him of his unworthiness. The impact of the colonial system leads to the disintegration of native society and with it the personality of the native. The argument thus far is built around a series of oppositions: colonizer/colonized, West/non-West, settler/native, disintegrated/integrated. At first these cancel each other out; they are equally false, as Fanon remarks in one place. Then the argument shifts so that these dichotomies become the thesis and antithesis of a dialectic. A synthesis is therefore possible; it represents an escape from the colonial stalemate. The way out is through violence. Because the system was established and perpetuated through violence, it must be destroyed through violence. Fanon even makes the point that the more settlers there are, the more violence there will be. Only in this way can the native reintegrate his personality and the synthesis of the dialectic be achieved. The need for violence thus derives from the logical structure of

Fanon's argument. Violence is (in his theory) good therapy; it is also the best guarantee that the people will remain immune to the mystification of their leaders.

The subject of violence is resumed in the next chapter, but treated from a slightly different angle. There, we learn that violence, while it may be an understandable response to colonial domination, is far from being an adequate one. The phase of spontaneous violence must be quickly superseded. For a war of national liberation to be successful, violence must be disciplined to its needs; it cannot be left uncontrolled. Fanon, as a psychiatrist, was well aware of the destructive impact that violence can have on its perpetrators as well as on its victims. He presents the case histories of a number of torture victims and of their torturers. The former are Algerians, the latter are French. Both suffer lasting psychological damage. He begins his discussion of the psychological impact of torture with the case of an African nationalist who, during the independence struggle, planted a bomb which took the lives of a number of Europeans. Years later, he was still tormented by anxiety and suicidal impulses on the anniversary of the deed. Even in a just cause, we learn, violence is not liberating.

A second myth to emerge from *The Wretched of the Earth* is that of the peasantry as the primary revolutionary force in the colonial world. Based on a misreading of the wider relevance of the Algerian revolutionary experience, Fanon's analysis on this point appears to have led astray more than one would-be guerrilla leader. Why does Fanon select the peasantry? The answer is clear when we examine the text more closely; the logical imperatives of his argument require it. The peasants, as opposed to the bourgeois leadership of the nationalist movement and the urban working classes (both of which have lost contact with the old ways and are therefore the most inclined to individualistic behavior), are the most integrated and thus the best disciplined group. They are therefore most suited to be in the vanguard of the revolution. The original argument of the liberating qualities of violence has been transformed, but the interplay of opposites continues here: integrated/disintegrated, rural/urban, bourgeois/peasant. Fanon's assertion of the primacy of the peasantry in wars of national liberation thus stems from a logical rather than a sociological analysis of the colonial situation.

It is now all but forgotten that Fanon's views of the peasantry were received with ridicule and disbelief. French Communists stoutly condemned the heretical notion that the peasantry, and not the working class, would produce the revolution. Western liberal analysts systematically discounted the rural populations, placing their bets instead on the development of political parties in the cities. Only later, as knowledge of the Chinese and Vietnamese revolutions began to spread and the Cuban revolution came to power through the mobilization of the rural masses, did this consensus begin to change. Algeria was clearly a case of a peasant-based revolutionary movement, and Fanon sought to underscore this fact in his analysis, the better to make some polemical points.

Given Fanon's commitment to the cause of Algerian independence, it was not surprising that he tended to use the Algerian model in his views on the decolonization of the rest of Africa. This has earned him a great deal of adverse criticism, for conditions in Algeria were in important ways quite different from those that pertained in most of black Africa. Juridically part of France, Algeria had almost a million European settlers in 1954 (and some nine million Muslims). The European impact on native society was vastly greater than elsewhere in Africa, and the regime was far more discriminatory and repressive. The prospects for a peasant uprising on anything like the Algerian scale were minimal in other parts of Africa. It is even possible to question Fanon's understanding of the Algerian situation, for his knowledge of Arabic was rudimentary at best and his grasp of the intricacies of Algerian Arab-Islamic culture seems on some points to have been rather precarious. Given Fanon's intentions and the level of generalization on which *The Wretched of the Earth* is written, these are not crippling weaknesses, but they do lessen confidence in his judgment.

One of the most prescient parts of the book is the analysis of the national bourgeoisie. Most of French Africa had been independent for only a few years when Fanon wrote his scathing denunciation of the nationalist elite who had come to power there: the new leaders of Africa are notable chiefly for their ability to manipulate slogans, the better to profit from their office. The people, when they realize that their leaders are primarily interested in filling their pockets, cry treason. But, says Fanon, the treason is not national, it is social. From this, he draws two conclusions. The first of them is that one does not have to be white to be an exploiter, the second, that nationalism is not in itself a sufficient program. Fanon's penetrating criticism of bourgeois nationalism is one of the great achievements of the book. But while we credit Fanon with uncommon foresight in his analysis of the bourgeoisie, we must also recognize that he seriously underestimated its power. According to his analysis, the national bourgeoisie occupied no productive function in the life of the nation and was thus simply an ersatz class whose early disappearance could be anticipated. Time has not borne this out. Today Lumumba is dead, and it is Mobutu who rules Zaire in a grisly parody of the authentic revolution.

One of Fanon's greatest weaknesses lay in his impatience with the study of social and economic structures. This led him to underestimate the staying power of the national bourgeoisie, in particular its connections with the army and its access to external sources of support against domestic rivals. At a time when three quarters of Africa is ruled by military men, it seems in retrospect remarkable how little Fanon has to say on the role of the army in his new Africa. In all fairness, however, others writing at the time were not notably more perceptive.

The first of what was to become an avalanche of military coups did not take place until 1963 in Togo.

Fanon had some proposals about how a country might hope to avoid domination by its national bourgeoisie and pursue a different political path. Basically, Fanon's suggestions are unremarkable. They are the standard ones proposed by theorists of revolution. Having first demonstrated the inadequacies of spontaneous violence, he then indicates how the bourgeois nationalist, by virtue of his class interests, will be unable to address the real problem—namely, social inequality. In order to bring about a more just socio-political system, Fanon suggests, first, that a trustworthy political party be formed, one that will genuinely represent the people (and not merely one that claims, like the bourgeois parties, to represent them); second, that the party's decision-making apparatus be decentralized insofar as possible, in order to place power in the hands of the people; third, that the intellectuals come into close contact with the people, but in such a way that the people still feel that they are in charge; and fourth, that political education be undertaken. Fanon states, "The purpose of political education is to invent souls." The phrase is borrowed from Césaire. Here, the argument shifts abruptly. The party now becomes nothing less than the mechanism that will create the new man; his appearance will mark a new beginning in the history of mankind. This new man—political man—is the creation of the intellectuals. It is totally an accident that just where Fanon is being the most straightforwardly descriptive, we suddenly find ourselves plunged into his utopian dream of the revolution?

It is characteristic of Fanon's thought that in the end he should opt for culture rather than material conditions as the crucial factor in bringing about the revolution. This is made clear in the chapter "On National Culture." It has been a source of debate among Marxists. It is perhaps a reflection of Fanon's consciousness of the fragility of political order in the new Africa that for him the crucial problem is that of legitimacy. If the political legitimacy of the government of national liberation is not to be called into question, then it must be supported by an authentic national culture. Fanon takes great pains to distinguish between the kind of revolutionary culture he is speaking of and the pseudo-national cultures most African states have contented themselves with: folklore, *négritude,* a truncated and self-interested version of the national past. The revolution, if it is not to lose itself in chauvinism, racism, or other errors, must seek to evolve a national consciousness which can transcend narrow nationalism. Only thus, Fanon argues, will it be possible to attain a new humanism. Unlike those who view the struggle in strictly political terms, he sees the revolution above all as a cultural phenomenon, a position approaching that of Mao Tse-tung, or perhaps more appropriately here, the Guinean President Sékou Touré. It is Fanon at his most theoretical, but also at his most universalist and humanitarian.

The Wretched of the Earth is a book of a particular moment in history, but also a stage of development of political consciousness in the Third World. With the liberation of most of Africa, its popularity is in decline and its utopian vision no longer seems convincing. The two major myths to which the book gave rise, that of the liberating qualities of violence and that of the primacy of the peasantry in the liberation struggle, still have their adherents, but they lack persuasive force in the harsher political environment of the mid-seventies. Yet while the book has reduced appeal, its language still has a capacity to startle and capture the attention of new discoverers. The upheaval in the Third World and among American domestic minorities persists, although new forms of struggle have emerged. It seems safe to predict that Fanonist ideas will continue to find supporters among the desperate and the downtrodden. To a remarkable degree, *The Wretched of the Earth* can still put us in touch with the hopes and fears of an age and with its lost illusions. In its pages that springtime of the nations, the nineteen-fifties and early -sixties, lives again. Because of its rhetorical brilliance, but also its universalism, *The Wretched of the Earth* will continue to be read long after other more parochial writings from this period and perspective have been forgotten. (pp. 127-35)

> *Edmund Burke III, "Frantz Fanon's 'The Wretched of the Earth',"* in Daedalus: Journal of the American Academy of Arts And Sciences, *Vol. 105, No. 1, Winter, 1976, pp. 127-35.*

FURTHER READING

Abrash, Barbara. "Frantz Fanon." *Africana Library Journal* 11, No. 3 (Autumn 1971): 9-12.
    Bio-bibliography of Fanon, with a discussion of *The Wretched of the Earth.*

Bondy, Francois. "The Black Rousseau." *The New York Review of Books* VI, No. 5 (March 1966): 26-7.
    Review of *The Wretched of the Earth,* describing it as a work that elevated Fanon to "the rank of hero and saint of 'negritude'."

———. "Frantz Fanon." *Encounter* XLIII, No. 2 (August 1974): 25-9.
    Evaluates Fanon's views about political liberation. Characterizing Fanon as the "Black Orpheus" of revolutionary intelligentsia, Bondy states: "[Fanon] was more a creature of the European system than he would ever know or admit, although he wanted to free a whole continent from it. Outside this system, and apart from the societies and cultures where it obtains, he is quite incomprehensible."

Forsythe, Dennis. "Frantz Fanon: Black Theoretician." *The Black Scholar* 1, No. 5 (March 1970): 2-10.

Lauds Fanon as a great hero, stating: "Fanon's presence was not only felt during the Algerian Revolution but this messianic and prophetic image today energizes contemporary liberation movements from French Canadian Nationalism, Women Liberation Movements, to the Civil Right Movements stretching from Harlem to Africa."

Geismar, Peter. *Fanon.* New York: The Dial Press, 1971, 214 p.

Critical biography of Fanon. Geismar writes: "The major part of this book was drawn from interviews.... Fanon's own writings, however, formed an essential part of the biography."

Gendzier, Irene L. *Frantz Fanon: A Critical Study.* New York: Pantheon Books, 1973, 300 p.

Biography of Fanon, from his early days on Martinique to his militant activities in Algeria. Gendzier concludes with a discussion of Fanon's influence in the Third World.

Hansen, Emmanuel. "Frantz Fanon: Portrait of a Revolutionary Intellectual." *Transition* 9, No. 46 (October/December 1974): 25-36.

Profile of Fanon, focusing on his life and work as a "professional revolutionary."

Kessous, Naaman. "Fanon and the Problem of Alienation." *The Western Journal of Black Studies* 11, No. 2 (Summer 1987): 80-91.

Examines the connection between colonialism and alienation in Fanon's *Black Skin, White Masks* and *The Wretched of the Earth.*

Nursey-Bray, Paul. "Race and Nation: Ideology in the Thought of Frantz Fanon." *The Journal of Modern African Studies* 18, No. 1 (March 1980): 135-42.

Discusses Fanon's ideas on race and national culture.

Obiechina, Emmanuel. "Frantz Fanon: The Man and His Works." *Ufahamu* III, No. 2 (Fall 1972): 97-116.

Explores Fanon's impact in the Third World, concluding: "Fanon provides such profound insights into the questions of racism, colonialism and post-colonial reconstruction that no sensitive person in the modern world can afford to ignore his pronouncements. His life and works constitute one of the great landmarks in the recent history of Africa and the Third World."

Zolberg, Aristide R. "Frantz Fanon." In *The New Left: Six Critical Essays on Che Guevara, Jean-Paul Sartre, Herbert Marcuse, Frantz Fanon, Black Power, R. D. Laing,* edited by Maurice Cranston, pp. 119-36. New York: The Library Press, 1971.

Discusses a selection of essays from Fanon's *The Wretched of the Earth.*

Nuruddin Farah

1945-

Somali novelist, dramatist, short story writer, and translator.

An important figure in contemporary African literature whose fiction is informed by his country's turbulent history, Farah combines native legends, myths, and Islamic doctrines with a journalistic objectivity to comment on his country's present autocratic government. His criticism of traditional Somali society—in particular, the plight of women and the patriarchal family structure—has made him an "enemy of the state," and he has lived in voluntary exile in England and Nigeria. Kirsten Holst Petersen described Farah's "thankless task" of writing about the oppressed: "Pushed by his own sympathy and sensitivity, but not pushed too far, anchored to a modified Western bourgeois ideology, he battles valiantly, not for causes, but for individual freedom, for a slightly larger space round each person, to be filled as he or she chooses."

Farah was raised in Kallafo, Somalia, the son of Hassan, a merchant, and Aleeli, a poet. His mother's poetry, composed in the oral tradition, inspired Farah. He recalled in a 1987 interview: "I used to watch her compose her poems . . . she used to pace up and down, wherever there was some space in the courtyard, thinking about her poems, and all I could actually hear were murmurs of her own whispers to herself. And then I used to be amazed with the final result: a poem to be sung, chanted to music." After working for the Ministry of Education of the then-recently established Republic of Somalia, he traveled to India to study philosophy and literature. Farah returned to teach in Somalia but left in 1974. According to Josef Gugler, "He still lives in exile, as he has done since 1974 when he left behind his four-year-old son—to whom each of the three novels [of the *Variations on the Theme of an African Dictatorship* trilogy] is dedicated—his only child, Koschin."

"Like all good Somali poets," commented Farah in a 1981 interview, "I used women as a symbol for Somalia. Because, when the women are free, then and only then can we talk about a free Somalia." He depicted the inferior status of women in Somali society in his first novel, *From a Crooked Rib* (1970), the first work of fiction to be published in English by a Somali author. This book presents the story of a rural Somali girl, Ebla, who flees her family to escape her impending marriage to an elderly man. Seeking refuge in Mogadishu, the capital of Somalia, Ebla is unable to adjust to the city's fast-paced environment and is eventually forced to become a prostitute in order to survive. According to Petersen, who has called Farah "the first feminist writer to come out of Africa," *From a Crooked Rib* will likely "go down in the history of African literature as a pioneering work, valued for its courage and sensitivity."

Other critics believe the work is substandard, however. Florence Stratton wrote: "Stylistically and technically, *From a Crooked Rib* is a most unsatisfactory piece of work. It does not prepare the reader for the elegant prose, intricate structures, or displays of technical virtuosity of the later novels." Farah's next novel, *A Naked Needle* (1976), revolves around a British-educated young man, Koschin, whose search for a comfortable existence in post-revolutionary Somalia is complicated by the arrival of a former lover from England who intends to marry him. Reinhard W. Sander observed: "Next to Wole Soyinka's *The Interpreters,* [*A Naked Needle*] is perhaps the most self-searching [novel] to have come out of post-independence Africa."

Farah's best-known novels form the trilogy *Variations on the Theme of an African Dictatorship.* These works document the demise of democracy in Somalia and the emerging autocratic regime of Major General Muhammad Siyad Barre, referred to as the "General" in this series. The first volume of the trilogy, *Sweet and Sour*

Milk (1979), focuses upon a political activist whose attempts to uncover the circumstances of his twin brother's mysterious death are thwarted by his father, a former government interrogator and torturer. *Sardines* (1981), the next installment, depicts life under the General's repressive administration and examines social barriers that limit the quest for individuality among modern Somali women. This novel centers on Medina, a young woman who loses her job as editor of the state-run newspaper for refusing to support the General's domestic policies. Medina must also contend with her mother-in-law's insistence that she allow her eight-year-old daughter to be circumcised, as decreed by tribal law. Critics admired Farah's realistic evocation of his heroine's tribulations. Charles R. Larson stated: "No novelist has written as profoundly about the African woman's struggle for equality as has Nuruddin Farah." *Close Sesame* (1982), the final volume of the trilogy, concerns an elderly man who spent many years in prison for opposing both colonial and postrevolutionary governments. When his son conspires to overthrow the General's regime, the man's attempts to stop the coup cost him his life. According to Peter Lewis, "*Close Sesame* analyses the betrayal of African aspirations in the postcolonial period: the appalling abuse of power, the breakdown of national unity in the face of tribal rivalry, and the systematic violation of language itself."

Farah's next novel, *Maps* (1986), is set during Somalia's war against Ethiopia in the late 1970s. In this work, Farah examined conflicts between nationalism and personal commitment through his story of Askar, a Somali orphan who is raised by an Ethiopian woman. As Askar approaches adulthood, he is forced to choose between enlisting in the army and caring for his ailing adoptive mother, who is suspected of being a spy. Although some reviewers faulted *Maps* for awkward prose and confusing shifts in chronology, Christopher Hope concluded: "[It] is always the sincerity of the emotions and [Farah's] ability to make them palpable that distinguish this tantalizing and original novel, and make it a journey into what [he] calls the 'territory of pain' and what we, rather loosely perhaps, call Africa."

Farah is currently working on a novel tentatively titled *Letters*. In a 1987 interview he described it as "about society coming out of the oral tradition into a written form. It's about the power of the word in its written or oral form on the psyche." Farah hopes to move eventually into filmmaking, using the medium to continue championing the rights of individuals in Somalia. Stratton concluded: "He has faith in the ability of individuals to develop the capacity for self-regulation, and although he does not seem to anticipate an immediate change in conditions in Somalia, he does envisage a time in the future when a collective effort will bring into being a nation which truly nurtures its people."

(For further information about Farah's life and works, see *Contemporary Authors*, Vol. 106 and *Contemporary Literary Criticism*, Vol. 53.)

PRINCIPAL WORKS

A Dagger in a Vacuum (drama) 1969
From a Crooked Rib (novel) 1970
A Naked Needle (novel) 1976
*Sweet and Sour Milk (novel) 1979
*Sardines (novel) 1981
*Close Sesame (novel) 1982
Maps (novel) 1986

*These works are collectively referred to as Variations on the Theme of an African Dictatorship.

Kirsten Holst Petersen (essay date 1981)

[*In the following excerpt, Petersen examines Farah's role among contemporary African writers, arguing that his singularity can be found in his rejection of aspects of traditional African culture.*]

Nuruddin Farah sifts the modern Somali experience through an exceedingly sensitive mind, and it is not surprising therefore that he eschews easy solutions and instead poses a set of questions. The questions he asks are to a very large extent the questions asked by the majority of modern African writers, and his authorship is very much part of the established African literary tradition in which the educated elite takes a "critical-and-yet" view of their societies.

Nuruddin Farah's three published novels, *From a Crooked Rib, A Naked Needle,* and *Sweet and Sour Milk* as well as *Sardines* (to be published shortly) deal with the role (or perhaps plight) of women in a Muslim society, the role of the educated elite, the corruption of the political elite and the repressive nature of the Somali revolution. Both by virtue of his educated background and his themes Nuruddin Farah conforms to the established canon of African writing, and a useful angle from which to investigate his work would seem to be to try and discover if he has added any new insight to it. Looked at in that way he is at least interesting when he discusses the tribalism and corruption of the military/political elite. His description of the alcohol, cars and fast women syndrome adds nothing to the already existing picture, except perhaps a well-chosen quote from Clemenceau to the effect that America "in only one generation" had "ceased being referred to as a barbaric nation and had qualified itself to be labelled decadent." The quotation is used with reference to Africa, but maintains the characteristic ambiguity found in all of the novels. (p. 94)

The naked needle in the book of the same name is Koschin, a young Somali, living in Mogadiscio during the early days of the revolution. In the prelude, which is written in first person narrative, he states the two events which are causing him his present concern and which are the two interwoven themes of the book. They are the revolution "to which I am loyal" and the fact that an English girlfriend, Nancy, whom he has invited to Somalia "on the whim of a day" has just sent a telegram announcing her arrival. These two events on their different levels are forcing him to make decisions, a thing he has never been able to do. This state of affairs is not much improved in the course of the book. On the political level he assesses means and ends by way of an image: "A revolution, y'know, is a pill that tastes bitter, the benefits of which are felt only when one has gone through the preliminary pain and pestilence." Loyalty to the revolution is considered necessary, and towards the end of the book a somewhat toothless and pompous stance is made. "Whoever will do any good for this country and for Africa, I shall back till I die. Go up to the pulpit, do something good and I shall certainly be on your side. If these fail to do what they owe us, I shall declare war against them, singlehanded even though I am." The author is, of course, hiding behind his character, and there is no precise indication of his attitude towards him. On the personal level Nuruddin Farah discusses the problems of a small group of Somali/white couples to which Koschin belongs. This is given a political dimension, not in relation to Somali, although it is stated that white wives are a handicap, but in a wider perspective of sexual power-relations between races. However, here also there is a lack of a final point of view. The first half of the Somali man/American woman love story is very much in the vein of Armah's *Why Are We So Blest,* but the second part blames the man for trapping the woman in an alien society by not telling her the truth beforehand. The moral, as pronounced by Koschin is to make sure not to be trapped. "I prefer whoring to marrying, I, for one, feel free." There is nothing wrong with that as a solution, but the whole incident is yet another example of an irritating tendency in the book to touch on vital topics only to drop them in an offhand manner. The style also suffers from this indecision. Sentences like "I . . . blinded to his wishes by a belief that may be killed no sooner than tomorrow" leave one visionless.

Although some of these flaws are still present in *Sweet and Sour Milk* the higher degree of firmness in both character development and statements of opinion makes it a more rewarding book to read. The book centres on a pair of identical twins, Soyaan and Loyaan, and their different attitudes to the revolution. The tone of the book is much more sinister, and arrests, imprisonments, tortures, informers and generally an atmosphere of fear prevail. Soyaan dies mysteriously in the beginning of the book under circumstances which indicate that he has been poisoned by the regime. Trying to ascertain the truth his brother traces Soyaan's movements using the few clues left to him—cryptic notes and coded messages found in his pocket. This is reminiscent of the detective story technique, but as well as finding out some facts about his brother . . . . [Loyaan] is driven by a personal wish to vindicate his brother, but the insight he gains into the machinations of the regime eventually force him to accept the validity of his brother's vision and try to incorporate it into himself. In a situation of stress he tells himself, *"you must help encounter and then fuse the talents of Soyaan and Loyaan; in you must encounter the forces of life (Loyaan) and death (Soyaan)."* To a reader who is used to more heroic stances against oppression, like, for example, Armah's *Two Thousand Seasons,* Loyaan's political maturing may seem excessively slow and naive, but Nuruddin Farah shares with Ngugi a concern for the doubts and failings of ordinary people who find themselves in extraordinary situations with which they cannot quite cope. Unlike Ngugi's characters, however, Nuruddin Farah's do not reach a definite point of view as a result of their deliberations. At the end of the novel Loyaan, despite his new insight, is still unable to act and the reader is still not certain just how much insight he has gained. The two novels represent a small and somewhat timid beginning of a crucial awareness which, however, in the Somali context, is enough to keep Nuruddin Farah in exile.

A critical view of present political powers, whether black or white, is a theme which in modern African literature is often combined with a search for roots, an affirmation of the validity of traditional society and its potential as a source for a new beginning which should replace the society under attack. One could mention writers like Achebe, Soyinka, Kofi Awoonor, Armah, and Ngugi. In this respect Nuruddin Farah differs radically from the established canon. He finds no virtue in traditional Somali social organization: indeed his two pet hatreds seem to be the patriarch in the traditional Somali Muslim family and the concomitant subjection of women. The patriarch or head of an extended family group as represented by Loyaan's and Soyaan's father is a petty tyrant with unlimited power over the members of his family, and in the larger context of the society he is a cowardly police informer. In [*Sweet and Sour Milk*] Nuruddin Farah connects these two social levels through a quotation from Wilhelm Reich: "In the figure of the father the authoritarian state has its representative in every family, so that the family becomes its most important instrument of power." This juxtaposition of negative aspects in traditional and modern society amounts to a heresy in African writing. It is closely connected with Nuruddin Farah's unique sensitivity towards the situation of women in traditional Somali society. Ironically, he would seem to be the first feminist writer to come out of Africa in the sense that he describes and analyzes women as victims of male subjugation . . . . The detached view of Nuruddin Farah's book, which coincides with the ideology and anger of the Western feminist liberation movement, has only become possible in West Africa with a second generation of writers, some of whom have gained enough self confidence to question and reject aspects of their heritage. The Nigerian writer Buchi Emecheta's description of the subjugation of women in traditional Ibo society is a result of this development and so far the only approximation to Nuruddin Farah's work. *From A Crooked Rib* will I think go down in the history of African literature as a pioneering work, valued for its courage and sensitivity.

Due to a mixture of Islamic law and the needs and hardships of nomadic life the position of women in traditional Somali society would seem to be extremely low. A woman is the property of a patriarch. As such she has no individual rights, but she is protected as a member of her lineage group against outside abuses. Thus blood compensation in slaughtered camels is demanded if she is murdered, even though the amount is only half of the blood compensation demanded for a man. Marriages are arranged by the patriarch who also settles the bride price. Nuruddin Farah incorporates into **From A Crooked Rib** the ethnographical information which is necessary for an understanding of the dilemma of the main character. This information coincides with what one can learn from reading an ethnographical survey, but his use of it is strongly coloured by his attitude. The information that "the engagement and marriage are ratified by a series of presentations" is expressed in the following way in **From A Crooked Rib:**

> From experience she knew that girls were materials, just like objects, or items on the shelf of a shop. They were sold and bought as shepherds sold their goats at market-places, or shop-owners sold the goods to their customers. To a shopkeeper what was the difference between a girl and his goods? Nothing, absolutely nothing.

The main character in the novel, Ebla, a young nomad girl, is sold several times in the course of the story, and when she understands the connection between her human value and money she draws the logical conclusion. "She scratched her sex, then chuckled 'This is my treasure, my only treasure, my bank, my money, my existence.'" This realization is made probable by the story. In order to avoid a forced marriage to an old man, Ebla flees from her nomadic kinship group to the city. By doing this she becomes a woman who is not owned by anybody, and as such she has no legal protection. She joins the marginal group of widows, spinsters and divorced women whose only means of survival is prostitution or shades of it. Ebla marries a student who soon after leaves for Italy, and she is left to fend for herself. Marriage is the purpose of her life, but she has confused ideas about it, and the book is somewhat contradictory on this point.... After the consummation of her marriage (which, incidentally, according to tradition is preceded by her husband beating her up), Ebla wishes that she were either an old woman or a man so that the experience would not have to be repeated. None of her problems are solved in the course of the book, but the reader is left with a very clear vision of the narrow space within which a Somali woman can define herself, and the virtual impossibility of breaking down the walls of tradition and widening the space.

With no sympathy for traditional society and a critical attitude towards the Revolution, Nuruddin Farah must be a lonely man in Somalia. Pushed by his own sympathy and sensitivity, but not pushed too far, anchored to a modified Western bourgeois ideology, he battles valiantly, not for causes, but for individual freedom, for a slightly larger space round each person, to be filled as he or she chooses. It is a thankless task, and Nuruddin Farah stands guard over liberty in Somalia like the camel owner of an anonymous traditional Somali song:

> One of my she-camels falls on the road
> And I protect its meat,
> At night I cannot sleep,
> And in the daytime I can find no shade.

(pp. 95-100)

Kirsten Holst Petersen, "The Personal and the Political: The Case of Nuruddin Farah," in Ariel: A Review of International English Literature, *Vol. 12, No. 3, July, 1981, pp. 93-101.*

J. I. Okonkwo (essay date 1984)

[*In the following excerpt, Okonkwo discusses Farah's groundbreaking portrayals of women in* From a Crooked Rib, A Naked Needle, Sweet and Sour Milk, *and* Sardines.]

Perhaps it was inevitable that in their presentation of African society, most African writers, being males, have tended to project an exclusively male, distorted view of that society, although one of the earliest Caribbean novels, Claude McKay's *Banana Bottom* (1933), has a woman, Bita Plant, as its central character. Since the proclaimed objective of African writing, especially in its early manifestations, was a reclamation of an African world view that was already on the eclipse, few had sufficient knowledge of the genuine society to question seriously, at the time, the authenticity of the executed re-creations in literature.... One aspect of African social existence whose portrayal remained unchallenged for a long time is the life of women within the societies depicted in these creative works. Not only were women characters few, but when they appeared they did so in subservient and insignificant roles. Even then, very little effort was made to illuminate their lives in any detail within the circumscribed role assigned them in traditional society. (pp. 215-16)

The African writer who has done the greatest justice to female existence in his writing, in the number of female characters he projects and the variety of roles accorded them as well as in the diversified attitudes toward life represented, is the Somali author Nuruddin Farah.... The perspective from which Farah projects his women is almost unique within the context of African creative writing. With the possible exception of Ousmane and Armah, whose women possess some vision on which they base their actions, Farah seems virtually alone among African writers in depicting the progress which women have made within the constricting African social landscape. Problems there may be, and for some they are insurmountable. Nevertheless, a good many women are succeeding in scaling the hurdles; and Farah exhibits them, together with their achievements and the challenges with which they are confronted. So pervasive and consistent is his espousal of the female cause that he has been described as "the first feminist writer to come out of Africa in the sense that he describes and analyses women as victims of male subjugation" [see essay dated 1981].

Farah's championing of the cause of women is part of his crusade against tyranny and victimization not just of women, but of all who are denied their legitimate rights—social and political, private and public.... With his novels *From a Crooked Rib* (1970), *A Naked Needle* (1976), *Sweet and Sour Milk* (1979) and *Sardines* (1981), we are introduced to yet a new trend in the large corpus of modern African creative writing, particularly the novel. The central feature of this new trend is the demythification of the traditional and communal concept of African life, the generally glorified African past, which overidealized the beauty, dignity and excellence of African culture. Farah, like Ekwensi and Soyinka (in his novels), is completely immersed in the present. His novels offer an incisive picture of contemporary African realities compounded with vestiges of tradition and elements of modernism. He sees his function as the molding of opinion (through authentic information) against social and political oppression. He champions the cause of individual freedom and exposes such aberrations as nepotism, misused tribal allegiances, female suppression and stifling materialism, which are responsible for the debasement of humanity and the standard values of the modern African. The first novel, *From a Crooked Rib,* discusses the feminine plight and the general odds which weigh against the female in a traditional Islamic cultural environment. The first two books of his proposed trilogy, *Sweet and Sour Milk* and *Sardines,* give prominent places to women and highlight the repressive and horrifying aspects of the Somali military regime.

The basic female problem, the uncomplimentary status accorded her in African society, is given a general treatment in *From a Crooked Rib.* Although the major character of the novel, Ebla, sets out to extricate herself from the imprisoning women's role in traditional society, her reflections on the matter delve into the general female predicament which exists in modern societies. The novel deals with Ebla's moral and intellectual growth, detailing her progress as she quests for personal freedom and dignity. Escaping from the imminent imprisonment of an arranged marriage to Giumalel (who is old enough to have been her father, and whose two sons had earlier courted her), she is nearly pawned to another consumptive man. But she has sufficient intelligence and strength of character to gradually work out her own destiny.

Ebla is introduced in a prologue through her grandfather's musings about her flight from home; we also learn that she is a member of a Jes (a unit of several nomadic families living together). She and her brother were orphaned early and were entrusted to their grandfather's care.... She is presented as intelligent, philosophical and self-willed. Her revolutionary outlook on life makes her question the application of Koranic teachings to every detail of social life. One is surprised that, despite her rural nomadic background, she is capable of examining not only her individual plight, but also the place of women vis-a-vis the male in society. Ebla ponders over many issues.

Such intelligence and individualism are at complete variance with the prescribed confinements of Ebla's cultural and religious environment. Her flight from home is not just a simple matter of not wanting to marry Giumalel; it is her desire to assert her individuality, and also to be understood and appreciated as a human being. (pp. 217-18)

Farah tells the story of Ebla's journey to discovery in a straightforward narrative style. His adroit manipulation of the naive narrator through whose voice we hear Ebla's story is impressive. The focus on Ebla unveils the deep recesses of her mind in this picaresque adventure. Her innocent ingenuity is conveyed not only in her own thoughts and utterances, which pervade the novel, but also in the naivete of the narrative voice itself....

The action of [*From a Crooked Rib*] takes its cue from an epigraph, a Somali proverb which emphasizes the subordinate existence of women: "God created Woman from a crooked rib; and any one who trieth to straighten it, breaketh it." Ebla's revolt is aimed at the refutation of this guiding proverb, a male-chauvinist slogan. The title, like Buchi Emecheta's *Joys of Motherhood,* is ironic, for Ebla succeeds in demonstrating the feminine capability of self-assertion and independence. This subtly ironic device, curiously unobtrusive though pervasive, stems from Farah's detachment, which allows the style slowly to reveal the deeper meaning of the novel. (p. 218)

Asha, the landlady with whom Ebla comes in contact after her marriage to Awill, presents another face of woman in this novel. Although she is immoral and greedy, her strong personality is striking. She is a confident and psychologically stable matron who has fought her way to survival in the modern, urban, dog-eat-dog environment. Farah creates a strong feminine independence in Asha in order to portray the potential of individual female achievement in a world dominated by men. Asha has a house in town which she rents on a tenement basis. Apart from the maternal role she adopts toward her tenants, like Awill, she also controls them, manipulates their love lives and purse strings. She tutors Ebla on how to take her revenge for her husband's infidelity.

The widow and Aowrolla, on the other hand, are victims of the rigid Muslim culture. Both appear passive and indifferent to the plight of women. The widow has been subjected to Muslim peremptory divorce, and Aowrolla experiences the painful, agonizing chastisement of childbirth. Together they represent all women who have accepted the age-long inequality of the sexes, with a reward that comes only through children.

Female characters in **From a Crooked Rib** are relatively few, but their varied outlooks and roles are sufficient to illustrate Farah's ability for comprehensive portrayal of women's roles and characters. In his fiction generally, it is possible to identify three distinct categories of women: the traditional African, the emancipated modern African and the foreigner or West European.

The traditional woman has already been observed in the persons of the widow and Aowrolla of **From a Crooked Rib**. Further characterizations are Qumman, Ladan and Beydan of **Sweet and Sour Milk** and Idil (Medina's mother-in-law) and Fatima bint Thabit (Medina's mother) of **Sardines**. They play a striking part as instruments whereby the repressive regimes of their setting are highlighted. They are the suppressed, second-class citizens of traditional Muslim culture, presented in the stifled protests of their private home backgrounds. Qumman is the typical mother, loving and all-caring, patient and wearily self-sacrificing for her family. Deeply superstitious and religious, she upholds the family reputation against what she considers an importunate assault from Margaritta's relationship with her late son Soyaan. The victim of physical abuse by her husband Keynaan, she exists solely for her children. Because of them, she endures Keynaan's mistreatment and neglect of her. The influence of Qumman and her kind ensures the perpetuation of the social status quo, for they assist in stifling any type of deviation from the pattern they know and accept. Qumman is already bringing up Ladan to be like herself; and through loyalty, service and emotional hold over sons and husbands, Qumman's generation of women, deeply conservative, militate against individual freedom and progress. Loyaan, for instance, determined to demonstrate his aversion to the General's regime by exempting himself from the hypocritical show of solidarity symbolized in communal sweeping of the "Rendezvous of the Brooms," is persuaded by Qumman, Ladan and other women of the clan to conform. (pp. 218-19)

Beydan is a helpless victim, the second wife who acts as the perennial enemy and scourge of the first. She is aptly used by Keynaan to further divide and rule his family. Completely abandoned by Keynaan in her state of pregnancy, her only succor is her co-wife's grown sons. Her life is sacrificed during childbirth. Beydan is a pathetic figure in her helplessness. Suspected by Qumman of poisoning her son Soyaan, deprived of money and attention, she was already haunted by her tragedy in dreams.

Idil and Fatima bint Thabit react to the restrictions of Muslim religion and the traditional cultural norms by channeling all their emotional resources toward the nurture and protection of their children. Their emotional ties to these children work as a type of blackmail. Idil, for instance, is domineering, and her love for Xaddia and Samater is overbearing. Her interference is responsible for the breakup of Xaddia's and Samater's marriages. She is so obsessed to have a grandchild from Xaddia that she consults an herbalist on Xaddia's behalf and goes into an uncontrollable rage when she discovers that Xaddia has been taking pills to prevent pregnancy. Her insistence on having Ubax, Medina's daughter, circumcised drives Medina and Ubax away from their home. In Medina's absence, she takes complete control of the household and attempts to marry off an uneducated and, in her view, more docile and malleable wife to her son—a move similar to the ploys of the mothers-in-law in Mariama Bâ's *So Long A Letter* and one which ultimately estranges her from Samater. Hers is the typical, traditional mother-in-law syndrome.

Fatima, Medina's mother, is obscure and quiet .... She is firmly rooted in tradition, sanctified by name and property. She is chained ankle, wrist and foot to the solidity of her homestead—a typical matriarch born into a slave-owning family. Fatima is of the opinion that the younger generations, no matter how hard they try, can never create any "culture-substitute as faultless and whole as the one Somali society has developed in the past few centuries, any substitute with which to replace the traditional culture." Economic dependence on their men is shown as partly responsible for the submission of these women. Beydan is constantly in need of money. Aowrolla's husband Gheddi takes care of the purchasing of food-stuffs himself. Idil's dependence on her son Samater and even on Medina helps to check her excesses. Psychological factors also contribute, because it is difficult to purge oneself of ideas that have been imbibed throughout one's life. Therefore the Qummans and Fatima bint Thabits cannot release themselves from their bondage. (p. 219)

Farah carries the fight for women's rights into the corridors of power in **Sardines,** a novel which highlights the activities of ... [the] new breed of Somali women. The novel revolves around Medina's search for "a room of one's own. A country of one's own. A century in which one was not a guest." This type of woman character has already been encountered in Margaritta, Soyaan's mistress in **Sweet and Sour Milk** who, with independent means of livelihood, pursues her own interests—intellectual, social, romantic and political. She does not even make any claims on Keynaan for the son she has by Soyaan (a cause of anxiety for Qumman). Margaritta is engaged in research, which absorbs most of her time and energy. After a disastrous first marriage, she has avoided any permanent attachment to a man. This, to a large extent, ensures her freedom. Mulki, Soyaan's secretary, also belongs to this class of women.

Needless to say, this new type of woman is thoroughly rejected by the Qummans and Idils of society .... With Western education, public employment and economic self-sufficiency, these emancipated Somali women hold their own through public and political activity. They are very much at home in the so-called corridors of power through their own merit. Farah's female characters in **Sardines** reach out, each in her characteristic way, for freedom of expression and action. These women of various ages and sociocultural backgrounds engage in unique and intricate systems of relationships and search for new meanings and social definitions of themselves. Their efforts symbolically represent Somalia's search for freedom. The enslavement of Somali women is analogous to the political repression of the people, and until women are completely emancipated, Farah sees no political freedom for the country. As Joyce Cary observed, the root cause of Africa's stagnation is the backwardness, ignorance and suppression of its women. Since women's influence upon the young is enormous, how these future leaders of society are brought up will determine their capacity for handling their country's destiny.

Through his portrayal of educated women like Medina, Sagal, Amina and their associates, Farah presents a penetrating study of the conflict between traditional Muslim culture and the encroaching Western influence. Medina, from all indications, is very emancipated, as are the other female characters in her group, to a certain extent. They all enjoy some degree of personal freedom, having been liberated from ignorance of the intellect—a major effect of education. They are also free from economic dependence.... Medina has the benefit of a university education and the exposure consequent upon the fact that she is the daughter of an ambassador. She is privileged to have been uprooted early from her traditional background and nurtured in the glittering society of many European capitals. She is lucky to enjoy the love and understanding of a humane husband and her country's recognition of her talents, which earns her the editorship of Somalia's national daily newspaper. Indeed, Medina has a country, and an enviable identity. Her efforts, therefore, are for the silent majority who submit to the oppressive laws of the fascist state. She regards her mother-in-law, her clan's traditions and the General as obstacles in her ideal world. They are as much her enemies as the General's militiamen or the security services. As an active member of a revolutionary group that is not only critical of the General's regime but also actively opposed to it in *Sweet and Sour Milk,* her finest hour comes when she is made the editor of the government's main propaganda machinery. Her genuine revolutionary tendency propels her to challenge the editorial policy of daily singing the General's praises. (p. 220)

From Margaritta, Medina and their like, it is only one step forward to the total freedom of Western women, first encountered in Barbara, Mildred and Nancy of *A Naked Needle.* These white women, attached to African men through marriage and friendship, are having difficulty in adjusting to African realities, especially those which concern the position of women in society. One distinctive feature about them is their sexual freedom, which makes them extremely permissive in their relationships with men. The meeting between Nancy and Koschin [of *A Naked Needle*], for example, is illustrative. Koschin met Nancy accidentally in "a crowded pub, in London. She had been looking for her boyfriend in the pub." She is presented as a stereotype of the liberated woman of modern Western society as she competes favorably with men in the pub: "She drank

lavishly, almost crazily, until in the end, when she was ready to leave, she ordered another drink. I saw that the contents of her Mexican straw-bag wouldn't settle the bill." Koschin settles her bill. They meet by chance some days later in a jammed discotheque "near the University." Nancy is again stood up by another boyfriend. It is unusual, according to African culture, that Nancy, after a few dates with Koschin, suggests marriage. It is her permissiveness that makes her accept, "at a whim of a day," to return to Africa to marry Koschin, should both be unmarried after two years.

The meeting between Mohamed and Barbara is equally casual; and even though their marriage is stable, Barbara, in a fit of revenge, sleeps with Barre, Mohamed's friend. Mildred's sexual infidelity has become scandalous and a source of concern and dishonor for her husband, Barre. These women, as well as Sandra the American lady, storm every citadel that men consider sacred to themselves.

One fact about Medina [of *Sardines*] is that in spite of her commitment to her freedom, she is never shown as indulging in irresponsible behavior. She is circumspect in her relationships with men and is amused at all the speculations of friends as to the reason for the temporary separation between her and Samater. Invariably, some sexual conflict is suggested. But for Medina, a woman's freedom does not necessarily involve an acceptance of sexual promiscuity. Even Margaritta, who as a single woman feels free to keep lovers, is still portrayed as applying restraint in her associations with men. The other Western types make one dizzy in their relentless pursuit of the male. With them the man has become the sexual victim. But they have drive and exhibit great acumen in the discharging of their duties. In the Somalia of *A Naked Needle,* Somali men, or at least the elite among them, seem to prefer these Western white women to their own women as wives—a fact which arouses the discomfort of Koschin. (pp. 220-21)

The realistic feature of Farah's portrayal of women is that they are seen to take active part in various forms of life around them. Even when they are cast in the traditional mold, like Qumman or Idil, they are active in those areas where they are permitted to operate.... More than this, Farah illuminates the changing role of women in a changing society. He even shows some of the men discussing the plight of women.... For such a commitment to the cause of women, Nuruddin Farah is unique among African creative writers. (p. 221)

J. I. Okonkwo, "Nuruddin Farah and the Changing Roles of Women," in World Literature Today, *Vol. 58, No. 2, Spring, 1984, pp. 215-21.*

Christopher Hope (essay date 1987)

[*Hope is a South African writer. In the following review, he praises Farah's portrayal of turmoil in Africa in* Maps.]

This is a novel about the politics of desire as well as a lyrical evocation of childhood—but above all, **Maps** is a book about borders, boundaries and territorial ambitions, what Nuruddin Farah calls "pastures of the imagination." The novel sets out to delineate, with a cartographer's scrupulousness, the anguish of living on a continent where national boundaries have been drawn by foreign hands, where geography merges with politics and where, even though the old imperialists have departed, their successors have inherited not only their powers but their maps. In short, this is a novel of modern Africa, in which the growing pains of the orphan boy, Askar, and his inchoate, fragmentary memories of his dead parents reflect the wider tragedy of a dismembered Somalia—a country split among the competing owners of its various territories . . . .

The most notable feature of this strange, poetic, passionate narrative is the extraordinary way in which Nuruddin Farah transforms what might in other hands be an angry political treatise into a sensitive account of an orphan of the storms that in Africa pass under the name of politics. And although the novel is set in the Horn of Africa, it has applications that reach as far as my own country, South Africa, where questions of "homelands" have violent political repercussions, and where the drawing of lines between people, the making of maps and the meaning of words are ultimately matters for the police and the army.

Among the powers possessed by the boy Askar is his ability to move backward and forward in time, to be present at his own birth and to peer into the future. His relationship with Misra, the woman who adopts him, is described with savage tenderness and a brilliant accumulation of intimate detail. Mr. Farah, who was born in 1945 and has written several novels, has considerable lyrical gifts. Askar is a kind of wonder child, a boy-man, in some ways the Somali messiah, the "wise child of his people," obsessed with the circumstances of his birth, possibly his own midwife, perhaps even his own creator, since the existence of his parents is problematical. Askar enjoys a relationship with Misra so close as to be almost incestuous and sufficiently powerful to cut them off from the rest of the world.

However, it is Askar's growing recognition that he must begin to discover his own independence that sets him on the path to political awareness and maturity. It is no coincidence that Misra is not a Somali but an Ethiopian, and it is Askar's destiny to fight against Ethiopian domination of his mother country. Such personal and political consonances are handled with great delicacy and imagination. Misra herself is a remarkable creation, warm, motherly, shrewd, but at the same time sexually submissive, devious and possibly a traitor to the Somali cause. Even so, the intense relationship between orphan and foreign mother provides the underlying strength of the novel and knits the whole together. Among the richly woven incidents of their mutual dependence, Askar's observation of an abortion performed on his

stepmother is one of the outstanding moments in the novel, a description spare, pungent, unforgettable.

But their relationship is doomed by geography and politics. Two events begin the inevitable separation of Askar and Misra; there is his circumcision and the presentation to him of an atlas in which the topography of his desire becomes clear. Askar begins deliberately to reunite the sundered sections of his "homeland," redrawing "the map of the Somali-speaking territories, copying it curve by curve."

Both as a child, and then as a young man in Mogadishu, by now a supporter of the Western Somali Liberation Front, Askar must contemplate the personal tragedy of the Somali people, scattered across Africa, delivered by geographers into the hands of foreign armies. And he must also confront the wider, equally familiar struggle in Africa between the new imperialists, the Russians in Ethiopia or the Cubans in Angola, and live with the bitter knowledge that Africa is once again little more than a "playfield," where African armies are simply part of the "reserve," to be drawn on by the major powers in their new scramble for Africa. Of course this is true and has a familiar ring to anyone alarmed by the spectacle of African countries caught in the trap between domestic incompetence and international interference.

Such is the force of Mr. Farah's anger that it sometimes overshadows the delicate portraits at the heart of the novel. And his allusive, playful style in which the narrative moves between past and present with great rapidity, is not always easy to follow. But it is always the sincerity of the emotions and his ability to make them palpable that distinguish this tantalizing and original novel, and make it a journey into what Mr. Farah calls the "territory of pain" and what we, rather loosely perhaps, call Africa.

Christopher Hope, "Boundaries of Desire," in The New York Times Book Review, *November 15, 1987, p. 40.*

Barbara Turfan (essay date 1989)

[In the following excerpt, Turfan closely examines Farah's Variations on the Theme of an African Dictatorship *trilogy, focusing on the author's portrayal of Somali politics.]*

The ruling regime is continuous throughout the [**Variations on the Theme of an African Dictatorship**] trilogy in the sense that the ruler, known as "the General", continues uninterruptedly in power. The irony is that the ideological basis of his rule changes from the Russian-backed "Socialism" of the first two books to the American-backed "democracy" of the third, yet nothing changes in the country other than the substitution of western for eastern aid and technicians. The iron hand of the General does not relax its grip over the ruled: suppression of information and oppression of individual opinion and action is the rule; arrest and imprisonment without charge, torture and even execution are so commonplace that few families or clans remain untouched and inviolate. It is the first two novels that convey directly and succinctly the methods of the government in its efforts to establish total control over its citizens. Soyaan and Ibrahim ("Il Siciliano"), two of the founder members of the opposition group, have prepared a subversive Memorandum which, but for Soyaan's mysterious and untimely death, they would have circulated clandestinely. The Memorandum is called "Dionysius's Ear" after the legend of the Syracusan tyrant who constructed a cave in the shape of an ear which echoed the secret whispers of his prisoners:

> Soyaan and I saw a similarity between this and the method the General has used so far. The Security Services in this country recruit their main corps from illiterates, men and women who belong to an oral tradition, and who neither read nor write but report daily, report what they hear as they hear it, word by word . . . They need no warrant to arrest anybody. Everything is done verbally . . . We've found that two thirds of the prisoners have no files, that over two thirds of them are serving indeterminate prison sentences . . . We say in our Memo that the General (with the assistance of the Soviets) has had an ear service of tyranny constructed.

The universal use of spies and informers is bound to create an atmosphere of suspicion, fear and isolation—an atmosphere heightened by laws such as ban the assembly of more than five people except at an Orientation Centre (at which civil servants and their families must attend thrice-weekly programmes of orientation on pain of losing their jobs) or to chant the praises of the General. Tension and suspicion are almost tangible throughout the trilogy, even after the switch to a western alliance with its insistence on at least the forms of democracy if not the spirit. Indeed, **Close Sesame** dwells no less than do the preceding novels on the strangers who approach one in the street to open up a conversation and prove one's political allegiances—the security men nicknamed the "pederasts" by Medina because " . . . they walk with the ease of a pederast scouring the streets they've always hunted in". The feeling of an omnipresent uncertainty and tension is deftly evoked also in conversations, conversations which leave out more than they include but form, with the speaker's unspoken thoughts, a continuous stream to which the reader, but not the other participants, has access. The conversational style is, like Farah's narrative, further enhanced by symbols and metaphors which enrich the most banal of exchanges and lend a profundity and a dignity to the characters themselves.

Another characteristic of the regime of which Farah clearly tries to make the reader aware is that of its dependence upon foreign powers, be they from the eastern or the western bloc, both to support its continued existence against subversive activity and, more fundamentally, to provide the very ideological foundation on which it bases its validity. There is not necessarily an identity between real and "validating" ideology. For example, the General espouses socialism and re-

ceives aid in the form of huge prisons built by the East Germans and medical doctors sent by China and the Soviet Union; yet he relies upon traditional tribal loyalties and family ties in selecting his ministers and administrative officers, always alert to the threat of ideological ties developing between members of different tribal groups and creating a dangerous potential "national" awareness and "nationalist" opposition. Yet is this not a major contradiction in terms? How can a regime truly espousing an ideological cause seek to deny the development of an ideological awareness among its own populace? How can it seek instead to graft the official ideological superstructure on to an unprepared tribal, or clannish, infrastructure? But of course the General is depicted as not truly seeking to graft the ideology he ostensibly espouses on to a society being educated to understand and embrace it. For him, socialism is merely a means to an end and can be dropped when other, more useful means come to hand—as indeed occurs. As Nasser writes to his sister, Medina, while there can be no doubt that the Soviets used the General for their own purposes, " ' . . . he used them too. He made them train his clansmen; he used them to build himself a system of security as tight as the KGB.' "

As for tribal loyalty, this is a theme to which Farah returns time and time again. In **Sweet and Sour Milk,** Loyaan's father rounds on him for his misplaced "self-importance":

> "The General fears tribal chieftains or men of his own age. Not you, nor Soyaan, nor anyone of your generation. You have no common ideology and no principles. You work for the interests of the countries in which you received your academic training. Some for Western Europe, some for Russia."

Sardines turns on the appointment of Samater as Minister of Constructions, a post he is reluctant to take up since it is incompatible with his subversive inclinations as a member of the group, but which he feels obliged to accept, against the group's instructions, in the face of open threats against his tribe and his duty as a clan member to save them. It is, we find, for Samater's ambivalent behaviour—his reluctance to condemn his kinsmen in order to uphold a principle—that his wife, Medina, leaves him until he has faced his own conscience and made his own decisions. Again, the plot of the final novel, **Close Sesame,** revolves around the relationship between four young opponents of the regime who are drawn from different tribal backgrounds. The aim of the General after the first, abortive assassination attempt is to isolate Mahad's tribe and family (in that order) and to play down the likely involvement of Mukhtaar, a member of the General's own clan and "the water he cannot swallow" of Somali lore. As the opposition realize, should more than one tribe be seen to be involved, the plot would assume ideological implications and hence nationalist proportions not possible in a purely tribal incident. Deeriye, the father of one of the four, has proved himself a long-standing and staunch opponent of oppression at the hands of the Italian colonialists and the succeeding Somali dictatorship; his friendships have been formed across the clan barriers, against all advice, and it is perhaps to establish beyond all doubt the nationalist, non-tribal basis of the ineptly managed assassination attempts of the four youths as much as to avenge the death of his own son in one of those attempts that Derriye himself dies in a futile but extremely public attempt on the life of the General. Clearly, Farah sees the clash between traditional tribal and modern national awareness as a major flaw in the development of a modern, independent nation-state:

> Must everything be interpreted according to the code of clan-, class- or group-interest, must everything be seen in this light? . . . This country hasn't a tradition of protest movements, trade unions or organised groups of any kind. There is no tradition such as there is in Egypt, Ethiopia or Sudan, of student movements which can help form or unform governments or shape public opinion.

One of the "group-interests" seems to be that of religion, again presented as an inconsistency in present-day Somali political life. For the traditional religion of Somalia, Islam, provides a firm cultural foundation for the society at large, a foundation, like tribalism, which is incompatible with a genuinely socialist superstructure. Yet the General has been able to distort his subjects' interpretation of Islam, bribing or coercing the sheikhs to support his rule and to lead their followers in singing his praises and comparing him, grotesquely, with the Prophet or even with Allah. In *Sweet and Sour Milk,* the dead Soyaan is posthumously turned into a "Hero of the Revolution" whose last words are given out as "Labour is Honour and there is no General but our General"—a perversion of the most fundamental tenet of the Islamic faith. The sheikhs are in total confusion, those who support the General being rewarded with stipends and honours, those who refuse being imprisoned, tortured, even executed. The provision of an Islamic legitimacy for a dictatorial, Marxist-Leninist regime is something the General obviously finds of extreme importance in securing at least the passivity and at best the full support of the populace. Much care is taken in the pursuit of this aim, to the extent of hiring the best and most famous popular singers; such is Dulman (*Sardines*)—the "Lady of the Revolution"—hired to sing praise-songs in his name both at home and on propaganda tours of Europe and the Middle East where she is reviled by the numerous Somalis in exile. But Farah's own attitude towards Islam is by no means hostile. Rather, it is the distortion of Islam by its practitioners and by those who seek to use it to their own advantage that provokes his criticism. His portrayal of strongly religious figures, such as the older women (particularly Medina and Nasser's mother, Fatima bint Thabit), may not always show them up in a particularly good light but nor does his portrayal of the bright young atheistic generation they have spawned. The chief character in *Close Sesame*—to my mind Farah's best, richest and most human novel to date—is the aged, asthmatic and devout Deeriye, a tribal elder who has spent his life in the

struggle against oppression or actually in prison for his beliefs. He is most sympathetically drawn as a character and is shown as a man who has come to terms with himself, who knows who he is and where he stands unlike so many of the confused and rootless adolescents and young people of Farah's novels (and whom, perhaps, Farah himself represents?), and especially of *Sardines.*

Sardines stands rather alone in the trilogy in that while it is, like the others, very much about personal relationships, it is particularly female—and most of all mother/daughter—relationships that form the texture of the book. And it is among the younger women that the confusion and rootlessness seem most prominent. To me, the adolescent Sagal stands out as the epitome of this; Sagal, described by various of his friends and relations in terms of flowing water:

> Sagal is a river changing course, country, beds, master and lover. She is the river which floods the farms it has watered. Where will she go? To Budapest, then London? It's not the first time she's talked of that. No nothing will surely come of it: she will not paint the dawn walls with slogans against the General . . .

Sagal is bright, alert, intelligent. Yet she is curiously transient in her attachments, with only a superficial interest in her enthusiasms; for example, she has on her wall stills of Marlon Brando in the film "Queimada" but is unable to explain to her questioning mother such basic points as who was the hero? What was the revolt he led? What other revolutions were taking place at that time in other places, especially Africa? Then it turns out that in Somalia only a very heavily censored version of the film was shown, and that for just one night—moreover, Sagal had not even seen it! " 'So why must you hold the banner of the revolutionary when you are not properly initiated . . . ?' " queries Ebla, her mother. Besides Queimada, Sagal has the usual poster of Che Guevara, records of Stevie Wonder, pictures of Malcolm X and Martin Luther King; she bubbles with flippant, revolutionary remarks, her naivete and insincere enthusiasm as transparent as the pyjamas which so dismay her mother:

> "All the men worth falling in love with either live in exile or are in prison. Both categories are outside my reach. That's why I want to go abroad: to join the ones already in exile."
>
> "And if you can't?"
>
> "I'll paint the morning leaves with slogans and go to prison. Possibly I shall meet some of them there."

Medina herself, the chief character of this book, is a more interesting personality. The daughter of a Somali ambassador, she has grown up in numerous European and African capitals, attended an Italian university and published occasional papers, speaks four European languages fluently as well as Arabic and writes two of them well, and was, albeit for a very brief period, editor of Somalia's only daily newspaper. She is cosmopolitan, relaxed in mixed company—indeed is never debarred from any group or activity on account of her sex, a characteristic shared by few women—and is one of the leading members of the original clandestine group of ten. She is deeply critical of the General and his regime which, as a declared Marxist-Leninist, she pronounces Fascist and intolerable; she is evidently sincerely concerned with her country's problems. She is a thinker, yet not profound enough to realize that it is a mistake to underestimate and despise one's enemy and is thus responsible for the split in the group between those like herself who consider the General an evil buffoon of no historical significance and those who believe the General to be following a definite policy and to be a foe worthy of circumspect observation and careful planning. She shuns convention wherever and whenever she finds the opportunity, bringing up her daughter, Ubax, is a way that scandilises not only her detested mother-in-law but also her own mother and even, at times, her liberal minded, co-revolutionary brother, Nasser. Yet she wonders why she feels like a "guest" in her own country, her own home, unable metaphorically to move the "furniture" without being invited to do so. She seeks a place for herself and longs to fit. In the view of the reviled Idil, her mother-in-law:

> "I am the product of a tradition with a given coherence and solidity; you [she is speaking to her son, Samater], of confusion and indecision. I have Allah, his prophets and the Islamic saints as my illustrious guides. For you, nothing is sacred, nothing is taboo. You are as inconsistent as your beliefs and principles are incoherent."

A remark such as this could be made of most of the youthful protagonists opposing the regime, in all three books. Indeed, we come across the same characters again and again as the novels unfold. All told, the youth portrayed in these pages are, to my mind, a reflection of a greater or lesser degree of the spoilt, rich, urban elite of western Europe and America with their fancy toys and gadgets, their expensive tastes, their passion for new and exotic experiences and their playing at revolution. Yes, playing; for while one by one the opposition group and their companions are eliminated from the struggle by imprisonment, exile or death—and they are certainly prepared to suffer and die for the cause—they none of them seem to have a clear idea of what they actually want to replace the hated General and his system with, nor do they have a clear idea of how to achieve their immediate objective of removing the General as a political force. It appears almost as if, for some of them at least, it is more important to strike a blow and win a heroic martyrdom than to achieve a positive gain for their peers, let alone for the "suffering masses". Loyaan, in *Sweet and Sour Milk,* is caught up by events on the mysterious death of his activist twin, Soyaan; he has no course mapped out in his mind except that of defending his brother's name against the encroachments of state propaganda which is claiming Soyaan for its own. Medina is a leader of the ten, but in her extremism misuses her one major opportunity to influence the state's propaganda as editor of Somalia's single newspa-

per, is sacked and refused permission to publish anything at all. She criticizes the General for ignoring her on the grounds that she is a woman and therefore insufficiently important. Yet other women are imprisoned and tortured, as we hear from Dr. Ahmed-Wellie's graphic accounts in *Sweet and Sour Milk* as well as the case of Ibrahim's sister, Mulki, and as we see in *Sardines* with the arrest of Sagal's chief rivals in swimming, Cadar and Hindiya. In *Close Sesame,* Deeriye is caught up, in the twilight of his life, in the activities of his son and three others; Deeriye, a man who has always professed his belief in non-violent opposition, eventually comes round to sharing Mursal's faith in "lex talionis", or the right of the victim of state oppression to exact personal vengeance on the state itself in the form of the General, its leader. The four plotters in this final part of the trilogy are the most coherent in their ideological grounding; they have based their argument upon Qur'ānic teaching (Mursal has a doctorate in the political relevance of the Qur'ān in an Islamic state and engages his father as well as his colleagues in long debates) and have clearly laid their plans in a systematic way. But like previous attempts, it is all rather "otherworldly" and is bungled from start to finish. These idealistic youths are no match for the worldly realism of the General and his state machinery. Similarly naive were the opposition group's original plans to collect information for a common pool and disseminate the information to the populace at large:

> "We can foretell", we added, "that the written word, more powerful than the gun, will frighten them [the government]. In the chaos ensuing from that, and just as they start their purge, we will announce our clandestinity and publish a leaflet of our intention, and you will see that more people will adhere to it. Then we will baptize it as a movement, we will give it a name."

● ● ● ● ●

I have tried so far to show how the regime is seen by the young subversive activists and what the background and views of the members of this group are. It appears that Farah's movement consists of a group of young intellectuals who belong to a small elite of educated, cosmopolitan and sophisticated Mogadiscans, sincere, idealistic and not very competent in practical terms. What then, may we ask, is Farah's intention in writing these novels? What does he wish to achieve? What point is he trying to drive home? Does he find action against state oppression pointless, in the sense that it cannot succeed? If he does believe there can be a solution to African oppression, does he offer any clues to this solution in his fiction?

I would aver that there are two principal themes present in *Variations on the Theme of an African Dictatorship.* The first is hinted at in the inclusion of "African" in the title of the trilogy. While, as we have seen his protagonists are sophisticated and cosmopolitan—apparently more versed in chic European modes of thinking than in their own society's—and many Europeans appear and have their say in the pages of these novels, Farah's fundamental concern does appear to be the position of Africa (and of Somalia in particular) in relation to colonial and neo-colonial powers. Somalia, indeed, provides a good case-study for European interference in African development—first as an Italian colony, later a Soviet Russian satellite and still later an ally of "Western democracy." Farah seems to be pleading for a native settlement of native problems and a native development within a native-inspired framework. While he is critical of governmental reliance upon the economic aid and ideological format of foreign powers, there is surely also present an indictment of an opposition's reaching likewise for foreign ideologies as remedies to be applied wholesale in the fight against tyranny.

This is the core of the clash between Medina and her erstwhile friend and co-revolutionary in Italy, Sandra. Medina's antagonism dates from the occasion when Sandra told her not to include Italy in their discussions about imperialism and socialism since as a foreigner Medina cannot and will never be able to understand Italy. When Medina takes her to task, therefore, for discussing Africa without restraint, she is brusquely told:

> "I'm not talking about Africa. I'm talking about Marxist theory, the Marxist ideology which is basically European, both in its outlook and philosophical development. Hegel, Marx, Engels, Lenin. They are all European."

This I believe to be the crux of the matter. That it is in the minds of Farah's opposition group is clear from the oath of the intellectuals and professionals who created the clandestine movement" ... to serve not the interests of any superpower but this nation's ... ", and also from Deeriye's response to his daughter's query whether he would not inevitably become a dictator if he were head of state:

> "I am not a black ape imitating the monkeys who trained me. For no man trained me. I did not learn what I know from a white man whose ways I hold sacred."

Is not Farah—himself cosmopolitan, multilingual, rootless—then questioning the relevance of foreign ways and ideologies to African countries? There can be no doubt that the foreign supporters of a regime do so in their own interest and assist in the development of those aspects of the state that accrue to their own advantage; there are, indeed, numerous references to such a view in the novels, from Loyaan's irrelevant training in Italy as a dentist when Somali teeth have not yet suffered enough from the diet of "civilization" to require the services of dentists to the statistics of infant mortality and the unequal distribution of economic aid between vast state prisons, unimportant public buildings and monuments, and vital hospitals for the population at large.

But is there not also implicit in the novels the idea that changes arising out of the wholesale adoption of alternative foreign ideologies and economic systems will compound rather than solve the existing problems, and that therefore the idealistic revolutionaries are in their own way just as culpable as the regime they oppose for the ills of Somalia? As Idil argues:

> "What is more, your generation hasn't produced the genius who could work out and develop an alternative cultural philosophy acceptable to all the members of your rank and file; not genius to propose something with which you could replace what you've rejected."

Just as socialism is seen not to have been appropriate for Somalia, especially so in the distorted version foisted upon the nation, so do Deeriye and his daughter, Zeinab, discuss the more tempting bait of "western democracy" in order to expose it as a sham, a fraud and an instrument of repression, particularly when applied by those "western" powers of African states.

Hence, throughout his trilogy, Farah seems to me to be making the point that African countries, including Somalia, must solve their own problems, work out their own destinies, not rely on wholesale importations from the outside world of ideas and methods evolved for the specific needs of other societies. The outside world will neither act from disinterested motives in promoting the well-being of African states or citizens, nor are the ideologies themselves, as the products of European thought geared to European situations, relevant to Africa.

As for the second theme of the trilogy, I feel that Farah may be preoccupied with a related problem—that of the position of the intellectual in a modern African state. As I have attempted to show, most of the prominent characters in these novels, that is those of the younger generation who have been brought up and educated in the "modern" Somalia or abroad, do not appear to have a firm grounding in their own society. Moreover, the Somalia portrayed by Farah is an extremely limited one, that of a narrow circle of "privilegentzia" in Mogadiscio who all know one another, are well-to-do, sophisticated, widely travelled. It is interesting that despite the noble ideals they profess, our subversive figures rarely, if at all, mention the poor, the under-privileged or the harsh and worsening conditions of drought and warfare in the rural areas; and this in spite of the fact that they all have clan relations and therefore connections in different parts of the country. Indeed, when Deeriye refers to " ... the natural famine [which] claims lives daily and a nationalist war in the Ogaden ... " it comes as rather a shock to the reader who has been fed almost wholly on a diet of very personal and very abstract problems so far. There is, I must admit, more comment on the urban mal-development of Mogadiscio—the traffic problems, the violence and the beggars—but these are more closely related to the lives of the urban elite with their fast cars, vouchers to avoid queuing for essential stores and food, and all the other modern gadgets that make life easier for those who can afford them. The reader gets the impression that most of these elite neither know nor care about their fellow countrymen except in the most abstract way, but are far more absorbed in their selfish, cosmopolitan interests and pursuits. Sagal, for example, practices her swimming every day and hopes to represent her country internationally as a swimmer, and this in a land where drought is endemic—yet she never mentions it and we can only assume that it never crosses her mind. One is reminded of the criticism of Jane Austen, that the War is never mentioned in her novels even though she lost a brother in it; either she is not interested in that side of life or she writes simply to entertain. I don't think Farah is writing simply to entertain, but it is not clear in these novels whether he himself is not interested or whether it is his characters that are so. This is an imbalance in Farah's work that is to a large extent redressed in his most recent novel, **Maps,** which does focus upon the very topics of famine, drought, poverty and war along the Somali/Ethopian border. Nevertheless, this weakness in *Variations on the Theme of an African Dictatorship* remains, I think, a very real one.

More questions, indeed, arise from speculation along the same lines. Is this evasion in *Variations* of important aspects of Somalia's existence as an independent state what Farah deliberately intends? Is such a morally ambiguous position avoidable for such an elite as he portrays? What, moreover, *is* the position of the intellectual in a modern African state? What of Farah's own position as a Somali intellectual living abroad and therefore even more cut off from his countrymen? For such an intellectual wishing to impart his own knowledge and communicate to his less-advantaged citizens his desire to help them and his country advance and prosper, what are the channels when he has no obvious links with them at any level? If one bases one's judgement on some of the popular heroes on the books and posters mentioned in these novels, Pablo Neruda, for example, or Che Guevara, the parallels seem ominous; the peasants whom Guevara came to liberate seemed not to appreciate his intentions but saw him as an interfering foreigner and he died unfulfilled, while the Chilean regime was able to corrupt Neruda's poetic idealism by appointing him ambassador to France—a technique also used by the Somali government in Farah's trilogy. Would a sophisticated "modern" Somali in the mould of Medina, Nasser, Sagal, Soyaan or Loyaan fare any better than a Guevara in the remoter parts of rural Somalia? And the question arising from this would of course be: to what extent can the intellectual and social elite seek to change and advance a society with which they have no real contact or identity? Such a question is clearly related to my previous discussion of whether a foreign ideology can or should be implanted in a developing state, for how can the country's intellectuals produce a home-grown remedy if they are steeped in the ways of societies not their own?

• • • • •

All these questions seem to me to be highly pertinent to Farah's novels of present-day Somalia. Perhaps it is partly for this reason that I find the last book of the trilogy, *Close Sesame,* the most satisfying. For unlike the earlier ones, which present the reader with a segment of the society quite out of context, *Close Sesame* has a historical dimension and a cultural context in which to weigh the principal figures. Indeed, the selection of the elderly Deeriye as the chief character is invaluable in this respect; he does not follow Farah's more usual pattern of brash and youthfully cosmospolitan protagonists. That Farah should portray a rather narrow section of society does not in itself merit criticism—witness Anthony Powell's *A Dance to the Music of Time,* for example, in British literature—but if he is trying to hint at something broader and more significant, as I think he is, then such an oblique angle of vision might be construed as a weakness.

To conclude, I find Farah's trilogy in many ways extremely convincing and powerfully written. He is, for example, an artist in the use of language which he makes almost tangible at times; he has a knack of offering slightly off-key metaphors and similes which strike one all the more vividly for this reason, and he can be very gentle and sensitive in his treatment of such minor characters as Beydaan and Dulman, who draw from the reader an instinctive compassion. Moreover, Farah's writing provokes much thought on topics wider than the subject matter might intitially suggest. Yet, I feel some doubt as to the underlying aims of his work in *Variations on the Theme of an African Dictatorship*—I am not certain whether he intends to provoke some of the lines of thought I have picked up or whether these have been provoked unwittingly by Farah's falling into the very trap that I have suggested he may be pointing out for us to observe. And it is in this ambivalence, perhaps, that Farah's main weakness lies. He cannot be putting over his message sufficiently clearly if the reader remains uncertain as to what that message actually is. (pp. 173-84)

Barbara Turfan, "Opposing Dictatorship: A Comment on Nuruddin Farah's 'Variations on the Theme of an African Dictatorship'," in Journal of Commonwealth Literature, *Vol. XXIV, No. 1, 1989, pp. 173-84.*

FURTHER READING

Bardolph, Jacqueline. "Time and History in Nuruddin Farah's *Close Sesame*." *The Journal of Commonwealth Literature* XXIV, No. 1 (1989): 193-206.
    Investigates the use of events in Somali history in the narrative of *Close Sesame*. Bardolph examines "how these known data are interwoven in the reflexion and dreams of the imaginary characters, how the apparently timeless waiting inside the household is examined and given meaning by the vast panorama of facts, myths and memories...."

Gugler, Josef. "African Literary Comment on Dictators: Wole Soyinka's Plays and Nuruddin Farah's Novels." *The Journal of Modern African Studies* 26, No. 1 (March 1988): 171-77.

> Surveys Wole Soyinka's and Farah's methods of protesting African dictatorships in their works.

Mnthali, Felix. "Autocracy and the Limits of Identity: A Reading of the Novels of Nuruddin Farah." *Ufahamu* 17, No. 2 (Spring 1989): 53-69.

> Analysis of Farah's works. The critic asserts that the themes of authoritarianism in the Somali family and autocracy in the Somali government, coupled with the characters' search for identity, "form the alternating and often interlocking angles of vision towards which the fiction of Nuruddin Farah is moving."

Sparrow, Fiona. "Telling the Story Yet Again: Oral Traditions in Nuruddin Farah's Fiction." *The Journal of Commonwealth Literature* XXIV, No. 1 (1989): 164-72.

> Examines orality in Farah's novels. Sparrow argues that although Farah writes in English, the oral tradition is particularly strong in his work, evidently because his native language has only been a written language since 1972, when it acquired a Roman script.

Stratton, Florence. "The Novels of Nuruddin Farah." *World Literature Written in English* 25, No. 1 (Spring 1985): 16-30.

> Overview of Farah's novels. Stratton determines that the "main thrust" of the works is "an exposition of the social and political realities in present-day Somalia."

Wright, Derek. "Unwritable Realities: The Orality of Power in Nuruddin Farah's *Sweet and Sour Milk*." *The Journal of Commonwealth Literature* XXIV, No. 1 (1989): 185-92.

> Explores the power of the written word and the "oppressive surveillance-techniques" of the spoken word under the Somali regime in *Sweet and Sour Milk*.

Jessie Redmon Fauset

1882-1961

American novelist, editor, short story writer, critic, essayist, poet, and writer of children's stories.

An integral figure of the Harlem Renaissance—a period of great achievement in black American art and literature that took place following World War I—Fauset earned recognition for her work on the *Crisis,* a progressive magazine published by the National Association for the Advancement of Colored People. As literary editor of the *Crisis,* Fauset discovered and published early works by such authors as Langston Hughes, Jean Toomer, and Claude McKay. She also wrote short stories and novels that were originally categorized as romantic melodramas but are now regarded as pioneering advocations of feminism and civil rights. Tracing the lives of upper middle-class black families, Fauset often centered upon a light-skinned heroine's efforts to gain economic security and social status by passing for white. Many of Fauset's protagonists subsequently suffer anguish as a result of bringing false values upon themselves and their families. Fauset challenged conventional literary portraits of females by featuring women who actively pursued careers and sought equality in their relationships with men. Although critics have noted limitations involving Fauset's themes and subject matter, her discussions of racial and sexual discrimination are considered insightful social commentaries. Joseph J. Feeney declared: "Miss Fauset's novels picture a mixed world of romance and prejudice, success and humiliation. . . .There is also a strong, underlying social purpose: to portray the educated black middle class and thereby uncover American racial prejudice."

Fauset was born to Reverend Redmon, an outspoken African methodist preacher, and Annie (Seamon) Fauset in Philadelphia in 1882. The Fausets, according to biographer Carolyn Wedin Sylvander, were poor, but cultured. Fauset attended Philadelphia public schools and was graduated from the High School for Girls in 1900. She enrolled at Cornell University and became the first black woman at the university to win Phi Beta Kappa honors upon her graduation. For the next fourteen years she taught at various schools, including Douglass High School in Baltimore and Dunbar High School in Washington, D. C. In 1919 she received a Master of Arts degree from the University of Pennsylvania, the same year she joined the staff of the *Crisis.* As its literary editor, she encouraged and promoted the works of Harlem Renaissance writers Langston Hughes, Nella Larsen, Countee Cullen, Claude McKay, and Jean Toomer as well as publishing her own short stories, essays, and poems. Along with W. E. B. Du Bois, she also produced *The Brownies' Book,* a monthly magazine for black children, to which she contributed many of her own stories. In 1921 Du Bois sent Fauset to Europe to cover the second Pan-African Congress in London, Brussels, and Paris; she was so enamored of Paris that she remained there for a year, studying French at the Sorbonne. Upon her return to the United States, she quit her position at the *Crisis* and, unable to find employment as a "publisher's reader" or a "social secretary" as she had hoped, returned to teaching in 1926. She married Herbert E. Harris, an insurance agent and businessman, several years later. Toward the end of her life she traveled extensively and taught English at Hampton Institute and Latin and French at Tuskegee Institute. She died in Philadelphia in 1961.

Fauset's career as a novelist began after reading T. S. Stribling's *Birthright,* a highly regarded novel about a mulatto Harvard graduate's inability to bring cultural refinements to the residents of his Tennessee hometown. When *Birthright* was first published in 1922, critics praised it as "the most significant novel on the Negro written by a white American." Dismayed by the "fallacies" she found in Stribling's book, Fauset resolved to write a book about Negro life: "A number of us started writing at that time.... Nella Larsen and Walter White, for instance, were affected just as I was. We reasoned, 'Here is an audience waiting to hear the truth about us. Let us who are better qualified to present the truth than any white writer, try to do so'." In 1924 Fauset published her first novel, *There Is Confusion*. The work depicts two wealthy black Philadelphia families who are brought together by the marriage of their children. Instead of focusing on the differences between black and white society, however, Fauset portrayed their similarities. While some critics faulted the book for an enigmatic narrative and melodramatic dialogue, the numerous characters, storylines, and details in *There Is Confusion* prompted William Stanley Braithwaite to describe Fauset as "the potential Jane Austen of Negro literature." Sylvander observed: "By taking the traditional *Bildungsroman* and family novel patterns and adapting them to study the peculiar confusion, learning, and ultimate understanding of American Blacks, Fauset has revealed insight into the human experience."

Fauset's second work, *Plum Bun: A Novel Without a Moral* (1929), is regarded as her finest literary achievement. Illustrating the conflict between the aspirations of blacks and the realities of a society dominated by whites, this novel portrays the consequences of Angela Murray's decision to advance her artistic career by passing for white. Although Angela's strategy proves successful, she becomes embarrassed by her deceptive actions and angry over society's unequal treatment of women. Fauset contrasted the emptiness of Angela's life with that of her sister, who embraces her black heritage by marrying a dark-skinned man and becoming a teacher in Harlem. When Angela is awarded a trip to Paris for her artistic accomplishments, she seizes the opportunity to proudly reveal her racial identity to a group of reporters. In *The Chinaberry Tree: A Novel of American Life* (1931), Fauset again explored the psychological consequences of racism on blacks. This book revolves around three characters of mixed racial ancestry who are denied social respectability by narrow-minded residents of a small town. While Fauset's blend of tragedy and romance garnered complimentary reviews upon the novel's publication, later critics have noted numerous plot deficiencies in the work and have identified it as her weakest literary effort.

In Fauset's final novel, *Comedy, American Style* (1933), the theme of passing is implemented through the character of Olivia Cary, whose pathological desire to be white alienates her entire family. After her light-skinned husband refuses to pass, Olivia emotionally destroys her daughter by forcing her to marry an insensitive white professor and leads her dark-complexioned son to suicide by masquerading him as a Filipino houseboy while entertaining white friends. Phebe, Olivia's daughter-in-law, serves as the antithesis of Olivia's obsession with skin color. Although blond and blue-eyed, she is passionate about her black heritage and refuses to marry a rich white man whom she does not love. The novel ends with a miserable and isolated Olivia successfully passing in Paris. While not as popular as *Plum Bun, Comedy, American Style* nonetheless received positive reviews; Hugh Gloster, for example, called it "the most penetrating study of color mania in American fiction."

Fauset is considered a minor, though pivotal, figure of the Harlem Renaissance. Critics who dismiss her novels as "trivial," "dull," and "vapidly genteel" readily acknowledge her discovery and promotion of important early black writers. Describing her role in helping shape the field of black literature, Langston Hughes remarked: "Jessie Fauset at the *Crisis*, Charles [S.] Johnson at *Opportunity*, and Alain Locke in Washington were the three people who mid-wifed the so-called New Negro literature into being. Kind and critical—but not too critical for the young—they nursed us along until our books were born."

(For further information about Fauset's life and works, see *Black Writers; Contemporary Authors*, Vol. 109; *Contemporary Literary Criticism*, Vols. 19, 54; and *Dictionary of Literary Biography*, Vol. 51: *Afro-American Writers from the Harlem Renaissance to 1940*. For related criticism, see the entry on the Harlem Renaissance in *Twentieth-Century Literary Criticism*, Vol. 26.)

*PRINCIPAL WORKS

"Emmy" (short story) 1912
"Rondeau" (poetry) 1912
"My House and a Glimpse of My Life Therein" (short story) 1914
"Again It Is September" (poetry) 1917
"'There Was One Time': A Story of Spring" (short story) 1917
"Mary Elizabeth" (poetry) 1919
"The Return" (poetry) 1919
"After School: A Poem" (poetry) 1920; published in periodical *The Brownies' Book*
"Dedication" (juvenile literature) 1920; published in periodical *The Brownies' Book*
"New Literature on the Negro" (essay) 1920
"Oriflamme" (poetry) 1920
"The Sleeper Wakes: A Novelette in Three Installments" (short story) 1920
"That Story of George Washington: A Poem" (poetry) 1920; published in periodical *The Brownies' Book*
"Turkey Drumsticks: A Thanksgiving Story" (short story) 1920; published in periodical *The Brownies' Book*
"Cordelia Goes on the War Path: A Story" (short story) 1921; published in periodical *The Brownies' Book*
"Ghosts and Kittens: A Story" (short story) 1921; published in periodical *The Brownies' Book*
"Impressions of the Second Pan-African Congress" (essay) 1921
"What Europe Thought of the Pan African Congress" (essay) 1921
"Dilworth Road Revisited" (poetry) 1922
"La Vie C'est La Vie" (poetry) 1922
"Song for a Lost Comrade" (poetry) 1922
"When Christmas Comes" (short story) 1922

"Double Trouble" (short story) 1923
"Here's April!" (poetry) 1924
"Rain Fugue" (poetry) 1924
"Rencontre" (poetry) 1924
There is Confusion (novel) 1924
"The Enigma of the Sorbonne" (essay) 1925
"The Gift of Laughter" (essay) 1925
"Stars in Alabama" (poetry) 1928
"'Courage!' He Said" (poetry) 1929
Plum Bun: A Novel Without a Moral (novel) 1929
The Chinaberry Tree: A Novel of American Life (novel)
    1931
Comedy, American Style (novel) 1933

*Unless otherwise indicated, all of Fauset's short stories,
poetry, and essays appeared in the periodical *Crisis*.

Robert Bone (essay date 1965)

[*Bone is an American authority on African-American
literature. He has said of himself: "A white man and
critic of black literature, I try to demonstrate by the
quality of my work that scholarship is not the same
thing as identity." He is the author of* The Negro
Novel in America *(1958; rev.ed.,1965). In the following essay from this work, he negatively assesses
Fauset's novels, stating that they are "sophomoric,
trivial, and dull."*]

Viewing the Negro Renaissance in retrospect, Richard
Wright has written caustically of "the prim and deco-
rous ambassadors who went a-begging to white America,
dressed in the knee-pants of servility, curtsying to show
that the Negro was not inferior, that he was human, and
that he had a life comparable to that of other people."
Without a doubt, one of the prime offenders whom
Wright had in mind was Jessie Fauset. Yet with all her
primness, Miss Fauset presents something of a paradox,
for in her editorial work on the *Crisis* she often
championed the young rebels of the Harlem School.
Unlike DuBois, who was a Philistine and objected to the
Harlem School on moral grounds, she showed a genuine
interest in the development of Negro art even when its
main current ran counter to her own social prejudices.

Claude McKay writes of Jessie Fauset in his autobiography, "All the radicals liked her, although in her social
viewpoint she was away over on the other side of the
fence." But if Miss Fauset won personal acceptance
among Harlem's colorful Bohemians, in her novels she
maintained an irreproachable decorum. Her literary
career was inspired, as a matter of fact, by the publication of T.S. Stribling's *Birthright* (1922), a "respectable"
novel of middle-class Negro life. "Nella Larsen and
Walter White," Miss Fauset remarks, "were affected
just as I was. . . . We could do it better." From the first,
therefore, her literary aspirations were circumscribed by

her desire to convey a flattering image of respectable
Negro society.

Jessie Fauset was the most prolific of the Renaissance
novelists, publishing four novels during a ten-year
period from 1924 to 1933. But in spite of an admirable
persistence, her novels are uniformly sophomoric, trivial, and dull. *There is Confusion* (1924) is nothing if not
well titled, for it is burdened with a plethora of
characters whose complex genealogy leaves the most
conscientious reader exhausted. *Plum Bun* (1928) is a
typical novel of passing, structured around the nursery
rhyme.

> To market, to market, to buy a plum bun;
> Home again, home again, market is done.

The Chinaberry Tree (1931) seems to be a novel about
the first colored woman in New Jersey to wear lounging
pajamas. *Comedy American Style* (1933) is an account of
a colored woman's obsessive desire to be white, not
unlike the novels which condemn passing in its nationalist implications.

Undoubtedly the most important formative influence
on Miss Fauset's work was her family background. An
authentic old Philadelphian (known as "O.P.'s" in the
colored society of that day), she was never able to
transcend the narrow limits of this sheltered world. It
accounts for her gentility, her emphasis on heredity and
genealogy, and her attitude toward race. Miss Fauset's
characters are bred to "rise above" racial discrimination, to regard it merely as "an extra complication of
living." Yet "the artificial dilemma," as she calls it, is
always present as an obstacle to gracious living, and is
the real antagonist of her novels. Racial protest, be it
ever so genteel, is an irrepressible feature of bourgeois
nationalism. (pp. 101-02)

> *Robert Bone, "The Rear Guard," in his* The
> Negro Novel in America, *revised edition,
> Yale University Press, 1965, pp. 95-108.*

Hiroko Sato (essay date 1972)

[*In the following excerpt, Sato reviews* There Is
Confusion, Plum Bun, The Chinaberry Tree, *and*
Comedy, American Style, *describing them as "novels
of manners of the Negro upper class."*]

In 1892, when the first novel by a black writer after the
Civil War came out, the author, Mrs. Frances Ellen
Watkins Harper, added the humble statement at the end
of the novel, *Iola Leroy, or Shadows Uplifted:*

> From threads of fact and fiction I have woven a story
> whose mission will not be in vain if it awakens in the
> hearts of our countrymen a stronger sense of justice
> and a more Christian humanity in behalf of those
> whom the fortunes of war threw homeless, ignorant
> and poor, upon a threshold of a new era. Nor will it
> be in vain if it inspires the children of those upon
> whose brows God has poured the chrism of the new
> era to determine that they will embrace every

opportunity, develop every faculty, and use every power God has given them to rise in the scale of character and condition, and to add their quota of good citizenship to the best welfare of the nation. There are scattered among us materials for mournful tragedies and mirth-provoking comedies, which some hand may yet bring into literature of the country, glowing with the fervor of the tropics and enriched by the luxuriance of the Orient, and thus add to the solution of our unsolved American problem.

The race has not had very long to straighten its hand from the hoe, to grasp the pen and wield it as a power for good, and to erect above the ruined auction block and slave pen institutions of learning . . . .

Thirty-five years later, young artists like Langston Hughes, Zora Neale Hurston, Gwendolyn Bennett, Aaron Douglas, and Wallace Thurman got together and published a magazine, *Fire 11.* In the "Foreword" of the magazine they wrote:

FIRE . . . weaving vivid, hot design upon an ebon bordered loom and satisfying pagan thirst for beauty unadorned . . . the flesh is sweet and real . . . the soul and inward flush of fire . . . . Beauty? . . . flesh of fire—on fire in the furnace of life blazing . . .

What had happened between the timid and humble statement of Mrs. Harper and the bold declaration of the young artists was the explosion of the black energy called the Harlem Renaissance. (pp. 63-4)

Of course, this flowering of the black arts did not come as suddenly as it seemed. The war and the great migration of the black people to Northern cities had something to do with it . . . . In a way, the Harlem Renaissance and the literature of the so-called Lost Generation came from the same social situation—the breaking down of the old ideals and sense of value. Those young artists, black and white alike, widened their world into that of physical sensations. Also, while the whites exiled themselves to Europe and looked back toward their homeland and tried to find its meaning, the blacks turned their eyes to Africa and tried to find their ties to the vast continent . . . . With the widening of the horizon of the black world of America, it seemed to some of the black people that the boundaries of American consciousness as a whole were enlarged. W.E.B. DuBois proudly points out:

We black folk may help for we have within us rare new stirrings; stirrings of the beginning of a new appreciation of joy, of a new desire to create, of a new will to be; as though in this morning of group life we had awakened from some sleep that at once dimly mourns the past and dreams a splendid future; and there has come the conviction that the Youth that is here today, the Negro Youth, is a different kind of Youth, because in some new way it bears this mighty prophecy on its breast, with a new realization of itself, with new determination for all mankind.

This movement was the restoration of "some of the things we thought culture had forever lost." There was no longer the need to be "over-assertive and over-appealing." The black artists felt that the American public had to acknowledge their full share in the world of art. (pp. 65-6)

Among those who helped this movement was Jessie Fauset, the literary editor of *The Crisis* from 1919 to 1926 . . . . Though she did "a yeoman's work for the Negro Renaissance," most of her own literary activities were done during the period of the Harlem Renaissance. And the significance of the fact that her first novel, *There Is Confusion,* came out in 1924, almost simultaneously with Toomer's *Cane,* will be discussed later.

The publication of her first novel was a memorable event in the Negro literary world. W.E.B. DuBois greeted its arrival with the following words:

The novel that the Negro intelligentsia have been clamoring for has arrived with Jessie Fauset's first novel, *There Is Confusion.* What they have been wanting, if I interpret rightly, is not merely a race story told from the inside, but a cross section of the race life higher up the social pyramid and further from the base-line of the peasant and the soil than is usually taken.

William Stanley Braithwaite comments: "Miss Fauset in her novel *There Is Confusion,* has created an entirely new milieu in the treatment of the Race in fiction. She has taken a class within the Race, given it an established social standing, tradition, culture, and shown that its predilections are very much like those of any civilized group of human beings."

This statement coincides with the author's attitude expressed in the preface to her third novel, *The Chinaberry Tree.*

I have depicted something of the home life of the colored American who is not being pressed too hard by the Furies of Prejudices, Ignorance, and Economic Injustice . . . . And behold he is not so vastly different from any other Americans.

As it has become clear from these statements, Jessie Fauset's novels can be regarded as novels of manners of the Negro upper class, and her attitude is to emphasize the similarity between the blacks and the whites, rather than the difference. Yet the words in the same preface, "To be a Negro in America posits a dramatic situation," cannot be ignored. (pp. 66-7)

Several reasons can be given why Miss Fauset chooses the people of her circle for the characters of her novels—tales of the "non-cabareting, churchgoing Negroes, presenting in all their virtue and glory and with their human traits, their human hypocrisy and their human perversities glossed over." The first one is, of course, that these are the people she knows best; secondly, according to her own words, the publication of T.S. Stribling's *Birthright* in 1922 stimulated her into fiction writing. This novel about a mulatto boy, a Harvard graduate, who, with an idealistic ambition, tried to improve his own people in a small town in Tennessee and failed, was considered as "the most significant novel on the Negro written by a white

American" at the time of its publication. However, the techniques are poor and ideas about the race questions are stale. In an interview Jessie Fauset tells what she thought of the book at its publication: "A number of us started writing at that time . . . . Nella Larsen and Walter White, for instance, were affected just as I was. We reasoned, 'Here is an audience waiting to hear the truth about us. Let us who are better qualified to present the truth than any white writer, try to do so.' " Whether or not this kind of novel was what the audience of the time had been waiting for becomes clear if we consider the difficulties Miss Fauset encountered in her efforts to find a publisher for her first novel. Publishers rejected her manuscript because "it contains no description of Harlem dives, no race riot, no picturesque, abject poverty." This shows the real attitude of the white world to the blacks.

Jessie Fauset's four novels have a similar plot—the heroine's pursuit of happiness. At the beginning of each novel the heroine has a rigid idea about the means to attain what she thinks to be happiness. The story evolves around the idea and a reader is told how her experiences in life affect and change it, or if not, what consequences the rigidity of her attitude has brought to her. In her first novel, *There Is Confusion,* the heroine, Joanna Marshall, was haunted with the idea of greatness. Even before she was five she determined that she would be someone great . . . . Joanna tried her best to be a great singer and dancer, but in spite of her extraordinary talent, she could attain only a mild success because of her color. She forced her sweetheart, Peter Bye, who had the tendency to be easily discouraged, to be a surgeon, the hardest road to take. Joanna even interfered with her brother's marriage to Maggie because Maggie was poor and without any family connections. Finally Joanna came to realize her mistake—that greatness, fame, and material success were not happiness. The most important thing was love. She and Peter were united in marriage and the novel ends with Joanna's declaration, "My creed calls for nothing but happiness."

Of course, this novel has more than this story. As Robert Bone severely says, "*There Is Confusion* is nothing if not well titled" [see excerpt dated 1965]. The author puts too many events in the novel to give it an artistic unity and coherence. There is the whole history of the white and black Bye family, with the story of miscegenation and exploitation, which explains Peter's subdued temperament. This story comes to its climax at Peter's encounter with his white kinsman, Merriwether Bye, on the boat to France, at Merriwether's death in the war, and with it the extinction of the Bye family on the white side, at Merriwether's grandfather's wish to acknowledge the son of Peter and Joanna as his heir, and their proud refusal. There is also a story of a short engagement of Peter and Maggie while both of them were separated from their true loves. A brief but moving tale is about Vera Manning, who could pass, and her lover, Harlet, who could not, and their final separation. When William Stanley Braithwaite calls Jessie Fauset "the

potential Jane Austen of Negro literature," the comparison seems well taken. The subject matter is the same, and the social status of the characters is the upper middle class. But when we think of what creates the dramatic situations in the fiction of these two writers, we come to realize the vast difference between them. In Jane Austen's case, what moves the plot is a certain temperament created in each character by the manners and morals of the class he or she belongs to. In Jessie Fauset's case, though she chooses a certain class of negro people, what really moves the story is not what is inherent to that class and hence to the character but what is imposed upon the person from outside. Miss Austen looks into the character's mind and creates humorous situations contrasting various temperaments and prejudices. In the Negro writer's novels the author's concern tends to be not psychological but social; and all the situations are serious. In a sense, Jessie Fauset's novels are those of social protest. (pp. 69-71)

In her next novel, *Plum Bun,* there is a great improvement in technique: William Braithwaite calls this novel "her most perfect artistic achievement." If we regard this novel as a melodramatic story of a girl who searched for a true love, fighting against adverse fate, it is the best conceived among Miss Fauset's four novels. She forms her novel around the nursery rhyme:

> To Market, to Market
>   To buy a Plum Bun;
> Home again, Home again,
>   Market is done.

She divides the novel into five parts, "Home," "Market," "Plum Bun," "Home Again," and "Market Is Done," to express the five stages of the heroine Angela Murray's ambition to attain happiness through passing, acquisition of wealth, her realization of the falseness of her idea, and the final happiness with her true lover. (p. 72)

To the parents, Junius and Mattie Murray, "who had known poverty and homelessness, the little house on Opal Street represented the *ne plus ultra* of ambition." But to the elder of their two daughters, Angela, the house seemed "the dingiest, drabbest" place. Angela thought that the shortest way to "the paths which lead to broad thoroughfares, large, bright houses, delicate niceties of existence" is to cross the color line and to live as a white girl. After her parents' death she cut off her family ties and even denied her only sister, Virginia, who showed color. She came to New York from Philadelphia and studied painting. The reason she chose art was not that she was interested in painting but because, through her study of art, she could meet interesting and wealthy people who would serve her purpose. She was gifted but "her gift was not for her the end of existence; rather it was an adjunct to life which was to know light, pleasure, gaiety and freedom." She found out that the surest way to accomplish her ambition was to marry a rich white man. She met a very wealthy young man, Roger Fielding, and tried every means to attract him and make him love her, though she was attracted to a quaint fellow

EDITORIAL ROOMS OF
THE CRISIS

69 FIFTH AVENUE
NEW YORK, N.Y.

W. E. B. DU BOIS, EDITOR
JESSIE FAUSET,
LITERARY EDITOR

January 26/ '26

Dear Mr. Spingarn:

I'm on the loop—out for a new position. My connection with this office will terminate February 28. I shall still have a piece of research work for Dr. Du Bois but shall start on a new position March 1.

I'm writing to ask you if you can assist me in any way. I should like

1. To be a publisher's reader (if remunerative enough)

2. To be a social secretary in a private family, preferably for a woman.

3. To be connected with one of the foundations here in New York.

You know something of my training—(A.B.; A.M.; ΦBK). I speak French more than fairly well and write it a little better than the average foreigner. I really know a great deal about magazine make-up. I type but very well although I know nothing of short hand.

Please do not think I'm making no effort to help myself. I've already taken the examination in French for the junior-high School but even if I should have passed there would be a lapse of time before an appoint—

Fauset's letter to Joel Spingarn, written shortly before Fauset's resignation from the Crisis.

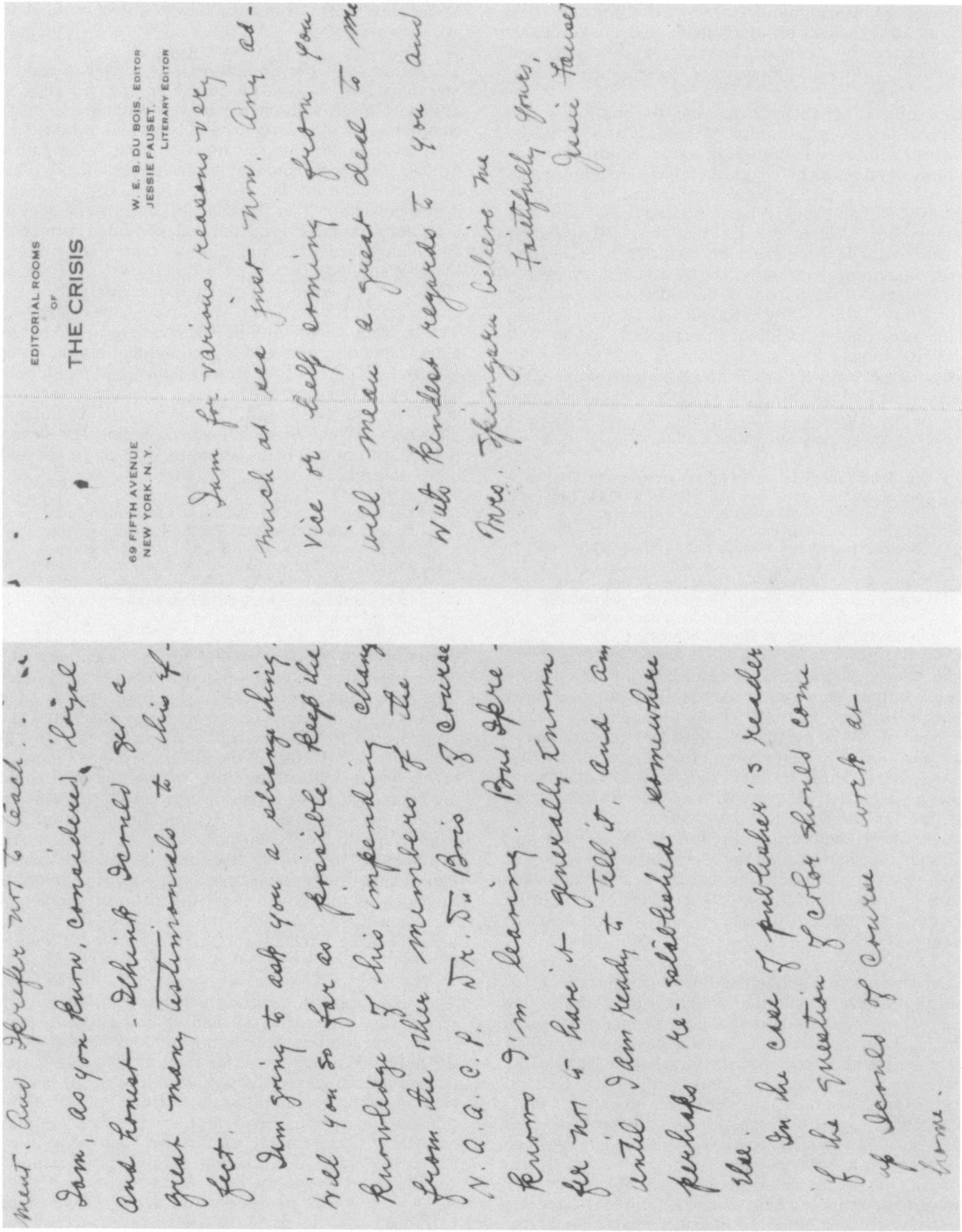

EDITORIAL ROOMS

OF

THE CRISIS

69 FIFTH AVENUE
NEW YORK, N.Y.

W. E. B. DU BOIS, EDITOR
JESSIE FAUSET,
LITERARY EDITOR

[handwritten letter, cursive]

student at Cooper Union, Anthony Cross. However, the result was that Roger only made her his mistress, because he did not care to marry a poor girl, and eventually threw her away when he was tired of her.

As a subplot, Miss Fauset describes the contrasting life of Angela's younger sister, Virginia, who came to Harlem and found happiness in teaching music to black children and in her marriage to Mathew Henson. Angela thought, "Jinny had changed her life and been successful. Angela had changed hers and had found pain and unhappiness. Where did the fault lie?" Miss Fauset seems to say that the fault lies in the fact that Angela used everything, her family, her friends, her profession, for the sake of her pursuit of happiness—she exploited everything, while Jinny always tried to serve others. This preaching of Christian virtues of service and sacrifice seems a little strange, but quite acceptable, for Miss Fauset's novels are in the tradition of the eighteenth- and nineteenth-century novels in subject and technique. However, the explanation she gives for Angela's selfishness surprises a reader:

> In all her manifestations of human relationship, how selfish she had been! She had left Virginia, she had taken up with Roger to further her own interest . . . . She had been too intent always on happiness for herself. Her father, her mother and Jinny had always given and she had always taken. Why was that? Jinny had sighed: "Perhaps you have more white blood than Negro in your veins." Perhaps this selfishness was what the possession of white blood meant: the ultimate definition of Nordic Supremacy.

This stereotyping of the white race as a kind of white fiend startles us when it comes from an intelligent person like Miss Fauset. Yet she never blames Angela for her most significant act—passing—for she knows the meaning of the expression "free, white and twenty-one." Also, though Harlem is gay and full of life and energy, it is "after all a city within a city." The problem of crossing the color line has been treated by several black writers before her: Frances E. W. Harper and Charles Chesnutt are among them. Mrs. Harper's attitude toward this question is that the near-white people have to cast their lot with their Negro race. Miss Fauset's attitude to the race solidarity is ambivalent. (pp. 72-4)

She even tries to describe the difference which the black blood made to people like Anthony and Angela—the near-white people. Yet when it comes to the question of the black intellectuals' role in the advancement of their race, her attitude becomes skeptical. She clearly shows the idea of the talented tenth, and treats the less fortunate of her race as if they were an inferior kind. Van Meier, one of the characters of *Plum Bun,* said: "Those of us who have forged forward, who have gained the front ranks in money and training, will not, are not able as yet to go our separate ways apart from the unwashed, untutored herd. We must still look back and render service to our less fortunate, weaker brethren." The standard of her judgment is that of the white world.

Miss Fauset fails to present a new aesthetic peculiar to her own race.

Her third novel, *The Chinaberry Tree,* is considered by many critics as the weakest among her four novels. . . . This novel deals with the narrow-mindedness of a black community in a town in New Jersey, Red Brook. The story evolves around the huge chinaberry tree that Colonel Halloway brought from the South for his lifelong lover, Aunt Sal, his mother's maid. Though he could not marry her because of her color, he did everything possible for Aunt Sal and their beautiful daughter, Laurentine. Aunt Sal was contented with her life, though she suffered a great deal from the prejudices of the white people and the moral accusation of the black people, for she knew what love meant to her. . . . Yet the black community of Red Brook regarded her as a degenerate woman and treated her and her daughter as pariahs. They said the strange family had bad blood. The most galling experience to Laurentine happened when she was a little girl. One of her friends stopped playing with her all of a sudden. Seeing the friend playing with other girls, Laurentine went up to her and asked the reason.

> Lucy stared at her, her eyes large and strangely gray in her dark face. "I wanted to Laurentine," she answered, "but my mumma say I dasn't. She say you got bad blood in your veins." Abruptly she left her former friend, ran to the table and came back with a tiny useless knife in her hand. "Don't you want me to cut yo' arm and let it out?"

Through her twenty-four years of life, Laurentine came to have an indelible complex about her birth, and every time something went wrong with her life she put the blame on it, and most of the time she was right. She wanted, above anything else, security in life. She tried in vain to make Phil Hacket, the richest Negro youth of the town, with a political ambition, marry her. Phil could not because he knew her strange parentage would be an obstacle to his career. Laurentine finally found her happiness with Dr. Denlaigh. As usual, Miss Fauset uses a subplot in this novel, describing the life of Melissa Paul, Laurentine's younger cousin. If there is anything to blame in this novel, it is this artificial subplot of incestuous love—obviously influenced by Greek tragedies—between Melissa and her half-brother, Malory Forten.

The main point of this novel, however, is to show a reader why colored people had to be rigid with their moral code and how Laurentine and Melissa, though in different ways, had to suffer from it. Though full of descriptions of elegant lives of wealthy colored people, we cannot help feeling what a strong influence the problem of race has had in forming black people's mentality. One example of this is, when black boys started to fight at a skating carnival, the minister complained: "Now boys, boys, don't start nothin'. Too many white folks here for that. We don't what this kind of thing closed to us." They have to be decent and moralistic to avoid the deprecating criticism of the whites. In spite of the unfavorable criticism, this book presents a deeper and subtler problem—the impact of the racial discriminations and prejudices by the whites on the black society in the long run.

Her last novel, *Comedy: American Style,* is a curious one. So far as the techniques are concerned, this is the most elaborate of Miss Fauset's novels.... The first two chapters show us the family background, social circumstances, and so forth, concerning the heroine, Olivia Cary, her children, and their friends. Olivia, who firmly believed that every advantage in the world can be attained only through the possession of white skin, forced her two older children, Chris and Teresa, to pass. Chris rebelled against her and, ignoring her wish, found his happiness with Phebe, a Negro girl with white skin and golden hair who remained faithful to her mother's race. But Teresa, after she was forced to denounce her handsome but brown-skinned lover, Henry Bates, came to realize that she was too much of her mother's making to rebel against her. When confronted by Henry as to whether she would choose him or her mother, she almost unconsciously said: "I was thinking, I was wondering—your Spanish, you know. Couldn't you use it most of the time and... and pass for a Mexican? In that way we could avoid most inconveniences...." This suggestion for passing hurt Henry deeply and their relationship ended. Teresa succumbed to her mother's wish and married a petty and miserly French linquist, Aristide Pailleron, in Toulouse, and led a miserable life. Oliver, the youngest and most beautiful child, had brown skin. His mother never showed him love and somehow contrived never to be seen with him on the street. When she had white women for tea at home— Olivia herself had passed into the white world—she treated the child as if he were a houseboy. When he found out that his mother thought that he was an obstacle to the happiness of other members of the family, he killed himself. Even after this tragedy Olivia was adamant in her belief. Finally, she went away to France, and the book ends with a picture of Olivia, bleak and lonely, living in a dingy Paris pension. When we finish reading the book, Olivia's coldness toward her family is unbelievable. Also, there are some unnatural situations: How could Olivia hide that she and her family were Negroes, when her husband, Dr. Cary, was practicing in the black community in Philadelphia, even though he had white skin? Yet a reader somehow is made to feel that the blame should not be placed totally on Olivia. All through this novel sufferings of the gifted and brilliant young people, like Phebe, Chris, Nicholas, and their friends—prejudices and discriminations in education, in profession, and in human relationships— are shown. You are almost convinced that you have to have white skin to enjoy living. I think the author's intention lies there, judging from the ironical title of the book.

This is the only book among her four novels with a depressing ending. Except for one slight light of Chris and Phebe's life, everything is under a dark shadow. Olivia, trying to cheat the world, cheated herself, her husband, and her family. In spite of many unnatural situations in the novel, a reader will readily accept William Braithwaite's comment on Olivia:

> She is the symbol of a force that must ultimately be acknowledged and discussed frankly by both races in America and when that discussion takes place there will be concessions and revisions on the part of white Americans which will make it possible to draw her like again as a warning.

And it seems symbolic that Jessie Fauset ended her literary career on this tragic portrayal of Olivia Cary.

Jessie Fauset is not a first-rate writer. First of all she failed to attain what Alain Locke called "the buoyancy from within compensating for whatever pressure there may be of conditions from without," though she was not unconscious of what was happening in the Negro world of the 1920s. Her appreciation of Negro musicals like *Shuffle Along* shows that she was aware of the new stirring of the black energy.... Yet this is a far cry from the younger artists' positive affirmation of the blackness. (pp. 75-9)

In a way, she shows the tragic situation which faces many of the black intellectuals: they are making too much of the white world, so that they can never escape its influence. Even if they try to create works unique to their race, they do not possess means to express them. They are deprived of the black soul. Jessie Fauset has never known the life of the black people of the rural South, nor the ghettos of the Northern cities. She came from a well-to-do old Philadelphia family, was educated at Cornell University, where she majored in French and was elected a member of Phi Beta Kappa. She did her graduate work at the University of Pennsylvania, and had been to France three times by the time of the publication of her first novel. The only thing she could do as an artist was to produce "uniformly sophomoric, trivial and dull" novels [see excerpt by Robert Bone dated 1965] with almost painful persistency, to show the world the goodness of the black people and to ask justice for the race. In her ideas she belongs to the older school of black writers like Mrs. Harper and Mrs. Hopkins, who wrote novels to "raise the stigma of degradation from [my] race." (pp. 79-80)

Miss Fauset does not have anything to do with "the investigation of the human soul" and her interest lies solely on the social level, yet there is one saving grace: the soundness of her judgment on racial situations in this country.

When we reflect upon the fact that her four novels came into the world between 1924 and 1934, and that the final picture she presents is the tragic product of the society of the white supremacy—Olivia Cary—we cannot deny that Miss Fauset had never drunk of the heady illusion of the Harlem Renaissance that affected many young blacks: the whites were accepting the black primitivism as a part of their civilization and hence the blacks as their equals. It was just a fad, exploited by commercialism, which came to its sudden end with the financial crash of 1929. Langston Hughes writes as follows:

> We were no longer in vogue, anyway, we Negroes. Sophisticated New Yorkers turned to Noel Coward. Colored actors began to go hungry, publishers politely rejected new manuscripts, and patrons found other uses for their money.

Jessie Fauset's observation on the social scene of the United States of the time is sane and sound. (pp. 80-1)

At the beginning of the discussion of Jessie Fauset's novels I said that the fact that Jean Toomer's *Cane* and Jessie Fauset's *There Is Confusion* came into the world almost simultaneously was important. What I mean is that the kind of novels Jessie Fauset wrote could have been nourishment and root for the flowering of quite different kinds of works represented by *Cane,* until these two tendencies are united in one and bring about the establishment of the black culture. Unfortunately, the white world took up only one side, because it coincided, in a way, with their conception of the black people, and ignored the other. This pattern in the treatment of the black arts has been repeated again and again, and the black arts have had several false flowerings without bearing any fruit. (p. 82)

> *Hiroko Sato, "Under the Harlem Shadow: A Study of Jessie Fauset and Nella Larsen," in* The Harlem Renaissance Remembered, *edited by Arna Bontemps, Dodd, Mead & Company, 1972, pp. 63-89.*

Joseph J. Feeney, S. J. (essay date 1979)

[*In the following excerpt, Feeney—contending that Fauset's works are rich with "double structure"— examines the "dark world of prejudice, sadness, and frustration" in* Plum Bun, The Chinaberry Tree, *and* Comedy, American Style.]

[There is] far more to Jessie Fauset than melodrama, romance, conventionality, and middle-class material.... A deep pain and anger affect both the form and content of her novels. They are not at all as conventional as they have appeared. Except for her rambling first novel, all her books have a double structure. On the surface they read as conventional middle-class love stories with happy endings; underneath these developing romances, though, lies a counterstructure which expresses either the souring of childhood hopes, or a near-tragedy, or sardonic comedy. Each counterstructure complicates, shadows, and darkens the love story.

In content and tone, too, a similar ambivalence prevails. On one hand there is happiness and self-confidence.... But life in Miss Fauset's novels is not always so romantic: sisters are estranged through skin color, scholarships are unfairly withdrawn, a darkskinned teenager kills himself. Just as there are two structures in Miss Fauset's novels, there are two visions of black experience. One views an upper world of success, love,

and middle-class comfort while the other stares at a lower world of pain, suicide, and prejudice. The balanced critic cannot ignore either vision.

Miss Fauset has too easily been named a conservative writer of traditional romances. Critics and historians have unfairly stressed her conventionality; they have paid scant attention to the anger, the tragedy, the sardonic comedy, the disillusioned hopes, the bitterness against white America. (pp. 366-67)

Only *There Is Confusion,* Miss Fauset's rambling first novel, is constructed conventionally. Despite an oversupply of characters and subplots, with a blurring of focus, the book basically tells the love story of Joanna Marshall and Peter Bye.... The book has a few subplots, some melodramatic scenes, and a few dramatically gratuitous incidents. But it is not structurally complex; there is no tension between the love story and some counterstructure. Miss Fauset's first novel, though diffuse, has the clear form of a romance.

Her next novel, *Plum Bun,* is more complicated and plays its romantic story line against a counterstructure suggested by its title. Its main plot also involves love and marriage.... But *Plum Bun* is more than a romance, for it also has a counterstructure, that is, some major organizing factor in opposition to the plot. In *Plum Bun,* this alternate structure is a children's rhyme:

> To Market, to Market
> To buy a Plum Bun;
> Home again, Home again.
> Market is done.

Besides providing the novel's title, the verse appears on the title page. More importantly, it provides titles and motifs for each of the book's five sections.... The irony of the counterstructure lies in this: what black children sing about and what Angela desires—the fun of going marketing and the pleasure of a delicious plum bun—are really the pleasures of whiteness.... By using this rhyme as a counterstructure the novel suggests that even the simplest desires of American blacks—even the small pleasures children sing about while at play— demand whiteness; the longed-for plum bun turns bitter for a woman born with Negro blood. Though on the surface *Plum Bun* is a romance with a happy ending, its ironic counterstructure shows the frustration of childhood hopes and the pain of being black in America.

The Chinaberry Tree, Miss Fauset's third novel, tells two happily ending stories of love, but also involves a near-tragedy in the Greek mode.... Both love stories end happily and the book closes with the whole family having a picnic under their chinaberry tree. Yet *The Chinaberry Tree* only seems a conventional romance, for Greek tragedy lies below the surface. Laurentine and some townspeople sense a curse in "that bad Strange blood" and both the Strange and Forten families feel that they suffer from some old family curse. Consequently, their actions seem designed and ruled by fate; the growing love of Melissa and Malory, in particular, appears fatally determined. A sense of doom and tragic inevitability dominates the book and leads to a series of recognition scenes in which the various characters, and last of all Melissa and Malory, realize the horror of their incestuous romance. Melissa is even terrorized by a recurring nightmare of the Greek comic and tragic masks, where she sees the comic mask reviling her with a leering grin.... The tragedy of incest is barely averted; at the end Laurentine's fiance comments that "there actually is such a thing as Greek Tragedy even in these days ... We were almost swamped with it. But the wave missed us." Despite the happy ending of both romances the narrator notes that the leading characters are only "enjoying a brief span of peace in the tragic disorder of their lives.".... (pp. 367-70)

In Miss Fauset's last novel, *Comedy: American Style,* a sardonic three-act comedy competes with the usual love story. The bitter comedy, in fact, dominates the novel's structure since the book is divided into six sections entitled "The Plot," "The Characters," Act I ("Teresa's Act"), Act II ("Oliver's Act"), Act III ("Phebe's Act"), and "Curtain." Miss Fauset maintains her traditional happy ending only by keeping the book's one happy story for Act III, and in this novel (her most jaundiced and interesting one) love, loneliness, and boredom combine to make the comedy's ending complex, ambiguous, and (from a black point of view) grotesquely American.

This tone grows naturally out of the story. The central character, though she is given no act of her own, is the ambitious Olivia Cary. She and her husband, middle-class Negroes, both have light skin. Olivia herself likes to be thought of as white because white Americans have more freedom and opportunities. She is proud of the light skin of their first two children, Teresa and Christopher, but Oliver, her handsome and talented third child, is born bronze. Each act of this "comedy" then focuses on one of the children. (p. 370)

Thus this "American-style" comedy offers ironic variations on blackness in America. Much human pain is caused by the American fixation on skin color. Two light Negroes leave the country where they might have "passed" but their European freedom hardly makes them happy. Those of lighter hue who stay in America live happily in the colored community and freely admit their Negro blood but still suffer from the national prejudice towards the Negro. The dark son dies because he is rejected by his mother and sister. Color, or the lack of it, is the source of pain and death in this peculiarly American comedy. The love story of Chris and Phebe is eclipsed by the dark comedy.

In designing her novels, then, Miss Fauset began as a writer of plain romance, developed through two books with double structures, and ended with *Comedy: American Style,* where the counterstructure dominated the romance. She had come to write the bitter comedy of a black in America, where happy endings were not common. (p. 371)

[Those] critics who speak of her middle-class respectability and her "genteel lace-curtain romances" miss the dark world of prejudice, sadness, and frustration just below the surface of her novels. There are two worlds in Jessie Fauset: the first is sunlit, a place of pride, talent, family love, and contentment; the other world is shadowed by prejudice, lost opportunities, a forced choice between color and country. (pp. 371-72)

This upper world of Miss Fauset's cosmos ... is a world of light and hope. Its inhabitants are young, talented, successful, and proud of their families and their blackness. They are educated, independent, and self-confident both as individuals and as members of a race that has come far and will progress yet farther. They feel at home in their city of Harlem but can also live at ease in the white world. Having accepted themselves and their color, they are confidently ready with money and talent to help their younger brothers and sisters. They are content, in short, with being black Americans, and Miss Fauset's reputation as a conventional, middle class novelist is based on her pictures of this comfortable, assured world. Even in this world, though, entrances to an underworld gape open: a sense that things are better in France and South America, a belief that being black is like being poor or deformed, a feeling that the colored are driven to basics earlier and more frequently than white Americans. (pp. 376-77)

In Miss Fauset's underworld the past meant slavery and lynchings; contemporary life offers insults, prohibited places, lost opportunities, denials of progress. Blacks fear and hate white prejudice but schizophrenically also admire white standards and model themselves on white values. Some must decide whether or not to pass, but all face problems of identity, prejudice within the black community, and unfairly different choices. Their exhaustion, their escapes, their stoicism, their bitterness are the fruits of this land of pain and suffering.

Miss Fauset, through structure and content, has offered a far more complex and harrowing portrait of American black life than the critics have recognized. She is far more than a conventional writer of middle-class romances, and her reputation must be revised accordingly. It cannot be denied that there is conventionality and sentimentality in her books. Her style was formal and she wrote novels about the Negro middle class. She wrote romance and melodrama and occasionally manipulated probability. She was not a major writer. But she cannot be dismissed as "vapidly genteel" or "sophomoric" [see excerpt by Robert Bone dated 1965]. In the construction of her novels and in her vision of the Negro world, she displayed a sensibility which comprehended tragedy, sardonic comedy, disillusioned hopes, slavery, prejudice, confusion, and bitterness against America. (p. 382)

Joseph J. Feeney, S. J., "A Sardonic Unconventional Jessie Fauset: The Double Structure and Double Vision of Her Novels," in CLA Journal, Vol. XXII, No. 4, June, 1979, pp. 365-82.

Barbara Christian (essay date 1980)

[*In the following review essay, Christian discusses the theme of passing—the identification or acceptance of oneself as a white person though having some black ancestry—in Fauset's novels.*]

[Jessie Fauset] was one of the intellectuals who "midwifed" the Harlem Renaissance, to which end she wrote articles covering a wide range of interests, from Pan-Africanism to blacks in the American theater. Her article **"The Gift of Laughter"** is an incisive analysis of the black actor as the "funny man" of America. She quickly grasped in this article the paradox of this gift of laughter that the American Negro is contributing to the American theater:

> In passing one pauses to wonder if this picture of the black American as a living comic supplement has not been tainted in order to camouflage the real feeling and knowledge of his white compatriot. Certainly the plight of the slaves under even the mildest of masters could never have been one to awaken laughter. And no genuinely thinking person, no really astute observer, looking at the Negro in modern American life, could find his condition even now a first aid to laughter. That condition may be variously deemed hopeless, remarkable, admirably inspiring, depressing; it can never be dubbed merely amusing.

Yet, although she knows the image of the laughing Negro to be partly a ploy, she does not discount the quality of zest and the love of life that the black actor brings to the stage:

> The remarkable thought about this gift of ours is that it has its rise, I am convinced, in the very woes which beset us. Just as a person driven by great sorrow may finally go into an orgy of laughter, just so an oppressed and too hard driven people breaks over into compensating laughter and merriment. It is our emotional salvation.

Fauset, however, seldom mentions the depressing conditions under which most turn-of-the-century blacks lived in her novels. Her fiction is peopled by characters who are "trying for a life of reason and culture," culture in this case being Western refinement. Her novels insist that the upper-middle-class Negro has the same values as the upper-class white. This indeed may be true, and a presentation of upper-class Negro life is certainly interesting material for fiction. The problem with Fauset's novels is that she gives us this particular Negro exclusively and as the representative of what the race is capable of doing. "She records a class in order to praise a race." Her Negroes become apologists for the race, indicators of the heights of refinement blacks might attain, given the opportunity. (pp. 41-2)

Jessie Fauset could certainly write with authority about the upper-middle-class Negro of the day. She herself came from an old Philadelphian family and, in contrast to most black women of the day, received an extensive formal education.... She traveled extensively in Europe and was as aware of the European culture as she was of upper-class American Negro life. Nor was she a "puff" of refinement.... She wrote consistently about the problems and aims of the Negro, translated poems of French West Indians into English, and was committed to the betterment of the race. She was in many ways a fine example of W.E.B. DuBois's "talented tenth." (pp. 42-3)

[Fauset] had at her disposal, because of her intimate knowledge of her class and because she was not fooled by the fad of primitivism, unique and significant subject matter. But because she was so conscious of being an image maker and because she accepted wholesale American values, except on the issue of race, her novels hardly communicate the intellectual depth that some of her articles do. Her fiction does not capture the essence of the upper-middle-class Negro society, a subject that certainly would show the relationship of class to race in America, because her characters lack critical insight and complexity, and because her plots seldom rise beyond the level of melodrama. In other words, her stories become bad fairytales in which she sacrifices the natural flow of life to the thesis that she feels she must prove—that blacks are as conventional as whites. Upper-middle-class blacks may have been as conventional, but Fauset's novels are so conditioned by her narrow mind set—the glorification of this position—that she does not allow her characters to become themselves.

Given her orientation, it is not surprising that Fauset's novels accepted the literary conventions of the nineteenth-century black novel. Her heroines are proper light-skinned women who unquestionably claim propriety as the highest ideal. They pursue the values of material success through marriage and inevitably believe that refinement is a reflection of spirituality. As a result, her heroines, like Laurentine Strange in *The Chinaberry Tree* and Angela Murray in *Plum Bun,* suffer crises because of a social mishap, either of birth or deportment. Nor does Fauset exercise any critical distance toward the unimportance of her heroines' major crises. She, too, believes that not being able to take up with the "right people" is a tragedy.

Her heroines, of course, are always beauties, according to the norms of the day. Light-skinned, long-haired, fine and graceful, they resemble princesses from a children's story who but for the complications of haphazard Negro birth would live happily ever after. *The Chinaberry Tree,* for example, is the story of Laurentine Strange, who is unfortunate enough to be the daughter of an ex-slave, Aunt Sal, and her former master, Captain Halloway. Far from having a primarily physical relationship, her parents were passionately in love with each other. "Halloway was a lad of serious bent but of tearing tyrannical passion. He loved her...he could not marry her." Aunt Sal, a straight, brown-skinned woman, lives in the glow of her memorable passion, the only traces of which are her daughter Laurentine and her house protected by the chinaberry tree. The tree is ever present throughout the novel as comforter and solidifier until one wonders if Captain Halloway's spirit has entered it.

Although Aunt Sal might have been a woman of passion, her mulatta daughter Laurentine is a lady, except for her manner of birth and the strained strangeness that seems to come form her mixed blood. Appropriately, she is the finest beauty in the town, who except for the sordidness of her birth would have few social difficulties in life. But Laurentine Strange's background alienates her from upper-middle-class society to which, by virtue of shade and taste, she rightfully belongs. The novel is, to a large extent, the measure of her ability to step softly and straight, so she might be admitted into its shelter.

Fauset's novels also employ the theme of "passing," a phenomenon that exemplifies the shakiness of the upper middle class. If upper-middle-class blacks could successfully compete with whites, why then would they have to resort to passing? Ironically, passing is a major theme of the 1920s when race pride was supposedly at a peak. One might at first think that this theme fed into the American belief system that it is better to be white than black. In actuality, the theme, as it was presented in the twenties, heightened the white audience's awareness of the restrictions imposed upon talented blacks who then found it necessary to become white to fulfill themselves. Talented blacks, however, in the novels of Walter White, as well as Jessie Fauset, are the mulattoes, who are distinguished from other blacks by their restiveness and frustration, a motif reminiscent of the rebellious mulattoes of the abolitionist novels. Inevitably, though, in Fauset's novels as well as in most novels of the Renaissance, the passer returns to her race convinced that her loss of identity, as well as the values she must adopt to be in the white race, are too high a price to pay. Assailed by passion, the taint or glory of her black blood, depending on your point of view, these mulattas also resemble the tragic mulattas of antebellum novels.

It is significant, too, that the passer is often a woman who believes that through her marriage to a wealthy white man, she might gain economic security and more freedom of mobility. The process of passing could have peculiarly feminine overtones, for a woman can often cement her future according to the man she marries. This theme is so inordinately prevalent during this period, engaging the attention of black writers and white writers alike, that one is tempted to wonder if it offered vicarious wish fulfillment, as well as amusement for those blacks who would pass if they could, and titillating drama for a largely white reading audience. Sterling Brown summarized the characteristics of the passer in the Harlem Renaissance novel, underlining the difference in interpretation, according to the novelist's race:

> We have thus seen that the mulatto who "passes" has been a victim of opposing interpretations. Negro novelists urge his unhappiness, until he is summoned back to his people by the spirituals, or their full-throated laughter, or their simple, sweet ways.... White novelists insist upon the mulatto's unhappiness for other reasons. To them he is the anguished victim of a divided inheritance. Mathematically they work it out that his intellectual strivings and self-control come from his white blood, and his emotional urgings, indolence and potential savagery come from his Negro blood. Their favorite character, the octoroon, wretched because of the "single drop of midnight in her veins," desires a white lover above all else, and must therefore go down to a tragic end. The white version is nearly a century old; the negro version sprang up recently.

In spite of their many social traumas, Fauset's heroines have great faith in America and in the American dream—that through hard work you can achieve equality. They even go one step further. They accept the precept that blacks must be superior to whites in their accomplishments to qualify. For what do they qualify? They qualify for freedom, yes, but not the freedom to experiment or experience. They want the highest of all American values: security. (pp. 43-5)

We must remember that Fauset exemplified the dominant position of the Harlem intellectuals of her day. Her works were praised by critics and her images exalted. However, her values also posed a serious threat to the New Negro Philosophy. If blacks were culturally no different from whites except when downtrodden, how could anyone posit a unique Negro genius, a specifically different culture? If Fauset's novels were to be believed, the Negro's peculiar contributions to America were a result of oppression rather than the consequence of a different cosmology or tradition. Also, what should one do with the issue of class? Why should lower-class

Fauset, Langston Hughes, and Zora Neale Hurston at Tuskegee Institute in 1927.

Negroes rise up and change their situation if they only replaced one master with another, black like them, but master nonetheless. Fauset's novels indirectly pose the question of whether one could really be conservative about all things except race unless one were sitting in a position of relative comfort. (p. 47)

> Barbara Christian, *"The Rise and Fall of the Proper Mulatta,"* in her Black Women Novelists: The Development of a Tradition, 1892-1976, *Greenwood Press, 1980, pp. 35-61.*

Deborah E. McDowell (essay date 1981)

[*In the following excerpt from an essay originally published in* Afro-Americans in New York Life *in 1981, McDowell explores what she terms the "neglected dimension" of Fauset's work: "her examination of the myriad shadings of sexism and how they impinge upon female development."*]

Jessie Fauset's novels are generally read as novels of manners of the black middle class, the refined intelligentsia, written to emphasize that, except for the biological accident of color, blacks are no different from whites and should therefore enjoy all the rights and privileges that whites enjoy.... [She] was traditional to some extent, both in form and content, but as Gary de Cordova Wintz rightly observes, "in spite of her conservative, almost Victorian literary habits," Fauset "introduced several subjects into her novels that were hardly typical drawing room conversation topics in the mid-1920s. Promiscuity, exploitative sexual affairs, miscegenation, even incest appear in her novels. In fact prim and proper Jessie Fauset included a far greater range of sexual activity than did most of DuBois's debauched tenth."

When attention is given Fauset's introduction of these challenging themes, it becomes possible to regard her "novels of manners" less as an indication of her literary "backwardness" and more as a self-conscious artistic stratagem pressed to the service of her central fictional preoccupations. Since many of Fauset's concerns were unpalatable to the average reader of her day and hence unmarketable in the publishing arena, the convention of the novel of manners can be seen as protective mimicry, a kind of deflecting mask for her more challenging concerns. Fauset uses classic fairy tale patterns and nursery rhymes in a similar fashion; however, although these stratagems are consciously employed, they are often clumsily executed.

In addition to the protective coloration which the conventional medium afforded, the novel of manners suited Fauset's works in that the tradition "is primarily concerned with social conventions as they impinge upon character." Both social convention and character—particularly the black female character—jointly form the nucleus of Fauset's literary concerns. The protagonists of all of her novels are black women, and she makes clear in each novel that social conventions have not sided well with them but, rather, have been antagonistic.

Without polemicizing, Fauset examines that antagonism, criticizing the American society which has institutionalized prejudice, safeguarded it by law and public attitude, and in general, denied the freedom of development, the right to well-being, and the pursuit of happiness to the black woman. In short, Fauset explores the black woman's struggle for democratic ideals in a society whose sexist conventions assiduously work to thwart that struggle. Critics have usually ignored this important theme which even a cursory reading of her novels reveals. This concern with exploring female consciousness and exposing the unduly limited possibilities for female development is, in a loose sense, feminist in impulse, placing Fauset squarely among the early black feminists in Afro-American literary history. It is this neglected dimension of Fauset's work—her examination of the myriad shadings of sexism and how they impinge upon female development—that is the focus of this discussion. A curious problem in Fauset's treatment of feminist issues, however, is her patent ambivalence. She is alternately forthright and cagey, alternately "radical" and conservative on the "woman question." On the one hand, she appeals for women's right to challenge socially sanctioned modes of feminine behavior, but on the other, she frequently retreats to the safety of traditional attitudes about women in traditional roles. At best, then, we can grant that Fauset was a quiet rebel, a pioneer black literary feminist, and that her characters were harbingers of the movement for women's liberation from the constrictions of cultural conditioning. (pp. 86-8)

[Fauset's short story] **"The Sleeper Wakes"** is crucial to an understanding of [her] concern with female psychology and socially-conditioned female role patterns. In this story Fauset sets the pattern that she will return to, in varying degrees, in each of her novels. She positions her major character in the adolescent stage . . . to demonstrate that her possibilities for development and attainment of freedom, well-being, and happiness are sorely limited in range. These limited possibilities are due both to how she perceives herself, based on socialization, as well as to how society perceives her. This early protagonist, like those to follow, aspires to "grow up" and marry, an orthodox female vocation, but she has extremely romantic notions not only about marriage, but also about life and human relationships in general. To dramatize her character's romanticism, Fauset uses patterns and imagery from classic fairy tales.

It is apparent even as early as 1920 that Fauset was aware of how folk literature—particularly fairy tales—serves to initiate the acculturation of children to traditional social roles, expectations, and behaviors, based on their sex. Marcia Lieberman has cogently explored this concept in "'Some Day My Prince Will Come': Female Acculturation Through the Fairy Tale," where she outlines the fairy tale patterns and demonstrates how they condition women to limited roles and expectations. Lieberman points out that central to the fairy tale is a beautiful girl who is finally rewarded by marriage to a handsome prince.... Lieberman concludes that "since girls are chosen for their beauty, it is easy for a child to infer that beauty leads to wealth, that being chosen means getting rich." Thus "the system of rewards in fairy tales ... equates these three factors: being beautiful, being chosen, and getting rich." These fairy tale patterns clearly operate in **"The Sleeper Wakes,"** which Fauset modeled on the classic tale, "Sleeping Beauty," for Amy, the protagonist, exists in a state of suspended animation, passively waiting for her prince to come. Unlike the classic Sleeping Beauty, however, Amy's "prince" does not bring her a "happily-ever-after" existence, but only the temporary illusion of happiness. Fauset inverts the classical ending to demonstrate that women's traditional attitudes and expectations about marriage are romantic and impractical. Moreover, the corresponding marital role-playing dictated by convention keeps women in stasis preventing their development of independence and autonomy.

When the story opens, Amy, a mulatto foster child, is growing up with the Boldins, a black family of modest means. She is youth personified, associated predominantly with the color pink, a symbol of innocence and femininity. We first see her in a dress shop, arrayed in a pink blouse, about to try on an apricot-colored dress. Her face is a "perfect ivory pink," highlighted by her "smooth, young forehead. All this made one look for softness and ingenuousness." Amy's physical appearance mirrors her perceptions. She sees life through the proverbial "rose-colored" lens, living totally in the realm of fantasy, fed by fairy tales, "the only reading that had ever made any impression on her," and movies of poor, beautiful girls who married "tremendous rich" men who gave them everything. Mr. Boldin's warning to Amy that "pretty girl pictures are not always true to life" does nothing to shake her persistent belief that "something wonderful" will happen to her, a belief that demonstrates a passive ("female") rather than active orientation. Following her talk with Mr. Boldin, Amy goes upstairs to her room for her flight into fantasy. She "lit one gas jet and pulled down the shades. Then she stuffed tissue paper in the key hole and under the doors, and lit the remaining gas-jets. The light thus thrown on the mirror of the ugly oak dresser was perfect .... In the mirror she apostrophized ... the beautiful, glowing vision of herself." The passage is important for exposing Amy's tendency to refract the harsh light of reality (suggested by the "ugly oak dresser") through her romantic imagination (suggested by the light from the gas jets). Amy believes that this image of herself reflected in the mirror will bring her happiness.... Deciding that her home environment with the Boldins is stifling, Amy runs away to New York, "Altogether happy in the expectation of something wonderful, which she knew some day must happen."

At the end of her second year in New York, Amy meets Zora Harrison; their developing friendship is a study in contrasts, a technique Fauset uses in each novel. The developing protagonist is foiled by more sophisticated characters who introduce her to alternative ways of thinking and behaving. While Amy is soft and pliable, Zora is hard and callous. Amy's "blonde, golden beauty" contrasts with Zora's dark beauty. Amy is passive and naive, Zora, active and worldly. In other words, while Amy is content to be more acted upon than acting, Zora actively goes after what she wants in life with a selfish and hardened determination. She first encourages Amy to marry the wealthy Stuart James Wynne (his name has a regal sound) and then to divorce him should she become dissatisfied. A retired and wealthy stockbroker of fifty-five, Wynne is instantly attracted to Amy. She "seemed to him everything a girl should be—she was so unspoiled, so untouched." He proposes marriage and Amy accepts, thinking that he is her prince, her "dream come true."

In her marriage Amy is nothing but an adornment, a doll for Wynne's amusement. (It is obvious that Fauset is also adapting Ibsen's *A Doll's House* to the special problems of a black woman.)... Their relationship is founded on inequality, analogous to that of vassal and lord, child and parent. Her sole activities are reading to Wynne and affecting her " 'spoiled child air,' as he used to call it. It was the way he liked her best." Amy is perfectly content to act as a spoiled child, fearful of upsetting her placid, "doll house" existence, ruffled only by Wynne's coarse insults to their black servants. Although Amy is passing for white, she intensely identifies with the servants and finally begins to wonder how Wynne would react should he discover that she is black. She confidently assures herself that her beauty has an unshakable hold on him .... Amy's assurance and security are soon shattered, however, for in a violent argument between Wynne and one of the servants, Amy confesses her blackness. To her chagrin, her beauty is not a stay against her husband's consuming racial prejudice, for he wants to divorce her immediately after she reveals her heritage.

Amy moves to New York and is supported by Wynne's alimony payments, but her financial ease does nothing to assuage her feelings of emptiness and loneliness.... Amy's solitude precipitates a period of introspection during which she reviews her past and slowly rejects her lifelong assumption that her beauty was her pass to a world of infinite possibilities. Admitting to herself that "amazingly [her] beauty availed her nothing," she begins to make plans for her future as a woman single and alone. She contemplates going to Paris to try her hand at dress designing.

One afternoon while she works on a design, Wynne comes to visit. In his characteristic manner, he commands that she come back to live with him, attempting to entice her with jewels as he had before. Amy mistakes his gesture for a marriage proposal but he quickly explains that he merely wants a mistress.... Thus Amy, the sleeper, wakes to the harsh reality of a "prince" transformed into a consummate racist and sexist. Having discovered that Amy is black, Wynne—

consistent with the white male's history of sexual exploitation of black women—regards remarriage to her as unthinkable. His attack reveals Fauset's understanding of a sexist society that often makes a marriage a form of prostitution, a vulgar financial arrangement that rewards women for being creatures of artifice and ornamentation and forces them to assume degrading forms of behavior.

With Wynne's insults Amy wakes from her romantic illusions about men and marriage, and to a realization of her own resources kept in dormancy by the dictates of convention. Whereas she had stifled the talent that would earn her a livelihood while relying instead on the supposed advantage of her beauty, Amy vows never more "to take advantage of her appearance to earn a living." She then releases her servants, refuses any more alimony from Wynne, and begins work as a dress designer to pay back all money received from Wynne to this point. When she has paid the sum in full, she feels "free, free! she had paid back her sorry debt with labor, money and anguish. From now on she could do as she pleased." Amy's freedom from monetary debt parallels her psychological freedom from her former slavish conformity to society's most invidious assumptions about blacks and women. Consistent with that nascent freedom, she makes plans to visit the Boldins, finally recognizing that they represent the regenerative virtues and riches of the black experience which she had rejected in pursuit of what was only a figment of happiness. More importantly, however, she makes plans to establish her own business, the returns on which will be not only financial solvency, but also the beginning of the self-reliance and autonomy that is impervious to society's assault. Fauset has thus inverted the classical fairy tale ending. "Happily-ever-after" is not marriage to a handsome, wealthy prince but realization and acceptance of the virtues of the black cultural experience as well as a realization and rejection of conventional social relationships that are injurious to the growth of selfhood.

Early in her career, then, Fauset is challenging sexual stereotypes and criticizing the conditions that give rise to them. In tracing Amy's growth from a fantasy-orientation to a realistic one, Fauset challenges some of society's most cherished sexist beliefs that women have bought wholesale, beliefs that have insured their marginality in society. Amy's story is a criticism of women who rely preeminently on beauty, which requires nothing of them, save for sitting and looking pretty. In so doing, they reinforce and perpetuate conventional stereotypes of women as passive sexual objects. Moreover, Fauset criticizes a society that encourages women to dissemble, to assume, uncritically, insulting and degrading forms of behavior in exchange for the so-called privilege of marriage. For all women who feign childishness and frivolity, who repress their talent and intelligence out of deference to an ideal of woman which men have largely created and maintained, Fauset has a message. These masquerades, she makes clear, are performed at great price. Stereotyped sexual roles, by

their very nature, deny human complexity and stifle growth, completeness of being, a state toward which Fauset aims all of her women characters. Inasmuch as this role-playing is, more often than not, a prerequisite to marriage, as well as a requirement during marriage, Fauset questions an institution that demands that women remain locked in growth-retarding roles. Therefore, at least in its more conventional forms, marriage can work to limit women's possibilities for self-realization and autonomy, a position that Fauset curiously repudiates in her first novel, *There Is Confusion.*

There Is Confusion chronicles the development of the protagonist, Joanna Marshall, tracing primarily her ambition to become a stage success as a singer-dancer and the trials she encounters in the process. (pp. 88-93)

The multiple stylistic weaknesses of *There Is Confusion* . . . are somewhat compensated for by its strengths in content. As usual, critics have missed the essential point of the novel, reading it as a formulaic apology for the black middle class and a plea for acceptance by whites. These critics ignore Fauset's continued exploration of the circumscribing effects of sexism on women.

Throughout the novel Joanna is described as self-assured, cool, practical, egotistical, and independent. It seems evident from the beginning of the novel that she has neither desire nor intention to accept or conform to conventional images of women, an option encouraged by the general run of the Marshall household where Joanna's mother "insists on each child's [girls and boys] learning to do housework." The female-related fixation with physical beauty and the cosmetics that are so-called beauty aids is equally unappealing to Joanna. Rather, "she had the variety of honesty which made her hesitate and even dislike to do or adopt anything artificial, no matter how much it might improve her general appearance. No hair straighteners, nor even curling kits for her." Even dolls that have traditionally oriented female children toward roles as wives and mothers fail to appeal to Joanna. Her dolls were usually in her sister Sylvia's care while Joanna was "reading the life of some exemplary female," "notable women of color." Reading of these important women inspires in Joanna a "fixity of purpose." (p. 93)

Although Joanna is inspired by the notable examples of her female ancestors, she is initially unaware that racist and sexist practices, deeply entrenched in the social structure, work to frustrate her ambitions. Her father's success as a caterer has instilled in her the American success ethic, and she mistakenly believes that any ambition is realizable if one is diligent and industrious. The success ethic doesn't work for all, Joanna soon discovers, for when she isn't plagued by occupational barriers because of her race, she is because of her sex. Her perennial struggles finally convince her that "it was women who had the real difficulties to overcome, disabilities of sex and of tradition." . . . Fauset is suggesting that sexual discrimination, more so than racial, is responsible for Joanna's occupational difficulties. (p. 94)

Fauset's oblique and ambivalent treatment of women's roles in **"The Sleeper Wakes"** and in *There Is Confusion,* respectively, is less apparent in her next three novels, *Plum Bun, The Chinaberry Tree,* and *Comedy: American Style.* She continues her exploration of women's roles, their lives' possibilities, and her criticism of social conventions that work to restrict those possibilities by keeping women's sights riveted on men, marriage and motherhood. These domestic and biological facets, Fauset suggests, while important, are just one dimension of a woman's total being, one aspect of her boundless capacities and possibilities. Seen in this light, then, fairy tale illusions about life give way to mature realities, and women, instead of waiting for their imaginary princes, aggressively take charge of their lives and move toward achieving authentic selfhood.

The idea of Fauset, a black woman, daring to write—even timidly so—about women taking charge of their own lives and declaring themselves independent of social conventions, was far more progressive than critics have either observed or admitted. Although what Fauset attempted in her depictions of black women was not uniformly commensurate with what she achieved, she has to be credited with both presenting an alternative view of womanhood and a facet of black life which publishers, critics, and audiences stubbornly discouraged if not vehemently opposed. Despite that discouragement and opposition, Fauset persisted in her attempt to correct the distorted but established images of black life and culture and to portray women and blacks with more complexity and authenticity than was popular at the time. In so doing, she was simultaneously challenging established assumptions about the nature and function of Afro-American literature. Those who persist, then, in regarding her as a prim and proper Victorian writer, an eddy in a revolutionary literary current, would do well to read Fauset's work more carefully, to give it a more fair and complete appraisal, one that takes into account the important and complex relationship between circumstances and artistic creation. Then her fiction might finally be accorded the recognition and attention that it deserves and Fauset, her rightful place in the Afro-American literary tradition. (p. 100)

> *Deborah E. McDowell, "The Neglected Dimension of Jessie Redmon Fauset," in* Conjuring: Black Women, Fiction, and Literary Tradition, *edited by Marjorie Pryse and Hortense J. Spillers, Indiana University Press, 1985, pp. 86-104.*

Deborah E. McDowell (essay date 1984)

[*In the following excerpt from the 1984 introduction to a 1985 edition of* Plum Bun, *McDowell favorably reviews the novel, describing it as a "rich tapestry."*]

On its face, *Plum Bun* is just another novel of racial passing. It has all the generic features of the passing novel: Angela Murray is the typical mulatto protagonist who, seeking to avoid the constraints of color prejudice in America, decides to cross the color line and pass for white, a deception, fraught with anxieties and frequently discovered. After learning that life on the other side is not without its difficulties, she develops an appreciation of black life and culture, and returns "home," psychically if not physically, to the black community and embraces its values.

But while *Plum Bun* certainly shows these most salient features of the novel-of-passing, to read it simply as such is to miss the irony and subtlety of its artistic technique. The novel is a richly-textured and ingeniously-designed narrative, comprised of plots within plots and texts within texts that cross refer to and comment upon one another in multiple and intricate combinations. In this rich tapestry, the passing plot is just one thread, albeit an important one, woven into the novel's over-arching frame, the *bildungsroman,* or novel of development.

While the passing plot forms a major stage in Angela Murray's coming-of-age, in the narrative's configuration and economy, that plot is backgrounded and handled with dispatch in order for Fauset to focus more sharply on the marriage plot. That plot forms, perhaps, the major phase of Angela's development as well as the structural core of the novel. Angela's obsessions with getting married are frustrated and complicated by the realities of sex-role stereotyping, the politics of sexuality, and the limitations of her own romantic assumptions. Although she is making plans to marry at the novel's end, it is not because she believes marriage to be "the most desirable end for a woman." Rather, she has developed from the adolescent crippled by romantic assumptions about marriage to a woman who understands the limitations of these assumptions. In that *bildungsroman* frequently combines elements of fantasy and romance with social realism, it is an appropriate genre within which to chronicle such a development.

Combining passing and marriage as ingredients in a novel of female development is a clever artistic choice and one that well serves Fauset's controlling theme: the unequal power relationships in American society. These two plots (which we might designate "racial" and "female" plots respectively), could not be more appropriate in a narrative about power, for both passing and marriage are naïve, fantasy-ridden attempts by blacks and women to avoid the structural inequalities that disempower them. In other words, both marriage and passing are the means by which these two disenfranchised groups hope to gain access to power. As the narrative makes clear, their expectations are frequently unfulfilled. (pp. x-xi)

Plum Bun baits the reader with a range of familiar expectations of women, found both in and out of literature, but then refuses to fulfill them, particularly those that perpetuate and reinforce stereotypes and sex-role expectations, that perpetuate and reinforce women's powerlessness. At the same time that she takes Angela through a developing and educating process about blacks and women, Fauset takes the reader. As Angela adjusts to the disappointment of limited and limiting expectations, so does the reader.

We can say, then, that **Plum Bun** has the hull but not the core of literary conservatism and convention. Like Angela's it is the case of mistaken identity. It passes for conservative, employing "outworn" and "safe" literary materials while, simultaneously, remaining suspicious of them. The novel moves toward dismantling the fantasy of racial passing, but more importantly, it moves toward de-idealizing romantic love and criticizing those literary and cultural structures that reinforce and promote that idealization. In other words, **Plum Bun** dares to explore questions about unconventional female roles and possibilities for development using the very structures that have traditionally offered fundamentally conservative answers to those questions. Fauset's answers were risky, in the literary marketplace, but powerful, liberating alternatives nevertheless, both for herself as a writer and for the image of blacks and women in literature. (p. xxii)

> *Deborah E. McDowell, in an introduction to* Plum Bun: A Novel without a Moral, *by Jessie Redmon Fauset, Pandora Press, 1985, pp. ix-xxii.*

FURTHER READING

Brown, Beth. Review of *Plum Bun*, by Jessie Redmon Fauset. *The Black Scholar* 17, No. 4 (July-August 1986): 58-9.
  Brief, positive review of *Plum Bun*.

Feeney, Joseph J. "Greek Tragic Patterns in a Black Novel: Jessie Fauset's *The Chinaberry Tree*". *CLA Journal* XVIII, No. 2 (December 1974): 211-15.
  Examines Fauset's use of "Greek tragedy elements" in *The Chinaberry Tree*. The critic remarks: "[Fauset] used many techniques of Greek tragedy to add a dimension of universality and bloodless horror to a story of love and domestic life among comfortable Blacks in a small north Jersey town.... There is Greek tragedy in *The Chinaberry Tree* but it is alloyed with much conventional sentiment."

Harris, Violet J. "Race Consciousness, Refinement, and Radicalism: Socialization in *The Brownies' Book*." *Children's Literature Association Quarterly* 14, No. 3 (Winter 1989): 192-96.
  Discusses the role of Fauset and W. E. B. Du Bois in creating *The Brownies' Book*, "one of the first literary manifestoes to explicate the socialization function of literature for Black children."

Johnson, Abby Arthur. "Literary Midwife: Jessie Redmon Fauset and the Harlem Renaissance." *Phylon* 39, No. 2 (Summer 1978): 143-53.
  Focuses on Fauset's work at the *Crisis* and her contributions to black literature. The critic notes: "As literary editor of *Crisis* and as a novelist, Fauset performed a valuable service in the Negro Renaissance.... Fauset was not a radical, by most estimates, but she did help to raise black consciousness...."

Lupton, Mary Jane. "Clothes and Closure in Three Novels by Black Women." *Black American Literature Forum* 20, No. 4 (Winter 1986): 409-21.
  Exploration of the "Cinderella Myth" in Fauset's *Comedy, American Style*, Alice Walker's *The Color Purple*, and Toni Morrison's *Tar Baby*.

Singh, Amritjit. " 'Fooling Our White Folks': Color Caste in American Life." In his *The Novels of the Harlem Renaissance: Twelve Black Writers, 1923-1933*, pp. 89-104. University Park: Pennsylvania State University Press, 1976.
  Considers the theme of passing in *Plum Bun*.

Rudolph Fisher

1897-1934

American short story writer, novelist, dramatist, critic, and essayist.

In his brief career, Fisher distinguished himself among Harlem Renaissance authors by writing novels and short stories noted for their narrative ingenuity and satirical objectivity. With masterful attention to detail, he captured the gradations of Harlem speech patterns and lifestyles during the 1920s and early 1930s. Fisher was one of the first "New Negro" writers to satirize both black and white society. He also explored the serious problems of the newly migrated black southerner in Harlem, examining interracial and intraracial prejudices and the conflict between traditional and modern mores.

Born in Washington, D.C., to middle-class parents, Fisher attended primary and secondary schools in New York City and in Providence, Rhode Island. After being graduated from Brown University with B.A. and M.A. degrees, he was graduated with honors from Howard University Medical School and continued his education at Columbia University. Not a professional writer, Fisher published his first short fiction while still a medical student. He continued to write fiction and literary criticism, as well as scholarly articles for medical journals, throughout his medical career. He died at the age of thirty-seven from a chronic intestinal ailment.

In the early years of the Harlem Renaissance, writers like Claude McKay and Jean Toomer accepted the portrayal by white writers of black characters as "primitives"; examples include Eugene O'Neill in his *The Emperor Jones* and Carl Van Vechten in *Nigger Heaven*. Reacting against this stereotyping, black novelists such as Jessie Fauset and Nella Larsen tried to present respectable black characters while still appealing to white readers. Embracing neither of these ways of representing black Americans, Fisher portrayed his characters with an unbiased but sympathetic detachment. He maintained a tone of impartiality in stories like "The City of Refuge" and "Miss Cynthie," leaving moral judgments about Harlem and its people to the reader.

The examination of class, color, and cultural distinctions recurs throughout Fisher's short stories: in "Blades of Steel," the low class "rats" and rich "dickties" are pitted against one another; in "High Yaller," a "white" black girl, taunted when she appears in public with her boyfriend, crosses the color line to escape both black and white prejudice. While white prejudice is a secondary issue in Fisher's works, of primary concern are the divisive influences of money and skin color within Harlem as well as the negative reaction of black Americans to "outsiders" like Africans and West Indians. In "Common Meter," as in several other stories,

music symbolizes the common bond among black people. Using a dance to bring together otherwise nonsocializing factions of the community, Fisher vividly illustrated class conflicts and the potential for resolution of conflict within Harlem society.

Often considered his best story, "Miss Cynthie" combines two of Fisher's principal concerns—the contrasting value systems of traditional Southerners and modern Northerners, and the value of music as a form of cross-cultural communication and reconciliation. Cynthie, initially disappointed to find that her grandson's success is achieved as a disreputable, "sinful" cabaret performer and not as a doctor or "at least" as an undertaker, gradually changes her opinion of his profession. Reconciliation results when the grandson reminds Cynthie that it was she who first taught him about the joy and self-expression that he could achieve through music.

Aside from his short stories, Fisher wrote two novels. *The Walls of Jericho* (1928), written after his short stories had met with some success, brings together Harlem insiders and outsiders at a General Improvement Association dance. In this dramatic comedy of manners Fisher satirized the angry new negro, professional uplifters, thrillseekers from downtown, and organizations like the NAACP. *The Conjure Man Dies* (1932), written two years before Fisher's death, is notable as the first fully developed detective novel known to have been written by a black author. Critics consider it typical of the genre in style and quality. Like his short stories, Fisher's novels display strong characterizations. Old time preachers, newly migrated black Southerners, West Indians, and city-slick Harlemites are vividly portrayed through their personal and cultural dialects. Sensitive to the subtle gradations of slang and dialect, Fisher has been compared to American humorist Ring Lardner for his manipulation of spoken idioms. His novels and short stories, which are liberally laced with puns and inventive personifications that animate the Harlem cityscape, sustain subtle humor even when they treat serious themes. Fisher's works thus faithfully render their Harlem setting—from the Sugar Hill bourgeoisie to the "rats" below—complete with schools, hospitals, night clubs, and barber shops on streets that have distinct class associations.

Langston Hughes called Fisher the "wittiest of these New Negroes of Harlem, whose tongue was flavored with the sharpest and saltiest humor." While other Harlem Renaissance writers used satire directed at whites, Fisher's satire was directed at the black community. Critics of the time recognized this as a skillful and sophisticated innovation. Fisher took a stand for neither the "common" individual, as did Claude McKay, nor the "respectable," often servile, middle class depicted by such writers as Jessie Fauset. This detachment, which some attribute to Fisher's distance from the masses of black people because of his social class and education, contributes to the quality of documentary realism in Fisher's fiction. Because of this realism, some commentators have found his works to be important historical documents as well as accomplished literary creations. While most have praised Fisher for writing about aspects of Harlem that other writers neglected, some critics, notably W.E.B. Du Bois, objected to his treatment of low-life blacks. In his review of *The Walls of Jericho,* Du Bois criticized Fisher for presenting the "low class" Linda and Shine as detailed, well-developed characters while leaving his "own kind," the "better class negroes," sketchy in their development. Du Bois nonetheless considered the novel "a strong, long, interesting" step up from the works of Claude McKay and Carl Van Vechten.

Though some critics view stories such as "Blades of Steel" and "Dust" as contrived and constructed solely to reveal surprise endings reminiscent of O. Henry, many others agree with Robert Bone that, at their best, Fisher's stories contain "isolated passages that are unexcelled in their depictions" of Harlem life. Fisher wrote: "Outsiders know nothing of Harlem life as it really is. What one sees in a night club or a dance hall is

nothing, doesn't scratch the surface—is in fact, presented solely for the eyes of the outsider." Many believe that Fisher had not reached his full potential as a writer when he died at age thirty-seven. Yet he stands as one of the few Harlem Renaissance writers who emphasized intraracial conflict without bitterness or blame, and who sought to emphasize the common experiences of black people.

(For further information about Fisher's life and works, see *Black Writers; Contemporary Authors,* Vol. 107; *Dictionary of Literary Biography,* Vol. 51: *Afro-American Writers from the Harlem Renaissance to 1940;* and *Twentieth-Century Literary Criticism,* Vol. 11.)

PRINCIPAL WORKS

"The City of Refuge" (short story) 1925; published in periodical *Atlantic Monthly*

"High Yaller" (short story) 1925; published in periodical *The Crisis*

"Ringtail" (short story) 1925; published in periodical *Atlantic Monthly*

"The South Lingers On" (short story) 1925; published in periodical *The Survey Graphic Number;* also published as "Vestiges: Harlem Sketches" [revised edition] in *The New Negro,* 1925

"The Backslider" (short story) 1927; published in periodical *McClure's Magazine*

"Blades of Steel" (short story) 1927; published in periodical *Atlantic Monthly*

"The Caucasian Storms Harlem" (essay) 1927; published in periodical *American Mercury*

"Fire by Night" (short story) 1927; published in periodical *McClure's Magazine*

"The Promised Land" (short story) 1927; published in periodical *Atlantic Monthly*

The Walls of Jericho (novel) 1928

"Common Meter" (short story) 1930; published in periodical *Baltimore Afro-American*

"Dust" (short story) 1931; published in periodical *Opportunity*

The Conjure Man Dies (novel) 1932

"Ezekiel" (short story) 1932; published in periodical *Junior Red Cross News*

"Ezekiel Learns" (short story) 1933; published in periodical *Junior Red Cross News*

"Guardian of the Law" (short story) 1933; published in periodical *Opportunity*

"Miss Cynthie" (short story) 1933; published in periodical *Story 3*

"John Archer's Nose" (short story) 1935; published in periodical *The Metropolitan*

*Conjur' Man Dies (drama) 1936

The City of Refuge: The Collected Stories of Rudolph Fisher (short stories) 1987

**This drama is an adaptation of the novel *The Conjure Man Dies.*

The Times Literary Supplement (essay date 1928)

[*In the following 1928* Times Literary Supplement *review, the anonymous critic offers a highly favorable assessment of* The Walls of Jericho.]

Mr. Rudolph Fisher, one of the most interesting of contemporary negro writers, has given in **The Walls of Jericho** a sympathetic and extraordinarily impressive account of negro thought and habit. As a storyteller he holds the reader's attention from first to last; his story has vigour and naturalness, and it is told with unfailing and pungent humour. But it is hard to dissociate the literary virtues of the narrative from its merit as a piece of evidence touching social and racial psychology in the United States. Mr. Fisher has no point of view to labour; on the contrary, he is impatient of systematic efforts to solve the negro "problem" and rather scornful of those people who look for a solution in endless discussion and futile organization. His concern is rather with the everyday characteristics of the negro temperament and with their impact on the development of negro society. The unusual thing about his novel is that its modes of thought and feeling, patiently spontaneous, are such as no "white" man could achieve; their truth to life is never in doubt, but it is quite plain that they are characteristic of the negro consciousness. The language of the story is the language of Harlem (the "expurgated and abridged" glossary of terms at the end of the book is fascinating reading), but every idea or sentiment it conveys is just as obviously "Harlemese."

At either end of the social scale the negro's tastes and experience, it seems, are in flat opposition to custom and privilege. Fred Merrit, the wealthy lawyer, bought a house in a street in one of the residential quarters in New York in which no negro had as yet dared to plant himself. Joshua Jones, known to his fellows as Shine, helped to move Merrit's furniture into the house, and in so doing observed a negro housemaid entering a house a few doors away. Neither fact may appear particularly significant, but together they provide Mr. Fisher with the means of illustrating the entire outlook of the negro on his ambitions and personal behaviour, and on his place in American society. Merrit's house is duly burned down, not by his neighbours, however, but by another negro who bears him a grudge. And Shine proceeds to become better acquainted with the housemaid. Into this seemingly ordinary narrative pattern Mr. Fisher has contrived to set a brilliant and cunningly diversified picture of negro character. Merrit, confessedly rabid on the subject of race, whose chief joy is in making white people uncomfortable, presents an illuminating contrast with Jinx and Bubber, Shine's fellow-workers, who have not a thought about the negro question between them, and whose racy, colloquial humour forms a pleasant feature of the novel. But it is Shine himself, a massive giant of a man, distrustful of people, white or black, resolved to keep every act "sentimentally air-tight," who best brings out the potential strength and philosophy of character the author has discovered in the inhabitants of Harlem.

A review of "The Walls of Jericho" in The Times Literary Supplement *No. 1388, September 6 1928, p. 630.*

W.E.B. Du Bois (essay date 1928)

[*Du Bois was a leading twentieth-century black author and thinker. In addition to writing novels, poetry, and sociological studies, he also edited the magazine* Crisis, *in which the following review of* The Walls of Jerich *originally appeared in 1928.*]

[**The Walls of Jericho**] is another story of Harlem, following the footsteps of *Nigger Heaven* and *Home to Harlem*. The casual reader wading through the first third of the book might think it nothing else but a following of these pathfinders into the half-world north of 125th Street. But a little persistence and a knowledge of what Rudolph Fisher has already accomplished in his remarkable short stories, will bring reward. For the main story of a piano mover and a housemaid is a well done and sincere bit of psychology. It is finely worked out with a delicate knowledge of human reactions. If the background were as sincere as the main picture, the novel would be a masterpiece. But the background is a shade too sophisticated and unreal. Mr. Fisher likes his two characters, Jinx and Bubber, and lingers over them; but somehow, to the ordinary reader, they are only moderately funny, a little smutty and certainly not humanly convincing. Their conversation has some undoubted marks of authenticity, for this kind of keen repartee is often heard among Negro laborers. But neither of these characters seems human like Shine.

Mr. Fisher does not yet venture to write of himself and his own people; of Negroes like his mother, his sister and his wife. His real Harlem friends and his own soul nowhere yet appear in his pages, and nothing that can be mistaken for them. The glimpses of better class Negroes which he gives us are poor, ineffective make-believes. One wonders why? Why does Mr. Fisher fear to use his genius to paint his own kind, as he has painted Shine and Linda? Perhaps he doubts the taste of his white audience although he tries it severely with Miss Cramp. Perhaps he feels too close to his own to trust his artistic detachment in limning them. Perhaps he really laughs at all life and believes nothing. At any rate, here is a step upward from Van Vechten and McKay—a strong, long, interesting step.

W. E. B. Du Bois, in a review of "The Walls of Jericho," in The Crisis *Vol. 35, No. 1, November, 1928, p. 374.*

Sterling Brown (essay date 1937)

[*Brown was a poet, folklorist, critic, and educator. He is perhaps best known for his critical studies of Harlem Renaissance writers, and his anthologies of black authors are considered major contributions to the field of black literature. In the following excerpt from his* The Negro in American Fiction, *Brown sees traces of* *mystery writer Octavus Cohen's burlesque character Florian Slappey in Fisher's slapstick characterizations of Jinx and Bubber. The wise-cracking duo appears in both of Fisher's novels,* The Walls of Jericho *and* The Conjure Man Dies.*]

Rudolph Fisher portrays Harlem with a jaunty realism. **The Walls of Jericho** deals with types as different as piano-movers and "race-leaders." The antics of Jinx and Bubber are first-rate slapstick, and though traces of Octavus Roy Cohen appear, most of the comedy is close to Harlem side-walks. Fisher is likewise master of irony. Miss Cramp, the philanthropist, who believes that mulattoes are the result of the American climate, is caricatured, but the picture of the Annual Costume Ball of the G.I.A. (General Improvement Association) is rich comedy of manners. He deftly ridicules the thrill-seekers from downtown who find everything in Harlem "simply marvelous." Satiric toward professional uplifters, **The Walls of Jericho** still has the New Negro militancy. Merrit is an embittered "New Negro"; he believes that the Negro should let the Nordic do the serious things, and spend his time in "tropic nonchalance, developing nothing but his capacity for enjoyment," and then take complete possession through force of numbers. Fisher likewise shows the spirit of racial unity between the "dicties" and the masses—"Fays don' see no difference 'tween dicky shines and any other kind o' shines. One jig in danger is ev'y jig in danger." It is significant, however, that the wrecking of a Negro's house in a white neighborhood is the work of a disgruntled Negro, the villain of the book.

But Fisher was less interested in the "problem" than in the life and language of Harlem's poolrooms, cafes, and barber shops. **The Conjure Man Dies** . . . , the first detective novel by a Negro, brings Jinx and Bubber back to the scene to help solve one of Harlem's grisliest murders. A high-brow detective, an efficient Negro police sergeant and an erudite doctor of voodoo are interesting new characters. The novel is above the average in its popular field and was followed by a Harlem tenement murder mystery solved by the same detective.

Before his untimely death, Fisher became one of the best short story writers of the New Negro movement. **"The City of Refuge,"** containing a good description of the southern migrant's happy amazement at Harlem, and **"Blades of Steel"** are first-rate local color of the barber shops, dance-halls and cafes. **"Vestiges"** and **"Miss Cynthie,"** for all of their light touch, have an unusual tenderness and fidelity to middle class experience. Fisher was an observer with a quick eye and a keen ear, and a witty commentator. At times his plots are too neat, with something of O. Henry's trickery. His Harlem is less bitter than McKay's, but it exists; and his realism, as far as it goes, is as definite as that of any of the numerous writers who took Harlem for their province. (pp. 135-36)

> *Sterling Brown "The Urban Scene," in his*
> The Negro in American Fiction, *Negro*

Poetry and Drama, *Arno Press, 1969, pp. 131-50.*

Arthur P. Davis (essay date 1974)

[*In the following excerpt, Davis explores theme and style in a selection of Fisher's works.*]

Rudolph Fisher, a Harlem physician and roentgenologist, viewed the black community with an understanding and amused eye. To him, it was a place where all kinds of Negroes—good, bad, and indifferent—from several areas—the South, the West Indies, and Africa—found a haven from the hostile white world. Fisher knew Harlem intimately—its con men, its numbers barons, its church goers, its night-life people, its visitors from the outside white world, and, above all else, the new migrants from the South, who found Harlem a miraculous city of refuge. His short stories and novels belong, with Cullen's *One Way to Heaven* and McKay's *Home to Harlem,* to the literature of the black ghetto; but his picture of Harlem is fuller than that of either McKay or Cullen. A comic realist, he laughed at the foibles of all classes of Harlemites from the "rats" (ordinary Harlem folk) to the "dickties"; but this laughter is healthy and therapeutic. It comes from a deeper-than-surface knowledge of and a fondness for the inhabitants of the black city. (p. 98)

Fisher's first Harlem short story ["**City of Refuge**"] was written while he was in medical school. . . . The story deals with a theme expressed in its title—a theme which appears often in Fisher's work—the wonder, pleasure, protection, and pride the black newcomer finds in Harlem. (p. 99)

["**The South Lingers On**"], republished in [Alain Locke's] *The New Negro* as **"Vestiges,"** consists of five sketches or vignettes showing the impact of Harlem on the Southern Negro. The first of the five deals with a Negro preacher whose flock has left one by one for Harlem. He finds them again, by accident, and reclaims them from a charlatan. The second sketch (which does not appear in *The New Negro*) concerns the faith which an unskilled Negro worker, in spite of disappointments and rebuffs, still has in the promise of Harlem. The third vignette deals with that much-used character, the Negro grandmother, who is the family anchor. Unsuccessfully trying to keep her granddaughter from the sinful ways of the city, the old lady in her defeat has only one recourse left—prayer. The next deals with the ambitions of a Negro girl who wants to go to college but whose Southern-born father feels that graduation from high school is enough. "Too much learnin' ain' good f' nobody." Pride causes him to change his mind when his daughter wins a scholarship to Columbia Teachers' College. The last story concerns two Harlem men about town who drop in on a tent revival just for kicks. The preaching and the praying are too much for one of the young men. He has not lost as much of his Southern upbringing as he had thought. In these sketches Fisher gives a nonsensational look at the deep imprint which the South has left on its sons and daughters who made their way North. In these simple and uncontrived vignettes he has shown Harlem to be, not the fun city of downtown white thrill seekers, but, actually, a transplanted Southern community, bigger and brassier, of course, but still essentially a slice of the South.

The best of Fisher's transplanted-Southerners stories is **"Miss Cynthie."** . . . It, too, has one of those strong, colorful grandmothers, in this case a spry and positive old lady known in her native town by black and white alike simply as Miss Cynthie. (p. 100)

In several of Dr. Fisher's stories, color prejudice within the Negro group plays a significant part. Fisher, unlike McKay, does not overplay the issue, but he does not ignore or sidestep it. Moreover, he shows that all of the bias is not on one side. One of the most revealing stories of this type is **"High Yaller."** . . . It concerns the hard road a light-colored Negro girl has to travel in a community of dark-skinned persons. Trying to make an adjustment, she dates a black boy and gets into trouble with her dark-skinned Negro "friends" on the one hand and white people on the other. Discouraged and disgusted, she gives up the battle for acceptance and crosses over the line . . . .

Although both Claude McKay and Langston Hughes have written a larger amount of short fiction than Fisher, their works lack the controlled intensity, the suggestiveness, the subtlety, and the overall artistry that his short stories have. (p. 101)

Fisher's style in [his novels *The Walls of Jericho* and *The Conjure-Man Dies: A Mystery Tale of Dark Harlem*] is clear and uncomplicated. If there is a weakness, it is a tendency to write like a professor on occasion; but he does not have any trouble in making his characters talk convincingly and naturally. One notes that in both these novels, large segments of each dealing with lower-class life, there is absolutely no use of four-letter words and no sex. Fisher, like Du Bois and other New Negro authors, believed in putting one's best foot forward. There were some things that one just did not parade for the white folks to see. McKay had shown the "debauched Tenth" and was condemned for it—by Negroes. Although Dr. Fisher could easily have played *up* the primitive side of Harlem life, he preferred to play it *down*. It was part of the price one's dual-inheritance demanded. (pp. 102-03)

> *Arthur P. Davis, "Rudolph Fisher," in his* From the Dark Tower: Afro-American Writers, 1900 to 1960, *Howard University Press, 1974, pp. 98-103.*

Robert Bone (essay date 1975)

[*Bone is the author of* The Negro Novel in America *(1958) and* Down Home: A History of Afro-American Short Fiction from Its Beginnings to the End of the Harlem Renaissance *(1975). Bone has said of himself:*

"A white man and critic of black literature, I try to demonstrate by the quality of my work that scholarship is not the same thing as identity." In the following excerpt from Down Home, *he examines Fisher's short fiction.*]

The best of local-color fiction strives to transcend the merely picturesque, and when it succeeds, it moves in the direction of pastoral . . . .

Fisher's most mature stories, **"Common Meter"** and **"Miss Cynthie,"** are concerned with reconciliation, within a pastoral framework, of the classes or the generations which divide the black community. (p. 141)

In a story called **"High Yaller,"** Rudolph Fisher gives us a brief glimpse of his Harlem boyhood:

> Over One Hundred and Thirty-fourth Street's sidewalks between Fifth and Lenox Avenues Jay Martin's roller-skates had rattled and whirred in the days when that was the northern boundary of Negro Harlem. He had grown as the colony grew, and now he could just recall the time when his father, a pioneer preacher, had been forever warning him never to cross Lenox Avenue and never to go beyond One Hundred and Thirty-fifth Street; a time when no Negroes lived on or near Seventh Avenue and when it would have been almost suicidal for one to appear unarmed on Irish Eighth.

This fictional account of Fisher's boyhood encompasses the chief ingredients of his imagination. The notion of a *boundary*, an artificial barrier creating a forbidden territory, and thereby denying access to experience, is basic to the impulse of the picaresque. The taboo, moreover, is enforced by the boy's father, whose paternal authority is associated with the Negro church. Several of Fisher's stories are concerned thematically with the crossing of forbidden boundaries, or in theological terms, with snatching Experience from the jaws of Sin. Their rogue-heroes bear witness to the fact that they derive from the tradition of the picaresque.

At the same time, the passage has profound historical reverberations. All the tensions and hostilities of the Great Migration are embodied in the clash between the Negroes and their Irish neighbors. The exposed position of the blacks, making racial solidarity imperative, is the source of Fisher's pastoral romances. Throughout his work, divisive tendencies within the black community are mollified and harmonized. His primary effort is to bridge the gap between the classes, but differences arising out of regional, generational, or (in the case of West Indians) former national affiliation are likewise subject to the healing qualities of pastoral. (pp. 150-51)

Harlem is the stamping ground of Fisher's imagination; without exception it provides the setting of his tales. (p. 152)

Fisher's intimate knowledge of the Harlem scene led him to exploit its possibilities as local color. His stories contain isolated passages that are unexcelled in their depiction of the Harlem cabaret, the rent party, the barbershop, the dance casino, and the Sunday promenade on Seventh Avenue. Good social history, however, is not necessarily good literature. If presented for its own sake, such material may detract from the author's larger purposes. In the end Fisher pays a heavy price for his reliance on local color. As the novelty of his Harlem settings wears thin, his imagination falters, and he tends to repeat himself.

Two metaphors convey Fisher's essential relation to the Harlem scene. In several of his stories the protagonist looks down upon the spectacle of Harlem life from an upper box, upper window, or upper balcony. This spatial metaphor embodies the social perspective of the black bourgeoisie, which overlooks the Harlem scene from the lofty eminence of Sugar Hill. In other stories Fisher seems to be conducting a guided tour of Harlem for a party of visitors from downtown. The name of the tour is "Adventures in Exotic Harlem," and it includes observations on the quaint customs of the country, helpful hints for fraternizing with the natives, and a Berlitz phrase-book for the comprehension of contemporary Harlemese.

The psychological setting of Fisher's stories—the interior landscape to which he compulsively returns—is a state of intolerable estrangement from his father. Several of his tales are concerned with dramatizing this estrangement, and effecting a symbolic reconciliation. "The Backslider" and "Fire by Night" . . . , for example, are variations on the theme of the Prodigal Son. In these stories a backsliding, ne'er-do-well, and potentially criminal youth is rescued from his self-destructive impulses and restored to middle-class respectability.

In essence there are two Rudolph Fishers: a conforming and rebelling self. The conformist is the middle-class child who obeys his parents when they warn him not to play with roughnecks. He is the brilliant student who is Class Day Orator at Brown, who graduates *summa cum laude* from Howard, and establishes his professional identity as Dr. Fisher. The rebel is Bud Fisher, frequenter of speakeasies and cabarets, who has always envied the bad kids on the block and who writes about them in his fiction. The rebel self, however, is more mischievous than dangerous, and after a period of bohemian adventures settles into middle-class routine. Such is the psychodrama at the heart of Fisher's cruder tales.

In a second group of Fisher tales, the theme of breach and reconciliation is projected outward on the social plane. Here the author strives to repair various divisions that threaten to destroy the black community. Thus "Ringtail" is concerned with the enmity between West Indian and native-born American; "High Yaller," with the potentially disruptive force of a light complexion; "Blades of Steel" and "Common Meter" with the social class division that separates the "rat" from the "dicky." In each of these contexts, Fisher's aim is to exorcise the demons of disruption and cement the ties of racial solidarity. (pp. 152-54)

The object of his fiction is precisely to provide a common ground, to bind the social classes in racial confraternity, and thus to rescue union from diversity. A favorite setting for his fiction is the ballroom scene, where all of Harlem gathers for the communal rite of the Saturday night dance. The action of "Common Meter," for example, takes place in a dance casino symbolically denominated "The Arcadia." For the ballroom and its ethnic music qualify as common ground, where the mediating force of pastoral can work its magic spell.

Fisher's "Arcadia" is modeled on the old Savoy, where two jazz bands played nightly for the Harlem throng. A lusty paganism fills the hall: the Pipes of Pan are jazz trumpets, at whose prompting nymphs and satyrs cavort across the floor. Metaphorically at least, it is a sylvan scene: "a brace of young wild birds double-timed through the forest, miraculously avoiding the trees." . . . Against this background a rivalry develops between two band leaders for the favors of a lovely girl. As appropriate to pastoral romance, however, the contest is contained within a ritual frame. The two musicians and their bands will compete for "the jazz championship of the world," with the tacit understanding that the victor wins the girl.

Two styles of musical performance thus provide the main dramatic contrast of the tale. Fess Baxter's work is flashy but inauthentic; his music is full of tonal tricks and false resolutions. Bus Williams' stuff, on the other hand, is the genuine down-home blues. Threatened with defeat in honest competition, Baxter slits his rival's trapdrum with a knife. Our heroine, however, saves the day, by instructing Williams' band to beat time with their feet, thus converting the blues performance to a shout. This ancestral form, handed down through generations from the tribal past, so stirs the crowd that opposition fades, abandoning the field to love.

At the center of the story is a pastoral inversion. The smart money hits the canvas; the city slicker is confounded; country music and elemental honesty combine to win the girl. The superiority of blackness is the point: to be possessed of soul is precisely to be capable of improvising, of winning the contest *without* your drums. At bottom, Fisher is warning the black community to guard itself against a certain kind of spiritual loss. Don't abandon your ancestral ways when you move to the big city; don't discard the authentic blues idiom for the shallow, trivial, flashy, meretricious values of the urban world.

A third group of Fisher stories is explicitly concerned with the Great Migration. As the author's imagination reaches out to embrace the historical experience of millions, his art assumes a greater density of texture and complexity of vision. On the plane of history, moreover, Fisher's divided self proves to be an asset: it enables him to project and then to mediate the central value conflict of his age. For the split personality of the Baptist preacher's son mirrors the divided soul of the Southern migrant. Both are torn between a set of standards that are traditional, religious, and puritanical, and a series of temptations that are novel, secular, and hedonistic.

Fisher's strength lies in the fact that he is genuinely torn between these value systems. His very ambivalence allows him to achieve a delicate balance of rural and urban, traditional and modern values. His divided psyche generates a powerful desire to mediate, or reconcile, or find a middle ground, which is the source of pastoral. He is therefore able to encompass the paradoxes of change and continuity, of spiritual loss and gain, which are the essence of the Great Migration. He is able to record the disappointments and defeats of the Southern migrants, and yet to celebrate the hope which survives their disillusionment.

"The City of Refuge" . . . is Fisher's first attempt to treat the paradoxes of the Great Migration. King Solomon Gillis, a greenhorn from the South, is bamboozled by a Harlem gangster and left to face a twenty-year sentence for peddling dope. His arrest by a black policeman, however, reconciles him to his fate, for he perceives that Harlem, while it may betray the Southern migrant, also offers him the possibility of manhood. The final scene where Gillis stands erect, exulting in his newborn sense of dignity and racial pride, is a powerful epiphany of the New Negro. Unhappily the story as a whole, which is riddled with bad writing, does not match the brilliance of its dénouement.

"The Promised Land" . . . is a more successful treatment of the migratory theme. As the story opens, a spiritual and a blues are contending for supremacy from opposite sides of an airshaft. The words of the spiritual ask, "How low mus' I bow / To enter in de promis' land?" Fisher's subject, then, is the social cost of the Great Migration. Divisiveness is the price the black community must pay to enter in the promised land. Urbanization brings division between the generations; between skilled and unskilled black workers; between established and more recent immigrants; between the partisans of gospel music and the blues.

These divisions are dramatized by the conflicts between Mammy and her grandsons; between the cousins, Sam and Wesley; and between the country cousins and Ellie, the city girl. Mammy is the first of several matriarchal figures who embody the old-fashioned virtues in Fisher's tales. In a memorable scene, she tosses the family Bible through a window of the opposite apartment to restrain her grandsons from fighting over Ellie. She represents the unifying, mediating force of pastoral, and she supplies whatever of cohesiveness and continuity the migratory family is able to achieve. Yet in the end she fails, and one of her grandsons is a sacrificial victim to the gods of racial progress.

"Miss Cynthie" . . . is the best of Fisher's stories, by virtue of a crucial technical advance. Having given us a gallery of static characters, he suddenly discovers how to *interiorize* his dramatic conflicts, so that his protagonists have an opportunity to grow. The title character, Miss Cynthie, is thereby able to embody in her own person the spiritual agony of the Great Migration. Painfully, reluctantly, and only after a sharp internal struggle, her old-fashioned morality bends and stretches to accommodate the new. Fisher's theme is the emergence of new moral codes, appropriate to new historical conditions. (pp. 155-58)

The aim of pastoral is reconciliation. In this instance it is not so much a matter of reconciling rural and urban values, or of mediating a conflict between the generations, as of bridging a gap between the black artist and the black middle class. The secret theme of **"Miss Cynthie"** is the reconciliation of bourgeois success norms with the unconventional and slightly suspect enterprise of art. David is a projection of Fisher's artist-self. The folk material that each employs as the basis of his art is suspect in the eyes of the black elite. To reconcile Miss Cynthie to her grandson's métier is thus to reconcile the black bourgeoisie to a certain kind of "lowlife" art.

Beyond these public meanings, the story serves a private end. The symbolic action indicates that Fisher has resolved the basic conflict of his adolescence and achieved the integration of a perilously fractured self. In the love and mutual respect of David and Miss Cynthie, his rebelling and conforming selves are harmonized. The result is an impressive gain in poise and equilibrium. **"Miss Cynthie"** constitutes, in short, a psychological as well as an artistic triumph. Published in the shadow of impending death, it testifies to Fisher's inner growth and aggravates our loss of his maturing powers. (pp. 158-59)

> *Robert Bone, "Three Versions of Pastoral."*
> *In his* Down Home: Origins of the Afro-American Short Story, *Columbia University Press, 1988, pp. 139-70.*

Thomas Friedmann (essay date 1976)

[*In the following excerpt, Friedmann argues that Fisher's short story "Common Meter" exhibits a prescient "consciousness of blackness," stating: "By fully fifty years, Fisher anticipates the notions of 'Black is beautiful'."*]

Although its appearance in Abraham Chapman's *Black Voices* . . . does not represent the first printing of **"Common Meter,"** the story is still not well known. Neither is its author, Rudolf Fisher, prominent in the gallery of Black writers, although he published two novels and many short stories during his lifetime. Perhaps this neglect is due to the fact that he has been dead for more than forty years and that younger writers are addressing themselves to contemporary issues in language more familiar to today's generation. Be that as it may, one reads this half century old story with a shock of recognition. Hardly could one find issues more contemporary than those examined in this story. More important, the terminology used to discuss those issues is up to date as well. By fully fifty years, Fisher anticipates the notions of "Black is beautiful," and uses the blackness of a man's skin to indicate his goodness much the same way that the vintage Western informed us of the hero's sterling character through the glaring whiteness of his hat. As such, **"Common Meter"** is a valuable source for those who look for early indications of the change in Black consciousness and for those who search literature for positive uses of the color black. As one goes about trying to reverse "the bigotry of language" which associates white with good and black with bad, scarcely a better source for examples is available than **"Common Meter."**

Set in a dance hall, "The Arcadia," on Harlem's Lenox Avenue, **"Common Meter"** is the story of two men, leaders of jazz bands, who compete for supremacy in music and in love. The object of their affection is Jean, one of the dance hall hostesses. The essence of their musical contention is the proper place of rhythm in jazz. To the cynical modern reader, the outcome is possible only in a fairy tale. The winner is the most noble and upright character, the jazz musician who prizes rhythm above all else and the man whose skin is darkest. The less cynical reader can appreciate the prophetic vision of the author who acknowledges and even encourages the fairy tale quality but is realistic enough to be ironic and optimistic enough to believe in the triumph of a black consciousness.

Our first sight of Bus Williams, leader of the "Blue Devils," presents the criteria for his ethical and amatory standing. His face is "jolly" and "round," and it "beamed" down on the crowd. The description is clearly positive, particularly in contrast to the one applied to Fessenden Baxter. The leader of the "Firemen" has an impersonal "countenance," unlike Bus's human "face." His features are presented as being much harsher as well. They are "blunt," where Bus's were round; glaringly "bright," where Bus was softly beaming.

More important, however, in our search for "color-coded" identification, Bus is a brown man while Fess is the "cheese colored," specifically "Swiss-cheese." The yellowish-white skin color thus ascribed to Fess places him at the far end of the spectrum. The middle ranges of this dark to light spectrum are occupied by Jean, a girl literally and figuratively "in the middle," whose skin is amber—brownish yellow—and by Curry, the manager of the dance hall, who is "yellow." Just as the skin color of these people ranges from dark to light, so does their moral character. Where the traditional association would have been from low to high moral standing, in **"Common Meter"** a new tradition is begun. In this story the lighter the skin color the lower the moral character of the individual.

Fessenden Baxter is guilty, of course, of sins and errors that bear no connection to his color. He tries to seduce Jean, for example, "talking her up" during their dance together with only dishonorable intentions in mind. Then he brags of conquering her, crudely announcing, "Yea. And I says, 'I'm a cash customer, baby. Just name

your price.'" Threatened by Bus to declare which girl it was that he claims "fell," to him, the cowardly Fess retracts his claim. He is also vain, "surreptitiously adjusting his ruffled plumage," a thief, rearranging other people's music and claiming it as his own, and a cheat, sabotaging the musical instruments of the rival band in his attempts to win the "battle of the bands." Those shortcomings of character do not, however, relate to the author's color scheme.

Fisher uses color to denote character when Fessenden's crimes are committed against color itself. He declares Fess guilty of rejecting his blackness. His indictment is thorough. Fess has "straightened brown hair," he tells us, stressing the fact that his hair, as his attire and music, are not natural. Consistent with his rejection of blackness of feature, Fess avoids the black elements in his jazz. Denying the association of blackness and rhythm, Fess Baxter "considered rhythm a mere rack upon which to hang his tonal tricks." Fisher's description of the Baxter style stresses the deliberately non-rhythmic aspect of his jazz. The price he plays during the contest is "dizzy with sudden disharmonies," is filled with "dissonances," contains "twists" and "false resolutions."

What is wrong with this philosophy, explains Fisher, is that it is a false representation of the race. Where Bus's rendition of the blues is genuine, "the nakedest of jazz," interpreting for his people "like leaden strokes of fate," their dissatisfaction with their lot, Baxter's music attempts to mislead and misdirect them, not merely helping them forget their existence but insisting their perceptions of it to be incorrect. His music exhausts his listeners, "distorting" and "etheralizing" their emotions. Fisher declares his contempt through Bus, stressing Fess Baxter's lack of black consciousness. "The cream-colored son of a buzzard!" Bus exclaims, bleaching that Swiss-cheese colored, yellowish-white skin into still a lighter shade.

In contrast to Fess Baxter's whiteness is Bus William's blackness, in color, music, and identity. As with Baxter, Bus's character is established with no reference to color. He displays his forthrightness and honesty by honorably proposing to marry Jean, by defending her reputation and by creating his own music, unlike Baxter, who often makes use of some "rearrangement." This behavior makes Bus a good man. His sense of being a black, on the other hand, also gives him nobility.

It is in his philosophy and interpretation of music that Bus displays his black consciousness. In theory, he values rhythm, holding tone to be "merely the vehicle" for rhythmic patterns. For Fisher, the black musician as the black man, yearns for harmony, for "unfaltering common rhythm." And as Bus begins to play, Fisher makes clear that the harmony Bus achieves is the harmony with the self. His music enables his listeners to forget, just as Fess Baxter's playing did. But where Baxter's jazz put his listeners out of touch with their emotions, Bus's enables them to get in tune with their feelings. When Baxter plays, the dancers sweat against one another. When Bus Williams plays jazz, the dancers "forget their jostling neighbors" and become aware instead "that some quality hitherto lost had at last been found."

What the listeners find in true black jazz, argues Fisher, is their origin. "Two hundred years ago they had swayed to that same slow fateful measure," Fisher tells us, then lets the music lead us further back, "They had rocked so a thousand years ago in a city whose walls were jungle." Bus Williams plays a music that was "not a sound but an emotion that laid hold on their bodies and swung them into the past."

Fisher is not, however, simply a nostalgiac, reaching into the past for sentimental memories. The virtue of this swing into the past is that it refreshes. More, returning, the "blueness itself, the sorrow, the despair, began to give way to hope," until the transformation into genuine human feeling is complete. Filled with a sense of possibility by the sound of the jazz, the black men and women in the Arcadia dance hall, "A restless multitude of empty, romance-hungry lives," do so by dipping deep into their racial consciousness, for a moment, while the spell of the music remains, it creates "an all-pervading atmosphere through which seared wild-winged birds." The illusion of freedom suggested by the ironic "Arcadia," becomes real; the dance hall is that pastoral place where people can soar as freely as wild birds.

And the way, declares Fisher, is clear. It is the way of blackness, in physical, historical and spiritual acceptance of blackness.

The story ends with Bus Williams being declared winner by Jean's spontaneous gift to him of her love and loving cup. The message is thus underlined once more by this prophetic writer. In the battle between Bus, the black man who accepts color and Fess, the black man who rejects it, the winner is Bus, his genuineness irresistible to Jean, the amber colored girl "in between." In the fight to vibrate "like nearing thunder," the source of the power is consciousness of blackness. That this was how the story would end was made clear of course from our very first glimpse of the "color-coded" antagonists, a color scheme that shows goodness in blackness. How truly Rudolf Fisher, in **"Common Meter,"** was a man of clear and far-seeing vision. (pp. 8-9)

> *Thomas Friedmann, "The Good Guys in the Black Hats: Color Coding in Rudolph Fisher's 'Common Meter',"* in *Studies in Black Literature, Vol. 7, No. 2, Spring, 1976, pp. 8-9.*

Leonard J. Deutsch (essay date 1979)

[*In the excerpt below, Deutsch discusses Fisher's short stories as mirrors of the geography and history, as well as the "morals and manners," of Harlem in the 1920s.*]

The argument can be made that more fully than any other chronicler of the manners and morals of Harlem in the 1920s, Fisher captures the breadth of black experience—and American and universal human experience—during a spectacularly dynamic era.

The Harlem Renaissance was occasioned, as observers have remarked, by a "demographic shift of the Black population that is perhaps the most crucial fact of Afro-American history in the twentieth century." Fisher took a lively look at this "crucial fact" and explored many of its consequences and manifestations in his short stories.

By his own admission, he saw himself as an interpreter of Harlem. Just as F. Scott Fitzgerald took "East and West Egg" for his milieu, so Fisher took Harlem for his. He succeeded in charting the physical and moral topography of Harlem during the Renaissance period as no writer has ever done. (p. 159)

In terms of physical topography, Fisher reconstructs the black community block by block. Practically every story is set on a specific street or cluster of streets. And when those streets are revealed to the reader, they are presented in both graphically realistic and metaphorically imaginative terms.

Fisher's favorite figurative device is personification and his personified analogies imbue each street with a precise and appropriate life of its own, ranging from glamorous to sordid. In **"Ringtail,"** for example, "Harlem's Seventh Avenue was dressed in its Sunday clothes," for this is where the dicties paraded themselves; but Lenox Avenue, in **"Fire by Night,"** is like a corpse divested of its fine clothes. The sights and smells of each street are there: 133rd Street in **"Guardian of the Law"**; 135th Street in **"Blades of Steel"**; "a wide open lot, extending along One Hundred and Thirty-Eighth Street almost from Lenox to Seventh Avenue, sharing the mangy backs of a long row of One Hundred and Thirty-Ninth Street houses" in **"The South Lingers On."** **"Miss Cynthie"** provides a tour of the ritzier sections of the city-within-a-city; and so on.

Fisher virtually creates a verbal map of Harlem containing a great many of its hospitals, schools, cabarets, and apartment buildings. He even delineates the neighborhoods in **"Fire by Night"** and indicates the territorial disposition of the various classes—that "dictydom," for example, was located "west of Seventh Avenue" in the 1920s, and Harlem's middle class lived between Lenox and Seventh Avenues.

But most of all, Fisher presents Harlem's people.

His first story, **"The City of Refuge,"** was published in the *Atlantic Monthly* (February, 1925) and was chosen for inclusion in Edward J. O'Brien's *The Best Short Stories of 1925*. It establishes the literary mode most characteristic of Fisher's work: irony. King Solomon

Gillis is neither powerful nor rich nor wise; he is simply green around the gills and easily gulled.... Gillis falls victim to the myth of Harlem. It may seem to be a city of and for blacks, a place where "you had rights that could not be denied you; you had privileges protected by law. And you had money. Everybody in Harlem had money. It was a land of plenty." But Harlem is the locus of intraracial exploitation (a black operator named Uggam muses, "Guess you're the shine I been waitin' for"); it is a battlefield of intraracial hostility (Gillis, hardened by his exposure to city values, derisively yells "Monkey-chaser!" at a West Indian); and it is the stalking ground of undiminished interracial enmity ("They's a thousand shines in Harlem would change places with you in a minute jess f' the honor of killin' a cracker"). Harlem is a place where one can become rich quickly, if like Tom Edwards, he becomes a drug pusher and pays off the police. Finally, the land of plenty offers Gillis a room "half the size of his hencoop back home," replete with all the sights, sounds, and smells of a sewer. More a city of refuse than refuge. (pp. 160-61)

In March of 1925 Fisher's second story appeared, **"The South Lingers On,"** reappearing later that year under the title **"Vestiges: Harlem Sketches,"** in Alain Locke's famous volume, *The New Negro*. Just as his first story depicts a newcomer's evolving response to Harlem—his naivete, his disillusionment, his gradual hardening—here, too, Fisher presents vignettes indicating the ways "the South lingers on" in Harlem for those who have recently arrived. The South lingers on in terms of attitudes toward religion, education, and morality. (p. 161)

[**"Ringtail"**] returns to the theme of intraracial conflict announced in **"The City of Refuge."** Cyril Sebastian Best, a dandified black from the British West Indies, is called a "ringtail monkey-chaser" by some black Harlemites; Best, in turn, holds Negro Americans in contempt. Although a character named Eight-Ball may complain: "You jigs are worse 'n ofays.... You raise hell about prejudice, and look at you—doin' just what you're raisin' hell over yourselves," even Eight-Ball seems to be won over by his cronies who believe a West Indian is naturally inclined to maniacal revenge. The resolution of Fisher's story—Cyril Sebastian Best kills the Harlemite who insulted him—seems to demonstrate the veracity of the conventional saying. The plot of **"Ringtail"** represents a rare instance when Fisher countenanced stereotyping. Despite some fine writing and a number of interesting passages, the story is further weakened by Fisher's use of the romantic triangle; here it is simply too contrived.

"High Yaller," awarded the Spingarn Prize of 1925, is a more complicated tale. It tackles the dual themes of intraracial and interracial enmity. Evelyn Brown's problem is that she is colored but looks white—there is "nothing brown about her but her name." At first she is accused of having "yellow-fever," that is, favoring fair skinned individuals and choosing her friends on that basis. The charge rankles and she laments that she is not

Title page of The Walls of Jericho *(1928), Fisher's first novel.*

darker (an inversion of Emma Lou's obsessive desire to become white in *The Blacker the Berry* by Wallace Thurman). Her response is to throw herself more fully into the black community by dating a black youth, Jay Martin.... When her dark-skinned mother dies, Evelyn decides to pass for white. Fisher shows with trenchant candor the vicious pressures that drive Evelyn to her decision to pass. It was undoubtedly this candor that led an early black critic to condemn the story for its "sensationalism." For Fisher, it is an uncharacteristically sardonic story. (p. 162)

[**"The Promised Land"**] demonstrates that terrestial Harlem is as far from the celestial heaven as death is from life. Interwoven in the texture of the tale are the blues and the melody of a spiritual: "one was a prayer for the love of man, the other a prayer for the love of God." In the city, with its philosophy of "ruthless opportunism," the secular blues take dominance over the otherworldly hymns. Harlem is no more a promised land than it is a city of refuge; it makes promises that it does not keep. And so Mammy, a living symbol of the generation gap, succeeds in stopping one fight involving her two grandsons by flinging a Bible between them, but must watch one kill the other over a girl (who is every bit as shallow and unworthy as Fitzgerald's Daisy Buchanan). The migrants have evaded misery in the South only to find tragedy in the North. But some become so callous that they fail to recognize the tragic dimensions of their behavior....

"Blades of Steel" is a brutal story which pits gambling-man Eight-Ball against knife-wielding Dirty Cozzens; Eight-Ball wins after his girlfriend, Effie, teaches him a trick with a "safety" razor blade. Despite the violence and occasional gore of the action, the story contains Fisher's full quota of puns and Harlemese. In a tale which plays upon the "blades of steel" motif we learn that "whoever whittles [Dirty Cozzens] down will be a hero," and that "Effie's tongue had cut like steel." The locale shifts from a barber shop to a dance hall, to a bar-and-grill, and in so doing Fisher utilizes music (jazz from a "low down" orchestra at the dance hall, Tessie Smith's blues from a phonograph at the bar-and-grill) both as background and as commentary upon the story's action. (p. 163)

[**"Fire by Night"**] sets elements from Harlem's three social classes against each other. Rusty Pride, the son of a beloved and upstanding preacher, is born a member of the temperate, respectable middle class but, made "swaggering, regardless, and worldly-wise" by the first World War, he returns from the service and rejects his middle class values; he rebelliously submerges himself in the life of the lower class (the so-called rats). It is not an attractive picture that Fisher presents of this class or its milieu—the "tameless corner of Harlem." These are the tough men and their heirs who "protected the colony in its infancy by their skill with pistols and knives and fists."... (pp. 163-64)

The so-called So-and-Sos tend to be snobbish and are not treated very sympathetically by Fisher either. They are comparable to the Blue Vein Society in Charles Chesnutt's "The Wife of his Youth," and Fisher satirizes the type again in *The Walls of Jericho*. Attending the dance at the *New Casino* thrown by the So-and-Sos— but standing apart from their aristocratic pretensions— is Roma Lee, the patient girlfriend of Rusty, who rescues her when he appears on the scene. Together they seek refuge in a dwelling which, all too patly, turns out to be Reverend Pride's parsonage. Symbolically, the two youths are saved when they come home to the safety and sanity of the God-fearing middle class (as Turpin's Club burns like a Satanic inferno in the background). The conclusion of the story suggests that Rusty is no longer going to wander around like a billiard ball, aimlessly ricocheting from one meaningless experience to another. Perhaps his father's prayers have been answered; perhaps Rusty has found God. At least he has found himself....

[In 1927, Dr. Fisher wrote] an essay for *American Mercury* entitled **"The Caucasian Storms Harlem."** Fisher's major point in this historical guide through

Harlem is that the formerly black cabarets have begun catering to whites—almost to the exclusion of blacks. "Why, I am actually stared at, I frequently feel uncomfortable and out of place" in these cabarets, he confesses. He not only explores the phenomenon by contrasting the way cabarets used to be when he first came to Harlem with the way they were becoming later in the decade; he also tries to account for this change, this new "active and participating interest" in Negroes. While not a story itself, **"The Caucasian Storms Harlem"** serves as a useful companion piece to the fiction providing, as it does, factual background on famous clubs in Harlem and sketches of such black stars as Ethel Waters, Florence Mills, and the comedy team of Miller and Lyles (possible prototypes of Bubber and Jinx—two characters in both of Fisher's novels). (p. 164)

Fisher explored the ways of love and the techniques of jazz in **"Common Meter."** At the Arcadia Ballroom Fess Baxter's Firemen and Bus Williams's Blue Devils vie with each other for the jazz championship and for Jean Ambrose, the contested girl. The story centers on their conflicting philosophies of jazz and sportsmanship.... To the delight of his readers, Fisher includes a great deal of winning badinage and felicitous phrasing—such as when Bus Williams's endeavor "to drain the girl's beauty with his eyes" is described as "a useless effort since it lessened neither her loveliness nor his thirst." In addition, Fisher makes thematic use of bird imagery. For example, Williams's baton droops "like the crest of a proud bird, beaten"; when Baxter faces defeat he must adjust "his ruffled plumage"; and when the men fight it out through their music, they look like "two roosters bearin' down on the jazz." But Williams finally beats the "buzzard" when "the unfaltering common meter of [his] blues" take off and soars like "wild-winged birds." With this last metaphor, Fisher neatly merges his bird imagery and his allusions to music. It might be added that his motif of interwoven blues lyrics to comment on the action reminds one of the poems of Langston Hughes. (p. 165)

[**"Dust"**] is the single story by Fisher not set in Harlem. Pard and his girl Billie are driving along in the Connecticut countryside; when Pard's black-and-white roadster is passed by a spunky yellow sport coupe with a Georgia license plate, Pard curses the unseen "cracker" and makes it a point of honor to overtake him. In so doing he almost wrecks both cars only to discover—to his utter astonishment—that the other driver is a black man too. Here misplaced racial animosity produces comical results (by contrast, in *The Walls of Jericho* the results are tragic for Fred Merrit). Still, Billie's observation that prejudice is a horrible thing makes the serious point of the story. **"Dust"** is very short but it offers an exciting chase, inventive metaphors, and a concluding sentence which in itself would have made the rest of the story worthwhile: "A far hill covered the face of the sun, like a hand concealing a grin." (pp. 165-66)

"Ezekiel" is a psychological study of a Southern boy's first day in "the Negro colony of New York City"; the story charts his inner struggle from self-doubt to growing self-assurance. . . . Having been sent North "so that he might attend the excellent New York schools," his education in self-knowledge has begun on the streets of Harlem. **"Ezekiel"** is a slight but pleasant performance by Fisher.

So is **"Ezekiel Learns,"** which appeared the following year, 1933. Ezekiel, by this time, has acclimated himself to all the wonders of Harlem, including the "proud parade of uniformed societies" which had been Marcus Garvey's legacy, as well as the "occasional riots between oddly excited mobs and grimly determined policemen." He has also witnessed the incredible sights of the rest of the city. But the one enduring memory is of an experience which gave him a glimpse into the enigma of his own personality. Fisher proceeds to tell the story of Ezekiel's clever and judicious response to the spiteful vengefulness of a mischievous playmate. Except for a relatively few word-plays, such as "the vendor disgustedly turned from a *fruitless* search of Sam," a suspect in the theft of a plum—except for this, **"Ezekiel Learns"** presents its anecdotal tale in a straightforward manner. Thematically it is similar to the poem, "Incident," written by Fisher's friend, Countee Cullen; in both, one seemingly little incident leaves a deeper impression on the sensibility of a young boy than all of his other experiences put together. (p. 166)

"Guardian of the Law" is notable for its humorous badinage; for its wry descriptions (as Sam and his adversary, Grip Beasley, fight they are described as "embracing each other with enthusiasm"); also notable is the story's use of personification ("a battered piano whose key-board grinned evilly at her"); and the characterization of Grip Beasley as a hoodlum who had "too much Harlem in him." Also of interest is the skillful use Fisher makes near the beginning of the story of a quasi-stream-of-consciousness technique ("comment pursued comment" across Grammie's mind "like successive windflaws sweeping the surface of a pool"). In addition, there is the fascination of the recent migrants with the idea that blacks could become symbols of authority—police officers. Gillis in **"The City of Refuge"** thinks with awe of becoming a policeman, a position never open to a black "down home"; Sam simply becomes one. (p. 167)

The image Fisher creates of Harlem [in **"Miss Cynthie"**] is closer to Claude McKay's lusty Harlem in *Home to Harlem* than Gillis's meretricious Harlem in **"The City of Refuge."** Here the black colony is a colorful and "tireless carnival." The very atmosphere exudes "laughter, abandoned strong Negro laughter." It was a Harlem which, historically, it would seem, had passed from the scene by Depression-haunted 1933, and a Harlem which, even in the twenties, had been able to offer such ostentatious luxury to very few (Dave's car is "a robin's egg blue open Packard with scarlet wheels"; his apartment is stunningly furnished). Also pre-Depression in spirit is Dave Tappen, an unself-conscious and uninhibited man like Jake in McKay's novel (and

wealthy besides) who seems to be one of those exceptional cases. His lifestyle certainly was not typical of Harlem's life in general.

Still, the change from life in the South to life in Harlem had appeared dramatic. When the female dancers in **"Miss Cynthie"** return to the stage of the Lafayette Theater after their cotton-fields number, they wear "scant travesties on their earlier voluminous costumes—tiny sun-bonnets perched jauntily on one side of their glistening bobs, bandanas reduced to scarlet neck-ribbons, waists mere brassieres, skirts were gingham sashes." . . . (p. 168)

A genre that Fisher introduced to Black Literature and perfected all in one strike is the detective novel. An unusual and ingenious work, *The Conjure Man Dies,* appearing in 1932 to solid critical applause, is a classic with all the standard ingredients and complications of the suspenseful novel of detection. It holds up remarkably well and seems not at all dated. In this novel Fisher introduces Sergeant Perry Dart, the professional detective, and his associate, Dr. John Archer, an amateur sleuth, who is the more sagacious of the two. Fisher enjoyed writing about these two characters so much that he intended "to use them in at least two more mystery novels—we'll call it the Dart-Archer series," he said. Fisher did not live to realize this goal but he did dramatize *The Conjure Man Dies* (which was produced posthumously) and he did finish a fine story featuring Dart and Archer [**"John Archer's Nose,"** the author's longest story]. . . . It is practically as good as the novel and it illustrates Fisher's inexhaustible fascination with policework. In it Dr. Archer denounces the kind of superstition and backwardness which resists the benefits of modern medical technology. A father, he tells Dart, has refused X-ray treatment for his sick baby, relying instead on a charm consisting of human hair fried in snake oil supplied by a conjure woman. The baby had worn the charm but, of course, he had died—the victim of superstition. . . . In a supremely clever and witty story, Fisher shows how "superstition killed Sonny." (pp. 168-69)

Just as William Faulkner, in his saga of Yoknapatawpha, creates an interrelating matrix of characters and places, so too does Fisher people his literary landscape with characters who recur in different stories. Spider Webb, for example, appears in both **"The Backslider"** and *The Conjure Man Dies.* Jinx and Bubber (based upon popular vaudeville teams of the twenties) appear in both novels. (p. 169)

There are undeniable lapses into stock types—matriarchal grandmothers, awed country bumpkins, and Jinx and Bubber in his novels—but they never remain one-dimensional stereotypes. It is also true that some of Fisher's characters are cartoons. But in most cases his caricaturing serves the aims of penetrating satire.

If there is comic exaggeration of character in Fisher's stories, there is rigorous realism of place. As has already been noted, Fisher delineates Harlem—lovingly and accurately—street by street. **"Miss Cynthie"** presents one perspective on Harlem—Harlem as race capital and mecca. Most of the other stories, however, present a less sanguine perspective. In **"The South Lingers On,"** Majutah's grandmother sees Harlem as a "great, noisy, heartless, crowded place where you lived under the same roof with a hundred people you never knew." Much like Gillis's room in **"The City of Refuge,"** Mammy's apartment in **"The Promised Land"** is compared to "a fifth-story roost on the airshaft of a seven-story hencoop," and Lil in **"The Backslider"** likens her room to a clothespress. As people move into the flats of Harlem their prospects—at least for some of them—turn flat too, even if the pace of their lives speeds up.

The citizens of Harlem certainly have not left all of their old problems behind. In **"High Yaller,"** school for Jay "had been a succession of fistfights with white boys who called him nigger," and he must remember never to cross Lenox Avenue or go beyond 135th Street or venture on or near Seventh Avenue because "it would have been almost suicidal for [a Negro] to appear unarmed on Irish Eighth." And where old problems have been left behind, they have often been replaced by new ones; for Harlem was a place "where there was so much more for one to quarrel about and resent"—as Sam and Wesley (who have such disparate salaries in **"The Promised Land"**) discover. If Fitzgerald's geography of East and West symbolically represents corruption and hope, respectively, Fisher's geography of North and South, more often than not, has the North representing disappointed hopes and expanding anxieties. And yet there is always the pulse of excitement and the counterbalance of new hopes and opportunities in Harlem.

Fisher's language is the medium of a rich style which informs while it entertains and elates. The author had appended a glossary of Harlemese to **The Walls of Jericho** but the stories burst with definitions too—some serious and helpful, others wry and ironic. If the reader does not know what a *dicty,* the *dozens,* a *rent party,* the *camel walk,* and other artifacts of black culture are, he will be enlightened by reading the stories in which they are explicitly defined. (pp. 169-70)

Always—whether he is being informative or entertaining—Fisher's language sings. His stories are filled with imaginative puns, inventive personifications, and other playful twists of language (as when he paradoxically describes Harlem apartment buildings as "mountains of flats"). In addition, the stories are a gold-mine of lines and stanzas from old hymns, blues, and popular songs. The collection, moreover, offers a compendium of Harlem idioms and dialects, the old-time preacher's sermons; the West Indian speech pattern; the people of Harlem bantering in Harlemese. It is no wonder that Langston Hughes considered Fisher "the wittiest of [the] New Negroes of Harlem." Hughes asserted that Fisher "could think of the most incisively clever things to say," and confessed, "I used to wish I could talk like Rudolph Fisher."

In 1933 Fisher averred: "Outsiders know nothing of Harlem life as it really is. What one sees in a night club or a dance hall is nothing, doesn't scratch the surface—is in fact presented solely for the eyes of outsiders. . . . But what goes on behind the scenes and beneath the dark skins of Harlem folk—fiction has not found much of that yet." Fisher was an insider who scratched deeply. The stories reveal his love for the people of Harlem and the diversity of talents they represent. They also help us to understand the quality of life of Harlem during the Renaissance period. (pp. 170-71)

> *Leonard J. Deutsch, "The Streets of Harlem: The Short Stories of Rudolph Fisher," in* PHYLON: The Atlanta University Review of Race and Culture, *Vol. XL, No. 2, second quarter (June, 1979), pp. 159-71.*

Margaret Perry (essay date 1987)

[*In the following excerpt, Perry places Fisher's short stories within the context of Harlem in the 1920s and 1930s.*]

It is not surprising that little of the work done in the short story form by Rudolph Fisher (1897-1934) is known; there has never been a collection of all his short stories, and this hampers the scholar in pursuit of a unified view of Fisher's themes and style. In the early part of our century, short stories written by black authors had little appeal to the primary reading public, which was white; Fisher seems to have been the exception to this, however. Although his stories were published frequently in Negro publications, he also appeared in non-Negro publications such as *Atlantic Monthly* and *McClure's,* and thus was able to reach a wider audience of short-story readers. Despite this, little space is devoted to Fisher in critical histories of the American short story. Indeed, the central metaphor of Black Invisibility can be said to have been operating among critics of the short story in America. In an effort to rectify this neglect, the present article explores the stories of Rudolph Fisher, both published and unpublished, and places them within the context of the times in which he lived. The precise time in history, as well as the place—Harlem, its spirit—were significant elements in Fisher's fiction; indeed they were perhaps the reasons he felt impelled to capture his world within the strictures of the short-story form. Full of wit, irony, humor, and some acerbity, Fisher has enriched the world of literature in a medium Frank O'Connor has called our "national art form." (pp. 253-54)

Fisher's first published story, **"City of Refuge,"** was written while he was still in medical school, and appeared in *Atlantic Monthly* during February 1925. In addition to unpublished stories, Fisher wrote two plays, **The Vici Kid** and **Golden Slippers,** neither of which was ever published or produced. According to his sister, the late Pearl M. Fisher: "like most writers, Dr. Fisher's ambition was to write the great Negro novel." Though Fisher did publish two novels—his second one, **The**

Conjure Man Dies, was the first detective novel by a Black American—it is through his short stories that he presented the widest view of Black American life in Harlem. In a radio interview, Fisher stated the following: "Harlem is the epitome of American Negro life...I intend to write whatever interests me. But if I should be fortunate enough to become known as Harlem's interpreter, I should be very happy."

Harlem's interpreter—this was his expressed desire, and this was the goal he achieved through all of his fiction, as well as in his articles. The reading public responded to Fisher's role as a reflector of the life in the nation's Black capital during the 1920s, for one newspaperman wrote: "De Maupassant used Paris for his chess-board, while Fisher moves his dusky pawns over the field of Negro Harlem, a location quite as interesting as 'dear Paree.'" At last the reading public would be entertained with literature that reflected the informing spirit of the Afro-American race, the cultural *temenos* sustaining the unique character of Black life from country to town to city, in particular, Harlem. The model of life, the white life, was to be just another version of real life rather than the version that would overpower the Black reality of living. Sometimes, of course, the evil or injustice evolving from what white *could impose* upon blacks is treated with satiric strokes by Fisher, such as in **"High Yaller."** Still, Fisher seems, in his portraits of life in Harlem, to have realized what Octavio Paz observed when writing about the majority and minority in Mexico: "Without otherness there is no oneness." So Fisher was, indeed, "Harlem's interpreter."

Fisher's fascination with Harlem came with the times, and his only regrets seemed to be the effects of white incursion into Harlem's places of entertainment. He hoped that the whites would also venture to explore more than this obvious part of Harlem and learn to understand Black life in general: "Maybe," he wrote, "they are at least learning to speak our language." Not really—but as long as the writings of Rudolph Fisher exist, everyone, Black and white, can learn to enjoy the sights and sounds of Negro Harlem during the 1920s, the city that King Solomon Gillis first viewed with wide-eyed joy and fascination by saying: "Done died an' woke up in Heaven." It was a little of everything, and Fisher's canvases faithfuly paint the people and places in its mosaic of dark and light hues.

The short stories of Rudolph Fisher have a sense of literary history behind them, for he ploughed the same fields as the masters of this art, such as Poe, Gogol, and James. There are times, indeed, when Fisher gives the impression that he went from studying the nineteenth-century writers directly to his desk to write, ignoring practitioners of the art who were his own contemporaries. In an earlier review of Fisher's work I noted that "Both stories [**'City of Refuge'** and **'Miss Cynthie'**] illustrate Fisher's ability to transform life into art through control of characterization, plot, and diction, and insistence on a single effect at the story's conclusion." Fisher was a traditionalist in form, then; but he was also one in point of view, in his themes, and in the values he stressed through the major characters he created. One might also venture to say that Fisher often wrote in the mode of dramatic comedies, eschewing tragedy in any case even in the stories that end unhappily.

Fisher writes comedy in the classical sense, as Gilbert Murray states in *the Classical Tradition in Poetry,* comedy that has at its core "a union of lovers." This re-creation of acts and emotions, mimesis, moves from conflict to resolution within the very special milieu of Black Harlem. The over-all impression one gets of Fisher's use of the short story form is that he engages the reader in a positive, comic view of life which arises from the lyric impulse to sing mainly about triumph, about the possibility of being saved or renewed. Once again, to quote Murray: "Tragedies end in death. Comedies end in marriage." Murray is not referring to marriage as a legal procedure, but is alluding to the joy that issues from a harmonious end to the strife and conflict within the imaginative work. It seems he is seeking not only the melody but also the harmony, as Shelley wrote in his famous *Defence of Poetry.* One is always conscious of an ordered universe in Fisher's world; he writes about the ruptures that are brought on by disharmony, the disjointedness that must be replaced at the denouement by order.

There are important non-literary elements in Fisher's stories that should also be noted, because he emphasizes them consistently. He was a satirist and social historian through the medium of the short story; thus, we have an accurate portrait of Harlem during the 1920s, whether or not one believes this is the proper function of imaginative literature. Fisher portrays the life of the "rats" and the "dickties" as well as the criminal element and the ordinary wage-earner. We see how life is played out in the cabaret, at rent parties, and we witness the city version of religion as it struggles to recapture the joy and spontaneity of the "down home" mode of expression. As a critic of the city—the city as duper, the city as destroyer of the immigrated Black—Fisher's stories act out the ritual of ruin in which so many men and women were immolated. For some, the family unit is disrupted, as in **"The Promised Land"** or in **"The South Lingers On"**; while others, seeking safety and freedom, like King Solomon Gillis in **"City of Refuge",** find that exploitation, confinement and racism are not limited to the South. In the latter story, Gillis encounters a new sort of racism, explored in several other Fisher stories—the prejudice of black against black, particularly Afro-American vs. British West Indian.

The relationship, or more aptly, the animosity, between the American Black and the West Indian Black is portrayed sharply in several of Fisher's stories; indeed, this topic is the major element of conflict in **"Ringtail."** Sociologically, there were several reasons for this real and sometimes imagined dislike among the two groups: to many American blacks it seems that the West Indians were arrogant about their "British" background—and many West Indians, like Cyril Sebastian Best in **"Ringtail,"** lorded this so-called advantage over American Blacks. Then, it did appear that West Indians who immigrated to the United States fared better economically and in a shorter length of time. As one character in **"Ringtail"** says: "'...they stick too close together an' get ahead too fast. They put it all over us in too many ways...Same as ofays an' Jews.'"

There was also the movement of "Back to Africa," carried on with parade and pomp, electrifying the masses with a thesis none of them wanted in reality. Going back to Africa and "chasing monkeys" wasn't the dream of American Blacks; so the detractors had a ready-made phrase to coin about Marcus Garvey, leader and symbol of this abortive movement. His fellow-West Indians fell prey to the same expression and it is still used privately to this day by many American blacks (and probably less privately in non-bourgeois society).

There are strains of satire, light in most cases, lurking among Fisher's descriptions of life in Harlem. The picture of Cyril Sebastian Best (**"Ringtail"**) is satirical, particularly at the opening when he is parading in his finery. Fisher mocks the concerns of the "dickties" for the false trappings of bourgeois habits, such as the So-and-So's "supper dansant" described in **"Fire by Night."** He mocks the fragility of the dickties further in this story when, at the height of a brawl at the "dansant," the women scurry to save their fur coats from invading pool-hall scavengers: "girls who had saved for two years to buy seal wraps; wives who had wheedled for months to get a caracal like Mrs. Jones; women who had undertaken payment for their Persian lambs by installments." There is the hypocrisy of the religious exposed in **"The Backslider,"** and even a hint of satire in the minor appearance of the Goldman brothers in **"Miss Cynthie."**

Imagery of a world of confinement and darkness—the black world on earth, not Hell (although that is one point, i.e., that Harlem frequently is Hell)—characterizes Fisher's fictional domain. Sometimes there is no value judgment implied in the painting he presents, e.g., "The pavement flashed like a river in the sun" (**"Ringtail"**); but most often his images and figurative language are undergirded by Fisher principles and points of view.

Langston Hughes, Charles S. Johnson, E. Franklin Frazier, Rudolph Fisher, and Herbert Delaney.

A large proportion of Fisher's imagery derives from his use of similes and metaphors such as "the thoughts that gathered and throbbed like an abscess were suddenly incised" (**"High Yaller"**); the "roadster . . . snorted impatiently" (**"Dust"**); "A young bronze giant" (**"Guardian"**); or, the "ambulance gong was like receding derisive laughter." (**"Ringtail"**). In a comprehensive sense, the image we have of Harlem is one of "a stage upon which one looked as from an upper box" (**"Guardian"**). Fisher places Harlem in an open-air theatre so the reader can view the high and the low, the very fine Seventh Avenue as well as Lenox Avenue, "the boulevard of the unperfumed." In painting scenes with colors as well as with sound, Fisher gives the reader what Mammy, in **"The Promised Land,"** sees from her window: "a screen upon which flashed a motion picture oddly alive and colorful." Often Fisher invests inanimate objects with human traits (e.g., the "keyboard grinned evilly"—**"Guardian"**) to indicate a point of view, the author's moral stance. The Blacks, frequently living in "hencoops," the white downtown in "kingly dwellings," the good and the bad, common and uncommon, the city itself, all enter upon a stage set up by Fisher and perform their roles in a pageant of contrasts and disharmonies that will eventually end in an orderly resolution. It is difficult to categorize Fisher's treatment of the rent party phenomenon, whether it is sadness or satire when he writes (in **"The Promised Land"**), "You provide music, your friends provide advertisement, and your guests, by paying admission, provide what your resources lack." Certainly, Fisher saw that the underlying reason for this Northeastern version of the "shindig" was in most instances exploitation, because people were having to pay more than a fair price for apartments. In any case, Fisher was unable to avoid the satiric touch from time to time as a technique for pointing out the meaninglessness of certain habits and concerns in the Black community.

In highlighting the special qualities that composed life in Harlem at every stratum, Fisher dramatically portrayed the obsession of blacks with their color. He turned his self-absorption into an artistic mode with moral as well as social implications. It has been noted by another critic that Fisher uses color to differentiate between good and bad characters, that "the lighter the skin color the lower the moral character of the individual." This differentiation is made in several of Fisher's stories, notably **"Blades of Steel"** and **"High Yaller."** Fisher offers readers a gallery of "good" guys and "bad" ones, most often designated by skin color—dark equaling good and yellow for the low-down cad. Consider for example, the following characters:

> "His coarse granular skin was dingy yellow and scarred . . . " (**"Fire by Night"**);

> "Eight-ball . . . was as dark as it is possible for skin to be, smooth and clean as an infant's . . . " (**"Blades of Steel"**);

> "Bus Williams' jolly round brown face beamed down on the crowd . . . " (**"Common Meter"**).

In between the absolute dark and light we have women who are "amber" (**"Common Meter"**), or "red-brown" (**"Guardian of the Law"**), or "golden-skinned" (**"Miss Cynthie"**); the women, in any case, are never black. The darkest woman of importance in his short stories is Effie Wright in **"Blades of Steel,"** who is described as having an "almost luminous dark complexion called 'sealskin brown'." With this obvious attention to color, Fisher reflects the self-consciousness of the decade toward the various shades of 'Blackness.'

It cannot be said that Fisher accomplished every goal he attempted in his short story writing, for there are some structural and linguistic imperfections that do not go undetected. Fisher, with his balanced and sane approach to the difficulties in life, wanted to demonstrate the effects of illusion on individuals. People continually misread the motives of self and other, and thus the seeds for conflict are scattered. Here we have the necessary elements for a good story—action, reaction, and resolution. If the exposition complements these elements, then the production proceeds as it should to a successful completion. This does not always occur, however, in Fisher's stories; there are some weaknesses that are apparent.

One weakness, which appears to derive from Fisher's occasional desire to preach or educate, is that of author intrusion. In **"Dust,"** which is one of his least effective stories, he succumbed to the urge to teach rather than to entertain; he did not move toward the effect he wanted, he commenced with it and rode it to death.

Adopting the role of the totally omniscient author, of course, allowed Fisher to write as he pleased. Still, he was good enough as a short-story writer to understand the necessity of removing unneeded words, the necessity of keeping the movement "tight" yet, more than once, he placed himself as writer into the middle of a story.

Another weakness was a general tendency to write by formula, making a Fisher situation and/or ending predictable, and sometimes too slick or facile. As one critic [Thomas Friedmann; see excerpt dated 1976] has written about **"Common Meter"**: "To the cynical modern reader, the outcome is possible only in a fairy tale. The winner is the most noble and upright character, the jazz musician who prizes rhythm above all else and the man whose skin is darkest." Of course, this conforms to Fisher's basic comic style, which anticipates the "happy ending."

Generally, however, Fisher goes swiftly to the heart of his story—moves the reader into the conflict, clearly points to the cast of characters and their features, and concludes the story tidily—leaving no doubt in the mind of the reader concerning the meaning of the tale. A certain stylistic stiffness in Fisher's expository mode sometimes impedes the smooth movement of the story, but this is an authentic feature of his writing. His use of idiomatic Harlem language is another characteristic feature, a strength in terms of authenticity, but also another weakness if taken as it has been by one critic in the following observation: "his use of the Negro idiom, Harlemese, (is) . . . self-conscious."

Despite these weaknesses, Fisher was successful in portraying his fellow black Americans from all strata of Negro life, from the "rats" to the "dickties," and he achieved his goal to a greater degree than any other writer of this period. The last of Fisher's short stories to be published in his lifetime, **"Miss Cynthie,"** leads one to postulate that he was moving closer to the real art of short fiction writing. As Robert Bone has noted, "'**Miss Cynthie**' constitutes . . . a psychological as well as an artistic triumph. Published in the shadow of impending death, it testifies to Fisher's inner growth and aggravates our loss of his maturing powers" [see excerpt dated 1975].

The importance of **"Miss Cynthie"** in the canon of Fisher literature does not obscure his lesser tales; but this story is the exemplum of Fisher's overriding concern for the motifs of love and reconciliation, of harmonious union between opposing elements, for that "union of lovers" in the most boundless sense. To say that "Class consciousness is perhaps the single most consistent theme in Fisher's work" is to mistake the means for the goal. Other themes are also found among Fisher's major concerns, such as the futility of prejudice (the irony of it, the waste), or the effects of the lure of the city upon people and the city's power to destroy individuals. Added to his themes is Fisher's employment of language to underscore the characterizations and settings. This wholeness of themes, characterizations, settings, and language exemplify the concerns of Rudolph Fisher to render the life he witnessed and lived in the transformed manner of mimetic art through the short story.

Fisher is predictable and consistent in his language, in descriptions, exposition, and dialogue. He uses words of confinement frequently, e.g., hencoop, airshaft, underground railroads, suffocation, a religious vocabulary in connection with characters acutely aware of sinfulness, and lastly—Fisher's special forte (or, as has been pointed out, also a weakness)—the language of Black Harlem, "Contemporary Harlemese," to use his own expression.

"City of Refuge" demonstrates Fisher's concern for the tidy progression of a tale from beginning to middle to end; the six sections of the story each lead Gillis closer to his fate. Just as he emerges like Jonah from the whale into Harlem (after being in the "hell" of the subway), he is caught at the end in a cabaret, which is another hell, and truly the place for the lost victims of the city, such as Gillis.

The end of **"The City of Refuge"** reflects the tendency of the modern short story, starting in the 1920s in fact, to place the protagonist in a situation where he receives some illumination as to the truth of his actual plight—a mini-epiphany, as it were—a moment of obvious re-

versed fortunes but without the insight into his own flawed character as one would have it in Aristotelian tragedy. There is passivity in King Solomon's acceptance of his "mistakes;" that his character has weaknesses does not occur to this protagonist, however. In this fashion, Fisher was certainly part of the mainstream of short story writers during his period of creativity—a time when there was, a short story writing, an underplaying of plot, reversals, total change, or complete insight into the self (or a need to do anything about an internal problem when it was discovered). In part, then, Fisher was writing in the mode of his contemporaries. Also, the fact that **"The City of Refuge"** has a comic rather than a tragic ending does not lessen the emotional poignancy of Gillis's situation unless, of course, the reader finds untenable Gillis's naiveté and gullibility.

Optimism is integral to the fiction of Fisher, a bourgeois-based belief that an optimistic philosophy of life, a firm Christian faith, and clear comprehension finally of human needs and motives can result in a harmonious conclusion to life's inversions. Because Fisher's aim was to be instructor as well as interpreter, this adoption of a positive and sanguine attitude gave him a limited point of view and made some of his work press too hard upon "a willing suspension of disbelief." Rather than demonstrating alienation from or despair with his group, Fisher—even when satirizing his race—chose to construct his stories around moral principles that served to emphasize the redemptive spirit. As in the case of all writers, of course, the choice was his to make; but the choice vitiated the effectiveness of his avowed wish to be an interpreter of his people.

The intent of his writing, however, cannot be overlooked at any time; and, apparently because he kept his aim clearly in mind, he succeeded. In a sense, he made the leap from individualizing his artistic concerns to informing about a group experience in his literary corpus; he sought to apply universal qualities to a special group and thus tamed "The artist's struggle with his vocation . . . a version of a universal human struggle: of genius with Genius, and of genius with genius loci (spirit of place)." And in demonstrating a manner of bond between his characters and their setting Fisher captures the cultural *temenos* of that Black capital.

What we have in Fisher's stories, then, is a polished portrait of the varied life in Harlem, written in a quick, sometimes witty, sometimes satiric, sometimes acerbic-sounding style. The conflicts between social and moral questions inform many of Fisher's stories—e.g., **"The Blackslider," "Higher Yaller,"** or **"The Promised Land"**—which highlights his aim to be not only entertaining, but enlightening as well. The social historian works hand-in-hand with the creative artist; the man of conscience stands behind the stories. A descendant of Emerson, Fisher stresses in his stories the notion that the God-loving, God-fearing person can triumph over adversity. If the short story is, as Mark Schorer has said, "an art of moral revelation" (whereas the novel is "an art of moral evolution"), then Fisher accomplished what he wished as an artist practicing this literary genre. His keen observations of life and manners in Harlem, couched in a literary form, demonstrate his very American concern for probing those flaws in our character which he felt could be ameliorated. The personal conflicts of his characters illustrate, once again, a major American concern—the problems stemming from belief versus action; a testing, it seems, of the theory of the American way of life versus the reality of how life is acted out day by day.

Unlike many of the white writers of the 1920s (e.g., Sherwood Anderson, Hemingway), who frequently chose protagonists who were unattractive and second-rate, Fisher for the most part eschews this sort of character in a principal role and emphasizes the redeeming features of the "good guy." One prominent exception is **"Ringtail,"** although it is not clear to me what attitude Fisher has or the precise point of a story such as this, where the main character certainly succeeds in evildoing. But in each case where there is a repugnant individual in a Fisher story, a contrasting figure is provided in the balance to represent the author's moral point of view. This, too, is an essential element of his art—to make sure that nothing, then, is left to the reader's inference: characters, setting, theme, point of view, resolution of the plot come together in a conclusion calculated tidily to furnish a panorama of Harlem as painted by a master interpreter of black life in this mecca of multicolored inhabitants. (pp. 254-62)

> *Margaret Perry, "A Fisher of Black Life: Short Stories by Rudolph Fisher," in* The Harlem Renaissance Re-examined, *edited by Victor A. Kramer, AMS Press, 1987, pp. 253-63.*

FURTHER READING

Bone, Robert. "The Harlem School." In his *The Negro Novel in America,* rev. ed., pp. 65-108. New Haven: Yale University Press, 1965.
> Brief discussion of Fisher as the forerunner of black self-satirists.

Brawley, Benjamin. "The New Realists." In his *The Negro Genius: A New Appraisal of the Achievement of the American Negro in Literature and the Fine Arts,* pp. 231-68. New York: Biblo and Tannen, 1937.
> Summarizes Fisher's novels and stories, commenting that "with keen perception and a fine sense of irony [Fisher] had also the detachment of the artist, and could employ humor when he pleased or be serious without being heavy."

Chamberlain, John. "The Negro As Writer." *The Bookman,* New York, LXX, No. 6 (February 1930): 603-11.
> Compares Fisher to Ring Lardner "as a manipulator of native idiom," remarking that each of the stories "The City of Refuge" and "Blades of Steel" "turns on a trick, but the tricks depend on character for their effectiveness."

Emanuel, James A., and Gross, Theodore L., eds. "Rudolph Fisher, 1987-1934." In their *Dark Symphony: Negro Literature in America,* pp. 110-11. New York: The Free Press, 1968.
> Introduction to a reprinting of "Miss Cynthie," arguing that "Fisher is particularly effective in evoking the saturnalian quality of Harlem life, but he attempts more than mere local color; he humanizes the corrupt as well as the innocent figures in his stories, and he suggests the great influence of place in the morality of his characters."

Henry, Oliver Louis. "Rudolph Fisher: An Evaluation." *The Crisis* 78, No. 5 (July 1971): 149-54.
> Summarizes Fisher's novels and short stories, with commentary and brief biography.

Kent, George E. "Patterns of the Harlem Renaissance." In *The Harlem Renaissance Remembered,* edited by Arna Bontemps, pp. 27-50. New York: Dodd, Mead and Co., 1972.
> Brief critical sketch of Fisher's novels and short stories, stating that Fisher "gave us pictures of the ordinary workaday black who was largely neglected by other Renaissance writers."

McCluskey, John, Jr. "'Aim High and Go Straight': The Grandmother Figure in the Short Fiction of Rudolph Fisher." *Black American Literature Forum* 15, No. 2 (Summer 1981): 55-59.
> Approaches Fisher as an author who, unlike many of his peers, treated the concerns of the workaday Harlemite rather than the dilemmas of members of the professional class.

———. "Healing Songs: Secular Music in the Short Fiction of Rudolph Fisher." *CLA Journal* XXVI, No. 2 (December 1982): 191-203.
> Examines Fisher's portrayal of music, particularly ragtime, jazz, and urban blues, in his short fiction.

———. Introduction to *The City of Refuge: The Collected Stories of Rudolph Fisher,* by Rudolph Fisher, edited by John McCluskey, Jr., pp. xi-xxxix. Columbia, Mo.: University of Missouri Press, 1987
> Biographical sketch, with commentary on Fisher's place in the history of African-American fiction.

Tignor, Eleanor Q. "The Short Fiction of Rudolph Fisher." *The Langston Hughes Review* I, No. 1 (Spring 1982): 18-24.
> Overview of Fisher's life and literary career, emphasizing the author's short fiction. Tignor concludes: "Fisher moved most of his short stories toward a happy or optimistic resolution, frequently with an O. Henry-style surprise twist. Detached but at the same time accepting of human foibles and able to see the comic side of human nature, Fisher was a sympathetic recorder and translator of Harlem life of the 1920's and early 1930's."

———. "Rudolph Fisher: Harlem Novelist." *The Langston Hughes Review* I, No. 2 (Fall 1982): 13-22.
> Explores theme, plot, and narrative structure in *The Walls of Jericho* and *The Conjure-Man Dies.*

Charlotte L. Forten

1837?-1914

(Born Charlotte Lottie Forten; assumed married name Charlotte L. Forten Grimké in 1878; also wrote as Miss C. L. F. and Lottie) American diarist, poet, essayist, and translator.

The Journal of Charlotte L. Forten: A Free Negro in the Slave Era (1953) is a record of the intellectual coming-of-age of a genteel black woman in the 1850s and 1860s. Forten kept the diary from the ages of 16 to 26, an exciting decade in her life and a turbulent era in American history. A revealing testimony to the psychological impact of racial hatred on a sensitive and idealistic person, *The Journal* is also an important historical document that details the progress and setbacks of the abolitionist movement and provides portraits of such notable movement figures as William Lloyd Garrison, Wendell Phillips, and John Greenleaf Whittier.

Forten was born into one of Philadelphia's most prominent and politically active black families. Her grandfather, James Forten, was a free-born man who became a wealthy sail maker and a prominent abolitionist; consequently, Forten grew up in a household dominated by discussions of slavery and America's racial policies—discussions that significantly influenced her perspective on the country's social and political practices. When Forten was still a young girl her mother died, and the youngster divided her time between her father's home and that of her aunt and uncle, Harriet and Robert Purvis, who lived in suburban Byberry. Purvis, a black abolitionist who had inherited substantial wealth from his English father, owned an estate where political meetings were held, runaway slaves were offered sanctuary, and traveling agents for various antislavery associations were lodged. Forten enjoyed the excitement and sense of righteousness such activities brought to her surroundings and also welcomed the chance to be with her cousins; previously, her exposure to other children had been limited because her father had chosen to have her privately tutored rather than send her to Philadelphia's segregated schools. In 1854, however, when Forten was sixteen or seventeen, she was sent to the Salem, Massachusetts, home of Charles and Amy Remond, who were to act as her foster parents while she attended the integrated Salem Grammar School.

Remond, his brother, and his sister Sarah lectured as agents of the American Anti-Slavery Society, a position to which Forten aspired. In the childless home a bond like that between mother and daughter developed between Forten and Sarah, who was twenty-three years her senior. The Remond home was congenial, and Forten welcomed the challenge offered by her new school, writing in her diary at the semester's end that "this year has been a very happy one. Happy because

the field of knowledge, for the first time has seemed widely open to me; because I have studied more, and, I trust, learned more than during any other year of my life.... I feel an earnest desire to become very much wiser...." She was further encouraged by her friendship with her teacher, a woman she admired even more when she learned of her abolitionist sympathies. Forten remained distant from her classmates, however, and was sensitive to the hypocrisy of white students who were friendly within the confines of the classroom but who refused to acknowledge her presence in public. "These are but trifles," she wrote, "certainly, to the great, public wrongs which we as people are obliged to endure. But to those who experience them, these trifles are most wearing and discouraging." Such behavior on the part of others gave Forten additional reason for wanting to excel; through her personal accomplishments she believed she could prove that black people deserve the respect afforded other Americans. She proved to be an exemplary student, embarking on a course of self-improvement that included teaching herself French, Latin, and German and attending lectures on literature and politics. During a single year, her diary shows, Forten completed a reading list of over one hundred books, including works by Charles Dickens, Elizabeth Barrett Browning, and Ralph Waldo Emerson, whom she heard lecture on several occasions. Her appraisals of literature and of lecturers were based not only on literary merit or oratorical excellence but also on the degree to which the writers and speakers reflected liberal sentiments about black people and women. Nevertheless, despite her diligence in pursuing her goals, and her obvious achievement, Forten remained modest to the point of self-deprecation, even hesitating to take credit for a poem that was accepted for publication by Garrison's antislavery journal *The Liberator.*

Because of her excellent work and genteel demeanor, Forten was accepted as a student at the Salem Normal School, where she prepared for a teaching career. However, her happiness at her graduation in 1856 was marred by the illness and subsequent death of Amy Remond. Forten remained in the Remond home for over a year after Amy's death, teaching at a local grammar school, but was forced to move in with another family when Charles Remond became irritable and difficult to live with; an orator of international reputation who was considered by many to be the leading spokesman for black Americans, Remond never accepted the secondary role assigned him in the abolitionist movement after the rapid rise of Frederick Douglass. During this period Forten tired of teaching and longed for a life devoted to cultural and intellectual pursuits. In 1858 she left Salem and returned to Pennsylvania, where she remained for four years, reading, studying, and recovering her strength after recurrent attacks of tuberculosis. Although she published several poems in antislavery periodicals during these years, she decided to return to teaching. In 1862 she applied for a position on St. Helena Island, South Carolina, in an experimental project designed to prove that former slaves could be educated and become valuable citizens.

St. Helena, an island in Confederate territory, had been taken by the Union army; with the approach of that army, 8,000 slaves had been deserted by the local land owners. The former slaves, who were isolated from the mainland, spoke Gullah (a dialect that combines various African languages) and were suspicious of the outsiders who poured onto the island. Forten found her young, undisciplined students a striking contrast to the white students she had instructed in Salem, but the unusual language, their love of music, and the challenge of helping them gave her a deep satisfaction. Forten particularly enjoyed the children's singing; a letter on their vocal abilities to Whittier, whom Forten had met along with many other celebrated persons while living with the Remonds, inspired the poet to compose a special Christmas hymn for her charges. Correspondents for several years, Forten and Whittier admired one another for their dedication to the cause of abolition, and when Forten sent him an essay about the project on St. Helena Island and the beauty of the natural sur-

roundings, Whittier saw that it was published in *The Atlantic Monthly.*

In her diary Forten demonstrated as much concern for the black regiment that was formed from among the Island's inhabitants as she did for her students. She therefore recorded the history of the soldiers' battles with the Confederate army. On one occasion she wrote, "They say the black soldiers fought the rebels bravely;— . . . I can think of nothing but this reg[iment]. How proud of it I am!" Despite such feelings of pride, Forten still considered Independence Day celebrations and other forms of patriotism hypocritical in a nation that had enslaved people for centuries: "*Patriotic* young America kept up such a din in celebrating their glorious *Fourth,* that *rest* was impossible. My soul is sick of such a mockery." In May 1864, suffering again from ill health, Forten returned to Philadelphia, well satisfied with the success of the experiment on St. Helena Island. For the next decade she lived a quiet life writing essays and poetry and taking an occasional teaching position.

In addition to recording her reactions to the abolitionist movement, slavery, and the Civil War, Forten also wrote about her personal loneliness, her desire to feel completely at ease with her numerous white friends, and her belief that no man would ever love her. "Though I had *almost* resolved to forbear committing sad thoughts and gloomy feelings to my pages, dear Journal, . . . to-night I long for a confidant—and *thou* art my only one . . . . I am *lonely* to-night . . . . I long for the pressure of a loving hand in mine, the touch of loving lips upon my aching brow . . . . There is none, for me, and never will be. I could only love one whom I could look up to, and reverence . . . . " Forten was to find such a man in Francis Grimké, the son of a South Carolina plantation owner and his slave, and the nephew of Sarah and Angelina Grimké, famous and ardent abolitionists and feminists. After a youth of enslavement, escape, imprisonment, and liberation, Francis Grimké became the valedictorian of his graduating class at Lincoln College and went on to Princeton Theological Seminary, earning a degree in theology. He and Forten married in 1878. With her husband, who was thirteen years her junior, Forten led what appears to have been a satisfying life of social work and cultural enrichment.

Forten is considered a minor creator of sentimental verse and a competent if not exceptional essayist. Her highest praise came from contemporaries who knew and admired her as a person and were therefore influenced by her sincerity as much as by her admittedly meager talents. However, her journal, which was composed as a personal document with no intention of publication and was not published until 1953, remains an outstanding accomplishment. One of only a few such surviving works composed by black Americans during her era, *The Journal* is an important human and historical document. According to Ray Allen Billington, *The Journal* is Forten's "bequest to humanity . . . which could reveal to a later generation her underlying belief in human decency and equality."

(For further information about Forten's life and works, see *Black Writers; Contemporary Authors*, Vols. 117, 124; *Dictionary of Literary Biography*, Vol. 50: *Afro-American Writers before the Harlem Renaissance;* and *Twentieth-Century Literary Criticism*, Vol. 16)

*PRINCIPAL WORKS

"To W. L. G. on Reading His 'Chosen Queen'" (poetry) 1855; published in periodical *The Liberator*

"Poem" (poetry) 1856; published in periodical *The Liberator*

"Glimpses of New England" (essay) 1858; published in periodical *National Anti-Slavery Standard*

"The Two Voices" (poetry) 1859; published in periodical *National Anti-Slavery Standard*

"The Wind among the Poplars" (poetry) 1859; published in periodical *The Liberator*

"In the Country" (poetry) 1860; published in periodical *National Anti Slavery Standard*

"The Slave Girl's Prayer" (poetry) 1860; published in periodical *The Liberator*

"Life on the Sea Islands" (essay) 1864; published in periodical *The Atlantic Monthly*

The Journal of Charlotte L. Forten: A Free Negro in the Slave Era (journal) 1953

*Selections of Forten's poetry have appeared in *An Anthology of American Negro Literature; The Black Man; Cavalcade; Life and Writings of the Grimké Family; Negro Poets and Their Poems;* and *The Rising Son.*

Charlotte L. Forten (journal date 1855-60)

[*In the following excerpts from her journal, Forten examines her attitudes concerning racism and friendship, commenting as well on her desire to improve herself through "thorough self-examination."*]

Wednesday, Sept. 12 [1855]. To-day school commenced.—Most happy am I to return to the companionship of my studies,—ever my most valued friends. It is pleasant to meet the scholars again; most of them greeted me cordially, and were it not for the thought that *will* intrude, of the want of *entire sympathy* even of those I know and like best, I should greatly enjoy their society. There is one young girl and only one—Miss [Sarah] B[rown] who I believe thoroughly and heartily appreciates anti-slavery.—*radical* anti-slavery, and has no prejudice against color. I wonder that every colored person is not a misanthrope. Surely we have everything to make us hate mankind. I have met girls in the schoolroom [—] they have been thoroughly kind and cordial to me,—perhaps the next day met them in the street—they feared to recognize me; these I can but regard now with scorn and contempt,—once I liked them, believing them incapable of such meanness. Others give the most distant recognition possible.—I, of course, acknowledge no such recognitions, and they soon cease entirely. These are but trifles, certainly, to the great, public wrongs which we as a people are obliged to endure. But to those who experience them, these apparent trifles are most wearing and discouraging; even to the child's mind they reveal volumes of deceit and heartlessness, and early teach a lesson of suspicion and distrust. Oh! it is hard to go through life meeting contempt with contempt, hatred with hatred, fearing, with too good reason, to love and trust hardly any one whose skin is white,—however lovable, attractive and congenial in seeming. In the bitter, passionate feelings of my soul again and again there rises the questions "When, oh! when shall this cease?" "Is there no help?" "How long oh! how long must we continue to suffer—to endure?" Conscience answers it is wrong, it is ignoble to despair; let us labor earnestly and faithfully to acquire knowledge, to break down the barriers of prejudice and oppression. Let us take courage; never ceasing to work,—hoping and believing that if not for us, for another generation there is a better, brighter day in store,—when slavery and prejudice shall vanish before the glorious light of Liberty and Truth; when the rights of every colored man shall everywhere be acknowledged and respected, and he shall be treated as a *man* and a *brother!*

September. This evening Miss B[rown] and I joined the Female Anti-Slavery Society. I am glad to have persuaded her to do so. She seems an earnest hearted girl, in whom I cannot help having some confidence. I can only hope and pray that she will be true, and courageous enough to meet the opposition which every friend of freedom must encounter.... (pp. 62-3)

Saturday, May 11 [1856]. All day I have been worrying about that poem. That troublesome poem which has yet to be commenced. Oh! that I could become suddenly inspired and write as only great poets can write. Or that I might write a beautiful poem of two hundred lines in my sleep as Coleridge did. Alas! in vain are all such longings. I must depend upon *myself* alone. And what can that self produce? Nothing, nothing but *doggerel!* This evening read Plutarch's Lycurgus.—(pp. 68-9)

Tuesday, July 22 [1856]. This afternoon we were examined in "School and Schoolmaster." Essays were read. Miss Pitman's D[issertation], My poor poem, and Lizzie's V[aledictory]—which is a beautiful production; charming as dear Lizzie's self. Crowds of people were there. Our diplomas were awarded. I was lucky enough to get one. This evening we had a delightful meeting at the school house,—our last. It was one of the pleasantest meetings we have had. And now I realize that my school days are indeed over. And many sad regrets I feel that it is indeed so. The days of my N[ew] England school life, though spent far from home and early friends, have still been among the happiest of my life. I have been fortunate enough to receive the instruction of the best and kindest teachers; and the few friends I have made are warm and true.—New England! I love to tread thy soil,—trod by the few noble spirits,—Garrison, Phillips and others,—the truest and noblest in the land; to breathe the pure air of thy hills, which is breathed by them; to gaze upon thy grand old rocks, "lashed by the fury of the ocean wave," upon thy granite hills, thy noble trees, and winding, sparkling streams, to all of which a greater charm is added by the thought that *they* the good and gifted ones, have gazed upon them also. (p. 71)

Monday, Aug. 10 [1857]. I scarcely know myself to-night;—a great and sudden joy has completely dazzled—overpowered me. This evening Miss R[emond] sent for me in haste saying a gentleman wished to see me. I went wondering who it *could* be, and found——— Whittier! one of the few men whom I truly reverence for their great minds and greater hearts. I cannot *say* all that I *felt*—even to *thee,* my Journal! I stood like one bewildered before the noble poet, whose kindly, earnest greeting *could* not increase my love and admiration for him;—my heart was full, but I *could* not speak, though constantly tormented by the thought that *he* would think me very stupid, very foolish;—but after a few simple words from him I felt more at ease, and though I still could say but very little, and left the talking part to Miss R[emond] who can *always talk,* it was such a pleasure to listen to *him,* to have *him* before me, to watch that noble, spiritual face, those glorious eyes—there are no eyes like them—that I felt *very, very* happy.—The memory of this interview will be a life-long happiness to me.—Shall I try to tell thee, my Journal, *something* of what he said? First we spoke of my old home and my present home. He asked me if I liked N[ew] E[ngland]— it was *such* a pleasure to tell him that I loved it well,—to see the approving smile, the sudden lighting of those earnest eyes! In comparing P[ennsylvani]a and N[ew] E[ngland] he spoke of the superior richness of the soil of the former, but said that here, though there were fewer and smaller farms, larger crops were raised on the same extent of ground, because vastly more labor and pains were bestowed upon its cultivation. Then I remembered that the poet was also a *farmer.* By some strange transition we got from *agriculture* to *spiritualism.* Whittier said that he too (having read them) thought that Prof. F[elton's] views were most uncharitable. Though *he* cannot believe in it; he thinks it wrong and unjust to condemn all interested in it.—The transition from this subject to that of the "future life" was easy. I shall never forget how earnestly, how beautifully the poet expressed his *perfect faith,* that faith so evident in his writings, in his holy and consistent life.—

At his request I took him to see Miss S[hepard]. The joy and surprise were almost more than she could bear. I stayed but a little while, then left them together. The poet gave me a cordial invitation to visit him and his sister at their home. God bless him! This is a day to be marked with a white stone . . . . (pp. 93-4)

Monday, Aug. 17 [1857]—My twentieth birthday.— Very, very fast the years are passing away,—and I,—Ah! how little am I improving them. I thought so to-day after I had finished "Jane Eyre," which has so powerful-

ly interested and excited me. The excitement was not a healthy one, I know—and reason told me I *ought* to have been better employed.—But we have so much company now that it is impossible to accomplish anything.—This afternoon was regularly bored, victimized by two dull people.—I do wish they would leave us to the enjoyment of our own family circle, which is such a pleasant one now.—Twenty years! I have lived. I shall *not* live twenty years more,—I feel it. I believe I have but a few years to live.—Them I *must,* I *will* improve.— I will pray for strength to keep *this* resolution;—I have broken so many. *This* I *must* keep . . . .

Thursday, Aug 20. . . . Went to see Miss S[hepard], and had a long talk with her about her noble Whittier. He has been pleased to speak most approvingly of my poor attempts at letter writing. I thank him, with all my heart. Miss S[hepard], with her usual great kindness, has made several plans for our mutual enjoyment, during vacation . . . . (p. 94)

Friday, Sept. 4. Very hot morning . . . . I have been examining myself, to-night,—trying to fathom my own thoughts and feelings; and I find, alas! too much, too much of *selfishness!* And yet I know that, in this world of care and sorrow, however weary and sad the heart may be, true *unselfishness* must ever be a source of the purest and highest happiness. Every kindly word, every gentle and generous deed we bestow upon others,—every ray of sunshine which penetrates the darkness of another's life, through the opening which *our* hands have made, *must* give to us a truer, nobler pleasure than any self-indulgence can impart. Knowing this, feeling it with my whole heart,—I ask thee, Oh! Heavenly Father! to make me truly *unselfish,* to give to me a heart-felt interest in the welfare of others;—a spirit willing to sacrifice *my own;—to* live "*for the good* that I can do!" . . . (p. 95)

Tuesday, June 15 [1858]. Have been under-going a thorough self-examination. The result is a mingled feeling of sorrow, shame and self-contempt. Have realized more deeply and bitterly than ever in my life my own ignorance and folly. Not only am I without the gifts of Nature,—wit, beauty and talent; without the accomplishments which nearly every one of my age, whom I know, possesses; but I am not even *intelligent.* And for *this* there is not the *shadow* of an excuse. Have had many advantages of late years; and it is entirely owning to my own want of energy, perseverance and application, that I have not improved them. It grieves me deeply to think of this. I have read an immense quantity, and it has all amounted to nothing,—because I have been too indolent and foolish to take the trouble of *reflecting.* Have wasted more time than I dare think of, in idle day-dreams, one of which was, how much I should *know* and *do* before I was twenty-one. And here I am nearly twenty-one, and only a *wasted life* to look back upon.—Add to intellectual defects a disposition whose despondency and fretfulness have constantly led me to look on the dark side of things, and effectually prevented me from contributing to the happiness of others; whose contrariness has often induced me to "do those things which I ought *not* to have done, and to leave undone those which I *ought* to have done," and *wanted* to do,—and we have as dismal a picture as one could look upon; and yet hardly dismal enough to be faithful. Of course, I want to *try* to reform. But how to begin! Havn't the least spark of order or method in my composition, and fear I'm wholly incapable of forming any regular plan of improvement. Wish I had some of the superabundant energy and perseverance which some whom I know possess, just to enable me to *keep* the good resolutions which are so easily made and so very easily broken.... (p. 106)

Tuesday, Aug. 17 [1858]. My birthday. Twenty-one to-day! It grieves me to think of it;—to think that I have wasted so many years. I dare not dare not dwell upon the thought! Saw to-day a book of leaves from Rome, and all the "hallowed shrines" of Italy. They were beautiful; and ah what a passionate longing—as ever—did such names as the Coliseum, The Forum, the Tomb of Juliet, Venice, St. Peter's, Florence, awake in this too restless,—eager soul of mine. Sacred, sacred spots! Scared to genius and beauty and deathless fame, ah little did I think, years ago, that twenty-one summers should pass over me without my realizing the cherished all-absorbing dream of my heart—the dream of beholding ye! And now when all hope of such happiness should have flown, the dream still lingers on. Foolish, foolish girl! When will you be strong and sensible!

I suppose I *ought* to rejoice to-day for all the city seems to be rejoicing. The Queen's message arrived safely through the wonderful submarine telegraph, the bells are pealing forth merrily. But *I cannot* rejoice that England, my beloved England should be brought so very near this wicked land. I tremble for the consequences, but I will *hope* for the best. Thank God for Hope!... (pp. 107-08)

Monday, Nov. 15 [1858]. A gloomy, chilly, and, to me, most depressing day. We have our first snow. It is an earnest of Winter, which I dread more than I have words to express. I am *sick* today, sick, sick, at heart;—and though I had *almost* resolved to forbear committing sad thoughts and gloomy feelings to my pages, dear Journal, and have very rarely done so, yet, to-night I long for a confidant—and *thou* art my only one. In the twilight—I sat by the fire and watched the bright, usually so cheering blaze. But it cheered me not. Thoughts of the past came thronging upon me;—thoughts of the loved faces on which I used to look so fondly;—of the loved voices which were music to my ear, and ever sent a thrill of joy to my heart—voices now silent forever. I am *lonely* to-night. I long for one earnest sympathizing soul to be in close communion with my own. I long for the pressure of a loving hand in mine, the touch of loving lips upon my aching brow. I long to lay my weary head upon an earnest heart, which beats for me,—to which *I* am dearer far than all the world beside. There is none, for me, and never will be. I could only love one whom I could look up to, and reverence, and that *one* would never think of such a poor little ignoramus as I. But what a selfish creature I am. This is a forlorn old maid's

reverie, and yet I am only twenty-one. But I am weary of life, and would gladly lay me down the rest in the quiet grave. There, alone, is peace, peace!... (p. 109)

Salem, Jan. 1, 1860. Can it be possible that so many months have elapsed since my pen last touched thy pages, old friend! Carelessly enough we say "time flies." Do we, after all, realize *how* it flies? How the months, days and hours *rush* along, bearing us on—on upon their swift, unwearying wings! To me there is something deeply impressive in this strange flight of Time. Standing now upon the threshold of another year, how solemn, how strangely solemn seem the Past and the Future; the *dead* and *newly born* year;—memories, gladdening and sorrowing of the one, eager hopes, desires, resolves for the other;—how they crowd upon us now! Do they avail aught? I ask myself. Alas! too often, I fear they do not. Too often past experiences, and high resolves for the Future; are forgotten swallowed up in the excitement of the Present moment. Have been reading to-day Arnold's History of Rome. How it thrills one to know of those heroic deeds done "in the brave days of old." And how blessed it is that all the wealth of the ages can be ours, if we choose to grasp it! That we can live, not in this century, this corner of the world, alone, but in every century, and every age, and every clime! That we can listen to the words of orators, poets and sages; that we can enter into every conflict, share every joy, thrill with every noble deed, known since the world began. And hence are *books* to us a treasure and a blessing unspeakable. And they are doubly this when one is shut out from society as I am, and has not opportunities of studying those living, breathing, *human* books, which are, I doubt not, after all, the most profoundly interesting and useful study. From that kind of pleasure, that kind of improvement I am barred; but, thank God! none can deprive me of the other kind. And I will strive to be resigned during the little while we have to stay here.—and in that higher sphere do I not *know* the cruelty the injustice of man ceases? There do Right, and Justice and Love abide. (pp. 113-14)

Charlotte L. Forten, in her The Journal of Charlotte L. Forten, *edited by Ray Allen Billington, The Dryden Press, Publishers, 1953, 248 p.*

Ray Allen Billington (essay date 1953)

[*Billington was an American historian and editor. In the following excerpt from his introduction to* The Journal of Charlotte L. Forten, *he discusses Forten's personal aspirations as they are revealed in her journal and comments on her opinions concerning race relations in America.*]

Charlotte L. Forten was a delicate young woman of sixteen when in 1854 she left her native Philadelphia to launch the educational and teaching career described in the... *Journal.* Her interests were those of other intelligent girls reared in that calm Quaker city during its antebellum days; she read widely and with a catholic taste that embraced everything from the classics to sentimental poetry, attended lectures avidly, listened rapturously to the musical recitals of wandering artists, gazed worshipfully on the steel engravings that passed for art among unsophisticated Americans, and took mild pleasure in the ailments that were the stock in trade of all well-bred females during the Victorian era. Yet one thing distinguished Charlotte Forten from other Philadelphia belles. She was a Negro, destined to endure the constant insults that were the lot of persons of color in pre-Civil-War America.

That no other influence was so strong in shaping Charlotte Forten's thoughts is amply revealed in the *Journal* . . . . When she began keeping that record, on a warm May morning in 1854, she had just arrived in Salem, Massachusetts, from Philadelphia . . . . [As] the pages of her *Journal* disclose, she was destined to long periods when "lung fever" forced her to forsake her studies and teaching. But on that May morning illness was furthest from her thoughts. Ahead lay the adventure of learning, and that was exciting enough to justify the diary she was beginning.

Miss Forten could not know, as she traced the opening words in a fine, bold hand, that she was starting a uniquely human document. Nor did her first entry reveal the unusual nature of the entries to follow: "A wish to record the passing events of my life, which, even if quite unimportant to others, naturally possess great interest to myself, and of which it will be pleasant to have some remembrance, has induced me to commence this journal." This, even in its stilted phrases, might have launched any one of the thousands of diaries kept by young women of that era. Yet the *Journal* that unfolded during the next decade bore no resemblance to any other. Instead it served as a moving record of the reactions of a sensitive young Negro to the white world about her.

For her race was always uppermost in Charlotte Forten's thoughts. The color of her skin determined her attitude toward her fellow humans, toward her country, and toward her God. From the accident of pigmentation stemmed even her driving ambition. She *must* excel among the students of the Salem grammar school in which she first enrolled or the normal school where she completed her education. She *must* read constantly; tucked among the pages of her manuscript *Journal* was a yellowed paper listing more than one hundred books completed in one year. She *must* master French, German, and Latin in addition to her regular school work. Every lesson learned well was a triumph not only for herself but for the oppressed Negro people of mid-century America. By excelling in all things she could help convince a hostile world that Negroes were as capable of self-improvement as whites.

That this was the source of her ambition was abundantly revealed in Miss Forten's *Journal.* "Would that there were far more intelligent colored people!", she wrote at one time. "And yet we could hardly expect more of those, who have so many unsurmountable difficulties to contend with. But despite them all let our motto still be 'Excelsior' and we cannot fail to make some improvement. At times I feel it almost impossible not to despond entirely of there ever being a better, brighter day for us. None but those who experience it can know what it is—this constant, galling sense of cruel injustice and wrong. I cannot help feeling it very often,—it intrudes upon my happiest moments, and spreads a dark, deep gloom over everything." Miss Forten was plunged into equal despair whenever a Negro failed to excel in competition with whites. (pp. 1-2)

Every page of Charlotte Forten's *Journal* reflected her determination to excel in all things. She was vexed, on the morning she began her diary, that the sun had risen before her, even though she had awakened before five o'clock. A few months later, as she looked back over her first seventeen years on the occasion of a birthday, she asked herself: "Have I improved them as I should have done?" Overcritical as always, she felt that she had not. "I feel grieved and ashamed to think how very little I know to what I should know of what is really good and useful. May this knowledge of my *want* of knowledge be to me a fresh incentive to more earnest, thoughtful action, more persevering study." Little wonder, in view of this attitude, that progress seemed alarmingly slow. Charlotte Forten might impress others with the catholicity of her literary tastes or with her rich knowledge of the past, but she was always more conscious of the tasks remaining than of those accomplished. (p. 3)

If ambition was one of Miss Forten's virtues, modesty was another. "When I read of the great and gifted ones of the earth," she confided in her *Journal,* "I feel more deeply my own ignorance and inefficiency.—How very little after the most diligent and persevering study can I hope to resemble them." Later triumphs did not decrease her humility. Thus she could not believe that her poetic efforts were worthy of the name, despite the publication of her verses in magazines and newspapers. "How often," she complained, "have I invoked in vain the 'spirit of song'; the muse is always most unyielding, despite my assurances, that should she deign to bless me, my first offering would be upon the shrine of Liberty." Even her friendships were marred by the fear that her presence was distasteful to others. Once, on leaving Salem briefly, she said her good-bys to a favorite teacher who "gently reproved me when we were parting, for not returning her embrace. I fear she thought me cold, but it was not so. I know not why it is that when I think and feel the most, I say the least, I suppose it is my nature, not to express by word or action how much I really feel."

Charlotte Forten's conflicts—between modesty and talent, ambition and apparent lack of realization, affection and shyness—all stemmed from her constant awareness that she was a Negro. A product of generations of discrimination, she could never hope to establish bonds of perfect friendship with whites, no matter how unprejudiced those whites might be. Between the two races, in

Charlotte Forten—seated and holding the open book—with her husband and three prominent women of the Washington, D.C., intellectual world.

that day of slavery, was a barrier that neither could completely remove. (pp. 3-4)

This racial consciousness endows Miss Forten's *Journal* with an importance in the twentieth century that it scarcely enjoyed in the nineteenth. Enlightened individuals today have dedicated themselves to a crusade for equality and human decency. Yet how few among them—how few among the nonpersecuted, that is—can know the effect of prejudice on its victims. Miss Forten's *Journal* makes this effect terrifyingly clear. Whenever she was barred from the railroad cars or an "ice cream saloon" or a museum or a school because of the color of her skin she returned home, sick at heart, to pour out her resentment on the pages of her diary. No believer in the golden rule can read that record today without reawakening to the need for decency among men. (p. 4)

Try as she did to counsel patience to the oppressed, Charlotte Forten found the practice more difficult than the preaching—and little wonder. Each new insult drove her to more outspoken rebellion. In the end prejudice drove this sensitive girl, who was an ardent patriot and a zealous Christian, to the point where she could denounce her country and almost deny her God.

That she should denounce the United States for sanctioning the institution of slavery was almost inevitable. Every Fourth of July celebration allowed her to contrast, in her *Journal,* the boast of liberty made by orators with the grim reality of the slave system. "The *patriots,* poor fools, were celebrating the anniversary of their vaunted *independence,*" she wrote on one occasion. "Strange! that they cannot feel their *own* degradation—the weight of the chains which they have imposed upon *themselves.*" . . .

To Miss Forten life in England seemed vastly preferable to life in a land where her countrymen were held in bondage. "Oh! England," she confided in her *Journal,* "my heart yearns towards thee as to a loved and loving friend! I long to behold thee, to dwell in one of thy quiet homes, far from the scenes of my early childhood; far from the land, my native land—where I am hated and

oppressed because God has given me a *dark skin.*" ...
(p. 5)

The hatred of discrimination that drove Charlotte Forten to the point where she denied her national heritage almost forced her, on one gloomy day, to renounce her God. "Hatred of oppression," she confessed, "seems to me so blended with hatred of the oppressor that I cannot separate them. I feel that no other injury could be so hard to bear, so very hard to forgive, as that inflicted by cruel oppression and prejudice. How *can* I be a Christian when so many in common with myself, for no crime suffer so cruelly, so unjustly? It seems in vain to try, even to hope."

That the racial question should constantly intrude on Charlotte Forten's consciousness as she wrote her *Journal* was not surprising; for sixteen years she had been regularly reminded that her dark skin doomed her to an inferior social station. When she was still a child, she and her parents had been barred from stores and denied service in restaurants. They had been forced to sit in segregated sections of omnibuses and railroad cars. They had been turned away from lectures and theaters. They had heard thoughtless white men refer to them as "niggers" without even realizing the insulting sting of that word. From behind drawn curtains in her grandfather's spacious Philadelphia home on Lombard Street the youthful Charlotte had watched terror-stricken as runaway slaves were hounded by mobs or returned in shackles to their masters. The continual recurrence of these incidents was enough to convince any young women of sensitivity that nothing else in the world was so important as the battle against prejudice.

The environment in which she lived was not the only factor that led Miss Forten to dedicate her life to the cause of decency. Equally influential was her immediate background. From the time that she lisped her first words she heard talk of Negro rights about the family table; from the time she could first comprehend she listened to abolitionists as they plotted freedom for the slaves while gathered in the Forten living room. Reared in an atmosphere of crusading zeal, she was predestined to play a minor yet significant role in the contest that ended with Abraham Lincoln's Emancipation Proclamation. Most influential among those who turned her youthful mind in that direction was her grandfather, James Forten. A man of wealth, idealism, and determination, he cast his shadow over the two generations of Fortens who followed in his footsteps. (pp. 5-6)

For a generation the Fortens' Philadelphia home was a mecca for abolitionists. So warm was their hospitality and so persuasive their charm that the great poet of abolitionism, John Greenleaf Whittier, immortalized them in a poem, "To the Daughters of James Forten" .... (p. 13)

Little wonder that when Miss Forten was ready to launch her own career she was so steeped in the cause that the plight of the slave transcended all other interests in her life. (p. 15)

Having decided on a career as a teacher, Miss Forten enrolled in the Salem Normal School, from which she was graduated, in the language of the *Salem Register,* "with decided éclat" in July, 1856. Through the intercession of the principal of the normal school, Richard Edwards, and with the hearty support of her grammar-school teachers, she immediately became a teacher in the Epes Grammar School of Salem. Despite the prejudice that existed among the less enlightened townsmen, her appointment was accepted by both school board and pupils without even a flurry of excitement, and Miss Forten soon found herself immersed in the routine of classes, lecture-going, and study that was the lot of village teachers a century ago.

The next two years were among the happiest in Charlotte Forten's life. Although she never enjoyed teaching, Salem offered plentiful opportunity for her to pursue her real interests: abolitionism and learning. (pp. 17-18)

From the time her **"Parting Hymn"** was acclaimed at [her] grammar-school graduation [Miss Forten] produced a succession of sentimental poems and essays which ranged from a hymn sung at the semiannual normal-school examination in 1856 through such poetic effusions as **"The Two Voices," "The Wind Among the Poplars," "The Angel's Visit,"** and **"The Slave-Girl's Prayer."** Perhaps her literary style was best portrayed in an essay, **"Glimpses of New England,"** which was published in the *National Anti-Slavery Standard:*

> The beach, which is at some distance from the town, is delightful. It was here that I first saw the sea, and stood 'entranced in silent awe,' gazing upon the waves as they marched, in one mass of the richest green, to the shore, then suddenly broke into foam, white and beautiful as the winter snow. I remember one pleasant afternoon which I spent with a friend, gathering shells and seaweed on the beach, or sitting on the rocks, listening to the wild music of the waves, and watching the clouds of spray as they sprang high up in the air, then fell again in snowy wreaths at our feet. We lingered there until the sun had sunk into his ocean bed ....

Perhaps wishful thinking occasioned a contemporary to remark that her writing, "for style and true poetical diction, is not surpassed by anything in the English language." (p. 18)

Charlotte Forten, bearing a letter from John Greenleaf Whittier, went before the Boston Educational Commission in August, 1862, asking to be sent to Port Royal as a teacher ....

Miss Forten found much to interest her when she reached her new home on St. Helena Island. She was fascinated by the tropical vegetation, the warm winter days, and the great plantation houses. She was entranced by the children who flocked to her school. She was captivated by the older Negroes and never tired of recording their quaint speech or their religious songs. But most of all she was intrigued with the social experiment that had brought her to Port Royal. She and her fellow teachers were destined to prove that Negroes were as capable of self-improvement as whites! Here was a cause worth any sacrifice, when the future of a whole race depended on the outcome. Little wonder that no other subject was treated in such detail in the pages of her *Journal*.

The experiment was just being launched when Charlotte Forten arrived at Port Royal. The teachers and officials hoped to demonstrate two things. One was the ability of the former slaves to learn; Miss Forten and her fellow workers labored mightily to instruct their charges in the three R's and exhibited unrestrained delight whenever success crowned their efforts. The other was the bravery of the Negro men; General Saxton wanted to show that they fought as fearlessly as their white-skinned brethren. Miss Forten was as interested in the Negro troops as she was in the youngsters who crowded her schoolroom. Intimately acquainted with both the soldiers and their officers, she recorded their experiences with an enthusiasm that she had formerly reserved for abolition meetings. (p. 25)

The Negro troops did not have to wait long before showing their mettle, for during the summer of 1863 the long-awaited attack on Charleston plunged them into one of the war's bloodiest battles. (p. 26)

Charlotte Forten witnessed these stirring events from the comparative safety of Port Royal. She cheered the Negro troops as they sallied out to raid the enemy coast, rejoiced when they returned triumphant, and tearfully recorded the loss of their dead. She thrilled as the fleet sailed away to attack Charleston, suffered while awaiting news of the assault, and mourned when she learned that the Fifty-Fourth Massachusetts Regiment had been cut to pieces and its brave leader, Colonel Shaw, had been killed. Yet Miss Forten never forgot the principal task before her. Even in the midst of battle she found time to care for her school, initiate former slaves into the mysteries of reading and writing, and comfort the Negro troops stationed at Port Royal. Her only reward was the knowledge that the social experiment was successful. Dispatches indicated that more and more freedman were buying land on the Sea Islands, that two thousand children were enrolled in schools, that thousands of adults were receiving instruction in the churches before the Sunday-morning services. Charlotte Forten could return north in May, 1864, knowing that Negroes were as capable of progress as whites. (pp. 28-9)

Ray Allen Billington, in an introduction to The Journal of Charlotte L. Forten, *The Dryden Press, Publishers, 1953, pp. 1-32.*

Joanne M. Braxton (essay date 1988)

[*In the following excerpt, Braxton surveys Forten's life and works.*]

Charlotte Forten Grimké (1837-1914), turn-of-the-century black woman poet, scholar, teacher and translator, is remembered chiefly for a version of four of her five manuscript diaries edited by Ray Allen Billington and published as *The Journal of Charlotte L. Forten, 1854-1862.* As a young black woman poet reading the *Journal* in the early 1970s, I was put off by the diarist's romantic language, as well as her class pretensions, and I resisted all identification with her.

Years later, when I read Anna Julia Cooper's typed transcriptions of all five diaries, I began to see their nature as a series of interrelated texts sustaining progression and development. Restoring Billington's editorial omissions presented a more rounded view of Charlotte Forten's day-to-day life, beyond her commentary on matters of political and historical significance; I began to view the published edition of the diaries as a mutilated text. Yet even when I read the typed copy with omissions restored, Forten seemed aloof and distant; she refused to speak with me.

In the hope of improving my relationship with the subject of my interest, I began to read what Forten read. Shakespeare, Blake, Keats, Wordsworth, Lydia Maria Child, Emerson, the Brownings, and the Brontës. And I read what she wrote: her **"Life on the Sea Islands,"** her **"Personal Recollections of Whittier,"** the dozen or so poems published during her lifetime, and *Madame Therese, or the Volunteers of '92,* a novel by Emilie Erckmann and Alexander Chartrian, which Forten translated from the French for Scribners.

When I returned to the Moorland-Spingarn Research Center at Howard University to read the original handwritten manuscript diaries for possible omissions, Charlotte began to smile on me. And when I held the slender, leather-bound volumes, each covered with a graceful marble paper, and when I read the delicate, faded black ink handwriting, I could feel the tension of pen against paper, and I could hear a voice. It was, unmistakably, the voice of a poet, struggling to be heard—the voice of Charlotte Forten.

Forten's first and second diaries cover the periods from 24 May 1854 to 31 December 1856 and from 1 January 1857 to 27 January 1858. These diaries, which Forten kept between the ages of seventeen and twenty-one, describe her life as a schoolgirl in Salem, Massachusetts, as a young abolitionist, and as an aspiring poet and writer. The third and fourth diaries cover the span from January 1858 to February 1863 and from February 1863 to May 1864, respectively. In these Forten records her continuing personal development and her participation in the historic "Port Royal Experiment" on the South Carolina Sea Islands during the Civil War. Forten began her fifth diary in November 1885 and made her final entry in July 1892, twenty-two years before her death in 1914. The final diary, which remains unpublished, presents a view of Forten's thirty-five-year marriage to the Reverend Francis J. Grimké, a distinguished black Presbyterian minister, who was also the nephew of white feminist abolitionists Sarah and Angelina Grimké Weld, the son of their brother and a slave woman, Nancy Weston.

Forten's five manuscript diaries show an intelligent black and female cultural sensibility struggling to balance political, intellectual, and emotional conflicts and to forge a public voice. Although Forten intended her diaries as a private record, her private autobiographical act relates to the development of a public voice in the move to objectify and take control of experience through the writer's craft; in the pages of her diaries, she gains distance between herself as subject and as object. This essay examines Forten's use of the diary as a tool for the development of her political and artistic consciousness and as a means of self-evaluation; for Forten, the diaries also represent a retreat from potentially shattering encounters with racism and a vehicle for the development of a black and female poetic identity, a place of restoration and self-healing.

The product of an environment that was both abolitionist and feminist in nature, Charlotte Forten grew up in the Philadelphia home of her paternal grandfather, James Forten, a wealthy and respected free black who advocated abolition and women's rights. In 1837, the year Charlotte was born, her aunts Sarah and Margaretta Forten, both active in the Philadelphia Female Anti-Slavery Society, organized a national convention of black women abolitionists.

The Fortens were cultured and well-educated, yet, like other free blacks in the "city of brotherly love," they found themselves excluded from museums, stores, ice-cream parlors, and restaurants. Predictably, the Fortens chose a private tutor over a segregated public school education for Charlotte. Stifled by years of living primarily in her grandfather's house and by being shut out from much of the typical social routine in which other girls participated, Charlotte Forten grew into an intensely introspective adolescent, continually examining and reexamining her intellectual and literary development. Thus she grew up separated from the dominant culture by race, and from much of the black community by economic and educational privilege, or by class and culture.

In 1854, Robert Bridges Forten responded to his daughter's developing isolation by sending her to the Higginson Grammar School in Salem, Massachusetts, where she lived with Charles Lenox Remond family. Significantly, Forten began her first diary with the advent of her stay in Salem, marking the initial separation from her home and Philadelphia.

But even in "free" Massachusetts, Forten felt the sting of white racism:

> I wonder that every colored person is not a misanthrope. Surely, we have everything to make us hate mankind. I have met girls in the classroom—they have been thoroughly kind and cordial to me,—perhaps the next day met them in the street—they feared to recognize me; these I can but regard now with scorn and contempt. (12 Sept. 1854)

When encounters such as these threatened her sense of self, Forten sought refuge in the pages of her diary, looking back on the incidents from her own perspective and laying claim to her experience in the language of her private diary. Here, Forten confronted the dominant white culture in small, homeopathic doses, analyzing and gaining psychological distance. On 17 July 1854, Forten entered: "I am hated and oppressed because God gave me a *dark skin*. How did this cruel, this absurd prejudice ever come to exist? When I think of it, a feeling of indignation rises in my soul too deep for utterance." For Charlotte Forten, the diary became a private (and therefore defensible) "territory" of the mind and a retreat from the racism and sexism of the dominant culture.

Forten's first and second diaries also demonstrate her quest for literary models. In Salem, she read voraciously and attended an impressive number of readings, lectures, and antislavery fairs. Caught in the 1850s surge of politics and romanticism, she found Hawthorne's Gothic tales "thrilling" and enjoyed walks by the sea and in the moonlight. On Christmas Day 1858, she came away from Ralph Waldo Emerson's lecture "On Beauty" feeling "much pleased" (25 Dec. 1858, diary 3). Quaker poet John Greenleaf Whittier, a special friend, sought Forten out for nature walks and for talks on farming and spiritual development.

Among Forten's favorite writers were Blake, Keats, Wordsworth, Emerson, the Brontës, and Lydia Maria Child. Forten apparently accepted Child's promotion of "a love of reading as an unspeakable blessing for the American female." Engaged in the quest for literacy and self-respect, Forten found books a means of knowing a world from which she felt excluded, a route to transcendence of her perceived cultural isolation:

> And hence are *books* to us a treasure and a blessing unspeakable. And they are doubly this when one is shut out of society as I am, and has not opportunities of studying those living, breathing, *human* books, which are, I doubt not, after all, the most profoundly interesting and useful study. (1 Jan. 1860, diary 3)

Forten, as a young abolitionist in 1854, read and reread Elizabeth Barrett Browning's powerful feminist-abolitionist polemic, "The Fugitive Slave at Pilgrim's Point," as "most suitable to my feelings and the times." On 30 May 1854, she added this commentary to the diary: "How earnestly and touching does the writer portray the bitter anguish of the poor fugitive as she thinks over all the wrongs and sufferings that she has endured, and of the sin the tyrants have driven her but which they alone must answer for!" (diary 1). Hence, the young black writer identified both with the literary sensibility of the white author of the poem and with the feminine heroism of its narrator, an outraged mother who rebels against her rapist master by murdering the child she has borne him.

Naturally, Forten's heroes and heroines included the fugitive slaves whose experiences were beginning to come to light, not only through polemical poetry and fiction, but through first-hand narratives and the camera. One entry in her second diary describes her reactions on being shown:

> a daguerreotype of a young slave girl who escaped in a box .... My heart was full as I gazed at it; full of admiration for the heroic girl, who risked all for freedom; full of bitter indignation that in this boasted land of liberty such a thing *could occur*. Were she of any other nation her heroism would receive all due honor from these Americans, *but as it is,* there is not even a single spot in this broad land, where her rights can be protected,—not one. (5 July 1857, diary 2)

Perhaps there is a sense in which the girl in the box can be viewed as a metaphor for Forten's own experience of separateness from and of isolation within the dominant culture, for although she herself was free, Forten recognized the interrelatedness of her oppression with the bondage of the slave woman.

Determined to live a full and expansive life, to *live out herself*, Forten responds to a feeling of restlessness which portends the rise of modernism in black women's writing. "I wonder," she wrote in her third manuscript diary on 2 January 1858, "why it is that I have this strange feeling of not *living out myself*. My existence seems not nearly full or expansive enough—This longing for—something, I know not what?" What Forten seeks, without her conscious knowledge, is, in the words of critic Margaret Homans, [in her *Women Writers and Poetic Identity* (1979)], "a return to her proper origins," the place where her identity (and her own subjective voice) reside.

Like other black women writing autobiography in nineteenth-century America, Forten discusses family, society, her profession, and her duty to her race; she also writes of her longing for an image of her deceased mother. "How I love to hear of her," Forten wrote. "What a pleasure it would be if I had an image of her, my own dear mother!" (15 Apr. 1858, diary 2). Lacking such a portrait, Forten set out to paint her own, and she would create her images with words.

Forten's poetry, noted for "its quiet simplicity and controlled tension," might well qualify her as "literary lady." Although she never published more than a handful of poems, some of these received critical acclaim. Praising Forten's **"The Angel's Visit"** (1860), William Wells Brown wrote [in *The Rising Sun; or, The Antecedents and Advancements of the Colored Race* (1874)]: "For style and poetic diction, it is not surpassed by anything in the English language (475). "Were she white," Brown commented, "America would recognize her as one of its brightest gems" [see Further Reading]. Although minor in the dominant tradition, Forten's poetry possesses rich descriptive imagery, intense lyricism, and sheer dramatic power.

Given the choice of a public voice and a private one, Forten, in a different time and in a culture where she did not bear the dual stigma of race and gender difference, might have blossomed as a poet. In Forten's third and fourth diaries, she gains the desired distance between self as subject and object, making a clearer distinction between the public and the private voice. During these years, Forten published more actively than at any other period, placing **"Two Voices"** (1858), **"The Wind among the Poplars,"** **"The Slave Girl's Prayer,"** and **"The Angel's Visit"** (all ca. 1860) in the *National Anti-Slavery Standard* and *The Liberator*. In **"The Angel's Visit,"** the poet's angel-mother/muse returns to plant the kiss of tradition and restore a childhood sense of wholeness threatened by the "cruel wrongs" which might destroy the motherless child who drifts from her roots:

> A sudden flood of rosy light
>   Filled all the dusky wood,
> And, clad in shining robes of white,
>   My angel mother stood.
>
> She gently drew me to her side,
>   She pressed her lips to mine,
> And softly said, "Grieve not, my child"
>   A mother's love is thine.
>
> I know the cruel wrongs that crush
>   The young and ardent heart;
> But falter not; keep bravely on,
>   And nobly bear thy part.

In this public creative act Forten, as the motherless speaker of the poem, claims the identity of both poet and daughter, still attempting to come to terms with the vocation of poethood as well as her experience of race and gender difference. In **"The Angel's Visit,"** the speaker of the poem recovers the "maternal origins" of her "feminine creativity" and creates a vehicle for the potential realization of her black and female poetic identity. That Charlotte Forten never realized her literary goals may be attributed, in part, to what Margaret Homans has called a pressure "to conform to certain ideas of ideal womanhood, none of which included a poet's vocation." To add that racial conflicts intensified Forten's confusion may be redundant, for as Claudia Tate has written [in *Black Women Writers at Work* (1983), "Nowhere in America is the social terrain more rugged than where a social minority and a 'weaker' gender intersect."

Providing a testing ground for the development of Forten's poetic identity and her public voice, diaries three and four also narrate her participation in the "Port Royal Experiment" during the Civil War. Forten's attraction to this experiment, designed to prove the fitness of former slaves for freedom, may be explained in part by her strong sense of duty to her race. Early in 1862, U.S. general Rufus Saxton, commander of the military district comprised of Port Royal and the South Carolina Sea Islands, wrote to the War Department to request instructors to teach former slaves. Forten answered the call immediately but was turned away, ostensibly because she was a woman.

Despite her disappointment, Forten showed her determination to go to Port Royal. Refused in Boston, she applied to the Philadelphia Port Royal Relief Association, where she was again discouraged because of the dangers facing a woman working in a war zone. However, John Greenleaf Whittier interceded in Forten's behalf, and on 27 May 1862 she sailed from New York aboard the steamship *United States* as an accredited agent of the Philadelphia Port Royal Relief Association (27 May 1862, diary 3).

In terms of her inner life, the experiment, viewed romantically as part of her duty to her race (and her transcendental or higher purpose), promised a partial solution to her predicament of isolation, a reconciling of intellect and a sense of Christian duty with the so-called cult of true womanhood. An inscription written in pencil inside the front cover of diary four confirms this interpretation. Speaking of her experience as a teacher at Port Royal, Forten comments: "This is what the women of this country need—healthful and not too fatiguing outdoor work in which are blended the usefulness and beauty I have never seen in women." Forten speaks of her labor as "healthful"; it might also be viewed as *health-building* in that it offered her opportunities to work for the sublime balance between usefulness and beauty.

Forten's diaries modify the impulse toward self-sufficiency with the Christian ideal of duty and service. On her twenty-fifth birthday, Forten made this reflective entry:

> The accomplishments, the society, the delights of travel which I have dreamed of and longed for all my life, I am now convinced can never be mine. If I can go to Port Royal, I will try to forget all these desires. I will pray that God in his goodness will make me noble enough to find my happiness in doing my duty. (17 Aug. 1862, diary 3)

Always something of a self-apologist, Forten makes use of the apology as a type of literary strategy, for she does not wish to appear presumptuous or self-serving. Moreover, doing one's Christian duty absolves a woman of the need to conform to the cult of true womanhood and opens up new avenues of identity.

Many entries in diaries three and four have a lyrical, poetic quality. Forten describes her romantic vision of the voyage to Port Royal in an entry written on white letter paper and headed by the title "At Sea—1862":

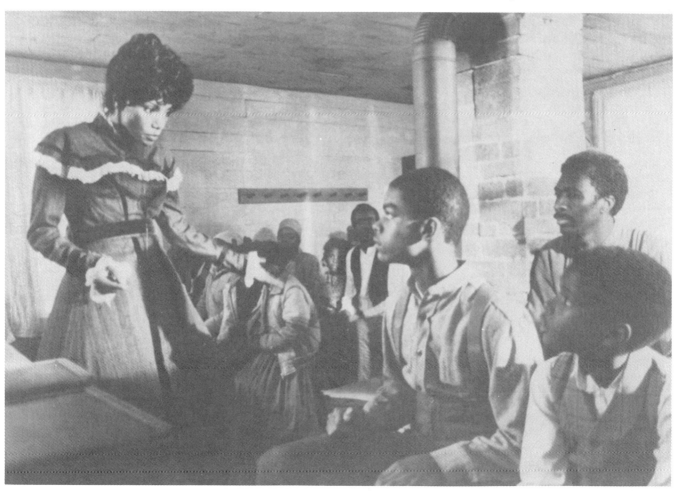

Melba Moore as Charlotte Forten in the 1985 American Playhouse production of "Charlotte Forten's Mission: Experiment in Freedom."

Oh, how beautiful those great waves were as they broke upon the sides of the vessel, into foam and spray, pure and white as new fallen snow. People talk of the monotony of the sea. I have not found it monotonous for a moment, since I have been well. To me there is "infinite variety," constant enjoyment about it.... One of the most beautiful sights I have yet seen is the phosphorescence in the water at night—the long line of light in the wake of the steamer, and the stars, and sometimes balls of fire that rise so magically out of the water. It is most strange and beautiful. (12 Oct. 1862)

Here, once again, the diary becomes a testing ground for the development of Forten's poetic identity, as she explores her experience in language.

Simultaneously, Forten continues her use of the diary as a tool of personal restoration and self-healing. An entry made on her arrival at Port Royal provides an example of this use. Here Forten "overheard" a conversation between two white Union officers, a conversation she judges deliberately calculated to disturb her: "The word 'nigger' was plentifully used, where upon set them down as *not* gentlemen. Then they talked a great deal about rebel attacks and yellow fever, and other alarming things. We saw through them at once" (28 Oct. 1862, diary 3). Maintaining an admirable detachment, Forten finds refuge in the pages of her diary, balancing her encounter with these racists with a lyrical description of the singing black boatmen who rowed her from St. Helena to Port Royal:

The row was delightful. It was just at sunset—a grand Southern sunset; and the glamorous clouds of crimson and gold were reflected in the waters below, which were as smooth and calm as a mirror. Then as we glided along, the rich sonorous tones of the boatmen broke upon the evening stillness. The singing impressed me very much. It was so sweet and strange and somber. (28 Oct. 1862, diary 3)

Transforming and transcending, Forten brings the values of romantic poetry to her text as she comments on the power of black spirituals to "lift [her] out of [her]self."

A parallel between the diarist's romantic mode of self-expression and the "transcendental present" of the slave spiritual emerges here, and Forten responds to both oral and literary traditions as she seeks her own voice: "The singing was very beautiful. I sat there in a kind of trance and listened to it, and while I listened looked through the open windows into the grove of oaks with their moss drapery. 'Ah w'ld that my tongue c'ld utter the thoughts that arise in me'" (2 Nov. 1862, diary 3). Yet, despite a sensitivity to black communication styles and the language of feeling, Forten remained an outsider. From the viewpoint of her own standard English voice, the lyrical orality of the slave spiritual was still foreign to the New England-educated diarist; she stood outside the veil of the black folk experience.

Although Forten generally reserved her diary entries as a record of the growth of her own mind, she did send an excerpt to John Greenleaf Whittier "for private perus-al." Whittier submitted **"Life on the Sea Islands"** to the *Atlantic Monthly,* where it was published in two segments in May and June 1864. The published article, subtly different from the form of the private journal entries, displays more thematic and topical development than the strictly chronological diaries. Likewise, this account shows more detailed analysis and seems more publicly autobiographical, giving focused attention to Forten's role as a teacher of former slaves. Significantly, she refers to her young scholars as "my children," seeking a public persona that would redeem her in the eyes of the "cult of true womanhood."

By the time Forten comes to the end of her fourth and final Port Royal diary, the entries have become less frequent; however, they display the thematic and topical development which distinguishes diary four from the earlier diaries. Thus diary four is more reflective and coherent and adheres more closely to the form of what has traditionally been called a journal than any of the earlier diary texts, where organization is strictly chronological and sometimes fragmentary. Oddly, diary four omits Forten's reaction to her father's death in April 1864. (James Forten died in Maryland, where he was recruiting black troops for the Union army.) Although the completion of the fourth diary coincides roughly with her father's death, Forten makes no comment about it—a very curious omission indeed. After her father's death, Forten returned to Philadelphia, where she remained for seven years before moving to Washington, D.C.

An interruption of twenty-two years ensues between the fourth and fifth diaries. During most of these years, Forten attempted to support herself as a writer of children's stories and as a translator of novels from the French and German. It was a point of honor with her to support herself solely by her own efforts—literary efforts. In these years, Whittier played an active role as Forten's mentor and protector, but her requests for help of various kinds eventually exhausted him. After one of Forten's continuing bouts with illness, Whittier wrote: "I am pained to hear of Charlotte Forten's illness. I wish the poor girl could be better situated—the wife of some good, true man who could appreciate her as she deserves."

In 1878 Forten married such a man. After moving to Washington, Forten taught for a year at the Summer School and after worked as a clerk in the U.S. Treasury Department; she also joined the Fifteenth Street Presbyterian Church and later married a pastor, the Rev. Francis James Grimké. Called the "black Puritan," Grimké upheld ideals of black womanhood as well as black manhood, exposing the sexual double standard of the South and attacking it in his sermons. As the son of a slave woman and her white master, he was well qualified to do so.

Despite the fact that Charlotte Forten was thirteen years older than her husband, the two were drawn together by the magnetism of like minds: both Francis Grimké and

Charlotte Forten were isolated by the tensions of race and intellect; both faced the "crisis of confidence" confronting ministers and literary women in mid-nineteenth-century America and as defined by Ann Douglas in *The Feminization of American Culture.* According to Douglas, both literary women and ministers shared a feminizing "impulse toward articulation and change," but they were "confined to the kitchen and the pulpit" and "forbidden to compete in the markets of the masculine world." In reaction, Douglas argues, these ministers and literary women often stressed illness "as a way . . . to dramatize their anxiety that their culture found them useless and wished them no good." They also used their illnesses "as a means of getting attention, of obtaining psychological and emotional power even while apparently acknowledging the biological correlatives of their social and political unimportance." Perhaps this parallel development explains, in part, Forten's life-long invalidism as well as the continual ill health of her beloved husband Francis; in this sense, Forten's experience reflects that of other literary women of nineteenth-century America who chose to marry ministers.

During the years of her marriage, Charlotte Forten continued to write poetry, but although her craft improved, her perspective changed substantially with age. Gone is the rebellion and conflict of the early poems, replaced by a tone of reflection and contemplation, as seen in her poem **"Wordsworth,"** stylistically reminiscent of that poet's "Prelude":

> In youth's fair dawn, when the soul, still untired,
> Longs for life's conflicts, and seeks restlessly
> Food for its cravings in the stirring songs,
> The thrilling strains of more impassioned bards;
> Or, eager for fresh joys, culls with delight
> The flowers that bloom in fancy's fair realm—
> We may not prize the mild and steadfast ray
> That streams from thy pure soul in tranquil song
> But, in our riper years, when through the heat
> And burden of the day we struggle on,
> Breasting the stream upon whose shores we
>   dreamed.

No longer the dreaming youth, the poet has entered "the riper years," "breasting the stream" of the dominant tradition, meeting, opposing, and balancing against it at the crest. She has grown, in her own words, "Weary of all the turmoil and the din / Which drowns the finer voices of the soul;" and weary of her struggle against the tide. Seeking now "the finer voices of the soul" she turns to the hierophant in his temple, speaking in a neutral voice but embracing symbolic polarities she avoided in her earlier poems.

> We turn to thee, true priest of Nature's fane,
> And find the rest our fainting spirits need,—
> The calm, more ardent singers cannot give;
> As in the glare intense of tropic days,
> Gladly we turn from the sun's radiant beams,
> And grateful hail fair Luna's tender light.

Associating the sun with the active "masculine" principle and the glaring heat of the struggle, the poet seeks a retreat into a "feminine" radiance symbolized by "fair Luna's tender light." Charlotte Forten retreated into the inner solaces of a marriage that would be, for her, a source of renewal and rejuvenation.

Together, the Grimkés braced each other, finding in their marriage a retreat from the anxieties of constant confrontation with the dominant culture. Here she found the balance, the communion she had achieved earlier only in the pages of her diary. Charlotte Forten found love, not the glaring love of subordination and domination that passes with the day, but a radiant, tender, and enduring one—a higher marriage.

Although Forten maintained diary five in a bound notebook of 140 pages, she apparently used only 43. Pages 44 to 100 are empty and unfortunately, pages 1 and 2 have been lost. Had they not been, they might have furnished insight into the reasons that Forten returned to keeping her diary. We may speculate that she found life with Mr. Grimké in "The High Ranks of Afro-America" to be another adventure, or that she may have been influenced by watching the reverend keep his own diary. On the other hand, it is possible that Forten returned to diary keeping to objectify her many personal losses and the separations from her husband occasioned by her ill health. Although the diary includes the years January 1885 to July 1892, there are fewer and fewer entries as Forten's health worsens. Most of the entries occur between 1885 and 1889. There are no entries for 1890 or 1891 and only one for 1892.

The fifth and final diary has a very different character from that of the first four. This diary represents the work of a mature woman who has become a chronic invalid, but one who has also found personal happiness in her marriage with Francis Grimké—a noble man who apparently possessed all of the gentleness and kindness of his slave mother and none of the faults of his white master/father. In this as yet unpublished diary, Forten writes of her 1885 move to Florida and her desire "to accomplish something" in "missionary labor" as well as to "direct church work . . . among the lower classes" (29 Nov. 1885). For although the Grimkés clearly saw themselves as part of a black elite, they must set an example.

Although the Grimkés held themselves a bit above many of the less fortunate in the small town in which they lived, they were warmly received into the new parish. One evening while they were still living at a boarding house, they were asked to come to church and were then escorted to their new home, provided by the congregation. The Grimkés found the cottage "beautifully lighted," with a "sitting room and bedroom very comfortably furnished . . . besides a handsome writing table for F's study, and a kitchen table, plates, and other useful articles." Their home, the classic "dog-trot" of southern architecture, had been built with "a hall through the center,—a style," Forten remarked, "I have always liked,—a study and a bedroom on one side, sitting room and kitchen on the other. Our pictures and books make the place very homelike" (15 Nov. 1885). But there was no study for Charlotte Forten, and no desk either.

The idealized view of her marriage that Forten presents in diary five may be justifiable, but the critic must ask why, as the wife of Francis Grimké, Forten never found fulfillment in her own work. Perhaps the answer lies in the restrictions placed on her as a minister's wife and in her reluctance to assume a public voice.

Greatest among the losses sustained by the Grimkés— including the deteriorating health of Whittier and the death of family members and other friends from the old abolitionist network—was the death of their only child, a daughter, Theodora Cornelia, who died less than a year after she was born. On 19 December 1885, Forten made this reflective entry:

> We have been married seven years today,—they would have been seven happy years had it not been for that one great sorrow! Oh my darling, what unspeakable happiness it would have been to have her with us to-day. She would be nearly six years old, our precious New Year's gift, how lovely and companionable I know she would have been. But I must not mourn. Father, it was Thy will. It *must* be for the best. I must wait.

Forten, already cut off from her primary link to black women's culture through the early death of her mother, was further separated from that tradition because the loss of her daughter denied her the possibility of acting out the role of mother. Her reflections centered on the idea that Theodora would have been "lovely and companionable," a creature balanced in beauty and intellect, another potential source of identity for the mother herself. When she writes "I must wait," Forten—already nearing the end of her biological generativity and still childless—probably does not mean that she must wait for another child. Rather, she must wait *on the Lord* for an understanding of the inherent ironies of her life. She continues to use her diary for restoration and self-healing, a tool for readjusting her psychic balance.

During the Grimkés's many separations, Charlotte's diary was still her best companion and possibly her only confidant. During the spring and summer of 1887, she found it necessary to go north "for her health," spending May in Washington and June and July at Newport. "Beautiful, beautiful Newport!" she wrote in July 1887. "In spite of illness I enjoy the sea and the rocks." "If my dear, dear F. were only here to share the happiness with me," she added. The next entry, dated October 1887, begins: "Back home with my dearest F. How glad I am to see him and find him well. I hope we shall not be separated again."

In several entries, Forten notes that she was "too unwell" to attend evening service. In fact, her illness prevented her from maintaining her diary with any regularity. "I having been able to write only at long intervals in my journal. My head and eyes are so bad that I can't use them much of the time" (October 1887). In April 1888 she suffered in the Florida heat, complaining of mosquitoes and fleas. "If one could only spend six months here, and the remainder of the year at the North! Sometimes I become dismayed at my almost continual ill health. It unfits me for work, and there is so much to be done here."

Although a physician examined Forten in Newport in July 1888, "he could find no organic disease,—only weakness." This diagnosis reminds us of Ann Douglas's discussion [in *The Feminization of American Culture* (1977)] of the "cultural uses of sickness for the nineteenth century minister and his lady." Certainly it could be argued that Forten, the invalid, used her ill health to dramatize her anxiety over a culture that found her useless (as the very appellation *invalid* implies). Francis Grimké was affected to a lesser degree; he developed a competent public voice in his highly articulate sermons. His wife, on the other hand, became more and more retiring, publishing less and less and making fewer entries in her diaries as her headaches increased and her vision dimmed.

There are few entries for 1889, the year Grimké resumed his ministry of the Fifteenth Street Presbyterian Church in Washington, and none for 1890 or 1891. In 1892 Forten made only one entry, in Lenox, Massachusetts, during the month of July. "The last three years have been full of work and of changes, but on the whole, happy ones," she wrote. "The greatest drawback has been constant ill health, which seemed to culminate this summer, and I was obliged to leave [W]ashington with its intense heat, sewer gas, and malaria, before it was time for Frank to. I was sorry to leave him, but hope he will join me next week." This entry, typical of those made by Forten during the years of her declining health, proved to be her last. She died of a cerebral embolism in Washington, D.C., on 23 July 1914, twenty-two years after her last entry.

On his wife's death, Francis Grimké wrote a testament of praise for the years of their marriage. "Not only my love for her, but my highest respect for her remained to the very last," he wrote shakily. "I have always felt that I was very fortunate in being thrown into such close and intimate company with so rare and beautiful a spirit." In thirty-five years of marriage, he wrote, he had never been able to detect anything "little, mean, contemptible, or unbecoming about her." He found his wife "an unusual woman, not only of great strength and character, but also sweet of temper, gentle, loving, full of the milk of human kindness."

Poet Angelina Weld Grimké, daughter of Francis Grimké's brother Archibald, remembered her "Aunt Lottie" with a poem entitled "To Keep the Memory of Charlotte Forten Grimké." The Grimké poem attempts to place Forten's "gentle spirit" in the stream of eternity:

Where has she gone? And who is to say?
But this we know: her gentle spirit moves
And is where beauty never wanes,
Perchance by other streams, mid other groves;
And to us here, ah! She remains
A lovely memory
Until eternity.
She came, she loved, and then she went away.
(*The Crisis,* 9 Jan. 1915)

Wherever she has gone, Charlotte Forten Grimké did not die without leaving her mark on a tradition of black women's writing. Her private autobiographical act portends the rise of literary forms less restrictive than most nineteenth-century narratives by black American women, and the diaries themselves offer untold insight into one black woman's search for a poetic identity and a public voice. In her own words:

Knowing this, toil we unwearied.
With true hearts and purpose high;—
We would win a wreath immortal.
Whose bright flowers ne'er fade and die.
(**"Poem,"** *The Liberator* 23 [24 August 1856])

(pp. 254-69)

Joanne M. Braxton, "Charlotte Forten Grimké and the Search for a Public Voice," in The Private Self: Theory and Practice of Women's Autobiographical Writings, *edited by Shari Benstock, The University of North Carolina Press, 1988, pp. 254 71.*

FURTHER READING

Barksdale, Richard, and Kinnamon, Keneth. Headnote to "Two Black Women Serve and Observe: From *Journal of Charlotte Forten.*" In *Black Writers of America: A Comprehensive Anthology,* edited by Richard Barksdale and Keneth Kinnamon, pp. 275-76. New York: Macmillan, 1972.
  Brief assessment of the literary and historical value of Forten's journal. The critics state: "[Forten's] style is lilting and her descriptive imagery at times quite effective. These effects, along with her candor, combine to make the *Journal* a remarkable piece of writing for a young Black girl who lived on the fringe of a slave culture."

Brown, William Wells. "Charlotte L. Forten." In his *The Black Man, His Antecedents, His Genius, and His Achievements,* pp. 190-99. 2d ed. New York: Thomas Hamilton, 1863.
  Brief biographical sketch. Brown, personal friend of Forten's and a fellow abolitionist, concludes: "Miss Forten is still young, yet on the sunny side of twenty-five, and has a splendid future before her. Those who know her best consider her on the road to fame. Were she white, America would recognize her as one of its brightest gems."

Cooper, Anna Julia. *Life and Writings of the Grimké Family.* 2 vols. Privately printed, 1951.
  Contains selections from Forten's writings, as well as biographical information.

Dannett, Sylvia G.L. "Charlotte L. Forten." In her *Profiles of Negro Womanhood,* Vol. 1, pp. 86-93. New York and Philadelphia: M. W. Lads, 1964.
  Brief biography, with excerpts from Forten's works.

Gaither, Frances. "The Will to Serve." *The New York Times Book Review* LVIII, No. 15 (12 April 1953): 6, 22.
  Reviews Ray Allen Billington's 1953 edition of Forten's journal, labeling the work "a valuable contribution to the most momentous chapter in American Negro history."

Longworth, Polly. *I, Charlotte Forten, Black and Free.* New York: Thomas Y. Crowell Company, 1970, 248 p.
  Re-creation of Forten's life and experiences, based upon *The Journal of Charlotte L. Forten.* Intended for young readers.

The Negro History Bulletin X, No. 4 (January 1947): 75, 79, 95.
  Historical information about the Forten, Grimké, and Purvis families. The article includes the poem "To Keep the Memory of Charlotte Forten Grimké," written by Forten's niece Angelina Grimké.

Sherman, Joan R. "Charlotte L. Forten Grimké." In her *Invisible Poets: Afro-Americans of the Nineteenth Century,* pp. 88-96. Urbana: University of Illinois Press, 1974.
  Studies Forten's prose and poetry, concluding that while Forten was not a great writer, her mature works show sensitivity and creativity.

Sumner-Lewis, Janice. "The Forten-Purvis Women of Philadelphia and the American Anti-Slavery Crusade." *The Journal of Negro History* LXVI, No. 4 (Winter 1981-82): 281-88.
  Documents the Forten-Purvis family's involvement with the Philadelphia Female Anti-Slavery Society and other abolitionist organizations from the 1830s to the 1860s.

Review of *The Journal of Charlotte L. Forten,* by Charlotte L. Forten. *The United States Quarterly Book Review* 9, No. 2 (June 1953): 113-14.
  Review of Ray Allen Billington's edition of *The Journal of Charlotte L. Forten.* The anonymous critic writes: "The full personal record of an intelligent and sensitive Negro girl, the journal is especially valuable because there are so few human documents of its kind. It shows Miss Forten's inmost thoughts about racial prejudice, her burning sense of injustice, and her never-ceasing concern for the betterment of her people."

Vaught, Bonny. "Trying to Make Things Real." In *Between Women: Biographers, Novelists, Critics, Teachers, and Artists Write about Their Work on Women,"* edited by Carol Ascher, Louise De Salvo, and Sara Ruddick, pp. 55-69. Boston: Beacon, 1984.
  Brief biography, with extensive commentary about how Forten's journal helped the critic better under-

stand what it was like to be a black woman in nineteenth-century America.

Wilson, Edmund. "Northerners in the South: Charlotte Forten and Colonel Higginson." In his *Patriotic Gore: Studies in the Literature of the American Civil War,* pp. 239-57. New York: Oxford University Press, 1962.

Account of the St. Helena Island experiment. Wilson briefly discusses Forten and her family background but gives a lengthy discussion of Colonel Thomas W. Higginson, Forten's friend and the leader of the regiment composed of former slaves from St. Helena Island.

Charles Fuller

1939-

(Full name Charles H. Fuller, Jr.) American dramatist, short story writer, and scriptwriter.

Fuller, an American playwright, is widely known for his 1982 Pulitzer Prize-winning drama *A Soldier's Play* (1981). His plays, which explore racism and discrimination, tackle social issues while striving to appeal to a wide audience. According to Esther Harriott in her *American Voices: Five Contemporary Playwrights in Essays and Interviews,* Fuller is "almost alone among contemporary American playwrights in focusing attention on social issues."

Born in Philadelphia, Fuller grew up comfortably amidst many foster children taken in by his parents, Charles H. Fuller, Sr. and Lillian Anderson Fuller. He became interested in literature when his father, a printer, let his son proofread his work. While at Roman Catholic High School in Philadelphia, Fuller and his friend Larry Neal, who himself became a dramatist and critic, vied to be the first to read every book in the library. But it was at a Yiddish theater that Fuller first became infatuated with drama. "It was fascinating!" he told Jean Ross in an interview. "Certainly I attribute my joy in theatre to that first experience—and I didn't understand a word of Yiddish!"

After attending Villanova University from 1956 to 1958, Fuller worked as an Army petroleum laboratory technician in Japan and Korea for four years. He is reticent about this army experience, preferring to reveal his views about military life in his plays. After his return to civilian life, he attended LaSalle College from 1965 to 1968 while continuing to write. Fuller generally accords little attention and praise to these early short stories and plays. Critics agree that he showed promise, however, in *The Village: A Party* (1968), a play in which a community of interracial couples murders its leader, who has fallen in love with a woman of his own race. This, his first professionally produced play, drew critical attention. With *The Brownsville Raid* (1976), however, commentators began to recognize Fuller's skill as a dramatist.

The Brownsville Raid is based on a 1906 shoot-up—by unknown assailants—in the town of Brownsville, Texas, that resulted in the dishonorable discharge of 167 soldiers from the all-black 25th Infantry stationed nearby. Fuller's documentary-like recounting of the incident generally garnered praise for its authenticity, and several critics applauded the play's conclusion, in which the names of the discharged soldiers and their respective fates are read in roll-call fashion. Fuller's *Zooman and the Sign* (1980) likewise drew acclaim, and the off-Broadway production won two Obie Awards. The play recounts a quest for justice after a young black

girl accidentally dies at the hands of Zooman, a black teenager. Because the girl's neighbors will not identify the killer, her family places a sign in their window reading: "The killers of our daughter Jinny are free because our neighbors will not identify them." The production of *Zooman* inspired Gerald Weales to write in *The Georgia Review* that Fuller is "an obviously talented playwright, ambitious in his attempt to deal with difficult and complex themes." Yet Weales agreed with other critics when he conceded that *Zooman* "never quite succeeds in the ambitious terms in which it is conceived...."

With his next production, *A Soldier's Play,* Fuller became the second black dramatist to win the Pulitzer Prize for drama since Charles Gordone received the honor in 1970. Herman Melville's *Billy Budd* influenced Fuller's story of the murder investigation of Technical Sergeant Vernon Waters, a martinet in charge of a unit of black soldiers stationed in Louisiana during World War II. Many critics believe Waters is Fuller's most interesting and complex character to date. A black non-commissioned officer decorated in World War I for his heroism, Waters is nevertheless discriminated against by fellow white officers. Yet Waters intentionally echoes Hitler when he suggests that C.J., an affable southern black soldier under his command, is a detriment to their race. When C.J. commits suicide, Waters undergoes a transformation, recognizing the futility of his efforts to fully integrate into society. Several critics believe the mystery of Waters' murder, discovered to be perpetrated by one of his black soldiers to avenge C.J.'s suicide, makes audience members examine their own prejudices in their choice of a murderer. *A Soldier's Play* ran in New York for more than a year, and Fuller received a 1984 Academy Award nomination for his screenplay adaptation of the play, *A Soldier's Story.*

A Soldier's Play also provoked controversy, however. Amiri Baraka, a dramatist and leading figure in the Black Arts and Theater Movement of the 1960s, accused Fuller of fulfilling the dreams of the white power structure in *A Soldier's Play* and consequently working against his own race. Fuller had long been associated with a rival organization of the Black Theater Movement, the Negro Ensemble Company, which built a theater off Broadway. As Harriott wrote in her *American Voices:* "The [Black Theater] Movement demanded black plays in black theaters in black communities, but Douglas Turner Ward, the actor and director who founded the Negro Ensemble Company in 1967, argued that until the ghettoes were rebuilt, their theaters would be islands." In his essay "The Descent of Charlie Fuller into Pulitzerland and the Need for African-American Institutions," Baraka opposed the Negro Ensemble Company, arguing that it "became a real force in the black community by means of the bourgeoisie's money." He added: "When negro artists say, as did Ward and Fuller recently, that they wanted 'a theatrical rather than a polemical event,' they lie. The have created as political a theater as any in the Black Arts Movement, only it is the politics of our enemies!" Other critics defended the Negro Ensemble Company, however, and praised Fuller for not producing "propaganda" or "agitprop."

Since *A Soldier's Play,* Fuller has opened two seasons for the Negro Ensemble Company with three plays in an intended five- or six-play series on the black experience during the Civil War and in postbellum America. *Sally* and *Prince,* performed jointly under the title *We,* and *Jonquil* opened successive seasons for the Company. Although these plays have received only moderate praise at best, Fuller has continued to portray the plight of blacks in a racially biased society through his drama.

(For further information about Fuller's life and works, see *Black Writers; Contemporary Authors,* Vols. 108, 112; *Contemporary Literary Criticism,* Vol. 25; and *Dictionary of Literary Biography,* Vol. 38: *Afro-American Writers after 1955: Dramatists and Prose Writers.*)

PRINCIPAL WORKS

The Village: A Party (drama) 1968
An Untitled Play (drama) 1970
In My Many Names and Days (drama) 1972
The Candidate (drama) 1974
First Love (drama) 1974
In the Deepest Part of Sleep (drama) 1974
The Lay Out Letter (drama) 1975
The Brownsville Raid (drama) 1976
Sparrow in Flight (drama) 1978
Zooman and the Sign (drama) 1980
A Soldier's Play (drama) 1981
*Sally (drama) 1989
*Prince (drama) 1989
Jonquil (drama) 1990

*These works were performed as *We* in 1989.

Harold Clurman (essay date 1976)

[*In the following review, drama critic and theater director Clurman praises* The Brownsville Raid *for its honestly drawn characters.*]

The Negro Ensemble Company has done itself proud with its production of Charles Fuller's *The Brownsville Raid....* Text, acting, direction are all of a piece and all good. I express my opinion in this blunt fashion because there is something so direct, compact, decisive and simple about the event that one leaves the theatre with a sense of having been informed by a statement so definitive and convincing that any further gloss on it becomes redundant.

In 1906, during Theodore Roosevelt's Presidency, a company of black U.S. Army soldiers was stationed in the town of Brownsville, Texas. They were all enlisted men and their ranking member, Sgt. Maj. Mingo Saunders (admirably played by Douglas Turner Ward), had been in the service for more than twenty years and several times engaged in action (in Cuba and the Philippines). One night a shooting took place in which a Mexican and a white man were killed. Exactly what provoked the violence, or who was responsible for it, was unknown. The townsfolk were sure that a black soldier, perhaps more than one, was guilty. No one in authority doubted this, but no concrete evidence was adduced.

The company's white captain insisted that Mingo discover the culprit. All the men claimed to have been asleep in their bunks at the time of the incident, and no one came forward to admit any participation in the matter. The War Office in Washington sent down a major and then a general to investigate. They were unable to elicit the slightest indication of who, if any, among the soldiers might have been involved.

The investigators decided that their inability to root out the guilty party constituted a conspiracy of silence on the part of the whole company. To prove his men innocent Mingo requested an open trial. The request was categorically rejected. The Army, with the President's indignant concurrence, ordered the entire company—including Sergeant Mingo—to be dismissed without an honorable discharge.

One of the soldiers was suspected by several of the men and by the Sergeant. He had been seen returning to the barracks immediately after the shooting, but there was no conclusive evidence that he was in fact implicated. The men agreed, one of them reluctantly, that if justice was to be done, they themselves would have to put the suspected soldier on trial, just as the company as a whole should have received similar treatment. But since they could not conduct such a trial, they decided not to voice suspicion of their comrade in arms. They were therefore obliged to submit to the blanket discharge.

What makes the play stirring is that all its characters—the white officers as well as each of the blacks—are honestly, incisively and often humorously drawn. The writing is apt: there are no routine or wasted words, no bathos, no special pleading or false heroics, not even an invidious portrayal of the white officers. Each figure is a truly observed person. We are confronted with facts which are not merely faithful to the record but fleshed in the living matter of authentic individuality.

The social and political background—especially in the scenes where a canny and adroit representative of the Booker T. Washington forces comes to plead with the President to delay peremptory action—add to our understanding of the situation, not alone as a single incident but as an historical phenomenon of broad connotations. The entire cast is excellent; the direction by Israel Hicks exemplary. (pp. 701-02)

> *Harold Clurman, in a review of "The Brownsville Raid," in* The Nation, *New York, Vol. 223, No. 22, December 25, 1976, pp. 701-02.*

Richard Gilman (essay date 1982)

[*In the following review, Gilman argues that* A Soldier's Play *was instrumental in helping the Negro Ensemble Company to change and grow.*]

After fourteen seasons, the Negro Ensemble Company can no longer be regarded as an exotic enterprise on the fringe. The N.E.C. came into being because the established American theater didn't seem to have any place for the black experience. So the group proceeded to carve such a place for itself, with determination if not always a clear notion of what it was doing. Its stance was either aggressive, that of an adversary, or defensive, which meant insular and self-validating; it stumbled, fell, rose and kept going.

Never quite a true ensemble, in that it frequently brings in performers for particular productions, the company has had difficulty creating an identifiable style, a way of doing things unmistakably its own. If it still has that difficulty, at least its repertory has become much more flexible, so that its socially oriented realism has lost some of the pugnacious, parochial quality that once marred it.

Charles Fuller's *A Soldier's Play,* the opening production of the N.E.C.'s fifteenth season, is exemplary of this change and, as I see it, this growth. A flawed but estimable play, it's about the black experience but is supple enough in its thematic range and social perspectives to treat that experience as part of a complex whole, as part of American reality in its widest sense. To be released from an adversary position may mean a loss of fierceness—it certainly means a reduction in ideological thunder—but it can make for an increase in subtle wisdom and intellectual rigor.

Not that *A Soldier's Play* is a triumph of the dramatic imagination. But it is intelligent and morally various enough to overcome some basic uncertainties and remnants of the N.E.C.'s older confrontational manner, and so commend itself to our attention. Set in a Louisiana army camp in 1944, the play deals with the fatal shooting of a black sergeant (reflecting the times, blacks are called "negroes" or "coloreds"), a martinet who, out of shame at his people's seeming acceptance of their inferior status, is tougher on his own men than are their white officers.

He's far from likable, but when he's killed and the culprits aren't found, the mood turns ugly among the black soldiers. At first, the Klan is suspected, then some white officers, but the brass wants no trouble and the incident is shunted aside. Finally, an investigator is sent from Washington, a black lieutenant with a law degree from Howard University. His relationship with the white captain previously in charge of the case makes up the moral and psychological center of the drama, which on one level proceeds as a moderately absorbing detective story.

The captain, an earnest liberal, is convinced he knows who the killers are but feels his hands are tied, and he grows impatient with the black officer's slow, careful inquiry. The real problem, however, is the dislocation the captain experiences in his abstract good will. "I can't get used to it," he tells the black man, "your uniform, your bars." Still, he comes to accept the investigator, whose mind is much more in tune with reality than his own and who eventually brings the case to a surprising conclusion. Along the way there are some deft perceptions about both political and psychological matters, and a jaunty historical sense: "Look out, Hitler," a soldier says, "the niggers is comin' to get your ass."

The biggest burden the play carries is the direction of Douglas Turner Ward, the N.E.C.'s artistic director, who is also a well-known playwright. Ward manages the many flashbacks, through which the action is propelled, with a heavy hand: lights go up or down with painful slowness, figures from the past *take their places* obediently in the present. There are also some soft spots among the performances and an unpleasant ending, or coda, in which the black officer gratuitously reminds his white colleague of the lessons taught and learned. Yet in its calm concern for prickly truths and its intellectual sobriety, *A Soldier's Play* elicits the audience's approval, if not its boisterous enthusiasm. (pp. 90-1)

> Richard Gilman, in a review of "A Soldier's Play," in The Nation, *New York, Vol. 234, No. 3, January 23, 1982, pp. 90-1.*

Charles Fuller with Esther Harriott (interview date 1982)

[*Harriott is the author of the 1988 study* American Voices: Five Contemporary Playwrights in Essays *and Interviews. She interviewed a harried Fuller in May 1982, just after he was awarded the Pulitzer Prize for drama. Fuller's responses, delivered with a combination of "amusement, good nature, and fatigue," concerned his works, his thoughts about being a black dramatist, and his current project, the screenplay adaptation of the prize-winning* A Soldier's Play.]

[Harriott]: *Do you have certain obligations as a black playwright? Is there pressure put on you to be a spokesman?*

[Fuller]: No. There never has been any pressure put on me to be a spokesman for anybody. No one has ever come to me and said to me, "Do this. Why don't you consider this or why don't you try looking at this or why aren't you looking at that?" I have been very fortunate in not ever having to deal with that.

So that when you write you're not trying to do anything in your writing other than to write what's inside of you?

I'm trying to capture my experience. I'm translating the kind of contact that I've made with people, most of them black. But how I would write anything that is presumptuous enough to masquerade as being something that speaks for black people is beyond me. I'm just not that sort of person.

What about addressing the audience? I guess that's what my question was getting at. Are you trying to make your audience change in any way?

Oh, of course. There are lots of things that have to change. How people see black people must change. That we are two-dimensional, length-and-width type people that have no depth is simply not true. And I think it's important to display that sense of having more to us than simply the stuff of protest or of being victimized. There's much more to us than that. I'm simply expressing what is real, not what people like to think we are. So far we've been the victims of a compendium of stereotypes about ourselves. The very idea that black people

are complex psychological beings is simply not dealt with.

Don't you think that anybody has dealt with that at all? Ralph Ellison, for example?

Yes. But part of the problem with the novel is that it takes a long time to be read by lots of people. The one advantage of working in the theater is that I know I'm going to get an instant response.

On the other hand, if someone writes poetry or fiction, he can count on more people reading him than a playwright can count on people seeing him. And if a play isn't produced, nobody at all is going to know what you've written.

Well, that's never happened. I also don't believe in an age of this great visual explosion that we have, that a whole lot of people take the time to go to a bookstore to find a book. The number of black publications produced every year will certainly attest to that fact. People are not reading a whole lot of black material. But if there's a play that you can come to, sit for two hours, and be moved in some way, and get up and tell your friends, that's a lot easier than spending a week with a book. And then a writer isn't quite sure, after you've read it, what you've got out of it. I'm fairly certain when an audience walks out whether they like or dislike what I've done. I don't want to wait six months, having written for six years.

Do you think, speaking of the visual explosion, that television and movies have hurt the theater?

They might have, but it hasn't been my experience. I think there's a place for all of it. We tend to be very drastic in the way we see things. We say television or the movies are hurting the theater and putting it out of business. The money that the long-running shows have made seems to me to belie the fact that television has cut across a lot of it. Certainly it has taken some money out of the box offices. But there's room enough for everybody. (pp. 112-13)

How will you approach your script to make it into a screen play?

What I do is make notes about what I am looking at, and what are some of things that are going to make sense in terms of this play being translated into pictures. Just pictures, flat, two-dimensional pictures. What do you do to make that happen, as opposed to making it three-dimensional, with depth, and with people moving about, who may trip one night and not trip another? What do you do with something that's always going to be the same every time you look at it?

I read your penciled questions on your script, and one of them that I really liked was "Would I like Davenport?" Do you remember that?

Yes.

Why would you explore his character more for a movie than for a play?

There's more room to do it in. He's the protagonist of the piece. Now when we talk about doing a movie, he's going to be much more real than when we watched him on the stage. And that's the person they're going to put all the money in. And the characters have to be explored more in the film because when their faces are on the screen they're about 40 feet wide and 20 feet high. The concerns that I had with the play are not the concerns that I'll have with the movie. I know the story is going to be the same, but how do you make sure that the people in the seats stay in the seats? That's what I'm basically saying, whatever I'm doing.

You do that very well in the theater. The tension and mood shifts seem to be just right. In movies, though, there's so much less language.

Yes, I know. So, there's that to be considered, too. How do you display this intention without two hundred words, without unnecessary babble, the babble of the theater? (p. 115)

Writers have been treated very badly in Hollywood.

Yes. I think that you can be treated better. But no one told any writer he can direct a motion picture better than a motion picture director can.

It's just that in the theater the playwright is very important. In the movies you hardly even know who the screenwriter is. In the theater, it's your *play.*

But if you are willing to go into that world and stay there, then you have to suffer those consequences. I have no interest in spending the rest of my life writing movies. Every now and then it might be nice to do that, but going to Hollywood and making a career out of writing movies doesn't interest me at all. I want to write them certainly, but I'm not going to lose any sleep over it. Rest assured. I'm 43 years old, and I know I will never be as good at anything else as I am as a writer. There's not enough time. If I began now, there's not enough time to get as good at being a doctor, for example, as I am as a writer. The older I get the less likely it is that I'm going to have the dexterity necessary to handle an operation. But by reading I can always improve my mind and get better at being a writer. So, I don't concern myself with getting good at being a director or getting good at being this or that. What I'm concerned about is trying to produce the best literary material America has ever seen.

That's pretty ambitious.

Yes, it is. But it's what I'm trying to do. And I think that is an ennobling desire. And I don't think there's anything wrong with it. And I'm not interested in being these other things.

I wonder what will happen to you. You've just won a Pulitzer Prize and sold film rights and are going to

Hollywood. *The world is running to you, right? I wonder if that could be very seductive and distracting?*

Not really. I have a lovely home, two sons that I'm in love with, a wife I love very much, a lifestyle that isn't confusing. It doesn't need all of this. It's nice and very wonderful, but it's not something I'd like to pursue as a life's work. I have more important things to do. I mean, this morning it was so interesting, you know, I was on the Today Show. I thought, "God forbid that my life would depend on having to be on these things every morning." Everyone asks, how can you turn it off? How can you *not?* Remain who you are. After all, it's *that* that I'm concerned about the most, not television, movies. I know that if I write plays there's a reasonable chance that two out of three will get done. That's not a bad average. I won't hassle that. I'm always challenged by the things that I'm doing anyway. So I'm not terribly worried about losing my interest in things.

Did you get discouraged during the period when you didn't think your plays were good?

No. I knew I was doing something different, and that people just didn't like it. It didn't bother me terribly. I was trying to do something enormous. I'm dissatisfied because I wasn't able to do what I set out to do. And it is just discouraging not to make any money. But so what? I keep wondering sometimes if the myth about American writers is of their own making or the public's.

Which myth?

The myth about being so discouraged and hurt and beaten when your work doesn't succeed. Of course there's pain and problems, but you keep on working. If that stops you, then . . .

Then you're not really a writer?

It's not painful enough to dwell on for any great length of time. I think it's something in the myth we have about writers, that we want them to be more feeling, more compassionate, more everything than we really are. And the truth of the matter is, we simply do something well that very few people can do—put human beings up on the stage. It's a difficult job to do. I don't perceive it as being anything other than that. Suffering is not an unusual human characteristic. You know what I mean? The specialness of writing is simply that not a whole lot of people do it. It's a small category in human affairs. A lot has been written, for not a whole lot of people wrote it. Certainly the things that have been remembered have been written by a very few people. (pp. 117-19)

Every other black artist I've talked to has been bitter, and it would seem to me that that's unavoidable. But that doesn't seem to be what you're saying.

Well, being bitter would imply that I'm not getting something that I should be getting, or that I feel inadequate somehow. In the reality that I'm faced with there is nothing about me that is not in any way adequate to anything that I have to face. So I'm not afraid of anyone.

I mean a collective bitterness.

About what?

About "the madness of race in America," to use your phrase in **A Soldier's Play.**

Yes, that's part and parcel of the United States. Anyone who wakes up in the morning and doesn't think that racism exists in the United States is crazy. But I don't have time to spend the rest of my life being angry about it. What will serve me, and benefit, certainly, my people more, it seems to me, is actively functioning in a way that everything I do and produce implies that all the nonsense of racism—certainly the stereotyping of racism—is not true. My argument is on the stage. I don't have to be angry. O.K.? I get it all out right up there. There's no reason to carry this down from the stage and into the seats. And it does not mean that I am not enraged at injustice or prejudice or bigotry. It simply means that I cannot be enraged all the time. To spend one's life being angry, and in the process doing nothing to change it, is to me ridiculous. I could be mad all day long, and if I'm not doing a damn thing, what difference does it make?

It could also be very destructive to the art. Not the anger itself, but if it becomes an axe to grind.

I think it can strangle you to death. But I'm certain that every now and then it's important to let people know that things have not been forgotten. Certainly *A Soldier's Play* lets you know that, yes, we lived in a country at one time when the whole army was segregated. But let's not think that oppressing means that the people who are oppressed are not human. O.K.? That is to believe what white people have believed about us. I don't believe that, I'm the human being here. I don't need you to tell me that I'm alive or that I'm human or that I have feelings. But to be angry at the fact that you said that I don't have feelings certainly doesn't mean that I stop feeling, or that I believe you, or care what you say. That's still believing that white people decide for you who you are, or what your impulse is going to be in the future. That's nonsense, and insulting to begin with. I mean, what makes anyone think I cannot do with language all the things they can? And I'm perfectly calm and contented doing it. It's ludicrous.

So many sad, angry people spend so much time arguing this question, and they don't get their work done. They get angry about not being received the way white writers have been received, about not getting the kind of support that white writers have gotten, never understanding that our function in this society has been, since we've been in it, to change how people see things. To go on changing, to go on making America a better place to live in, because the landscape is broad enough for everybody to be on it. If you were to see a black man standing there, you would say, yes, that's the American experience too. That the American experience is not just a white experience. It's black experience and Indian experience, Puerto Rican experience. For anyone to believe that anyone can, by simply telling you that you're no good, make you no good, that's nonsense. My argument is with the people who really believe that only white people have done things that are artistically sensible. That very fact that we create the things that we create simply proves that that's not true. Why should I argue with them all my life? That's nonsense.

It is important that we do things that seem to me to be beneficial to our people, and by doing so, benefit the larger landscape of America. It seems to me that making people more human in their presentation on stage is one way of doing that, rather than making them so two-dimensional that all they do is confront each other in violent terms. That doesn't speak to anything, doesn't move us anywhere. You learn nothing about you, and I learn nothing about me. Finally, I must make it somehow sensible for my sons to live in the twenty-first century. I believe that if I don't do something about that, I've failed. (pp. 120-21)

> *Charles Fuller and Esther Harriott, in an interview in* American Voices: Five Contemporary Playwrights in Essays and Interviews, *by Esther Harriott, McFarland and Company, Inc., Publishers, 1988, pp. 112-25.*

Amiri Baraka (essay date 1983)

[*Baraka is a major figure in the development of contemporary black literature. As a leading dramatist in the Black Arts and Theater Movement of the 1960s, he received worldwide acclaim for his first professional production,* Dutchman *(1964); his subsequent plays have provoked both praise and controversy. In the following essay, he condemns Fuller's "descent into Pulitzerland" with* A Soldier's Play, *a work that Baraka claims caters to the wishes of whites instead of championing blacks.*]

When I saw Charlie Fuller's *Brownsville Raid* in 1976, produced by the Negro Ensemble and directed by Doug Ward, I was generally impressed. Even Ward's acting, which I find rather stylized, was not too much to take that night.

Before that, I had read **"Love Song For Seven Little Boys Called Sam"** in *Liberator,* Larry Neal and I had even anthologized it in *Black Fire*. The story had a certain poignance that wanted to poke through in the telling of a confrontation between some black youth and white supremacy.

Somehow I always got Charlie Fuller mixed with writer Charlie Russell (maybe because both wrote for the *Liberator* for a minute); at any rate I always try to hook up Fuller to Russell's *Five on the Black Hand Side,* which was a pretty awful movie, an extremely superficial look at the contradictions in the black community, particularly between the "integrationist" sector and the cultural nationalists. What the deep concerns of the majority African American community are—democracy, equality, self-sufficiency—and how different sectors of the black community look at these concerns and why they look at them differently—these would have been what *Five* was about, were it fully drawn. But I could not have written such a play then either. Although Theodore Ward did with his *Big White Fog* almost forty years before. I even had to go back and look through film books to make sure that Fuller did not write *Five*. But, whereas **"Love Song"** is a sensitive look at the struggle and trauma involved with the desegregation of U.S. society and the African American mind, *Five* simply establishes that its author has not taken enough time to know the black community in any really profound depth.

"Love Song" does deal with the deep feelings of the black community, through the focus of black youth coping with white supremacy, intimidation, and violence, certainly in a more profound and compelling way than does Russell's script. He takes some of the legitimate concerns of the black community and tests them in the context of young black life struggling to develop. This short story was good enough so that when I saw Fuller's *Brownsville Raid* I was prepared for the quality and depth I saw in **"Love Song."** (If Fuller *had* written *Five on the Black Hand Side* I might have been prepared for what happened after *Brownsville*!)

With *The Brownsville Raid,* it seemed to me that Fuller had grown enormously. Suddenly, I became aware of who he was, of how his mind, articulated through the drama, worked. *Brownsville* was not so slight or so superficial as the other examples of Fuller's work I had seen. It was fully drawn, within the limitations it had set for itself—a courtroom drama with other penetrations. In some ways, *Brownsville* was very much like *A Soldier's Play.* The United States' segregated army was not a metaphor for the U.S.; it was the U.S. black soldiers who, pushed past their limits in remaining "disciplined"—i.e., placid before national oppression— (even unto the murder of their fellow soldiers), rise up to fight against this bloody oppression and are themselves murdered, legally: They are court-martialed and shot for roaring into town in trucks, shooting everything in sight, trying to even the score after some Southern racists have killed one of their number while he was in town on a pass.

The racist process and white supremacy court and government proceedings penetrate to the heart of apartheid America. It shows us America as a courtroom where black people are on trial endlessly with always the same sentence: death by white supremacy! Death comes more swiftly if the victims resist or struggle against it, or demand liberation. Plus, it is always perfectly justifiable and most of the time "legal."

The memory of *Brownsville* stayed with me a long time: I often wished I could see it again. Given this situation, I was completely unprepared for the Negro Ensemble's production of *Zooman and the Sign.* Suddenly here was Charlie Fuller as the voice of the most reactionary sector of the black middle class.

Zooman marked a new low ideologically in black theater. Chas Gordone's abortion *No Place To Be Somebody* could be understood almost as the creation of racists who wished to counter the statements made by the theater of the Black Arts Movement. The awarding of a Pulitzer Prize to Gordone, who is not even a playwright, marking the first time an African American received the award, is pure anti-Black Liberation Movement politics. When Gordone's main character shoots the black gangster figure (Black Power) and then gets into drag announcing he is ecstatic because black militancy has been killed forever, it makes the hair stand up on the back of your neck, but it's obvious that white supremacy is fighting back. Gordone has never even identified as black, much less become a playwright. Just in terms of the conventions of written drama, *No Place* would get a D in any writing class.

Zooman brought this idea back to me, uglier than ever. Zooman is the black teenage "animal" racists see black youth as. This "animal" epithet is what the sick cops scream as they pump bullets into the back of these kids' heads. It's what the white cops screamed at me as they opened my head with their gun butts and sticks during the 1967 Newark rebellion.

Fuller has his middle-class negroes talk like the most backward negroes on the block. (And I use the term *negro* advisedly.) Because that is what Charlie Fuller seems to want to represent in *Zooman: the Negro Consciousness,* the consciousness of the black people who have been so washed out mentally by white supremacy that they think other blacks are the problem!

Their child has been killed by this black youth, Zooman, but the rest of the community is too frightened to identify him. Fuller's negroes put up a sign accusing the black community of cowardice, in not turning in the youth. The youth comes to take the sign down, and one of Fuller's negroes kills him.

There is no attempt to lay out just what the real causes of black national oppression are, or the ghettos and pathology created by oppression. There are only animals, Zoomen, and they can only be stopped by blacks having the courage to kill them. What about the courage to kill off white supremacy? What about the courage to destroy racism and monopoly capitalism forever? What about even the courage to organize black artists so that they can take an open adversary relationship to this hellish system that has traditionally enslaved and tortured us? No, the only "courage" Fuller speaks of is the "courage" necessary for middle-class negroes to see themselves as a beleaguered elite, beset by a bunch of black animals!

It is no wonder that Chemical Bank immediately put out money to advertise *Zooman,* with huge ads in the *Village Voice, New York Times,* and other newspapers, and initiated a campaign to keep *Zooman* open (to shield it from the problems that most black theater has) so that its "intelligent" message could be spewed out even more broadly.

Zooman not only is backward but, like Gordone's monstrosity, is poorly written as well. Fuller could get maybe a D+ for the writing of *Zooman.* It is awkward and simplistic with old static forms—characters coming to the footlights, etc. Despite its obvious drawbacks, the white supremacists made a great deal of fuss about *Zooman,* all the time allowing as how it could have been written, etc.

But with *A Soldier's Play,* they scored. It is what such types long for: a play as reactionary as *Zooman* (even more so in the long run) but one well-written, which, as Mao said, makes it even more dangerous since reactionary ideas couched in attractive forms can draw unsuspecting people in.

ASP draws some of its form and thrust from *The Brownsville Raid,* but it is ideologically way on the other side. Fuller says he modeled the play, in some ways, on Melville's *Billy Budd.* This idea alone was enough to send negro critic Stanley Crouch into veritable ecstasies. "You know we's into somethin' now, when we can imitate Melville," I can hear him saying.

But the real deadliness of *ASP* is Fuller's point of view. Again, it is the most backward sector of the black middle class, the voice of the negro heard loud and clear.

Adolph Caesar plays a black-hating sergeant who would be at home with a great many negroes, even famous ones, saying, "Stop thinkin' like a nigger," or "You bring us down, boy; we're gonna get rid of you, boy— one less fool for the race to be ashamed of." These comments are said by this sergeant to a young blood from the deep South who represents the oldest, blackest folk ties of the African American. Caesar's character hates this Southern blackness that connects, through slavery, directly back to Africa. When Caesar causes this naive young boy to commit suicide, he is killed. This creates a kind of whodunit mystery aspect to the play and also provides an opening for Fuller's real hero (who he says was modeled on Larry Neal—When? is what I would ask), a black, or is it negro, officer, a captain, who serves as Melville's narrator and at the same time Fuller's prototype of the negro in high places who is qualified to get the job despite the obstruction of white supremacy.

The connection of the black middle class and black bourgeoisie to the black masses is the fact of national oppression. Yes, the qualified negro can be stopped from advancing to his or her proper place, or receiving his or her deserved recognition, by a society based on white supremacy and black national oppression. Caesar's character has been made sick by such obstruction. He, like the negroes in *Zooman,* thinks that the obstruction is other black people, especially Southern black

ones who sing the blues. When he is killed, another negro comes on the scene, fundamentally to prove that he is qualified to be an officer in "the man's army."

Of course, the captain is resented and obstructed, even threatened, but in the end he overcomes. He finds the sergeant's murderer, who turns out to be none other than Malcolm X! Not really or literally Malcolm, although the sergeant's killer is the company black militant, a young actor who had played Malcolm X, just weeks before, not so coincidentally, in Laurence Holder's play *When the Chickens Come Home to Roost,* about the conflict between Malcolm X and Elijah Muhammad. Denzel Washington still looked very much like Malcolm—close haircut, glasses, and all.

But what is important, aside from such non-concidences, is that this black militant, the very opposite of the black-hating sergeant, is given to making militant speeches and condemning the sergeant—although the sergeant takes him out and beats him in a one-on-one combat (you know that all negroes can beat militants). And when the sergeant causes the young boy's suicide, the militant kills the sergeant.

The captain tracks the militant down, condemning him because he lacks compassion for the black-hating sergeant. Fuller says that is our real problem, that the black militants lack compassion for black-hating negroes. Though, interestingly enough, there is no real denouement to the play's ideology. One would expect that there would be the final flaming conflict between Fuller's mouthpiece, the competent, skilled, qualified negro captain, and the militant, in which Fuller would lay out his argument and shoot holes into the concept of black political militance and radicalism. But he does not. There are a few brief remarks, and the militant is led away. No scene of raging ideological confrontation occurs because Fuller hasn't the courage to say, really, anything directly in defense of negro reaction, except what he does say by way of the play's ending.

But then check this as his shattering statement, one he has sneaked away from open ideological confrontation (as even Shakespeare, Dante, or Melville would provide): The negro captain proves his right to be among the white officers by uncovering the militant. Now he belongs. Despite white supremacy, he has proved his mettle, his ultimate worth. He is a soldier, and it is a soldier's play. A soldier "in the man's army"—that's the ultimate aspiration of these reactionary negroes: to be soldiers in the man's army. And their whole lives are nothing but a soldier's play.

The negro captain (Charles Brown, a clumsy quasi-actor) is Fuller and company going off into the sunlight, having proved their right to belong. And let's look at the scorecard: black folk symbol=dead; black folk symbol-hating negro (openly pathological)=dead; black militant=court-martialed, locked up; intelligent, efficient, qualified negro captain=belongs, goes off into the sunlight. Hey, but what about the rest of the troops, the other soldiers, the black masses in the army? Well, they go off to the war, to fight Hitler, to fight against fascism, and they are all killed—to a man, the narrator says! Only I alon⌐ lived to tell the tale, said Ishmael (Reed?): the lone surviving negro, who survives because he is an officer in the man's army. All those other non-officer, non-negro blacks perished, fighting white supremacy. Only the negro alone survived to tell the tale and, by the way, win the second Pulitzer Prize any colored playwright ever got!! And Chemical Bank beat the drum louder and longer than ever!! (pp. 51-3)

> Amiri Baraka, "The Descent of Charlie Fuller into Pulitzerland and the Need for African-American Institutions," in Black American Literature Forum, *Vol. 17, No. 2,* Summei, 1983, pp. 51-4.

William W. Demastes (essay date 1987)

[*Demastes is the author of the 1988 study* Beyond Naturalism: A New Realism in American Theatre. *In the following essay, originally published in* Studies in American Drama 1945-Present *in 1987, he responds in part to Amiri Baraka's critique of Fuller's career (see excerpt dated 1983); asserting that Fuller's strength is his ability to translate "his black experience into an idiom that can be more broadly termed an 'American' experience."*]

Charles Fuller's recent work as a playwright has marked him as a new voice for an element of American society greatly underrepresented in mainstream theatre today—the black American community. Fuller's talents make him a worthy spokesman, but such a labeling is an uncomfortable one for any artist to bear, given the political implications attached to being a "representative" of such a vastly heterogeneous group. Despite the difficulties, though, Fuller's work has been favorably received by both the general black community and the mainstream theatre world. In fact, Fuller's most noteworthy contribution may be his success at translating his black experience into an idiom that can be more broadly termed an "American" experience.

Throughout his playwriting career, Fuller has been closely connected with the Negro Ensemble Company (NEC), a group that was founded in the late 1960s (first play produced December 1967) because, as critic Richard Gilman puts it, "the established American theater didn't seem to have any place for the black experience." Gilman continues: "So the group proceeded to carve such a place for itself, with determination if not always a clear notion of what it was doing. Its stance was either aggressive, that of an adversary, or defensive, which meant insular and self-validating." Charles Fuller is one of the playwrights responsible for bringing the NEC into mainstream theatre. His *Soldier's Play* (1981; Pulitzer Prize, 1982) has capped that struggle to prove beyond an adversarial posture and has succeeded at presenting something more than a work that "self-validates" the black perspective. But the result of such a theatre as Fuller and the NEC have created is that there is, as

Gilman notes, "a loss of fierceness ... a reduction in ideological thunder" [see excerpt dated 1982]. It is this lack of thunder that has led one faction of the black community to reject the efforts of the NEC.

Perhaps the most outspoken of that faction is dramatist/activist LeRoi Jones/Amiri Baraka, who, in an essay attacking *A Soldier's Play* in particular, makes the following observation of the NEC in general:

> An oppressed people demand that all their resources be put to the service of liberating them, no matter what these resources are. Certainly art and culture must be seen in such a light. Either we are trying to fashion an art of liberation, whatever its forms, or we are creating an art that helps maintain our chains and slave status (even high, giggling, or in ecstasy). The Negro Ensemble has been, in the main, a skin theater, offering only colored complexion but not sustained thrust in concert with the whole of the BLM [Black Liberation Movement] to liberate ourselves. It has been fundamentally a house slave's theater, eschewing struggle for the same reason that the house niggers did—because they didn't have it so bad [see essay dated 1983].

Baraka himself approaches the "black condition" advocating one option, "revolutionary violence," as W. D. E. Andrews notes in his study of Baraka's Marxist theatre. Baraka's is an approach that considers "reformism" or "revisionism" nothing more than "bourgeois doubletalk" assisting the white oppressors rather than helping the black oppressed. For Baraka, any approach other than his own is worthy of nothing but contempt, as the above passage clearly illustrates. But upon closer scrutiny, Baraka's theory of art as revolutionary tool has its own limitations. For example, to more clearly draw the line between the perceived antagonists, Baraka's works have relied heavily on "generality and sloganeering," a tactic most noticeable in Baraka's more recent works. And as such, his art becomes didactic and dogmatic, tendencies that Andrews notes damages two of Baraka's more recent dramatic products: "Both *The Motion of History* [1978] and *S-1* [1978] are plays which do not allow the spectator to make his own discoveries or to draw his own conclusions."

Closed to the fuller freedoms that art is capable of utilizing, Baraka has slipped into a realm that may conform to his revolutionary political designs, but one that has also led him to create questionable "art." Fuller's art, on the other hand, is not at all revolutionary in intentions, given Baraka's designs, but neither is it designed to concede the current black condition, as Baraka claims it does. Rather, Fuller's strategy illustrates a subtlety that practitioners such as Baraka either fail to see or fail to acknowledge, a subtlety that, if successful, would bring about its own type of revolution. And it is not a strategy dependent on unsupported generalizations or didacticism. Fuller's dialectic is neither directly confrontational nor in any real sense "agitprop." But though Fuller's works may lack "fierceness" or "thunder," it's a concession that Fuller seems willing to make in order to suggest another approach to the race issue.

The process of change that Fuller advocates begins first with his portrayal of a whole spectrum of character types, revealing subtleties and complexities that black characterization rarely receives, both positive and negative. Such an approach to his characterizations in turn argues that for Fuller the black experience has itself attained a self-assurance and sense of identity that will allow it to be fully included in mainstream American culture without fear of losing itself in the process. Baraka would argue that such a process actually entails losing that black identity, but Fuller's works prove otherwise.

The most noticeable effect of this process is that Fuller helps to break a long tradition of stereotyping blacks—particularly black men—in literature, cinema, drama, and television. Fuller describes the tradition he is challenging as one that portrays blacks as "[i]neffectual types who just can't get themselves together, the kind Hattie McDaniel used to chase out of the kitchen.... We speak [in traditional portrayals] one abominable language—hip; we have one interest—women. Our lives have no beginning, no ending. We're highly emotional in terms of reactive violence, and we do not use our minds in any way." Fuller's plays do include such characterizations, but also many others that awaken the audience to a more rounded understanding of blacks as individuals who perhaps have been brought up in different cultural circumstances but who should not be considered some group fundamentally different from others and therefore easily "ghetto-ized."

Fuller's characters, therefore, are no longer racially limited and assume a more "universal" quality. Fuller argues, "I can't see how any growing people would want to be continually portrayed as sweet and innocent," for breaking one stereotype to establish another is not the answer. Stereotypes of any sort isolate people from true understanding, and finally . . . Fuller contends that it is blacks who "have more to lose by staying remote from the White community." Fuller completes the thought: "[Y]ou change or they change or, if nobody changes, somebody loses in this equation, and I'm thinking it's us." Fuller's approach leads to an equation that asks both sides to see and both sides to change. The result is that whites and blacks are shown their common humanity rather than being shown some racial "difference," which is the type of "revolutionary" exacerbation of the

The Negro Ensemble Company production of A Soldier's Play.

factions that Baraka's art must strive for. And it seems Fuller has succeeded. Though at one level blacks and whites are seen as two communities, Fuller is striving to illustrate another level where the two communities are, or should be, one.

Fuller's arrival at this conclusion in *A Soldier's Play* is the result of an evolution that can be seen in the thematic progress of his three most successful works, *The Brownsville Raid* (1976), *Zooman and the Sign* (1980), and finally *A Soldier's Play* (1981).

The Brownsville Raid portrays blacks as a minority oppressed by the hatred and misunderstanding of the white majority. Fuller takes an historical event (1906) in which a predominantly white town, Brownsville, Texas, is attacked by a band of unidentified marauders shortly after an all-Negro infantry battalion is bivouacked on its outskirts. The circumstances suggest that the blacks were the marauders. But though the ensuing action, historically and in the play, fails to prove that the blacks were involved in the raid, the black battalion is disbanded in disgrace.

Within this clash of blacks and whites lies a trademark of Fuller's. Amid the public accusations and denials, Fuller has inserted a reasonable cause for private suspicion among the blacks that in their midst may be a guilty party. The richness of ambiguity leaves serious doubt as to who is to blame—retaliating blacks or conspiring whites—and the result in the play is not some reductive "finger pointing" but a more general condemnation of the suspicion itself, the result of mistrust and lack of communication existing between blacks and whites. Interestingly, Baraka applauds the "message" of *The Brownsville Raid,* arguing that "it was the U.S. black soldiers who, pushed past their limits in remaining 'disciplined'... rise up to fight against this bloody oppression and are themselves murdered, legally." Baraka, unfortunately, has seen the play without noting the subtleties of doubt and suspicion among the blacks that will more notably mark Fuller's later works. Baraka sees it as merely a play documenting the injustices blacks have suffered at the hands of the white power structure.

Zooman and the Sign is the play that at least partially clarifies any misinterpretation of Fuller's designs, and understandably Baraka condemns it. The confrontation becomes more focused in *Zooman and the Sign,* virtually eliminating any black-white opposition in favor of studying one half of the problem, namely the struggle within the black community itself. Baraka says of the play, "Suddenly here was Charlie Fuller as the voice of the most reactionary sector of the black middle class." As noted above, however, the action of the play is not a "sudden" shift but a clearer sign of Fuller's designs.

Again an actual event is the germ of the play, a report of a senseless, violent killing of a small black girl by a black hood in the streets of Philadelphia. Frank Rich reports that the play does not illustrate a reactionary black middle-class capitulation to comfort, as Baraka claims, but

> an indictment of black Americans who capitulate to tyrannical punks within their midst. Yet it is much to the playwright's credit that his compassion is not merely reserved for the heroic Reuben Tate [the girl's father]. He also has sympathy for Reuben's frightened friends—and for Zooman, a kid driven into psychosis by the social circumstances of poverty. In *Zooman and the Sign* there are no real villains, only victims. Every character is locked in the same cycle of terror, and it's a nightmare only courage can end.

Fuller's play does not argue that since blacks are trapped by white institutions, it is the whites' responsibility to enact change or even that it is the blacks' responsibility to rebel against the system. Rather, it is a treatment of human courage that argues the need to take responsibility for one's life, inasmuch as one can—a message that in fact transcends racial considerations. And Fuller's sensitivity extends to all in this complex situation, victims as well as victimizers. On a more specific level, though, it is a fair but hard and analytic focus on the black community and on the interactions—shortcomings included—of its black residents, and failing to include whites in the action has led to some criticism, Baraka's included.

With *A Soldier's Play,* Fuller strikes the balance that he seems to have been striving for throughout his early works. In very clear terms we see the hatred and prejudices of whites, but more specifically we see the interactions of blacks within that circle. Both halves of the problem are reunited, the result being a study of broad social structures as in *The Brownsville Raid* and a scrutiny of both blacks and whites in a way that included only blacks in *Zooman and the Sign.*

This play has no actual historical source, but Fuller does return to a military setting, for it offers him the opportunity, as he says, to have "men confront men" more honestly, since "[y]ou can't call a man a fool whose principal function is to defend his country." In this camp, set in Louisiana during World War II, an investigation is being conducted into what seems to be a racially motivated murder of a black sergeant. A black investigator, initially convinced of a white conspiracy, eventually discovers the murderer to be a black soldier formerly under the murdered sergeant's charge. In essence the play is a mystery, and designedly so.

A Soldier's Play works to investigate and evaluate racial tensions that have been intensified by the conditions established in the play; for this the mystery form is appropriate. As such, a typical formula would be to look for extreme—and atypical—conditions that would aid in unearthing the mystery: radical blacks confronted by KKK whites, for example. The play, however, challenges the standard, comfortable assumptions that tensions exist only between such radical elements of both races. To overturn such oversimplified assumptions, Fuller works to challenge the cool foundations of reasoned abstraction that lead to these conclusions. The way he challenges these notions is to present standard clues, allow classic and typically stereotypical assumptions to develop—among the investigators—into simple conclusions. Fuller then reveals previously unperceived complexities in the situation, which in turn show how complacent, comfortable solutions/approaches are rooted, finally, in a subtle but pervasive prejudice. The result is that in addition to a murderer's confession and indictment, the process brings out "indictments" of a sort against the entire cast of characters for prejudice and racial/racist behavior.

The modified mystery plot contributes to this unexpected and more encompassing end, but it also has an additional twist. Because audiences are standardly involved in their own process of solving murder-mysteries, if this play succeeds, it will engage the audience, forcing the members to utilize critical instincts—or more accurately, prejudices—which will lead to a complicity similar to that of the onstage investigators. So the play is less concerned with unfolding facts identifying the murderer than it is a work revealing subtle causes of the event under scrutiny that in turn eventually force not only the onstage investigators but also the audience into admitting having taken a superficial approach to the issue, assisted by prejudice and stereotypical assumptions. For Fuller, the play's the thing wherein he will catch the conscience of his audience.

Walter Kerr argues that the play's "particular excitement . . . doesn't really stem from the traditional business of tracking down the identity of the criminal. It comes instead from tracking down the identity of the victim." Fuller focuses on the central character, the murdered Tech/Sergeant Waters, a use of the mystery form that temporarily draws attention away from solving the mystery and toward analyzing a complex and troubling character who is working to improve the image of "his people" but in the end does more to hurt that image.

Waters is a character who has taken upon himself the job of refashioning the black image, assuming a missionary zeal and adopting what he considers a self-justifying posture almost similar to an "amoral" stance of declaring war, where the ends unquestionably justify the means. In World War I, he distinguished himself in actual combat, as did many blacks, but as he says, "[t]he First War, it didn't change much for us," and he feels the time has come for change, though his military background of violent action misdirects him. His intention of bringing about change may be a noble one, but the strategy becomes obsessive to the point of near megalomania. He recounts one event that occurred during the "First War":

> Do you know the damage one ignorant Negro can do? (Remembering) We were in France during the First War . . . . We had won decorations, but the white boys had told all the French gals we had tails. And they found this ignorant colored soldier. Paid him to tie a tail to his ass and parade around naked making monkey sounds . . . . And when we slit his throat,

you know that fool asked us what he had done wrong?

This formative incident in Waters's life is followed by others which in turn lead up to Waters's radical act within the play that in turn leads to Waters's murder. That crucial act in the play is Waters's assault on the easygoing C. J., which dramatizes Waters's current as well as former modus operandi.

C. J. is a Southern black, a sort of Billy Budd, by Fuller's account. This innocent "handsome soldier" is a natural athlete (emphasis on natural), the best ball player on the black baseball team, and a simple, unlettered youth who best expresses himself with his guitar, country imagery, and soulful song. His simplicity is the quality that marks him an "ignorant colored soldier" in Waters's eyes.

Waters works to frame the naive and innocent C. J. with an elaborate plot and has him stockaded, thereby singly succeeding in eliminating one more "geech" from the public eye. Waters triumphantly comments:

> I waited a long time for you, boy, but I gotcha! And I try to get rid of you wherever I go. I put two geechies in jail at Fort Campbell, Kentucky—three at Fort Huachuca. Now I got you—one less fool for the race to be ashamed of.

This scheme of purifying his race and the methods used are unethical at best and are especially noted as such when presented with Nazi Germany in the background, complete with the connotations of its own system of purification. But Waters is made to be more complex than this initial response suggests. When discussing his family, for example, we see more precisely the motives behind Waters's actions: to improve the world for future black generations, not necessarily for himself:

> When this war's over [World War II], things are going to change . . . . and I want him [Waters's son] to be ready for it—my daughter, too! I'm sendin' bot' of 'em to some big white college.

So though he appears sinister in executing his plan against C. J., Fuller refuses to offer Waters as a pure source of evil, instead allowing him to be human and even allowing him eventually to express keen remorse upon the ultimate realization of the inhumanity of his plan. Unable to survive walled up in the stockade, C. J. commits suicide, and Waters is driven to drink because he sees the flaws in his "master plan" and realizes he is to blame for this man's death. At first he internalizes the grief, but finally he challenges the source that has so twisted him into his obsession: the white establishment. In a drunken stupor he confronts and attacks two white officers on the night of his murder:

> Followin' behind y'all? Look what it's done to me!—I hate myself . . . . I've killed for you . . . . And nothin' changed! . . . I've tried everything! Everything.

Waters finally realizes his ends in fact have failed to justify the means. He has been misdirected all along. That Waters is murdered/executed in the play is a sort of justice, retribution for all his past crimes, and finally something he himself likely welcomed.

As Kerr says, uncovering the personality of Waters is an intriguing process. Fuller has created a complex "villain" whose rich character can actually trigger a variety of mixed emotions within the audience. This very complexity of character, this creation of an intriguing human being who also happens to be black, greatly contributes to the overall complexity of the issues presented in the play and sheds light on the complexities of trying to "solve" the race problem in general. We accuse and possibly condemn him, only to have to reevaluate at a later time. This mixed reaction occurs throughout the play, onstage as well as offstage, in the audience. And the audience is given its lead by the characters onstage because the structure of the play is such that uncovering the character of Waters occurs throughout the action of the play, through a process of interviewing the various suspects and having their recountings take the form of flashbacks on stage. The audience in turn, engaged in an investigation of its own, responds to the suspects' reactions to Waters as presented on stage.

Within the play, the variety of responses to Waters's character is presented by introducing a variety of characters as suspects, another convenience afforded by selecting the mystery form. Throughout the several interviews, suspicion continually shifts. Any of a variety of suspects could have committed the crime, we realize, and the effect is that uncovering the actual criminal again becomes less important than uncovering the variety of violent responses to Waters's life and what it represents. Presented are white bigots, stereotypically malleable blacks, radically sophisticated blacks, etc. That P. F. C. Peterson, a black, is finally revealed to be the actual culprit is thematically significant, presenting an argument by Fuller that a dangerous "enemy" lies within black ranks rather than without. But it is also a sort of dramatic trick since his guilt is unexpected, which allows for the investigation to continually "misfire" and for the on- and offstage investigators to question the motives for their finally unsupportable conclusions.

A murder of such a nature leads to instant assumptions that it was racially motivated. To a point, it in fact is so motivated, since the death of C. J. was racially motivated and since Waters's murder was the result of C. J.'s death. But that complexity is not at issue in the early investigation, which duly takes the predictable turn of assuming white complicity. The two white officers that Waters confronted on the night of his murder are interrogated, one of whom presents the standard white bigot's view, first insisting that Waters broke with military protocol and then revealing formerly hidden feelings:

> Look—the goddamn Negro was disrespectful! He wouldn't salute! Wouldn't come to attention! And where I come from, colored don't talk the way he spoke to us—not to white people they don't.

But the simple solution of accusing a white is not the actual solution, though it is seriously posed and considered until late in the play, a strategy that succeeds at arousing and keeping alive suspicion that whites are the guilty party. Such serious suspicions stem from prejudiced leanings toward an easy solution, thoughts that Fuller develops in his on-stage investigators and seems to want to allow to develop in the audience, if the tendency exists. Vindicating the whites late in the play gives such presumptions freedom to grow.

The next logical suspect is Private Wilkie, a black man busted to private by Waters from the rank of sergeant, which took him ten years to earn. The revenge motive is there, but Wilkie instead subordinates himself to the will of Waters, a fact not immediately revealed to the audience. This quality leads Waters to take advantage of Wilkie, using him to help frame C. J. That he is such a character, and not some "typically" revenge-ridden emotional stereotype, again provides the opportunity to misinterpret. With Wilkie, too, no simple solution is offered. Wilkie is innocent of murder, though guilty of complicity in framing C. J., guilty of betraying a fellow for his own advancement.

P.F.C. Peterson, the man who finally confesses (along with an accomplice by association, a minor character), places an ironic sense of closure on the mystery. He is strong and opinionated, in many ways the kind of man Waters is trying to make out of all his men. Unlike Waters, though, Peterson maintains his attachment to his black heritage: he's a man from "Hollywood, California—by way of Alabama." But unlike C. J., the suicide from Mississippi, Peterson is a Southerner who has been introduced to a more sophisticated world and has developed the tools to defend himself, to stand up for himself. The confident self-reliance is what Waters admires; the sense of separatism is what Waters wants to beat out of him. The two men's conflicting perspectives on "black destiny" lead first to a fist fight and finally to Peterson murdering Waters for destroying C. J. C. J. represents a kind of innocence that Waters was ashamed of and that Peterson seemed anxious to stand up for and wanted to preserve. The hatred stemming from the confrontation eventually leads to mutual elimination.

To one degree or another, *all* the characters are guilty of racially motivated violence (with the exception of C. J.) an implicit indication that such prejudices are pervasive and not merely restricted to reported acts of violence. Having the least likely suspect turn out to be the actual murderer serves two purposes, as noted above. With Peterson, Fuller makes a statement about the efficacy of a militant stand, a theme he developed in his earlier works. But more significantly, having Peterson be the murderer provides opportunities for misdirected accusations to fly, accusations which are invariably the product of prejudicial conclusions and which condemn the accuser even more than the accused. On stage the accusations come from the two investigators of the murder, men whose efforts to solve the crime force them to come to terms with their own personal prejudices,

prejudices that surface because of the work at hand. And if the murder-mystery form succeeds in engaging the audience, the investigators become onstage representatives of their audience equivalents.

To come close to creating audience representatives on stage, Fuller creates two "Everyman" types, characters of equal rank, one white, the other black. The two are the white Captain Taylor and the black chief investigator, Captain Davenport, who is brought in especially to solve the case, and who may have the credentials of an "equal" but who is afforded few of the privileges of his rank, a condition he must continually fight against and which colors his perceptions, almost against his will. Both men's rational attempts to determine the guilty party are constantly clouded by overt prejudices that neutralize their formal efforts to uncover the truth. Taylor considers himself to be a fairly liberal white, concerned about blacks as human beings, though he still considers them his social inferiors, a belief stemming from his "comfortable" upbringing. As a result, his attempts at honesty and sincerity are both comical and revealing: "Forgive me for occasionally staring, Davenport, you're the first colored officer I've ever met." And his observations are stereotypically naive: "Listen, Waters didn't have a fifth grade education—he wasn't a schemer! And colored soldiers aren't devious like that." Blinded by a consequent overzealousness to do right, Taylor falls into a sort of "liberal" trap and overreacts to the facts presented him. In the second interview with the two suspected white officers, he is the one to charge them with murder, proceeding only on an unsound suspicion that the men, obvious bigots, are lying. The charge comes despite Taylor's own earlier insistence that the men had sound alibis: "Consider yourself under arrest, 'gentlemen'! . . . You think I believe that crap—." Davenport, however, at this point releases them.

Though rational during this particular interview, Davenport is not much different from Taylor at other points. For example, feeling like a crusader for his race, Davenport first considers the KKK until common sense evidence eliminates it as a possible force: Waters's insignia would have been stripped from his uniform. Then, even before Taylor does, Davenport attacks the white officers with a conspiracy charge. He blindly argues against fact, claiming that their alibis are "nothing more than officers lying to protect two of their own." When the conspiracy theory extends to having to accuse the camp commander of complicity, Davenport still rages, "They're all lying!" He does eventually settle into looking at the facts, letting the officers go, and finding the actual murderer, almost by accident. Once the crime is solved, he offers a fitting eulogy to those men destroyed by the event and a fitting condemnation to those blinded by color, himself ironically included:

> Two colored soldiers are dead—two on their way to prison. Four less men to fight with—and none of their reasons—nothing anyone 'said' or 'did,' would have been worth a life to men with larger hearts—men less split by the madness of race in America.

The madness, in fact, has captured all in the play—blacks and whites—and has not just affected the four men directly involved.

But finally what happens onstage, the formal "lesson" Davenport provides, is not nearly as profound as what is hoped to occur in the audience. Fuller turns very specifically to the audience with the final event reported in the play. Davenport reports to the audience that the case itself was subsequently buried and forgotten under more important matters involving the war effort. Also, "[t]hrough a military foul-up," Waters was given a hero's burial, so the affair itself is formally buried. And finally Davenport reports that "the entire outfit—officers [the whites] and enlisted men—was wiped out in the Ruhr Valley during a German advance." Davenport alone is left to tell the tale. It seems that the lessons of the play are to die with the end of the play. None are left to disseminate the lesson unless, of course, the audience itself is to be considered. So, quietly working its way into the audience throughout the course of the production, the play clearly moves into the auditorium at play's end.

The process is ingenious and effective. The murder-mystery plot first forces upon the audience a dramatically leading curiosity to know the victim and to understand the complexities of a conscientious but misguided man in his search for a racial identity. But the stereotypical dramatic expectations (those concerning the murder plot) go further, drawing out hidden prejudices from the investigators onstage and from those "investigators" in the audience as well since they all string together information along a line of individually preconceived notions, which are in turn challenged by the outcome of the event, leaving the various investigators troubled by the various racial prejudices surfaced by the play. And finally the play detaches itself from its stage life and reaches out into the auditorium asking that the audience accept its legacy. Manipulating what may at first have been considered merely a "form of entertainment" is an alarmingly disarming and finally effective technique.

A Soldier's Play deals with a wide variety of "causes" of the race problem, but the "argument" moves to break through prejudices, to shatter barriers, not abstractly but on a personal level. The underlying assumptions are clear. Understanding and psychological change must come on an individual level for any change to be permanent. Group militancy is not the answer. That Waters and Peterson self-destruct clearly argues against either of their brands of militancy and may in fact be read as a subtle comment by Fuller on the inevitable results of the "destiny" that leaders like Baraka are trying to create for blacks. Fuller seems to argue that such visions as Baraka's have their limits and are dreams that are themselves destined to self-destruct.

In *A Soldier's Play,* Fuller has manipulated a theatrical formula to subtly achieve his ends: social awareness not preached but experienced. And with *A Soldier's Play,* Fuller and the Negro Ensemble Company have broken from those former defensive and insular postures to present a work that confidently creates not just a black experience, but an "American" experience. (pp. 43-56)

William W. Demastes, "Charles Fuller and 'A Soldier's Play': Attacking Prejudice, Challenging Form," in Studies in American Drama, 1945-Present, *Vol. 2, 1987, pp. 43-56.*

Richard Hornby (essay date 1989)

[*In the following excerpt from the essay "Minority Theatre," originally published in* The Hudson Review *in 1989, Hornby offers a mixed review of* We—two *plays,* Sally *and* Prince, *in a series Fuller plans to create on the Civil War and postbellum race relations.*]

Some of the best theatre in New York is produced by minority groups. Blacks, Puerto Ricans, Jews, French, Italians, Irish, homosexuals, find theatre the best medium for exploring their problems because, despite McLuhan and the mystique of electronic media, it is the most efficient way such groups have of communicating among themselves. Film and television are potentially much cheaper per audience member, but only when audiences are very large, because of the enormous capital investment required. The need for large audiences also means that film and television drama inevitably become homogenized; Hollywood executives have little interest in producing the work of minority writers or actors. ("The Cosby Show" is the exception that proves the rule; it does provide work for black actors, but has little to do with the realities of black life in America.)

Theatre, however, requires only three boards and a passion, as Lope de Vega put it (though nowadays he'd have to throw in some lighting equipment as well). A stage play can be put together quickly and relatively cheaply; reaching audiences in the thousands rather than the millions, it can be frank, localized, and topical, or even parochial and jargonistic, if the performers and the audiences want it that way.

Charles Fuller's two new plays, *Sally* and *Prince,* produced in repertory by the Negro Ensemble Company under the joint title *We,* deal with black history, but are anything but parochial. Skillfully directed by Douglas Turner Ward on a small, bare, sloping stage (Lope de Vega would have been pleased), the two plays provide a panoramic view of the American Civil War and its aftermath from an African-American perspective. The large casts, the numerous, wide-ranging locales, and the episodic form of the works would seem to make them more suited to film than the stage, but theatre is a wonderfully flexible performance medium. With a bit of imagination and skill, it can suggest a vastness that film could only show literally, at considerably more expense.

Sally begins in South Carolina in the middle of the war. Its opening scene is an encounter between some black

Union soldiers and a slave boy they stumble across. This is solidly based in history; there were indeed black troops in the Union army (Abraham Lincoln praised their bravery), and Fuller is imaginative enough to see the dramatic possibilities in such a confrontation, which must have happened frequently as the Northern armies advanced. The soldiers are tough, well trained, disciplined; their sergeant, Prince, is a thorough professional, completely at home in the army. His general, whose life Prince saved in battle, describes him as the best soldier in his command, black or white. The slaves, on the other hand, are naive and ignorant; there is a greater gulf between them and the black soldiers than between the soldiers and their white officers.

Though ignorant, the slaves are anything but stupid. Seeing the Northern army as their ticket to freedom, some, including the slave boy from the opening scene, join up; others become hangers-on, trading with the soldiers or, in the case of some of the former slave women, taking up with them. Sally, a young widow with a sixteen-year-old son, takes up with one of Prince's men, but becomes attracted to Prince himself. She yearns for some land, a man of her own, a secure family life. Prince, however, is a free-spirited fellow with no intention of settling down; he dreams of traveling west after the war, reaching the Pacific, seeing the world. Unlike Sally, whose black, and slave, heritage is inescapable, Prince seems part of the nineteenth-century American mainstream, with the same kind of ambitions and fantasies common to white men.

The central action of the play brings out the latent conflict between the white and black aspects of Prince's character. Congress decides to maintain the pay of black soldiers at three dollars a month less than that of whites. (This is again historically accurate.) The black soldiers go on strike. Their general, though sympathetic to their plight, sees this as a dangerous rebellion against his authority; forcing Prince to identify the ringleaders, he has them shot.

Several features emerge here that are common to both *Sally* and *Prince,* and to some of Fuller's other plays as well. Though some of his white characters are outright racists, most of the white authority figures are tolerant or even respectful of blacks; they typically do damage in spite of basically good intentions. Here, the General unwittingly imposes an agonizing moral dilemma on Prince, who must betray either his fellow black soldiers or the army system that he approves of and has flourished under. In Fuller's plays, the focus is on the injuries blacks do to blacks, which always result ultimately from the racist infrastructure in which they find themselves. It is the Aristotelian pattern of a tragic incident, performed at least partly in ignorance, "between those who are near and dear to one another."

In *Prince,* the title character has been transferred to guard duty at an army prison in Virginia. Guarding a Southern spy, who taunts him ruthlessly, he shoots the man dead. The scene shifts to a nearby farm, where ex-slaves are picking cotton for the North. There is also a fascinating black entrepreneur, a woman named Lu, who had been sold five times as a slave, and separated from her child. Now she has become a tough, yet generous, businesswoman, who makes a living selling sweetcakes and longs to own her own store. Again the plot turns on money; the fieldworkers' pay is long overdue. One of the blacks, Burner, complains that it is like slavery all over again. The well-intentioned, gentle, but benighted Northerner running the plantation sees this as a betrayal of the Union cause, and has him thrown in the prison. Not realizing that Prince is on the run, Lu insists that he free Burner, her lover. When Prince declares his intention to pursue his dream of heading west instead, Lu stabs him in a rage. The play is open-ended; Prince is apparently dead (Lu even shows his body to another character), but in the final scene he appears wounded but alive, on his way to the frontier. Fuller plans three more plays in the series, which will no doubt continue to deal with Prince's fortunes.

The outlines of both plays above are simplified; there are subplots, atmospheric scenes, and dozens of characters. Fuller is writing the kind of Brechtian "Epic" drama, with historical scope and episodic structure, that our white playwrights today shun, partly for financial reasons (only a subsidized American theatre company, like the Negro Ensemble, can afford to produce plays with such large casts), and partly from an obsession with individual psychology at the expense of historical or political perspective.

Fuller's sense of history is rather bookish and stilted, however, especially in contrast to August Wilson, who is not only our leading black playwright but probably the best American playwright writing today. Wilson has more feel for the atmosphere of an era, like the restless energy and feeling of uprootedness at the turn of the century in his *Joe Turner's Come and Gone,* or the jazzy insouciance of the twenties in *Ma Rainey's Black Bottom.* In *Sally* and *Prince,* however, the history is often merely unloaded, as if in an awkward lecture. When Fuller's soldiers discuss the Congressional debate about their pay, they sound like TV commentators, and when the Emancipation Proclamation is mentioned, we get it complete with date. Similarly, the dialogue at times sounds anachronistic, which it never does with Wilson; Fuller's characters here use jarring modern phrases like "Don't dicker around with me," "I don't give a damn," or "not too keen on." Such flaws weaken the dramatic thrust of the plays, though they certainly don't destroy it. Fuller has a firm awareness of the inherent moral dilemmas imposed on blacks by the Civil War, the way in which freedom involved terms and conditions that often forced them to deny themselves. He also, as usual, provides a vivid picture of army life—the boredom, the camaraderie, the gossip, the obsession with rank, and the sudden, almost unreal moments of violence. He is very good at depicting personal relationships too, especially friendship and marital love. Despite the historical setting, the ultimate

subject of *Sally* and *Prince* is not history but ethics, but they are very good ethical plays indeed.

The acting of the members of the Negro Ensemble Company, one of the oldest theatre companies in New York, was of a consistently high standard. A number of performances were especially notable, including Ed Wheeler's plain, honest Burner and Hattie Winston's intense, commanding Lu. Samuel L. Jackson was tall, lean, strong, and, above all, soldierly as Prince, with particularly expressive eyes. I found Charles McClennahan's set to be too steeply raked to be always effective, though director Ward, as noted, used it well, aided by Arthur Reese's fine lighting, the principal design element for establishing the many locales. Judy Dearing's costumes, often appropriately ragged but always individualized, were equally beneficial. (pp. 283-86)

Richard Hornby, "Minority Theatre," in The Hudson Review, *Vol. XLII, No. 2, Summer, 1989, pp. 283-89.*

FURTHER READING

Asahina, Robert. "Theatre Chronicle." *The Hudson Review* XXXV, No. 3 (Autumn 1982): 439-46.
> Examines Fuller's motives behind the characterization and setting of *A Soldier's Play,* concluding, "It's not that I suspect Fuller's motives—it is just that I don't know what they are."

Demastes, William W. "New Voices Using New Realism: Fuller, Henley, and Norman." In his *Beyond Naturalism: A New Realism in American Theatre,* pp. 125-54. New York: Greenwood Press, 1988.
> Explores Fuller's use of realism in *A Soldier's Play.*

Harriott, Esther. "The Quest for Justice." In her *American Voices: Five Contemporary Playwrights in Essays and Interviews,* pp. 101-11. Jefferson, N.C.: McFarland and Company, 1988.
> Study of *The Brownsville Raid, Zooman and the Sign,* and *A Soldier's Play.*

Hughes, Catharine. "Soldiers at Sea." *America* 147, No. 17 (1 May 1982): 343.
> Laudatory review of *A Soldier's Play.*

Hughes, Linda K., and Faulkner, Howard. "The Role of Detection in *A Soldier's Play.*" *Clues* 7, No. 2 (Fall/Winter 1986): 83-97.
> Examines the mystery in *A Soldier's Play,* determining that "the play ultimately asks whether the detective's traditional quest for truth is possible when conducted amidst a racist society."

Oliver, Edith. "A Death in the Streets." *The New Yorker* LVI, No. 44 (22 December 1980): 55-6.
> Favorable review of the off-Broadway performance of *Zooman and the Sign.*

————. "A Sergeant's Death." *The New Yorker* LVII, No. 42 (7 December 1981): 110, 113-14.
Praises *A Soldier's Play,* noting that Fuller "moves from strength to strength" with each of his plays.

————. "Fuller's Civil War." *The New Yorker* LXIV, No. 47 (9 January 1989): 82.
Reviews *Sally* and *Prince,* determining, "Although non-vintage Fuller, they can be considered the groundwork for what lies ahead."

————. "Post-Bellum." *The New Yorker* LXV, No. 50 (29 January 1990): 83.
Mixed review of *Jonquil,* "a sometimes awkward, sometimes murky play."

Sauvage, Leo. "Plays That Got Away." *The New Leader* LXV, No. 14 (12-26 July 1982): 21-22.
Praises the production of *A Soldier's Play.*

Simon, John. "Maybe in Allentown." *New York* 22, No. 2 (9 January 1989): 56-7.
Pronounces Fuller's *We,* consisting of the plays *Sally* and *Prince,* a "mighty disappointment."

Weales, Gerald. "American Theater Watch, 1981-1982." *The Georgia Review* XXXVI, No. 3 (Fall 1982): 517-26.
Analyzes Fuller's claim that *A Soldier's Play* parallels Melville's *Billy Budd.*

White, Frank, III. "Pushing Beyond the Pulitzer." *Ebony* XXXVIII, No. 5 (March 1983): 116-18.
Profiles Fuller's life and writing.

Ernest Gaines

1933-

American novelist and short story writer.

Known chiefly for *The Autobiography of Miss Jane Pittman* (1971), Gaines is one of the most popular contemporary novelists in the United States. Yet some critics lament that he "has not received anything like the attention he deserves, for he may just be the best black writer in America." His stories of rural Louisiana have garnered glowing reviews for their gentle depictions of blacks struggling for dignity in the face of numerous obstacles. Reviewer Melvin Maddocks observed: "Gaines is first and last a country-boy writer. He sets down a story as if he were planting, spreading the roots deep, wide and firm. His stories grow organically, at their own rhythm. When they ripen at last, they do so inevitably, arriving at a climax with the absolute rightness of a folk tale."

Gaines was born on a Louisiana plantation during the darkest days of the Great Depression. When he was nine years old, he began contributing to the family's welfare by working in the fields, digging potatoes for fifty cents a day. He spent his happiest times with his Aunt Augusteen Jefferson, a remarkable woman, according to Gaines, who had no legs but who still managed to care for the family: "She crawled on the floor, as a seven or eight-month-old would crawl. She washed our clothes, cooked our food, kept our lives together. After her nap, she'd go outside to work her garden. She was the bravest, most courageous person I've ever known." He would later base Miss Jane Pittman, the title character of his best-known novel, on this beloved aunt.

Unable to escape poverty in Louisiana, Gaines's family moved to Vallejo, California, when Gaines was fifteen. "After we moved to California," he explained to *Washington Post* interviewer Joseph McLellan, "I used to hang around on the corner with the boys, and my father, who was in the merchant marine, told me, 'Get off the block or you're going to get into trouble.' I had a choice of two places to spend my time—the YMCA or the library. I had never been in a library in Louisiana, so I went there looking for books about my people—blacks, especially southern blacks—and I didn't find much. Eventually I started to write about my old home; if the book you want doesn't exist, you try to make it exist." In his quest to write books about his people, Gaines enrolled at San Francisco State University and took writing courses at Stanford University. In 1964 he published his first novel, *Catherine Carmier,* the story of Jackson Bradley, a young, black man who falls in love with Catherine, the daughter of a Creole sharecropper. His next novel, *Of Love and Dust* (1967), is also a love story; it centers on the forbidden romance between Marcus Payne and Louise Bonbon, the wife of a Cajun overseer. Both romances fail, critic William E. Grant

suggested, because the characters are "caught up in a decadent social and economic system that determines their every action and limits their possibilities. . . ." Gaines turned to writing short stories in the late 1960s. In 1968 he published the collection *Bloodline,* followed by *A Long Day in November* in 1971. Although Gaines himself considered these "better than anything else I had written," critics gave them little attention. Due to the success of his later novels, however, they are enjoying renewed interest.

In 1971 Gaines completed what many scholars consider to be his masterpiece, *The Autobiography of Miss Jane Pittman.* A novel he described as "folk autobiography," it was adapted for television in 1974 and won nine Emmy Awards. In the work, Miss Jane Pittman—well over one hundred years old—relates a personal history that begins during the Civil War and culminates with the civil rights movement of the 1960s. *The Autobiography of Miss Jane Pittman* contains four sections: "The War Years," "Reconstruction," "The Plantation," and

"The Quarters." Together, they cover Miss Jane's early life as a newly-freed slave, her marriage, her experiences among poor blacks during the 1920s and 1930s, and her stance against white oppression in the 1960s. "To travel with Miss Pittman from adolescence to old age is to embark upon a historic journey, one staked out in the format of the novel," remarked Addison Gayle. "Never mind that Miss Jane Pittman is fictitious, and that her 'autobiography,' offered up in the form of taped reminiscences, is artifice," added Josh Greenfield, "the effect is stunning. I know of no black novel about the South that exudes quite the same refreshing mix of wit and wrath, imagination and indignation, misery and poetry. And I can recall no more memorable female character in Southern fiction since Lena of Faulkner's *Light in August* than Miss Jane Pittman herself." Readily acknowledging the influence of William Faulkner and Ernest Hemingway on his work, Gaines portrayed Jane Pittman as the embodiment of the black experience in America. Reviewer Jerry H. Bryant commented: "Jane's story is an epic poem. Literally , it is an account of Jane's life. Figuratively, it is a metaphor of the collective black experience. . . ." Keith E. Byerman likewise noted that "Jane captures the experience of those millions of illiterate blacks who never had a chance to tell their own stories." *The Autobiography of Miss Jane Pittman* is, according to most critics, a brilliant novel, deserving of wide readership.

In his fourth novel, *In My Father's House* (1978), Gaines focused on a theme that appears in varying degrees throughout his fiction: the alienation between fathers and sons. As the author told interviewer Paul Desruisseaux: "In my books there always seems to be fathers and sons searching for each other. That's a theme I've worked with since I started writing. Even when the father was not in the story, I've dealt with his absence and its effects on his children. And that is the theme of this book." *In My Father's House* tells of Phillip Martin, a prominent civil rights leader and reverend who, at the peak of his career, is confronted with a troubled young man named Robert X. Although Robert's identity is initially a mystery, eventually he is revealed to be one of three offspring from a love affair the reverend had in an earlier, wilder life. Martin hasn't seen or attempted to locate his family for more than twenty years. Robert arrives to confront and kill the father whose neglect he sees as responsible for the family's disintegration: his sister has been raped, his brother imprisoned for the murder of her attacker, and his mother reduced to poverty, living alone. Although the son's intent to kill his father is never carried out, the reverend is forced to undergo a long and painful odyssey through his own past.

A Gathering of Old Men (1983), Gaines's most recent novel, presents a cast of aging Southern black men who, after a life of subordination and intimidation, make a defiant stand against injustice. Seventeen of them, together with the 30-year-old white heiress of a deteriorating Louisiana plantation, plead guilty to murdering Beau Boutan, a hostile member of a violent Cajun clan.

While a confounded sheriff and vengeful family wait to lynch the black they've decided is guilty, the group members—toting recently fired shotguns—surround the dead man and "confess" their motives. "Each man tells of the accumulated frustrations of his life—raped daughters, jailed sons, public insults, economic exploitation—that serve as sufficient motive for murder," noted Byerman. "Though Beau Boutan is seldom the immediate cause of their anger, he clearly represents the entire white world that has deprived them of their dignity and manhood. The confessions serve as ritual purgings of all the hostility and self-hatred built up over the years." Fifteen or so characters—white, black, and Cajun—advance the story through individual narrations. Reynolds Price commented that the black narrators "are nicely distinguished from one another in rhythm and idiom, in the nature of what they see and report, especially in their specific laments for past passivity in the face of suffering." The accumulated effect, observed Elaine Kendal, is that the "individual stories coalesce into a single powerful tale of subjugation, exploitation and humiliation at the hands of the landowners."

Assessing Gaines as a writer, Alice Walker wrote that Gaines "claims and revels in the rich heritage of Southern Black people and their customs; the community he feels with them is unmistakable and goes deeper even than pride. . . . Gaines is mellow with historical reflection, supple with wit, relaxed and expansive because he does not equate his people with failure." Gaines has been criticized by some, however, for not focusing more directly on problems facing blacks. Gaines responded to this criticism: ". . . too many blacks have been writing to tell whites all about 'the problems,' instead of writing something that all people, including their own, could find interesting, could enjoy." He also remarked that more can be achieved than strictly writing novels of protest. In an interview he stated: "So many of our writers have not read any farther back than [Richard Wright's] *Native Son*. So many of our novels deal only with the great city ghettos; that's all we write about, as if there's nothing else." Gaines continued: "We've only been living in these ghettos for 75 years or so, but the other 300 years—I think is worth writing about."

Writing about what matters to him most—the Louisiana folk people—Gaines has established himself as one of the most popular and critically acclaimed novelists in America. He once stated that his ambition is "to learn as well as I can the art of writing (which I'm sure will take the rest of my life)." He now lives in San Francisco, but he still writes—"five hours a day, five days a week"—about his boyhood Louisiana, trying to perfect his art.

(For further information about Gaines's life and works, see *Black Writers; Contemporary Authors,* Vols. 9-12; *Contemporary Authors New Revision Series,* Vols. 6, 24; *Contemporary Literary Criticism,* Vols. 3, 11, 18; *Dictionary of Literary Biography,* Vols. 2, 33; and *Dictionary of Literary Biography Yearbook,* Vol. 80.)

PRINCIPAL WORKS

Catherine Carmier (novel) 1964
Of Love and Dust (novel) 1967
Bloodline (short stories) 1968
The Autobiography of Miss Jane Pittman (novel) 1971
A Long Day in November (short stories) 1971
In My Father's House (novel) 1978
A Gathering of Old Men (novel) 1983

———————————

Jerry H. Bryant (essay date 1972)

[*In the following review essay, Bryant discusses the influence of Ernest Hemingway and William Faulkner on Gaines's novels. He also examines Gaines's development as a writer, focusing on* The Autobiography of Miss Jane Pittman.]

In 1963, *The Sewanee Review* published "**Just Like a Tree**," one of Mr. Gaines's first stories. Since then, Dial Press has brought out two novels, *Catherine Carmier* (1964) and *Of Love and Dust* (1967), and a collection of short stories, *Bloodline* (1968). His first two novels are competent, promising pieces of fiction. The five stories in *Bloodline* are of high quality, confirming the potential of *Catherine Carmier* and *Of Love and Dust.* With the appearance of *The Autobiography of Miss Jane Pittman*, eight years after the publication of his first story, Gaines makes the leap from promising competence to mature achievement. It is, in my opinion, one of the finest novels written since World War II in America and a distinguished contribution to our national literature. Its publication calls for a critical interpretation and assessment of all Gaines's work, particularly the stylistic and thematic relationships between this latest brilliant novel and his earlier pieces.

I am going to start with what I take to be the weaknesses in the first two novels, but I want to emphasize that whatever I say that is derogatory, in the long run weighs little on the scales of Gaines's total merit. I can think of no other contemporary American novelist whose work has produced in me anything like the sense of depth, the sense of humanity and compassion, and the sense of honesty that I find in Gaines's fiction. It contains the austere dignity and simplicity of ancient epic, a concern with man's most powerful emotions and the actions that arise from those emotions, and an artistic intuition that carefully keeps such passions and behavior under fictive control. Gaines may be one of our most naturally gifted story-tellers. Hopefully, we may look to him for many more years of increasing satisfaction, for he is only thirty-eight years old.

The trouble with having a native talent in an age so self-conscious as ours is that there are too many temptations to ignore that talent and imitate abilities of others who have already succeeded. This temptation especially assails the young and inexperienced. The Gaines of *Catherine Carmier* and *Of Love and Dust* is relatively young and inexperienced, and he succumbs to the power and the achievement of Hemingway and Faulkner. From Hemingway, he borrows the familiar clipped, journalistic sentence structure, understatement and repetition, and simple, concrete diction. These qualities come naturally to Gaines, but when he attempts to implement them through Hemingway, too much of Hemingway and not enough of Gaines remains. Furthermore, underlying the Hemingway style is the Hemingway philosophy, a tough but sentimental stoicism whose highest good is the display of individual grace under pressure, the deliberate seeking out and meeting death with courage.

The spirit of Hemingway is inappropriate to Gaines. Gaines's perception of the world may contain some stoicism, but it is a less theatrical stoicism than that of Hemingway, less self-conscious, less colored by a self-indulgent sense of grievance. The inappropriateness of the Hemingway spirit is most obvious when Gaines attempts to capture Hemingway's combination of toughness and sentiment in passages dealing with romantic love:

> Maybe what she really wanted was to feel his arms around her, their bodies pressed together, his mouth on her mouth. No, not maybe, this is what both of them wanted.

When he is not imitating, Gaines writes much better than this. His dialogue suffers too:

> "You know it's wrong, don't you? Don't you know it's wrong? All we can do is hurt each other, don't you know that?"
> "Say you don't love me, Catherine, and I'll never see you again. Say you don't love me, and I'll never bother you again."

Because neither Gaines's talent nor his vision harmonizes with those of Hemingway, it is no wonder that he has incompletely adapted his model's techniques and attitudes to his own. Simplicity, understatement, repetition are all admirable qualities of Gaines's prose at its best—not when they descend from Hemingway, but when they emerge directly from Gaines.

Faulkner has had an even stronger and more pernicious hold on Gaines's abilities. One of the most characteristic features of Faulkner's writing is his sense of history. He is famous for the way in which he expresses this sense in his long sentences, ranging through the present, the past, the future, through parenthetical remarks and qualifying subordinate clauses, identifying ownership and family ties. The success of these sentences is achieved by his genius for combining the serious with the humorous. He counters his stately evocation of vast historical significance with mocking parody. The vision of man such sentences convey is that of a creature at once dignified and noble, and mean and ignominious.

It does not work this way for Gaines. "One summer afternoon," he writes in *Catherine Carmier,* "Robert Carmier rode up to the plantation store (the store was still being managed by the Grovers then) and asked Mack Grover for the house. (Antoine Richard, who was at the store, brought this version of the story into the quarters.)" In the first place, these sentences are too short to convey the great tides of history we find in Faulkner. More important, Gaines does not have Faulkner's particular sense of historical and human ambiguity. What in Faulkner is a combination of opposites that elicits the laughter of the gods, in Gaines is youthful seriousness lacking in depth. This seriousness leads him to respond to another fatal temptation: "explaining" the significance of his story. Too often we get from the characters interpretations of the action that should have been left unspoken. For example, in *Of Love and Dust,* after eliciting from the reader an ambivalent judgment of rebellious young Marcus Payne, Gaines has his narrator, Jim Kelly, settle our minds with a positive evaluation. These are the shortcomings of an inexperienced writer lacking in confidence, who does not trust the concrete action to convey its own meaning. Faulkner leans in this direction too, but his aim is to intensify the ambiguity he perceives in the world. He generally uses the context of his explanations to undercut their validity. The explanations in *Catherine Carmier* and *Of Love and Dust,* though expressed by the characters in context, seem to come from Gaines himself.

It is understandable how Gaines could have put himself into such deep debt to Hemingway and Faulkner. Hemingway's popularity reached a peak in the 1950's when Gaines was going to college. And Faulkner is, like Gaines, a native Southerner. Few Southern writers who write about the South can escape his influence. But of course Gaines need imitate no one. The five stores in *Bloodline* are proof of this. Showing very little awareness of either Hemingway or Faulkner, in this collection Gaines advances stylistically from his first two novels, making greater use of the dialect he knows so well—that of the Louisiana bayou country where he grew up—and introducing a greater sharpness and liveliness in the language of his narrators. His phraseology takes on the quality of that of the black preacher, and derives from the poetic language of black folk forging their perceptions of the world with simple, unlettered directness. In "**Just Like a Tree,**" old Aunt Fe eases

> back on the bed—calm, calm, calm.

Her passing will be like the cutting down of a beautiful old tree, which leaves

> a big hole in the ground . . . and you get another big hole in the air where the lovely branches been all these years.

A character speaks of the fate of old people in the face of growing black unrest and increasing civil rights demonstrations:

> A big wind is rising, and when a big wind rise, the sea stirs, and the drop o' water you see laying on top the sea this day won't be there tomorrow.

There is repetition, understatement, simplicity, and poetry here, but it is Gaines's, not Hemingway's.

Because the stories in *Bloodline* were written before or during the composition of *Catherine Carmier* and *Of Love and Dust,* we might assume that the difference in the quality of their styles is due to a predilection in Gaines for the short rather than the long narrative. The disproof of this assumption comes with *The Autobiography of Miss Jane Pittman.* Here Gaines finds his true voice. I can think of no other novel by a black author in which a black Southern dialect is so successfully sustained over a long narrative. What is most impressive is the dialect's authenticity. Artists in all media have always been fascinated by the art and language of the folk. Theocritus, Virgil, Longus, Chaucer, Spenser, Wordsworth—all have attempted to render the spirit of the common speech of simple people. Keats and Yeats adapted the form of the medieval folk ballad to their own artistic purposes. In each case, however, the adapting poet was educated in a culture and a language widely different from that of the poets whose forms they tried to imitate. The ballads of Keats and Yeats are "art" rather than "folk" ballads, and the pastorals of Virgil and Spenser reflect what educated, sophisticated men assume to be the simple expressions of country life rather than exact renderings of that life. Gaines bridges the gap between the folk artist and the cultured artist of formal education. He is both. His is not, therefore, an "art" narrative, but an authentic narrative by an authentic ex-slave, authentic even though both are Gaines's inventions. So successful is he in *becoming* Miss Jane Pittman, that when we talk about her story, we do not think of Gaines as her creator, but as her recording "editor."

Miss Jane's art is that of the primitive minstrel. Her interests are events and her feelings about those events rather than motives and psychology. She is a completely honest reporter, who does not like "retrick." She throws away good lines and ignores contrived climaxes. Her narrative runs evenly, with few peaks and valleys, as if her vantage point of a century of living has brought her a peace and serenity which erases the turbulence of her recall. Her contempt for literary self-consciousness is the contempt of the person for whom talking is neither a recreation nor a polemical device, but a very precarious means for communicating precious values from one person to another, from one generation to the next. The world we view is Jane's world, but many of the details come from her friends who gather around the imaginary tape recording of Gaines's imaginary "editor," so her story is a communal effort. Jane is, therefore, for all her powerful uniqueness, a representative character. And her story is a representative story, the collective account of the collective black since emancipation, told by Jane when she is 110 years old, just a hundred years after she is freed from slavery.

All of these aspects of the novel produce Gaines's most mature work. Only the cumulative effect of reading through the entire chronicle can convey the substance of

Gaines's stylistic achievement. But a short sample can suggest the quality of Jane's language. The following is her comment about the collapse of Reconstruction and the cruelty with which lawless bands of whites treated those blacks who sought to make a living by farming their own small plot of land. Such groups, says Jane,

> rode all over the state beating and killing. Would kill any black man who tried to stand up and would kill any white man who tried to help him. Just after the war many colored people tried to go out and start their own little farm. The secret groups would come out there and beat them just because their crops was cleaner than the white man's crop. "What you growing there, Hawk?" they would ask him. "Corn, Master," Hawk would say. "That look like grass out there to me, Hawk," they would say. "But 'fore day in the morning I surely get it out—if the Lord spare." "No, you better start right now, Hawk," they would say. Then they would make you get down on your hands and knees and eat grass till you got sick. If they didn't get enough fun out of watching you throw-up, they would tie you to a fence post or to a tree and beat you. "Tomorrow night we come back again, Hawk," they would say. "And you better not have no grass out there, you hear?" Or, "Tomorrow night we come back and you better have some grass in that field, hear, Charlie?"

From the beginning, Gaines has worked to put into an appropriate form his own sense of history, a sense which has both dictated and arisen from his central subject, the blacks and the whites who live in and around his imaginary town of Bayonne, near Baton Rouge, and who work the land of the plantations that still survive. Gaines has the special feeling for these people and this land that comes from having grown up among them, and having absorbed the quality of their lives without exercising any analytical selectivity as to what he absorbed. Thus, his feelings are strongly attached to the sheer physical texture of this country, and it pervades his fiction: the hot summer sky filled with a hazy sun; the freezing, sleet-ridden days of winter; the monochromatic hues of a brilliantly white sky meeting a brilliantly white earth; the winter darkness in whose heavy overcast the distinction between the earth and the sky are obliterated. Gaines has the intuition of D. H. Lawrence and Thomas Hardy. Like them, he feels a permanent spirit residing in the land, which transcends time and space. His characters are born with the past in their bones, and their lives, whether they stay or leave this place, are dominated by it—this "place" in which the past is embedded.

It is not surprising that Gaines failed effectively to cast these responses in forms created by Faulkner. Faulkner sees in the past an admirable simplicity and strength, whose resting place is the ancient wilderness. That past is not without its evil, but by far the greater evil for Faulkner is the intrusion of the new into the old, to the destruction of the former. Gaines's conception of the past does not simply and diametrically oppose that of Faulkner. Had it done so, he would not have mistaken Faulkner's forms as appropriate vehicles for his own fiction. Gaines's vision entails a deep conflict of values.

In the past, he sees much to love and to cherish, especially in the figures of his old "aunts," whose lives are manifestations of that past. For example, Aunt Charlotte in *Catherine Carmier* and Aunt Margaret in *Of Love and Dust,* patiently submit to the slave mentality and the absolute power of the whites, and find their satisfaction and contentment in that submission. Submission is virtually a religion for them. They find the threat of change not only repugnant, but full of forebodings of cosmic doom, the disruption of the heavens, and the onset of chaos. Their own lives having been so precarious and unsure, they cling to the nearest and most accessible certainty, the Southern code of *de facto* slavery. They are strong and courageous, however, and fiercely determined to survive. For them Gaines has the love of a son for his mother, a love so ambivalent as to be painful, divided between gratitude for the mother's unconditional love and always welcoming arms, and rejection of the dependence and love which means destruction of dignity and pride, indeed, of one's very self.

In the present Gaines sees much to reject, especially as it appears in the figures of some of his rebels against the old order. Jackson Bradley and Marcus Payne, for example, from *Catherine Carmier* and *Of Love and Dust* respectively, make overt attempts to bring down the old structures. While such attempts may be desirable in the abstract, in these particular cases our approval of them is deeply equivocal, as is Gaines's. Jackson is too strident an accuser of the plantation world, concentrating too much on condemning it while justifying himself and insisting upon his own innocence. Marcus looks for grievances, too, and is quick to find them. His means of seeking redress, however, are ill-conceived and hasty and endanger not only himself but other innocent people.

Gaines is torn between his love for the *persons* of his "aunts" but a rejection of their submission to the past, and a rejection of the persons of his "rebels" but approval of their defiance of the Southern code. Consequently, in *Catherine Carmier* and *Of Love and Dust,* his main theme is the conflict between changing the inheritance from the past and resistance to that change. He cannot follow Faulkner in an affirmation of the old, nor can he turn away from Faulkner in an affirmation of the new. He is left with a deep split. Faulkner's sense of history tells him that the new will inevitably replace the old. The acceptance of this inevitability makes it possible for Faulkner to shape his controlling irony, the clash between his nostalgic wish to perpetuate what is good in the past and his realistic recognition that the present denies him that wish. This kind of paradox, since it is embedded in nature, is subject to satisfactory fictional balance. For Gaines, however, the past with its implications of slavery cannot be thought of as worth preserving. Nor can the present with its implications of thoughtless, self-centered revolution be thought of as repugnant enough to reject.

In *Catherine Carmier* and *Of Love and Dust,* Gaines has worked out neither an ethical nor an esthetic resolution to these contradictions, that satisfactorily reflects his own intuition. Instead, he invests the two novels with a classical inevitability similar to Faulkner's, except that for Gaines the victor is the past, the world of slavery. Jackson Bradley loses his beloved Catherine and with her, as he puts it, new life and fresh air. Marcus Payne loses his bid to get revenge against Sidney Bonbon, the white plantation overseer, by running off with Sidney's wife, Louise. It is as if the will of the gods supports the Southern code, as if some transcendent force embraces the destiny of all the characters and no puny human can thwart that destiny. Those who struggle are defeated. The Aunt Charlottes and the Aunt Margarets have tuned into the controlling forces, but in their submission to them, they too are defeated. All of the characters seem to be victims, either unable to bring about salutary change or determined to resist change.

These novels suggest that the past is too strong to fight against it. From this, we can infer their significance. They are inventions of images of failure, seeing and experiencing which the reader may better know the true nature of his condition. This is pessimistic determinism, similar to the assumptions of Hemingway and Faulkner, and it does not quite embody Gaines's own convictions. These novels tell us what they do because of the disharmony between Gaines's intuitive vision and the vision he hammered out to fit his literary models. His intuitive vision is that, though much of men's lives may be determined, in the instance of slavery the slave past must not be either valued or preserved, and need not be. This vision says that there is no god-like force preventing us from bringing about change. In *Of Love and Dust,* Gaines shows signs of liberating himself from determinism. Presiding over the fates of Bonbon and Marcus is Marshall Hebert, the white owner of the plantation on which the two black men work. Hebert manipulates them for his own benefit, and wins. But Hebert is not a god, and James Kelly becomes aware of this in the course of the novel. Hebert is vulnerable. And because he is, the possibility of destroying his power and introducing change is no dream or illusion doomed by irresistible necessity. However many reservations Gaines has about Marcus as a rebel, he has Kelly conclude that Marcus, in his defiance of the Southern code, is to be admired for "starting something that others would hear about, and understand, and follow."

The increasing maturity of Gaines's style is an index to the increasing clarity with which he perceives his theme. Thus, in *Bloodline,* not only does he have his style under better control than in his first two novels; he also works out an effective metaphor, whose form expresses his conception of history, the possibility that the present may work to make the future better than the past. Very generally, the metaphor is organic life, for which growth and change are the signs of life's greatest strength and highest good. In *Bloodline,* each of the stories represents a stage of growth, in this case the growth of the black man in a black community toward a courage strong enough to fight a repugnant past in order to bring about a better future. The first story, "**A Long Day in November,**" is about the failure of six-year-old Eddie spiritually to be born into the process of growth. His world is cold and wintry; money is scarce, pleasures few, and light and warmth in short supply. It is not this world, however, that blocks the commencement of Eddie's growth. It is the reversal of the roles of his parents. His mother Amy has the strength and determination his father should have. But Amy does not use her strength to help Eddie face his world, but to protect him from it. As the story closes, Eddie is back in bed, where he began the story, essentially unchanged, luxuriating in the protective warmth of the covers and fantasizing daring deeds which would take courage he has not yet learned.

The growth process does not start until the next story, "**The Sky is Gray.**" Octavia, like Amy, is strong and determined, but unlike Amy, she teaches her son James to meet the world with courage and dignity. "You not a bum," she tells James as she orders him to put down his coat collar even against a freezing drizzle, "you a man." Procter Lewis, the nineteen-year-old narrator of the next story, "**Three Men,**" whose title picks up the theme of "**The Sky is Gray,**" carries the growth process another step. Convinced that if he allows a powerful white man to secure his release from jail he will never again belong to himself, Procter determines to refuse any such offer, hoping to acquire by such a refusal the awareness, self-dignity, and strength that Octavia sought to inculcate in James. To acquire these manly qualities is inherently valuable and desirable, but it also means a growth of immense importance to the collective black man. Such qualities prepare him to contribute to the growth of his people by assuming the courage necessary for trying to destroy lingering slavery. This is precisely the aim of Copper Laurent, the firebrand mulatto son of the late Walker Laurent, in the title story "**Bloodline.**" Copper returns to his father's plantation, where ten years before he had been treated like a slave, without any rightful claims as Walter's son. He proclaims himself a "general," and announces that he plans to lead his "army" not only against those who are denying him his just inheritance, but those general rapists, murders, and plunderers of his people. Copper may be a little mad, and Gaines may have his suspicions about him, but his vitality injects into the sick atmosphere of the decaying Laurent plantation the irresistible strength of health and confidence in the future.

The growth process depicted in these stories culminates in "**Just Like a Tree,**" which is ironic, since of the work I have been discussing it is one of Gaines's first pieces. A young black militant has become active in the civil rights movement, and in doing so, he has endangered the lives of many of those he loves, including Aunt Fe. One of Aunt Fe's nieces decides to bring the old lady North with her to live. Before she leaves, Aunt Fe's friends gather to say goodbye. Most of them resent the young militant for the same reason many of the blacks in *Of Love and Dust* resent Marcus, for disrupting the superficial calm of their precarious lives. They are all skeptical and afraid of change. But this rebel is no Marcus Payne. He dislikes what he is doing, knowing that it causes trouble for the people he loves. But he cannot give it up, for he is riding a wave of pride and strength and determination. He approaches his participation in the struggle for freedom fully aware that it is a sword that cuts two ways. He commits himself having decided that his belief in change outweighs the dangers change implies.

Aunt Fe belongs to a generation that cannot follow its young into the new world. She can neither go North and leave the land she has spent her life on, nor stay on that land in her old situation. She does not, however, like Aunt Charlotte and Aunt Margaret, warn her young descendent to beware the wrath of the gods lest he be destroyed for disobedience. Her time has come and she knows it; she does not attempt to preserve it beyond its term. She crawls into her bed the night before she is to leave, and dies. With her death, Gaines completes a natural cycle, which the stories in *Bloodline* trace, the entrance of the new, the exit of the old, the death of the past and the birth of the future. In this metaphor, Gaines resolves his ambivalent attitudes towards his "aunts." We may lament the passing of Aunt Fe, but we cannot deny the validity of the young rebel's commitment, and the hopeful possibilities of the future for which he is risking both himself and his brothers and sisters. This natural cycle does not lock man into the tragedy of death and the destruction of a valuable past. It supports life, and works to the advantage of the blacks who pattern their lives after its forms.

Bloodline shows Gaines struggling to reconcile his love for his "aunts" and the past they belong to with his rejection of that past and the affirmation of the "rebel." He achieves that reconciliation by examining the process through which the black male acquires the strength and the courage to attempt to modify the past. What is lacking in the process expressed in *Bloodline* is the female element, which until now Gaines has seen merely as the determination to survive and associated it with submission to the past. In *The Autobiography of Miss Jane Pittman,* he introduces into the metaphor of *Bloodline* the female element that was lacking, and brings that metaphor to its completion. His sight clearer and his confidence stronger, he abandons the melodramatic superstructure of classical doom in his first novels and turns to the simple, authentic earnestness and understatement of Jane. She is a transformed version of Aunt Charlotte, Aunt Margaret, and Aunt Fe. In her new manifestation, she is both a repository of womanly endurance and a vehicle for the change sought by her men. What has been an unresolved clash between the male and the female, and the new and the old, becomes in *Miss Jane Pittman* a dialectic of re-enforcing opposites which work for life.

The form of Jane's narrative fits Gaines's theme perfectly. Like the separate stories in *Bloodline,* each episode in Jane's story marks a stage in the growth of Jane's life

and that of the collective black which she mirrors. The first episode is an account of her spiritual birth, in which two bands of soldiers, one Confederate, one Yankee, stop to rest at the plantation where Jane is a ten-year-old slave. The Confederates are weary, hungry, defeated; and they treat Jane with the bitterness of the vanquished. The Yankees are ebullient, optimistic, full of victory, and thoughtful of "Ticey," Jane's slave name. From one of these Yankees, Corporal Brown, Jane takes a new name, Jane Brown, and symbolically is born into freedom. Later, when she leaves the plantation with a group of ex-slaves, she will see them do the same thing, slough off the old and put on the new.

These acts of birth contain a certain amount of exhilaration and hopefulness. But they also contain depression and disappointment. Like the North as a whole, Corporal Brown professes to make Jane free simply by giving her a new name. He excites in Jane, as the North did for all Southern blacks, a dream of freedom and equality that are synonymous with the North. Thus, when the war ends and they are freed, Jane and her companions embark upon a quest for freedom, associated in their minds with an actual place. In Jane's case, it is Ohio, the home of Corporal Brown. But Jane soon realizes that, as a gentle white lady tells her, "there is no Ohio." Gaines has always been moved by the gap between this dream and the reality. Marcus and Louise intend to go North where they supposedly will be free of the prejudices of the Southern code. Aunt Margaret tries to warn them that there is no such North, but Marcus refuses to listen to her. Jane learns for herself, and something more besides. For all the bitter disappointment engendered in the black by the North's unfulfilled and irresponsibly made promises, something of great value is achieved by them. Jane and her people develop an unprecedented impulse toward growth and freedom. More important, Gaines suggests that the only way Jane can complete her quest is to remain in the South.

In other novels dealing with blacks in an oppressive white society, Jane's resigned decision to stay in Louisiana would be the signal for either the pessimistic ending of the story, or the beginning of a detailed account of further outrages committed against the black by the white, an account cast in the voice of social protest. The absence of this familiar note in Jane's narrative is one of the things that makes *The Autobiography* such a milestone in American fiction. Gaines does not avoid having Jane report white atrocities, but he does not allow her to use the propagandistic and sociological stridency that characterizes so many earlier novels.

The second main episode depicts the first attempt of the freed slaves to test their freedom. It is a tragic failure, but it is not a dead end. Before the little band leaves the plantation, they conduct an archetypal discussion, in which emerge the original lines of separation between the young, hot-headed militants, and the old conservative compromisers. The conservative position is expressed, not by one of Gaines's "aunts," but by old Unc

Isom, who tries to persuade the younger blacks to use caution:

> "You telling us to stay here?" somebody young said.
> "Them who want stay, stay," he said. "Them who must go, go. But this is no time for weeping. Rejoice now."
> "We leaving out," somebody young said. "If the old people want stay here, stay. We free, let's move."
> . . . .
> "You free from what?" Unc Isom said. "Free to do what—break more hearts?"
> "Niggers hearts been broke ever since niggers been in this world," somebody young said.

Unc Isom argues that what is past cannot be helped, and that to demand a redress of past grievances is futile. He says that he is talking wisdom. The young reject his wisdom and move on, Jane among them.

Their decision is fatal. That night, deep in the swamp, they are attacked by a band of outlaw whites, and everyone but Jane and six-year-old Ned is murdered. They cut themselves off from the protection of the plantation and find only death in freedom. They are like children; unused to the responsibilities of independence and intoxicated by their new sense of identity, they do not submit easily to the social imperative of making voluntary concessions. They squabble; they fight; a "slow-wit" tries to rape Jane. They cannot afford such conflict when they are so vulnerable to enemies. When darkness falls, Big Laura, their leader, prepares to light a fire. Silently, everyone gathers around her while she strikes the iron against the flint, draws sparks, starts the flame. It is a fine scene. But this first assertion of black freedom, in which the blaze of consciousness defies the dark swamp, serves only to expose them, and they are killed.

But something of the fire remains. The massacre is not an unequivocal disaster. Little Ned is Big Laura's son, and he has been made the custodian of the flint and iron, the instruments of light and warmth. They become previous symbols for Ned and Jane. Jane's survival is also significant. Big Laura is the original black mother, whose courage, determination, and stamina transfuse blood-strength into her people. But all of her strength is not sufficient to save the little band. The reason it is not is suggested by the pairing off of Ned and Jane. Jane, only a ten- or eleven-year-old child herself, also suffers from a body stunted and sterilized by slavery. But her spirit compensates for what she lacks physically. Jane takes from Laura the position of the black mother, and in caring for Ned as a foster child, demonstrates her willingness and ability to assume the responsibility for succouring and preserving the race. Big Laura had to fail, for she tried to combine the male's explosive strength and drive toward dignity with the female's instinct for preservation and longevity. In Ned and Jane, these qualities are properly divided, though not separated or conflicting. Thus, from the slaughter of the innocents, Jane and Ned emerge as the bearers of a new consciousness, of flint and iron, of manhood and motherhood.

From here on, Jane becomes the preserving woman and Ned (together with Jane's other men) becomes the explosive, courageous male. The several main episodes that constitute the rest of the novel grow out of this relationship. Of these, the pivotal one is that in which Jane marries Joe Pittman and accompanies him from central Louisiana to a ranch near the Texas border, where he has taken a job breaking wild stallions. This is dangerous work, and eventually Jane's fear for his life activates her preserving instinct. When a great black stallion is captured and Jane sees death waiting for Joe on the horse's back, she sets the great beast free. It is impossible, however, for her to protect Joe, just as it is impossible for Aunt Charlotte and Aunt Margaret to protect Jackson and Marcus. It is fortunate that it is so. The character of Joe is a real breakthrough for Gaines, representing a possibility he did not quite formulate in his earlier stories. Joe is the archetypal rebel, but one with whom Gaines can go along unequivocally without sacrificing respect for his old "aunts." Joe is their praiseworthy counterpoint. Echoing Wilson in Hemingway's "The Short Happy Life of Francis Macomber," Joe tells Jane that every man signs a contract when he is born, accepting death as the basic condition of life. If his life and his death are to have any substantial meaning, he must pass his life doing the best way he can whatever he can do best. In Joe we see the emergence of black manhood, which, in accepting the possibility of death, brings freedom and self-respect, which cannot be achieved by following the pleas of the protective black woman.

The stallion is the force of nature, with which man must voluntarily struggle if he is to make his life worthwhile, if he does not want to become a passive slave to himself and his fears. The tragedy in this relationship is that these forces must eventually break each other, even though to be so broken is, especially for the human, a precious honor. When Joe goes after the stallion and dies in attempting to recapture it, he fulfills his potential. He dies in freedom, grandly and nobly. Jane would rather have him alive and less vividly charged with intensity than have him dead and beyond her arms. We can sympathize with her, and wonder if Joe's commitment to his leviathan job is worth what it returns, whether there is not something terribly wasteful in this warfare between great powers, a squandering of marvelous energy. Yet, even Jane knows without doubt that Joe will never be replaced in her life. His existence shines with the glow of true mettle, enlivens Jane with its display of courage. He is a man. And while he shortens their years together by meeting the obligations of his manhood before his obligations to her, neither she nor we could value him nearly so highly had he done it differently.

In this episode, Gaines shows us that death lies constantly across life, and that the confrontation between the two frequently gives life meaning. Joe's struggle with the stallion is analogous to the fire lighted by Big Laura in the swamp. Both are assertions of the black presence against a world that would extinguish that presence. Both contain death because that assertion makes them vulnerable. Even so, the assertion is supremely valuable. All of this sounds like Hemingway. But Hemingway stops with the value of individual assertion. Gaines goes further and suggests that the individual assertion is the value-giving booster to the longevity carried by Jane, the black woman. From that assertion, the black race absorbs intensified life.

Ned inherits the spirit of Joe. Just before Jane goes with Joe to west Louisiana, Ned is forced to run away to Kansas for having joined a black activist movement. Jane makes no secret of her desire that he stay and give up the dangerous activism. But he goes, unable at this point either to die for the cause or to submit as Jane wishes him to do. Ten years after Joe's death, he returns, and begins to preach the words of Frederick Douglass. Work together, he tells his people, but do not condemn all whites. Walk with dignity and do not be afraid to die. We sense that, had not Joe Pittman demonstrated the possibilities, Ned could not have acquired the courage he needs. Joe did not defeat death, but he defeated the fear of it, and for the black man that is the important thing. The new Ned is the spiritual son of Joe. If one must die, he says, echoing Joe, "wouldn't you rather die saying I'm a man than to die saying I'm a contented slave?" And Ned does die, at the hands of a Cajun hired by whites for the job.

Joe and Ned illustrate two of the forms freedom and the pursuit of it take. Both are based on personal courage. Joe faces nature; Ned faces a social system. Joe faces natural necessity in a struggle that ennobles himself and his antagonist. Ned faces a degenerate, demeaning artificiality, a social apparatus that clothes its neurotic fears and mean weaknesses in piety and righteousness. Joe's struggle is universal, the great model of other specific instances. Ned's struggle takes its form from the larger universal. Joe's is an act performed in freedom. Ned's is an act in which freedom must be torn from an oppressive society.

Over half a century after the death of Ned, Jimmy Aaron drives home the importance of Joe's and Ned's example. He returns to his native country around Bayonne as the point man for a civil rights organization. As in *Of Love and Dust,* the blacks on the plantations are frightened and slightly angered by Jimmy's defiant intentions, though he is no hot-head following ill-conceived plans. But Jimmy manages to win many of them over, convincing them to march in a demonstration he has planned for execution in Bayonne. The morning of the march Jimmy is killed by the local whites. The scene in which the plantation blacks gather to start for Bayonne is the climax to all of Gaines's work and thinking to the present. Jane herself has agreed to participate, indicating the profound change she has undergone in these last few years of the century she has been describing. When the news of Jimmy's death

arrives, the gathered blacks go through several minutes of uncertainty, made more difficult by the fact that the white plantation owner, Robert Samson, has come to dissuade them from going. There are now, however, more Joes and Neds and Jimmys. Alex Strut steps forward to declare his intention of going into Bayonne to rendezvous with Jimmy's spirit. Still the group hesitates, and then Jane speaks: "I will go with Alex."

With these words, Jane heals the old split between the old and the young, and brings the leading male and the following female into harmony. She has, like the classical black mother, sought to teach her men the protective coatings of obedience and submission. More than that, she has borne one of the essential principles of life, continuity and survival. She has agonized and grieved over the death of her men, but she has never given up nor lapsed into despair. Now she turns onto a new path. She does not counter Alex's determination to go into Bayonne with the advice of Unc Isom or Aunt Charlotte or Aunt Margaret. She joins her longevity with the intensity of Alex. Probably Alex will die, but if he does, as have Joe, Ned, and Jimmy, it will be in the service of the black race's life principle.

The male and female are equally important. The woman preserves, the man makes worthwhile what she preserves. The longevity of the woman contains no vivifying intensity of honor and self-respect and freedom (a generalization from which Jane must be excepted). The explosiveness and intensity of the male contains too little longevity for its value to be satisfactorily grasped. Only when the longevity of the woman and the intensity of the man merge can there be anything like worthwhile life, can the black look forward to a transformed existence.

There is also a lesson in this concept of life and growth for the white American. Robert Samson, the white plantation owner, attempts to prevent his black workers from going to Bayonne. He represents a dead culture. He is one of the last of a long line of white Southerners who have maintained an inflexible resistance to change and growth. Just as Southern whites fought for the re-establishment of a white supremacist rule after the Civil War, so do they fight for its perpetuation in the face of a growing civil rights movement. Just as Colonel Dye takes over the Bone plantation, on which Jane works, upon the collapse of Reconstruction and orders the black hands either to accept the return of the old order or get out, so does Robert Samson tell his black workers that he will throw anyone out of the house he occupies on Samson land if he participates in the Bayonne demonstration. Colonel Dye is an accurate forecast of Robert Samson. Between them there is no growth. While the whites have sought to hold the line, they have been dying, and while the blacks have died in the struggle against containment, they have been growing into a new life. The Southern white, unexercised in movement and risk, has allowed his muscles to atrophy and his energies to dissipate.

The consequences of the white's failure to grow are made clear in the episode which precedes and prepares for the final confrontation between Jane and Robert Samson. Tee Bob Samson, Robert's son, contains the potential for a new white man, but the atmosphere he lives in is airless and his potential is stunted. In a significant reversal from *Catherine Carmier* and *Of Love and Dust,* white Tee Bob falls in love with Mary Agnes LeFabre, black. Mary Agnes knows that Tee Bob's origins and the culture they both live in absolutely deny any success for Tee Bob's love. Tee Bob, however, like a white Jackson Bradley or Marcus Payne, persists in the belief that the old rules can be transcended by love. For the Southern white, however, there can be no such transcendence, no change, no growth. Tee Bob searches for some break in the container of his culture that hermetically seals him into stasis. Finding none, he commits suicide, for he cannot live without new air.

Like Joe and Ned, Tee Bob presses against an antagonist. Ironically, the class to which he belongs, which maintains nearly absolute physical power over the black man, cannot give Tee Bob any strength. His opponent is in a sense himself, and he dies by his hand. Wise old Jules Raynard, Tee Bob's "parrain" and an old friend of the Samson family, is the kind of man upon whom a new South might be based. He understands that Tee Bob's death is the result of cultural stagnation, for which everyone, including Jane, is to blame. Tee Bob, he says, had to pay for the sins of them all. He does not mean that Tee Bob is an instrument of salvation, through which the sinful may be relieved of their sins, but that he is the inevitable consequence of their sins—the failure to solve racial differences and enter into a new cycle. Tee Bob's literal death prefigures Robert Samson's symbolic one.

Whether it is intuitive or learned, Gaines's perception of the world resembles that of a biologist, who sees each living organism passing through time, occupying stages, crossing boundary lines into new and unfamiliar territory. Organic life is postulated on the oscillation between life and death, and these are the realities which Gaines fastens onto. The two states transmit to each other a vitality, which, when fused in the unity of the organism, presuppose growth, the *sine qua non* of life. Out of death grows life, which spreads through time to the edge of its identifiable being. If that being cannot tolerate the leaping of its own boundaries, or lacks the strength to make those leaps, it must die without hope of new life. If it dares to make that crossing, it snatches—from the death implied in the crossing—new life. Similarly, the female impulse toward survival and the male impulse toward brief but vivid intensity have, as Gaines suggests in *The Autobiography of Miss Jane Pittman,* promoted growth in the collective black, the metaphor of whose unity is the living organism. This conviction Gaines drives home in the last sentence of Jane's chronicle. Standing face to face with Robert Samson, the embodiment of a hundred years of white resistance to change, Jane, the embodiment of a hundred years of black growth, pauses in her move toward Bayonne and the

demonstration. "Me and Robert," she says, "looked at each other a long time, then I went by him."

This sentence may become one of the most trenchant expressions of our period's spirit. Soon after speaking this sentence into the tape recording of Gaines's "editor," Jane dies. But like the death of Aunt Fe in **"Just Like a Tree,"** Jane's death marks a beginning rather than an end. With this last sentence, she expresses the end of the first great cycle of American life since emancipation. If the Robert Samsons are all but dead; if they do not dare to move into the unknown beyond their old limits; Alex and Jane *are* alive and they *do* dare to make that crucial move. And if whites learned nothing from the blacks for that hundred years, perhaps now, with the advent of a new life cycle, the black can teach the white to enter that cycle with a new vitality.

Jimmy Aaron, from the time of his birth, is thought by his people to be "the One," the leader, the incarnation of his people's aspirations. But only upon his death do his people realize they are ready for him. We are also ready for him, because Gaines has brought us through a century of growth. The nature of the new area into which Jane will move when she and her companions march into Bayonne is unknown. Perhaps it holds death. But that is the nature of life, and anyone who wants to live it completely must be prepared to die out of the old and be born into the new. The development of that preparedness in the spirits of the black American is the main subject of *The Autobiography of Miss Jane Pittman,* and the growth from death to life as its main lesson. (pp. 106-20)

> *Jerry H. Bryant, "'From Death to Life': The Fiction of Ernest J. Gaines," in* The Iowa Review, *Vol. 3, No. 1, Winter, 1972, pp. 106-20.*

Jack Hicks (essay date 1977)

[*In the following excerpt, later published as a chapter in his* In the Singer's Temple: Prose Fictions of Barthelme, Gaines, Brautigan, Piercy, Kesey, and Kosinski *(1981), Hicks favorably appraises* The Autobiography of Miss Jane Pittman, *describing it as a "powerful folk history of Afro-American life."*]

The Autobiography of Miss Jane Pittman is fiction masquerading as autobiography, but mostly, it is a powerful folk history of Afro-American life from the Civil War to the mid-1960s. If such comparisons are helpful, it is a novel and a racial repository as well, *sui generis* like W. E. B. DuBois's *The Souls of Black Folk* and Jean Toomer's *Cane.* Jane Pittman's life is a framing metaphor, complex and vibrant, like Toomer's sugar cane. Her life and his field are poetically imagined, specific and concrete; people go in and out of them, they can be sweet and raw, can harbor love and lust, spawn tragedy and hatred. And like DuBois and Toomer, Ernest Gaines taps the languages and forms and powers of black folk-rooted art forms. The bones of his book are communal, oral and rhetorical: spirituals, black folk sermons, slave narratives, biblical parables, folk tales, and primitive myths. These are spoken, declaimed forms, issuing from a collective human voice. As the putative "editor" tells us in his "Introduction," the novel is built on a series of interviews with Miss Jane Pittman, a one hundred-ten-year-old former slave, and many of her friends. The "friends" is important, for her being is truly a repository of Southern black life since the Civil War. As our editor notes of those "wonderful people" and their relation to Miss Jane, "Miss Jane's story is all of their stories, and their stories are Miss Jane's."

There are four sections to *Miss Jane Pittman:* "The War Years," covering the years 1865-1866 and the child Ticey's (Jane's slave name) wanderings as a newly-freed slave; "Reconstruction," extending from 1876-*circa* 1912, in which Reconstruction fails, Jane is married, and loses her husband—one of the early black cow-boys—and her adopted son; "The Plantation," moving from 1912-the 1930s, during which she comes to Samson Plantation and experiences the very different declines of poor Blacks and ruling Whites; and "The Quarters," an unbroken memoir running from the 1930s to the book's present, drawing events of those years about the life of Jimmy Aaron, "The One." Summary serves few fictions well, and here it is particularly inappropriate. The power of the book lies precisely in the way Gaines dramatizes concretely a vision of human history and black community, and so thoroughly absorbs his materials and their modes of expression, that what results is a truly unique creation. But there are deep structures and patterns of experience that we might examine with minimal reduction. (p. 16)

[The] power of *The Autobiography of Miss Jane Pittman* does not lie in the patterns and motifs of recurring characters, actions, themes. There are familiar patterns, to be sure: black leaders are consistently thrust up, only to be slain and dash the hopes they inspired; and again and again, Jane and her people take to the road on still another exodus, in search of still another homeland. But there is less of a concern with shoring-up the structure of the novel, and a much greater willingness on Gaines's part to allow his material its own natural course— indeed the richness of the fiction lies in the momentary eddies and pools into which the narrative stream is deflected. When Gaines speaks of Richard Wright's decline, he attributes it to an inability to continue writing from a black "American soil, not out of a European library." In his own writing, he demonstrates his strong suspicion that the traditional techniques of the novel are too analytical, schematic, do not properly define his materials or express his vision of the natural history of black people. Gaines seems to agree with his contemporary William Melvin Kelley's assessment that "to carry the weight of our ideas, the novel has got to be changed. We are trying to tap some new things in a form which is not our form."

That power lies in Gaines's careful assimilation of Afro-American folk materials, particularly those of the South, in which his historical vision is absorbed and vivified. His debt is to the rich fund of customs and folkways of black American pasts, to the unique forms grown out of them—to the spirituals, determination songs, church music like Jane's "Done Got Over," urging a rock-like perseverance even as "they tell," heard by W.E.B. DuBois, "of death and suffering and unvoiced longing toward a truer world, of misty wanderings and hidden ways." From the church he also draws on folk sermons and church talks, adapting them to his own more secular uses; to these, a debt for the compelling rhetorical power running through Ned Douglass and Jimmy Aaron, and a broad, historical apology for pain and suffering. And to slave narratives—like that of Frederick Douglass—testi-fying to the moral diseases incipient in human bondage, and to the psychic devastations resulting in both Black (Black Harriet) and White (Cluveau and Tee Bob). A more regional Louisiana folk heritage is spun out in the presence of hoo-doo Madame Eloise Gautier and the many webs of prophecies bound in dreams, visions, superstitions. Their presences suggest a world more alive and mysterious beyond our own, and are borne earlier in the folk tale, as in the remarkable account of Albert Cluveau's suffering and death, "The Chariot of Hell." Many of Gaines's figures are familiar to black myth: Singalee Black Harriet and her return to the shelter of her homeland via insanity; the hunter in search of his mother, pausing in the swamps to trap food for Ticey and Ned. To this rich stream, played through Gaines's own shaping contemporary imagination, we owe the spectrum of Afro-American life and language set loose in *Miss Jane Pittman.*

His direct concern with history and those who record it is apparent from the start. The putative "editor" is a teacher of history, and explains to Jane and her friends that her life will help students to better learn their lessons. "'What's wrong with them books you already got?'" her friend asks. "'Miss Jane is not in them,'" is his reply. Teachers are important throughout Jane's story, and good ones such as Ned Douglass and Mary LeFabre are treasures; the lessers, like Miss Lilly and Joe Hardy, are quietly indicted—and damned simply—as being among "the worst human beings I've ever met."

But it is not easy to teach: we are often reminded of the difficulty of knowing a truth, of daring a vision of history. Jane is first made aware of this painful fact by a riddling old man in whom a world of mystery was refracted. Discouraging her trek to Ohio in search of a kind "Yankee soldier name Brown," he images a detailed and exhausting account of her fruitless travels, concluding: "'And the only white Brown people can remember that ever went to Luzana to fight in the war died of whiskey ten years ago. They don't think he was the same person you was looking for because this Brown wasn't kind to nobody. He was coarse and vulgar; he cussed man, God, and nature every day of his life'." And as long as man can speak it and shape it, history can deceive, can be a weapon against one's foes.

Remembering Herbert Aptheker's adage that "History is mighty," especially for the oppressor, we listen to Jules Raynard's account of Robert Samson's suicide. His reading of the past is historically myopic, consciously blurring the pattern of cause and effect. In his account of slavery, for example, the lion and the lamb lie down together, and each is equally guilty and helpless before the fated retribution for the sins of a common past. Raynard drives Jane home from the plantation to the old slave quarters, and she listens quietly from a back seat, suspicious of his version of "the gospel truth." For all his decency, Raynard is still another white man whose dream of the past makes those in the present impotent; history is a wall for him, before which master and serf can do little but surrender.

For Ernest J. Gaines, like his creation Jimmy Aaron, there is immense power in language, and its use is a sacred trust. And like Aaron, he assumes his obligations cautiously and naturally. Aaron's simple skills to read and write family letters and papers, and his rhetorical talents that serve him later; Gaines's powers to create fiction: each is a way a people are preserved, a heritage passed on. Ned Douglass's last text is a popular folk sermon, adapted from the "Vision of Dry Bones," in Ezekiel, in which it is taught that words can bring a past to life, put flesh on bones and a seed in the soil. "Son of man, these bones are the whole house of Israel: behold, they say. Our bones are dried up, and our hope is lost; we are clean cut off" (Ezekiel 37:11). Ernest Gaines writes from this lament, and *The Autobiography of Miss Jane Pittman,* his finest work, is his mighty attempt to open the graves, make these bones live, and re-unite a people. (pp. 18-19)

> *Jack Hicks, "To Make These Bones Live: History and Community in Ernest Gaines's Fiction," in* Black American Literature Forum, *Vol. 11, No. 1, Spring, 1977, pp. 9-19.*

Reynolds Price (essay date 1983)

[*In the following essay, Price reviews* A Gathering of Old Men, *noting that it is more a "pageant, a morality play, even a film script, than a novel."*]

Ernest Gaines has won a sizable audience with his stories of the black and white Louisiana of his childhood. In a number of short stories and in novels like the early and tender *Catherine Carmier* and *The Autobiography of Miss Jane Pittman* (the latter the basis of an excellent television film), he has built handsomely on his firsthand knowledge of, and intensely ambivalent feelings for, that landscape. *A Gathering of Old Men* is again set in the bayou country of central Louisiana and employs characters closely related to those in his previous books. But in a crucial way, the new novel is distinctly different from the earlier work and is not so immediately attractive. If Mr. Gaines's old readers fail to adjust to its innovative method and conclusion, they may well be disappointed.

The time is roughly the present, although in so stable a society and so bare a fictional texture it takes a little calculation by the reader to establish a date. Beau Boutan—the elder son of Fix Boutan, a Cajun notorious for racial violence—is murdered one morning in the black quarters of a large cane plantation. The young white female proprietor of the plantation unaccountably claims responsibility for the crime and summons nearly 20 elderly black men of the community to join her beside the corpse before the arrival of the racist sheriff. These men, too, will claim a role in the shooting in order to confuse the sheriff and the inevitable nightriders.

The old men gather slowly with their ancient hunting guns during a long and tense day. In the confrontation that follows (the first time the vigilantes have been challenged by blacks), suffocated years of communal guilt and hatred are revived and aired before violence breaks out. Two more men are killed (one of them Beau Boutan's murderer) and many others wounded. The oddly comic trial of both vigilantes and blacks with which the novel concludes achieves a surprising but just resolution of the tragic events.

Mr. Gaines's narrative method has largely dictated his achievement. He has chosen to tell a complex and heavily populated tale through 15 first-person narrators, each of whom advances the plot in short, chronological monologues. Ten of them are black, most of them are male, none of them proves to be implicated in the heart of the action. They are nicely distinguished from one another in rhythm and idiom, in the nature of what they see and report, especially in their specific laments for past passivity in the face of suffering. Some of them, especially at the beginning, are a little long-winded and repetitive, in the manner of country preachers. But a patient reader will sense the power of their stories through their dead-level voices, which speak not from the heart of a present fear but from lifetimes of humiliation and social impotence. They are choosing now to take a stand, on ground where they've yielded for centuries—ground that is valuable chiefly through their incessant labor.

A good oral narrator is always ruthless with detail, with the décor and the visual atmosphere that have become such large components of the realistic American novel. Since the majority of Mr. Gaines's characters are oral narrators who, because of their rural Southern heritage, have adopted some elements of the entertainer's arsenal, they selectively exaggerate certain aspects of the larger story or omit others—in particular, the look of the landscape to which their lives have been devoted: the plantation house, the red-neck tavern and the Cajun home that are the settings of the action. Mr. Gaines's method has forced him to sacrifice these potentially humanizing particulars, and the book that ensues is profoundly shaped by the choice.

What results is more nearly a pageant, a morality play, even a film script, than a novel. The imagining eye of a camera, to be sure, would provide us silently with dimensions that the reader normally expects from a writer. Would those palpable dimensions have impaired the meaning Mr. Gaines appears to have wished to convey? My own guess is that his meaning—some sense of conclusive battle (part victory, part rout) at the end of the meeting of long-entwined white and black lives; some leftover resonance of eventual wry justice in the lives of a few younger witnesses—would have been richer and almost certainly more accessible. Mr. Gaines has dangerously entrusted the work of visualization to the reader.

Still, in *A Gathering of Old Men* he has built, with large and single-minded skills, a dignified and calamitous and perhaps finally comic pageant to summarize the history of an enormous, long waste in our past—the mindless, mutual hatred of white and black, which, he implies, may slowly be healing. Though the idea that propels his action and characters is often disconcertingly apparent, Mr. Gaines's unflagging commitment is to a breadth, even grandeur, of grasp and comprehensiveness. At a time when American fiction is increasingly a matter of infinitely detailed reports from the locked interiors of minds any sane man would flee at first meeting, such ambition is as quietly startling as it is welcome. It may even prove true and durable.

> Reynolds Price, "A Louisiana Pageant of Calamity," in The New York Times Book Review, *October 30, 1983, p. 15.*

Ernest Gaines with Mary Ellen Doyle (interview date 1983)

[*In the following 1983 interview, Doyle and Gaines discuss Gaines's short stories and the novels* Catherine Carmier, In My Father's House, The Autobiography of Miss Jane Pittman, *and* A Gathering of Old Men. *In a preface to this interview, the critic states: "A writer who knows his own goals and methods, knows his right to maintain them, and does so with tenacity and good humor—this is Ernest J. Gaines in public and private interviews. As a guest of the 1982 River City Contemporary Writers series at Memphis State University, Gaines was questioned by a panel from several Memphis colleges and by the audience. Later, he answered my further questions by letter and telephone in three interviews in 1983 at his home in San Francisco."*]

[Doyle]: *My first question is really an invitation to speak of your own aims and motives. Your work was first published in the sixties, the era primarily of militant writers. Your basic tone seems significantly different from theirs, although you have several militant characters truthfully drawn, and you certainly "tell it like it is." Would you comment on this difference and on your aims?*

[Gaines]: Well, most of the writers of the sixties were younger than I, and I started when I was sixteen—in 1949; and I haven't changed much what I wanted to do then. The sixties were just another time to continue what I'd thought about all through the early fifties, when I first got out of the Army and went to San Francisco State and later on a fellowship to Stanford. I knew I wanted to write about my rural Louisiana, the people I knew—their personal daily lives, their dreams, accomplishments. I began writing seriously, I'd say, about 1955, and I started publishing in college magazines as early as 1956. So by the sixties, I'd discovered—decided—what I wanted to deal with, and I never did alter it.

I was living in San Francisco in the late sixties, and I had friends and relatives and critics tell me I should be writing about what was going on at San Francisco State (when Mr. Hayakawa let the cops on campus—things of that sort). I was writing *The Autobiography of Miss Jane Pittman* then, and I know most people thought I should be writing something more contemporary. But I stuck to my ground—to writing my particular book. I felt I had already set the goals for my writing, and I intended to go on. I followed the work of the sixties, read a lot of it—criticized a lot of it. But I established my direction before they started.

Are you saying that you want to break with the tradition of protest associated with Richard Wright and his followers?

What I've always been saying is that the blueprint for Black literature is not *Native Son,* that something existed a hundred years before Chicago in 1940. In my writing, I just refuse to accept the idea that everything started in Harlem or Chicago, that we must write only about the big city, urban northern ghetto life, say. I know there are other things to write about. I know there's bravery and courage, and love and hate and fear and singing and dancing. These things were happening many many years before the naturalistic novel came about with Richard Wright. Jean Toomer wrote about them in *Cane*, a fantastic book. Before Alex Haley called it *Roots,* I was trying to do something like that, to write about our past, where we come from. Each book I've written, except the last one, has gone farther back: *Catherine Carmier* starts with the sixties; the *Bloodline* stories were set in the forties up to the sixties; *Of Love and Dust* was a story of the forties; then *Miss Jane,* of course, went back to 1862. So I'm constantly going back and back and back, trying to show that all Black stories don't have to be in Memphis or Harlem or wherever.

This sounds like the concept of the novelist as ghost-writer of history. Does this concept interest you, and if so, what history are you trying to write?

Well, I don't know that I'm writing history. I try to write about my background, the people I come from. They have lived in the same area, on the same plantation, for five generations, and they have not been written about. Most white writers treated only the romantic things of the South and I think many Black writers of the fifties, sixties, and seventies also thought rural life was not worth writing about; they preferred urban life, the big city. I'm trying to write about a people I feel are worth writing about, to make the world aware of them, make them aware of themselves. They've always thought literature is written about someone else, and it's hard to convince them that they are worthy of literature. I keep repeating this over and over, to convince them.

Do you try to educate white readers about Blacks?

No, I think too many Blacks have tried to do that—to write to educate whites. No, I don't. I—really, I write because I must write. I write because I don't want to stay drunk all the time or don't want to climb mountains or start fights—or anything like that. So I write—I write to keep my sanity really. I'm always asked who I write for, and if I had to write for any particular group—if I *had* to do it—someone had a machine gun and said, "You'd better write for someone; tell us," I'd say, "Well, I write for Black youth, especially of the South." And if they said, "OK, give us two groups," I'd say, "For the Black and white youth of the South." But I'm not really writing for any one group of people—just as I never did join "schools." If I joined a school, I'd have to write according to what was going on around me, and I refuse to have to do that. So I just write as honestly as I possibly can and put it out there and hope you read it. It's a lonely position to be in, but there are lonelier, I suppose.

I'd like to comment that your work also reaches very significantly the northern urban youth, primarily Blacks, but also whites, because you deal with precisely that area of Black experience, from 1860 to 1960, that they cannot personally remember. I knew I'd crossed the generation gap when I first met students who had little or no living memory of Martin Luther King or the civil rights revolution. And your work brings that experience alive for these students who are not from the South and not from the time period that you write about. But the inevitable question: if you choose to write about rural Louisiana, why do you choose to live in San Francisco?

Well, you see, I'm always in Louisiana even though I'm not living there. And that's not unique. Other writers left a certain area to write about it. I can shut my eyes and see—especially the things I write about. If I wrote about the oil wells popping in Louisiana right now, maybe it'd be better if I were in Louisiana. But if I'm writing about something that happened forty years ago, I can face the wall in San Francisco and see it as well or better than I would if I sat in an apartment or a house in Louisiana and looked out at oil wells; they would distract me. Looking at the blank wall, I can see any kind of world I want to see there. But I do go back there every year; I go back to be with the people, to be with the land, to talk, eat the food, go to the bars—that sort of thing.

Do you ever write about other places?

No, I can only write about Louisiana. I've written several manuscripts about San Francisco, but they're very bad. I have about five manuscripts—on the Beat thing, all kinds of live stories—but they just didn't come out. So I picked my own back yard—and there's nothing

wrong with that. After all, Yoknapatawpha County was good enough for Faulkner. I want to write about Louisiana because I think we have enough material in Louisiana to outlast me. I haven't touched it yet. So I concentrate as much as possible on that little area. That's enough.

Then do you write from experience?

Well, people ask me that, and I say, yes, I write from direct experience and vicarious experience. I use the rural Louisiana material—rural and Baton Rouge. I can't even write about New Orleans because I never spent enough time in New Orleans. I've been there twenty-five times, I suppose, but I have not stayed there. I can get a lot of books—history, travel guides—but I'd rather not do that. So I can have characters go to New Orleans and do things, but then they must leave because I don't know the structure of things there. They have to go back to Baton Rouge, back out to the country as fast as possible, to the small town. I know that feeling there.

If you write only from your experience, how can you write about an old woman or whites? Or, on the other hand, how can writers stick to their own experience and not be limiting themselves as artists?

I don't write only about things I've done; I said I use both direct and vicarious experience. I don't know a woman's feeling about different things; I've read enough and heard them talk about it. I don't know living conditions before the forties, but I had to write about Miss Jane Pittman in the 1860s—through reading and reading and reading. I wrote about white characters during that time through reading and reading about what was going on at that time. I've been praised for some of the things. But I've had the same sort of criticism about my Black characters: they are too harsh or too mean, or they are bowing and scraping. I think the writer's success depends on how much talent he has, how much work he does, how well he wants to do this; if he's a poor writer, no matter how well he wants to do it, he won't write well even about his own situation, his own people.

Can you tell us about the research you did for **Miss Jane Pittman?**

Yes, I went to the archives at LSU, the library at Southern, and the State library. I bought books, and the library in San Francisco got books from other libraries. I would read just enough of any books for the particular thing I wanted Miss Jane to know—just the passage I needed. The single book that I think helped me most was a collection of interviews by ex-slaves in the 30s, called *Lay My Burden Down.* Through that book, I got a common language; I got how the ex-slaves of a certain area spoke, what they ate, the number of pieces of clothes, what freedoms they did have—that sort of thing. The other books were technical histories. I also read biographies—autobiographies—journals. I even read *The Diary of Anne Frank* to see what a young girl

Dust jacket of Gaines's most recent novel.

would think about when she's alone—almost anything to try to get to Miss Jane.

I remember—speaking of research—I remember the Huey Long chapter. I read three books on Long, and knew that when he was shot, it was a Sunday and was raining; I knew that when he died on Tuesday, it was raining. But no one had written what the weather was on Thursday, the day of his burial, so I went out to the fields and asked the people about it. Some people would say it was raining, others that the sun was shining. So I went back to LSU and asked the research librarian for all she could find on the days after Huey Long's assassination. She brought out a pile of manila folders—yea high—and said, "Well, it's somewhere in there." I went through it for three or four hours, and a little passage in an Arkansas paper, about three inches long said there were intermittent showers. So both groups of people I'd spoken to were right. But I had to find out for myself. And after I'd spent four hours in there, I didn't even use the material because when Miss Jane came to narrate her little chapter, the detail was not necessary. But I had to get it. Using historical information like that, you have to digest it and then give it back to a little lady who is illiterate—very intelligent—brilliant, but illiterate. She's never read a book; she cannot write. So

that was a problem; I had to get all this information, and then I had to come back and get a language for all this information, and then I had to come back and get a language for her. I remember Twain said, "Read, then distort." You must know everything, then give it to someone like Huckleberry Finn.

Let's go more into your reading. What contemporary novelists do you read?

I don't read too many contemporary novelists. As a matter of fact, I only read contemporary novels by friends of mine—James Allen McPherson, Alice Walker, Maya Angelou. There are so many other books that I like reading over and over. I can always pick up *War and Peace* and read a chapter. I can't do that with contemporary novels. Once I've seen them I don't read them any more. (I shouldn't say that because I'm writing now!)

What reading would help a beginning writer today? Would contemporary writing help most?

If it is experimental writing, I think it would not be as helpful to the young writer as good established past writers. I can't think of a better book for a young writer to read about war, say, than *All Quiet on the Western*

Front. Tolstoy's *War and Peace* might be too big. I think for structure, there's not a better book for a young writer, whether he likes the subject matter or not, than *Gatsby*—for first person point of view and the structure. Or Twain's *Huckleberry Finn.* Or Flaubert's *Bovary.* Or Turgenev's *Fathers and Sons.* I think the young writer should know these books. I think he should read them and then come up to contemporary novels. If the novel is going in a different direction (and I'm not sure of that), I don't know when it's going to get there. If we knew that in 1988 a novel would differ from what we know as the novel form, I would say, well, maybe read the experimental books today. But I think a writer should have a base of these other established novels. I think he should have that.

But of course, I do something very different from the experimental novel; my characters still say "Yes" and "No" and they say it in separate sentences, and I use commas and periods a lot. I don't use way-out adjectives and adverbs and long, "subconscious" sentences and all. I still like well structured paragraphs and end them with a period. All these dashes and parentheses and little drawings and symbols—I can't do things like that. If anyone can, let him do it. It depends on the individualism of the writer. I can just give a few hints on how to get started.

Can we talk a little about process? Do you rewrite a lot? How much can you write in a typical day?

Of course, I rewrite a lot. Dialogue is very easy for me to write; I can write, say, ten pages of it a day. Of course, I may rewrite it ten times to get it exactly the way I want it, but I can revise dialogue very fast. Descriptive passages give me some problem; I might write only one page of descriptive work a day. How much work I can do in any day's time depends on what the situation is, whether I have a group of people I'm writing about, or one or two people talking or moving, what part of a scene I'm doing. Instead of trying to write a certain number of pages or a certain number of words a day, I try to get in a certain amount of time a day—about five hours. I start at nine in the morning and work until about two in the afternoon. I stop in the middle for coffee or water, but I try to get in that much time each day, five days a week. If I get two pages today, maybe I get five pages the next day, and the next day only two or three paragraphs. It depends on the problem of the book that I'm working out.

Are there any things about the process that you fear?

No, I don't have any fear of the process—I'm just trying to think—no, I just get up and I go to that desk.

Someone talks about how characters begin to take the writer over as if the personalities of the characters are floating around out there and the writer doesn't really always know what they will do or say next. Is it that way with you?

I think Faulkner once said the characters take over on page 114 unless the book ends on page 113. I do think that they take over. Miss Jane took over. I have a problem with the omniscient point of view because I'm constantly overseeing everything. I had this difficulty with my first novel, **Catherine Carmier,** and with **In My Father's House.** But in those stories where I use the first person point of view, the characters do sort of get control. There's no way you can change them; there's no way in the world I could have kept that little old lady from trying to get to Ohio. I knew she would never get there, but I couldn't keep her from going. She had to go as far as she did till she got very, very tired, and I couldn't do anything about that. Yes, they do take over. But you have to get up every morning at nine o'clock and sit at the desk and write for five or six hours or they won't take over.

I'd like to pick up on your comment on viewpoint because I find that to be one of the most interesting technical features of your writing. Usually first person narration is in the past tense; the event is over. But in several stories, you have narrators, including children, who use present tense, as if the event is in progress, as if they are "thinking their lives" as they go. For instance, in "The Sky is Gray": "We stand and wait for the bus and the bus is coming. . . ." This is done even when the child is coming out of a waking dream. It struck me as a technical innovation. Is it, or is it a kind of dialectical use of the present tense?

I never thought of making changes in technique. I think I must have read if somewhere. I think Faulkner uses it in the first part of *The Sound and the Fury,* with Benjy's immediate feelings. And it was a way to deal with a kid six or eight years old.

Well, Lewis in "Three Men," too, at least part of the time, is thinking-narrating as the action occurs. It does create tremendous immediacy. Whatever your technical viewpoint, your stories seem to use the mind's eye as a camera which is always very closely on the character.

I think the best writers of the present are those who concentrate on the people very closely. And I do try to develop characters to make them as real as possible. My aim in literature is to develop character, not only the character in the book, but my character as well as yours, so that if you pick up the book, you will see something you feel is true, something not seen before, that will help develop your character from that day forward.

My students ask about some of your strong characters, especially your very strong, even tough, mothers. In "The Sky is Gray," for instance, the mother insists her young son endure the bitter cold without his collar turned up. Not only does she not coddle him, she does not accept what most of us consider a child's ordinary demonstrations of affection. Why?

In that story, the father was in the Army, and whether he would ever come back she did not know. She was just disciplining this kid to be able to face that tough life out there, and what she required wasn't any tougher than what many children have had to go through at that time, children who went into the fields at seven or eight years old, had to work whether it was hot or cold. But until I started going around to schools, I never thought she was harsh in any way. She disciplined him, and the kid could take it. But it was discipline with love.

I find that students recognize that love, and they recognize that James recognizes it and, in some very real sense, understands. But it is the other adults in his life who explain her requirements to him. What they come to is, "OK, I understand, but why must it be that tough?" And another question they ask is why the mother in **"Long Day in November"***—another strong woman!—insists at the end that her husband beat her. That gives a lot of trouble; wife-beating under any circumstances is a bit hard to explain!*

She insisted on that because she knew the people would laugh and make fun of her husband for having to burn up his car just to get his wife back home again. And the last thing she wanted, I think the last thing any woman wants—I'm not up to date on what women think and feel, but I *think* the last thing they want is for someone to laugh at their mates. And she says, "OK, if you put a mark on me with this switch and you hurt me, then they will not have anything to laugh at: they'll see that you are a man after all, 'cause most of them said you were not."

They acknowledge her motive but still ask why she had to use that method. That story ends in a clearly positive resolution. And most of your novels leave the reader, I think, with a strikingly positive view of human life. Yet, paradoxically, most of them end with ambiguous or very tentative projections of a better future for the protagonist—if he/she is even alive. Can you comment on this paradox?

I think some of us will make it, due to the tenacity of our nature. And this is what I try to say in my books, and that is what my protagonists are saying: "I will make it, I will make it, I will make it." Ten percent or so do make it, the other ninety percent don't. For every Miss Jane Pittman who made it, nine other Black women either went insane or died inside long before they were physically dead and put in the ground. It is the ten percent I choose to write about. That is why most of my leading characters are super brave and must take risks—to help themselves or others, even though the risk may cause his or her death.

Before we turn to specific novels, will you tell us something about your still uncollected short stories? So far, I have found listed: **"Boy in the Double Breasted Suit," "Chippo Simon," "Mary Louise," "My Grandma and the Haint," "The Turtles,"** *and* **"The Comeback."** *Will you eventually collect some of these as you did those in* **Bloodline***? Or have they been incorporated into later stories?*

The stories you mentioned were written while I was at San Francisco State and Stanford. They are the only published stories of mine other than those in the **Bloodline** collection. One day I should hope that a "small press" or a university press would take an interest in my "college stories." As of now, no one has requested permission to publish them in a collection. Too bad. Because I think they are pretty good stories, and they show the ideas of the young writer.

May we talk about specific novels now? **Catherine Carmier** *seems to me an amazing first novel. Was it written while you were at Stanford?*

One version was written much earlier; when it came back from New York, I just burned it up. Then, at Stanford, a visiting New York editor told the class you could never make money on short stories, which I was writing at the time. I thought I'd never have a penny when I left Stanford, so I'd better write a novel. And the only thing I could recall was the idea I'd had before. I wrote and rewrote that for five years. Many more things were in it: more background, more characters; the people in the quarters and Catherine's aunts were more involved. It was about the problems of Black and mulatto people on either side of a stream of water. And it was the story of Jackson and Lillian coming home for the last time to tell people they were moving out. In the original draft, they had a long conversation on the bus without his knowing who she was. But then I wanted to make them tragic lovers, and that wouldn't work. The tragedy was not their love but what had already happened to them. Lillian wasn't mature enough; Catherine was the mature one on the place. My agent, who has done more for me as a writer than anyone, said she could not see how Lillian and Jackson could have anything mature, especially after she saw that Jackson and Catherine had been very close as children but didn't know they loved each other. Eventually, I saw them being close again. So all these things made the book very big; I was developing them all, but nothing dramatic was happening. Finally, I cut it down to size because I believe in form in my books, and I was not getting it.

The title suggests that the story is Catherine's. Yet in reading, I felt a balance of interest between Catherine and Jackson, with Lillian in a supporting secondary role.

It's titled **Catherine Carmier** because I finally couldn't think of a better title. I called it "A Little Stream" once; part was published once as **"Barren Summer."** But I don't see it as Catherine's story more than Jackson's or even Lillian's.

I think viewpoint affects our sense of its form. That is basically omniscient, but in a few places, I wasn't sure whether I was hearing the narrator's comments or Jackson's thoughts.

You have both, also others. This novel was originally done from multiple viewpoints; Lillian, Della, Catherine, Mary Louise, different people in the quarters would each have a section. When I shifted to the omniscient, some of those voices or views were kept. But writers do that unconsciously; as you look over the shoulder of characters, you slip into their minds.

Then how much do you want the reader to see the old people and the quarters as Jackson sees them? Is the "deadness" in him or in them?

In him—well, in both. The place is stagnant, and the people have their little lives and problems. But when he sees the garden drying up and says, "No more than my soul," that's true; it's in both. Catherine doesn't see the life around her as he does; why not take her viewpoint or Mary Louise's? I don't want any one character's viewpoint to be taken as the whole story, and Jackson has an obvious prejudice.

So when he described the old people as trees or rocks, "never understanding, never giving," that is his view?

Yes, that's his view. I disagree with him.

What about Jackson and his aunt? He was evidently very close to her as a boy; now he can't talk to her.

You come back ten years later and I don't know that you can talk to people. The religion that held you together, the place, the road and the river, all the old people—he can't relate to any of them. He loves Brother and Mary Louise, and he can't talk to them. Madame Bayonne's the only one because there he's dealing with reasoning, not emotion. And he can leave her; nothing keeps him. He can't do that with Aunt Charlotte. She wants him to be the typical Black schoolteacher, go to church, listen to the old people; he can't do that anymore.

He comes across as a character in great pain—very moving. You project in the book a very sensitive feeling for his difficulty of having gone to California for an education and then come back. Did that come to some extent from your own experience?

I can tell his feeling, but his life and mine are not parallel. I left Louisiana, left aunt and friends, and I would not exchange San Francisco now; but that's all.

Why has Lillian kept coming back for six years or more?

Well, she loves her sister, and she hasn't made a final decision not to come. Also, the people in New Orleans were worse on the "Creole, Creole" business than her people at home and she probably hated them worse.

At one point, Jackson thinks of her as "deep and evil," and this seems somehow true. She seems hard, stifled in feelings, and evil in trying to manipulate others' lives.

Many people are like her, and she did not make the world that formed her character. I cannot criticize her; she saw Jackson's taking Catherine as revenge for all three of them—not only on her family but on the whole system.

Would you talk about the relation of Raoul and Catherine?

People have interpreted that all wrong. Raoul depends on Catherine but not for sexuality, and surely she has no desire for him. After his wife becomes unfaithful, she's just dead, and his whole life is for his daughter. And Catherine knows that if she stays, she can put some sun in both their lives. Raoul needs her more than Della.

I saw Raoul as very possessive; I did not see real incest. Yet his sister's words suggest at least an unacknowledged substitution for a relation with a woman.

I think she says that because he turned down Bertha. But that's the last thing that *I* had in mind.

Catherine's staying home to be the companion her father demands—it may look like unselfishness, but is it? And isn't it in some sense hurting Della? Suppose she'd gone with Jackson—might not Raoul have turned to his wife again?

No, no. I don't know that just because Catherine left, Della would have had any better life. And she stays not only for her father but her mother too,—and Lillian, she keeps coming back. I know two women who lived like that with their families, and I think both cases were mistakes. But the South needs these women. Faulkner and Tennessee Williams and I wouldn't have anything to write about if these neurotics weren't there. Not that Catherine is neurotic; she's very strong. I have a brother whose wife had to look after her own family, her brothers and their children, her mother, who had only one leg, her father and an old aunt. Without her there, I don't know how they'd ever have gotten along. As a matter of fact, I based Della somewhat on her mother, a beautiful woman who used to laugh and talk a lot.

I'd like to talk about the ending. Della says that Raoul needs her now, that he will make Catherine go, and that she will send her to Jackson; that seems like a final word and judgment. But then the narration says Jackson waited for Catherine to come out and "she never did." And this seemed to be a wide "never" and a different final word. To me, it's ambiguous.

Della says Raoul needs her; he hasn't said that. He probably will make Catherine leave, but then he'd just as soon die. Another thing—when Jackson and Catherine are driving back from the dance, he keeps saying, "I need you, it will be just you and me," and that reminds her that life and marriage can't be "just us"; Jackson could possess her just as much as her father. But all that's another story. When Catherine goes into the house, that's the end of the story. I suppose it is ambiguous. It may be the writer just wasn't mature enough at that time to know how to end it.

I was struck more on second reading with the beauty of the book, yet it does seem that the later books have greater depth of characterization.

Oh yes, this is a very young man's book, a college book in which you try to put everything your instructors have told you to make viewpoint and form right. Later you write with everything you've learned from your reading, from baseball to bars, from all life experience.

I hope to see more critical comment on **In My Father's House,** *which seems to me very significant in its themes and characterization. Will you comment on this novel, your purpose in it, its thematic meaning?*

That book is a hard one for me to talk about. I don't ever read from it when I go to colleges and universities. It is a book I had to write because I was haunted by the idea. It cost me more time (seven years) and pain than any other book I've written. It is the story of a minister and his son, one of the children he's fathered as a young man but never even seen in the many years since their mother left him. Until he found God, this was just "something that happened," that happened to many Black males then. When he realized his responsibility, he tried to make it up by becoming the "new man" with a new family, and still forgot the old. When the past catches up, he goes to God for an answer but finds it can't be fixed in a few days. There is an old Negro saying, "God isn't always there when you call him, but he's always on time." But his Christian belief is shaken, cracked. God helped the minister to help other people, but when he needed God to bring himself and his son together, God failed.

And his work in civil rights is not enough to make him a success as a man.

Not really. When Johanna left because he would not care for her and the children, he really wanted to get up and go after her. That's what he wanted to do, but being the kind of person he was at that time, he could not do it. And his dream says he still cannot do it; he runs but cannot catch up. When he falls, he cannot get up. He can lead people to a voting booth, to demonstrate in stores, but what she wanted, he cannot do, not with her. He can do it with the little family he has now, in a way he can.

And the civil rights revolution as such cannot repair the breach in families, between fathers and sons?

No way! That's the next point I wanted to make in the book. Sitting at a counter with whites does not bring father and son together. Just because they are sitting there does not mean they are communicating. Billy says that: he and his father get along "average. . . . I don't bother him, he don't bother me." That's a main theme of the story.

The father-son relation is central to **In My Father's House** *and to several short stories. Would you comment further on your ideas about it?*

The father and son were separated when they were brought to this country over three centuries ago. The white man did not let them come together during slavery, and they have not been able to reach each other since. Despite the revolution, the Black father is in a position of non-respectability, and the white is still in control. The Black man is seldom the owner, still is not

the public defender in court, not the judge. The young Black man almost always sees a white in these positions, not an older Black man, not his father. You can always hear a professional football player say the most important male in his life was his coach—usually white; that was the father-figure who would stand by him in trouble. We expect the same in the military, a white officer. So the son cannot and does not look up to the father. The father has to look up to the son. That is not natural. And the cycle continues, and continues, and continues. A few of our Black fathers make it, but the majority do not—and I doubt they will in our time.

How do you react to reviews that see him as a weakened Martin Luther King?

Some people thought I attacked King because I named him Martin. Martin is a common name along False River where I come from. If I have six heroes, Martin Luther King is one of them. Phillip Martin had done a lot. But twenty years earlier he had made a mistake with his own family, and when he had a second chance, he made the same mistake; when he fell, he didn't try to get up, he didn't explain. That's the whole story—not what he failed to do in the town.

A most interesting aspect of the book is his continuing inadequacy as a husband in important ways; he does not trust Alma enough to involve her; she says this to him: you want me for the bed, to take care of the children and go to church.

That's most common, but he couldn't do even that much for Johanna.

When he's talking to Robert in the car after getting him out of jail, he says he couldn't do it because he went by the rules left from slavery. Isn't this his rationalization? In 1950, lost of Black men did take responsibility for their women and children.

Yes, but Phillip Martin is not included in the "lots." He says I was never allowed to respect my woman; I just continued the rules. Until he finds God, he continues.

How did you intend sympathy to go in the scene of his demotion as civil rights leader? I found mine going back and forth; on one hand, he deserves what he gets. . . .

Well, my sympathies were much more with the people than with him. I have no sympathy with a man who is supposed to be a leader, to take care of the people and puts one person above them. And yet, as a father, he had to go the other way. He'd done all the other things they wanted; now he had to try to catch up with what he'd lost long ago.

In the chapter of his search for Chippo, he seems to be making a journey into the past. Was that the purpose of prolonging that chapter, bringing in all those people? Why couldn't he just go to Baton Rouge and find Chippo?

That would be too simple, just as it would be to cross the room to his son. The old preacher has to say, "Just pray," so he can say if that was all that was needed, the trouble would have been solved long ago. Then he meets Billy who says to just leave everything to the roaches and start over, and he disagrees with him. And waiting for Adeline is not the answer either. So on his search for his son, he has to meet all kinds of people—almost like what Miss Jane had to go through for her conversion.

He has to look at all the options of the past and reject them, also the future option of burning the whole place down. It seems to me Beverly puts the answer in front of him: you have done something for the people, they aren't afraid any more. And there's Patrick, you do have a son and a future. And she's young enough to represent the future.

That's what I wanted Beverly to do. And Shepherd's name—he's sort of Shepherd of the flock. That's why I brought in the young lovers. You can't change what is gone by, but you can pick up and do a little better. They will do what Johanna and Phillip might have done at their ages. And I'm sure I had that symbolism in mind for his son Patrick.

One other question about the ending—one gap about it in my mind: was there any idea in your mind that part of this starting over would be to reach out to Johanna, to tell her of her son's death, take some responsibility for her present poverty and misery?

I really don't know that. Maybe. It's over when Alma says "We have to start again." But I would think that after this he would reach out to her, go to California, explain to her, then come back and start over with Alma.

A few questions about structure. Why did you withhold any direct introduction to Phillip until Chapter 4? We hear of him from others, get a physical view of him, but don't see him act or get into his mind.

The first few chapters are devoted to the boy: Martin's name comes up only to get the reader interested in his character. Until the confrontation it's not necessary to bring out what he really was.

It struck me that the withholding makes the reader hear first the positive views of him—Virginia's, Elijah's, Beverly's. Only then do you find out for sure his relation to Robert. I felt prepared to look at his past without just wiping him out of my sympathy because I'd seen what those people see, and that was necessary to balance the intense sympathy for Robert that is built up in that first part.

(laughing) Well, you've just explained it better than I could. I agree, because they did see just one side, and the people who knew the other—Chippo and Nanane—were not there. And I wanted that positive side seen; he's done some very positive things.

Phillip's conversion was obviously central in his life. Did you ever put in a conversion scene of any kind?

I did in the original and tore it up because it was narrated by Chippo when I was telling the story from multiple points of view. Then I found that was impossible because I could never have Phillip Martin or the boy as narrators. But if they couldn't be narrators, I couldn't tell the story because it's about them and no one else could tell it. So I had to switch to omniscient point of view and cut out Chippo's telling the conversion.

Could Phillip have remembered it as he does Johanna's leaving him?

No, it wouldn't have been keeping the form together.

I have the feeling that it is formally right that the scene not be dramatized, but I haven't figured out why. A last question on this book. In a 1975 interview you said it was "giving me more hell than anything I've ever written." Do you want to say why?

I don't know. It was like a cold you have to get rid of that takes a long time. It was something I'd always wanted to do—to write a tragedy that has a lot to do with the Black male and his history in this country.

Your last novel, **A Gathering of Old Men,** *seems to have a similar theme: the second chance to be a man. Yet it seems to have no central character.*

The old men as a group are the protagonist. The central motif is that they had not acted manfully in the past, and here was God giving them a second change to stand up one day. So it's not Mathu or any one person; it's the men. In an early version, a mulatto who is really a first cousin of Candy's was going to be the leading character. Then I realized I was playing something I didn't want to get into, that I really wanted the men to be important, wanted to concentrate on them. The other character would divide the interest.

I read about twenty-five pages of an early version in Callaloo. *There it seemed that the narration was going to be entirely through Lou Dimes. Was that your original intention?*

The original idea was that Lou Dimes was a "liberal white guy" who's played basketball with Blacks, who sees a relationship between Candy and Mathu and between Mapes and Mathu, sees something about these old men, and from a liberal viewpoint is learning and trying to understand and tell it. So I began with the first-person viewpoint, but after going over it a few times, I realized that Dimes could not get all the information needed and especially not the language I wanted: the child's or the old women's, Janey's or Miss Merle's, or the men fishing. So I dropped Lou Dimes as sole narrator and went to multiple narrative.

In checking out the narration, I noticed that none of the "main," the most involved characters, do any of the narration. Candy, Mathu, Fix, Charlie, Luke Will, Gilbert—none of them do. It's Janey and Snookum, the whites in the store, and the old man.

I just felt those people, as observers, could do much better than the people involved. Mathu and Candy can't narrate or the reader would know too much. It wasn't important for Fix to narrate because the young man tells what went on, and when he's visited by his son we know what he thinks and feels. In one draft, I had Mapes narrating; he's on his way fishing when he gets the call and starts talking and talking.

The order of narration seems significant. The first several sections are Black-white-Black; then it's all given over to the memories of the Black men, and then you switch to a series of white narrators.

In the first part, I didn't intend the Black-white-Black; I was just building up the plot, and there was no better way than having the boy run messages around. Once I got to the men, I had to arrange their stories so I would not have two tear-jerkers following each other but have it paced. I had stories for twice as many men, but my editor said we can get the feeling of the thing with only four or five of them. The point is that it's not just Fix; he represents everything that has happened to these people whether he was involved or not.

The long chapter of their reminiscences is one of the most powerful in the book, and it is striking that immediately after it you switch to the white Tully who goes to Fix's house. And suddenly, just after all those horror stories, there is Fix with his grandchild in his lap, grieving for his son. I expected to see him organizing a lynching—which, in a sense, he was—but the impact is of his grief. And even more powerful is the moment when Luke Will, who has nothing to redeem him or what he's doing, asks someone to take care of his wife and children. You never seem to deny anyone his moment of humanity.

My agent brought that up, too; she had seen all the drafts and Luke had never said anything like that. It's a normal thing; I think Klansmen could love their children. For me to be fair as a writer, I cannot deny Fix or Will his humanity, and I don't know anyone totally without feeling. Maybe I was feeling good that morning. I know I had written several drafts and not written that speech of Luke's.

But another thing—Fix is thirty years late. His son is playing football now. The Klan doesn't come on horses as nightriders now, you have pick-up trucks and CB radios. So Fix's kind of vigilante vengeance is dying out, but there will be the new Luke Will type. The Luke Wills are in the police department. Fix is seventy or eighty and can't shoot straight, but Luke will do it for him.

In 1979, the story time, would a sheriff slap old men around as Mapes does, and would they answer him back as they do?

They had not answered him back before, because before they were afraid to die. But that day, they came to live or die for a cause—"for once in my life, I'm going to do something and then I die." So they'll say anything. I don't know that Mapes would typically knock them

around, but there are people like him who don't know any other way to get information. But I've never seen just this situation.

So this scene was the product of your creative imagination. Were any of the episodes based on actual events?

None, really. Some of the ones I cut out were. I had heard of a fight between a Black and a white sharecropper racing to the derrick with their sugar cane. I had heard of a sixteen-year-old young man electrocuted for supposedly killing a white man; he was partially insane. A man there told me the electric chair didn't work and they garrotted him, choked him to death. I had that in the story once, and my agent advised me to change it. I had heard these stories not from Blacks but from whites. Another woman told me of going to town with her little girl, a fair-skinned child; an insane white woman tried to take the child because she was "too beautiful to be a nigger." They had a fight over it, I knew them. In the book, one of the mulatto men tells this, how they fought and fought until the white woman got the child and slammed its head on the ground and killed it. The killing did not occur, in fact, though the fight did. I cut that story out. The point of all the stories was that these things happen; if Fix didn't do it, somebody did.

I would like you to talk about the killing that does occur—the shoot-out. Obviously Charlie has to come out and take his stand. But does he come out to end this scene if Luke doesn't shoot him, so that they'd both be alive, or does he not believe what Luke said and come out to shoot to kill?

Well, I sent him out to do that because he knew durn well that Luke Will would come out to kill. When he came back from the swamp, he didn't know Luke Will would be there with a shotgun, but he knew he was going to live as a man and then die. So he stood up to die at that moment rather than prolong it.

When Luke says, "Let us give up," does he mean it or is it a trick?

No, no, he knew they couldn't get away so he wanted to give up.

Then my question is—and here's where I got stuck in that episode—wouldn't it have been the humane thing and just as much a victory to have let him give up?

How does Charlie know what Will means? I'm telling you, but Charlie doesn't know that. He knows he's going to die, so Luke's wanting to give up doesn't mean anything to him, not now. He may believe in Lou Dimes, but he doesn't believe in any real justice. I cut out a part where Lou says, "Charlie, I got me and Candy here and we know what happened," and he says, "Yes, but you won't be the jury. I'm going to die anyhow." So he has to come out fighting. They chose the battleground, and he has to fight.

Then, were we to respond to all the shooting and killing as a sign of manhood over cowardice or as a tragic necessity that so many should die? Well, only two die, but the possibilities were enormous.

Oh no, never was, because the old men couldn't see anything, and the other bums were drunk. I knew that; that's why I got them drunk. I could have had complete chaos, but I didn't want that; I just wanted those old men to stand one day.

After all the grandeur and tragedy, so to speak, of Charlie's stand, why the switch to the great comedy of the trial?

The tragedy is over; it was told in eight hours, one day, as in Greek tragedy. The whole book meant one thing to me, that day of standing up. After that, I had to get them buried and have some kind of hearing; but as far as I was concerned, once they walk around and touch Charlie's chest, it's over. Gilbert is back sitting with his family, Candy leans on Lou, Mathu is back with the people and has achieved an independence of Candy, and Mapes will be embarrassed for the rest of his life; but these are sort of comic things. It was not their day; it was the old men's day.

It struck me that all those characters except Mathu have undergone some degree of change and progress.

Mathu has too, and he says it at the end: "I never thought I would see a day like this. I always felt above you because you never did anything. I hated those people because they never let me be an American, and I hated you because you never tried."

Candy seems to undergo a learning process about Mathu and the people, to realize she can't be the old-time patron because they won't take her protection any more. She understands why Mathu goes home from the courthouse with the other people.

I really don't think she does understand that. She knows she needs Lou for support; that's why she reaches for his hand when Mathu leaves. But Mathu's turned his back on her, and I don't think she knows why. Lou tells her in the car; that's why she slaps him, because she doesn't want to understand. In another draft, she gives a big speech, "When you needed medicine, who went to the store? When you went to the doctor, who took you? When you were hungry, who fed you?" And they must all say, Yes, Candy did it. I cut that out, but I hope people can still get the feeling of her role.

Mapes also seems to move from his kind of contempt to some respect at the end.

Yes, I think so. He's always respected Mathu, but the rest were just darkies or niggers. They'd never do anything. But at the end, he has to give them, especially Charlie, some respect. And he means it.

Why did you change the title from The Revenge of Old Men?

Well, I didn't see them doing anything for revenge. I thought "Gathering" sounded better, too. I've tried to use "Revenge" in several titles. I once called *In My Father's House* Revenge in St. Adrienne. Just didn't work.

Do you see any changes and developments in your overall purpose and tone from your early work to your latest?

None. Absolutely none. Just got better, I hope. (pp. 59-81)

> Ernest J. Gaines and Mary Ellen Doyle, in an interview in MELUS, Vol. 11, No. 2, Summer, 1984, pp. 59-81.

FURTHER READING

Bryant, Jerry H. "Politics and the Black Novel." *The Nation* 212, No. 14 (5 April 1971): 436-38.
    Reviews *The Autobiography of Miss Jane Pittman*, describing it as an "epic poem." The critic writes: "Literally, it is an account of Jane's life. Figuratively, it is a metaphor of the collective black experience. . . ."

Burke, William. "*Bloodline:* A Black Man's South." *CLA Journal* XIX, No. 4 (June 1976): 545-58.
    Summarizes *Bloodline,* noting of the work: "The five stories in [this] collection demonstrate their excellence in two ways; they are human stories—moving, humorous, ironic; and they are symbolic—which tradition tells us is a quality of all great literature."

Callahan, John F. "A Moveable Form: The Loose End Blues of *The Autobiography of Miss Jane Pittman.*" In his *In the African-American Grain: The Pursuit of Voice in Twentieth-Century Black Fiction,* pp. 189-216. Urbana: University of Illinois Press, 1988.
    Review of *The Autobiography of Miss Jane Pittman,* concluding: "As a writer of his people, Gaines keeps faith with the oral tradition—a tradition of responsibility and change, and, despite violent opposition, a tradition of citizenship. In turn, his novel's spirit of call-and-response invites readers to pick up the loose ends, join in the storytelling, and, like Miss Jane Pittman, come home."

Gaudet, Marcia, and Wooton, Carl. "An Interview with Ernest J. Gaines." *New Orleans Review* 14, No. 4 (Winter 1987): 62-70.
    Interview with Gaines. The discussion focuses on *The Autobiography of Miss Jane Pittman* and *A Gathering of Old Men* and their subsequent television adaptations.

Griffin, Joseph. "Ernest J. Gaines's Good News: Sacrifice and Redemption in *Of Love and Dust.*" *Modern Language Studies* XVIII, No. 3 (Summer 1988): 75-85.
    Examines the character of Marcus Payne in *Of Love and Dust* as a "messianic figure."

Harper, Mary T. "From Sons to Fathers: Ernest Gaines' *A Gathering of Old Men.*" *CLA Journal* XXXI, No. 3 (March 1988): 299-308.

> Appraises *A Gathering of Old Men,* focusing on the character development from "men-children" to "fathers."

Hicks, Jack. "Afro-American Fiction and Ernest Gaines." In his *In the Singer's Temple: Prose Fictions of Barthelme, Gaines, Brautigan, Piercy, Kesey, and Kosinski,* pp. 83-137. Chapel Hill: The University of North Carolina Press, 1981.

> Overview of Gaines's work, stating: "The movement from his first work, *Catherine Carmier* (1964), to his most recent, *In My Father's House* (1978), is a movement from history rendered as a kind of bondage, an existential nightmare of dead ends from which a solitary black man finds no escape, toward history sensed as a natural cycle, wheeling slowly through the rebirth of a people and their inevitable liberation."

Roberts, John W. "The Individual and the Community in Two Short Stories by Ernest J. Gaines." *Black American Literature Forum* 18, No. 3 (Fall 1984): 110-13.

> Discusses the conflict between community values and individual needs in "A Long Day in November" and "The Sky Is Gray."

Shelton, Frank W. "Ambiguous Manhood in Ernest J. Gaines's *Bloodline.*" *CLA Journal* XIX, No. 2 (December 1975): 200-09.

> Analysis of *Bloodline,* focusing on recurring themes in Gaines's short stories.

Vinson, Audrey L. "The Deliverers: Ernest J. Gaines's Sacrificial Lambs." *Obsidian II* 2, No. 1 (Spring 1987): 34-48.

> Examines the protagonists in Gaines's fiction, describing them as "sacrificial lambs."

Washington, Mary Helen. "The House Slavery Built." *The Nation* 238, No. 1 (14 January 1984): 22-4.

> Reviews *A Gathering of Old Men,* criticizing Gaines's portrayal of women in the book. Washington writes: "In exploring this vital issue of how black people can exert control over their history, why does Gaines so thoroughly deny the power of the women who contributed equally to that history?"

Marcus Garvey

1887-1940

(Full name Marcus Moziah Garvey, Jr.) Jamaican essayist, orator, editor, journalist, and poet.

Garvey was a major twentieth-century black activist and orator. He is best known for founding the "back to Africa," or Garveyist, political and social movement among African- and West Indian-Americans at the end of World War I. In his essays, poems, and speeches Garvey advocated racial separatism and encouraged African-Americans and others of African heritage to achieve economic and cultural unity and to form an independent nation in Africa. A highly controversial, flamboyant, and charismatic figure, Garvey drew the scorn of many prominent black intellectuals, notably W. E. B. Du Bois, who saw him as an antagonistic demagogue. Nevertheless, Garvey attracted an immense following among the disaffected working class, who rallied behind his calls for racial pride and African home rule. He is today remembered as one of the most important black political theorists of the twentieth century.

Garvey was born into a working-class family in St. Ann's Bay, Jamaica, in 1887. His family's financial difficulties forced Garvey to leave school and find work at the age of fourteen. He became a printer's apprentice in the Jamaican capital of Kingston and soon involved himself in political oratory and labor politics. In 1907 he led a printer's union strike and in 1910 founded his first periodical, *Garvey's Watchman*. After this venture failed, Garvey spent two years traveling in Central America, where he developed several radical journals and tried unsuccessfully to lobby white business owners to improve the working conditions of black laborers; this embittering episode hardened his desire to agitate for black rights on an international level. In 1912, while traveling in Great Britain, he read *Up from Slavery* by Booker T. Washington, whose philosophy of black economic and social self-reliance inspired Garvey to found a black nationalist movement. In Garvey's words, "my doom—if I may so call it—of being a race leader dawned upon me. . . . I asked: 'Where is the black man's Government?' 'Where is his King and his kingdom?' 'Where is his President, his country, and his ambassador, his army, his navy, his men of big affairs?' I could not find them, and then I declared, 'I will help to make them.'"

Returning to Jamaica, Garvey failed in his attempt to found a school modeled on Washington's Tuskegee Institute. He subsequently traveled to New York in 1916, hoping to find a more receptive audience for his ideas. Within three years Garvey was well known as a lecturer and had sufficient financial backing and contacts to establish the Universal Negro Improvement Association (UNIA) and its journalistic organ, the weekly *Negro World* newspaper. Garvey wrote editorials for the paper and gave speeches calling for an independent African state; he claimed that only through such independence could blacks worldwide gain the power needed to win social equality. In 1919, to further African nationhood, he organized the Black Star Line, a fleet of ships owned and operated by black Americans. Operating between New York and Africa, the ships carried many passengers who were seeking repatriation in Africa. Garvey envisioned colonies of African-Americans bringing Western technology to help native Africans gain self-sufficiency and eventually independence from European colonial powers. Having gained popular and financial support from blacks around the world, Garvey negotiated with the government of Liberia for land grants to settlers and was elected provisional president of Africa by the 25,000 delegates at the international UNIA convention in 1920. He also began to formalize the political, theological, economic, and aesthetic aspects of his pan-Africanist philosophy in essays and manifestos collected in 1923 in *The Philoso-*

phy and Opinions of Marcus Garvey; or, Africa for the Africans.

In spite of the successful sale of shares of stock in the Black Star Line, the company suffered a series of financial and nautical setbacks that proved a crippling drain on UNIA resources. After an attempt to raise money through a mail soliciting campaign, Garvey was arrested for postal fraud in 1922. He represented himself in court, staging a dramatic and eloquent but legally inept defense, and was convicted. In 1927 he was released from prison and deported to Jamaica. There he established the periodical *Black Man,* began a mail-correspondence school of African philosophy, and ran an unsuccessful campaign for a seat in the Jamaican legislature. With his reputation tarnished by his imprisonment, and pan-African activism dampened by the more immediate concerns of the Great Depression, Garvey's influence steadily decreased until his death in London in 1940.

Garvey's most highly regarded statements of his ideals and social philosophy are contained in his speeches and essays, particularly those collected in *Philosophy and Opinions.* Garvey's separatist philosophy was a radical break from previous civil rights movements, which had advocated equality with whites socially, politically, and financially within the same milieus. Such integrationist groups as W. E. B. Du Bois's National Association for the Advancement of Colored People (NAACP) criticized Garvey's ideas as counterproductive and his business plans as foolish. Garvey, however, argued that no race would willingly relinquish power and that black citizens who attempted integration were doomed to second-class status. He therefore maintained that only the existence of a separate, free, and powerful African state could ensure rights and security for black people living outside of Africa. He further charged that the African-American intelligentsia was elitist and dominated by mulattoes who sought preeminence for those with light complexions rather than dark. Garvey frequently maligned Du Bois's racially mixed heritage and quipped that NAACP stood for "National Association for the Advancement of Certain People." Critics have suggested that Garvey thus needlessly alienated black leaders who might have helped him.

Paralleling Garvey's call for African political nationalism was his development of a black theology and aesthetic. Garvey argued that black people had been cowed into submission by such institutionalized propaganda of white superiority as the anthropomorphism of God as white and the slight attention paid to black historical achievements. He called on blacks to reject the white aesthetic and to adopt African standards of physical and artistic beauty instead. However, he also rejected as elitist the literature of the Harlem Renaissance, much of which contained lyrical celebration of the black body and drew on images of Africa as a spiritual touchstone. Instead, he used the *Negro World* as a vehicle for black authors whose work he believed more relevant to the masses. In the mid-1920s Garvey's

advocacy of separatism and racial purity grew more radical, and he endorsed the aims of white supremacist groups including the Ku Klux Klan; Garvey asserted that these groups opposed miscegenation, as the UNIA did, and he stated that he regarded "the Klan, the Anglo-Saxon Clubs, and White American Societies . . . as better friends of the [black] race than all other groups of hypocritical whites put together."

Scholars generally agree that even though Garvey's concrete contributions to civil rights were few, his ideological impact was tremendous. His calls for Afrocentric scholarship and the rediscovery of a black aesthetic strongly influenced such groups as the Black Arts Movement of the 1960s. Garvey's development of a black theosophy and ideology of separatism presaged the efforts of later black nationalist and Black Muslim leaders, including Elijah Muhammad and Malcolm X. Critics also credit Garvey's pan-Africanist political thinking for increasing the scope of the American civil rights movement, which had been largely isolationist, and also for influencing such African liberation leaders as Jomo Kenyatta. While many critics fault Garvey for the impractibility of some of his goals and for allying with white racist groups, others argue that the novelty and audacity of his methods were precisely what helped him fire the imagination of the greater public; even Garvey's detractors have conceded that Garveyism succeeded as few other movements have in galvanizing and restoring racial pride to African-Americans. An editorial in the integrationist *Messenger* magazine in 1922 conceded that, as much as he proved a scourge to the black intellectual mainstream, "Garvey has done much good work in putting into many Negroes a backbone where for years they have only had a wishbone."

(For further information about Garvey's life and works, see *Black Writers* and *Contemporary Authors,* Vols. 120, 124.)

PRINCIPAL WORKS

The Philosophy and Opinions of Marcus Garvey; or, Africa for the Africans. 2 vols. (essays) 1923-25
The Tragedy of White Injustice (poetry) 1927
The Poetical Works of Marcus Garvey (poetry) 1983
The Marcus Garvey and Universal Negro Improvement Association Papers. 6 vols. (essays and journalism) 1983-87

John Edward Bruce (essay date 1922)

[*An American journalist, essayist, and short story writer, Bruce was a vocal and witty proponent of black nationalism. In his newspaper columns, written under the pseudonym "Bruce Grit," he argued for black pride and against miscegenation. In the 1920s he*

I have been studying Marcus Garvey for the past four years, and I have studied some of his opponents for thirty or forty years, and find that my estimate of Marcus Garvey is much higher than it is of many of those whom I have personally known in all these years. To me, two of the tests of true leadership are the absence of the love of money and a desire to help the masses to get on and up. I haven't discovered such altruism in the ethics of many of these leaders whom Mr. Garvey is putting out of business by his straightforward methods and bull-dog tenacity.

When Mr. Garvey first came to this country from his island home in Jamaica, B.W.I., I was one among the first American Negroes, on whom he called. I was then residing in Yonkers on the Hudson, New York. He was a little sawed-off and hammered-down Black Man, with *determination* written all over his face, and an engaging smile that caught you and compelled you to listen to his story. Like all other Negroes who feel deeply the injustices of the White Man, whether they are committed by individuals or by the State, he had a grievance, and I listened with interest to its recital, which is much too long to repeat here, but the substance of which was, that the Negroes in the West Indian Island, from which he came, were not receiving fair play at the hands of the Whites, either in the matter of education or in the industries, in that the school facilities were inadequate, and that the workers were underpaid, thus preventing them from doing for themselves what they would like to do to improve their educational and economic condition. All they needed was a fair opportunity and the Organization which he was then endeavoring to form, he believed would give them, in some slight measure, this opportunity, if the Negroes on this side of the World would lend a helping hand.

Mr. Garvey is a rapid-fire talker, and two reporters are necessary to keep up with him at his meetings here in Liberty Hall on Sunday Nights, when he speaks to audiences of 5000 or more; I was able to catch enough from his rapidly spoken story, however, to convince me that he had a real mission, and I promised him such aid in the furtherance of his plans as I could give him, morally and substantially. We parted the best of friends. I had given him a list of names of our leading men in New York and other cities, who, I felt, would encourage and assist him. Some of them were Clergymen; some professional men; and some of them private citizens. He called on some of these, and among them, Prof. Du Bois, who did not think well of his plan, but he kept on.

The Jamaica Club of New York City hired St. Mark's Hall on 138th Street, near Lenox Avenue, for a public meeting and announced that Mr. Garvey would speak on his favorite subject. He spoke with so much vigor and earnestness that he stepped off the platform to the floor. The tickets were $5.00 and I gladly purchased one and went to hear him. Since I had seen him in Yonkers, he had been *seeing things* in and around New York, and his vision had become enlarged. His address in St. Mark's Hall indicated, from its tenor, that his plan for Racial uplift was not to be wholly confined to his Island Home. The problems which it embraced were universal, because the Negro in the United States of America was but little better off than the Negro in the West Indies. Later on, he *reasoned* that the Negroes throughout the World had as much to complain of as those of Jamaica, and to prove that he was right, he made a trip into our *Southern Shambles,* and mingled freely with the humble and lowly classes, "who, in the Halcyon days of politics, served as 'meal tickets,'" for the scalawags of the White Race, seeking office and power through their Black accomplices, in the dirty game of American politics, which has at last come to a period in that section of the Country, and left the Negro political leader on the outside looking in.

Among these leaders were many men calling themselves ambassadors of God, who made a good living out of the political game, by using their Congregations as weavers use a shuttle-cock, for their personal gain. Garvey saw all the rottenness and deceptions of both White and Black leaders. He saw his Race being used as a plaything by these men, who had no other aim than to advance themselves politically at the expense of these Blacks, and then to pose as their Champions and defenders. Their hollow pretensions, their mock heroics, their false zeal and their rank hypocrisy set him to thinking, and after months of travel in the West Indies and the United States, where he used his eyes and kept his own counsel, he finally changed his plans, and began a vigorous soapbox campaign in Negro Harlem, out of which grew the Universal Negro Improvement Association, the original membership of which was thirteen (13), and which now numbers four millions in the United States, with 800 Divisions throughout the United States and the World which include Africa, the West Indies, and South and Central America. The Divisions which are established are growing by leaps and bounds in every part of the World where Negroes are to be found.

In the incipiency of this newer Movement of Garvey, the old leaders paused, and snorted; the preachers, who found their Congregations thinning out and slipping away from them, and the Professional leaders for Revenue only, discovering that majorities for the candidates who had paid them to get results in Negro districts were growing more and more uncertain, combined and united in a campaign of slander and abuse of the Garvey Movement, and threw all sorts of obstacles in the way, to prevent the accomplishment of his plans. But they continued to develop, despite these handicaps, and, like the proverbial steamroller of the G.O.P., they will all of them be flattened out, if they wait long enough.

Mr. Garvey is very busy now working out the larger details of his plan, jailing crooks who have robbed his Association, and finding and fitting men to take up the

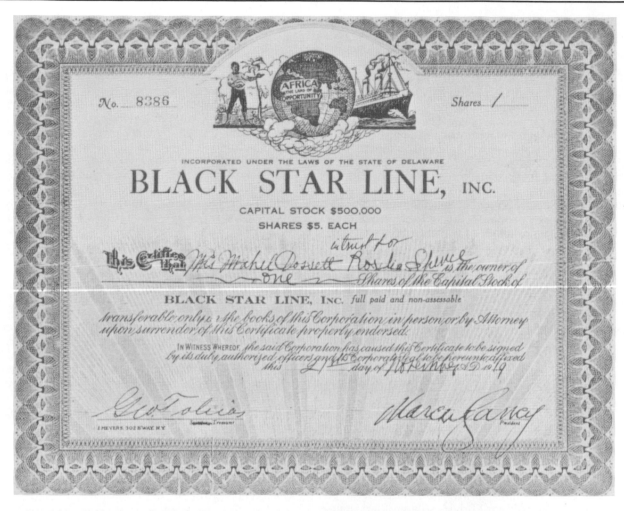

A certificate of stock in the Black Star Line, the shipping company Garvey founded to repatriate African–Americans.

work of spreading the Gospel of the U.N.I.A., among those who sit in darkness.

I was among those who opposed him at the start and who wrote against him, and I tried my best to defeat his aims, which, I confess, I did not then thoroughly understand. They seemed to me wild, chimerical and impossible of accomplishment. I stood, one night, at a corner of Lenox Avenue and 135th Street, when Garvey standing on an especially built platform—a step ladder—with which he could take liberties without falling, unfolded, in part, the plan of his Organization, which was to draw all Negroes throughout the World together, to make one big brotherhood of the Black Race for its common good, for mutual protection, for commercial and industrial development, and for the fostering of business enterprises. This sounded not only good to me, but practical. The things he proposed were easy of accomplishment under a leader as full of his subject as he, and, "Why not?" I said to myself, "let him try out his plan; since no one else has submitted a better one, why oppose him?" and from that cold night, in October, I ceased writing and talking against Garvey.

His street corner audiences were larger than those of the Socialist Orators on the other corners a few blocks away, and they stayed longer. The people hung upon his words, drank in his messages to them, and were as enthusiastic and earnest about this business as their doughty little Black Orator. To me, this connoted that Marcus Garvey was more than the average Street Corner Orator and that his work and mission had more than an ordinary significance. The people to whom he spoke heard him gladly, pondered his words, and acted wisely by organizing what is today the most powerful Negro Organization in the World. There is absolutely no corner of the earth where there is a Black or Brown or Yellow face, where there is not a Branch of the U.N.I.A. There are branches in Germany, London, Wales, Scotland, and recently, I saw a letter from far off Peru, requesting the literature of the Organization. What does this mean? It means clearly, that Mr. Garvey has caught the vision, that the people of Color, throughout the World, believe in his leadership and want him to lead them. Nothing could be plainer.

The old leaders were not able or were too lazy or indifferent or both, to work out a plan for the redemption and regeneration of the Race, as attractive and practical from any angle in which it is viewed, as that of Marcus Garvey. It has progressed too far now for any of them singly or all of them combined to stop it, and it will be a hazardous undertaking for those who think they are powerful enough to do so. They have had their chance and failed, and the wisdom of prudence suggests that they let Garvey alone. Let him carry on the work to which he has put his hands and to which he, in the greatness and bigness of his heart, is inviting them now to put their hands, their brains, and their money to make the Big Negro World Brotherhood, the accomplished *fact* that he intends it to be, with or without the consent of any Negro leader or leaders who now think they are IT.

Garvey is neither a rum drinker, a user of tobacco in any form, a social bug, nor a grafter. He is scrupulously honest in the handling of the funds of the Organization, and exacts the strictest accounting of its funds from those holding subordinate positions in the Organization, and through whose hands its money passes. "His spear knows no brother." The man caught stealing the people's money is promptly cut off the payroll and headed for jail, if the offense is sufficient to justify such action. He is branded a thief in the "Negro World," and must change his name and complexion to do business elsewhere. Garvey is relentless with crooks and fakers, and he is the idol of the masses of the common people, of whom he is one (pp. 167-70)

> *John Edward Bruce, "Marcus Garvey and the U.N.I.A.," in his* The Selected Writings of John Edward Bruce: Militant Black Journalist, *edited by Peter Gilbert, Arno Press, 1971, pp. 167-70.*

Charles Willis Simmons (essay date 1961)

[*In the following excerpt, Simmons assesses criticisms of Garveyism made by the black intelligentsia, arguing that Garvey was taken more seriously by intellectuals than some have contended.*]

This article represents an attempt to assay the attitudes and opinions of Negro intellectuals with reference to Marcus Garvey's To Africa Movement. The intellectuals referred to herein are those scholars, politicians, editors and leaders who, during and after Garvey's era, expressed their attitudes in print. The impression one might gain from reading the general works dealing with this period of the Negro's history in America is that Garvey was regarded by Negro intellectuals as a buffoon, a rascal, and an object of disdain. Such was not the case. (p. 33)

In the opinion of some observers, early opposition of Negro intellectuals to the movement was based upon envy over " . . . the striking success of an upstart foreigner," but as time passed the intellectual opposition to

Garvey and his movement sprang from far more reasonable grounds.

Garvey, seemingly, had bred within himself a strong dislike for and distrust of mulattoes. When the Negro leadership, which was primarily mulatto, voiced its opposition to his program because it would, if successfully carried out, have destroyed the policies and plans which Negro leaders had outlined as the road which would lead to first class citizenship, Garvey turned upon them, calling them " . . . opportunists, liars, thieves, traitors and bastards." Garvey charged that Dr. W. E. B. Du Bois and the National Association for the Advancement of Colored People; the successor to Booker T. Washington, Dr. R. R. Moton and his followers; the Negro clergy; The Negro politicians of New York; and the mulattoes of Jamaica, did not want any new organization among Negroes to succeed.

Garvey declared that the mulatto was not a Negro. He charged that the failure of the Negro in the United States was a result not of the action of the white man, but was a result of the conduct of the Negro intellectuals who were traitors and enemies of the Negro race. The intellectuals, he said, were not in sympathy with the black people of America. He promised that the Universal Negro Improvement Association would " . . . put the National Association for the Advancement of Colored People to shame for employing only the lightest of the race." Among the mulatto opponents who aroused strong feelings of animosity in Marcus Garvey was Du Bois whom Garvey went so far as to brand a minion of the white man who was leading a movement which had as its objective the denial of independence to the American Negro.

This clever propagandist's description of the Negro intellectuals intensified their opposition to him and to his program, perhaps because the description contained a germ of truth. Of the Negro intellectuals, Garvey wrote:

> The present day Negro or 'colored' intellectual is no less a liar and a cunning thief than his illustrious teacher. His occidental collegiate training only fits him to be a rogue and a vagabond, and a seeker after the easiest and best by following the line of least resistance. He is lazy, dull and uncreative. His purpose is to deceive the less fortunate of his race, and by his wiles ride easily into position and wealth at their expense, and therefore agitate for and seek social equality with the creative and industrious whites.

In "**An Appeal From Marcus Garvey**" he stated that "There are some Negroes who think themselves too educated, too successful to lend an ear to the common plea. . . . these people are indeed narrow minded and have no vision." Garvey then proceeded to describe the futility of the search for first class citizenship in the United States. "There is no guarantee of the safety of any such Negro, because by mob violence and lynch law, the outcome of race prejudice, one's success can be overthrown overnight, and one transformed from a prosperous subject or citizen, to a refugee." The hand-bill demonstrated an improved understanding on the part of Garvey of the American's Negro's attitude toward color. An improved understanding reflected in Garvey's statement that the program of the UNIA "... is for everybody, so long as you have one drop of Negro blood in your veins."

Some Negro intellectuals were sufficiently interested in the Garvey movement to ally themselves with it at one time or another. Emmett J. Scott, Registrar at Howard University, for example, became "Duke of the Nile" in Garvey's African Empire; but the majority of the intellectuals bitterly opposed the movement. The opposition was led by such men as Du Bois, A. Philip Randolph and Robert S. Abbott, editor of the influential newspaper, The Chicago *Defender.*

Garvey's telegram endorsing President Warren G. Hardings' 1921 Birmingham speech about the Negro's place in American politics and society aroused a storm of protest from Negro intellectuals. The telegram stated that "... true Negroes were against social equality and that the Negroes should develop along their own social lines." Garvey, perhaps, had no intention of arousing even stronger opposition to his movement, but he "... had stumbled headlong into the hornet's nest of the Northern Negro intelligentsia." The southern whites of that era regarded social equality as the equivalent of amalgamation, whereas northern Negro leaders interpreted the phrase to mean equal opportunity in industrial, educational, political and other avenues of American life. Garvey, the West Indian Negro, had used the phrase in its West Indian sense, in interpretation identical with that of the southern white.

The Chicago *Defender* in its news columns and on its editorial pages strongly opposed the To Africa Movement and its founder. The newspaper's cartoonist frequently ridiculed the movement. The September 2, 1922, editorial page contained a cartoon showing a dignified and manly Negro holding a scrawny midget in the air by means of a firm grip on the seat of the trousers. The midget was being admonished: "The best thing you can do is stay right here and fight out your salvation." The *Defender* a few months later editorially suggested that UNIA "... stands for Us Nonsensical INVITERS to Africa." Soon after the movement gained prominence the newspaper in a "Back to Africa" editorial, sarcastically stated:

> It might be interesting to count noses and see just how many there are among us who hail from Africa. How many who know anything about Africa by reason of setting foot on African soil. Very, very few, and yet we hear much about "going back home". And by the way when we invest in a piece of property in this country we insist upon having a deed for same. Will those who hold deeds for the land they have purchased in Africa please rise. As no one seems to leave his seat, we will sing the doxology. Use all the doors please.

Du Bois, editor of the *Crisis,* and a NAACP leader, wrote of Garvey: "He is not attacking white prejudice, he is grovelling before it and applauding it, his only attack is on men of his own race who are striving for freedom."

George S. Schuyler, then a young man, but later a severe journalistic critic of the foibles of the American Negro, in a letter to the editor of *The Messenger,* wrote of Garvey:

> An ass was created to be ridden. Keep on riding Garvey by all means. Remember the much quoted maxim of Mr. P. T. Barnum and don't let up on brother Marcus as long as he continues in his mess, lest more foolish Negroes be taken in by this sable Ponzi.

When William Pickens, field organizer for the NAACP, was offered a position in the UNIA, he refused, saying, "I cannot feel myself quite bad enough to accept any honor or alliance with such organizations as the Ku Klux Klan or the Black Hand Society... You compare the aim of the KKK in America with your aim in Africa—and if that be true, no civilized man can endorse either of you."

Later Pickens gave additional expression to his contempt of the alliance between Garveyism and the Ku Klux Klan:

> When the invisible government of Africa came to an understanding with the invisible empire of America... the terms... had to be held secret, but they are easily inferred from Garvey's voluminous speeches immediately following his visit to Atlanta where he conferred with the Imperial Wizard. The KKK was to be given America, so far as Garvey was concerned, and in return for his preaching to his followers that this is a "white man's Country", he and his followers were to be allowed to take Africa, so far as the Imperial Wizard was concerned.

After Garvey's arrest on the charge of using the mails to defraud, his trial was postponed a number of times. Negro intellectuals, perhaps seeking an end to Garvey and Garveyism, repeatedly requested that the Justice Department prosecute Garvey. George W. Harris, editor of the New York *News,* Robert S. Abbott, publisher of the Chicago *Defender,* John E. Hall, New York realtor, William Pickens and Robert W. Bagnall, NAACP officials, Chandler Owens, editor of the *Messenger* magazine and others in a signed petition urged that Garvey be tried, imprisoned and then deported.

During and after Garvey's trial, imprisonment and deportation, Negro intellectuals frequently expressed admiration for the man or for the ideas which he advocated. The Chicago *Defender,* during Garvey's trial, was moved to comment editorially, "At times even a degree of admiration must be felt at the nerve of the man in shattering court customs. Were it not for the fact that he has so evidenced his total unfitness to lead a colossal movement such as he has set in motion... it is certain that some of the man's action should be admired."

Dr. Du Bois in later years described the movement as a "grandiose and bombastic scheme, utterly impractical as a whole,...," but Du Bois considered the movement sincere and said of Garvey that he "...proved not only an astonishingly popular leader but a master of propaganda." Displaying even greater admiration for the leader of the UNIA and seemingly refusing to acknowledge that the profound impact of that organization had fallen upon United States Negroes, Du Bois wrote that Garvey had "...made vocal the great and long suffering grievances and spirit of protest among the West Indian peasantry." He described the UNIA as "...one of the most interesting spiritual movements of the modern world."

E. Franklin Frazier, in 1926, commenting upon Garvey and his movement, wrote: "As a leader of a mass movement among Negroes, Garvey has no equal." Later, 1949, Frazier described Garvey as being the "...leader of the most important, though ephemeral, nationalistic movement among Negroes."

Alain Locke, in the *New Negro* saw in Garveyism "...the sense of a mission of rehabilitating the race in world esteem from the loss of prestige for which the fate and conditions of slavery have so largely been responsible. Garveyism may be a transient, if spectacular, phenomenon, but the possible role of the American Negro in the future development of Africa is one of the most constructive and universally helpful missions that any modern people can lay claim to."

A. Philip Randolph, one of Garvey's persistent opponents, pointed out that the UNIA "...had stirred Negroes to the realization of a need for organization and had demonstrated the ability of Negroes to organize under Negro leadership." Randolph credited Garvey and his organization with having aided in the destruction of the "...slave psychology which throttles and strangles Negro initiative."

One Negro intellectual, observing the impression which Garvey was making upon the American Negro said that "...whatever may happen to his grandiose schemes of finance and politics, he is the best point at which to study what is going on inside the hearts of ten million colored people of the United States."

James Weldon Johnson believed that if Garvey had possessed a more tactful personality and had used more moderation he would have been successful in his To Africa Movement. "He had," wrote Johnson,

> ...energy and daring and the Napoleonic personality, the personality that draws masses of followers.... he had great power and possibilities within his grasp, but his deficiencies as a leader outweighed his abilities. To this man came an opportunity such as comes to few men, and he clutched greedily at the glitter and let the substance slip from his fingers."

Garvey's frequent assertion that black men should be proud of their color and that black was the symbol of honor might have been the source of a new concept of color among Negroes. "Before his time, such things as colored dolls or calendars with colored families and heroes were a rarity: today they are commonplace. Garvey didn't get many Negroes back to Africa, but he helped to destroy their inferiority complex and made them conscious of their power."

The UNIA and its founder in the opinion of the Negro intellectuals of that era were a Jekyll and Hyde creature. The Negro leaders, while strongly opposed to the To Africa Movement, frequently but reluctantly were forced to express admiration of the personality and some of the methods of its captain. Even so distinguished a contemporary Negro American as the Nobel prize-winner, Ralph Bunche, has said of Garveyism, "No other American Negro organization has been able to reach and stir the masses of Negroes to the same degree, or receive from them such generous financial support." (pp. 33-5)

> *Charles Willis Simmons, "The Negro Intellectual's Criticism of Garveyism," in* The Negro History Bulletin, *Vol. 25, No. 1, October, 1961, pp. 33-5.*

Richard Hart (essay date 1967)

[*In the following excerpt, Hart outlines the major points of Garvey's political philosophy and explores his impact on black national consciousness.*]

The central core of Garvey's agitation was what he called the regeneration of Africa. He believed that if only Africa could become a strong united national state the Negro would obtain the respect of the white world and come into his own. To achieve this 'regeneration' he urged that all Negroes in the western world possessing talent and energy should 'return' to Africa, the land of their forefathers.

The copy of the Manifesto of the organisation Garvey formed in Jamaica in 1914 is the first record we have of his views about Africa. We owe its preservation to the chance circumstance that he sent a copy to Booker T. Washington.

The manifesto is interesting in that it shows not only the germ of Garvey's central idea, but also his woeful ignorance about Africa. He appears to have accepted fully the picture of 'darkest Africa,' needing a civilizing western Christian influence, currently being popularised by the imperial powers. Here is how he expressed this in the aims of his organisation.

> To establish a Universal Confraternity among the race; to promote the spirit of race pride and love; to reclaim the fallen of the race; to administer to and assist the needy; to assist in civilising the backward tribes of Africa; to strengthen the imperialism of independent African states; ... to promote a conscientious Christian worship among the native tribes of Africa ...

Within a few years Garvey had obviously gained a better appreciation of Africa's historical contributions to world culture and civilisation. But he does not appear to have done much study of African history. Judging from the absence of references to them in his writings, he was probably only vaguely, if at all, aware of the level of civilisation reached in the ancient empires of Ghana and Mali. These facts were available and would have been extremely useful to him had he done more detailed research. As it was, most of his examples of Africa's greatness were drawn from ancient Egypt and Ethiopia.

An article entitled **'Who and What is a Negro',** written on 16 April 1923, furnishes an example of how effectively Garvey used historical references to instill racial pride into his audiences:

> Every student of history, of impartial mind, knows that the Negro once ruled the world, when white men were savages and barbarians living in caves; that thousands of Negro professors at that time taught in the universities in Alexandria, then the seat of learning; that ancient Egypt gave the world civilisation and that Greece and Rome have robbed Egypt of her arts and letters, and taken all the credit to themselves.
>
> It is not surprising, however, that white men should resort to every means to keep Negroes in ignorance of their history, it would be a great shock to their pride to admit to the world today that 3,000 years ago black men excelled in government and were the founders and teachers of art, science and literature.
>
> The power and sway we once held passed away, but now in the twentieth century we are about to see a return of it in the rebuilding of Africa; yes, a new civilization, a new culture, shall spring up from among our people, and the Nile shall once more flow through the land of science, of art, and of literature, wherein will live black men of the highest learning and the highest accomplishments.

In his **'Declaration of Rights of the Negro Peoples of the World,'** adopted at the UNIA convention held in New York in 1920, Garvey developed his idea of a united African nation:

> We believe in the freedom of Africa for the Negro people of the world, and by the principle of Europe for the Europeans and Asia for the Asiatics; we also demand Africa for the Africans at home and abroad.

Garvey, in ceremonial military dress, participates in a 1920 UNIA parade.

We believe in the inherent right of the Negro to possess himself of Africa, and that his possession of same shall not be regarded as an infringement on any claim or purchase made by any race or nation.

We strongly condemn the cupidity of those nations of the world who, by open aggression or secret schemes, have seized the territories and inexhaustible natural wealth of Africa and we place on record our most solemn determination to reclaim the treasures and possession of the vast continent of our forefathers.

In an article dated 24 March 1923 Garvey wrote:

The mission of the Universal Negro Improvement Association is to arouse the sleeping consciousness of Negroes everywhere to the point where we will, as one concerted body, act for our own preservation. By laying the foundation for such we will be able to work toward the glorious realisation of an emancipated race and a constructed nation.

Nationhood is the strongest security for any people . . . while others are raising the cry of a white America, a white Canada, a white Australia, we also without reservation raise the cry of a 'Black Africa' . . .

Out of this very reconstruction of world affairs will come the glorious opportunity for Africa's freedom.

. . . We can be as loyal American citizens or British subjects as the Irishman or the Jew and yet fight for the redemption of Africa, a complete emancipation of the race.

Oddly enough, although Africa became the focus of his agitation throughout his life's work, Garvey never visited Africa and remained blissfully innocent of the political structure of the African states and the customs, languages and religions of the people of Africa. A beautifully over-simplified conception of Africa as a single whole to be established under his leadership was the image he held before the eyes of his followers, even when he was at the crest of his power and influence. He drew up an elaborate constitution for his 'United States of Africa' and had himself elected, at his International Convention in New York in 1920, as 'Provisional President of Africa'. His constitutional model was, of course, the constitution of the U.S.A.

Garvey was much attracted by the glamour of the British nobility and decided that his regenerated Africa also should have an aristocracy. But it was not to be merely idle and parasitic:

It will be useless . . . for bombastic Negroes to leave America and the West Indies to go to Africa, thinking that they will have privileged positions to inflict upon the race that bastard aristocracy that they have tried to maintain in this Western world at the expense of the masses. Africa shall develop an aristocracy of its own, but it shall be based upon service and loyalty to the race.

Garvey does not seem to have paid much regard to the traditional aristocracy that already existed in a number of African countries and one wonders whether he even

bothered to inform himself of their existence. He proceeded to create a number of 'Lords', 'Ladies' and 'Knights' and other dignatories by personal appointment.

He adored regal pomp and ceremony. In *The Blackman* of 24 August 1929 appears a report of what is described as a 'Court Reception' at Edelweiss Park in Jamaica, which opens as follows: 'His Highness the Potentate, Hon. Alfred Potter arrived in regal attire.' There follows an account of the presentation to him of the visitors and delegates. Then the report continues as follows:

All interest however was centered in the arrival of the Hon. Marcus Garvey, the principal figure of attraction . . . Precisely at 8.10 p.m. the greatest Negro Leader of modern times accompanied by Mrs. Amy Jacques-Garvey and an Aide-de-Camp of the Legions, arrived wearing the uniform of the Provisional President of Africa. The Band played the African Anthem 'Ethiopia the land of our fathers'. After acknowledging the Royal Salute the President General was escorted . . .

To the American Negro intellectual of the period all this was inexcusable buffoonery to which he could never be reconciled. But Garvey had little use for the Negro intelligensia. He knew that his pageantry, his processions and uniforms, had an irresistible appeal for the masses he was bent on stirring out of their apathy.

Garvey made a valiant effort to produce a new unified religion for his followers with a black God and a black clergy. At first he thought in the rather limited terms of a black Christianity. Rev. George Alexander McGuire, a prominent Episcopalian, left his Boston pulpit to become Chaplain General of the UNIA. In September 1921 he was ordained a bishop by dignitaries of the Greek Orthodox Church and consecrated as head of a new 'African Orthodox Church'. Some progress was made, particularly after the 1924 Convention, in pushing the idea of replacing the pictures of the white Christ and Madonna by black ones.

By the Jamaica Convention of 1929, however, it appears that Garvey had run up against the problem that there were probably as many or more Negro Muslims in the world than there were Christians. He accordingly made a speech which is reported in *The Blackman* of 31 August 1929 under the following headline: 'Speech of Hon. Marcus Garvey outlining discussion on formulating of plans to unify the Religious Beliefs and practises of the Entire Negro Race'. The speech was exploratory and thought-provoking only. It laid down no definite line and Garvey does not seem to have pushed this project any further.

Garvey believed that one of the impediments to the development of the Negro's self respect was his acceptance of the white man's standards of beauty and consequent failure to see any beauty in his own form. He worked aggressively to correct this. Speaking at his welcome meeting in Jamaica on his deportation from the U.S.A. he said:

I would be untrue to my Gods if I did not stand upon a platform of racial righteousness, of racial truth, of racial honour, of racial self respect. Why there is no beauty in the world except it looks like me!

There is beauty in our women, there is beauty in our children, because God made us in His image, as there is beauty in every race. Anglo-Saxons see beauty in themselves to the exclusion of all others. The people of Mongolia, the Chinese, the Japanese see beauty in themselves to the exclusion of all other beauty. I shall teach the black man to see beauty in himself to the exclusion of all others, and be hanged to the man who says: 'It shall not be so.'

During his period of activity in the U.S.A., Garvey was strongly opposed by all significant leaders of thought among American Negroes and also by all progressive and left orientated organisations. The main reason for this was his strong opposition to any attempts at social and economic integration of the Negro into American life. He openly conceded that the U.S.A. is a white man's country and that the Negro had no right to demand equality within it.

A fairly full exposition of his views on this subject, addressed to the American people, is to be found in an undated article published in the **Philosophy and Opinions** collection:

Hitherto the other Negro movements in America, with the exception of the Tuskegee effort of Booker T. Washington, sought to teach the Negro to aspire to social equality with the whites, meaning thereby the right to inter-marry and fraternize in every social way. This has been the source of much trouble and still some Negro organisations continue to preach this dangerous 'race destroying doctrine' added to a programme of political agitation and aggression.

The Universal Negro Improvement on the other hand believes in and teaches the pride and purity of race. We believe that the white race should uphold its racial pride and perpetuate itself, and that the black race should do likewise. We believe that there is room enough in the world for the various race groups to grow and develop by themselves without seeking to destroy the Creator's plan by the constant introduction of mongrel types.

The unfortunate condition of slavery, as imposed upon the Negro, and which caused the mongrelisation of the race, should not be legalised and continued now to the harm and detriment of both races. The time has really come to give the Negro a chance to develop himself to a moral-standard-man, and it is for such an opportunity that the Universal Negro Improvement Association seeks in the creation of an African nation for Negroes, where the greatest latitude would be given to work out this racial ideal . . .

The time is opportune to regulate the relationship between both races. Let the Negro have a country of his own. Help him to return to his original home, Africa, and there give him the opportunity to climb from lowest to the highest positions in a state of his own.

If not, then the nation will have to hearken to the demand of the aggressive 'social equality' organisa-tion known as the National Association for the Advancement of Coloured People, of which W. E. B. DuBois is leader, which declares vehemently for social and political equality, viz: Negroes and whites in the same hotels, homes, residential districts, public and private places, a Negro as president, members of the Cabinet, Governors of States, Mayors of cities, and leaders of society in the United States . . .

All these, as everybody knows, are the Negroes constitutional rights, but reason dictates that the masses of the white race will never stand by the ascendency of an opposite minority group to favored positions in a government, society and industry that exist by the will of the majority, hence the demand of the DuBois group of coloured leaders will only lead, ultimately, to further disturbances in riots, lynching and mob rule. The only logical solution therefore, is to supply the Negro with opportunities and environ-ments of his own, and there point him to the fullness of his ambition.

In an article written on 31 March 1923 Garvey says:

We of the Universal Negro Improvement Association cede to the white man the right of doing as he pleases in his own country, and that is why we believe in not making any trouble when he says that 'America is a white man's country', because in the same breath and with the same determination we are going to make Africa a black man's country.

Not surprisingly this doctrine endeared Garvey to the leaders of the Ku Klux Klan. Garvey's vehement denunciations of miscegenation, his glorification of racial purity, his concession that the U.S.A. was a white man's country, his advocacy of the Negro's migration to Africa—all this was closely paralleled by Ku Klux Klan doctrine on the desirability of racial purity for whites. Speakers from the KKK and other white racialist organisations were welcome at UNIA headquarters in New York. There is ample evidence of this in the **Philosophy and Opinions.**

On 28 October 1925 Garvey introduced a speaker from one of the white racialist organisations to a UNIA audience in Harlem in these terms:

In the great American confusion of races it is hard to discern our friends, but as a people we have not been entirely friendless. When I speak of friendship I mean that which is sturdy, honourable and sincere. Such a friendship I desire to apprise you of in the introduction of Mr. John Powell, of the Anglo-Saxon Clubs of America.

Mr. Powell represents a body of men and women for whom I maintain the greatest respect because of their honesty and lack of hypocrisy. They represent the clean-cut and honest section of the white race that uncompromisingly stands for the purity of their race, even as we unhesitatingly and determinedly agitate and fight for the purity of the Negro race.

All races should be pure in morals and in outlook, and for that we, as Negroes, admire the leaders and members of the Anglo-Saxon Clubs. They are honest and honourable in their desire to purify and preserve the white race even as we are determined to purify and standardize our race.

Mr. Powell and his organisation sympathize with us even as we sympathize with them. I feel and believe that we, the two organisations, should work together for the purpose of bringing about the ideal sought— the purification of the races, their autonomous separation and the unbridled freedom of self-development and self-expression. Those who are against this are enemies of both races, and rebels against morality, nature and God.

Garvey advised American Negro workers that so long as they remained in the U.S.A. their best interests did not lie in fighting for equal job opportunities and wages with white workers and equal civil rights. The employers were predominantly white, he said, and it was unreasonable to expect them to do other than show a preference for their own kind. The salvation of the Negro worker, he said, lay in the emergence of Negro owned businesses and a Negro employing class. In the meanwhile he advised Negro workers to stay out of inter-racial trade unions and political organisations and offer their services to the existing employers at lower wage rates than the white workers in order to ensure survival.

In an article entitled **'The Negro, Communism, Trade Unionism and His (?) Friend'**, Garvey wrote:

If I must advise the Negro workingman and labourer, I should warn him against the present brand of Communism or Workers Partizanship as taught in America, and to be careful of the traps and pitfalls of white trade unionism, in affiliation with the American Federation of white workers or labourers . . .

The capitalist being selfish—seeking only the largest profit out of labour—is willing and glad to use Negro labour whenever possible on a scale 'reasonably' below the standard white union wage. He will tolerate the Negro in any industry (except those that are necessarily guarded for the protection of the whiteman's material, racial and assumed cultural dominance) if he accepts a lower standard wage than the white union man; but, if the Negro unionizes himself to the level of the white worker and in affiliation with him, the choice and preference of employment is given to the white worker, without any regard or consideration for the Negro.

Such reactionary ideas of course delighted the Negro bourgeois elements striving to gain a foothold in the employing class, and roused the implacable opposition of all socialists and other progressives. The Communist International categorised Garveyism as a reactionary bourgeois philosophy, as indeed in part it was.

What then did Garvey leave behind him when he left the U.S.A.? The really progressive element in Garvey's teaching in the U.S.A. was that he successfully challenged the imperialist doctrine of Negro inferiority which millions of Negroes in the Western world had themselves come to accept. In making this challenge he used techniques which fired the imagination of simple people.

Garvey stirred dispirited and downtrodden millions into motion and they never became still again. The intelligensia and the Marxists and other socialists had started the thought processes whirring in the minds of mere thousands, causing hardly a ripple on the placid sea of the Negro masses. Paradoxically enough, the militant mass movement of American Negroes for social integration today owes much to the fact that Garvey's agitation, which preceded it, troubled the waters. Thanks partly to Garvey, those who organise today are getting a response because they are no longer speaking to sheep.

Others appealed to the intellect with sane and logical reasoning and won to the path of struggle a dedicated handful. Garvey spoke less logically, more emotionally; he spoke from less knowledge but more convincingly. Garvey used flamboyant methods that fired simple imaginations. And Garvey stirred millions of the apathetic into action who but for him might have slumbered on.

Today, even among those who could not bring themselves to support him during his years of maximum influence in the U.S.A., his contribution is generally recognised. Few indeed are the voices of coloured Americans today who do not now acknowledge the American Negro's debt of gratitude to him.

It is as well that Garvey passed from the scene at the time he did. What Garvey had to offer to his followers, once he had stirred them into awareness and self respect, would have been of negligible value. But he it was who first stirred the masses up and they will never be the same again. (pp. 229-35)

> *Richard Hart, "The Life and Resurrection of Marcus Garvey," in* Race, *Vol. IX, No. 2, October, 1967, pp. 217-37.*

Henry J. Young (essay date 1977)

[*In the following excerpt, Young analyzes the religious elements of Garveyism, including the theological beliefs expressed in Garvey's writings and speeches.*]

The program of The Universal Negro Improvement Association and The Black Star Line was not directed toward seeking freedom and liberation for blacks in America; it was directed toward a mass movement of taking blacks back to their homeland Africa. Garvey contended that blacks were strangers in America and were children of captivity. As children of captivity, he argued that blacks looked forward to a new day when they would possess the land of their fathers, the land of refuge, the prophets, the saints, and the land of God's crowning glory. He said that blacks should gather together their children, treasures, and loved ones, and, like the children of Israel who by the command of God left Egypt and went to Canaan, the promised land, blacks should leave American and return to Africa, their promised land. Garvey felt that the black race and white race were competitive and could not live permanently side by side without friction and trouble; the white race wanted a white America and the black race wanted a black Africa. Garvey did not want social equality in America between blacks and whites. He wanted to have a nation owned, determined, and controlled by blacks so that blacks could reestablish a culture and civilization exclusively theirs.

Garvey believed that Africa was the legitimate moral and righteous home of all blacks. He argued that blacks and whites would learn to respect one another if they ceased to be competitors in the same country for the same things in politics and society. By having independent countries, he firmly believed that blacks and whites would be friendlier and more helpful toward each other because "the laws of nature separated them to the extent of each and every one developing by itself." Garvey called for this right to be practiced and the desire to be instilled in blacks to govern and rule themselves without fear of being encumbered and restrained. "We form a majority in Africa and we should naturally govern ourselves there. No man can govern another's house as well as himself."

In his strong emphasis on black Americans' returning to Africa, he clearly indicated that his program was not based on hate toward whites. He said that the Universal Negro Improvement Association was organized for the purpose of enhancing the condition of blacks industrially, commercially, socially, religiously, and politically. He said, "We are organized not to hate other men, but to lift [blacks] and to demand respect of all humanity." He believed that his program was righteous and just. He, therefore, declared that Africa must be free and that the entire black race must be emancipated from bondage and that Africa be made their homeland. Garvey made every effort to build his program on religious principles.

Garvey conceived of God in a way that facilitated the goals and aspirations of the Universal Negro Improvement Association—namely, the independence and redemption of Africa. For Garvey the objective essence of God was colorless in that he was conceived as a spirit. But in terms of the essential appropriation of God, Garvey argued that God for blacks must be conceived as "the God of Ethiopia, the everlasting God—God the Father, God the Son and God the Holy Ghost." Garvey's main concern was to demythologize the black man's conception of God and to redefine God in light of Pan-Africanism. He did not see how blacks could be true to the cause of black liberation's adhering to a conception of God that emerged from the white community. He felt that blacks should view God through the black experience and that whites should view God through their own experience. To view God, as Garvey argued, through the black experience did not mean that God literally becomes black. But it meant that when blacks view God, he takes on the identity and particularity of the black experience.

Garvey did not think of God as a passive, uninvolved reality. He viewed God as a God of both war and peace.

God becomes a God of war, he continued, when man transgresses his power and interferes with his authority.

He believed that as long as man worked in the interest of justice, righteousness, and the improvement of his race and humanity, God was on his side. But to accomplish this Garvey realized that man had to assert himself and make use of power. The black race in America was powerless in terms of independence and self-determination. In the attempt to help the black race realize their potential, Garvey told them that God was on the side of the powerful and the strong. By this he meant that blacks must become strong and powerful as a race, and by so doing God would work in their behalf.

Did God create any superior and inferior races? Garvey responded negatively to this question and asserted that God created all men equal, regardless of their color. Black people, white people, yellow people, and all other people were created as equals. Therefore, for any race to feel that they could not accomplish what another race had accomplished would be an insult to the Almighty God who created all races equal.

It was Garvey's contention that God made man lord and ruler of the earth. Since every man was given this responsibility, Garvey felt that whether man was white, yellow, brown, or black, nature had provided a place for each and every one. Garvey referred to geographical location: "If Europe is for the white man, if Asia is for the brown and yellow man, then surely Africa is for the Black man." He compared the black man's quest for nationhood with that of other nations, saying that the white man fought for the preservation of Asia, and blacks should be willing to shed blood for the redemption of Africa and the emancipation of blacks everywhere. He believed that every race must find a home because this was what God intended. The Jews found Palestine; the Irish found Ireland; the Indians found India; and he saw Africa for the Africans.

For Garvey, God did not create any man or race without a goal or purpose in mind. He created every man with possibilities for achievement, and for man to think that he was created only to be what he is and not what he has the possibilities of becoming is to misunderstand God's reason for making man. Why did God create the black man? Did he create him to be a slave? Garvey answered in the following manner: "God Almighty created us all to be free. That the Negro race became a race of slaves was not the fault of God Almighty, the Divine Master, it was the fault of the race." For God to have been responsible for the enslavement of blacks, he would have had to control and direct history in a providential manner. It is clear that Garvey did not perceive God as the director and controller of history and human affairs.

According to Garvey, for man to know who he really is means for him to realize that he has no human master. He took the position that the only master that man had was God. Man, in terms of his rightful place in creation, was conceived by Garvey as a sovereign lord. This applies both to individual men and to races. Garvey said

Garvey under escort by federal officers following the rejection of his appeal of his 1923 mail fraud conviction.

that this position made man courageous, bold, and impossible to enslave. What does it take then to be a man? To be a man in Garvey's eyes meant never to give up, never to depend upon others to do what one ought to do for oneself, and to be one who will not blame God, nature, or fate for one's condition. But the real man, said Garvey, goes out and makes conditions to suit himself. Garvey called upon blacks to know themselves and to realize that in them is a sovereign power, an authority that is absolute.

Marcus Garvey's eschatology was grounded first and foremost in the relentless quest for the ultimate freedom and liberation of the black race throughout the world and the acquisition of Africa as the homeland for blacks. He was not concerned with an otherworldly hope, nor did he believe that God would vindicate the black race for their sufferings. It was not his contention that God would intervene in the distant future and liberate the black race. In fact, he blatantly condemned the view held among some black leaders at the time that the problem of black and white polarization in America would work itself out and that all the black man had to

do was to be humble, submissive, and obedient, and everything would work out well in the sweet bye and bye. To the contrary, Garvey argued that if the black race is to be free, they must assert themselves with all their might and in every respect. They cannot depend upon God to free them, they cannot depend upon any other race for freedom, and they cannot hope for conditions to improve without human effort. But with the help of God, Garvey declared that the time had come for the black race to carve out a pathway for themselves in the course of life. He said that the black race "shall go forward, upward and onward toward the great goal of human liberty" and that it was his determination that all barriers placed in the way of the progress of the black race must be removed and cleared away by blacks themselves because the light of a brighter day had come. This brighter day, as Garvey perceived it, was the eschatological vision of an independent African nationality for the black race.

There are many significant and sustaining theological motifs that emerged from Marcus Garvey and that are existentially relevant for contemporary black Americans. He did not think of God as a reality detached and removed from the black-liberation struggle. He conceived of God as a reality whose metaphysical nature made his existence an integral part of the liberation struggle. God-talk, for Garvey, emerged out of the context of existential blackness and, therefore, functioned in the interest of black Americans. Garvey did not think of God in a way that minimized the efforts of black Americans toward liberation. But rather his contention was that God was a God of power, and if blacks were to be free, they must work from the perspective of social, economic, political, educational, and religious power. He felt that God would only help black Americans achieve freedom if they would utilize all their resources to the maximum capacity. Garvey developed theology organically in light of such sustaining ideas as self-assertions, independence, self-determination, nationhood, courage, strength, love, justice, righteousness, and corporate consciousness.

In spite of the many weaknesses of the Garvey movement, we cannot overly emphasize the importance of Marcus Garvey and the Garvey movement. He saw a need within the black community and devoted his life to trying to satisfy it. He continued the great legacy of black nationalistic consciousness and the development of black pride and self-respect. Regardless of what others may do in aiding blacks in America and throughout the world toward liberation, Garvey realized that if blacks were to be truly free they must take the initiative in the process. All of Garvey's theological motifs were geared toward the actualization of the freedom and liberation of blacks throughout the world. (pp. 155-62)

> *Henry J. Young, "Marcus Garvey (1887-1940)," in his* Major Black Religious Leaders: 1755-1940, *Abingdon Press, 1977, pp. 152-62.*

Tony Martin (essay date 1983)

[*An American educator and historian, Martin has written several scholarly and biographical works on Garvey and Garveyism. In the following excerpt from his* Literary Garveyism: Garvey, Black Arts, and the Harlem Renaissance, *he examines the influence of Garvey and the* Negro World *on black literature.*]

The Garvey Movement in general, and the *Negro World* in particular, played a role in providing a potential infrastructure for the Harlem Renaissance, which needs take second place to none. The *Negro World* reached many more people every month than the *Crisis, Opportunity* and *Messenger* combined. At its peak circulation of 200,000 it reached more people weekly than those three reached in a month.

It pioneered a regular, fully developed book review section. Its literary competition of 1921 significantly predated those of *Opportunity* and the *Crisis.* (p. 156)

Yet it can be argued that the potential infrastructure that the Garvey Movement helped build for the Harlem Renaissance remained, to some extent at least, just that—a potential infrastructure. It was an infrastructure composed of a large international Black community united by the Garvey aesthetic. What the Harlem Renaissance proper too often provided was a group of talented Black artists writing or performing under the direction of white mentors and publishers and largely for white audiences. There were no large publishing houses satisfying the special needs of the *Negro World* readership, despite their numbers. If Garvey had been left alone perhaps he would have filled this need. But from his conviction in 1923, the UNIA was too preoccupied trying to keep him out of jail. From 1925 to 1927, he was *in* jail. And in 1927 he was deported.

Between Garvey's potential infrastructure, then, and the superstructure of the Harlem Renaissance, there remained a missing link. It is not correct to say (even as some *Negro World* contributors said) that there was no sufficient Black market for Black literature. The *Negro World* proved that such a market existed—and it was a large market. But the Harlem Renaissance superstructure was by and large not sufficiently addressing that market. The superstructure was largely hijacked away from that market by the lure of white acceptance. In vain did Harrison and Garvey (and eventually DuBois) complain of the disdain of big publishers towards the Black reading public and the unreasonable demands they made on their Black authors. In vain, because there were no alternative publishing houses of equal power and stature. So Garvey's potential infrastructure could do nothing but stand helplessly by as one after another of the gifted Black writers either got unhitched from it or studiously avoided it altogether. (p. 157)

Alain Locke, always more clear-headed than most of his Renaissance protégés . . . saw the Harlem Renaissance for the transient fad that it was—a fad propelled largely by a white bohemian desire for the sensual and the exotic. Locke knew that this was no basis upon which to build a people's literature. "The proportions [of the Renaissance]," he wrote, "show the typical curve of a major American fad, and to a certain extent, this indeed it is." He continued, "We shall not fully realize it until the inevitable reaction comes; when as the popular interest flags, the movement will lose thousands of supporters who are now under its spell, but who tomorrow would be equally hypnotized by the next craze." If anybody knew the inner realities of the Harlem Renaissance it had to be Locke, for he had been its mentor for a long time. But now he sadly admitted that "to win a hearing, much exploitation has had to be tolerated. There is as much spiritual bondage in these things as there ever was material bondage in slavery." All he could do at this stage was wistfully hope that out of the ashes of the Harlem Renaissance there would arise a more durable Black literature, one with firmer roots in its own community. Garvey had provided the infrastructure for such a literature, but Locke's protégés had chosen not to see it.

Locke's observations found a belated and pathetic echo in Claude McKay, who eventually discovered, with the benefit of much hard hindsight, that "The Harlem Renaissance movement of the artistic '20's was really inspired and kept alive by the interest and presence of white bohemians. It faded out when they became tired of the new plaything."

Garvey himself, in a historically most unusual way, became the literary and artistic symbol par excellence of both major tendencies within the Black cultural world of the 1920s and 1930s. Those who subscribed to his aesthetic showered him with poetic praise. He was the single most popular subject of *Negro World* poetry. Some, like Ethel Trew Dunlap, wrote not one but several poems in his honor. Some of these poems were set to music and Arnold Ford composed the Garvey hymn, "God Bless Our President." Not even in prayer could the creative expression of pro-Garvey sentiment suffer restraint. From South Africa to Cincinnati, Garvey made his way into the religious expression of Black people.

In music and drama too, Garvey recurred as a noble theme. The photographs of Van Der Zee and the sculpture of Augusta Savage added visual supplement to this riot of positive artistic portrayal. Garvey even loomed heroic in *The Flaming Sword,* a long novel by the notorious Afrophobe, Thomas Dixon. However much he disliked Black folk, Dixon could find no fault with one who seemed to manifest no interest in generalized social intermingling between the races.

This artistic fascination with Garvey did not fade away after his deportation from the United States in 1927 or even after his death in 1940. But with the Black Power movement of the 1960s, coupled with the elevation of Garvey to national hero of Jamaica in 1964, it again assumed vast proportions. And although Black Power subsided in the 1970s, the Garvey revival has continued to grow. The Jamaican reggae singers of the 1980s now take the place of the *Negro World* poets of the 1920s. Garvey is an ever repeated theme in their lyrics. He has also begun to make his way into the calypsoes of Trinidad.

All over the Caribbean and Afro-America there has recently taken place what can only be described as an explosion of popular, often anonymous, Garvey-inspired artwork. Street murals, posters, silk-screenings and buttons of all description, paintings, here and there a poem, at least one novel—and the list keeps growing. It is only a matter of time before somebody attempts a serious film on the life and work of Marcus Garvey. Some of Afro-America's best known artists have also joined the street artists and the poster makers in building works around Garvey's red, black and green.

The elevation of Garvey to the position of positive literary and artistic symbol did not go unchallenged in his own time. Those who disputed the Garvey aesthetic made a determined effort to do the reverse—to portray Garvey as a buffoon, criminal and lunatic. Zora Neale

Hurston sent a copy of her anti-Garvey story to Carl Van Vechten and he must have liked it. For his *Nigger Heaven* took a negative view of Garvey, though not as wittily so as Hurston's story had done. Wallace Thurman and Willard Jourdan Rapp's *Jeremiah the Magnificent* did not get off the ground, though its intent was the same. Eric Walrond made his contribution, via literary criticism. Theodore Ward's off-Broadway play, *Big White Fog* (1940) took a somewhat unsympathetic view of Garvey. And it was inevitable that someone would sooner or later compare Garvey to the buffoonish Emperor Jones. James Weldon Johnson of the NAACP obliged. As far as he was concerned, the Emperor Jones was but a modest fool compared to Garvey. Within a brief ten years, Johnson argued, "a Black West Indian, here in the United States, in the twentieth century, had actually played an imperial role such as Eugene O'Neill never imagined in his *Emperor Jones.*"

The most elaborate effort to build a work of fiction around a negative image of Garvey came, not unnaturally, from W.E.B. DuBois. Alain Locke, reviewing DuBois' 1928 novel, *Dark Princess,* thought he could discern therein "perhaps a thinly varnished Garvey." Locke was absolutely correct.

Anyone familiar with DuBois' anti-Garvey utterances would have recognized the fictitious Garvey of *Dark Princess.* DuBois had long characterized Liberty Hall as a "low, rambling basement of brick and rough stone." He had long insisted on seeing in the UNIA only an alien movement not representative of Afro-Americans. He had described Garvey, in a major white magazine, as a "little, fat black man, ugly, but with intelligent eyes and big head. . . ." All of this and more was repeated under the guise of fiction in *Dark Princess.*

Garvey was transformed into Mr. Perigua, "a thin, yellow man of middle size," but his physical features were foisted onto Perigua's sergeant-at-arms, "a short, fat, black man" given to "intense declamation." Perigua's offices were on 135th Street in Harlem, the same as Garvey's and every bit as run-down as DuBois' vision of Liberty Hall. One approached them via "an ill-kept hall and up dirty and creaking stairs, half-lighted. . . ." Perigua's followers were congregated in a room "hot with a mélange of smoke, bad air, voices and gesticulations." They seemed often "on the point of blows, but blows never came." All of this puzzled the character Matthew, "until he caught their broad *a*'s and curious singing lilt of phrase. He realized that all or nearly all were West Indians. . . . They were to him singular, foreign and funny."

Perigua's followers seemed to love him very much. For without much provocation they suddenly broke into "a song with some undistinguishable rhyme on 'Perigua forever'"—undoubtedly DuBois' caricature of "God Bless Our President."

Matthew's overall opinion of Perigua was a synopsis of DuBois' anti-Garvey statements from the *Crisis* and elsewhere. "This man was no leader," he thought, "he was too theatrical. . . . Matthew had at first thought him an egotistic fool. But Perigua was no fool. He next put him down as an ignorant fanatic—but he was not ignorant. He was well read, spoke French and Spanish, read German, and knew the politics of the civilized world and current events surprisingly well. Was he insane? In no ordinary sense of the word; wild, irresponsible, impulsive, but with brain and nerves that worked clearly and promptly." (pp. 158-62).

Garvey's own personal involvement in building his potential infrastructure was as immense as could be expected from a busy political leader and one, moreover, who was under constant pressure from all manner of adversaries. His interest in literature and the arts predated the UNIA, and went back to his formative years in Jamaica. He himself was the first literary editor of the *Negro World* (and he never ceased to be its managing editor). It was he who laid down the political line upon which the Garvey aesthetic was built.

This ultimately political underpinning of all criticism, this Garvey aesthetic, this Black aesthetic 1920s style, provided the Garveyites with a tool for artistic analysis. It was a constant. It never changed. It could be applied with equal effect to poetry, drama, fiction, music or art or anything else. Did the piece of work contribute positively to the race's knowledge of itself?—to the way in which it was perceived by other races? Or, alternatively, did the work at least not demean the race, not hold it up to ridicule? Was it technically proficient? Or, if not, then did it at least represent a creditable tentative effort worthy of encouragement? Was its plot or theme consistent with the notions of race first, self-reliance, and nationhood? These are the questions that can be deduced from the artistic writings of the Garveyite group. (p. 163)

It was the Garvey aesthetic that provided the essential difference between Garvey's potential infrastructure and the superstructure of the mainstream writers. The wealthy dilettantes who patronized the Renaissance loved exotic Harlem and genial Claude McKay and witty Zora Neale Hurston and jazz and speakeasies and Negro melodies and brown-skinned chorus lines; but they could not love Garvey. Garvey was not out to entertain anybody. (p. 164)

> *Tony Martin, in his* Literary Garveyism: Garvey, Black Arts and the Harlem Renaissance, *The Majority Press, 1983, pp. 156-64.*

FURTHER READING

Boulware, Marcus H. "The Marcus Garvey Period, 1916-1927." In his *The Oratory of Negro Leaders, 1900-1968,* pp. 54-62. Westport, Conn.: Negro Universities Press, 1969.

Discusses black oratory within the context of the Garveyist movement.

Brisbane, Robert H. "His Excellency: The Provincial President of Africa." *Phylon* 10, No. 3 (Third Quarter 1949): 257-64.
    History of Garvey and his movement, concluding that Garvey "adversely affected the slow but definite integration of the Negro into American society."

——. "Some New Light on the Garvey Movement." *The Journal of Negro History* 36, No. 1 (January 1951): 53-62.
    Outlines Garvey's rise to prominence and examines his impact on subsequent black intellectuals. Brisbane credits Garvey with revitalizing black racial consciousness but concludes that his economic ideas benefited blacks little.

Burkett, Randall K. *Garveyism as a Religious Movement.* Metuchen, N.J.: The Scarecrow Press, Inc. and the American Theological Library Association, 1978, 216 p.
    Examines the religious ideas embodied in Garvey's work, arguing that Garveyism comprised a Christian religious movement with its own theological and eschatological beliefs.

Chaka, Oba. "Marcus Garvey: The Father of Revolutionary Black Nationalism." *Journal of Black Poetry* 1, No. 14 (1970-71): 82-96.
    History of the Garveyist movement, with discussion of its influence on later black nationalist movements and leaders.

Clarke, John Henrik, ed. *Marcus Garvey and the Vision of Africa.* New York: Random House, 1973, 496 p.
    Offers a broad sample of essays on Garveyism, including several by Garvey.

Cronon, E. David. *Black Moses: The Story of Marcus Garvey and the Universal Negro Improvement Association.* Madison: University of Wisconsin Press, 1955, 278 p.
    Highly regarded biography of Garvey.

"A Black Moses and His Dream of a Promised Land." *Current Opinion* 70, No. 3 (March 1921): 328-31.
    Profile of Garvey and the UNIA.

Du Bois, W. E. B. "Marcus Garvey." *The Crisis* 21, Nos. 2, 3 (December 1920; January 1921): 58-60, 112-15.
    Questions the feasibility of Garvey's economic plans and the desirability of his nationalist objectives, but commends him for creating a black business initiative.

——. "The Black Star Line." *The Crisis* 24, No. 5 (September 1922): 210-14.
    Account of Garvey's trial for fraud, implicitly criticizing Garvey's business practices and organizational methods.

Edwards, William A. "Racial Purity in Black and White: The Case of Marcus Garvey and Earnest Cox." *The Journal of Ethnic Studies* 15, No. 1 (Spring 1987): 117-42.
    Examines Garvey's intellectual collaboration with Earnest Sevier Cox, a white supremacist theorist, on the basis that both opposed racial assimilation and miscegenation.

Fierce, Milfred C. "Economic Aspects of the Marcus Garvey Movement." *The Black Scholar* 3, Nos. 7, 8 (March-April 1972): 50-61.
Discusses Garvey's philosophy of black economic independence.

Frazier, E. Franklin. "Break with the Traditional Background: The Renaissance That Failed." In his *Black Bourgeoisie: The Rise of a New Middle Class in the United States,* pp. 103-07. 1957. Reprint. New York: Collier Books, 1962.
Briefly examines the Garveyist movement, noting its lack of support among the rising black bourgeoisie of his time.

Garvey, Amy Jacques. *Garvey and Garveyism.* New York: Octagon, 1978, 336 p.
Biography of Garvey by his wife.

Graves, John L. "The Social Ideas of Marcus Garvey." *The Journal of Negro Education* 31, No. 1 (Winter 1962): 65-74.
Discusses Garvey's social theory and conjectures how he would view contemporary racial issues.

Hill, Robert A. "'The Foremost Radical among His Race': Marcus Garvey and the Black Scare, 1918-1921." *Prologue* 16, No. 4 (Winter 1984): 215-31.
Describes efforts by the U.S. Federal Bureau of Investigation to suppress the political activities of Garvey and the UNIA.

Kahn, Robert M. "The Political Ideology of Marcus Garvey." *The Midwest Quarterly* XXIV, No. 2 (Winter 1983): 117-37.
Extensive analysis of Garvey's political philosophy as expressed in the author's *Philosophy and Opinions.*

Langley, Jabez Ayodele. "Garveyism and African Nationalism." *Race* 11, No. 2 (October 1969): 157-72.
Examines the influence of Garveyism on nationalist politics in Africa during the 1920s.

Levine, Lawrence W. "Marcus Garvey and th Politics of Revitalization." In *Black Leaders of the Twentieth Century,* edited by John Hope Franklin and August Meier, pp. 105-38. Urbana: University of Illinois Press, 1982.
Includes biographical discussion of Garvey and describes his political and social theories.

————. "Marcus Garvey's Moment." *The New Republic* 191, No. 18 (29 October 1984): 26-31.
Surveys Garvey's career and evaluates *the Marcus Garvey and Universal Negro Improvement Association Papers.*

Lewis, Rupert. *Marcus Garvey: Anti-Colonial Champion.* Trenton, N.J.: Africa World Press, 1988, 301 p.
Study of Garvey's philosophy, stressing its opposition to European colonialism in the Third World.

Martin, Tony. *Race First: The Ideological and Organizational Struggles of Marcus Garvey and the Universal Negro Improvement Association.* Westport, Conn.: Greenwood Press, 1976, 422 p.

Analyzes Garvey's ideology and describes the political struggles of the UNIA against such political opponents as the Communist party, the black integrationist movement, and the governments of the United States and the European colonial powers.

————. "The Economic Programs of Marcus Garvey." *The Black Collegian* 9, No. 1 (September-October 1978): 12, 14, 16.
Outlines the business ventures of the UNIA, particularly the Black Star Line enterprise.

Matthews, Mark D. "Perspective on Marcus Garvey." *Black World* 25, No. 4 (February 1976): 36-48.
Argues that Garvey incorporated much Marxist-Leninist analysis into his philosophy.

Okonkwo, R. L. "The Garvey Movement in British West Africa." *The Journal of African History* 21, No. 1 (1980): 105-17.
Examines the UNIA's influence on black nationalist movements in British West Africa during the early twentieth-century.

Padmore, George. "Black Zionism or Garveyism." In his *Pan-Africanism or Communism,* pp. 65-82. Garden City, N.Y.: Doubleday and Co., 1971.
Describes Garvey's career, focusing on the UNIA's failed dealings with the government of Liberia.

Rogers, J. A. "Marcus Garvey: 'Provisional President of Africa' and Messiah, 1887-1940." In his *World's Great Men of Color,* Vol. II, edited by John Henrik Clarke, pp. 415-31. New York: Collier Books, 1947.
Biographical survey of Garvey's career.

Rudwick, Elliott M. "Du Bois Versus Garvey: Race Propagandists at War." *The Journal of Negro Education* XXVIII, No. 4 (Fall 1959): 421-29.
Examines the vociferous rivalry between Garvey and W. E. B. Du Bois.

Runcie, John. "Marcus Garvey and the Harlem Renaissance." *Afro-Americans in New York Life and History* 10, No. 2 (July 1986): 7-28.
Considers the antagonism between Garvey and many of the authors of the Harlem Renaissance, offering a number of explanations for Garvey's rejection of the literary movement.

Weber, Shirley N. "Black Nationalism and Garveyist Influences." *The Western Journal of Black Studies* 3, No. 4 (Winter 1979): 263-66.
Assesses various black nationalist movements, asserting that Garveyism was one of the most successful at integrating economic, social, and political aspects of black empowerment.

Weisbord, Robert G. "Marcus Garvey, Pan-Negroist: The View from Whitehall." *Race* 11, No. 4 (April 1970): 419-29.
Examines the British government's reaction to Garvey and the UNIA.

Nikki Giovanni

1943-

(Born Yolande Cornelia Giovanni) American poet, essayist, editor, and author of children's books.

Giovanni gained widespread popularity during the 1960s for her revolutionary poems in *Black Feeling, Black Talk* (1968) and *Black Judgment* (1968), two works that feature rhythmic, often angry verse. She made her poems accessible to a multi-generational and international audience through public readings at universities and best-selling recordings accompanied by gospel music. In much of her work, Giovanni focuses on the individual's search for love and acceptance, reflecting what she considers a general struggle in the black American community. Concentrating on themes of family, blackness, womanhood, and sex, Giovanni's poetry is conversational and strongly influenced by rhythm and blues music. Although many early admirers faulted her for later taking a more domestic and personal stance toward societal change, the author herself contends that the evolution of her ideas reflects her own changing attitudes as well as changes in the world she observes. John W. Conner commented: "[Giovanni] sees her world as an extension of herself, she sees problems in the world as an extension of her problems, she sees herself existing amidst tensions, heartache, and marvelous expressions of love. But the tensions, heartaches, and expression of love do not overwhelm the poet. She controls her environment— sometimes with her mind, often with her heart."

Giovanni was born in Knoxville, Tennessee, but grew up in Lincoln Heights, Ohio, a predominantly black community. Her happy childhood, spent partly with her grandparents in Tennessee, became a major theme of her poetry. The author received her bachelor's degree in history from Fisk University in 1967. While at Fisk, she was strongly influenced by a creative writing workshop taught by novelist John Oliver Killens. She also rejected her formerly conservative views in favor of the radicalism she encountered in fellow classmates. *Black Feeling, Black Talk* and *Black Judgment,* her first two volumes of poetry, reflect the anger and enthusiasm of a 1960s community of writers and political activists with whom Giovanni early became involved. This group included such poets as LeRoi Jones (Amiri Baraka), H. Rap Brown (Jamil Abdullah Al-Amin), and Don L. Lee (Haki R. Madhubuti). One of Giovanni's best known poems, "The True Import of the Present Dialogue, Black vs. Negro," from *Black Feeling, Black Talk,* is typical of her early work: a call to black Americans to destroy the whites who oppress them as well as the blacks whose passivity and compliance contribute to their own oppression. Adopting this revolutionary stance, Giovanni advocated open violence and expressed her impatience for change. "Nikki Rosa," which

recounts Giovanni's contented childhood, is often considered the author's signature poem. Speaking affectionately of her supportive family, the poet asserts that happiness is dependent on love, not material possessions, and this love is the staple of unity within the black community. *Black Feeling, Black Talk* and *Black Judgment* were well received, and Giovanni quickly gained recognition as an important contemporary poet.

Giovanni maintained the personal perspective of "Nikki Rosa" in her next volume, *Re:Creation* (1970), and in her essays in *Gemini: An Extended Autobiographical Statement on My First Twenty-Five Years of Being a Black Poet* (1971). Two events, the birth of her son in 1969 and her increasing passion for rhythm and blues music, influenced these pieces, which are less angry than her previous work. Here, the poet viewed the black revolution as a personal rather than a collective movement. Both volumes received negative appraisals from some formerly enthusiastic critics. Ruth Rambo McClain, for example, stated: "[Regrettably], Nikki

Giovanni, my sparkling gnat throwing huge fiery sun poems into the Black Heavens, [has been] transformed (re:created?) into an almost declawed, tamed Panther with bad teeth." Commentators also claimed that the author manipulated the language in *Re:Creation* to conform to song-like rhythms at the expense of the poems' content. Overall, however, reviewers praised Giovanni for verse that appealed to an audience that had previously been alienated by militant black poetry. In a 1972 collection, *My House*, Giovanni depicted personal and public lives as complementary forces working toward change. The work, which is divided into two sections, "The Rooms Inside" and "The Rooms Outside," received mixed reviews. While some critics felt that the dichotomy between public and private in *My House* was forced, most commentators agreed that Giovanni successfully characterized the shared relationship of the individual to society, and vice versa. *The Women and the Men* (1975), Giovanni's next collection, contains poems from *Re:Creation* and *Black Judgment*, as well as new works.

Giovanni explored new themes in *Cotton Candy on a Rainy Day* (1978), a somber collection that addresses isolation and loneliness. Many critics claimed that this volume reflects the poet's disappointment with the loss of the idealism of the 1960s. Paula Giddings noted: "Giovanni has evolved to be that creature which often finds itself estranged from the history which created it." Despite her disillusionment in the opening poems of the collection, however, the author ultimately reaffirmed her belief in the possibility of change, and she closed *Cotton Candy on a Rainy Day* with poems about friendship and love. And, critics agree, even when one takes into account the many thematic variations evident in Giovanni's poems, the poet's work is unified by a consistently personal and often revealing voice. William J. Harris observed: "On the whole what is most striking about Giovanni's poetry is that she has created the charming persona of 'Nikki Giovanni.' This persona is honest, searching, complex, lusty, and, above all, individualistic and charmingly egoistical."

(For further information about Giovanni's life and works, see *Black Writers*; *Children's Literature Review*, Vol. 6; *Contemporary Authors*, Vols. 29-32; *Contemporary Authors Autobiography Series*, Vol. 6; *Contemporary Authors New Revision Series*, Vol. 18; *Contemporary Literary Criticism*, Vols. 2, 4, 19; and *Dictionary of Literary Biography*, Vols. 5, 41.)

PRINCIPAL WORKS

Black Feeling, Black Talk (poetry) 1968
Black Judgment (poetry) 1968
Night Comes Softly: An Anthology of Black Female Voices [editor] (poetry) 1970
Re:Creation (poetry) 1970
Ego Tripping and Other Poems for Children (poetry) 1971

Gemini: An Extended Autobiographical Statement on My First Twenty-Five Years of Being a Black Poet (essays) 1971
Spin a Soft Black Song: Poems for Children (poetry) 1971
My House (poetry) 1972
A Dialogue: James Baldwin and Nikki Giovanni (dialogue) 1973
A Poetic Equation: Conversations between Nikki Giovanni and Margaret Walker (dialogue) 1974
The Women and the Men (poetry) 1975
Cotton Candy on a Rainy Day (poetry) 1978
Vacation Time: Poems for Children (poetry) 1980
Those Who Ride the Night Winds (poetry) 1983
Sacred Cows . . . and Other Edibles (essays) 1988

––––––––––––

Don L. Lee (essay date 1971)

[*An American poet, essayist, critic, and publisher, Lee (also known by his Swahili name Haki R. Madhubuti) has written widely about African-American life and culture. In the following excerpt, he commends the political expression in* Black Feeling, Black Talk *and* Black Judgment, *identifying Giovanni as an important developing poet.*]

Nikki Giovanni has published two thin volumes of poetry, **Black Feeling, Black Talk** and **Black Judgement,** which reflect her awareness of the values of Black culture as well as her commitment to the revolution. In **"The True Import of Present Dialogue"** she asks the Black male / warriors to "kill the nigger" in themselves, to let their "nigger mind die," to free their black hands and "learn to be Black men." Like many of us, Miss Giovanni is concerned that Black men have been sent out of the United States to kill other "colored" peoples of the world when the real enemy is here. She expresses this same concern in **"Of Liberation,"** where she points out that there is an international bond between all peoples of color. Stress is placed on unity, the need to work together for mutual progress.

"Poem (No Name No. 3") mentions leaders of the Black revolution who have been either silenced permanently or at least hampered seriously in their efforts to increase the awareness and involvement of our people and help them to effect a means to cast off the chains. Cautioning, warning the apathetic, Miss Giovanni states: "if the Black Revolution passes you bye its for damned sure / the white reaction to it won't."

In the autobiographical **"My Poem,"** the poet tells us that she has been robbed, that because of her involvement in the movement she expects at any time a deliberate, planned attack on her very person. In spite of harrassment and personal danger, however, she expresses her conviction that the killing / silencing of one revolutionary will not stop the onward movement of our people . . . .

Nikki writes about the familiar: what she knows, sees, experiences. It is clear why she conveys such urgency in expressing the need for Black awareness, unity, solidarity. She knows how it was. She knows how it is. She knows also that a change can be affected. (p. 70)

Traditionally, most people think of poetry as writing that has certain prescribed forms and that revolves around a "poetic," light theme. This point of view is concomitant with the "art-for-art's-sake" concept Nikki rejects. In **"For Sandra,"** she lets us know why her subject and form are what they are. She says that she

> . . .wanted to write
> a poem
> that rhymes
> but revolution doesn't lend
> itself to be-bopping

She then thought of writing a "tree" poem, but couldn't find a model to view in order to make a fit description, for "no trees grow in manhattan"—only asphalt. Then she thought to write "a big blue sky poem / but all the clouds have winged / low since no-Dick was elected."

> so i thought again
> and it occurred to me
> maybe i shouldn't write
> at all
> but clean my gun
> and check my kerosene supply
>
> perhaps these are not poetic
> times

These are hard lines that force thought. These are the lines that suggest the writer has a real, serious commitment to her people and to the institutions that are working toward the liberation of Black people.

Her sharpness shines through like the sheen of a sister's greased-up dark limbs. Yet, she has serious problems with many of her longer "militant" poems, such as **"Of Liberation."**. . . [Some lines] read like a first outline of a college freshman's essay. What is perhaps more important is that when the Black poet chooses to serve as political seer, he must display a keen sophistication. Sometimes Nikki oversimplifies and therefore sounds rather naive politically. For example, are brothers like Imamu Baraka and Larry Neal to be excluded from black revolutionary leadership because they have "white degrees?" (Or Nikki herself, for that matter!)

In some cases she has used contradictory mis-information, as in **"Ugly Honkies, or The Election Game and How to Win It."**

The lines

> the obvious need is a new liberal white party
> to organize liberal and radical honkies

are contradicted seven lines later with

> the worst junkie or black businessman is more
>   humane
> than the best honkie.

If the last statement is true, why organize whites? The emphasis on organization should be aimed at the weaker Blacks. The poem is a street corner rap, not a poem. The poet's longer works often look like first or second drafts needed to fill up the pages.

Nikki is at her best in the short, personal poem. She is definitely growing as a poet. Her effectiveness is in the area of the "fast rap." She says the right things at the right time. Orally this is cool, but it doesn't come across as printed poetry. (pp. 72-4)

> *Don L. Lee, "Nikki Giovanni," in his* Dynamite Voices I: Black Poets of the 1960's, *Broadside Press, 1971, pp. 68-73.*

June Jordan (essay date 1972)

[*Jordan is an American poet, novelist, essayist, and author of children's books. In the following excerpt, she compares* Gemini *to autobiographical works by other black Americans.*]

Well, this "extended autobiographical statement" by Nikki Giovanni is not an autobiography. It may therefore disappoint many among her plentiful followers who will buy a copy, hoping to find out about their poet. If you read through the 13 separate essays [in **Gemini: An Extended Autobiographical Statement on My First Twenty-five Years of Being a Poet**], you can conclude that Nikki Giovanni came from a middle-class background: Both parents were college graduates and pursued professional careers. She grew up in Knoxville, Tenn. She took her own undergraduate degree at Fisk University. She loved her grandmother, and her mother, especially, loves her son, Thomas, loves her sister, Gary, and liked to fight for her, from when she was 4 years old. Her family has long regarded Miss Giovanni as a genius, and she has long regarded herself as a genius. More than that, of an autobiographical nature, her fans will not learn—not here.

The reader never hears of any real trouble in her life; she must have had some. There are no Giovanni word-dealings with personal pain, or anguish. And where are the men who have figured in her life? (Even her father and grandfather receive comparatively incidental mention, before disappearing from the page.) And who are the people who have helped her with her career? And who are her friends? And so forth.

That's enough about what's missing. What you do have is a collection of essays with titles such as **"Spiritual View of Lena Horne," "On Being Asked What It's Like to Be Black,"** and **"Don't Have a Baby Till You Read This."** Compared to the autobiographical writings of Maya Angelou, or of Alice Walker in "To Hell With

Dying," or of Julius Lester, in "Search for the New Land," this is light stuff. Still, it is an entertaining collection of mostly high-spirited raps. Its interest is guaranteed by Miss Giovanni's status as a leading black poet and celebrity.

All the essays are first person, "I"—writings. Some of them are enjoyable—jive pieces of pure jive. Witness "**Revolutionary Tale**," where the reader is promised the story of how and why Miss Giovanni arrived "late," to join "The Movement." Instead, the reader is taken on a float among the laughing bubbles of a really tall tale.

Over-all, the style of the book poses some difficulty; paragraphs slide about and loosely switch tracks on the reader. But, now and then, she can make you laugh. And two of the essays are unusual for their serious, held focus and for their clarity. These two, "**The Beginning Is Zero**" and "**Black Poems, *Poseurs* and Power**," stand apart from the rest; they do not blur and drift.

"**The Beginning Is Zero**" gives us a grateful look at Charles Chesnutt, 19th-century black novelist. Guided by Miss Giovanni, we consider the man, his influence and his revolt. We come to understand how he has remained important to white and black literature. We learn, for example, that "Chestnutt [sic], by making the Black man innocent and the white man his executioner, introduced Jesus as a Black man into the American context." This is a useful piece of scholarship and tribute.

"**Black Poems, *Poseurs* and Power**" offers the reader an engaging piece of self-criticism, in the sense that it questions where we, black folks, are heading, how we are handling the trip, and why. Miss Giovanni believes: "There is a tendency to look at the Black experience too narrowly." This can lead to a blacker-than-thou kind of non-think: Black may discriminate against black, for instance, if the brother or the sister is not wearing the "right" the "Black" clothing of the moment. Or, such non-think may lead to the Last Poets performing "Die Nigga," which as Miss Giovanni points out, is negative and "just not the same concept as 'kill.'" In short, she wants to call off the asinine sanctimony that sets black against black and lets the real enemies rest, laughing, at the sidelines.

From this, she proceeds to condemn the "latent militarism of the [black] artistic community" as "despicable." She remembers the abundance of black artists, equipped with military "guard," who appeared at the 1968 Black Power Conference at Philadelphia. ("Even the guards had guards.") Here the non-think resulted in black becoming the enemy of black. Miss Giovanni comments, "It's a sick syndrome with, again, the Black community being the loser."

One more essay must be mentioned, her last: "**Gemini— A Prolonged Autobiographical Statement on Why**." This will prove particularly interesting to everyone familiar with the author's poems. When you compare the poetry with the ambivalence and wants expressed in this essay,

it becomes clear that a transition is taking place inside the artist.

She has written in one poem: "Nigger / Can you kill . . . . Can we learn to kill WHITE for BLACK / Learn to kill niggers / Learn to be Black men." Now, in this final essay she is a woman writing: "I don't want my son to be a warrior . . . . I don't want my son to be a George or a Jonathan Jackson . . . . I didn't have a baby to see him be cannon fodder." Whatever the depth of the transition, the uncertainties are real and plainly spoken: "Perhaps Black people don't want Revolution at all. That too must be considered. I used to think the world needs what I need. But perhaps it doesn't." And, the final, two lines of the book: "I really like to think a Black, beautiful, loving world is possible. I really do, I think."

To be sure, that is a puzzling conclusion. Is it the black part, or the beautiful, or the "loving world" part, that leaves her unsure—or all of them? Maybe that was the goal, to raise more questions about herself, at the age of 27, than she would or could answer. At 27, that might seem fair enough, and a lot less surprising than an honest-to-God autobiography. (pp. 6, 26)

> *June Jordan, in a review of "Gemini," in* The New York Times Book Review, *February 13, 1972, pp. 6, 26.*

Donez Xiques (essay date 1972)

[*In the following review essay, Xiques discusses apparent contradictions in the tone and message of* Gemini.]

Gemini, the first book of prose by a talented young poet, Nikki Giovanni, is a collection of thirteen essays subtitled "An Extended Autobiographical Statement on My First Twenty-Five Years of Being a Black Poet." For many readers these essays will serve as an introduction to an intellectually astute, witty and persuasive writer who once referred to herself as a "revolutionary poet in a pre-revolutionary world."

In an interview Nikki Giovanni remarked, "If you have a population where there is suffering, you are all suffering." In this collection of essays she wields prose in an endeavor to probe the reader. She asks, " . . . is there such a thing as normal in an abnormal world run by subnormal people?" The negative reply explains why she can say, "Nobody's trying to make the system Black; we're trying to make a system that's human so Black folks can live in it."

Her essays are concerned with change and challenge needed to affect the system. She believes that "the state of the world we live in is so depressing. And this is not because of the reality of the men who run it but because it doesn't have to be that way. The possibilities of life are so great and beautiful that to see less wears the spirit down." Four chapters in this book are devoted to those who are involved with articulating the vision for change—artists, writers, musicians. Here she explores blackness as a cultural entity and discusses the role of the artist in relationship to the community at large.

Despite Nikki Giovanni's considerable talent, in the final analysis, *Gemini* struck me as a book that did not need to be written. It has all been said before—more incisively, more humorously, more poignantly. This is not to imply, however, that the book is worthless. But there are real stylistic weaknesses in it. The author is uneven and inconsistent.

At times, what purports to be the voice of black awareness emerges as downright silliness. The reader finds it impossible to take her seriously when she writes passages such as the following one: "Why would Dostoevski need to write *Crime and Punishment?* For the same reason Shakespeare needed to write—not to pass information but to pass time. There are no great honkies—anything that excludes our existence is not great."

One is uneasy, too, about the contradictory statements in *Gemini.* When Nikki Giovanni points simultaneously in two different directions, the result is only confusion. One cannot follow her, nor can one be confident of her leadership. She writes: "Most of us accept responsibility of / for living. It's very worrisome when we find black people committing suicide by dope, self-hatred and the actual taking of life. It means we have gotten away from our roots. This is when the poet must call." In another passage, however, we read: "We need to get rid of whitey. I mean, if we can't kill a whitey, how can we ever justify killing a brother? . . . We can only justify offing a brother if we have already offed twenty whiteys—that's the ratio, I told him, for offing a brother."

And, finally, when a black writer admonishes the black community to beware of wearing "*wigs*" and to get their own thing together, then I, for one, cannot understand why the revolutionary writer, Nikki Giovanni, entrusted *Gemini* to a white publishing company. (pp. 186-87)

> *Donez Xiques, in a review of "Gemini," in* America, *Vol. 126, No. 7, February 19, 1972, pp. 186-87.*

John W. Conner (essay date 1973)

[*In the following excerpt, Conner commends Giovanni for a controlled representation of her environment in* My House.]

[In *My House*, the] poet Nikki Giovanni looks upon her world with a wide open penetrating gaze. She sees her world as an extension of herself, she sees problems in the world as an extension of her problems, she sees herself existing amidst tensions, heartache, and marvelous expressions of love. But the tensions, heartaches, and expressions of love do not overwhelm the poet. She controls her environment—sometimes with her mind, often with her heart.

My House is the poetic expression of a vibrant black woman with a special way of looking at things. A strong narrative line runs through many of the poems: a familiar scene is presented, and the poet comments upon the people or the events. The poems are short, the language is simple; each poem contains a single poignant image. The people in Nikki Giovanni's poems are insulated from one another by carefully constructed walls of personal superiority: the old lady in "**Conversation**" is proud of the knowledge she assumes she has because of her advanced age; the woman in "**And Another Thing**" maintains an uncertain status by constantly talking.

When a reader enters *My House,* he is invited to savor the poet's ideas about a meaningful existence in today's world. Without reducing their importance, the poet places all instances of cultural, social, and political strife in appropriate perspective—as effects which must not be allowed to consume an individual.

> *John W. Conner, in a review of "My House,"* in English Journal, *Vol. 62, No. 4, April, 1973, p. 650.*

Suzanne Juhasz (essay date 1976)

[*Juhasz is an American poet, essayist, and critic. In the following excerpt, she examines the themes of love and power in Giovanni's works.*]

[Nikki Giovanni] comes to her art knowing that she is as female as she is black and that somehow she must, in her own life and art, express how these aspects of herself come together and define her. She has always defined herself as a black woman, seeing Women's Liberation as a white woman's movement; seeing black women as different from both white women and black men: "But white women and Black men are both niggers and both respond as such. He runs to the white man to explain his 'rights' and she runs to us. And I think that's where they are both coming from . . . . We Black women are the single group in the West intact." But her ideas about the black woman's role in the movement have changed over the past several years, I think, moving from a more traditional view (black womanhood comes second to black revolution) to one that is stronger and more individualistic. (p. 155)

As a woman, as a black, as a black woman, Giovanni defines herself in terms of two primary factors, which she sees as related: power and love . . . .

Power and love are what are at issue in Nikki Giovanni's poetry and life. In her earlier poems (1968-1970), these issues are for the most part separate. She writes of personal love in poems of private life; of black power and a public love in political poems. She won her fame with the latter. (p. 157)

In poems such as ["**The True Import of the Present Dialogue, Black vs. Negro**"], Giovanni speaks for her people in their own language of the social issues that concern them. Her role is that of spokeswoman for others with whom she is kin except for the fact that she possesses the gift of poetry: "i wanted to be / a sweet inspiration in my dreams / of my people . . ." ("**The Wonder Woman**"). The quotation is from a later poem in which she is questioning that very role. But as she gains her fame, the concept of poet as "manifesting our collective historical needs" is very much present.

In defining poetry as "the culture of a people," Giovanni, in [a] statement from *Gemini,* uses "musician" and "preacher" as synonyms for "poet." All speak for the culture; all *speak,* with the emphasis on the sound they make. Making poems from black English is more than using idioms and grammatical idiosyncrasies; the very form of black English, and certainly its power, is derived from its tradition and preeminent usage as an oral language. So in Giovanni's poems both theme and structure rely on sound patterns for significance.

> i wanta say just gotta say something
> bout those beautiful beautiful beautiful outasight
> black men
> with they afros
> walking down the street
> is the same ol danger
> but a brand new pleasure

In the opening stanza of "**Beautiful Black Men (with compliments and apologies to all not mentioned by name)**," the idiom ("outasight") is present, so is the special syntax ("they afros"), but more centrally are the rhythms of speech employed to organize the poetic statement. The statement is political, because the poem, like many of hers from this period, is meant to praise blackness: in praising, to foster, to incite. For the proper pride in and achievement of blackness is revolutionary. The poem is not a treatise, however; it is an emotionally charged utterance that, as it develops, creates through its own form the excitement about which it is speaking. In the first stanza, the repetitions, the emphases that the pause at line breaks creates, the accelerations within lines because of lack of pauses, all achieve the tenor of the speaking voice. As the poem progresses, the excitement that the speaker feels as she describes her subject is communicated by her voice on the page. (p. 157-58)

A sense of humor is never lacking in Giovanni's poetry—serious purpose does not negate the ability to laugh! [In "**Beautiful Black Men (with compliments and apologies to all not mentioned by name)**"], she mocks with affection the black male's love of splendor as it accompanies his dislike of cleanliness. What comes through in her tone is love as well as clear-sightedness, both qualities giving her the right to appreciate "beautiful, beautiful, beautiful black men." From wanting to say, having to say, something about beautiful black men, the poem moves, gathering speed and intensity as it goes, to a scream, a stamp and a shout that impel the person reading to likewise shout, likewise praise—to *feel* as the speaker feels . . . . (p. 159)

[Giovanni's] love poems are private and describe the woman enacting rather than criticizing the socially prescribed female role. They speak for Giovanni only and are not meant to incite anybody to any kind of revolution. Such a private / public dichotomy in her work may be neat, but it contains too great a degree of ambivalence for a woman poet like Giovanni to feel comfortable with it or to maintain it for long. How can the woman who sees herself as a sweet inspiration of her people and the woman who has been trained not only to sit and wait but also to need and to value interpersonal, private relationships be the same poet? In "**Adulthood**" (*Black feeling, Black talk / Black judgement*), she writes about going to college and learning that "just because everything i was was unreal / i could be real"—not from "withdrawal / into emotional crosshairs or colored bourgeois / intellectual pretensions," "But from involvement with things approaching reality / i could possibly have a life." What about not merely black reality, but her own reality? And what is the relation between them? Especially as through her poetry she becomes a genuine public personality, she needs to ask these questions. And what about the revolution?

A poet may be musician, preacher, articulator of a culture, but she or he is also a dreamer. In a series of poems about herself as dreamer, Giovanni explores the conflicting and confusing relations between her roles as poet, woman, and black.

In "**Dreams**" (*Black feeling, Black talk / Black judgement*), she describes her younger years—"before i learned / black people aren't / supposed to dream." She wanted, she says, to be a musician, a singer, a Raelet or maybe Marjorie Hendricks, grinding up against the mike screaming "baaaaaby nightandday." But then she "became more sensible":

> and decided i would
> settle down
> and just become
> a sweet inspiration

(The significance of the black singer—the musician as articulating the culture—appears throughout her work, as in "**Revolutionary Music**": "you've just got to dig sly / and the family stone / damn the words / you gonna be dancing to the music". . ."we be digging all / our revolutionary music consciously or un / cause sam cooke said 'a change is gonna come.'")

A few years later, in "**The Wonder Woman**" (*My House*), she must deal with the fact of having become that sweet inspiration. "Dreams have a way / of tossing and turning themselves / around," she observes; also that "the times / make requirements that we dream / real dreams." She may have once dreamed of becoming a sweet inspiration of her people:

> . . . but the times
> require that i give
> myself willingly and become
> a wonder woman.

The wonder woman is a totally public personage who cannot—must not—integrate her personal needs and experiences into that role if they do not coincide. Giovanni makes this clear in poems about female stars, like Aretha Franklin, and in poems about herself, such as "**Categories**" (*My House*) . . . . (pp. 165-66)

"**Categories**" [questions] black/white divisions (political and public), if they can—and they do—at times violate personal reality, describing in its second stanza an old white woman "who maybe you'd really care about" except that, being a young black woman, one's "job" is to "kill maim or seriously / make her question / the validity of her existence."

The poem ends by questioning the fact and function of categories themselves (". . .if this seems / like somewhat of a tentative poem it's probably / because i just realized that / i'm bored with categories"), but, in doing so, it is raising the more profound matter of the relations between society and self. The earlier "**Poem for Aretha**," 1970 (*Re:Creation*), begins with a clear sense of the separation between public and private selves:

> cause nobody deals with Aretha—a mother with
>   four children—having to hit the road
> they always say "after she comes
> home" . . .

Again Giovanni explains the significance of the musician/artist to society: "she is undoubtedly the one person who puts everyone on / notice," but about Aretha she also says, "she's more important than her music—if they must be / separated." (It is significant that the form of both these poems is closer to thought than speech. No answers here, only questions, problems.)

One means of bridging the gap between public and private is suggested in "**Revolutionary Dreams**," 1970 (*Re:Creation*) . . . . "Militant" and "radical" are poised against "natural" here, as they were in "**Categories.**" But this poem makes the connection to gender: the "natural dreams," of a "natural woman" who does what a woman does "when she's natural." The result of this juxtaposition is "true revolution." Somehow the black woman must be true to herself as she *is* to be both a poet and a revolutionary, for the nature of the revolution itself is in question. Revolutions are not only in the streets, where niggers must be asked if they can kill. Revolutions do not occur only in male terms, as Giovanni had begun to understand, humorously, in "**Seduction**" (*Black feeling, Black talk/Black judgement*), in which the male keeps talking politics ("The Black . . ."; "The way I see we ought to . . ."; "And what about the situation . . ."; "the revolution . . .") while she is resting his hand on her stomach, licking his arm, unbuckling his pants, taking his shorts off. The poem is, however, set in some hypothetical future: "one day." It concludes with that future:

> then you'll notice
> your state of undress

and knowing you you'll just say
"Nikki,
isn't this counterrevolutionary . . .?"

The implicit reply is no, but it is not until her 1972 volume, *My House,* that Giovanni can make this answer with self-confidence. In the poems of *Black feeling, Black talk/Black judgement* and of *Re:Creation,* the doubts are present, and possibilities for solution occur and disappear. However, *My House* as a book, not only the individual poems in it, makes a new statement about the revolution, about the very nature of political poetry, when the poet is a black woman.

Earlier, in "**My Poem**" (*Black feeling, Black talk/Black judgement*), she had written:

> the revolution
> is in the streets
> and if i stay on
> the 5th floor
> it will go on
> and if i never do
> anything
> it will go on

Perhaps, but it will not be the same revolution, she has realized; and she has also come to understand that it will take place, as well, on the fifth floor.

In "On the Issue of Roles," Toni Cade, editor of one of the first collections of essays about being black and female, *The Black Woman,* makes a comment that seems to me to be a valuable gloss to the statement of Giovanni's *My House.*

> If your house ain't in order, you ain't in order. It is so much easier to be out there than right here. The revolution ain't out there. Yet. But it is here. Should be. And arguing that instant-coffee-ten-minutes-to-midnight alibi to justify hasty-headed dealings with your mate is shit. Ain't no such animal as an instant gorilla.

Ida Lewis points with a different vocabulary to the same phenomenon: "A most interesting aspect of her [Giovanni's] work is the poet's belief in individualism at a time when the trend in the Black community is away from the individual and towards the mass." In *My House,* Giovanni is trying to be a natural woman doing what a woman does when she's natural—in doing so, dreaming natural dreams, having a revolution. She is integrating private and public; in doing so, politicizing the private, personalizing the public. This action is occurring in poetry.

My House is divided into two sections, "The Rooms Inside" and "The Rooms Outside." The inside rooms hold personal poems about grandmothers, mothers, friends, lovers—all in their own way love poems. "**Legacies**," in which the poet describes the relationship between grandmother and granddaughter, is a very political poem . . . . Black heritage is explained in personal terms. The little girl in the poem recognizes an impulse to be independent, but the speaker recognizes as well the importance of the old woman, of her love, to the grandchild in achieving her own adulthood. Although the poem ends by observing that "neither of them ever / said what they meant / and i guess nobody ever does," it is the poem itself that provides that meaning through its understanding.

Overtly political are poems like **"Categories"** or **"The Wonder Woman,"** but also political are the gentle love poems (**"The Butterfly," "When I Nap"**), and indeed all the poems that are about Giovanni as private person. (pp. 166-70)

The poems of the rooms outside are not calls to action from the public platform; they are dreams, some funny, some apocalyptic, of old worlds and new. In each of these poems, *My House*'s equivalent to the earlier poems of black feeling and black judgment, the poet stresses the element of personal vision. (p. 170)

This artist has begun to learn—through a process of coming to terms with herself as black woman, black poet, that art can create as well as reflect reality, as revolutions do.

It is fitting to the purpose of *My House* that its final poem, which is in "The Rooms Outside," is **"My House."**...

The first stanza follows Giovanni's familiar oral structure. Phrases stand against one another without the imaginative extensions of figurative language: word against word, repeating, altering, pointing. A love poem, to one particular lover. It starts in a tone reminiscent of both **"Beautiful Black Men"** and **"all i gotta do"**—the woman is there to adore her man: "i only want to / be there to kiss you"; "as you want"; "as you need." But although the gentle tone persists, an extraordinary change is rung with a firm emphasis on the personal and the possessive in the last three lines: "where i want to kiss you," "my house," "i plan." She is suiting his needs to hers as well as vice versa. (p. 171)

Nonetheless, she makes it clear that she is still very much of a woman, using the traditionally female vocabulary of cooking and kitchens to underscore her message. But this woman is active, not passive: she means, wants, bakes, calls, runs. She orders experience and controls it. The element of control asserts itself not only through direct statement—"cause i run the kitchen"—but through vocabulary itself: "i mean"; "[i] call them yams" (in the latter phrase asserting blackness itself through control of language: "yams" and not "sweet potatoes"). She controls not only through need and desire but through strength, ability: "i can stand the heat."...

The house and its elements . . . assume symbolic proportions, surely emphasized by the fact that the poem [continually calls] attention to its existence as a poem. The house is a world; it is reality . . . . (p. 172)

> english isn't a good language
> to express emotion through
> mostly i imagine because people

> try to speak english instead
> of trying to speak through it
> i don't know maybe it is
> a silly poem.

I am making a message, both poet and poem are insisting; and now they explain how messages work. "Trying to speak through" language rather than speaking it means that word and thing are not identical: that words are not yams, and thus language frees the poet to create realities (dreams) and not just to copy them. So that somehow this not-very-silly poem is carrying out a revolution . . . . (p. 173)

The act of naming, of using language creatively, becomes the most powerful action of all—saying, calling. Calling fudge love, calling smiling at old men revolution is creative (rather than derivative) action that expresses more than her own powers as woman and poet. In "Seduction" there was a significant gap between language (rhetoric) and action, between male and female. In that fable, men and words were allied with action (love), but she was, in the poem, mute. The man calls her action "counterrevolutionary." Now, in **"My House,"** the woman's action, love (an overt expression of the personal, private sphere), is allied to language. Giovanni brings her power bases together in this poem, her dominion over kitchens, love, and words. No longer passive in any way, she makes the food, the love, the poem, and the revolution. She brings together things and words through her own vision (dream, poem) of them, seeing that language (naming) is action, because it makes things happen. Once fudge has been named love, touching one's lips to it becomes an act of love; smiling at old men becomes revolution "cause what's real / is really real." Real = dream + experience. To make all this happen, most of all there must exist a sense of self on the part of the maker, which is why the overriding tone of the poem is the sense of an "i" who in giving need feel no impotence from the act of taking (both become aspects of the same event). Thus this is *her* house and he makes her happy, thus and only thus—"cause" abounds in this poem, too: this, her poem, can be his poem. Not silly at all.

In bringing together her private and public roles and thereby validating her sense of self as black woman poet, Giovanni is on her way towards achieving in art that for which she was trained: emotionally, to love; intellectually and spiritually, to be in power; "to learn and act upon necessary emotions which will grant me more control over my life," as she writes in *Gemini*. Through interrelating love and power, to achieve a revolution—to be free. (pp. 173-74)

Suzanne Juhasz, "'A Sweet Inspiration . . .of My People': The Poetry of Gwendolyn Brooks and Nikki Giovanni," in her Naked and Fiery Forms: Modern American Poetry by Women, A New Tradition, *Harper Colophon Books, 1976, pp. 144-76.*

Michele Wallace (essay date 1979)

[*Wallace is an American critic, essayist, short story writer, and poet. In the following excerpt, she discusses Giovanni's influence on American women.*]

Nikki Giovanni, a kind of nationalistic Rod McKuen, was the reigning poetess of the Black Movement during the sixties. Most of us remember her best for poems like ["**The True Import of Present Dialogue, Black vs. Negro**"] written in 1968 . . . . (p. 235)

She attached herself to a black poets' movement in New York that had been started by LeRoi Jones [Amiri Baraka]. The poems generally exhorted blacks to return to their roots and to partake in revolutionary action like killing honkies. There were a great many men and very few woman involved; Giovanni was one of the few that lasted.

She had a remarkable facility for riding the tide of public opinion. When it became obvious that (1) the black male poets were going to shut her out and that (2) she could not depend upon a black female audience as long as her poems advocated outright violence, she began to speak positively of the church and to focus more on having babies and loving the black man. Her albums sold quite well. She herself had a baby and refused to disclose the name of the father. Early in the seventies she told young black women to become mothers because they needed something to love. She also told young black people that school was useless and a waste of time—despite her own years of education at Fisk University. Soon after, she backed away from these positions, amending her original statement about having babies to you-should-only-have-one-if-you-could-afford-to-take-care-of-it-like-she-could, and actually encouraging blacks to go back to school. Concomitantly, she began to make a lot of money on the college lecture circuit. She received an award for her work with youth from the *Ladies' Home Journal*. It was presented by Lynda Bird Johnson on national television.

Both [Angela] Davis and Giovanni represented the very best black women had to offer, or were allowed to offer, during the Black Movement. They carved out two paths for women who wished to be active. Davis's was Do-it-for-your-man. Giovanni's was Have-a-baby. Neither seemed to have any trouble confining herself to her narrow universe.

Unfortunately, and I believe unintentionally, Davis set a precedent for black female revolutionary action as action that could never be self-generated. When I visited Riker's Island several years ago, I met a few female revolutionaries suffering the consequences of that example. The run-of-the-mill female prisoner was there because of her man—her pimp, her dope supplier, or the man she had accompanied on a stickup. The political women were there for the same reason.

But only the most adventurous were ready to follow Angela Davis's lead. The majority took Nikki Giovanni much more seriously. She was the guiding light for those who had been left behind in the flurry and chaos of the revolution. No doubt she prompted many by word and deed to have babies so that they could have "something to love." By the time she advised them later to first make sure they had enough income to support the child, a lot of women were already on welfare. (pp. 236-38)

Although she rarely chose to reflect it in her work, Giovanni did realize the black woman's dilemma to some extent. A line from one of her later poems ["**all i gotta do**"] is unfortunately more typical: "what i need to do/is sit and wait/cause i'm a woman . . ." (p. 239)

> *Michele Wallace, in an excerpt in her* Black Macho and the Myth of the Superwoman, *Dial Press, 1979, pp. 235-39.*

Nikki Giovanni with Claudia Tate (interview date 1983?)

[*Tate is an American essayist and short story writer. In the following excerpt from an interview published in her 1983 collection* Black Women Writers at Work, *she and Giovanni discuss literature's importance as a reflection of reality and the poet's role in society.*]

[Tate]: *Your earlier works,* **Black Feeling, Black Talk, Black Judgment** *and* **Re:Creation,** *seem very extroverted, militant, arrogant. The later work,* **The Women and the Men** *and* **Cotton Candy on a Rainy Day,** *seem very introverted, private, lonely, withdrawn. Does this shift in perspective, tone, and thematic focus reflect a conscious transition?*

[Giovanni]: I'll tell you what's wrong with that question. The assumption inherent in that question is that the self is not a part of the body politic. There's no separation.

I'm not a critic of my own work. It's not what I'm supposed to be about. I think literary analysis gives academics something to do. Books are generally amusement parks for readers. They will ultimately make a decision about which book to ride. But as for critics, they have to write a book as interesting as the one they're criticizing or the criticism is without validity. If they succeed, then the book they're writing about is only their subject; it is not in itself necessary. The critics could have written about anything. And after all, they've got to have something to do. It's Friday and it's raining, so they write a critique of Nikki Giovanni. It's not serious. And I'm not denigrating myself; it's just that it's no more serious than that.

Is there a black aesthetic? If so, can you define it?

It's not that I can't define the term, but I am not interested in defining it. I don't trust people who do. Melvin Tolson said you only define a culture in its decline; you never define a culture in its ascendancy. There's no question about that. You only define anything when it's on its way down. How high did it go? As long as it's traveling, you're only guessing. So too with the black aesthetic.

As the black-aesthetic criticism went, you were told that if you were a black writer or a black critic, you were told *this* is what you should do. That kind of prescription cuts off the question by defining parameters. I object to prescriptions of all kinds. In this case the prescription was a capsulized militant stance. What are we going to do with a stance? Literature is only as useful as it reflects reality. I talk about this in *Gemini;* I also say it's very difficult to gauge what we have done as a people when we have been systematically subjected to the whims of other people. (pp. 62-3)

Is there validity to For Colored Girls Who Have Considered Suicide When the Rainbow Is Enuf *and* Black Macho and the Myth of The Superwoman, *and the subsequent criticism these works incite?*

Evidently there is validity or it wouldn't fly. You're essentially asking does it have a motor? It's got to have a motor or it wouldn't fly. Otherwise it'd just sit out on the runway. I have problems with this man-woman thing because I'm stuck on a word. The word's "boring." (p. 66)

I wrote a poem about a black man, and Don Lee wrote the most asinine thing I've ever read. His criticism was that Nikki Giovanni's problem is that she's had difficulty with a man. *Kirkus Review's* critical response to *The Women and the Men* was "Oh she's just in love." My life is not bound in anything that sells for $5.95. And it will never be. No matter what you're seeing, it's not me. If I'm not bigger than my books, I have a problem. I have a serious problem. I don't take my books personally because they're not personal. They reflect what I have seen, and I stand behind them because they are about reality, truth. I'm not America's greatest writer, but I'm credible.

The truth I'm trying to express is not about my life. This is not an autobiography we're talking about. *Gemini* is barely one, and it comes close. It was what I said it was, an autobiographical essay, which is very different from autobiography. Even autobiographies are not real because we only remember what we remember. And the truth has to be bigger than that, and if it isn't there's something wrong with your life. What we remember is only a ripple in a pond. It really is. And where does the last ripple go and who sees it? You never see the end of your own life. We put too much emphasis in the wrong places. And what we do to writers, particularly, is we try to get away from what is being said. We brand them. Of course, I'm back to the critics again.

The point of the writer is to remind us that nuclear energy, for example, is not just some technical, scientific thing, not that Pluto is the last planet and it's freezing, but that such things are comprehensible to the human mind.

We've got to live in the real world. If we don't like the world we're living in, change it. And if we can't change it, we change ourselves. We can do something. If in 1956 I didn't like the way the world was, it was incumbent upon me to at least join a picket line. I didn't have to join a picket line happily. I didn't have to join it with full knowledge of what this could mean to me. None of that was required of me. It was only required that I try to make a change so that ten years later I'll be able to go to Knoxville, Tennessee, and I'll be able to walk down Gay Street without having to move aside for some cracker. And in ten years we did. That was a limited goal, but I won. All I'm trying to say is, okay, if you can't win today, you can win tomorrow. That's all. My obligation is to win, but winning is transitory. What you win today, you start from ground zero on the next plateau tomorrow. That's what people don't want to deal with.

You're only as good as your last book. And that's what writers have a problem with. You say you wrote a book twelve years ago. Hey, I'm real glad, but I want to know what you are doing now. I complained about [Ralph] Ellison in *Gemini* in this regard. And I think it's a valid complaint. God wrote one book. The rest of us are forced to do a little better. You can't live forever on that one book. No matter how interesting, or how great, or how whatever, you are forced to continue, to take a chance. Maybe your next book won't be as good as your last. Who knows?

A lot of people refuse to do things because they don't want to go naked, don't want to go without guarantee. But that's what's got to happen. You go naked until you die. That's the way it goes down. If you don't want to play, you're not forced to. You can always quit. But if you're not going to quit, play. You've got to do one or the other. And it's got to be your choice. You've got to make up your own mind. I made up my mind. If you're going to play, play *all* the way. You're going to sweat, and you're going to get hit, and you're going to fall down. And you're going to be *wrong.* Probably nine times out of ten you're going to be wrong, but it's the tenth time that counts. Because when you come up right, you come up right beautifully. But after that you have to start again. We as black people, we as people, we as the human species have got to get used to the fact we're not going to be right most of the time, not even when our intentions are good. We've got to go naked and see what happens. (pp. 67-9)

What makes a poet different from a John Doe who's cleaning gutters?

The fact that I write poetry and do it well makes me different. I dare say I probably wouldn't clean gutters nearly as well. Though if it came to cleaning gutters, I could do it. If I am a better poet, it's because I'm not afraid. If artists are different from ordinary people, that's because we are confident about what we are doing. That's the difference between what I would consider to be a serious artist and those who are in it for the fun. A lot of people are always into thinking they can become famous. Kids are always asking how one becomes famous. Well, I don't know. You know if you're talking fame, you're not a serious person. (p. 72)

You know people write me and say, "I want to be a writer. What should I write about?" How the hell should I know what one should write about?

Nobody's going to tell me what to write about because it's about me dancing naked on that floor. And if I'm going to be cold, it's going to be because I decided to dance there. And if you don't like to dance, go home. It's that simple. So the artistic attitude is that you take your work seriously. However, we writers would all be better off if we didn't deceive ourselves so frequently by thinking everything we create is important or good. It's not. When you reread something you need to be able to say, "Gee, that wasn't so hot. I thought it was really great ten years ago." But sometimes you can say, "Hey, it's not so bad."

What about the prose?

I don't reread my prose because I'm kind of afraid. I suppose one day I will. At least I would like to think so. But I'm very much afraid to be trapped by what I've said. I don't think life is inherently coherent. I think what Emerson said about consistency being the hobgoblin of little minds is true. The more you reread your prose the more likely you're going to try to justify what you've said. I don't really object to being an asshole. I don't take it personally.

If I never contradict myself then I'm either not thinking or I'm conciliating positions and, therefore, not growing. There has to be a contradiction. There would be no point to having me go three-fourths of the way around the world if I couldn't create an inconsistency, if I hadn't learned anything. If I ever get to the moon, it would be absolutely pointless to have gone to the moon and come back with the same position.

That's been a quarrel I've had with my fellow writers of the sixties. If you didn't learn anything what was the point of going through a decade? If I'm going to be the same at thirty-eight as I was at twenty-eight, what justifies the ten years to myself? And I feel that's who I've got to justify it to—ME.

Though I don't reread my prose, I do reread my poetry. After all that's how I earn my living.

How do you polish the poems?

A poem is a way of capturing a moment. I don't do a lot of revisions because I think if you have to do that then you've got problems with the poem. Rather than polish the words, I take the time to polish the poem. If that means I start at the top a dozen times, that's what I do. A poem's got to be a single stroke, and I make it the best I can because it's going to live. I feel if only one thing of mine is to survive, it's at least got to be an accurate picture of what I saw. I want my camera and film to

record what my eye and my heart saw. It's that simple. And I keep working until I have the best reflection I can get. Universality has dimension in that moment.

Do you have a particular writing method—a special place, a special time for writing?

One thing for sure I can say about me is that if my book is going to bust, it's going to bust in public. It is either going to be so bad or so good. That's true of most of my books. Nothing is ever half way with me. It's shit or it's great. That's my attitude. I think that's the only way to go. Now other people are much more cautious. They'll do the safe thing and handle it right. Jean Noble put twelve years into *Beautiful Are the Souls of My Black Sisters*. Jean's book is beautiful, and I'm glad she did. Alex put twelve years in *Roots*. I couldn't be happier he did. I'm glad for Alex; I'm glad for me because I've got galleys. But I could no more put twelve years into anything. Nothing is worth twelve years to me. I can't grow a garden. I can't see waiting that long just for some vegetables. Some people can do it; I'm not one of them. I believe in accepting the limits of my competency.

That's a weakness. Yeah, I'll admit it. I just don't get a thrill out of seeing tomatoes grow. I do get a thrill seeing my poems, and I will take the time for them. But if after a year I was working on a poem, not a book but a poem, I would say something's wrong with either the poem or me. That's probably not the best way to be a writer. I wouldn't even want to consider myself an example. I'm essentially undisciplined. I do a lot of thinking, a lot of reading, but I wouldn't recommend my writing method. On the other hand I can't be like Hemingway and get up at six o'clock every morning and write for two hours. He had a wife who got up and cooked his breakfasts. I don't have time to sit there and write for two hours whether I have something to say or not. I write when it's compelling.

I'm not good at moving. I understand why Andrew Wyeth felt that if he left Brandywine he wouldn't be able to paint. It's very difficult for an artist to move. Richard Wright moved to Paris, and people said his work suffered. He didn't live long enough to reestablish his connection with his new place. I think people really overlook this. I never knew Wright, but I'm sure there was a lack of connection. It was very difficult for me to move from Cincinnati to New York. And it was equally difficult for me to move from New York back to Cincinnati. I have to feel at home in order to write. No matter what kind of little shack home is; I have to be at home. I'm very territorial.

How do you regard your audience?

I have always assumed that whoever is listening to a reading of mine, whether it be from my first book [*Black Feeling, Black Talk*] to the most recent, whether a kid or a senior citizen, deserves to hear my best. I think a lot of writers make the assumption that the people in the audience are not generally very bright. So they don't give them their best because they think they won't

Dust jacket for the 1974 transcription of a conversation between Giovanni and poet Margaret Walker.

understand it. I also think there ought to be improvement in every subsequent piece of work.

We were talking about my writing habits. If my next book isn't at least an emotional improvement over my last book, I would never submit it to a publisher. I like to think there's growth. If there's no growth, there's no reason to publish. But I think the people who read me are intelligent. That's one reason I continue to be read because I do make this assumption: if you're reading, me, you've got something going for yourself. That's arrogant. Writers are arrogant.

I would really feel badly if somebody said, "Well, I read you in '69 and I'm glad to say, you haven't changed." That would *ruin my day.* That would send me into a glass of something, and I don't drink. I'd have to say who are you and what have you read because I think I've changed. (pp. 72-5)

I have a heavy foot. And the advantage of that is not necessarily that I speed. It's that I will go in the wrong direction fast enough to recognize it and turn around and still beat you. We're going to make mistakes. It's not

what so-and-so says that defines a mistake. It's what I decide is an error: that was wrong; that was dumb; that was insensitive; that was stupid . . . . But I've got to go on and try again. That's the only thing we really have to learn.

I'd like to beat the winners. That's the only fun. I wouldn't want to be the only black poet in America. It's not even interesting. I want to be among the best. And it's going to take a lot of poets because we don't even have enough to make a comparison. I'm looking for a golden age, and I would very much like to be a part of it. But there's no race now. In twelve years I produced fifteen books. That's not bad. I would like to have a little more attention.

I'm looking for a golden age, and the only way that's going to happen is for a lot of people to have a lot of different ideas. We don't need just one idea. That's my basic quarrel with some writers, and it remains. We don't need somebody telling us what to think. We need somebody to encourage us to think what we want to think. That was the problem with the black aesthetic.

That's why *Negro Digest* went out of business—because it was boring.

On this level you critics do bear responsibility. I'm going to be very clear about this. You critics really praise what you understand. The fact that you understand it is almost suspect. Because once you get the critics all saying, "Well, that's really good," then you have to know something's wrong. If the ideas and concepts of a work are all that comprehensible, then the work hasn't broken any new ground. There has to be something new. (p. 76)

> *Nikki Giovanni and Claudia Tate, in an interview in* Black Women Writers at Work, *edited by Claudia Tate, Continuum, 1983, pp. 60-78.*

Paula Giddings (essay date 1984)

[*Giddings is an American journalist known for her writings about the history of black women in America. In the following excerpt, she examines the dominant themes in Giovanni's works.*]

It was the publication of *Black Feeling, Black Talk, Black Judgement* (1968, 1970) that began [Giovanni's] rise to national prominence. She captured the fighting spirit of the times with such lines as "Nigger can you kill?" (in **"The True Import of Present Dialogue, Black vs. Negro"**) and "a negro needs to kill / something" (**"Records"**). These poems were distinguished more by the contrast between the words and the image of their author than by anything else. Also in the volume were a number of personal poems, including gentle satires on sexual politics, and introspective, autobiographical ones, such as **"Nikki-Rosa,"** still one of her best. It talked about growing up, the value of a loving childhood and challenged the stereotype of the angry militant: " . . . they'll/probably talk about my hard childhood / and never understand that / all the while I was quite happy," she wrote.

From the beginning, the personal, feeling poems were juxtaposed against those of violent militancy. But in subsequent books she spurned the latter completely. Her vision in *Black Feeling* which saw "our day of Presence/When Stokely is in/The Black House" (**"A Historical Footnote to Consider Only When All Else Fails"**) narrowed, in her autobiographical essays *Gemini* (1971), to the conclusion that "Black men refuse to do in a concerted way what must be done to control White men." In any case, as she wrote in *My House* (1972), "touching" was the "true revolution" (**"When I Die"**).

But Giovanni's books after *Black Feeling* did more than repudiate violence. As critic Eugene Redmond pointed out, they offered her views from a new perspective: that of the rite of passage toward womanhood. The growing-up motif is a common one in literature, especially among women writers. It has provided some of their

most memorable work and, in Giovanni's case, a unifying theme in her work.

In *Gemini,* she is the feisty woman-child who, to the consternation of her mother, defies middle-class convention and gets suspended from Fisk. She traces her relationship with her older sister, that evolves from shameless idolatry to the realization that love "requires a safe distance." In these essays we are introduced to other members of her family, including a wise and warm grandmother and a newly born son, who reappear in later books.

As the title suggests, *My House* continues this theme, and Giovanni explores the legacies passed from generation to generation; and the lighthearted pleasures of love and mischief. Sex sans politics does allow more playfulness; in the book's title poem, she writes about kissing you "where I want to kiss you / cause it's my house / and i plan to live in it."

The evolvement away from the political poems had a significant impact on her career. Her work became distinguished from that of others in her generation at a time when it was propitious to stand out from the rest. By the early seventies, the Black movement was in disarray, factionalized, and largely reduced to internecine bickering. Giovanni, however, could still maintain an appeal across ideological lines. (pp. 212-13)

Pursuing the rite-of-passage theme eventually leads to becoming a woman; an adult, graced or burdened with the responsibilities of maturity. *The Women and the Men* recognized a coming of age. For the first time, the figure of the woman-child is virtually absent. In **"The Woman"** section, the dominant theme is the search for identity, for place, in the community of Black women. In the poem **"The Life I Led,"** whose title is already suggestive, the poet even envisions her physical aging process: "i know my arms will grow flabby / it's true / of all the women in my family." The free-spirited love poems are grounded in the concern that "my shoulder finds a head that needs nestling." Although there are fewer poems in this volume that get a rise from an audience, the collection is clear and definite in its tone. It is as if the search for identity and womanhood had come to fruition. In place of the nervous, mercurial relationships of youth, there is a relaxation evident. Now the poet is capable of "lazily throwing my legs / across the moon" (**"I Want to Sing"**).

In each of Giovanni's books, there is a poem or two which signals the direction of a subsequent book. In *The Women and the Men,* **"Something to Be Said for Silence"** contains the lines "somewhere something is missing/ . . . maybe i'm just tired"; and in **"December of My Springs,"** another poem, Giovanni looks forward to being "free from children and dinners / and people i have grown stale with."

The next book, *Cotton Candy on a Rainy Day* (1978), recognizes the completion of a cycle. ". . . Now I don't fit beneath the rose bushes anymore," she writes, "anyway they're gone" ("**The Rose Bush**"). The lines are indicative of the mood of this book, which talks about a sense of emotional dislocation of trying "to put a three-dimensional picture on a one-dimensional frame," as she wrote in the title poem. She has evolved to be that creature which often finds itself estranged from the history which created it: a bright Black female in a white mediocre world, she notes in "**Forced Retirement.**" The consequences are an emotional compromise to a bleak reality, for compromise is necessary to forestall inevitable abandonment. Although the men in her life "refused to/be a man," Giovanni writes in "**Woman**," she decided it was "all/right." The book is immersed in a world-weary cynicism, as the lines, "she had lived long and completely enough/not to be chained to the truth" suggest ("**Introspection**").

Cotton Candy does have its upbeat poems, but it is the rain dampening the spirit of another time which prevails. There is an emotional as well as a physical fatigue in the "always wanting/needing a good night's rest" ("**Introspection**").

The same mood dominates Giovanni's latest book, *Those Who Ride the Night Winds* (1983), but in a different way. Frankly, this collection is so hollow, the thinking so fractious, that it makes a reader ask new questions about the author. One of the needling problems in Giovanni's books, particularly those published after 1975, is that as her persona matured, her language, craft, and perceptions did not. Although lyricism, and profundity were never her forte, the simplistic, witty vocabulary in her earlier work were appropriate for the observations of the woman-child. But more is needed from a fortyish woman who contemplates the meaning—or meaninglessness—of life. The symptoms which appeared sporadically in earlier books, of a poet losing control of her theme, completely engulf *Night Winds.* Perhaps it is because even greater resources are needed to pass through the life stage of introspection to commenting on the world around her.

From the first page of the book we know that Giovanni will take on such subjects as art and the human condition. In the preface she tells us: "The first poem . . . ever written . . . was probably carved . . . on/a cold damp cave . . . by a physically unendowed cave man/ . . . who wanted to make a good impression . . . on a physically endowed/ . . . cave woman . . . ." Already it is evident that she is in over her head. The poem "**Love: Is a Human Condition**" is typical of the quality of thought in this book—which often borders on the incoherent. It begins, "An amoeba is lucky it's so small . . . else its narcissism would lead/to war . . . since self-love seems so frequently to lead to self-righteousness . . . ." What does size have to do with narcissism? And isn't self-righteousness often a function of the lack of genuine self-love? Of course the fundamental question is what an amoeba has to do with the poem's title in the first place. One must ask, she says, "if the ability to reproduce oneself efficiently has/anything to do with love . . . ."

Unfortunately, in terms of imagery and craft, similes like this one are all too common: "Lips . . . like brownish gray gulls infested by contact with/polluted waters circling a new jersey garbage heap . . . flap in/anticipation . . ." ("**Mirrors**"). In search for some philosophical meaning of her life (one assumes), the poet subjects her readers to lines like "My father . . . you must understand . . . was Human . . . MY mother/ . . . a larva . . . and while I concede most Celestial Beings . . . have/taken the bodies of the majority . . . I chose differently . . . No/one understands me . . . ." ("**A Word for Me . . . Also**"). Little wonder. Although the poet concedes confusion in the succeeding stanza, Giovanni doesn't seem to understand that even "non-sense" poems must have some internal logic and meaning to justify their existence.

Even the love poems, which were once entertaining, are flat and uninspiring in this book. The same concepts, words, and even phrases which once described the gleam-in-the-eye flirtations are superimposed on what seems to be more meaningful relationships. The result is an overwhelming sense of triviality.

We look for relief in the poems written in the names of the artist Charles White, the playwright-activist Lorraine Hansberry, and the slave poet Phillis Wheatley. What more fertile subjects for a politically conscious poet? But there is no relief from the lack of substance, the lack of structural and aesthetic power, the trite philosophizing.

Underlying the problems in *Night Winds* may be Giovanni's own philosophy of writing. It was conceived at a time when we were generous, some could call us loose, in our definition of poetry. Seduced by the content of the writings of many young Turks, we bestowed the label of "poet" as a reward. Few demanded that poetry weave emotion and creative imagination with the mastery of language. Few exhorted that the use of "free verse" required even greater skill than more traditional forms. Then, the message, not the medium, was important.

In *Gemini,* written at a time when many believed that intellectualism eroded the spirit, Giovanni wrote: "I couldn't see anywhere to go intellectually and thought I'd take a chance on feeling." Convinced that too many Black writers had been stymied by the self-conscious quest for perfection, she said in *Poetic Equation:* "I am perfectly willing to expose a great deal of foolishness [in my work] because I don't think infallibility is anything to be proud of." The point, she continued, was to learn from mistakes and go on. It is a philosophy which has made her a highly prolific writer. It is also one which allowed her to touch the rapid, irregular pulse of an earlier time. The appeal of the early Giovanni, as a poet and a media personality, was her highly individual way of thinking and feeling, her maverick attitude toward respectability, her concern for the elderly, her "silly" love poems, and a confessed fallibility in the face of humorless ideological dictates. Her lack of concern with craft and technique—even in literary circles—was not unappealing when the prevailing ethos was protest, whether in the form of political or personal rebellion. But as times and her own focus changed, Giovanni's lack of growth combined with a diminution of creative energy and spirit has made her latest book a sad parody of earlier ones.

Looking over her entire career, Nikki Giovanni's achievements are many. Not the least of them is chronicling the life passages of a young Black woman imbued with the sensibilities of the sixties. But her greatest challenge, as a poet, lies ahead in the eighties. One hopes that she will be able to fulfill an earlier promise. (pp. 214-17)

> *Paula Giddings, "Nikki Giovanni: Taking a Chance on Feeling," in* Black Women Writers (1950-1980): A Critical Evaluation, *edited by Mari Evans, Anchor Press/Doubleday, 1984, pp. 211-17.*

William J. Harris (essay date 1984)

[*Harris is an American poet, essayist, and editor. In the following excerpt, he contends that Giovanni has been unfairly underrated by critics.*]

Even though Nikki Giovanni has a large popular audience, she has not gained the respect of the critics. Michele Wallace calls her "a kind of nationalistic Rod McKuen"; Eugene Redmond claims her poetry "lacks lyricism and imagery"; Haki Madhubuti (Don L. Lee) insists she lacks the sophistication of thought demanded of one with pretensions of a "political seer" and finally, Amiri Baraka and Saunders Redding, united on no other issue, declare in their different styles that she is simply an opportunist. These critics illustrate the problem of evaluating Nikki Giovanni dispassionately. Her limitations notwithstanding, there is a curious tendency of normally perceptive critics to undervalue her, to condescend to her rather than to criticize her.

When Michele Wallace compares Giovanni to McKuen, she is suggesting that both are popular poets. This is true enough, but still there is a crucial difference between them: McKuen is a bad popular poet; Giovanni is a good one. He is a bad popular poet because he presents conventional sentiments in a shamelessly sloppy form. His retellings of conventional stories in conventional ways, without a trace of thought or feeling, have won him a ready audience. In essence, he is the genius of the unexamined life; he is the opposite of a serious artist who is dedicated to the exploration of his life. The serious artist deals in fresh discoveries; McKuen in clichés. Giovanni, on the other hand, is a popular poet but also a serious artist because she tries to examine her life honestly. (p. 218)

Giovanni is a good popular poet: she is honest, she writes well-crafted poems, and, unlike McKuen, she pushes against the barriers of the conventional; in other words, she responds to the complexities of the contemporary world as a complex individual, not as a stock character in anybody's movie about Anyplace, U.S.A. In fact, much of Giovanni's value as a poet derives from her insistence on being herself; she refuses to go along with anybody's orthodoxy. Since she is always reacting to her multifarious environment, it is not surprising that her career has already gone through three distinct stages: first, the black militant; then the domestic lover; and now the disappointed lover. Therefore, it is clear that her move from Black militant poet to domestic woman poet is not a contradiction, as some critics maintain, but only a response to her times: the seventies and eighties call for different responses than did the sixties. Unlike Madhubuti she is not doctrinaire; she does not have a system to plug all her experiences into. She examines her time and place and comes to the conclusions she must for that time and place.

Giovanni does have weaknesses. At times she does not seem to think things through with sufficient care. Furthermore, she often does not bother to finish her poems; consequently, there are many unrealized poems in her oeuvre. Finally, not unlike a movie star, she is possibly too dependent on her public personality. In other words, she can be self-indulgent and irresponsible. Paradoxically, her shortcomings do grow out of the same soil as her strengths, that is, out of her independence of mind, her individuality, and her natural charm.

Since her first book in 1968, Nikki Giovanni has published a number of volumes of poetry, including ***Black Feeling, Black Talk, Black Judgement*** (a combined edition, 1970), ***Re:Creation*** (1970), ***My House*** (1972), ***The Women and the Men*** (1975), and her most recent work, ***Cotton Candy on a Rainy Day*** (1978), and even though her attitudes have changed over the years, the books are unified by her personality. Like many poets of the period she is autobiographical and her personal stamp is on all her work. There is also a consistency of style, even though there is a change of mood: the poetry is always direct, conversational, and grounded in the rhythms of Black music and speech. Her poems are also unified in that they are written from the perspective of a Black woman. Moreover, her themes remain constant: dreams, love, Blackness, womanhood, mothers, children, fathers, family, stardom, fame, and sex. In addition to her poetry books, she has published an autobiography, ***Gemini,*** two extended interviews—one with Margaret Walker, one with James Baldwin—and a number of children's books.

In Giovanni's first stage she wrote several classic sixties poems expressing the extreme militancy of the period. These include "**The True Import of Present Dialogue, Black vs. Negro,**" and "**For Saundra.**" In 1968 Giovanni spits out:

> Nigger
> Can you kill
> Can you kill
> Can a nigger kill
> Can a nigger kill a honkie

The poem these lines are taken from, "**The True Import of the Present Dialogue, Black vs. Negro**," is intended to incite violence by asking for the literal death of white America. It captures the spirit of the sixties, that feeling that Armageddon, the final battle between good and evil, is imminent. It is informed by the example of Frantz Fanon, the Black revolutionary author of *The Wretched of the Earth*, whose book Eldridge Cleaver called "the Bible" of the Black liberation movement. In it, Fanon declares: "National liberation, national renaissance, the restoration of nationhood of the people, commonwealth: whatever may be the headings used or the new formulas introduced, decolonisation is always a violent phenomenon." Cleaver correctly claims that Fanon's book "legitimize[s] the revolutionary impulse to violence." No matter how romantic that moment now seems, there was then a sincere feeling that it was a time of revolution; and Giovanni, along with Madhubuti, Baraka and others, expressed these revolutionary ideas in their poems. Furthermore, Giovanni's poem "**The True Import of Present Dialogue, Black vs. Negro**" embodies more than the literal demand for the killing of whites: it also expresses a symbolic need on the part of Blacks to kill their own white values:

> Can you kill the nigger
> in you
> Can you make your nigger mind
> die

Eliot has said that poetry should not deviate too far from common speech; these Black revolutionary poets—in a sense Eliot's heirs—demonstrate that they have absorbed the subtleties of their language. For example, in the above poem Giovanni exploits the complex connotations of the term "nigger"; she uses it in this stanza to suggest the consciousness that wants to conform to white standards; consequently, to kill the "nigger" is to transform consciousness. In more general terms, the entire poem is cast in the form of a street chant: the rhythm is intended to drive the reader into the street, ready to fight. In fact, the source of much of the form utilized in the 1960s Black Arts Movement is street language and folk forms such as the chant and the dozens, a form of ritualized insult.

Giovanni's "**For Saundra**" provides the rationale for the New Black Poetry:

> i wanted to write
> a poem
> that rhymes
> but revolution doesn't lend
> itself to be-bopping
>   . . .
> maybe i shouldn't write
> at all
> but clean my gun

In short, Giovanni is saying that the times will not allow for poems which are not political in nature, which do not promote revolution. In the 1960s art had to subordinate itself to revolution. Ron Karenga insisted: "All art must reflect and support the Black Revolution."

Even though such revolutionary figures as Karenga and Baraka stressed collective over individual values, Giovanni remains an individual, implicitly questioning the call for revolutionary hatred in the very titles of such poems as "**Letter to a Bourgeois Friend Whom Once I Loved (and Maybe Still Do If Love Is Valid).**" She feels the tension between personal and revolutionary needs—a tension that runs throughout her work in the revolutionary period. Baraka demands: "Let there be no love poems written / until love can exist freely and cleanly." Giovanni understands that there are times of hate but also realizes that to subordinate all feeling to revolutionary hate is too abstract and inhuman.

Yet Giovanni's independence can be irresponsible. At times she seems a little too eager to gratify human desires at the expense of the revolution. She confides in "**Detroit Conference of Unity and Art**" (dedicated to former SNCC leader H. Rap Brown):

> No doubt many important
> Resolutions
> Were passed
> As we climbed Malcolm's ladder
> But the most
> Valid of them
> All was that
> Rap chose me

Even a nonrevolutionary reader would question the political commitment of the above lines. If one is going to set herself up as a serious poet-prophet—and Giovanni has—one had better be concerned about the revolutionary business at a meeting, not one's love life. This is the sort of frivolousness that Giovanni's critics, such as Madhubuti and Wallace, rightfully attack. However, at other times, Giovanni's frivolousness was refreshing in those tense and serious days of revolt. "**Seduction**" delightfully points out that the revolution cannot be conducted twenty-four hours a day. The poem centers around a brother so earnestly involved in the revolution that he does not notice that the poet has stripped both of them. The poem concludes:

> then you'll notice
> your state of undress
> and knowing you you'll just say
> "Nikki,
> isn't this counterrevolutionary . . .?"

Part of Giovanni's attractiveness stems from her realization that for sanity, there must be sex and humor, even in revolutionary times.

When the revolution failed her, Giovanni turned to love and began writing a more personal poetry, signaling the onset of the second stage of her career. The literature of the seventies was quite unlike those of the hot and hopeful sixties . . . . For Giovanni . . ., idealism of the sixties had been replaced by the despair of the seventies . . . . The sixties stood for endless possibility; the seventies for hopelessness and frustration. However, in *My House* she seeks an alternative to public commitment and finds one in domestic love. Giovanni is not the only Black figure to seek new alternatives in the seventies: Cleaver found God; Baraka found Marxism; Julian Bond shifted allegiances from the activist organization SNCC to the staid NAACP. (pp. 219-23)

Giovanni has exchanged the role of revolutionary Mother Courage, sending her Black troops into battle, for the role of domestic Black woman, making fudge for her Black man. While the poem may make the reader uncomfortable—has it set the feminist movement back fifty years?—one can sympathize with Giovanni's desire to retreat into domestic comforts in the face of a disappointing world. In "**My House**" she declares her domesticity loudly, militantly, perhaps to give herself confidence in her new role. Later she will celebrate the domestic more quietly and convincingly . . . .

[In "**Winter**" from *Cotton Candy*], Giovanni gathers supplies to retreat from the cold world; however, it is only for a season. And unlike "**My House**," this poem creates a snug place one would want to retire to; Giovanni has become more comfortably at home in the domestic world of "**Winter**" than in the brash "**My House.**"

If she implicitly questioned "pure" revolution earlier, in the seventies she questions all ideologies that try to define or categorize her . . . . It is not surprising that this maverick does not want to be fenced in by anybody—friend or foe. She will not go along with anybody's orthodoxy.

By the third stage of her career, love, too, has failed Giovanni. In the title poem from *Cotton Candy on a Rainy Day* (1978), she notes:

> what this decade will be
>   known for
> There is no doubt it is
>   loneliness

and in the same poem she continues:

> If loneliness were a grape
>   the wine would be vintage
> If it were a wood
>   the furniture would be mahogany
> But since it is life it is
>   Cotton Candy
>   on a rainy day
> The sweet soft essence
>   of possibility
> Never quite maturing
>   . . .
> I am cotton candy on a rainy day
>   the unrealized dream of an idea unborn

Cotton Candy is Giovanni's bleakest book and reflects the failure of both revolution and love in the late seventies. Possibility has become stillborn.

Cotton Candy's bleak title poem provides good example of the problems the reader faces in trying to evaluate Giovanni. Even though the poem is not a total success, it is better than it appears on casual reading. At first the title seems totally sentimental: "cotton candy" conjures up images of sticky, sappy love—it seems to catapult us into the world of Rod McKuen . . . . Despite the poem's sometimes vague language which suggests the conventional popular poem, "**Cotton Candy**" has serious moments which save it from the world of pop songs and greeting cards. When we look closely at the cotton candy image we see it refers to a world of failed possibility; and the language, at least for a few lines, is stately and expressive of a generation. (p. 223-26)

A curious aspect of Giovanni's appeal has little to do with her language per se but with the sensibility she creates on the page. It isn't that she does not use words effectively. In fact, she does. Not only did she use Black forms effectively during the sixties; in the seventies she mastered a quieter, less ethnic, free verse mode. However, on the whole what is most striking about Giovanni's poetry is that she has created the charming persona of "Nikki Giovanni." This persona is honest, searching, complex, lusty, and, above all, individualistic and charmingly egoistical. This is a verbal achievement having less to do with the surface of language than with the creation of a character, that is, more a novelistic achievement than a lyric one.

Giovanni's lust is comedic (see "**Seduction**") and healthy; it permeates her vision of the world . . . . A source of her unabashed lustiness could be the tough, blues-woman tradition. She could be following in the footsteps of Aretha Franklin's "Dr. Feelgood." The following Giovanni poem explicitly exploits and updates the blues/soul tradition:

> its wednesday night baby
> and i'm all alone
> wednesday night baby
> and i'm all alone
>
>   . . .
>
> but i'm a modern woman baby
> ain't gonna let this get me down
> i'm a modern woman
> ain't gonna let this get me down
> gonna take my master charge
> and get everything in town

This poem combines the classic blues attitude about love—defiance in the face of loss—with references to contemporary antidotes to pain: charge cards.

The poem "**Ego Tripping**," one of her best poems, grounded in the vital Black vernacular, features her delightful egotism. The poem is a toast, a Black form where the hero establishes his virtues by boasting about them. Her wonderfully healthy egotism, which is expressed succinctly in these witty lines: "show me some one not full of herself/and i'll show you a hungry person" abounds in "**Ego Tripping**". . . . In a way "**Ego Tripping**" is an updating of Hughes' "The Negro Speaks of Rivers" from a woman's perspective. Hughes' poem is a celebration of the collective Black experience from the primordial time to the present. Giovanni's poem creates a giant mythic Black woman who embodies and celebrates the race across time. The poem doesn't only claim that Giovanni is Black and proud: it creates a magnificent Black woman whose mere gaze can burn out a Sahara Desert and whose casual blowing of her nose can provide oil for the entire Arab world. In a word, she is "bad!" Since it is not Giovanni speaking personally but collectively, it is not a personal boast but a racial jubilee.

Giovanni is a frustrating poet. I can sympathize with her detractors, no matter what the motives for their discontent. She clearly has talent that she refuses to discipline. She just doesn't seem to try hard enough. In **"Habits"** she coyly declares:

> i sit writing
> a poem
> about my habits
> which while it's not
> a great poem
> it's mine

It isn't enough that the poem is hers; personality isn't enough, isn't a substitute for fully realized poems. Even though she has created a compelling persona on the page, she has been too dependent on it. Her ego has backfired. She has written a number of lively, sometimes humorous, sometimes tragic, often perceptive poems about the contemporary world. The best poems in her three strongest books, **Black Feeling, Black Talk, Black Judgement, Re:Creation,** and **Cotton Candy,** demonstrate that she can be a very good poet. However, her work also contains dross: too much unrealized abstraction (flabby abstraction at that!), too much "poetic" fantasy posing as poetry and too many moments verging on sentimentality . . . . Giovanni must keep her charm and overcome her self-indulgence. She has the talent to create good, perhaps important, poetry, if only she has the will to discipline her craft. (pp. 226-28)

> *William J. Harris, "Sweet Soft Essence of Possibility: The Poetry of Nikki Giovanni," in* Black Women Writers (1950-1980): A Critical Evaluation, *edited by Mari Evans, Anchor Press/Doubleday, 1984, pp. 218-28.*

Marita Golden (essay date 1988)

[*In the following excerpt, Golden, an American journalist, autobiographer, poet, and novelist, reviews Giovanni's* Sacred Cows and Other Edibles.]

In **Sacred Cows and Other Edibles,** Nikki Giovanni—poet, personality, social critic, iconoclast and raconteur—exhibits the best and the worst uses of the essay as a vehicle for expression, verbal performance and exploration of the mundane and the special. The articles that make up this collection have previously been published in publications as varied as the *Boston Globe, Essence* and *USA Today.* The topics Giovanni submits to her unique brand of analysis are as different as the stances she assumes. Tennis, termites, game shows, black politi-

cal leaders, literary politics, the profession of writing, odes to fellow writers and the proper celebration of national holidays are some of the subjects Giovanni explores with humor that is street and worldly wise, and with occasional insights that, in the best Giovanni style, turn a neat phrase too.

The problem with **Sacred Cows and Other Edibles,** however, is that it falls short precisely because Giovanni's glib, wise-cracking overly conversational style (which has made her poetry so popular) is ill-suited to the intellectual requirements of the essay. These pieces mildly entertain more than they probe; more often than not, the reader is merely reminded of what is obvious rather than introduced to another way of seeing things.

Giovanni is at her best in the selection titled **"Reflections on My Profession"** and **"Four Introductions"**—pieces dedicated to writers, among them Paule Marshall and Mari Evans. In **"An Answer to Some Questions on How I Write"** Giovanni asserts, "I don't have a lifestyle. I have a life," which made me want to cheer this hearty refutation of categories and oversimplification of the human equation. And puncturing the vague pomposity of the current hot cliché, the "role model," Giovanni says: "When people do not want to do what history requires, they say they have no role models. I'm glad Phillis Wheatley did not know she had no role model and wrote her poetry anyway." And she sums up the job of the writer with a feisty confidence saying, "We write because we believe that the human spirit cannot be tamed and should not be trained." This is Giovanni at her best—sparkling *and* thoughtful.

But the overall quality of this collection is marred by the author's penchant for digression. Several pieces cry out loudly for editing. In one essay ostensibly on the writer's profession, Giovanni wanders over an unruly terrain that detours to a discussion of Vanessa Williams, the Miss America Pageant, Bob Guccione, her son Tom and her dog Bruno. She apologizes for the "tendency to digress" without much conviction, blaming it on having passed her 40th birthday. The longer the essay, the more Giovanni seems to glory in her ability to free-form associate a host of incompatible ideas and examples so that it becomes like reading a conversation with someone who has 100 opinions on a single topic.

Politically, Giovanni adopts a neo-black conservatism—knocking special privileges, and racial and sexual quotas. I've no problem with her political views, but whatever Giovanni's political beliefs or how long they last, they deserve stronger justification than "Life seems so unfair lately to those of us who are ordinary."

Black conspicuous consumption, buppies and materially successful blacks come in for special praise. Giovanni long ago decided she was a winner and so she has spun gold in most of her career endeavors, exhibiting little patience with those too busy complaining to hustle up some luck. She criticizes black political and social leaders for promoting a perception of the black community as weak, fragmented and hopelessly mired in despair, all she asserts quite convincingly, for the sake of their corporate and foundation-supported bread and butter.

Sacred Cows and Other Edibles is quintessential Nikki Giovanni—sometimes funny, nervy and unnerving with flashes of wisdom. But this collection will be appreciated most by those already among the converted, rather than those searching for someone to follow.

> *Marita Golden, "Tennis, Termites, Game Shows and the Art of Writing," in* Book World—The Washington Post, *February 14, 1988, p. 3.*

FURTHER READING

Brooks, A. Russell. "Power and Morality as Imperatives for Nikki Giovanni and James Baldwin: A View of *A Dialogue.*" In *James Baldwin: A Critical Evaluation,* edited by Therman B. O'Daniel, pp. 205-09. Washington, D.C.: Howard University Press, 1977.
  Compares Giovanni's and Baldwin's opinions on power and morality as expressed in *A Dialogue: James Baldwin and Nikki Giovanni.*

Elder, Arlene, and Giovanni, Nikki. "A MELUS Interview: Nikki Giovanni." *Melus* 9, No. 3 (Winter 1982): 61-75.
  Interview with Giovanni, focusing on other contemporary authors as well.

Giovanni, Nikki. "An Answer to Some Questions on How I Write: In Three Parts." In *Black Women Writers (1950-1980): A Critical Evaluation,* edited by Mari Evans, pp. 205-10. Garden City, N.Y.: Anchor Press, 1984.
  Giovanni discusses herself as a writer, emphasizing the influence borne by history, politics, and race upon literary works.

Salaam, Kalumu Ya. Review of *My House,* by Nikki Giovanni. *Black World* (July 1974): 64-70.
  Review of *My House,* which Salaam claims lacks a strong authorial commitment to critical social analysis.

Thompson, M. Cordell. "Nikki Giovanni: Black Rebel with Power in Poetry." *Jet* XLII, No. 9 (25 May 1972): 18-24.
  Biographical overview of Giovanni's career, including discussions of the poet's involvement in political organizations.

Donald Goines

1937?-1974

(Also wrote under pseudonym Al C. Clark) American novelist.

Goines is known for grim novels about drug users and prostitutes in Detroit, Michigan, and other American cities. In his brief five-year literary career, he wrote about the lives of underworld ghetto blacks, inventing, according to critic Greg Goode, a new literary genre, the "Black experience novel." Wrote Goines's biographer Eddie Stone in 1988: "[Goines] was on the cutting edge of the life he depicted in his books and saw the cancer spreading. It's a pity that not too many people took him seriously those nearly twenty years ago. As a writer, it certainly can be said that Goines didn't have great skills. But as a social observer he was light years ahead of most of the rest of us."

Goines was born in Detroit in 1937 (some sources say 1935 or 1936) and attended Roman Catholic schools there, proving himself an earnest and cooperative student. In his mid-teens, however, he abruptly left school and joined the Air Force. In joining the service he lied about his age, an act that may account for the later discrepancy regarding his actual birthdate. During the Korean War, Goines was stationed in Japan. There he became a frequent drug user, and when he returned home in 1955 he was a heroin addict.

For the next fifteen years Goines supported his drug habit by pimping, robbing, and smuggling. He was arrested fifteen times and served seven prison terms. While in jail—where he apparently quit using heroin for a time—he was introduced to the writings of Robert "Iceberg Slim" Beck, a pimp-novelist who enjoyed substantial popularity among inmate readers. Inspired by Slim's *Trick Baby,* Goines, who had earlier attempted to write westerns, produced *Whoreson: The Story of a Ghetto Pimp* (1972), a semiautobiographical novel about a pimp and his clashes with other seedy criminals. The world of *Whoreson* is an unsparing one where weakness or error inevitably leads to death. Goines circulated the manuscript of *Whoreson* among his fellow inmates, soliciting their opinions of the work. Upon the advice of one particularly enthusiastic convict, Goines sent *Whoreson* to Iceberg Slim's publisher, California-based Holloway House. The company, known for specializing in black literature, readily accepted Goines's manuscript and requested additional works. Though still in prison, Goines quickly produced *Dopefiend: The Story of a Black Junkie* (1971), which became his first published work. In *Dopefiend* he presented a graphic account of the drug addict's sordid life, tracing the degeneration of two middle-class blacks. In a *Village Voice* assessment of Goines's writings, Michael Covino described *Dopefiend* as a "relentless" depiction of loathsome and disgusting individuals. Particularly

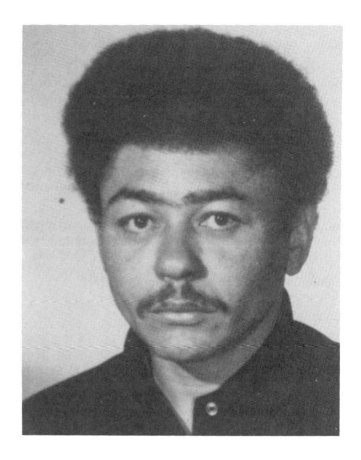

memorable is Porky, a vicious drug dealer first presented examining a pornographic magazine amid bloody squalor while a desperate addict jabs a syringe into her groin. *Dopefiend* abounds in such repellent situations. In one episode a pimp taunts a syphilitic prostitute, threatening to incorporate her into a sex show featuring animals; another passage details Porky's plan for killing two addicts who had robbed him. For Covino, the unsettling *Dopefiend* is "Goines's best book."

With advances from Holloway House for both *Dopefiend* and *Whoreson,* Goines could afford to concentrate on writing after he left prison in 1970. But by 1971 he had resumed heavy drug use. He wrote only in the mornings, spending the rest of each day indulging his heroin habit. In 1972 he nonetheless published a third novel, *Black Gangster,* about a cynical hoodlum who establishes a civil-rights organization as a front for prostitution and extortion. After publishing this novel, Goines moved to Los Angeles for greater access to

Holloway House and to the nearby film industry, which he hoped to interest in his works.

In 1973 Goines published three more novels, including *White Man's Justice, Black Man's Grief,* an indictment of what he viewed as rampant racism in the American judicial system. The novel tells of two inmates who conspire to commit a burglary after leaving prison. When one inmate is freed, he attempts the crime unassisted and kills a witness. Upon apprehension the killer names his black co-conspirator as the mastermind of the robbery and thus his accomplice in murder. The black convict is then tried and sentenced for murder even though he was in prison when the crime transpired.

Goines wrote eight more novels in 1974, including several works under the name of his friend Al C. Clark. Four of Goines's novels as Clark feature the ambitious militant Kenyatta, who rises from small-time hoodlum to leader of a two-thousand-member organization. With his military gang, Kenyatta hopes to eliminate all white police officers and rid the black ghetto of drugs and prostitution. Through considerable violence, he nearly succeeds. But in *Kenyatta's Last Hit*—the final work in a series that also features *Crime Partners, Death List,* and *Kenyatta's Escape*—he is killed while plotting the murder of a wealthy Los Angeles businessman dealing drugs.

Before writing *Kenyatta's Last Hit,* Goines returned to Detroit, having apparently disliked vast, unfamiliar Los Angeles. He settled with his common-law wife in nearby Highland Park. They were murdered there in October, 1974. Police suspected that robbery was the motive behind the slayings, though there were indications that Goines had once again involved himself in drug use. The case remains unsolved.

Goines's novels have continued to prove profitable for Holloway House, which reprinted his entire canon after his death and has reported total sales surpassing five million copies. Critical recognition, however, has been minimal. Mainstream publications ignore Goines's work, and more offbeat periodicals and literary journals rarely acknowledge his achievements. Nevertheless, as biographer Stone noted in 1988, "Goines has become America's Number One best selling black author. If anything, nearly a quarter of a century after the publication of his first book, Goines is more popular than ever, even more so than when he was alive."

(For further information about Goines's life and works, see *Black Writers; Contemporary Authors,* Vols. 114, 124 and *Dictionary of Literary Biography,* Vol. 33: *Afro-American Fiction Writers after 1955.*)

PRINCIPAL WORKS

Dopefiend: The Story of a Black Junkie (novel) 1971
Black Gangster (novel) 1972
Whoreson: The Story of a Ghetto Pimp (novel) 1972
Street Players (novel) 1973
Black Girl Lost (novel) 1973

White Man's Justice, Black Man's Grief (novel) 1973
Crime Partners [as Al C. Clark] (novel) 1974
Cry Revenge! [as Al C. Clark] (novel) 1974
Daddy Cool (novel) 1974
Death List [as Al C. Clark] (novel) 1974
Eldorado Red (novel) 1974
Kenyatta's Escape [as Al C. Clark] (novel) 1974
Never Die Alone (novel) 1974
Swamp Man (novel) 1974
Inner City Hoodlum (novel) 1975
Kenyatta's Last Hit [as Al C. Clark] (novel) 1975

Greg Goode (essay date 1984)

[*In the following excerpt, Goode surveys Goines's career as a novelist, crediting to him the invention of a literary genre, the "Black experience novel."*]

Donald Goines is the foremost example of a cultural phenomenon possible no earlier than the 1970s—a successful Black author of mass market fiction written by and about Blacks. Unlike the mass market fiction of Black authors such as Samuel R. Delany and Frank Yerby, the majority of whose readers are white and are intended to be white, the books of Donald Goines are devoured by legions of Black Americans everywhere, from the inner city to American military bases abroad.

Goines's books, all paperback originals, have never been out of print since their original publication; they have sold more than five million copies and have been on option to several movie studios and independents. They are recommended reading at some urban high schools. In 1974 Goines was so prolific that his publisher asked him to adopt a pseudonym, which he did, taking the name of a friend, Al C. Clark. Primarily through Goines, his Los Angeles-based publisher Holloway House has made a name for itself in mass market publishing and has even invented a new literary genre, the "Black experience novel," of which Goines is termed the master. In spite of all this, Goines's books are largely unknown to white readers.

Goines's sixteen books, all slice-of-ghetto-life crime novels with Black characters, have ostentatious, lurid, concrete titles such as *Swamp Man, Street Players, Death List* and *White Man's Justice, Black Man's Grief.* The characters, and very often the protagonists, are whores, pimps, thieves, pushers, card sharps, gangsters, bootleggers, numbers operators, hit men and dope addicts. With the exception of *Swamp Man,* the books are all set in the inner city ghettos of Goines's home city Detroit, or Watts, Harlem, or the Southwest.

Goines himself loved the ghetto street life and pursued most of these professions and activities at one time or another until his murder on October 21, 1974, and so was well qualified to write authoritatively about them.

In his short 37-year life Goines was addicted to heroin off and on for over twenty years. He was arrested fifteen times, jailed seven times, spent a total of six and a half years incarcerated, but nevertheless published sixteen books in his last five years. Like Chester Himes, Goines wrote his first novel in jail and later wrote a prison novel.

Future popular literary sociologists will find a goldmine of material in Goines. His characters exhibit patriarchal, male chauvinist values. Men are to lead, women are to follow, obey, and speak only when spoken to. The dark is the good. With a very few exceptions, the white men who appear are short, fat, ruddy-faced, middle aged, balding, tastelessly dressed and poorly endowed sexually. White women are prizes for Black conquest. Black men are tall, strong, handsome, well dressed even if poor, and are well-equipped sexual gladiators. Black women are beautiful, especially if dark, but are subservient to the men.

The 1960s provided a fertile and formative literary climate for Black experience writers such as Goines, and his early books are fictionalized vest pocket versions of earlier well known Black memoirs and autobiographies such as *The Autobiography of Malcolm X* (1964), Claude Brown's *Manchild in the Promised Land* (1965), Melvin Van Peebles' *A Bear for the FBI* (1968), and George Jackson's *Soledad Brother* (1970). While in Jackson State Prison in 1965, Goines, who had for a long time wanted to be a writer, tried to write Westerns and, according to his friends, failed miserably. But in the same prison again five years later, he was introduced to the work of the founding father of the Black experience novel, Iceberg Slim (the pseudonym of Robert Beck), who had gained notoriety earlier from his memoirs and novels about pimps. Within just four weeks of his reading Slim's books and seeing that his own sorts of life experiences were publishable, Goines had finished **Whoreson, The Story of a Ghetto Pimp** (1972), a tribute to Slim's book *Trick Baby* (1967). Goines handed his **Whoreson** manuscript around to his fellow inmates for criticism; they suggested that he send it off to Iceberg Slim's publisher, Holloway House. In two weeks Goines had from the publisher an offer to publish and a cry for more. Four weeks later he sent them **Dopefiend, The Story of a Black Junkie** (1971), his second book. From then on Goines was off and running, having decided to become a professional writer.

With respect to the standards of literature, the books of Donald Goines are not considered subliterary, for they are not even considered. They are offensive to many because of the obscenity, sex, and violence, all well before their time in graphic explicitness. The titles, and, in early printings, the naive bullet-and-blood style cover art, make the books appear to be utter trash. They are poorly written for the most part, in an uneasy mix of Black English and misspelled, ungrammatical Standard English. The descriptions, transitions, plots, and narrative voice are sandpaper rough. Nevertheless the Goines *corpus* is important because it is perhaps the most

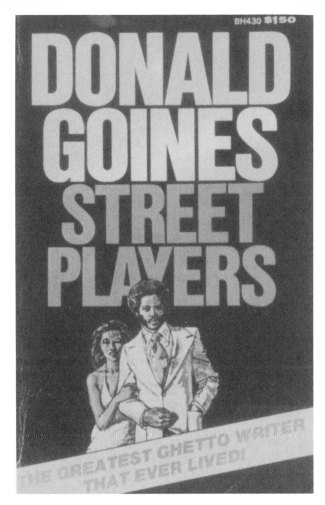

Front cover of Goines's 1973 novel Street Players.

sustained, realistic, multifaceted, widespread fictional picture ever created by one author of the lives, activities, and frustrations of poor urban Blacks. Goines's eye for interracial social subtleties is acute. And although he describes characters as briefly as possible, his descriptions go to the heart of the matter, so we learn a character's greatest hopes, assets, and fears, even if Goines has not told us so much as what the character is wearing. Some of Goines's passages are touching, such as the occasional portrayal he gives of family devotion, or of lovers enjoying a moment of serenity in the eye of the ghetto storm. Such scenes are well and seriously done for a writer of Goines's caliber, and demonstrate that his books are neither purely cynical stories of hate for the world of the ghetto nor action/exploitation potboilers.

Because Goines's ghettos are like zero-sum-game societies in which one man's gain must be another's loss, his characters cannot thrive or even survive without breaking the law. His books are automatically crime novels similar to the way in which *Caleb Williams* is a crime novel. The law broken is sometimes the white man's legal code, and sometimes the Ghetto Golden Rule, "what goes around comes around." Often, therefore, the sadistic pimp loses his best woman, the murderer dies, the hustler gets sent to jail, and a sort of automatic inner city justice is maintained. In other books, all the major characters die. In these books Goines seems to be expressing the hopelessness of life in the ghetto.

Goines's first several books were the most roughly written and unsentimental, but among them are his best books and those for which he will be remembered the longest. *Whoreson, The Story of a Ghetto Pimp,* Goines's first, is the first-person story of Whoreson Jones, the child of a Black prostitute and a white john. Abandoned by his father, having at age thirteen lost his mother to heroin addiction, Whoreson had to "come up" alone in the ghetto. The story tells of his early rise at age sixteen to a fulltime pimp, and demonstrates the ruthlessness, the abuse of friends and associates that are necessary for his survival. The book ends with Whoreson in jail, vowing to go straight and give up street life. The best example of the cold harshness of Goines's world is Whoreson's reaction to the misfortune suffered by one of his prostitutes who had gotten pregnant. When he is told by a doctor that she has had a miscarriage and is in danger of dying, Whoreson, cooler than ice, thinks,

> The last thing I wanted to do was lose a good whore. After waiting all this time for her to get streamlined, I didn't want to lose her now that she was ready for the track.

But later Whoreson gains insight into the sort of person he has become and realizes that the conditions of his immediate surroundings cause people striving for success to become brutal animals who, "faced with poverty on one side, ignorance on the other . . . exploit those who are nearest."

The book which Goines's publishers call his best in *Dopefiend, The Story of a Black Junkie* (1971), his second. It is the graphically vivid story of a young Black couple who sink from the respectability of the Black middle class deeper and deeper into the muck and degradation of heroin addiction. *Dopefiend* contains some of Goines's most repulsively memorable settings and characters. Besides recounting the insane desperation and labyrinthine rationalizations of the frantic junkie who will do anything to cop a hit to ward off the sickness, Goines describes in close-up technicolor detail the gruesome horrors of the dope house and its owner. The dope house, a 1970s version of Sax Rohmer's turn-of-the-century opium dens, is where the heroin addict buys dope, shoots up, and nods off. To read Goines's description is to imagine a bloody, pustulant cross between a pharmacy, an operating room and a torture chamber, where sick junkies frantically stab themselves with rusty, clogged needles trying to hit a track. Goines's personal ruler over this hell is Porky the dealer, to whom every possible vice and degradation is attributed. Porky, also Black, is a blubbery 380 pound bestial exploiter of female addicts, a cowardly, greedy, pitiless, perverted sadistic overseer of this vicious chamber of horrors.

About the only vice not attributed to Porky is dope, for he does not use.

Other books of Goines's early period are *Black Gangster* (1972), *Street Players* (1973), and *White Man's Justice, Black Man's Grief* (1973). *Black Gangster* is the cynical account of Prince, a hustler who struggles from a young age to become number one in the ghetto. Prince exploits the rise in Black consciousness to serve his own ends by organizing a criminal gang under the guise of a revolutionary group, most of whose members are utterly fooled. While well intentioned Blacks cry "Black is Beautiful," Prince lines his pockets with money. He feels justified, for the Blacks will revolt anyway, white man's justice is biased and means JUST US, so Prince might as well use these social phenomena to his own advantage. In *Street Players* (1973), Goines tells the depressing story of Earl the Black Pearl, a wealthy pimp and pusher whose world finally crashes down around him: his woman and best friend are maimed and murdered, and he loses his wealth and finally his life.

White Man's Justice, Black Man's Grief (1973) is perhaps a tribute to Chester Himes's prison novel *Cast the First Stone,* published twenty years earlier. Goines even gave his protagonist a name similar to that of Himes, that is Chester *Hines.* Goines's book is an indictment of the American criminal justice system and contains an angry preface which argues that the combination of false arrests and bail bonding is disproportionately harmful to Blacks. Chester Hines is sentenced to county jail, then to four years of prison for carrying a concealed weapon. In addition to containing sadistic, closely described scenes of jailhouse sex and violence, the book contains a final irony. Hines, still in jail, is tried for a murder committed 400 miles away on the outside by a former cellmate. The man had bungled a robbery, shot a guard, and had accused Hines of planning the job. Hines is convicted and sentenced to life imprisonment.

Such were Goines's early books, brutal, harsh, realistic and often chillingly cold. In what could be a period of development, Goines infused the next several books (with one exception) with a slight sense of freshness and hope. His writing was also improving from book to book. The one exception is *Swamp Man* (1974), Goines's worst book. It is set in the swamps of an unnamed southern state and is notable only for its inconsistent, muddled character motivations, and overlong scenes of sadistic sex and violence which carry no message and are not even redeemed through revenge. Other than *Swamp Man,* subsequent books were probably influenced by positive events in Goines's life, such as the birth of a baby girl, his only legitimate child, and his move to Los Angeles from Detroit, both of which occurred in 1972. Goines felt very tender about his baby girl and quite hopeful about his move, for he wanted to settle down into a respectable family life, kick his heroin habit, and perhaps even break into movies as a writer. His books began to display some of this tenderness, such as *Black Girl Lost* (1973), the relatively touching story of a girl growing up virtually alone in the ghetto from age eight, and *Daddy Cool* (1974), which tells of a successful hit man who is enriched but finally defeated by the strong love he feels for his daughter.

The most interesting and ambitious project of the later Goines is his creation of a Black revolutionary series hero, probably the only such hero in fiction. Just as the literary and cultural climate of the 1970s fostered Black memoirs and autobiographies, that of the early 1970s was suitable for a new breed of violent Black heroes who worked outside the law, and often, against it. For unlike earlier Black heroes such as Ed Lacy's Lee Hayes, Chester Himes's Coffin Ed Johnson and Grave Digger Jones, John Ball's Virgil Tibbs, and Ernest Tidyman's John Shaft, all of whom were professional detectives fighting on the side of the law, the new breed of Black heroes fought against the law most of the time. Outlaw cinema heroes such as Sweet Sweetback, Slaughter, Trouble Man, The Mack, Willie Dynamite, Black Gunn, Black Caesar, the Black Godfather, Black Samson, and Blackbelt Jones included pimps, hustlers, gangsters, outlaw private detectives, and even a revolutionary. Black pulp-fiction heroes such as B.B. Johnson's Superspade, Joseph Nazel's Black and Iceman characters, Roosevelt Mallory's Radcliffe and Joseph Rosenberger's Murder Master included renegades, vigilantes, and political fixers, but were primarily hit men working against organized crime and other corruption of inner city conditions.

Donald Goines took this extralegal trend several steps further and created a Black militant hero with an African name, Kenyatta, and a pseudonym under which he wrote Kenyatta's saga. Kenyatta's goals are to rid all American ghettos of drugs and prostitution, and to kill all white policemen, beginning in Detroit. His organization of Black militants starts with 40 members and ends up with over 2000; it branches from Detroit to Watts, as Kenyatta becomes a recognized leader. Murders, slayings, and executions in the series abound, and there is even one massacre of Blacks by police. With true collective revolutionary zeal, Kenyatta's organization kills anyone who might possibly hinder them, and will even kill Blacks, if by doing so they can kill significantly more whites.

In the four book Kenyatta series, *Crime Partners* (1974), *Death List* (1974), *Kenyatta's Escape* (1974), and *Kenyatta's Last Hit* (1975), all written under Goines's "Al C. Clark" pseudonym, Kenyatta establishes his goals, plans the robbery of a food stamp agency, buys a list of top Detroit drug dealers, and starts killing them and police men one by one. Kenyatta keeps a training camp on the outskirts of Detroit where he trains his members in martial arts and Marxist-Muslim philosophy. When the police catch on to their Detroit activities, Kenyatta and several trusted aides hijack a plane to Algiers but crashland in Nevada. From there Kenyatta migrates to Watts and sets up his larger organization. When he learns the identity of the Las Vegas finance tycoon who is responsible for the flow of narcotics into Watts, Kenyatta goes after him with a small army. A bloody battle ensues, the

tycoon escapes in a helicopter, and Kenyatta dies, as do most of Goines's heroes.

This seems the stuff of pulps, a leap into urban fantasy fiction. In fact, however serious and ambitious Goines may have been in creating a hero to clean up the ghettos, something his hero does through organized violence because no one else does it by any means, the style of his books places them in literary limbo. They are more violent and more poorly plotted than other Black hero fiction, yet there is not enough serious or substantial philosophical treatment in them to be instructive or to warrant the action. It is even possible that Goines had mixed motives in writing this series—though Goines may have been in favor of Kenyatta's intentions, the fact that Kenyatta had to do battle in the streets against police and gangsters, and the fact that Goines killed him off might indicate that Goines thought that even organized violent means would ultimately fail.

Shortly before writing *Kenyatta's Last Hit,* Goines became discouraged with his Los Angeles lifestyle. He did not like the sprawling, spread-out geography of Los

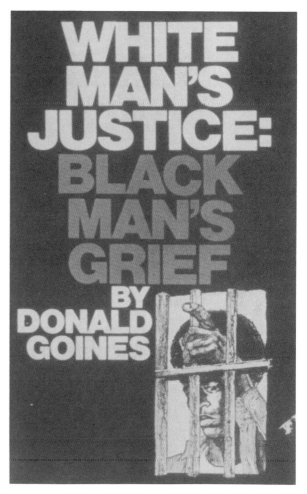

Front cover of Goines's 1973 novel White Man's Justice, Black Man's Grief.

Angeles, which seemed to him to lack a center of action. He had not kicked his hundred dollar-a-day heroin habit. He was being bothered and harassed too much by the police. And he had not succeeded in breaking into the Hollywood film industry—in spite of some mild interest shown by a few studios, he had received no offers to write for the movies. So in autumn of 1974, Goines decided to take his common-law wife Shirley and his two young daughters (one his, one hers) and drive back to Detroit. After leaving the Southern California area, Goines stopped in Las Vegas to rest and indulge in some recreation gambling. But in Vegas he lost his entire fund of cash, some $1500, and had to call Holloway House in Los Angeles to send him money, an advance on his next book. Holloway House complied, through a contact of theirs in Vegas. But the episode was shattering to Goines, and served only to further sour his opinion of the West coast. Perhaps this helps explain why a bit later, in *Kenyatta's Last Hit,* Goines has Watt's main drug supplier living in Las Vegas, and why Goines set the final confrontation there, in which his series character perishes. In any case, after his gambling losses Goines finished his trip to Detroit and set up house-keeping there.

On October 21, 1974, at his Detroit home, Goines received two white "visitors" who were known to his wife Shirley, who answered their knock at the front door. According to police reports, presumably based in part on the eyewitness testimony of Goines's daughters, the two men came into the kitchen, where Shirley was popping popcorn, and shot her several times. Next they came into Goines's study and shot him over his typewriter. To this day, the crime remains unsolved. The Detroit police department does not even know the motive for the crime, though there are several theories, such as that Goines had sold some bad dope and was being "punished" for it, or that Goines, like Superfly, was planning one last score, one last caper, and was found out by his potential victims.

Goines's last book, *Inner City Hoodlum* (1975), was found sitting in manuscript form on a shelf in his study after his death. It is a story of vengeance wrought by a pair of teenage hoodlums on Watt's premier hustler. It represents a return of Goines's relatively more subdued stories, and lacks even the inflated, improbable sense of hope exhibited in the Kenyatta series. It is interesting to speculate on the direction Goines's writing would have taken had he lived, since he was the most prolific, popular writer of a quickly growing publisher, but unfortunately this question cannot be answered. Subsequently there have been imitators, almost all better writers than Goines. But no writer, before or since, can be compared to Goines in the breadth of criminal experience, and the prolific intensity with which he put his experience to paper. (pp. 41-8)

Greg Goode, "From 'Dopefiend' to 'Kenyatta's Last Hit': The Angry Black Crime Novels of Donald Goines," in MELUS, Vol. 11, No. 3, Fall, 1984, pp. 41-8.

Eddie Stone (essay date 1988)

[*Stone is the author of* Donald Writes No More: A Biography of Donald Goines *(1974). In the following 1988 epilogue to a reissue of this work, he assesses Goines's place in the history of black literature.*]

It has now been fourteen years and some days, as of this writing, since Donald Goines and Shirley Sailor were murdered in their Detroit apartment on a cool October evening (the 21st) in 1974. Think about it. Fourteen years—Richard Nixon had only recently resigned from office—and the sixteen books Goines wrote are still in print and still selling. "Each new generation discovers him," a Holloway House executive was quoted as saying in the Detroit *News* in March, 1987: "Each generation discovers him anew. We still get fan letters from readers, a lot of them from teenagers who don't realize that he is dead. We also get at least one manuscript weekly that is an attempt to knock off Donald Goines' style and an endless stream of letters from guys who are offering to write us books 'like Donald Goines only better.'

"Holloway published several of those Goines knock offs in the three or four years after he died and some of them were written by better writers, at least technically, than Goines was. But they were *not* Goines and never were going to be and the readers knew it. Forget about that old saw that imitation is the sincerest form of flattery; it is not."

Before Goines' literary voice was silenced that night in his Detroit apartment, he'd produced sixteen books. With the exception of *Swamp Man,* a little sex-and-violence for the sake of sex-and-violence number that he knocked off because he was extremely hard up for money, all of Goines' books are set in the inner city ghettos of Goines' home city Detroit, or Watts, Harlem, or a never named city in the Southwest that sometimes resembles Las Vegas, where the writer spent a few weeks. The books were *Dopefiend; Whoreson; Street Players; Black Gangster; Eldorado Red; Black Girl Lost; White Man's Justice, Black Man's Grief; Never Die Alone; Inner City Hoodlum; Daddy Cool; Crime Partners; Death List; Cry Revenge; Kenyatta's Escape* and *Kenyatta's Last Hit.*

And here, in the winter of 1988-89, all sixteen books are out in new editions and have never been out of print and Goines has become America's Number One best selling black author. If anything, nearly a quarter of a century after the publication of his first book, Goines is more popular than ever, even more so than when he was alive. His books are reprinted over and over and the entire package (with the exception of *Swamp Man*) is under option for a television mini-series. "Hardly a month goes past," a Holloway House executives says, "that we don't have to rush print one of Goines' books. More and more he's become required or recommended reading at the high school and college level and where that used to happen among just a few urban inner-city high schools, now it's happening in the South as well as in some very prestigious Eastern universities."

Critics, and Goines has always had his critics, keep asking "Why?"

As in "Why on earth is he still popular? And how did he ever become popular in the first place? He wasn't really a very good writer and what he wrote would seem to have such a limited appeal to readers."

Well, yes. With the help of others, let's see if we can, in retrospect, answer some of those questions. Let's try this one from Greg Goode, writing in *Melus,* a journal of literary criticism, in the fall of 1984 [see excerpt dated 1984]: "Donald Goines is the foremost example of a cultural phenomenon possible no earlier than the 1970s—a successful Black author of mass market fiction of Black written by and about Blacks. Unlike the mass market fiction authors such as Samuel R. Delany and Frany Yerby, the majority of whose readers were white and are intended to be white, the books of Donald Goines are devoured by legions of Black Americans everywhere, from the inner city to American military bases abroad."

That certainly is one answer to that "why?" question but we've never believed it was the entire answer. There is probably not one entire answer. But as the years have gone on, important "mainstream" critics as well as scholars have discovered Goines and more papers have been and are being written about the writer and his work. Hardly a month goes past that Holloway House doesn't receive a request for a press kit from some author somewhere in the country where still another article is being written on Donald Goines, his books and his career.

Maybe that fails to impress you but look at it in this light: it now has been a decade since the movie studio 20th Century Fox sent out a press kit on Marilyn Monroe (that was her "home studio") or, for that matter, bothered to produce one to be sent out!

Something about the writings of Donald Goines struck a nerve; still strikes a nerve with a large audience that has been referred to by some journalists as a "cult" following.

Perhaps it was no more than his painfully raw honesty. And perhaps that, alone, explains why Goines remains popular with young people of high school and college age, as well as with older people year after year, decade after decade.

Greg Goode of the University of Rochester expanded on one theory when he wrote: "In his five-year literary career, Donald Goines provided perhaps the most sustained, multifaceted, realistic fictional picture ever created by one author of the lives, choices, and frustrations of underworld ghetto blacks. Almost single-handedly, Goines established the conventions and the popular momentum for a new fictional genre, which could be called 'ghetto realism.'"

Well, perhaps. If what Goines did really did become the "ghetto realism" school of fiction, Donald Goines was just about the only writer who ever practiced it. Dozens of other black writers (and a couple of white ones), as mentioned before, tried to become "another Donald Goines." Eventually a few of them found their own voice and made a niche for themselves in the world of black street experience fiction. Still others, fine writers such as Odie Hawkins and Joe Nazel, tested the waters of "ghetto realism" and decided their calling lay elsewhere and that their writing talents could be put to, for them, better use.

And when it comes to comparing Goines, Hawkins and Nazel, we're sort of discussing oranges, apples and pears. Hawkins, in particular, writes honest realism that is sometimes painfully so. Hawkins is a much more lyrical writer but often just as gritty as Donald Goines. But he also writes from and about a broader range of experience and there is no way anyone can honestly ever refer to him as a "ghetto" writer of any sort.

Nazel, on then other hand, sometimes uses the ghetto (Watts) as a setting for his books and has ventured into such places as Las Vegas and Miami for his good-guys-against-the-bad-guys crime stories. But Nazel's books aren't so much about the ghetto as they are about corruption and, in particular, individual and political corruption. He is, in one manner, a broader writer than either Goines or Hawkins. He has written several biographies (Richard Pryor, Paul Robeson, Jackie Robinson) and other books closer to "mainstream" American fiction than either Hawkins or Goines.

It is also true that neither Hawkins or Nazel choose to deal with the violence on a level or in the oftentimes sickeningly realistic manner in which Goines did.

And the focus on the protagonist, or main character, differs. Goines gave his characters the same illegal professions he himself had practiced. Setting almost all his books in urban ghettos where the dominant moral standard was "what goes around comes around," Goines wrote about the pecking order of the workings of ghetto criminal elements; the big fish swallowing the smaller fish. There are not a helluva lot of "self-made" men in Goines' works and those that are there mostly "self-made" it through some highly illegal activities.

As Greg Goode has written: "The overall theme of the Goines corpus, however, seems to be that the ghetto life of the underprivileged black produces a frustrating, dangerous double-bind effect. One has only two choices, neither wholly desirable. One may settle for membership in the ghetto's depressed, poverty-stricken silent majority, or opt for dangerous ghetto stardom. Goines' characters do the latter; they become pimps, prostitutes, pushers, numbers operators, thieves, gangsters, and contract hit men. This choice extracts its price, for the characters, even those who have the reader's sympathy, lose their humanity as they gain success. Because 'what goes around comes around' and because even the novels' protagonists are forced to exploit, cheat and kill even loved ones in order to survive, it is not uncommon that most of Goines' major characters die violent, often horrible deaths."

In comparing Goines' work to that of the two most popular Holloway House writers to follow him—Hawkins and Nazel—there is an immediate and apparent difference in *who* meets a violent death and just how violent that death may be.

In Goines' *Daddy Cool,* for instance, the violence is relentless. The protagonist, Larry "Daddy Cool" Jackson, is, in Goines' words, "one of the deadliest killer the earth has ever spawned." He kills with a knife and does it often; his first victim is an old man who has worked as an accountant for the numbers organization and has ripped them off for $125,000. It is a contract murder for which Daddy Cool is paid $10,000.

The only warm spot in the heart of this "deadly killer" seems to be for his beautiful young and rebellious daughter, Janet. He does not harbor the same sentiments for his son, Buddy, and certainly not for his stepson, Jimmy. Nor for his wife either, for that matter. He tells us that he'd long since gotten rid of her if it wasn't for the fact that Janet needed a mother and another woman around the house. Some mother, but that sort of shading of detail never got in Goines' way of telling a story.

They all live together in an expensive home in an apparently well-to-do section of Detroit. Daddy Cool covers up his real occupation by posing as a successful dry cleaning store owner, which is run by his old and trusted friend, Earl. (Shades of Goines' own background; he grew up in a nice, middle-class area of Detroit, the son of a successful dry cleaning establishment owner.)

Ah, but in a twist that is typical of Goines ("what goes around comes around"), Daddy Cool isn't the only bad odor in this corner of middle-class paradise. Janet's good looking young man just happens to be a pimp; and a particularly odious one that is despised by Daddy Cool (who considers all pimps to be nothing more than parasites).

Janet and her father fight over her dating the pimp, Ronald, one night after she stays out way past curfew. The next morning Janet is gone, bag and baggage; brother and stepbrother having watched her run off with Ronald during the night to "go become a whore."

And where she has gone is to a fleabag hotel in a seedy part of town with Ronald. And Ronald, true to character, has her turning tricks ("just this one time so we can have some money") so quickly that one has to wonder about Janet's smarts. But, then, Janet is a typical act-on-instinct-and-think-later Goines character.

Daddy Cool sends Buddy, Jimmy and Earl out to find Janet but son (Buddy) and stepson (Jimmy) decide, somewhere along the way, to go into business for

Front cover of Goines's eighth published novel, Swamp Man *(1974).*

themselves, along with their sleazeball friend, Tiny. Of course the numbers house they decide to rob belongs to one of Daddy Cool's oldest and best friends. And, yes, of course his thirteen-year-old daughter just happens to have stopped by for her allowance a few minutes beforehand so that Tiny and Jimmy can brutally rape her (up against one of those old steel heat radiators!). And yes, "what goes around comes around." The father runs a numbers game, the little girl gets gang raped while her father has to watch.

And who does the numbers runner call as the instrument of his revenge? Daddy Cool, of course. Good friend, paid hit man and "one of the deadliest killers the earth has ever spawned." And he's hired to go after the two men who raped the numbers kingpin's daughter—one of whom just happens to be his own stepson he learns when he's given film of the entire episode that was taped by hidden cameras. And, in another twist that is typical of Goines, he learns that his own son was not only there but did nothing to stop the rape of the child.

Daddy Cool tracks the three down, kills both Tiny and stepson Jimmy (with one of his trusty homemade knives in the back of each as they flee in panic). However, he lets son Buddy live but tells him to leave Detroit and never return.

Meanwhile the trusted friend Earl, a giant of a man, has tracked Janet and her pimp down to the sleazebag hotel where she is now turning tricks at a hot and heavy pace. Ronald has set her up as a working prostitute, Janet realizes, when he will no longer kiss her. Earl watches, realizes how far she has fallen (or how far Ronald has pushed her) and kills the pimp with his bare hands. Daddy Cool is hot on the trail and arrives about the time the police do Earl in for being a "psycho killer."

In the final confrontation between Janet and Daddy Cool at the death scene, he watches as she goes for the knife she wears in the halter between her shoulder blades (just as he wears his own). He taught her himself to reach for it, grip the hand and throw it in one fluid movement. He knows that Janet is distraught and blames himself, and that he is the target but he is "somehow pleased to see Janet close the distance between them," and thinks "she's so much like I used to be..." Ha! That doesn't surprise him one bit. In fact, he thinks, "she makes me proud, moving so smooth, so easy."

He goes for his knife and thinks: "Wonder if I can beat her from here? I got to do something to protect her. If she kills me straight out, she'll end up facing a first degree murder charge. Got to make my move, not to hurt her, just to save her from the law."

With knife in hand, Daddy Cool shouts: "You're wrong, Janet!"

He doesn't try to dodge Janet's knife—and hopes the police see it as self-defense for his daughter.

Instead of throwing his own knife, he grips it tighter. At the last instant he knows he would have had plenty of time to get his toss off...

If he had really wanted to.

The book ends with Janet crying over the body of Daddy Cool; nearby is the body of Earl. Back in the hotel is the body of lover/pimp Ronald.

No one really wins.

No one ever really wins in a Donald Goines book.

Adds Goode: "The violence in Goines' novels is like an uncontrollable contagious disease, affecting everyone who comes into contact with it. That is partly why the books are not cleanly plotted tales of crime or revenge, but realistic character stories in which motives are mixed, people act at the mercy of panic, frustration, and rage, and the effects of their actions are blurred by happenstance."

It can also be said of Odie Hawkins' novels that the actions of some of his characters are "blurred by happenstance." However, Hawkins has much more control over his material and his characters. Hawkins, as a matter of fact, if a very skilled writer, a craftsman where Goines wrote from an emotional viewpoint that was either a facet of his own personality and street experience or of that of someone he had encountered on his journeys through the dark side of the urban ghetto.

Joe Nazel, on the other hand, is always in total control. Nothing ever happens to a character in a Joe Nazel book that has not been planned, plotted and well thought out.

The comparison is given because we are discussing three of the best selling black novelists ever and it is important that we not compare them so much as to celebrate each for being his own man. Hawkins and Nazel came along after Goines and chose not to try "to be another Donald Goines" as so many have done but, instead, to develop their own voices. They have both done so successfully.

Most of the writers who attempted to "become another Donald Goines" quickly found there was room for only one. Even today Holloway House is submitted several manuscripts each month by people who not only blatantly attempt to copy Goines' style and cover the same territory, but invariably will state that they're "writing like Goines, only better."

Writing recently in *The Village Voice,* Michael Covino stated [see Further Reading]: "All those (other black) writers, no matter how well they dealt with black experience, appealed largely to an educated, middle-class, largely white readership. They brought news of one place to the residents of another. Goines' novels, on the other hand, are written from ground zero. They are almost unbearable. It is not the educated voice of a writer who has, so to speak, risen above his background; rather, it is the voice of the ghetto itself."

Perhaps there will be "another Donald Goines" one day. But it will not be a clean-cut, handsome and somewhat shy young man named Donald Goines, Jr. However, if Donny Junior, as his family calls him, makes it as a writer, and he shows great promise, it will be doing it the same way as his father did; writing about the things he knows.

And Donny will quickly tell you that he doesn't know about the things his father knew and wrote about; they are from different worlds and eras. Donny has not yet published a book but those of us who have seen his work can attest to the fact that he has the makings of an excellent writer.

He also realizes there are dozens (hundreds of them over the years) of people who have tried to "become another Donald Goines" by copying his father's style.

Donny has never tried. "I know I couldn't if I did try," he has said. He has a good command of language (better than his father's actually) and his writing is lyrical, even poetic.

"There was Donald Goines and there won't be another," he has said. "He wrote from his experience and brought to that an emotion and discipline that was uniquely his own. It would not only be a waste of my time but I'd feel I was cheating by trying to use his experience and copy his style to write my own book. My books have to come from me and from what I know and experience."

There may be another person who, in a great burst of energy and/or need, will write sixteen novels in only four years that will make a last impact as Donald Goines did. Hopefully, there will be. But he will be, like Donny Goines, from another time and another age.

Wrote Michael Covino in *The Village Voice:* "Goines caught the menace of the young bloods who kill with malign indifference, the anarchism and nihilism of the ghetto streets, well before *Time, Newsweek,* and the rest of us got there in recent years with stories about the ghetto epidemic of black-on-black killings, the horrifying statistics (a white male has one chance in 186 of becoming a murder victim, a black man one in 29), the armchair analyses of social pathology .... Goines, neither an intellectual nor a social protestor, wrote about that 'quarantined area'" of black ghetto experience that was not only foreign, in his time, to most whites but to a majority of blacks.

Covino offered as an example, a scene from *Black Gangster* when an older man is insulted by a youth: "Some instinct warned him that Donnie was searching for trouble. His whole being cried out to meet it, but a small voice in the back of his mind told him it wasn't like it used to be. The kids nowadays didn't fight anymore, they believed in killing."

In his *Village Voice* "Motor City Breakdown" article, Covino summed up Goines work thusly: 'Goines depicted the poverty, the random violence, the casualness about going to prison, the unemployment, the female-headed households, the birth out of wedlock, the child abuse, the pervasive drug culture, the rage, the indifference, the frustration, the cold cynicism. He depicted it all as a matter of course. His message, if he can be said to have one, perhaps lies in the very relentlessness, the magnitude, the savagery, the fury, the luminous power of pessimism. Any life that can inspire such pessimism cries out to be changed."

Early in 1988, the motion picture *Colors* was released, starring Sean Penn and Robert Duvall, and directed by Dennis Hopper. The movie focused on drugs and gang culture and brought howls of protest, especially from the self-appointed "black leadership," some of whom accused the movie of being racist, others of promoting the drug/gang culture; still many others found various other aspects wrong with the film. The movie upset such people, so much, that a movement to boycott the film ensued.

Of course such people have never read Donald Goines. As a matter of fact some such people have demanded that Goines' books be withdrawn from school and public libraries for his use of "swear words."

Observing such antics, Joe Nazel wondered what the shouting was all about: "Those people (gang members like those in *Colors*) are out there but they are worse than anything depicted in that movie," he stated.

Yes, those people are out there. That life is out there. And it is what Goines was writing about long before anyone else wanted to think about it. He was on the cutting edge of the life he depicted in his books and saw the cancer spreading. It's a pity that not too many people took him seriously those nearly twenty years ago.

As a writer, it certainly can be said that Goines didn't have great skills. But as a social observer he was light years ahead of most of the rest of us. (pp. 225-37)

> *Eddie Stone, in his* Donald Writes No More: A Biography of Donald Goines, *Holloway House Publishing Co., 1988, 237 p.*

FURTHER READING

Covino, Michael. "Motor City Breakdown: Donald Goines's Tales from Ground Zero." *The Village Voice* 32, No. 31 (4 August 1987): 48-9.
> Surveys Goines's writing career. Covino notes: "Goines's novels ... are written from ground zero. They are almost unbearable. It is not the educated voice of a writer who has, so to speak, risen above his background; rather, it is the voice of the ghetto itself .... [Goines's] message, if he can be said to have one, perhaps lies in the very relentlessness, the magnitude, the savagery, the fury, the luminous power of his pessimism. Any life that can inspire such pessimism cries out to be changed."

Nicolás Guillén

1902-1989

(Full name Nicolás Cristobal Guillén y Batista) Cuban poet, journalist, prose writer, and editor.

Named National Poet of Cuba by Fidel Castro in 1961, Guillén remains an important figure in West Indian literature. He was one of the first writers to affirm and celebrate the black Cuban experience, beginning with his celebrated and controversial *Motivos de son* (1930). With Marxism as a dominant influence, Guillén chronicled the turbulent social and political history of his native land, addressing what he perceived to be the injustices of imperialism, capitalism, and racism. Robert Márquez characterized Guillén's work as "a poetry which is explicit, deceptively simple in style, militant in its assumptions, one which reaches out to the Third World and looks forward to liberation, then peace."

Guillén, a mulatto from the Cuban provincial middle class, was born in Camagüey to Argelia and Nicolás Guillén. His father, a journalist and Liberal senator, was assassinated in a "political skirmish" in 1917. According to Vera M. Kutzinski, after his father's death "the young Guillén became increasingly interested in poetry and journalism." He left the University of Havana, forsaking a career in law in order to write. Kutzinski continued: "By 1930 he had not only published his first book of poems, *Motivos de son* [*Son* Motifs], but had also established a reputation as a journalist."

Motivos de son introduced to a literary audience the *son*, a sensual Afro-Cuban dance rhythm. "The stir these poems provoked," wrote Kutzinski, "remains unparalleled in Cuban literary history: while their reception was largely enthusiastic, some critics were also disturbed by the aesthetic and social implications of Guillén's literary use of the *son*, a popular musical form with a strong black component." With the rhythmic patterns of the *son*, Guillén evoked the energetic flavor of black life in and around Havana. Poems like "Negro bembón" (translated by Langston Hughes, a friend of Guillén, as "Thick-Lipped Cullud Boy") prompted some readers to accuse Guillén of promoting negative images of black Cubans. Nevertheless, critics praised the poet for his originality and his blend of Afro-Cuban idioms and traditional verse. Guillén expanded his focus in his next volume of poetry, *Sóngoro cosongo* (1931). In this volume he emphasized the importance of mulatto culture in Cuban history. Guillén explained in the prologue to *Sóngoro cosongo* that Cuba's "African injection is so profound, and in our well-irrigated social hydrography so many bloodlines crisscross, that one would have to be a miniaturist to unravel that hieroglyph."

Following the demise of the corrupt government headed by Gerardo Machado in 1933 and the increasing indus-

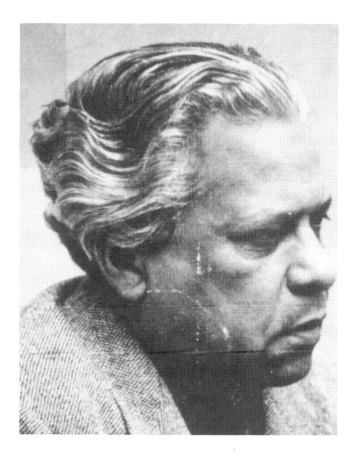

trial and political presence of the United States in Cuba, Guillén began to write poetry with overtly militant implications. In *West Indies, Ltd.* (1934), a collection of somber poems imbued with anxiety and frustration, he decried the social and economic conditions of the Caribbean poor. Guillén attacked imperialism through his recurring description of the region as a vast, profitable factory exploited by foreign nations. The poet's commitment to social change grew when he traveled to Spain in 1937 to cover the civil war for *Mediodia* magazine and participated in the anti-fascist Second International Congress of Writers for the Defense of Culture. That year he joined the Cuban Communist Party and produced an extended narrative poem chronicling the Spanish Civil War entitled *España: Poema en cuatro angustias y una esperanza* ("Spain: A Poem in Four Anguishes and a Hope"). In 1937 Guillén also published *Cantos para soldados y sones para turistas* ("Songs for Soldiers and *Sones* for Tourists"), a volume of poetry denouncing the escalating military presence in Cuban society. He employed biting satire in poems that contrast the darkness and squalor of Cuba's ghettos with the garish ambience of downtown tourist establishments.

Guillén spent much of the 1940s and 1950s in exile in Paris and Buenos Aires during the height of the Fulgencio Batista y Zaldívar regime. His works of this time reflect his opposition to Batista's repressive policies and denounce racial segregation in the United States. The poems in *La paloma de vuelo popular* (1959; "The Dove of Popular Flight") favor revolution, praising the activities of such political figures as Castro and Ché Guevara. Guillén returned to Cuba following Batista's expulsion in 1959 and helped found the Cuban National Union of Writers and Artists (UNEAC), over which he presided for more than twenty-five years. In 1964 he published *Tengo*, a volume of poetry celebrating the triumph of the Cuban revolution and extolling Cuba's abolition of racial and economic discrimination. In 1981 Guillén garnered Cuba's highest honor, the Order of José Martí, and he became a member of the Central Committee of the Communist Party of Cuba in his later years. He died after a long illness in 1989.

Many commentators have distinguished between Guillén's early *poesía negra*, or Afro-Cuban-influenced poems, and the poems he produced after converting to Communism. There is little agreement among critics, however. As Richard Jackson noted, "Some critics have focused on Guillén as an exponent of Afro-Cuban poetry while others have viewed him as a poet having little to do with Africa. Some perceive a black aesthetic in his poetry; others say he is the most Spanish of Cuban poets. Some see him as a poet who stopped writing black poetry; others declare that he never wrote black poetry at all." Despite this controversial transition in Guillén's poetry, many scholars have found coherence in his oeuvre. Kutzinski argues: "Perhaps the best way to describe Guillén's poetic ventures is as processes of unraveling the intricate hieroglyphics of Cuban (and Caribbean) culture: his poetic texts are engaged in the forging of a literary tradition from the many disparate elements that constitute the cultural landscape of that region, and he is well aware that such a tradition can be established only on the basis of a perpetual reconciliation between black and white cultures."

(For further information about Guillén's life and works, see *Black Writers; Contemporary Authors*, Vols. 116, 125, 129; and *Contemporary Literary Criticism*, Vol. 48.)

PRINCIPAL WORKS

Motivos de son (poetry) 1930
Sóngoro cosongo: Poemas mulatos (poetry) 1931
West Indies, Ltd.: Poemas (poetry) 1934
Cantos para soldados y sones para turistas (poetry) 1937
España: Poema en cuatro angustias y una esperanza (poetry) 1937

Cuba Libre: Poems by Nicolás Guillén [edited and translated by Langston Hughes and Ben Frederic Carruthers] (poetry) 1948
Elegía a Jacques Roumain en el cielo de Haití (poetry) 1948
Versos negros (poetry) 1950
Elegía a Jesús Menéndez (poetry) 1951
Elegía cubana (poetry) 1952
La paloma de vuelo popular: Elegías (poetry) 1958
Buenos días, Fidel (poetry) 1959
Prosa de prisa; crónicas (prose) 1962
Poemas de amor (poetry) 1964
Tengo (poetry) 1964
    [*Tengo*, 1974]
Ché Comandante (poetry) 1967
El gran zoo (poetry) 1967
    [*¡Patria o muerte! The Great Zoo and Other Poems by Nicolás Guillén*, 1972]
Cuatro canciones para el Ché (poetry) 1969
El diario que a diario (poetry) 1972
La rueda dentada (poetry) 1972
Man-Making Words: Selected Poems of Nicolás Guillén (poetry) 1972
El corazón con que vivo (poetry) 1975
Poemas manuables (poetry) 1975
Prosa de prisa: 1929-1972 [edited by Angel Augier] (prose) 1975-76
Cerebro y corazón (poetry) 1977
Por el mar de las Antillas anda un barco de papel (poetry) 1977
Música de camara (poetry) 1979
Páginas vueltas: Memorias (memoirs) 1982
Sol de domingo (poetry) 1982

Robert Márquez (essay date 1972)

[*Márquez edited and translated an anthology of Guillén's poetry entitled* ¡Patria O Muerte! The Great Zoo and Other Poems *(1972). In the following excerpt from the introduction to this work, he briefly surveys Guillén's poetry.*]

Despite the current vogue among publishers for all forms of neo-African literature and a complimentary flowering of interest in writers from the Third World, Nicolás Guillén's name is still generally unfamiliar to the American reading public. This is unfortunate, for along with Pablo Neruda, César Vallejo, and García Lorca, all already widely translated, Guillén, poet laureate of revolutionary Cuba, represents the very best in Hispanic poetry and is at the same time the undisputed leader of an important trend in contemporary Latin American letters. Guillén is also an open stylist whose manner does not simply anticipate a coterie audience. The publication of this anthology-translation [*¡Patria o Muerte! The Great Zoo and Other Poems*] is therefore timely and particularly satisfying.

Since his first widely acclaimed *Motivos de son* (1930), Guillén, a mulatto, has been regarded as the major exponent of Black poetry in the Spanish-speaking world. But his thematic scope is wide, and although primarily known as a poet of folk rhythms, Black and popular themes, he is also recognized for his humor, for his artistic refinement, for the sensitivity of his love ballads, and for the compassionate poignancy of his political and revolutionary verse. He is not, strictly speaking, a poet of Negritude. Unlike Aimé Césaire and the poets of the French and English Caribbean, his concern with Negro culture and his condemnation of white hypocrisy and injustice do not include a direct repudiation of European (in this case Spanish) cultural traditions. Guillén is more properly the poet of a people and his principle concern has been the creation of a poetry with a distinctly Cuban flavor, one which reflects—and helps consolidate—the Cuban national identity. (pp. 13-14)

Guillén, like the majority of the writers of his generation, began his poetic career in the shadow of Rubén Darío. But it was "the worst Darío," he later confessed, "the Darío of tintypes and enamels, with swans, fountains, abbots, pages, counts, marchionesses, and all those other knick-knacks." . . . [By] 1922 [Guillén] had managed to complete his first small book of poems, a collection whose rather unpoetic title, *Cerebro y corazón* (*Head and Heart*), hinted at the author's tragic ambivalence. It was a derivative work of little poetic distinction which, to the writer's credit, he never published [until 1964, when it appeared as an appendix to the first volume of Angel Augier's biography, *Nicolás Guillén: Notas para un estudio biográfico-critico*], but which does give us some sense of Guillén's developing technical and rhythmic expertise and of his skeptical and misanthropic outlook at the time. "Lord, Lord, . . . why is humanity so evil?" he pleads in a tone reminiscent of the decadent poets. *Cerebro y corazón* also evinced a tendency to evade reality, an avoidance of the mundane and the popular, and a conception of art that is aristocratic and romantically formalistic. (pp. 15-16)

When Guillén's next book, *Motivos de son,* appeared, it therefore heralded the appearance of a new authenticity and was an immediate and scandalous success. These eight poetic monologues for the first time allowed the Negro to speak for himself and from his own perspective. They were at the same time based on the repetitive rhythms of the *son,* were therefore deeply rooted in the Cuban folk tradition, and spotlighted the daily world of the Black *habanero.* In the prologue to the book, Guillén made it clear that unlike those who came before, he intended to

> incorporate into Cuban literature—not simply as a musical motif but rather as an element of true poetry—what might be called the poem-*son* . . . My *sones* can be put to music, but that does not mean they were written precisely for that purpose, but rather with the aim of presenting, in what is perhaps the most appropriate form, representative scenes created with two brush strokes . . . ordinary people just as they move around us. Just as they speak, just as they think.

Nevertheless, Guillén's first published book of poems was not entirely unrelated to the work of his predecessors in the *negrista* movement. The total effect of the collection is comic and picturesque. The poet's vision of the world of his creations is a mixture of roguishness and sympathetic amusement. He also focuses on the sensual and frivolous features of that world, and though he faithfully transmits the nuances and subtleties of popular Black speech, he highlights the entertaining characteristics of its linguistic distortions of the normative language. Yet the book contains an implicit, compassionate, critique of life in Havana's Black slums—a social dimension almost entirely lacking in the earlier *negrista* poetry. The purists considered the book an affront, but their opposition to it—which was not entirely literary—was dismissed and Guillén's reputation as a poet became firmly established.

A year later (1931) he reissued *Motivos de son,* along with a series of eight new poems, under the title *Sóngoro cosongo.* The new poems did not abandon the sensual accents of the earlier work (e.g., **"Madrigal"** and **"The New Woman"**) but indicated something of a shift in emphasis and perspective. Guillén dropped the comic distortions of speech which gave the first poems their distinctive flavor in favor of a more normative poetic language that relied on onomatopoeia and *jitanjáforas,* [a word of no particular meaning invented by the artist and used for its suggestiveness], to suggest the totemic and rhythmic world of Africa in Cuba, in combination with the *romance* and other meters more typical of the classical Spanish literary tradition. This gave the poet a new freedom, a broader poetic scope, and with it appear the first insinuations of a poetry of social protest. In **"Sugarcane,"** for example, the reader is given a terse glimpse of the anti-imperialist feelings which are to become one of the major preoccupations of Guillén's later poetry. The Negro, moreover, had ceased to be a superficial personality out of popular folklore and had become a character of some depth, part of the national dilemma, an indispensable part of the national heritage. Guillén was moving toward a clearer definition of his role as the poet of a people. He became concerned with the elaboration of a genuinely Cuban poetry, a poetry which would reflect the true history and racial composition of the island. (pp. 18-20)

The publication of *West Indies, Ltd.* (1934), immediately after the revolution which deposed the dictatorship of Machado (1925-1933), marks a significant transition in the development of Guillén's poetry. *Motivos de son* exposed the reader to the anecdotal and purely external; *Sóngoro cosongo* penetrated deeper into the world of the Black but spoke to the whole Cuban nation. With *West Indies, Ltd.,* the poet expands his area of concern to encompass the entire Antillean archipelago. Furthermore, here the elements of social protest come into prominence. . . . [These] strikingly lyrical poems are clear indictments against the abuses and injustices to which the people of the Antilles—and particularly Cubans and Blacks—are collectively subjected under imperialism. The tone is anguished and bitterly elegiac and the mood, though somber, mirrors the frustrations of the incipient revolutionary (see particularly **"Riddles"** and **"Guadeloupe, W.I."**). It is the first important step in Guillén's evolution toward Marxism and toward an art of unambiguously militant convictions, although at this stage his protest is a purely visceral indignation, rooted in broadly nationalist and humanitarian ideals with little specific ideological content. **"Sabás,"** however, does offer some indication of the direction in which his thinking will go and of the militancy which will become characteristic of Guillén's verse after 1934.

In 1936 the Spanish Civil War broke out. A year later Guillén, like artists from all over the world sympathetic to the Republican cause, traveled to Spain as one of the Cuban delegates to the antifascist Second International Congress of Writers for the Defense of Culture. In that same year, 1937, he joined the Communist Party and, under the impact of the war, wrote *España, poema en cuatro angustias y una esperanza* (*Spain: A Poem in Four Anguishes and a Hope*), a poem of epic proportions in which—as in works on the same theme by César Vallejo and Pablo Neruda—the poet laments the Spanish tragedy. He also published his *Cantos para soldados y sones para turistas* (*Songs for Soldiers and Sones for Tourists*), poems in which the *son,* once limited to the realm of the anecdote and the dance, is turned into an instrument for mocking the American tourist in prerevolutionary Cuba and for denouncing the more salient features of American colonialism on the island. The various *cantos* see the soldier—Cuban or European—as a pawn in the service of imperialism whose role will qualitatively change only with a change in the social structure. The tone of these poems is solemn and accusatory and it is clear that Guillén's allegiance is to the great mass of Cuba's dispossessed—although he also shows a genuine compassion for those victims who, like his soldiers, are unaware of the reality of their own situations. This is as clear in **"Why, Soldier, does it seem to you . . ."** as his anti-fascism is in **"Soldiers in Abyssinia."** (pp. 21-3)

[*El son entero (The Entire Son)*] brought together the different elements of theme and style which had by now become representative of the poet's work: the *son,* the "mulatto poem," the atmosphere of pain and accusation. There was also the strict identification with the Negro, wherever he might be, although, as in **"Sweat and the Lash,"** the author had progressed far beyond an interest in the merely picturesque literary motif: "I deny the art that sees in the Negro only a colorful motif and not an intensely human theme," he explained during one of his lectures in 1947. He did not want his readers to forget that, particularly in the United States, the Negro was still being denied his most elemental human rights. He wanted his poems to transmit that reality and, to the degree that it was possible, to incite his public to change it. (p. 23)

El son entero was followed in 1958 by *La paloma de vuelo popular (The Dove of Popular Flight)* and *Elegías (Elegies),* in which the melancholic undertones of his

previous books and the already implicit identification of Cuba with the rest of Latin America were crystallized. These two books (usually published together) also provide the reader with the substance of Guillén's hopes for the future and with his vision of the revolution as the only real possibility for Cuba's—and by extension, Latin America's—liberation. These are simple songs

> of death and life
> with which to greet a future drenched in blood,
> red as the sheets, as the thighs,
> as the bed
> of a woman who's just given birth.

Implicit in Guillén's concept of a "mulatto poetry" was the universalist premise that, after 1934, had led him to see the Negro as part of the great mass of the disinherited. It was now quite evident that for Guillén—as for Frantz Fanon—the "Negro problem" was not a question of Black men living among whites, but of Black men systematically oppressed by a society that was racist, colonialist, and capitalist, but only accidentally white.

In an effort to combat that society—a society symbolized by the international and domestic policies of the United States—more successfully, Guillén began to employ a number of techniques which, although foreshadowed in his earlier poetry, were used with increasing frequency in his later books. He began, for example, to sprinkle his verse with words and phrases from standard American English with an intent that recalls the hidden meanings behind the title of *West Indies, Ltd.* Many of these poems are addressed directly to the racial and political situation in the United States as well as other parts of the world (see **"Puerto Rican Song"**), and, as a result, figures from contemporary politics begin to make their appearance. The specificity with which Guillén indicts individuals like Eisenhower, Nixon, Orville Faubus, and a host of others is contrasted with the use of symbolic and anonymous names—"John Nobody," "John Blade," or simply "John"—to indicate the great mass of ordinary people with whom his sympathies lie. After the success of the Cuban Revolution, the interest in current affairs and Yankee political figures was complemented by the appearance of figures out of Cuba's revolutionary past and present (Antonio Maceo, José Martí, Fidel Castro, Che Guevara), with whom those less palatable individuals were contrasted. In *La paloma de vuelo popular,* the playful humor of Guillén's earliest works turned to irony and a wry sarcasm. In the *Elegías,* on the other hand, a sense of loss was added to the sense of outrage. These were in the main laments on the death of friends and victims or—as in **"My Last Name"**—for an entire history. In addition to the poet's usual stylistic vehicles, a variety of forms and meters were juxtaposed.

With the triumph of the Cuban Revolution, Guillén saw the fulfillment of his hopes and prophecies. He embraced the Revolution wholeheartedly, and its unfolding, along with the personalities who led it, immediately became a major theme of his poetry . . . . The poet was filled with a new serenity, while the expressiveness of his poems reached a peak of revolutionary fervor. All this is manifest in *Tengo* (1964), and is nowhere more evident than in the poem that gives that book its title. Its very simplicity—"I Have"—already reflects the new sense of pride in and comradeship with the Cuban people. The new spirit of exuberance is unmistakable as the poem unfolds and Guillén's collective protagonist, at first surprised and bewildered by the sudden turn of events, is moved to take stock of his new relationship to reality. He concludes that he has finally come into possession of his birthright as a man: "I have, let's see: / I have what was coming to me." (pp. 23-6)

Guillén's celebration of the Cuban Revolution is more implicit in his latest collection of poems, *El gran zoo* (1967). By then the Revolution was an irrevocable fact of history, and from the perspective of that particular reality Guillén's witty little book treats the reader to an ironic interpretation of the contemporary—and particularly the capitalist—world which is now considered part of Cuba's bleak pre-history. Guillén therefore takes his audience on a tour of a symbolic zoo and introduces a mosaic of characters, animal, mineral, and vegetable, which reveal to the reader-tourist a vision of the universe in microcosm. The author's invitation to follow him through this menagerie, is not, however, entirely disinterested: on the one hand, we are invited to tour a zoo and see the "animals" in it; on the other hand, and more significantly, we are given a peculiarly Cuban tour of that zoo. More important than seeing just exactly what is caged is the realization that it is Cuba, and Guillén the guide, who are free and *not* caged and who interpret and reflect upon what *is*.

This is a volume which, in structure and style, is unique in Guillén's work. At the same time that the symbolic device of a zoo serves to create an organic totality, the poet moves away from the modes and forms of his previous works in favor of a stylized and elemental language in which everything is reduced to personification and metaphor. The lines are generally very short, the style clipped; rhyme is infrequent and the meter is inconsistent and at times reminiscent of free verse. The intent is to mimic the impersonal tone of plaques and of official notices and announcements, although alternating notes of pride, concern, amusement, and distaste creep into the comments of our host. The total effect of each of the poems is largely dependent on their interrelationship with each other and, although the great majority could stand alone, there are some which have no particular *raison d'être* except in terms of the book.

Guillén's major preoccupations are still present, although they are more pointedly synthesized: his uncompromising allegiance to Cuba and his rejection of a world ruled by greed and imperialist aggression are present in **"The Caribbean," "The Usurers,"** and **"The Eagles"**; his concern for the total liberation of the Black man is clear in **"Lynch"** and **"KKK"**; implicit in **"Tonton-Macoute"** is the poet's revolutionary vision of a more humane world. (pp. 26-7)

His most recent poems, some of which have been published in various Cuban journals ... have been collected in a soon-to-be-published volume entitled *La rueda dentada* (*The Serrated Wheel*). It is clear from such poems as **"I Declare Myself an Impure Man," "Problems of Underdevelopment,"** and **"Propositions on the Death of Ana,"** that Guillén intends to continue writing, from a particularly Cuban perspective, a poetry which is explicit, deceptively simple in style, militant in its assumptions, one which reaches out to the Third World and looks forward to liberation, then peace. (p. 28)

> *Robert Márquez, in an introduction to* ¡Patria O Muerte! The Great Zoo and Other Poems *by Nicolás Guillén, edited and translated by Robert Márquez, Monthly Review Press, 1972, pp. 13-29.*

Lloyd King (essay date 1975)

[*In the following excerpt, King examines the social and political content of Guillén's poetry.*]

Nicolás Guillén is Cuba's most honoured poet. There is little doubt that most of his aspirations as a political activist and 'social protest' poet have been realized since the Cuban Revolution. Within Cuba itself his most popular collection of poems is his *Songs for Soldiers and Ballads for Tourists (Cantos para soldados y sones para turistas)* which he originally published in 1937. These poems are anticipatory blueprints of the relationship between the people's militia, formed since the Revolution as part of Cuba's embattled response to U.S. aggression, and the Cuban people. Written at a time when the soldier seemed rather to be the tool and guardian of U.S. interests and the power hunger of Fulgencio Batista, they yet called on the soldier to recognize his links with the ordinary folk who were the victims of exploitation and political gimcrackery, and the need to forge fraternity with the oppressed masses. The *sones para turistas* expressed the repugnance felt by many Cubans towards the insensitive American tourist, and sought to dramatize the resentment and bitterness towards him as an insane but all too visible symbol of the rigorous and painful grip on Cuba's monoculture economy by American imperialist-capitalist interests.

As is well known, the Cuban Revolutionary leadership ran out the tourists and the capitalists and aligned itself with the Cuban Communist Party, of which Guillén had been a member since the thirties. The Revolution also acted swiftly to eliminate a feature of Cuban life against which Guillén had campaigned both in verse and prose, namely racial discrimination; it desegregated the schools and the beaches and provided equal educational opportunity for all. Guillén has expressed his recognition of this reality in a poem **"Tengo" ("All is mine")** .... (p. 30)

When Guillén wrote **"Tengo"** in the post-revolutionary period, it must have seemed to him that he and other militant Cubans—artists, trade unionists, ordinary

Langston Hughes, Mihail Kolstov, Ernest Hemingway, and Guillén, 1937.

folk—had reached the end of a long process of struggle and desperate affirmation during a dark night of dictatorship and violence, to bring in the dawn of a socialist state in the Americas. For Guillén it was a process which had always had to do with the achievement of an integrated national personality, based on a discovery of the common Cubanness of whites and blacks in Cuban society. But equally Guillén realized that this objective could not possibly take shape until external capitalist interests were tamed along with their capacity for disruptive activity. Thus the two constants of his verse were related to internal racial integration and socialist militancy. His verse therefore came to be prophetic of some of the main objectives of the Cuban Revolution itself. (p. 31)

[In 1930], Nicolás Guillén published eight 'negrista' poems in the newspaper *Diario de la Marina* with the general title *Son Motifs (Motivos de son)* and in 1931 included them again with others in book form, with the title *Sóngoro Cosongo.* Guillén was immediately recognized as a writer who had his finger on the pulse of folk sensibility.... Guillén seemed instinctively to realize the opportunity to blend the scribal and oral traditions and derived the rhythms of his verse from a popular musical form, the 'son', which had been born of the contact between African rhythms and the creole environment, a form which had long been frowned on by polite Cuban society. In one long magical moment Guillén came to prefigure some of the obsessions of future Caribbean writing. (pp. 35-6)

The poems of *Son Motifs* explored a variety of folk urban situations. Two of the poems **"Ay negra, si tu supiera"**, ("Aye, black lover, if you only knew") and **"Búscate plata"** ("Go and look for bread") deal with women abandoning their lovers because they have no money, a situation related to the effects of the Depression. Two others **"Ayer me dijeron negro"** ("Yesterday I was called nigger") and **"Mulata"** refer to the antagonism between mulatto and black. In **"Yesterday I was called nigger"**, Guillén strikes what was to be a recurring note of his verse suggesting to some person who passed for white that he has African/black blood:

> Tan blanco como te bé,
> y tu abuela· sé quién é.
> Sácala de la cocina,
> Sácala de la cocina,
> Mamá Iné.
>
> (As white as you look
> I know your grandma (the cook)

Bring her out of the kitchen
Bring her out of the kitchen
Mamma Inés.)

This Caribbean picong uses the sharp-edged social barb to puncture the pride along the colour and class line. The most disturbingly ironic of the poems is **"Negro Bembón"** (**"Thick-lipped Nigger"**). The speaker, Caridad, is presented telling her Negro boyfriend with thick lips not to allow himself to be wounded by the mocking intent of those who call him 'negro bembón', and seeking to turn the epithet into a term of endearment. Hers is in a certain sense a Négritude position, for she urges the man to assume freely a term which the society uses in a 'denigratory' manner:

Por qué te pones tan bravo
cuando te dicen negro bembón
se tienes la boca santa
negro bembón.

(Why do you get so vexed
When people call you big-lipped nigger
Since your mouth is very attractive
You thick-lipped nigger, you?)

However the poem cannot sustain a Négritude interpretation because in the last two lines we learn that the 'negro bembón' is really living off his mistress's earnings, whatever her line of work may be.

When he widened the collection of poems in *Sóngoro Cosongo,* it was noticeable that many of the poems dealt with the self-contained violence of the low-life of Havana. **"Velorio de Papá Montero"**, (**"Wake for Papa Montero"**) was inspired by a popular 'son' of the time, and evokes with a mix of irony and sadness the death in a drunken brawl of a folk character. **"Chévere"** (sweetman) is a short dense image of concentrated violence, orchestrating the movement of a man's rage till he slices his unfaithful woman to death. (pp. 36-7)

Guillén's ghetto images were not calculated to win the approval of coloureds who were seeking to project an image of respectability, and in an interview with Antonio Fernández de Castro in the newspaper *La semana,* we find him denouncing those who were unwilling to acknowledge the 'son' as a part of their culture. These attitudes of shame and self-contempt were particularly striking, Guillén noted, since the 'son' was popular in Paris and even in Cuba was now accepted in the most exclusive society, and yet many Negroes demonstrated public hostility to this popular art form because it was lower-class and 'incompatible with their spiritual delicacy and their grade of culture'. (pp. 37-8)

One of the most hostile critics of the influence of Afrocuban folk forms on the wider Cuban sensibility was Ràmon Vasconcelos, a Cuban journalist resident in Paris. A self-styled watchdog of Cuban culture, he wrote from Paris to discourage Guillén from the idea that the Cuban 'son' could be used and become popular in the way that the American 'blues' had been, since it was not at all suitable for social commentary or serious pur-

poses . . . . Vasconcelos's attitude was so outrageous that one would have expected a stinging reply, but Guillén's answer was quite mild. He explained that his use of the 'son' was simply in line with the world-wide interest in popular forms, and that the 'son' poems were not in the majority in *Sóngoro Cosongo.* He even went on to lament that it was a pity that to use the speech rhythms of the folk seemed to require heroism.

This moderate reply to Vasconcelos exposes the weakness in Guillén's mulatto position. One senses that he has always been a little afraid of being called a black racist. Thus in an interview with Keith Ellis, published in the *Jamaica Journal* in 1973, Guillén when asked about his attitude to Négritude, at first dismissed it contemptuously, then went on to admit that the assertion of blackness and of neo-African values was certainly necessary in a colonial situation. But he sees it as above all 'one of the manifestations of the class struggle'. In other words, he felt that 'black assertiveness' in post-revolutionary Cuba was wrong, but even before this he always rejected the use of the term 'Afrocuban'. One need not be a black racist in order to question Guillén's attitude. (pp. 38-9)

It is not a little amazing that Guillén was never tempted to adopt a Négritude position, particularly as even sympathetic white Cuban critics were not persuaded by his claim that Cuba's was mulatto. (p. 39)

In *Sóngoro Cosongo,* Guillén had captured something of the downbeat of ghetto life, a sense of its cynicism and violence, the rhythms of its speech. His next collection of poems, *West Indies Ltd.* (1934) shows that his political awareness had sharpened, for these were the years of the Depression and of the inept and brutal dictatorship of General Machado who finally fell from power in 1933. Behind him, there was already the example of another mulatto poet, Regino Pedroso, who had been converted to Marxism and the Communist Party in the twenties. In one of his better known poems, "Hermano Negro" ("Brother Black"), Pedroso called upon his black brothers to acquire a right consciousness and to recognize that race prejudice was secondary to economic exploitation. They ought to reconsider their role as entertainers for the western world and understand that they were a part of the exploited proletariat . . . . Once Guillén got the message, his folk characters assume the elemental posture of exploited men. The poet's own posture is that of a member of the revolutionary vanguard, sharpening the consciousness of the masses. The movement in tone and perspective anticipates the classical transferral of aggression which Fanon analysed in *The Wretched of the Earth,* whereby that violence which the sub-culture practised against itself, as exemplified in poems such as **"Chévere"** and **"Velorio de Papá Montero"**, must now be directed outwards against the colonialist exploiter and the bourgeoisie. Such poems as **"Caminando"** and **"Sabás"** reflect this new mood and show Guillén undertaking the task of political education. In **"Sabás"**, the poet calls upon Sabás, servile because reduced to penury in the Depression days, to recognize his moral and economic rights and to understand that when the society will not allow him the dignity to survive as a human being, he must be prepared to claim his rights violently if necessary. The irony is both sharp and bitter:

> Porqué Sabás la mano abierta?
> (Este Sabás es un negro bruto)
> Coge tu pan pero no lo pidas;
> Coge tu luz, coge tu esperanza cierta
> como a un caballo por las bridas.
>
> Why Sabás do you hold out your hand?
> (This Sabás is really a foolish nigger)
> Take your bread, don't beg for it
> Take hold of your senses, take firm hold of your
>   hopes
> As of a horse under sure command.

In 1937, Guillén published his *Cantos para soldados y sones para turistas,* and although his earlier collection *West Indies Ltd.* (1934) and later *El son entero* (1943) have a better selection of poems, they were not greeted with as good a press as the *Songs for soldiers.* Guillén's Party colleague Juan Marinello... hailed the *Songs for soldiers* as a definitive triumph of the American melting pot. What strikes one about this claim in relation to the poems is the fact that Guillén here abandoned the Afrocuban stance which is so easily picked up in the other collections. One must therefore conjecture that there was possibly some pressure on the poet to move away from his 'negrista' image, perhaps to come closer to Marti's dictum that 'Cuban was more than black, more than white'. Perhaps also a bland poem like **"Balada de los dos abuelos"**(**"Ballad of the two grandfathers"**) in which slave-owning conquistador grandfather and enslaved African grandfather are reconciled in the poet's dream, has been played up by some critics for the same kind of reason. There was a lot of truth in Cintio Vitier's judgment on Guillén that 'the new theme is not just a fashion, a subject for literature, but the living heart of his creative activity'. But because he has always been sensitive to the charge of black racism and to the ideological posture of the Party in Cuba, he has also had to react to the association of his name with Négritude.

This is confirmed by a poem **"Brindis"** (**"Cheers!"**) which he wrote in 1952 but which has never appeared in book form till the recent publication of his *Obra poética.* "Brindis" is addressed to the famous black American singer Josephine Baker who in her day was the toast of Paris and who met with racial discrimination on returning to the United States. In disgust and anger, the poet tells la Baker that she might well have been lynched and he introduces a mood of violence which again anticipates one response of black militants which eventually came to pass .... In a few lines, Guillén evokes the long hot summer, the incendiary fury which would take place in ghettos like Watts years later. What is equally interesting, however, is that Josephine Baker had also visited Cuba, and there had also been refused a hotel room by a racist management. But the Cuban incident had drawn from Guillén an article written in sadness rather than in anger. It can be argued, and quite rightly, that Cuba did not have a Ku Klux Klan and that white Cuban racism was milder; but it is also clear that it was felt to be 'politic' to focus on the more extreme brutalities which occurred in the United States. The poet could both deliver a blow against racism and associate it with imperialistic capitalism.

One way in which Guillén tried to hit at the Cuban bourgeoisie was by insisting that most of its members had some concealed African ancestry, for example in the poem **"Canción del bongó"** (**"Bongo song"**):

> Y hay titulos de Castilla
> con parientes en Bondó.
>
> (There are those with patents of nobility from Castille. Who yet have relatives in Bondó.)

Guillén in such poems was striking an embarrassing note for whereas in Latin countries those who can pass for white are considered white, in the United States a drop of African blood makes a man black. The Cuban bourgeoisie who identified their interests so closely with American capitalists and American standards would therefore not particularly appreciate what the poet was taking pains to advertise.

In 1943, Guillén published *El son entero* with a number of negrista poems, **"Sudor y látigo"** (**"Sweat and the whip"**), **"Ebano real"** (**"Royal ebony"**), **"Son número 6"** (**"Son No. 6"**), **"Acana"**, and even a rather embarrassing poem which calls upon Shango and Ochun to guard Stalin whom 'free men accompany singing, "Una canción a Stalin"'. These poems do not add anything new to his output although they show once again how strongly influenced by the oral tradition Guillén was. A much more interesting later poem is **"El apellido"** (**"The surname"**) in which Guillén again worries about the way in which the African connection is vulnerable to the Hispanic mould, even in such things as names.... Finally one must mention a not-too-good poem **"Qué color"** which was provoked by a comment of the Russian poet Yevtushenko on the death of Martin Luther King that his soul was white as snow. Guillén insists rather that Luther King's soul was as black as coal, 'negro como el carbón'. **"Qué color"** shows the way in which Guillén and the Cuban Revolution are solid supporters of men who struggle against oppression and imperialism everywhere. Amílcar Cabral and Angela Davis are very popular in Cuba. Nevertheless, Guillén would never write of a *Cuban* that his soul was black as coal, on the basis that the Revolution has abolished the emotive connotations of colour.

The Marxist attitude to colour, which is Guillén's own attitude, is that it is irrelevant in a socialist state. It counts upon Revolutionary policy of equal opportunity to reverse a variety of instinctive attitudes about race, bred during more than one hundred and fifty years of Cuban history in the context of the white racist attitudes of western civilization. At the primary level of what we accept as the basic human needs and rights, the right to a balanced diet, educational development, etc. no one can disagree with the Cuban perspective. However, at a second level of reference, that of cultural formation and a variety of subtle attitudes, this writer, whose experience is that of the English-speaking Caribbean (where black men have attained the highest offices) and who has seen how readily a Euro-oriented environment can twist and confuse men of African ancestry, must express some reservations about the Cuban Revolution's desire to straighten out the kinks and achieve a determined uniformity in Cuban cultural life. (pp. 40-4)

> *Lloyd King, "Nicolás Guillén and Afrocubanismo," in* A Celebration of Black and African Writing, *edited by Bruce King and Kolawole Ogungbesan, Ahmadu Bello University Press, 1975, pp. 30-45.*

Constance Sparrow de García Barrio (essay date 1977)

[*In the following excerpt, Sparrow de García Barrio examines Guillén's portrayals of black men as rejections of the prototypes of the early twentieth century and as figures new to Spanish-American literature.*]

Prior to the beginning of the twentieth century, the image of blacks in Spanish-American literature had been limited to a few prototypes. This repertoire included the black as a physical dynamo, the meek and loyal slave, the sexually stirring mulatto woman, and the brave Afro-Spanish-American soldier fighting in the service of colonial authorities. Blacks themselves, during the colonial period, were rarely in a position to contribute to the making of their own literary image. They found themselves hindered by the lack of means to become literate since their learning to read and write was discouraged. If they managed to gain these skills, societal and governmental restrictions compelled them to write on themes alien to their own situation. (p. 105)

About 1900, a Negro vogue began in Europe. It seemed to provide an external stimulus for the study of blacks in Latin America, and their incorporation in literary works. In the late 1920s and early 1930s, Cuban writers, especially poets, avidly sketched black protagonists, but hardly ventured beyond the caricatures and customs presented in colonial literature. Moreover, for most of these writers, the inclusion of black characters represented no more than a parenthesis in their careers.

The Cuban mulatto poet Nicolás Guillén . . . proves an exception. He is the only major practitioner of Negroid poetry in whom the figure of the black man outlives the vogue of the first third of this century. Furthermore, during his career the poet has created black figures new to Spanish-American literature. These creations dynamically express the intense social concern and heightened political consciousness of the author. (pp. 105-06)

In 1930 Nicolás Guillén published his first collection of Negroid poems, *Motivos de son.* In it, he offers a potpourri of dark island types. While highly chromatic,

this presentation of the lower strata of Cuban blacks is quite traditional in its predominant eight-syllable line, and in its reproduction of the peculiarities of the Spanish spoken by these islanders as well:

Por qué te pone tan bravo,	Why do you get so mad,
cuando te dicen negro bem-	when they call you "Big-Lips,"
bón,	
si tiene la boca santa,	because your mouth is sweet
negro bembón?	Big-Lips?
Bembón así como ere	Big Lips just as you are
tiene de to	you have everything
Caridad te mantiene,	Caridad supports you
te lo da to.	you have everything.

As significant as the dropping of the final *s* of *pones, tienes,* and *eres,* and the reduction of *todo* to *to* is the theme of identity. The *bembón,* or big-lipped Black, objects to the epithet in spite of its accuracy. The poet contends that the bembón's mouth is large but sweet, and he has no grounds for complaint since he is being supported by his sweetheart Caridad. In another poem, Guillén reproves a mulatto woman who has laughed at his broad nose and called it a *nudo de corbata,* knot of a necktie. He replies that he would prefer his black gal to her any time.

In his next collection, *Sóngoro Cosongo* (1931), Guillén seems to divide his efforts between traditional black characters, and the shaping of new types. **"Rumba"** and **"Secuestro de la mujer de Antonio"** both capture the sexual implications of the rumba danced by a mulata. The knife-wielding *chévere,* prefigured in the *negro curro* of colonial literature, is the subject of **"Velorio de papá montero."** The poem **"Chévere"** provides a briefer statement on the same type. Although *Sóngoro Cosongo* and *Motivos de son* share traditional elements, the former lacks the apparent lightheartedness of the latter. This new sobriety is conveyed in the elimination of dialect, in an ironic address to the question of racial identity, and in a concern over the exploitation of Cuba by the United States. One of the most striking poems in *Sóngoro Cosongo* is **"Caña."** Its terse lines denounce American economic control, its effect on the land where sugar cane is grown, and the anonymous black who cultivates it.

Guillén examines the United States from another vantage point in **"Small Ode to a Cuban Boxer."** He warns the boxer, who is about to travel to New York, that, "The North is wild and crude." The boxer's English is precarious, and his Spanish not much less so, but the poet tellingly suggests that the fighter's fists are what he will need to "speak black Truth." (pp. 106-07)

Three years later, in *West Indies Ltd.* (1934), the poet's attitude has become much more aggressive. Allusions to the clenched fist, later to be the symbol of the Black Power Movement, fill this collection. He asks why the fists of the dock workers haven't been raised in a single decisive gesture:

> Oh strong fist, elemental and hard!
> Who restrains your open gesture?

In **"Ballad of Simón Caraballo,"** a black beggar sings his sorrows, but the lines that spotlight his hands reveal anger and potential violence:

> I
> black Simon Caraballo,
> sleep on a door step now;
> a brick is my pillow
> my bed is on the ground.
> . . . . .
> . . . . .
> I don't know what to do with my arms
> but I'll find something to do
> I,
> black Simon Caraballo,
> have my fists closed,
> have my fists closed,
> and I need to eat!

In describing another black, Sabás, who begs from door to door, the poet poses the question three times: "Why, Sabás, the open hand?" He urges Sabás to demand what he needs, and discard his open-handed attitude . . . . (pp. 107-08)

Guillén chose to invest another poor black character with his most urgent message in 1937, when *Songs for Soldiers and Tunes for Tourists* was published. This

Drawing of Guillén by Samuel Feijóo.

figure is distinctive in his immunity to the venality associated with the tourist trade. A musician, he warns the tourists that his song, unlike that of many of his countrymen, will not soothe them like the rum they drink because José Ramón Cantaliso—perhaps the artist's self-portrait—is a singer-of-truths . . . . (p. 108)

The model of the singer-of-truth, whose voice has grown more strident, reappears in **"Son venezolano,"** from *El son entero* (1947). This time he bears the name Juan Bimba, and makes a frontal attack on foreign exploitation of Cuban and Venezuelan products:

> I sing in Cuba and Venezuela,
> a song that comes out of me.
> What bitter oil,
> caramba,
> oh, how bitter this oil,
> caramba,
> that tastes like Cuban sugar!

In *El son entero,* Guillén pours the seething anger of the beggars into a new vessel, that of the rebellious slave. The enslaved black, who has been recovering from a beating, rises to slay his master in **"Sweat and Whip":**

> Then the silent sky,
> and under the sky, the slave
> stained in the blood of the master.

Violent self-assertion would inform some of Guillén's later black figures too. This position is summarized in **"Sports,"** a poem from *La paloma de vuelo popular* (1958). The poem contains a catalogue of black prize fighters from both Americas,

> But above all, I think
> of the Patent-Leather Kid, the great king without
>   a crown
> and of Chocolate, the great crowned king,
> and of Black Bill, with his rubber nerves.

Guillén implies that their victories as individuals are enhanced by the pride they inspire in other blacks. Repeated mention of the Cuban chess grand-master José Raul Capablanca seems to countervail the importance given to physical stamina. Intellectual vigor is also necessary.

During this period, racism in the United States, with its concomitants of segregation in schools and lynching, claimed Guillén's attention. In **"Little Rock"** and **"Elegy to Emmett Till,"** the poet gives voice to his indignation. **"Elegy to Emmett Till"** was written for a fourteen-year-old black who was lynched in Greenwood, Mississippi, in 1955. It minutely describes a "danse macabre" over the mutilated body of the boy . . . . (p. 109)

In 1959, the revolution of Fidel Castro triumphed. One of its goals, the eradication of racial discrimination, was accomplished through the immediate integration of schools and all public facilities. Guillén jubilantly reflects on the changes wrought by the revolution in *Tengo,* written in 1964:

I have, let's see
that being a black man
no one can stop me
at the door of a bar or of a dance hall
Nor in the vestibule of a hotel
scream at me that there's no vacancy.

(p. 110)

Still directing his attention towards the United States, Guillén included a poem in praise of the will and militancy of Angela Davis. Although it appears in *La rueda dentada* (1972), it depicts the heroine as being made of the same elemental stuff that gave strength to the **"New Woman"** of 1931 . . . . [**"Qué color,"** a] poem dedicated to Martin Luther King also appears in this volume. It comes as a reply to the Russian poet Evtushenko, who described King as a black man with " . . . a most pure soul like white snow." Guillén, in his violent rejection of this image, ends his poem by saying that King's soul was "black like coal." Guillén was understandably provoked by the use of the words "white snow" to describe a black man who had lived many of the ideals that Guillén saw as essential. For more than forty years, Nicolás Guillén has forcefully treated blacks in his poetry. During that time, one can observe a transition from the presentation of the usual black figures, speaking in a typically distorted manner, poured into the traditional octosyllabic lines, to the naissance of startling new blacks, whose profiles are often etched in free verse.

Guillén seems to begin by making plastic his vision of ideal men and women in **"Arrival"** and **"New Woman."** Once the ideal has been described, the poet proceeds to grapple with raw reality. Thus emerge the black beggars. Guillén would make of his poems a *maraca* or *güire,* a percussion instrument whose beat would awaken the beggars to a sense of self-worth and the need to fight. He tells them to demand a share of society's goods rather than beg for them. The tone of this poetry grows increasingly tense and combative, and may be summed up in the clenched fist, an image which appears repeatedly.

A third new black figure is the singer-of-truth, José Ramón Cantaliso. Poverty has made him hypersensitive to the economic ills that the tourist trade has brought to Cuba. His song stresses the suffering of poor Cubans, and while the tune does not please the tourist's ear, it cannot be changed by their dollars. Later, the song of Juan Bimba, a character in every way similar to José Ramón Cantaliso, denounces parasitic foreign business interests in the Caribbean.

In much of Guillén's later poetry, there seems to be a conformity between the black figures he has drawn earlier and the concrete men and women whom he makes the subject of his poems. The premium which Guillén places on physical strength and an indomitable spirit is incarnated in Kid Charol, Kid Chocolate, Johnson, and Black Bill, all of whom are boxers. These traits are also seen in Jesús Menéndez, who sought

power for the Cuban sugar workers through organization. His mission was parallel to that of Cantaliso, who aimed to jar tourists and islanders out of the old pattern with his song. Angela Davis and Martin Luther King also provide living examples of the militancy and purpose that Guillén has placed in some of his fictional figures.

In assessing Guillén's contribution to Spanish American literature, Cuba's long colonial status must be kept in mind. In 1898, the island was freed from Spanish domination only to immediately become a functional protectorate of the United States. Frantz Fanon, in discussing the shift from colonial mentality to national consciousness [in *The Wretched of the Earth*], states that the change is usually accompanied by a break with past artistic expression. (pp. 111-12)

Although Guillén has forged new types, he has written a variety of other poems of ethnic content as well. On occasion, he has delved into Afro-Spanish folklore and religion. He also wrote a lullaby for a black baby, conspicuous because of its late date of publication, 1958. The question of racial identity is handled in various guises throughout his career. Guillén never loses historical perspective, as **"Noche de negros junto a la catedral"** (1966) reveals. His creation of new figures and the cultivation of other Afro-Spanish themes measure the depth of his commitment. (p. 112)

> *Constance Sparrow de García Barrio, "The Image of the Black Man in the Poetry of Nicolas Guillén," in* Blacks in Hispanic Literature: Critical Essays, *edited by Miriam DeCosta, Kennikat Press, 1977, pp. 105-13.*

Richard L. Jackson (essay date 1979)

[*In the following excerpt from his 1979 study* Black Writers in Latin America, *Jackson explores the "blackening process" Guillén underwent in his poetry.*]

[Nicolás Guillén] has lived long enough . . . to become the premier black poet writing in Spanish. Guillén's earlier poetry was definitely non-black and largely inconsequential, of interest to contemporary readers only as illustrations of his early expertise and technical domination of traditional Spanish verse forms, particularly those in vogue during and just after the literary reign of Rubén Darío, and as contrast they illustrate, as well, how far he has come in the blackening process he underwent from *Cerebro y corazón* (1922) to *Motivos de son* (1930). Before this metamorphosis, Guillén's literary output in the twenties, with only a very few exceptions, followed European models. Literary historians who want to "de-blacken" him or turn him into a nonblack poet can find ample evidence in these adolescent poems to support their view which, as best expressed by Luis Iñiguez Madrigal, is that Nicolás Guillén is not—nor has he ever been—a black poet in language, style, or theme. Madrigal has another view, namely, that Nicolás Guillén is not even a predominantly social poet, but one who writes primarily on "other" themes. Madrigal can find some evidence in these early poems to support both his views, as Guillén's pre-*Motivos de son* work is dominated by such universal or colorless themes as love, death, nature, religion, and other abstract head and heart ("cerebro y corazón") subjects.

But a turning point came early in Guillén's literary career when he decided to focus his attention on the true black experience in the New World, starting with his native Cuba, where he saw the black as the one most affected by imperialist exploitation and other evils.... Guillén abandoned the white muse he had followed in his youth and infused his literature with a black sensibility which has permeated his work for more than forty years.... The appearance of his *Motivos de son* in 1930, an authentic literary happening, was upsetting, unsettling and controversial, partly because they broke momentarily with traditional Spanish verse expression and partly because they dealt with authentic black characters, but largely because they brought to literature a new and genuine black concern, perspective, and poetic voice, which even some blacks misunderstood.

The *Motivos de son* had a strong impact on black and white Cubans alike. White readers, after getting over the initial shock of seeing authentic blacks in literature, were pleased to see them appear because, on the surface, Guillén in *Motivos de son* seemed to highlight the comic and picturesque side of the black locked into an uneducated happy-go-lucky lower class image. Black readers were quick to react negatively against the *Motivos de son* largely for the same reason. They were not pleased to see the *negro bembón* given center stage in literature nor were they pleased to see what appeared to be the perpetuation of stereotyped images of the black. Both groups, however, soon came to realize that Guillén's *Motivos de son* went far deeper than racial insult and superficial entertainment.... It was soon recognized that the *Motivos de son* incorporated into formal poetic structure distinctive oral forms from the musical heritage of black people, but popular song and dance forms (the *son*) that were familiar to all Cubans. Black and white Cubans came to understand that Nicolás Guillén was using black talk and black rhythms to set escape motifs like wine, women, and song against a harsh background of unemployment, poverty, prejudice, and misery while making, in effect, a subtle plea for black pride and racial identity as well as for more awareness of social inequities, and of the growing presence of the United States in Cuba.

Although many critics prefer to hasten through this black period in the poet's development, moving on to what they think are his less racial stages, we cannot overestimate the importance of Guillén's work in the late twenties and early thirties. In these years Guillén laid the groundwork that gave his later work meaning and direction, rejecting the white aesthetic whether adhered to by whites, mulattoes, or blacks. It is also

during this period that he first declared the black to be as Cuban as anyone else. Guillén attacked in particular during this period the black's own propensity to abrogate his rights by forfeiting them to white Cubans who, though not always backed by law, were willing to take advantage. To Guillén the black's own black phobia, that is his own fear of being black and of identifying with his *son,* his *rumba,* and his *bongó,* was the first obstacle to overcome as he sought ways to restore value to a people long denied it. Rejection of the white aesthetic and a plea for black recognition are really the keys, paradoxically, to his theory of *mulatez,* of a mulatto Cuba. In essence this theory represents the elevation of the black to the level already occupied by whites. Guillén's desire to write Cuban poetry, and not black poetry, is really the culmination of that elevation since Cuban poetry after Guillén can never again mean solely white or European poetry. Moreover, Guillén's subsequent rejection of the term Afro-Cuban paradoxically is the most pro-black statement he could make. To him the term "Cuban" already includes the "Afro," for the term has come of age and been elevated to the highest degree. Without the black, in other words, there would be no theory of *mulatez;* instead, there would only be white poetry in Cuba. Guillén, then, forces the black man into social recognition, and the white Cuban's acceptance of that theory is in effect a compromise.

Guillén's blackening process, his metamorphosis from a white escapist poet to a black poet, represents a rejection of the white aesthetic in general. More specifically, though, his defiant turnabout can be seen as a black reaction to a poetic Negrism, which was a local movement staffed by white intellectuals largely in the Caribbean whose interest in things black in the late twenties and early thirties coincided with the black as *nouvelle vogue* in Europe and America. Rather than associate Guillén with poetic Negrism, we should see his dramatic conversion to blackness in the late twenties and early thirties as a reaction against this white literary fad that was sweeping the world, one Guillén himself defined as

> circumstantial tourism which never penetrated deeply into the human tragedy of race, being more like excursions organized for photographing coconut trees, drums and naked Negroes, whilst there existed the seething drama of the flesh and blood Negro bearing the scars of whiplashes, a Negro now fused with the whites to produce an indelible mulatto imprint on the Cuban social scene.

(pp. 80-3)

By drawing directly from the black experience and by giving black reaction to that experience in the *Motivos de son,* Guillén pits the black as speaker from his own environment against the superficial interest in blacks, thus revealing a closeness to the subject, scene, or emotion depicted in each *poema-son* not found in poetic Negrism. It is this closeness, together with Guillén's understanding of his subject, that gives the *Motivos de son* their startling authenticity and Nicolás Guillén the title of authentic black poet.

Guillén lost little time in reaffirming that his conversion to blackness was not a passing fancy. One year later, in *Sóngoro cosongo* (1931), his second volume of black verse, he again set himself apart from the *negrista* craze.... The poems in this volume almost without exception continue to deal with the black experience in Cuba. Just as the semblance of self-mockery and black insult had helped gain respectability among the white *literati* for the *Motivos de son,* so too does his use of the term mulatto (which gives the white a share in blackness) for his black verse, help protect *Sóngoro cosongo* against white backlash.

If anything, the black racial nature of Guillén's poetry intensifies in *Sóngoro cosongo.* The language changes a bit, becoming less colloquial, and the form moves closer to recognizable Spanish verse. The emphasis, though, is the same: black pride, the black experience, and black types continue to dominate his poetry.... But unlike the *Motivos de son* where the black is largely the speaker and singer, in *Sóngoro cosongo* the black, for the most part, is spoken about. The *Motivos de son,* in other words, is closer to black speech and black song (*son*) in poetic form, while *Sóngoro cosongo* is closer in several poems to the Spanish *romance* or ballad form, but with *son* elements. *Sóngoro cosongo* represents growth as Guillén includes variations on the *son* form while enlarging the black world he is introducing by bringing in black folklore, superstitions, even negative types. The black world of the time he represents was not always a pleasant one, but his point is clear: the black has arrived and literature must recognize this fact.

Perhaps the best illustration of this point can be seen in **"Llegada"** ("The Arrival").... In this lead-off statement which ostensibly describes the arrival of the black as slave to the Island, Guillén repeatedly writes as refrain "¡Aquí estamos!" ("Here we are!") as the poem develops into yet another expression of black racial affirmation. **"Pequeña oda a un negro boxeador cubano,"** which Guillén first published in 1929, one year before the *Motivos de son,* has the same turning-point impact. This poem, like **"Mujer nueva"** whose black woman figure "trae la palabra inédita" ("brings new knowledge"), is a strong call for racial pride and black identity. To be sure, **"Pequeña oda a un negro boxeador cubano"** can be read on several levels: (1) as a poem about a black boxer; (2) as a poem where the black boxer acts as symbol for all blacks in struggle; and (3) as a poem about a struggle between nations, more specifically, about impending conflict between Cuba and the United States. But it is the final verse of that poem, where the poet exhorts the black to "hablar en negro de verdad" ("speak in real black talk")—a phrase that certainly refers to more than just black dialect—that underscores the authentic blackening of the poet in this early period. From the black fist of the boxer in **"Pequeña oda a un negro boxeador cubano"** to the black fist of the slave rower in **"Llegada,"** who has now exchanged his oar for a knife..., there is really very little distance. These three poems, **"Pequeña oda a un negro boxeador cubano," "Llegada,"** and **"Mujer nueva,"**

and others in *Sóngoro cosongo* are very black indeed even though they do not contain any of the phonetic speech characteristic of his *Motivos de son.*

In 1934 Guillén published **West Indies Ltd.,** a volume widely hailed as his first volume of social (as opposed to racial) protest poetry. But it is in this volume in which Guillén widens his perspective or attack that he, at the same time, deepens the blackening process begun in the late twenties.... It is evident that Nicolás Guillén focuses as well on the dispossessed white, "Dos niños: uno negro, otro blanco...ramos de un mismo árbol de miseria" ("Two children: one black, one white...two branches from the same tree of misery"), to illustrate yet another victim, like the black, of United States imperialism in the Antilles, but it would be a mistake to accept that Guillén's concern for the black in this volume is only a symbolic one. The poet continues to depict specific black figures and black folklore, and he also continues his program of instilling black pride in those blacks like Sabás—in a poem of the same name—who continue to go about with their hands out begging rather than shaking the strong black fist.... Guillén perhaps more insistently than in his two previous volumes of black verse makes himself the focal character in many of the poems as time and again he emphasizes his own black identity. In **"Palabras en el trópico,"** the poet speaks of his "dark body," his "curly hair." In **"Adivinanzas"** "the black" becomes "I." Either he or other blacks like "I, Simón Caraballo the black" in **"Balada de Simón Caraballo"** or "The blacks, working" in **"Guadalupe W.I."** are the stars. Most importantly in **"West Indies Ltd.,"**... it is clear that Guillén's concerns have moved beyond Cuba, but it is equally clear that the poet of black pride admonishing Sabás is the same poetic voice speaking at times in the sarcastic tone of an intelligent observer and at other times through the *son* sung at intervals throughout the poem by Juan el Barbero. This is a point the poet does not want the reader to miss, as he closes this poem with the words, "This was written by Nicolás Guillén, *antillano,* in the year nineteen hundred and thirty-four."

Despite Guillén's ever-widening circle of concerns that he has pursued throughout his long career, he has never left the black man behind or out of his poetry. In one of the few published studies of its kind, Constance Sparrow de García Barrio recently traced Guillén's creation of new black characters through his later poetry that includes poems, for example, on such contemporary black figures as Martin Luther King and Angela Davis [see essay dated 1977]. In *Tengo* (1964), Guillén, significantly, speaks specifically as a black man in praise of Castro's Cuba where some allege, including Guillén himself, racial identity is no longer important. Throughout his career it has been his insistence on elevating the black that has given his poetry the extra dimension and excitement that makes him a "classic poet" who "has a clear understanding of his art and an absolute control of his technique, as well as something to say." It is this "something to say" that distinguishes his *Motivos de son* and his later poetry from his earlier nonblack work and that sets his verse off from the *negrista* poetry of his white contemporaries. It is also this "something to say" that had a profound effect on Fernando Ortiz, the white Cuban specialist on things black, whose racist research had provided source material and orientation to white *negrista* poets *prior* to Guillén's appearance and domination of the Cuban literary scene in the late twenties and early thirties.

Guillén not only turned himself and *negrista* poetry around but his theory of *mulatez* seems to have been instrumental in turning Ortiz away from a rather clinical examination of the black largely as isolated criminal and slave and more toward the integration of blacks and whites in Cuba, the essence of Ortiz's well-known concept of *cubanidad,* which he developed in the forties.... Before Guillén's conversion to and insistence on blackness in Cuba, Ortiz was known in part for his *Glosario de Afronegrismos* (1923), a collection of African words and words that sound African that, because of their rhythmic quality, proved useful to the *negrista* poets. He was known also for what can be called his "unholy trinity," a series of works on "el hampa afro-cubano": *Los negros brujos* (1906), *Los negros esclavos* (1916), and "Los negros curros," a lecture he gave in 1911 whose title he had planned to give to a third volume in the trilogy.... Before Guillén, in short, Ortiz's emphasis was on the Cuban black, not on the black Cuban or the mulatto Cuban, and on the "Afro" part of the term "Afro-Cuban"—an isolated, negative part at best.

Guillén's decision, then, during the late twenties and early thirties to write as a black about blacks and to blacks, and to whites and mulattoes, too, was an influential one that represented a new departure for himself and for his contemporaries. But what was the immediate impulse that brought him to that new commitment? Literary historians and Nicolás Guillén, too, usually point to a moment in 1930 when the words and rhythm of *negro bembón* came to the poet in a dreamlike trance after which the **Motivos de son** were written, dashed off, as it were, in white hot heat. But what put him in that trance in the first place?... We know that his turning point was inspired in part by his own personal experiences of racism, by his awareness of worsening economic conditions for blacks in Cuba, and by the control of the black literary and cultural image that was being taken over by white intellectuals like Fernando Ortiz and the *negrista* poets. We know also that Guillén had many local black models to emulate, including his father.... But most of all, I believe, the black model or example set by Langston Hughes provided one of the most immediate sparks.

Langston Hughes, the dean of black poets in the United States, was already famous when he made his second trip to Cuba in February 1930. Guillén met Hughes on this trip, showed him around, and as a journalist published an interview he had with him that he called **"Conversation with Langston Hughes."**... For a black writer who had already begun to see that the black

problem was really a white problem, the black pride and racial flavor of Langston Hughes' verse and manner had to have an impact on any black, certainly on one who writes. I think what moved Guillén deeper into his blackening process was Langston Hughes' physical or somatic appearance. In Guillén's words, Hughes, "looked just like a little Cuban mulatto. One of those dandies who spends all his time organizing little family parties for two dollars a ticket." This description, of course, is negative, but Guillén's appraisal of "this great Black poet," "one of the souls most interested in the black race," is overwhelmingly positive. The impact for Guillén, I believe, comes with the realization that Hughes, a mulatto like himself, could genuinely identify with blacks with a dedication so intense that his only concern "is to study people, to translate their experience into poetry, to make it known and loved." When Guillén says that Langston Hughes is unique, we have to understand this statement to mean both Hughes' total concern "with everything related to blacks" and the fact that this concern can come from a mulatto. (pp. 83-8)

It is not surprising, then, that Guillén's conversion to blackness becomes complete shortly after Hughes' departure from the Island.... Nor is it surprising to see

Photo of Guillén and Langston Hughes taken by Carl Van Vechten.

the *Ltd.* of Hughes' *Scottsboro Ltd.* (1932) reappear in Guillén's title **West Indies Ltd.** (1934), or to see Guillén try the *son*-form, which sometimes has a blues effect, considering Hughes' earlier success with blues and jazz forms in poetry. One also can see the striking similarity between Guillén's black credo in the prologue to his *Sóngoro cosongo* (1932), especially the part where Guillén says that it does not matter if people are not pleased with what he is doing, and Hughes' own well-known declaration of artistic and racial commitment published five years earlier. He wrote in that piece, "If white people are pleased we are glad. If they are not it doesn't matter . . . If colored people are pleased we are glad. If they are not their displeasure doesn't matter either." Were it not for such credos firmly rooted in black ethnic identity, it is possible that the later revolutionary vision these two poets developed might not have been so intense. (pp. 89-90)

I see a compatibility between Guillén poet of negritude and Guillén poet of revolutionary Cuba. Guillén need not have continued with the black talk of the *Motivos de son* to be considered a poet of negritude . . . . Nor was it necessary for him to abandon the black man to be considered a universal poet. Although Guillén now rejects the term negritude that he insists on seeing in its strictest sense, there can be little doubt that he was just as much a forerunner of the term in its strictest racial sense as he is now a leading exponent of what I have called elsewhere the negritude of synthesis, which is negritude understood in a broader sense that does not reject "a quest for an antiracist, possibly universal culture, 'the culminating point of the dream of every serious advocate of Negritude,' a universal brotherhood in which the black man will establish solidarity with all mankind." The organization of this section on the Major Period reflects the central role Guillén played in the development of black consciousness and black literature in Latin America in the thirties and forties, when—under his influence—the black as author became just as visible as the black as subject. This period is major because of the high visibility given the black as author through the appearance of works like Pilar Barrios' *Piel negra* (1947) and Virginia Brindis de Salas' *Pregón de Marimorena* (1947) in Uruguay, Juan Pablo Sojo's *Nochebuena negra* (1943) in Venezuela. Adalberto Ortiz's *Juyungo* (1943) in Ecuador, and Jorge Artel's *Tambores en la noche* (1940) and Arnoldo Palacios' *Las estrellas son negras* (1949) in Colombia. These works and others such as Guillén's *El son entero* (1947) that follow his initiative of the thirties, made the forties especially a fertile decade for black writers in Latin America. (pp. 90-1)

> *Richard L. Jackson, "The Turning Point: The Blackening of Nicolás Guillén and the Impact of His 'Motivos de son'," in his* Black Writers in Latin America, *University of New Mexico Press, 1979, pp. 80-92.*

Nicolás Guillén with Laurence E. Prescott (interview date 1984)

[*Prescott joined Guillén on April 5, 1984, in Medellín, Colombia to conduct the following interview. It originally appeared in a 1987 edition of* Callaloo *devoted to Guillén and criticism of his works. Here, Guillén discusses the black elements of his writing.*]

[Prescott]: *I know that when you began to publish your works* **Motivos de son, Sóngoro cosongo, West Indies, Ltd.** *in 1930, 1931, and 1934, the political situation in Cuba was very bad.*

[Guillén]: Not very comfortable.

That's right. I would like to know, then, how you were able to publish works with an obvious social intention during such a difficult period?

What happened was that there was no intention to publish those books right away. On the other hand, the social intention was dissimulated by the rhythm, the picturesque elements, etc., which made the people laugh although, in the case of one or two poems, it forced people to think. (p. 352)

Do you believe that the poems by José Zacarías Tallet, Ramón Güirao, and Palés Matos about the dances, the dancing blacks, gave a false image of blacks?

No, no. In fact, that false image appeared as a consequence of those poems, because they were badly focused. That's the problem. In Palés Matos, what emerges is a black, how can I put it, a superficial black, a black man without any human problems at all, like the black woman [in "Danza negra"] who sings, "bambú y calabú." These are things that belong, I presume, to the surrealist period in literature. There is where you have to look for him, but in any case, his position toward life was really very limited, and he was satisfied with the rhythmic thing, which, by the way, is very beautiful, there is no doubt, but he did not go any deeper than that. He did not devote himself to that anymore, but above all he failed to give it a human content, and when there is no human content, horrible things come out. It isn't that one must be carrying a torch to lead the way to the struggle. If you don't have the temperament to fight, all right, don't fight, although you should. But, you understand, you must nevertheless assume a dignified position. And Palés Matos was another disillusioned one, a man who showed up the monstrosity of United States imperialism in his country, Puerto Rico, and did not do anything to fight it, to go against it, to lend his name and his prestige to the struggle.

Why did you stop using the peculiar language of Cuba or of Cuban blacks?

It was very limited. It was absolutely limited. I could use it in several poems, like for example, ah, it does not matter which, one of the many poems. It produced a language that could not express everything that needed to be expressed. That's why the "**Canción del bongó**" was written. In the **"Canción del bongó"** the resources are broader, although it uses folkloric elements, too. But it goes beyond them, it goes beyond other poems.

I know that since the thirties and forties you have published elegies and other poems dealing with the situation of blacks in the United States.... How do you see the situation of blacks in the United States today from your point of view?

The worst thing American blacks have is American whites. But actually, that is not true. There are many whites who are friends of blacks, who are consistent, who are cordial, and for me to generalize in such a way would be unjust and unpolitical. But, naturally, the problem would be solved and will have to be solved through a revolution, what do you think of that? Only a revolution, only a struggle in the social realm, even only an armed struggle, because it all depends on the degree of development, because we are not going to follow here Trotsky's idea that revolution should be made anywhere at anytime. One has to make the revolution where conditions allow it, and that's why there is no permanent revolution. There are different stages in one and the same revolution which have a given intensity in a given place and another intensity in another place, all determined by the economic and social circumstances that prevail in a given country.

Yesterday I participated in the meeting of the Committee for Culture, and we spoke, among other things, about the role of culture in the search for peace, and I believe that all of us agreed that culture in the countries that are at war, the so-called developing countries, must exist as a function of the struggle for the liberation of those countries.

There is nothing that can oppose that. Was there a culture under Hitler? There wasn't any. Wherever there is an aggressive nucleus, culture becomes weakened and eventually disappears. Remember that phrase by Goebbels, "When I hear the word culture, I pull out my gun." Or did Hitler say that? I think more than Hitler, it was Goebbels. That gives you a picture of the relationships that can exist between culture and non-culture, that is, the efficacy of culture and the inefficacy of non-culture. That gives you idea of what culture is good for. (pp. 353-54)

> *Nicolás Guillén and Laurence E. Prescott, in an interview in* Callaloo, *Vol. 10, No. 2, Spring, 1987, pp. 352-54.*

FURTHER READING

Berry, Faith. "A National Poet Sings of the Revolution." *Freedomways* 15, No. 4 (1975): 282-84.

Praises *Tengo,* "a lasting tribute to the accomplishments of the Cuban Revolution."

"Nicolás Guillén: A Special Issue." *Callaloo* 10, No. 2 (Spring 1987).
    Issue devoted to Guillén, edited by Vera M. Kutzinski. Includes poetry and translations; Jay Wright's reading of Guillén, a drama entitled *Daughters of the Water;* and critical essays and a short interview with Guillén.

Cobb, Martha K. "Concepts of Blackness in the Poetry of Nicolás Guillén, Jacques Roumain and Langston Hughes." *CLA Journal* XVIII, No. 2 (December 1974): 262-72.
    Brief study of Guillén, Jacques Roumain, and Langston Hughes because "their works reflect the continuities and parallels of black experiences generated by slave dispersions that spanned Africa and the Americas."

Hughes, Langston. "Langston Hughes: Six Letters to Nicolás Guillén." Translated by Carmen Alegría. *The Black Scholar* 16, No. 4 (July-August 1985): 54-60.
    Letters from Hughes to Guillén, outlining "one of the longest and most significant literary friendships" of the twentieth century.

Jackson, Richard. "Nicolás Guillén in the 1980s: A Guide to Recent Scholarship." *Latin American Research Review* XXIII, No. 1 (1988): 110-22.
    Surveys critical studies of Guillén published in the 1980s.

Kutzinski, Vera M. "Poetry and Politics: Two Books on Nicolás Guillén." *Modern Language Notes* 98, No. 2 (March 1983): 275-84.
    Review of two books on Guillén published on the occasion of his eightieth birthday. Kutzinski finds Nancy Morejón's *Nación y mestizaje en Nicolás Guillén* flawed but more complete than Lorna V. Williams's *Self and Society in the Poetry of Nicolás Guillén.* She concludes, "As it is, there is much work to be done on Guillén in either language."

———. *Against the American Grain: Myth and History in William Carlos Williams, Jay Wright, and Nicolás Guillén.* Baltimore: Johns Hopkins University Press, 1987, 298 p.
    Finds a coherence other than Marxism in Guillén's poetry, determining that "what underlies Guillén's carnival is not a Marxist dialectic but an irreducible intercultural dialogue, a dynamic ritual of transculturation that represents the very foundations of Cuban (and New World) culture."

Márquez, Roberto. "Racism, Culture and Revolution: Ideology and Politics in the Prose of Nicolás Guillén." *Latin American Research Review* XVII, No. 1 (1982): 43-68.
    Examines Guillén's "long-neglected" prose, the merits of which Márquez finds considerable.

Williams, Lorna V. *Self and Society in the Poetry of Nicolás Guillén.* Baltimore: Johns Hopkins University Press, 1982, 177 p.
    The first English language book-length study of Guillén's work. The first part is devoted to the effect of

the past on Guillén's writing, and the second part concerns his visions for the future of Cuban society.

Willis, Susan. "Caliban as Poet: Reversing the Maps of Domination." In *Reinventing the Americas: Comparative Studies of Literature of the United States and Spanish America,* edited by Bell Gale Chevigny and Gari Laguardia, pp. 92-105. Cambridge, U.K.: Cambridge University Press, 1986.

Probes similarities in poets of the Caribbean.

Alex Haley

1921-

(Full name Alex Murray Palmer Haley) American
journalist, essayist, and historical novelist.

Haley is the celebrated author of *Roots: The Saga of an
American Family* (1976). This work is seldom mentioned without the word "phenomenon" tacked on.
Combined with the impact of the televised mini-series,
Roots has become a "literary-television phenomenon"
and a "sociological event," according to *Time* magazine.
By April 1977 almost two million hardcover copies of
the book had been sold and 130 million people had seen
all or part of the eight episode television series. *Roots* is
thus considered by many critics a classic in African-
American literature and culture.

Haley, who was born in Ithaca, New York, and raised in
the small town of Henning, Tennessee, became interested in his ancestry while listening to colorful stories told
by his family. One story in particular, about an African
ancestor who refused to be called by his slave name
"Toby" and declared instead that his name was "Kin-
tay," impressed Haley deeply. Young Haley was so
fascinated by this account that he later spent twelve
years researching and documenting the life of "Kunta
Kinte," the character in his famous *Roots*. School
records indicate that Haley was not an exceptional
student. At the age of eighteen he joined the U. S. Coast
Guard and began a twenty-year career in the service. He
practiced his writing, at first only to alleviate boredom
on the ship, and soon found himself composing love
letters for his shipmates to send home to their wives and
girlfriends. He wrote serious pieces as well and submitted them to various magazines.

Upon retiring from the Coast Guard, Haley decided to
become a full-time writer and journalist. His first book,
The Autobiography of Malcolm X (1965), which he
cowrote with Malcolm X, was widely acclaimed upon its
publication. The work sold over five million copies and
launched Haley's writing career. Malcolm X was at first
reluctant to work with Haley. He later told the writer: "I
don't completely trust anyone...you I trust about
twenty-five percent." Critics praised Haley for sensitive-
ly handling Malcolm X's volatile life, and the book
quickly became required reading in many schools. Two
weeks after *The Autobiography of Malcolm X* was
completed, Haley began work on his next project, *Roots*.
Roots chronicles the life of Kunta Kinte, a proud
African who is kidnapped from his village in West
Africa, forced to endure the middle passage—the brutal
shipment of Africans to be sold in the Americas—on the
slave ship *Lord Ligonier*, and made a slave on the
Waller plantation in the United States. To authenticate
Kunta's life and that of Kunta's grandson, Chicken
George, Haley visited archives, libraries, and research
repositories on three continents. He even reenacted

Kunta's experience on the *Lord Ligonier*. "[Haley]
somehow scourged up some money and flew to Liberia
where he booked passage on the first U. S. bound ship,"
an *Ebony* interviewer related. "Once at sea, he spent the
night lying on a board in the hold of the ship, stripped to
his underwear to get a rough idea of what his African
ancestor might have experienced."

Although critics generally lauded *Roots*, they seemed
unsure whether to treat the work as a novel or as a
historical account. While the narrative is based on
factual events, the dialogue, thoughts, and emotions of
the characters are fictionalized. Haley himself described
the book as "faction," a mixture of fact and fiction.
Most critics concurred and evaluated *Roots* as a blend of
history and entertainment. Despite the fictional characterizations, Willie Lee Rose suggested in the *New York
Review of Books* that Kunta Kinte's parents Omoro and
Binte "could possibly become the African proto-parents
of millions of Americans who are going to admire their
dignity and grace." *Newsweek* applauded Haley's decision to fictionalize: "Instead of writing a scholarly

monograph of little social impact, Haley has written a blockbuster in the best sense—a book that is bold in concept and ardent in execution, one that will reach millions of people and alter the way we see ourselves."

Some voiced concern, however—especially at the time of the television series—that racial tension in America would be aggravated by *Roots.* While *Time* did report several incidents of racial violence following the telecast, it commented that "most observers thought that in the long term, *Roots* would improve race relations, particularly because of the televised version's profound impact on whites.... A broad consensus seemed to be emerging that *Roots* would spur black identity, and hence black pride, and eventually pay important dividends." Some black leaders viewed *Roots* "as the most important civil rights event since the 1965 march on Selma," according to *Time.* Vernon Jordan, executive director of the National Urban League, called it "the single most spectacular educational experience in race relations in America." Speaking of the appeal of *Roots* among blacks, Haley added: "The blacks who are buying books are not buying them to go out and fight someone, but because they want to know who they are.... [The] book has touched a strong, subliminal cord."

For months after the publication of *Roots* in October 1976, Haley signed at least five hundred copies of the book daily, spoke to an average of six thousand people a day, and traveled round trip coast-to-coast at least once a week. Scarcely two years later, *Roots* had already won 271 awards, and its television adaptation had been nominated for a recordbreaking thirty-seven Emmys. Over eight million copies of the book were in print, and the text was translated into twenty-six languages. In addition to fame and fortune, *Roots* also brought Haley controversy. In 1977 two published authors, Margaret Walker and Harold Courlander, alleged separately that Haley plagiarized their work in *Roots.* Charges brought by Walker were later dropped, but Haley admitted that he unknowingly lifted three paragraphs from Courlander's *The African* (1968). A settlement was reached whereby Haley paid Courlander $500,000. The same year other accusations also arose. Mark Ottaway in *The Sunday Times* questioned Haley's research methods and the credibility of his informants, accusing Haley of "bending" data to fit his objectives. Gary B. and Elizabeth Shown Mills also challenged some of Haley's assertions. Writing in 1981 in *The Virginia Magazine of History and Biography,* they cited evidence that there was indeed a slave named Toby living on the Waller plantation. He was there, however, at least five years before the arrival of the *Lord Ligonier,* supposedly with Kunta on board.

Haley's supporters maintain that Haley never claimed *Roots* as fact or history. And even in the presence of controversy, the public image of *Roots* appears not to have suffered. It is still widely read in schools, and many college and university history and literature programs consider it an essential part of their curriculum. According to Haley himself, *Roots* is important not for its

names and dates but as a reflection of human nature: "*Roots* is all of our stories.... It's just a matter of filling in the blanks...; when you start talking about family, about lineage and ancestry, you are talking about every person on earth." Indeed, Haley's admirers contend, *Roots* remains a great book because it is the universal story of humankind's own search for its identity.

(For further information about Haley's life and works, see *Black Writers; Contemporary Authors,* Vol. 77-80; *Contemporary Literary Criticism,* Vols. 8, 12; and *Dictionary of Literary Biography,* Vol. 38: *Afro-American Writers after 1955: Dramatists and Prose Writers.*)

PRINCIPAL WORKS

The Autobiography of Malcolm X [with Malcolm X] (autobiography) 1965
"In Search of the African" (essay) 1974; published in periodical *American History Illustrated*
"My Search for Roots" (essay) 1974; published in periodical *Reader's Digest*
**Roots: The Saga of an American Family* (historical novel) 1976
"What Roots Mean to Me" (essay) 1977; published in periodical *Reader's Digest*
"Sea Islanders, Strong-Willed Survivors Face Their Uncertain Future Together" (essay) 1982; published in periodical *Smithsonian*

*This work was televised as a mini-series in January 1977.

Colin MacInnes (essay date 1966)

[*In the following excerpt, MacInnes reviews* The Autobiography of Malcolm X, *noting that "the modest hero of [the book] is really Alex Haley."*]

The modest hero of [*The Autobiography of Malcolm X*] is really Alex Haley, who provides, in his introduction, a frank and just appreciation of Malcolm X, and whose task it was, at snatched moments over two hectic years, first to win Malcolm's confidence and then persuade him to tell his story fully. The result is beyond praise, for one must instantly feel that though this is, technically, a 'ghosted' book, it is Malcolm's thought and voice we are hearing all the time....

Malcolm foresaw his martyrdom and he knew his heroic mould. And it is impossible to read this book without becoming convinced that Malcolm was a hero....

The cause of the break with the muslims isn't satisfactorily explained even in this frank book, and one suspects that Malcolm, in talking to Haley, still had reticences....

I suspect many English readers will dismiss Malcolm as a fanatic who preached the sword and perished by it.

But any such reader can have no comprehension whatever of the virulent despair and aggression of the American Negro....

What Malcolm achieved was to give coherence to the feelings of millions. Until and unless absolute economic and social equality are won by Negroes, these feelings will remain and grow. Internationally, they are allied to all those of non-white peoples throughout the world. If anyone doubts this, and doubts the anger of it, Malcolm's biography will be a corrective.

> Colin MacInnes, "Malcolm," in The Spectator, *Vol. 216, No. 7196, May 27, 1966, p. 668.*

Arnold Rampersad (essay date 1976)

[*In the following excerpt, Rampersad—a noted American scholar—offers a mixed review of* Roots, *stating that the narrative is "a work of extremely uneven texture but unquestionable final success."*]

A narrative history of the family from the birth of Kunta Kinte to the maturity of Haley himself, *Roots* is a hybrid work. It links the detective skills of a superior investigative reporter to the powers of a would-be fiction writer, and the product is a work of extremely uneven texture but unquestionable final success. (p. 23)

Haley's search for his ancestors is not conducted to discover unvarnished truth but rather, from one perspective, to justify the history of blacks in America—as if that history needed justification. There is a dominant angle of vision in *Roots;* almost the entire story is seen from the vantage point of a belief in the necessity of social and political justice, which is the principal romantic illusion to inform the text. From an artistic and intellectual point of view there is what may be for some readers a fateful shift of emphasis from the pathos and ingenuity of the author's search for his family toward the elevation of its members to mythical level as accurate representatives of the black race in America, with Kunta Kinte as the archetypal African warrior prince. Side by side in the book, then, exist these twin desires for the illumination of truth and the cultural propaganda. What further complicates this odd combination is the absence of radical political belief on the author's part; Haley's values, except concerning the worth of black people, are those of the masses of Americans, to whom the book is in fact dedicated.

In one sense Haley's ancestral family bears its mythic burden well; with the exception of Kunta Kinte, after all, the members are really ordinary. But it is on Kinte that the book is based. Though Haley's account of his hero's African childhood sometimes reads like a dramatization of a master's thesis on childhood and youth among the Mandinko people in the mid-18th century, more often it is suffused in the light of Haley's reverence for the Africa of his ancestors and his loving account of their society. His recreation of Kinte's middle-passage journey in the hold of a slave ship is harrowing, the major place in the book where facts are incontrovertibly alchemized into vivid narrative; and his presentation of Kinte's unfolding consciousness of the strange new white world of America is brilliant, yielding startling insights into the psychological process of American slavery, and into aspects of American culture then and now. Kunta Kinte's rage for freedom—one foot is cut off after his fourth attempt to escape—impressed on succeeding generations a respect, however muted, for the integrity of their origins and their dignity as well.

On the other hand, the middle of the book is dominated by the flamboyant figure of Kinte's grandson, Chicken George, reared by his white father—and owner—to be an expert trainer of gamecocks. Haley's accounts of cockfighting in the South in the 19th century are lively (though there are too many of them), but Chicken George himself is about as interesting as a plucked bird. Survival and endurance replace defiance as the central concern of Kunta Kinte's clan, and it is at this point that its members become History. Haley's integration of personages and events from the American past into his narrative is the stuff of pageants or some other moribund medium, such as television, and fails to conceal the fact that uncovering the truth about the past does not necessarily make it interesting.

The solemnity of the basic theme of *Roots* also cannot obscure the fact that the Afro-American novel is too accomplished in its basic skills for *Roots* to pass as a well wrought novel or romance. Technically, the work is so innocent of fictive ingenuity that it seldom surpasses the standards of the most popular of historical romances. Haley's ability to write dialogue and dialect is competent at best, and stilted and artificial far too often. Nor is the work helped much by the strange and fitful dramatic strokes its author casts into the void (Kinte, for example, does not sleep with a woman until he marries at the age of 39...). Similarly, sociological and historical scholarship on both West Africa and the American slave centuries is too developed for Haley's uncoverings to be met as revelations. Undoubtedly the book will make history and sociology more familiar to its readers, but that role in itself can hardly be the reason for the possibly long-lasting consequence of this narrative.

One pushes through *Roots,* sometimes swiftly, sometimes laboriously, as often captivated as irritated by the limitations of its concern with form. But there is no denying the extraordinary force of individual passages and episodes or—more importantly—the exhilaration with which one bursts forth, as from the underbrush of dried fact and tangled genealogical vines, into the present time and the living presence of the author. For one dazzling moment, from which it seems impossible to recover, the past becomes the present, and the present becomes the past, and there is a sense of circularity, of completeness, of integration of sensibility within the black American experience that is unparalleled, to my knowledge, in either fiction or scholarship concerning Afro-America.

The primary effect of **Roots** is not, however, partisan, if only because the implied relationship between the sense of political identity imposed by racism on the American black and the sense of genetic identity with Africa is minimal in its intellectual dignity. **Roots** is the record of the voluntary location of an individual in the context of the past. Haley may have intended to make the justification of Afro-America the locus of his effort; he has succeeded, in spite of his intentions and his personal reticence, in making himself, as an individual, vital to the book's meanings. The peculiar essence of **Roots** is that the author, prostrating himself before the past, is himself called upon to justify his existence before the power of history and the court of the past.... And it is this test of the individual life before the sacrifices and disasters of a common ancestry that Haley passes most movingly. In the display of intelligence, industry and humanity out of which the substance of the book evolves—its limitations as fiction are really insignificant in comparison—one finds preserved not pride of family or race or a smattering of heirloomed words but those qualities of spirit that, as Kunta Kinte knew in preferring mutilation to servility, make freedom not a privilege but a necessity. When Haley stands at the end of **Roots** before his African country-cousins and feels himself "impure" because of their richly black skin, there is behind the tedious racial romanticism the felt truth of a confrontation between the individual and his—and in this case—personified past. Haley has nothing to be ashamed of, at least not in this book; Kunta Kinte would have respected him. (pp. 24, 26)

Arnold Rampersad, in a review of "Roots," in The New Republic, *Vol. 175, No. 23, December 4, 1976, pp. 23-4, 26.*

Howard F. Stein (essay date 1977)

[*In the following excerpt, Stein favorably assesses* Roots, *noting that the work is "an American epic that Black and White men and women of good will might read and watch and discuss together."*]

For all its moving, tender, and grisly historic vividness, **Roots** remains what psychologists call an "ambiguous stimulus," one which is selectively restructured by the observer who is participant. This is not to despair in solipsism, but to emphasize the omnipresence of subjectivity in the never-detached observer; and to stress equally that that subjectivity can be a tool either for unself-conscious *indulgence,* or for *disciplined* engagement. (p. 12)

For me, what is refreshing about Haley's **Roots** is that reality is not ... cavalierly held in contempt. While there is much absolutistic either-or in the tale, Haley's world of human bondage does more than outrageously simplify into good guys and bad guys. I would go further: his is an *American* epic that Black and White men and women of good will might read and watch and discuss *together.* For while Haley does lamentably indulge in stereotyping, which I shall consider later, the over-all effect of

Roots is, for me, a transcendent one, not a one-sided victory. In a sense, **Roots** taps the core of the American experience with its focus on the journey from whence we come, where we are now, where we aspire to, and the ever-new and constantly renewing pioneer settling of a new-found-land in freedom. "We" becomes everyone, not a single race. Haley is not fixated on the past: the past is simply, and starkly, and dramatically, the Proud Beginning. Haley does not rest complacently with an origin myth: for roots is *process,* not place. Roots lie not only in the past—but in the present and future as well.

Those who view Haley's message as exclusively a look backward have missed the dramatic unfolding toward the *future.* A sinking and spreading of roots takes place throughout the odyssey. (pp. 11-12)

The American dream became a new image of rootedness. The American cultural value on "Don't give up hope," that "If I can't attain it, I will help my children to get it," these values, in Haley's script, become transformed into *Afro*-American values, making for convergence, congruence, synthesis in cultural aspirations. (p. 13)

The new rootedness is not without anguish and sacrifice and risk. Kunta Kinte must choose among divided loyalties: his choice reveals what sort of man he is, his values, his priorities. He must decide between acting upon his vow to be a free man at any cost, and remaining with his new family.... Ultimately, it required greater courage for Kunta Kinte to choose to remain behind, to establish new roots, than it would have been to make a daring escape. To the maturing Kunta Kinte, the freedom of dogged ideological adherence to the individualism of the past became less attractive than commitment to those who were by love and promise of the future committed to him. He found new reward in meeting the new demands and opportunities of family life. There were other ways of fighting slavery than fleeing it.

Kunta Kinte chooses the limits and different freedoms of responsibility, mutuality, and devotion. Like his future descendant Alex Haley, he is more self-disciplined than self-indulgent. Selfhood is deepened, not suffocated, in relation and commitment—all the more dramatically poignant when the imminence of the master's whim renders impermanent any human relationship. (pp. 13-14)

Haley does frequently indulge himself oversimplifying and overdrawing racial differences to the point of caricature. This results in a reversal of White stereotypes, popular and sociological, and obscures much of the interpersonal complexity and internal anguish in those both Black and White caught *together* in the "American Dilemma." Thus Africans and Afro-Americans are portrayed as strong, courageous, loving, alive, patient, compassionate, determined, proud, moral, having integrity, knowing who they are, resorting to deception and obsequious cunning only out of the necessity of survival. Whites, excepting Old George, are cruel, inhuman, immoral, pretentiously mannered, inured to human suffering, calloused in their emotions, obsessed with property and propriety and order. Freedom in Africa is contrasted with Slavery in America, as though African slavery not only did not antedate White slavers but did not exist. Neither Kunta Kinte, nor Chicken George, nor others in the later succession of Black males, were weak, passive, docile, fatalistic, resigned. For survival they may have feigned what submission the credulous master and mistress needed for their own dehumanizing entertainment. But everything was a finely rehearsed outward act.... Defiance was the underlying flame that made brokenness and despair impossible. Rootedness endured....

If in some ways, Haley simplifies history, in other ways, his dramatic autobiographic odyssey of personal lineage is congruent with the findings of current historians of the antebellum South. (p. 14)

With insight and grace, Haley is able to articulate contradictions and ambivalences that less self-aware writers would make a matter of either-or. With empathic historical relativism, he successfully (for me) tries to imagine himself and his audience back in the eras he depicts.... There is no denying the human holocaust of American slavery. Yet even in the constraints of such degradation, there was some mutuality, some warmth, some caring, some commitment, some sense of reciprocal obligation. All was not feigned. Haley conveys much of this, even as he exaggerates the virtues and frailties and failings of his characters.

I find and identify with in *Roots* a struggle and process that is incomplete, one which I suspect cannot be finalized without foreclosing or violating the life-long development of identity. Here is where *Roots* parts company with most personal histories, self-disclosures, and autobiographic-ethnic confessionals of the contemporary genre. For if I hear Haley correctly, *Roots* does not denote exclusively African origins. Kunta Kinte is not his protagonist, but a vehicle for the *dramatic unfolding* which is the true protagonist, one of a search for wholeness. I do not find in Haley's agonized itinerary a tale of primeval innocence, despite frequent lapse in characterization. I do not hear an apologia for ethno-racial separatism, since Haley's and *Roots'* odyssey is inextricably Black and White. I do not find Black pride purchased exclusively at the expense of White shame and guilt. Haley is not altogether clear here, but the direction of his resolution is what compels my identification. He is, after all, the biographer of Malcolm X who just before his assassination, transcended the hate-ridden phase of "White Devils" hortatory rhetoric in his pilgrimage to Mecca, discovering that all men could be brothers irrespective of race. *Roots* serves as a reminder that not only is Black history bound up with White, but that White history is inseparable from Black. In a word, Haley's integrity and authenticity outweigh his sins of omission and commission. He has held a mirror before us, one in which we have chosen to peer attentively. Haley has chosen not the deceptive

luxury of cozening himself and us into a fixation on the past, but has with sensitivity and self-discipline documented and embellished a continuum of culture and history that is common to the *American* experience.

Roots concludes with homage to the past and hope for the future, a future founded on a fresh start—something peculiarly American. (pp. 15-16)

[This] fairy tale in historical form is designed to make a point. And the degree to which it has touched us, made us more whole, is the extent to which Haley's odyssey is ours also, his hope, ours. In the end, there remains the unanswered questioned: Quo vadimus? Is it still possible to overcome together? (p. 16)

> *Howard F. Stein, "In Search of 'Roots': An Epic of Origins and Destiny," in* Journal of Popular Culture, *Vol. XI, No. 1, Summer, 1977, pp. 11-17.*

Alex Haley with Jeffrey Elliot (interview date 1978)

[*In the following 1978 interview, Haley and Elliot discuss the writing of* Roots *and examine how the success of the book has changed Haley's life. Describing Haley, Elliot observed: "[Haley] is an extraordinary man. He is a man of strength, courage, and determination, a man who lives and loves as though life and love were one.... He is a man of decency and dignity, a man who is able to see beyond all of the nonsense which parades as truth. In sum, Haley is what his book,* Roots, *is: a striking testimonial to the goodness and nobility of the human species."*]

[Elliot]: *Numerous reviewers have heralded* **Roots** *as one of the most significant books of our time. What makes it such an important work?*

[Haley]: I've heard numerous erudite explanations of the *Roots* phenomenon, several of which are probably correct in one way or another. In my own mind, however, I tend to go back to something my grandmother said many years ago—that is, "The Lord might not come when you expect him to, but he will always be on time." That's the best answer I know how to give you.

Is there something about the book or, perhaps, its subject matter, which helps to explain the public response to **Roots**?

Yes. Looking back over the project, I tried to orchestrate the story prior to actually writing the book. Indeed, the book was significantly enhanced by the fact that I devoted considerable attention to the architecture of the story long before I started writing. My aim was to try to strike a responsive chord in the reader. I started with a little boy, Kunta Kinte, and focused on him from the time he was born. The reader literally shared his birth. He grew up and, like all little boys, he was universal. You can't help but like a little boy romping around playfully, enjoying life, experiencing its wonders. We watched him, we loved him, we pulled for him. As he grew up, I tried to weave the story around him and his orbit. I attempted to relate what I had learned about the African culture which had spawned him. And so, we became beguiled by him as we shared his journey through life. When I say, "we" I mean I was as beguiled as anyone else in recounting the story of his life. There were many times when I would catch myself at the typewriter or with pen in hand, feeling as though I were standing off somewhere at the edge of the village watching Kunta doing the things I was writing about at the time. I was totally caught up in his youthful adventures. In another sense, it was a very personal experience. I so enjoyed my own childhood in Henning, Tennessee, that sometimes I wish I had never grown up. I had a ball. And so, in a way, I was Kunta Kinte, reliving my own childhood through his boyhood experiences. As Kunta continued to mature, we watched him grow into teenage, a nice youngster, still. He was disciplined, respectful, hard working, and reverent of his parents. You can't help but like that kind of youngster. He had his dreams, his hopes, his aspirations. And then he went off to manhood training, coping with the problems that it entailed. By the time Kunta returned home, only to be captured, slavery ceased to be impersonal. Indeed, it became highly personal to millions of readers who identified with him in human terms, very much as I did. As a brief aside, I would admit that in a structural sense, that portion of the book dealing with Africa is too long in terms of balance. One of the contributing reasons, however, is that when it came time for Kunta to be captured, I just hated to see it happen. So I took him off on another trip with his little brother, Lamin, to keep that from happening for awhile. When he finally was captured, I felt as though I had been hit in the head with a two-by-four. In fact, I was so broken up over his capture, that I quit writing for several weeks. I just didn't want to go back to the book. Before I could actually begin the next section, I had to go off and get my head together.

Much of your time these days is spent in promoting **Roots***. Has the massive publicity generated by the book significantly affected your private life?*

In some ways, it exploded what had been my previous private life. After the initial publication of **Roots,** when there were strong signs that it was going to be an unusual book, various public relations and media people would say to me, "You're going to lose your privacy." And I would say to myself, "That's what you think. It will never happen." At the time, their warning was abstract. I didn't quite know what they meant. I do now, however. Somehow you don't seem to appreciate your privacy until you lose it. And then, of course, it's too late. The process itself is a subtle one. Suddenly, you don't have time to do things you did previously as a matter of course. In a metaphorical sense, nothing really affects the twenty-four-hour-day. It's fixed in time and space. Meanwhile, the demands, the requests, the mandatories, that are part of your new-found success, seem to grow geometrically in comparison to what they were previously. For example, there was one period when in

three days, I gave thirty-three interviews—television, magazine, radio, newspaper, etc. I scarcely ate or slept, and the demands of the press grew almost beyond physical endurance. Moreover, it was often the case that when you were tired, really tired, someone in the press would come in and zing you. I'm not complaining about the press. It's simply a matter of fact. After all, each of these reporters is looking for something which will make his or her story a little bit different. For instance, I can recall a good example which illustrates my point. One morning I awoke, having had only two hours sleep the night before, after what seemed like dozens of interviews. Some reporter in a group asked me to comment on a criticism of **Roots** that was raised at the time. I said something like, "Very few books which have received the praise that **Roots** has, are not without their critics, including Homer or even the Bible." That afternoon I was astonished to see a story on the AP wire which read, "Haley, turning the opposite of humble, today compared his book, **Roots,** to Homer and the Bible." It wasn't what I meant at all, and the reporter knew it wasn't what I said. But the point is, he was able to get an unusual slant to his story, even if it was at my expense. There's much more I could say on this point. However, I feel uncomfortable complaining about the pressures of success. After all, I'm never very far from the fact that previous to all this, I had worked for over twenty years praying to God that one day, just a piece of what has happened to me would come true. It was that fantasy which sustained me all those years at the typewriter, pecking away day-after-day, just hoping for the right break. When a thing like that finally happens, however, it catches you off guard. At one point, I can remember giving seventy-three speeches in sixty days in forty-two states. It was like being in a maze. I can recall during that period, making a point of trying to establish in my mind where I was, lest I slip and mention the wrong city. Overall, it's a test, a challenge, something you learn to cope with as best you can. One of the things that most distressed me was my inability to answer the mail, something I always prided myself on before. After **Roots** was published, I was on the road for the next ten months. I was almost never home. In fact, in those first seven months, I was home something like twenty-two nights. I spent the rest of the time in various hotels around the country. As the public response to **Roots** began to mount, the correspondence came in canvas sacks. It piled up and up and up. I suppose I probably have 25,000 pieces of unanswered mail. I was simply, physically, unable to do anything about it. It was easy enough to hire secretaries to get the mail out, but I had to read it, at least I thought I did. I would feel awfully uncaring if I simply hired someone to answer it all, particularly after people were nice enough to write and tell me how much they enjoyed the book. Perhaps that would be better than not answer the letters at all, but it's still my hope to be able to answer as much of it as I possibly can within the next few months. For example this morning I dictated correspondence until around 3:30 a.m. And I plan to dictate for several more hours this afternoon. When all of this happened, I fantasized that I could become identical triplets—one of me would be chained to the typewriter and fed at periodic intervals; another would devote full-time to answering the correspondence, telephone calls, personal requests, etc.; and the third would make all of the public appearances, which is a full-time job in itself. Right now, on my desk as of last week, there were approximately 800 speaking requests, all of which are slated for the next six months. That will give you some idea of what it's like. And yet, that's only part of it. I wouldn't even call it the negative side, but rather a facet of the situation. There are also the beautiful things that have happened. Perhaps the most beautiful of all, is how many times people pass me, wave to me, recognize me, and cry out, "thank you." That just warms me to the bottom of my feet. The emotional, positive responses of people—black, white, yellow, brown—are an incredible thing to behold. In fact, one of the greatest wonders to me is how *Roots* has literally transcended all ethnic groups. The identification of Chicano people, of Oriental people, of Indian people, is something I never would have anticipated. They have the feeling that somehow, *Roots,* is a good thing for them, too. White people of various ethnic extractions have responded extremely well to the book. It shows itself in many ways, too numerous to go into now. However, it's all I can do to keep from crying. People don't know it, but I'm often that way. For instance, when I go into a room where I'm scheduled to speak, it's not uncommon for everyone to stand up when I enter. You don't know what that does to me. I have to force myself to keep from crying. It's something that almost overwhelms you when it happens. As a result I go around pretty emotional these days.

Not only has **Roots** *brought you fame and fortune, but it has also cast you in the role of a major black leader. Do you enjoy that role?*

Well, I would quibble with the word, "leader," I just don't feel like a leader. I have become a prominent black voice on account of the tremendous media exposure I've received. But I don't have organized followers or anything of that nature, and that's about the last thing I'm seeking. In any event, I will accept the term, "voice,"; the "leader," I don't feel. I suppose I could have some influence in one direction or another if I went out and spoke for some cause or some candidate. But I don't choose to exercise that role as such. Each person has a role to play. Mine is, hopefully, to write books. That's my number one priority.

As you view the public response to **Roots,** *what do you see as its greatest impact?*

If I had to boil it down to a sentence or two, it would be that on a worldwide basis, and I say that because *Roots* is being translated into twenty-four languages, that the "Tarzan" and "Jungle Jim" images, as pervasive world symbols of Africa and African people, will be replaced by Kunta Kinte and his brave people. That's the biggest thing *Roots* could ever do. The pernicious effort of these

stereotypes transcends all the adjectives I know. Beyond that, I hope it will give a new sense of pride to black people. Moreover, I hope it will help to foster a renewed feeling of appreciation and respect for black people to take greater pride in the slaves, and Uncle Tom, and Aunt Hager, because they did the most vital thing in the world—they survived. If they hadn't done that, then, we, who descend from them wouldn't be doing all the things we're doing today.

Did you ever envision that **Roots** *would have such an enormous impact on the American psyche?*

At the time I wrote *Roots,* I didn't think it would have an enormous impact on anything. Of course I had a great hope for the book, but the extent of my dreams was quite limited. I didn't go around doing a lot of dreaming. I was more obsessed with finishing the book. In fact, I probably never spent more than a total of six hours projecting its results. I had great faith in the book, obviously, since I had twelve years invested in it, but I never dreamed it would create the sensation it has in terms of the public response. It is said by some people that *Roots* is the most important book in terms of social change since *Uncle Tom's Cabin.* If that's true, I can only be humbled by that fact. That's all you can be. You would have to be the worst kind of fool to go around thinking, "I'm going to write a book that will change the world." The most one can do, I think, sensibly, is to write the best book that one is capable of writing. You never quite know what it's going to do. Writing a book is very much like having a baby. Once it's published, it takes off and becomes its own entity. That's happening now with *Roots.* Not a week passes but that I don't get letters, or my agents get letters, from people all over the world, who propose some business proposition involving *Roots*—either the book or something derivative of the book—that I've never heard of before. There's really no way to know what's going to happen. You just have to sit back and wait.

To what extent can **Roots** *be viewed not only as the saga of your own search for identity, but in larger terms, as man's search for identity?*

I think there's a lot of that in the book and in the public response to it. Obviously, the book and the film, but especially the book, touched something deep in all people. It cut across all lines—age lines, color lines, nationalistic lines, ethnic lines, etc. It literally touched something of a DNA-nature. And so, I think your question probably answers itself. In essence, *Roots* touched man's universal quest for identity. Let me give you an example. Not long ago I was in Paris for a speech. Something happened there which really astonished me. One day some people were taping an outdoor interview with me. I was walking alongside the host, who was talking to me at the time. All of a sudden there was this enormous cry, "Alex Haley!" And what it turned out, there was literally a bus load of white people, Americans, who piled out of the bus and came running over to where we were standing. Needless to say, the interview stopped in the midst of the confusion. It turned out that these were people from Kentucky who had not known each other a year before, but who had, spurred on by *Roots,* begun researching their family backgrounds in Kentucky and discovered themselves to have French ancestry. Indeed, it was in the genealogical reference places that they had met each other and uncovered their French backgrounds. They had come to France, as a group of sixty-five people, to dig up their records in remote villages and towns. And I happened to walk by as they piled out of their bus. You want to know how that makes you feel?

Has the success of **Roots** *helped or hurt your ability as a writer—that is, has it type-cast you or given you greater creative leeway*?

I certainly don't think it has type-cast me. The first person who would have to feel type-cast is the writer himself or herself. If I felt I could only write another *Roots* or *Roots*-related book, then I would have type-cast myself. In truth, that's the last thing I think. I'm extremely excited over books down the line which, in a sense, have nothing to do with *Roots* or *Roots*-related material. What has happened, however, is that the success of *Roots* has significantly cut into my personal life in so many ways, and to such an extent, that I'm no longer able to write as I once did. Sadly, and I must face it, my life has changed in dramatic ways. It used to be that my main problem was to simply get up enough money so that I could afford to get on a ship, which is my favorite place to write, and sail off for two or three months. The problem now isn't raising the money, but getting the two or three months. I would cheerfully, happily, eagerly, pay someone, if this sort of thing were possible, $10-an-hour to sleep for me, if I could get the benefit of the eight hours sleep a night. Unfortunately, it doesn't work that way. As a result I have found writing, serious writing, hard to do since *Roots* was published.

Why did your family history fascinate you so, particularly to the extent of investing so many years in trying to understand it?

My family was always deeply interested in its own history. From my earliest recollections, I can remember sitting on the back porch and listening to my grandmother and others reminisce about the family history. They loved to regale each other with the various stories they knew. The stories themselves were new only to me. I can recall those back porch discussions quite vividly. My grandmother, who lived in Henning, would invite all of the family to her home, where they would sit around and discuss the family history. I listened to everything very intently. I didn't realize it at the time but my family coalesced around its history. As I think about it, my family has always been proud of knowing who they were, and they loved to talk about it. It was kind of natural, therefore, that I would pick it up later as I grew up and became a writer. Actually, I didn't think about writing a book dealing with my family history until I began digging into ancestral records at the

National Archives that tended to corroborate what they had talked about on my grandmother's back porch in Henning.

As you think about the development of **Roots,** *was there a moment when the idea, the dream, the concept, came alive in your mind?*

It never came together in a composite way, as I gather you mean. It came in wisps, in nuances, in unrelated happenings. From the time I first began, when I discovered the material in the National Archives, to the time I actually decided to write the book, probably a year elapsed. Considerably more time went by as I conceptualized the book in my mind, but again, only in vague form. I had no idea what direction the book would take as I began my research. At the outset, I thought of the book simply in terms of doing a family history. I had no thought of going to Africa to trace my roots. I thought I would merely write a book about my family in this country, which I knew like the back of my hand. But as time went on, I got the idea of going to Africa. Even with the family lineage slant, there wasn't enough material to put together a book. And I wasn't sure whether I should try to write an abstract history of the black family or something more personal. Finally, after thrashing it around in my head, and scribbling down some thoughts on paper, I decided that the best way to tell about a people is through an individual, or a family, with whom a reader could identify in personal terms. Eventually, it boiled down to focusing the book around the life of Kunta Kinte—his people, his community, his village, and his culture.

Did you ever envision that it would take you twelve years to complete the book?

No, never. I doubt I would have given it a second thought had I know that beforehand. I couldn't have afforded to invest twelve years to a project of that type. The only reason I did was because I got hooked. I had a tremendous investment in the project, not so much in monetary terms, because I didn't have much money to invest, but my emotional investment was such that I couldn't let go. And believe me, I must have tried to give up the whole project at least twenty times. But I just couldn't do it. I always found myself easing right back into it again. I would take a job to write an article or something, and it was like a canker in my stomach, just thinking about something else.

What lessons would you hope black people might learn from your own search for identity? What about white people?

Insofar as black people are concerned and, to an extent, white people as well, the biggest single lesson is that we black people do indeed have an identity, a rich, prideful heritage. We must make a concerted effort to cast off the negative images that have been applied to us throughout history and which have, in various ways, come to represent an almost self-fulfilling prophecy. If you tell a people that they have no history, that they have nothing of which to be proud, that they are innately inferior, then they will eventually come to believe it. It's that kind of legacy that we must cast off.

Has your own quest for identity made you more proud of being black?

No, I'm not sure I would say that. As I indicated before, I come from a family that has a long history of being proud of who they are, and that includes, of course, being black. I can never recall a time when I was ashamed of being black. We were always taught to be proud of who we were. The search for **Roots** did, however, increase my sense of responsibility in being black, particularly now, in that I'm often held up as a role model, or a voice, or a person who is a contributor to the shaping of culture.

You have used much of the money from the sale of **Roots** *to establish the Alex Haley Roots Foundation. What is the purpose of the Foundation?*

The Foundation is a reflection of the responsibility I feel as a result of the success of **Roots.** I very much want to do something constructive with the profits from the book. I have no desire whatsoever to own a yacht, or a mansion, or a limousine, or anything else like that. I'm just not interested in those things. Instead, I've established the Alex Haley Roots Foundation. It only bears my name because of the shoe company which has a similar name. Basically, it's an outgrowth of my desire to put into practice what I believe. I think it's vitally important that black people, particularly those in positions of responsibility, do what they can to help others who aren't quite as fortunate. As a result, I've set into motion this Foundation. It's arranged so I can donate the legal maximum to insure its continued operation. I was fortunate to secure the assistance of my friend, Mr. James Dyer, who will head the Foundation. Mr. Dyer, who is a Harvard graduate, worked previously for both the Urban League and the Carnegie Corporation. He has, with the blessings of the Carnegie Corporation, agreed to become the Director of the Alex Haley Roots Foundation, which will be headquartered in New York. It will begin operation in October, 1977. The purposes of the Foundation are still being worked out. However, we hope to provide scholarships for post-graduate students who are working in the thematic area which encompasses **Roots.** In addition, we would like to help disseminate course materials at the primary and secondary levels, on a national basis, dealing with solid information concerning black history. Finally, we want to work in connection with Africa and, in particular, with The Gambia, to help build bridges between black Africans and black people in this country. As you can see, we have an ambitious agenda before us.

Are you concerned about the excessive commercialization of **Roots,** *what some people might call the "poster-t-shirt craze?"*

Well, I'm certainly not pleased by it. At the outset, I did everything I could to discourage it. My lawyers and I wrote letters to all sorts of people. We soon discovered, however, it was like standing in a shower trying to protect ourselves from getting wet with our hands. It just got out of hand. And so we quit that. We realized there was no way to stop it. You could spend all your time trying to track down this t-shirt or that poster-maker or whatever. The best I could do was to personally refrain from contributing to the commercialization of **Roots** by refusing to lend my name to any product associated with it. The biggest single thing I did was to turn down an offer, which would have netted me $250,000 for merely signing my name on a contract in exchange for endorsing a product as the author of **Roots.** Now, once you do that, it's not so difficult to turn down other offers involving lesser amounts. The real test for me, however, was not the $250,000 as such, but that I could have put the money in my Foundation. However, I decided to turn it down and others like it because I felt they weren't compatible with what I took to be the dignity of **Roots.**

Finally, you are now involved in several projects designed to capitalize on the public response to **Roots.** *What are you working on at the present time?*

Right now, most of the projects I have in mind involve films of one kind or another. We're now putting together a one-hour documentary entitled, "The Phenomena of Roots," which will air as a network special in January, 1978. We also have in the works a feature film called, "Roots—The Next Generation," which will premiere on Easter, 1978. We also have another miniseries, much the same as the last one, which is scheduled for sometime in 1979. Those are the three films with which I'm deeply involved at the present time. Together with that, I have a book to write, *Search,* which should be completed this coming January, 1978. That book will deal with the story, or rather the drama, of the twelve years it took me to write **Roots.** You see, **Roots** is told from the point of view of the characters in the book. That let me explore their minds, but it also limited me to what they could know. For example, Kunta Kinte, imprisoned in the slave ship, bound in chains, couldn't even know the name of the ship, much less anything about it. But I, on the other hand, through my research, know a great deal about that ship, that voyage, about slaving in general. Seen overall, the drama of those twelve years is a highly suspenseful detective story, encompassing three continents, not to mention nearly fifty libraries, archives, repositories, etc. In addition, I plan to write a book entitled, *Henning,* which is the little town in Tennessee where I was born. I like one-word titles, as you can gather. I think if you can find the right word that captures what you want to write about, then that's the ideal title. *Henning* will be the story of that small town from the perspective of a young boy, me, as I grew up there. Symbolically, it's the story of small towns all over the South, which are similar in many ways. As such, I think the book will capture the nostalgia associated with small towns. I have another book in mind, although I know very little about it, except that the concept itself excites me. I'm extremely interested in

Dust jacket for Haley's celebrated Roots.

Africa—physically, the second largest continent in the world. And yet, we scarcely know the extent, the depth, or the breadth of its wealth; its minerals, its culture, its history, etc. For a writer, Africa is a pure piece of heaven in terms of material. After the book, *Henning,* I propose to go to Africa, build a home in The Gambia, and travel extensively throughout the continent. I have no idea what form the book will take. It could be a novel, or nonfiction, or whatever. I just don't know. But I feel there is an exciting book awaiting me in Africa. (pp. 782-85)

> *Alex Haley and Jeffrey Elliot, in an interview*
> *in* The Negro History Bulletin, *Vol. 41, No.*
> *1, January-February, 1978, pp. 782-85.*

Albert E. Stone (essay date 1982)

[*In the following excerpt, Stone praises Haley for capturing the complexity and urgency of Malcolm X's life in* The Autobiography of Malcolm X.]

Haley's book [*The Autobiography of Malcolm X*] deserves unstinting admiration, first of all, for recapturing both the vertical and horizontal axes of the unique yet deliberately representative life of a contemporary urban black man. "How is it possible to write one's autobiog-

raphy in a world so fast-changing as this?" is Malcolm X's initial and ultimate question. Many celebrity autobiographies raise the same question, but Haley and his subject explore it with a terrible urgency. *The Autobiography* records changes in this life of such bewildering rapidity and magnitude as to throw into sharp relief the slower-paced, more one-dimensional lives of the Sioux holy man [Black Elk] and the Alabama farmer [Nate Shaw]. There is a sharp poignance in [John G.] Neihardt's description of Black Elk and his friends on the Pine Ridge reservation. "Little else but weather ever happened in that country—other than the sun and moon and stars going over—and there was little for the old men to do but wait for yesterday". Malcolm X comments to his collaborator on the radically different circumstances in his urban experience. "With the fast pace of newly developing incidents today, it is easy for something that is done or said tomorrow to be outdated even by sunset on the same day". "Sunset" indeed came while Malcolm X was in the throes of a rapid personal transformation. Before the assassination, however, he and Haley had fixed at least the outlines of a new identity born in the tumult of the 1960's. Yet this new self is also firmly anchored in the personal past. Malcolm X once remarked: "why am I as I am? To understand that of any person, his whole life, from birth, must be reviewed. All of our experiences fuse into our personality. Everything that ever happened to us is an ingredient". Had Alex Haley not been at his side, Malcolm X might never have grasped the basic patterns and interactions of his violently changing inner and outer worlds.

To test this judgment, we must take note of the writer's crucial role as revealed in the biographical Epilogue. There Haley records not only Malcom X's last months but traces in some detail the process of collaboration interrupted by the assassin's bullets. "Nothing can be in this book's manuscript that I didn't say", the subject insisted, "and nothing can be left out that I want in it". In return, Haley won an equally significant concession: "I asked for—and he gave—his permission that at the end of the book I could write comments of my own about him which would not be subject to his review". As Malcolm X pointedly remarked, "a writer is what I want, not an interpreter". But the Epilogue reveals that such a distinction is illusory. Though Haley made extraordinary efforts to subordinate himself to his partner and subject, his more vital achievement was to get Malcolm X to *see, say,* and *believe* the changes and continuities in his life and character which Haley had come to see. Such self-awareness is the crucial consequence, is it not, of any successful autobiographical act? How can we know that, even in the true autobiography, illumination has not come this way?

Their cooperation began coolly enough. Skepticism and mistrust abounded on both sides—as it also existed in many readers' minds of 1965—and perhaps still exists in 1981. For at the time of his death Minister Malcolm X of the Nation of Islam was widely (though falsely, as I think this book shows) depicted as a dangerous, rigid, and violent racist. For his part, Malcolm X was probably right to distrust Haley who, after all, was a thoroughly middle-class black, associated with white magazines whose viewpoints on race were little different from other mass media. Later, in their midnight sessions in Greenwich Village, Haley's adroit questioning gradually won over his suspicious subject while encouraging him to probe more deeply into the violent past and the problematic present. All the while, Malcolm X was living through the agony of his break with his leader and father-figure, the Honorable Elijah Muhammad. The temptation was great to revise the past just as it was being recovered. This Haley perceived as a great danger. Not only would it rob his story of dramatic interest and suspense, but would undermine the chief trait revealed in Malcolm X's character: this ability to move and live fully in each stage and milieu of his life, his capacity to reenter each part of the past with sympathy yet with moral judgment. *Then* seen from *now* is, of course, the perspective of all autobiography. Haley succeeded brilliantly in getting Malcolm X to balance memories of his sinful past and his initial conversion in prison against more recent changes—including the hegira to Mecca and his second conversion there to a larger, raceless vision of mankind and society.

In this intricate interaction, Malcolm X's passionate desire to historicize his existence, to tell the "raw, naked truth" about the "life of only one ghetto-created Negro" is not bypassed but actually sharpened by Haley's psychological probings. When, for instance, Haley got his collaborator to talk about the women in his past, some deepseated fears rose to the surface. "I don't *completely* trust anyone", he tells Haley. Malcolm X looked squarely at me. "You I trust about twenty-five percent"! The full significance of this emerges months later when Malcolm X blurts into the phone, "Alex Haley?... I trust you seventy percent". This dramatic shift in one relationship throws all the others into sharp relief. Quite simply, trust and mistrust is the root problem in this man's life and mind. These contending attitudes might never have been juxtaposed so effectively into an explanatory pattern if Haley, the second consciousness here, had not encouraged his partner to make connections between his social and psychic life. As the record of an often unpleasant inward journey of self-definition, *The Autobiography of Malcolm X* illustrates the consequences as historical truth-telling of two men's collaboration.

These ideological and confessional dimensions are established in Malcolm X's re-created voice and words. Through Haley, the reader participates in imagination, as the midnight monologist paces the floor of Haley's flat and *talks* the spectres of his violent past into reappearance.

As a wide-ranging dramatic monologue—one filled with an urgency unlike either *All God's Dangers* or *Black Elk Speaks—The Autobiography of Malcolm X* is knit together as a history-discourse by a rich pattern of metaphors of self. The commonest of these unifying tropes is Malcolm X as secular traveler and spiritual pilgrim. A string of names, nicknames, and aliases mark the successive stages on this life-journey, just as clothing and personal belongings become its emblematic images. But what encapsulates most inclusively Malcolm X's entire life, including his not-so-brief partnership with Haley, is the repeated pattern of two persons face to face—one a dark-skinned Negro, the other a light-skinned or white partner or opponent. The variations of this vivid pairing are numerous: Malcolm Little's father and almost-white mother arguing and fighting; his mother and black-skinned Ella Collins embracing at the insane asylum; Malcolm Little dancing with black Laura and then, on the same evening, with white Sophia; his last handshake at the traffic-light with the white man, on his return from Mecca. These are actual figures from the past. But they also dramatize deep emotions struggling for balance in one man's memory and psyche. They are metaphors, that is, of the ceaseless, though changing tension between bitter distrust and guarded trust, domination and love, physical violence and words in all his personal and public relationships. If this emblematic and actual battle between dark and light begins with his murdered father and insane mother, it is eventually resolved in Malcolm X's vision in the prison cell, where the shadowy figure in the corner "wasn't black and...

wasn't white". Essential aspects of this black man's identity are clarified by two disparately defined figures from the past fighting but always somehow communicating. Haley is at once participant, outsider, and manager of this self-defining dialectic. In each role he stands in for the reader who, as in all autobiographical encounters, joins in the recreation of a subject first by *distrusting* and then coming to *trust* the words on the page. The brutal fact of Malcolm X's assassination renders the reader's experience of this process particularly poignant as well as socially relevant. Death indeed cut Malcolm X off in the midst of self-transformation. Alex Haley perceived, furthered, and eventually got Malcolm X himself to see this change as a continuity in his own life and character. Just before that tragic death—in which we, as white Americans and Europeans are very much implicated—this vital black man and driven human being became, in the words of the poet Robert Hayden, "much more than there was time to be". (pp. 159-63)

> Albert E. Stone, "Collaboration in Contemporary American Autobiography," in Revue Française d'Études Américaines, No. 14, May, 1982, pp. 151-65.

Harold Courlander (essay date 1986)

[*In 1977 Courlander accused Haley of plagiarizing from his work,* The African *(1968). Haley later conceded to the charges and Courlander was awarded $500,000 in a court settlement. In the following excerpt, Courlander points out ethnological errors in* Roots, *arguing that Kunta Kinte is far from being an "authentic African."*]

Haley aspired for Kunta [in **Roots**] not only to be an authentic African, but the African par excellence, the real and true African who would not be seduced from "Africanness," the natural-man African who would stubbornly resist transformation from what he was at the time of his capture, a figure symbolic of the cultural greatness of Africa. He was to be the ideal against which goodness and evil, spirit, fortitude, uncompromising courage, or surrender could be measured, with his Gambian village and heritage an ever-present backdrop.

Yet what struck me forcibly in numerous readings of **Roots** is how un-African Kunta is most of the time, and the extent to which Haley unwittingly derogated the ideal he sought to celebrate. Kunta's behavior, perceptions, and explanations of self frequently are untrue to African personality, African knowledge of people and the world around them, African technology and capability, and the disciplines and sophistication of most African societies.

The 148-page overture to the narrative is devoted to the Mandinka village setting. Its purpose is to reveal and establish the African psyche and cultural richness in preparation for what comes later, and to explain the basis of Kunta's trauma after his capture. We are introduced to Mandinka mores and attitudes which condition Kunta, so that we will know him to be a true African. Nevertheless, once he departs from his village of Juffure we hardly recognize him as the same person, and on occasion he appears to be an African in blackface.

One of the disturbing aspects of Kunta's character is Haley's concept of him as a primitive being, which actually derogates both the protagonist and the level of his tribal culture. Kunta emerges as a young man too often baffled by non-African things that probably would not have perplexed the average Mandinka of his age and times. On many occasions he is immoderately slow in interpreting what he observes; in early parts of the book, at least (and sometimes in later parts), his overriding responses to difficult situations are giant-sized anger and blind rage; he is much too sexually innocent (even prudish) for a person of his age, African or not; he has an animal-like sense of smell that is paramount over his other senses; and though he often thinks and speaks of the disciplines of his Mandinka culture, they are never truly integrated into his nature. It is not easy to appreciate Kunta as an African. Haley repeatedly reminds us that he is, and Kunta repeatedly insists that he is, while rarely showing or persuading us that he is.

Haley perceives his protagonist as the product of an isolated Islamic-African community scarcely touched by alien influences. In response to critical comments noting that the village of Juffure in reality had been intruded upon by European traders and slavers even before Kunta's day, and thus had knowledge of at least some European ways and material things, Haley responded that he had exercised a writer's prerogative to dramatize the conflict between the old and the new. We accept his right to redesign Juffure and, to an extent, history in the interest of shaping his novel. However, the Mandinka, like the Bamana, Soninke and other peoples of the region, were far more sophisticated about Europeans and products of Europe than Haley suggests. They knew of sailing ships, cannons and muskets, for example. Wars of the period between towns and kingdoms often utilized European-made weapons, while muskets and even gunpowder were made by local craftsmen. The Mandinka, like other peoples of the Sudan, were familiar with glass and glass products brought in along the northern trade routes. They knew the technology of smelting and metal forging, and their goldsmiths were capable of shaping wires and chains from gold, silver and brass.

Yet Kunta fails to recognize a musket when he sees it and does not have the words to identify a white man's ship as a ship or a sail as a sail. Many other commonplace objects are deemed by Haley to be totally outside his character's experience. This assessment of Kunta's intelligence and awareness is distressing. It would have greatly amazed other boys or young men of Juffure.

When Kunta is first brought to the slave ship he perceives it only as "a great dark thing" having "tall poles with thick wrappings of coarse white cloth." A little later, in terror, he becomes aware that "this place was moving." Eventually he comes to terms with it as a "big canoe" or a "great canoe." When the sails are hoisted, what Kunta senses from the hold is "some very heavy object being creaked very slowly upward." And days later he is allowed to go on deck and notes that "the cloths seemed to be filled up with the wind."

To Kunta, a razor is a "narrow, gleaming thing" rather than a special variety of knife. A musket is "some kind of heavy metal stick with a hole in the end." A shipboard cannon is "a huge, terrible looking metal thing." Just about every European object encountered by Kunta is represented as exotic and mysterious, giving him little opportunity to demonstrate that he is a reasoning human being with normal African perceptions and knowledge.

A sailor playing an accordion is seen by Kunta as "a toubob pulling out and pushing in between his hands some peculiar folding thing that made a wheezing sound," rather than as a man operating a bellows that produced unusual musical tones. It is still less flattering to Kunta (and by extension to his people) that he characterizes a violin as "an even more oddly shaped light wooden thing with a slender black neck and four taut, thin strings running almost its length," since stringed musical instruments, some bowed, some plucked, were known to even the smallest Sudanic villages. Equally astonishing is Kunta's mental reference to the "blowing of a strange sounding horn" which turns out to be a conch trumpet, ubiquitous in Africa as a musical or signalling device. When the *Lord Ligonier* docks at the end of its journey, it "bumps hard against something solid and unyielding," and on land Kunta sees "some kind of a marketplace" in which there are objects that "seemed to be fruits and vegetables."

Kunta's ignorance of, or uncertainties about, things that would be recognized or quickly reasoned out by his Mandinka peers is almost without end. On the plantation he observes someone weaving dried cornshucks "into what [he] guessed was a broom." When he sees glass he knows only that it is "something clear and shiny," although African people near the trade routes were quite familiar with it. He characterizes wire, a regular trade item in the Sudan, as "a kind of metal twine." And he refers to the horse as "a strange animal," though horses had been a part of the scene in Sudanic Africa for centuries.

Can Kunta really be the African through whom we are supposed to glimpse the breadth and depth of African achievement and knowledge?

Haley appears to have believed that while his Gambian Africans lacked so much knowledge about the outside world they had an enormously developed sense of scent, the power to smell and identify things where sight and sound failed. In this respect he placed his protagonist in the same class with leopards and other wild creatures of the bush. It is understandable, of course, that he would

want to convey to the reader something of the foulness of the slave ship's hold and its effect on the captives. And so we have, page after page, such phrases as "his nose was assaulted by an unbelievable stink"; "he could feel and smell his own vomit on his chest"; "cursing, gasping and gagging in the stink"; "the stench smelled even worse than before"; and so on, ad infinitum.

Much of this, particularly on the slave ship, can simply be charged to overkill. But as event follows event, the reader begins to feel that Kunta's perceptions are dominated by his olfactory powers, and that most of the smells are unpleasant or evil. Shortly after his capture he wonders why he had not smelled the toubob slavers coming after him. On shipboard he experiences "some indescribable smell" from a slave woman's private parts. On land he is revolted by the smell of filthy swine, and, again, his "nose stifled at the smelling spread of guts" when a pig is killed. He can distinguish by smell, even at a distance, the bodies of American-born plantation slaves: "he heard the voices of what he smelled were many black people"; "he could smell the black one he had choked"; and "he knew from the smell that he [a certain slave] was the one who held the rope after Kunta had been trapped by the dogs." He smells a dog approaching.

Time and again Kunta reacts to the noxious smell of whites (One cannot help wondering whether there is a subtle act of reprisal here for white stereotypes of the smell of blacks). Thus we read: "almost choking with the awful toubob stink"; the mass smell of a crowd of whites hits "like the blow of a giant fist in Kunta's face"; "Kunta could smell the bodies of many unfamiliar toubob." He sees two Indians on the road and observes to himself that they smell different from whites and Africans.

The power of, and obsession with, smelling that Haley imposes on his African ancestor is an unending lietmotif. The unfortunate subliminal effect is to place Kunta on a level with an animal order of being rather than with advanced though scent-diminished humans—something Haley surely did not intend.

For the first 148 pages of **Roots** we see Kunta Kinte as a normal, alert Mandinka boy not too different from other boys, learning and absorbing the social controls, relationships and traditions that make a village community possible. But after his capture we see him as a personality compounded of rages. There are, to be sure, gross provocations. He suffers all the misery consonant with cruel captivity, the same misery experienced by his comrades. But mere endurance of misery, it seemed to Haley, would not be worthy of his ancestor-hero. Never mind that so many slaves, once in secure captivity, accept the physical reality of their condition even while reflecting privately on their fate, and perhaps on possibilities of escape or retribution. Haley aspired for Kunta to be exceptional, and one of the ways he did so was by endowing him with a propensity to rage exceeding that of his shipmates. Thus Kunta becomes and remains the undiluted Mandinka warrior, in contrast to his more typical shipboard companions and the docile fellow slaves on the plantation. Rage, much of it reflexive and unthinking, becomes a component of his character. Regrettably it does not enhance the concept of a warrior hero to see him thrashing about mindlessly in situations where the momentary odds are greatly against him.

Bound tightly by stout ropes while in the slave coffle, he does not reflect and ponder the possibilities of escape. Instead, "in wild fury, Kunta lunged back and forth trying to break his bonds." Again, "Kunta struggled and howled with fury." And yet again we see Kunta "springing and lunging amid shouts and screams." On shipboard, "his mind screamed . . . 'Kill the Toubob'"; "he felt himself about to burst with rage"; "he felt like he wanted to *bite* through his chains"; " . . . an explosion of rage. With his throat ripping out almost an animal's cry, Kunta lunged"; "so great was his fury"; "his heart throbbed with lust to murder"; "he came up snarling with rage and terror." (In fairness, Haley sometimes allowed other shipboard captives to share in the screaming and thrashing: "Men started shouting all around him, screaming to Allah and His spirits, banging their heads against the planking, thrashing wildly against their rattling shackles").

But Kunta's wild fury is not drained in the coffle and on shipboard. It accompanies him to the plantations: he has the impulse "to leap for the throats of the four blacks"; he "leaped up in a rage, snarling like a leopard"; he "sat staring with cold fury"; "he let his eyes bore with hatred"; "exploded upward—his hands clamping around the driver's big throat like the bone-cracking jaws of a hyena"; "a rage flooded him such as he had never felt before." And chained down in a hut after an attempt to escape, he tries putting one of the [iron] rings in his mouth and biting is as hard as he could" until one of his teeth cracks.

There is nothing in the Haley family chronicles to suggest that Kunta Kinte was a chain biter. African cultures have proverbs that in effect warn against biting what is unbiteable. Circumstances can motivate blind rage and irrational violent action. But surely Kunta's architect could have provided him with more subtle and reasoning responses for use on occasion.

It is puzzling why Haley decided to make his protagonist sexually innocent for such a long period of his life. There is nothing in Kunta's early background, as revealed to us, to make it reasonable. Mandinka culture? Islamic teachings? Advice of the elders, either African or Afro-American? Some unusual event in his childhood or youth? Nothing explains it. Kunta's sexual innocence is totally out of tune with prevailing African attitudes; with the weeks of manhood training through which young Mandinka boys must go; with the word of mouth interchanges between boys growing into puberty in Juffure; and with the normal opportunities to catch sight of an uncovered female body.

Kunta is captured in his sixteenth year. In the slave coffle he sees three girl captives "all naked," and we are told that "Kunta could only avert his eyes; he had never seen a naked woman before." On the slave ship he is much affected by the nakedness of both women and man. Of course Haley is attempting to stress the cruel indignity perpetrated on the slaves by taking their clothing away, but he does not just state it and leave it. He repeats it over and over. On three consecutive pages reference to nakedness appears nine times. Clearly it has something to do with Kunta's state of mind.

On the plantation, Kunta leads a life of emotional stresses and crises, but there are no sexual incidents until his thirty-ninth year (The television production invented an interim incident, no doubt to make his life more plausible). Older men on the plantation sometimes slyly tease him about his totally unsexual life. But finally, when Kunta is nearly forty, the great thing happens; "Bell's hand suddenly grasped his, and with a single motion she blew out both of the candles and swiftly with Kunta feeling as if he were a leaf borne by a rushing stream, they went together through the curtained doorway into the other room and lay down facing one another on the bed. Looking deeply into his eyes, she reached out to him, and they drew together, and for the first time in the thirty-nine rains of his life, he held a woman in his arms."

Was it the author's oversight that kept Kunta virginal to such an age? Or an idea that sexuality would place him on the same plane as the plantation slaves he generally despised? We are told that Mandinka men generally married around the age of thirty, but that does not mean they were sexually inactive before that time. Whatever the literary reason, if there was a reason, Kunta's behavior does not ring African or true.

Haley's basic theme is that despite the pressures of two New World cultures—the white master society and black slave society—Kunta forever remains an unreconstructed African. The idea came, Haley says, from the tidbits of oral tradition passed on to him by his grandmother and others of her generation to the effect that Kunta (Toby) never forgot his original homeland and even in his later years continued to speak of it and insist that his real name was "Kin-tay." That is what Haley built on. But the fictional Kunta goes far beyond the wispy family allusions.

It might be reasonably supposed that after living so many years in America, Kunta would come to comprehend that his slave companions, even though not African born and reared, were people to whom he need not condescend. One may understand, and even forgive, Kunta's initial reactions to the black "pagans" who did not know how to do things the correct African way, who had forgotten so much about their origins, and who even smelled different from Africans. After all, he was only sixteen on his arrival, and he had the adolescent capacity for contempt as well as prejudices fostered by his Mandinka/Islamic training. On the other hand, his youth should have given him flexibility for swift acculturation and development.

So it is more discouraging than inspiring to see Kunta twenty-odd years later still trying to separate himself from the taint of New World blackness. At the age of thirty-seven, Kunta is vowing to himself "that now more than ever his dignity must become a shield between him and all of those who called themselves 'niggers'." There is only snobbery in his repetitious thought that the other blacks "knew nothing of their ancestors," while he could recite "the names of Kintes from the ancient clan in old Mali down across the generations." What Kunta regards as dignity in reality is intolerance.

Haley placed great value on keeping his African ancestor pure, heroic, faithful to Africa and the African way, and contemptuous of those slaves who had adapted and found their own ways of surviving. But common sense tells us that, even while remembering and preserving some of his old ways (in particular, religious teachings), Kunta would have had to develop new awareness between his sixteenth year and his thirty-seventh. He had lived a greater span of time in the new environment than in the old. And we know from documented cases that Muslim Africans apparently did acculturate and adapt, even while the more devout among them preserved elements of their Islamic beliefs. Nevertheless, uncompromising "Africanness" was the theme, and Kunta was doomed to play out this unrelenting role to the end. While there are black individuals whom Kunta learns to respect and even love, as a group the black community remains beyond his acceptance.

There is a curious point-of-view intrusion into the narrative, in which Kunta—seeking reasons for his rejection of most of the slaves—becomes in effect an ethnologist. It is natural enough that he should be aware of differences between Juffure ways and those of the plantation, but not likely that a person in his circumstances would take such detailed note of the similarities. For similarities between people are generally taken for granted. Someone in a strange land would not think it at all noteworthy that the people around him drink water from some kind of cup, generally cover themselves with some kind of clothing or decoration, work to grow food, or take care of their young. If African women generally carry infants on one hip it should not be a revelation to Kunta that slave women do the same. But Kunta becomes obsessed with what Bell, the cook in the Big House, like an academic Africanist, calls "Africanisms." And so, early in his New World experience, he attains an ethnological perspective. He observes:

> Ignorant as they were, some of the things they did were purely African, and he could tell that they were totally unaware of it themselves. For one thing, he had heard all his life the very same sounds of exclamation, accompanied by the very same hand gestures and facial expression....

> And Kunta had been reminded of Africa in the way that black women here wore their hair tied up with strings into very tight plaits, although African women

often decorated their plaits with colorful beads. And the women of this place knotted cloth pieces over their heads, although they didn't tie them correctly....

> Kunta also saw Africa in the way the black children here were trained to treat their elders with politeness and respect. He saw it in the way that mothers carried their babies with their plump little legs straddling the mothers' bodies....

As he has done with various other characters in *Roots,* Haley has thus placed in Kunta's mind the observations and knowledge of generations of scholars. Kunta's ethnological reflections do not make him seem more African, but more synthetic.

To breathe new life into the theme of Kunta's undiminished "Africanness," some twenty years later another first-generation African is introduced, an older man named Boteng Bodiako who identifies himself (curiously) as a Ghanaian. Kunta is up at the Big House, and he hears the sound of a percussion instrument being played not far off. He knows from the "sharpness and power" of the playing that the musician is not a plantation black, but a genuine countryman. He races to where a crowd of slaves are dancing and discovers "a lean, gray-haired, very black man" playing some kind of gourd instrument. There is instant, mystical recognition between them: "As they flicked glances... Kunta's eyes met his—and a moment later they all but sprang toward each other, the other blacks gawking, then snickering, as they embraced. 'Ah-salakium-salaam!' 'Malakium-salaam!' The words came as if neither of them had ever left Africa."

This scene is the grossest kind of overkill. The plantation witnesses have a right to snicker. Boteng is not the first live African Kunta has seen in the New World, nor is Kunta the first Boteng has seen. It is not a case of long separated brothers finding each other, but two men who left Africa when they were very young, one a Mandinka and the other a "Ghanaian." Later on, the two meet again to recall the Africa they remember, and Boteng becomes a kind of father figure to Kunta.

Nowhere in *Roots* is there any visible fear of overdoing Kunta's "Africanness." When he is beyond forty and his daughter Kizzy is born, we are told: "Kunta felt Africa pumping in his veins." Regrettably, allusion to this mystic plasma does not make Kunta appear more African, nor does it help us to know him better, or reveal any larger dimension or deeper truth.

Some of the various questions raised about *Roots* (though not all) resulted from its misrepresented and ambiguous genre. Once it became generally accepted that the book is essentially a fictional work, even while including genealogical facts, the question of historical veracity has diminished importance. But as a novel, the literary elements loom larger and veracity or credibility of the central character becomes paramount. (pp. 294-302)

Harold Courlander, "Kunta Kinte's Struggle to be African," in PHYLON: The Atlanta University Review of Race and Culture, *Vol. XLVII, No. 4, December, 1986, pp. 294-302.*

FURTHER READING

Adams, Russell. "An Analysis of the *Roots* Phenomenon in the Context of American Racial Conservatism." *Présence Africaine* 116, No. 4 (1980): 125-40.
   Explores factors that contributed to the success of *Roots.*

Baker, John F. "PW Interviews: Alex Haley." *Publishers Weekly* 210, No. 10 (6 September 1976): 8-9, 12.
   Haley and Baker discuss the creation of *Roots* and its subsequent television adaptation.

Blayney, Michael Steward. "*Roots* and the Noble Savage." *North Dakota Quarterly* 54, No. 1 (Winter 1986): 1-17.
   Contends that *Roots* was popular "not because it inspired black pride . . . but because it struck a responsive chord in its ninety per cent white audience."

Marsh, Carol P. "The Plastic Arts Motif in *Roots." CLA Journal* XXVI, No. 3 (March 1983): 325-33.
   Examines the motif of "plastic arts"—carving, weaving, and blacksmithing—in *Roots.*

Mills, Gary B., and Mills, Elizabeth Shown. "*Roots* and the New 'Faction': A Legitimate Tool for Clio?" *The Virginia Magazine of History and Biography* 89, No. 1 (January 1981): 3-26.
   Examines apparent genealogical errors in *Roots.*

"Satan in the Ghetto." *Newsweek* LXVI, No. 20 (15 November 1965): 130, 132.
   Summary and review of *The Autobiography of Malcolm X.*

Nichols, Charles. "The Slave Narrators and the Picaresque Mode: Archetypes for Modern Black Personae." In *The Slave's Narrative,* edited by Charles T. Davis and Henry Louis Gates, Jr., pp. 283-98. Oxford: Oxford University Press, 1985.
   Claims *The Autobiography of Malcolm X* as "probably the most influential book read by this generation of Afro-Americans."

Othow, Helen Chavis. "*Roots* and the Heroic Search for Identity." *CLA Journal* XXVI, No. 3 (March 1983): 311-24.
   Describes *Roots* as the embodiment of the "feverish search for meaning in an alien universe."

Jupiter Hammon

1711?-1800?

American poet and essayist.

Although Phillis Wheatley has often been called America's first black author, twentieth-century scholarship has now determined that Hammon was almost certainly the first black American whose work appeared in print. His first poem, *An Evening Thought: Salvation by Christ, with Penetential Cries,* appeared in 1761 and antedates Wheatley's verse by at least nine years. Hammon's best known work, *An Address to the Negroes in the State of New-York* (1787), promises a just spiritual reward for obedient slaves, depicting a heaven where white masters and black slaves will be judged as equals.

Hammon's birthdate is believed to be October 11, 1711, though many sources place his birth nearly ten years later. He was born a slave on the estate of Henry Lloyd on Long Island and served the Lloyd family for three generations. As a household slave, Hammon was given many privileges not available to other slaves: he attended primary school with Lloyd's children and learned to read and write. In 1733 Hammon purchased a Bible from Mr. Lloyd and began the religious studies that greatly influenced both his poetry and prose. The inspirational hymns of Charles Wesley, John Newton, and William Cowper also profoundly affected Hammon's verse. *An Evening Thought,* which strongly resembles eighteenth-century devotional hymns, reflects Hammon's evangelical preoccupation with salvation, righteousness, and eternal life.

After the death of Henry Lloyd in 1763, Hammon became the property of Lloyd's son Joseph, who fled with his family to Connecticut when the British took control of Long Island. In Hartford, Hammon produced four works, the most noteworthy being *An Address to Miss Phillis Wheatly* [sic]. Printed in 1778, this poem suggests that Wheatley's enslavement in Ethiopia, arrival in America, and conversion to Christianity were the product of divine will. The other works printed during Hammon's years in Connecticut include two essays that are commonly referred to as sermons: *An Essay on the Ten Virgins* (1779), of which no copy is known to exist, and *A Winter Piece: Being a Serious Exhortation, with a Call to the Unconverted, and a Short Contemplation on the Death of Jesus Christ* (1782). A third essay, *An Evening's Improvement: Shewing the Necessity of Beholding the Lamb of God* (1783), was also printed in Hartford. It includes a dialogue in verse, entitled *The Kind Master and Dutiful Servant,* which recommends that all slaves show dutiful servitude.

Following the death of Joseph, Hammon returned to Long Island as the property of Joseph's nephew, John Lloyd, Jr. Hammon produced only one work after his return to the Lloyd estate, although it is possible that other pages of manuscript were never discovered. *An Address to the Negroes in the State of New York* became Hammon's most popular piece. Two editions were issued during his lifetime, and a third was published by members of the Pennsylvania Society for Promoting the Abolition of Slavery after Hammon's death.

Hammon is not widely known. Many critics find his syntax weak and his use of language and theme repetitive. Still others feel that his verse is forced and imperfect in meter and rhyme. The primary reason for Hammon's obscurity, however, is most likely what Vernon Loggins called the author's "conciliatory attitude towards slavery." Hammon was not an avid abolitionist, although he did urge manumission—the emancipation of black children and adolescents—in his *Address to the Negroes in the State of New-York.* Hammon himself, however, preferred to remain in servitude. Citing his advancing age, he stated that he "should hardly know how to take care of [himself]."

While he is still little known today, Hammon remains important as the first black American author to appear in print. His verses are considered the forerunners of Negro spirituals and abolitionist dialogues. After more than a century of neglect, twentieth-century critics are now beginning to recognize Hammon's important contribution to early black American literature.

(For further information about Hammon's life and works, see *Dictionary of Literary Biography,* Vols. 31, 50 and *Nineteenth-Century Literature Criticism,* Vol. 5.)

PRINCIPAL WORKS

An Evening Thought: Salvation by Christ, with Penetential Cries (poetry) 1761
An Address to Miss Phillis Wheatly [sic] (poetry) 1778
An Essay on the Ten Virgins (essay) 1779
*A Winter Piece: Being a Serious Exhortation, with a Call to the Unconverted, and a Short Contemplation on the Death of Jesus Christ (essay and poetry) 1782
†An Evening's Improvement: Shewing the Necessity of Beholding the Lamb of God. The Kind Master and Dutiful Servant (essay and poetry) 1783
An Address to the Negroes in the State of New-York (essay) 1787
America's First Negro Poet: The Complete Works of Jupiter Hammon of Long Island (essays and poetry) 1970

*This work includes *A Poem for Children, with Thoughts on Death.*
†The publication date of this work is uncertain.

Oscar Wegelin (essay date 1915)

[*Wegelin is responsible for discovering Hammon's* An Evening Thought, *thus allowing him to suggest that Hammon merits precedence over Phillis Wheatley as one of the first black American writers. In the following excerpt, he concludes that Hammon's work is "commonplace" but notes that had Hammon received a formal education, he might have "ranked as (Miss Wheatley's) equal if not her superior."*]

As a poet Hammon will certainly not rank among the "Immortals." His verse is stilted, and while some of his rhymings are fairly even, we can easily comprehend that they were written by one not well versed in the art of poesy. They have a sameness which is wearying to the reader and there is too much reiteration, in some cases the same or nearly the same words being employed again and again.

His verse is saturated with a religious feeling not always well expressed, as he did not possess the ability to use the right word at the proper time. Hammon was undoubtedly deeply religious, but his religion was somewhat tinged with narrowness and superstition, a not uncommon fault of the time in which he lived and wrote.

Although grammatically almost perfect, it seems certain that an abler and more experienced hand than his own was responsible for this.

Compared with the verses of Phillis Wheatley, his lines are commonplace and few would care to read them more than once. When we consider, however, that this poor slave had probably no other learning than what he had been enabled to secure for himself during his hours of relaxation from labor, it is surprising that the results are not more meagre. Although his rhymings can hardly be dignified by the name of poetry, they are certainly not inferior to many of the rhymings of his day and generation.

As before noted, his lines breathe a deep religious feeling and were written with the hope that those who would read them would be led from the ways of sin to righteousness. (pp. 19-21)

He was fond of using certain words, and "Salvation" was one of his favorites, it being made use of twenty-three times in his earliest known publication....

Hammon was also fond of using marginal references from Scripture and in some of his writings they are found at every second line. (p. 21)

When we consider that he was probably without any education whatsoever, we marvel that he accomplished as much as he did. Had he had the advantages of learning possessed by Miss Wheatley, it seems possible that as a poet he would have ranked as her equal, if not her superior. His prose writings were also above the mediocre, but from the testimony of one of his printers he was evidently deficient as a speller.

He stands, however, unique in the annals of American Poetry and his works must not be too harshly judged. The disadvantages under which he composed them were probably far greater than we can imagine.

It seems, however, too bad that his verse is entirely of a religious nature. Much would have been added to its interest had he written about some of the events that were transpiring all around him during the War for Independence and the years that followed that struggle.

He seems to have been content to sing the praises of the Master whom he longed to serve and whose reward he some day expected to receive, and with that end in view he labored to instill the blessings of religion into his less fortunate brethren.

For this his memory should be honored and let the broken lines which fell from his pen be cherished, if for no other reason than that they were written by the first American Negro who attempted to give expression to his thoughts in verse. (pp. 21-2)

> *Oscar Wegelin, in his* Jupiter Hammon, American Negro Poet: Selections from His Writings and a Bibliography, *1915. Reprint by Books for Libraries Press, 1969, 51 p.*

Vernon Loggins (essay date 1931)

[*In the following excerpt, Loggins examines external influences on Hammon's literary work.*]

It is an interesting coincidence that most of Hammon's poetry was published at Hartford at a time when that Connecticut town was the literary capital of America. But if the neoclassical "Hartford Wits" [a literary circle which included John Trumbull and Timothy Dwight] read his poems, they no doubt looked upon them as chaotic effusions of crude thoughts poured out in a verse not inappropriate to the cheapest balladry. To the twentieth-century mind, which places a high value on the artlessness of folk poetry, Jupiter Hammon's work takes on a new meaning. There is a strength of wild and native religious feeling in what he wrote, a strength which he achieved without conscious effort. From hearing evangelical sermons and from reading the bible according to his own untrained fancy, he picked up strange notions regarding salvation, penitential cries, redeeming love, tribunal day, the Holy Word, bounteous mercies. His mystic Negro mind played with these notions; and, endowed with the instinct for music which is so strong in his race, he sang out his impressions in such meters as he had become familiar with in the hymns of Charles Wesley and Augustus Montague Toplady, and in such rimes as for the moment pleased his ear. Indeed, his method of composition must have been that of the unknown makers of the spirituals.

Like the spirituals, the poems of Jupiter Hammon were composed to be heard. There is evident in his verse that peculiar sense for sound which is the most distinguishing characteristic of Negro folk poetry. A word that appeals to his ear he uses over and over again, in order, it seems, to cast a spell with it. In *An Evening Thought* the word *salvation* occurs in every three or four lines. Any impressionable sinners who might have heard Jupiter Hammon chant the poem when in the ecstasy of religious emotion no doubt went away to be haunted by the sound of the word *salvation* if not by the idea.... [The] metrical arrangement is that of the ballad stanza with alternating rimes, a verse form which is often found in the early Methodist hymns.... Hammon followed this pattern in all of his poems, though not without marked irregularities. There are numerous cases of wrenched accents demanding an outrageous pronunciation.... [The] most interesting irregularities are the strange rime combinations—such as, *word* and *God, Lord* and *God, call* and *soul, sound* and *down.* Since we know little about how English was spoken by the Negroes on Long Island in the eighteenth century, we cannot determine how far astray Jupiter Hammon's ear was in hearing exact times in such combinations. We can say with definiteness that the riming words which he selected are always sonorous.

While the imagery in Hammon's poems is in general restrained, often taken bodily from the New Testament, there are unexpected turns in the thought which suggest the wild extravagance of the spiritual. The unusual association of ideas in the following stanza from *An Address to Miss Phillis Wheatly* is probably the result of a necessity for rimes:

> God's tender mercy brought thee here;
>   Tost o'er the raging main;
> In Christian faith thou hast a share,
>   Worth all the gold of Spain.

(pp. 11-13)

It must not be supposed that Jupiter Hammon was only primitive and naïve, merely a folk poet incapable of consistent and orderly reflection. *An Address to Miss Phillis Wheatly,* his second poem, written eighteen years after his first spontaneous and chaotic effort, *An Evening Thought,* shows a balanced structure of ideas.... Both this poem and **"A Poem for Children with Thoughts on Death"** are provided with scriptural glosses, and in each the thought association with the Biblical citations is fairly logical and exact. While the two earlier prose pamphlets, *A Winter Piece* and *An Evening's Improvement,* intended as sermons, are rhapsodic and incoherent, the *Address to the Negroes in the State of New-York* displays a regular and firm organization. (pp. 14-15)

[However, Hammon's] attempts at thoughtful composition, such as *An Address to the Negroes in the State of New-York,* fall low in the class of the subliterary. It is his poetry, with all of its artlessness and crudeness, which makes his name important. As the product of the uncultivated Negro imagination and temperament, his verse, slight as the body of it is, forms a unique contribution to American poetry in the eighteenth century. The reader of today is likely to find a more sincere feeling in it than in most religious verse written

in America during Hammon's age. It is a quaint prelude to the rich and varied songs which were to burst spontaneously from the Negro folk a little later, songs which make up the great gift from Africa to the art of America. (pp. 15-16)

> *Vernon Loggins, "The Beginnings of Negro Authorship, 1760-1790," in his* The Negro Author: His Development in America to 1900, *1931. Reprint by Kennikat Press, Inc., 1964, pp. 1-47.*

Jean Wagner (essay date 1962)

[*A French author and critic, Wagner has written authoritative works about black and Southern writers of the United States. In the following excerpt from a work originally published in French in 1962, he praises the "bold syncopations" in Hammon's poetry, commenting that the author's verse was "destined to be heard rather than seen and read."*]

If the quality of [Jupiter Hammon's] verse were the only criterion we might consign him to oblivion forthwith, for his poems, inspired by the Methodist hymns of the period and taking over their phraseology, are crudely composed. Yet Hammon deserves mention above all for his first poem, **"An Evening Thought: Salvation by Christ with Penitential Cries"** ..., which is very close in tone to folk poetry. It represents a halfway stage between the guileless art of the unknown composers of spirituals and the already much wordier manner of the black popular preacher.... [Hammon] can readily be imagined using this poem to appeal to his fellows, until the sonorous repetition of the word "salvation" at regular intervals finally stirs the rhythm that has so often channeled the religious emotions of Negroes.... A shifting of tonic accents and even bold syncopations characterize a poem destined to be heard rather than seen and read. Employing a subtle, complex rhythm, the preacher's voice beings the verse to life, and so he can with impunity set aside the traditional rules of prosody. Hammon probably relied on the extraordinary precision of his auditory sensibility, while remaining unaware of the process. Yet his experiment should be borne in mind, for the black poets of the twentieth century will take it up again.

One can find much less to praise in Jupiter Hammon's religious fervor, which overlaid a strange torpor in his racial sensitivity. For here we are confronted with a neophyte who has been carefully indoctrinated by his entourage and whom kindly treatment has rendered docile. He ultimately ceases even to long for the future restoration of his freedom. More curious still are his endeavors to lull to sleep the same desire in his fellow slaves by turning their thoughts away from terrestrial realities and directing them toward the joys of eternity. In **"The Kind Master and Dutiful Servant,"** basically a dialogue on salvation and God's mercy, the great gap that separates master and slave is conscientiously insisted upon, on the lines of the "aristocratic contempt for the sodden mass of the people," a feature of the Calvinistic outlook that Hammon adopted with a somewhat naïve enthusiasm.... (pp. 17-18)

This passiveness and resignation obscure the genuineness of Hammon's religiosity, so that today we view his Christian faith as something alien to him. His morality also remains undeveloped, and seemingly restricted to Saint Paul's admonition: "Slaves, obey your masters!" He lets fall not a word that might be taken to criticize slavery, in which he sees only the manifestation of divine foresight and mercy. Thus the deportation of Africans to America becomes a kind of providential pilgrimage toward knowledge of the one true God. (pp. 18-19)

> *Jean Wagner, in an introduction to his* Black Poets of the United States: From Paul Laurence Dunbar to Langston Hughes, *translated by Kenneth Douglas, University of Illinois Press, 1973, pp. 3-36.*

Kenny J. Williams (essay date 1970)

[*In the following excerpt, Williams evaluates Hammon's poetry, concluding that the author's work mirrors much of eighteenth-century American religious poetry.*]

Although much of his poetry was published at Hartford at a time when the Hartford Wits were attempting to aid in the creation of a national literature, there is a great deal of difference between any of their works and the existing poems by Hammon. His poetry was not hampered by the rules of neo-classicism as was the work of the Hartford Wits, neither was his poetry pallid imitations of current English modes. Rather, his poetry is closer in spirit and technique to the poetry of the earlier century of New England, the poetry produced by the New England Puritans of the seventeenth century.... There is in Hammon's poetry a religious feeling which resulted in an intensity which he apparently achieved without conscious effort. From hearing evangelical sermons and from reading the Bible according to his own interpretations, he adapted his ideas regarding salvation, penitence, redeeming grace, God's mercy, death, and judgment day to his poems. He recorded his ideas and impressions in a poetic meter which is designed to be heard. A word which appealed to him is repeated until the very word itself seems to cast a spell. In **"An Evening Thought..."** the word *salvation* appears so often that the sound of the word becomes far more important than the message of the poem. (pp. 10-11)

[In **"An Evening Thought...,"**] Hammon used a variation of the ballad stanza, a verse form which is often found in Methodist and in Baptist hymnals and which is the basic pattern of [Michael Wigglesworth's] *The Day of Doom.* This pattern consists of quatrains whose first and third lines are iambic trimeter; the four-line stanza has a usual rhyme scheme of abcd. Although Hammon followed this pattern in most of his poems, there are instances of irregularities which can be seen in **"An Evening Thought...."** In addition to his adaptation of the ballad rhyme pattern to abab, there are examples of distorted accents as well as of syncopation which occur most frequently in the iambic trimeter lines. To the twentieth century reader, Hammon's poetry seems similar to so much of eighteenth-century poetry for his work tends to employ unusual rhyming patterns and combinations.... When odd uses of poetic diction occur, they often result because his choice of language is an immediate outgrowth of an apparent need for rhyming patterns. (pp. 13-14)

It is apparent that most of Hammon's religious poetry is characterized by a certain naivete, and his art of versification seems little more than spontaneously rhymed doggerel; but this is the same charge which is frequently hurled at Michael Wigglesworth who also used poetry as a means of instruction and as a means of simply stating basic religious concepts. The difference between these two poets, however, rests in the difference between the complexity of the religious dogma of Puritanism which is explained by Wigglesworth and the simplicity of the more primitive forms of Protestantism. In the eighteenth century complexity of dogma and creed was not a characteristic of the Methodist and Baptist movements.... These more primitive groups stressed "religion by faith" as opposed to the Puritan emphasis on "religion by reason." Wigglesworth—for example—in attempting to simplify Puritanism made its doctrines appear harsh and terrible when he placed them into ballad form; while Hammon, on the other hand, in attempting to capture the tone of primitive Christianity, seems extremely childlike in his wonder and in his awe. (pp. 14-15)

Hammon has been condemned because of his acceptance of the institution of slavery; yet, it must be remembered that he was in no position to understand it in its fullest impact. With his limited experiences in Long Island and in Hartford and with his own lot being much better than that of the average workingman of the period, it is no wonder that he tended to place all of his attention on matters of religion. While his poems are far superior to his prose works, his poetry is, after all, eighteenth-century religious poetry and does not differ too greatly from other such works of the period. His infrequent references to slavery and to his race are the only distinguishing marks of his work. The chaos of the rhythmic structure and the distortions of rhyme which appear, the sudden bursts of religious fervor, the sometimes strained poetic diction coupled with apparent sincerity are characteristics of religious poetry in America during the seventeenth and eighteenth centuries. (pp. 16-17)

> *Kenny J. Williams, "A New Home in a New Land," in her* They Also Spoke: An Essay on Negro Literature in America, 1787-1930, *Townsend Press, 1970, pp. 3-49.*

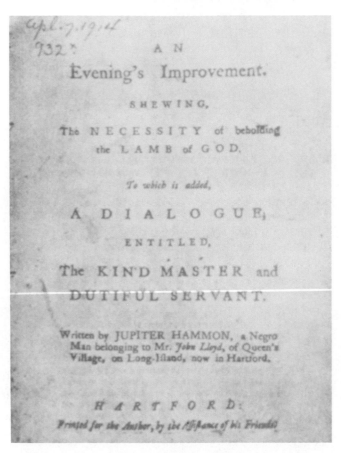

Title page of the sermon in which Hammon promised his fellow slaves, "if we love God, black as we be, and despised as we are, God will love us."

Writing about Black Literature (essay date 1976)

[*The following excerpt was written by an unidentified student of Chester J. Fontenot, Jr., who revised the piece for publication in* Writing about Black Literature. *The critic's opinion differs sharply from that of some other commentators, who have maintained that* An Evening Thought *reveals Hammon's personal resignation to slavery. According to the author of this essay, Hammon "uses ambiguous language and symbols to create a poem which subtly protests against . . . (slavery)."*]

In **"An Evening Thought"** Jupiter Hammon uses ambiguous language and symbols to create a poem which subtly protests against the inhuman conditions which slavery created. Hammon's language is characterized by the repetitive use of words such as "thy," "only," and "true," to suggest an emphasis on salvation from God and opposed to the corrupted version of salvation the slavemaster offered, and by the use of ambiguous words such as "salvation," "king," "spirit," "preparation," and "nation." These characteristics lead one to think that Hammon's poem has a dual quality: (1) on the surface the poem seems to be addressed to those who either are sinners, or who are simply misled by false versions of salvation; (2) on another level, the poem seems to be addressed to the slaves in an attempt to move them from a passive stance with regards to the master to an active, rebellion's position. (p. 116)

Hammon begins **"An Evening Thought"** by introducing the reader to the concept of salvation. He says, "Salvation comes by Christ alone! The only Son of God." The concept of salvation here is ambiguous—with the knowledge that Hammon was a slave, one might conclude that he is talking about salvation in two senses: (1) as a transcendence from the secular world; and (2) as an escape from slavery. If we place emphasis on certain words in the first two lines of the poem (alone and only), we can see that the second sense of salvation may be the one that Hammon is talking about here . . . . Hammon continues his usage of ambiguous language in lines 4-8; they read as follows:

> Dear Jesus we would fly to thee,
> And leave off every sin,
> Thy tender mercy well agree,
> Salvation from our King

I think that by using the word "we," Hammon is talking about slaves. The metaphor he uses to suggest union with Christ—"we would fly to thee"—implies freedom from bondage of some sort. Hammon's use of "sin" is also ambiguous. Sin can mean two things here: (1) the original sin which all men are *born* with; and (2) the sin of being *born* black. I think Hammon is using sin in the latter sense. His use of "King" to suggest both God and the slavemaster here is important. "King" suggests the slavemaster because Hammon says, "Salvation from our King." This is an ambiguous line: It can mean that God will give man salvation, or that the slaves need to be saved from the slavemaster. (pp. 116-17)

Hammon shifts his stance from that of mediator between God and slaves (or mankind) to that of a slave. He says:

> We cry as sinners to the Lord
> Salvation to obtain
> It is firmly fixt his holy word,
> Ye shall not cry in vain

The significance of this shift is that Hammon moves the poem from a critique of social conditions to an appeal to the slaves for insurrectionary action. Again, Hammon emphasizes "We cry as sinners to the Lord," as opposed to an appeal for freedom to the slavemaster . . . .

Hammon's appeal though does not seem to be in the form of a passive prayer, but of an invocation of the "nations" for action. He asks God to "turn our dark benighted souls;/ Give us a true motion." One might ask here if the souls are "dark" and "benighted" because of their sins, or because of the color of their skins? If we assume the latter choice, it seems that Hammon is calling for inspiration—divine or otherwise—for all himself and other slaves to plot their paths to freedom. Hammon's language suggests freedom. He says, "O let our prayers ascend on high." The notion of upward movement combined with his previous use of the metaphor suggesting flight ("Dear Jesus we would fly to thee"), suggest transformation of social conditions and not transcendance to another ethereal world. (p. 118)

Hammon seems to write as if [a] revolution is occurring while he is writing his poem. He says..., "Lord unto whom now shall we go,/ Or see a safe Abode." These two lines imply that the slaves are searching for alternatives to slavery (perhaps that they are considering escape by means of the underground railroad). "Unto whom now shall we go," and "safe abode," seem to suggest that the slaves are searching for a plan for escape, perhaps even for places and people to aide them in their escape. In any case, these two lines are illusions to escape from slavery by some means.

Hammon also tries to reverse the stereotypical image of the black person as damned, as not fit to sit in the presence of the Lord. He does this by referring to the slaves as "Blessed of the Lord," and by insisting that their "souls are fit for Heaven." He asks that the slaves accept the true Word of God, and that they move toward an acknowledgment of their plight. (p. 119)

Hammon's use of ambiguous language and symbols gives this poem a dual quality. I think that the poem is addressed to slaves. Hammon uses dual language and symbols to mask his intentions from the slaveholders. The poem is, only superficially, addressed to believers in Christianity who are in need of salvation. (pp. 119-20)

> "'An Evening Thought' as a Protest Poem,"
> in Writing about Black Literature, edited by
> Chester J. Fontenot, Jr., Nebraska Curriculum Development Center, 1976, pp. 116-20.

Bernard W. Bell (essay date 1977)

[*In the following excerpt, Bell claims that Hammon's poetry and prose reflect Hammon's apolitical stance on slavery and black independence.*]

In the case of Jupiter Hammon, we see the influence of the Bible and slavery in shaping an otherworldly view of liberty and equality that distorted his social vision. (p. 176)

Lacking the originality, ironic tension, graphic imagery, and call and response pattern of black American spirituals, [*An Evening Thought*] reveals Hammon's personal resignation to slavery and the inspiration of the Psalms and Methodist hymnals....

The repetition of "Salvation" in twenty-three of the poem's eighty-eight lines does not significantly elevate the prosaic quality of the verse. (p. 177)

Hammon's unimaginative use of the meter, rhyme, diction, and stanzaic pattern of the Methodist hymnal combined with the negative image of Africa and concil-

iatory tone of [his] early poems reveal the poet's limitations and the costly sociopsychological price he paid for the mere semblance of cultural assimilation....

The lessons of the Bible and slavery had taught him that for body and soul, black and white, individual and nation, freedom was God's alone to grant. (p. 178)

Hammon's reference to himself and his people as "Africans by nation" [in *A Winter Piece*] reflects his awareness of the duality of his identity, a duality he unfortunately sought to transcend rather than synthesize through religiosity. Appended to the sermon is the seventeen quatrain *Poem for Children with Thoughts of Death* as further testimony to the poet's piety.

The sermon and poem believed to have been written soon after *A Winter Piece* contain references to "the Present War." In *An Evening's Improvement. Shewing the Necessity of Beholding the Lamb of God*...Hammon is true to his apolitical, religious philosophy of life.... [In] the second half of **"A Dialogue Intitled the Kind Master and the Dutiful Servant,"** the two-page poem concluding the sermon, the poet stands above [a] battle praying for peace.... Banal, bloodless, unoriginal, and nonracial, these lines on Christian virtue tell us as much about the theology whites imposed on colonial blacks as they do about Hammon's warped sense of identity and poetry.

The most decisive evidence of the poet-preacher's exploitation by those who found his religious convictions a model for African-American character and behavior is found in Hammon's final discourse, *An Address to the Negroes of the State of New York*.... With an uncommon if not unnatural faith in God and white people, whose sinful habits, he believed, did not in God's eyes and his own condone the slaves, Hammon preaches against the sins of disobedience, stealing, lying, swearing, and idleness. Consciousness of the irony of his people's oppression by those who had waged a costly and bloody war to end their own oppression is expressed but quickly suppressed by personal resignation to slavery and otherworldliness.... Jupiter Hammon's importance as a poet is essentially historical and sociological, for his blind faith in the benevolence of whites and the kingdom of heaven is a vivid illustration of the ambiguous political role of too many early African-American integrationist writers and preachers whose double-consciousness was both a blessing and a curse in the struggle of blacks for independence. (pp. 179-80)

> Bernard W. Bell, "African-American Writers," in American Literature, 1764-1789: The Revolutionary Years, edited by Everett Emerson, The University of Wisconsin Press, 1977, pp. 171-94.

FURTHER READING

Baker, Houston A., Jr. "Terms for Order: Acculturation, Meaning, and the Early Record of the Journey." In his *The Journey Back: Issues in Black Literature and Criticism,* pp. 1-26. Chicago: The University of Chicago Press, 1980.
> Addresses the role of religion in Hammon's poetry. Baker maintains that religion is used by Hammon as a means of conforming to and surviving in eighteenth-century white society.

Brawley, Benjamin. "The Pioneers." In his *The Negro Genius: A New Appraisal of the Achievement of the American Negro in Literature and the Fine Arts,* pp. 16-31. New York: Dodd, Mead & Co., 1937.
> Includes a brief account of Hammon's life and works.

Brown, Sterling. "Early American Negro Poetry." In his *Negro Poetry and Drama and the Negro in American Fiction,* pp. 4-14. New York: Atheneum, 1969.
> Considers the significance of Hammon's verse in the development of black American literature.

Kaplan, Sidney. "The Emergence of Gifts and Powers: Jupiter Hammon." In his *The Black Presence in the Era of the American Revolution: 1770-1800,* pp. 171-80. Greenwich, Conn.: The New York Graphic Society, 1973.
> Overview of Hammon's life and works. Kaplan uses extracts from Hammon's poetry and prose to illustrate the poet's views on slavery and the American Revolution.

Ransom, Stanley Austin. Introduction to *America's First Negro Poet: The Complete Works of Jupiter Hammon of Long Island,* by Jupiter Hammon, edited by Stanley Austin Ransom, pp. 11-19. Port Washington, N.Y.: Kennikat Press, 1970.
> Brief biographical introduction to Hammon and his works. Ransom describes Hammon's poetry as "sincere and enthusiastic" and asserts that his later prose "unquestionably served the cause of freedom."

Lorraine Hansberry

1930-1965

(Full name Lorraine Vivian Hansberry) American dramatist and essayist.

The first African-American and the youngest woman to win the New York Drama Critics Circle Award, Hansberry is best known for her play *A Raisin in the Sun* (1959). The story of a black working-class family and their decision to move into a white neighborhood, *A Raisin in the Sun* helped pioneer the acceptance of black drama by Broadway producers and audiences. Although dismissed by some militant blacks as assimilationist, *A Raisin in the Sun* nevertheless garnered praise for its sensitive and revealing portrait of a black family in America. Anne Cheney observed: "A moving testament to the strength and endurance of the human spirit, *A Raisin in the Sun* is a quiet celebration of the black family, the importance of African roots, the equality of women, the vulnerability of marriage, the true value of money, the survival of the individual, and the nature of man's dreams. A well-made play, *Raisin* at first seems a plea for racial tolerance or a fable of man's overcoming an insensitive society, but the simple eloquence of the characters elevates the play into a universal representation of all people's hopes, fears, and dreams."

Hansberry was born into a middle-class family on Chicago's Southside in 1930. She recalled that her childhood was basically a happy one: "[The] insulation of life within the Southside ghetto, of what must have easily been half a million people, protected me from some of the harsher and more bestial aspects of white-supremacist culture." At the age of seven or eight, Hansberry and her family moved into a restricted white neighborhood, deliberately violating the city's "covenant laws" that legally sanctioned housing discrimination. When ordered to abide by the law, Hansberry's family, with the help of the NAACP, took their case to the Illinois Supreme Court, which struck down the legislation as unconstitutional. During litigation, white neighbors continually harassed the Hansberry family; in one incident, a brick thrown through their living room window barely missed Hansberry's head. "Lorraine's character and personality were forged in this atmosphere of resistance to injustice," observed Porter Kirkwood. "Both of my parents were strong-minded, civic-minded, exceptionally race-minded people who made enormous sacrifices in behalf of the struggle for civil rights throughout their lifetimes," Hansberry herself recalled.

Hansberry became interested in the theatre while still in high school. "Mine was the same old story—" she recollected, "sort of hanging around little acting groups and developing the feeling that the theatre embraces everything I liked all at one time." Hansberry attended the University of Wisconsin, where she became further

acquainted with great theatre, studying the works of August Strindberg, Henrik Ibsen, and Sean O'Casey. She studied painting in Chicago and abroad for a time but moved to New York City in 1950 to begin her career as a writer.

Politically active in New York, Hansberry wrote for Paul Robeson's *Freedom* magazine and participated in various liberal crusades. During a protest at New York University, she met Robert Nemiroff, a white writer and himself a pursuer of liberal politics. A romance developed and in 1953 they married. Nemiroff encouraged Hansberry in her writing efforts, going so far as to salvage her discarded pages from the wastebasket. One night in 1957, while the couple was entertaining a group of friends, they read a scene from Hansberry's play in progress, "A Raisin in the Sun." The impact left by the reading prompted Hansberry, Nemiroff, and friends to push for the completion, financing, and production of the drama within the next several months.

Enjoying solid success at tryout performances on the road, *A Raisin in the Sun* made its New York debut in March 1959 at the Ethel Barrymore Theatre. It was the first play written by a black woman to be produced on Broadway and the first to be directed by a black director in more than fifty years. When *A Raisin in the Sun* won the New York Drama Critics Circle Award, Hansberry became the youngest writer and the first black artist ever to receive the honor, competing that year with such theatre luminaries as Tennessee Williams, Eugene O'Neill, and Archibald MacLeish. In June 1959 Hansberry was named the "most promising playwright" of the season by *Variety*'s poll of New York drama critics.

Hansberry originally named her play "The Crystal Stair" after a line in the Langston Hughes poem "Mother to Son," but she later changed its title to *A Raisin in the Sun,* an image taken from another Hughes piece, "A Dream Deferred." Set in a modest apartment in Southside Chicago after World War II, the play focuses on the Younger family: Lena, the matriarch; her son Walter Lee, a chauffeur; her daughter Beneatha, a college student; Walter Lee's wife, Ruth; and their son, Travis. In the opening scene, Ruth rouses her family on an early Friday morning. Ruth is described by Hansberry as "a settled woman" whose disappointment in life clearly shows in her demeanor. Walter, conversely, is a lean, intense man whose voice always contains "a quality of indictment." His second question of the morning—"Check come today?"—immediately reveals the central conflict of the play. Walter's father has died, leaving a ten thousand dollar insurance policy to Lena. Walter plans to persuade his mother to give him the money so that he, along with two other men, can invest it in a liquor store. Lena, however, uses part of the money as a down payment on a house in another neighborhood. Yet when a white representative from the neighborhood the family plans to move to offers to buy back their home, Walter refuses. He submerges his materialistic aspirations—for a time, at least—and rallies to support the family's dream. The play ends as the Youngers close the door to their apartment and head for their new home. For Walter, whose desires are frustrated, this ending leaves unsettled the question posed by Hughes in "A Dream Deferred": "What happens to a dream deferred? / Does it dry up / like a raisin in the sun? / Or fester like a sore— / and then run? / Does it stink like rotten meat? / Or crust and sugar over— / like a syrupy sweet? / Maybe it just sags / like a heavy load. / Or *does it explode?*"

Because the play explores a universal theme—the search for freedom and a better life—the majority of its first-run audience loved the work. According to Gerald Weales, *A Raisin in the Sun* reflects neither the traditional Negro show—folksy and exotic—nor the reactionary protest play, with black characters spouting about the injustices of white oppression. Rather, *A Raisin in the Sun* is a play about a family that just happens to be black. *New York Times* critic Brooks Atkinson admired *A Raisin in the Sun* because it explores serious problems without becoming academic or ponderous. "[Hansberry] has told the inner as well as outer truth about a Negro family in Chicago," the critic observed. "The play has vigor as well as veracity and is likely to destroy the complacency of anyone who sees it." Weales labeled *Raisin* "a good play" whose "basic strength lies in the character and the problem of Walter Lee, which transcends his being a Negro. If the play were only the Negro-white conflict that crops up when the family's proposed move is about to take place, it would be editorial, momentarily effective, and nothing more. Walter Lee's difficulty, however, is that he has accepted the American myth of success at its face value, that he is trapped, as Willy Loman was trapped, by a false dream. In planting so indigenous an American image at the center of her play, Miss Hansberry has come as close as possible to what she intended—a play about Negroes which is not simply a Negro play."

A Raisin in the Sun ran for 530 performances. Shortly thereafter, in 1961, a film version of the drama was released, starring Sidney Poitier and Claudia McNeil. Hansberry won a special award at the Cannes Film Festival and was nominated for Screen Writers Guild award for her screenplay. She then began work on a second play about a Jewish intellectual who vacillates between social commitment and paralyzing disillusionment. Entitled *The Sign in Sidney Brustein's Window* (1964), the play ran on Broadway for 101 performances despite mixed reviews and poor sales. "Its tenure on Broadway parallels the playwright's own failing health," Kirkwood noted. The play closed on January 12, 1965, the day Hansberry died of cancer at the age of thirty-four.

Although Hansberry and her husband divorced in 1964, Nemiroff remained dedicated to the playwright and her work. Appointed her literary executor, he collected his ex-wife's writings after her death in the autobiographical *To Be Young, Gifted and Black: Lorraine Hansberry in Her Own Words* (1969). He also edited and published her last three plays, which were subsequently produced after 1970: *Les Blancs,* a psychological and social drama about a European-educated African who returns home to protest colonialism; *The Drinking Gourd,* a black woman's story of slavery and emancipation; and *What Use Are Flowers?,* a fable about an aging hermit who, in a ravaged world, tries to impart to children his remembrances of a past civilization. "It's true that there's a great deal of pain for me in this," Nemiroff told Arlynn Nellhaus about his custodianship, "but there's also a great deal of satisfaction. There is first-class writing, and the joy of seeing [Lorraine's] ideas become a contemporary force again . . . [is] rewarding . . . . She was proud of black culture, the black experience and struggle . . . . But she was also in love with all cultures, and she related to the struggles of other people . . . . She was tremendously affected by the struggle of ordinary people—the heroism of ordinary people and the ability of people to laugh and transcend."

A Raisin in the Sun is ranked with Arthur Miller's *Death of a Salesman,* Tennessee Williams's *Glass Menagerie,* and Eugene O'Neill's *Long Day's Journey into Night* as a classic in American theatre. Recently the play has attracted a new generation of admirers. In 1984 Nemiroff published an expanded, twenty-fifth anniversary edition of the play. With the restoration of scenes and text originally removed from the first production, *A Raisin in the Sun* was also adapted for television in 1989, starring Danny Glover, Esther Rolle, and Kim Yancey. Critic Ed Siegel called the expanded version "a major American work of art, as gritty as it is poetic, as specific as it is universal, and as contemporary as it is ... visionary. [It] is a bristling, unqualified triumph." Although Hansberry wrote other plays, they pale in comparison to *A Raisin in the Sun*. Full of power, compassion, and emotional appeal, *Raisin* is, without question, Hansberry's best work. As Siegel concluded: "[Hansberry] may, in the end, have been just a one-play playwright. But what a ... play."

(For further information about Hansberry's life and works, see *Black Writers; Contemporary Authors,* Vols. 25-28; *Contemporary Authors New Revision Series,* Vol. 109; *Contemporary Literary Criticism,* Vols. 17, 62; and *Dictionary of Literary Biography,* Vols. 7, 38.)

PRINCIPAL WORKS

A Raisin in the Sun (drama) 1959
The Movement: Documentary of a Struggle for Equality (essays) 1964; also published as *A Matter of Colour: Documentary of the Struggles for Racial Equality in the USA,* 1965
The Sign in Sidney Brustein's Window (drama) 1964
To Be Young, Gifted and Black: The World of Lorraine Hansberry [adapted by Robert Nemiroff] (drama) 1969; also published as *To Be Young, Gifted and Black: Lorraine Hansberry in Her Own Words,* 1969; also published as *To Be Young, Gifted and Black: Lorraine Hansberry in Her Own Words, An Informal Autobiography of Lorraine Hansberry,* 1970; also published as *To Be Young, Gifted and Black: A Portrait of Lorraine Hansberry in Her Own Words* [acting edition], 1971
Les Blancs [adapted by Robert Nemiroff] (drama) 1970
†*Les Blancs: The Collected Last Plays of Lorraine Hansberry* (dramas) 1972

---

*This drama, an assemblage of Hansberry's letters, speeches, plays, and essays, was posthumously adapted for the stage by Hansberry's former husband Robert Nemiroff.
†This work includes *The Drinking Gourd* and *What Use Are Flowers?*

Gerald Weales (essay date 1959)

[*In the following excerpt, Weales offers a generally favorable assessment of* A Raisin in the Sun, *conclud-*

ing: "Despite an incredible number of imperfections, Raisin *is a good play."*]

The playwright who is a Negro is faced with a special problem. Broadway has a tradition of Negro shows, inevitably folksy or exotic, almost always musical, of which the only virtue is that Negro performers get a chance to appear as something more than filler. The obvious reaction to such shows is the protest play, the Negro agitprop, which can be as false to American Negro life as the musicals. A playwright with serious intentions, like Miss Hansberry, has to avoid both pitfalls, has to try to write not a Negro play, but a play in which the characters are Negroes....

Having suggested that objectivity is impossible with respect to ***A Raisin in the Sun,*** I should like to make a few objective remarks about it. The play, first of all, is old fashioned. Practically no serious playwright, in or out of America, works in such a determinedly naturalistic form as Miss Hansberry in her first play.... *Raisin* is the kind of play which demands the naturalism that Miss Hansberry has used, but in choosing to write such a play, she entered Broadway's great sack race with only a paper bag as equipment. Her distinction is that she has won the race this year, which proves, I suppose, that narrow naturalism is still a possible—if anachronistic—form....

[The] play itself—in its concentration on the family in society—recalls the 30's and Clifford Odets.... The conflict within the play is between the dreams of the son, Walter Lee, who wants to make a killing in the big world, and the hopes of his mother and his wife, who want to save their small world by transplanting it to an environment in which it might conceivably flourish. The mechanical means by which this conflict is illuminated—the insurance money, its loss, the representative of the white neighborhood association—are completely artificial, plot devices at their most devised. (p. 528)

Of the four chief characters in the play, Walter Lee is the most complicated and the most impressive. He is often unlikable, occasionally cruel.... The play is concerned primarily with his recognition that, as a man, he must begin from, not discard, himself, that dignity is a quality of men, not bank accounts. Walter Lee's penchant for taking center stage has forced his wife to become an observer in his life, but at the same time she is an accusation. For most of the play she wears a mask of wryness or the real cover of fatigue, but Miss Hansberry gives her two scenes in which the near-hysteria that lies beneath the surface is allowed to break through. The mother is a more conventional figure—the force, compounded of old virtues and the strength of suffering, that holds the family together. She is a sentimentalized mother figure, reminiscent of Bessie Burgess in *Awake and Sing,* but without Bessie's destructive power. The daughter, who wants to be a doctor, is out of place in this working-class family. Not that her ambition does not belong with the Youngers, but her surface characteristics—the flitting from one expensive fad to another—

could not have been possible, on economic grounds alone, in such a household . . . .

Despite an incredible number of imperfections, *Raisin* is a good play. Its basic strength lies in the character and the problem of Walter Lee, which transcends his being a Negro. If the play were only the Negro-white conflict that crops up when the family's proposed move is about to take place, it would be an editorial, momentarily effective, and nothing more. Walter Lee's difficulty, however, is that he has accepted the American myth of success at its face value, that he is trapped, as Willy Loman was trapped, by a false dream. In planting so indigenous an American image at the center of her play, Miss Hansberry has come as close as possible to what she intended—a play about Negroes which is not simply a Negro play.

The play has other virtues. There are genuinely funny and touching scenes throughout. Many of these catch believably the chatter of a family—the resentments and the shared jokes—and the words have the ring of truth that one found in Odets or [Paddy] Chayefsky before they began to sound like parodies of themselves. (p. 529)

> Gerald Weales, "Thoughts on 'A Raisin in the Sun'," in Commentary, *Vol. 27, No. 6, June, 1959, pp. 527-30.*

Lorraine Hansberry (essay date 1959)

[*In the following excerpt, Hansberry examines critical reaction to* A Raisin in the Sun.]

Some of the acute partisanship revolving around *A Raisin in the Sun* is amusing. Those who announce that they find the piece less than fine are regarded in some quarters with dramatic hostility, as though such admission automatically implies the meanest of racist reservations. On the other hand, the ultra-sophisticates have hardly acquitted themselves less ludicrously, gazing cooly down their noses at those who are moved by the play, and going on at length about "melodrama" and/or "soap opera" as if these are not completely definable terms which cannot simply be tacked onto any play and all plays we do not like.

Personally, I find no pain whatever—at least of the traditional ego type—in saying that *Raisin* is a play which contains dramaturgical incompletions. Fine plays tend to utilize one big fat character who runs right through the middle of the structure, by action or implication, with whom we rise or fall. A central character as such is certainly lacking from *Raisin.* I should be delighted to pretend that it was *inventiveness,* as some suggest for me, but it is, also, craft inadequacy and creative indecision. The result is that neither Walter Lee nor Mama Younger loom large enough to monumentally command the play. I consider it an enormous dramatic fault if no one else does. (p. 7)

All in all, however, I believe that, for the most part, the play has been magnificently understood. In some cases it was not only thematically absorbed but attention was actually paid to the tender treacherousness of its craft-imposed "simplicity." Some, it is true, quite missed that part of the overt intent and went on to harangue the bones of the play with rather useless observations of the terribly clear fact that they are old bones indeed. More meaningful discussions tended to delve into the flesh which hangs from those bones and its implications in mid-century American drama and life.

In that connection it is interesting to note that while the names of Chekhov, O'Casey, and the early Odets were introduced for comparative purposes in some of the reviews, almost no one—with the exception of Gerald Weales in *Commentary* [see excerpt dated 1959] discovered a simple line of descent between Walter Lee Younger and the last great hero in American drama to also *accept* the values of his culture, Willy Loman. I am sure that the already mentioned primary fault of the play must account in part for this. The family so overwhelms the play that Walter Lee necessarily fails as the true symbol he should be, even though *his* ambitions, *his* frustrations, and *his* decisions are those which decisively drive the play on. But however recognizable he proves to be, he fails to dominate our imagination and finally emerges as a reasonably interesting study, but not, like Arthur Miller's great character—and like Hamlet, of course—a summation of an immense (though not crucial) portion of his culture.

Then too . . . we must not completely omit reference to some of the prior attitudes which were brought into the theatre from the world outside. For in the minds of many, Walter remains, despite the play, despite performance, what American radical traditions *wish* him to be: an exotic. Some writers have been astonishingly incapable of discussing his purely *class* aspirations and have persistently confounded them with what they consider to be an exotic being's longing to "wheel and deal" in what they further consider to be (and what Walter never can) "the white man's world." Very few people today must consider the ownership of a liquor store as an expression of extraordinary affluence, and yet, as joined to a dream of Walter Younger, it takes on, for some, aspects of the fantastic. We have grown accustomed to the dynamics of "Negro" personality as expressed by white authors. Thus, de Emperor, de Lawd, and, of course, Porgy, still haunt our frame of reference when a new character emerges. We have become romantically jealous of the great image of a prototype whom we believe is summarized by the wishfulness of a self-assumed opposite. Presumably there is a quality in human beings that makes us *wish* that we *were* capable of primitive contentments; the *universality* of ambition and its anguish can escape us only if we construct elaborate legends about the rudimentary simplicity of *other* men.

America, for this reason, long ago fell in love with the image of the simple, lovable, and glandular "Negro."

We all know that Catfish Row was never intended to slander anyone; it was intended as a mental haven for readers and audiences who could bask in the unleashed passions of those "lucky ones" for whom abandonment was apparently permissible. In an almost paradoxical fashion, it disturbs the soul of man to truly understand what he invariably senses: that *nobody* really finds oppression and/or poverty tolerable. If we ever destroy the image of the black people who supposedly do find those things tolerable in America, then that much-touted "guilt" which allegedly haunts most middle-class white Americans with regard to the Negro question would really become unendurable. It would also mean the death of a dubious literary tradition, but it would undoubtedly and more significantly help toward the more rapid transformation of the status of a people who have never found their imposed misery very charming.

My colleagues and I were reduced to mirth and tears by that gentleman writing his review of our play in a Connecticut paper who remarked of his pleasure at seeing how "our dusky brethren" could "come up with a song and hum their troubles away." It did not disturb the writer in the least that there is no such implication in the entire three acts. He did not need it in the play; he had it in his head.

For all these reasons then, I imagine that the ordinary impulse to compare Willy Loman and Walter Younger was remote. Walter Lee Younger jumped out at us from a play about a largely unknown world. We knew who Willy Loman was instantaneously; we recognized his milieu.... Willy Loman was a product of a nation of great military strength, indescribable material wealth, and incredible mastery of the physical realm, which nonetheless was unable, in 1946, to produce a *typical* hero who was capable of an affirmative view of life.

I believe it is a testament to Miller's brilliance that it is hardly a misstatement of the case, as some preferred to believe. Something has indeed gone wrong with at least part of the American dream, and Willy Loman is the victim of the detour.... His predicament in a New World where there just aren't any more forests to clear or virgin railroads to lay or native American empires to first steal and build upon, left him with nothing but some left-over values which had forgotten how to prize industriousness over cunning; usefulness over mere acquisition, and, above all, humanism over "success." The potency of the great tale of a salesman's death was in our familiar recognition of his entrapment which, suicide or no, is *deathly*.

What then of this new figure who appears in American drama in 1958; from what source is he drawn so that, upon inspection, and despite class differences, so much of his encirclement must still remind us of that of Willy Loman? Why, finally, is it possible that when his third-act will is brought to bear, *his* typicality is capable of a choice which *affirms* life? After all, Walter Younger is an American more than he is anything else. His ordeal, give or take his personal expression of it, is not

extraordinary but intensely familiar like Willy's. The two of them have virtually no values which have not come out of their culture, and to a significant point, no view of the possible solutions to their problems which do not also come out of the self-same culture. Walter can find no peace with that part of society which seems to permit him and no entry into that which has willfully excluded him. He shares with Willy Loman the acute awareness that *something* is obstructing some abstract progress that he feels he *should* be making; that *something* is in the way of his ascendancy. It does not occur to either of them to question the nature of this desired "ascendancy." Walter accepts, he believes in the "world" as it has been presented to him. When we first meet him, he does not wish to alter *it;* merely to change *his* position in it. His mentors and his associates all take the view that the institutions which frustrate him are somehow impeccable, or, at best, "unfortunate." "Things being as they are," he must look to *himself* as the only source of any rewards he may expect. Within himself, he is encouraged to believe, are the only seeds of defeat or victory within the universe. And Walter believes this and when opportunity, haphazard and rooted in death, prevails, he acts.

But the obstacles which are introduced are gigantic; the weight of the loss of the money is in fact, the weight of death. In Walter Lee Younger's life, somebody *has* to die for ten thousand bucks to pile up—if then. Elsewhere in the world, in the face of catastrophe, he might be tempted to don the saffron robes of acceptance and sit on a mountain top all day contemplating the divine justice of his misery. Or, history being what it is turning out to be, he might wander down to his first Communist Party meeting. But here in the dynamic and confusing post-war years on the Southside of Chicago, his choices of action are equal to those gestures only in symbolic terms. The American ghetto hero may give up and contemplate his misery in rose-colored bars to the melodies of hypnotic saxophones, but revolution seems alien to him in his circumstances (America), and it is easier to dream of personal wealth than of a communal state wherein universal dignity is supposed to be a corollary. Yet his position in time and space does allow for one other alternative: he may take his place on any one of a number of frontiers of challenge. Challenges (such as helping to break down restricted neighborhoods) which are admittedly limited because they most certainly do not threaten the basic social order.

But why is even this final choice possible, considering the everpresent (and ever so popular) vogue of despair? Well, that is where Walter departs from Willy Loman; there is a second pulse in his still dual culture. His people have had "somewhere" they have been trying to get for so long that more sophisticated confusions do not yet bind them. *Thus the weight and power of their current social temperament intrudes and affects him, and it is, at the moment, at least, gloriously and rigidly affirmative.* In the course of *their* brutally difficult ascent, they have dismissed the ostrich and still sing, *"Went to the rock, to hide my face, but the rock cried out:*

'No hidin' place down here!'" Walter is, despite his lack of consciousness of it, inextricably as much wedded to his special mass as Willy was to his, and the moods of each are able to decisively determine the dramatic typicality. Furthermore, the very nature of the situation of American Negroes can force their representative hero to recognize that for his *true* ascendancy he must ultimately be at cross-purposes with at least certain of his culture's values. It is to the pathos of Willy Loman that his section of American life seems to have momentarily lost that urgency; that he cannot, like Walter, draw on the strength of an incredible people who, historically, have simply refused to give up.

In other words, the symbolism of moving into the new house is quite as small as it seems and quite as significant. For if there are no waving flags and marching songs at the barricades as Walter marches out with his little battalion, it is not because the battle lacks nobility. On the contrary, he has picked up in his way, still imperfect and wobbly in his small view of human destiny, what I believe Arthur Miller once called "the golden thread of history." He becomes, in spite of those who are too intrigued with despair and hatred of man to see it, King Oedipus refusing to tear out his eyes, but attacking the Oracle instead. He is that last Jewish patriot manning his rifle in the burning ghetto at Warsaw; he is that young girl who swam into sharks to save a friend a few weeks ago; he is Anne Frank, still believing in people; he is the nine small heroes of Little Rock; he is Michelangelo creating David and Beethoven bursting forth with the Ninth Symphony. He is all those things because he has finally reached out in his tiny moment and caught that sweet essence which is human dignity, and it shines like the old startouched dream that it is in his eyes. We see, in the moment, I think, what becomes, and not for Negroes alone, but for Willy and all of us, entirely an American responsibility.

Out in the darkness where we watch, most of us are not afraid to cry. (pp. 7-8)

> Lorraine Hansberry, "Willie Loman, Walter Younger, and He Who Must Live," in The Village Voice, *Vol. IV, No. 42, August 12, 1959, pp. 7-8.*

C. W. E. Bigsby (essay date 1968)

[*In the following excerpt, Bigsby reviews* A Raisin in the Sun *and* The Sign in Sidney Brustein's Window, *arguing that the latter play is better than the former.*]

[The central factor of *A Raisin in the Sun*] is not poverty but indignity and self-hatred. The survival of the family is dependent on their ability to accommodate themselves to the white world. (p. 156)

Hansberry's play is set in the same locale [as Richard Wright's *Native Son*]. Its sense of desperation is the same. . . . Yet where Wright created in Bigger Thomas a hardening of the stereotype . . . , Hansberry, writing

some twenty years later, is concerned with demonstrating human resilience. The gulf between the two writers is in part that dictated by the changing social position of the American Negro but more fundamentally it is indicative of Lorraine Hansberry's belief in the pointlessness of despair and hatred. Indeed Hansberry's play is essentially an attempt to turn Wright's novel on its head. Where he had examined the potential for violence, Hansberry sees this as a potential which once realised can only lead to stasis. (p. 157)

The dreams of the Youngers are sharpened and pointed by the indignity and self-hatred which is their racial inheritance. Walter dreams of owning a store and thus becoming independent of the system of which he is the victim, while his [sister], impressed by the need for compassion, wants to become a doctor. (p. 158)

Walter Younger's sullen cynicism, which, like Willy Loman's confused mind, grants value only to wealth and power, is balanced by his [sister's] passionate belief in the feasibility of change and the need for compassion. Beneatha has a strong sense of racial pride compounded with humanistic commitment. Intensely aware of her racial origins she associates with Asagai, an African student, and steeps herself in the culture of her forbears. When Asagai gives her the nickname Alaiyo, 'one who needs more than bread', it is both an ironical comment on her intensity and an indication that Hansberry's concern is less with the poverty of the Youngers than with the need for spiritual replenishment which can only come with a return of dignity. Yet when Walter squanders the money which was to have paid for her medical training Beneatha lapses into despair and the compassion which she had shown evaporates as had Ruth's hope and Walter's ambitions. Like Sidney Brustein in Hansberry's second play, forced to confront present reality, she slips into the cant of nihilism. She projects her personal disappointments onto a universal scale and Asagai identifies the questions which obsess her. 'What good is struggle; what good is anything? Where are we all going? And why are we bothering?' (pp. 158-59)

The personal and familial crises are finally resolved by the open challenge offered by the white world. . . . [The white community representative's] insult is delivered with courtesy but it stings Walter into a response which simultaneously gives him back his dignity and commits him to an involvement which he had sought to escape. Thus in a sense this is a fulfillment of Asagai's prophesy. In speaking of his own political future in Africa he had said, 'They who might kill me even . . . actually replenish me!' (p. 159)

Yet while leaving the Youngers committed to 'new levels of struggle' Miss Hansberry brings about this partial resolution through something of a specious *deus ex machina*. Although she is as antipathetic towards a life printed on dollar bills as Odets had been, it is clear that the spiritual regeneration of the Younger family is ultimately contingent on a ten thousand dollar check, for it is only the money which makes it possible for them to challenge the system under which they have suffered. In making it the necessary prerequisite for their return to dignity and pride Hansberry would seem to demean the faith in human potential which she is ostensibly endorsing. Walter, again like Willy Loman, far from rejecting the system which is oppressing him wholeheartedly embraces it. He rejects the cause of social commitment and compassion and places his faith in the power of money. It is the unintentional irony of this play however that he proves to be right .... Walter's final conversion, or, as Hansberry would put it, the eventual realisation of his potential, is itself as unconvincing as Biff's similar conversion in *Death of a Salesman.* Her true declaration of faith is, however, embodied in the person of Asagai, the least convincing of the play's characters. This African revolutionary is used by Lorraine Hansberry as a point of reference—as the realisation of the dignity and commitment which exists in Walter only as potential .... Yet Asagai's self-assurance remains untested. His confident assertion of progress and redemption remains unreal precisely because we do not see him, as we do the Youngers, brought face to face with frustration. (pp. 159-60)

Asagai has no validity outside of [the convention of Africa as a land of primal innocence]. If Hansberry mocks the naïvete with which Beneatha tries to adopt African modes of dress and general culture she leaves unchallenged the assumption that those values stem from a purer source. Yet Asagai's vitality and enthusiasm spring from his own dreams which differ in kind from Walter's only in magnitude and in the fact that they are never put to the test .... Asagai's declaration of the inevitability of change built on courage and compassion, a declaration which clearly represents Lorraine Hansberry's own faith, remains as unconvincing as do the circumstances of Walter's change of heart .... (p. 161)

Lorraine Hansberry dedicates her second and last play, **The Sign in Sidney Brustein's Window** to 'the committed everywhere' and in doing so expresses not only her own personal philosophy but also her conception of the purpose of art. From her play, however, it becomes apparent that commitment does not mean for her exactly what it had for [Bertolt] Brecht or even [Elmer] Rice and Odets, neither does it mean that intransigent alignment with sectional interests which undermines the drama of LeRoi Jones. The commitment of which she speaks is one to life rather than death, hope rather than despair and to human potential rather than human failure. Her enemy is thus neither the rich industrialist nor the racial bigot but rather the indifferent and the self-deceived. In terms of art her enemy is [Albert] Camus and the theatre of the absurd so that **The Sign in Sidney Brustein's Window** is as much a statement of artistic responsibilities as of social inadequacies. Indeed in many ways it is a dramatic equivalent of [Kenneth] Tynan's assault on [Eugène] Ionesco for while he was working, like Brecht, from a Marxist premise, Hansberry's rejection of the absurd is based on a similar desire (already noted in the drama of confrontation of which

this play is essentially a part) to re-constitute the humanist heresy of belief in man.

The Sidney Brustein of the title is a liberal who fluctuates between the two poles of liberalism; Thoreauesque dissociation and enthusiastic political involvement. The play effectively spells out the inadequacies and ultimately the futility of both these extremes. In essence Sidney Brustein is but another of the American heroes in search of primal innocence waging a holy war and deeply wounding those around him. (p. 162)

Sidney's liberalism is the exercise of conscience without attendent responsibility ....

Lorraine Hansberry's portrait of bewildered liberalism, however, far from constituting an attack on liberals ..., lies at the very centre of a drama which is essentially concerned with the plight of the individual in a society in which commitment is considered passé. (p. 163)

If Hansberry is critical of liberalism which is nothing more than naive self-expression she is equally critical of disinterest which masquerades under the guise of liberal tolerance. Iris epitomises this attitude which constitutes the other side of the liberal coin. It takes Mavis to point out the implications of this moral disengagement. When Iris takes as her maxim, 'Live and let live, that's all' Mavis retorts, 'That's just a shoddy little way of trying to avoid responsibility in the world.' ... This desire for non-involvement is further emphasised, rather too pointedly, by Iris's surname, Parodus, an implication which Mavis again underlines. Parodus, as she points out, is the Greek word for chorus .... (pp. 164-65)

Lorraine Hansberry's involvement with the plight of the Negro is subsumed here in a more general concern. The human failure which is evidenced in the hardening of prejudice in racial matters becomes for her indicative of a more fundamental failure which underlies alike the capricious enthusiasm of Sidney Brustein and the disaffiliation of Iris. The commitment which she urges, and in which all the play's characters fail, is a devotion to humanity which goes beyond a desire for political and moral freedoms. Gloria Parodus, Iris's sister, becomes the focus of Miss Hansberry's call for compassion .... (p. 165)

When Sidney underlines the racial nature of Alton's failure his concession is equally an admission of the fatuity of an intellectual commitment unsupported by emotional engagement, 'I know it—*(Touching his head)* here!' ... His liberalism thus stands revealed as an irrelevant pose and the expansive humanity of his principles is subverted by an inability to transform it into political action. This gulf between intellectual commitment and a genuine involvement rooted in passion lies at the very heart [of this book] .... (pp. 165-66)

The extent of this gulf is demonstrated by the fact that Gloria is failed not only by Alton but equally by Sidney, Iris and Mavis as well. (p. 166)

Gloria's death brings Sidney to [an understanding of himself]. This, together with his realisation of the true nature of his liberalism, constitutes that moment of 'momentous enlightenment' which [Edward] Albee and [Arthur] Miller had been concerned with portraying....

The sign which hangs in Sidney Brustein's window is not an ironical comment on the impossibility of achieving anything in what Iris sees as this 'dirty world'. It represents the public face of a man whose vision of the world is radically simplified and who, until brought to the point of confrontation, has failed to understand what Hansberry conceives as the nature of commitment. The sign becomes, as Iris puts it, like spit in his face.... (p. 167)

The Sign in Sidney Brustein's Window constitutes one of the most complete disavowals of absurdist drama which has yet been made. In its concern with the nature and purpose of art it goes beyond the introspection of *The Connection* and even the self-conscious dramas of [Luigi] Pirandello. Clearly Sidney's attack on the callow prophesies of [William] Golding and [Samuel] Beckett represents the credo of a dramatist who believes passionately in the validity of insurgence and the redeemable nature of man. The play is the voice of social protest, no longer touched with the embarrassing simplicity of the thirties but rather redolent with the cutting sophistication which Albee had introduced into the American theatre. It is a protest not, like *A Raisin in the Sun,* against the suffocating actuality of existence inside a coloured skin but against a defeatism ingrained in postwar man and finding expression in modern literature. Lorraine Hansberry is in rebellion against a vision of man which destroys hope and which asserts, as does Golding, that moral regression is as inevitable as physical and mental advance.... She avoids the temptation to transmute racial bitterness into universal anguish and enervating fatalism, granting an ambivalence to her characters which would have been foreign to Wright and which stems from her passionately held faith in human potential. Mavis Parodus's racial prejudice does not nullify her genuine humanity neither does Alton Scales' colour justify his brutality. Miss Hansberry weds an understanding of historical causality to a genuine belief in the possibility of change—a faith which necessarily rejects art formed out of despair and finding its genesis in individual suffering. (pp. 167-69)

Lorraine Hansberry's death at the age of thirty-four has robbed the theatre of the one Negro dramatist who has demonstrated her ability to transcend parochialism and social bitterness. (p. 172)

> *C. W. E. Bigsby, "Lorraine Hansberry," in his* Confrontation and Commitment: A Study of Contemporary American Drama, 1959-66, *University of Missouri Press, 1968, pp. 156-73.*

Gerald Weales (essay date 1969)

[*In the following excerpt, Weales negatively reviews* To Be Young, Gifted and Black, *arguing that the play—"pieced together by Robert Nemiroff" —makes a mockery of Hansberry's talents.*]

To Be Young, Gifted and Black, as everyone knows by now, is a patchwork play pieced together by Robert Nemiroff from the produced and unproduced works, the letters, the speeches, the articles of Lorraine Hansberry. Subtitled "The World of Lorraine Hansberry," it is an attempt to present Miss Hansberry, the writer, and the background which produced her and provided the material for her work....

Whatever Nemiroff intended, the play made a mockery of Miss Hansberry's talents, destroyed everything that is good and subtle in her work. (p. 542)

For her... human possibility was what counted.... *The Sign in Sidney Brustein's Window* was primarily an attack on a particular kind of fashionable determinism, the assumption that nothing can be done about the evils of the world and the resulting "great sad withdrawal from the affairs of men," as one of the characters puts it.

Despite her need to *say* something, to make a social point, she did not want to sacrifice art to argument, to go agitprop as a few of the young black playwrights have recently done. She was forced, then, to embrace the traditional American realism, to do as serious American playwrights from James A. Herne to Arthur Miller have done, to use plot to make her points and character to express her sense that it is all more complicated than it seems. There are traps in the form, the temptation of easy devices... and pat character reversals.... There are virtues, however—characters, like Sidney Brustein and Walter Lee in *Raisin,* which transcend stereotype, become so rich and suggestive that the message itself is always about to be swallowed in human complexity.... It is impossible to guess how she might have grown as a writer, but her two plays indicate that she had wit and intelligence, a strong sense of social and political possibility and a respect for the contradictions in all men; that she could create a milieu (the family in *Raisin,* the Greenwich Village circle in *Sign*) with both bite and affection; that she was a playwright—like Odets, like Miller—with easily definable flaws but an inescapable talent that one cannot help admiring.

What has *To Be Young, Gifted and Black* got to do with the playwright described above? Very little, I am afraid. If Nemiroff's mosaic were taken at face value, it would be necessary to assume that Miss Hansberry was a gushy little girl, oohing and ahing in much the same voice over Wisconsin snow and ghetto courage, a dramatist who turned out clumsy genre pieces or broad comedy putdowns.... None of the new material is likely to add much to Miss Hansberry's reputation. (pp. 542-43)

Gerald Weales, "Losing the Playwright," in Commonweal, *Vol. XC, No. 20, September 5, 1969, pp. 542-43.*

Jordan Y. Miller (essay date 1969)

[*In the following excerpt, Miller praises Hansberry's skills as a dramatist, citing* The Sign in Sidney Brustein's Window *as proof that Hansberry was not an "accidental" success.*]

To explain, a decade after the fact, to a college class in American drama how neatly *A Raisin in the Sun* fits into a logical evolution within the theatre, to justify its dramatic viewpoint, and to praise its creator for her skill in writing a black . . . play without "blackness," remaining all the while a black writer who refuses to call attention to the fact, will raise instant challenges. The accusations are many. Is not Lorraine Hansberry an Uncle (Aunt?) Tom? Is not *A Raisin in the Sun* a sellout to the white power structure? Are not the Youngers really betraying themselves and their own? Is not their attempt to assimilate themselves into the white society, and to force themselves, however peacefully, into the neighborhood where they are so obviously unwanted, simply a gratuitous attempt to become white? . . . Therefore, to discuss, to attempt to teach the plays of Lorraine Hansberry in terms of the "colorless" world in which she at one time seemed to belong becomes a greatly complicated matter. To justify what once was regarded as part of a highly favorable development in the commercial theatre now raises spectres of pandering to the white viewpoint, avoiding the inevitable and necessary confrontation. (p. 160)

Structurally, Lorraine Hansberry remains essentially within the bounds of the conventional realistic well-made play, something almost anachronistic amidst the styles of the 1960s. . . . Plot in Miss Hansberry's plays is of secondary importance, for it is not her main dramatic purpose. Nonetheless, because the audience has considerable interest in *what* is happening as well as *to whom*, both *A Raisin in the Sun* and *The Sign in Sidney Brustein's Window* are thoroughly enhanced by well-ordered revelation of the events which are so important in the lives of the characters. The straightforward telling of a story remains a thoroughly honorable literary accomplishment, and Miss Hansberry has practiced this ancient dramatic art with eminent respectability. Moreover, the scene, incident, and dialogue are almost Ibsenesque, avoiding overt stylization for its own sake and performed within the standard "box" set that progressively becomes more rare.

To one like myself who welcomes theatrical innovation and will tolerate a lot of nonsense if it has some underlying legitimacy in valid experimentation, it is still a pleasure to experience a play constructed in Miss Hansberry's style, watching fairly "normal" people confront themselves with those around them on the basis not of social revolt and upheaval, nor because of excessive emotional hangups, but on the basis of their

fundamental human decency, expressed in commensurately decent language. . . . [Her characters] are very little people, performing in a world of other little people, and their confusion and their anger have solid basis in their irritations at the refusal of the world to behave the way it should. They never become sentimentally maudlin. . . . On the other hand, inhabiting an essentially sanc if not always rational world, they never become the puzzled but game little people of [James] Thurber's wacky universe. They are, in short, attractively and convincingly real people, for whom no excuses are made and none sought.

Lorraine Hansberry's success with her characters is, I think, accomplished through her ability to make us become very very interested in every one of them from the beginning, and as each assumes his identity the interest is consistently maintained. The author's dramatic techniques show up best in the ensemble portrayal of the members of the Younger household and the beneficiaries of the Brustein's open door policy. Each person is clearly individualized and none are able to dominate the others. (pp. 161-62)

[The] beautifully executed patterns of interrelationships evidenced in both plays are major factors in their attractiveness. The absence of a hero or a heroine is no flaw, as Chekhov so well demonstrated. Thus in *Raisin* Hansberry offers us in equal portions Lena, Walter, Ruth, and Beneatha, and though comparatively undeveloped but hardly of less importance, George Murchison, Asagai, and of course Linder the white intruder. Nobody in *Sidney Brustein* remains peripheral. Although Sidney and Iris are on stage almost continually and it is "their" play, they simply do not emerge as any more important than the next person. Nobody is their foil and what they are and what they become are parts of what Mavis, Alton, David and Gloria are. We must listen to Sidney's ideas more because he talks more, but his affirmation of some of the more old fashioned values is no more significant in the play's development than David's revolt against Ibsen or Gloria's pitiful race toward her own destruction. Who, in either play, has the most to say? . . . To whom does the playwright prefer we listen? (p. 163)

Miss Hansberry provides ample possibilities to satisfy [critics who demand a single protagonist] . . . . But the playwright will not have it so, for she is far more concerned with the commitment of her characters to finding themselves as individuals and as a family, rather than to the Absolute and Ultimate Confrontation which is so quickly and shockingly brought to their door. The Big Scene is not to be allowed. (pp. 163-64)

The Sign in Sidney Brustein's Window, on the other hand, while lacking the opportunity for the melodramatic moment provided because of the racial theme in *A Raisin in the Sun,* tosses together as separately articulated a group of dramatic "types" as one could want, places them in Greenwich Village where anything can happen and generally does, and proceeds, once more, to blend all together with such evenness that nobody is permitted the privilege of major emphasis.... Miss Hansberry mixes everyone into a potentially explosive collage of characters, but try as one may, one cannot cite a single one of the many fine scenes as better than another. (pp. 164-65)

If this form of dramatic structure is so seriously flawed as to bother the viewers of *Sidney Brustein,* I fail to see it. There are high points as well as low, and the uniformity of emphasis on character does not by any means prevent the development of a satisfactory dramatic rhythm. This sort of writing, like the appeal of Chekhov or some of Odets, may not exactly be everybody's cup of tea, but it meets the author's requirements for what the plays are designed to do....

If any segment of Hansberry's well-made play technique is open to question it could well be the *deus ex machina* of the $10,000 insurance check in *A Raisin in the Sun*.... The situation here, however, is saved by the expedient of setting all the action after the fact, so that to condemn the insurance check is, to all intents and purposes, to condemn the entire play. The insurance money is expected and cannot under any circumstance serve as the sudden reverser of fortune which the routine 19th century meller would demand. (p. 165)

The great miracle of *A Raisin in the Sun* is, I firmly believe, that Lorraine Hansberry has presented one of the most volatile of our society's problems, telling it precisely "like it is," within the most conventional of dramatic frameworks, without rancor and without violence. The play *is* a problem play, and the problem is blackness in a white society. The underlying humanity of the characters, however, and the decency of their struggle because and in spite of their blackness, will prevent the dream from drying up. (pp. 167-68)

In 1964 with *The Sign in Sidney Brustein's Window* Lorraine Hansberry became more than a black playwright in the American theatre. She stood apart as an important American playwright who happened to be black. This play, even more than *A Raisin in the Sun,* would also place her completely outside the world of racial dogma and protest, for it had even less of a social bone to pick than her first.... This second play had shown plainly that *A Raisin in the Sun* was not an accident and that she was a dramatist of considerable skill whose sense of theatre, notwithstanding race, ethnic identification or social background, was superb....

It is a charming, delightful, and touching play, and furthermore, it is a very moral play. In its straightforward old-fashioned way, *Sidney Brustein* goes somewhere, says something, and arrives at a conclusion, all of which seems, in the midst of the turmoil of the 1960s, a mighty good way to have it. (p. 168)

Since those who walk so freely in and out of the Brustein's attractively cluttered apartment are of little significance in the way the world turns . . . they are going to have to be made significant to those who watch if the play is to have any meaning at all. What we have, I think, is a significant look at ourselves.... Throughout the play runs that constant plea to make the important and painful elements of others' lives a bit more important to ourselves, with the companion warning that there is considerably more to life than our own narrow visions. It's all been said many times before, and Miss Hansberry discovers absolutely nothing new, but her ability to make use of the varied group of individuals she pulls together to say it makes the renewal well worth the effort. (pp. 169-70)

> *Jordan Y. Miller, "Lorraine Hansberry," in his* The Black American Writer: Poetry and Drama, Vol. II, *Everett/Edwards, Inc., 1969, pp. 157-70.*

Doris E. Abramson (essay date 1969)

[*In the following excerpt, Abramson surveys theme and plot in* A Raisin in the Sun.]

A Raisin in the Sun is the first play by a Negro of which one is tempted to say, "Everyone knows it." Thousands of Americans have seen it on the stage in New York, in other large cities, on college campuses, and in community theatres. Many more thousands have seen in on the screen. And, finally, millions of American who might not seek it out have seen the movie on their television screens. (It is fascinating to speculate that the majority of white Americans have had Negroes in their homes *only* via television.) Americans who read could have read *A Raisin in the Sun* in hardcover, in a very inexpensive paperback, printed alone or in anthologies. (p. 241)

It hardly seems necessary, then, to analyze the play scene by scene in order to remind the reader/viewer of those elements that are reflections of American Negro existence. It will be sufficient to pull out moments in the play that demonstrate Lorraine Hansberry's use of Negro problems in creating a play that has become for many white people an introduction to the contemporary Negro.

Much has been written about *A Raisin in the Sun,* about Lorraine Hansberry (who died of cancer in 1965), and about the implications of her Broadway success, but neither the critics nor Miss Hansberry ever acknowledged her debt to Richard Wright's *Native Son* (novel or play), although surely one existed. Both plays are set in Chicago's Southside. Bigger Thomas and Walter Younger are both chauffeurs, black men who feel caged in a white society. And they both "explode" because of a "dream deferred." Walter's explosion, to be sure, is not so fatal as Bigger's, but it erupts from much the same frustration and confusion. Both plays even begin with the same sound—the ringing of an alarm clock. To press comparisons much further would not be fair; it is enough to say that the influences of *Native Son* on *A Raisin in the Sun* are striking. What the later play has

A scene from A Raisin in the Sun, *starring Sidney Poitier as Walter Lee and Claudia NcNeil as Lena Younger.*

that the earlier one lacked is warmth and humor as well as characters who never become categories.

The living room in which the action of *A Raisin in the Sun* takes place is scrupulously described by the playwright; she wants it to be known that the shabbiness comes from the fact that the room has had to accommodate "too many people for too many years." The Negroes who live here, like any other poor family, live with old furniture that reflects their own weariness and poverty. (pp. 241-42)

Three generations in three rooms can lead to various complications. It is soon evident, for example, that the apartment has always been Mama's, with the result that Walter is no more the "head of a household" than a much younger Bigger Thomas was in a meaner apartment in the same part of Chicago. Not much is made of it by the playwright, but the little boy, Travis, has no single authority figure, and so he plays all three adults off against each other and is, as a result, "spoiled." This kind of domestic situation is common among the poor, black and white. There is, however, an added burden placed upon the Negro adult male; not only is he

unmanned by the fact that frequently his wife and mother can more readily find work than he can, but he is also subject to a dominant white society that would keep him a "boy," keep him harmless and "in his place."

A Raisin in the Sun is set up to demonstrate the clash of dreams, a clash between generations, between men and women, and even—because for all its commonality with domestic dramas about white people, and in spite of Miss Hansberry's statement to the contrary, it *is* a Negro play—the clash between black and white. (p. 243)

Lena Younger is the old-fashioned Negro mother (we have already seen her in *Harlem*, in *Native Son*, and in *A Medal for Willie*) who has over the years worked hard, attended church, and made sacrifices for a family and a future in which she has always had faith. Early in the play Ruth tries to speak in favor of Walter's business plans: "Like Walter say—I spec people going to always be drinking themselves some liquor." ...Mama tells Ruth that she will not be responsible for people drinking liquor; she has no desire to have that on her conscience at this late date.

What Mama wants to do with the insurance money is to put some of it away for Beneatha's schooling and then to make a down payment on a "little old two-story somewhere, with a yard where Travis could play in the summertime." Hers is a simple desire for a home that is the reward of her labors. And lest we think that she will capitulate easily to youth, there are two scenes that show Mama's strength as she stands up first to her daughter and then to her son.

Although Beneatha is a twenty-year-old medical student, she is quite adolescent in her behavior. She is fresh, full of talk about dates and "forms of expression." When she speaks of playing the guitar and riding horseback, one cannot help thinking more of the black bourgeoisie than of a lower-class family. Nor is it surprising to read that Lorraine Hansberry once said of Beneatha, "She's me eight years ago. I had a ball poking fun at myself through her." Beneatha calls her rich boy friend, George Murchison, "shallow" and dismisses her own brother as an "elaborate neurotic."

At one point, when Mama says that her daughter will be a doctor, "God willing," Beneatha answers drily, "God hasn't got a thing to do with it." At first Mama tries gently to get Beneatha to retract her statement, but the girl persists in saying that she is sick of hearing about God. Mama warns her that she is about to get her "fresh little jaw slapped," but Beneatha feels compelled to state her modern position. She assures her mother that she will not go out and commit crimes or immoral acts simply because she no longer believes in God. But she is tired of having God get all the credit for everything the human race achieves. As far as Beneatha is concerned there is only man, and he is the maker of miracles.

Mama slaps her daughter across the face and after a moment of silence, forces her to repeat, "In my mother's house there is still a God." Beneatha does as told, but when her mother is out of earshot, she says quietly to Ruth, "All the tyranny in the world will never put God in the heavens!" Commenting further on her personal relationship to Beneatha, Lorraine Hansberry said, "I don't disagree with anything she says. I believe science will bring more rewards for our generation than mysticism and all that jazz."

Beneatha takes her slap and goes her independent way. It is Walter who will inevitably clash with his mother. Medical school, after all, is more compatible with the Protestant ethic than Walter's highly suspect business adventure.

Some wonderfully warm, humorous scenes involve Beneatha and her African boy friend, Asagai. (Interestingly enough, much of the message of the play is embedded in the lighter speeches.) When she first tells her mother that an African student, an intellectual, will be coming by, Mama says that she has never met an African before. Beneatha is worried that Mama will ask ignorant questions because, like most Americans, she knows the dark continent only from seeing Tarzan movies. "Why should I know anything about Africa?"

Mama asks indignantly. Beneatha reminds her not of her people's history but of the missionary work she has supported to save Africans from heathenism. Then, modern young woman that she is, she adds that they need salvation from colonialism, not from heathenism.

Asagai turns out to be a sophisticated young African who is delighted by Beneatha. He brings her a gift of colorful Nigerian robes and records of tribal music. Having draped the robes properly, he admires her, as he says, "mutilated hair and all." She tries to defend her straightened hair, but he reminds her that when they met she told him that she was looking for "her identity." To him she looks more like a queen of the Nile than like a Hollywood queen. She is both flattered and disturbed.

Beneatha protests when Asagai accuses her of being an assimilationist, and yet she seems disturbed by what he is awakening in her. She does not want to be "someone's little episode in America." He bursts into laughter, telling her that she is like all American women; white or black, they are not so liberated as they proclaim themselves to be. (pp. 243-46)

As soon as the check is an actuality, a check that can be held in the hand, Walter is frantic to get his mother to agree to his business plans. Mama is particularly adamant in her refusal because she not only has her old convictions on her side, but she also knows that Ruth has become desperate enough to plan the abortion of a baby Walter has had no knowledge of. To the old woman this is a sign of how ugly their life has become. To her way of thinking liquor stores could only make it uglier.

Finally, in an effort to make her see his dissatisfaction with his job—"Yes, sir; no, sir; very good, sir; shall I take the Drive, sir?"—Walter speaks to her seriously, but with little hope, he says, of being understood:

> Sometimes it's like I can see the future stretched out in front of me—just as plain as day. The future, Mama. Hanging over there at the edge of my days. Just waiting for me—a big, looming blank space— full of nothing. Just waiting for me. (*Pause*) Mama— sometimes when I'm downtown and I pass them cool, quiet-looking restaurants where them white boys are sitting back and talking 'bout things . . . sitting there turning deals worth millions of dollars . . . sometimes I see guys don't look much older than me—

She interrupts him to ask why he talks so much about money. "Because it is life, Mama!" he says passionately. To which she answers, almost to herself, "Once upon a time freedom used to be life—now it's money." Walter disagrees, saying that it was always money, but "we just didn't know about it." (Psychologists have described the basic Negro personality as "a caricature of the corresponding white personality, because the Negro must adapt to the same culture, must accept the same social goals, but without the ability to achieve them.")

Although it accomplishes nothing, Mama tells Walter about the old days in the South when to stay alive was a goal. And for her it has been enough to work and save, to give her children the freedom allowed in the North. Walter cannot make her understand his frustration. Here, as in *Take a Giant Step*, the generations cannot communicate their different dreams. "The dream deferred is Walter's dream," Max Lerner once wrote, and then he observed:

> Examine it—the dream of getting away from his despised job, of setting up a business with a liquor license, of building it up big, of having pearls to hang around the neck of his wife, of enabling his young son to drive to school in a taxi—and you will see that it isn't particularly Walter's dream as a Negro, nor yet an intensely private one. It is a dream that comes out of the larger culture of the whites, in which Walter is caught up.

Not their disagreement about money or even his refusal to say that he will accept the responsibility of another child, but rather the events that follow persuade Mama to look at Walter in a different light. He stops going to work. If he is at home, he is drinking beer. When he is out, he drives around Chicago in a borrowed car or walks all over the Southside, just looking at Negroes—unemployed ones like himself.

In the midst of a drunken scene in which Walter stands on the table, swaying to Beneatha's recording of African music and speaking to a tribe that he can see in fantasy, George Murchison arrives. ("The Murchisons are honest-to-God-real-*live*-rich colored people, and the only people who are more snobbish than rich white people are rich colored people.") A completely convinced assimilationist, he would be the last one to understand a wild parody of African ritual. George calls Beneatha eccentric, and when she accuses him of being ashamed of his heritage, he reminds her that her heritage is "nothing but a bunch of raggedy-assed spirituals and some grass huts." Although she counters with a proud reference to the Africans "who were the first to smelt iron on the face of the earth," she does agree to change from her Nigerian robes for their date.

Walter has drunk enough beer and had sufficient discouragement about his business prospects to welcome a chance to attack the privileged young Murchison. First he makes fun of the college boy's clothes. Then he goes into a sardonic appreciation of George's "old man," someone who "thinks big." When he suggests that he and George should sit down for a talk sometime, the boy's skepticism and boredom are very evident. Walter is offended to the point of belligerence. He attacks George for not learning anything important in college, not learning to run the world, only to read books, to speak properly, and to wear "fairyish-looking white shoes." George, who has remained aloof until this time, cannot resist saying to Walter, "You're all wacked up with bitterness, man." Walter replies, through clenched teeth:

> And you—ain't you bitter, man? Ain't you just about had it yet? Don't you see no stars gleaming that you can't reach out and grab? . . . You contented son-of-a-bitch . . . . Bitter? Man, I'm a volcano. Bitter? Here I

am a giant—surrounded by ants! Ants who can't even understand what it is the giant is talking about.

And soon after this scene Walter learns that his mother has made a down payment on a house in Clybourne Park, in what is a white, not a Negro, neighborhood. Walter turns on his mother then, accusing her of running her children's lives as she wishes. "So you butchered up a dream of mine," he says to her, "you—who always talking 'bout your children's dreams."

It is in response to his bitterness and the despair that she reads in her son's growing alienation from his family that Mama finally admits to Walter that she has been wrong. "I been doing to you," she tells him, "what the rest of the world been doing." Now she tries to make it up to him by giving him the $6500 left after the down payment on the house, for him to put in the bank—$3,000 for Beneatha's education and the rest for his own checking account. He is astonished to hear her say, "I'm telling you to be head of this family from now on like you supposed to be." This moment is a turning point in Walter's fortunes and in the play itself.

The crucial scene in Act II, a scene that begins with enthusiasm and ends in despair, introduces the one white character in the play, a middle-aged man named Karl Lindner. He interrupts a lighthearted scene in which the Youngers (all but Mama) are packing their things in anticipation of the move to their new home. As chairman of the New Neighbors Orientation Committee of the Clybourne Park Improvement Association, Lindner announces that he has come to see the Youngers in order to "give them the low-down" on the way things are done in Clybourne Park. Commenting on the background of the members of the community, Lindner says that there is no question of racial prejudice. "It is a matter," he explains, "of the people of Clybourne Park believing, rightly or wrongly . . . that for the happiness of all concerned that our Negro families are happier when they live in their *own* communities." The welcoming committee turns out to be nothing more than an attempt to bribe the Youngers to stay out of a white neighborhood. . . . Walter, rising to his role as head of the family, orders him out of the apartment.

The young people are quite amused by the whole idea of the welcoming committee. When Mama is told of the white man's visit, she asks, "Did he threaten us?" Beneatha's answer serves to show youth's relaxed attitude toward what was and is very serious to their parents:

> Oh—Mama—they don't do it like that any more. He talked Brotherhood. He said everybody ought to learn how to sit down and hate each other with good Christian fellowship.

The relaxed atmosphere of the early part of the scene is easily recaptured, but it is interrupted once again by a doorbell. (The playwright has a sure sense of the dramatic value inherent in shattering moods in this fashion.) When Walter opens the door, it is to admit a frightened little man named Bobo, who confesses to

Walter before his astonished family that another partner has disappeared with their money.

Walter cries out in sheer madness now, praying and cursing, begging an absent Willy to bring back the money that was *"made out of my father's flesh."* He falls to the floor sobbing, and he is there when his mother goes to him to ask if all the money is gone. Lifting his head slowly he says, "Mama . . . I never . . . went to the bank at all." His money and Beneatha's, all of it is gone. When Mama has taken in the enormity if his act, she tells her children about their father, who worked himself to death for the money that Walter has given away in a day. Standing over her son, she prays, "Oh, God . . . Look down here—and show me the strength."

On the page this climactic scene seems both melodramatic and sentimental, but it is doubtful that many members of the theatre audience could resist the performance of Claudia McNeil [in the original production of *A Raisin in the Sun* in 1959]. (pp. 246-50)

Act III, in one scene, is short and still in a melodramatic vein. It begins quietly with an episode that further defines Beneatha and Asagai. She tells her African friend about Walter's treachery, and Asagai expresses his concern for her future. Beneatha tells him that she may have stopped caring about being a doctor, about curing hurt bodies. He questions her original impulse if she can so easily give up helping the ailing human race because of her brother's childish mistake. He wants to know why she does not continue to struggle for the future. Disillusioned, she turns the questions back to him and to the Africa of which he dreams; she wants to know what he plans to do about all the crooks and stupid men "who will come into power and steal and plunder the same as before—only now they will be black and do it in the name of the new independence."

His reply is that he is living the answer to her question by getting an education for leadership. And he acknowledges the fact that there will be retrogression before there is progress. Like a good revolutionary, he knows that even his own death could represent an advance for his people. When Asagai asks Beneatha to go home to Nigeria as his bride, she asks for time to consider his proposal. Something about her hesitation implies that she will not go "home to Africa." The tug toward the exotic was present earlier in the play, and while even now she seems flattered by his attention, Asagai remains, for Beneatha, a symbol of the past, not a portent of the future.

The balance of Act III belongs to Walter. It depicts his temptation to accept compromise and then a reversal that leads him into real nobility. At first he announces that he is ready to make a deal with Lindner's welcoming committee. As he explains to Mama, life is divided up between "the takers and the 'tooken.'" He has been among the "tooken," but he has learned to keep his eye on what counts. One of the most moving statements in the play is made by Mama when she says to Walter in response to his decision:

Son—I come from five generations of people who was slaves and sharecroppers—but ain't nobody in my family never let nobody pay 'em no money that was a way of telling us we wasn't fit to walk the earth. We ain't never been that poor . . . that dead inside.

Walter's only answer is that he did not make the world the way it is, and he does a heartbreaking imitation of a begging darky: "Yasssssuh! Great White Father, just gi' ussen de money, fo' God's sake, and we's ain't gwine come out deh and dirty up yo' white folks neighborhood."

And yet, by the time Lindner arrives, Walter has had time to consider his mother's words and his own humiliation, and he tells the astonished white man:

We have all thought about your offer and we have decided to move into our house because my father—my father—earned it . . . . We don't want to make no trouble for nobody or fight no causes—but we will try to be good neighbors . . . . We don't want your money.

When Lindner tries to appeal to Mama's good sense, she says that her son speaks for all of them.

The play ends with Walter's coming into his manhood and the family moving on to a future that promises to be bright only because it is predicated on the strength of the characters as we have come to know them. It is interesting to note Robert Nemiroff's contention that *A Raisin in the Sun* does not have a happy ending, "only a commitment to new levels of struggle," an idea that he says escaped most of the play's critics in 1959. Such an oversight is understandable in view of the fact that critics had nothing but the play before them, not Miss Hansberry's political statements or social proclamations.

John Davis, executive director of the American Society of African Culture, has said that the Negro writer's basic problem has been that "he must write for a non-Negro market which often is also the object of his protest." It would be difficult to disagree with this general statement. He went on, however, to call *A Raisin in the Sun* "social protest" that is "such consummate art" that audiences applaud the very protest that is directed against them. A few observations should be made about both the art and the protest in Lorraine Hansberry's play.

In the first place, members of the Negro community supported this Broadway production of a Negro play as they had supported no other; there were nights, even in New York, when the audience was almost half Negro. This particular Broadway play, then, was not performed for the usual white middle-class audience. Also, the play is not what is generally termed a protest play. The values of white society may have warped Walter Younger . . . , but it is not a play overtly protesting those values. Members of the audience, both white and black, could appreciate the play because Walter's rebellion is meliorated by the conservative values of Mama. In fact, he is shamed into maturity by his mother, which is to say that he is persuaded to accept her version of middle-class values.

Henry Hewes felt that the nearest thing to a message in *A Raisin in the Sun* was spoken by Asagai, the Nigerian revolutionist: "I know that we cannot allow life to depend on accidents." But few Americans would hear in this statement, as the critic did, a condemnation of sudden success and overnight acquisition of wealth in our society. Hewes concluded that Negroes are becoming a part of the illusion sometimes called the American myth of success. "Like the rest of us," he predicted, "some will be destroyed by it. But *A Raisin in the Sun* would seem to suggest that when the bubble bursts the families with the most courageous pasts will be best equipped to pick up the pieces."

Other critics were less concerned with social commentary and more concerned with art. Brooks Atkinson wrote that *A Raisin in the Sun* could be regarded as a Negro *Cherry Orchard*. No matter how different the social scale of the characters, he observed, "the knowledge of how character is controlled by environment is much the same, and the alternation of humor and pathos is similar." Kenneth Tynan's main reservation about the Hansberry play was in connection with its sentimentality, "particularly in its reverent treatment of Walter Lee's mother....I wish the dramatist had refrained from idealizing such a stolid old conservative." But, like Max Lerner, he could compare the play favorably with those of Clifford Odets.

Some critics—Miss Hansberry agreed with them, according to a stage manager who knew her a few years after the original production of *A Raisin in the Sun*—called the play a soap opera. It abounds in types: Mama is a tyrannical but good-natured matriarch; Walter, a frustrated young man surrounded by too many women; Beneatha, a free-thinking college student; the African Asagai, a poetic revolutionary; and the one white man, a cliché-ridden suburbanite. The interest in them lies chiefly in the fact that the central characters are Negroes, which is something new to soap opera. Tom Driver went so far as to say that this play would have done well to recover its investment if it had been written by a white woman about a white family. Of the play he concluded:

> As a piece of dramatic writing it is old-fashioned. As something near to the conscience of a nation troubled by injustice to Negroes, it is emotionally powerful. Much of its success is due to our sentimentality over the "Negro question."

After everything is said that can be said about the form and content of the play, one must agree with Harold Clurman about the importance of the Broadway production of *A Raisin in the Sun*. As he put it, "The play is organic theatre: cast, text, direction are homogeneous in social orientation and in sentiment, in technique and in quality of talent." (pp. 250-54)

> *Doris E. Abramson, "The Fifties," in her*
> Negro Playwrights in the American Theatre

1925-1959, *Columbia University Press,* 1969, pp. 165-266.

Julius Lester (essay date 1972)

[*In the following excerpt, Lester evaluates Hansberry's literary work, concluding that* Les Blancs *is the author's finest play.*]

The subject matter of *A Raisin in the Sun* may make it appear outdated. The action taking place in what now seems like a long past time—the days before Black Power, antiwar protests, student uprisings and black rebellions. The play concerns itself with the Younger family: Mama Younger, who has survived and won; her son, Walter, the pivotal character of the play, the black male castrated by the blade of the American dream but who blames the castration on his wife; Ruth, Walter's wife, who sees the wound and is unable to stanch the bleeding and, like her Biblical namesake, can say, "Whither thou goest, I will go"—but Walter will not lead; Beneatha, Walter's sister, a college student, a black militant in a day before there was a name for her; and, Joseph Asagai, an African student, with a vision of a black-ruled Africa. Within one apartment, Lorraine Hansberry capsulized so much of black life on a myriad of levels. Here is the black male-black female conflict presented in all its painful rawness in Walter and Ruth; and here too is a history of black women, all of them beautiful in totally different ways, all of them strong in totally different ways. (pp. 4-5)

Walter has been taught that he should want the world, but because he is black he has been denied the possibility of ever having it. And that only makes the pain of the desire that much more hurting....But Mama Younger has not let America define her. She has defined herself. (p. 7)

[It] is this difference in values [between Mama and Walter] that the play is about. Perhaps that would be clearer if Lorraine Hansberry had not chosen to write about material needs and aspirations so concretely. *A Raisin in the Sun* is no intellectual abstraction about upward mobility and conspicuous consumption. It goes right to the core of practically every black family in the ghettos of Chicago, New York, Los Angeles and elsewhere.... *A Raisin in the Sun* is most definitely about "human dignity" because Lorraine Hansberry is concerned with the attitude we must have toward material things if we are to be their master and not their slave. (pp. 8-9)

Few see the heroism in Walter's simple act of assertion [in rejecting the white neighborhood association's offer to buy them out]. Indeed, how many who have seen the play or the movie have not thought that Walter was a fool for *not* accepting the money? How one views Walter's act is a direct reflection of how much one accepts the American dream. And there is the significance of the fact that the play ends with the Youngers moving into a "white" neighborhood. To see this as a confirmation of the American dream is to accept the myth that blacks have wanted nothing more than to be integrated with whites. In actuality, the fact that the neighborhood is white is the least important thing about it. It merely happened to be the neighborhood in which Mama Younger could find a nice house she could afford. And it is this simple, practical element which has always been mistaken by whites as a desire on the part of blacks to be "integrated." But why, the question could be raised, would the Youngers persist in moving into a neighborhood where they are not wanted, where they may be subjected to harassment or even physical violence? They persist, as all blacks persist, not because it is any great honor to live among whites, but because one cannot consider himself a human being as long as he acquiesces to restrictions placed upon him by others, particularly if those restrictions are based solely on race or religion. If Walter had accepted the money, he would have been saying, in graphic language, You are right, we are niggers and don't have the right to live where we can afford to. But, with that earthy eloquence of a black still close to his roots, Walter says, "We have decided to move into our house because my father—my father—he earned it." And, in that realization, Walter learns also that it was not a black woman who castrated him. It was America and his own acceptance of America's values. No woman can make him a man. He has to do it himself.

He is a hero, a twentieth-century hero. (pp. 11-12)

The Younger family is one particular black family living in a very particular place. And because she draws them with such precise fidelity, they are true to the social, cultural and political environment in which they live and, by being so, they become universal—as Leopold and Molly Bloom become universal. (p. 15)

The Sign in Sidney Brustein's Window was a conscious warning, a plea to her white intellectual counterparts to prepare to pick up the gauntlet and return to the field. (*A Raisin in the Sun* is a conscious warning to the black middle class and those of the lower class with middle-class aspirations not to exchange the lessons bequeathed them by their parents for a mess of pottage.) (p. 20)

Sometimes, [her] enormous faith [in the potential of each human being for struggle and growth] could lead her to indulge in sentimental excesses, as with *What Use Are Flowers?* ... It is not a good play, but it helps us all the more to appreciate how good Lorraine Hansberry was when she was good .... The audience of a Lorraine Hansberry play left the theater feeling a little better than when it entered. They left with a little more hope; and while *What Use Are Flowers?*, is a momentary failure of craft, it is not a failure of vision. (pp. 23-4)

[Her identification with black people] gets its most complex treatment in *Les Blancs,* her finest play. (p. 25)

Les Blancs is the story of a group of individuals caught in a very particular situation, a situation to which they must respond, regardless of their desire not to. And who

Dust jacket for the posthumous collection of Hansberry's plays.

they are as human beings will be determined by how they respond to that situation—black liberation.

Tshembe, the black intellectual, is Sidney Brustein's counterpart; but the fact that he is black compounds the intellectual's disease of alienation. He is suspended between the part of him rooted in Africa and the part of him which has set down roots, personal and cultural, in Europe. (pp. 26-7)

Some of the sharpest and most pointed dialogue Lorraine Hansberry wrote occurs between Charlie Morris, the reporter, and Tshembe. Charlie, like all white liberals, does not want to recognize his share in the collective responsibility for a radically defined society. He insists that he is not all white men, but simply Charlie Morris. And it is on that basis that he wants to have a relationship with Tshembe, unaware that no relationship between a black and a white can be that simple. Tshembe knows that Charlie is a person, an individual in his own right. He also knows, however, that Charlie *is* all white men and, sadly, there is nothing either of them can do about it. Not unless Charlie becomes radicalized. (pp. 27-8)

Lorraine Hansberry had no illusions about revolution. She had no illusions about people. In some way or another, all of the characters in *Les Blancs* have a little of the truth. None of them are all bad or all good. We must recognize both the humanity and inhumanity of Major Rice as well as of Peter. But, above all, we must recognize that the necessity of black liberation takes command of the lives of its bearers and its victims. And, because it does, one "emits an animal-like cry of grief." One does not glorify or romanticize revolution. One cries.

Les Blancs is no catharsis for bloodthirsty blacks or masochistic whites. One leaves it with a profound sorrow in the soul. Yet because of the magnificent examples of humanity in Tshembe and Madame Neilsen, one also leaves saying Yes, that is the way it is and, maybe, I have a little more strength to accept it now . . . .

It is a masterful play, an almost pure distillation of Lorraine Hansberry's personal/political philosophy. (p. 31)

> *Julius Lester, in an introduction to "Les Blancs": The Collected Last Plays of Lorraine Hansberry, edited by Robert Nemiroff, Random House, 1972, pp. 3-32.*

W. Edward Farrison (essay date 1972)

[*In the following excerpt, Farrison briefly reviews Hansberry's last plays:* The Drinking Gourd, Les Blancs, *and* What Use Are Flowers?]

The Drinking Gourd, a three-act drama well suited for television presentation, is what may be called in television jargon a documentary on American plantation slavery. It is a compact yet comprehensive, authentic, and vivid portrayal of the "peculiar institution," correctly called the sum of all villainies, as it was especially in the cotton kingdom on the eve of the Civil War. The action in the drama is framed between a long prologue and a brief epilogue both of which are spoken by a soldier "perhaps Lincolnesque" in appearance. The prologue kaleidoscopically reviews the history of American slavery from its beginning to the middle of the nineteenth century. The epilogue avows that by that time the Civil War had become necessary to keep slavery from destroying the United States. (p. 193)

Rissa [the plantation cook] is indeed a faithful representation of the matriarchal heads of slave families—as far as slave families were allowed to exist—and to some extent she is also a prototype of Lena Younger, the widow and *mater familias* in *A Raisin in the Sun.* (p. 194)

Imaginative, unified, easily documentable, and intensely interesting story that it is, and being good theater as well as good dramatic literature, *The Drinking Gourd* is in the best tradition of historical dramas—much more so than *Les Blancs,* which is also an historical drama. In both of these works, nevertheless, as in the drama which first won her acclaim as a playwright, Miss Hansberry skillfully used original and vivid dialogue to reveal character and develop action. In *Les Blancs* she wrote all of the dialogue in standard informal spoken English, having no reason to use any other kind. In *The Drinking Gourd* she used the same kind of English to represent the speech of literate characters but changed to substandard usage to represent the speech of semiliterate and illiterate people. This she did convincingly . . . .

Miss Hansberry first described *What Use Are Flowers?* as "a bit of a fantasy thing about war and peace." As this brief drama now stands, war and peace are involved in it only by implication. Indeed the work is less of a fable—an imaginative work that conveys a specific moral—than a fantasy whose objective, according to Nemiroff, is the affirmation of "the value and purpose of life." . . . (p. 196)

What Use Are Flowers? is a brave venture into philosophical drama, which, although it added variety to its author's works, left her reputation as a noteworthy playwright resting on the other four plays she completed. (p. 197)

> *W. Edward Farrison, "Lorraine Hansberry's Last Dramas," in* CLA Journal, *Vol. XVI, No. 2, December, 1972, pp. 188-97.*

Amiri Baraka (essay date 1987)

[*A leading black dramatist of the 1960s, Baraka (who wrote until 1967 under his given name LeRoi Jones) is considered a seminal figure in the development of contemporary black literature. Often called the "Malcolm X of literature," he once dismissed* A Raisin in the Sun *as "middle class." In the following excerpt, he reappraises the work, now lauding the "imposing stature, continuing relevance, and pointed social analysis" of the play.*]

In the wake of its twenty-fifth anniversary, Lorraine Hansberry's great play *A Raisin in the Sun* is enjoying a revival of a most encouraging kind. Complete with restorations of the text of scenes and passages removed from the first production, the work is currently being given a new direction and interpretation that reveal even more clearly the play's profoundly imposing stature, continuing relevance, and pointed social analysis. At major regional theaters in city after city *Raisin* has played to packed houses and, as on the night I saw it, standing ovations. It has broken or approached long-standing box office records and has been properly hailed as "a classic," while the *Washington Post* has called it succinctly: "one of the handful of great American dramas . . . in the inner circle, along with *Death of a Salesman, Long Day's Journey into Night,* and *The Glass Menagerie.*"

For a playwright who knows, too well, the vagaries and realities of American theater, this assessment is gratifying. But of even greater significance is the fact that *A Raisin in the Sun* is being viewed by masses of people, black and white, in the light of a new day.

For *Raisin* typifies American society in a way that reflects more accurately the real lives of the black U.S. majority than any work that ever received commercial exposure before it, and few if any since. It has the life that only classics can maintain. Any useful re-appreciation of it cannot be limited, therefore, to the passages restored or the new values discovered, important though these are: it is the play itself, as a dramatic (and sociopolitical) whole, that demands our confirmation of its grandeur.

When *Raisin* first appeared in 1959, the Civil Rights Movement was in its earlier stages. And as a document reflecting the *essence* of those struggles, the play is unexcelled. For many of us it was—and remains—the quintessential civil rights drama. But any attempt to confine the play to an era, mind-set, an issue ("Housing") or set of topical concerns was, as we now see, a mistake. The truth is that Hansberry's dramatic skills have yet to be properly appreciated—and not just by those guardians of the status quo who pass themselves off as dramatic critics. For black theater artists and would-be theorists especially, this is ironic because the play is probably the most widely appreciated—particularly by African Americans—black drama that we have.

Raisin lives in large measure because black people have kept it alive. And because Hansberry has done *more* than document, which is the most limited form of realism. She is a *critical realist,* in a way that Langston Hughes, Richard Wright, and Margaret Walker are. That is, she *analyzes* and *assesses* reality and shapes her statement as an aesthetically powerful and politically advanced work of art. Her statement cannot be separated from the characters she creates to embody, in their totality, the life she observes: it becomes, in short, the living material of the work, part of its breathing body, integral and alive.

George Thompson in *Poetry and Marxism* points out that drama is the most expressive artistic form to emerge out of great social transformation. Shakespeare is the artist of the destruction of feudalism—and the emergence of capitalism. The mad Macbeths, bestial Richard III's, and other feudal worthies are actually shown, like the whole class, as degenerate—and degenerating. (pp. 9-10)

Hansberry's play, too, was political agitation. It dealt with the very same issues of democratic rights and quality that were being aired in the streets. It dealt with them with an unabating dramatic force, vision, political concreteness and clarity that, in retrospect, are awesome. But it dealt with them not as abstractions, fit only for infantile-left pamphlets, but as they are *lived.* In reality.

All of *Raisin*'s characters speak *to* the text and are critical to its dramatic tensions and understanding. They are necessarily larger than life—in impact—but crafted meticulously from living social material.

When the play opened on Broadway, Lena Younger, the emotional adhesive of the family, was given a broad, aggressive reading by Claudia McNeil. Indeed, her reading has been taken as the model and somewhat institutionalized in various productions I've seen.

The role itself—of family head, folksy counsel, upholder of tradition—has caused many people to see her as the stereotyped "black matriarch" of establishment and commercial sociological fame. Carrying with them (or rebelling against) the preconceived baggage of that stereotype, and recalling the play through the haze of memory (or from the compromised movie version), they have not bothered to look more closely at the actual woman Hansberry created—and at *what* tradition she in fact upholds. (p. 11)

[In the recent New York revival of the play, Olivia Cole's reading of Lena] was revelation and renewal.

Ms. Cole came at the role from the inside out. Her Lena is a woman, black, poor, struggle-worn but proud and loving. She was in the world *before* the rest of the family, before many of us viewing the play. She has seen and felt what we have not, or what we cannot yet identify. She is no quaint, folksy artifact; she is truth, history, love—and struggle—as they can be manifest only in real life. (p. 12)

Similarly, the new interpreters of Walter Lee . . . are something "fresh," like our kids say. They bring a contemporary flavoring to the work that consists of knowing—with more certainty than, say, Sidney Poitier could have in the original—the frustration and rage animating the healthy black male, *post*-civil rights era. They play Walter Lee more aggressively, more self-consciously, so that when he does fall we can actually hate him—hate the frivolous, selfish male-chauvinist part of ourselves. And when he stands up at the finale and will not be beaten, we can cry with joy.

Part of the renewed impact of the play comes with the fresh interpretation of both director and actors. But we cannot stop there! The social materials that Hansberry so brilliantly shaped into drama are not lightweight. For me this is the test of the writer: no matter the skill of the execution—*what* has been executed? What is it he or she is talking about? Form can never be dismissed, to say the least, particularly by an artist. But in the contradiction between form and content, content must be the bottom line—though unless the form be an extension of (and correctly serve) that content, obviously even understanding of the content will be flawed.

Formalist artists must resort to all kinds of superficial aberrations of form because usually they have nothing to say. Brecht said how much safer the red is in a "non-objective" painting than the red of blood rushing out of the slain worker's chest . . . . And it is one reason why some critics will always have a problem with the realism of a Hansberry—and ignore the multilayered richness of her form.

A Raisin in the Sun is about *dreams,* ironically enough. And how those psychological projections of human life can come into conflict like any other product of that life. For Lena, a new house, the stability and happiness of her children, are her principal dream. And as such this is the completion of a dream she and her late husband—who has literally, like the slaves, been *worked* to death—conceived together.

Ruth's dream, as mother and wife, is somewhat similar. A room for her son, an inside toilet. She dreams as one of those triply oppressed by society—as worker, as African American, and as woman. But her dream, and her mother-in-law's, conflicts with Walter Lee's. He is the chauffeur to a rich white man and dreams of owning all and doing all the things he sees "Mr. Arnold" do and own. On one level Walter Lee is merely aspiring to full and acknowledged humanity; on another level he yearns to strut his "manhood," a predictable mix of *machismo* and fantasy. But Hansberry takes it even further to show us that on still another level Walter Lee, worker though he be, has the "realizable" dream of the black petty bourgeoisie. "There he is! *Monsieur le petit bourgeois noir*—himself!," cries Beneatha, the other of Lena Younger's children. "There he is—Symbol of a Rising Class! Entrepreneur! Titan of the system!" The deepness of this is that Hansberry can see that the conflict of dreams is not just that of individuals but, more importantly, of classes. Not since Theodore Ward's *Big White Fog* (1938) has there been a play so thoroughly and expertly reflective of class struggle within a black family.

Beneatha dreams of medical school. She is already socially mobile, finding a place, as her family cannot, among other petty bourgeois aspirants on the rungs of "education," where their hard work has put her. Her aspiration is less caustic, more attainable than Walter's. But she yearns for something more. Her name Beneatha (as who ain't?) should instruct us. She is, on the one hand, secure in the collegiate world of "ideas" and elitism, above the mass; on the other, undeceived by the myths and symbols of class and status. Part militant, part dilletante, "liberated" woman, little girl, she questions everything and dreams of service to humanity, an identity beyond self and family in the liberation struggles of her people. Ah, but will she have the strength to stay the course?

Hansberry has Beneatha grappling with key controversies of the period, but also some that had yet to clearly surface. And she grapples with some that will remain with us until society itself is changed: The relationship of the intellectual to the masses. The relationship of African Americans to Africans. The liberation movement itself and the gnawing necessity of black self-respect in its many guises (e.g., "straightened" hair vs. "the natural"). Written in 1956 and first seen by audiences in the new revivals, the part of the text in which Beneatha unveils her hair—the "perm" cut off and she glowing with her original woolly crown—precedes the "Afro" by a decade. Dialogue between Beneatha and her mother, brother, Asagai and George Murchison digs into all these still-burning concerns.

Similarly, Walter Lee and Ruth's dialogues lay out his male chauvinism and even self- and group-hate born of the frustration of too many dreams too long deferred: the powerlessness of black people to control their own fate or that of their families in capitalist America where race is place, white is right, and money makes and defines the man. Walter dreams of using his father's insurance money to buy a liquor store. This dream is in conflict not only with the dreams of the Younger women, but with reality. But Walter appreciates only his differences with—and blames—the women. Throughout the work, Hansberry addresses herself to issues that the very young might feel only *The Color Purple* has raised. Walter's relationship to his wife and sister, and Beneatha's with George and Asagai, gives us a variety of male chauvinism—working class, petty bourgeois, African.

Asagai, the Nigerian student who courts Beneatha, dreams of the liberation of Africa and even of taking Beneatha there: "We will pretend that . . . you have only been away for a day." But that's not reality either, though his discussion of the dynamics and dialectics of revolution—and of the continuity of human struggle, the only means of progress—still rings with truth!

Hansberry's warnings about neo-colonialism and the growth (and corruption) of a post-colonial African bourgeoisie—"the servants of empire," as Asagai calls them—are dazzling because of their subsequent replication by reality. As is, above all, her sense of the pressures mounting inexorably in this one typical household, and in Walter Lee especially, and of where they must surely lead. It was the "explosion" Langston Hughes talked about in his great poem "Harlem"—centerpiece of his incomparable *Montage of a Dream Deferred,* from which the play's title was taken—and it informs the play as its twinned projection: dream or coming reality.

These are the categories Langston proposes for the dream:

> Does it dry up
> Like a raisin in the sun?

Dried up is what Walter Lee and Ruth's marriage had become, because their respective dreams have been deferred. When Mama Lena and Beneatha are felled by news of Walter Lee's weakness and dishonesty, their life's will—the desired greening of their humanity—is defoliated.

> Or fester like a sore—
> And then run?

Walter Lee's dream has festered, and in his dealings with the slack-jawed con man Willie (merchant of the stuff of dreams), his dream is "running."

We speak of the American Dream. Malcolm X said that for the Afro-American it was the American Nightmare. The little ferret man . . . is the dream's messenger, and the only white person in the play. His name is Lindner (as in "neither a borrower nor a Lindner be"), and the thirty or so "pieces of silver" he proffers are meant to help the niggers understand the dichotomous dream.

"But you've got to admit that a man, right or wrong, has the right to want to have the neighborhood he lives in a certain kind of way," says Lindner. Except black folks. Yes, these "not rich and fancy" representatives of white lower-middle America have a dream, too. A class dream, though it does not even serve them. But they are kept ignorant enough not to understand that the real dimensions of that dream—white supremacy, black "inferiority," and with them ultimately, though they know it not, fascism and war—are revealed every day throughout the world as deadly to human life and development—even their own.

In the post-civil rights era, in "polite" society, theirs is a dream too gross even to speak of *directly* anymore. And this is another legacy of the play: It was one of the shots fired (and still being fired) at the aberrant white-supremacy dream that is American reality. And the play is also a summation of those shots, that battle, its heightened statement. Yet the man, Lindner, explains him/them self, and there is even a hint of compassion for Lindner the man as he bumbles on in outrageous innocence of all he is actually saying—that "innocence" for which Americans are famous, which begs you to love and understand me for hating you, the innocence that kills. Through him we see this other dream:

> Does it stink like rotten meat?
> Or crust and sugar over—
> Like a syrupy sweet?

Almost everyone else in the play would sound like Martin Luther King at the march on Washington were we to read their speeches closely and project them broadly. An exception is George Murchison (merchant's son), the "assimilated" good bourgeois whose boldest dream, if one can call it that, is to "get the grades . . . to pass the course . . . to get a degree" en route to making it the American way. George wants only to "pop" Beneatha after she, looking good, can be seen with him in the "proper" places. He is opposed to a woman's "thinking" at all, and black heritage to him "is nothing but a bunch of raggedy-ass spirituals and some grass huts." The truth of this portrait is one reason the black bourgeoisie has not created the black national theaters, publishing houses, journals, galleries, film corporations, and newspapers the African American people desperately need. So lacking in self-respect are members of this class of George's, they even let the Kentucky Colonel sell us fried chicken and giblets.

The clash between Walter Lee and George, one of the high points of class struggle in the play and a dramatic tour de force, gives us the dialogue between the *sons* of the house and of the field slaves. (pp. 12-18)

When *Raisin* appeared the movement itself was in transition, which is why Hansberry could sum up its throbbing profile with such clarity. The baton was ready to pass from "George's father" as leader of the "Freedom Movement" (when its real muscle was always the Lena Youngers and their husbands) to the Walter Lees and Beneathas and Asagais and even the Georges.

In February 1960, black students at North Carolina A & T began to "sit in" at Woolworth's in a more forceful attack on segregated public facilities. By the end of 1960, some 96,000 students across the country had gotten involved in these sit-ins. In 1961, Patrice Lumumba was assassinated, and black intellectuals and activists in New York stormed the United Nations gallery. While Ralph Bunche (George's spiritual father) shrank back "embarrassed"—probably more so than by slavery and colonialism! But the Pan African thrust had definitely returned.

And by this time, too, Malcolm X, "the fire prophet," had emerged as the truest reflector of black mass feelings. It was of someone like Malcolm that Walter Lee spoke as in a trance in prophecy while he mounts the table to deliver his liquor-fired call to arms. (Nation of Islam headquarters was Chicago where the play is set!) Walter Lee embodies the explosion to be—what happens when the dream is deferred past even the patience of the Lena Youngers.

Young militants like myself were taken with Malcolm's coming, with the immanence of explosion. (pp. 18-19)

We thought Hansberry's play was part of the "passive resistance" phase of the movement, which was over the minute Malcolm's penetrating eyes and words began to charge through the media with deadly force. We thought her play "middle class" in that its focus seemed to be on "moving into white folks' neighborhoods," when most blacks were just trying to pay their rent in ghetto shacks.

We missed the essence of the work—that Hansberry had created a family on the cutting edge of the same class and ideological struggles as existed in the movement itself and among the people. What is most telling about our ignorance is that Hansberry's play still remains overwhelmingly popular and evocative of black and white reality, and the masses of black people dug it true.

The next two explosions in black drama, Baldwin's *Blues for Mr. Charlie* and my own *Dutchman* (both 1964) raise up the militance and self-defense clamor of the movement as it came fully into the Malcolm era . . . . But neither of these plays is as much a statement from the African American majority as is *Raisin.* For one thing, they are both (regardless of their "power") too concerned with white people.

It is Lorraine Hansberry's play which, though it seems "conservative" in form and content to the radical petty bourgeoisie (as opposed to revolutionaries), is the accurate telling and stunning vision of the real struggle . . . . The Younger family is part of the black majority, and the concerns I once dismissed as "middle class"—buying a house and moving into "white folks' neighborhoods"—are actually reflective of the essence of black people's striving and the will to defeat segregation, discrimination, and national oppression. There is no such thing as a "white folks' neighborhood" except to racists *and to those submitting to racism.*

The Younger family is the incarnation—*before* they burst from the bloody Southern backroads and the burning streets of Watts and Newark onto TV screens and the *world* stage—of our common ghetto-variety Fanny Lou Hamers, Malcolm X's, and Angela Davises. And their burden surely will be lifted, or one day it certainly will "explode." (pp. 19-20)

> *Amiri Baraka, "A Raisin in the Sun's' Enduring Passion," in* 'A Raisin in the Sun'; *and* 'The Sign in Sidney Brustein's Window', *by Lorraine Hansberry, edited by Robert Nemiroff, New American Library, 1987, pp. 9-20.*

Steven R. Carter (essay date 1991)

[*In the following excerpt from his* Hansberry's Drama: Commitment amid Complexity *(1991), Carter compares two unproduced filmscripts—written by Hansberry herself—of* A Raisin in the Sun. *He concludes: "The filmscripts are literary works of a high order that have much to offer readers . . . ."*]

When Hansberry sold the film rights for *A Raisin in the Sun* to Columbia Pictures in 1959, she insisted on writing the screenplay to ensure that the integrity of her work was preserved. As she knew uncomfortably well, Hollywood had a long history of presenting degrading and stereotyped images of blacks and often depicted them as exotic creatures with simple desires very different from those of the rest of humanity, and she was fearful that her Younger family might be similarly debased. This fear was perhaps intensified during a Chicago television show in 1959 by Hansberry's confrontation with Otto Preminger, whose exotic portrayal of blacks in *Carmen Jones* deeply offended her. Moreover, he had just finished directing *Porgy and Bess,* which was based on a novel in which the treatment of blacks was equally demeaning and distorted in Hansberry's eyes. Preminger's insensitivity and unwillingness to listen to legitimate complaints about the handling of black characters in films during the impromptu debate must have been an additional warning about what could happen to the film version of her play in the hands of the wrong director or writer.

However, Hansberry had an additional reason for wanting to do the screenplay. She was keenly aware of the differing demands of the stage and film and longed for the chance to re-imagine her story in filmic terms, giving it a panoramic sweep not possible in the original version. She was filled with ideas about how to take the Younger family into their community, thereby focusing on several additional problems that blacks face in daily life and heightening viewers' awareness of the Youngers' role as representatives of a large, embattled minority. With these objectives in mind, she wrote two filmscripts which, retaining all the basic plotlines, included many new scenes that added significant dimensions and nuances to her characters and themes. Equally important, these filmscripts also lovingly detailed a vital and wide-ranging visual depiction of black life. (pp. 70-1)

Both screenplays retain all the primary and secondary plots of the play, including Ruth's down payment on an abortion and Beneatha's courtship by Asagai and Murchison. Both contain roughly equivalent versions of a large number of new scenes, such as Lena's last morning at work, her confrontation with a white clerk at a ghetto market, Walter's discussion of the liquor business with a white store-owner, his conference with Willy Harris and Bobo at a bar, Beneatha's meeting with Asagai at a student lounge, Lena's encounter with the drunken Walter at the Green Hat bar, and the family's visit to their new house.

The first filmscript, however, conceived as a preliminary draft for discussion purposes, is forty-six typewritten pages shorter than the second, largely because it omits extensive portions of dialogue from the play, such as Beneatha's early morning banter with her brother and Asagai's discussion with Beneatha about the loss of the money. This brevity inevitably places greater emphasis on the new scenes and therefore on the Youngers' involvement with their city. The longer filmscript, as one might expect, offers a fuller statement of Hansberry's ideas, not only restoring Asagai's philosophical speeches, for example, but also adding new lines to them along with the best of his old lines in some of the early drafts. The second filmscript contains most of the dialogue from the play plus most of the new scenes from the first filmscript and some scenes and speeches never staged from early drafts. Three notable restorations from early drafts are included in the second filmscript. (1) Beneatha tells Murchison that, unlike the rest of her family, who "are all sort of rushing around trying to be like everybody else," she wants "the right to be *different* from everybody else—and yet—be a part too." (2) Asagai provides a Marxist analysis of Beneatha's folly in lamenting the loss of money that she did not earn and comments that "there is something wrong when all the dreams in this house—good or bad—had to depend on something that might never have happened if a man had not died" (a comment which, in slightly different form, was restored in the twenty-fifth anniversary edition of *A Raisin in the Sun*). (3) Asagai praises Lena because "she moves, she acts, she changes things."

The two filmscripts also differ in organization, the most significant change being the placement of Lena's dialogue with her employer, Mrs. Holiday, during her last morning at work. The first script begins with this confrontation, then moves to the scene from the play in which the Youngers get up, thus creating some confusion about whether the two scenes take place on the same day. Scattered references to Lena's last half-day at work add to the muddle. In the second filmscript, however, the wake-up scene comes first, leaving no doubt that this is the morning of Lena's last day as a maid. In the event of the publication of the second, stronger, filmscript, three scenes from the first version should be included as an appendix because they differ markedly from those in the second and are highly interesting in themselves, both artistically and socially.

The most remarkable of the scenes is a black nationalist speech by a man on a ladder to a street crowd that includes Walter and Asagai, who are unaware of each other because they have never met. A much shorter version appears in the second filmscript, with only Walter looking on. Although the fuller version is much more readable and effective as a speech, it was obvious from the beginning that it would never be filmed, and the shorter version proved equally unacceptable to Columbia executives. In the first filmscript, the speaker begins by describing the typical black man from the South, who imagines that Chicago is the Promised Land but finds that to get a job he must go "to the very man who has stolen his homeland; put him in bondage; defamed his nation; robbed him of his heritage!—The White Man," and that the White Man's response will be to give him a broom. The speaker then points to the insurgency of African blacks and asks when American blacks will follow their example, a comment and question that apply to both Asagai and Walter. The man on the ladder concludes that American blacks "are the only people in the world who are the completely disinherited" and asks a question that disturbs Walter: "Where are our factories, where are our mills, where are our mighty houses of finance!" Of the four-page scene, only the half-page concluding statement on disinheritance remains in the second filmscript.

On the other hand, the shorter version of the black nationalist speech in the second filmscript is more carefully placed within the framework of the story and is preceded by several images that help to visualize some of the points that the original speech made verbally. The second version of the speech is thus an advance in cinematic terms over the first and shows Hansberry making an effective use of her medium. The first version of the speech was preceded only by images of Lena making a down payment on the house and Walter walking the streets and encountering the man on the ladder. This version thus stands starkly by itself, and attention focuses sharply on the speaker's words and on the presence of Walter and Asagai, for both of whom the message obviously has considerable, although not necessarily the same, relevance. Before the second version of the speech, however, is the scene in which Walter angrily denounces his mother for buying the house and butchering his dream of owning a liquor store, followed by his period of despair, when he wanders the city and its environs, unable to work or think about anything except his loss. The images of this period accentuate Walter's sense of how he and so many others like him have been forcibly kept out of the mainstream of American life. After a shot of Walter drinking alone, we see him driving out to the steel mills, where "he simply stands staring at the industrial landscape; the muscles of his jaws working in anguish." Then we follow him to the stockyards, where he leans on a ramp and watches the animals. Finally, after observing him drink alone again, we discover "him sitting on a curb in the early morning shadow of the Negro soldier's monument in a square at 39th and South Parkway," a reminder of the blacks who died defending the United States in segregated units under white commanders. With these images freshly before our eyes (had this film had been made), we could readily understand Walter's overwhelming pain when the speaker refers to American blacks as "completely disinherited" and asks "Where are your textile or steel mills? Heh? Where are your mighty houses of finance—?" The speaker seems to be voicing Walter's own thoughts. With Asagai missing, the focus is entirely on Walter, and the context ensures sympathy and understanding. Although much of value from the original speech has been lost, more has been gained by the second version. Nevertheless, the first version is strong enough to deserve publication in its own right.

The second scene that should be preserved from the first filmscript occurs immediately after Lena has confronted an impudent white clerk over the inferior produce offered in his ghetto store—upending a bag of apples that look like "they was left over from the Last Supper." Mrs. Johnson, who overhears the argument, asks Lena whether she is "still out there trying to change the world," and Lena further discusses her argument. In the second filmscript, Hansberry deleted the scene in favor of one in which Lena meets Mrs. Johnson in front of a fruit stall on the other side of town and explains why she has chosen to shop there, even though it is so far away, instead of at the greatly overpriced ghetto market.

The third memorable scene is Lindner's encounter with Walter, Ruth, and Beneatha at their new house (an encounter that takes place at their apartment in the second filmscript). It includes some new speeches by all three and some notable screen directions that do not appear in the second filmscript. For example, when Walter mentions that it is the first time he and his family have seen the house, Lindner is surprised into asking how they like it. Ruth, whom the directions describe as "in the final analysis, the most quietly perceptive of the three," responds with the double-layered message that they "are going to like living here very much, thank you." When Walter orders Lindner out of his house, the directions inform us that he is not being "heroic" but simply "disgusted and annoyed" and that "his commands mean only that—that he wishes the pathetic little human being would get out of his sight."

Several of the scenes appearing in both filmscripts enlarge the portrait of Lena and afford a clearer view of her relationship to her society. The scene on her last morning at the Holidays', for example, indicates volumes about the conditions Lena has had to work under all her life and how she feels about them. Part of her work for the Holidays has been taking care of the six-or-seven-year-old daughter. She is gruffly affectionate in bidding the girl farewell, yet she is adamant in resisting Mrs. Holiday's attempt to use this affection to convince her to stay on. She stands equally firm against Mrs. Holiday's plea that if Lena retires she will be forced to leave "the agency" to look after her daughter. Lena is not prepared to sacrifice herself for her employers, no matter how kindly or pleasantly they have treated her, and she says emphatically that she is sixty-five years old and tired. After having worked steadily from the age of twelve for a total of fifty-three years, she understandably feels that she "had to start too early and keep on too long." Almost against her will—it means inconvenience and even hardship for her if Lena goes—Mrs. Holiday says that she is glad Lena can finally retire. Now that the young white woman has become a wholly sympathetic listener, Lena tells about a former employer who "like to had a heart attack" when, after twenty-two years of service during her younger days, Lena asked for a raise. "A brutal if accurate mimic," she recalls the old woman's response, "Why, *Lee-na,* I never thought to hear *you-ou* talk as if you thought of this as a job!" Lena quit that non-job the same day. She also describes how she and Big Walter, a railroad porter, tried to get jobs as welders in a defense plant during World War II, because "nobody would spend their life being a domestic if there was something better they could get to do, child." Because both of them were in their fifties, it was not easy for them to learn something new, and Lena was intimidated by "one thing there" that "all but shook my dentures out." However, Big Walter learned, "and he was so proud not to never have to be a porter no more . . . ." Lena too remains proud of him for this and tells Mrs. Holiday that she has a son who is just like Big Walter, whereupon the scene shifts to a view of Walter in his chauffeur's uniform.

The later scene, common to both filmscripts, in which Lena expresses outrage over the white clerk's selection of apples that "look like they was on the scene when Moses crossed over" and at the clerk's impudent responses to her just complaints demonstrates once again her refusal to accept injustice passively. It also demonstrates, as Lena observes, that "the South Side is the garbage dump of this city where you can sell all the trash don't nobody else in America want." Her only alternative is to take a street car to the "Open Markets" of the far South Side where she encounters Mrs. Johnson and explains that "it's worth the carfare just to be able to shop decent." On her way back, she sees the type of house that she eventually buys, and "an expression of unabashed longing" fills her eyes. Thus, a connection is suggested between her rebellious visit to the distant market and her defiant purchase of the house in a white neighborhood, both aimed at seizing a better deal from life, even at the cost of much hardship. There is also an implication that the encounter at the market helped shape Lena's mood when she goes to the real estate office.

In both filmscripts, Hansberry juxtaposes the scene of Lena on the bus looking at the house with a scene of Walter on another bus looking at a liquor store, highlighting the obvious clash of their dreams. Moreover, it is significant that Lena and Walter are each enclosed in a boxlike structure that is rapidly moving past the dream, a visual symbolism not possible on the stage. This scene is followed by one in which Walter visits the liquor store to ask the white owner, Herman, about the details of running the business. Herman, who knows Walter as a steady customer, finds it hard to take him seriously at first and, when he realizes that Walter does mean to go into the business, strongly advises against it. The directions in the second filmscript stress that "there is nothing 'racist' in Herman's attitude to Walter Lee. He is genuine, helpful, is simply voicing a typical shopkeeper's plaint." They also note "the irony of non-communication between two men." Herman, "who, somehow, believes every word," argues that it is better to have a "nine to five job" as Walter does than to put in long hours and pay high overhead costs in a business of one's own. Walter sees this as a mixture of condescension and hypocrisy and asks why Herman doesn't sell his store and get a nine-to-five job. Herman's explanation that his wife has "got a vocabulary of one word: 'Gimme'" implies that he is making money, thus justifying—in part—the anger that makes Walter leave the store so abruptly.

Later, when Walter describes this encounter to Willy Harris and Bobo at the Green Hat, Willy comments that "that's the way the greys are. They figure if you join 'em, you beat 'em. Last thing they want to see is a Negro going into business." Walter also explains that the reason he is having trouble getting his part of the money for the liquor store is that he has to face "three women at the barricades" and that "if there is somebody who cannot be persuaded to take a larger view in this world, it is a woman!" Both Willy and Bobo agree with this view of women, thereby establishing an atmosphere of male conspiracy around their deal.

One other new scene in both filmscripts that involves Walter and Lena, a scene actually used (at least in part) in the film, takes place when Lena comes to get her son at the Green Hat after she learns that he has not shown up at work for three days. It is, of course, ironic that Walter is drinking his way to self-destruction because of his mother's refusal to give him the money to buy a liquor store. Lena orders him out of the bar and they continue their conversation in a luncheonette. How long will it be, she asks him, before she has to pick him up from the sidewalk? She is "used to a man who knew how to live with his pain and make his hurt work for him. Your daddy died with dignity; there wasn't no bum in him." However, Walter surprises her by inquiring why she left the South. Once she is sure that he is not incoherent from drunkenness but genuinely wants to know, she explains that she thought that she might be able to do better for herself in the North. Walter then demands: "But you didn't give nobody the right to keep you there when you decided you had to go, did you

Mama? Even if you wasn't really goin' no place at all—you felt like you was, didn't you, Mama, didn't you? Then why in the name of God couldn't you let me get on my train when my time came!" The question is crucial because it forces her to compare her own ambitions with her son's as well as heightens her understanding of his desperation, and, "at once defeated and resurrected," she gives him all her remaining money.

Other new scenes in the two filmscripts pertain to Ruth and Beneatha. In a variation on the scene in the play in which he requests money to take to school for some unspecified purpose, Travis now needs the 50 cents each month for books on "the poor-Negroes-in-history." After determining from Travis that his teacher really does say "poor Negroes" all the time, Ruth asks why "there got to be *special* books" and argues that "the man who writes the rest of the books ought to get around to writing the Negro part." Travis throughout remains innocently unaware of the condescending liberalism of both his teacher and the books, but Ruth has assessed them accurately. The result is the same as in the play; Ruth tells Travis that she does not have the money and Walter gives it to him.

Beneatha's new scene is with Asagai at the campus lounge. As he does all during the play, Asagai is teasing her, and Beneatha, offended, asserts that he seems to regard her as a "circus clown." Asagai's deliberately unreassuring response is that she delights him "for a lot of reasons—including being a clown." Later, he explains that he cannot take women very seriously, and Beneatha inquires if he is "really so proud about being so backward about women?" At another point in their discussion, she asks if he is a revolutionary and he replies that "all Africans are revolutionaries today, even those who don't know that they are. It is the times. In order to survive we must be against most of what is." When Beneatha affirms that she would like to be an African too, he guesses that she desires this because she would like to be "a revolutionary." Her answer: "Yes, and a nationalist, too."

In addition to the new scenes, the two unproduced filmscripts contain extensive analyses of characters and settings, bonuses for readers. Among the most provocative and insightful is Hansberry's commentary on the Youngers' apartment. From it, the reader learns that Travis, who sleeps in the living room now that his grandfather is dead, previously had a bed behind a screen in his grandparents' bedroom. This "unhappy arrangement" "bitterly antagonized" the family for many years, but was considered necessary because the only alternative was to place the "almost grown aunt" in the same room with her father. The commentary also notes that "not indolence, not indifference and certainly not the lack of ambition imprisons them—but various enormous questions of the social organization around them which they understand in part; but only in part." Other illuminating remarks abound throughout, helping to clarify Hansberry's interpretation of her work.

The filmscripts are literary works of a high order that have much to offer readers already familiar with the play and those who know nothing about it. Both for the dimensions they add to one of the great dramas of this century and for their own special power and perceptiveness, they should be published as rapidly as possible. And, perhaps, someday a great director, reading them, will be inspired to create a movie version of *A Raisin in the Sun* that illustrates the full range of Hansberry's vision. (pp. 72-8)

> *Steven R. Carter, in his* Hansberry's Drama: Commitment amid Complexity, *University of Illinois Press, 1991, 199 p.*

FURTHER READING

Brown-Guillory, Elizabeth. "Black Women Playwrights: Exorcising Myths." *Phylon* XLVIII, No. 3 (Fall 1987): 229-39.
> Compares *A Raisin in the Sun* to dramas by Alice Childress and Ntozake Shange.

Cheney, Anne. "Measure Him Right: *A Raisin in the Sun*." In her *Lorraine Hansberry,* pp. 55-71. Boston: Twayne Publishers, 1984.
> Detailed explication of *A Raisin in the Sun*.

Davis, Arthur P. "Lorraine Hansberry." In his *From the Dark Tower: Afro-American Writers 1900-1960,* pp. 203-07. Washington, D. C.: Howard University Press, 1974.
> Brief overview of Hansberry's career.

Dedmond, Francis. "Lorraine Hansberry." In *American Playwrights Since 1945,* edited by Philip C. Kolin, pp. 155-68. New York: Greenwood Press, 1989.
> Provides a brief assessment of Hansberry's career as well as an overview of *A Raisin in the Sun*.

Freedomways 19, No. 4 (1979).
> Special issue devoted to Hansberry, including essays by James Baldwin, Nikki Giovanni, and Alex Haley.

Hooks, Bell. "*Raisin* in a New Light." *Christianity and Crisis* (6 February 1989): 21-3.
> Contends that Hansberry and her work continue to inspire African-Americans thirty years after the debut of *A Raisin in the Sun*.

Nemiroff, Robert. Introduction to *A Raisin in the Sun,* by Lorraine Hansberry, pp. ix-xviii. New York: Signet/New American Library, 1987.
> Reappraisal of *A Raisin in the Sun* by Hansberry's former husband. Nemiroff focuses on sequences removed from the original production and restored in a recent revival of the play.

Norment, Lynn. "*Raisin* Celebrates Its 25th Anniversary." *Ebony* XXXIX, No. 5 (March 1984): 57-60.
> Production history of *A Raisin in the Sun,* featuring photographs of the original staging.

Olauson, Judith. "1950-1960." In her *The American Woman Playwright: A View of Criticism and Characterization,* pp. 77-99. Troy: The Whitston Publishing Company, 1981.
   Analysis of *A Raisin in the Sun,* focusing on characterization.

Peerman, Dean. "*A Raisin in the Sun:* The Uncut Version." *The Christian Century* (25 January 1989): 71-3.
   Discusses material excised from the original production of *A Raisin in the Sun.*

Wilkerson, Margaret B. "The Sighted Eyes and Feeling Heart of Lorraine Hansberry." *Black American Literature Forum* 17, No. 1 (Spring 1983): 8-13.
   Brief biographical and critical survey of Hansberry's career, centering on *A Raisin in the Sun.*

————. "*A Raisin in the Sun:* Anniversary of an American Classic." *Theatre Journal* 38, No. 4 (December 1986): 441-52.
   Article celebrating the enduring qualities of *A Raisin in the Sun.*

Frances Ellen Watkins Harper

1825-1911

(Born Frances Ellen Watkins; also wrote as Effie Afton)
American poet, novelist, essayist, and short story writer.

Harper, a celebrated orator and social activist, was one of the most popular black poets of the nineteenth century. Her works are considered transitional: while she wrote against slavery, she also broke away from the purely propagandistic mode of the antislavery poet and became one of the first black writers to focus on national and universal issues. Today, she is considered a minor poet of the abolitionist era whose works possess historic rather than artistic significance.

Born of free parents in the slave state of Maryland, Harper was raised by an aunt and uncle after her parents' early deaths and educated at her uncle's school for free blacks. Her first job, at thirteen, was caring for the children of a bookseller; there she began composing poems and reading the popular literature of the period. Intent on living in a free state, Harper moved to Ohio, where she worked as a teacher. A subsequent move to Little York, Pennsylvania, acquainted her with the Underground Railroad, and she quickly aligned herself with the antislavery movement. Her first abolitionist speech was a marked success; preaching social and political reform and moral betterment, Harper spent the next several years lecturing against slavery and offering readings from her *Poems on Miscellaneous Subjects* (1854). This, the poet's most popular book, sold several thousand copies and saw at least twenty editions. Containing her most-acclaimed abolitionist poem, "Bury Me in a Free Land," it firmly established Harper's literary reputation.

Married to a farmer when she was thirty-five, Harper retired from public life and bore a child but soon returned to lecturing when she was widowed. Following the Civil War she traveled south for the first time and was appalled by the unfair treatment of freed blacks; she saw flagrant voting rights violations, meager educational opportunities, and overt physical abuse. Particularly stirred by the plight of black women—whose subjugation had not only continued, but had grown worse with emancipation—the poet determined that "a free people could be a moral people only when the women were respected." Ignoring the advice of friends, and despite failing health and dwindling financial resources, Harper continued to speak before black and white audiences—often without a fee—throughout the still-dangerous South. Until her death she remained active in such religious and social organizations as the Women's Christian Temperance Union, the National Association of Colored Women, and the American Woman Suffrage Association. She died at age 85 in Philadelphia.

Like Paul Laurence Dunbar, Harper was extremely popular with both black and white audiences. Most critics believe that her popularity as an orator was largely responsible for the favorable reception of her *Poems on Miscellaneous Subjects*. Imitative of the works of Henry Wadsworth Longfellow and John Greenleaf Whittier, the poems in the volume are primarily antislavery narratives. Although Harper believed that black writers "must write less of issues that are particular and more of feelings that are general," most of her poetry nevertheless is about the abolition of slavery.

Moses: A Story of the Nile (1869) and *Sketches of Southern Life* (1872) are considered Harper's best works, though they are not as well known as *Poems on Miscellaneous Subjects*. Published fifteen years after her first collection, *Moses* chronicles the Hebrew patriarch's life, stressing the personal sacrifices he made in order to free the Israelites. Most critics consider this a nonracial work, but the poem's emphasis on leadership and self-sacrifice is consistent with Harper's often-stated hopes for black leadership and unity. *Sketches of Southern Life,* a collection of poems, is narrated by ex-slaves Aunt Chloe and Uncle Jacob. With wit and charm, they provide a commentary on the concerns of Southern blacks: family, education, religion, slavery, and Reconstruction. The narratives are written in African-American vernacular speech—"a new idiom in black poetry," Joan R. Sherman elaborated, "which ripens into the dialect verse of [James Edwin] Campbell, [Daniel Webster] Davis, and Dunbar in the last decades of the century." While critics J. Saunders Redding and Kenny J. Williams praised the book's colloquial, though non-dialect, idiom, Jean Wagner argued that Harper's "language and humor are far from being authentically of the people."

In addition to her poetry, Harper published short stories and the novel *Iola Leroy; or, Shadows Uplifted* (1892). The stories are generally considered artistically weak, but one, "The Two Offers," is historically significant as the first short story known to have been published by a black American. While the stories went virtually unnoticed in Harper's lifetime, *Iola Leroy* received favorable attention; contemporary critics praised the work, although modern critics consider it contrived and sentimental. The story of light-skinned Negroes who reject "passing" as whites in order to work and live among their people, *Iola Leroy* expresses the author's belief that sacrifice is essential to black progress. Today the novel is considered important chiefly for its positive portrayal of black characters.

Harper has lately sparked renewed interest among twentieth-century scholars, who recognize her as a figure of more historic than artistic importance. Described variously as an early feminist, one of the first African-American protest poets, and—in the words of Patricia Liggins Hill—"a major healer and race-builder of nineteenth-century America," Harper nonetheless made aesthetic contributions of pioneer significance. In a *Crisis* editorial following the poet's death, W. E. B. Du Bois reflected: "It is, however, for her attempts to forward literature among colored people that Frances Harper deserves most to be remembered. She was not a great singer, but she had some sense of song; she was not a great writer, but she wrote much worth reading. She was, above all, sincere. She took her writing soberly and earnestly; she gave her life to it."

(For further information about Harper's life and works, see *Black Writers; Contemporary Authors,* Vols. 111, 125; *Dictionary of Literary Biography,* Vol. 50: *Afro-American Writers before the Harlem Renaissance;* and *Twentieth-Century Literary Criticism,* Vol. 14.)

*PRINCIPAL WORKS

†*Forest Leaves* (poetry and prose) 1845
Eventide [as Effie Afton] (poetry and prose) 1854
‡*Poems on Miscellaneous Subjects* (poetry and essays) 1854

"The Two Offers" (short story) 1859; published in periodical *Anglo-African Magazine*
Moses: A Story of the Nile (poetry and prose) 1869
Poems (poetry) 1871
Sketches of Southern Life (poetry) 1872
"The Colored Woman of America" (essay) 1878; published in periodical *English Woman's Review*
Iola Leroy; or, Shadows Uplifted (novel) 1892
Atlanta Offering: Poems (poetry) 1895
Poems (poetry) 1895
Idylls of the Bible (poetry) 1901
The Poems of Frances E. W. Harper (poetry) 1970
Complete Poems (poetry) 1988

*Works before 1860 were published under Harper's maiden name, Frances Ellen Watkins.
†This work is sometimes known as *Autumn Leaves.* The publication date is uncertain.
‡This work was published in at least twenty editions during Harper's lifetime, with various additions made throughout its publishing history.

William Still (essay date 1893)

[*In the following excerpt, originally published in 1893 as the introduction to* Iola Leroy; or, Shadows Uplifted, *Still—a personal friend of Harper and the author of a biographical study of her that appeared in 1871 in his* The Underground Railroad *(see Further Reading)—endorses the novel as the "crowning effort" of Harper's achievements.*]

I confess when I first learned that Mrs. Harper was about to write "a story" on some features of the Anglo-African race, growing out of what was once popularly known as the "peculiar institution," I had my doubts about the matter. Indeed it was far from being easy for me to think that she was as fortunate as she might have been in selecting a subject which would afford her the best opportunity for bringing out a work of merit and lasting worth to the race—such a work as some of her personal friends have long desired to see from her graphic pen. (p. 1)

And now I am prepared to most fully indorse her story [*Iola Leroy, or Shadows Uplifted*]. I doubt whether she could, if she had tried ever so much, have hit upon a subject so well adapted to reach a large number of her friends and the public with both entertaining and instructive matter as successfully as she has done in this volume.

The grand and ennobling sentiments which have characterized all her utterances in laboring for the elevation of the oppressed will not be found missing in this book.

The previous books from her pen, which have been so very widely circulated and admired, North and South—*Forest Leaves, Miscellaneous Poems, Moses, a*

Story of the Nile, Poems, and *Sketches of Southern Life* (five in number)—these, I predict, will be by far eclipsed by this last effort, which will, in all probability, be the crowning effort of her long and valuable services in the cause of humanity. (pp. 2-3)

[Being] widely known not only amongst her own race but likewise by the reformers, laboring for the salvation of the intemperate and others equally unfortunate, there is little room to doubt that the book will be in great demand and will meet with warm congratulations from a goodly number outside of the author's social connections.

Doubtless the thousands of colored Sunday-schools in the South, in casting about for an interesting, moral story-book, full of practical lessons, will not be content to be without *Iola Leroy, or Shadows Uplifted.* (p. 3)

> *William Still, in an introduction to* Iola Leroy; or, Shadows Uplifted *by Frances E. W. Harper, second edition, James H. Earle, Publisher, 1893, pp. 1-3.*

J. Saunders Redding (essay date 1939)

[*Redding was a distinguished critic, historian, novelist, and autobiographer. His first book,* To Make a Poet Black *(1939), is a scholarly appraisal of black poetry and is considered a landmark in criticism of black writers. In the following excerpt from this work, he discusses* Poems on Miscellaneous Subjects *as a product of the propagandist school of antislavery poetry.*]

In 1854, while Douglass was climbing in importance as the spokesman and ideal of the Negro race, there appeared in Philadelphia a thin volume called *Poems on Miscellaneous Subjects,* by Frances Ellen Watkins. The title is significant, for it indicates a different trend in the creative urge of the Negro. Except for Jupiter Hammon and Phillis Wheatley, Negro writers up to this time were interested mainly in the one theme of slavery and in the one purpose of bringing about freedom. The treatment of their material was doctrinal, definitely conditioned to the ends of propaganda. A willful (and perhaps necessary) monopticism had blinded them to other treatment and to the possibilities in other subjects. It remained for Miss Watkins, with the implications in the title of her volume, to attempt a redirection. (pp. 38-9)

In 1861, Mrs. Harper (Frances Ellen Watkins) wrote to Thomas Hamilton, the editor of the *Anglo-African,* a monthly journal that had been established the year before: "If our talents are to be recognized we must write less of issues that are particular and more of feelings that are general. We are blessed with hearts and brains that compass more than ourselves in our present plight. . . . We must look to the future which, God willing, will be better than the present or the past, and delve into the heart of the world." (p. 39)

To what degree Frances Ellen Watkins followed her own advice can be judged from her writings. In one sense she was a trail blazer, hacking, however ineffectually, at the dense forest of propaganda and striving to "write less of issues that were particular and more of feelings that were general." But she was seriously limited by the nature and method of her appeal. Immensely popular as a reader ("elocutionist"), the demands of her audience for the sentimental treatment of the old subjects sometimes overwhelmed her. On the occasions when she was free "to delve into the heart of the world" she was apt to gush with pathetic sentimentality over such subjects as wronged innocence, the evils of strong drink, and the blessed state of childhood.

Poems on Miscellaneous Subjects was published when Miss Watkins was twenty-nine years old. It is evident from the poems in this volume that she had not thought out the artistic creed later indited to Thomas Hamilton. Her topics are slavery and religion, and these first poems mark her as a full-fledged member of the propagandist group. (p. 40)

At first she was sometimes tense and stormy, as in **"Bury Me In a Free Land."** . . . After *Moses* Miss Watkins tended more frequently to the maudlin. Her later volumes show her of larger compass but of less strength than does the first. Though she held conventional views on most of the social evils of the day, at her best she attacked them in a straightforward manner. (pp. 40-1)

Miss Watkins wrote a great many sentimental ballads in obvious imitation of the ballads which appeared with monotonous regularity in *Godey's Lady's Book* and other popular monthlies. The ballad form was well suited to some of her material and was an excellent elocutionary pattern. Even now the recitation of the piece **"The Dying Bondman"** has not lost its effectiveness. (p. 41)

Practically all the social evils from the double standard of sex morality to corruption in politics were lashed with the scourge of her resentment. Her treatment of these topics never varied: she traced the effects of the evil upon some innocent—a young and dying girl, as in **"A Little Child Shall Lead Them,"** or a virtuous woman, as in **"The Double Standard,"** or a sainted mother, as in **"Nothing and Something."** But her treating these evils at all entitles her to respect and gratitude as one who created other aims and provided new channels for the creative energies of Negro writers.

In some of Miss Watkins's verse one thing more is to be noted especially. In the volume called *Sketches of Southern Life* the language she puts in the mouths of Negro characters has a fine racy, colloquial tang. In these poems she managed to hurdle a barrier by which Dunbar was later to feel himself tripped. The language is not dialect. She retained the speech patterns of Negro dialect, thereby giving herself greater emotional scope (had she wished or had the power to use it) than the humorous and the pathetic to which it is generally acknowledged dialect limits one. In all of her verse Miss

Watkins attempted to suit her language to her theme. In *Moses* she gives her language a certain solemnity and elevation of tone. In her pieces on slavery she employs short, teethy, angry monosyllables. Her use of dialectal patterns was no accident. She anticipated James Weldon Johnson.

Miss Watkins's prose is less commendable than her poetry, though here, too, she made a departure by trying the short story form. Her prose is frankly propagandic. The novel *Iola Leroy; or, Shadows Uplifted,* published in 1893, was written in "the hope to awaken in the hearts of our countrymen a stronger sense of justice and a more Christlike humanity in behalf of those whom the fortunes of war threw homeless, ignorant, and poor, upon the threshold of a new era." It is a poor thing as a novel, or even as a piece of prose, too obviously forced and overwritten, and too sensational to lift it from the plane of the possible to the probable. Her short stories, two of which were published in the *Anglo-African,* were no better in kind. Her knowledge of slave life and of slave character was obviously secondhand, and the judgments she utters on life and character are conventional and trite. As a writer of prose Miss Watkins is to be remembered rather for what she attempted than for what she accomplished.

In general Miss Watkins was less confined than any of her contemporaries. Her poetry can be grouped under four heads—religious poems, traditional lyrics of love and death, antislavery poems, and poems of social reform, of which the antislavery group is not the largest. Her poetry was not unduly warped by hatred. . . . [She] gave to some of her pieces a lightness of touch that was sadly lacking in most of the heavy-footed writing of her race. A great deal of her poetry was written to be recited, and this led into errors of metrical construction which, missed when the poems are spoken, show up painfully on the printed page. In all but her long, religious narrative, *Moses,* simplicity of thought and expression is the keynote.

She was the first Negro woman poet to stand boldly forth and glory in her pride of race, but she was not too vindicative. Her ambition to be the pivot upon which Negro writers were to turn to other aims, to compass more than themselves in their racial plight, was not accomplished. But before her death in 1911, the movement of which she had been the first champion had a brief and brilliant revival. (pp. 42-4)

> *J. Saunders Redding, "Let Freedom Ring,"
> in his* To Make a Poet Black, *1939. Reprint
> by McGrath Publishing Company, 1968, pp.
> 19-48.*

Kenny J. Williams (essay date 1970)

[*In the following excerpt, Williams surveys Harper's poetry, concluding that although* Poems on Miscellaneous Subjects *is self-consciously didactic, it is Harper's greatest contribution to American letters.*]

[Francis Ellen Watkins Harper's] *Poems on Miscellaneous Subjects,* first issued in 1854, went through several editions. In 1857 she added to the collection, and by 1871 it was published as the "twentieth edition." It seems apparent from the letters of the day that she distributed this book during her many lectures in order to gain additional funds for her work in the anti-slavery movement. Such widespread distribution may well explain her popularity as a poet during the period. A large number of the poems which appear in *Poems on Miscellaneous Subjects* are narrative; however, there are a few lyrics included. Just as Wheatley demonstrated great fidelity to Pope, her literary model, so Harper demonstrated an equally faithful fidelity to Longfellow, her selected literary mentor. She also published two collections simply entitled *Poems.* One appeared in 1871 and included short verse which had not been included in her first volume. The other appeared in 1900 and contained what she considered to be her best work.

Moses: A Story of the Nile represents her most ambitious and her most symbolic work. Published before 1869, it never mentions the Negro's position in America nor the problems which immediately occurred as a result of the Emancipation Proclamation; yet it is quite obvious that the poem is an attempt to use the story of Moses very much as the poets of the spirituals had done in order to emphasize the need for a racial leader. The poem begins as a dramatic one; however, the narrative element soon becomes dominant. . . . The effectiveness of the poem is considerably heightened by the symbolic interpretation of Moses' contribution to and for the freedom of his people.

Perhaps of all of her work *Sketches of Southern Life,* which first appeared in 1872 and subsequently in 1888 and 1896, is the most original. While much of her poetry tends to be didactic and to use characters only as a means for getting a "message" to the reader, in *Sketches of Southern Life* Harper is far more subtle. The work consists of a series of poems which are unified through two characters: Aunt Chloe and Uncle Jacob. Both of these characters are similar to some of Dunbar's in the sense that they capture the essence of primitive life in America. Yet Aunt Chloe, who tends to comment on the major issues of the day, and Uncle Jacob, who is the more mystical of the two, do not use dialect. In this respect Harper anticipates James Weldon Johnson who also rejected dialect in favor of what he was later to define as the "Negro idiom."

The more consciously anti-slavery poems appear in her first volume. Two poems appear entitled **"The Slave Mother."** In one a mother laments as her child is taken away and is given to a slave trader. In the other a fugitive mother kills her baby when she senses that she is to be recaptured and sent back into slavery. Both are effective anti-slavery ballads because they concentrate upon the very emotional relationship between mother and child; however, both are somewhat marred by the author's own deliberate intrusion as she comments on the action. **"The Fugitive's Wife"** recounts the terror and agonizing despair of a female slave whose husband is planning to make a run toward freedom. The experiences of a slave who had heard of a plot to escape but who had elected to be beaten to death rather than reveal the secrets of his fellow slaves is simply told in **"The Tennessee Hero."** In all of these poems Harper is able to penetrate the feelings of a people haunted and broken by the chains of slavery. Unlike the typical abolitionist she does this without becoming mawkishly sentimental. In each poem she builds her case by letting each tragic example of the effects of slavery serve as an indication of the broken bodies and broken spirits which resulted because of slavery's inhumanity to man. In **"The Slave Auction,"** for example, she presents the impact of human sales upon families and concludes the poem by pointing out the terror of such sales. (pp. 120-23)

Mrs. Harper's faith in the eventual solution of human problems is perhaps best exemplified by **"The Present Age"** which, though one of her later poems, is most reminiscent of Longfellow. (p. 125)

In **"A Grain of Sand"** is demonstrated Harper's characteristic of finding a lesson or a moral in everything around her.... **"Truth"** also shows her ability to find a moral lesson from ordinary objects; at the same time the poem also indicates her attempt to vary her stanza pattern by shifting from the trochaic rhythmic structure of **"A Grain of Sand"** to the more common iambic tetrameter. As is frequently typical in didactic poetry of this name, the poet permits an image—in this case the image of the rock and the seed—to occupy the bulk of the work; then in the last stanza the meaning of the image is revealed. (pp. 127-28)

Occasionally Frances Harper used the ballad meter with varying degrees of success. In the ballad of **"Vashti"** she was able to adhere more strictly to the form; however, in **"The Dying Bondman"** she tells the story of a dying slave with the simplicity which is characteristic of her anti-slavery poems. This is one of the few poems in which she does not insert her own comments. Both of these ballads are indicative of her strong interest in contemporary problems. Long a supporter of women's rights, Harper tells in **"Vashti"** the story of a young woman who dared to disobey her husband who was also her king. In both ballads the central characters are intent upon gaining freedom. (pp. 130-31)

When she died in 1911, Frances Ellen Watkins Harper had lived and worked through the last days of slavery, through the Civil War, through Reconstruction with all of its attendant problems, and on into the twentieth century. She was essentially optimistic in the Longfellow tradition, but her optimism was not totally unjustified. She had seen progress being made, and as a popular lecturer and poet she had played an important role in that progress. If her poetry appears too moralistic for the modern temperament, it must be remembered that didactic poetry was at one time the most popular poetic type. If she appears too concerned about the contemporary problems of her day, it must be remembered that

she belonged to a poetic tradition which maintained that poetry was not a form separate from the ordinary materials and concerns of everyday life. She was a woman who believed in causes. When the Civil War was over and abolitionism was no longer relevant, she turned her attention to women's rights and to the Women's Christian Temperance Union. She did not wholly ignore the problems of the freedmen, but she felt—as did others then—that these problems were well on the way to being solved. Her greatest contribution, however, remains in the area of anti-slavery literature, and when she wrote **"Bury Me In a Free Land,"** she had no doubt that America would one day be a completely free country. (pp. 134-35)

> *Kenny J. Williams, "And the Poets Came Forth: Tendencies in Nineteenth-Century Negro Poetry," in her* They Also Spoke: An Essay on Negro Literature in America, 1787-1930, *Townsend Press, 1970, pp. 115-52.*

Joan R. Sherman (essay date 1974)

[*In the following excerpt, Sherman assesses Harper's poetry, noting: "Mrs. Harper's verse is frankly propagandist, a metric extension of her life dedicated to the welfare of others."*]

Mrs. Harper's verse is frankly propagandist, a metrical extension of her life dedicated to the welfare of others. She believed in art for humanity's sake.... (p. 67)

Her poems were "songs to thrill the hearts of men / With more abundant life," "anthems of love and duty" for children, and songs of "bright and restful mansions" for the "poor and aged" (**"Songs for the People,"** 1894). Except for *Moses* ... and *Sketches of Southern Life,* ... Mrs. Harper's lyric and narrative poetry varies little in form, language, or poetic technique.

Her numerous religious poems embrace both New and Old Testament ideologies and imagery, honoring their respective God heroes, a gentle Redeemer and a fiery Jehovah. The former brings "comfort, peace and rest," "changes hearts of stone / To tenderness and love" through grace, and offers a "crown of life" hereafter to all who trust in him. This God of light and mercy appears in several early poems like **"That Blessed Hope"** and **"Saved by Faith,"** ... in poems of the middle years when, following the loss of her husband in 1864, Mrs. Harper seems preoccupied with death (twelve of the twenty-six selections in *Poems* ... concern dying or life after death), and in the 1890's the same God of love dominates some two dozen poems such as **"The Refiner's Gold," "The Sparrow's Fall," "The Resurrection of Jesus,"** and **"Renewal of Strength."** Mrs. Harper's fervid commitment to Christian virtues and her faith in a "gloryland" are moving, but poetically more interesting is her allegiance to a dynamic warrior God who "hath bathed his sword in judgement," who thunders in "whirlwinds of wrath" or swoops with a "bath of blood and fire" to redress injustice in *this* world. It is the God of the Israelites who will free her people, as in **"Ethiopia."**...In poems like [**"Lines," "Retribution,"** and **"The Martyr of Alabama"**], Mrs. Harper invokes the God of Moses not only as a militant redeemer, but also as the scourge of men and nations who "trample on His children." She wrote to John Brown in prison in 1859: "God writes national judgements on national sins." Thus when men of Cleveland returned a young fugitive girl to slavery to "preserve the union," Mrs. Harper prophesied the coming chaos in one of her best poems, **"To the Union Savers of Cleveland."** ...Mrs. Harper seldom shows such righteous indignation as gives power to this poem, and even less often is she bitter or cynical. However, these emotions do invigorate such poems as **"The Bible Defense of Slavery,"**...**"The Dismissal of Tyng,"**...and **"A Fairer Hope, A Brighter Morn"**...in which the poet denounces white "prophets of evil" who weave phantom fears of miscegenation out of their own guilt in order to oppress the race they formerly enslaved.

In many other poems on racial themes, such as **"Eliza Harris"**...and **"The Slave Auction,"**...Mrs. Harper describes the anguish of slave mothers, the heroism of black men, and the suffering of fugitives and captives. As in most abolitionist verse, emotions of fear, pain and pity are generic, like the situations, detached from both poet and poetry. Without Mrs. Harper's dramatic recitations they remain superficial, sentimental period pieces. On the other hand, when the poet speaks in her own voice, as in **"Bury Me in a Free Land,"**...true passion is felt, and the poem succeeds.... More objective and intellectual than the abolitionist verses are Mrs. Harper's postwar appeals for freedom's rights. Although often militantly urgent in tone, they express conciliatory sentiments. **"Words for the Hour"**...is addressed to "Men of the North."....**"An Appeal to the American People"**...reminds white Americans of the black soldiers' heroism, chides them for ignoring these "offerings of our blood," and appeals to their manhood, Christian principles, and honor to see justice done in the nation. There are no suggestions of black separatism in these poems; rather, the poet optimistically envisions racial brotherhood and national progress.... (pp. 67-70)

As black and white work together for mutual betterment, their souls must be pure and their hearts consecrated to Christian morality and social welfare. In some three dozen "reform" ballads Mrs. Harper weeps for families ruined by King Alcohol, and she gushes over innocent children and helpless women threatened or ruined by a sinful world. Her lecture audiences were captivated by these catalogues of human frailty which now seem maudlin. Nevertheless, such ballads on issues of national concern represent a unique and significant movement by a black poet, a breaking away from exclusively racial protest themes to write "more of feelings that are general...and delve into the heart of the world."...In **"The Drunkard's Child"**...a boy dies of neglect in his besotted father's arms. A ruined bride, mother, and child regain happiness through "the gospel and the pledge" in **"Signing the Pledge"**...; a dozen

unsuspecting people are destroyed by drink in the melodramatic **"Nothing and Something"**...; and a typical father repents at the sight of his child's empty Christmas stocking in **"The Ragged Stocking."**...Mrs. Harper was also an outspoken champion of women's rights. In **"A Double Standard"**...a deceived young girl speaks:

> Crime has no sex and yet today
>   I wear the brand of shame;
> Whilst he amid the gay and proud
>   Still bears an honored name.
>   . . . .
> No golden weights can turn the scale
>   Of Justice in His sight;
> And what is wrong in woman's life
>   In man's cannot be right.

Other oppressed women are victims of economic injustice, as in **"Died of Starvation"**..., or martyrs to man's pride like Vashti, Queen of Persia. Occasionally Mrs. Harper projects her own moral and spiritual strength into biblical heroines, creating appealing individuals, warm, courageous, loving women who transcend the cause they espouse. In poems like [**"Rizpah, the Daughter of Ai," "Ruth and Naomi," "Mary at the Feet of Christ,"** and **"Vashti"**]...emotions tied to specific crises are conveyed in simple, direct language, giving the poems a vibrant immediacy as well as lasting human validity.

Most of Mrs. Harper's religious, racial, and reform verse resembles the typical nineteenth-century work in Rufus W. Griswold's *Female Poets of America* (1848, 1873), possessing by today's standards more cultural and historical than aesthetic value. Generally her diction and rhymes are pedestrian; the meters are mechanical and frequently dependent on oral delivery for regularity, and the sentiments, however genuine, lack concreteness and control. However, Mrs. Harper attains notable artistic success with ***Moses: A Story of the Nile***...and the Aunt Chloe poems in ***Sketches of Southern Life***.... ***Moses,*** a forty-page narrative in blank verse recounting the career of Israel's leader, was no doubt inspired by the Emancipation and Lincoln's death. Through a dramatic dialogue of Moses and Charmian, the poet describes Moses' departure from the Pharaoh's court. Then her narrative moves briskly through the Old Testament story to Moses' death. Mrs. Harper handles the blank verse skillfully, bringing the biblical events to life with vivid imagery.... In grisly detail, the ten plagues descend on Egypt: "every fountain, well and pool / Was red with blood, and lips, all parched with thirst, / Shrank back in horror from the crimson draughts / "; frogs "crowded into Pharaoh's bed, and hopped / Into his trays of bread, and slumbered in his / Ovens and his pans."...The poem's elevated diction, concrete imagery, and formal meter harmoniously blend to magnify the noble adventure of Moses' life and the mysterious grandeur of his death. Mrs. Harper maintains the pace of her long narrative and its tone of reverent admiration with scarcely a pause for moralizing. *Moses* is Mrs. Harper's most original poem and one of considerable power.

She shows a similar talent for matching technique and subject in the charming series of poems which make up most of *Sketches of Southern Life* .... Aunt Chloe, the narrator, is a wise, practical ex-slave who discusses the war and Reconstruction with earthy good humor, as Uncle Jacob, a saintly optimist, counsels prayer, "faith and courage." These poems are unique in Mrs. Harper's canon for their wit and irony; the colloquial expressions of Aunt Chloe's discourse form a new idiom in black poetry which ripens into the dialect verse of Campbell, Davis, and Dunbar in the last decades of the century.... The Aunt Chloe series is successful because a consistent, personalized language and references to everyday objects give authenticity to the subjects while directly communicating the freedmen's varying attitudes of self-mockery, growing self-respect, and optimism without sentimentality. Serious issues sketched with a light touch are rare in Mrs. Harper's work, and it is unfortunate that Aunt Chloe's fresh and lively observations were not enlarged.

Mrs. Harper wrote a great quantity of poetry during half a century, all of it in moments snatched from her public life as lecturer and reformer. Possibly *Moses* and *Sketches* were composed during her brief marriage, only four years out of eighty-seven that might be called leisure time. Her race protest and reform verse, combined with her lectures, were effective propaganda; she takes honors as well for the originality and harmony of poetic form and language in *Moses* and the innovative monologues of Aunt Chloe. In short, Mrs. Harper's total output is the most valuable single poetic record we have of the mind and heart of the race whose fortunes shaped the tumultuous years of her career, 1850-1900. (pp. 70-4)

> Joan R. Sherman, "Frances Ellen Watkins Harper," in her Invisible Poets: Afro-Americans of the Nineteenth Century, *University of Illinois Press, 1974, pp. 62-74.*

Patricia Liggins Hill (essay date 1981)

[*In the following excerpt, Hill offers a thematic discussion of Harper's poetry.*]

Very little has been written about Frances Watkins Harper, the major black female literary figure and "the most popular nineteenth-century poet before Dunbar." As a poet and a public lecturer for various social reform causes, the Abolitionist Movement, the Underground Railroad, the Women's Suffrage Movement, and the Women's Christian Temperance Union, Harper has been hailed as "the Bronze Muse" of the antebellum period. She has been described by S. Elizabeth Frazier as "having attracted more attention by her poetic productions than any Negro woman since Phyllis Wheatley."

Harper's popularity, unlike Phyllis Wheatley's however, is not based on conventional notions of poetic excellence. In her handling of poetic forms and her major subject matter—race (abolition in particular), religion, and women's rights—she is considered generally to be less a technician than either of her contemporary abolitionist poets, James Whitfield and George Moses Horton. According to Benjamin Brawley Harper's earlier poems, especially *Poems on Miscellaneous Subjects* ... and *Poems* ..., in which she relies primarily on the ballad stanza and rhymed tetrameter, reveal the heavy influences of Henry Wadsworth Longfellow, John Greenleaf Whittier, and Felicia Dorothea Hemans. With the exception of *Moses: A Story of the Nile* ... and *Sketches of Southern Life* ..., Harper's poetry varies little in form, language, and poetic technique.

Harper's fame as a poet, instead, rests on her excellent skills in oral poetry delivery. Her oratorical talents have been attested to by her contemporaries and modern critics alike.... As Gloria Hull in "Black Woman Poets from Wheatley to Walker" has astutely observed, Harper's

> popularity stemmed from the fact that she took her poetry to the people just as did the young black poets of the 1960's and 70's. As a widely traveling lecturer of the Anti-Slavery Society, who spoke to packed churches and meeting halls, giving dramatic readings of her abolitionist poems which were so effective that she sold over fifty thousand copies—an unheard figure—of her first two books.

Indeed, there are similarities between Frances Harper's poetry and the verse of the new black poets—Imamu Baraka (LeRoi Jones), Madhubuti (Don L. Lee), Nikki Giovanni, Lalia Mannan (Sonia Sanchez), and others. Just as these latter-day poets base their oral protest poetry primarily on direct imagery, simple diction, and the rhythmic language of the street to reach the masses of black people, Harper relies on vivid, striking imagery, simplistic language, and the musical quality and form of the ballad to appeal to large masses of people, black and white, for her social protest. Moreover, she, like the new black poets, embraces an "art for people's sake" aesthetic, rather than a Western Caucasian aesthetic assumption, "an art for art's sake" principle. In her poem **"Songs for the People"** which is her closest statement on aesthetics, Harper makes this point clear.... Clearly, in this poem and in her other works, Harper assumes the stance of a poet-priestess whose "pure and strong" songs serve to uplift the oppressed in particular and humanity as a whole. The corpus of her poetry indicates that she, like the new black poets, however, is primarily concerned with uplifting the masses of black people. According to William Still the question as to how Harper could best serve her race lay at the very core of her literary and professional career.... She answers this question early in her career when she writes to Still in 1853 that she has decided to devote her life to the liberation of her people. As she expresses to him, "It may be that God Himself has written upon both my heart and brain a commissary to use time, talent, and energy in the cause of freedom." ... This intrinsic concern for black liberation led her to envision herself as a race-builder, the black shepherd who will provide leadership for her flock of sheep (the black masses). In her February 1870 letter to Still, Harper states, "I am standing with my race on the threshhold of a new era ... and yet today, with my limited and fragmented knowledge, I may help my race forward a little. Some of our people remind me of sheep without a shepherd." ... (p. 60)

Harper's poetry is essentially a product of this vision. In this regard, she focuses the majority of her poems on abolition and postwar appeals for freedmen's rights, suffrage, and racial equality. Even her major religious poetry such as *Moses: A Story of the Nile* reflects her concern for the liberation of blacks. Also, as a race-architect, Harper undertakes the black woman's cause and women's rights as a whole. As Larsen Scruggs points out, Harper reminds the Southern freedwomen who had been victims of physical abuse that "they had rights which all men should regard and that a free people could be a moral people only when the women were respected." Thus, in several of her poems she champions the cause of women's rights and stresses the important roles that women must play in the black liberation struggle.

The major theme of Harper's abolitionist poems is the evils of slavery. Even though she was born free in Baltimore, Maryland, in 1825, and was educated in the North in Pennsylvania and Ohio, she identifies readily with the brutalities of the Southern slavery system. As Linda Riggins makes clear, because Harper herself was orphaned at the age of three and was in constant contact with slaves while working in the Underground Railroad, she "easily identifies with the emotional loss accompanying the break up of a family." Consequently, most of her abolitionist verse deals with the tragic impact of the slavery system upon the black nuclear family.

In **"The Slave Auction"** from **Poems** ..., for instance, Harper uses harsh, graphic imagery to bring attention to this tragic emotional loss. In this poem, she portrays the anguish of the slave mothers who are standing defenselessly watching their children sold away.... She concludes her poem by insisting that only those who are slaves themselves can fully understand the deep sense of loss.... (pp. 60-1)

Again, using emotionally charged language and imagery, Harper depicts the break up of the black slave family in two other abolitionist poems, **"The Slave Mother I"** and **"The Fugitive's Wife"** from **Poems on Miscellaneous Subjects.** "The Slave Mother I," ... which is very similar to **"The Slave Auction,"** tells of a mother's parting from her son who is to be sold to a slave trader....

In **"The Fugitive's Wife,"** ... Harper varies her theme slightly. This poem depicts the agony of a slave woman whose husband is planning to escape. Even though she is suffering because he must leave her, she encourages him to escape to freedom....

Unlike **"The Fugitive's Wife,"** the slave woman in Harper's **"Eliza Harris"** ... shares the fortune of not being totally separated from her family. In this poem, which Vernon Loggins postulates the ballad influence of both Longfellow and Whittier, the poet tells of the experiences of Harriet Beecher Stowe's character Eliza who escapes to the North with bloodhounds at her heels.... However, Harper portrays in another poem, **"Slave Mother II,"** ... the ill fate of a slave mother who attempts to escape with her children. In this ballad, the poet reflects a theme that was prevalent in the nineteenth-century slave narratives—that death is preferable to slavery....

Harper repeats the "death is preferable to slavery" theme in **"The Tennessee Hero."** ... As she relates in the introduction to the poem, this work tells of a black male slave who "heard his comrades plotting to obtain their liberty and, rather than betray them, he received 750 lashes and died." ...

Indeed, to Harper, the worst evil that has befallen the black race is that of slavery. In one of her best abolitionist poems, **"Bury Me in A Free Land,"** ... in which her own poetic voice is clearly heard, she expresses that the worst fate that she could suffer would be to be buried in a land of slaves.... (p. 61)

Harper's abolitionist poems only marked the beginning of her struggle for black liberation. Her postwar appeals for freedmen's rights can be found in her many lectures, her novel *Iola Le Roy,* ... and her several volumes of poems, [*Moses: A Story of the Nile, Poems, Sketches of Southern Life, The Martyr of Alabama and Other Poems, The Sparrow's Fall and Other Poems, Atlanta Offering Poems, Poems,* and *Light Beyond the Darkness*].... Her post-Civil War literature stems primarily from her extensive travels throughout the country.... She observed the violations of voting privileges, the lack of education and educational facilities, and the physical abuse of black people.... (pp. 61-2)

These concerns are reflected in her postwar poetry. For instance, in **"Word for the Hour,"** she appeals to the "Men of the North" to help to uplift the Southern black in terms of education and voting rights....

In **"An Appeal to the American People,"** ... Harper calls on white America to improve the conditions of the black soldiers who fought side by side with the white infantry during the Civil War....

The continued physical abuse of blacks also lies heavily on Harper's mind. In another poem, **"The Martyr of Alabama,"** ... she protests the actual death of Tim Thompson, a black Alabama boy, who was killed because he refused to dance for some Southern white males.... The poet uses vivid, descriptive imagery to unfold this horrifying event....

Even though Harper realizes the wrongs and crimes committed by white Americans to blacks, she advocates interracial brotherhood, rather than black separatism as the solution to the black liberation problem. Her poem, **"The Present Age,"** . . . expresses her optimism for racial equality. . . .

Much of Harper's optimism about the black liberation struggle stems from her strong religious beliefs in Christian brotherhood and social equality. In this respect, her major religious poems deal also with the black liberation cause. One such poem is *Moses,* . . . a forty-page blank verse narrative on this religious leader's life and death, which Joan R. Sherman considers to be Harper's best poem and one of considerable power [see excerpt dated 1974]. This work was obviously inspired by the Emancipation and the death of Abraham Lincoln. As Still has observed, Harper frequently praises Moses and compares black people to Israelites in bondage. . . . In addition, in her April 19, 1869, correspondence to him, Harper compares Moses to Lincoln. . . .

Just as Harper believes that Lincoln has been summoned by God to free her people, she portrays Moses, in this moving poem, as the great Liberator of the Israelites. . . .

The God of Moses is evoked again by Harper in **"Retribution."** He appears as the scourge of men and nations who "trample on his children." (p. 62)

On the whole, Frances Harper's postwar appeals for freedmen's rights are more effective than her abolitionist verse. Essentially, the former are less emotional, more objective than the latter. For instance, in *Moses* there is less moralizing than in her earlier verse. In addition, such poems as **"An Appeal to American People"** and **"The Present Age"** give a more balanced, optimistic view of the race problem than her early poems.

Besides her strong religious convictions in Christian brotherhood and social equality, Harper draws much of her optimism about the race problem from her postwar tour of the South. . . .

Harper's Southern experiences convinced her that her social purpose concerning women must be two-fold: on the one hand, she must champion the cause of women's rights, while on the other hand, she must appeal to the women of both races, black and white, to become actively involved in the uplifting of the black race. After her 1867-1871 Southern tour, Harper spent a substantial portion of the last forty years of her life attempting to accomplish this purpose. Harper championed the women's rights cause as a lecturer and member of the National Association of Colored Women and the National Council of Women in the United States. In the latter organization, May Wright Sewall, Susan B. Anthony, and Harper were the most active members. On February 22, 1891, for example, Harper delivered an eloquent, moving speech, **"Our Duty to Dependent Races,"** in which she represented the black race, not as a dependent race, "but as a member of the body politic who asks simple justice under the law, the protection of

human life, education and complete citizenship." . . . Throughout her discourse, she urged also black and white women to improve the social/political status of the black race as well as their own social conditions.

These passionate pleas are apparent in Harper's poetry as well. Above all, her women's poetry stresses that woman/womanhood must be respected by man and society as a whole. In her poem, **"A Double Standard,"** . . . which Eugene Redmond observes has "the stirrings of feminism," Harper makes the point clear. Her protagonist, a seduced woman, scorns society for excusing the male's social behavior in the affairs of love while holding the female responsible for hers. . . . She insists, in her concluding stanza, that the same moral standards which apply to women should apply to man. . . .

The "respect for womanhood" theme is also evident in Harper's **"Vashti."** . . . In this poem, her biblical heroine Vashti, Queen of Persia, falls victim to her husband's male pride. Her tyrant-husband commands her to unveil her face which, in return, will bring shame to her womanhood. Harper projects her own moral strength and courage into Vashti, who decides instead to give up her throne rather than shame herself and all other Persian women as well. (p. 63)

While such poems as **"Vashti"** and **"A Double Standard"** help to advance the women's rights cause, other poems point out the significant roles that Harper feels both black and white women must play in the black liberation struggle. Her Aunt Chloe poems from *Sketches of Southern Life,* which form a new idiom in black poetry that ripens into the dialect verse of Campbell, Davis, and Dunbar, emphasize Harper's views on how the black woman can best serve her race during the antebellum period.

As with Vashti, Harper projects her own moral strength, courage, and social/political statements into Aunt Chloe, her charming, witty black protagonist, who has survived slavery and the separation from her two sons, and who has dedicated the remainder of her life to race-building during the Reconstruction era. In this regard, Aunt Chloe functions much like Harper herself: she exhorts the freedmen to gain education, to be independent, responsible, voting citizens, and to build strong black communities based on mutual cooperation and Christian morality.

In order to serve as an inspiration for other blacks in her small Southern town community to obtain their education, Aunt Chloe teaches herself to read. . . .

Besides emphasizing the need for the Southern blacks to obtain an education, Aunt Chloe appeals to the freedmen to become responsible, voting citizens. In **"The Deliverance,"** . . . she chides several of the black males for selling their votes. She reveals that some of them sold their votes for "three sticks of candy," while others such as David Rand "sold out for flour and sugar / The sugar was mixed with sand." Yet, Aunt Chloe is quick to point out that the David Rands are exceptions to the rule.... She makes clear that most of the freedmen understood "their freedom cost too much / For them to fool away their votes / For profit or for pleasure." However, until more freedmen vote responsibly, Aunt Chloe maintains that black female activists like herself must continue to intervene in the political process on behalf of the race....

Above all, Aunt Chloe stresses that black males and females must work together for the betterment of the race. In **"Church Building,"**...for example, she tells that her male confidante and companion, Uncle Jacob, advises the black community after Emancipation "all to come together / And build a meeting place." The church is eventually built because the people "pinched and scratched and spared / A little here and there."

While, in the Aunt Chloe poems, Harper emphasizes how the black woman can help uplift her race, she addresses white American women in her poem **"An Appeal to My Countrywomen"**...to help advance the black freedom cause. She reminds them that while they are praying for "the sad-eyed Armenian[s], the exile[s] of Russia" and others who are suffering throughout the world, black men and women are suffering in this country.... In order to persuade them to take up the black liberation cause, Harper appeals to them as women, sisters, and mothers. First of all, she asks them to pity men who are the ones who cause wars.... Then, she calls them as sisters of black women to have compassion for and to identify with the freedwomen who are still suffering throughout the South.... And, finally, Harper appeals to their motherhood, insisting that they pray not only for the black race but also for their own sons who must pay for their fathers' sins.... (p. 64)

There are feminist overtones in her women's poetry as a whole. In this poem, Harper appeals to white females to form a bond of sisterhood with black females to help to correct the social ills of white males. And, in the Aunt Chloe series, the protagonist and other black women radicals are seen rectifying the political mistakes committed by black males. In addition, her poem **"A Double Standard"** establishes her clearly as the first black feminist poet. However, these poems, like Harper's other works, are essentially a product of her concern for social equality. In **"A Double Standard,"** she wishes simply for males and females to be judged on equal terms, by the same moral standards. Furthermore, her intention in such poems as the Aunt Chloe series and **"An Appeal to My Countrywomen"** is to draw from women the leadership qualities and talents necessary to insure the rights of the freedmen. As an example, in **"The Deliverance,"** she champions the black suffrage rather than women's suffrage cause. This poem, like her other works, reveals that her major concern remains that of black race-building. In this regard, Harper effectively uses both her black and feminine consciousness and her special literary talents as a black female artist to accomplish this end. (pp. 64-5)

For her poetic and other literary achievements, Frances Watkins Harper deserves honor as a major healer and race-builder of nineteenth-century America. Her own words express the contributions she has made to black America and to America as a whole. In her essay **"Our Greatest Want,"** she declares:

> We [black people] need men and women whose hearts are the homes of a high and lofty enthusiasm and a noble devotion to the cause of emancipation, who are ready and willing to lay time, talent and money on the altar of universal freedom.

No words more aptly describe Harper who devoted unselfishly most of her adult life and literary talents for this cause. Her numerous poems and other works attest to this complete devotion. Her abolitionist verse and postwar appeals for freedmen's rights are effective propaganda: these "songs stir like a battle cry / Wherever they are sung." Her poem *Moses,* that has rhythms which liberate the minds and spirits of her readers, audiences, and her people as a whole, is the most natural and original verse that she produced. And her Aunt Chloe poems, which put her a century ahead of other black feminist poets, have a colloquial naturalness of speech and truth to black characterization achieved by no other poet before Dunbar. In essence, as Sherman makes clear, Harper's total output "is the most valuable single poetic record we have of the race whose fortunes shaped the tumultuous years of her career, 1850-1900" [see essay dated 1974]....

However, in spite of Harper's literary achievements, she is relatively unknown today. Like many other black literary artists and race-builders, her deeds and achievements, for the most part, have been forgotten. Soon after her death in 1911, her volumes of poetry disappeared from print and only occasional mention of her works appears in major black literature anthologies.

Whatever may be the reason for her present obscurity, Frances Watkins Harper and her poetry deserve serious literary/critical attention. As the editor of *Crisis* [W. E. B. Du Bois] reminds us: "It is however for her serious attempts to forward literature among colored people that Frances Harper deserves to be remembered. She was a worthy member of that dynasty beginning with dark Phyllis in 1773...." Like Wheatley, Harper, the Black Muse of her age, has made significant contributions to black poetry. As the "Bronze Muse," an early black social protest poet, and the major black female poet of the nineteenth century, Harper has helped to lay a sound aesthetic foundation upon which much of contemporary black poetry is based. (p. 65)

Patricia Liggins Hill, "'Let Me Make the Songs for the People': A Study of Frances Watkins Harper's Poetry," in Black American Literature Forum, *Vol. 15, No. 2, Summer, 1981, pp. 60-5.*

FURTHER READING

Brown, Hallie Q. "Frances E. W. Harper." In her *Homespun Heroines and Other Women of Distinction*, pp. 97-103. 1926. Reprint. Freeport, N.Y.: Books for Libraries Press, 1971.
    Biographical sketch focusing on Harper's career as an orator and her work with the Underground Railroad.

Dannett, Sylvia G. L. "Freedom Lectures." In her *Profiles of Negro Womanhood: Volume I, 1619-1900*, pp. 94-109. New York: M. W. Lads, 1964.
    Biography and critical comment. Dannett's laudatory remarks about Harper's poetry and the novel *Iola Leroy* are secondary concerns in the essay.

Montgomery, Janey Weinhold. "Analysis of Selected Speeches from 1851 to 1875" and "Conclusions." In her *A Comparative Analysis of the Rhetoric of Two Negro Women Orators—Sojourner Truth and Frances E. Watkins Harper*, pp. 46-92, 92-4. Hays: Fort Hays Kansas State College, 1968.
    Examines the significance of voice, subject, audience, and other factors in Harper's lectures. Montgomery also compares the oratory techniques of Harper and Sojourner Truth.

Robinson, William H., Jr. "Frances E. W. Harper." In his *Early Black American Poets: Selections with Biographical and Critical Introductions*, pp. 26-38. Dubuque: Wm. C. Brown, 1969.
    Selection of Harper's poetry, with a short biographical introduction to her life and works.

Still, William. "Frances Ellen Watkins Harper." In his *The Underground Railroad*, pp. 755-80. 1871. Reprint. New York: Arno Press and The New York Times, 1968.
    Biographical essay. Still, a contemporary and personal friend of Harper, is considered the authoritative biographical source on Harper. He includes excerpts of letters written to him by Harper and newspaper reviews of her lectures.

Robert Hayden

1913-1980

(Born Asa Bundy Sheffey) American poet, editor, essayist, and dramatist.

Although Hayden is now recognized as a major American poet, he suffered critical and popular neglect during most of his career. He considered himself the "best *unknown* American poet in the country" and added: "I'm in trouble with the Afro-Americans *also,*" alluding to his conflict with proponents of the Black Arts Movement, a period during the 1960s of literary and cultural revival for black writers and artists. Unlike the writers most closely associated with this movement, Hayden argued that black poets should be judged by the same criteria as other poets, thus rejecting the notion of a "Black Aesthetic." He further warned against "ghettoizing" writers and maintained that separating black writers from the the rest of the literary world limited their audience. Despite the dearth of attention formerly paid to his experiential and often mystical poetry, Hayden is now considered an innovative and principled literary craftsman and poet.

Hayden was born Asa Bundy Sheffey in the ghetto neighborhood of "Paradise Valley" in Detroit, Michigan. His mother, Gladys Ruth Finn Sheffey, left her husband Asa Sheffey to move to New York—but not before giving her eighteen-month-old baby to her neighbors, William and Sue Ellen Hayden, who rechristened the boy Robert Hayden. The Haydens never legally adopted Robert, but they provided him with a home and an education. Hayden later acknowledged the Hayden's efforts in two poetic tributes, "The Ballad of Sue Ellen Westerfield" and "Those Winter Sundays." Young Hayden remained in close contact with his biological parents: he was enthralled with his beautiful, vivacious mother, and his father gave him lavish gifts. Hayden attended Detroit City College (now Wayne State University) and the University of Michigan, where he studied with poet W. H. Auden. As a student Hayden read and admired the works of the Harlem Renaissance. He especially favored authors Countee Cullen, Langston Hughes, and Orrick Johns, but he also studied the works of other renowned poets of the period, including Carl Sandburg and Edna St. Vincent Millay. The Bahá'í religion also influenced his development as a poet: in 1943 he became a Bahá'í and adopted their belief in the unity of all religions and worldwide brotherhood. After being graduated from college in 1944, Hayden embarked on an academic career; he considered himself "a poet who teaches in order to earn a living so that he can write a poem or two now and then." Hayden taught for over twenty years at Fisk University in Tennessee, where he became a professor of English, and ended his career at the University of Michigan. He died in 1980.

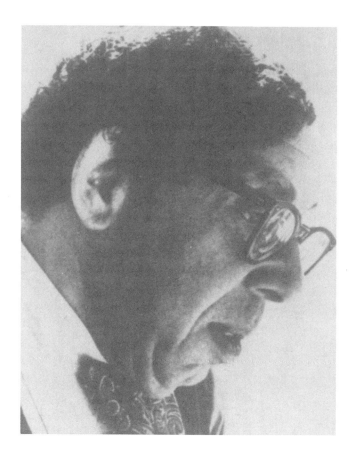

Hayden's early work is based on traditional poetic forms and is not considered technically innovative. Nevertheless, some of the author's most famous poems appear in his first three collections: *Heart-Shape in the Dust* (1940), *The Lion and the Archer* (1948), and *Figure of Time: Poems* (1955). In "Middle Passage," a poem about the shipping of enslaved Africans to the Americas, Hayden used ship logbooks, personal narratives, and court testimony to depict the famous mutiny on the slave ship *Amistad.* Two other well-known poems of the period also treat racial themes: "Runagate Runagate" (a corruption of the word "renegade") is about the underground railroad, and "Frederick Douglass" is an unrhymed sonnet commemorating the great black leader. Hayden received little critical attention for these poems, however. According to William Rice, "It would be unfair to lay Hayden's ill luck with critics to his refusal to endorse" the Black Arts Movement. "Nevertheless," Rice added, "his name would probably be more familiar if he had not resisted the militant doctrines that were in the air in the 1960s, the pivotal years of his career." In keeping with his Bahá'í beliefs, Hayden rejected any narrow racial classification of his work. He termed work by militant writers of the 1960s "separatist Negro poetry" and labeled it an "ideological weapon." A noted proponent of the Black Arts Movement, Don L. Lee (later Haki Madhubuti), responded in *Negro Digest:* "Mr. Hayden, what are television, radio, movies . . . and weekly news magazines if not ideological weapons— white ideology?" Hayden refused to adapt his somewhat formal, traditional poetry to counteract charges that he was an "Uncle Tom." In a foreword to Hayden's *Collected Prose* (1984), William Meredith determined: "In the 1960s, Hayden declared himself, at considerable cost in popularity, an American poet rather than a black poet, when for a time there was posited an unreconcilable difference between the two roles. . . . He would not relinquish the title of American writer for any narrower identity."

With the publication of *Selected Poems* in 1966 Hayden began to enjoy greater success with American literary critics. One reviewer noted that *Selected Poems* showed Hayden to be "the surest poetic talent of any Negro poet in America; more importantly, it demonstrated a major talent and poetic coming-of-age without regard to race or creed." The same year Hayden won the grand prize for poetry at the first World Festival of Negro Arts in Dakar, Senegal, for his *A Ballad of Remembrance* (1962). With succeeding volumes of verse—*Words in the Mourning Time* (1970), *The Night-Blooming Cereus* (1972), and *Angle of Ascent: New and Selected Poems* (1975)—he broadened his range of topics. While still devoting many poems to images of the black experience, Hayden began to write about travel, art, family, and the Bahá'í religion. John S. Wright maintained that this later poetry is "less embossed, less erudite, more serene even when dealing with the violence and chaos of the time, unguardedly conversational, and measurably freer." In 1976 Hayden was appointed poetry consultant to the Library of Congress, a position once described as "the American equivalent of the British poet laureate designation." He was the first black writer to hold this position—a fact that helped confirm his stature in American literature.

American Journal (1978) continued Hayden's exploration and celebration of the history and achievements of black Americans. This volume includes poems about pioneering black poets Phillis Wheatley and Paul Laurence Dunbar and a tribute to Matthew Hensen, the explorer who traveled to the North Pole with Admiral Robert Peary. In "Elegies for Paradise Valley" Hayden depicted scenes from his Detroit neighborhood, and in "American Journal" he presented the United States through the eyes of a visitor from another planet. Robert G. O'Meally called *American Journal* "a book of unforgettable images of America and her people, a prayerful report from one of our most hauntingly accurate, and yet hopeful, recorders." Hayden's posthumous publications include *Collected Prose* and *Robert Hayden: Collected Poems* (1985), which Edward Hirsch suggested "should become one of our exemplary poetic texts."

Although Hayden was not an especially prolific writer, his poems have become an integral part of black literature. He mastered many techniques, forms, and styles of poetry, and critics have come to appreciate both his facility as a poet and his insight as an observer of black life in the United States. Michael S. Harper commented: "Hayden has been called a stellar poet of remembrance with a symbolist bent for mysticism and for the cryptic phrasings of the bizarre and the occult, but most folks saw him as a consummate storyteller who had the pace, coloration and detailed finish of a romantic, with an iconoclastic air." Frederick Glaysher, editor of Hayden's *Collected Prose,* simply concluded that Hayden is "the most outstanding craftsman of Afro-American poetry."

(For further information about Hayden's life and works, see *Black Writers; Concise Dictionary of American Literary Biography,* 1941-1968; *Contemporary Authors,* Vols. 69-72, 97-100; *Contemporary Authors Bibliographical Series,* Vol. 2; *Contemporary Authors New Revision Series,* Vol. 24; *Contemporary Literary Criticism,* Vols. 5, 9, 14, 37; *Dictionary of Literary Biography,* Vols. 5, 76; *Major 20th-Century Writers;* and *Something about the Author,* Vols. 19, 26.)

PRINCIPAL WORKS

Heart-Shape in the Dust (poetry) 1940
The Lion and the Archer [with Myron O'Higgins] (poetry) 1948
Figure of Time: Poems (poetry) 1955
A Ballad of Remembrance (poetry) 1962
Selected Poems (poetry) 1966
Words in the Mourning Time (poetry) 1970
The Night-Blooming Cereus (poetry) 1972
Angle of Ascent: New and Selected Poems (poetry) 1975
American Journal (poetry) 1978; enlarged edition, 1982
Collected Prose [edited by Frederick Glaysher] (prose) 1984
Robert Hayden: Collected Poems [edited by Frederick Glaysher] (poetry) 1985

Robert Hayden with John O'Brien (interview date 1973)

[*The following excerpt is from an interview that originally appeared in O'Brien's* Interviews with Black Writers *in 1973. Here, Hayden discusses his development as a poet.*]

[O'Brien]: *Are you sometimes struck by the mystery of your art?*

[Hayden]: I've always felt that poetry and the poetic process are pretty mysterious. What is it that makes one a poet? What are you doing when you write a poem? What is poetry? The feeling of mystery is no doubt intensified because you can't deliberately set out to be a poet. You can't become one by taking courses in creative writing. You are born with the gift, with a feeling for language and a certain manner of responding to life. You respond in a particular way to yourself, to the basic questions that concern all human beings—the nature of the universe, love, death, God, and so forth. And that way of responding, of coming to grips with life, determines the kind of poetry you write. Once you discover you're a poet—and you have to find out for yourself—you can study the art, learn the craft, and try to become a worthy servitor. But you can't *will* to be a poet. This is an age of overanalysis as well as overkill, and we've analyzed poetry and the poetic process to a point where analysis has become tiresome, not to say dangerous for the poet. And for all our investigations, mysteries remain. And I hope they always will.

Do you see a progression in your work? Do you realize that you are writing poetry today that you could never have succeeded with ten years ago?

I've been very much aware of that. Yes. I think I'm now writing poems I couldn't have written ten or fifteen years ago. But I should add that some of my best-known

Hayden at age eight in Detroit.

poems were written back then. But there've been changes in outlook and technique since, and so I'm able to accomplish, when I'm lucky, what I once found too difficult to bring off successfully. I didn't know enough. Still, there are elements, characteristics in my work now, that seem always to have been present. Certain subjects, themes, persist, and—perhaps—will continue to give my work direction. My interest in history, especially Afro-American history, has been a major influence on my poetry. And I have a strong sense of the past in general, that recurs in much of my work. I don't have any nostalgia for the past, but a feeling for its relationship to the present as well as to the future. And I like to write about people. I'm more interested in people than in things or in abstractions, philosophical (so-called) ideas. In heroic and "baroque" people especially; in outsiders, pariahs, losers. And places, localities, landscapes have always been a favorite source for me. I once thought of using *People and Places* as the title for one of my books. Despite changes in outlook and technique over the years, the qualities I was striving for as a younger poet are the same ones I'm striving for today, basically. I've always wanted my poems to have something of a dramatic quality. I've always thought that a poem should have tension—dramatic and structural. And I've always been concerned with tone, with sound in relation to sense or meaning. I sometimes feel that I write by the word, not by the line. I'm perhaps oversensitive to the weight and color of words. I hear my words and lines as I write them, and if they don't sound right to me, then I know I'll have to go on revising until they do. I revise endlessly, I might add.

Did you ever fear that you might stop developing as a poet, that perhaps in another year or two years you would have exhausted yourself?

Oh, yes. A year or so ago—before I'd completed **The Night Blooming Cereus**—I was afraid I'd never be able to write a new poem again....I went stale, felt I was repeating myself, had nothing more to say. I've been through all this before, many times in fact. *Cereus*...was a breakthrough for me, and no doubt that's why it's my favorite book up to now. Writing it released me, also confirmed ideas and feelings I'd had before, but distrusted. I began to move in a new direction and to consolidate my gains, such as they were.

When you first started writing, were there poets that you tried to imitate and hoped you would be as good as, some day?

When I was in college I loved Countee Cullen, Jean Toomer, Elinor Wylie, Edna St. Vincent Millay, Sara Teasdale, Langston Hughes, Carl Sandburg, Hart Crane. I read all the poetry I could get hold of, and I read without discrimination. Cullen became a favorite. I felt an affinity and wanted to write in his style....All through my undergraduate years I was pretty imitative. As I discovered poets new to me, I studied their work and tried to write as they did....I reached the point, inevitably, where I didn't want to be influenced by anyone else. I tried to find my own voice, my own way of seeing. I studied with W. H. Auden in graduate school, a strategic experience in my life. I think he showed me my strength and weaknesses as poet in ways no one else before had done. (pp. 116-18)

*I know that your religion has greatly affected your poetry. Have your religious views changed since writing **"Electrical Storm,"** where you recorded a near encounter with death? There seems to be a skepticism in that poem, absent in your most recent volume of poetry, **Words in the Mourning Time.***

No, not actually. I'm only suggesting the skepticism I might have felt earlier in my life. This wasn't a factor at the time I wrote the poem. I've always been a believer of sorts, despite periods of doubt and questioning. I've always had God-consciousness, as I call it, if not religion.

Do you think that there is a religious dimension to the work of the poet? Is there a special role that he must play in a century like ours?

Being a poet is role enough, and special enough. What else can I say? I object to strict definitions of what a poet is or should be, because they usually are thought up by people with an axe to grind—by those who care less about poetry than they do about some cause. We're living in a time when individuality is threatened by a kind of mechanizing anonymity. And by regimentation. In order to be free, you must submit to tyranny, to ideological slavery, in the name of freedom. And, obviously, this is the enemy of the artist; it stultifies anything creative. Which brings me to my own view of the role of the poet, the artist. I am convinced that if poets have any calling, function, *raison d'être* beyond the attempt to produce viable poems—and that in itself is more than enough—it is to affirm the humane, the universal, the potentially divine in the human creature. And I'm sure the artist does this best by being true to his or her own vision and to the demands of the art. This is my view; it's the conviction out of which I write. I do not set it up as an imperative for others. Poetry, all art, it seems to me is ultimately religious in the broadest sense of the term. It grows out of, reflects, illuminates our inmost selves, and so on. It doesn't have to be sectarian or denominational. There's a tendency today—more than a tendency, it's almost a conspiracy—to delimit poets, to restrict them to the political and the socially or racially conscious. To me, this indicates gross ignorance of the poet's true function as well as of the function and value of poetry as an art. With a few notable exceptions, poets have generally been on the side of justice and humanity. I can't imagine any poet worth his salt today not being aware of social evils, human needs. But I feel I have the right to deal with these matters in my own way, in terms of my own understanding of what a poet is. I resist whatever would force me into a role as politician, sociologist, or yea-

sayer to current ideologies. I know who I am, and pretty much what I want to say.

There's an impersonal tone in almost all of your poetry. You're removed from what you write about, even when a poem is obviously about something that has happened to you.

Yes, I suppose it's true I have a certain detachment. I'm unwilling, even unable, to reveal myself as directly in my poems as some other poets do. Frequently, I'm writing about myself but speaking through a mask, a persona. There are troublesome things I would like to exteriorize by writing about them directly. One method for getting rid of your inner demons sometimes is to be able to call their names. I've managed to do so occasionally, but not very often. I could never write the confessional poems that Anne Sexton, Robert Lowell, John Berryman have become identified with. And perhaps I don't honestly wish to. Reticence has its aesthetic values too, you know. Still, I greatly admire the way Michael S. Harper, for example, makes poems out of personal experiences that must have been devastating for him. He's a marvelously gifted poet. I agree that poets like Harper and Lowell do us a service. They reveal aspects of their lives that tell us something about our own. One of the functions of poetry anyway. I think I tend to enter so completely into my own experiences most of the time that I have no creative energy left afterward. (pp. 119-21)

Do you think of yourself as belonging to any school of poetry? Do you place yourself in a romantic tradition as well as a symbolist?

I don't know what to say to that. I suppose I think of myself as a symbolist of a kind, and symbolism is a form of romanticism by definition. I've often considered myself a realist who distrusts so-called reality. Perhaps it all comes down to my being a "romantic realist." How would I know? Leave classification to the academicians. I do know that I'm always trying in my fumbling way to get at the truth, the reality, behind appearances, and from this has come one of my favorite themes. I want to know what things are, how they work, what a given process is, and so on. When I was writing **"Zeus over Redeye,"** for instance, I studied the booklets I picked up at the Redstone Arsenal so I'd learn the correct terminology, get the facts about rocket missiles. I scarcely used any of this information, but it gave me a background against which my poem could move. (p. 121)

Except when you are dealing with an obvious historical situation, you depend upon the present tense in your poems.

I've made a superficial—very superficial—analysis of the recurrence of the present tense in my poems, and I think I may be using it to achieve dramatic immediacy and because in a sense there is no past, only the present. The past is also the present. The experiences I've had in the past are now a part of my mind, my subconscious, and they are there forever. They have determined the present for me; they exist in it.

There appears to be a progression in your long poem **"Words in the Mourning Time."** *The first few sections catalogue the madness of our age, particularly that of the 1960s. Yet love enters in the last section and restores what appeared to be a hopeless condition. I'm not sure how you move from the vision of the evils to one of love. Were you suggesting that love comes after the violence and killing, or perhaps because of them?*

The final poem is the culmination, the climax of the sequence. For me, it contains the answers to the questions the preceding poems have stated or implied. If I seem to come to any conclusion about injustice, suffering, violence at all, it's in the lines about man being "permitted to be man." And it's in the last poem, written originally for a Bahá'í occasion. Bahá'u'lláh urged the absolute, inescapable necessity for human unity, the recognition of the fundamental oneness of mankind. He also prophesied that we'd go through sheer hell before we achieved anything like world unity—partly owing to our inability to love. And speaking of love, I try to make the point, in the elegy for Martin Luther King in the section we're discussing, that love is not easy. It's not a matter of sloppy sentimentality. It demands everything of you. I think it's much, much easier to hate than to love. (pp. 123-24)

In **"Monet's 'Waterlilies'"** *you refer to "the world each of us has lost." Is it a world of innocence, of childhood?*

I'm absolutely cold to the voguish and overused theme of "lost innocence." Maybe I'm just too pseudo-Freudian. I might have been thinking about childhood, though surely not about innocence. But no, I can't honestly say I was even thinking about childhood. I grant you the poem could be so interpreted without doing too much violence to its meaning. Certainly, children, as we all know, live in a fantasy world, in a realm of the imagination that's forever lost to them when they grow up. But each of us has known a happier time, whether as children or as adults. Each of us has lost something that once gave the world a dimension it will never have again for us, except in memory. A botched answer, to be sure, but the best I can offer at the moment.

Is it through art that one is able to recapture it or at least become highly conscious of it?

Sometimes. That particular Monet helps me to recapture something—to remember something. I would say that one of the valuable functions of all the arts is to make us aware, to illuminate human experience, to make us more conscious, more alive. That's why they give us pleasure, even when their subjects or themes are "unpleasant." (pp. 127-28)

Robert Hayden and John O'Brien, "A 'Romantic Realist'," in Collected Prose *by Robert Hayden, edited by Frederick Glaysher,* The University of Michigan Press, 1984, pp. 115-28.

Michael S. Harper (essay date 1981)

[*Harper is, according to Hayden, a "marvelously gifted" American poet. In the following excerpt, Harper pays tribute to Hayden.*]

[Robert Hayden] was a man of considered reserve, with an unsuppressible elegance, his bowties, watch-chain and old man's comforts giving him the glow of a courtly preacher who was summoned to give the word, and well he did, recalling his early childhood testifying days in Detroit's "Paradise Valley", scenes captured by the images of a sanctified Second Baptist Church Service in his **"Witch Doctor"** poem, which conjured up the *high-falutin'* church talk of a would-be saviour in the tradition of a Daddy Grace. Hayden spent his early days in the 'save your sight' school program, sometimes playing the violin, and picking up the lore of his adopted parents, the Haydens; and when he was to 'finish' Detroit City College (later Wayne State University) as a Spanish major, and do research on the WPA's Federal Writers Project gathering the folkstuff of his people, he spoke of the neighbors who slipped him book money, small coins and, on rare occasions, a dollar bill, to help him get through school—they made him proud as he made them sing in poetry. Hayden has been called a stellar poet of remembrance with a symbolist bent for mysticism and for the cryptic phrasings of the bizarre and the occult, but most folks saw him as a consummate storyteller who had the pace, coloration and detailed finish of a romantic, with an iconoclastic air. His poetic heroes, Dunbar and Keats, pushed him toward *The Tempest* and the ancestors: Pa Hayden for one, whom Hayden memorialized in the sonnet, **"Those Winter Sundays":**

> Speaking indifferently to him,
> who had driven out the cold
> and polished my good shoes as well.
> What did I know, what did I know
> of love's austere and lonely offices?

Hayden said, in an interview, that he wrote **"Frederick Douglass,"** his great accentual sonnet of religious American possibility, for the future, when 'man was permitted to be man.' He dreamed of freedom and literacy, a perennial dream of humane transformation. There is no lost Eden in Hayden's *oeuvre;* he was a most elegant prognosticator of the future—a Baha'i for almost forty years—and a craftsman par excellence. His knowledge of poetic traditions led him beyond many of the experiments steeped in a conscious modernism; his **"Middle Passage,"** a poem in eight voices which borrowed from ships' logs and court testimony, slave and master, was written, in part, to answer Eliot's *The Waste Land* with the addition of a broad and pungent social reality—'Voyage through death / to life upon these shores'. His recalling the schizoid past's brutalities was always shaped to light the future. He was a poet of the discovery of self as art, not a proponent of the confessional mode, but a poet of design who saw patterns of consciousness in the foibles and fascinations of the most public and private surfaces. These surfaces that Hayden polished always opened through a trapdoor to a 'striptease of reality'—no "deep image" for him but the deep pit, lest the poet—"squalored in that pit"—forget his wings. His last poems display utter candor and embossed technique, with no self-consciousness; the poems **"A Letter From Phillis Wheatley"**... and **"Paul Laurence Dunbar"**... are talismans of his inheritance, and his possibility. The unknown visitor from elsewhere in his title poem, **"American Journal,"** is more than any observer ("must be more careful item learn to use 'okay'/their pass word 'okay'") and less than any spokesman for the country, though his voice suggests the inner reexamination of that *quiddity* hidden in the word made flesh, those sacred documents that brought form and geography together.... (pp. 231-33)

Hayden's ballads reveal a story told, offhandedly, of a storytelling people, for he was a national poet in the voicings he could capture in a phrase; he could also recall Wallace Stevens and take us into that hidden arena of transcendence.... (p. 233)

Hayden has been working as a liberator in the only world he knew, ours. That spiritual realm he refers to in his poems is glow and afterglow of rockets and science fiction. The poem he was working on, and to which he hoped to return, at the end, was for Josephine Baker; his notes and drafts might tell us one day whether he made that deadline. As a figure who, increasingly, will earn his rightful place in our hearts, in our minds and libraries and anthologies, his epitaph ought be the poems he gave us.... (pp. 233-34)

> *Michael S. Harper, "Remembering Robert E. Hayden," in* The Carleton Miscellany, *Vol. XVIII, No. 3, March 2, 1981, pp. 231-34.*

Vera M. Kutzinski (essay date 1986)

[*In the following excerpt, Kutzinski examines the poem "Middle Passage" as a reinterpretation of history.*]

Robert Hayden gives a poetry reading at the Library of Congress in 1971.

Hayden's best poems are preoccupied with processes of displacement, both in historical and in literary terms. For example, he displaces traditional concepts of order (unity) and of time (linearity) as they manifest themselves in the form of certain literary and historical (or historiographical) conventions. We may call Hayden's poetry a consistent "experiment in disorder" (to borrow a phrase from Octavio Paz) or incoherence, as long as we do not associate incoherence with unintelligibility. Hayden's incoherence is a strategy to free language from static, fixed meanings. **"Middle Passage"** is a fine example of this strategy which, as we shall see, effectively links historical with literary revisionism.

The poem's title already refers to a very specific historical process of geographical, social, and cultural dislocation: the Middle Passage. This context is rendered more concrete by references to the transatlantic slave trade throughout the poem, including lists of actual names of slave ships and lengthy "quotations" from logbooks and other seemingly authentic historical documents. A transition from freedom to slavery, the crossing from Africa to the New World is indeed a "Voyage through death," a "voyage whose chartings are unlove." But Hayden is hardly content to enumerate the horrors of the slave trade and to condemn the injustices of slavery. His is a more ambitious goal: to change the very texture of history, to alter the insidious design the dark ships have created:

> Shuttles in the rocking loom of history,
> the dark ships move, the dark ships move,
> their bright ironical names
> like jests of kindness on a murderer's mouth.

Hayden's use of a metaphor of weaving as a figure for writing is most significant: for him, the pattern of crisscrossing lines connecting Africa with the Americas constitutes the charts or "chartings" of Afro-American history, that is, its official text(s), represented in the poem by the fragmented "quotations" from what at first glance appear to be historical documents. **"Middle Passage"** as a whole is a careful reading of those official texts, one that unravels the threads of their fabric to weave them together in very different ways. Hayden is indeed a most diligent and skillful weaver of poetic textures, of designs that revise official historical charts and offer correctives or alternatives to historical documentary. Resituated in a new context, the texts Hayden purports to quote lose not their appearance of authenticity but their historical authority. Broken up into textual fragments, they are no longer capable of offering a coherent, unified historical narrative. They become voices among many other, competing voices, or better perhaps, images of language, of the discourse of slavery, without claims to representational authority and historical truth.

This displacement, and in fact effacement, of authority indicated by the conspicuous absence of a central, controlling consciousness or "voice" in the poem, is significantly reinforced by the fact that these "documents" are not just general accounts of the slave trade.

They all have to do, directly or indirectly, with slave mutinies:

> "10 April 1800—
> Blacks rebellious. Crew uneasy. Our linguist says
> their moaning is a prayer for death,
> ours and their own . . . ."

Hayden has carefully "selected" passages reporting various "misfortunes" that interfere with the steady course of the slavers: Ophthalmia ("It spreads, the terrifying sickness spreads. / Its claws have scratched sight from the Capt.'s eyes"); suicides; fires; and stormy seas. All these interferences build up to a lengthy narrative of the famous *Amistad* rebellion (1839) in the poem's final section.

On its way from Havana to Puerto Principe (today's Camaguey), the schooner *Amistad,* with fifty-four blacks and two passengers on board, was taken over by the Africans under the leadership of Cinquez (or Cinque). Their intention was to reverse the course of the vessel, using as navigators the two Spaniards they had spared. But instead of returning to the African coast, the *Amistad,* after several months of aimless zigzagging due to the deception of its navigators, finally reached the Connecticut shoreline. The mutineers, seized by the local authorities, were taken first to New Haven and then to Hartford to await the trial that would determine whether they were to be freed or returned to their owners. Due to the involvement of prominent New England abolitionists such as Lewis Tappan, as well as of former President John Quincy Adams, the *Amistad* case became something of an international incident. In short, the Court ruled that the Africans be freed and returned to their native land on the grounds that their enslavement and transport to Cuba had been in violation of international treaties banning the transatlantic slave trade.

I am not offering this brief sketch of the *Amistad* affair in lieu of a reading of Hayden's poem; nor is it simply intended as background material. At least some familiarity with this event is crucial to an understanding of the historical bases of Hayden's literary strategies of displacement in **"Middle Passage."** It should further be noted that the *Amistad* case not only created considerable publicity for the New England abolitionists; it also generated a substantial body of writing in the form of legal documents and newspaper reports, not to mention the numerous historical studies it has inspired since. Finally, it set a legal precedent that literally reversed the direction of the Middle Passage and the "laws" that continued to sanction, albeit implicitly, the illegal trade in slaves.

Hayden's account of the *Amistad* mutiny and the subsequent trial merits detailed scrutiny . . . . Although cast in the form of a citation, presumably from Pedro Montez' court testimony, Hayden's narrative bears little resemblance to contemporary transcripts of that report. One of the most striking deviations from those documents is the emphasis Hayden places on the storm that delayed the vessel's scheduled arrival. While this information was obviously not relevant to the trial, Hayden explores the way in which it served to rationalize the success of the mutiny:

> "But for the storm that flung up barriers
> of wind and wave, *The Amistad,* señores,
> would have reached the port of Principe in two,
> three days at most; but for the storm we should
> have been prepared for what befell.
> Swift as the puma's leap it came. There was
> that interval of moonless calm filled only
> with the water's and the rigging's usual sounds,
> then sudden movement, blows and snarling cries
> and they had fallen on us with machete
> and marlinspike. It was as though the very
> air, the night itself were striking us.
> Exhausted by the rigors of the storm,
> we were no match for them. Our men went down
> before the murderous Africans . . . . .

(pp. 173-76)

Insofar as the *Amistad* revolt epitomizes the successful struggle against an unjust institution and thus the achievement of freedom from bondage, it serves Hayden as an historical paradigm for throwing off course conventional notions of history and of time. History, for him, is not a unilinear progression, an orderly procession of events regulated by laws of causality. The *Amistad* case is of particular interest to Hayden, the revisionist, because it successfully disrupts the official design of Afro-American history by reversing the direction of the Middle Passage, not just in geographical terms, but, even more importantly, in conceptual ones: it literally changes the conceptual and ideological structures, the "laws," that define the power relationships upon which the slave trade is predicated: the idea of European racial and cultural supremacy. Within this context, Montez' fictionalized account of the mutiny becomes a self-indictment mainly because of his attempt to rationalize that ideology as "lawful." What Hayden illustrates brilliantly and subtly in the following passage is a significant discrepancy between "lawful" and just.

> Now we
> demand, good sirs, the *extradition* of
> Cinquez and his *accomplices* to La
> Havana. And it distresses us to know
> there are so many here who seem inclined
> to *justify* the mutiny of these blacks.
> We find it paradoxical indeed
> that those whose wealth, whose tree of liberty
> are rooted in the labor of your slaves
> should suffer the august John Quincy Adams
> to speak with so much passion of the *rights
> of chattel slaves* to kill their *lawful masters*
> and with his *Roman rhetoric* weave a hero's
> garland for Cinquez. I tell you that
> we are determined to return to Cuba
> with our slaves and there *see justice done.* Cin-
>   quez—
> or let us say 'the Prince'—Cinquez shall die."

(my italics)

The legalistic rhetoric of this passage, particularly evident in the words and phrases I have emphasized, is clearly a more aggressive attempt at rationalization than the previously employed references to the storm. A noticeable change in tone announces the shift from the impressionistic description of the revolt and its presumed causes to an interpretation of the legal case; Montez' voice in that latter passage is tellingly conflated with that of the Spanish Minister. An important connection exists, however, between the two rhetorical modes Hayden employs here: On the one hand, the speaker's strategic emphasis on the storm implies that the uprising of the slaves was simply another "misfortune," a lamentable interference in the "natural" course of events; on the other hand, he treats it as a criminal act that requires punishment. The projected expectation is that order will be restored, that justice will be done. The question is, What order and whose justice? This is not an ethical problem as the speaker seems to imply; it is a legal and a rhetorical one. Neither the Middle Passage as representative of the process of enslavement nor the distinction between master and slave is a "natural" phenomenon. Both are social conventions, and the way in which they define the idea of justice is as paradoxical as the image of the "tree of liberty" rooted in slave labor. These same conventions define the struggle for freedom as a crime (as evidenced by the terms "extradition" and "accomplices") against laws that conceive of slavery and, for that matter, of the proposed murder of Cinquez, as acts of justice.

The exposure of the internal contradictions that characterize the discourse of slavery and result from the confusion and conflation of natural laws with ideological precepts is one of the trademarks of abolitionist rhetoric, which provides a kind of subtext in this passage. But even the language of abolitionism is not free from inconsistencies: what is at issue here for Hayden is clearly not the paradox of defending "the right of chattel slaves to kill their lawful masters," but the contradictions inherent in the very distinction between *chattel* slaves and *lawful* masters. Hayden added these two qualifiers (the original reads "the right of slaves to kill their masters") to strengthen the point he is making: that the rhetoric of slavery seeks carefully to conceal its internal contradictions. If slavery poses as a "natural" institution (that phrase already a contradiction), then the discourse of slavery poses as a "natural" language, thus detracting from the ideological assumptions on which it rests. This is precisely what Hayden's subtle changes in language emphasize in this instance.

By making these seemingly authentic texts part of the poem, Hayden draws further attention to the problematic truth-value of historical documents. In the same way that "justice" is a matter of conforming to certain laws, historical truth is a function of rhetorical conventions. **"Middle Passage"** both exposes and unsettles such conventions in order to redefine and reinscribe the idea of history and historical truth. (pp. 177-78)

Vera M. Kutzinski, "Changing Performances: Historical and Literary Revisionism in Robert Hayden's 'Middle Passage'," in Callaloo, *Vol. 9, No. 1, Winter, 1986, pp. 171-83.*

FURTHER READING

Campbell, Charles R. "A Split Image of the American Heritage: The Poetry of Robert Hayden and Theodore Roethke." *Midamerica* XII (1985): 70-82.

> Examines the poetry of Hayden and Theodore Roethke, determining: "Both Hayden and Roethke were searching for a heritage; Hayden seeking a reality to be found in brotherhood, in others, in the people he met, and in history; Roethke almost always seeking for himself within himself."

Cooke, Michael G. "Intimacy: The Interpenetration of the One and the All in Robert Hayden and Alice Walker." In his *Afro-American Literature in the Twentieth Century: The Achievement of Intimacy,* pp. 133-76. New Haven, Conn.: Yale University Press, 1984.

> Explores "intimacy"—a concept in which "the Afro-American protagonist (male or female, pugilist or philosopher, activist or ascetic) is depicted as realistically enjoying a sound and clear orientation toward the self and the world"—in Hayden's poetry and Alice Walker's fiction.

Fetrow, Fred M. *Robert Hayden.* Boston: Twayne Publishers, 1984, 159 p.

> First book-length biography and critical study of Hayden.

————. "Portraits and Personae: Characterization in the Poetry of Robert Hayden." In *Black American Poets Between Worlds, 1940-1960,* edited by R. Baxter Miller, pp. 43-76. Knoxville: University of Tennessee Press, 1986.

Analyzes Hayden's poetic representations of such figures as Frederick Douglass, John Brown, Malcolm X, Phillis Wheatley, and Paul Robeson, maintaining that the poet "disguised" himself in these portraits.

Glaysher, Frederick. "Re-Centering: The Turning of the Tide and Robert Hayden." *World Order* 17, No. 4 (Summer 1983): 9-17.

> Examines the influence of the Bahá'í faith on Hayden's "matchless" poetry, which Glaysher believes has "justly won international acclaim."

Hatcher, John. *From the Auroral Darkness: The Life and Poetry of Robert Hayden.* Oxford, England: George Ronald, 1984, 342 p.

> Acclaimed work on Hayden. Provides a critical biography of the poet, an assessment of his conflicts with literary movements and trends, and an analysis of his major works of poetry.

Hirsch, Edward. "Mean to Be Free." *The Nation* 241, No. 21 (21 December 1985): 685-86.

> Lauds *Collected Poems,* declaring that it "should become one of our exemplary poetic texts."

Oehlschlaeger, Fritz. "Robert Hayden's Meditation on Art: The Final Sequence of *Words in the Mourning Time.*" *Black American Literature Forum* 19, No. 3 (Fall 1985): 115-19.

> Analysis of *Words in the Mourning Time,* a poetry collection that Oehlschlaeger believes "responded directly to one of the most violent decades in American history"—the 1960s.

Rice, William. "The Example of Robert Hayden." *The New Criterion* 8, No. 3 (November 1989): 42-5.

> Explores Hayden's place in literature, surveying the poet's opposition to the militancy of many black writers in the 1960s.

Williams, Pontheolla T. *Robert Hayden: A Critical Analysis of His Poetry.* Urbana: University of Illinois Press, 1987, 241 p.

> Examines Hayden's development as a poet of the American experience.

Bessie Head

1937-1986

(Born Bessie Amelia Emery) South African-born Botswanan novelist, short story writer, and nonfiction writer.

One of Africa's most renowned women writers, Head explored the effects of racial and social oppression and the theme of exile in her novels and short stories. She was a person of mixed race, and she experienced menacing discrimination both in her birthplace, South Africa, and in her adopted land, Botswana. Her novels, unlike many other works of protest literature, cast a distinctly feminine perspective on the ills of social injustice and the psychological costs of alienation. Head, however, refused to be called a feminist, insisting instead that she abhorred all oppression—racial, sexual, and political. "She hated labels—political or otherwise," Head scholar Huma Ibrahim observed. "South African literary critics are very unhappy with Head, claiming she is not political. I claim that she goes beyond the political without hiding from political issues. She is political in a very large sense. She does not just want to change South Africa, she wants to change the world...."

Head had a "curious history," according to Ibrahim. She was born the daughter of an upper-class white woman and a black stablehand. When her mother was found to be pregnant, she was committed to a mental hospital and labeled "insane." Head was born in the asylum but was quickly sent off to live with foster parents; later, she was placed in the care of white missionaries. Head's mother committed suicide when Head was still a young girl. "Her name was Bessie Emery," Head wrote in *Ms.* magazine, "and I consider it the only honor South African officials ever did me—naming me after this unknown, lovely, and unpredictable woman." Head was trained as a teacher and taught elementary school children for several years in South Africa. In 1961 she married a journalist but divorced shortly thereafter. At age twenty-seven she left for Botswana with her young son because, in her words, she could no longer tolerate apartheid in South Africa. Conditions in Botswana were not much better for her. For the next fifteen years she lived as a refugee at Bamangwato Development Farm, barely fighting off poverty. Betty McGinnis Fradkin described Head's meager existence after a particularly lean year: "There is no electricity yet. At night Bessie types by the light of six candles. Fruit trees and vegetables surround the house. Bessie makes guava jam to sell and will sell vegetables when the garden is enlarged." Despite her impoverished circumstances, the regularity of her life among 30,000 blacks and fifty "white faces" gave Head—for the first time ever—a sense of community: "In South Africa, all my life I lived in shattered little bits. All those shattered

bits began to grow together here.... I have a peace against which all the turmoil is worked out!" Her sense of peace was further enhanced by her writing. She produced three novels: *When Rain Clouds Gather* (1969), *Maru* (1971), *A Question of Power* (1973); a short story collection, *The Collector of Treasures and Other Botswana Village Tales* (1977); and two historical chronicles, *Serowe: Village of the Rain Wind* (1981) and *A Bewitched Crossroad: An African Saga* (1984).

Critics have analyzed Head's novels in terms of their thematic concerns and their thematic progression. Suggesting that the works "deal in different ways with exile and oppression," Jean Marquard noted that "the protagonists are outsiders, new arrivals who try to forge a life for themselves in a poor, under-populated third world country, where traditional and modern attitudes to soil and society are in conflict." Unlike other African writers who are also concerned with such familiar themes, observed Marquard, Head "does not idealize the African past and...she resists facile polarities, emphasizing personal rather than political motives for tensions between victim and oppressor." *When Rain Clouds Gather* focuses on Makhaya, a black South African man victimized by apartheid in his country of birth and then as a refugee in Botswana. *Maru,* which depicts racism within a black society, centers on the lives of Margaret Cadmore, an orphaned Masarwa (Bushman), and the two men who love her, Maru and Moleka. Head's third novel, *A Question of Power,* is considered the author's most introspective and complex work. It relates the story of Elizabeth, a young woman who must "journey through disintegration and madness in order to integrate the warring parts of self and flee the tyranny of absolutes," according to Linda Susan Beard. Some critics have proposed that Elizabeth's search for wholeness symbolizes the wider struggle against intolerance in South Africa. "It is precisely this journeying into the various characters' most secret interior recesses of mind and...of soul," Arthur Ravenscroft observed, "that gives [*When Rain Clouds Gather, Maru,* and *A Question of Power*] a quite remarkable cohesion and makes them a sort of trilogy."

Head's collection of short stories, *The Collector of Treasures and Other Botswana Village Tales,* which was considered for the *New Statesman*'s Jock Campbell Award, explores several aspects of African life, especially the social condition of women. Likening Head to the "village storyteller of the oral tradition," Michael Thorpe noted that her stories are "rooted, folkloristic tales woven from the fabric of village life and intended to entertain and enlighten, not to engage the modern close critic." In its yoking of present to past, the collection also reveals the inevitable friction between old ways and new. The world of Head's work "is not a simply modernizing world but one that seeks, come what may, to keep women in traditionally imprisoning holes and corners," wrote Valerie Cunningham. "It's a world where whites not only force all blacks into an exile apart from humanity but where women are pushed further still into sexist exile."

Head's last two books, *Serowe: Village of the Rain Wind* and *A Bewitched Crossroad: An African Saga,* are historical chronicles that combine true accounts with the folklore of the region. The collected interviews in *Serowe* focus on the eras of Khama the Great (1875-1923) and Tshekedi Khama (1926-1959) through the Swaneng Project beginning in 1963 under Patrick Van Rensburg, "a South African exile who, like Head herself, has devoted his life in a present-day Botswana to make some restitution for white rapacity," wrote Thorpe. Calling the work a "quasi-sociological account," Charles R. Larson described *Serowe* as "part history, part anthology and folklore." "Its citizens give their testimonies, both personal and practical, in an unselfconscious way," added Paddy Kitchen, "and Bessie Head—in true African style—orders the information so that, above all, it tells a story." *A Bewitched Crossroad* examines in a broader scope the African tribal wars of the early nineteenth century. In this work Head exalted human

ideals and peace-loving efforts over ancestor-worship and the use of physical force.

Explaining the manner in which she worked, Head revealed: "Every story or book starts with something just for myself. Then from that small me it becomes a panorama—the big view that has something for everyone." At the time of her death in 1986 from hepatitis, she was working on her autobiography. Head endured rampant racism and near-debilitating poverty and deprivation during her life; yet despite her rejection of and by South Africa as well as the hardships of her exiled existence, she emerged with two firm convictions: "that love is really good...and...that it is important to be an ordinary person." She added: "More than anything I want to be noble." According to Kitchen, "a great deal has been written about black writers, but Bessie Head is surely one of the pioneers of brown literature—a literature that includes everybody."

(For further information about Head's life and works, see *Black Writers; Contemporary Authors,* Vols. 29-32, 109; *Contemporary Authors New Revision Series,* Vol. 25; and *Contemporary Literary Criticism,* Vol. 25.)

PRINCIPAL WORKS

When Rain Clouds Gather (novel) 1969
Maru (novel) 1971
A Question of Power (novel) 1973
The Collector of Treasures and Other Botswana Village Tales (short stories) 1977
Serowe: Village of the Rain Wind (nonfiction) 1981
A Bewitched Crossroad: An African Saga (nonfiction) 1984

Arthur Ravenscroft (essay date 1976)

[*In the following excerpt, Ravenscroft appraises Head's novels, focusing on characterization, technique, and theme.*]

[Bessie Head's novels] are strange, ambiguous, deeply personal books which initially do not seem to be 'political' in any ordinary sense of the word. On the contrary, any reader with either Marxist or Pan-Africanist political affinities is likely to be irritated by the seeming emphasis on the quest for personal contentment, the abdication of political kingship—metaphorically in **When Rain Clouds Gather,** literally in **Maru,** and one might say wholesale in **A Question of Power.** The novelist's preoccupations would seem to suggest a steady progression from the first novel to the third into ever murkier depths of alienation from the currents of South African, and African, matters of politics and power—indeed in **A Question of Power** we are taken nightmarishly into the central character's process of mental breakdown, through lurid cascades of hallucination and a pathological blurring of the frontiers between insanity and any kind of normalcy. It is precisely this journeying into the various characters' most secret interior recesses of mind and (we must not fight shy of the word) of soul, that gives the three novels a quite remarkable cohesion and makes them a sort of trilogy.... It seems to me that with Bessie Head... each novel both strikes out anew, and also re-shoulders the same burden. It is as if one were observing a process that involves simultaneously progression, introgression, and circumgression; but also (and here I believe lies her particular creative power) organic growth in both her art and her central concerns. For all our being lured as readers into the labyrinth of Elizabeth's tortured mind in *A Question of Power,* and then, as it were, left there to face with her the phantasmagoric riot of nightmare and horror, one nevertheless senses throughout that the imagination which unleashes this fevered torrent resides in a creative mind that is exceedingly tough. It is not just that the fictional character emerges worn down yet regenerated and incredibly alive still after her long ordeal, but that her experience at the narrative level is also a figuring of the creative imagination in our time— that that process is both part of the multi-layered theme *and* the method of its communication. And that process as an embodiment of the novelist's art is a tough, demanding labour. (p. 175)

There are two major clues to the overall homogeneity of Bessie Head's novels. It is impossible to avoid noticing how frequently the words 'control' and 'prison' (and phrases and images of equivalent value) occur in all three novels, in many different ways certainly, and probably not as an altogether conscious patterning. 'Control' occurs in contexts tending towards the idea of control over appetites felt as detonators that set off the explosions in individual lives, no less than in the affairs of mankind, which leave those broken trails of blasted humanity that are a peculiar mark of our times. 'Prison' occurs in more varied uses, but most often related to a voluntary shutting of oneself away from what goes on around one. Sometimes it may be straight escapism or alienation, but more often it suggests a willed control over a naturally outgoing personality, an imprisonment not for stagnation but for recollection, and renewal—a severely practical self-imposed isolation which is part of natural growth. Like the silk-worm's cocoon, it is made for shelter, while strengths are gathered for outbreak and a fresh continuance. (p. 176)

To the characters [in *When Rain Clouds Gather*], Golema Mmidi may be a kind of pastoral retreat after their earlier rough encounters with life, but the haven is a place of tough, demanding labour, of recurrent crises, of improvisation and ingenuity, of the constant threat of disruption from a power-hungry, resentful local chief. Their co-operative efforts constitute an image of creativity in which sweat and imagination, harsh reality and an ultimate dream to be fulfilled are mixed in just about equal proportions. Out of this creative, co-operative enterprise of constructive energy Bessie Head generates a powerful sense of potential fulfilment for characters

who have jealously guarded, enclosed, shut up tightly their private individualities. Against a political background of self-indulgent, serf-owning traditional chiefs and self-seeking, new politicians more interested in power than people, the village of Golema Mmidi is offered as a difficult alternative: not so much a rural utopia for the Africa of the future to aim at, as a means of personal and economic independence and interdependence, where the qualities that count are benign austerity, reverence for the lives of ordinary people (whether university-educated experts or illiterate villagers), and, above all, the ability to break out of the prison of selfhood without destroying individual privacy and integrity.

Makhaya's quest for personal freedom was a flight not only from South Africa's police-van sirens and the burden of oppression, but also from the personal demands upon him of his immediate relations. The last thing he is looking for when he enters Botswana is a new network of intimate relationships or a new struggle against a different oppression. And of course he finds both. That is why the 'peaceful haven' idea in the book is really very deceptive. Golema Mmidi is no Garden of Eden, even if its potentialities are indeed richer than the South African life Makhaya left behind could offer him. (p. 177)

Makhaya does find innocence, trust, and respect, though not as unqualified absolutes. He has to give of himself both in physical labour and in the opening of the cell door to his private sanctum. His marriage to Paulina Sebeso near the end of the novel is, of course, also a finding of himself, with the ghosts of his former 'gray graveyard' life no longer visible, now, in the merciful darkness of Paulina's hut.... (p. 178)

The precise relationship between individual freedom and political independence, and between a guarded core of privacy and an unbudding towards others, may seem rather elusive, perhaps even mystical, in my reading of the novel, and I see it as one of the weaknesses of *When Rain Clouds Gather.* It is a straightforward narrative with no unexpected tricks of technique and very down-to-earth in the minutiae of an agricultural hard grind of a way of life.... There are moments of melodrama and excessive romanticism, but the real life of the novel is of creativity, resilience, reconstruction, fulfilment. Of the six major characters, four are themselves Batswana but all are in one sense or another handicapped exiles, learning how to mend their lives in the exacting but ultimately viable sands of Golema Mmidi. It is the vision behind their effortful embracing of exile that gives Bessie Head's first novel an unusual maturity. (pp. 178-79)

[*Maru*] immediately proclaims itself as technically a very different sort of book. The first six pages present the outcome of the events narrated in the rest of the novel, and, though they are essential for our adequate grasp of how those events unfold, they don't make sense at first, not until one has read to the end. The opening is thus both a species of sealed orders for the reader and an epilogue. And are we sure, at the end, that the two chief male characters, Maru and Moleka, who are close, intimate friends until they become bitter antagonists, are indeed two separate fictional characters, or that they are symbolic extensions of contending character-traits within the same man? (p. 179)

Maru's methods, 'cold, calculating and ruthless', are the normal methods of those who seek and wield power, and yet Maru's role in the novel is the very antithesis of power-wielding. He renounces the kingdom of political power in favour of the kingdom of love. But before he does so, he manipulates, engineers, 'fixes' the delicate relationships among himself, his sister Dikeledi, his friend Moleka, and Margaret the Masarwa woman, with whom both he and Moleka are in love. With the help of his three spies, Maru is able to manoeuvre Moleka against his real will to marry Dikeledi, who loves him; Maru is then able to marry Margaret, whom Moleka really loves. And Maru can exert such a persuasive influence upon Margaret that she begins to learn to love him, though it is Moleka with whom she has been secretly in love since her arrival in the village. (p. 180)

Maru's almost god-like perspicacity justifies his seemingly devious methods of preventing Moleka from obtaining Margaret's love. Maru knows that because his kingdom is of love, he has the strength to marry Margaret and live by all the consequences. (pp. 181-82)

Maru is no god. He remains a man with doubts. We know from the beginning that he and Margaret have not got away to another Garden of Eden. Rich and fulfilled and symbolically healthful as their life together is, it nevertheless has shadows and questions over it. Though Maru has obeyed the voices of the gods in his heart and trusts them, the closed door in Moleka's heart still hides an uncertainty....

This doubt and with it his willingness to give up Margaret, despite his deep love for her, if he should one day be proved wrong about Moleka, comes in those pages of introductory epilogue that I mentioned earlier, and throughout the novel influences our view of Maru and his actions.

On the one hand Maru's marriage is a deeply personal thing. He knows he 'could not marry a tribe or race.' ... On the other hand the marriage also carries a considerable political symbolism. (p. 182)

Much more that *When Rain Clouds Gather, Maru* is a novel about interior experience, about thinking, feeling, sensing, about control over rebellious lusts of the spirit; and, ironically, ambiguously, in Bessie Head's comprehending vision, it is also a more 'political' novel than *When Rain Clouds Gather.* I am not sure that the two things are satisfyingly fused, even whether it is the sort of novel in which they *should* be so fused, but I am much impressed and moved by the power with which they are conveyed. That power resides in the vitality of the enterprise, which projects the personal and the

political implications in such vivid, authentic parallels that one feels they are being closely held together, like the lengths of steel on a railway track, which fuse only in optical illusion and are indeed useless if they don't maintain their divided parallelism....

Bessie Head's most recent novel, *A Question of Power,* is clearly more ambitious than its two predecessors, and less immediately accessible, and altogether a more risky undertaking. The movement here is even deeper (and more disturbingly so) into the vast caverns of interior personal experience. (p. 183)

Bessie Head's common-sensical rootedness in the earthy level of everyday reality is still there to anchor for the reader the terrifying world of Elizabeth's hallucinations, but it is the events of that world that dominate the book. Even more than in the two earlier novels, one finds an intimate relationship between an individual character's private odyssey of the soul and public convulsions that range across the world and from one civilization to another. To see Bessie Head's handling of Elizabeth's mental instability as a clever literary device to make possible an epic confrontation between Good and Evil within the confines of a realist novel, is to underestimate the achievement. One wonders again and again whether the phantom world that comes to life whenever Elizabeth is alone in her hut could have been invented by a novelist who had not herself gone through similar experiences, so frighteningly and authentically does it all pass before one's eyes. But there is no confusion of identity between the novelist and the character, and Bessie Head makes one realize often how close is the similarity between the most fevered creations of a deranged mind and the insanities of deranged societies. (pp. 183-84)

The characteristic Bessie Head irony comes out in the fact that even as Elizabeth, the South African coloured refugee among the Batswana, finds herself screaming in her nightmares that she hates black Africans, she is none the less in what appears to her the almost dream-like world of her workaday activities in the co-operative vegetable garden, forging, steadily and genuinely, links of personal regard and affection with the Batswana villagers and with the foreign helpers. The last words of the novel are 'a gesture of belonging'...as Elizabeth settles herself for her first untortured night's sleep in three years, annealed both spiritually and socially, as in imagination she places one soft hand over her land.

I do not believe that Bessie Head's novels are offering anything as facile as universal brotherhood and love for a political blueprint for either South Africa or all of Africa. In *Maru* common sense is described as the next best thing to changing the world on the basis of love of mankind. What the three novels do say very clearly is that whoever exercises political power, however laudable his aims, will trample upon the faces and limbs of ordinary people, and will lust in that trampling. That horrible obscenity mankind must recognize in its collective interior soul. The corollary is not liberal abstention from action, but rather modest action in very practical terms, and with individual hearts flushed and cleansed for collective purpose. The divinity that she acknowledges is a new, less arrogant kind of humanism, a remorseless God who demands that iron integrity in personal conduct should inform political action too. Of course the novels don't sermonize like this, but grow out of a moral basis of this kind of order. (p. 185)

In the development of the South African novel, this disturbing toughness of Bessie Head's creative imagination returns to us that gesture of belonging with which *A Question of Power* ends. All three novels are fraught with the loneliness and despair of exile, but the resilience of the exiled characters is even more remarkable. Bessie Head refuses to look for the deceiving gleam that draws one to expect the dawn of liberation in the South, but accepts what the meagre, even parched, present offers. (p. 186)

> *Arthur Ravenscroft, "The Novels of Bessie Head," in* Aspects of South African Literature, *edited by Christopher Heywood, Africana, 1976, pp. 174-86.*

Jean Marquard (essay date 1979)

[*In the excerpt below, Marquard examines thematic development in Head's three novels.*]

[Bessie Head's three novels] deal in different ways with exile and oppression. The protagonists are outsiders, new arrivals who try to forge a life for themselves in a poor, under-populated third world country, where traditional and modern attitudes to soil and society are in conflict. These are familiar themes in African writing but Bessie Head may be distinguished from other African writers in at least two respects. In the first place she does not idealize the African past and in the second she resists facile polarities, emphasizing personal rather than political motives for tensions between victim and oppressor. She moves beyond the stereotype of white oppressing black to show, particularly in *Maru,* systems of privilege and discrimination working solely within black society.

Makhaya, the hero of *When Rain Clouds Gather* is an exile from South Africa who has fled across the border to Botswana, having served a prison sentence for alleged political activities with banned organizations. He seeks, we are told in the opening paragraph, 'whatever illusion of freedom lay ahead'. Thus it is clear from the outset that independent Africa will not necessarily offer the victim of apartheid an easier life than the one he has left behind.... Makhaya, himself an exponent of modern, Western ideas, rejects tribalism as a barbarous system in which women are discriminated against and in which the village witchdoctors perpetuate their power over the community by encouraging superstition and ignorance. (pp. 54-5)

Makhaya settles in Golema Mmidi, a village distinguished from others in Botswana by its system of permanent settlement.... (p. 55)

In the creation of Golema Mmidi Bessie Head combines fictive metaphor—the village as Eden—with realistic social detail. The Utopian qualities of the village are balanced by hard realities. Thus the dream of creating a garden in the desert is constantly eroded by poverty, the lack of rain, (staple currency in Botswana is the *pula,* a Tswana word meaning rain) and by prejudice and corruption in local government.

In Golema Mmidi Makhaya meets Gilbert, an idealistic Englishman.... (p. 56)

Makhaya and Gilbert are spokesmen for reason, hard work and the abolition of tribal habits in favour of science and progress. Under the influence of Gilbert, Makhaya abandons 'hate-making political ideologies' as ultimately retrogressive and turns instead to agriculture 'for his salvation'. (pp. 56-7)

Factual social detail is closely integrated into the movement of the plot and is seldom merely digressive or episodic. At the same time a good deal of writing is devoted to accurate analysis of climate, crops, cattle diseases and the problems of land enclosure. This concern for practical bread-and-butter issues is a striking feature of all [Bessie Head's] work and even in the short stories the reader is supplied with accurate social, domestic and economic detail. (p. 57)

In *Maru* Bessie Head continues to explore the conflict between change and tradition in rural Southern Africa. The heroine of this novel is Margaret Cadmore.... Margaret's actual superiority over those who regard her as socially inferior [because she is a Masarwa or Bushman by birth] is given repeated emphasis. She has had a better education than anyone else in the village, she is more beautiful and more refined, she is a talented artist with visionary powers, she is affectionate and patient, animals love her, people are drawn to her in spite of their prejudices. Not surprisingly therefore, the two most powerful men in the village, Maru and Moleka, both fall in love with her. Moleka suppresses his love in conformity with social decorum, but Maru, who is paramount chief elect, abdicates his position in order to marry Margaret. Thus in *Maru* the conflict between freedom and the closed system is explored in the context of love and marriage rather than agriculture. (p. 58)

The idea that social change is brought about by the action of powerful individuals rather than gradual temporal evolution (the winds of change are not seen as 'natural' or arbitrary forces) motivates much of the action of *When Rain Clouds Gather.* In her second novel Bessie Head explores this idea in more subtle ways. Maru, to all appearances, decided to renounce the world for love. But his choice is equally the enactment of the individualist principles by which he lives.... Maru obeys his gods even when they tell him to deceive his rival. (pp. 58-9)

The sources of power are more fully explored in Bessie Head's third novel, as the title suggests. The semi-autobiographical tone of **Maru** becomes more explicit in **A Question of Power** where parallels between the protagonist and the writer include their mutual South African 'coloured' origins, their attempts to form new beginnings in Botswana and, more significantly, their temporary break-down as a result of the mental stresses of exile and loneliness. Although these correspondences are frankly outlined Bessie Head does not allow the subjective involvement which gives a particularly vivid sense of authenticity to Elizabeth's interior life to diminish the broader theme this life exemplifies. Elizabeth's private sufferings are assimilated to the historical sufferings of mankind through a network of wide-ranging images, the seemingly random nature of which points to their inclusiveness.

This universalizing expression, with its attendant extravagance, is balanced by a steady concentration in the novel on Elizabeth's inner life which ranges from 'the elegant pathway of private thought' to the agony of madness. Thematic development in Bessie Head's three novels reveals a consistent movement inwards from a social to a metaphysical treatment of human insecurities and in the last novel the problem of adaptation to a new world, or new schemes of values, is located in the mind of a single character. It is still Africa's problem however and the ideal garden is once again cultivated on a cooperative basis. Once more the dream of prosperity is in close touch with the necessity for hard work. As in **When Rain Clouds Gather,** the pioneer of the new schemes for Africa is a white immigrant, this time a South African. The heroine's task is to integrate the external world of innocent productivity, burgeoning growth and friendship in a mini-international community (Golema Mmidi reappears in this novel as Motabeng) with her chaotic inner experience. For Elizabeth, as for Makhaya, sanity means making friends. Those sections of the novel that deal with Elizabeth's madness dramatize her struggle to exorcise feelings of inferiority and resentment which breed estrangement. Each of her two nervous breakdowns is preceded by racial aggression, first against the indigenous population and then against one of the European volunteers. In the creation of two shadowy male figures called Dan and Sello who plague Elizabeth's dreams, forms of oppression, or power are depoliticized, identified as the desire for either spiritual or sexual domination over others.... The lesson to be learnt thus, in all three novels, is that love and humility lead the exiled consciousness from estrangement, 'pride and arrogance and egoism of the soul' to 'an identification with mankind' or, as the author expresses it in the novel's last sentence, 'the warm embrace of the brotherhood of man'. These phrases...are condemned when used as slogans by political opportunists. In **A Question of Power,** however, where the writing is spare, concentrated and tough, they are invested with the meaning of Elizabeth's painful

quest for peace of mind. Throughout the novel the process of 'becoming' African is double edged, involving not only the assumption of social identity but also purification of the spirit. Bessie Head's treatment of Africa is both realistic and symbolic. In one sense the large, empty, barren desert that is repeatedly invoked is a mind landscape too, the storm clouds gather in the individual psyche, Africa becomes a way of being. In the concluding sentence of **A Question of Power,** Elizabeth is described as placing 'one soft hand over her land'. And finally, we are told, 'It was a gesture of belonging.'

It is also a private gesture, with a deeply personal meaning and it exemplifies Bessie Head's achievement in fusing the ideal of community and brotherhood with a belief in the value of the one over the many. **A Question of Power** is the first metaphysical novel on the subject of nation and a national identity to come out of Southern Africa. (pp. 59-61)

Jean Marquard, "Bessie Head: Exile and Community in Southern Africa," in London Magazine, *n.s. Vol. 18, Nos. 9 & 10, December-January, 1978-79, pp. 48-61.*

Bessie Head with Linda Susan Beard (interview date 1982)

[*In the following 1982 interview, Head and Beard discuss how Head's self-exile from South Africa has affected the writer's work. The editors of* Sage *magazine note: "[Beard] interviewed Bessie Head in 1982 as part of a Rockefeller Humanities Fellowship Project entitled 'The Human Cost of Apartheid.' Beard refers to this interview as 'a sort of extended obituary for a most incredible talent'."*]

[Beard]: *You chose exile from South Africa. One of the most complex facets of your life must have been your reactions to exile.*

[Head]: You know, it is such a complicated answer. Such a complicated answer. First of all, I never had feelings of sentiment about South Africa. The country, the life that had emerged there, the fact that we had the experience of white domination—it was such a choking, throttling, death-like kind of world. In contrast, there's a certain aspect to my life in Botswana which is full and rich. The difference is that for the 27 years I lived in South Africa, I had the experience of a Black South African—the poverty-stricken, slum-dweller; the feeling that there was no way in which you could look around and breathe and feel the air. There was nothing there. Black people had been so completely dispossessed that there was nothing there that Black people owned. Even the air choked you. It was so stressed, so stressed. In whichever direction you looked, there were notices. The best and most privileged places had notices: FOR WHITES ONLY. There was total dispossession. Black people were totally dispossessed from ownership of the land. In fact, what was very striking in my 27 years in South Africa is that there was never a thought—I never

ever felt it—that this is my land. This is my land. No, the link is such a subtle one: this is my land, this is my country. It had been so successfully seized by whites that there was nothing left for Black people. I had that experience for 27 years and then I came to another experience.

I came to Botswana when it was still the British Bechuanaland Protectorate moving into independence. That was '64. What is very startling, and I think it mostly startles you because Africa is so huge, is that barely a day's journey separates one country from the other. What is very significant is that Botswana was, for 80 years, under British control, but with a completely different historical experience. The British presence was barely visible. In the village where I lived in Serowe, there was a very tentative kind of administration. The Black population was 30,000, and whatever white faces you saw in the village amounted to about 50. The Black presence, the Black historical treasure really, or things that people have been able to keep for themselves, was very dominant. So that I was faced, after living for 27 years with a sense of complete dispossession as a Black person, with a community that possessed the land. The British had been a presence that had not disrupted the old, traditional way of life, the old African traditional way of life. Coming from one situation of complete dispossession to something like that, I did not fail to notice that.

I think what I'm really trying to say is that there has to be a very serious assessment made of this colonial experience. It has so many variations, to a certain extent. If British colonialism tended to be different, it was because the gains were not too high. A country like the old Bechuanaland Protectorate presented the British with a vista of a land that was dry and unproductive, and they were completely disinterested in it. I do not think they would have lacked interest had the country offered them resources because British colonialism tended to be very commercial. But, what was valuable for me, with my South African Black background, was to find a society where the African experience is continuous and unbroken.

Is that the reason, in **Collector of Treasures,** *that you focus on characteristics of traditional life?*

Well, you know, a book grows with you. You make certain decisions about the next book and why you're going to write it. What I could say about *The Collector of Treasures* is that it was like a kind of resumé of 13 years of living entirely in village life. And village life is particularly enchanting. In actual fact, all of the stories are based on real life happenings. The village is like this: it's *very* peaceful and everyday. There's one story, **"Life,"** which describes the rhythm almost as monotonous. One day is just the same as another, but human beings are so similar all over the world. Suddenly, a great drama explodes. Now you wake up and take your shopping basket and walk down the road and people say: 'Oh, have you heard....' So that most of the

stories have this odd combination of gentleness and violence. The reason is that most of the stories came to be written because they actually happened. They may be decorated and interpreted and so on, but you go out and people say, 'Have you heard....' And then, because it surrounds a dramatic death, a murder, or a very painful court case, you get to know all the details. In a village, it's so vivid. It's so vivid.

In reality, all I simply did was record stories that had happened and had been told to me and described to me. Most of the stories there are based on reality; they're not inventions. They happened; they are changed. They are decorated; they are interpreted. But there's a basis there in fact, in reality.

Why do you prefer living in Serowe?

Gaborone never existed. When it was known that the country would be independent, a capital had to be built. It was one of those situations where the British had the capital of the country outside the country. The former capital of Botswana was Mafeking. And then, Mafeking is in South Africa, the border of the old Protectorate. So there was then a decision made that a capital of a country can't be outside. Gaborone was chosen because I think there was a permanent water supply from a river or a tributary. There was no such thing as Gaborone when I came here in 1964. The bulk of the country had villages like Serowe and life there is rich, meaningful and purposeful.

Did you have problems with the government of Botswana? Many South African exiles here seem to have serious problems with the government.

As an individual I prefer very simple choices and decisions. I like a peaceful life. There's two things that face a human being—two lives a person lives, one that you feel is under your control. As an individual I like things to be orderly, honorable, neat, tidy, without pain and complications, without any sense of shame. I do admit that I'm the sort of a woman who wants to be happy every day. I prefer that kind of life where everything is lived in the open, in the sunlight. I do very badly with intrigues, doubledeals, lies. I'm one of those sorts of people who cannot lie. If I do, I tremble and shake and quake. So, the way my temperament is, a plain, straightforward life is very essential for me. I get ill when complications develop, especially if I feel dark shadows have fallen over my life. But that's all very well. Life isn't going to offer you something so simple. There's areas of your life that you do not control.

To make a long story short, there's a certain relationship Botswana has to South Africa, and if it had a favorable attitude towards South African refugees, it would be attacked. So, the government long ago adopted a policy of using the refugees as pawns. That is my personal view. So that there has been a kind of cat-and-mouse game with refugees. You know—they walk a kind of tightrope. That is, being Black, we assume the government of Botswana is sympathetic to the plight of Black people in South Africa. But, if it came to a crunch, that is, the country versus the plight of a South African refugee, the government wouldn't give a damn. They would and they *have* deposited refugees back in South Africa because of the kind of interplay between the two countries to reassure the Boers that they'll give them back South Africa's enemies if they want them.

I now am a Botswana citizen, but for 13 years I had refugee status—when I felt suffering like most South African refugees have experienced. You might like to ask me how I got my citizenship. I applied after 13 years and they wrote back very quickly and said: "Dear Madam, your application for citizenship has been unsuccessful." So I did nothing further. I just kept silent. Two years later I opened my post office box, in February 1979, and there was another letter. (I had never asked again.) "Dear Madam, we are pleased to inform you that your application has been successful." I decided to take it because having a valid passport is much better than a United Nations Travel Document. You don't travel far with a UN Refugee Travel Document. And when it's a question of other human beings being dependent on you for passports...I took the Botswanan citizenship because it simplified my life, but I acquired it in that manner.

Do you feel at home here?

You know, I'm a writer and something of me goes into my books. But then I feel, from my own experience, that I've never been able to write about South Africa. I feel that writing, in some way, is based on a feeling that roots are present in the society. I don't think that writers, who sort of grow into an environment that is fairly secure, concentrate so much on this sense of continuity of roots; I do as a South African. In that sense, I've always been drawing on something in this society: the feeling that the roots go deep and that the historical sequence was not broken and disturbed by the British. And I think it made sense of my life. There's that aspect. And then, when the book is eventually assessed, a person says, I notice I do it myself, that it still comes down to you, your talent, what you are putting into it so that it's original. But then you also draw on your environment. It's so many subtle combinations. If it had only been me and my choices, as I have said, life would have always been beautiful and simple, but other things beyond your control intrude on you as a human being.

How accurate is it for a reader to take **Question of Power** *as an autobiographical journal? Is Elizabeth, Bessie?*

There's no way in which I can deny that that was a completely autobiographical novel taking a slice of my life, my experience, and transcribing it verbatim into novel form. It was maybe the way in which I interpreted experience. It *was* an experience I went through and, if the book can be faulted, it is because of the interpreter. It was the type of experience that needed interpretation and analysis. If there is a fault in it, it is possibly because the interpretation sounds confused.

What about the autobiographical content of **Maru**?

The two are very closely linked, but **Maru** has much more inventiveness. I used certain personal material. I would state, for instance, that my beginnings and background can be found in the girl Margaret Cadmore, but I wouldn't really say that **Maru** is as autobiographical as *A Question of Power.* Bits were borrowed, but otherwise **Maru** is inventive fiction. Central to my decision to write it was the astonishing similarity between racial prejudices. You see, in South Africa, the white man says of us (and it's so painful and bitter to read it—it's even in historical records), "They don't think. They don't know anything." And then they treat you that way. When they see a Black person, they automatically either look through you or above your head because you're a non-thinking "it" or something. But when I came to Botswana, the Botswana people's reaction to a tribe they oppressed, the Masarwa, was similar. You find, you know, that racial prejudice is so standardized. What was so shocking and surprising was to hear them use terminology white people used toward Black people in South Africa. Botswana said to me: "Oh, the Masarwa, they don't think; they don't know anything." How human beings can do that to human beings beats me! I thought, well, it's not that hard for me to put myself into the shoes of the Masarwa. **Maru** is not like *A Question of Power,* but it's borrowed elements from my own life.

I thought I may as well say that I could be a Masarwa. I then portrayed parts of my own early experience because I was reared by missionaries and the early beginnings were very much my life under missionaries. So, instead of saying Bessie Head, South African, I only had to say Bessie Head, Masarwan. It came to the same thing. **Maru** was bits borrowed with observations and learnings.

Does **Serowe: Village of the Rain Wind** *indicate a new direction in your writing?*

Everybody says, "Oh, is she going to write another **Question of Power?**" You feel such a sense of continuity because you produce the work. If I take on a job it's because I love it. That's all. It isn't change—just the one job is finished. You've done as much as you could. It's just your own sense of continuity and direction.

Do you continue to have any *sense of connectedness to South Africa?*

You know, that's what's so difficult. I personally tend to have a very cut-off life. Very kind of remote, cut-off life. And I am only in touch with literary trends in South Africa insofar as I'm asked to contribute to journals and so on. I have been aware; I have contributed to some journals in South Africa, most notably Ravan Press. But I have lived far too remotely from current trends. Serowe is a very remote village; to subscribe to newspapers and periodicals takes an enormous amount of money which I haven't got. So I keep in touch only if I'm asked to contribute. By making these contributions I became aware that there's sort of a literary explosion in South Africa. It was started by Ravan Press. I contributed to something; I was sent the magazine. So much vigor and intellectual life there considering that oppression has become more severe. I think there's two possible explanations: one is the fact that Africa is almost totally independent. Now there's only Namibia and South Africa where these things are going to be worked out. The other I'm very interested in because I've met some of the young people. The sense of vigor I attribute to something that's not of my generation, but belongs to the young people—that's the Black Consciousness Movement. (pp. 44-6)

Why is it difficult for you to write about South Africa?

I think it is because I was so sensitive to my environment. On one hand, I am a very highly individualistic person and I'm sure my books have borne that out. On the one hand, there's this strong individualist apparently above environment and everything. And then, on the other hand, I feel comfortable blending in with my surroundings. And I never felt happy, I never felt happy about South Africa. I think I was so sensitive to that question of dispossession. (p. 47)

> *Bessie Head and Linda Susan Beard, in an interview in* Sage: A Scholarly Journal on Black Women, *Vol. III, No. 2, Fall, 1986, pp. 44-7.*

FURTHER READING

Bazin, Nancy Topping. "Feminist Perspectives in African Fiction: Bessie Head and Buchi Emecheta." *The Black Scholar* 17, No. 2 (March-April 1986): 34-40.

Examines the novels of Bessie Head and Buchi Emecheta "to determine what the nature of the black African women's experience is and how this experience can be analyzed . . . ."

Chetin, Sara. "Myth, Exile, and the Female Condition: Bessie Head's *The Collector of Treasures.*" *The Journal of Commonwealth Literature* 24, No. 1 (1989): 114-37.

Thematic discussion of Head's short story collection *The Collector of Treasures,* focusing on the importance of myth in the work.

Geurts, Kathryn. "Personal Politics in the Novels of Bessie Head." *Présence Africaine* 140, No. 4 (1986): 47-74.

Explores the political nature of Head's novels.

Johnson, Joyce. "Metaphor, Myth and Meaning in Bessie Head's *A Question of Power.*" *World Literature Written in English* 25, No. 2 (Autumn 1985): 198-211.

Explains Head's use of myths and metaphors in *A Question of Power.* The critic writes: "In telling Elizabeth's story, Head draws a parallel between the situation of the individual who has suffered from the forces of prejudice and social oppression and that of a society which has been exploited by external forces."

Sarvan, Charles Ponnuthurai. "Bessie Head: *A Question of Power* and Identity." *Women in African Literature Today* 15 (1987): 82-8.

Overview of *A Question of Power,* concluding: "The novel is the work of an honest, sensitive and courageous writer."

Thorpe, Michael. "Treasures of the Heart: The Short Stories of Bessie Head." *World Literature Today* 57, No. 3 (Summer 1983): 414-16.

Appraises *The Collector of Treasures,* noting that "in Bessie Head's telling there is pain enough, but it is pain relieved constantly by the clear light of a compassionate, understanding heart."

Chester Himes

1909-1984

(Full name Chester Bomar Himes) American novelist, short story writer, autobiographer, and essayist.

Himes is best known for the serial detective novels he wrote toward the end of his career. While his earliest novels are often identified as works of social protest, his later writings are regarded as pleas for social reform. His works, though often violent, have been commended for their satire and impartial approach to volatile issues. James Sallis noted: "[Himes] is a marvelous observer and prodigious inventor, working by instinct and feeling towards his singular vision.... I do not know of any other American writer who has created vivid, memorable scenes in the quantity Himes has, scenes which are hard-edged and durable like a footprint in cement, and with an astonishing economy of dialogue and language."

Himes was born in Jefferson City, Missouri, but his family moved throughout the South before settling in Cleveland, Ohio, when he was fifteen. His mother, a light-skinned black who berated and humiliated her dark-skinned husband and children, was to inspire a dominant character in his novels: the belligerent white woman. While enrolled at Ohio State University, Himes established a raucous reputation that led to his dismissal. He became involved in gambling and drugs and committed petty thefts and forgeries. He was arrested for armed robbery in 1928 and sentenced to twenty years in prison. While incarcerated, he began writing short stories based on his experiences behind bars. "To What Red Hell," which appeared in a 1934 issue of *Esquire,* concerns the 1930 fire that killed over three hundred convicts in the Ohio State Penitentiary. Other stories, including "Crazy in the Stir" (1934) and "The Night's for Cryin'" (1937), examine loneliness and fear in the brutal, angry prison environment. Granted parole after serving seven years, Himes moved to California to find a job. His ill fortune and encounters with blatant racism there formed the basis of his first novel, *If He Hollers Let Him Go* (1945), which has been described as Himes's most embittered work.

Written in Southern black dialect and set in Los Angeles during World War II, *If He Hollers Let Him Go* centers on Bob Jones, a young black man who is demoted from his factory supervisory position for retaliating against Madge, a coarse white woman who abuses him verbally and taunts him sexually. Bob vows to punish Madge by raping her but rejects her after realizing that she has always desired him. When Bob attempts to apologize to Madge, the scorned woman screams that he is raping her. Madge eventually drops the fabricated charges, and the book ends as Bob is forced to join the army to fight overseas. Himes continued his exploration of interracial relationships in *Lonely Crusade* (1947), the story of a

black man, Lee Gordon, who becomes involved with a white woman, Jackie Falks.

In *Cast the First Stone* (1952), a highly autobiographical work with a white protagonist, Himes began to balance his racial themes. Set entirely in an unidentified jail, the story focuses on Jim Monroe, a young man from Mississippi who is incarcerated for armed robbery. Jim discusses the inhumanity of both the prisoners and the guards and, in a sequence reminiscent of "To What Red Hell," describes a fire that nearly destroys the jail. Jim breaks prison rules by having a homosexual affair with another inmate. In order to receive a lighter sentence, he concedes that the relationship was a mistake. His lover later commits suicide. In *The Third Generation* (1954), Himes scrutinized the racial strife he experienced during his childhood. The Taylors, a thinly disguised version of Himes's family, are constantly embroiled in familial and class struggles. Although Mr. Taylor is a respected college professor, his ancestors were slaves, and his wife considers her white lineage and light skin color to be more impressive than his career achievements. She urges her three sons, particularly the youngest, Charles, who narrates the story, to ignore black culture. The psychological turmoil that Mrs. Taylor creates ultimately destroys the entire family. Himes's next work, *The Primitive* (1955), again focuses on an interracial relationship. Jesse, a black man, and Kriss, a white woman, are old friends who reunite for a weekend of celebration when Jesse gets a cash advance for his novel. Quite drunk, Kriss demands sexual favors of Jesse, whom she has always envisioned as the stereotypical libidinous black man; Jesse, who has pictured Kriss as the personification of white feminine beauty, complies. Neither can fulfill the other's expectations, however, and Jesse murders Kriss in an angry, drunken stupor. The novel ends as Jesse telephones the police to inform them that a black man has killed a white woman.

Frustrated by racism, Himes left the United States in 1954 and traveled throughout Europe, eventually settling in Spain, where he lived until his death in 1984 from Parkinson's disease. As an expatriate, Himes wrote more freely of racial concerns. He achieved international success with *Pinktoes* (1961), his only nonviolent novel. Again, Himes confronted racism, but through a radically different thematic approach. A sex farce, this novel probes the doctrines of Mamie Mason, a white society matron who believes that she can end prejudice by hosting desegregated sexual orgies. In reality, the guests are merely interested in interracial sex and not social change. Widely popular in France, where readers were amused with the satire of American high society, *Pinktoes* is regarded as Himes's most daring work of fiction. During this time, Himes was encouraged by his agent to write the series of detective novels that would become his most famous works. Between 1957 and 1969, he published nine books, all of which, with the exception of *Dare-dare* (1959; *Run Man, Run*), are set in Harlem, New York, and feature the same pair of black detectives, Coffin Ed Johnson and Grave Digger Jones. The two are fiercely loyal to each other and to the white and black Harlem residents they protect. Of the series, James Sallis asserted: "I admired their singular voice, the precise economy of Himes' imagery and description, the outlandish rightness of his characterizations and the velocity he generated in his narratives, their sheer force of imagination."

Throughout the detective novels, Himes depicted oppression within black society as the detectives' gravest problem. Each plot involves an enigmatic object or an amount of money that the detective duo inevitably locate. The formula is reminiscent of the novels of Raymond Chandler, whose works Himes admitted to reading and admiring while in prison. Extreme violence, vivid descriptions, and dry wit characterize the series, of which *Retour en Afrique* (1964; *Cotton Comes to Harlem*) is perhaps the best known volume. In this work, Coffin Ed and Grave Digger must recover the eighty-seven thousand dollars that Harlem families lost as a result of a swindle by a religious group. The story's light, farcical style contributed to its overwhelming success, as

did Himes's ability to enrich the tale with symbolism and elements of African-American history. A film version of *Cotton Comes to Harlem* was produced in 1970. Himes's earlier novel, *A Rage in Harlem* (1965; originally published as *For Love of Imabelle* in 1957)—about the misadventures of Jackson and his lover, Imabelle—was adapted for film in 1991. The production stars Robin Givens, Gregory Hines, and Danny Glover.

In addition to detective novels, Himes wrote *Black on Black* (1973), an acclaimed volume of short stories. This work includes "Baby Sister," a brutal tale of an incestuous affair between a poverty-stricken brother and sister. He also published an autobiography in two volumes, *The Quality of Hurt* (1972) and *My Life of Absurdity* (1976). Of *The Quality of Hurt*, Richard H. Gaines commented: "[Not] only does one discern in these pages the spirit of vengeful evil that seems to assist Himes in achieving his goals ... but the presence of innate good. He is at once menacing and admirable, darkly tragic and luminously human." At the time of his death, Himes was working on another novel, *Plan B*. It was published in French in 1983.

Chester Himes wrote successfully in many genres, including short stories, autobiographies, and popular crime thrillers. But whatever form his writing took, it was always dedicated to one subject—"racism, the hurt it inflicts, and all the tangled hates," according to Stephen F. Milliken. Himes wrote about racial oppression with a bitter, unrelenting anger. This sense of rage and the unforgiving strokes with which Himes painted both black and white characters alienated many readers of both races; as a result, Himes was for years almost unknown in this country. American readers are, however, rediscovering Himes and his novels of social protest.

(For further information about Himes's life and works, see *Black Writers; Contemporary Authors*, Vols. 25-28; *Contemporary Authors New Revision Series*, Vols. 22, 114; *Contemporary Literary Criticism*, Vols. 2, 4, 7, 18, 58; and *Dictionary of Literary Biography*, Vols. 2, 76.)

*PRINCIPAL WORKS

"To What Red Hell" (short story) 1934; published in
    periodical *Esquire*
If He Hollers Let Him Go (novel) 1945
Lonely Crusade (novel) 1947
Cast the First Stone (novel) 1952
The Third Generation (novel) 1954
The Primitive (novel) 1955
For Love of Imabelle (novel) 1957; also published as *A
    Rage in Harlem* [revised edition], 1965
Couché dans le pain (novel) 1958
    [*The Crazy Kill*, 1959]
Il pleut des coups durs (novel) 1958
    [*The Real Cool Killers*, 1959]
Dare-dare (novel) 1959
    [*Run Man, Run*, 1966]

Tout pour plaire (novel) 1959
  [*The Big Gold Dream*, 1960]
Imbroglio negro (novel) 1960
  [*All Shot Up*, 1960]
Ne nous énervons pas (novel) 1961
  [*The Heat's On*, 1966; also published as *Come Back, Charleston Blue*, 1967]
Pinktoes (novel) 1961
Une affaire de viol (novel) 1963
  [*A Case of Rape*, 1984]
Retour en Afrique (novel) 1964
  [*Cotton Comes to Harlem*, 1965]
Blind Man with a Pistol (novel) 1969; also published as *Hot Day, Hot Night*, 1970
The Quality of Hurt: The Autobiography of Chester Himes (autobiography) 1972
Black on Black: Baby Sister and Selected Writings (short stories) 1973
My Life of Absurdity: The Autobiography of Chester Himes (autobiography) 1976
Plan B (unfinished novel) 1983

* All of Himes's works were originally written in English. Most of the author's detective novels, however, were translated and published first in France.

Chester Himes with John A. Williams (interview date 1969)

[*The following interview was conducted at the home of Chester and Lesley Himes in Spain in 1969. Here, Himes and Williams discuss the author's literary career and readers' reactions to his detective fiction. In the preface to the printed interview, Williams—a personal friend of Himes—noted: "Himes and I talked endlessly in the room he uses as a study, in the living room with its balcony that overlooks the city and the port, and on walks down to and along the promenade. There was never a time when I dared to be without the recorder, for out of Himes pours so much, at any time and at any place. He's slower getting about than he used to be, but intellectually he is as sharp as ever and his opinions as blunt and honest as always.*"]

[Williams]: *Well, how would you place yourself in American letters? [Himes laughs.] You're sixty-one years old now, you've been writing long before* **If He Hollers** *came out—You've been writing now for thirty-four years.*

[Himes]: Yes, I've been writing since 1934. Let's see, how long is that? My first story in a national magazine was published in *Esquire* in 1934. That's thirty-five years. Well, I don't know where to place myself actually on the American scene of letters because America has a highly organized system of reputation-making which I'm afraid would place me in the bottom echelon. The American communications media are very well organized about what they intend to do and how they intend

to show that this person is of great importance and that person is chickenshit. So they work this out and they make reputations. Not only do they make reputations of writers, which is insignificant, but they take people like Roosevelt and they will set out systematically to break his place in history. They'll spend millions of dollars to do so if they wish. And the same thing happens with the literary scene. That's why I never contemplate it, because I realize the Americans will sit down and they will take a white writer—he will be one that appeals to their fancy, one that has been abroad and clowned around, like Hemingway—and they will set him up and they will make him one of the most famous writers on the face of the earth. And not because of anything he has written, because his work is not that important, but because they wish to have an American up there at the top of the world literature. Anyone reading him will realize that Hemingway is a great imitator of the styles of Ford Madox Ford, James Joyce and D. H. Lawrence. As a matter of fact, if you have read the works of these four writers, you can see the lines, you can see the exact imitation. So there's nothing creative about even Hemingway's form. This was borrowed, as Gertrude Stein says.

But the Americans set out and they made him a legend. Now, it's very difficult for me to evaluate any of the people on the American scene, because if I take my information from the American white communications media then, of course, it is slanted to whatever way they wish to slant it. So one can't form any opinion, unfortunately.

Do you foresee the time when you'll ever quit writing?

Well, no, no I don't foresee it. I mean writing is like . . . I remember I have a line in a book—I've forgotten now what book it was—where I quote [Max] Schmeling. He said a fighter fights, and I went on to say " . . . and a writer writes." That's what I do, that's all I do, and I don't foresee that I will quit, as long as I'm able to write. No. I do foresee the fact that age will deteriorate my writing, as it does everyone else's writing. I don't foresee the fact that because age will deteriorate my writing, and that I will realize that I can't do what I could do when I was young (I know damn well that I can't do what I could do when I was young), that I am going to blow out my brains like Hemingway did when he discovered that.

It seemed to me when I started reading the first couple of pages of your autobiography, **The Quality of Hurt,** *that you were sort of preparing yourself for the time when you wouldn't write any more. But then I also noticed that this is Volume I, the carbon that I have. How many volumes do you foresee in this autobiography?*

I imagine there will just be another volume in which I will write about the change in my writing habits or change in my attitudes toward the entire American scene, and my change from pessimism to optimism. I became much less subject to the inroads of the various attitudes of people that I didn't particularly respect. I know that I will write another volume that will concern my beginning to write detective stories, and then my beginning to write the last ten or twelve books that I have written.

In one of your letters you said—and you've mentioned it since I've been here—that you were working on the bloodiest book that you have ever worked on, that you'd ever conceived, but you didn't expect (you said in this letter) to have it published in America, that it would be difficult to have published. Do you remember that?

Well, yes, because I can see what a black revolution would be like. Now, first of all, in order for a revolution to be effective, one of the things that it has to be, is violent, it has to be massively violent; it has to be as violent as the war in Vietnam. Of course, in any form of uprising, the major objective is to kill as many people as you can, by whatever means you can kill them, because the very fact of killing them and killing them in sufficient number is supposed to help you gain your objectives. It's the only reason why you do so.

Now, when you have resorted to these means, this is the last resort. Well, then, all dialogue ceases, all forms of petitions and other goddamned things are finished. All you do then is you kill as many people as you can, the black people kill as many of the people of the white community as they can kill. That means children, women, grown men, industrialists, street sweepers or whatever they are, as long as they're white. And this is the fact that gains its objective—there's no discussion—no point in doing anything else and no reason to give it any thought.

Now a soldier, if he would have to think about the morality of going out and killing the enemy, or if he had to consider his feelings about killing people, he would be finished. To do so, he would get court-martialed or shot on the scene. A soldier just goes out and kills; no one thinks anything about it; that's his objective. The objective for a foot soldier is to kill the enemy, and that's all. It's very simple. There's nothing else to be added to it or subtracted from it.

Well, that's what a revolution by the black people in America will be; that's their only objective. Their objective is not to stand up and talk to the white man and to stand him in front of a gun and say, "Now you did so and so to me"; the only objective is to blow out his brains without a word, you see. So I am trying to show how this follows, how the violence would be if the blacks resorted to this. Even individually, if you give one black one high-powered repeating rifle and he wanted to shoot it into a mob of twenty thousand or more white people, there are a number of people he could destroy. Now, in my book all of these blacks who shoot are destroyed. They not only are destroyed, they're blown apart; even the buildings they're shooting from are destroyed, and quite often the white community suffers fifty or more deaths itself by destroying this one black man. What I'm trying to do is depict the violence that is necessary so that the white community will also give it a little thought, because you know,

they're going around playing these games. They haven't given any thought to what would happen if the black people would *seriously* uprise.

The white community gets very much upset about the riots, while the black people haven't seriously undertaken in advance to commit any great amount of violence; it's just been forced on them. What little violence they have done has actually been for protection; it's been defensive, you know. So what I would hope is to call to mind what *would* happen, what *should* happen, when the black people have an armed uprising, what white people should expect. It seems that the whites don't understand this.

Because one thing is sure—I have said this and I keep on saying it over and over again—the black man can bring America down, he can destroy America. The black man can destroy the United States. Now, there are sensible people in America who realize this, regardless of what they might think about the black man. The black man can destroy America completely, destroy it as a nation of any consequence. It can just fritter away in the world. It can be destroyed completely. Now I realize of course that the black man has no money, he has very little equipment to do this, he has very little fire power, he has lots of things against him, he hasn't been trained particularly. Even a Southern white cracker colonel . . . I remember a Southern white cracker colonel in the army in the Second World War got up and he made this famous speech about the black people, saying, "You have never been taught to use violence and you have never been taught to be courageous, but war calls for these things and you must learn them." Well, he's right. That's the most right thing he ever said.

Do you think the publishers will be . . .

I don't think . . . I don't know what the American publishers will do about this book. But one thing I do know, Johnny, they will hesitate, and it will cause them a great amount of revulsion, because the scenes that I have described will be revolting scenes. There are very few war books written that have ever described actual scenes of war, 'cause in war people are killed and blown to pieces, and all. Even when they just say "blown to pieces" that doesn't describe what they *look* like blown to pieces. When a shell hits a man in a war, bits of him fly around, half of his liver is flying through the air, and his brains are dribbling off. These are actual scenes, no one states these outright.

How do you think the majority of white readers react to your books and other books by black writers?

The white readers read into a book what they wish, and in any book concerning the black people in the world, the majority of white readers are just looking for the exotic episodes. They're looking for things that will amuse or titillate them. The rest of it they skip over and pay no attention to. That was one of the remarkable things about Richard Wright's autobiography—that the white community was willing to read his suffering and poverty as a black man. But it didn't move them, didn't move them one bit. They just read it and said, "Tsk, tsk, isn't it awful?"

Well, you know, I sometimes have the feeling that when they read books like that, they say to themselves, "Boy, ain't we a bitch! Look what we're doing to them people."

[Laughs.] Yeah, something like that. They're thinking along those lines; certainly they're not thinking in the ways you'd like for them to think. That's one of the saddest parts about the black man in America—that he is being used to titillate the emotions of the white community in various aspects. Now I couldn't say exactly how he titillates them, but in any case it's titillation in a way that's not serious. America is a masochistic society anyway, so they probably just like being given a little whipping, enough to get a feeling out of it, a sensation, but not enough for them to be moved. I want these people just to take me seriously. I don't care if they think I'm a barbarian, a savage, or what they think; just think I'm a serious savage.

There's a rash of books, I hear (I haven't read them)— detective books—in which there are black detectives, and of course one of these books was made into a movie with Poitier, In the Heat of the Night. *Do you feel that these people are sort of swiping your ideas?*

No, no. It's a wonder to me why they haven't written about black detectives many years ago. It's a form, you know, and it's a particularly American form. My French editor says, the Americans have a style of writing detective stories that no one has been able to imitate, and that's why he has made his *Série Noire* successful, by using American detective story writers. There's no reason why the black American, who is also an American, like all other Americans, and brought up in this sphere of violence which is the main sphere of American detective stories, there's no reason why he shouldn't write them. It's just plain and simple violence in narrative form, you know. 'Cause no one, *no one,* writes about violence the way that Americans do.

As a matter of fact, for the simple reason that no one understands violence or experiences violence like the American civilians do. The only other people in the white community who are violent enough for it are the armed forces of all the countries. But of course they don't write about it because if the atrocities were written about the armies of the English and the French in Africa, they would make among the most grisly stories in the history of the world. But they're not going to write about them. These things are secret; they'll never state them.

American violence is public life, it's a public way of life, it became a form, a detective story form. So I would think that any number of black writers should go into the detective story form. As a matter of fact, I feel that they could be very competent. Anyway, I would like to see a lot of them do so. They would not be imitating me because when I went into it, into the detective story

field, I was just imitating all the other American detective story writers, other than the fact that I introduced various new angles which were my own. But on the whole, I mean the detective story originally in the plain narrative form—straightforward violence—is an American product. So I haven't created anything whatsoever; I just made the faces black, that's all.

You know, I'm always amazed when I read your books. Here you've been out of the country for twenty years, but I'm always amazed at your memory of things and how accurate you are in details, like the guns that the cops use. In rereading the screenplay last night, there was the business of the drop slot in the car. How do you come by all this knowledge?

Well, some of it comes from memory; and then I began writing these series because I realized that I was a black American, and there's no way of escaping forty some odd years of experience, so I would put it to use in writing, which I have been doing anyway. I had always thought that the major mistake in Richard Wright's life was to become a world writer on world events. I thought that he should have stuck to the black scene in America because he wouldn't have had to live there—he had the memory, so he was still there, but it was subconsciously, which he discovered when he went back to write *The Long Dream* and the sequel (which was never published, I don't think).

Well, then, I went back—as a matter of fact, it's like a sort of pure homesickness—I went back, I was very happy, I was living there, and it's true. I began creating also all the black scenes of my memory and my actual knowledge. I was very happy writing these detective stories, especially the first one, when I began it. I wrote

Himes (seated, far right) with his parents and older brothers.

those stories with more pleasure than I wrote any of the other stories. And then when I got to the end and started my detective shooting at some white people, I was the happiest. (pp. 42-50)

Chester Himes and John A. Williams, in an interview in Amistad, *Vol. I, February, 1970, pp. 25-94.*

John M. Reilly (essay date 1976)

[*In the following excerpt, Reilly examines Himes's "Tough-Guy" novels, proposing that the author's detective fiction is a microcosm of American culture.*]

Chester Himes began writing Tough-Guy fiction in 1957, . . . and the most striking of his "new angles" is the fact that his stories take place almost entirely in *Black* America. The detectives, the setting, the themes, the plots, and the viewpoint are all Black. (p. 936)

In several ways Himes' nine Harlem novels constitute a cycle. Characters reappear, predominantly his two police detectives Coffin Ed Johnson and Grave Digger Jones, similar events occur, and incidents and persons in one novel are referred to in others. Fundamentally, however, the stories form a cycle because they are controlled by Himes' perception of Black American life, a perception that can be readily outlined by a brief examination of the works making up the cycle. (p. 937)

Details of character behavior in combination with the wild sequence of events convey Himes' essentially violent view of Harlem reality. Grave Digger and Coffin Ed are a basic part of the scene, using violence themselves to get information and to catalyze events. Their Tough behavior encourages the belief among Harlem's citizens that they would "shoot a man stone dead for not standing straight in line." . . . Whenever they want to control people they draw their long barreled nickel plated guns while Grave Digger shouts "straighten up!" and Coffin Ed adds "Count Off!" Their complicity in violence is undeniable, but their use of it contrasts with others' in that their purpose is to introduce order. From that perspective the organized underworld is not their problem, since it functions in a predictable fashion most of the time, but small time hoodlums and strangers working a con game disrupt people's lives excessively. In such circumstances morality is situational, and the Good often becomes a matter of choosing lesser evil, because the environment of Harlem determines people to live on an elemental level. . . . (p. 938)

Even though Harlemites prey on each other, their elementally violent life connects with life elsewhere. The fraud of the bill "raising" and other cons are images of capitalist business and a version of the American dream of quick riches. Likewise, physical murder is the overt complement of the social violence that maintains a cramped ghetto where human misery, denied a salutary assault upon its cause, turns in frustration upon the nearest vulnerable people. In conjunction with these

points of theme Himes' prolific use of visually comic scenes becomes very serious business. Those scenes depend upon exaggerated action and unexpected slapstick, and with their violent content they appear to be almost sur-real. But they are in no way incongruous, for actual life in Harlem, as Himes describes it, has the significance of profound absurdity. (p. 939)

By the time of his third Harlem Tough-Guy novel, *The Crazy Kill,* Himes had his formulas well-established. An opening scene of violence rendered in predominantly visual terms depending upon the unexpected physical event, as in film comedy, involves a number of Harlem characters in a crime that is apparently inexplicable. The remainder of the novel then reveals the motives that explain the crime and relate the characters to each other. While the motives are often psychological in nature, they are intensified and complicated by their presence in residents of Harlem; therefore, they must be interpreted by Coffin Ed and Grave Digger who understand that the conditions of Black life give rise to unique social relationships. As they put it, people in Harlem do the same things other folk do—deceive, rob, and kill—but for different reasons and in different ways. (pp. 939-40)

Run Man Run, Himes' fourth Tough-Guy novel, omits Coffin Ed and Grave Digger from the cast of characters and transfers the crime to downtown New York, but despite that the story retains the characteristic viewpoint that links the novels in a cycle. In particular this novel underlines Himes' perception of the risky life led by Blacks in a white society. (p. 940)

Besides the tough guys themselves another notable omission in *Run Man Run* is the visual comedy. But Himes' intention cannot be taken as different on that count. . . . The story . . . takes place in the context of white society where the appearance of categorical reason is a chief value rather than in Black Harlem where unexpected slapstick physical action is the objective correlative of the disorder induced by racial oppression.

One of the intrinsic interests of Naturalistic fiction for the reader is the detail of workaday life. In Tough-Guy fiction the work is often illegal, and in Himes' contribution to the genre enormous ingenuity marks the big and little rackets that consume the energy of the characters. *The Big Gold Dream,* his fifth Tough-Guy novel, is especially full of such detail. (pp. 940-41)

The sixth Tough-Guy novel *All Shot Up* varies Himes' formula only with the introduction of a prominent national political figure into the cast of characters. There is an exploration of the Gay sub-culture and a series of complicated impersonations emphasizing the dubiousness of reasonable order, but had Himes ended his Harlem cycle in 1960 with *All Shot Up* one might have thought he had lost interest in the Tough-Guy form. True, the possibilities for telling stories of people involved in fraud seem innumerable, but Himes has always been intensely concerned with conveying social themes and while the cumulative effect of the first six novels provides readers a strong commentary on the conditions of Harlem, the vehicle that carries those themes has become too formulaized.... The result of his continuation [with the cycle] has been the production of what are possibly the most interesting of his Harlem Tough-Guy stories.... [The] cause of their interest is their topicality. In a burst of social creativity Black Americans have built a liberation movement and invigorated a culture to carry its message. Himes could not fail to be affected by this, and in consequence his three most recent Tough-Guy novels have been devoted to commentary on issues of the sixties. (pp. 941-42)

Himes' characterization of his detectives [in *The Heat's On*] becomes fuller, because they are animated by broader moral convictions than in earlier novels. It's as if Ed and Digger had raised their intuitive loyalty to Black people and their commitment to order up to the level of a conception and begun to develop the general principles of their actions and commentary. (p. 942)

The events in [*Cotton Comes to Harlem*] are a projection of Himes' belief that Blacks must make their way in the culture in which they find themselves, that is to say, neither in Africa nor in the idealized past but in present-day Afro-America.... [In this novel both] the Back to Africa movement and the Back to the Southland chicanery are viewed by Coffin Ed and Grave Digger as frauds..., a social problem, as well as a police matter.

Satiric tone is the indicator of this view.... Comic physical scenes and irony in the earlier novels interpret, but they do not ridicule. In *Cotton Comes to Harlem* the pairing of a Back to Africa movement with a Back to the Southland movement makes it impossible to imagine a serious ideal behind the phoniness.

A further development in the character of Ed and Digger that accompanies Himes' introduction of specifically topical material is their appearance as appreciative commentators on Black culture. As defenders of Black people and interpreters of their ways, they have been appreciative of course, but in *Cotton Comes to Harlem* a reader begins to notice scenes with the purpose of involving Ed and Digger in Black cultural life. (pp. 942-43)

With the publication of his ninth Tough-Guy novel *Blind Man With a Pistol* Chester Himes fulfilled the internal logic of his Harlem cycle by bringing the American racial conflict that underlies each of the books into the story as the explicit principle of structure and theme. (p. 943)

[*Blind Man With a Pistol* contains Himes' fullest exploration of race politics.] The plot involves a collection of fools and charlatans offering the people of Harlem competing solutions to the "Negro Problem." (p. 944)

Himes' satiric description ridicules [their] non-revolutionary panaceas for American racism simply by describing them.... [Ed and Digger observe] that a younger generation of Blacks takes equality seriously whereas earlier generations, like their own, had been resigned to their condition. A talk with Michael X of the Black Muslims certifies this perception. The Muslims receive no ridicule from Himes or his detectives; they are genuinely committed to their people. So when Michael X says that what Whitey doesn't understand is "that there are Negroes who are not adapted to making white people feel good,"... it's an accurate analysis of the mood of the streets. (p. 945)

Himes tells a parable-like incident involving a blind man aggravated to try to kill at least one white man. Trapped as he is in blindness he shoots instead a Black minister who is admonishing the whites and Blacks to behave like brothers.

The parable relates to many other episodes in the Tough-Guy novels. The rapid sequence of unanticipated violence is on one level comic. On a more profound level the absurd actions are understandable consequences. Himes extends the significance of the parable further, though, by a brief preface to the novel in which he explains that an anecdote ... about a blind man with a pistol made him think of "some of our loudmouthed leaders urging our vulnerable soul brothers on to getting themselves killed," and "further that all unorganized violence is like a blind man with a pistol."

The operative word in the preface is *unorganized*. The violence throughout Himes' Harlem cycle and the violence of riots is defensive. It has been forced upon Blacks. The Black community, after all, is where it takes place, and the instigation is clearly from the white community. In an interview with John A. Williams Himes makes clear his belief that a change to *organized* violence would be salutary:

> It's just an absolute fact that if the blacks in America were to mount a revolution in force, with organized violence to the saturation point, that the entire black problem would be solved ... So the point is that the white people are jiving the blacks in America ... whites want the blacks to find a solution where the blacks will keep themselves in a secondary state.

In the light of these remarks Himes' Tough-Guy novels must be seen as an effort to describe necessity. Upon reflection one finds no reason for surprise at Himes' convictions about violent Black revolution. To resist the possibility that the books would be read for titillation (according to Williams this is Himes' favorite word to describe the usual white response to Blacks), he has included the full measure of the violence he perceives in America and tried to demonstrate that it is congenital. In the three most recent books he has become more explicit and increased the topicality, because like other Black Americans he grows justly impatient.

Perceiving the stories of the Harlem detectives as a cycle allows us to see that the commentary Himes intends in *Blind Man With a Pistol* is implicit throughout the cycle. Sometimes critics confuse a Naturalistic writer's credo with his technique and take his intention to describe things the way they really are, to him, as indication that his narrative will provide uncritical portrayal for its own sake. Truly, writers themselves will add to the confusion by their insistence upon their own dispassion or their bleak representation of helplessly determined characters, and it must be said that some of the earlier novels in the cycle independently appear to stress the detectives' coolness and the hopelessness of life in Harlem. Read as cycle, however, Himes' Tough-Guy novels demonstrate how every detail of Naturalistic writing can make an assertion. His descriptions of physical setting, the overcrowded decaying buildings, the rooms filled with the cast-off furnishings of white people or over-priced junk, and the paradoxical streets, emphasize the status of Harlem as an internal colony. The characters reduced to elemental living or channeling their virtues of loyalty and organization into a struggle for survival represent social relations determined by exclusion and oppression. The plots initiated by fraud or delusion and proceeding through a sequence of unanticipated violent events represent the experience of living in a contradictory world where, on the one hand the majority espouses equal social mobility, and on the other hand actually grants the power of self-determination according to the pattern of rigid castes. Together these essentials of his Tough-Guy novels add up to Chester Himes' assertion of the true nature, not just of Harlem but the entire American culture of which Black society is inextricably a part. (pp. 945-46)

> *John M. Reilly, "Chester Himes' Harlem*
> *Tough Guys," in* Journal of Popular Culture,
> *Vol. IX, No. 4, Spring, 1976, pp. 935-47.*

Stephen F. Milliken (essay date 1976)

[*In the following excerpt, Milliken appraises Himes's non-detective novels, stating: "Racism, the hurts it inflicts, and all the tangled hates, is the dominant subject of the literary works that Chester Himes actually did produce."*]

The bitter laugh of the dedicated satirist runs through much of Himes's work, but nowhere is there to be found the limpid moral certainty of the greatest satirists. And Himes's laughter is jubilant and gay as often as it is bitter.

His favorite subject was pain, and it screams in naked release on almost every page he has written, but justice, easily the most turgid and pompous of literary subjects, is invoked only slightly less often. (p. 4)

Himes's work is social, personal, symbolic, and frankly commercial. It is bleak tragedy, sophisticated parody, hearty folk humor, and storytelling for the sheer excitement of story itself. It operates on many levels, unleashing echoes from abysmal psychic depths, and the raffish charm of the huckster out to capture a popular audience, on his own terms. (p. 5)

Like Jesse Robinson [of *The Primitive*], Himes is determinedly "ungracious." If his humor does not always make his readers cry, it at least never fails to make them acutely uncomfortable, and he does routinely supply, for their further discomfort, "a vise of despair and bitterness." More important, he too rejected the narrow limitations he felt publishers tried to impose on the black writer, and their low horizon of expectations where black writers were concerned implied in their special use of the term *protest*. Like the stubbornly argumentative Jesse, Himes possessed the massive ego of the consciously talented and aspired to comparison with the greatest figures of Western literature. (p. 8)

The anger that Chester Himes's characters express is his own anger, and more often than not, it is aimed directly at the reader. Power, the shocking immediacy of personal confession, is purchased at the expense of aesthetic distance.

The black writer's "difficult" humor is also rooted directly in his special experience. This humor that merges in perfect harmony with the harshest and most despairing views of human life is closely related to a gut-level existentialism that the black man has no need to formulate in intellectual terms, an unshakable conviction that the world is indeed absurd based on a lifetime of absurd experience. (p. 11)

The Third Generation is perhaps Himes's least contrived work. It flows easily, irresistibly, organically, retracing the course of Himes's troubled childhood and youth, seemingly driven solely by its own internal forces, without apparent management or manipulation. The characters develop freely, moving toward fates that they must both invent and discover, and the novel is shaped by them . . . .

His novel reduces the traumas generated within the black American community itself by the pressures of racism to the story of a single black family, rent by the conflict between a black-hating mother and a black-accepting father, and the sons caught in between—Himes's own story. (p. 139)

The characters of *The Third Generation* have a largeness of size that is without parallel in the rest of Chester Himes's fiction. They are creatures of epic, of romance, of allegory—and of life itself, remembered with love and anguish. (p. 140)

The novel's title, "The Third Generation," has, like almost all of Himes's titles, a hidden edge of irony. On the one hand, it refers to Charles and his brothers, the third generation from slavery, the grandsons of the freed slaves. But the novel's epigraph is a quotation from Exodus, "For I the Lord thy God am a jealous God, visiting the iniquity of the fathers upon the children unto the third and fourth generation of them that hate me." . . . Lillian's god, the chastiser of peoples, races, generations, is a very real presence in the novel. A kind of cosmic malevolence seems to stalk the Taylor family, inflicting crippling accidents upon them, blinding them to every possibility of tenderness, turning their loves to bitterness and hate. (pp. 144-45)

[*Cast the First Stone*] is the most selectively focused of Himes's three autobiographical novels. It explores one sharply defined segment of Himes's experience in great depth. (p. 159)

[In] making Jimmy Monroe white, Himes effected an even more drastic narrowing of scope. He eliminated the entire subject of racism, the central theme of his first two novels. It is the most radical change imaginable, a basic alteration in the nature of the reality portrayed. But racism is not an easy truth for an artist to handle. It is a lurid, obtrusive, noisy truth, usurping to itself all of the center stage. It distorts and obscures all lesser or subtler truths. The most obvious of these distortions—in evidence whenever a black writer accepts racism as his central subject—involves the depiction of white characters. In any account of a racist society seen from the victim's viewpoint, the white characters, as oppressors, are automatically reduced in stature, diminished, to the point that they appear scarcely human. (p. 160)

Although the narrative point of view in *Cast the First Stone* is first person, Himes, as usual, introduced a number of complex variations into the basic approach. Jimmy Monroe is both the narrator and the convict described, but the qualities that the first-person narrator unintentionally reveals in himself, the qualities implied by the narrative style itself, tend to differ slightly from the traits of character that are all too clearly implied by the recorded acts and statements of the young convict Jimmy Monroe. The single important trait that Jimmy Monroe's two avatars, narrator and protagonist, have in common is a confusing volatility. Both seem to be forever in a state of change. (p. 162)

The protagonist is too busy attempting to dodge the slings and arrows of outrageous fortune, usually unsuccessfully, to betray any capacity for humor, but the narrator finds many subjects for dry, wry humor in the general prison scene, and even in various traits of the battered psyche of young Jimmy Monroe, his childlike vanity in particular.... (p. 163)

[*The Primitive*] is a very short novel, less than seventy thousand words, but it is as richly packed and complex a book as the sprawling *Lonely Crusade*. It is the most intricately patterned piece of fiction Himes ever produced. The narrative approach is officially third-person omniscient, but the anonymous, all-knowing narrator is far more than an expedient technical device, the most convenient way to bring a variety of facts before the reader.... The book is overflowing with "symbols"; the characters live surrounded by things, crowded on all sides by objects of every kind, objects that seem to exist solely for the sake of the resonances they create in the minds of the protagonists, their mysterious capacity to jar loose vagrant fragments of almost forgotten memories or to inspire vague premonitions of dread, a sense of malevolent forces at work beneath the surface of things. (pp. 184-85)

The characterization of Kriss in *The Primitive* is the most complete exposition [Himes] gave in his writing of his conviction that the hurts of the white woman are at least comparable to those of the black man, and that she endures a roughly similar, and equally pitiable, minority status.... Kriss epitomizes "the female condition," as Himes saw it, the unique quality of defeat a sadistic society has reserved for its women: "Not defeated like a man in battle, but like a woman who is defeated by her sex, by the outraged indignity of childbearing, menstrual periods, long hair and skirts." Kriss's minority status, the dues she has paid for a place in the foremost ranks of the outraged and insulted, is a prime factor in maintaining and insistently stressing the parallelism of the novel's two central characterizations. (p. 186)

In the novel's most patently surrealistic twist, the electronic pseudomiracle of a chimpanzee that talks is complemented by the authentic miracle of genuine, precise, detailed prophecy.... Himes's chatty and omniscient chimpanzee seems to have been created primarily to remind the reader, and perhaps the writer, that fictional worlds are at best only pale copies of an awesomely mysterious reality, and, again like Shakespeare's Fool, the chimpanzee, with his clear view through the fictional fabric to the greater outside, is totally unable to communicate with the other characters in the work, each one lost in his own private rut, surrounded by impenetrable walls. The chimpanzee is also, however, perhaps a bit too obviously, an element in Himes's satire of the highly "advanced" consumer culture that produced Kriss and all her lamentable sisters and stranded them in the meaningless void of a social order whose only positive value is material productivity. (pp. 188-89)

The Primitive is not an easy book to evaluate.... The book has evident faults—constant shifts in tone, an uncomfortable density of texture, a narrator who philosophizes, often gratuitously, and an organizational structure that is stiff and symmetrical to a point of obvious artificiality—but each of these, according to the reader's individual tastes, might equally well be regarded as virtues. *The Primitive* is, however, beyond question, the autobiographical novel in which Himes achieved the greatest degree of control over his material, perhaps because the events covered had hurt him less, marked him less profoundly, than the memories of childhood, adolescence, and prison he had dealt with in the two earlier novels. Himes did succeed, as he had not quite succeeded with Charles Taylor and Jimmy Monroe, in making Jesse Robinson a purely novelistic creation, an effective vehicle for the expression of his own deepest insights into the human condition in general. *The Primitive* is, of the three autobiographical novels, the least dependent on autobiographical interest. Its hold on the imagination is that of a novel, a product of the creative imagination, rather than that of an autobiography, a chronicle of facts, a simple act of self-revelation. Every reader is left free to find some aspect of the incredibly complex, multilayered Jesse Robinson, a compound of rage, despair, love, and hope, that he can personally identify with. (pp. 205-06)

The Quality of Hurt was a kind of summing up, a tying together of loose ends, more a casual "rap" about a few random segments of his past than a rigidly organized autobiography, primarily offering vivid sketches of the handful of characters and incidents important in his life that he had not already "used" in his three autobiographical novels. (p. 270)

Himes was determined to show that hurt, like mercy, has an almost inexhaustible variety of forms, all of which are rooted deep in the human heart. If mercy is a human quality that it behooves the race of masters to explore in depth—as Portia instructs her audience of Jew haters and unimaginatively legalistic bureaucrats—hurt is a quality that the oppressed, seldom through choice, invariably come to know in its full complexity. The autobiography of a talented man who is a member of an oppressed minority cannot help but be a valuable guide, a veritable textbook on the intricacies, the "quality," of this singularly unpleasant emotion. Himes was only too painfully aware that he was passing in review experiences and human relationships that had been damaged or destroyed, poisoned, embrued with a unique quality of hurt, by the racist pressures that had impinged at every point on his life. It is his unifying theme. (p. 272)

The ending of this passionate account of a passionate affair is singularly satisfying, both esthetically and emotionally, a kind of ending that life, and autobiographies, seldom afford. (p. 277)

Racism, the hurts it inflicts, and all the tangled hates, is the dominant subject of the literary works that Chester Himes actually did produce. He did not choose the subject. It was thrust upon him. He did not at first even choose the literary forms that he used. But he drove deeper into the subject than anyone ever had before. He recorded what happens to a man when his humanity is questioned, the rage that explodes within him, the doubts that follow, and the fears, and the awful temptation to yield, to embrace degradation.... [He] has produced, in the form of a long series of novels, both heavy and light, what was, arguably, the most complete and perfect statement of the nature of native American racism to be found in American literature, and one of the most profound statements about the nature of social oppression, and the rage and fear it generates in individuals, in all of modern literature. (pp. 306-07)

Stephen F. Milliken, in his Chester Himes: A Critical Appraisal, *University of Missouri Press, 1976, 312 p.*

A. Robert Lee (essay date 1978)

[*In the following excerpt, Lee evaluates Himes's* A Case of Rape, Black on Black, The Quality of Hurt, *and* My Life of Absurdity.]

Just as [his] earlier fiction was neither as solemn nor monotone as had casually been supposed so Himes's use of the thriller genre, ostensibly all pantomime and knock-about, could be seen to mask serious and long-held preoccupations. In changing from high to popular form Himes hadn't altered his basic sense of direction.

But if his themes have arguably been of a piece, Himes's overall achievement presents more difficult problems. His very best writing can give way to weaknesses of a quite blatant kind. He can sound clumsy, flat-footed, too strident. His style has often been uneven and the pressure of his own feelings has shown through. Yet within writing which exhibits all of these deficiencies, as well as others, he has scored clear and attractive triumphs. (p. 100)

Himes's command of black argot and street idiom in the thrillers, in which some thought they heard traces of Hemingway and of Dashiell Hammett, together with the pace and sheer inventiveness of their violence, helped to establish a vision uniquely and utterly his own. Perhaps the violence, a pre-occupation which carries over from his earlier fiction, spoke directly to an age of assassination, black shoot-outs, riot, cities burnt and burning. Himes had turned to considerable imaginative profit his insights into the whole ecology of Harlem ghetto and underworld life: the soul talk, the dope, the food, the Jazz and Blues, the daily dramas of putting on the Man, the store-front prophets, the black crime perpetrated against other Blacks, the chippies and their pimps, the shysters of every type and sex. (pp. 102-03)

Himes's only other published novel, *Une Affaire de Viol* [*A Case of Rape*] (1963), remaindered immediately after publication (and now something of a collector's item), has never appeared in English, only in French translation. It has suffered almost total eclipse. A short and intriguing tale which views post-war Paris through a particularly caustic eye, it nevertheless lacks the general vitality of the Harlem scenarios—though more, one is bound to suspect, because of the slightly flat-sounding French of the translation than because of Himes's original style. (p. 104)

Une Affaire de Viol anticipates various of the formal hallmarks of Himes's thrillers—a crime wrongly construed, a syndrome of apparent black rape and arrest, the need to resift evidence, a cluster of contrasts in racial point of view—but Himes works these into a more seriously pitched effort than any of the Coffin Ed/Grave Digger volumes. The book takes the shape of a court transcript, fiction as written evidence or historical witness. In choosing this quasi-judicial or "detective" format, Himes moves easily between past and present, between a specific instance of racism now and the larger historical framework to which it belongs.

Though it perhaps promises more than it delivers, *Une Affaire de Viol* concerns two related kinds of disaffiliation, one that of the artist, the other racial.... *Une Affaire de Viol* thus tells a contemporary fable and acts as a theatre of racial memory. Garrison finds himself caught in a particularized racial web, and the larger web of America's racial past.

The human focus of *Une Affaire de Viol* falls upon the writers, painters, newsmen and intellectuals who, willingly or not, inherit custody of the image of the black American expatriate in Europe. The descendants of slaves are hosted uneasily by the descendants of old European slavers. Certainly, Himes displays few illusions in the novel about French racial enlightenment. Among other things, *Une Affaire de Viol* registers the guilty truce which allows selected black Americans, mainly jazzmen and writers, to fraternize with Paris intellectuals, but leaves unchecked French colonial racism and the exploitation of immigrant black and Arab workers.... Yet Himes refrains from turning his victims into simple models of virtue. He matches their frailties with those of their hosts. Just as it examines French racism, the novel dares to tackle black racism. If guiltless of murder, Himes's four expatriates aren't free of other taints. (pp. 105-06)

Black on Black (1973), makes available in one binding nineteen of Himes's stories written between 1937 and 1969, four of his angry war-time essays, and the scenario he wrote for a film montage on Harlem, **"Baby Sister,"** which his French admirers not unfairly called "Greek Tragedy." ... (p. 107)

Though funny, and in parts as quick-witted and surreal as the thrillers, **"Baby Sister"** tells essentially a black city lament over spoilt life.... The whole moves to a lively pace, stage cartoon almost, in the manner of Brecht's *Arturo Ui.* **"Baby Sister"** again shows Himes's authority in capturing the spirit of Harlem life: the tinsel amid the poverty, the contrary styles of a people crowded into an urban box.

The piece enacts the fall of a dynasty. The Louis family isn't a house brought down in classical Troy, however, or the Verona of *Romeo and Juliet,* but deep inside the city heat of black Manhattan. The route to collapse is firmly sign-posted: in Himes's racially-crossed lovers, the hints of destructive incest, the family's increasing failure to hold together and in the ritual shoot-outs with white cops. Similarly, **"Baby Sister"** offers not so much Homeric catalogues of high chivalric arms and errantry, but Harlem's own distinctive iconography, that of vice, poverty, switchblades, guns, dilapidated houses, numbers, black matrons and street brothers, the Apollo Theatre and shiny big cars. (pp. 107-08)

[Like] the thrillers, **"Baby Sister"** amounts to far more than a few vivid pages of black spectacle. Himes blends into his "down-home" folk idiom just the right dash of *kitsch* to suggest the glittery vulnerability of his heroine and all she represents. **"Baby Sister"** tells a sermon and enacts a comedy of racial error....

If **"Baby Sister"** tells one version of Himes's *comédie humaine,* the short stories add considerably to the canvas. Given the thirty-year span of his selection, Himes might have been working to a single refrain, the old blues line he cites in his Foreword, "What did I do to be so black and blue?" Despite lapses, and some heavy-footedness in developing his ironies, Himes has

kept his style muscular, trim, clear for the most part of unnecessary freight. (p. 108)

With the publication of his two-volume autobiography, *The Quality of Hurt* (1972) and *My Life Of Absurdity* (1976), Himes has made a formidable attempt to tell his contrary history. And he tells, rather than builds a disciplined interpretation, of his life. Together, the volumes add up to a retrospect more than a thousand pages long. Both titles, the first with its adaptation of Shakespeare's "The quality of mercy...," call attention to traits he believes decisive in his life. The prose remains in fine order, fluent, as closely particular as ever, the instrument of a writer whose vision, in all its contrary imaginings of violence and absurdity, has basically always been serious. (p. 109)

Two observations in particular mark out [*The Quality of Hurt*]. In the first, Himes offers his stand as a writer.... The other, a run of insights made while describing the circumstances in which he wrote *The Primitive,* gives further measure of Himes's intense personal contrariness, and also something of his estimate of what blackness in America has meant. (p. 110)

My Life Of Absurdity continues the momentum: the moves back and forth between Europe and America, the Paris café circles once more.... Himes hasn't written a life which comes to any final point of order. Perhaps he finds that impossible. "No American," he says, "has ever lived a life more absurd than mine." His comments on blackness and the ways of expatriation, as well on the writer's craft and psychology, work more as counterpoint to the adventures of being Chester Himes than self-diagnosis.... That Himes remains, by all accounts, his own included, cantankerous, easily angered, as hard on black brothers as white Americans and Europeans, in all as contrary as ever, doesn't make a final assessment, even if that were desirable, any easier.

Himes has pursued his craft against hurt, absurdity, indirections of every sort and price, on the move and at rest. (p. 111)

> *A. Robert Lee, "Hurts, Absurdities and Violence: The Contrary Dimensions of Chester Himes," in* Journal of American Studies, *Vol. 12, No. 1, April, 1978, pp. 99-114.*

Robert E. Skinner (essay date 1989)

[*In the following excerpt from his* Two Guns from Harlem: The Detective Fiction of Chester Himes *(1989), Skinner analyzes the characters Grave Digger Jones and Coffin Ed Johnson—the two black detectives who appear in Himes's "Harlem Domestic" series.*]

Chester Himes had not had a great deal of experience writing about detectives when he met Marcel Duhamel in Paris. Criminals were more in his line of understanding. He had been one for a year and consorted with others for more than seven years of his life. Considering the reality from which he sprang, the fictional private eye probably would have appeared as a silly and romantic notion. His personal experience with police detectives was certainly not going to provide him with any heroic notions about them.

However, he did produce one story featuring detectives in his early career. In view of the path his writing took, it makes interesting reading today. **"He Knew,"** published in the December 2, 1933 issue of *Abbott's Monthly,* concerns a pair of tough and uncompromising Black police detectives. The story is much too short for much character development, but Himes created an interesting vignette in which he examined the problems faced by a working-class detective in resolving the conflict brought about by his loyalty to his job and the needs of his family.

Most detective story writers have avoided this conflict by keeping the detective single and unencumbered. Himes met this conflict head-on by spending much of the story inside his protagonist's head as he walked his beat. The detective (coincidentally named Jones), worries about how his children may be growing away from him and the values he has tried to instill in them.

In a somewhat predictable ending, Detective Jones and his partner unwittingly kill Jones' two teenaged sons during a gun battle in a darkened warehouse. Even before Jones realizes that it is his own sons he has killed, he voices some rather emotional and (for a detective hero) uncharacteristic feelings about the brutal realities of his work:

> A light, what he'd give for a light, Jones thought. He experienced a sudden distaste for his job—shooting men down in the darkness like rats, rats! For an instant he felt that he was going crazy.

Himes once related in an interview that the real impetus for the creation of Grave Digger Jones and Coffin Ed Johnson came from a pair of black police detectives that he knew in Watts during the 1940s. Himes described the pair as callous and brutal men who used an excess of physical force and emotional terror to keep the people in their precinct under control.

Himes' own first-hand experiences with the police, combined with his remembrance of the two brutal Los Angeles cops, must have been in force when he first conceived of Digger and Ed. Thus he probably did not intend them to be the main focus of his first detective novel. As if to underscore this feeling, his cynicism about policemen (of any color) comes out bluntly in this early description of them:

> Grave Digger and Coffin Ed weren't crooked detectives, but they were tough. They had to be tough to work in Harlem. Colored folks didn't respect colored cops. But they respected big shiny pistols and sudden death . . . They took their tribute, like all real cops, from the established underworld catering to the essential needs of the people—game keepers, madams, streetwalkers, numbers writers, numbers bankers. But they were rough on purse snatchers, muggers, burglars, con men, and all strangers working any racket.

In this unflattering yet sharply worded portrait, Himes is expressing his understanding of not only the detectives but also the world in which they operate. The detectives take bribes and protection money from gangsters and pimps, but their doing so is accepted on both sides of the fence. At the same time, they try not to interfere actively in any activity which the community tacitly supports, regardless of its technical illegality. Perhaps unwittingly, Himes was mimicking the traditional hard-boiled ethic which places justice over law.

While these policemen make up their own rules about upholding the law, they think nothing of terrorizing small-time criminals. Unlike the whores and gamblers, these criminals are prone to hurt someone physically while plying their trade, and the detectives consider this behavior off limits. Perhaps coincidentally, these petty criminals are also the only ones who are unlikely to be able to pay them off.

These attitudes Himes expresses may seem grotesque, but they are attitudes which are accepted in the Black netherworld about which he writes. By white standards, attitudes here are absurd, but it is an absurdity that the Negro inhabitants have lived with for so many years that it has become their reality. These are poor people with little hope. What little hope they have left they have invested in the short-term possibility of hitting the number for big money and the long-term possibility of getting into heaven.

A hero in Harlem is somebody who has beaten the system, risen above his origins, and yet remained a member of the community. A Johnny Perry (*The Crazy Kill*) who has served time on the chain gang for murder and survived to become the owner of a successful gambling club is someone to emulate. This is even more the case for flamboyant evangelists like Reverend Deke O'Malley (*Cotton Comes to Harlem*) and Sweet Prophet Brown (*The Big Gold Dream*). They have taken the Black man's salvation and turned it into a moneymaking business. They not only have wealth, power, and luxury, but also sit on the right hand of the Almighty.

Along with these flamboyant and, to white eyes, twisted visions of heroism and power, Himes' Black world also is filled with genuine grotesques. Writing in the same tradition as Dickens, Twain, and Faulkner, Himes created grotesque characters who, in their very absurdity, serve as models for certain kinds of human behavior. We may laugh at the tribulations of Jackson, Pinky, Dummy, and Reverend Short, but Himes makes it possible for the reader to understand their motivations and possibly even to recognize himself in their twisted bodies.

In a world like this, it is inevitable that any man who represents the white perspective, i.e. the established order, must be different. This is particularly true for a Black man. In Chandler's words, he must be "a complete man and a common man and yet an unusual man." That he will be considered an outsider is accepted from the outset.

In the classic tradition, the hard-boiled detective was a private agent, usually setting himself against the legally appointed or elected bureaucracy. His lack of status, power, and resources underscored the heroic fight of a lone hero against a corrupt power structure.

Digger and Ed, for all of Himes' attempts to make them seem a part of their grotesque backdrop, are much more outsiders in their world than the classic private eye is in his own. As Black cops in all-Black Harlem, they are worse than outsiders to others of their race: they are traitors, upholders of the white man's law. On the opposite side of the coin, although they represent the law, they are still Black men working within a white-dominated power structure. This is not so obvious when they are working alone, but it immediately becomes apparent whenever they find themselves working with white members of the force. The hostility and suspicion of the white officers is often so strong that they cannot ignore it. Many times they must act physically and violently, simply in order to assert themselves as men. An excellent example occurs in *All Shot Up* as the two Black men join a group of white officers at the scene of Black Beauty's death on Convent Street. A flip cop keeps using the word "nigger," in spite of warnings from Coffin Ed. When he uses the word one time too many, Ed beats the man to the ground.

At the beginning of *The Heat's On,* the two detectives find themselves trying to protect Pinky, an albino Negro who has turned in a false fire alarm, from a group of enraged firemen. When they try to calm the angry firemen down, the group of white men ceases to see them as cops, only as two Negroes trying to protect another one. They are nearly hurt in the melee.

Thus Digger and Ed are separate and apart from their fellow Blacks, the police department they serve, and the white power structure in which they try to work. It is one of the ironies of Digger and Ed's lives that they do not begin to really appreciate this apartness until they are on their last case, *Blind Man With A Pistol.* Here they find that they are completely unable to make any headway in the case because of the hostility and suspicion of their Black brethren (with whom they seem to be out of touch) and the prejudice and venality of their white superiors who actively inhibit their progress.

Like Chandler and Hammett, Himes came to the crime novel from a more traditional literary background. He had read widely in prison and was able to draw on other traditions in the creation of his work. Therefore the Harlem he created was not akin to the realistic California that so many fictional detectives walked in. Rather, it is closer to a Dickensian village that is separated by color and grotesque attitudes from the rest of the world.

Himes was frank in admitting to Maurice Duhamel that he knew nothing about detective stories. As a virtually self-educated man, it is probable that he had read very little of the genre he was about to enter. In some measure, this was to his credit, because it allowed him to start out unencumbered by the baggage of his predecessors.

When Grave Digger and Coffin Ed first make their appearance one-third of the way through *For Love of Imabelle,* the prior actions of the other characters already have prepared us for the bizarre figure that these men cut as they keep order in the Savoy ticket line:

> The famous Harlem detective team of Coffin Ed Johnson and Grave Digger Jones had been assigned to keep order.
>
> Both were tall, loose-jointed, sloppily-dressed, ordinary-looking dark-brown colored men. But there was nothing ordinary about their pistols. They carried specially made long-barreled nickel-plated .38-caliber revolvers, and at the moment they had them in their hands.

Himes makes a deliberate contradiction in this description. The shabbiness of the two detectives seems to cast them in the same proletarian mold of other detectives, but we can tell already that they are not as ordinary as Himes indicates. Having told us in the same breath that they are the "famous Harlem detective team," Himes deliberately invites us to take another look at them. It is clear that everyone in the Savoy ticket line knows them by sight, and it is equally clear that they command immediate respect by virtue of their presence.

In their tall lankiness there is something, too, of the western lawman who stands loosely in the dusty street with his gun held ready to do battle with evil. It is an image that Himes reinforces on a number of occasions. For example, when the pair arrive at the scene of Val's murder in *The Crazy Kill,* Chink Charlie is heard to say "Jesus Christ. Now we've got those damned Wild West Gunmen here to mess up everything!" Later in the same story this image of the small-town lawman is called up when Coffin Ed tells another character that " . . . me and Digger are two country Harlem dicks who live in this village . . . . "

So little is different about the two detectives that, in the early stories, they almost seem to be interchangeable. In *The Heat's On* Himes tells us:

> Both of them looked just as red-eyed, greasy-faced, sweaty and evil as all the other colored people gathered about, combatants and spectators alike. They were of a similar size and build to other "working stiffs"—big broad-shouldered, loose-jointed and flat-footed. Their faces bore marks and scars similar to any colored street fighter. Grave Digger's was full of lumps where felons had hit him from time to time with various weapons; while Coffin Ed's was a patchwork of scars where skin had been grafted over the burns left by acid thrown into his face by Hank.

In many ways, they seem like an inseparable pair of twins. They dress alike, usually in black alpaca suits and battered shapeless hats. Both wear their hair cut short and each speaks in a blunt, profane way.

They are also brothers-in-arms, and as if to prove it each carries an identical long-barrelled .38 special revolver built on a .44 frame. They carry these weapons in identical tan shoulder holsters which the detectives keep smeared on the inside with seal fat in order to facilitate a quick draw.

Himes seems to dwell more on these guns than he does on the lives and habits of detectives themselves. He has endowed these pistols with an almost supernatural aura. Jones and Johnson do not have to draw these weapons; they seem to appear in their owners' hands of their own volition and with miraculous speed. The two men brandish them like the weapons of medieval knights-errant and, indeed, they often seem to give the pair the same kind of invulnerability and invincibility as magic swords.

Significantly whenever one of the pair is *hors de combat,* the still-functioning partner makes a point of taking the fallen brother's revolver with him. Possibly it was Himes' way of allowing the missing partner to remain present in spirit during these crisis situations. In *For Love of Imabelle,* after Coffin Ed has acid thrown in his face by Hank, Grave Digger shoots Hank through the right eye with his own revolver and then through the left with Coffin Ed's before the killer can fall to the ground. Before firing the second shot Digger says "For you, Ed." After Digger is shot from behind in *The Heat's On,* Ed breaks into his friend's home to get his revolver before taking it to set a trap and kill their assailants.

In spite of the many obvious similarities between the two men, Himes eventually revealed subtle differences between them. It is likely that in the beginning Himes saw no need to differentiate between the two men. The briefest of readings of *For Love of Imabelle* reveals that the story could have been written without them. Although Himes gave the two detectives a greater part in his next book, the main emphasis was still on the relationship of Johnny and Dulcy Perry and the secrets kept by the half-mad Reverend Short.

By the time of the third book in the series (*The Real Cool Killers*), some obvious differences between the two detectives began to appear. The first tension in the story harks back to the time Coffin Ed was splashed with acid in *For Love of Imabelle.* It is clear from the beginning of *Real Cool Killers* that since this traumatic attack, Ed has not been the same man and his fear has made him erratic and dangerous.

Himes made this injury central to Ed's character from then on. Ed is a tough, resilient man who not only has been badly traumatized, but who also is no longer quite sane. His hatred of criminals is now tinged with more than a hint of hysteria, and his partner can no longer completely trust him in a tight spot. On more than one occasion, Digger has to restrain him physically to prevent the murder of someone who has unknowingly tripped Coffin Ed's deadly switch.

This quality is first brought into focus at the beginning of *The Real Cool Killers.* When Ed and Digger are in the street in the aftermath of the Greek's death, they attempt to question a group of teenagers dressed in Arab costumes. The teenagers, all members of a gang, are disrespectful to the two officers; at one point, one of them breaks wind in their faces. Ed is already angry when one boy attempts to splash him with the contents of a bottle. Wild with fear that the bottle may contain acid, Ed responds with gunfire that kills the boy and wounds an innocent bystander. Digger has to fight his friend to keep him from further violence and is hurt in the bargain. To Ed's chagrin and shame, they later learn that the bottle contained harmless perfume.

One of Ed's trademarks is a facial tic in the scarred side of his face. When the tic starts, it is a signal that he is likely to do anything. In *Cotton Comes to Harlem* he gets so angry during the questioning of Iris O'Malley that he almost chokes her to death before Digger can call him back to sanity.

As disturbed as Ed is, he is not insensitive to his problem. After he realizes he has not only killed the teen gangster in *Cool Killers* for nothing but also has wounded an innocent bystander in the process, he is flushed with embarrassment. After he nearly hurts Chink Charlie during an interrogation in *The Crazy Kill,* he goes out into the hallway and cries with shame.

When Ed's paranoia and hate are combined with guilt, he is at his most terrifying and sadistic. Believing Digger has been killed in *The Heat's On* because of his bad judgment, he launches himself on a mad chase all over town to track the killers. In the process, he threatens and beats a score of people before reaching Red Johnny's house.

Himes' capacity for depicting graphic violence and sadism is at a peak during this scene. When the pain— and guilt—crazed Ed fails to get the answers he wants from the pimp, he bashes the man's teeth in with the barrel of his revolver. Not content with this display of violence, Himes describes in sickening detail how the wounded man coughs up blood and bits of teeth. In an uncharacteristically humane gesture, Ed uses a spoon to grab the man's slippery tongue and keeps him from choking to death.

When Ed finally locates the two-timing Ginny, what little humanity he has left is fast disappearing. He strips the woman and throws her naked body on a couch and ties her down. With a knife he cuts the skin in a thin line six inches across her throat. To make certain she gets the point, he shows her what he has done in a hand mirror. Even her stark terror fails to move this implacable man to pity:

> He knew that he had gone beyond the line; that he
> had gone outside of human restraint; he knew that

what he was doing was unforgivable. But he didn't want any more lies.

Few fictional detectives have ever gone so far. For Ed, the job, his guilt, and his own personal thirst for vengeance have put the solving of the case before anything, even human decency. People whom he has regarded in the past with no more than casual contempt have ceased to rate even the slightest consideration in the face of his rage.

Strangely enough, even in this extreme Ed does not completely lose touch with the ideals that made him become a detective. When Ginny offers to cut him in on the loot if he will kill the members of the gang, Himes writes that:

> He was caught for a moment in a hurt as terrible as any he had ever known.

> "Is everybody crooked on this mother-raping earth?" It came like a cry of agony torn out of him.

In Ed, Himes has created a very complex character. He has been presented to us as a cynical, hard-nosed lawman whose pragmatic outlook on life has made him one of the most feared figures in Harlem. It is ironic that in Ed this pragmatism seems to be balanced with a simplistic belief in right and wrong, a fact that prevents him (and probably all cops) from realizing the ultimate uselessness of law (and lawmen) in a society that is governed completely by corrupt influences. Ginny's proposition is such a shock to him that, possibly for the first time, he realizes just how terrible his world, symbolized by Harlem, has become.

Another important incongruity in Coffin Ed's character is that, as brutal as he is with his enemies, he is at bottom a devoted family man with a boyish sense of humor. For example, when he and Digger visit the Great Man night club for dinner, they decide to have watermelon for dessert just as the floor show commences. The sight of the naked, jiggling bottoms of the four sepia-colored showgirls creates such a temptation in him that he begins spitting watermelon seeds at their backsides. Only the quick thinking of the more dignified Digger saves them from being embroiled in a free-for-all.

Ed owns a home next door to his partner in Astoria, Long Island. He has a teenaged daughter named Evelyn whom we meet only once in *The Real Cool Killers.* It is apparent that he is very fond of her: after he is temporarily suspended for the shooting of the teenaged

Himes in France, 1963.

"Arab," his first thought is to go home and spend some time with her or take her to a movie.

When he and Digger discover later that she is being held hostage by Sheik, the head of the teen gang, Ed has himself suspended by a wire around his ankles over the edge of the apartment building. He hangs there for 20 minutes with the wire cutting into his legs, waiting for the chance to shoot Sheik and save Evelyn. Afterwards, he does not chastise his daughter for her thoughtless rebellion but instead quietly takes her home. Possibly he has the insight to realize that he is partially responsible for her lapse in moral judgment.

We see very little else of Ed's or Digger's family life during the course of their adventures. Ed's wife is named Molly and we see her briefly with Digger's wife, Stella, after Digger is taken to the hospital in *The Heat's On.*

We see Digger's wife only one other time. She awakens him in *Cotton Comes to Harlem* when the word comes that Deke O'Malley has escaped and killed two cops. She fixes him Nescafe and warns him to be careful, although she seems far too wise to believe that he will. Digger has two young daughters whom we never meet. We hear at one point that they are away at summer camp, an experience that was once considered a luxury for the inner-city children of New York.

The fact that Digger and Ed have wives and families is something that sets them apart from most of the rest of the hard-boiled world. The time-honored tough guy ethic mandates that the job must be everything, that a detective doesn't really have the right to a family or the time to indulge one. Himes seems to make it possible for Digger and Ed to have families by placing them on a work shift that lasts from late afternoon through the early morning. These night-owl hours allow them to fight crime in the all-night world of Harlem while the respectable world in Astoria is asleep.

It is clear from the story line of *Real Cool Killers,* however, that Himes realized the strain that police work could place on a policeman's family. The horrors that Ed faces on a day-to-day basis, combined with the physical and emotional wounds that he must cope with, undoubtedly have a negative effect on his personal life and his relationship with his daughter.

Ed shows a spark of real individuality and one of the rare instances of independence from his partner when we discover another woman in his life near the end of *Blind Man With a Pistol.* There we discover that he has had, or is having, an affair with a beautiful light-skinned hooker named Barbara Tyne. The discovery comes as a shock to Digger, who expresses an uncharacteristic irritation with his partner. Peculiarly, Digger's irritation is more like what one would expect from a deceived wife than from a male work partner. His behavior seems to suggest that, to Digger, his relationship with Ed is supposed to enjoy that same sanctity. At the same time, Ed's failure to confide his infidelity to his partner shows

a rather provincial embarrassment and shame over his breach of societal rules.

Of the two detectives, Grave Digger Jones comes off as the more reasonable personality and the real brains of the team. Even after he is badly wounded in the line of duty himself, he never becomes as trigger-happy as Ed. Indeed, he takes the responsibility, unbidden, for calming Ed down at those times when he has gone off the deep end. It is equally characteristic of Digger that he does so at great personal risk.

Grave Digger is typically the spokesperson for the team, especially if they are called upon to report their findings or explain their actions to a superior officer. It is perhaps because Digger is the more thoughtful one that he often expresses pity or rage or anguish over the face of victims or the callous indifference on the part of the authorities to Black suffering. In *The Real Cool Killers* he responds to a white man's criticism with

> "I'm just a cop," Grave Digger said thickly. "If you white people insist on coming up to Harlem where you force colored people to live in vice-and-crime-ridden slums, it's my job to see that you are safe."

In *Cotton Comes to Harlem* Digger offers the corrupt precinct captain Brice a chance to crack the case by letting Iris O'Malley escape from jail but the cowardly Brice will not take the risk himself. However, he will allow Digger and Ed to carry out their plan if they are willing to take the heat if the plan goes awry. Digger tells Brice "I wouldn't do this for nobody but my own black people" before he storms out to get Iris.

Digger is something of an amateur sociologist. Possibly better than the professors in their ivory towers, he realizes what the race problem is all about. He sees the young lives corrupted every day by drugs, unemployment, and hopelessness. He sees the jobless turn to crime when there is no other way to put food on the table.

His realizations have turned him bitter, so bitter that he sometimes explodes with pent-up rage:

> We got the highest crime rate on earth among the colored people of Harlem. And there ain't but three things to do about it; make the criminals pay for it— you don't want to do that; pay the people enough to live decently—you ain't going to do that; so all that's left is let 'em eat one another up.

Digger's anger is much slower to come to the surface than is Ed's, but the warning signs are distinctive to those who know him. The swelling of his neck until the veins pop and the cottony, dry quality of his voice let the reader and his listener know that dynamite is about to explode.

Because he has a better grip on his emotions, Digger is much more ruthless and calculating than Ed. Never having been traumatized in the way his partner has, Digger has more control over his hatred and instinct for violence.

This control is graphically exemplified in *For Love of Imabelle* when Digger accidentally finds Imabelle (the eponymous heroine of the story) in the Harlem precinct station. He takes advantage of the fact that Imabelle doesn't recognize him and enjoys the preening, whorish performance she puts on for him before he slaps her out of the chair.

Only one time during his career does Grave Digger lose such complete control of himself that he attacks someone in a rage. This instance occurs near the end of *The Real Cool Killers* after he has arrested Ready Belcher and Big Smiley. Discovering that Sheik has barricaded himself in the apartment with hostages, the badly frightened Ready reveals that Coffin Ed's daughter, Evelyn, is in the apartment.

Digger has known for some time that Ready has been holding out a piece of vital information. Upon hearing this startling news, Digger has to be restrained to keep him from beating the craven pimp to death.

Under normal circumstances, however, Digger is capable of subtleties that would be beyond his violent partner. A typical example occurs in *Cotton Comes to Harlem* when Digger threatens to shoot Iris O'Malley through the head unless she reveals the whereabouts of the stolen money. With unquestioning loyalty, Ed immediately covers all of the other police officers in the room. The other officers know that Digger would never commit murder, but they also realize that the volatile Ed will shoot them if they dare to interfere with him.

As far as is known, Digger is faithful to his wife, Stella, but at least once he is severely tempted. When he meets the voluptuous Lila Holmes in *All Shot Up,* sparks fly between the two. Digger appraises her in an aggressive way that is completely out of character for him. In spite of her obvious sophistication and contempt for Digger's lowly position, Lila feels the heat of the meeting.

After Lila is badly wounded later helping the detectives rescue her husband, Casper, Digger comforts her while they wait for the ambulance and strokes her hair. In his typical fashion, Himes closes the door on his detectives' private lives, and we never find out if Digger and Lila consummate their passion for one another.

Following the tradition of other hard-boiled writers, Himes purposely kept the origins of Digger and Ed shadowy. We discover from Mamie Pullen in *The Crazy Kill* that the two grew up in Harlem and went to public school there. During *Blind Man With a Pistol* they mention having been in the army during World War II and reminisce about service in Paris.

How they got on the police force is less clear. A significant conversation takes place between them and Casper Holmes during *All Shot Up.* As they begin to annoy Casper by asking too many pointed questions regarding his activities, the powerful Black politician reminds them that he got them their jobs on the police force. Unwilling to allow him that power over them, the

detectives counter that their high marks on the civil service examination and their military service might have had just as much to do with their subsequent hiring. This assertion seems to indicate that the pair were decorated for distinguished combat experience.

Although they are native New Yorkers, their appetites are those of rural southern Negroes. In *Cotton Comes to Harlem* they twice go to their favorite restaurant, Mammy Louise's, for "soul food." The first time they order double orders of ribs with side dishes of black-eyed peas, rice, okra, collard greens with fresh tomatoes and onions, and deep-dish apple pie and vanilla ice cream. Later they return for a meal of barbecued opossum with candied yams, collard greens, and okra.

In *All Shot Up* they also visit Mammy Louise. They are devouring Mammy's specialty "chicken feetsy" when they get a radio call which brings them into the case. During *The Heat's On* they visit the Great Man night club where they enjoy New Orleans gumbo. The recipe, which is not the recipe used in most New Orleans restaurants, includes a bizarre mix of fresh pork, chicken gizzards, hog testicles, and giant shrimp in a base of okra, sweet potatoes, and twenty-seven varieties of seasonings, spices, and herbs.

Neither detective is a big drinker, but several times during their adventures they stop at bars for a whiskey or beer. When their car heater doesn't work during the terrible winter of *All Shot Up,* the pair drink from a bottle of whiskey to keep warm, and the normally sensible Digger gets rather frisky from it.

Although the detectives associate with any number of underworld characters with whom they are on good terms, the only person in their adventures who can come close to being called a friend is their immediate superior, Lieutenant Anderson. Anderson is a figure whose personality never really develops during the eight stories, although he is normally supportive of their actions. He seems to like the two Black detectives, and in turn they are good-natured and respectful with him. Often we see him trying, unsuccessfully, to use Black slang properly, and the pair either smile tolerantly or kid him good-naturedly about it.

Anderson is much more important to the stories than his position of "good" white man or titular superior would imply. His major function is often to supply an audience for the pair when they rage in frustration against a system that fosters and even encourages the corruption which they must constantly battle.

Anderson also serves as a moderating influence on the detectives. Since he seldom has to go out on the street, the rage and frustration that Digger and Ed feel never develop in his personality. Thus he tries to keep them (and himself) out of trouble with higher authority by reminding them that police, even in a violent society, have to answer to the public:

"I'm on your side. I know what you're up against here in Harlem. I know your beat. It's my beat, too. But the commissioner feels you've killed too many people in this area—" He held up his hand to ward off an interruption. "Hoodlums, I know—dangerous hoodlums—and you've killed in self-defense. But you've been on the carpet a number of times and a short time ago you had three months' suspensions. Newspapers have been yapping about police brutality in Harlem and now various civic bodies have taken up the cry."

Anderson often finds himself the man in the middle. His immediate superior is Captain Brice, a well-fed, white bureaucrat whose noticeable prosperity is the result of graft. Brice is far too interested in his own concerns to be bothered with the demands of justice. Brice comes very close to feeding Digger and Ed to the wolves on a couple of occasions, and Anderson does what he can to prevent his doing so.

Although he is an experienced police officer, Anderson never really gets used to Harlem or the seemingly senseless crimes that make running his precinct such an exercise in frustration. At times, he resembles a Greek Chorus as he describes the bizarre life that continues outside the walls of the station house:

> Man kills his wife with an axe for burning his breakfast pork chop . . . man sees stranger wearing his own new suit, slashes him with a razor . . . man dressed as Cherokee Indian splits white bartender's skull with homemade tomahawk . . . twenty-five men arrested for trying to chase all the white people out of Harlem—
> "It's Independence Day," Grave Digger interrupted.

Anderson comes off as a believable boss, even though we see very little of him. He listens to his detectives' reports and gives them their instructions in a business-like way. Once, when Coffin Ed shows a characteristic disregard for a killing, Anderson chews him out and sends him packing. This no-nonsense side of Anderson is balanced by the number of times we see him drinking with his men in a friendly atmosphere.

As the series comes to a close, Anderson is shown to be just as human and, by implication, just as weak as anyone else. During *Blind Man With A Pistol* it becomes clear that Captain Brice is about to retire and that Anderson has been promised command of the precinct. In order to win this promotion and the graft that goes with it, Anderson is forced to help his superiors prevent Ed and Digger from discovering the clues necessary to solving the crime. To allow them to succeed will open up a large-scale homosexual scandal which undoubtedly involves important public figures, possibly of both races.

Blind Man With A Pistol is the final story in the series, and it shows Himes at his most bitter and mistrustful. Anderson's fall from grace is the final blow that symbolizes a world so corrupt that even Digger and Ed can't save it. Their rambunctious zeal and their knowledge of underworld life are not sufficient weapons in a world where faceless and powerful men can manipulate both the legal machinery of a city and the emotions and actions of the common people.

Although Digger and Ed lack the polish of Marlowe and Parker's Spenser, they can be thinking detective none-theless. Although they seem rough and unlettered, they make it clear that they have read a book and understood what they have read. During their adventures they draw parallels between their cases and scenes from books such as Hemingway's *For Whom The Bell Tolls* and Maxim Gorky's *The Bystander.*

On several occasions they make rather startling deductions from clues other detectives have missed. The sight of a jacked up car near the scene of Snake Hip's bizarre death, for example, is enough to convince them that a local tire thief has probably witnessed the death. Furthermore, they reason, a man out stealing tires during a blizzard must have a "hot" woman to support. Both contentions prove to be true.

As Black men trying to lead meaningful lives in a white-dominated society, they have made as much of a success of their lives as they can. They have been able to purchase homes in a quiet, middle-class suburb and provide decent lives for their wives and children. At the end of their adventures, however, they are visibly aging, and after ten years they still have not been promoted from the lowest detective grade. Because their salaries have not kept pace with inflation, they still owe money on their houses, and it seems clear that they will remain in debt.

They have changed significantly from the two detectives who took protection money in *For Love of Imabelle.* Like the Continental Op, Philip Marlowe, and other classic detectives, they have joined what William Marling calls "the round table of parsimonious knights." In the world of the hard-boiled detective, it is necessary for the hero to remain poor if he is going to retain his essential honesty. True to that world, Digger and Ed have remained pure, rejecting the opportunities they are offered over the years to enrich themselves.

They have retained their honesty, often at the cost of their emotional security and the love of their families but they are affected by a tragic flaw. They have let the world in which they must live and work twist them into creatures who are sometimes more like beasts than men. Their success in solving crimes has been overbalanced by the sheer savagery with which they pursue criminals.

In a telling scene near the beginning of *All Shot Up,* Mammy Louise berates them for beating and killing so many people. Hurt by this accusation, Digger and Ed protest that the people they have hurt all have been criminals and that they are not by nature violent men. Suddenly, they have to leave the restaurant to answer a radio call in their car. Their precipitate rush causes Mammy Louise's nervous bulldog to jump at them, and without thinking, Digger nearly shoots the animal. Only

Mammy Louise's restraining hand prevents the foolish dog from becoming another of Digger and Ed's victims.

In his now-classic essay on Himes' detective fiction, Raymond Nelson summed up these characters and their saga by saying "if the vehicle itself is small, Himes's accomplishments within it are not, and the residual portrait left by these books—of Coffin Ed and Grave Digger outlines against the dull, lurid light of a criminal city—is one of the compelling images of our time."

It is possible that Nelson allowed himself to be a little too romantic in his assessment of these characters, but it is hard to fault him for it. In the work of the best writers of the hard-boiled detective thriller, the heroes have all been men who, for their own reasons, placed the safety of the innocent and the search for truth over and above their own prosperity and well-being. Himes has created two heroes who fit that mold and, at the same time, heralded the beginning of a third wave of hard-boiled heroes who have reshaped and given new life to one of the few truly American literary genres. (pp. 25-37)

> *Robert E. Skinner, in his* Two Guns from Harlem: The Detective Fiction of Chester Himes, *Bowling Green State University Popular Press, 1989, 190 p.*

FURTHER READING

Margolies, Edward. "Race and Sex: The Novels of Chester Himes." In his *Native Sons: A Critical Study of Twentieth-Century Negro American Authors,* pp. 87-101. Philadelphia: J. B. Lippincott Company, 1968.
> Critical overview of *The Third Generation, If He Hollers Let Him Go, Lonely Crusade, The Primitive,* and *Pinktoes.*

Nelson, Raymond. "Domestic Harlem: The Detective Fiction of Chester Himes." *Virginia Quarterly Review* 48, No. 2 (Spring 1972): 260-76.
> Evaluates Himes's detective novels, concluding: "Himes is a fighter, a sort of literary Muhammad Ali (or, perhaps more accurately, Jack Johnson), and he writes with the same intense ferocity with which he might knock a man down."

Rabinowitz, Peter J. "Chandler Comes to Harlem: Racial Politics in the Thrillers of Chester Himes." In *The Sleuth and the Scholar: Origins, Evolution, and Current Trends in Detective Fiction,* edited by Barbara A. Rader and Howard G. Zettler, pp. 19-29. New York: Greenwood Press, 1986.
> Compares Himes's detective novels with those of Raymond Chandler.

Willeford, Charles. "Chester Himes and His Novels of Absurdity." *American Visions* 3, No. 4 (August 1988): 43-4.
> Brief summary of Himes's novels. The critic observes: "Himes certainly deserves acclaim for the shrewd talent he brought to the detective genre.... *Lonely Crusade* and *The Primitive* are still the novels he will, in all probability, be remembered for...."

Pauline Elizabeth Hopkins

1859-1930

(Also wrote under pseudonym Sarah A. Allen) American novelist, dramatist, short story writer, editor, and biographer.

A minor black author of the late nineteenth and early twentieth centuries, Hopkins was one of the first writers to introduce racial and social themes into the framework of traditional nineteenth-century romance novels. In her most important publication, *Contending Forces: A Romance Illustrative of Negro Life North and South* (1900), she propounded the ideology of W. E. B. Du Bois, an early advocate of liberal education and political rights for black Americans. Throughout her work Hopkins examined racial injustice, challenged widely held notions about her race, and emphasized self-reliance as an important component of social advancement for black Americans.

Hopkins was born in Portland, Maine, and grew up in Boston, Massachusetts, where she attended public schools and graduated from Girls' High School. She was twenty-one when her musical drama *Slaves' Escape; or, The Underground Railroad* (1880) was produced, with Hopkins and members of her family in the cast. For several years following this production Hopkins toured as a singer with her family's performing group, the Hopkins' Colored Troubadors. During the 1890s she worked at various clerical jobs and as a public lecturer. In 1900 Hopkins's short story "The Mystery Within Us" appeared in the first issue of the *Colored American* magazine. The same year her first novel, *Contending Forces*, was published. During the early 1900s Hopkins served on the editorial staff of the *Colored American* and eventually became the magazine's literary editor. Her subsequent novels, short stories, and nonfiction appeared primarily in the *Colored American* between 1901 and 1903. Three of her novels, *Hagar's Daughter: A Story of Southern Caste Prejudice* (1901-02), *Winona: A Tale of Negro Life in the South and Southwest* (1902), and *Of One Blood; or, The Hidden Self* (1902-03), were first serialized in the magazine. Ill health caused Hopkins to leave the magazine's staff in 1904, but she continued writing and occasionally published fiction and nonfiction in black-owned journals while supporting herself largely through clerical work. She died in a fire in 1930.

Contending Forces is a historical romance tracing the experiences of one black family throughout the nineteenth century, from slavery in the West Indies and the American South to freedom in Boston and New Orleans. The novel illuminates the political, economic, and social problems encountered by blacks in antebellum America. Hopkins stated that she wrote *Contending Forces* in order to "faithfully portray the inmost thoughts and feelings of the Negro with all the fire and

romance which lie dormant in our history" and to help "raise the stigma of degradation" from her race—something that she maintained black people had to do for themselves. *Contending Forces* earned Hopkins neither literary fame nor financial success during her lifetime, and it began to receive critical attention only after her death. In an early survey of black American authors, Vernon Loggins considered *Contending Forces* overly complicated and sensational. In 1948 Hugh M. Gloster also pronounced Hopkins an untalented narrator, but he commended *Contending Forces* for providing "interesting sidelights on the struggles of a middle-class Negro family for education, employment, and social adjustment in post-bellum Boston."

Throughout her career Hopkins protested the inequities suffered by her race, advocating assimilation and integration with the white community as a remedy to racial injustice. Hopkins's presumption of the superior value of white culture and her advocacy of assimilation have been of particular interest to modern critics. Gwendolyn

Brooks, for example, criticized Hopkins for her assimilationist outlook and admiration of the dominant culture, and Joseph Rosenbaum has observed that in *Contending Forces* "beauty and success are judged by the white man's standard." Most commentators agree that *Contending Forces* is overplotted and confusingly constructed; nevertheless, they consider it an important historical and sociological document that portrays the effect of Du Bois's social and educational programs on the black community and sheds light on the role of black women in nineteenth-century America.

Hopkins remains an obscure figure in American literature. The critical neglect of her work has most often been attributed to her unexceptional narrative technique, although the relative unavailability of her works and the general neglect suffered by female authors have also been cited as reasons for her obscurity. Nevertheless, a number of commentators have argued that her fiction merits wider attention, and many have praised *Contending Forces* as a poignant reflection of Hopkins's era.

(For further information about Hopkins's life and works, see *Dictionary of Literary Biography*, Vol. 50: *Afro-American Writers before the Harlem Renaissance* and *Twentieth-Century Literary Criticism*, Vol. 28.)

PRINCIPAL WORKS

*Slaves' Escape; or, The Underground Railroad (drama) 1880; also published as *Peculiar Sam; or, The Underground Railroad* [revised edition]

Contending Forces: A Romance Illustrative of Negro Life North and South (novel) 1900

"The Mystery Within Us" (short story) 1900; published in periodical *Colored American*

Famous Men of the Negro Race (biographical sketches) 1901-02; published in periodical *Colored American*

Famous Women of the Negro Race (biographical sketches) 1901-02; published in periodical *Colored American*

Hagar's Daughter: A Story of Southern Caste Prejudice [as Sarah A. Allen] (novel) 1901-02; published in periodical *Colored American*

Winona: A Tale of Negro Life in the South and Southwest (novel) 1902; published in periodical *Colored American*

Of One Blood; or, The Hidden Self (novel) 1902-03; published in periodical *Colored American*

A Primer of Facts Pertaining to the Greatness of Africa (nonfiction) 1905

Topsy Templeton (novella) 1916; published in periodical *New Era*

---

*The publication date of the revised edition of this work is unknown.

Pauline E. Hopkins (essay date 1900)

[*In the following excerpt from the preface of* Contending Forces, *Hopkins discusses why she wrote this, her first novel.*]

In giving this little romance [**Contending Forces**] expression in print, I am not actuated by a desire for notoriety or for profit, but to do all that I can in an humble way to raise the stigma of degradation from my race.

While I make no apology for my somewhat abrupt and daring venture within the wide field of romantic literature, I ask the kind indulgence of the generous public for the many crudities which I know appear in the work, and their approval of whatever may impress them as being of value to the Negro race and to the world at large.

The colored race has historians, lecturers, ministers, poets, judges and lawyers,—men of brilliant intellects who have arrested the favorable attention of this busy, energetic nation. But, after all, it is the simple, homely tale, unassumingly told, which cements the bond of brotherhood among all classes and all complexions.

Fiction is of great value to any people as a preserver of manners and customs—religious, political and social. It is a record of growth and development from generation to generation. *No one will do this for us; we must ourselves develop the men and women who will faithfully portray the inmost thoughts and feelings of the Negro with all the fire and romance which lie dormant in our history*, and, as yet, unrecognized by writers of the Anglo-Saxon race. (pp. 13-14)

In these days of mob violence, when lynch-law is raising its head like a venomous monster, more particularly in the southern portion of the great American republic, the retrospective mind will dwell upon the history of the past, seeking there a solution of these monstrous outbreaks under a government founded upon the greatest and brightest of principles for the elevation of mankind. While we ponder the philosophy of cause and effect, the world is horrified by a fresh outbreak, and the shocked mind wonders that in this—the brightest epoch of the Christian era—*such things are.*

Mob-law is nothing new. Southern sentiment has not been changed; the old ideas close in analogy to the spirit of the buccaneers, who formed in many instances the first settlers of the Southland, still prevail, and break forth clothed in new forms to force the whole republic to an acceptance of its principles.

"Rule or ruin" is the motto which is committing the most beautiful portion of our glorious country to a cruel revival of piratical methods; and, finally, to the introduction of *Anarchy*. Is this not so? Let us compare the happenings of one hundred—two hundred years ago, with those of today. The difference between then and now, if any there be, is so slight as to be scarcely worth mentioning. The atrocity of the acts committed one hundred years ago are duplicated today, when slavery is supposed no longer to exist.

I have tried to tell an impartial story, leaving it to the reader to draw conclusions. I have tried to portray our hard struggles here in the North to obtain a respectable living and a partial education. I have presented both sides of the dark picture—lynching and concubinage—truthfully and without vituperation, pleading for that justice of heart and mind for my people which the Anglo-Saxon in America never withholds from suffering humanity. (pp. 14-15)

I have introduced enough of the exquisitely droll humor peculiar to the Negro (a work like this would not be complete without it) to give a bright touch to an otherwise gruesome subject. (p. 16)

> *Pauline E. Hopkins, in a preface to her* Contending Forces: A Romance Illustrative of Negro Life North and South, *1900. Reprint by Southern Illinois University Press, 1978, pp. 13-16.*

Cornelia A. Condict (essay date 1903)

[*In the following excerpt from a letter written to the* Colored American *magazine in 1903, Condict addresses the prevalence of interracial love affairs in the magazine's fiction and recommends a different focus. Hopkins, the magazine's literary editor, replied to Condict's letter in the same issue (see excerpt below dated 1903).*]

I have been taking and reading with interest the *Colored American* magazine.

If I found it more helpful to Christian work among your people I would continue to take it.

May I make a comment on the stories, especially those that have been serial. Without exception they have been of love between the colored and whites. Does that mean that your novelists can imagine no love beautiful and sublime within the range of the colored race, for each other? I have seen beautiful home life and love in families altogether of Negro blood.

The stories of these tragic mixed loves will not commend themselves to your white readers and will not elevate the colored readers. I believe your novelists could do with a consecrated imagination and pen, more for the elevation of home life and love, than perhaps any other one class of writers.

What Dickens did for the neglected working class of England, some writer could do for the neglected colored people of America. (pp. 398-99)

> *Cornelia A. Condict, in a letter to the editor in* The Colored American Magazine, *Vol. VI, No. 5, March, 1903, pp. 398-99.*

Pauline E. Hopkins (essay date 1903)

[*In the following excerpt, Hopkins replies to a letter from Cornelia A. Condict to the* Colored American *magazine (see excerpt above dated 1903), challenging Condict's perspective and explaining her rationale for the subject matter of her own fiction.*]

My stories are definitely planned to show the obstacles persistently placed in our paths by a dominant race to subjugate us spiritually. Marriage is made illegal between the races and yet the mulattoes increase. Thus the shadow of corruption falls on the blacks and on the whites, without whose aid the mulattoes would not exist. And then the hue and cry goes abroad of the immorality of the Negro and the disgrace that the mulattoes are to this nation. Amalgamation is an institution designed by God for some wise purpose, and mixed bloods have always exercised a great influence on the progress of human affairs. I sing of the *wrongs* of a race that ignorance of their pitiful condition may be changed to intelligence and must awaken compassion in the hearts of the just.

The home life of Negroes is beautiful in many instances; warm affection is there between husband and wife, and filial and paternal tenderness in them is not surpassed by any other race of the human family. But Dickens wrote not of the joys and beauties of English society; I believe he was the author of *Bleak House* and *David Copperfield*. If he had been an American, and with his trenchant pen had exposed the abuses practiced by the Southern whites upon the blacks—had told the true story of how wealth, intelligence and femininity has stooped to choose for a partner in sin, the degraded (?) Negro whom they affect to despise, Dickens would have been advised to shut up or get out. I believe Jesus Christ when on earth rebuked the Pharisees in this wise: "Ye hypocrites, ye expect to be heard for your much speaking"; "O wicked and adulterous (?) nation, how can ye escape the damnation of hell?" He didn't go about patting those old sinners on the back saying, "All right boys, fix me up and the Jews will get there all right. Money talks. Divy on the money you take in the exchange business of the synagogue, and it'll be all right with God." Jesus told the thing as it was and the Jews crucified him! I am glad to receive this criticism for it shows more clearly than ever that white people don't understand *what pleases Negroes*. You are between Scylla and Charybdis: If you please the author of this letter and your white clientele, you will lose your Negro patronage. If you cater to the *demands* of the Negro trade, away goes Mrs. —. I have sold to many whites and have received great praise for the work I am doing in exposing the social life of the Southerners and the wickedness of their caste prejudice.

Let the good work go on. Opposition is the life of an enterprise; criticism tells you that you are doing something. (pp. 399-400)

Pauline E. Hopkins, in a reply to a letter in
The Colored American Magazine, *Vol. VI,
No. 5, March, 1903, pp. 399-400.*

Gwendolyn Brooks (essay date 1978)

[*Brooks is an American poet, novelist, and educator
whose second volume of poetry,* Annie Allen *(1949),
won the Pulitzer Prize in 1950. In the following
excerpt, she compares Hopkins with other twentieth-
century black writers, examines Hopkins's view of the
dominant white culture of her time, and comments on
her assimilationist outlook.*]

No, [*Contending Forces*] is not *Native Son, Invisible
Man, Jubilee, Roots.* Pauline Hopkins is not Richard
Wright, Ralph Ellison, Margaret Walker, Alex Haley.
Unlike Margaret Walker, in the fire of *For My People,*
Pauline Hopkins is not ... urging that "martial songs be
written"; she is often indignant, but not indignant
enough to desire Margaret's "bloody peace." It is true
that Pauline Hopkins can and does involve herself with
black anger, but the texture, range, scope, the slashing
red and scream and curse and *out-there* hurt that
overwhelm us as Wright, Ellison and Haley deal with us,
are not to be found in *Contending Forces.* I am not
prepared to say that they are not "necessary." However,
this quaint little "romance"—as the author likes to call
it—keeps us with it, keeps us trotting, with quite some
tension, too, down its elder dust, and through its
quizzical mist.

Words do wonderful things. They pound, purr. They can
urge, they can wheedle, whip, whine. They can sing,
sass, singe. They can churn, check, channelize. They can
be a *"Hup* two three four." They can forge a fiery army
out of a hundred languid men. Pauline Hopkins, had we
met, might have said in answer to my questions that her
interest was *not* in Revolution *nor* exhaustive Revision.
But it is perfectly obvious that black fury invaded her
not seldom and not softly, and if she has not chosen
from her resources words and word jointures that could
make changes in the world, she has given us a sense of
her day, a *clue* collection, and we can use the light of it
to clarify our understanding and our intuition. We can
take the building blocks she does supply us and use them
to fill in old gaps. After association with her, some of
our concepts won't be quite as wobbly.

Pauline Hopkins had, and this is true of many of her
brothers and sisters, new and old, a touching reliance on
the dazzles and powers of anticipated integration. But
she would have been remarkable indeed if, enslaved as
she was by her special time and special temperament,
she had been forward enough to instruct blacks not to
rely on goodies coming from any source save personal
heart, head, hand. To ask them, to entreat them to
address themselves, rather than whites, to cherish,
champion themselves, rather than whites, to trust, try,
traipse with themselves, was not her inspiration nor
motivation.

Often doth the brainwashed slave revere the modes and
idolatries of the master. And Pauline Hopkins consistently proves herself a continuing slave, despite little
bursts of righteous heat, throughout *Contending Forces.*
She tells us, for example, what she really thinks of
"black beauty" over and over again, in passages like this
description of our paper-doll heroine, Sappho Clark:
"Tall and fair, with hair of a golden cast, aquiline nose,
rosebud mouth, soft brown eyes veiled by long, dark
lashes which swept her cheek, just now covered with a
delicate rose flush ... a combination of 'queen rose and
lily in one'." To which vision an *ordinary* black, Sarah
Ann, (fat, colloquial, ebony-hued), responds: "That's
somethin' *God* made, honey." (The accepted understanding being that one of the lower devils made the ilk
of Sarah Ann.) We are also treated to such outrages as
"there might even have been a strain of African blood
polluting the fair stream of Montfort's vitality"; and "In
many cases African blood had become diluted from
amalgamation with the higher race"; *and* "that justice of
heart and mind for my people which the Anglo-Saxon in
America never withholds from suffering humanity."

In her preface, the author suggests that *her* desire is to
give us the kind of "simple, homely tale ... which
cements the bond of brotherhood among all classes and
all complexions." But like most blacks, of whatever
persuasion, self-delusion, perverse ambition, or approximate "transformation," Pauline is unable to keep a
certain purely "native" rage *steadily* stomped down.
Certain things she does not mind us suffering through,
any more than does Alex Haley or Margaret Walker. We
get "cruelties ... such as to sicken the most cold-hearted
and indifferent. For instance: causing a child to whip his
mother until the blood ran; if a slave looked his master
in the face, his limbs were broken; women in the first
stages of their accouchement, upon refusing to work,
were placed in the treadmill where terrible things
happened, too dreadful to relate." And she is able to
make Will say—calmly—that agitation—never Revolution—"will do much. It gave us freedom; it will give us
manhood. The peace, dignity, and honor of this nation
rises or falls with the Negro."

As she says, and with more desperate truth than she
knows she says or feels, the reader is left to "draw
conclusions." (pp. 403-06)

Gwendolyn Brooks, in an afterword to Contending Forces: A Romance Illustrative of
Negro Life North and South *by Pauline
Elizabeth Hopkins, Southern Illinois University Press, 1978, pp. 403-09.*

Claudia Tate (essay date 1985)

[*In the following excerpt, Tate discusses the ways in
which Hopkins adapted nineteenth-century literary
conventions to document black concerns in* Contending Forces, Winona, *and* Of One Blood.]

Pauline Hopkins was an important writer who deserves serious attention because, in being both black and female, she documents the cross section of the literary concerns of two major groups of American writers: turn-of-the-century black writers, who primarily dramatized themes of racial injustice, and mid- to late-nineteenth-century white women writers, some of whom wrote sentimental and domestic novels that acclaimed Christian virtue. In some of these novels, a young girl is deprived of the family assistance she had depended on to sustain her throughout her life. The popular success of white women in depicting their heroines' necessity of making their own way in the world despite injustice provided a ready and fertile context within which black women writers might also place their fair-haired black heroines and dramatize racial protest. For many black women writers embellished the plot line of their white predecessors and contemporaries. They include Amelia Johnson, Sarah Allen, Emma Kelley, Ruth Todd, Marie Burgess Ware, Frances Harper, and J. McHenry Jones. In their work we find that the youth is black and may be male but is more often female. She believes herself to be white, obviously having no knowledge of her African ancestry. This knowledge is withheld so that she can enjoy the privileged life afforded her by her white father. Circumstances lead to his death, and as a result the child and her mother are subjected to the horrors of slavery. Both are abused by cruel slave masters, despite the fact that they are as white and as noble as any one of their former caste and more handsome than most. The child survives and eventually marries well, thereby concluding the tragedy of her plight. This marriage is not only based on love but forms a partnership for continued work in racial advancement and, thus, gives the union a high and noble purpose. But practically every one of these writers has been lost in out-of-print books and periodicals which have long ceased to be available. Their work must be retrieved in order to correct the now longstanding misconception that Phillis Wheatley and Frances Harper were the lone literary women of the eighteenth and nineteenth centuries, who all by themselves brought forth the generation of black women writers of the Harlem Renaissance.

Contending Forces, Hopkins's first and best-known novel, conforms to the basic plot structure I have outlined. The story begins in 1790 on the island of Bermuda, when Charles Montfort decides to move his family to North Carolina to invest in a cotton plantation in order to secure his fortune. All goes as planned until a jealous neighbor, Anson Pollock, suspects that Montfort's beautiful wife, Grace, has black blood. He conspires to kill Montfort, claim Grace as his slave mistress, make her two children—Charles and Jesse—chattel slaves, and steal a portion of Montfort's estate. The conspiracy is successful, and after Montfort's murder, Grace commits suicide in order to escape her fate. Charles is sold to an Englishman who subsequently frees him and takes him to England, while Jesse suffers under the abuse of Pollock, until he manages to escape to New England. He eventually marries the daughter of his black benefactor and fathers a large family in Exeter, Massachusetts.

These events comprise the background for the novel's central story, which concerns Jesse's grandchildren, Will and Dora Smith.

The central story is set in Boston. Will Smith is a philosophy student at Harvard College, and Dora assists her mother in running the family-owned rooming house. Among the roomers are Sappho Clark and John Langley. Will falls in love with Sappho, a beautiful, virtually white young woman with a mysterious, southern past. John Langley, who is engaged to Dora, also falls in love with Sappho, but his intentions are not honorable. He plots to force Sappho into becoming his mistress, while planning to marry Dora. Sappho escapes Langley, but in so doing she must abandon her lover Will. She leaves behind a letter for him, explaining Langley's intentions as well as her mysterious and tragic past. Will shares this information with Dora, who immediately breaks off her engagement to Langley. Will then tries to find Sappho, but she has left without a trace. In an effort to heal his broken heart, Will goes abroad to continue his studies after graduating from Harvard. Dora eventually marries her former childhood friend, Dr. Arthur Lewis, who is the head of a large industrial school for Negroes in Louisiana. The newlyweds move to Louisiana, and while Will is paying them a visit, he unexpectedly finds Sappho. They are united in marriage a few weeks later on Easter Sunday. Thus, the virtuous are rewarded with happy marriages, made even more fulfilling because of their commitments to racial progress, while the villainous John Langley dies in a mining accident, after having repented much too late for his "sins."

Hopkins's characters conform, as we would expect, to nineteenth-century conventions in that their inner virtues are reflected in their outward appearances. Dora Smith is described as an "energetic little Yankee girl" with a "delicate brown face" and "smooth bands of dark-brown hair." Will Smith, Hopkins's DuBois-like hero, is "tall and finely formed, with features almost perfectly chiseled, and a complexion the color of an almond shell. His hair is black and curly, with just a tinge of crispness to denote the existence of Negro blood." John Langley, on the other hand, is "shorter in stature and very fair in complexion. His hair is dark and has no indication of Negro blood in its waves; his features are of the Caucasian cut.... (But)...the strong manhood and honesty of purpose which existed in Will Smith are lacking in John Langley. He was a North Carolinian—descendant of slaves and Southern 'cracker' blood." Hopkins accounted for Langley's ignoble character as an inherent result of his poor ancestry, and in so doing, she further qualified the nineteenth-century notion that the mulatto was a degenerate by making degeneration the result not of miscegenation in and of itself but of poor-quality white blood.

When we turn our attention to the beautiful Sappho Clark, we find that her appearance conforms more readily to that of the mulatto heroine: "Tall and frail, with hair of a golden cast, aquiline nose, rosebud mouth, soft brown eyes veiled by long, dark lashes." Although

Sappho is fair enough to pass into the white world and secure herself a rich, handsome, white husband, she chooses instead to unite her plight to that of her black brethren. Her most important role, however, is not that of the "tragic mulatto" but that of Hopkins's spokeswoman for the political rights of black Americans. When her argument is combined with Will's contention that "No Negro college... ought to bestow a diploma upon a man who had not been thoroughly grounded in the rudiments of moral and natural philosophy, physiology, and economy," we have their combined social program for the advancement of the Negro. Their program is a fictionalized version of DuBois's position in the DuBois-Washington controversy. Washington, his opponent, argued for industrial education for the Negro and believed that this program could be best accomplished by not antagonizing whites over the black vote. Hopkins dramatized Washington's position through the character of Dora's admirer, Dr. Arthur Lewis. Whereas the real-life controversy was never resolved, Hopkins resolved her fictionalized version quite easily by joining the two programs in marriages at the novel's conclusion. As a consequence, we find that the Lewises promote industrial education for the Negro, while their in-laws, the Smiths, promote liberal academic education for the Negro and agitate for his political rights as well.

It is not surprising to find that Hopkins, being both black and female complemented her racial argument with her concern for women's issues. In the chapter entitled "The Sewing Circle," Hopkins characterized a "race woman" by the name of Mrs. Willis who is a proponent for the "evolution of true womanhood in the work of the 'Woman Question' as embodied in marriage and suffrage." Hopkins, through this spokeswoman, contends that women should chart their advance within the domain of marriage and with the assistance of the vote. Mrs. Willis further says that "the advancement of the colored woman should be the new problem in the woman question," and in order to pursue this inquiry she supports "the formation of clubs of colored women banded together for charity, for study, and for every reason under God's glorious heavens that can better the condition of mankind."

The advancement of the black woman was certainly an area of concern at the time of the publication of *Contenting Forces*. No doubt the women's clubs which were chartered in the late nineteenth century provided stimulation for the black women's development, although Hopkins had little more than tentative programs to propose, theories to assert, and positions to state. But she did have her spokeswoman, Mrs. Willis, insist that women construct their advancement on virtue and duty within the domain of marriage and with the responsibility of the vote. In addition, Hopkins had Mrs. Willis further reiterate an underlying theme of the entire novel, namely that blacks and women, especially, must be on constant guard to subdue the growth of any passion: "Enthusiasm for any one object or duty may become a passion. I believe that in some degree passion may be beneficial, but we must guard ourselves against a sinful growth of any appetite." Therefore, if we view *Contending Forces* as Hopkins's dramatized expression of a tentative program for the advancement of black Americans in general and black American women in particular, we can surmise that black men and women must be responsible for the course of their own advancement and that duty, virtue, carefully controlled emotions, the institution of marriage, and the vote are the key components for directing social progress and achieving results. (pp. 54-9)

Like *Contending Forces, Winona* conforms to the basic plot structure I have described. In 1849 an unknown white man joins the Indian tribes around Buffalo, New York, and eventually becomes their chief, taking the name of White Eagle. Buffalo is the last and, therefore, most important stop in the underground railroad, and as a result many fugitive slaves arrive there in pursuit of freedom. One such fugitive is a mulatto slave woman whom White Eagle marries and who dies shortly after the birth of their daughter, Winona. Another fugitive slave woman also dies shortly thereafter, leaving her small son, Judah, in White Eagle's care. The children grow up as brother and sister, totally unaware of their racial origin; in fact, they believe themselves to be Indians. They spend their days fully enjoying the adventures afforded by the forest, but they also heed the importance of securing a public-school education. In 1855 Warren Maxwell, an Englishman, comes to America in search of the heir to the Carlingford estate. On the first night of Maxwell's arrival, White Eagle is murdered by an unknown assailant. Maxwell learns of his death from Winona and Judah, to whom he immediately becomes attached, so much so that he plans to take them to England with him. But before they can leave, Maxwell has to complete his search, which will take him to another location. When he returns to make arrangements for their trip, he finds that the children have been claimed as chattel slaves by their mothers' owners under the Fugitive Slave Act of 1850 and subsequently have been taken to Missouri.

Two years later Maxwell, still searching for the missing Carlingford heir, visits Colonel Titus's plantation in Missouri, where he finds Winona and Judah in bondage. They plan an escape, and while Maxwell is awaiting their arrival, he meets Maybee, a friend, who is on his way to Kansas to join John Brown and his militia. When Winona and Judah arrive, they are taken to Brown's camp and left in his care. The next night Maxwell is taken prisoner by Thomson, who was White Eagle's murderer. Thomson subsequently tries Maxwell for inciting slave escapes and ultimately sentences him to be hanged. While he awaits his fate, Brown's men discover his whereabouts and he is rescued. The story comes to a quick conclusion when Maxwell learns that White Eagle was the missing Carlingford heir. As a result Winona and Judah, who are now both young adults, inherit his legacy. By this time, as we might have expected, Maxwell has fallen deeply in love with Winona and she with him. They return to England, a nation which Hopkins described as being beyond American caste prejudice, and they are married. Judah, who also accompanies them to England, is eventually knighted by the Queen. He grows prosperous and marries a woman from an old English family. Thus, the story concludes with both couples thriving in domestic bliss.

The structure of this novel conforms to basic conventions. But *Winona* is even more sensational than *Contending Forces* in that there are more incredible coincidences, swashbuckling adventures, and exaggerated heroic descriptions, all held together with a very sentimental love story. Winona's appearance, as we might expect, conforms to the tragic mulatto mold: "Her wide brow, about which the hair clustered in dark rings, the beautifully chiselled features, the olive complexion with a hint of pink." And her hero, Maxwell, is equally as handsome, though fair: "... a slender, well-knit figure with a bright, handsome face, blue eyes and a mobile mouth slightly touched with down on his upper lip." The virtuous pair are rewarded with prosperity and happiness, while the villain suffers a painful death.

Hopkins placed this novel into the genre of the fugitive slave story and identified her protest as that against the arbitrary segregation and subjection of black Americans:

> Many strange tales of romantic happenings in this mixed community of Anglo-Saxons, Indians and Negroes might be told similar to the one I am about to relate, and the world stand aghast and may try to find the dividing line supposed to be a natural barrier between the whites and the dark-skinned race.

Thus, as is the case with *Contending Forces*, the central issue of *Winona* is its protest against racial injustice, but unlike *Contending Forces, Winona* outlines no program of social reform other than that offered by escape. Whereas escape offered a possible resolution to the slave's dilemma prior to 1864, Hopkins's contemporary scene of 1901 afforded virtually no ostensible reason for her to write an abolitionist novel. Perhaps she wrote the novel as an exercise in nostalgia, intended to arouse sympathy for oppressed black Americans. There was, however, more than sufficient reason to condemn the practices of employment and housing discrimination, separate public accommodations, mob violence, and lynching, as she had done in *Contending Forces.* Whereas her first novel was very sensitive to the racial issues of 1900 and consequently addressed each of them, *Winona* seems to be essentially an escapist, melodramatic romance in which Hopkins used sentimental love as a means for supporting an appeal for racial justice. Though, granted, Hopkins does dramatize the fact that being black in America means being subjected to racial abuse, she offers little hope to those who cannot escape like Winona and Jude.

Women's issues, which were central to the argument of *Contending Forces,* have been abandoned entirely in *Winona.* Although marriage is depicted as woman's ambition in both *Contending Forces* and *Winona,* in the latter novel a woman's role is seen exclusively as finding a suitable husband and tending to his needs. Love is translated singularly into duty, and duty finds expression only on the domestic front. We do not see women, like Mrs. Willis of *Contending Forces,* who are their husbands' helpmates in the struggle for racial advancement. On the contrary, marriage offers women its own blissful escape in *Winona,* and marital love is portrayed as the balm which soothes their worldly wounds. When we turn our attention to the subject of the advancement of black women, we find no discussion of this topic at all. Although Hopkins was, nevertheless, a product of the nineteenth century's rising consciousness of women's concerns, it is surprising to find that this issue appears so inconsistently in her work.

The change in argument and setting in *Winona* may be a signal for Hopkins's own growing frustration with the effort to improve both the American racial climate and the quality of life for black American women. In 1899, when *Contending Forces* was written, Hopkins's argument concerned the advancement of black Americans in general and black American women in particular. In 1901, when *Winona* was written, her argument seems to focus on escape. Whereas escape is an incident of plot in *Winona* and love is, likewise, translated into domestic duty, both the themes of escape and love evolve into even more limited contexts in Hopkins's third novel, *Of One Blood, or the Hidden Self,* published in 1902/03. Here, the effort to escape becomes total and comprehensive, as the story moves beyond the American social scene to a mysterious Atlantis-like region of an underground city in Africa. And love is translated into racial imperatives on one hand and perversion on the other. Thus, instead of finding urgent social problems dramatized in a somewhat realistic fictional setting, we find the remote landscape of science fiction. Although it can be argued that much of this genre provides critical observations and predictions about the real world, in Hopkins's case, however, her science fiction novel seems almost entirely gratuitous. *Of One Blood* is, nonetheless, an extremely intriguing, imaginative, and provocative novel. (pp. 59-62)

Of One Blood is set in the stimulating climate of early twentieth-century scientific discoveries. William James and Sigmund Freud were advancing theories about the nature of the subconscious, while archaeological finds in Egypt were uncovering modern man's racial and cultural history. In this setting we find Reuel Briggs, a young black medical student who is particularly interested in mysticism and the powers of the subconscious mind. The story begins on one evening when he sees the face of a beautiful woman, whom he cannot seem to forget. A few days later, he attends a Negro concert with his best friend, Aubrey Livingston, and who should appear but the beautiful woman, singing a haunting melody. In this manner her racial identity is uncovered. Soon thereafter, Briggs is called upon to assist the victims of a railroad accident at a local hospital, and who should he find but this same young woman, who is presumed dead but who is actually in a catatonic sleep. Briggs succeeds in restoring her consciousness, although she can remember nothing of her past life. As we would expect, Briggs falls in love with the woman, whose name we learn is Dianthe Lusk. He marries her, but his financial situation is so strained that he decides to postpone its consummation until he can secure his fortune and make a name for himself as a member of an archaeological expedition headed to Meröe, Ethiopia. He leaves her care entrusted to his friend Livingston. But soon after Briggs's departure, Livingston expresses his passionate love for Dianthe, who finds that she is unable to resist the mysterious power he has over her. He plans to take her away, but he must first rid himself of his fiancee, Molly Vance. He conspires to arrange a boating accident in which Molly is drowned. He and Dianthe are presumed dead, although their bodies are never found.

Meanwhile the expedition arrives in Ethiopia, and Briggs is very uneasy because he has not heard from Dianthe. His concern grows to the point that he experiences a clairvoyant trance of the boating accident. As a result, Briggs is brokenhearted, and he becomes seriously ill. When his strength returns, he wanders into a mysterious pyramid in the hope that a man-eating beast may release him from his grief. While exploring the pyramid, he loses consciousness, and when he awakens he finds himself in a mysterious underground city. The populace proclaim him as their long-awaited monarch, King Ergamenes, and he is subsequently betrothed to Queen Candace. Together they are to bring forth a long line of monarchs who will reclaim Ethiopia's former glory. Despite his new life, Briggs cannot forget Dianthe, and while having another trance, he learns that she is still alive.

Meanwhile, Livingston has married Dianthe, who is distraught when she learns that Briggs is not dead, as Livingston has told her. She tries to escape but gets lost in the woods. An old black woman by the name of Aunt Hannah rescues her and immediately recognizes that she is her daughter Mira's child and, therefore, her own granddaughter. Hannah tells Dianthe that Mira was also the mother of Briggs and Livingston; hence, Dianthe learns in the span of a few moments that she, Livingston, and Briggs are all "of one blood" and that she has married not one but both of her brothers. As a result of this knowledge, Dianthe loses her mind and attempts to poison Livingston, but he discovers her plan and makes her drink the poison instead, which she does without regret. When Briggs finally traces the whereabouts of Dianthe and Livingston, he arrives only to find Dianthe dead. Soon afterward, Livingston commits suicide, and Briggs returns to the Hidden City with Aunt Hannah, his grandmother. There he spends the rest of his life with his Queen Candace, doing God's work to prove that "Of one blood has (God made) all races of men."

Like **Contending Forces, Of One Blood** has an early twentieth-century setting. No sooner has the story begun than we find the Fisk Jubilee Singers presenting a concert to a Boston audience, which provides the occasion for Dianthe's introduction. In addition, the startling scientific discoveries in psychology and ar-

chaeology of that era provide a launching point for the fantastic events which follow. In fact, the entire intellectual milieu from which the story arises gives Hopkins the opportunity to display the breadth of her knowledge in the arts and the sciences, as if she were using her own writing in a self-conscious attempt to prove that the inherent intellectual capacity of black Americans was equal to that of their Anglo-Saxon counterparts. Moreover, the archaeological expedition is the means by which Hopkins underscores her contention that the biblical references to Ethiopia as a former world power could have been, indeed, factual rather than mythic. In this regard, she spends considerable effort describing Ethiopia's past glory, in addition to arguing her underlying point that there is no scientific basis for the arbitrary separation of the races. Hopkins further contends that knowledge is a serious impediment to racial prejudice, and although readers of today may detect the naiveté of such a position, Hopkins and her contemporaries firmly believed that knowledge would eliminate social injustice of all kinds and improve the quality of human life.

Although most Afro-Americans came from West Africa and not East Africa, this geographical oversight does not offset Hopkins's basic argument that "Afro-Americans are," as she wrote, "a branch of the wonderful and mysterious Ethiopians who had a prehistoric existence of magnificence, the full record of which is lost in obscurity." Hopkins did not appear to be fundamentally concerned with providing a genealogical tree for modern-day American blacks but with presenting broad notions of cultural and racial origins for them specifically and for mankind in general. In this regard, the ambition to retrieve Ethiopia's lost record of glory provides the impetus for the unfolding story and forms the foundation for Hopkins's racial argument.

Hopkins focused most of her attention on dramatizing the racial argument in **Of One Blood,** and as a consequence little emphasis falls on women's issues. There are, however, references to two issues which are related topically to women. The first concerns Queen Candace's physical appearance, and the second concerns Hopkins's mandate that passion must be subjected to reason. Turning our attention first to Candace, we find that, although her name seems peculiarly inappropriate for an Ethiopian queen, her physical portrayal marks a very early appearance of the "brown" heroine in Afro-American fiction. Instead of the conventional olive-skinned heroine, Queen Candace, though she resembles Dianthe, has a "warm bronze complexion; thick black eyebrows and great black eyes." Interestingly enough, she is the means by which pigment is reintroduced into the royal line, inasmuch as Ergamenes (alias Reuel) lost that trait as a result of American miscegenation. Hence, pigment becomes a positive physical attribute measured in terms of feminine beauty more than sixty years prior to the coinage of the slogan "Black is Beautiful." The second issue which finds repeated expression is Hopkins's admonition for restraining passion with reason and for not equating passion to love. This theme consistently appears in all of Hopkins's work, as well as in that of her

Advertisement for Hopkins's most popular work.

female contemporaries. Its repeated expression measures the extent of their concern that women avoid being viewed merely as passionate creatures but be seen instead as rational human beings capable of serious thought. Hopkins also makes repeated references to marriage as the proper social domain for both men and women. In this regard, marriage is characterized as the distinctly harmonious setting in which good works abound, and Omnipotence directs good works, in her novels, toward the elimination of caste prejudice and the elevation of racial pride.

Of One Blood brings Hopkins's major themes, which were dramatized in her earliest play to this her last novel, full circle. In each work we find that she habitually insisted that black men and women be responsible for the course of their own advancement and that duty, virtue, carefully controlled emotions, and the institution of marriage are the key components for directing social progress. Her excessively episodic and melodramatic techniques resulted in her failure to meet twentieth-century critical standards; nevertheless, she was a serious writer, who wrote three novels at the turn of the century. This fact, alone, demands that we retrieve her work from obscurity. (pp. 62-5)

> *Claudia Tate, "Pauline Hopkins: Our Literary Foremother," in* Conjuring: Black Women, Fiction, and Literary Tradition, *edited by Marjorie Pryse and Hortense J. Spillers, Indiana University Press, 1985, pp. 53-66.*

Hazel V. Carby (essay date 1987)

[*In the following excerpt from her* Reconstructing Womanhood: The Emergence of the Afro-American Woman Novelist *(1987), Carby surveys Hopkins's "political fiction," focusing on characterization in* Contending Forces.]

Hopkins's first novel, *Contending Forces,* was the source of figures and narrative devices that developed throughout her later work; her use of history to rewrite an American heritage and question the boundaries of inheritance was important in her fiction and shaped her political perception. The actions and destinies of Hopkins's characters were carefully related to the condition and actions of their ancestors; the consequences of events initiated at some specific moment in history constituted a significant aspect of Hopkins's fictional strategy. (p. 128)

Contending Forces was a novel about the period in which it was written, but it opened with a chapter entitled "A Retrospective of the Past." This first story was set in the decade between 1790 and 1800: the years of political agitation in Britain for the abolition of slavery in the West Indies. Hopkins reproduced the history of the British abolitionists in the interests of being "instructive" as well as "interesting" and to preface the story of Charles Montfort, a West Indian planter who had moved his family and estate of slaves from Bermuda to

North Carolina to avoid emancipating them. Hopkins delineated the "instructive" aspect of this decision as the perversion of morality in favor of commercial interest and profit:

> Nature avenges herself upon us for every law violated in the mad rush for wealth or position or personal comfort where the rights of others of the human family are not respected. If Charles Montfort had been contented to accept the rulings of the English Parliament, and had allowed his human property to come under the new laws just made for its government, although poorer in the end, he would have spared himself and family all the horrors which were to follow his selfish flight to save that property.

It was the economic profitability of the system of slavery which was established as being the cause of the events and conditions of the rest of the novel.

Hopkins used the move to North Carolina to establish a series of contrasts between the British and U.S. slave systems, a romanticized vision of the former set against the human misery within the latter. Montfort was criticized for his "liberality" as a master and his intention to free his slaves after he had made his fortune and could afford to retire to Britain. The local vigilante group decided to put an end to his bad example. Montfort's supposed liberality was used to set into relief the uncivilized and savage aspects of the American slave system, but the focus of the text quickly became the suspicion and subsequent rumor that the blood of Grace Montfort was "polluted" by an African strain. Hopkins made it clear that it was irrelevant whether Grace Montfort was a black or a white woman. Her behavior was a representation of "true womanhood," but her skin was a little too "creamy." The readers were left to guess her actual heritage; what was important was that the suspicion of black blood was enough cause for the ostracism of the whole family and Grace Montfort's transition from the pedestal of virtue to the illicit object of the sexual desire of a local landowner, Anson Pollock. The possibility that Grace might be black was responsible for the murder of Charles Montfort, the "rapes" of Grace and her black foster sister, Lucy, and the enslavement of the two sons, Jesse and Charles.

Grace Montfort rejected the sexual advances of Anson Pollock, who planned his revenge and the satisfaction of his sexual obsession. Under the pretense of an imminent rebellion by Montfort's slaves, Pollock and the vigilante group, "the committee on public safety," raided the Montfort plantation. Montfort was quickly dispatched by a bullet in the brain, leaving Grace prey to Pollock's devilish intentions. In a graphic and tortured two-page scene, Hopkins represented the brutal rape of Grace in the displaced form of a whipping by two of the vigilantes. Her clothes were ripped from her body, and she was "whipped" alternatively "by the two strong, savage men." Hopkins's metaphoric replacement of the "snaky, leather thong" for the phallus was a crude but effective device, and "the blood [which] stood in a pool about her feet" was the final evidence that the "outrage" that had been committed was rape.

Grace committed suicide to escape Pollock and was replaced as his mistress by her black maid and slave, Lucy. The actual and figurative ravishing of "grace" at the hand of Southern brutality established the link that Hopkins believed existed between the violent act of rape and its specific political use as a device of terrorism. Both Charles and Grace Montfort suffered because they threatened to break the codes that bound the slave system. The possibility that Grace Montfort was black represented the ultimate violation of the position of the white woman which necessitated the degradation of her and her offspring to use as chattel. Charles Junior was eventually bought from Pollock by an English mineralogist; Jesse escaped as a young man when on an errand to New York and made his way to Boston and eventually New Hampshire, where he was absorbed into the black community. One grew up "black" the other "white," which emphasized Hopkins's political intent of blurring the lines between the races.

This first tale took the first eighty pages of **Contending Forces** and acted as an overture to the main story which was set at the end of the nineteenth century, but it also contained all the narrative elements that eventually resolved the crises of the relations between the main characters. At the end of the novel the characters were finally made aware of the history which had shaped their lives; the Smith family inherited a tale which appeared remote from their everyday lives and retained significance only in the naming of children. Ma Smith, her husband dead, ran a lodging house with her son, William Jesse Montfort, and her daughter, Dora Grace Montfort. Two other main characters were lodgers, John P. Langley, engaged to Dora, and Sappho Clark, a woman with a mysteriously hidden past. The future of each of these characters was tied to and dependent on a revelation of their personal histories. These fictional histories were Hopkins's narrative displacement of the increasing separation of the races; issues of inheritance, heritage, and culture dominated the text, and blood lines between the races were so entangled that race itself became a subordinated concern. Crucial to the construction of this narrative was the historical importance of rape; because of the rapes of Grace and Lucy, white and black shared an interdependent destiny. John Langley was revealed to be the descendant of Anson Pollock and Lucy, and he was destined to repeat and relive his ancestor's sexual obsession.

However, the initial tale of slavery had a second important narrative function which situated the personal histories within a history of the relations between imperialist nations and their colonies, between colonizers and colonized. Hopkins wrote **Contending Forces** at a moment of intense debate concerning the consequences of acquiring and colonizing overseas territories. The Spanish-American War of 1898 had led to the secession of the Philippines, Puerto Rico, and Guam to the United States, and the Filipino resistance was brutally repressed. In 1899, Germany and the United States divided Samoa, and a year later the United States annexed Hawaii. By end of the nineteenth century the United States had acquired the basis of its empire, an empire that was and would continue to be "composed primarily of darker peoples, people of African, Indian, Polynesian, Japanese and Chinese extraction" [Robert L. Allen in *Reluctant Reformers,* 1975]. (pp. 130-33)

[In] **Contending Forces,** Hopkins reconstructed an interdependent history of the colonized and their colonizers as a narrative of rightful inheritance in which lynching and rape were the central mechanisms of oppression. Commercial interests and a desire for profit motivated Montfort to keep his slaves and move to the United States. The consequence in Hopkins's fictional world was that a debt needed to be paid on two levels: the debt that accrued within the family history of the Montforts and, by implication, a debt that was owed to the whole black community from the profits of the slave world.

The search for and establishment of kinship is a recurrent Afro-American literary metaphor. It had its source in slave narratives but recurred throughout the nineteenth century and expanded to become a figure for the dispersion of blacks throughout the diaspora. But Hopkins's particular use of this narrative device crossed racial boundaries. Ma Smith told the family tale to the British Charles Montfort-Withington, who then revealed himself to be a direct descendant of Jesse's brother, Charles. From Britain, Charles had successfully sued the U.S. government, and money had been left in trust for the heirs of Jesse, who were, of course, the Smith family. The rights of inheritance were established, and Ma Smith received $150,000. Lucy was found in Bermuda, with her granddaughter who identified John Pollock Langley as her son. Withington invested "a small annuity" on them both as they lived in total poverty, but Lucy, the only living witness to the original tale, died within days of being found. The fictional kinship network of the Montforts included an aristocratic British family, who acknowledged their intimate relation and paid the debt of history to their "American cousins." In relation to the Pollock kin, however, inheritance and heritage were given a negative emphasis. The young John Langley inherited none of the characteristics of his black family but was represented as being a carbon copy of his evil white grandfather, Anson Pollock. Hopkins repeated the story of the Montforts and the Pollocks in the story of the Smiths, John Langley and the mysterious Sappho Clark.

Sappho arrived at the Smith lodging house as a typist who had to work at home, for while her boss was willing to employ her he could not allow a black woman to work for him on his premises. She was represented as a tragic mulatta, and all members of the household fell in love with Sappho. Will formed a romantic attachment, while Langley, engaged to Dora, grew increasingly sexually obsessed with her. Langley, a lawyer ambitious to succeed politically, was a person in whom the "natural instinct for good had been perverted by a mixture of 'cracker' blood of the lowest type on his father's side." He accepted bribes from white Northern politicians to be an acquiescent and malleable black representative who exercised control over his community to prevent any form of organized political demonstration against lynching or any other form of outrage perpetrated on blacks in the South. Langley perceived Dora to be the most suitable choice of wife to further his ambitions, but he desired Sappho as his mistress. Sappho's need to hide her sexual history provided the occasion for Langley to blackmail her.

In preparation for the denouement which linked the personal history of Sappho to the history of black persecution in the South, Hopkins assembled all her characters for a meeting of the American Colored League, called in response to the increased number of lynchings in the South. Langley, as a white man's puppet, urged that no action be taken, but his conservative platitudes were countered by a new character, Lycurgus (Luke) Sawyer, who addressed the audience by defining the "contending forces" of Hopkins's title:

> I want to tell the gentlemen who have spoken here tonight that conservatism, lack of brotherly affiliation, lack of energy for the right and the power of the almighty dollar which deadens men's hearts to the sufferings of their brothers, and makes them feel that if only *they* can rise to the top of the ladder may God help the hindmost man, are the forces which are ruining the Negro in this country. It is killing him off by thousands, destroying his self-respect, and degrading him to the level of the brute. *These are the contending forces that are dooming this race to despair!*

Luke had two tales to tell. In the first a lynching was the central focus, in the second a rape. Both tales confirmed the primacy of these two violent acts in Hopkins's thesis of "contending forces." The first history was about Luke's father, whose success in trade resulted in competition with white traders, threats to his life, and eventually a mob attack on his house and family. Because Luke's father attempted to defend himself, he was lynched, and his wife and daughter were whipped and abused until they died. Luke's two baby brothers were seized by the mob, who "took them by the heels and dashed their brains out against the walls of the house."

The second tale followed from the first. Luke escaped into the woods, was found and rescued by a black, Beaubean, who took Luke into his home to raise as a son. Beaubean's white father had been his owner, and he had a wealthy and politically influential white half-brother who assumed a stance of paternal friendship toward Beaubean's daughter, Mabelle, which was a disguise for his real intention to rape her. When fourteen years old, Mabelle was kidnapped by her uncle, raped, and left a prisoner in a brothel. After weeks of searching, Beaubean found his daughter and confronted his brother with his crime. In his defense, the brother stated, "What does a woman of mixed blood, or any Negress, for that matter, know of virtue? It is my belief that they were a direct creation by God to be the pleasant companions of men of my race." He then offered Beaubean a thousand dollars. Beaubean threw the money back at his brother and threatened legal action in the federal courts. This threat was met with mob action; Beaubean's house was set alight and the family shot. Luke escaped with Mabelle and placed her in a convent.

At this point in the text, Hopkins tried to mold Sappho's history into a paradigm of the historical rape of black women. At the conclusion of the story, Sappho fainted, and Langley correctly identified her as Mabelle Beaubean. Armed with this information, he confronted Sappho and tried to blackmail her into being his mistress. Sappho at first misunderstood his intention and declined what she thought to be a proposal of marriage, but his response was clear: "who spoke of marriage? Ambitious men do not marry women with stories like yours." Hopkins molded Langley as an archetype, an embodiment of the cultural myth of the rise of the poor child to success and power. She re-created in this individual character what she understood to be a representative figure of the "Gilded Age," manipulating and monopolizing unbridled power:

> He had prospered. He had accomplished the acquisition of knowledge at the expense of the non-development of every moral faculty. He did not realize that he was a responsible being, or that morality was obligatory upon him. With him, might was right . . . . John had given no thought to the needs of his soul in his pursuit of wealth and position.

Langley embodied what Hopkins represented as the dominant characteristics of the South, which she felt needed "nothing less than a new moral code." In alliance with the white politicians who bought his allegiance, he was implicated in the social structure of "Southern arrogance, trusts, political bossism, and every other abuse waged against God's poor" against which Hopkins urged organized opposition.

Hopkins used the history of Anson Pollock, as representative of the oppressive power of slaveholders, with the contemporary characteristics of political, social, and economic opportunism, and produced a John Langley. The social forces that these two males, white and black, reproduced had particular consequences for the patriarchal control of women. Langley placed the responsibility for her rape on Sappho's own shoulders and could envision no possible future for her other than as concubine. Yet it was Langley and the patriarchal oppression he represented that had no future in Hopkins's fictional world. Langley was given a choice; he was offered an alternative path of action, much as the text itself attempted to pose alternative relations between dominant and subject peoples. A fortune-teller, Madame Frances, warned Langley that if he persisted in his machinations he would die in utter desolation and desperation surrounded by the wealth he so desired but which would be useless to him. The warning was disregarded, and Langley died in the final pages of the novel, in the middle of the Klondike gold fields, in a storm of snow and ice, surrounded by an immense fortune and the twenty-nine bodies of his companions.

Langley and the histories of Luke Sawyer and Mabelle Beaubean formed the story of the colonization of a people within the United States. But their stories were also a part of Hopkins's critique of the racism that structured the imperialist enterprise.... Hopkins tried to make visible this intrinsic framework of thought and reproduced through her characters and their histories of oppression the consequences of both the assertion of white supremacy and acquiescence in white supremacist practices.

The dominance of characterizations of mulattoes and octoroons in *Contending Forces* has been interpreted as an intention to glorify the possibilities of the black race if only it would integrate with and eventually lose itself within the white. But the presence of "mixed" characters in the text did not represent an implicit desire to "lighten" blacks through blood ties with whites. Hopkins wanted to emphasize those sets of social relations and practices which were the consequence of a social system that exercised white supremacy through the act of rape. Her use of mulatto figures engaged with the discourse of social Darwinism, undermining the tenets of "pure blood" and "pure race" as mythological, and implicitly exposed the absurdity of theories of the total separation of the races. But Hopkins also attempted to demonstrate the importance of social, political, and economic interests in determining human behavior in order to negate contemporary propositions of the danger of the degeneracy of a social group through its amalgamation with another. Hopkins addressed accusations that miscegenation was the inmost desire of the darker races of the earth, a conspiracy to weaken and debilitate the white race. Her response was to reconstruct miscegenation as white male rape and to deny that the black community wanted intermarriage. The character of Will Smith, who most frequently made political statements similar to the political opinions of Hopkins, stated categorically to the American Colored League, "Miscegenation, either lawful or unlawful, we do not want."

Hopkins used *Contending Forces* to demonstrate that the political issue behind the violence of lynching was not the threat of black sexuality but the potential power of the black vote: "Which race shall dominate ... south of Mason and Dixon's line? The negro if given his full political rights, would carry the balance of power every time. This power the South has sworn that he shall never exercise." Her presentation of rape and lynching as tactics of political terror to repress any attempt at black political, social, or economic advancement drew on the arguments and indictments of Ida B. Wells. The act of rape, Hopkins argued, had to be totally separated from the issue of violated white womanhood and situated as a part of the social, political, and economic oppression of black people:

> Lynching was instituted to crush the manhood of the enfranchised black. Rape is the crime which appeals most strongly to the heart of the home life.... *The men who created the mulatto race, who recruit its ranks year after year by the very means which they invoked lynch law to suppress,* bewailing the sorrows of violated womanhood! no; it is not rape. If the Negro votes, he is shot; if he marries a white woman, he is shot or lynched—he is a pariah whom the National Government cannot defend. But if he defends himself and his home, then is heard the tread of marching feet, as the Federal troops move southward to quell a "race riot."

In Hopkins's fictional representation of the social relations between white and black, she reconstructed a generational history across a century to situate the contemporary reassertion of the doctrine of white supremacy within a framework that demythologized the American story of origins. Democracy was exposed as an imperialist slavocracy. Hopkins's characters were created not as holistic individuals but as the terrain on which the consequences of her authorial interpretation of history were worked through, making the whole Smith family the bearers of the history of colonization and slavery. But perhaps Hopkins's political intention was at its clearest in the construction of the two identities of Sappho Clark.

The disguise in which history was hidden was Sappho, the poet of Lesbos, who was admired and loved by men and women, though her erotic poetry was addressed to women. The Sappho of Hopkins's text was the focus of admiration of all the occupants of the boardinghouse, indeed of everyone she met, men and women. To Dora, who occupied domestic space running the boardinghouse, Sappho was the independent woman who in their intimate moments together talked of the need for suffrage and the political activity of women. Sappho disrupted Dora's complacency with her existence that led her to "generally accept whatever the men tell me as right" and made her reassess the importance of friendships with women:

> There was a great fascination for her about the quiet, self-possessed woman. She did not, as a rule, care much for girl friendships, holding that a close intimacy between the two of the same sex was more than likely to end disastrously for one or the other. But Sappho Clark seemed to fill a long-felt want in her life, and she had from the first a perfect trust in the beautiful girl.

The feelings that Sappho created in Dora contrasted dramatically with Dora's emotional response to John Langley, her betrothed, who, she complained to Sappho, made her feel "unsexed."

But Sappho as an ideal embodiment of womanhood did not exist. In order to function, to work and survive, Mabelle Beaubean, a product of miscegenation and the subject of rape, had to bury her violated womanhood and deny her progeny. For, like Sappho of Lesbos, Sappho Clark had a child, "Whose form is like gold flowers." Sappho Clark fled the accusations of John Langley and returned south to New Orleans, telling no one of her whereabouts. Her journey to retrieve her own identity and understand and accept the consequences of her womanhood meant that she also had to acknowledge her position as mother and to accept the child she had denied, a child that represented her rape. In a chapter entitled "Mother-love," Harper exposed the consequences of rape: "the feeling of degradation had made her ashamed of the joys of motherhood, of pride of possession in her child." The passage toward acceptance of her motherhood retrieved and combined the elements of Sappho and Mabelle. This necessary transition preceded the final transformation into wifehood and marriage with Will. "Mother-love" was present in the text as a process of purification, a spiritual revival that could purge the circumstances of birth and that prepared Sappho for the future, "fitting her perfectly for the place she was to occupy in carrying comfort and hope to the women of her face."

The most significant absence in the network of social forces through which Hopkins delineated her characters was the black father. The father was a narrative figure who mediated patriarchal control over women. In Hopkins's text, as in texts by most nineteenth-century black women, patriarchal control was exercised by and mediated through the figures of white men who denied political, social, and economic patriarchal power to black men. Henry Smith was present only as a memory; his story was recounted as a life circumscribed by racism in every activity he undertook. Though the struggle of his life was constant, "he had no desire to contend with the force of prejudice". He had no active part in Hopkins's text, having died years before her contemporary tale began. His absence thus confirmed the denial of patriarchal power to black men, but in this space Hopkins created alternative figures of black men constructed in peer relations, as brothers or as potential partner/husbands. The black heroines did not become the subject of an exchange between black men in marriage; they are not transferred from father to husband in a passage from daughter to wife. As did Frances Harper's *Iola Leroy*, **Contending Forces** posed but did not explore the possibility of utopian relations between men and women.

What Hopkins concentrated on instead was a representation of the black female body as colonized by white male power and practices; if oppositional control was exerted by a black male, as in the story of Mabelle's father, the black male was destroyed. The link between economic/political power and economic/sexual power was firmly established in the battle for the control over women's bodies. Hopkins repeatedly asserted the importance of the relation between histories: the contemporary rape of black women was linked to the oppression of the female slave. Children were destined to follow the condition of their mothers into a black, segregated realm of existence from where they were unable to challenge the white-controlled structure of property and power. Any economic, political, or social advance made by black men resulted in accusations of a threat to the white female body, the source of heirs to power and property, and subsequent death at the hands of a lynch mob. A desire for a pure black womanhood, an uncolonized black female body, was the false hope of Sappho's pretense. The only possible future for her black womanhood was through a confrontation with,

not denial of, her history. The struggle to establish and assert her womanhood was a struggle of redemption: a retrieval and reclaiming of the previously colonized. The reunited Mabelle/Sappho was a representation of a womanhood in which motherhood was not contingent upon wifehood, and Will was a representation of a black manhood that did not demand that women be a medium of economic exchange between men. The figure of Mabelle/Sappho lost her father when he refused to accept that his daughter was a medium of cash exchange with his white stepbrother. Beaubean had his fatherhood denied at the moment when he attempted to assert such patriarchal control and was slaughtered by a white mob. Instead of representing a black manhood that was an equivalent to white patriarchy, Hopkins grasped for the utopian possibility that Will could be a husband/partner to Mabelle/Sappho, when he accepted her sexual history, without having to occupy the space of father to her child.

Contending Forces was the most detailed exploration of the parameters of black womanhood and of the patriarchal limitations of black manhood in Hopkins's fiction. In her following three novels, Hopkins would adopt the more popular conventions of womanhood and manhood that defined heroes and heroines as she produced a magazine fiction that sought a wide audience. Hopkins continued to write political fiction at the same time as she adopted popular fictional formulas and was the first Afro-American author to produce a black popular fiction that drew on the archetypes of dime novels and story papers. (pp. 136-44)

> *Hazel V. Carby, "'Of What Use Is Fiction?':*
> *Pauline Elizabeth Hopkins," in her* Reconstructing Womanhood: The Emergence of the Afro-American Woman Novelist, *Oxford University Press, Inc., 1987, pp. 121-44.*

FURTHER READING

Review of *Contending Forces: A Romance Illustrative of Negro Life North and South,* by Pauline Elizabeth Hopkins. *Choice* 15, No. 11 (January 1979): 1518.
   Maintains that *Contending Forces* is significant for its content despite Hopkins's adherence to outdated nineteenth-century literary conventions.

Rush, Theressa Gunnels; Myers, Carol Fairbanks; and Arata, Esther Spring. "Pauline Elizabeth Hopkins." In their *Black American Writers Past and Present: A Biographical and Bibliographical Dictionary,* Vol. 1, pp. 389-90. Metuchen, N.J.: Scarecrow Press, 1975.
   Sketch of Hopkins's life and career, including a bibliography of primary and secondary works.

Setnick, Susan E. Review of *Contending Forces,* by Pauline Elizabeth Hopkins. *Kliatt* XIV, No. 6 (September 1980): 7.
   Positive review of *Contending Forces.*

Shockley, Ann Allen. "Pauline Elizabeth Hopkins: A Biographical Excursion into Obscurity." *Phylon* XXXIII, No. 1 (Spring 1972): 22-6.

> Surveys Hopkins's life and career.

Smith, Albreta Moore. "Editorial and Publishers' Announcements." *The Colored American Magazine* III, No. 6 (October 1901): 478-79.

Praises *Contending Forces* as "undoubtedly the book of the century.... It is all absorbing from first to last.... In point of composition, plot and style of writing it cannot be excelled."

Langston Hughes

1902-1967

(Full name James Mercer Langston Hughes) American poet, short story writer, novelist, dramatist, autobiographer, editor, translator, and author of children's books.

A seminal figure of the Harlem Renaissance, a period during the 1920s and early 1930s of unprecedented artistic and intellectual achievement among black Americans, Hughes devoted his versatile and prolific career to portraying the urban experience of working-class blacks. Called "the Poet Laureate of Harlem" by Carl Van Vechten, Hughes integrated the rhythm and mood of jazz and blues music into his work and used colloquial language to reflect black American culture. Hughes's gentle humor and wry irony often belie the magnitude of his themes. Having been a victim of poverty and discrimination, Hughes wrote about being seduced by the American Dream of freedom and equality only to be denied its realization. He composed the poem "Dream Deferred" to symbolize his frustration: "What happens to a dream deferred? / Does it dry up / like a raisin in the sun? / Or fester like a sore— / And then run? / Does it stink like rotten meat? / Or crust and sugar over— / like a syrupy sweet? / Maybe it just sags / like a heavy load / Or *does it explode?*" Speaking of Hughes's wide-range of works, Theodore R. Hudson stated: "Dipping his pen in ink, not acid, [Hughes's] method was to expose rather than excoriate, to reveal rather than revile."

Hughes was born in Joplin, Missouri, to James Nathaniel and Carrie Mercer Langston Hughes, who separated shortly after the boy's birth. His father left the United States for Cuba and later settled in Mexico, where he lived the remainder of his life as a prosperous attorney and landowner. In contrast, Hughes's mother lived a transitory life, often leaving her son in the care of his maternal grandmother while searching for a job. Following his grandmother's death in 1910, Hughes lived with family friends and various relatives in Kansas and, in 1914, joined his mother and new stepfather in Cleveland, Ohio. Hughes attended Central High School, where he excelled academically and in sports. He also wrote poetry and short fiction for the *Belfry Owl,* the high school literary magazine, and edited the school yearbook. In the summer of 1919 Hughes visited his father in Mexico for the first time but soon became disillusioned with his father's materialistic values and contemptuous belief that blacks, Mexicans, and Indians were lazy and ignorant. Upon graduating from high school in 1920, Hughes returned to Mexico, where he taught English for a year and wrote poems and prose pieces for publication in the *Crisis,* the magazine of the National Association for the Advancement of Colored People. With the help of his father, who had originally urged him to study engineering in Switzerland or Germany, Hughes enrolled at Columbia University in New York City in 1921, favoring classes in English literature. Subjected to bigotry on campus—he was assigned the worst dormitory room because of his color—and teachers he found boring, Hughes often missed classes in order to attend shows, lectures, and readings sponsored by the American Socialist Society. Following his freshman year, Hughes dropped out of college and worked a series of odd jobs while supporting his mother, who had recently moved to Harlem. Hughes also published several poems in the *Crisis* during this period. In 1923 he signed on as a cabin boy on a merchant freighter en route to West Africa.

Hughes spent the majority of the following year overseas. After resigning his position on the *S. S. McKeesport* in the Netherlands, he lived in virtual poverty in France and Italy. Returning to the United States in 1925, he resettled with his mother and half brother in Washington, D. C. He continued writing poetry while working menial jobs, experimenting with language, form, and rhythms reminiscent of the blues and jazz compositions he had heard in Paris nightclubs. In May and August of 1925, Hughes's verse garnered him literary prizes from both *Opportunity* magazine and the *Crisis.* In December, Hughes, now a busboy at a Washington, D. C., hotel, attracted the attention of poet Vachel Lindsay by placing three of his poems on Lindsay's dinner table. Later that evening Lindsay read Hughes's poems to an audience and announced his discovery of a "Negro busboy poet." The next day reporters and photographers eagerly greeted Hughes at work to hear more of his compositions. Shortly thereafter, with the help of critic and art patron Carl Van Vechten, Hughes published his first book, *The Weary Blues* (1926), a collection of poems that reflect the frenzied atmosphere of Harlem nightlife. Most of the selections in this volume approximate the phrasing and meter of blues music, a genre popularized in the early 1920s by rural and urban blacks. In such pieces as "Jazzonia," "Cabaret," and "The Weary Blues," Hughes evoked the frenzied, hedonistic atmosphere of Harlem's famous nightclubs and speakeasies, while "The Jester" and "Mother to Son" comment upon racial conflict. Hughes also included several pieces about his travels in Africa, as well as "The Negro Speaks of Rivers," a much-anthologized poem Hughes wrote during his second visit to Mexico in 1920. The lines "I bathed in the Euphrates when dawns were young / I built my hut near the Congo and it lulled me to sleep" foreshadow the nationalist writings later popularized by other writers of the Harlem Renaissance and by young militant poets of the civil rights era. *The Weary Blues* received mixed reviews, with some critics questioning the motives and appropriateness of blues and jazz verse centering on Harlem life. Countee Cullen wrote: "I regard these jazz poems as interlopers in the company of the truly beautiful poems.... There is too much emphasis here on strictly Negro themes."

Shortly before the publication of *The Weary Blues,* Hughes enrolled at Lincoln University in Pennsylvania, where he continued publishing poetry, short stories, and essays in mainstream and black-oriented periodicals. In 1927, together with Zora Neale Hurston and other writers, Hughes founded *Fire!,* a literary journal devoted to African-American culture. The venture was unsuccessful, however, in part because a fire destroyed the editorial offices. In the spring of the same year, Hughes published his second collection of verse, *Fine Clothes to the Jew* (1927). In this volume he included several ballads and chose Harlem's lower class as his principal subject. This approach dismayed several leading black intellectuals and critics, who felt that Hughes's depictions of crap games, street brawls, and other unsavory activities would undermine their efforts to improve race relations. Alain Locke, however, held an opposing view: "[*Fine Clothes to the Jew*] is notable as an achievement in poetic realism in addition to its particular value as a folk study in verse of Negro life." During the late 1920s Hughes met Mrs. R. Osgood Mason, an elderly white widow who served as both his literary patron and friend. Strongly committed to developing the talents of young

black artists, Mason supported Hughes while he wrote his first novel, *Not without Laughter* (1930). Following this book's publication, however, Hughes and Mason suffered a dramatic and bitter break in their relationship. Hughes later reconstructed these events in his short story "The Blues I'm Playing."

In 1932 Hughes traveled to Moscow with other black Americans on an unsuccessful filmmaking venture that nevertheless proved instrumental to his short story writing. While working as a journalist in Moscow, a friend loaned Hughes a copy of D. H. Lawrence's short story collection *The Lovely Lady.* After reading the title story, Hughes was struck by the similarities between Lawrence's main character and Mrs. Mason, his former Park Avenue patron. Overwhelmed by what he felt was the power of Lawrence's stories, Hughes began writing short fiction of his own. By 1933, when he returned to the United States, he had sold three stories and had begun compiling his first collection, *The Ways of White Folks* (1934). Between 1933 and 1935 Hughes wrote the majority of his short stories, and, in 1943, the first of his "Simple" tales appeared in the black-owned *Chicago Defender* newspaper. His most noted short pieces, the Simple sketches center on Jesse B. Semple, known as Simple, who is a black Everyman. Simple is the quintessential "wise fool" whose experiences and uneducated insights capture the frustrations of being black in America. Arthur P. Davis declared that "Simple's honest and unsophisticated eye sees through the shallowness, hypocrisy, and phoniness of white and black America alike." The Simple sketches were very popular among black readers of Hughes's day, and they remain some of Hughes's best-loved works. The Simple stories are collected in *Simple Speaks His Mind* (1950), *Simple Takes a Wife* (1953), *Simple Stakes a Claim* (1957), and *Simple's Uncle Sam* (1965).

Although generally considered less significant than his poetry and prose, Hughes's work for the theater was also popular with black audiences. Using such innovations as theater-in-the-round and audience participation, Hughes anticipated the work of later avant-garde dramatists, including Amiri Baraka and Sonia Sanchez. In 1938 Hughes founded the Harlem Suitcase Theater and also helped establish the Los Angeles Negro Arts Theater and the Skyloft Players of Chicago. As with his work in other genres, Hughes's drama combines urban dialogue, folk idioms, and a thematic emphasis on the dignity and strength of black Americans. *Mulatto* (1935), his first play to be produced, *Little Ham* (1935), *Soul Gone Home* (1937), *Simply Heavenly* (1957), and *Tambourines to Glory* (1963) are among Hughes's most noted plays.

Despite his success in a variety of genres, Hughes considered himself a poet first. In the late 1930s, after producing numerous plays and short stories, he returned to writing poetry. These later collections of verse, however, show an increasingly bleak view of black America. In *Montage of a Dream Deferred* (1951) Hughes contrasted the drastically deteriorated state of

Harlem in the 1950s to the Harlem he had known in the 1920s. The exuberance of nightclub life and the vitality of cultural renaissance had given way to an urban ghetto plagued by poverty and crime. Parallel to the change in tone was a change in rhythm: the smooth patterns and gentle melancholy of blues music were replaced by the abrupt, fragmented structure of postwar jazz and be-bop. *Ask Your Mama: 12 Moods for Jazz* (1961) consists of twelve irreverent poems that comment on the political turbulence of the early 1960s. Intended to be read aloud with musical accompaniment, Hughes's verse offers acerbic solutions to segregation and the plight of Southern blacks. He also rendered an imaginary South in which civil rights leader Martin Luther King, Jr., is elected governor of the state of Georgia, and Orval Faubus, the Arkansas governor who defied federal court orders to desegregate public schools, becomes a mammy in charge of rearing black children. Hughes's final collection of verse, *The Panther and the Lash: Poems of Our Times,* was published posthumously in 1967. In such pieces as "Black Panther" and "The Backlash Blues," Hughes wrote bitterly and angrily about race relations in America. This volume received scant critical attention upon its publication; some reviewers viewed the work as a polemical effort that surrendered to political fashion. W. Edward Farrison, however, considered *The Panther and the Lash* an appropriate conclusion to Hughes's career: "From the beginning of his career as an author, Hughes was articulate in the Negro's struggle for first-class citizenship. It is indeed fitting that this volume with which his career ended is a vital contribution to that struggle as well as to American poetry."

Throughout his career Hughes encountered mixed reactions to his work. Many black intellectuals denounced him for portraying unsophisticated aspects of lower-class life, claiming that his focus furthered the unfavorable image of his race. Hughes, however, believed in the inherent worth of the common people and in the need to present the truth as he perceived it: "I didn't know the upper class Negroes well enough to write much about them. I knew only the people I had grown up with, and they weren't people whose shoes were always shined, who had been to Harvard, or who had heard of Bach. But they seemed to me good people, too." As the struggle for American civil rights became increasingly widespread toward the end of his life, Hughes was also faulted by militants for failing to address controversial issues. Nevertheless, Hughes's reputation with black readers has remained consistently strong, chiefly due to his poetry and short stories. Despite the criticism, Hughes's position in the American literary scene seems to be secure. David Littlejohn wrote: "[Hughes is] the one sure Negro classic, more certain of permanence than even Baldwin or Ellison or Wright.... His voice is as sure, his manner as original, his position as secure as, say Edwin Arlington Robinson's or Robinson Jeffers'.... By molding his verse always on the sounds of Negro talk, the rhythms of Negro music, by retaining his own keen honesty and directness, his poetic sense and

ironic intelligence, he maintained through four decades a readable newness distinctly his own."

(For further information about Hughes's life and works, see *Black Writers; Children's Literature Review,* Vol. 17; *Contemporary Authors,* Vols. 1-4, 25-28; *Contemporary Authors New Revision Series,* Vol. 1; *Contemporary Literary Criticism,* Vols. 1, 5, 10, 15, 35, 44; *Dictionary of Literary Biography,* Vols. 4, 7, 48, 51, 86; *Poetry Criticism,* Vol. 1; *Short Story Criticism,* Vol. 6; and *Something about the Author,* Vols. 4, 33.)

PRINCIPAL WORKS

"Negro Artist and the Racial Mountain" (essay) 1926; published in periodical *The Nation*
The Weary Blues (poetry) 1926
Fine Clothes to the Jew (poetry) 1927
Not without Laughter (novel) 1930
Dear Lovely Death (poetry) 1931
The Negro Mother and Other Dramatic Recitations (poetry) 1931
The Dream Keeper and Other Poems (poetry) 1932
Popo and Fifina: Children of Haiti [with Arna Bontemps] (juvenilia) 1932
Scottsboro Limited: Four Poems and a Play in Verse (poetry and drama) 1932
The Ways of White Folks (short stories) 1934
Little Ham (drama) 1935
Mulatto (drama) 1935
Soul Gone Home (drama) 1937
Don't You Want to Be Free? (drama) 1938
A New Song (poetry) 1938
The Big Sea: An Autobiography (autobiography) 1940
Shakespeare in Harlem (poetry) 1942
Freedom's Plow (poetry) 1943
Jim Crow's Last Stand (poetry) 1943
Lament for Dark Peoples and Other Poems (poetry) 1944
Fields of Wonder (poetry) 1947
One-Way Ticket (poetry) 1949
The Barrier (libretto) 1950
Simple Speaks His Mind (short stories) 1950
Montage of a Dream Deferred (poetry) 1951
Laughing to Keep from Crying (short stories) 1952
Simple Takes a Wife (short stories) 1953
The Sweet Flypaper of Life [with Roy De Carava] (nonfiction) 1955
I Wonder as I Wander: An Autobiographical Journey (autobiography) 1956
Simply Heavenly (drama) 1957
Simple Stakes a Claim (short stories) 1957
The Langston Hughes Reader (poetry and short stories) 1958
Tambourines to Glory (novel) 1958
Selected Poems of Langston Hughes (poetry) 1959
Ask Your Mama: 12 Moods for Jazz (poetry) 1961
The Best of Simple (short stories) 1961
Black Nativity (drama) 1961
Five Plays by Langston Hughes (dramas) 1963
Something in Common and Other Stories (short stories) 1963
Simple's Uncle Sam (short stories) 1965

The Panther and the Lash: Poems of Our Times (poetry) 1967
†*Mule Bone: A Comedy of Negro Life* [with Zora Neale Hurston] (drama) 1991

*This work was adapted for the stage in 1963.
†This comedy, completed by Hughes and Hurston in 1930, was first staged in 1991 with a prologue and epilogue by George Houston Bass.

Arthur P. Davis (essay date 1954)

[*An American authority on black literature, Davis is the author of* From the Dark Tower: Afro-American Writers 1900-1960 *(1974). In the following excerpt, he explores both the comic and tragic dimensions of Hughes's character Jesse B. Semple.*]

In his companion-works, **Simple Speaks His Mind** (1950) and **Simple Takes a Wife** (1953), Langston Hughes has given us one of the freshest and most fascinating Negro characters in American fiction. Mr. Jesse B. Semple, or Simple for short, is an uneducated Harlem man-about-town who speaks a delightful brand of English and who, from his stool at Paddy's Bar, comments both wisely and hilariously on many things, but principally on women and race. An unusual character in several respects, Simple's most appealing trait is that he is a Negro comic figure at whom Negroes themselves can laugh without being ashamed. Simple is so human, so believable, and so much like each of us that we are drawn to him in spite of ourselves. We laugh with Simple rather than at him; and our laughter is therapeutic because it tends to make us aware of our own cliché-thinking on the race question, a shortcoming which we all evidence at one time or another. (p. 21)

Accepting Simple for what he is, Hughes makes effective use of the contrast in viewpoint between Simple's segment of society and his own. He has made Simple the very highly articulate spokesman of the untrained-worker group and himself the voice of the educated Negro liberal. The merit of this arrangement is that the two attitudes tend to complement each other. Simple generally exemplifies the directness and singlemindedness of the untrained Negro and Hughes the sophisticated tolerance and broadmindedness of the black intellectual. The clash and interplay of these attitudes furnish much of the humor in Simple, but they also serve a deeper purpose; they point up and accentuate the two-level type of thinking which segregation tends to produce in all Negroes. And as we read these dialogues, we often find ourselves giving lip-service to the sophisticated Hughes side of the debate while our hearts share Simple's cruder but more realistic attitude. It is this "double" approach that appeals to the Negro reader because... the Negro in our country has to live a dual life—as a Negro and as an American.

But enough of this analysis of Langston Hughes' approach. Let us turn now to Simple himself. Our first impression of Mr. Jesse B. is that however unpredictable he may be in other things he is thoroughly consistent in one respect: first, last, and always, he is a "race man"—a fourteen carat, one hundred percent, dyed-in-the-wool race man. No professional Negro leader, no Harlem orator, no follower of Marcus Garvey is more concerned about the fate and well-being of the black brother than Simple. Morning, noon, and night and seven days a week, Simple thinks and talks and gripes about being colored. Whatever happens to him, if it is bad, Simple can trace to some remote origin in race. "No matter what a man does, sick or well," he tells us, "something is always liable to happen especially if you are colored." He constantly reminds that "a dark man shall see dark days"; and he can point with certainty to the cause of all his troubles: "I have been caught in some kind of riffle ever since I been black." When Hughes remonstrates with him and accuses him of always bringing up the race question, Simple's answer is that a black man does not have to bring up the race question; it is always present. "I look in the mirror in the morning to shave—and what do I see? Me." Brushing aside all fancy and sophisticated extenuations and commentary, Simple has brought the issue home to himself. A black face in our color-conscious world is the problem. Simple and every other Negro knows that.

It is this going to the heart of racial matters that amuses and intrigues us. Simple may be biased, but he is always realistic. For example, he and Hughes are discussing that much-discussed topic, race relations, one evening, and the latter insists that inter-marriage is not and should not be an important consideration in such relations. Simple ridicules the highfalutin' argument and as usual puts his finger on the real issue: "But if races are ever going to relate," he asserts ungrammatically, "they must also mate, and then you will have race relations." Again, as humorous and literal-minded as Simple's answer is, it makes sense. Or let us take Simple's discussion with his well-meaning downtown white friends concerning the progress Negroes have made (a typical topic of well-meaning whites): "Them white folks," Simple informs us, "are always telling me, 'isn't it wonderful the progress that's been made amongst your people. Look at Dr. Bunche.' All I say is Look at Me!"

Simple's comment is excellent social criticism. (pp. 22-3)

The squeamish reader may be unfavorably impressed when he finds that Simple is anti-white. As a working man living in a society in which a black face means an inferior position, Simple naturally and understandably has anti-white feelings, but one soon discovers that these feelings are neither morbid nor bitter, are not very deep, and as a matter of fact are not even consistent. But when you hear Simple holding forth from the stool at Paddy's Bar, he sounds like a rabid racist. In such cases, Simple is doing what most Negroes do on occasion; he exaggerates his anti-white feelings for the sake of the argument. For example, Hughes and Simple are discussing the "second coming" of Christ (they had read about a lecture being given on the subject), and Simple naturally added a racial angle to the debate. Christ, he maintained loudly and belligerently, should come back and "smite down" all of the white folks for the way they treated Negroes. "You don't mean all white folks, do you?" Hughes asked. "No," said Simple, "I hope he lets Mrs. Roosevelt alone." In this one short sentence Simple has expressed much of the inconsistency which characterizes the American Negro's anti-white tendencies. It would take volumes of sociology to explain all of the nuances of irritation and concession and extenuating circumstances which make up this attitude, but Simple has put it all into one humorous statement.

Simple is guilty of another inconsistency in his racial thinking. Although he tends to blame all of his troubles on being colored, yet he refuses to use race as an excuse for shoddiness on the part of Negroes. Therefore when he goes into a Harlem restaurant and gets bad service or into a 125th Street dime store and finds an impolite and inefficient Negro girl clerking he is vitriolic in his denunciation. In this respect Simple is typical not only

Hughes with friends (clockwise: Isidore Kaplow, "Wendel" Gomez, and Irwin Braverman) at Central High School, circa 1919.

of his class but of all decent, self-respecting Negroes. The severest criticism of Negro misconduct comes not from Negro-haters but from Negroes themselves, a fact often overlooked by whites. Simple's attitude stems from an awareness that the Negro group, unlike any other group in America, is often judged by each individual act; he is therefore always alert to any act that will stigmatize the race. His position is summed up in a very forthright declaration: "When my race does wrong, I say, No. But when they do right, I give 'em credit." And Simple is big enough to be objective about himself on this score. One day he and another "cat" were about to mix it up in a 125th Street store when an old Negro lady said to them: "Now, sons, sons, you-all are acting just like Negroes." Simple immediately regained control of himself. "That made me ashamed," he confesses ruefully, "so I cut out." (pp. 23-4)

The American Negro's propensity to laugh at as well as to criticize himself is nowhere better exemplified than in Simple; and this laughter usually has its source in certain "racial" characteristics and features which distinguish the Negro from whites. For example, the gradations of color among American Negroes is a perennial source of such laughter, and Hughes in his delineation of Simple has drawn heavily upon this reservoir of folk humor. Simple's description of himself is in this vein: "I am a light black," he tells us. "When I were a child, Mama said I were a chocolate, also my hair was straight. But that was my Indian blood." When a mild doubt is raised concerning Simple's redskin genealogy, he becomes almost indignant: "Anybody can look at me and tell I am part Indian." Knowing Simple's color and knowing also the thousands of real-life Simples who, in all seriousness, make such claims, we can appreciate the humor of such remarks, but it is almost impossible to explain that humor to an outsider. For one reason, it is a very grim sort of humor because underneath the fun is the harsh reality that color is all-important in America. Though they laugh at themselves for doing it, the Simples unconsciously seek any mythical alliance that will alleviate in some measure the full social and economic stigma of blackness. For instance, when Simple's girl friend Joyce takes him to the photographer's, she requests that Simple's portrait be made "a little lighter than natural." There is, of course, an extra charge for this service, but both Joyce and Simple know that "color" comes high in a world where "white is right." Humor of this sort has many tragic overtones; it is essentially defensive; it is the Negro laughing first at his own "differences" in order to remove the sting of outside ridicule.

Another aspect of Simple's racial humor is his language. The jive talk of ghetto Negroes, it seems to me, has its origin in social ostracism. Set apart from the whole community, the black segment tends to flaunt its exclusion by a kind of "inside" vocabulary—a vocabulary known only to the initiate. Mastery of this peculiar speech serves oftentimes as a badge of belonging, consequently when the uneducated migrant comes to a community like Harlem, he acquires the new speech pattern not only for purposes of communication but also as a sign of his having made the grade up North.

Simple impresses me as being typical in this respect. Like most Harlemites, he was born in the South, in his case, Virginia. He, therefore, has a twofold speech background—his native Southern and his acquired Harlem. His language, reflecting the conflict and the adjustment between the two, is made of good old-fashioned Southern idiom and Harlem jive talk. For example, when Simple says, "I am tired of trickeration. Also I have had too many hypes laid down on me. Now I am hep," he is blending both traditions. The first sentence is pure Southern; the rest pure Harlemese. But Simple's language is typical in yet another respect. The uneducated Negro is inclined to avoid usual words just because they sound too natural. Simple has this attitude towards "was" and "were." Why do you use "was" and "were" both in the same way, he is asked. His answer is a lesson in applied linguistics: "Because sometimes I were and sometimes I was, . . . I was at Niagara Falls and I were at the Grand Canyon. . . ." For Simple "was" denotes the immediate past and "were" the remote. This is Simple's explanation, but the real reason as we know is that Simple likes the sound of "were"; it is much more "proper" than plain old everyday "was" which any "downhome" boy could use. (pp. 25-6)

Simple's love of the black ghetto shines through every comment he makes. "Harlem," he boasts, "has got everything from A to Z. Here, like the song says, 'I have found my true love.'" Simple likes Harlem because it is "so full of Negroes." He feels the protection that black faces give from a predominantly white world, a world which is too often hostile. Simple works downtown, but he plays uptown. Harlem therefore means for him release from harsh and unpleasant duties; it means a chance to climb a bar stool or to ring a doorbell and say, "Baby, here I am." He loves Harlem because there are no time clocks or bosses to think about—just joy, relaxation and his girl friend. And although he does not state it bluntly, Simple loves Harlem because to him it is the only place in New York where a black man can find sanctuary; elsewhere in New York he is an alien. It is this sense of finding refuge that underlies much of his comment on the black city. "I will take Harlem for mine," he says emphatically. "At least if trouble comes, I will have my own window to shoot from." When Langston Hughes reminds him that most of the houses in Harlem are owned by whites, Simple is not disturbed: "I might not own 'em, but I live in 'em! It would take an atom bomb to get me out."

Even in his wildest dreaming, Simple cannot stay away from Harlem. Indulging his fancy one evening at Paddy's, Simple imagines himself a bird (black bird of course) flying away in the wild blue yonder following Jackie Robinson as the team moves from place to place. But as Simple envisioned himself flying over New York, he found that the pull of Harlem was too strong: "I fell in on Lenox Avenue like a fish falls back in the pool when it gets off the hook." In short, even in his dream world of escape, Simple can conceive of no place better than Harlem. But Simple knows that Harlem and New York can be a challenge to the peasant coming up from the South. All of them do not make it, he tells us. They come and they go. (pp. 26-7)

Simple is actually a displaced person as far as his native region is concerned. This accounts for his love of Harlem and for the fierce protective instinct that makes the Simples of Harlem such tragic characters deep down. As a matter of record, Simple in spite of his good nature and his ebulliency leads a very narrow and lonely existence. From Monday to Saturday he works downtown in an alien world. His real life uptown lies between his drab Third-Floor-Rear room and Paddy's Bar, with trips, of course, to see Joyce, his girl friend. This is his whole limited life. He has no friends—as he tells us—only barroom acquaintances. When he asks Hughes to be his best man at the June wedding, he confesses the real loneliness of his existence: "I likes to be rowdy myself, but don't like to run with rowdies. Why is that? I like to drink, but I don't like drunks. I don't have the education to mingle myself with educated folks. . . . So who are my buddies? You—and a couple of bartenders." (pp. 27-8)

In this light Simple is no longer a comic character but a black Pagliacci. Underneath all of his gaiety and humor there is the basic tragedy of the urban Negro and his circumscribed life. As such Simple becomes a symbol of all the limited and proscribed figures of all the black ghettos in America. The Simples talk gaily and laugh loudly, but they are really laughing to keep from crying.

Simple, however, like every other great fictional character is a complex and many-sided figure, and I do not wish to stress his tragic aspect to the exclusion of the more obvious one. Whatever else he may be, Simple is also exceptionally funny; and his greatness as a comic character lies, as I have said, in his averageness and typicalness. The Negro reader finds in him all of the slightly mixed-up racial thinking, all of the "twofold loyalties," and all of the laughable inconsistencies which the segregation pattern produces in us. The pressure of jim crow living is so uniform that even though Simple is an uneducated worker his responses to this pressure ring true for all classes. In this sense, Simple is the American Negro. If you want to understand the black brother, learn to know Simple. (p. 28)

> *Arthur P. Davis, "Jesse B. Semple: Negro American," in* PHYLON: The Atlanta University Review of Race and Culture, *Vol. XV, No. 1, first quarter (Spring, 1954), pp. 21-8.*

Webster Smalley (essay date 1963)

[*In the following excerpt, Smalley assesses Hughes's major dramas:* Mulatto, Soul Gone Home, Little Ham, Simply Heavenly, *and* Tambourines to Glory.]

[Langston Hughes] began writing during the Harlem literary renaissance of the twenties and is today, at the age of sixty, America's outstanding Negro man of letters.... No writer has better interpreted and portrayed Negro life, especially in the urban North, than Langston Hughes....

From his plays it is evident that Hughes has more and more identified with and written about the Negro community in Harlem. This crowded section of New York City, its vitality and variety, is his favorite setting.... (p. vii)

Not all of his writing is about Harlem and its inhabitants, of course.... His strong feeling for the Negro race and for the past and present problems of the Negro in America made inevitable his concern with the lot of the Negro in the South. This concern is strongly reflected in his first full-length play, **Mulatto,** for which Hughes chose as his subject the still explosive problem of racial intermixture and based the story on the plight of the son of a Negro housekeeper and a white plantation owner. (p. viii)

[*Mulatto*] was Langston Hughes' first professionally produced play and its text appears for the first time in [*Five Plays by Langston Hughes*]. (p. x)

While reading **Mulatto,** one should remember when it was written. It is very much a play of the thirties, an era when sociopolitical plays dominated American drama. The tendency was to oversimplify moral issues as in melodrama.... In **Mulatto,** the injustices suffered by Bert, by Cora, and by all the Negroes in the rural South are clearly and forcefully presented. The thesis is there clearly enough. But then the characters of Bert and Cora begin to dominate the action, and the play becomes something more than mere thesis drama. Bert Lewis, the rebellious son of a white plantation owner and his Negro mistress, is placed in an unhappy, untenable situation, but it is his own stubborn, unbending pride—inherited, ironically, from his father—that brings about his downfall and death. The patient love and rich dignity of Cora and Bert's final recognition of the totality of his tragic situation raise **Mulatto** above the level of a mere problem play. One forgives Hughes the sometimes obvious exposition of the opening scenes (as one does the early O'Neill in *Beyond the Horizon*) for the tragedy and power of the play's final scenes. If the reader finds "melodramatic" elements in the play, let him look to the racial situation in the deep South as it is even today: it is melodramatic.

Mulatto is the only play included [in *Five Plays by Langston Hughes*] in which a white character is more than peripheral. In the other plays, where white characters do appear, they are little more than symbols—evil, good, or, as in the one-act **Soul Gone Home,** indifferent. The conception of **Soul Gone Home** is that of fantasy, and it contains some ironically comic moments, but its impulse is far removed from comedy. In a vignette-like episode, Hughes creates with great economy the kind of play Zola called for in his preface to *Thérèse Raquin.*

Although a fantasy in concept and structure, its atmosphere and effects are those of naturalism. Like one of Hughes' poems, **Soul Gone Home** bristles with implications and reverberates with connotations. That which is unsaid becomes almost more important than what is put into the dialogue. The repressive dominance of the white culture is suggested only by the arrival of ambulance attendants, who are white as the mother knew they would be. The tragedy is that of a people so repressed that they can no longer love, and the ironic implications build to a shocking climax. Its impact is stark and uncomplicated, and it is a difficult play to forget.

Hughes does not always write in a serious vein, as readers of his stories and poems well know. His folk plays of urban Negro life, at once humorous and revealing, are a true contribution to American folk drama. The three included [in **Five Plays by Langston Hughes**]—*Little Ham, Simply Heavenly,* and **Tambourines to Glory**—are, if one must define them, comedies. But the triple specters of poverty, ignorance, and repression can be seen not far beneath the surface of the comedy. The "numbers racket," "dream books," and the "hot goods man" in **Little Ham,** Simple's wistful sadness that no Negro has seen a flying saucer, and Laura's attitude toward the "religion business" in **Tambourines to Glory,** all indicate the near poverty, the ignorance, and the superstition that prevail in the world of which Hughes writes. Nevertheless, it is a colorful, wonderful world he presents to us, and we cannot but admire the spirit and vigor of his characters. He gives us a dynamic view of a segment of life most of us will never know and can discover nowhere else. At times he may sacrifice dramatic action for the sake of portraying nothing more than the people of Harlem absorbed in living out their lives from day to day, but if the humor of the scene and Hughes' infectious interest in his characters carry us along with him, what more can we ask?

Little Ham, "a play of the roaring twenties," is the first of Hughes' urban folk comedies. Its setting is Harlem at the time of the "Negro Renaissance," of *Shuffle Along,* and of the Cotton Club, but it is unlikely that any of its characters knew the meaning of "renaissance," had seen *Shuffle Along,* or had been inside the Cotton Club (which catered to a white clientele). Completed in 1935, *Little Ham* is a period piece, and one should remember the short skirts, tassels, brocades, and bell-shaped trousers of the era as he reads.

The play concerns the affairs (the word is intentionally ambiguous) of Hamlet Jones, a fast-talking, colorful, pint-sized Negro who shines shoes for a living. Little Ham's world is crowded, almost too crowded at times, with Harlemites of every sort except those of conventional respectability and education. It is a lively world, a society of casual morality that the white community either ignores or makes no attempt to understand. Hughes understands it, and this is the Harlem he has made into a literary land exclusively his own. One should not search too hard for profundity in *Little Ham;*

it is a high-spirited revel and should be accepted as just that. Little Ham, Madam Bell, Lulu, and generously proportioned Tiny Lee are of the Harlem Hughes remembered as a young man, but are persons clearly recognizable today. If the characters in these folk comedies seem uncomplex, it is simply because these people are, in reality, direct and lacking in subtle complexity. Since they are unaware of the existence of Freud and Jung, Hughes has not hampered them with a burden of subconscious motivation.

Hughes creates his characters from life. He does not create character to fit a preconception, so he is not frightened if some of his creations do things and like things that Negroes are reputed to do and like. There is probably no group of people he dislikes more than the "passers" and pretenders of this world. He accepts, loves, and enjoys every aspect of his heritage and has the wisdom to recognize its richness. He does not write for those Negroes who have turned their backs on the spirituals and blues, nor for the people, Negro and white, who would bowdlerize *Huckleberry Finn*. He writes of what he sees, in his own way. (pp. xi-xiii)

Langston Hughes is a most eclectic writer. In his "Simple" books and in his play, *Simply Heavenly,* he has created a hero who is almost no hero at all. Jesse Semple, or "Simple," yields to temptation so innocently but means so well, that any audience will forgive him more quickly than does his fiancée. Simple is Hughes' most memorable comic creation. He is of the same dramatic stripe as Figaro in Beaumarchais' *Figaro's Marriage*—both constantly skirt calamity and get into a good deal of trouble before they finally succeed in marrying the girls they love, and each has a unique dignity in spite of their comic weaknesses. Like his comic compeer, Simple has more than his share of these. His power of reasoning is wonderful to follow, even when his conclusions are unanswerable . . . . Simple, like most of his friends in Paddy's Bar, seldom has much money. What the inhabitants of this "neighborhood club" lack in affluence, they make up for in high spirits and good humor. There are no villains in *Simply Heavenly* . . . . The values of this play are not built on dramatic clash and suspense, rather, they are inherent in Hughes' intimate and warmly affectionate picture of the unique inhabitants of this city within a city. (p. xiv)

Essie and Laura, in *Tambourines to Glory,* are presented as simply and forthrightly as are Ham and Simple, but there is no similarity of character. Essie and Laura are both strong individuals—Essie, in her goodness, and Laura, in her predilection toward chicanery. Symbolically, they represent two very real aspects of all revivalist, perhaps all religious, movements. The saint and the charlatan often live side by side, even in established religions, and sometimes exist in a single personality. Hughes chose to write a rousing musical melodrama about some aspects of Harlem religion. The result is a skillfully created, well-integrated musical play, written with humor, insight, and compassion. (p. xv)

Villains are not plentiful in Hughes' Harlem plays. Big-Eyed Buddy Lomax (who informs us that he is really the Devil) is unique. Even he is a threat only through Laura's weakness for him (and all he represents). Hughes is not as interested in a conventional conflict between protagonist and antagonist as in revealing the cracks in the self-protecting façades humans erect to conceal their weaknesses. His characters are never merely subservient to plot. Thus, even within the confines of melodrama, he is able to write a moving and honest play.

Tambourines to Glory is more than musical melodrama; it is a play of redemption. It is a Faust-like tale, told with the simplicity of a medieval morality play. Hughes tells the story with great good humor, but he never asks us to laugh derisively or to smile sardonically. Behind the laughter is a touch of pity and a great quantity of warm understanding. As broadly and simply as the characters are sketched, they are utterly believable. When they show weakness, their frailties stem directly from problems that plague the average Negro in our largest metropolis. Laura's grasping drive for material things, for example, is a natural reaction to the deprivation and poverty she has suffered all her life, and Essie's honest faith is a triumph over tribulation and temptation. Both characterizations are true.

Finally, this play is in effect a "dramatic song," to use one of Hughes' descriptive terms. It has a pervasive rhythm. The integration of action, original lyrics, traditional spirituals, and the gospel music of Jobe Huntley, adds to the richness of the drama and contributes to characterization. Music is central to the lives—one might say, even to the spiritual being—of these characters. Nowhere has Hughes more skillfully interwoven and integrated music into the fabric of drama. (p. xvi)

The dramatic world of Langston Hughes is a quite different world from that of any other playwright, and the discovery of that world is, in itself, an entertaining, wonderful, and enlightening experience. (p. xvii)

> *Webster Smalley, in an introduction to* Five Plays *by Langston Hughes, edited by Webster Smalley, Indiana University Press, 1963, pp. vii-xvii.*

David Littlejohn (essay date 1966)

[*Littlejohn is the author of* Black on White: A Critical Survey of Writing by American Negroes *(1966). In the following excerpt from this work, he praises Hughes's skills as a poet and a storyteller.*]

Not Without Laughter deserves notice . . . as an antidote to the many shrill and artificial Harlem Renaissance novels.

It is not easy to define Hughes' achievement without making him sound corny or soft. Formulations of his work come out like Faulkner's stodgy explanations of his own novels, even to the motifs of "affirmation" and "endurance." *Not Without Laughter* belongs with the fiction of its simpler time. It is a gentle sequence of well-sketched social views, like so many Negro novels of the period—the family gatherings, the colored ball, the pool hall. It even includes the standard caricature of the Episcopalian, anti-watermelon dicty.

Its special value, like that of DuBois' social essays, lies in its completeness and truth, its control and wide humanity. It is probably the most genuine inside view of Negro life available in the fiction of the period, comparable to later works like Ann Petry's. Like almost all of Hughes' work it is sad, to a degree, but never violent or bitter; it is touching, but never falsely sentimental. It is very small, really, in outline—a collection of the more or less connected stories of a family of very average, very attractive small-town Negroes in Kansas; but the stories flow with the warmth of genuine life. (p. 52)

Langston Hughes . . . remains the most impressive, durable, and prolific Negro writer in America. His voice is as sure, his manner as original, his position as secure as, say, Edwin Arlington Robinson's or Robinson Jeffers'. He is the one sure Negro classic, more certain of permanence than even Baldwin or Ellison or Wright. By molding his verse always on the sounds of Negro talk, the rhythms of Negro music, by retaining his own keen honesty and directness, his poetic sense and ironic intelligence, he has maintained through four decades a readable newness distinctly his own . . . . Hughes is a true professional, like the hero of his fictions only deceptively "Simple." . . . He has . . . produced, for the white reader, a convincing, singing source book on the emotional life-style of the lower-class urban Negro in America, as valid as the blues. (pp. 54-5)

Langston Hughes is as skillful and durable a storyteller as he is a poet, a master at the ironic little social comedies of Negro life—a type he seems almost to have invented, so sure now is his hold and possession. His work lives as a potent reminder to the critic of the enduring primacy of "the story." He is an ingenious and happy craftsman in the best tradition of Somerset Maugham or O. Henry; his stories can be read, enjoyed, and understood by the man of simple common sense who dwells, presumably, in everyone. It would be folly to condescend; to suggest, effetely, that one is past such things: one never is. There is much to be admired in a small perfect circle. If Langston Hughes' stories are not deeply, endlessly resonant, or are not richly laden with awesome suggestion, they are still honest, deft, amusing, and provocative, reading after reading. They endure. He is lesser than Ellison or Baldwin only because his scope is so much smaller, not because his work is cheaper or less complete. But comparisons are foolish for a writer so attractive and secure . . . . He really "tells stories" rather than writes fiction, and he rarely makes mistakes. Although he has written of many things, his most comfortable subject is the urban Northern American Negro, his jobs, his play, his churches, his women. He can deal with various classes, but seems most at home with the poor. His text for Roy de Carava's rich photo

essay, *The Sweet Flypaper of Life* (1955), is as total an example of Langston Hughes, of his bittersweet participation in the lives of his people, as anything else he has written. There seems to be no distance, really, between author and subject, no artist's detachment—which is doubtless the effect of very careful art.

His tone has that intimate, elusive, near-tragic, near-comic sound of the Negro blues, and is equally defiant of analysis. His theme is not so much white oppression, as the Negro's quiet resistance to it. His writings typify (and probably support) the famous and useful myth of Negro endurance—the knowing grin, half-smile half-smirk, of the bowing but unbeaten. They may thus not find favor with more militant Negroes, who regard the very myth of endurance as treacherously pacifist, supported if not invented by whites.

The "Simple" stories, one or two pages long, offer little barbed home truths about Harlem life, the cost of living, domestic unbliss, and especially the various ludicrous paradoxes of America's racial double standard. Jesse B. Simple is a sort of comic no-good (a stereotype turned to use, written by a Negro for Negroes) with perpetual lady troubles, cadging beers off the straight main who tells the stories in exchange for another of his twisty bits of folk wisdom about "the ways of white folks."

On the whole, Hughes' creative life has been as full, as varied, and as original as Picasso's, a joyful, honest monument of a career. There is no noticeable sham in it, no pretension, no self-deceit; but a great, great deal of delight and smiling irresistible wit. If he seems for the moment upstaged by angrier men, by more complex artists, if "different views engage" us, necessarily, at this trying stage of the race war, he may well outlive them all, and still be there when it's over. Much of the greatness of the three major Negro novelists derives from their singularity, their essential aloneness; Hughes' at least seems to derive from his anonymous unity with his people. He *seems* to speak for millions, which is a tricky thing to do. (pp. 144-47)

> *David Littlejohn, "Before 'Native Son': The Renaissance and After," and "Negro Writers Today: The Novelists II," in his* Black on White: A Critical Survey of Writing by American Negroes, *Viking Press, 1966, pp. 39-65, 138-56.*

James A. Emanuel (essay date 1968)

[*In the following excerpt, Emanuel provides a general overview of Hughes's short stories.*]

Justly esteemed for his versatility and competence as a writer, especially as a poet and humorist, Langston Hughes deserves close study as the author of sixty-six published short stories. (p. 170)

The ninety-odd reviews of *The Ways of White Folks* and the less numerous brief critical notices of his other collections of stories record as their main consensus that

Hughes's style is natural, humorous, restrained and yet powerful. The naturalness is largely found in his characters' talk, which merges incident, personality, and racial history into recurrent patterns. The dialogue is particularly true to facts of race, which authentically control cadences, accents, and ductile phrases. The realism and pathos in much of his work are not adequately recognized in published commentary; nor is his characteristic irony—a point of view that Negro reviewers have best understood. At least twenty-five other typical traits of the stories, including their linguistic play, lyrical exuberance, juxtapositions, and repartee, have been relatively unnoticed. Their rhythm even, not to mention their tension and imagery, has barely been subjected to analysis. Hughes's interspersed songs and Chekhovian endings, which suggest both racial history and modern impasses in social progress, enhance his virtues of style.

The comprehensiveness of his stories has been generally admitted, although not usually detailed. Using settings as different as Harlem and Hong Kong, Havana and Africa, Hollywood and the Midwest, Alabama and New England, and in the main limiting himself to ordinary Negroes, Hughes reflects all the crucial factual realities and psychological depths of Negro experience, especially in urban communities. The variety of themes, images, and symbols through which he mounts this large picture can be indicated by a few statistical and analytical references. Of his forty-odd distinct themes, his main theme is racial prejudice (the focus of thirty-eight stories); his much less intense thematic purposes are to present usually delinquent fathers, affection-seeking women, interracial love, the faddish misconceptions of Negroes by whites, religion and morality, the life of the artist, and jealousy. His images, classifiable into sixteen general types, are most vivid when he is treating nature, physical violence, and weariness. His symbols, usefully introduced in at least seventeen different varieties, into material approached with uncluttered directness, most effectively employ crosses, Negro voices and laughter, snow, coal, and steel.

Hughes's skill in plotting and in creating character demands some comment. The easy and lively movement of **"A Good Job Gone"** exemplifies what Sherwood Anderson meant in calling him a "natural story teller." Hughes's plots are never complicated, and flashbacks are usually handled with grace. Some of his plots are mere gossamer, as in the sketches that he calls his "prose-poems"; some are rather mechanical, like that of **"One Friday Morning,"** which he judges his most "contrived" story; and some are skillfully unified, like that of **"Little Dog."** Some tales invite the risibilities in the manner of sure-fire anecdotes, like **"Tain't So."** Only in such uncollected narratives as **"Saved from the Dogs"** does the usual interest lag.

Not ordinarily concerned with fully rounding his characters, Hughes intimately develops only ten (Cora Jenkins of **"Cora Unashamed,"** Mr. Lloyd of **"A Good Job Gone,"** Oceola Jones of **"The Blues I'm Playing,"** Clara Briggs of **"Little Dog,"** Colonel Norwood and Bert

of **"Father and Son,"** Carl Anderson of **"On the Way Home,"** and Professor Brown, Charlie Lee, and Flora Belle Yates in three other stories); and some details of appearance, activities, background, and range of emotion and attitude are missing even in these portraits. Characterization is Hughes's primary technical consideration, however: he said conversationally in 1961, "I do not analyze what goes into the story from the standpoint of emotion, but in terms of whoever I am writing about." Racially, his characters are rather well balanced, despite a few claims to the contrary. One Negro newspaper review of *The Ways of White Folks* asserts that "Hughes's characters are no Uncle Toms"; but old Sam in **"Father and Son,"** complete with multiple *yes, sah's,* chattering teeth, popping eyes, and moaning, justifiably fits the mold—and more are stationed in Colonel Norwood's kitchen. And the pompous Dr. Jenkins in **"The Negro in the Drawing Room"** impressively qualifies. It is true, however, that Hughes almost never subjects Negroes to his own ridicule; and he never attributes any unmitigated felonious activity to them.

Regarding his characterization of whites, which has been usually termed compassionate, even "generous," the author clarified his view in a letter to me in 1961:

> I feel as sorry for them as I do for the Negroes usually involved in hurtful . . . situations. Through at least one (maybe *only* one) white character in each story, I try to indicate that 'they are human, too.' The young girl in **'Cora Unashamed,'** the artist in **'Slave on the Block,'** the white woman in the red hat in **'Home,'** the rich lover in **'A Good Job Gone'** helping the boy through college, the sailor all shook up about his **'Red-Headed Baby,'** the parents-by-adoption in **'Poor Little Black Fellow,'** the white kids in **'Berry,'** the plantation owner in **'Father and Son'** who wants to love his son, but there's the barrier of color between them. What I try to indicate is that circumstances and conditioning make it very hard for whites, in interracial relationships, each to his 'own self to be true.'

Hughes's sense of personal identification with specific characters in **"Slave on the Block,"** **"Father and Son,"** **"On the Way Home,"** and five other stories, explained in the same letter, increases the importance of characterization to his reshaping of experience into fiction.

Hughes's demonstrable sympathetic characterization of whites stands in revealing conjunction with the bitterness observed by about one-fifth of the reviewers of the 1934 collection and by a somewhat smaller percentage of those commenting upon *Laughing to Keep from Crying* in 1952. This bitterness, emphasized in a *Phylon* review by the perceptive John W. Parker in 1952 as "unwavering pessimism," is generalized by another Negro critic, Blyden Jackson, in 1960 in *CLA Journal*, as the improverishing "ogre" of the ghetto-ridden substance of Negro fiction. The fact that it coexists, in the not unusual case of Hughes, with restraint of style—a characteristic attributed to *The Ways of White Folks* almost as often as bitterness—should invite psychologically oriented critics to explore ways in which Negro writings illuminate the creative process itself.

The nature of the bitterness in Hughes's stories throws light upon his art, his wisdom, and his realism. In the forty-one narratives in his first two collections, only two characters have personalities substantially weighted with bitterness: Bert in **"Father and Son"** and Charlie Lee in **"Powder-White Faces."** Both kill because of it. The bitterness in four other characters is modified: Johnny Logan, in **"Trouble with the Angels,"** gives in, only at the end, to a bitterness that is bound to subside into resignation; the bitterness of Bill, in **"Sailor Ashore,"** and of little Maurai, in **"African Morning,"** is too dispirited to merit the name, and is evanescent. The bitterness of the Columbia University-trained secretary, in **"The Negro in the Drawing Room,"** means less to him than his stewardship of the papers of an important man, and is merely occasional stimulation for his sense of virtue.

There remains only the bitterness of circumstance. Into this tight corner is pushed the meaning of what commentators have felt with a clarity often sharper than their powers of explanation. It is here that one understands how fully Hughes has accomplished what he stated as his purpose: "to explain and illuminate the Negro condition in America." The bitterness spreads throughout that condition, not as a definable mood of Negroes in the stories (and Hughes knows that the healthy mind cannot long sustain pure bitterness, however rational that attitude might be), but as a stern, incessant truth suffused through the countenance of factual life.

Ugly truth, when recorded by Negro authors, usually raises the blanket indictment of "protest writing," the persistent balderdash which Hughes disposes of in a reply to Rochelle Girson for one of her "This Week's Personality" features in *The Saturday Review* after the publication of *Laughing to Keep from Crying:*

> I have . . . often been termed a propaganda or a protest writer . . . . That designation has probably grown out of the fact that I write about what I know best, and being a Negro in this country is tied up with difficulties that cause one to protest naturally. I am writing about human beings and situations that I know and experience, and therefore it is only incidentally protest—protest in that it grows out of a live situation.

Some of Hughes's narrative sketches in his books about Jesse B. Semple that qualify as short stories (**"A Dog Named Trilby,"** a few pieces on Cousin Minnie, **"Banquet in Honor,"** and **"A Veteran Falls"**) ably combine social protest with humor, artistic restraint, and the bright accumulations of energetic wordplay for which Simple is famous.

A nighttime and pre-dawn writer who composed his average first draft in three days and his second and third drafts in an additional day or more, Hughes has reflected in his short stories his entire purpose as a writer. Early in his career, he knew what he wanted to accomplish in his art: to interpret "the beauty of his own people," a beauty, he wrote in 1926 in *The Nation,* that they were taught either not to see or not to take pride in. He sought to portray their "soul-world." Above the weaknesses of his stories (didacticism, dialogue from unseen "white folks" and other voices, and too many exclamations and parentheses) rise his humanity, his faithful and artistic presentation of both racial and national truth—his successful mediation, that is, between the beauties and the terrors of life around him.

One becomes alive to the vigor and delicacy, the fun and somber meaning, in Hughes's short stories only by reading them attentively. But it would be helpful to read or reread his best works mindful of certain themes, technical excellences, or social insights. **"Slave on the Block,"** available in *The Langston Hughes Reader* (1958), for example, a simple though vivid tale, reveals the lack of respect, and even human communication, between Negroes and those whites whose interest in them is only modishly superficial. **"Poor Little Black Fellow,"** found in *The Ways of White Folks,* satirizes religious, rather than social cant in race relations, treating corrosive varieties of self-deceit with a subtle complexity—although its consistent point is merely that Negroes, even little ones, want only to be treated like everyone else.

Hughes's best stories include four that portray racial violence, but his more comprehensive revelation of prejudices is woven, for the most part, into eleven other tales of uneven quality. Among the eleven, **"Professor,"** which is in *Something in Common, and Other Stories,* excels in its use of irony and ambiguity, and in its solid but artful attack on discrimination in education; **"Powder-White Faces"** and **"Sailor Ashore,"** reprinted in the same collection, deserve close reading too, the former for its meditative picture of the chaos that prejudice can swell in a Negro's mind, the latter for its exploration of a uniquely baneful government-tolerated prejudice, that suffered by military men.

Among the four well-written stories containing racial violence (all except **"Home"** reprinted in *Something in Common*), two employ religious themes and events. **"On the Road"** is a story perfectly conceived as both fantasy and reality, and poetically executed, using intense patterns of wintry images to join Christ and a black hobo in a brief adventure against systemized, prejudiced religion. **"Big Meeting,"** less artistically ingenious than **"On the Road"** but richer in racial meaning, pursues the theme of Negro identification with Christ more emotionally and picturesquely, using a green-coated, big revival preacher whose timing and histrionics are masterful. **"Home,"** published in *The Ways of White Folks,* ends with a savagery that tends to obscure the profound interplay between life and art which thematically deepens the action; the sensitive, gifted little Negro violinist who finds the world too "rotten" for his survival, is a doomed purveyor of beauty into the midst of European decay and hometown American racism. In **"Father and Son,"** Hughes works at a number of themes (psychopathic Southern violence, sexual exploitation of Negro women, Negro miseducation, and religious abuses) and uses effective symbols and striking arrays of atmospheric images; but the title itself underscores his strongest theme: the climactic encounters of steel will and frustrated love between a white father and his mulatto son.

One of Hughes's best stories, **"The Blues I'm Playing"** (collected in *The Ways of White Folks*), addresses itself not only to the Harlem "cult" of the Negro in the Twenties, but to the exploration of American Negritude as conceived by Hughes in that decade. Although this story, like **"Home,"** written in the same month, September, 1933, closely pictures the conflict between life and art, the blues-playing heroine represents life more so than art precisely because she is so much of a Negro, so close to the roots of art—the blues—in her own racial community experience. The last few pages of the story, almost chart-like in their clarity, support Negritude as an insistence upon the black artist's preservation of personal and racial integrity.

Two of Hughes's top stories, **"A Good Job Gone,"** and **"Little Dog,"** both available in *Something in Common,* cross the color line on the wings of interracial love. The former fast-moving tale, in which a "sugar-brown" with a suppressed hatred of bigots drives a promiscuous rich white man insane, remains as popular as the "hugging and kissing" with which Harlem's updated Luani of the Jungles works her charms. **"Little Dog"** is distinguished by Hughes's adept characterization of a lonely white spinster who falls in love with a "big and brown and kind looking" Negro janitor; the formidable task of presenting a wasted life without minimizing its integrity or ridiculing its belated humanity is handled admirably. **"Red-Headed Baby,"** reprinted in *The Langston Hughes Reader,* tells of a white sailor's carelessly destructive amours; it is unique for its ably used stream-of-consciousness passages, not attempted again, however, until twenty-eight years later, in **"Blessed Assurance."**

Two essentially nonracial stories, **"Cora Unashamed"** and **"On the Way Home,"** are among Hughes's best narratives. The former, twice published the same year, in *The Ways of White Folks* and *Best Short Stories of 1934* shows the ignoble defeat of both parental and carnal love; its tragedy is moderated only by the earth-rooted strength of a Negro maid whose simple thoughts ("And there ain't no reason why you can't marry, neither—you both white") free her of all but natural impulses. **"On the Way Home,"** reprinted in *Something in Common,* suggestively employing various images of wine and water, understandingly describes a young man's ambivalent responses to his mother's death; trapped in both guilty exhilarations and anguish, the dutiful son—who is never racially identified—struggles to be reborn.

Traveling throughout the world, Langston Hughes was always a man of the people, equally at home eating camel sausage in an Asian desert or tasting strawberries in a Park Avenue penthouse. He once said that he had lived much of his life in basements and attics. Metaphorically, his realism and his humanity derive from this fact. Moving figuratively through the basements of the world, where life is thickest and where common people struggle to make their way, he remained close to his vast public. At the same time, writing in attics like the one he occupied in Harlem for twenty years, he rose to the long perspective that enabled him to shine a humanizing, beautifying, but still truthful light on what he saw. His short stories form a world of fiction built with truth and a special love—a little civilization shaped by high purpose and steadfast integrity. (pp. 172-78)

> James A. Emanuel, "The Short Fiction of Langston Hughes," in Freedomways, *Vol. 8, No. 2, Spring, 1968, pp. 170-78.*

James Presley (essay date 1969)

[*In the following excerpt, Presley offers a personal tribute to Hughes's life and career.*]

Clarence Darrow said it and I remembered it when I learned in May, 1967, that Langston Hughes was dead at sixty-five: "I know that no man who ever wrote a line that I read failed to influence me to some extent. I know that every life I ever touched influenced me, and I influenced it." I had known Langston Hughes for the last seven years of his life. I recall vividly that dark winter's afternoon in San Antonio where I met him. I do not mean I met him in person, but I met him personally, in the pages of his autobiographical *I Wonder As I Wander* that I took from the public library. Through the years we corresponded and I read most of what he had published in books, and I wrote of his work. He had touched my life, me, a white man almost three decades his junior, across the light years separating my Texas from his Harlem.

Because he had touched my life, because we were friends by correspondence, it hurt to hear at his death, as I had heard through the years, that he was considered old-fashioned by a younger, very angry generation of Negroes. I had always thought of him as, most of all, honest, a man who could eat watermelon, if he wished to, without feeling embarrassed. His career had stretched from Ernest Hemingway and William Faulkner to Richard Wright and John Steinbeck to James Baldwin and Norman Mailer. He had, it seemed clear to me, been relevant to every decade he had worked in. Antiquated? Clinging to old customs, old ideas?

Langston Hughes?

But there was no doubt about it, he somehow hadn't touched the hearts of the black militant generation who had called him old-fashioned. The man who was "the poet laureate of the Negro people" by the nineteen-twenties wasn't fiery, polemical, and gut-burning enough to please them. Wasn't that it? To them, he was

Hughes, "The Negro busboy poet," working at the Wardham Park Hotel in Washington, D.C., where he left three poems on Vachel Lindsay's dinner table.

left over from the past, a man like Countee Cullen, also from the twenties, signifying another generation.

It is strange that in this time when folk music is being discovered and elevated, a man who devoted more than forty years of his life to writing stories, poems, plays and books of the Negro folk, rural and urban, is thought to be out-of-date.... Perhaps one day a renaissance will rediscover Langston Hughes and, especially, his poetry, for his poems came from the working-class Negroes, to whom he spoke in a language they—and I—understood, a talent that poets do not always exhibit. The folks back home understood Langston Hughes because his poetry was simple and powerful. He communicated with a folk poetry that outlives the elaborate and the gorgeous. Whether it was in children's gentle verses or blues or "protest" lines, he remained the poet of the people. This was his greatest strength. (pp. 79-80)

[He] made the best of a bad situation, possibly the worst situation: a black man in America writing for a living, most of the time when a man, because he was black, had a small and fickle public, if one at all. "I'm trying to conduct a major career on a minor income," Hughes

told one recent interviewer who called him, accurately enough, a literary jack-of-all-trades. Depending on grants, fellowships, ten cross-country lecture tours, recordings, teaching..., his columns in the *Chicago Defender,* and his royalties, he lived long enough to practice almost every literary form known to man: novels, autobiographies, poetry, plays, juveniles, anthologies, musicals, short stories, humor, journalism, histories, songs, and essays—adding up to thirty or forty books.

To be sure, his work at times was uneven and much of it less than his best. But who expects all of one's work to be uniformly fine? Even Balzac omitted some of his books from the *Comédie Humaine.* No man who had well over a dozen different publishers, as Hughes did, can have had an easy time of it as a professional writer, yet he did leave enough that was very good to earn his own niche in American letters. His poetry is almost always good, from *The Weary Blues* (1926) to *Jim Crow's Last Stand* (1943) to *Montage of a Dream Deferred* (1951) to *Ask Your Mama: 12 Moods for Jazz* (1961). (pp. 80-1)

Throughout his long career he wrote of life as he saw it. *Not Without Laughter* reflected his growing up in Kansas on the dark side of the color line. He moved easily into the mainstream of the protest literature of the thirties. *A New Song* (1938) was filled with poems of protest, among which his Whitmanesque **"Let America Be America Again"** is a classic pleading for the poor white, the Negro, the worker, the hungry—those underdogs who made this country with their hands.

> From those who live like leeches on the people's
> lives,
> We must take back our land again,
> America!

The class struggle, or the writing of it anyway, may appear old hat now. Yet one wonders how a later generation would respond if in the poet's warning to "all Nazis, Fascists, and Klansmen" in *Jim Crow's Last Stand* (1943) they substituted "racists," or Stokely Carmichael's "honkies." (pp. 81-2)

Ask Your Mama: 12 Moods for Jazz (1961), written to be read to jazz accompaniment, is a kaleidoscope of Negro names and Negro problems. Dreams follow nightmares. The poet dreams the Negroes of the South have voted out the Dixiecrats, made Martin Luther King governor of Georgia. Negroes sit on comfortable verandahs of pillared mansions, served by whites, their plantations worked by white sharecroppers, their colored children cared for by white mammies. "Culture," the poet quotes, "is a two-way street," and he admonishes the mammy to make haste with his mint julep. The jazz mood runs international, bringing in [Gamal] Nasser, [Fidel] Castro, [Sékou] Touré, [Jomo] Kenyatta, [Kwame] Nkrumah. In one mood, a Negro moves out to Long Island, where he is the only colored man, and becomes famous—"the hard way"—known downtown and across the world. For all the irritating questions that whites have for him about Negroes, he has one question-stopping reply, the theme, *Ask your mama.*

> THEY ASKED ME AT THANKSGIVING
> DID I VOTE FOR NIXON?
> I SAID, VOTED FOR YOUR MAMA.

(p. 82)

Hughes had his critics, white and black. One Negro reviewer called *Fine Clothes to the Jew* (1927) "trash," and the Negro press in general concurred. Bourgeois Negroes, proving that brown Babbits are no different from white Babbits, wanted Negro artists to depict educated, cultured Negroes—not the kind of people Hughes knew and loved and wrote about. A few, more perceptive, like James Weldon Johnson, praised the poems.

White critics frequently downgraded all of his work by labeling him a "protest" writer, the old technique of dismissing a Negro artist, and to a generation or two of *bigotis americanis* he was the radical agitator who went to Russia with a Negro company to film *Porgy and Bess* under the auspices of the Soviet Union. The movie was never made, but Hughes saw Russia. If that weren't enough, *A New Song* was published by the International Workers Order, since designated as a Communist-front organization by the U.S. Attorney General and the House Un-American Activities Committee. When McCarthyism swept this country, self-anointed textbook and library purgers found these facts to be powerful ammunition against his work.

Now, ironically, it seems he did not protest enough.

It is possible that it is the textbook Hughes, the writer of the twenties and the thirties now enshrined in anthologies, that obscures the view of the younger Negro. Each generation seeks its own image, from its own ranks. If that is so, I hope they will reread him, and read his later work. (p. 83)

Come what may, Langston Hughes, in the quarter of the Negroes, in the world of us all: a man should get credit for what he is, and what he has been, and what he does, and what he has done. Come what may, my friend.

> WHEN THEY ASKED ME IN MID-SUMMER
> IN THE QUARTER OF THE NEGROES,
> IS LANGSTON HUGHES OLD-FASHIONED?
> I SAID, ASK YOUR MAMA!

(pp. 83-4)

> *James Presley, "Langston Hughes: A Personal Farewell," in* Southwest Review, *Vol. LIV, No. 1, Winter, 1969, pp. 79-84.*

Edward E. Waldron (essay date 1971)

[*In the following excerpt, Waldron explores three themes common in Hughes's blues poetry: love, bad luck, and flight.*]

As a form of folk expression, the blues has come to occupy a justly revered spot in American music; at long last, recognition is being given to the artists—and the audience—that were instrumental in creating this art form. At the same time, many writers/poets have attempted for years to incorporate the essence of the blues into works outside the reference of music—i.e., into stories and poetry. One of the most successful poets in this endeavor was Langston Hughes, the "Poet Laureate" of Black America. In his blues poetry Langston Hughes captures the mood, the feel, and the spirit of the blues; his poems have the rhythm and the impact of the musical form they incorporate. Indeed, the blues poems of Langston Hughes *are* blues as well as poetry....

[The] blues reflects the trials and tribulations of the Negro in America on a secular level, much as the spirituals do on the religious level. Both expressions are, certainly, necessary releases. In one of his "Blues for Men" poems in *Shakespeare in Harlem,* Hughes dramatizes the necessity for this release. Lamenting the dirty treatment he has received from his woman, the singer of **"In a Troubled Key"** (the narrator of a blues poem *is* a singer, in effect) sings:

> Still I can't help lovin' you,
> Even though you do me wrong.
> Says I can't help lovin' you
> Though you do me wrong—
> But my love might turn into a knife
> Instead of a song.

Here we see the blues maker turning his despair into song instead of into murder; and, one has the feeling that the mood of the blues is often one step away from death—either murder or suicide—and that the presence of the blues form makes it possible for the anguished one to direct his sorrow inward into song and find happiness in the release. (p. 140)

The blues, as any art form, has definite patterns which are adhered to in its composition. In [an] introductory "Note on Blues," ... in *Fine Clothes to the Jew,* Hughes gives us the most common pattern:

> The *Blues,* unlike the *Spirituals,* have a strict poetic pattern: one long line repeated and a third line to rhyme with the first two. Sometimes the second line in repetition is slightly changed and sometimes, but very seldom, it is omitted.

In order to maintain a closer semblance to poetic form, Hughes breaks the first two lines into two lines each and also divides the final line, creating a six-line stanza. A typical stanza is this one from **"Po' Boy Blues."**

> When I was home de
> Sunshine seemed like gold.
> When I was home de
> Sunshine seemed like gold.
> Since I come up North de
> Whole damn world's turned cold.

The second stanza of the poem illustrates the change that often occurs in the repeated line(s):

> I was a good boy,
> Never done no wrong.
> Yes, I was a good boy,
> Never done no wrong.
> But this world is weary
> An' de road is hard an' long.

In the case of a line changed in repetition, sometimes a word of exclamation, such as the "Yes" of this example, is added, and sometimes a word or two might be omitted, if not the whole line. For example, consider this stanza from **"Bound No'th Blues"**:

> Goin' down de road, Lawd,
> Goin' down de road.
> Down de road, Lawd,
> Way, way, down de road.
> Got to find somebody
> To help me carry dis load.

Here we see both kinds of change taking place; the repeated first line has dropped a word, and the repeated second line has changed by dropping one word and adding others in its place. This changing of lines helps keep the flow of the poem going, without ruining the effectiveness of the repetition. (pp. 141-42)

As with any poetic style, the blues' form is directly related to its content. Although what a particular blues is about may vary from blues to blues, the basic content of the blues usually has to do with some form of disappointment, most commonly in love, but also in other areas of life—or maybe in just plain living. [E. Simms] Campbell may be going a little overboard when he states that the blues " . . . are songs of sorrow charged with satire, with that potent quality of ironic verse clothed in the raiment of the buffoon." Yet, he is close to the same concept of the blues that Hughes voiced in the "Note on Blues" in *Fine Clothes to the Jew:*

> The mood of the *Blues* is almost always despondency, but when they are sung people laugh.

This seemingly paradoxical statement reflects an essence that is found in almost every facet of Black American expression: the duality of laughing and crying at the same time or, as Hughes says it, "laughing to keep from crying." Laughing at trouble is a concept we may all try to adopt at one time or another, but Black American writers have wrought this fine ability into a grand motif that consistently runs through their works; and Langston Hughes is certainly qualified as an artist in weaving this quality into his poetry and other works. (p. 142)

An extensive treatment of the man's side of the lost-love blues is found in the "Seven Moments of Love" section of *Shakespeare in Harlem,* which Hughes subtitled "An Un-Sonnet Sequence in Blues." This is a progressive series of seven poems dealing with a man's state of mind after his woman has left him. At first (**"Twilight Reverie"**) he wants to shoot her, but his loneliness begins to take away that mood. By **"Supper Time"** his despair has advanced to the point where he can hear his "heartbeats trying to think" and his "footprints walking on the floor." **"Bed Time"** is even worse; he wants to go out and have fun, but his habits of being with his woman won't let him go: "A human gets lonesome if there ain't two." He wakes up the next day (**"Daybreak"**), miserable, and wonders "if white folks ever feels bad / Getting up in the morning lonesome and sad?" **"Sunday"** finds him thinking again about how "glad" he is to be "free"—"But this house is mighty quiet!" On **"Pay Day"** he recalls how he used to have to give his woman all the money, but now he is free to spend it all by himself. He is going to give up the furniture and things and go back to renting "a cubby-hole with a single bed." His dismay at his woman has the sound of frustrated humanity in it:

> Women's abominations! Just like a
> curse!
> You was the best—but you *the worst!*

Finally, he hears from Cassie and writes her a "Letter" telling her to come back: "I can't get along with you, I can't get along without." With this last echoing thought, a thought that permeates the blues of love, Hughes closes one of his more ambitious blues poetry experiments. Throughout this series of poems Hughes manages to maintain a sense of identity in the singer of the blues and keeps at work a progression that ties together all seven poems very neatly. (p. 143)

While men do get to sing some of the blues written by Langston Hughes, the women seem to find favor with the poet more frequently, and their reactions often are more severe. Two poems from *Fine Clothes to the Jew* state explicitly the blues singer's desire to kill herself. The first stanza in **"Suicide,"** as well as the title itself, makes the singer's intent quite clear:

> Ma sweet good man has
> Packed his trunk and left.
> Ma sweet good man has
> Packed his trunk and left.
> Nobody to love me:
> I'm gonna kill ma self.

The river usually serves as the focal point for the suicide's thoughts of self-murder, although this woman docs consider using a knife first. She rejects the blade, though, in favor of the water . . . . Of course, no one expects the blues singer to go out and commit suicide; after all, singing the blues is supposed to help relieve the hurt and act to channel the emotions away from self-directed or other-directed murder (see **"In a Troubled Key"** mentioned earlier).

In another woman's blues, **"Midnight Chippie's Lament"** (*Shakespeare in Harlem*), Hughes presents us with a blues person who seeks out the blues instead of death for her release:

> I looked down 31st Street,
> Not a soul but Lonesome Blue.

Down on 31st Street,
Nobody but Lonesome Blue.
I said come here, Lonesome,
And I will love you, too.

But "Lonesome Blue" rejects her offer, saying:

Woman, listen! Hey!
Buy you two for a quarter
On State Street any day.

Although Hughes ends this blues with a bit of sardonic humor ("Cry to yourself, girls, / So nobody can't low-rate you"), it still remains obvious that the woman singing this blues has reached a desperate level; she'd rather have the lonesome blues than *nothing* at all. (pp. 143-44)

[Love] is not the only subject of the blues, even though it does dominate as the main concern of the blues. Another common theme of the blues is bad luck. **"Hard Luck"** in *Fine Clothes to the Jew* is a good example of this kind of blues and gives the source of the title of that collection:

When hard luck overtakes you
Nothin' for you to do.
When hard luck overtakes you
Nothin' for you to do.
Gather up yo' fine clothcs
An' sell 'em to de Jew.

"De Jew" here is, of course, the local pawnbroker, the man to whom the desperate must turn in order to scrape up a few pennies with the last of their possessions. That the amount given for the goods received is rarely considered equitable is reflected in the second stanza:

Jew takes yo' fine clothes,
Gives you a dollar an' a half.
Jew takes yo' fine clothes,
Gives you a dollar an' a half.
Go to de bootleg's
Git some cheap gin to make you laugh.

(p. 145)

A final dominant theme in blues poetry is the idea of moving, of traveling, of getting away. **"Six-Bit Blues,"** an early poem which appeared originally in *Opportunity* (February, 1939), has this idea as its central theme:

Gimme six-bits' worth o' ticket
On a train that runs somewhere.
I say six-bits' worth o' ticket
On a train that runs somewhere.
I don't care where it's goin'
Just so it goes away from here.

The urgent need to move and to escape does not precede the need for love, but it makes that need somehow less binding:

Make it short and sweet, your lovin',
So I can roll along.

I got to roll along!

The final "tag" line, italicized for emphasis, reinforces the singer's urgent desire to get away. No explanation is given about why he wants to leave, but an explanation really is not necessary. In fact, given the nature of the blues, the question is probably irrelevant. (pp. 146-47)

Humor dominates in a few of the blues poems of Langston Hughes. **"Crowing-Hen Blues"** (*Poetry*, September, 1943) is a blues that is also pure folk humor. The singer, after a rough night of drinking, swears he hears his cat talking:

I had a cat, I called him
Battling Tom Mc Cann.
Had a big black cat, I called him
Battling Tom Mc Cann.
Last night that cat riz up and
Started talking like a man.

Waking up his "baby" to tell her the news, he gets a skeptical reaction: "I don't hear nothin' / But your drunken snorin', dear." Undaunted, the singer stands up for his right to drink and hallucinate all he wants.... (p. 147)

Another humorous blues poem by Hughes is **"Morning After,"** from the "Blues for Men" section of *Shakespeare in Harlem.* The subject of this blues, again a hangover and its effect on the singer, seems more the subject of a standup comedian than a blues maker, but the blues form does suit this particular poem. The first stanza establishes the man's problem:

I was so sick last night I
Didn't hardly know my mind.
So sick last night I
Didn't know my mind.
I drunk some bad licker that
Almost made me blind.

The humor gets very heavy-handed in the last two stanzas, as the man laments that his baby's "mouth was open like a well" and made enough noise for "a great big crowd." While this type of blues may not be as common as other blues, it does illustrate the wide possibilities of the blues form. Clearly, the mood of this blues poem is *not* despondency.

In addition to the more common subjects for blues that Hughes makes use of in his poetry, he also uses other, less common, subjects. A natural disaster would most likely find its way into a blues or a folk ballad, and Hughes took a terrible flooding of the Mississippi as the subject for his **"Mississippi Levee."** In the poem the singer cries out in anguish as the flood-waters keep coming in spite of his efforts to stop them.... A sense of hopelessness dominates this poem and is made clear in the final stanza:

Levee, Levee,
How high have you got to be?
Levee, Levee,
How high have you got to be?
To keep them cold muddy waters
From washin' over me?

Folk material has always made use of local natural disorders as subject matter, and this poem is in keeping with that tradition.

Finally, the blues themselves serve as the subject for some of the blues written by Langston Hughes, and the best single example of this type of poem is the title poem from **The Weary Blues.** In this poem, Hughes sets up a "frame" wherein he recalls the performance of a blues singer-pianist "on Lenox Avenue the other night":

> With his ebony hands on each ivory key He made
> that poor piano moan with melody—
>
> • • •
>
> Sweet Blues!
> Coming from a black man's soul.

After an exhausting performance, one that both drains and relaxes the blues man as only a creative act can, he quits his playing and goes to bed:

> While the Weary Blues echoed through his head.
> He slept like a rock or a man that's dead.

This form proves quite effective, since in it the reader receives not only the blues of the singer, but also a look at the creation of this blues from an outside source—the poet. In this way we become totally involved in the creative blues process.

The blues poetry of Langston Hughes, then, has a great deal to offer. Within this limited source of Hughes's creativity alone, we confront many of the themes that he develops more fully in other works. Loneliness, despair, frustration, and a nameless sense of longing are all represented in the blues poetry; and, these themes dominate not only the works of Hughes but also those of most Black American writers.

What direction Hughes's poetry of the blues might have taken thematically were he writing today is hinted at in the one traditional-form blues included in his last collection of verse, **The Panther and The Lash: "The Backlash Blues."** Once again Hughes underscores his concern with the social plight of the Black man in America in this poem, which also warns—

> I'm gonna leave you, Mister Backlash,
> Singing your mean old backlash blues.
>
> You're the one,
> Yes, you're the one
> Will have the blues.

While the blues traditionally have not concerned themselves *directly* with sociopolitical problems, and while Hughes follows this tradition fairly closely in his blues poetry, one sees in this, his final published blues poem the potential that Hughes might have developed in light of today's Black Power movement. Whether he would have gone in this direction or not is, of course, mere speculation, but his concern with the common man throughout his blues poetry—and other works—could have led him in this direction.

At any rate the blues poems we *do* have from this gifted poet illustrate quite well the effectiveness of this great American art form—even though his blues are read and not sung. Indeed, Hughes's sensitive reproduction of the language of the blues, which is the language of the common man/blues maker, and his ability to recreate the rhythmic effect of a sung blues make it difficult *not* to sing, however softly, the blues of Langston Hughes. (pp. 147-49)

> *Edward E. Waldron, "The Blues Poetry of Langston Hughes," in* Negro American Literature Forum, *Vol. 5, No. 4, Winter, 1971, pp. 140-49.*

Arthur P. Davis (essay date 1974)

[*In the following excerpt from his* From the Dark Tower: Afro-American Writers 1900-1960, *Davis surveys Hughes's literary career.*]

Poet, fiction writer, dramatist, newspaper columnist, writer of autobiography, anthologist, compiler of children's works, and translator, Langston Hughes was by far the most experimental and versatile author of the Renaissance—and time may find him the greatest.

A man of good will who believed that all races and groups are essentially the same in things that really count, Hughes fought the black man's fight for dignity and equality with rare insight, great tolerance, and a vast amount of humor. Always a protester, he was seldom if ever bitter; always a race author, he was never a racist. Keenly aware of the Negro's position in America, he never espoused separatism or black nationalism. "I too sing America" was not merely a verse of poetry to him, it was part of his credo.

Negro writing owes much to Hughes: he showed by example and experiment the importance of the folk contribution to black writing through his use of the blues, spirituals, ballads, jazz, and folk speech; he gave Negro drama a shot in the arm when it needed it most; he exemplified the kind of freedom, the breaking away from stereotypes which many New Negro authors preached but did not always practice; and he preserved, in the face of an increasing seriousness on the part of militant young black writers, a much-needed sense of tolerance and old-fashioned humor. (p. 61)

The bulk of Hughes's poetry is found in ten major publications, ranging from 1926 to 1967, the year of his death. During this span of over forty years he touched on many subjects and experimented with various techniques, but he never quite gave up any of the old approaches he used in the earliest works. One notes that in his last volume of poems, **The Panther and the Lash,** he has examples of works from all the previous volumes. With regard to subject matter, he was equally consistent. As a matter of fact, he really had but one theme during his entire poetic career, and that was to delineate the wrongs, the sorrows, the humor, and the enduring quality of the Negro. There are, of course, brief excursions into nonracial themes, but these are very rare.

His works may be divided into the following major categories: poems of protest and social commentary; Harlem poems; poems influenced by folk material; poems on African and negritude themes; and miscellaneous poems.... Naturally, there is some overlapping among these categories, but in the main they are valid. If there is one quality which characterized all Hughes's poetry—in fact all his works—it is simplicity: the plain acts of everyday people written in the uncomplicated language of their speech.

The protest-and-social-commentary theme runs through the whole body of Hughes's poetry. He freely acknowledged that he was a propagandist. One notes, however, that in his first two works, *The Weary Blues* and *Fine Clothes to the Jew,* there are very few protest poems. By the time of *One Way Ticket* (1949) the stream is flowing freely, and from this work on down to his last, social protest and commentary become increasingly important. Like other New Negro poets, Hughes used lynching as the supreme symbol of American injustice, and in *One Way Ticket* devotes a whole section of the work ("Silhouette") to lynch poems. His protest-and-social-commentary poems are usually topical, and if a reader were to put them all together, he would have a dramatic and revealing account of thc many glaring instances of injustice perpetrated by America on the black citizen—an account that would include the Harlem Riot of 1935 and the trials and tribulations of Stokely Carmichael and other recent Black Power leaders; an account which would perhaps give as much insight, if not more, than a library of sociological works.

Langston Hughes, like other young Negroes of the thirties and forties, saw hope for the oppressed in the Marxist position. Although he never became a Communist, many of his social poems during this period show leftist influence. But nothing could disturb for long Hughes's innate "coolness," his ability to see both sides of an issue. Characteristic of him is a late poem called **"Impasse"** in which he cleverly gets at the heart of the racial dilemma in America:

> I could tell you,
> If I wanted to,
> What makes me
> What I am.
> But I don't
> Really want to,
> And you don't
> Give a damn.

It is revealing to contrast Hughes's attitude toward racial protest poetry with that of Countee Cullen. During most of his career Cullen used to complain about being a *Negro poet.* "To make a poet black and bid him sing" was considered a peculiar kind of malevolence on the part of God. Hughes, on the other hand, seemed to glory in his mission as a black

propagandist, looking upon his protest poems as a weapon in the arsenal of democracy.

Called the poet laureate of Harlem, Hughes retained all his life a deep love for that colorful city within a city, and he never tired of delineating the changing moods of that ghetto. Except for one, there are specific poems on Harlem in every major poetical work. To Hughes, Harlem was place, symbol, and on occasion protagonist. It is a city of rapid transformation: the Harlem of the first two works is a gay, joyous city of cabaret life, the Harlem that jaded downtown whites seeking the exotic and the primitive flocked uptown to see. This Harlem of **"Jazzonia"** was never the *real* Harlem; that begins to appear in *One Way Ticket* (1949) after a riot and a depression have made the ghetto into an "edge of hell" for its discouraged and frustrated inhabitants, though still a refuge from the white man's world.

The fullest and best treatment of Harlem (and Hughes's best volume of poetry) is found in *Montage of a Dream Deferred* (1951). Actually one long poem of 75 pages, it employs a "jam-session technique" to give every possible shade and nuance of Harlem life. Very few cities have received such a swinging and comprehensive poetic coverage. The key poem of the work is prophetic in its implications:

> What happens to a dream deferred?
> Does it dry up
> like a raisin in the sun?
> Or fester like a sore—
> And then run?
> Does it stink like a rotten meat?
> Or crust and sugar over—
> like a syrupy sweet?
> Maybe it just sags
> like a heavy load.
> Or *does it explode?*

Although Dunbar and Chesnutt had tapped the reservoir of Negro folk material during the late nineteenth century, the New Negro writers were the first to make broad use of this important body of songs and literature. No longer interested in the dialect tradition, they fashioned new forms of expression based on the spirituals, the blues, the ballads, the work and dance songs, and the folk sermon. The most important and the most dedicated experimenter with these forms was Langston Hughes.

In his first works he emphasized the blues form, a form for which he had a special fondness probably because it was congenial to his style and to his temperament. The title poem of his first volume ["**The Weary Blues**"] has a bluestype form; seventeen of the poems in his second work are blues; and his first novel, *Not Without Laughter* and two of his best-known plays, **"Don't You Want to Be Free?"** and *Tambourines to Glory,* lean heavily on folk influence and folk blues and spirituals for artistic support. Hughes also employed ballad forms and on occasion dance rhythms, as in:

> Me and ma baby's

Got two mo' ways,
Two mo' ways to do de Charleston!
    Da, Da,
        Da, Da, Da!
Two mo' ways to do de Charleston!

The experimentation with folk forms and rhythms reached brilliant heights in two later works: *Montage of a Dream Deferred* and *Ask Your Mama: 12 Moods for Jazz*. In the first work Langston Hughes seeks to capture "the conflicting changes, sudden nuances, sharp and impudent interjections, broken rhythms, and passages some times in the manner of the jam session...." In short, he blends light and shadow, serious and comic, harmony and dissonance after the manner of jazz music to give the reader a unified picture of many-faceted Harlem. *Ask Your Mama* is a different type of experiment, and though not quite as impressive as *Montage*, it is still a successful work. For this volume the poet uses the traditional folk melody of "The Hesitation Blues" as a leitmotif. "In and around it," he tells us, "along with the other recognizable melodies employed, there is room for spontaneous jazz improvisation...." Printed in the margins beside each of the poems one finds elaborate directions for the musical accompaniment to the verse. It should be noted that Hughes, if not the first, as some critics claim was among the pioneers of the poetry-read-to-jazz movement.

Langston Hughes's treatment of the African-negritude theme changed and deepened over the years. Like other New Negro poets, he featured in his earlier poems the alien-and-exile theme.... This early treatment of Africa was little more than a literary pose, a kind of literary Garveyism, and neither the New Negro poets nor their readers took it seriously. Hughes's later African poems, however, are not conventional when he writes of a real and embittered Africa battling its way into freedom:

Lumumba was black
And he didn't trust
The whores all powdered
With uranium dust....

Lumumba was black.
His blood was red—
And for being a man
They killed him dead....

This concern with Africa brings to mind Langston Hughes's role in the negritude movement. Space will not permit a discussion of this question, but it should be noted that the poetry of Langston Hughes greatly influenced West African and West Indian negritude. He is counted among the fathers of that movement. Hughes was always deeply interested in Africa, but he never considered changing his name or metaphorically donning a dashiki. He never renounced his American citizenship—literary or otherwise. (pp. 62-6)

Arthur P. Davis, "First Fruits: Langston Hughes," in his From the Dark Tower: Afro-American Writers 1900-1960, *Howard University Press, 1974, pp. 61-73.*

Cary D. Wintz (essay date 1975)

[*In the following excerpt, Wintz discusses Hughes's development as a poet.*]

The most outstanding feature in [*The Weary Blues*] was the use of Negro music as a model for a number of poems. The blues and jazz, the distinctive music of Negro life, provided the form for the title poem and several others. This stylistic experimentation was one of the major elements in Hughes's work. In this first volume the young poet also introduced the two major themes that would characterize his poetry throughout his long career. First, he expressed a deep commitment to the Negro masses.... His verses reflected a keen insight into the life of the Negro masses, including a vivid picture of the poverty and deprivation of their life. (p. 60)

The second theme that Hughes introduced in his first volume of poetry was Harlem. Although he depicted Negro life in the rural South, and occasionally in his native Midwest, Hughes was essentially an urban poet, and life in the Negro metropolis was a basic element in his work throughout his career. (pp. 60-1)

More clearly than most other Renaissance writers he saw that beneath Harlem's glitter was an oppressive, melancholy slum; the excitement of jazz contrasted sharply with the weary blues.... (p. 61)

As Hughes developed his portrayal of the black lower classes and their ghetto environment, he became more and more preoccupied with the question of the Negro's racial identity. Hughes had begun his search for the meaning of the racial experience in America shortly after he graduated from high school. In his first mature poem, **"A Negro Speaks of Rivers,"** he found an analogy between the river that flowed through his native Midwest and the ancient rivers that watered the lands where his race was born.... (pp. 63-4)

Hughes continued this investigation in several directions. First, like many of his contemporaries, he looked to Africa, where he found few answers but a great many questions.... In his poetry Africa became a symbol of lost roots, of a distant past that could never be retrieved....

As one who had grown up in America's heartland [Hughes] seemed content with his conclusion that American blacks were Americans, not Africans, and consequently he focused his attention on the Negro's identity problems in this country. In particular, on several occasions he looked into the role of the mulatto in American society.... Very quickly, very directly, Hughes moved beyond anger and resentment to expose the isolation that was the real tragedy of the mulatto in a racist society. He followed [the early poem **"Cross"**] with an equally dramatic, but a more bitter examination in **"Mulatto."** Here he wove together two themes, an angry confrontation between an illegitimate youth and

181 West 135th Street,
New York, N. Y.
October 13, 1931.

Mr. William Pickens
N. A. A. C. P.
69 Fifth Avenue
New York City

My dear Mr. Pickens:

    I have had the feeling for sometime that the modern
Negro Art Movement in America has been largely over the heads,
and out of reach, of the masses of the Negro peoples. It's
appeal within the race has been mainly to a small group of
"intellectuals", and as for books, most colored folks have
not been able to pay two dollars or more for volumes of
novels or poems. In many cases the context, too, of Negro
books has been uninteresting or displeasing to a large part
of the race. They have not cared for jazz poetry or low-
down novels—and one can't blame them much—since they
usually know such things all too well in life.

    In recent Negro poetry, I have felt that there has been
a distinct lack of rhymed poems dramatizing current racial
interests in simple, understandable verse, pleasing to the
ear, and suitable for reading aloud, or for recitation in
schools, churches, lodges, etc. I have felt that much of
our poetry has been aimed at the heads of the high-brows,
rather than at the hearts of the people. And we all know
that most Negro books published by white publishers are ad-
vertised and sold largely to white readers, and little or no
effort is made to reach the great masses of the colored
people.

    I have written "THE NEGRO MOTHER" with the hope that my
own people will like it, and will buy it. If they do, I shall
write other booklets of both verse and prose in this unpre-
tentious fashion, to sell for as reasonable a price. I am
sending you this personal letter, not for publication, (please),
but merely to inform you of the raison d'etre behind this
little booklet. I would appreciate your comments on its
merit.

                              Sincerely yours,

                              Langston Hughes

Letter explaining Hughes's reasons for writing his 1931 collection of poems.

his white relatives, and a taunting description of the violent act of miscegenation.... (p. 64)

Given Hughes's interest in the problems of the lower classes and his attempt to uncover the difficulties of being black in the United States, it is not surprising that he occasionally turned his pen against racial and social injustice. Fortunately his protest poetry did not succumb to bitterness.... Instead, he approached the subject of racial oppression through satire, understatement, or wry, sardonic humor. The poem **"Cross"** was a clear example of his ability to expose an extremely controversial subject in a cool, matter-of-fact fashion. In **"Mulatto"** his language was angry and even inflammatory, but the impact of the poem remained controlled and powerful. This was also true of his most controversial protest poem, **"Christ in Alabama,"** which he wrote at the height of the Scottsboro case.... Hughes described this piece as "an ironic poem inspired by the thought of how Christ, with no human father, would be accepted if he were born in the South of a Negro mother." Its power, like that of most of his poetry, came through using inflammatory images to produce a cool, controlled anger.

Perhaps the most interesting feature of Hughes's poetry was his innovative style. Throughout his literary career he experimented with adapting black musical forms to his work.... As a result, he emerged as one of the few truly innovative writers to come out of the Harlem Renaissance, and in the process he uncovered a poetic style that was adaptable to a variety of circumstances. The blues form, for example, with its repetitive reinforcement, was a very effective technique to impart a subtle sense of suffering and despondency:

> When I was home de
> Sunshine seemed like gold.
> When I was home de
> Sunshine seemed like gold.
> Since I came up North de
> Whole damn world's turned cold.
> ....
> Weary, weary,
> Weary early in de morn.
> Weary, weary,
> Early, early in de morn.
> I's so weary
> I wish I'd never been born.

It is difficult to imagine a literary form that could capture the exhaustion and despair of the working class more effectively. (pp. 65-6)

Hughes used jazz rhythms and the tempo of black work music to achieve different effects. In **"Brass Spittoons,"** for example, work rhythms set the pace of the poem and captured the feeling of menial, methodical labor. In jazz he found a particularly fertile area for experimentation.... Hughes took this music with its choppy, breathless, almost chaotic tempo and recreated the bustling rhythms of city life and the boisterous atmosphere of the ghetto at night....

He refined his technique in his post-Renaissance poetry and applied it most successfully in his Harlem epic, ***Montage of a Dream Deferred,*** where he used jazz models to capture the full essence of Harlem life. (p. 66)

The weaknesses of [Hughes's novel ***Not Without Laughter***] are fairly obvious. Sandy [the protagonist] is never fully developed as a character, while the more interesting figures, Harriet and Aunt Hagar, remain on the periphery. The plot is also weak—in fact the novel essentially consists of a series of unrelated episodes in Sandy's life. Nevertheless the novel does have its strong points. The characters, while not fully developed, are believable. More importantly, Hughes's description of small town Negro life is unsurpassed. (pp. 67-8)

Not Without Laughter was the only serious attempt Langston Hughes made to examine the experience of blacks in the Midwest. After he completed the novel in 1930, his career changed dramatically. He continued to write prodigiously, but not about his own childhood, and he disassociated himself from the declining Harlem Renaissance. (p. 68)

Hughes's poetry also shifted to the left during the 1930's. Although he always had been concerned with the problems of blacks and of the poor, during the depression years he moved closer to Communism in his personal beliefs, and his poetry became angrier and more inclined toward propaganda. Unfortunately, as Hughes became more political, the quality of his work declined....

Fortunately, along with his other accomplishments Langston Hughes took the time at least once in his career to examine the Negro's life in small-town America. (p. 69)

> *Cary D. Wintz, "Langston Hughes: A Kansas Poet in the Harlem Renaissance," in* Kansas Quarterly, *Vol. 7, No. 3, June, 1975, pp. 58-71.*

Peter Bruck (essay date 1977)

[*In the following excerpt, Bruck provides social, literary, and historical perspective on Hughes's short fiction.*]

Langston Hughes (1902-1967), according to many critics "poet laureate of Harlem" and "Dean of American Negro Writers," began his literary career by winning a poetry contest sponsored by the black magazine *Opportunity* in 1925. **"The Weary Blues"** was noted by Carl Van Vechten, through whose sponsorship Hughes was able to get his first contract with the noted publisher Alfred Knopf. Van Vechten, who acted as a main ambassadorial advisor and patron of black literature to white publishing firms during the 1920's, not only paved the way for Hughes' literary career but also became the "chief architect of his early success." Just as with [Paul Laurence] Dunbar and [Charles Waddell] Chesnutt, white patronage played a decisive role in the literary emergence of Langston Hughes. The omnipresence of the white patron with his significant socio-literary influence on the black author was a discovery that the young Hughes was still to make; his gradual and painstaking emancipation from the grip of such white patrons was to become the major concern of his early phase and to play a dominant theme in his short fiction.

Starting to publish in the midst of the 1920's meant for Langston Hughes to be intrinsically involved in a debate over the function, theme, and aesthetic form of black literature. The problem became even more urgent when the 'Harlem Renaissance' period began and, at the same time, the widely acclaimed emergence of the "New Negro" confronted the black writer with the task of defining his role as a literary artist. In order to foster a critical discussion of these questions, the leading black magazine *The Crisis* organized a symposium, "The Negro in Art: How Shall He Be Portrayed?," throughout the March-November issues of 1926. Prior to this, Alain Locke, "father of the 'New Negro' and the so-called Harlem Renaissance," had attempted to define the cultural stance of the 'New Negro' in the following manner:

> He [the New Negro] now becomes a conscious contributor and lays aside the status of a beneficiary and ward for that of a collaborator and participant in American civilization. The great social gain in this is the releasing of our talented group from the arid fields of controversy and debate to the productive fields of creative expression. The especially cultural recognition they win should in turn prove the key to that revaluation of the Negro which must precede or accompany any considerable further betterment of race relationships.

Locke, who clearly pursued [W. E. B.] DuBois' philosophy of a "talented tenth," aspired to an attitude of cultural elitism that envisioned art and culture to be a bridge across the racial barrier; hence his calling for a "carefully maintained contact between the enlightened minorities of both race groups." This philosophy of culture undoubtedly presented a challenge to all those young black writers who were primarily concerned with expressing the new feeling of ethnic identity and racial pride. One of those willing to face this challenge was the young Langston Hughes who, on June 23, 1926, published an essay [in the *Nation*] that may not only be viewed as an indirect reply to Locke but also became known as the first significant black literary manifesto.

The importance of the **"Negro Artist and the Racial Mountain"** for the evolution of black literature cannot be overstressed. In the words of Charles S. Johnson, former editor of *Opportunity,* none other than Hughes with this essay "so completely symbolized the new emancipation of the Negro mind."

In outlining his stance as a black writer, Hughes placed particular emphasis on racial pride and ethnic identity:

> To my mind, it is the duty of the younger Negro artists . . . to change through the force of his art that old whispering, "I want to be white," hidden in the

aspirations of his people, to "Why should I want to be white? I am a Negro and beautiful."

Hughes' emphasis on blackness, which anticipated the present-day discussion of the possibilities of a black aesthetic, clearly signalled the renunciation of the well-known problem of "racial" vs. "universal" art. Instead Hughes turned to depicting the ordinary black American. . . . His extensive reliance on folk forms and rhythms and his application of oral folk culture to poetry highlight his innovating efforts and mark the beginning of the "reconciliation of formal black poets to their folk roots and grass roots audience." One of the most popular results of his preoccupations in terms of narrative fiction were the "Simple folk tales" that first appeared in the black weekly *Chicago Defender* in November 1942. (pp. 71-3)

From a socio-literary point of view, the Simple tales marked Hughes' first success in gaining a genuine black audience. In the late 1920's, however, this goal still proved utopian. . . . Whereas the bulk of his poetry is usually associated with the Harlem Renaissance, . . . [Hughes's] career as a short story writer did not begin before the wane of this epoch. Although his first stories, all reflecting the author's experiences as a seaman on a voyage along the West coast of Africa, were already published in Harlem's literary magazine *The Messenger* in 1927, it took another six years before Hughes really devoted himself to writing short fiction. From the spring of 1932 to the fall of 1933 he visited the Soviet Union and the Far East. It was during his stay in Moscow that he had a decisive reading experience [having read D. H. Lawrence's collection *The Lovely Lady*] which prompted him to devote himself to the short story . . . . The years to come were to see amazing results from this literary initiation. Between 1933 and 1934 he devoted himself exclusively to this genre. (pp. 73-4)

[*The Ways of White Folk*] which received rather favorable reviews, presents, thematically, a close examination of black-white relationships. Mostly satirical in tone, the stories try to unmask several manifestations of the Harlem Renaissance. Specifically, the theme of white patronage, as displayed in **"Slave on the Block," "Poor Little Black Fellow,"** and **"The Blues I'm Playing,"** is used to demonstrate the dishonesty of whites and the absurd notion of their paternalistic philanthropy. In this context, it is of particular socio-literary interest to note that Hughes' fictional treatment of the incipient dissociation from white predominance caused him no setback in magazine publication. Instead, his new literary efforts soon fount their way into leading periodicals. Whereas Hughes' poetry was usually printed in such black journals as *Opportunity* and *The Crisis* (he had complained in 1929 that "magazines used very few stories with Negro themes, since Negro themes were considered exotic, in a class with Chinese or East Indian features), four out of his five stories written in Moscow were now accepted and published by such noted periodicals as *The American Mercury, Scribner's Magazine* and *Esquire.*

This major breakthrough provided him with a nation-wide, non-parochial platform, allowing him to escape from his predicament, and opened up the opportunity of gaining a primarily white reading audience.

The reading of Lawrence's *The Lovely Lady* not only prompted Hughes to concentrate on the short story but also persuaded him to use the story's protagonist Pauline Attenborough as a model for the creation of Dora Ellsworth, the fictional representative of his former white Park Avenue patroness. **"The Blues I'm Playing,"** written after his return from the Soviet Union and first published in the May 1934 issue of *Scribner's Magazine,* was thus subject to an interesting combination of influence.

The impact of Lawrence's story becomes apparent when one compares the opening description of both women. Lawrence describes Pauline Attenborough as a woman who "could still sometimes be mistaken...for thirty. She really was a wonderfully preserved woman, of perfect *chic....* She would be an exquisite skeleton and her skull would be an exquisite skull." The narrator's mocking emphasis on her appearance, which she can change through a "mysterious little wire" of "will," exposes her artificiality. As a collector of art, Pauline is herself a "self-made object d'art." Dora Ellsworth is introduced in a similar way. Hughes' description, how-ever, is more mocking and obviously aims at unmasking his character's self-deception from the very beginning. Hence one common denominator of both figures seems to be hypocrisy:

> Poor dear lady, she had no children of her own. Her husband was dead. And she had no interest in life now save art, and the young people who created art. She was very rich, and it gave her pleasure to share her richness with beauty. Except that she was some-times confused as to where beauty lay .... She once turned down a garlic-smelling soprano-singing girl, who, a few years later, had all the critics in New York at her feet.

This passage reveals several central aspects of the narrative texture. The focus of interest, which is on Mrs. Ellsworth throughout the story, suggests that Hughes is primarily concerned with depicting the ignorance of the white philanthropist. This intention is underlined by authorial comments which, although sometimes quite devastating, are seldom strongly aggressive. Instead, Hughes pities his white character, thereby producing the particular reading process of **"The Blues I'm Playing."** By undermining the cultural status of his protagonist and exposing the absurdity of her judgements, Hughes creates in the reader's imagination the illusion of witnessing the forthcoming degradation of so-called superior white culture.

Satire hence sets the emotional tone throughout the story. Its function, autobiographically, is to unveil the devastating influence that Hughes' former patroness had on his creative impulses: "She wanted me to be primi-tive and know and feel the intuitions of the primitive. But, unfortunately, I did not feel the rhythms of the primitive surging through me, and so I could not live and write as though I did." On the cultural level, this conflict was representative of a whole range of dilemmas that had emerged during the Harlem Renaissance. The black writers' "search back to a national past," their literary journey of ethnic self-discovery, marked the beginning of a declaration of cultural independence, whose paradigm may be seen in Hughes' literary mani-festo **"The Negro Artist and the Racial Mountain."** Satire as employed in **"The Blues I'm Playing"** signals the end of white paternalism, thereby demystifying the 'cult of the primitive Black' that many whites took for granted during the 1920's.

This historical conflict is reflected in the antagonistic relationship of Dora Ellsworth and her black protégée, the pianist Oceola Jones. Both women represent oppos-ing points of view; [according to Robert Bone in his *Down Home*], this structural contrast manifests a clash between "two standards of morality," between a "white and a Negro code." The conflict itself evolves through-out five stages, each dramatizing their incompatible positions: the financial sponsorship is followed by increasing efforts on part of Mrs. Ellsworth to dominate the private life of her protegée; Oceola's return to Harlem and the announcement of her engagement to a black medical student cause a severe crisis and finally lead to a dissolving of their relationship.

The mocking irony with which the narrator emphasizes Mrs. Ellsworth's ignorance prevails through all these scenes. Her ignorance of art and artists is even excelled by her total lack of insight into black life and, in particular, Harlem: "Before going to bed, Mrs. Ellsworth told her housekeeper to order a book called 'Nigger Heaven'..., and also anything else...about Harlem." Here Hughes tries not merely to unmask the fakery of white patronage; he also scores Carl Van Vechten's *Nigger Heaven.* This novel, published at the height of the Harlem Renaissance in 1926, served as a kind of guide-book to Harlem for many white readers and was mostly rejected by blacks. DuBois' review [in the *Crisis,* 1926] perhaps sums up best the black reaction of that time: "'Nigger Heaven' is a blow in the face. It is an affront to the hospitality of black folk.... It is a caricature. It is worse than untruth because it is a mass of half-truths." Although Hughes' own criticism of *Nigger Heaven* and Van Vechten [in his autobiography, **The Big Sea**] was rather friendly, the satirical connota-tion of the passage quoted above seems to suggest that by 1934 Hughes felt free enough to denounce Van Vechten's patronage in the same way as he did that of his former Park Avenue patroness.

Moreover, the same passage reveals another important feature of Mrs. Ellsworth's personality. Her reliance on books instead of personal experience, her preference for a substitute for reality, demonstrates that she is unable to differentiate between substance and appearance. This failure is particularly emphasized in the scene where she drives Oceola to her Harlem home:

Mrs. Ellsworth had to ask could she come in. "I live on the fifth floor," said Oceola, and there isn't any elevator," "It doesn't matter, dear,' said the white woman, for she meant to see the inside of this girl's life, elevator or no elevator.

Devoid of any emotional and psychological perception, she mistakes the exterior for the interior, form for being, and thereby reduces life to a mere artifact. This attitude is equally apparent in her conception of art. Having substituted art for life, Mrs. Ellsworth, like Pauline Attenborough, becomes a self-made *objet d'art;* her stress merely on the refining, cultivating, and sublimating function of art not only separates art from life, but also deprives it of its vitality and reduces it to a dead object.

Mrs. Ellsworth's attitudes contrast with Oceola's character and music. Having grown up in the musical tradition of the black church, Oceola's life is firmly rooted in jazz and the blues. Her music, which derives its strength from her cultural identity, distinctly sets her apart from Dora Ellsworth, who conceives of art as essentially classical. The evolving conflict thus centers around the clash of two antagonistic modes of life. In contrast to her patroness' understanding of music, Oceola has kept an original sense of it, one that "demanded movement and expression, dancing and living to go with it." As an initial, spontaneous expression of black life and experience, the blues is devoid of "classical runs or fancy falsities." Rather, it becomes, as Ralph Ellison once remarked, a form of individual therapy:

> The blues is an impulse to keep the painful details and episodes of a brutal experience alive in one's aching consciousness, to finger its jagged grain, and to transcend it, not by consolation of philosophy but by squeezing from it a near-tragic, near-comic lyricism. As a form, the blues is an autobiographical chronicle of personal catastrophe expressed lyrically.

Oceola's music hence becomes not only an assertion and definition of her identity; it also links her, culturally, to that chain of black folklore tradition, which, as Ellison has pointed out, "announced the Negro's willingness to trust his own experience, his own sensibilities as to the definition of reality, rather than allow his masters to define these crucial matters for him." Oceola's "sheer love of jazz", her hatred of "most artists, . . . and the word art in French or English," gives voice to an attitude which considers music a manifestation of an experienced reality, thus merging both art and life. Her contempt for a philosophy that separates these two arises out of her primal emphasis on the affirmative and virile nature of music . . . .

The "bipàrtite structure" of this story, emphasizing two opposing ethnic codes and philosophies of art, is also equally apparent in the different geographical settings of the various scenes. From the very beginning of their relationship, the Park Avenue patroness tries to alienate Oceola from Harlem: "I must get her out of Harlem at once. I believe it's worse than Chinatown." Her efforts finally result in Oceola's moving to Greenwich Village,

and then for two years' study to Paris. The effects of her training in classical music are not, however, as sublimating as Mrs. Ellsworth had hoped. Returning from Paris, Oceola is determined more firmly than ever not to give up the black musical tradition. This is especially shown in her decision to move back to Harlem: "I've been away from my own people so long, I want to live right in the middle of them again." This symbolic rediscovery of her heritage, induced by a stay in Paris, is one of the earliest black reiterations of the Jamesian pattern. For it is in Europe that Oceola, to paraphrase a title of one of James Baldwin's essays, makes the discovery of what it means to be black.

The different settings hence express metaphorically the various stages of their relationship. The symbolic confrontation of Harlem with Greenwich Village and Paris ultimately demonstrates that the conflict is again dramatized on a personal as well as cultural plane. Her return to Harlem signals the attempt to preserve her black cultural identity. Significantly enough, it is only after she has accepted her lover's proposal that Oceola at a concert in a Harlem church suddenly lives up to her own musical intentions by "not sticking to the classical items listed on the program," for now she is able to "insert one of her own variations on the spirituals."

The inevitable separation of Oceola and Mrs. Ellsworth takes place one evening in the patroness' apartment, where Oceola had come to play for the last time "with the techniques for which Mrs. Ellsworth had paid." Again, the conflict is described in the contrasting images that are representative of the two different cultural spheres. Dora Ellsworth's position is almost entirely linked with exquisite, though lifeless antique objects, evoking the impression of her emotional sterility and deadness. These objects, acting as objective correlatives of her emotional state, cannot be reconciled with life. The vital, life-promising nature of Oceola's music, which grew "into an earth-throbbing rhythm that shook the lilies in the Persian vases of Mrs. Ellsworth's music room," ultimately exposes her limited point of view and suggests the final triumph, as it were, of black over white culture.

Because of her limited point of view, Dora Ellsworth remains unchanged. Even though she is dressed at the end in the same black velvet that Oceola used to wear, [James A.] Emanuel's reading this as "a symbolic fusion of herself and her protegée" seems to be an unwarranted conjecture. Rather, the story's ending calls for a reading [as Bone states] which views the two unreconciled positions as a re-emphasis of "the theme of cultural dualism which is basic to the Harlem Renaissance" and Hughes' position therein.

Oceola's self-conscious revolt against her patroness, which has strong autobiographical parallels, underlines historically the black's incipient ethnic assertion, his pride in his race and the rediscovery of his cultural heritage. Within this cultural context, **"The Blues I'm Playing"** may be considered a two-fold satire. One of its objectives, of course, is to unmask the hypocrisy of white patronage. In addition to this, the philosophy of black cultural elitism and the 'New Negro' seems to be equally under attack. By refuting the 'high culture' of the Renaissance champions, Hughes satirizes through his fictional character those attempts to bridge the gap between the two races by means of art. For this must, as he demonstrates through Oceola, inevitably lead to servility and a loss of black identity. In contrast to Emanuel's general dictum that "Hughes as a writer cannot be explained by references to the Harlem Renaissance," this particular short story echoes, both on the autobiographical and cultural plane, historical problems that were firmly rooted in this period; thus Hughes' delineation of Oceola may ultimately be conceived as a fictional representation of his own literary manifesto and the story as a satirical reaction to the Harlem Renaissance.

Within the bulk of Hughes' sixty-six published short stories, **"The Blues I'm Playing"** holds a unique position. In keeping with Emanuel, who classified Hughes' short fiction thematically, this story turns out to be his only genuine artist story. It marks one of Hughes' outstanding achievements in this genre and established him as a serious writer of satirical short fiction. Most stories in the collection *The Ways of White Folk* are retrospective, looking back to the 1920's and trying to unveil many of the manifestations of the Harlem Renaissance. The date of publication, however, suggests a further significance. For the year 1934 signals the end of Hughes' early phase. (pp. 74-80)

Despite favorable review, the first issue of *The Ways of White Folk* sold only 2500 copies. This meagre success may be accounted for not only by the fact that Hughes had not yet gained, as he was to do later with his "Simple Tales," a genuine black reading audience; the commercial failure also seems to demonstrate that with the end of the Harlem Renaissance the potential white audience no longer shared a larger enthusiasm in black literary products. From a historical and socio-literary perspective, however, the stories of *The Ways of White Folk* caused a major breakthrough in paving the way for a racially unrestricted audience. By re-examining the black-white relationships of the 1920's and by unmasking the falseness of the enthusiasm of whites for the 'New Negro,' [Donald C. Dickinson states that] Hughes "clarified for the Negro audience their own strength and dignity and . . . supplied the white audience with an explanation of how the Negro feels and what he wants." Six years after the publication of this collection, Richard Wright, in a review of Hughes' autobiography *The Big Sea,* perhaps summed up the importance of the early works of Hughes best. In his eyes, Hughes, on account of his extensive publications, had served as a "cultural ambassador for the case of the blacks." (pp. 80-1)

Peter Bruck, "Langston Hughes: 'The Blues I'm Playing' (1934)," in The Black American Short Story in the 20th Century: A Collection of Critical Essays, *edited by Peter Bruck, B. R. Grüner Publishing Co., 1977, pp. 71-84.*

Arnold Rampersad (essay date 1986)

[*An American educator and writer, Rampersad is the author of the two volume study* The Life of Langston Hughes *(1986, 1988), considered by many critics the definitive biography of Hughes. In the following excerpt, he analyzes* Fine Clothes to the Jew, *concluding that the work is "by far Hughes's greatest collection of verse."*]

As prolific as Langston Hughes strove to be in a variety of genres—poetry, fiction, drama, and essays notably—he saw himself from first to last primarily as a poet. Of his many collections of verse, nine must be considered major in his career by almost any accounting: *The Weary Blues* (1926); *Fine Clothes to the Jew* (1927); *Shakespeare in Harlem* (1942); *Fields of Wonder* (1947); *One-Way Ticket* (1949); *Montage of a Dream Deferred* (1951); *Ask Your Mama* (1961); and *The Panther and the Lash* (posthumously in 1967, the year of his death). To these efforts might be added the volume published by the leftist International Workers Order, *A New Song* (1938); although it contained no new poems, the verse in that slender pamphlet was unusually radical and had not been collected previously.

Of these volumes, the least successful both in terms of sales and critical reception, at least among black reviewers, was unquestionably *Fine Clothes to the Jew.* I would like to argue that, paradoxically, this volume was by far Hughes's greatest collection of verse, that the collection marked the height of his creative originality as a poet, and that it remains one of the most significant single volumes of poetry ever published in the United States. In fact, despite its failure to gain recognition, *Fine Clothes to the Jew* may stand in relationship to black American poetry in a way not unlike Walt Whitman's 1855 edition of *Leaves of Grass* stands in relationship to white American poetry, or to the poetry of the nation as a whole.

Fine Clothes to the Jew appeared almost ten years after Hughes first began to write poetry. While his work in Lincoln, Illinois (where by his own account he wrote his first poem, in 1916), is lost, almost all of his poems written in high school in Cleveland and thereafter are available to scholars. They may be found in the *Central High School Monthly, Crisis, Opportunity,* and other magazines published largely by blacks, as well as in white magazines that cover the broad ideological spectrum from *Vanity Fair,* on one hand, to the communist *New Masses,* on the other. The work of these first years culminated in the appearance from Knopf of Hughes's first book of any kind, *The Weary Blues. Fine Clothes to the Jew,* the next, built on elements found in the previous volume and in the magazines, but with such emphases and revision that it marked, in effect, an unparalleled rethinking by Hughes about poetry in the context of black America.

Once Hughes shed his most youthful approaches to poetry and felt the stirring influence of Walt Whitman, whose lines he echoed unmistakably in his first published free verse poem, **"A Song of the Soul of Central"** (*Central High School Monthly,* January 1919) and Carl Sandburg ("my guiding star"), his poetry fell almost inevitably into three distinct areas. The first area found Hughes dwelling on isolation, despair, suicide, and the like—conventional themes for a young, romantic poet, to be sure, but notions strongly felt by Hughes personally as he struggled to overcome the effects of his father's desertion and his mother's flighty compromise of her relationship with her son.... The second area, also present virtually from the start of Hughes's career as a poet and fiction writer, reveals an aggressive socialist, non-racial intelligence, as for example in the very titles of two poems written later, in 1932: **"Good Morning Revolution"** and **"Goodbye Christ."** The third area, for which Hughes is almost certainly best known, finds him creating in direct response to the needs of black people—epitomized by **"The Negro Speaks of Rivers,"** published in 1921. (pp. 144-45)

Fine Clothes to the Jew falls outside of these categories. Although all of the poems in the various categories naturally involve a poetic concern with the manipulation of form, *Fine Clothes to the Jew* is based in essence on what one might acknowledge as a separate aesthetic, a different approach to poetic art. In the other work, Hughes writes—in spite of his concern with race—as a poet impelled by the literary tradition as defined by certain major poets of the language—in particular, Walt Whitman and his epigones, notably Carl Sandburg and Vachel Lindsay. But in *Fine Clothes* Hughes attempted to work in a way no black or white poet had ever attempted to work: deliberately defining poetic tradition according to the standards of a group often seen as subpoetic—the black masses. (p. 145)

While *The Weary Blues* was in press and in the months following its appearance, Hughes went through certain experiences that revolutionized his aesthetic. First was his sojourn...among the black poor in Washington. Second was his entry into black Lincoln University a few days after *The Weary Blues* appeared, when for the first time since he was nine or ten, Hughes went to school with a majority of blacks (and all male)—an

Hughes in Atlanta during Negro History Week, 1947.

experience of incalculable effect on his sense of race. Third was the impact of the brilliant circle of young stars—the key members of the Harlem Renaissance—in Harlem at the same time: Aaron Douglass, Arna Bontemps, Wallace Thurman, Bruce Nugent, and Zora Neale Hurston, for whom Hughes's *Nation* essay of June 1926, **"The Negro Artist and the Racial Mountain,"** was manifesto; to these should be added the names of musicians Hall Johnson, Paul Robeson, Clarence Cameron White, and W. C. Handy (often called the father of the blues), with whom Hughes either worked or consulted in the summer of 1926, especially in connection with a musical, to star Robeson, called "O Blues!" (from **"The Weary Blues"**). The fourth experience was the reaction of the black press to Carl Van Vechten's Harlem novel, *Nigger Heaven,* and to the appearance of *Fire!!* magazine.

The younger writers in general enthusiastically approved of *Nigger Heaven* ("Colored people can't help but like it," Hughes had predicted; the novel read as if it were written by "an N.A.A.C.P. official or Jessie Fauset. But it's good"). To almost all the young black writers, Van Vechten's troubles were their own. The attack on him was an attack on what they themselves, or most of them, stood for—artistic and sexual freedom, a love of the black masses, a refusal to idealize black life, and a revolt against bourgeois hypocrisy. They decided to publish their own magazine, instead of relying on the staid *Crisis* and the like. For their pains, *Fire!!* received a withering reception in the black press. "I have just tossed the first issue of *Fire* into the fire," the reviewer in the *Baltimore Afro-American* fumed; Aaron Douglass had ruined "three perfectly good pages and a cover" with his drawings, while Langston Hughes displayed "his usual ability to say nothing in many words."

These experiences prompted Hughes to go where no poet had gone before; in the summer of 1926 he wrote poems that differed sharply from the spirit of **The Weary Blues** and that contested the right of the middle class to criticize the mores and manners of the black masses. (The rebellious campaign continued into the fall, when Hughes wrote his first short stories since high school, the "West Illana" sequence of stories set on a ship much like the one on which he had sailed to Africa in 1923. Hughes's fiction navigated more sensual waters than ever before; whatever their limitations as art, the stories that resulted steam suggestively of miscegenation, adultery, promiscuity, and the turmoil of sexual repression—subjects all taboo to the critics who hated *Fire!!.*) During the summer he wrote almost feverishly; back in Lincoln for the fall term, he soon gathered his new poems into what he hoped would be his second book.

On Sunday, October 3, he visited New York and delivered the manuscript to Carl Van Vechten, to whom the collection was dedicated. As with Hughes's first book, they went over each of the poems; exactly what part Van Vechten played now is unclear. Three weeks later, Langston presented the revised collection to him to take to Knopf. By this time it had a name: **Fine**

Clothes to the Jew, after a line from Hughes's **"Hard Luck"**:

> When hard luck overtakes you
> Nothin' for you to do
> Gather up yo' fine clothes
> An' sell 'em to de Jew...

Knopf accepted **Fine Clothes to the Jew,** but not without balking at the title (the firm had published *Nigger Heaven* apparently without difficulty). After Van Vechten personally defended the name, as he recorded in his journal, it was allowed to stand. Van Vechten perhaps had also chosen it, as he had chosen **The Weary Blues**. Certainly, Hughes had been thinking of using "Brass Spittoons," from one of his poems. The choice was unfortunate. Apparently no one alerted Hughes to the effect his title would have on sales, which proved to be opposite to the result of Van Vechten's own crudeness. But he later regarded the title as one of the main reasons for the failure of the book: it was "a bad title, because it was confusing and many Jewish people did not like it."

By mid-January, 1927, Hughes had copies of **Fine Clothes to the Jew.** The first reports were encouraging. Far from objecting to the title, his friend and supporter, Amy Spingarn, liked the book even more than **The Weary Blues,** because it seemed "more out of the core of life." Her brother-in-law, Arthur Spingarn, who was also Jewish, noted the title but found the book a "splendid" work, in which "Jacob and the Negro come into their own." The black conservative George Schuyler praised Hughes as "the poet of the modern Negro proletariat." But after the attacks on *Nigger Heaven* and *Fire!!,* Hughes was nervous. "It's harder and more cynical," he explained defensively to Dewey Jones of the Chicago *Defender,* and "limited to an interpretation of the 'lower classes,' the ones to whom life is least kind. I try to catch the hurt of their lives, the monotony of their 'jobs,' and the veiled weariness of their songs. They are the people I know best."

On February 5, just as he prepared to set out on a tour for Negro History Week, the black critics opened fire. Under a headline proclaiming Hughes a "SEWER DWELLER," William M. Kelley of the New York *Amsterdam News,* denounced **Fine Clothes to the Jew** as "about 100 pages of trash.... It reeks of the gutter and sewer." The regular reviewer of the *Philadelphia Tribune* adamantly refused to publicize it; Eustance Gay confessed that **Fine Clothes to the Jew** "disgusts me." In the *Pittsburgh Courier,* historian J. A. Rogers called it "piffling trash" that left him "positively sick." The Chicago *Whip* sneered at the dedication to Van Vechten, "a literary gutter-rat" who perhaps alone "will revel in the lecherous, lust-reeking characters that Hughes finds time to poeticize about.... These poems are unsanitary, insipid and repulsing." Hughes was the "poet 'low-rate' of Harlem." The following week, refining its position, the *Tribune* lamented Hughes's "obsession for the more degenerate elements" of black life; the book was "a study in the perversions of the Negro." It is questionable whether any book of American poetry, other than *Leaves of Grass,* had ever been greeted so contemptuously.

To these and other black critics, Hughes had allowed the "secret" shame of their culture, especially its apparently unspeakable or unprintable sexual mores, to be bruited by thick-lipped black whores and roustabouts. How could he have dared to publish **"Red Silk Stockings"**?

> Put on yo' red silk stockings,
> Black gal.
> Go out an' let de white boys
> Look at yo' legs.
>
> Ain't nothin' to do for you, nohow,
> Round this town,—
> You's too pretty.
> Put on yo' red silk stockings, gal,
> An' tomorrow's chile'll
> Be a high yaller.
> Go out an' let de white boys
> Look at yo' legs.

Or **"Beale Street Love"**?

> Love
> Is a brown man's fist
> With hard knuckles
> Crushing the lips,
> Blackening the eyes,—
> Hit me again
> Says Clorinda.

By pandering to the taste of whites for the sensational (the critics ignored their own sensationalism, demonstrable in the scandal-ridden sheets of most black weeklies), Hughes had betrayed his race.

In spite of this hostility, *Fine Clothes to the Jew* marked Hughes's maturity as a poet after a decade of writing, and his most radical achievement in language. While *The Weary Blues* had opened with references to the blues and poems written in dialect, before presenting the sweeter, more traditional lyrics, a prefatory note ("the mood of the *Blues* is almost always despondency, but when they are sung people laugh") now indicated the far greater extent to which *Fine Clothes to the Jew* falls deliberately within the range of authentic blues emotion and blues culture. Gone are the conventional lyrics about nature and loneliness, or poems in which the experience of the common black folk is framed by conventional poetic language and a superior, sometimes ironic poetic diction. Here few poems are beyond range of utterance of common black folk, except in so far as any formal poetry by definition belongs to a more privileged world. *Fine Clothes to the Jew* was the perfect companion piece to Hughes's manifesto, **"The Negro Artist and the Racial Mountain."**

As a measure of his deeper penetration of the culture and his increased confidence as a poet, three kinds of poems are barely present in *Fine Clothes to the Jew*— those that praise black people and culture directly, those that directly protest their condition, and those that reflect his own personal sense of desolation. For exam-

ple: **"Laughters,"** which celebrates blacks as "Loud laughers in the hands of Fate," is also probably the earliest piece in the book, having been published first as **"My People"** in June, 1922. **"Mulatto"** lodges perhaps the strongest protest, but is staged dramatically:

> ...The Southern night is full of stars,
> Great big yellow stars.
> > O, sweet as earth,
> > Dusk dark bodies
> > Give sweet birth
> To little yellow bastard boys.
>
> > *Git on back there in the night.*
> > *You aint white.*
>
> The bright stars scatter everywhere.
> Pine wood scent in the evening air.
> > A nigger night,
> > A nigger joy.
>
> *I am your son, white man!*
>
> > A little yellow
> > Bastard boy.

Only one poem, **"Sport,"** proposes life as an empty nothingness—as "the shivering of a great drum / Beaten with swift sticks."

Sorrow and despair dominate *Fine Clothes to the Jew,* but mainly through the expressive medium of the blues and its place in the lives of poor black men and women. In **"Hey!"** the blues is mysterious: "I feels de blues a comin', / Wonder what de blues'll bring?" It is also, as in **"Misery,"** soothing, or even cathartic.... (pp. 149-52)

In *Fine Clothes to the Jew,* the signers and mourners are mainly women. By comparison, men are almost shallow; one man (**"Bad Man"**) beats his wife and "ma side gal too": "Don't know why I do it but / It keeps me from feelin' blue." Men may be hurt in love, like the fellow in **"Po' Boy Blues"** who met "a gal I thought was kind. / She made me lose ma money / An' almost lose ma mind." But the blues are sung most often, and most brilliantly, by black women. Sometimes they sing to warn their sisters (**"Listen Here Blues"**).... Women lament being cheated, for having been done wrong by "a yellow papa," who "took ma last thin dime" (**"Gypsy Man"**); or, as in **"Hard Daddy,"** they grieve over male coldness:

> I cried on his shoulder but
> He turned his back on me.
> Cried on his shoulder but
> He turned his back on me.
> He said a woman's cryin's
> Never gonna bother me.

But the blues can reflect great joy as well as sorrow, as in **"Ma Man,"** where a black woman's emotional and sexual ecstasy is so overpowering it drives her into song.... The last stanza of this poem, the second to last in the book (as if Hughes tried to hide it), was among the most sexually teasing in American poetry—to those who understood that "eagle-rocking" was possibly more than a popular dance step. (pp. 153-55)

When the *Pittsburgh Courier* invited Hughes to defend himself against his critics, he did not hesitate. In **"These Bad New Negros: A Critique on Critics,"** he identified four reasons for the attacks: the low self-esteem of the "best" blacks; their obsession with white opinion; their *nouveau riche* snobbery; and their lack of artistic and cultural training "from which to view either their own or the white man's books or pictures." As for the "ill-mannered onslaught" on Van Vechten: the man's "sincere, friendly, and helpful interest in things Negro" should have brought "serious, rather than vulgar, reviews of his book." A nine-point defense of his own views and practices ended in praise of the young writers, including Toomer, Fisher, Thurman, Cullen, Hurston, and the Lincoln poet Edward Silvera. And Hughes himself: "My poems are indelicate. But so is life," he pointed out. He wrote about "harlots and gin-bibers. But they are human. Solomon, Homer, Shakespeare, and Walt Whitman were not afraid or ashamed to include them." (Van Vechten thought the situation easy to explain; "you and I," he joked to Hughes while making an important distinction, "are the only colored people who really love *niggers*."

Hughes was not without friends in the black press. The *New York Age* found the book evocative of the joy and pathos, beauty and ugliness of black Americans, if of the more primitive type. The poet Alice Dunbar-Nelson, once married to Paul Laurence Dunbar, compared the book to Wordsworth and Coleridge's once maligned yet celebrated venture, *Lyrical Ballads,* which used the lives and speech of the common people; Hughes was "a rare poet." Theophilus Lewis praised the book in the *Messenger,* and in the *Saturday Review of Literature* Alain Locke was deft about *Fine Clothes to the Jew:* "Its open frankness will be a shock and a snare for the critic and moralist who cannot distinguish clay from mire." And Claude McKay wrote privately to congratulate Hughes on having written a book superior to his first.

Among white reviewers, perhaps the most perceptive evaluation came from the young cultural historian Howard Mumford Jones [in The *Chicago Daily News*]. Using black dialect austerely, Hughes had scraped the blues form down to the bone, and raised the folk form to literary art. "In a sense," Jones concluded, "He has contributed a really new verse form to the English language." Although, like Wordsworth, he sometimes lapsed into "vapid simplicity." But if Hughes continued to grow, he was "dangerously near becoming a major American poet." (pp. 155-56)

The ignorant blasts of the black press were nicely offset when Hughes accepted an invitation ("a great honor for me") from the Walt Whitman foundation to speak at the poet's home on Mickle Street in Camden, New Jersey. Stressing Whitman's humane depictions of blacks in his poetry, Hughes went on to claim that modern free verse, and his own work, descended from Whitman's great example. "I believe," Langston told the little gathering, "that poetry should be direct, comprehensible and the epitome of simplicity." Suspicious of theory, Hughes had nevertheless identified one of the main ideas behind his theory of composition—the notion of an aesthetic of simplicity, sanctioned finally by democratic culture but having a discipline and standards just as the baroque or the rococo, for example, had their own. That simplicity had its dangers both extended its challenge and increased its rewards. The visit to Whitman's home left Hughes elated; to Van Vechten he mailed a postcard imprinted with an excerpt from Whitman's "Song of the Open Road": "All seems beautiful to me."

Although Hughes would place the emphasis in his poetry in a different direction in the 1930s, when he wrote his most politically radical verse, he continued to write the blues even during this period. After the Depression, when Knopf published his *Shakespeare in Harlem,* the blues dominated the volume. When in the late 1940s and 1950s he allowed first be-bop (as in *Montage of a Dream Deferred*) and then increasingly "progressive" jazz (as in *Ask Your Mama*) also to shape his poetry, he was applying a basic principle he had first learned in the context of the blues. He never abandoned the form, because the blues continued as perhaps the most fertile form of black expressivity; *Ask Your Mama,* for example, is explicitly based on the "Hesitation Blues."

His initiative in the blues remains the only genuinely original achievement in form by any black American poet—notwithstanding the excellence of much of the work of writers such as Countee Cullen, Melvin Tolson, Gwendolyn Brooks, Robert Hayden, and even the rebel Amiri Baraka (surely the greatest names in modern black poetry). Their art is largely derivative by comparison. Afro-American poets did not rush to build on Hughes's foundation; most remained black poets who wished to be known simply as poets. But some poets followed the lead. Sterling Brown's *Southern Roads,* the most distinguished book of verse by an Afro-American in the 1930s, was certainly indebted to Hughes.... Richard Wright, initially a poet, tried to write the blues, and even published one poem in collaboration with Hughes. Among whites, Elizabeth Bishop tried her hand at the form, with results certainly no worse than Wright's—the blues, they learned, is not as simple as it seems.

Black poetry, however, had to wait until the late 1960s and 1970s, with the emergence of writers such as Sherley Anne Williams, Michael S. Harper, and Raymond Patterson, to capitalize fully on Hughes's historic achievement. Ironically, because of the obscurity in which *Fine Clothes to the Jew* remains, and because the full extent of Hughes's artistic revolution has not been appreciated, many young black poets are unaware of the history of the form that they nevertheless understand as providing the only indisputably honorable link between their literary and cultural ambitions as blacks and the language compelled on them by history. (pp. 156-57)

Arnold Rampersad, "Langston Hughes's Fine Clothes to the Jew," in Callaloo, *Vol. 9, No. 1, Winter, 1986, pp. 144-58.*

FURTHER READING

Barksdale, Richard K. *Langston Hughes: The Poet and His Critics.* Chicago: American Library Association, 1977, 155 p.
    Surveys critical response to Hughes's works.

Bontemps, Arna. "Langston Hughes: He Spoke of Rivers." *Freedomways* 8, No. 2 (Second Quarter 1968): 140-43.
    Brief account of Bontemps's first meeting with Hughes during the Harlem Renaissance.

Brooks, Gwendolyn. "Langston Hughes." *The Nation* 205, No. 1 (3 July 1967): 7.
    Tribute to Hughes shortly after his death.

Dandridge, Rita B. "The Black Woman as a Freedom Fighter in Langston Hughes' *Simple's Uncle Sam.*" *CLA Journal* XVIII, No. 2 (December 1974): 273-83.
    Compares three women in *Simple's Uncle Sam*—Joyce, Lynn Clarisse, and Minnie—to the historical figures Booker T. Washington, Martin Luther King, Jr., and Malcolm X, showing their similarities as advocates of black liberation.

Davis, Arthur P. "The Tragic Mulatto Theme in Six Works of Langston Hughes." *Phylon* XVI, No. 2 (Second Quarter 1955): 195-204.
    Analyzes Hughes's portrayal of racially mixed individuals in his poetry, short fiction, and drama.

Emanuel, James A. *Langston Hughes.* New Haven, Conn.: College and University Press, 1967, 192 p.
    Literary biography of Hughes.

Farrison, W. Edward. "Langston Hughes: Poet of the Negro Renaissance." *CLA Journal* XV, No. 4 (June 1972): 401-10.
    Overview of Hughes's career, emphasizing his prominent role in the Harlem Renaissance.

Klotman, Phyllis R. "Jesse B. Semple and the Narrative Art of Langston Hughes." *The Journal of Narrative Technique* 3, No. 1 (January 1973): 66-75.
    Analyzes four narrative techniques in the Simple tales.

O'Daniel, Therman B., ed. *Langston Hughes: Black Genius—A Critical Evaluation.* New York: William Morrow and Co., 1971, 245 p.
    Collection of thirteen critical essays on Hughes, with a selective bibliography of criticism.

Presley, James. "The American Dream of Langston Hughes." *Southwest Review* XLVIII, No. 4 (Autumn 1963): 380-86.
    Discusses Hughes's belief in and disillusionment with the American Dream for blacks.

Rampersad, Arnold. *The Life of Langston Hughes: I, Too, Sing America, Volume I, 1902-1941.* New York: Oxford University Press, 1986, 468 p.
    Literary biography of Hughes up to the publication of his autobiography *The Big Sea.*

——. *The Life of Langston Hughes: I Dream a World, Volume II, 1941-1967.* New York: Oxford University Press, 1988, 512 p.
    Continues discussion of Hughes's life and career up to his death.

Randall, Dudley. "The Black Aesthetic in the Thirties, Forties, and Fifties." In *The Black Aesthetic,* edited by Addison Gayle, Jr., pp. 224-34. Garden City, N.Y.: Doubleday and Company, Inc., 1971.
    Examines black nationalism in Hughes's poetry and prose.

Short, Randall. "Just Folks." *Mirabella* (March 1991): 72.
    Discusses efforts to bring *Mule Bone* to the stage. The critic writes: "The play's brilliant comedy should make [*Mule Bone*] popular with contemporary audiences. Its rediscovery may change perceptions of the history of black theater in this country."

Zora Neale Hurston

1901?-1960

American novelist, folklorist, short story writer, autobiographer, essayist, dramatist, poet, and anthropologist.

Hurston is recognized as an important writer of the Harlem Renaissance, an era of unprecedented achievement in black American art and literature during the 1920s and early 1930s. Although she influenced such writers as Ralph Ellison, Toni Morrison, Gayl Jones, and Toni Cade Bambara, interest in her has only recently been revived after decades of neglect. In addition to her four novels, three nonfiction works, and numerous short stories and essays, she is acknowledged as the first black American to collect and publish African-American folklore. Lillie P. Howard stated: "[Hurston's] works are important because they affirm blackness (while not denying whiteness) in a black-denying society. They present characters who are not all lovable but who are undeniably and realistically human. They record the history, the life, of a place and time which are remarkably like other places and times, though perhaps a bit more honest in the rendering."

Hurston was born and raised in Eatonville, Florida, where, she later recalled, she "grew like a gourd and yelled bass like a gator." Eatonville was the first incorporated all-black town in America and became the setting for most of Hurston's fiction. At the age of thirteen Hurston was taken out of school to care for her brother's children. At sixteen she joined a traveling theatrical troupe and worked as a maid for a white woman who arranged for her to attend high school in Baltimore. Hurston later studied anthropology at Barnard College and Columbia University with the anthropologist Franz Boas—an experience that profoundly influenced her work. During this period, Hurston began publishing short stories and establishing friendships with many important black writers. In 1927, together with Langston Hughes and other artists, Hurston founded *Fire!*, a literary magazine devoted to African-American culture. The publication collapsed, however, after its premiere issue as a result of financial difficulties and a fire that destroyed the editorial offices. After graduation she returned to her hometown for anthropological study. The data she collected there would be used both in her collections of folklore and in her fictional works.

"I was glad when somebody told me: 'You may go and collect Negro folklore,'" Hurston related in the introduction to her short story collection *Mules and Men* (1935). "In a way it would not be a new experience for me. When I pitched headforemost into the world I landed in the crib of Negroism. From the earliest rocking of my cradle, I had known about the capers Br'er Rabbit is apt to cut and what the Squinch Owl says from the housetop. But it was fitting me like a tight chemise. I couldn't see it for wearing it. It was only

when I was off in college, away from my native surroundings, that I could see myself like somebody else and stand off and look at my garment. Then I had to have the spyglass of anthropology to look through at that."

Mules and Men was a popular success. The book includes many folktales, which the tellers call "lies." These "lies," which contain hidden social and philosophical messages, were an important part of the culture of Hurston's hometown region. Hurston also provided descriptions of voodoo practices and beliefs. Although many critics praised the book's readability and entertaining qualities, some cited an absence of scholarly analysis and comparative notations and an abundance of authorial intrusions. Others accused Hurston of ignoring racial oppression and exploitation in the South—accusations that recurred throughout her literary career. Recent commentators, however, have refuted these charges. Theresa R. Love asserted: "[Hurston's goal] was not merely to collect folklore but to show the beauty and wealth of genuine Negro material. In doing so, she placed herself on the side of those who saw nothing self-defeating in writing about the black masses, who, she felt, are more imaginative than their middle-class counterparts."

In her first novel, *Jonah's Gourd Vine* (1934), Hurston combined her knowledge of folklore with biblical themes. Loosely based on the lives of her parents, *Jonah's Gourd Vine* centers on John Pearson, a respected minister and town leader, and the life and death of his first wife, Lucy Potts. Written in the southern black dialect that Hurston used throughout her fiction, *Jonah's Gourd Vine* earned Hurston recognition for her "notable talents as a story teller." In *Moses, Man of the Mountain* (1939) Hurston used data obtained from her studies in folklore and voodoo. Basing her story on the premise that most black Americans view their heritage as similar to that of the Hebrews in ancient Egypt, Hurston wrote *Moses* as an allegorical novel of American slavery. Moses is portrayed not as a prophet but as a powerful magician and voodoo practitioner.

Most critics maintain that *Their Eyes Were Watching God* (1937) is Hurston's best work. The novel, now considered by some a classic in feminist literature, tells the story of a woman's quest for fulfillment and liberation in a society where women are objects to be used for physical work and pleasure. Upon publication, critical opinion of the novel varied. Otis Ferguson contended that the book "is absolutely free of Uncle Toms," while Richard Wright accused Hurston of manipulating white stereotypes of black people to attract white readers. Other black critics at the time attacked Hurston for what they considered her lack of racial awareness. Contemporary critics, among them Alice Walker and June Jordan, have refuted these charges, asserting that Hurston was acutely aware of the racial climate of the time and describing the novel as an affirmation of black culture. Jordan wrote: "Unquestionably, *Their Eyes Were Watching God* is the prototypical Black novel of affirmation; it is the most successful, convincing, and exemplary novel of Black-love that we have. Period. But the book gives us more: the story unrolls a fabulous, written-film of Blacklife freed from the constraints of oppression; here we may learn Black possibilities of ourselves if we could ever escape the hateful and alien context that has so deeply disturbed and mutilated our rightly efflorescence—*as people.* Consequently, this novel centers itself on Black-love—even as *Native Son* rivets itself upon white hatred."

By the mid-1940s Hurston's literary career had begun to fail badly. Novel after novel was rejected by publishers who sensed that Hurston's submissions lacked the depth and insight of her earlier work. Hurston set her last published novel, *Seraph on the Suwanee* (1948), in Florida, where she was then living. Critics view this as her most ambitious but least successful work of fiction. *Seraph on the Suwanee,* which is thematically similar to *Jonah's Gourd Vine* and *Their Eyes Were Watching God,* is the story of a neurotic woman's search for self-esteem and her attempt to return the love of her husband. In this work, Hurston's major characters are poor whites, not the black inhabitants of Eatonville found in her previous novels. This radical change in focus and the absence of dialect prose prompted some black critics to label Hurston an assimilationist.

In her autobiography *Dust Tracks on a Road* (1942), Hurston revealed her stance on race relations in America. She maintained that black artists should celebrate the positive aspects of black American life instead of indulging in what she termed "the sobbing school of Negrohood." Yet Hurston acknowledged racial prejudice and published essays on the problem in several journals and magazines. Her early play *Color Struck!* (1925) addresses bigotry within the black community, specifically the favoring of light-skinned over dark-skinned blacks. Recent studies have indicated that the original manuscript of *Dust Tracks on a Road* included severe criticism of American racial and foreign policy, but these sections were omitted because Hurston's editors feared that some readers might interpret her views as an attack on America's role in World War II.

In 1948 Hurston, then living in New York, was arrested and charged with committing an immoral act with a ten-year-old boy. The charges were later dropped—Hurston was able to prove that she had been out of the country when the alleged incident took place—but Hurston was devastated by the ensuing publicity. She wrote to a friend: "I care nothing for writing anything anymore.... My race has seen fit to destroy me without reason, and with the vilest tools conceived by man so far." By 1950 Hurston had returned to Florida, where she worked as a cleaning woman in Rivo Alto. Later in the year she moved to Belle Glade, Florida, and attempted to revive her writing career. During the remaining years of her life she worked variously as a newspaper reporter, librarian, and substitute teacher. She suffered a stroke in 1959 and was forced to enter the Saint Lucie County, Florida, Welfare Home, where she died penniless in January 1960. She was buried in an unmarked grave in Fort Pierce's segregated cemetery, the Garden of the Heavenly Rest.

Hurston was an ambiguous and complex figure with seemingly antipodal traits. Robert Hemenway described her in his *Zora Neale Hurston: A Literary Biography* as "flamboyant yet vulnerable, self-centered yet kind, a Republican conservative and an early black nationalist." Hurston was never bitter and never felt disadvantaged because she was black. She wrote in 1928: "I am not tragically colored. There is no great sorrow dammed up in my soul, nor lurking behind my eyes. I do not mind at all. I do not belong to the sobbing school of Negrohood who hold that nature somehow has given them a lowdown dirty deal and whose feelings are all hurt about it.... No, I do not weep at the world—I am too busy sharpening my oyster knife."

(For further information about Hurston's life and works, see *Black Writers; Contemporary Authors,* Vols. 85-88; *Contemporary Literary Criticism,* Vols. 7, 30; *Dictionary of Literary Biography,* Vols. 51, 86; and *Short Story Criticism,* Vol. 4.)

PRINCIPAL WORKS

Color Stuck (drama) 1925
The Great Day (musical revue) 1932
Jonah's Gourd Vine (novel) 1934
Mules and Men (short stories) 1935
Their Eyes Were Watching God (novel) 1937
Tell My Horse (nonfiction) 1938; also published as
    *Voodoo Gods: An Inquiry into Native Myths and
    Magic in Jamaica and Haiti,* 1939
Moses, Man of the Mountain (novel) 1939; also pub-
    lished as *The Man of the Mountain,* 1941
Dust Tracks on a Road (autobiography) 1942
*Polk County: A Comedy of Negro Life on a Sawmill
    Camp* [with Dorothy Waring] (drama) 1944
Seraph on the Suwanee (novel) 1948
*I Love Myself When I Am Laughing... and Then Again
    When I Am Looking Mean and Impressive: A Zora
    Neale Hurston Reader* (fiction and nonfiction)
    1979
The Sanctified Church (essays) 1981
Spunk: The Selected Stories of Zora Neale Hurston
    (short stories) 1985
*Mule Bone: A Comedy of Negro Life [with Langston
    Hughes] (drama) 1991

* This comedy, completed by Hughes and Hurston in 1930, was first staged in 1991 with a prologue and epilogue by George Houston Bass.

Robert Bone (essay date 1975)

[*A noted American critic, Bone is the author of the critical histories* The Negro Novel in America *(1958) and* Down Home: Origins of the Afro-American Short Story *(1975). In the following excerpt from* Down Home, *he surveys Hurston's short stories, emphasizing the tension that they demonstrate between urban and pastoral values. Bone asserts that Hurston's story "The Gilded Six-Bits" best expresses this concern and stands as her principal achievement in the short story genre.*]

The thirst for experience was always strong in Zora Hurston's soul. In her autobiography, *Dust Tracks on a Road,* she writes of herself as a child:

> But no matter whether my probings made me happier or sadder, I kept on probing to know. For instance, I had a stifled longing. I used to climb to the top of one of the huge chinaberry trees which guarded our front gate, and look out over the world. The most interesting thing that I saw was the

horizon. Every way I turned, it was there, and the same distance away. Our house, then, was in the center of the world. It grew upon me that I ought to walk out to the horizon and see what the end of the world was like.

Far horizon never ceased to beckon, and the urge to explore it formed the basis of her picaresque adventures. That urge was momentarily suppressed, however, by the stifling atmosphere of a provincial, racist, and male chauvinist society. Everywhere she turned she encountered restrictive boundaries which designated certain areas as "off limits" to a Southern black girl. These limits were enforced no less by the black than the white South; hence the abrasive conflict between this imaginative youngster and the black community. Again and again she was reminded by her elders that, being black, she must settle for a good deal less than far horizon. And she rebelled with every fiber of her being.

To escape from the cramped quarters of her childhood was the central thrust of Hurston's adolescence. This thrust toward freedom, whose literary mode is the picaresque, is dramatized in three early stories, **"Drenched in Light," "John Redding Goes to Sea,"** and **"Magnolia Flower."** At the same time, a conflicting impulse is apparent in Hurston's early fiction: namely, the urge to celebrate the singularity of Eatonville, the all-black town in Florida where she was born and raised. This local-color strain, which manifests itself in stories such as **"Spunk"** and **"Sweat"** flowers ultimately into pastoral. (pp. 141-42)

Eatonville is the roosting place of Hurston's imagination; it is what she counterposes to the modern world. Founded during Reconstruction by Northern abolitionists, this independent township was the breeding ground of the frontier virtues celebrated in her fiction. Six of Hurston's stories and two of her novels are set in Eatonville, and when she abandons this familiar setting she does so at her peril. Hers is an imagination bound to a specific landscape: its people, its folkways, and its pungent idiom. This deep attachment to the Florida lake country accounts for both the strengths and limitations of her art, since what she gains in density of texture she sometimes dissipates in the depiction of a purely surface world. (p. 144)

In approaching Hurston's short fiction it is well to bear in mind that this was her apprentice work. Six of her eight stories were published from 1924 to 1926, while she was still an undergraduate. Only **"The Gilded Six-Bits,"** which appeared in *Story Magazine* of August 1933, is representative of her mature achievement. Of the apprentice pieces of the 1920's, **"Magnolia Flower"** and **"Muttsy"** are hopelessly incompetent. **"John Redding Goes to Sea,"** and **"Sweat"** hover on the borderline of art and fantasy, while **"Drenched in Light"** and **"Spunk"** display something of the power that is generated by her best fiction.

"Drenched in Light" (*Opportunity,* December 1924) is a remarkable first story, whose impetus derives from the author's childhood. Here is the relevant passage from Hurston's autobiography:

> I used to take a seat on top of the gate-post and watch the world go by. One way to Orlando ran past my house, so the carriages and cars would pass before me. The movement made me glad to see it. Often the white travelers would hail me, but more often I hailed them, and asked, "Don't you want me to go a piece of the way with you?" They always did.

The story that derives from these materials is a portrait of the artist as a young girl. The plot depicts a high-spirited child, full of mischief and invention, in conflict with a Calvinist, repressive, and experience-prohibiting society. The white-shell road that beckons to the child's imagination is a symbol of experience. Her picaresque adventures, undertaken in defiance of adult authority, are emblematic of the budding artist's unavoidable collision with the narrow outlook of the folk community. Grandma Potts, who functions like the Widow Douglas in *Huckleberry Finn,* embodies this restrictive outlook, while the child-heroine, whose name is Isis, symbolizes joy, laughter, and the pagan attitude toward life.

One day, on the occasion of a village barbecue, Isis makes off with Grandma's new red tablecloth and wears it as a Spanish shawl. Thus adorned, she performs a gypsy dance to the delight of her immediate observers. Among them are two white men and a lady who befriend the vagrant child, take her "a piece of the way" in their car, and interpose themselves and their authority between the malefactor and her grandma's wrath. In the woman's confession that she is in need of brightness, while the child is "drenched in light," adumbrations of the myth of primitivism may be seen.

It is highly significant that the white upper class, in the person of Lady Bountiful, should support the child in her imaginative exploits, and her conflict with the folk community. This woman is the fictional projection of a series of white patrons who encouraged Zora Hurston's art. At a deeper level, the episode suggests that in Hurston's unconscious mind, having access to experience was tantamount to being white. Hurston makes much of the fantasies that she indulged in as a child, devoting an entire chapter to the subject in her autobiography. It is clear from **"Drenched in Light"** that one of her most potent fantasies—imaged as a princess, wearing stately robes and riding on a white horse to the far horizon—was that of being white.

"John Redding Goes to Sea" (*Opportunity,* January 1926) is essentially a sequel, taking up where **"Drenched in Light"** leaves off. The imaginative child—this time a boy—longs to go to sea and experience something of the world, but his desire is stubbornly opposed by his mother. Mrs. Redding, like Grandma Potts, embodies the narrow and provincial outlook of the folk community, which cannot cope with the artistic temperament. Images of stasis and stagnation dominate the tale, expressive of the fate awaiting John if he lacks the courage to be free. Grown to manhood, but still

intimidated by his mother, he is offered a chance to be a hero, when a bridge is threatened by a hurricane. In an ironic dénouement he drowns, escaping mediocrity only through a kind of crucifixion.

In his young manhood, John Redding is caught in an agonizing dilemma. To remain in Eatonville is to be trapped forever in superstitious ignorance, symbolized by his mother. But to depart is to be disloyal to the folk community where he was born and bred. This is the central dilemma of Hurston's life, and a common predicament among black artists. It is resolved, in Hurston's case, by her assumption of the bardic role. Guilty for having left the folk community in order to pursue her personal ambitions, Hurston seeks atonement through her art. She is determined to avoid stagnation by transcending her milieu, but equally determined to give voice to that milieu, to become its spokesman. The result is her bardic fiction, written in the local-color vein.

Two of these local-color stories, **"Spunk"** and **"Sweat,"** are closely related to the Brer Rabbit tales. In their central polarities between the cruel and powerful and the weak and oppressed, echoes of the master-slave relationship are unmistakable. Like the animal fables from which they are descended, these tales are exercises in the art of masking. The secret theme of **"Spunk"** is the violation of black womanhood; of **"Sweat,"** the deadly hatred nurtured in the hearts of the oppressed. The racial implications are effectively disguised by an all-black cast of characters, but the emotional marrow of these tales is a sublimated racial anger.

"Spunk" (*Opportunity,* June 1925) is concerned with two varieties of courage or definitions of manhood. Spunk Banks is a giant of a man who carries off his neighbor's wife and defies him to redress the injury. Joe Kanty, the aggrieved husband, hesitates to challenge his tormentor, but taunted by the village men, he attacks him from behind, only to be shot to death. The men function as a chorus, observing and commenting on the action. At the outset Spunk wins their admiration through his fearlessness, while Joe is despised for his apparent cowardice. In the end, however, a villager proclaims that "Joe was a braver man than Spunk." Amid the derisive shouts of his audience he explains that it requires a greater courage for the weaker to attack the stronger man.

Behind the two antagonists loom the archetypal figures of Brer Rabbit and Brer Bear. Joe Kanty, as his name suggests, would be helpless in an open test of strength; his only hope lies in a surprise attack. The story thus endorses the survival values of subterfuge and treachery, up to and including an assault from behind. Two conflicting codes, one "honorable" or Anglo-Saxon, the other "cowardly" or Negro, are juxtaposed. The story repudiates conventional morality and affirms the outlaw code imposed upon the black man by his social subjugation. Hurston thus invokes the ancient wisdom of the folktale to reconcile the frontier virtues of courage and manliness with the brutal facts of caste.

"Sweat" (*Fire,* November 1926) is a less successful tale. The heroine is Delia Jones, a long-suffering laundress whose life is made unbearable by a brutal, tyrannous, and flagrantly philandering husband. Sykes attempts to kill his wife by concealing a rattlesnake in her laundry basket, but in an ironic reversal, he is destroyed by his own villainy. Throughout the story, man and wife are locked in a mutual hatred so intense that it acquires the force of myth. Behind their murderous domestic quarrel we discern the ancient animosities of Brer Rabbit and Brer Wolf. Like the cruellest and most sadistic of the animal fables, this story serves to vent illicit feelings of hatred and revenge.

The story has an ending that can only be described as self-indulgent. In the episode depicting Sykes' ordeal, Hurston loses her composure and rejoices in the torture of her villain. "Sweat" is thus reduced to a revenge fantasy. While such fantasies are a common feature of the animal fables, a more sophisticated medium demands a commensurate advance in emotional control. Nor does the story succeed as a horror tale, for naming the emotion that a reader is supposed to feel is not the same as compelling him to feel it. Hurston is an amateur in horror, and compared to Eric Walrond's "The White Snake," this story is a visit with the children to the Bronx Zoo.

From stories in the local-color vein, Hurston's imagination flowered into pastoral. But not until her disillusionment with urban life was complete. "Muttsy" (*Opportunity,* August 1926) is her story of recoil from the black metropolis, similar in tone and psychological significance to Claude McKay's Harlem tales. "Drenched in Light" and "John Redding Goes to Sea" portray the self setting forth from its place of origin in quest of wider horizons. "Muttsy," Hurston's sole attempt to deal with the urban scene, depicts the self in jeopardy from false, urban values. "The Gilded Six-Bits" brings the theme full circle as the self, reconciled to its provincial origins, returns to its spiritual home in Eatonville.

"The Gilded Six-Bits" (*Story,* August 1933) is Hurston's principal achievement in the short-story form. The tale inaugurates the second and most creative phase of her career, which followed her return to Eatonville in 1932. She now was a mature woman: her ambivalent feelings toward the folk community had been resolved; her adolescent impulse to escape it, mastered. Her curiosity to witness something of the larger world had been appeased, and she was ready to accept her destiny. That destiny, she now perceived, was to embrace her folk experience and give it form. The fruit of self-acceptance was a burst of creativity, beginning with the present story and extending through three novels.

The story is concerned with a crisis in the lives of Joe and Missie May. They have been happily married for a year when Slemmons, an urbanized Negro from Chicago, opens an ice-cream parlor in Eatonville. Dazzled by his fancy clothes and city ways, Missie May forgets herself and takes him as a lover. Joe discovers the deception and drives Slemmons off, but it is many months before he can forgive his thoroughly remorseful wife. Structurally speaking, the woman functions as a pivot between two value systems: the one urban and "sophisticated," the other rural and elemental. At first she chooses falsely, but in the end the deep and abiding values of the countryside prevail.

"The Gilded Six-Bits" is essentially a drama of sin and redemption, a symbolic reenactment of the Fall. As the story opens, Joe and Missie May frolic in prelapsarian innocence. Their pastoral surroundings and simple way of life constitute a Paradise where "all, everything was right." Into this happy Eden comes the Tempter, Slemmons, who proffers not an apple but a ten-dollar gold piece suspended from his watch chain. That the gold should prove to be illusory is Hurston's bitter comment on the Great Migration. Through Slemmons the city is exposed as a repository of false values.

The shallowness of urban culture is conveyed through Slemmons' attitude toward time. In the modern world of progress and improvement, of which the ice-cream parlor is an emblem, time is a commodity. The capitalist ethos, with its obligation to convert time into money, is symbolized by Slemmons' golden watch charm. But the peasant world of Joe and Missie May responds to natural rather than artificial rhythms: "Finally the sun's tide crept upon the shore of night and drowned its hours." In this world, time has a moral and theological rather than economic significance. It is primarily a healing force, repairing the breach that guilt has opened in the human soul.

"The Gilded Six-Bits" thus reveals the central core of Hurston's values. In this story, written in the depths of the Depression, she attacks the acquisitive society from a standpoint not unlike that of the Southern Agrarians. For the first time her social conservatism, inherited from Booker Washington by way of Eatonville, finds in pastoral an appropriate dramatic form. At the same time that her values coalesce, her narrative voice assumes a new authority. A mature style emerges whose metaphors, drawn from folk speech, function as a celebration of agrarian ideals. Having discovered her subject and mastered her idiom, she turns to those longer works of fiction where, for the most part, her achievement as a writer lies. (pp. 144-50)

> *Robert Bone, "Three Versions of Pastoral," in his* Down Home: Origins of the Afro-American Short Story, *Columbia University Press, 1988, pp. 139-70.*

Alice Walker (essay date 1977)

[*An American novelist, short story writer, poet, and critic, Walker is noted for works that express her concern with racial, sexual, and political issues, particularly the black woman's struggle for spiritual and political survival. In the following excerpt from her foreword to Robert E. Hemenway's biography of Hurston, she testifies to the significance of* Mules and Men *as a work of literary art and an invaluable document of African-American folk culture.*]

I became aware of my need of Zora Neale Hurston's work some time before I knew her work existed. In late 1970 I was writing a story that required accurate material on voodoo practices among rural southern blacks of the thirties; there seemed none available I could trust. A number of white, racist anthropologists and folklorists of the period had, not surprisingly, disappointed and insulted me. They thought blacks inferior, peculiar, and comic, and for me this undermined—no, *destroyed*—the relevance of their books. Fortunately, it was then that I discovered **Mules and Men,** Zora's book on folklore, collecting, herself, and her small, all-black community of Eatonville, Florida. Because she immersed herself in her own culture even as she recorded its "big old lies," i.e., folktales, it was possible to see how she and it (even after she had attended Barnard College and become a respected writer and apprentice anthropologist) fit together. The authenticity of her material was verified by her familiarity with its context, and I was soothed by her assurance that she was exposing not simply an adequate culture, but a superior one. That black people can be on occasion peculiar and comic was knowledge she enjoyed. That they could be racially or culturally inferior to whites never seems to have crossed her mind. (p. xi)

When I read **Mules and Men** I was delighted. Here was this perfect book! The "perfection" of it I immediately tested on my relatives, who are such typical black Americans they are useful for every sort of political, cultural, or economic survey. Very regular people from the South, rapidly forgetting their southern cultural inheritance in the suburbs and ghettos of Boston and New York, they sat around reading the book themselves, listening to me read the book, listening to each other read the book, and a kind of paradise was regained. For Zora's book gave them back all the stories they had forgotten or of which they had grown ashamed (told to us years ago by our parents and grandparents—not one of whom could *not* tell a story to make us weep, or laugh) and showed how marvelous, and, indeed, priceless, they are. *This is not exaggerated.* No matter how they read the stories Zora had collected, no matter how much distance they tried to maintain between themselves, as new sophisticates, and the lives their parents and grandparents lived, no matter how they tried to remain cool toward all Zora revealed, in the end they could not hold back the smiles, the laughter, the *joy* over who she was showing them to be: descendants of an inventive, joyous, courageous, and outrageous people: loving drama, appreciating wit, and, most of all, relishing the pleasure of each other's loquacious and *bodacious* company.

This was my first indication of the quality I feel is most characteristic of Zora's work: racial health—a sense of black people as complete, complex, *undiminished* human beings, a sense that is lacking in so much black writing and literature. (In my opinion, only Du Bois showed an equally consistent delight in the beauty and spirit of black people, which is interesting when one considers that the angle of his vision was completely the opposite of Zora's.) Zora's pride in black people was so pronounced in the ersatz black twenties that it made other blacks suspicious and perhaps uncomfortable; after all, *they* were still infatuated with things European—*everything* European. Zora was interested in Africa, Haiti, Jamaica—and, for a little racial diversity (Indians), Honduras. She also had a confidence in herself as an individual that few people (anyone?), black or white, understood. This was because Zora grew up in a community of black people who had enormous respect for themselves and for their ability to *govern* themselves. Her own father had written the Eatonville town laws. This community affirmed her right to exist, and loved her as an extension of itself. For how many other black Americans is this true? It certainly isn't true for any that I know. In her easy self-acceptance, Zora was more like an uncolonized African than she was like her contemporary American blacks, most of whom believed, at least during their formative years, that their blackness was something wrong with them.

On the contrary, Zora's early work shows she grew up *pitying* whites because the ones she saw lacked "light" and soul. It is impossible to imagine Zora envying anyone (except tongue-in-cheek), and, least of all, a white person for being white. Which is, after all, if one is black, a clear and present calamity of the mind.

Condemned to a deserted island for life, with an allotment of ten books to see me through, I would choose, unhesitatingly, two of Zora's: **Mules and Men,** because I would need to be able to pass on to younger generations the life of American blacks as legend and myth, and **Their Eyes Were Watching God,** because I would want to enjoy myself while identifying with the black heroine, Janie Crawford, as she acted out many roles in a variety of settings, and functioned (with spectacular results!) in romantic and sensual love. *There is no book more important to me than this one.* (pp. xii-xiii)

> *Alice Walker, "Zora Neale Hurston—A Cautionary Tale and a Partisan View," in* Zora Neale Hurston: A Literary Biography, *by Robert E. Hemenway, University of Illinois Press, 1977, pp. xi-xviii.*

Cheryl A. Wall (essay date 1982)

[*In the following excerpt, Wall discusses Hurston's presentation of black verbal expression in* Their Eyes Were Watching God *and later works.*]

The developing tradition of black women's writing nurtured now in the prose and poetry of such writers as Toni Morrison and Alice Walker began with the work of

Zora Neale Hurston. Hurston was not the first Afro-American woman to publish a novel, but she was the first to create language and imagery that reflected the reality of black women's lives. Ignoring the stereotypes, social and literary, that her predecessors spent their energies rejecting, Hurston rooted her art in the cultural traditions of the black rural South. As a daughter of the region, she claimed these traditions by birthright. As an anthropologist, she reclaimed them through years of intense, often perilous, research. As a novelist, she summoned this legacy in her choice of setting, her delineation of character, and most devotedly in her distillation of language. Hers became the first authentic black female voice in American literature. (p. 371)

The critical perspectives inspired by the black consciousness and feminist movements allow us to see Hurston's writings in a new way. They correct distorted views of her folklore as charming and quaint, set aside misperceptions of her characters as minstrels caught, in Richard Wrights' phrase, "between laughter and tears." These new perspectives inform this re-evaluation of Hurston's work. She asserted that black people, while living in a racist society that denied their humanity, had created an alternative culture that validated their worth as human beings. Although that culture was in some respects sexist, black women, like black men, attained personal identity not by transcending the culture but by embracing it.

Hurston's respect for the cultural traditions of black people is the most important constant in her career. This respect threads through her entire oeuvre, linking the local-color short fiction of her youth, her ethnographic research in the rural South and the Caribbean (an account of her fieldwork in Jamaica and Haiti, *Tell My Horse,* was published in 1938), her novels, and the essays she contributed to popular journals in her later years. In all, she published more than fifty short stories and articles in addition to her book-length works. Because her focus was on black cultural traditions, she rarely explored interracial themes. The black/white conflict, which loomed paramount in the fiction of her black contemporaries, in Wright's novels especially, hardly surfaced in Hurston's. Poet and critic June Jordan [in *Black World* (August 1974)] has described how the absence of explicitly political protest caused Hurston's work to be devalued. Affirmation, not protest, is Hurston's hallmark. Yet, as Jordan argues, "affirmation of Black values and lifestyle within the American context is, indeed, an act of protest." Hurston appreciated and approved the reluctance of blacks to reveal "that which the soul lives by" to the hostile and uncomprehending gaze of outsiders. But the interior reality was what she wished to probe. In that reality, blacks ceased to be "tongueless, earless, eyeless conveniences" whose labor whites exploited; they ceased to be mules and were men and women.

The survival of the spirit was proclaimed first and foremost through language. As a writer, Hurston was keenly sensitive to the richness of black verbal expression. Like Langston Hughes and Sterling Brown, she had no patience with theories of linguistic deficiency among blacks; she ignored racist assumptions that rural blacks spoke as they did because they were too stupid to learn standard English. Hurston, whose father was a Baptist preacher, was well acquainted with the tradition of verbal elegance among black people. From her father's example, she perceived how verbal agility conferred status within the community. His sermons had demonstrated as well the power of his language to convey the complexity of the lives of his parishioners. Early in her career, Hurston attempted to delineate "characteristics of Negro expression." She stressed the heightened sense of drama revealed in the preference for action words and the "will to adorn" reflected in the profusion of metaphor and simile, and in the use of double descriptives (*low-down*) and verbal nouns (*funeralize*). To her, the "will to adorn" bespoke a feeling "that there can never be enough of beauty, let alone too much." Zora Hurston shared that feeling, as the beautifully poetic prose of her novels attests. The collective folk expression was the soil that nourished the individual expression of her novels. After a lengthy dialogue with her homefolk, Hurston was prepared to change some words of her own.

In one of her first published articles, Hurston declared:

> BUT I AM NOT tragically colored. There is no great sorrow dammed up in my soul, nor lurking behind my eyes. I do not mind at all. I do not belong to the sobbing school of Negrohood who hold that nature somehow has given them a lowdown dirty deal and whose feelings are all hurt about it . . . . No, I do not weep at the world—I am too busy sharpening my oyster knife.

The exuberant tone of the assertions in **"How It Feels to Be Colored Me"** suggests that they were more strongly felt than reasoned. Hurston locates the source of her feelings in her childhood experiences in Eatonville, Florida, the hometown to which she often returned in fiction and fact. Eatonville was an all-black town, the first to be incorporated in the United States. Hurston remembered it as a place of possibility and promise. She revered the wit and wisdom of the townspeople, admired the originality of their culture and their moral and aesthetic values, saw in their language drama and the "will to adorn." Having been insulated from racism in her early years, unaware of racial distinctions until she was nine, she professed herself "astonished" rather than angered by discrimination. The lingering astonishment accounts perhaps for the shortcomings of the article as self and racial definition; Hurston relied on "exotic primitive" myths popular in the twenties to round out the explanation of herself and her people.

During this time Hurston was studying anthropology at Barnard under the tutelage of Franz Boas. This study complemented by her fieldwork in Florida and Louisiana allowed her to appreciate her past intellectually as well as intuitively. No longer were her homefolk simply good storytellers, whose values were commendable, superstitions remarkable, and humor penetrating. As

Hurston on a folklore collecting trip, late 1930s.

such, they had been well suited for local-color fiction of the kind Hurston published in the 1920s. Now however [according to Robert Hemenway in his *Zora Neale Hurston*], "they became a part of cultural anthropology; scientific objects who could and should be studied for their academic value." The cultural relativity of anthropology freed Hurston from the need to defend her subjects' alleged inferiority. She could discard behavioral explanations drawn from racial mythology. Eatonville blacks were neither exotic nor primitive; they had simply selected different characteristics from what Ruth Benedict, another pioneering anthropologist trained by Boas, called the "great arc of human potentialities." (pp. 372-74)

With the publication of *Their Eyes Were Watching God,* it was clear that Zora Neale Hurston was an artist in full command of her talent. Here the folk material complements rather than overwhelms the narrative. The sustained beauty of Hurston's prose owes much to the body of folk expression she had recorded and studied, but much more to the maturity of her individual voice. The language of this novel *sings*.... Janie, the heroine of *Their Eyes,* is a fully realized character. During the

twenty-odd years spanned by the plot, she grows from a diffident teenager to a woman in complete possession of her self. Two recurring metaphors, the pear tree and the horizon, help unify the narrative. The first symbolizes organic union with another, the second, the individual experiences one must acquire to achieve selfhood. Early reviewers thought of the novel as a love story, but recent commentators designate Janie's search for identity as the novel's major theme. Following the pattern we have observed, Janie's self-discovery depends on her learning to manipulate language. Her success is announced in the novel's prologue when, as a friend listens in rapt attention, Janie begins to tell her own story.

The action of the novel proper begins when Janie is sixteen, beautiful, and eager to struggle with life, but unable to articulate her wishes and dreams. Her consciousness awakens as she watches bees fertilizing the blossoms of a pear tree. In the following passage, the narrative voice is not Janie's but the scene, like the novel as a whole, expresses her point of view:

> She was stretched on her back beneath the pear tree soaking in the alto chant of the visiting bees, the gold of the sun and the panting breath of the breeze when the inaudible voice of it all came to her. She saw a dust-bearing bee sink into the sanctum of a bloom; the thousand sister-calyxes arch to meet the love embrace and the ecstatic shiver of the tree from root to tiniest branch creaming in every blossom and frothing with delight. So this was a marriage! She had felt a pain remorseless sweet that left her limp and languid.

The lyricism of the passage mutes somewhat its intensely sexual imagery. Still, the imagery is remarkably explicit for a woman novelist of Hurston's time. Janie's response to the scene and her acceptance of its implications for her own life are instructive: "Oh to be a pear tree—*any* tree in bloom!" Janie acknowledges sexuality as a natural part of life, a major aspect of her identity. Before she has the chance to act on this belief, however, her grandmother interposes a radically different viewpoint.

To Nanny, her granddaughter's nascent sexuality is alarming. Having been unable to protect herself and her daughter from sexual exploitation, Nanny determines to safeguard Janie. Janie must repress her sexuality in order to avoid sexual abuse; the only haven is marriage. Marriage had not been an option for Nanny, who as a slave was impregnated by her master; her mistress had forced her to flee with her newborn infant. Her daughter was raped by a black schoolteacher, convincing Nanny that male treachery knows no racial bounds. The world has thwarted her dreams of what a woman should be for herself and her daughter, "Ah wanted to preach a great sermon about colored women sittin' on high, but they wasn't no pulpit for me," but she has saved the text for Janie. She envisions her on the pedestal reserved for southern white women, far above the drudgery that has characterized Nanny's own life—the drudgery that has made the black woman "de mule uh de world." She arranges for Janie to marry Logan Killicks, an old man whose sixty acres and a mule constitute his eligibility. "The vision of Logan Killicks was desecrating the pear tree, but Janie didn't know how to tell Nanny that." So she assents to her grandmother's wish.

Joe Starks offers Janie an escape from her loveless marriage. He arrives just after Logan Killicks, despairing of his efforts to win his wife's affection by "pampering" her, has bought a second mule and ordered Janie to plow alongside him. Perceiving that Killicks's command threatens to reduce her to the status her grandmother abhorred, Janie decides to escape with Joe. Their marriage fulfills Nanny's dreams. Eventually it causes Janie to understand that the old woman's dreams are not her own. Initially though, Joe Starks cuts a fine figure. Stylishly dressed and citified, he is a man of great ambition and drive. He is like no *black* man Janie has ever seen. He reminds her vaguely of successful white men, but she cannot grasp the implications of the resemblance. She can appreciate his big plans and the élan with which he courts her. Tempering her reservations that "he did not represent sun-up and pollen and blooming trees," Janie resolves, "he spoke for far horizon. He spoke for change and chance."

It quickly becomes apparent that, like Nanny, Joe has borrowed his criteria for success from the white world. He takes Janie to Eatonville because there, he believes, he can be a "big ruler of things." His ambition is soon realized. He buys property and opens a store which becomes the town's meeting place. He decrees that roads be dug, a post office established, a street lamp installed, and town incorporation papers drawn. Already landlord, storekeeper, and postmaster, Joe runs for mayor to consolidate his power. After his election, he builds a large white house that is a travesty of a plantation mansion, and then furnishes it in the grand manner right down to brass spittoons. His brashness elicits equal measures of respect and resentment from the townspeople. As much as they admire his accomplishments, they take exception to his manner. One citizen's observation is widely shared: "he loves obedience out of everybody under de sound of his voice."

Everybody naturally includes Janie. Joe assigns her the role of "Mrs. Mayor Starks." She must hold herself apart from the townspeople, conduct herself according to the requirements of his position. Under no circumstances must she speak in public. Starks first imposes this rule during a ceremony marking the opening of the store. The ceremony has occasioned much speechmaking, and toward the end, Janie is invited to say a few words. Before she can respond, her husband takes the floor to announce:

> Thank yuh fuh yo' compliments, but mah wife don't know nothin' 'bout no speech-makin'. Ah never married her for nothin' lak dat. She's uh woman and her place is in de home.

Joe's announcement takes Janie by surprise. Unsure that she even wants to speak, she strongly resents being denied the right to decide for herself. Joe's prohibitions increase. He forbids Janie to participate in the lying sessions held on the store porch; she is hustled inside when they begin. Janie loves these conversations and notes that Joe, while not deigning to join in, stays around to listen and laugh. Being forbidden to speak is a severe penalty in an oral culture. It short-circuits Janie's attempt to claim an identity of her own, robs her of the opportunity to negotiate respect from her peers. Barred from speaking to anyone but Joe, she loses the desire to say anything at all. "So gradually, she pressed her teeth together and learned to hush."

After seven years of marriage, Janie recognizes that Joe requires her total submission. She yields. As she does so however, she retains a clear perception of herself and her situation, a perception that becomes her salvation in the end. On one occasion after Joe has slapped her (for naturally, her submission has not slowed his verbal or physical abuse), she experiences the following revelation:

> Janie stood where he left her for unmeasured time and thought. She stood there until something fell off the shelf inside her. Then she went inside to see what it was. It was her image of Jody tumbled down and shattered. But looking at it she saw that it never was the flesh and blood figure of her dreams. Just something she had grabbed up to drape her dreams over. In a way she turned her back upon the image where it lay and looked further. She had no more blossomy openings dusting pollen over her man, neither any glistening young fruit where the petals used to be. She found that she had a host of thoughts she had never expressed to him, and numerous emotions she had never let Jody know about. Things packed up and put away in parts of her heart where he could never find them. She was saving up feelings for some man she had never seen. She had an inside and an outside now and suddenly she knew how not to mix them.

Facing the truth about Joe allows Janie to divorce him emotionally. She accepts her share of responsibility for the failure of the marriage, knowing now that if Joe has used her for his purposes, she has used him for hers. Yet she understands that her dreams have not impinged on Joe's selfhood; they have been naive but not destructive. By creating inside and outside selves, she hopes to insulate the core of her being from the destructive consequences of Joe's dreams. She cannot claim her autonomy, because she is not yet capable of imagining herself except in relationship to a man. Still, she is no longer willing to jeopardize her inner being for the sake of any such relationship.

Janie remains content to practice a kind of passive resistance against Joe's tyranny until he pushes her to the point when she must "talk smart" to salvage her self-respect. For many years, Joe has forced her to clerk in the store, taking every opportunity to ridicule her for minor mistakes. As he grows older, he adds taunts about her age to his repertoire of verbal insults. Sensing that her womanhood as well as her intelligence is under attack, she retaliates: "Humph! Talking' 'bout *me* lookin' old! When you pull down yo' britches, you look lak de change uh life." So unaccustomed is Joe to hearing his wife "specify" that he imputes nefarious motives to her words. Ill and suspicious, he hires a hoodoo doctor to counteract the curse he believes Janie is putting on him. No curse exists, of course, but Starks is dying of kidney disease and of mortal wounds to his vanity. As he lies on his deathbed, Janie confronts him with more painful truths. Again she reveals how well she comprehends the effect of his domination: "Mah own mind had tuh be squeezed and crowded out tuh make room for yours in me."

The attack on her dying husband is not an act of gratuitous cruelty; it is an essential step toward self-reclamation. Moreover, in terms of the narrative, the deathbed episode posits a dramatic break with Janie's past. She is henceforth a different woman. Independent for the first time in her life, she exults in the "freedom feeling." Reflecting on her past, she realizes that her grandmother, though acting out of love, has wronged her deeply. At base, Nanny's sermon had been about things, when Janie wanted to journey to the horizons in search of people. Janie is able at last to reject her grandmother's way and resume her original quest. That quest culminates in her marriage to Tea Cake Woods with whom she builds a relationship totally unlike the others she has had.

Tea Cake is a troubadour, a traveling bluesman, whose life is dedicated to joyful pursuits. With this character, Hurston explores an alternative definition of manhood, one that does not rely on external manifestations of power, money, and position. Tea Cake has none of these. He is so thoroughly immune to the influence of white American society that he does not even desire them. Tea Cake is at ease being who and what he is. Consequently, he fosters the growth of Janie's self-acceptance. Together they achieve the ideal sought by most characters in Hurston's fiction. They trust emotion over intellect, value the spiritual over the material, preserve a sense of humor and are comfortable with their sensuality. Tea Cake confirms Janie's right to self-expression and invites her to share equally in their adventures. She sees that he "could be a bee to a blossom—a pear tree blossom in the spring." Over the protests of her neighbors, she marries this man several years younger than she whose only worldly possession is a guitar.

They embark on a nomadic existence which takes them to the rich farmland of the Florida Everglades where both Tea Cake and Janie work on the muck and where both share household chores. Their cabin becomes "the unauthorized center of the job," the focal point of the community like the store in Eatonville. Here, however, Janie "could listen and laugh and even talk some herself if she wanted to. She got so she could tell big stories herself from listening to the rest." This is an important and hard-won accomplishment. Even Tea Cake, strongly idealized character though he is, has had difficulty accepting Janie's full participation in their life together. Zora Hurston knew that Tea Cake, a son of the folk

culture, would have inherited its negative attitudes toward women. She knew besides that female autonomy cannot be granted by men, it must be demanded by women. Janie gains her autonomy only when she insists upon it. Under pressure, Tea Cake occasionally falls back on the prerogatives of his sex. His one act of physical cruelty toward Janie results from his need to show someone else who is boss in his home. In the main though, Tea Cake transcends the chauvinistic attitudes of the group. He largely keeps his pledge to Janie that she "partake wid everything."

The marriage of Janie and Tea Cake ends in the wake of a fierce hurricane that is vividly evoked in the novel. In the process of saving Janie's life, Tea Cake is bitten by a rabid dog. Deranged, he tries to kill Janie, and she shoots him in self-defense. Despite these events, the conclusion of *Their Eyes Were Watching God* is not tragic. For, with Tea Cake as her guide, Jane has explored the soul of her culture and learned how to value herself. This fact is underscored in the prologue and epilogue of the novel, sections set after Janie's return to Eatonville following Tea Cake's death. In the former, she tells her friend Pheoby: "Ah been a delegate to de big 'ssociation of life. Yessuh! De Grand Lodge, de big convention of livin' is just where Ah been dis year and a half y'all ain't seen me." Having been to the horizon and back, as she puts it, she is eager to teach the crucial lesson she has learned in her travels. Everybody must do two things for themselves: "They got tuh go tuh God, and they got tuh find out about livin' fuh theyselves." This is Janie's text; the sermon she preaches is the novel itself. She has claimed the right to change her own words.

Hurston was never to duplicate the triumph of *Their Eyes Were Watching God.* In her subsequent novels, she changed the direction of her work dramatically. *Moses: Man of the Mountain* (1939) is a seriocomic novel which attempts to fuse Biblical narrative and folk myth. *Seraph on the Suwanee* (1948) is a psychological novel whose principal characters are upwardly mobile white Floridians. Although Hurston's willingness to experiment is admirable, the results are disappointing. Neither of her new settings is as compelling as the Eatonville milieu. Though the impact of black folk expression is always discernible, it is diminished and so is the power of Hurston's own voice. In these novels, the question of female autonomy recedes in importance, and when it is posed in *Seraph,* the answer is decidedly reactionary. What is of interest in terms of this essay is Hurston's reworking of themes identified in her earlier work.

Hurston's Moses is a combination of Biblical lawgiver and Afro-American hoodoo man. He is officially a highborn Egyptian, but according to legend, he is a Hebrew; Moses neither wholly rejects nor accepts the legend. The uncertainties about his identity complicate his quest for fulfillment. That quest conforms in part to the pattern we have outlined. Moses becomes a great manipulator of language, and much of his authority derives from the power of his words. As an educated man, he has been taught the formal language of the Egyptian elite. He later spends many years with the Midianites in spiritual preparation for his divinely appointed task; this period is somewhat comparable to John Pearson's stay in the work camp [in *Jonah's Gourd Vine*] and Janie's sojourn on the muck. With the Midianites, Moses adapts to the rhythms of a rural folk culture and learns to speak more colloquial English. The Hebrews speak in the black folk idiom, and when he becomes their leader, Moses masters their tongue. Moses is of course a man of action, and as befits a leader, he fights most often for the rights of those under his stewardship. Though he knows he would be more beloved as a king and more popular as a politician, Moses rejects the accouterments of power. He has as little use for class distinctions as Janie and Tea Cake. In Moses, Hurston developed a character who was already a certified hero, not only in the Judeo-Christian tradition, but according to her introduction, also among the peoples of Asia and Africa. What she adds are new points of emphasis, and these had precedents in her earlier work. The most important is implicit in her attempt to reconcile the Biblical Moses and her conception of Moses as conjurer. Hurston had been the first scholar ever to research hoodoo in America and had studied the more systematic religion of Vodun in Haiti. In both instances, she had noted the coexistence of seemingly antithetical religious beliefs in the lives of her informants. In *Moses: Man of the Mountain,* one looks in vain for a synthesis of the two belief systems to which the hero is heir. Hurston simply allows them to coexist. In a novel whose protagonist seeks and achieves cosmic fulfillment, the failure to explicate the spiritual sources of that fulfillment is serious indeed.

Moses is a very ambitious novel. If it fails in some respects, it succeeds in others. It offers a very effective satire on the transition from slavery to freedom for black Americans. Hurston drew on the long-standing identification of blacks with the enslaved Hebrews, the identification that had inspired the majestic spiritual "Go Down, Moses" and countless other sacred and secular expressions. Most dwelt on the sufferings of bondage and the joys of emancipation. Hurston's concerns were the responsibilities of freedom. In the novel, the people of Goshen are hesitant to rebel against slavery and unable to fully comprehend freedom. Hurston satirizes their ready assent to the commands of their slavemasters and their reluctance to follow Moses. She mocks the vainglory of self-appointed leaders and the failure of the people to understand the need for sacrifice. Their petty bickering and constant backbiting are also objects of her ridicule. Hurston's satirical sallies are invariably good-natured and often very funny. But her novel is not the serious statement about faith and freedom she seems to have intended.

Hurston did not publish another novel for nine years. In the interim, her political instincts grew markedly conservative. World War II and its Cold War aftermath hastened the rightward drift of her thinking. At the suggestion of her publisher, she revised the manuscript of *Dust Tracks on a Road* to eliminate sections critical of the American system; as it was published in 1942, her autobiography seemed a celebration of the American way. Through the decade, Hurston contributed a number of articles to the *American Mercury* and the *Saturday Evening Post* which developed patriotic themes. By the 1950s, her work was welcome in the pages of the *American Legion Magazine.* Not all of Hurston's articles were reactionary. Some applauded the achievements of blacks in various endeavors. Others reaffirmed her belief in the value of black folklore, though she had ceased her research in the field. A few pieces, written for *Negro Digest,* protested racism in diplomacy, publishing, and everyday life. On the whole, however, Hurston's political views, which she expounded more often in the 1940s than at any other time in her life, supported the status quo. The same charge might be leveled at her last work of fiction, *Seraph on the Suwanee.*

This novel restates the major themes of *Their Eyes Were Watching God,* perhaps in a misguided attempt to universalize them. Here the protagonist is Arvay Henson Meserve, who like Janie searches for self-identity. She is hindered in her quest by the deep-rooted inferiority she feels about her poor cracker background. For the wrong reason, she has come to the right conclusion. As Hurston depicts her, she is inferior to her husband Jim and the only identity she can attain is through accepting her subordinate role as his wife. Hurston endows Jim Meserve with a mixture of the attractive qualities found in Joe Starks and Tea Cake. He is more crudely chauvinistic than either of them, but this aspect of his character is treated with amazing tolerance. Early in the novel, Arvay reflects that if she married Jim, "her whole duty as a wife was to just love him good, be nice and kind around the house and have children for him. She could do that and be more than happy and satisfied, but it looked too simple." The novel demonstrates that it is much too simple, but at the conclusion the happiness Arvay supposedly realizes is achieved on exactly these terms. The problem is Hurston's inability to grant her protagonist the resources that would permit her to claim autonomy. Although Arvay "mounts the pulpit" at the end of the novel, she has no words of her own to speak.

Ultimately, Arvay's weakness may be less a personal problem than a cultural one. Though black characters play minor roles in the novel, black cultural traditions permeate the narrative. They influence everyone's speech, so much so that at times the whites sound suspiciously like the storytellers in Eatonville. Jim relishes the company of his black employees, whom he treats in a disgustingly condescending manner; and one of his sons, after being tutored by a black neighbor, leaves home to join a jazz band. Unlike the earlier protagonists, Arvay cannot attain her identity through a profound engagement with the folk culture, because she has no culture to engage. The culture of the people Arvay despises has supplanted her own. Seen from this perspective, *Seraph on the Suwanee* is not as anomalous or as reactionary a work as it otherwise appears.

From any vantage point, however, it represents an artistic decline. Hurston was at her best when she drew her material directly from black folk culture; it was the source of her creative power. Throughout her career, she endeavored to negotiate respect for it, talking smart then sweet in her folklore and fiction, proclaiming its richness and complexity to all who would hear. Her most memorable characters are born of this tradition. In portraying them, she was always cognizant of the difficulties in reconciling the demands of community and the requirements of self, difficulties that were especially intense for women. The tension could not be resolved by rejecting the community or negating the self. Hurston challenged black people to dig deep into their culture to unearth the values on which it was built. Those values could restore the balance. They could give men and women words to speak. They could set their spirits free. (pp. 384-92)

> Cheryl A. Wall, "Zora Neale Hurston: Changing Her Own Words," in American Novelists Revisited: Essays in Feminist Criticism, edited by Fritz Fleischmann, G. K. Hall & Co., 1982, pp. 371-93.

Michele Wallace (essay date 1988)

[*In the excerpt below, Wallace offers an overview of modern critical perspectives on Hurston and her work.*]

Habitually, Afro-American literary criticism has kept a strict lookout for backsliding to, say, the antebellum days when some free blacks wrote Southern state legislatures asking to be re-enslaved because their living conditions were so tenuous. The fear has been that because black writers had to please white audiences, editors, and publishers, a grotesque minstrelsy—discursively equivalent to Stepin Fetchit's shuffle—would surface in works of Afro-American literature, deadening the inevitable polemical sting. The prime exhibit for the prosecution was once Zora Neale Hurston, whose fiction and folklore collections have in the past been repeatedly dismissed by the black male literary establishment on the grounds that she was simply "cutting the fool" for white folks' benefit.

But as pioneer of the Harlem Renaissance's literary translation of the Afro-American oral tradition (blues and bebop, folklore, street language and Black English, toasts, jive, and the dozens), Hurston dared to laugh at racist stereotypes—even to risk verifying them—in order to make a point on behalf of "the folk farthest down." At a time when the Ku Klux Klan was still lynching blacks en masse, and the tone of racial wisdom, à la W. E. B. Du Bois and Richard Wright, was dignified and dramatic, Hurston rejected the racial uplift agenda of the Talented Tenth on the premise that ordinary bloods had something to say, too. As she wrote in her autobiography in 1942, among blacks "there was a general acceptance of the monkey as kinfolks. Perhaps it was some distant memory of tribal monkey reverence

from Africa.... Perhaps it was an acknowledgment of our talent for mimicry with the monkey as a symbol." How black intellectuals must have cringed. Then.

Now Afro-Americanist extraordinaire Henry Louis Gates calls Hurston's rebellion "signifying" or "critical signification" and proposes the Signifying Monkey—preeminent trickster of the Afro-American oral tradition—as a figure to evoke the patterns of imitation and reversal that enable black narrative to respond to and defy an exclusionary white culture. Gates describes the way Hurston's figure works as "the ironic reversal of a received racist image in the Western imagination of the black as simian-like, the Signifying Monkey—he who dwells at the margin of discourse, ever punning, ever troping, ever embodying the ambiguities of language." Gates readily concedes that no writer before Ishmael Reed better demonstrated the range of signifying strategies than Zora Neale Hurston.

As folklorist, anthropologist, and novelist, she was vigilant in her quest to render the Afro-American oral tradition and its characteristic "signifying" a permanent feature in the museum of American culture. And Gates suggests that in *Their Eyes Were Watching God,* Hurston was "the first author of the tradition to represent signifying itself as a vehicle of liberation for an oppressed woman, and as a rhetorical strategy in the narration of fiction." Which is why, despite the sexism that once clouded Afro-Americanists' view of Hurston's assets, Gates now leads a gang of black male Afro-Americanists who make pivotal use of Hurston's work in their most recent critical speculations.

They follow the lead of black feminist critics and novelists—Alice Walker, Sherley Anne Williams, Toni Cade Bambara, Mary Helen Washington, Barbara Christian—who first proclaimed Hurston, with the help of Robert Hemenway's biography [see Further Reading]. The change in her reputation is due, in part, to feminist enlightenment, but also to a general easing up: it's time to reassess Hurston's self-conscious manipulation of a kind of dialectical minstrelsy that may be the crucial mark of Afro-American cultural and artistic productivity.

Since slavery, Afro-Americans have produced culture in a peculiar limbo between languages, between nationalities. The integrity of the signifier (the Law of the Father or the Sacred Word) was always a scandal from the Afro-American point of view—as unobtainable as American justice. The resultant narrative funkiness, which can also look like political evasiveness, is what Ralph Ellison may have meant by "invisibility" in 1952. Remember in the beginning of *Invisible Man,* the grandson is instructed to "overcome'm with yeses, undermine'm with grins, agree'm to death and destruction..." Afro-American literary criticism has finally drawn substantial insight into the subtleties of race business from the literature itself.

Still, that Afro-American critics should be interested in an Afro-American writer, though she is female, seems to require no backbreaking explanation, even if it's never happened before, which it *never* has. Yet how do we explain the interest of Yale's Harold Bloom, godfather of a white, patriarchy-obsessed literary theory? Bloom, who is editing Chelsea House's vast series of critical anthologies, ominously entitled "Modern Critical Views," has devoted one of the early volumes to Hurston [see Further Reading]. How do we explain the work of Marxist critic Susan Willis, who has written *Specifying* [see Further Reading], a book on black women writers that takes its name from Hurston's use of the term in her autobiography, **Dust Tracks on a Road.** Or the two articles on Hurston in deconstructionist Barbara Johnson's new book, *A World of Difference* [see Further Reading]. Or even the emergence of a pseudo-black feminist criticism practiced by white feminists, the outstanding example of which is the introduction to *Conjuring: Black Women, Fiction and Literature,* where Marjorie Pryse appears to be attempting a codification of Alice Walker's "womanist" method. Last year's annual meeting of the National Women's Studies Association, which focused on "Women of Color," leads me to think that a host of other "modern critical views" will soon follow.

All well and good, you may say. About time. Literature needs a rainbow coalition—black, white, male, female, artists and academics, historicists and deconstructionists joining together to insure the preservation of Hurston's work and reputation. Except that canon formation has little to do with such benign cultural practice. Rather, Hurston's extraordinary textual ambivalence about race, class, nationality, sex, religion, and family, her cryptic, inscrutable subjectivity, offers a crucial vantage point on the crisis in signification which fuels postmodernism and haunts Western self-esteem—and which, not coincidentally, lies at the core of the Afro-American experience. So, like groupies descending on Elvis Presley's estate, critics are engaged in a mostly ill-mannered stampede to have some memento of the black woman who could mock the 1954 Supreme Court decision desegregating the schools, who simultaneously insisted upon substantive racial difference and no difference at all, who epitomizes our inability to revise the text of American racism, or to acknowledge its sexism. For what is at stake is the integrity and vitality of language, literature, and American thought, from the bottom up.

Remember how this whole Zora Neale Hurston thing got off the ground. Not how it started, which was when Hurston made the best move of her literary career by dying of stroke, poverty, and a profound lack of literary appreciation in a welfare home in Saint Lucie County, Florida, in 1960. Focus on Alice Walker's mystical attempt (documented in her essay "Looking for Zora") to locate Hurston's body in an abandoned cemetery overgrown with weeds by calling out to her, "Zora . . . I'm here. Are you?" When Walker's foot sank into a hole, she took it as a sign. In that spot, she installed a granite stone reading, "Zora Neale Hurston 'A Genius of The South' [she borrowed Jean Toomer's

poetic use of the phrase], 1901-1960, Novelist, Folklorist, Anthropologist." From 1960 to 1973, Hurston had been buried in an unmarked grave in a segregated cemetery in Fort Pierce, Florida, a place Hemenway calls "symbolic of the black writer's historical fate in America."

The current unceremonious exhuming of the Hurston corpse should be considered in the reflected glory of these two distinctly different memorials—the erasure, anonymity, and degradation of the unmarked pauper's grave and the double-whammy of canonization as signified by the gravestone that may have missed the mark, and that employs the term *genius* ambivalently and in quotes. Not only may we be canonizing a Hurston who never existed, or the wrong corpse, but it may simply be intrinsic to the process of canonization (think mummification) to lay waste to the symbolic and intellectual urgency of this or any other cultural object of our affections.

The efforts of Washington, Walker, Williams, Bambara, and Hemenway to resurrect and republish Hurston have certainly been useful (although I privately wonder about so much reverential awe for a woman who scorned the stuff), but what if their unwillingness to submit Hurston's signifying to rigorous examination invites others, who are not of the faith, to misuse her and derail the future of black women in literature and literary criticism? The time to consider such questions is upon us, for Hurston's cultural use has clearly passed beyond the control of black feminists/womanists.

Even when the opportunity obviously exists to describe and define the black woman in her own terms, her own voice, white male and female and black male expertise may persist in silencing her by unwanted sexual/textual acts. Take Harold Bloom's book on Hurston. Bloom means well, I suppose, but in an introduction almost too short to bother reading, he sweeps aside those critical challenges to the canon that first recovered Hurston's achievements from the dust heap of marginality: "Her sense of power has nothing in common with politics of any persuasion, with contemporary modes of feminism, or even with those questers who search for a black aesthetic."

Rather, he makes a case for Hurston's protagonist Janie, firmly locating her in the only tradition that matters to him—the one that began with Samuel Richardson's Clarissa and peaked with Dreiser's Carrie and Lawrence's Ursula and Gudrun. Predictably, he recasts *Their Eyes Were Watching God* as the story of a woman's struggle with repression. The blackness of virtually everybody in the book takes a backseat to the issue of Janie's beleaguered sexuality. Further, according to Bloom, it's another woman, the grandmother, who offers the largest obstacle to Janie's sexual fulfillment and self-articulation. Grandma's pretext, that she was raped in slavery and that her daughter, Janie's mother, fared not much better, is utterly ignored in Bloom's elegant but slapdash revision. He wraps it up by proposing that we see Hurston as the Wife of Bath, that anti-feminist mouthpiece proposed in the 14th century as a cure for priests who would choose marriage over celibacy. Cute, huh?

What follows in the book, you might wonder. Precisely the Afro-Americanist and feminist interpretations Bloom has just erased—the prefaces, introductions, and articles by Darwin Turner, Larry Neale, Hemenway, Walker, Williams, and Washington that have accompanied Hurston's republication these past 14 years.

The cumulative effect is of some kind of cosmic blunder: Bloom's introduction doesn't introduce but rather supersedes the text that follows. He morbidly objectifies Hurston in a sexually charged image of Western culture's embedded anti-feminism. Hurston's silent black body floats to the surface of systemic dilemma. The irony is that Afro-American studies and women's studies courses will constitute a captive audience for this book.

It was in my first narrative writing class at the City College of New York that I first encountered Hurston. In 1971, that twilight year of Black Power, on a campus at the margins of open enrollment and my native Harlem, I felt buried alive by the self-regard of black males and the blindness of the faculty's typical white male, who could not imagine a black feminist writer. Then my writing teacher, Mark Mirsky, pressed upon me a hardcover copy of **Mules and Men,** Hurston's deceptively simple presentation of black storytelling, the oral tradition, and voodoo in the '30s in the rural South.

Her unequivocal presentation of "rustic folk" as speaking subjects whose race was not compromised but informed by their sexuality was music to my ears. **Mules and Men** portrayed Afro-American oral tradition in three settings. In Hurston's hometown, all-black Eatonville, old friends treat her like long-lost family. Twice she makes extended visits to an impoverished sawmill camp in Loughman, Florida. The women in Loughman often engage in knife fights, and Hurston requires the constant protection of the roughest of them all, Big Sweet, who is described admiringly by one of Hurston's male informants as "uh whole woman and half uh man." Finally, there's the quasi-European, quasi-African New Orleans, where Hurston pursues several apprenticeships as a voodoo priestess.

Her archly heretical tone about such sacred cows as racial pride, skin color, slavery, the eating of watermelon, the singing of the blues and conjure—her skillful narrative flow into and out of dialect, and the multiple rhetorical strategies of her "native" informants—was a revelation to me. Not because I'd never heard such linguistic antics before—in Harlem, the crossroads of the African diaspora, such a medley of voices was not unfamiliar—but I'd never seen the attempt to write it down.

Soon after that, I read **Their Eyes Were Watching God** in connection with a newly inaugurated women's studies

program at CCNY and was thoroughly enchanted, although alarmed. On one hand, in a community deeply split over the appropriate use of black English, Hurston's confident handling of dialect gave this story the rigor and readability of a black *Alice in Wonderland.* On the other hand, I was disappointed that Janie didn't pursue intellectual curiosity, as Zora playing herself did in **Mules and Men,** barreling down the backroads of Florida in her Chevrolet in search of stories old and new, borrowed and blue. Instead of a career, Janie pursues the right kind of marriage and finally finds it with Tea Cake, who teaches her how to play checkers and beats her, then brags to his friends about how ladylike she is and how easily she scars.

Black feminists Alice Walker, Mary Helen Washington, and Sherley Anne Williams have suggested that it's wisest to see such moments in the plot as subsidiary to Janie's triumph of voice when she virtually loudtalks her second husband to death and achieves mastery in the telling of her own tale at the end of the book. It's true that concentrating on this symbolic resolution is more satisfying than dealing with how Hurston ultimately faced the conflict and left it unresolved. But Harold Bloom also defends the evolution of Janie in his ritual canonization of **Their Eyes.** In the process, he further consolidates the black female absence in a white male literary establishment—which suggests to me that other "critical views" more subversive than "modern" must be ventured.

The book I've read since 1971 that helped me to see both **Their Eyes Were Watching God** and Hurston's career in another light is **Dust Tracks on a Road.** Here is Hurston's recapitulation of the blues wisdom concerning black women, as opposed to "brown" women like Janie:

> They brought bad luck for a week if they came to your house of a Monday morning. They were evil. They slept with their fists balled up ready to fight and squabble even while they were asleep. They even had evil dreams. White, yellow and brown girls dreamed about roses and perfumes and kisses. Black gals dreamed about guns, razors, ice picks, hatchets and hot lye. I heard men swear they had seen women dreaming and knew these things to be true.

Here Hurston is at her signifying best. These remarks constitute a major transitional moment in a chapter called "My People! My People!" that discusses, or rather juggles, competing notions of "race." In a seductively entertaining way that makes you first think you're reading fluff, Hurston repeatedly assaults the concept of racial essence, revealing its basis as absurd and fundamentally rhetorical. She does this by exploring a series of rhetorical relations—between blacks and whites, the black middle class and the black poor, males and females, blacks and tans—what each says about the other in the process of defining the superior self. Hurston gives the impression of a constantly shifting perspective (much like Virginia Woolf's in *A Room of One's Own*) until it becomes clear that race is a game played with mirrors called words. While she's at it, she

Hurston's gravesite in Fort Pierce, Florida. Alice Walker had the marker erected in 1973.

gives W. E. B. Du Bois's celebrated "colorline," as in "the problem of the twentieth century is the problem of the colorline," a good working over.

Although she draws the rather obvious conclusion that blacks, therefore, are individuals, what's more important is the polyvocal and multidirectional terms in which the argument is made. Here's how she ends this chapter in her autobiography:

> *I maintain that I have been a Negro three times—a Negro baby, a Negro girl and a Negro woman. Still, if you have received no clear-cut impression of what* The Negro in America *is like, then you are in the same place with me. There is no* The Negro *here.*

Politics is less the issue than the amazing audacity of this woman who dared to challenge the rhetoric and posturing of a race. Hurston's work—the nonfiction writing on oral tradition in *Tell My Horse, The Sanctified Church, Mules and Men,* and *Dust Tracks on a Road,* as well as the fiction of *Their Eyes Were Watching God, Jonah's Gourd Vine, Moses, Man of the Mountain,* and the short stories—forms an essential complement to the occasional tunnel vision of Booker T. Washington, Jean Toomer, James Weldon Johnson, Alain Locke, Langston Hughes, Sterling Brown, and Richard Wright. Du Bois, Hughes, Brown, and Wright all expressed grave doubts about the viability of Hurston's writing—and

that's precisely why we ought to read her and them in tandem. She provides a funky footbridge between the lofty pronouncements of a public racial self-consciousness and a private (ordinarily anonymous) collective black sensibility, a sense that somebody/women had another view of things.

How peculiar that Hurston should be taught, read, and written about as though the context of Afro-American cultural and intellectual history did not exist. For one thing, Hurston was always signifying. If you don't know the boys, how do you know what she was signifying on?

In *Specifying,* Susan Willis announces the intention of historicizing the literature of contemporary black women writers. But not unlike Bloom's crypto-deconstructionism, Willis's "historicism" inserts "Hurston" where one might expect to read history. Her analysis of Hurston's rhetoric suffers the consequences. For instance, Willis takes the title of her book from a passage in *Dust Tracks on a Road* in which Hurston describes her first encounter with Big Sweet, who was in the process of "specifying" somebody:

> *Big Sweet broke the news to him, in one of her mildest bulletins that his pa was a double humpted camel and his ma was a grass gut cow, but even so, he tore her wide open in the act of getting born, and so on and so forth . . .*

Bypassing more complex explanations of the use of figurative language in the Afro-American oral tradition, some of which Hurston herself helped to supply, Willis settles upon "name-calling" to denote "specifying" and concludes that it "represents a form of narrative integrity. Historically, it speaks for a noncommodified relationship to language, a time when the slippage between words and meaning would not have obtained or been tolerated."

The translation of "specifying" that Hurston offers within the text is "putting your foot up" on somebody, which Big Sweet promptly does when a troublemaker in camp threatens Hurston with a knife. "Specifying," more like Gates's "Signifying," is a fluid, relational process unconcerned with original intent. If the slippage between signifier and signified is the problem, the writing of Zora Neale Hurston is not the cure, except to the degree that the cure is making the unconscious judgment apparent, re-establishing the severed links between "linguistic undecidability" and economic and political fact. Hurston often did this in her writing, not by forcing meaning to heel, but rather by tracking its proliferation/demise.

Willis makes valid observations, but her interpretation bears the unmistakable stamp of the tourist because of her failure to read Hurston in the context of Afro-American letters and her determination to cast black women's writing in polar opposition to the alienation and reification of white middle-class culture.

I don't mean to imply that you have to be a black feminist to do Zora Neale Hurston justice. A fine example of a way to tackle the territory is provided by Barbara Johnson in *A World of Difference.* Her approach is forthright from the beginning: "It was not clear to me what I, a white deconstructor, was doing talking about Zora Neale Hurston, a black novelist and anthropologist, or to *whom* I was talking . . . . Was I talking to white critics, black critics, or myself?" Johnson decides that the answer is "all of the above" and that her interest in Hurston's "strategies and structures of problematic address" does not have a single motivation. "I had a lot to learn then," she writes, "from Hurston's way of dealing with multiple agendas and heterogeneous implied readers."

Johnson recalls the double-voicing of the Afro-American literary tradition in terms of Du Bois's famous veil metaphor, which divides the Afro-American citizen, automatically assumed to be male, between contending allegiances to race and country. She illustrates Hurston's location in that discourse by quoting from Richard Wrights's review of *Their Eyes Were Watching God,* in which he wrote that "the sensory sweep of her novel carries no theme, no message, no thought." Johnson says of this statement, "the full range of questions and experiences of Janie's life are as invisible to a mind steeped in maleness as Ellison's *Invisible Man* is to minds steeped in whiteness."

Following black feminist readings, Johnson suggests that Janie's display of rhetorical mastery in the male-dominated world of an all-black town constructs a symbolic resolution of the dilemma that plagued Hurston's career. But she proposes, as well, that discussions of race or gender invariably rely upon an oppositional or dualistic logic that forces the black woman writer into a virtually untenable position in critical discourse.

As Johnson finally puts it, "The black woman is both invisible and ubiquitous; never seen in her own right but forever appropriated by the others for their own ends." Yet even in Hurston's nonfiction writing, ultimate resolution of the dilemma is always displaced, for as Johnson insists, "unification and simplification are fantasies of domination, not understanding" and "the task of the writer" is "to narrate both the appeal and the injustice of universalization, in a voice that assumes and articulates its own, ever-differing self-difference."

In Hurston's nonfiction writing, she insists that Afro-American oral tradition is unique and irreplaceable, thereby seeming to confirm the notion of an irreducible racial essence. At the same time, she makes the counterclaim that "race" as a way of categorizing and limiting a writer's domain simply shouldn't and doesn't exist. Although generalizations about Hurston are probably useless, her life offers a possible explanation of this apparent contradiction.

While Hurston's anchor in New York was her scholarship with Franz Boas in anthropology at Columbia, the road was rocky still. Besides the criticism of her male peers, constant financial troubles, and the increasing inaccessibility of publication, Hurston had bad luck

with husbands, didn't get along with her family, and couldn't keep a teaching job. Invariably, her response to "worriation" was to go on another folklore hunting trip in the South, or South America or the Caribbean. Financial and professional security were strangers to her all her life, which may explain why she never seemed to recover from the shock of the headlines in the *Afro-American,* a black Baltimore paper, reporting a morals charge in 1948 that accused her of sodomizing the teenage son of her Harlem landlady while she was, in fact, out of the city. Though she soon fled the North for the South's "heart of darkness," never to return, her writing became more politically conservative and color blind: she was clearly disillusioned with the racial politics of a Northern black bourgeoisie that had never offered her anything but torment anyway.

The biographical approach has its uses, but I like Johnson's take on Hurston's self-contradiction. For Hurston, she says, "Difference is a misreading of sameness, but it must be represented in order to be erased. The resistance to finding out that the other is the same springs out of the reluctance to admit that the same is other." The point here, it seems to me, is both political and literary: Black and white, and male and female exist in asymmetrical relation to one another, they are not neat little opposites to be drawn and quartered. We recognize the persistence of such measures in our narratives in order to dismantle them in our lives.

Forceful black female critical voices are needed to verify the crucial assault on the logic of binary oppositions of race, class, and sex already launched by contemporary black women novelists, poets, and playwrights. Scrutiny of Hurston's nonfiction writing could inspire us to take on this task. Instead, the thrust of black feminist writing on Hurston implicitly proposes her life and work as a role model for contemporary black female scholarship, intellectual curiosity, and literary production. The model is too narrow.

Black feminist criticism on Hurston may already be changing its tune, or so *Invented Lives: Narratives of Black Women 1860-1960,* edited and annotated by Mary Helen Washington, would seem to indicate. Washington's introduction to excerpts from Hurston's novels questions the viability of Janie as a heroic voice and suggests that Hurston's real sympathies lay with John Pearson, the protagonist of *Jonah's Gourd Vine.* Hurston depicts the oral tradition in the all-black town of *Their Eyes* as sex-segregated and male-dominated: Janie doesn't stand a chance. Is Washington's analysis a step in the right direction, or is it the inevitable swing of the pendulum back to a position dismissive of Hurston's work?

We need a re-evaluation of Hurston's re-evaluation, a running blow-by-blow commentary on the progress and health of the black female literary/critical voice and its relationship to the mainstream. As for role models, we might do ourselves greater service to choose among that school of black women writers flourishing now—Paule Marshall, Toni Morrison, Alice Walker, Audre Lorde, Toni Cade Bambara, Sonia Sanchez, June Jordan, Ntozake Shange, Gloria Naylor, Thulani Davis, Lucille Clifton, Sherley Anne Williams, Maya Angelou, critics Barbara Christian, Barbara Smith, Mary Helen Washington, Gloria Hull, Bell Hooks. It is now that black women are "writing themselves into history," as black feminist critic Hortense Spillers aptly puts it in her afterword to *Conjuring.*

Yet there are those of us who fear the proliferation of continental theory. Audre Lorde and Barbara Christian have said as much, on the grounds that "the master's tools cannot be used to dismantle the master's house," which makes me think the reluctance of black women writers to rise to the challenge of critical self-definition may not be only the fault of male and/or white intimidation. As Bell Hooks suggested recently, in an essay called "Talking Back," critical writing may hold a special terror for black women as a result of an anti-intellectual bias that is automatic, unconscious, and defensive in our upbringing.

To be more specific, little black girls are not encouraged at home or at school to value their own thoughts. To articulate them is often labeled "talking back" and even punished. The sense that black females should be either supportive or silent is carried over into adulthood. So, like Jane Austen hiding her novel-writing under blotting paper in the family room, black women, too, have been forced to conceal their best contemporary articulations of self under the cloak of fiction. Even our endless respectful tributes to our mothers' courage and endurance in the face of slavery and racial oppression may actually interfere with our intellectual growing up as daughters.

It's time to consider that the process of concealment, which was once essential to our collective survival, has outlived its usefulness. Although I'll grant you that talking back is a risky business, the alternative is that Afro-American women will continue to be objects, not subjects, in the global production of knowledge. So, hagiography is fine if you have the time, but more urgent matters call. It probably won't do any of us any good to make that childless trickster Zora Hurston into a madonna figure, whose arms we can lie in and be safe. Black women have written numerous autobiographies, among which *Dust Tracks on a Road* takes the prize for inscrutability. We do well to remember that when dust tracks blow away, they are impossible to follow. (pp. 18-21)

> Michele Wallace, "Who Dat Say Who Dat When I Say Who Dat?" in VLS, No. 64, April, 1988, pp. 18-21.

Sherley Anne Williams (essay date 1991)

[*Williams is an American critic, poet, novelist, and educator. In the following introduction to a 1991*

illustrated edition of Their Eyes Were Watching God, *she examines the historical importance of the novel and comments on the behavior and beliefs of the novel's protagonist, Janie.*]

I first encountered Zora Neale Hurston in an Afro-American literature course I took in graduate school. She was one of numerous authors surveyed in the two-semester course, which began with Lucy Terry in 1747 and ended with the Black Arts writers of the sixties. Hurston's works were studied as a sort of holdover from the Harlem Renaissance, the period that coincided, at least in part, with the jazz age and that witnessed the first concerted outpourings of formal artistic expression among Afro-Americans. The most important stylistic developments of the period were the attempt to use Afro-American folk culture as a basis for creating distinctive black contributions to serious or "high" culture, and the attempt to repudiate the false and degrading stereotypes promulgated in Anglo-American popular (and high) culture by exploring the individual consciousness hidden behind the enveloping Sambo mask. **Their Eyes Were Watching God** was published in 1937, almost ten years after the stock market crash of 1929, the date most often given as the end of the Harlem Renaissance. The book's rural southern settings, the use of dialect and folkloric materials, even its romantic theme represent much that was distinctive and significant about this period.

It would have been difficult for most of the students in that case to prove these statements. We "read at" Zora Neale in the same way we had read at most of the writers studied to that point (and quite a few that came after): in snatches. And although I'd never seen—much less read—an embarrassing number of the works discussed in the course, I felt lucky to be there. Afro-American literature was still an exotic subject then, rarely taught on a regular basis. Most of the works of the writers we studied had been out of print for a long time, and we relied on lectures, anthology selections (when available), what samplings could be garnered in a Saturday spent in a rare-book collection or an evening in the reserve-book reading room, and Robert Bone's *Negro Novel in America* for our impressions of William Wells Brown, Frances Harper, William Attaway, Jessie Fauset, and Zora Neale Hurston. We were fortunate to be in Washington, D.C., with its several large university and public libraries and the Library of Congress. But library holdings really couldn't make up for those out-of-print books. The few personal or library copies of this or that were shared around, but there were about forty students in the class, and by the time a person got the book, it had usually been discussed at least four weeks prior and the owner needed it back to write a paper. So, like many students in the class, out of sheer frustration I ended by concentrating on contemporary authors (i.e., Wright, Ellison, Baldwin), whose works were more readily available.

It did, however, finally become my turn to read **Their Eyes Were Watching God**, and I became Zora Neale's for life. In the speech of her characters I heard my own country voice and saw in the heroine something of my own country self. And this last was most wonderful because it was most rare. Black women had been portrayed as characters in numerous novels by blacks and non-blacks. But these portraits were limited by the stereotypical images of, on the one hand, the ham-fisted matriarch, strong and loyal in the defense of the white family she served (but unable to control or protect her own family without the guidance of some white person) and, on the other, the amoral, instinctual slut. Between these two stereotypes stood the tragic mulatto: too refined and sensitive to live under the repressive conditions endured by ordinary blacks and too colored to enter the white world.

Even the few idealized portraits of black women evoked these negative stereotypes. The idealizations were morally uplifting and politically laudable, but their literary importance rests upon just that: the correctness of their moral and political stance. Their value lies in their illuminations of society's workings and their insights into the ways oppression is institutionalized. They provide, however, few insights into character or consciousness. And when we (to use Alice Walker's lovely phrase) go in search of our mothers' gardens, it's not really to learn who trampled on them or how or even why—we usually know that already. Rather, it's to learn what our mothers planted there, what they thought as they sowed, and how they survived the blighting of so many fruits. Zora Neale Hurston's life and work present us with insights into just these concerns.

The date of her birth, like many of the facts of her life, is a matter of uncertainty. Robert E. Hemenway, in a first and much-needed biography, *Zora Neale Hurston* (Urbana: University of Illinois Press, 1977), cites January 7, 1901, as the date that makes the most sense. Eatonville, Florida, the small, all-black town where Zora was born, is the setting for two of her four published novels, *Jonah's Gourd Vine* (1934) and *Their Eyes Were Watching God*. The gatherings on the front porch of the town's general store came to symbolize for Hurston the richness of Afro-American oral culture, and she struggled for much of her career to give literary renderings of that oral richness and to portray the complex individuality of its unlettered, "uncultured" *folk* creators. Hurston studied cultural anthropology under Franz Boas, first as a student at Barnard College and later at Columbia University. In 1927 she returned to the South, where she lived off and on for the rest of her life, collecting examples of and participating in the dynamic culture created in the saw mills, turpentine camps, and small-town jook joints and cafés. She had at her command a large store of stories, songs, incidents, idiomatic phrases, and metaphors; her ear for speech rhythms must have been remarkable. Most important, she had the literary intelligence and had developed the literary skill to convey the power and beauty of this heard speech and lived experience on the printed page.

Hurston's evocations of the life-styles of rural blacks have not been equaled; but to stress the ruralness of her settings or to characterize her diction solely in terms of exotic "dialect" spellings is to miss her deftness with language. In the speech of her characters, black voices—whether rural or urban, northern or southern—come alive. Her fidelity to diction, metaphor, and syntax—whether in direct quotations or in paraphrases of characters' thoughts—rings, even across forty years, with an aching familiarity that is a testament to her skill and to the durability of black speech. Yet Zora's personality and actions were so controversial that for a long time she was remembered more as a *character* of the Renaissance than as one of the most serious and gifted artists to emerge during this period. She was a notable tale-teller, mimic, and wit, confident to the point of brashness (some might even say beyond), who refused to conform to conventional notions of ladylike behavior and middle-class decorum. To one of her contemporaries, she was the first black nationalist; to another, a handkerchief-head Uncle Tom. Larry Neal, in his introduction to her autobiography *Dust Tracks on a Road* (1942; rptd. New York; J. B. Lippincott, 1971), calls her a "kind of Pearl Bailey of the literary world . . . a conservative in her political outlook with a remarkable understanding of a blues aesthetic and its accompanying sensibility." To Alice Walker and others of our generation, Zora was a woman bent on discovering and defining herself, a woman who spoke and wrote her own mind.

Something of the questing quality that characterized Zora's life informs the character of Janie—without, of course, the forcefulness of Hurston's own personality. In this and other instances, the character is more conventional than the author, for despite obvious idealizations, Janie operates in a "real" world. Her actions, responses, and motivations are consistent with that reality and the growing assertiveness of her own self-definitions. Where Janie yearns, Zora was probably driven; where Janie submits, Zora would undoubtedly have rebelled. Author and character objectify their definitions of self in totally different ways. Zora was evidently unable to satisfactorily define herself in a continuing relationship with a man, whereas such definition is the essence of Janie's romantic vision and its ultimate fulfillment provides the plot of the novel. But in their desire and eventual insistence that their men accord them treatment due equals, they are one.

The 1978 University of Illinois Press reprint of *Their Eyes Were Watching God* sparked an intensive and wide-ranging reconsideration of Hurston and her work, in particular this second novel which had been so roundly, and wrongly, dismissed at its original publication. Much of this commentary has focused on the female quest in the novel—Janie's search for identity, fulfillment, and voice—and the implicit critique of marital norms. Hurston's sophisticated deployment of female archetypes, particularly the archetype of the green-world, that "special world of nature where women's desires for authentic self-hood" are realized, the green-world lover, the erotic figure associated with the hero's naturistic epiphany, and her play on enclosure imagery place the novel firmly within a tradition of women's literature. Inside houses (i.e., enclosures), as Henry Louis Gates observes [in *The Signifying Monkey: A Theory of Afro-American Literary Criticism* (1988)], people attempt to oppress Janie; so she dreams outdoors, in nature, in the green-world. In the final act of the novel, Janie harmonizes the dissonant aspects of her inner and outer-worlds by naturalizing the space within the "gloaty, sparkly white" "'big house'" inherited from her husband, "pull[ing] in her horizon like a great fish-net . . . drap[ing] it over her shoulder." The transformation of seemingly appropriate mates into guardians of the enclosures links the novel to such texts as Ruth Suckow's *Folks* (1934), Josephine Herbst's "Man of Steel" (1934), and Christina Stead's *Man Who Loved Children* (1940). Hurston was not unique among women writers of her generation in insisting on Janie's right to romantic love. Annis Pratt maintains [in *Archetypal Patterns in Women's Fiction* (1981)] that the attempt to wedge some modicum of equity and eros into the matrimonial enclosure was a significant part of the rebellion against patriarchy in the early years of the century.

Nellie McKay links Janie to a tradition of black women's travel narratives in which the journey is a vital part of the narrator's search for self and freedom, narratives that began with Nancy Prince in 1856 [*New Essays on "Their Eyes Were Watching God,"* ed. Michael Awkward (1990)]. Hurston's revisioning of the theme of black immersion in southern culture seems now an obvious commentary on the rendering of the same theme in the work of Renaissance contemporaries Jean Toomer (*Cane*, 1923) and Nella Larsen (*Quicksand*, 1928). In common with Toomer, Hurston pictured a southern soil that is a rick, yeasty, almost primeval humus rather than the quagmire Larsen suggested in *Quicksand*. Unlike Larsen and Jessie Fauset, another contemporary, Hurston saw female sexuality not as danger or even power but as potential, its open expression the goal of her hero's quest. Larsen's Helga is forced to pay for her unacknowledged sexual hungers with children, a baby almost every year. Janie's sexuality is an aspect of her womanhood, and Hurston's refusal to set Janie's sexuality within the context of maternity is another way of questioning what was then seen as an inevitable, and mostly desirable, consequence of female sexuality. The continuing influence of *Their Eyes* is particularly marked in the fiction of the eighties, from the foregrounding of southern rural culture as the modern folk culture in Toni Morrison's *Tar Baby* (1981) and Ntozake Shange's *Sassafrass, Cyprus and Indigo* (1982) to Terry McMillan's re-visioning of romance across class lines in *Disappearing Acts* (1989).

Recent criticism has focused also on Hurston's narrative strategies, her successful incorporation of black expressive principles—that is, principles of black orature—into the genre of the novel. *Their Eyes* is the first of what Gates has called Afro-American "speakerly texts," nov-els that give the illusion of oral narration. Hurston achieved in this novel a point of view that evokes the intimacy of a first-person, black vernacular voice within authoritative, third-person narration. Lionel Trilling has called such "shocking intimacy" a hall-mark of modernism. In this sense, then, *Their Eyes* is the mother text for such classic Afro-American works as Richard Wright's *Native Son* and Ralph Ellison's *Invisible Man*, whose achievements, in part, have to do with point of view and voice. *Their Eyes* is also the text signified on, or alluded to, by writers as diverse as Ishmael Reed and Alice Walker.

It may be, as Michele Wallace suggests [in *Invisibility Blues: From Pop to Theory* (1990)], that the unprecedented volume of criticism about the work of one black woman writer has had the effect of appearing to recommend Hurston's life and work as the preeminent role model for contemporary female scholarship, intellectual curiousity, and literary production. Such over-emphasis, if it exists, will no doubt be addressed in the inevitable ebb and flow of critical and popular fashion. Hurston's work, recovered now from the margins of tradition and brought to a more appropriate place within the main currents of American literature, is subject to inquiry and attack from all sides. It seems unlikely, however, that the torrent of commentary that *Their Eyes Were Watching God* and its author have inspired will vitiate its meaning or misappropriate the accomplishments of the fiercely independent Hurston. Janie's story has the simplicity and depth of classic blues; it will sustain multiple hearings and readings, and can survive even the most arcane critical theory.

Janie's narrative, the inner tale of her experience and maturity which dominates the novel, begins with her sixteen-year-old self beneath a pear tree that is clothed in the "snowy virginity of bloom." The pristine, almost prissy image of the blossoming pear tree attracting the "dust-bearing bee" is emblematic of Janie's yearning for romantic love. It is a startling contrast to the grim reality symbolized in the second image that Janie's grandmother, Nanny, calls "de mule uh de world." Black women, the double other of American culture, ubiquitous and everywhere disregarded, are the work animals of society and so can have no true self-consciousness, no hope for autonomy or community. Janie rejects the mule image in favor of the flowering tree that is her personal symbol, the secret emblem of herself. She protects this image from violation in her first marriage by running away, and in her second marriage by assuming a dutiful pose and silently "saving up feelings for some man she had never seen."

The fulfillment of Janie's hope of romantic love drew many black women to the novel in the early 1970s. *Their Eyes*, after all, as June Jordan observed [in *Black World* (August, 1974)], is "the most successful, convincing and exemplary novel of Blacklove that we have." Were sisters ready for Tea Cake? black women asked themselves, reading Janie's situation as archetypal. Janie was "classed off" by her looks and her husband's status, his "class," just as they were set apart by education and the putative class thus acquired. Janie chose voice over privileged objectivity, and her rejection of status was a refutation of the charges of materialism and racial assimilationism that middle-class black women in literature, and in life, stood accused of at the height of the black power movement in the late 1960s. Janie's story—a black woman searching for, and finding, a black man's love—was the stuff of black women's dreams and suggested some of their deepest uncertainties.

It seems impossible now not to have commented in 1978 on the presumption that "brothers" were better able to deal with a lover from a lower class than were black women, or on the obvious differences between the idealized Tea Cake, who asked Janie to work alongside him, and the militant lovers who were then demanding that black women walk ten paces behind their men when the women were not, in fact, under them. And if Tea Cake was not totally free of chauvinistic habits and Janie's growth from male-identified girl to self-asserted womanhood was possible only because she had no children, if Tea Cake himself, bitten by the mad dog of jealousy, was a cautionary image of what "love" did to even the best of men, well, the devices with which Hurston parodied or undercut her own romantic images were of less interest than the romance itself. Maybe Janie's solitary posture at the end of the novel really meant that Hurston thought it was impossible for a black woman simultaneously to be artist, lover, and mother, and so the wise woman chose her work. But black women have always had just that, "their" work, and what enchanted them was the romance of Janie's labor.

Scholars have actually published studies of the number of times Hurston mentions trees or uses tree imagery in **Their Eyes**. As Gates has shown in *The Signifying Monkey*, it is more than a matter of numbers. Indeed, he sees the tree as Janie's master trope, its use revealing precisely the point at which Janie's voice assumes control over the text's narration. This "lyrical trope of desire" returns when Tea Cake, the green-world lover, the veritable (or "Vergible") woods themselves, enters the text. The parallels between Janie and her emblem are not perfect. While Janie is not without a symbolic fecundity—in narrating her own life story to her friend, Pheoby, she gives us the fruit of her mind and in her own memories of love and light the fruit of her relationship with Tea Cake—unlike the pear tree, she bears no glistening or tangible fruit and is childless through her three marriages.

The beauty and fecundity of the tree is repeatedly contrasted with the bleak present and barren prospects of the mule, an image introduced in the present-tense frame of the novel and, like the tree, one that reappears throughout the interior tale. The first repetition of the mule image is the folktale Janie's grandmother tells the impressionable girl to school her in the history and destiny of black women: "Honey, de white man... throw down de load and tell de nigger man tuh pick it up. He pick it up because he have to, but he...hand it to his womenfolks. De nigger woman is de mule uh de world." The mule is the embedded image that haunts Janie through two marriages and becomes a metaphor for the roles she repudiates in her quest for self-fulfillment. It is the idea against which the book implicitly argues. Love, for the old ex-slave, is "de very prong all us black women gits hung on"; that is, as Nanny goes on to explain, love makes black women see substance in a "dressed up dude" who can't keep himself in shoe leather, much less provide for someone else; his women tote that burden for him. Love doesn't kill black women; it makes them "sweat." The character of Nanny inaugurates in Afro-American literature a tradition of unreliable older figures, mostly female, the untrustworthy surrogate parent who, under the guise of helping the hero to remain self-possessed, to achieve independence, actually tries to shape the hero to the demands of the racist and patriarchal culture as an art of survival.

Nanny's tale is almost actualized in the marriage she arranges for Janie; and, as Rachel Blau DuPlessis notes [in *New Essays*, ed. Awkward], it is the figure under which Janie's second marriage, to Joe Starks, unfolds. The metaphor of the mule is further reified in Joe's insistence that Janie tote his narrow, stultifying notions of what behavior is appropriate to her class and sex. Rooted at first only in the specificity of the Afro-American female experience, the metaphor has been transformed into one for the female condition; Janie's individual quest for fulfillment becomes, as Bessie Smith wailed a decade earlier, any woman's blues.

To link Hurston the writer with Smith the singer, as a number of others have done, is to suggest that the novel is a blues romance, an earthy allegory of sexual fulfillment as well as a paradigmatic commentary on the complicated social process of courtship and marriage. It is the blues—that is, black reality—that rounds out and individualizes the flat, fairy tale-like characters. Janie is Beauty, the old king's wife rather than his daughter. Logan Killicks and Joe Starks, her first two husbands, represent stolid conventionality. Although we see them only through Janie's unsympathetic eyes, both embody much that is "good"; they don't beat Janie (as a general rule), don't chase other women, don't drink. Starks raises Janie to the middle-class, "front porch" leisure that black women of the day were taught to admire, and to envy, in white women. Yet Janie is fast approaching middle age by the time she is aroused from the troubled sleep of two unsuccessful marriages by "Prince" Tea Cake, a wanderer with more than a hint of the outlaw about him (he actually escapes from a press gang). The class disparity between Janie and Tea Cake is settled not by the romantic uplift of fairy tale and domestic fiction but by a kind of egalitarian partnering that is as much at home in the blues as in novels of social protest.

Tea Cake's nickname is itself a polite play on "jelly roll," synonymous in the blues with sexual delight; in the self-consciously repressed world of Renaissance fiction Tea Cake represents an almost unbridled sensuality. Associated most vividly with the Everglades—"Ground so rich that everything went wild....Dirt roads so rich and black that a half mile of it would have fertilized a Kansas wheat field. Wild cane on either side of the road hiding the rest of the world. People wild too"—Vergible "Tea Cake" Woods is the catalyst for Janie's erotic longings, too powerful for society to assimilate, the "very prong," that is, (hetero) sexual fulfillment, that black women especially have been warned about. He is also meant to embody something of the passion, freedom, and self-discipline associated with the black musician (he frequently announces his presence with a song). He makes Janie feel as carefree as a child breaking rules; and he can work "lak uh dawg for two whole weeks" to get the money to take her to a picnic. A "bad" man as well as a ladies' man, Tea Cake is a gambler who cares more for the thrill of getting than the routine of holding; he is satisfied to rescue no more than changing clothes from his adventures. Tea Cake's disdain for material possessions and his attitudes toward work and play, as well as his dark complexion, contravene the notions of racial uplift exposed by many of the civil rights and social organizations of the day.

Barred by the prudish gentility of the times, *Their Eyes Were Watching God* is never as bawdy as the blues. But Hurston did portray her characters in concrete and often vivid physical terms: Janie's firm buttocks, the great rope of her hair, her pugnacious breasts; Tea Cake's purple lips, the lashes that curl away from his lazy eyes like drawn scimitars, his overpadded shoulders and narrow waist. These and the almost throwaway metaphors—Pheoby "switch[ing] a mean fanny round in a kitchen"; Janie "lacerated" by a kiss; communication described as "come kiss and be kissed"—let us know that we are in the realm of flesh and love. The trope of the kitchen ("Come on in my kitchen," one blues song of the period invites, "'cause it's going to be raining outdoors") reappears as a more openly sexual figure in Tea Cake's courtship of Janie.

The prim circumspection with which Hurston accommodated the blues values of her characters gives the story an aura of quaintness. Janie's sexual awakening is suggested through a revelation she has under the pear tree, the naturistic epiphany associated with the green-world archetype. She felt a pain "remorseless sweet that left her limp and languid." Her love of Tea Cake is consummated in "laughter" that rings out "first from the kitchen" and then "all over the house." It is significant that the first and only open quarrel between Janie and Joe Starks is precipitated by Joe's "talkin' under [Janie's] clothes," ridiculing her body under the guise of reprimanding her for some "fault." He has slashed at the flesh behind the dutiful pose, invaded with his big voice the interior sanctuary Janie had created for herself.

Janie, then, is an idealized black woman, a vision of the best a black woman might be without racist-inspired self-images: pretty, trusting, and self-confident, but still

willing to risk a dream. And it is as much Janie's ability to dream and to trust as her physical beauty that sets her apart from the other women in the novel. Certainly it is that ability that awakens her friend Pheoby to the potentials of her own marriage and therefore becomes Janie's legacy to the world.

In contrast to the social status that her previous marriages gave her, Janie's place in her relationship with Tea Cake is "down on the muck," a booming farming area, picking beans at his side. Janie has come "down," that paradoxical place in Afro-American literature that is both a physical bottom and the setting for the character's attainment of a penultimate self-knowledge. Down on the muck, Janie becomes a participant in the life that Nanny, Logan, Joe—conventional society—would have her believe is beneath her, and comes at last into her own, at home with herself, her lover, and her world. This unity is symbolized in a final play on the black-woman-as-mule image. Tea Cake asks Janie, and she consents, to work in the fields with him, because neither wants to be parted from the other even during the working day. Their love for each other makes the stoop labor of bean picking seem almost like play. The differences between the initial and successive images of the mule and this reversal are obvious: Tea Cake has asked, not commanded; his request stems from a desire to be with Janie, to share every aspect of his life with her, rather than from a desire to coerce her into some mindless submission. It isn't the white man's burden that Janie carries; it is the gift of her own true love. (pp. xiii-xxix)

Sherley Anne Williams, in an introduction to an illustrated edition of Their Eyes Were Watching God *by Zora Neale Hurston, University of Illinois Press, 1991, pp. xiii-xxix.*

FURTHER READING

Benesch, Klaus. "Oral Narrative and Literary Text: Afro-American Folklore in *Their Eyes Were Watching God*." *Callaloo* 11, No. 3 (Summer 1988): 627-35.

Close analysis of *Their Eyes Were Watching God*. Benesch concludes that Hurston's "emphasis on communication and community is representative not only of [her] affirmative attitude toward Afro-American oral culture, but also of a frequently misunderstood narrative strategy: the merging of *literary* and *oral* style."

Bethel, Lorraine, "'This Infinity of Conscious Pain': Zora Neale Hurston and the Black Female Literary Tradition." In *All the Women Are White, All the Blacks Are Men, but Some of Us Are Brave*, edited by Gloria T. Hull and others, pp. 176-88. Old Westbury, N.Y.: The Feminist Press, 1982.

Feminist reevaluation of Hurston's literary career, focusing on her short stories and her novel *Their Eyes Were Watching God*.

Bloom, Harold, ed. *Zora Neale Hurston.* Modern Critical Views. New York: Chelsea House Publishers, 1986, 192 p.
Contains nineteen biographical and critical essays on Hurston, including pieces by Langston Hughes, Fannie Hurst, Larry Neal, and Alice Walker.

Gates, Henry Louis, Jr. "Why the 'Mule Bone' Debate Goes On." *The New York Times* (10 February 1991): H5, 8.
Review of the debut production of *Mule Bone,* a drama cowritten by Hurston and Langston Hughes. Gates, an educator and critic noted for his studies of African-American literature, discusses the play's use of black folklore and black vernacular English.

Hemenway, Robert. *Zora Neale Hurston: A Literary Biography.* Urbana: University of Illinois Press, 1977, 371 p.
Critical biography of Hurston.

Hite, Molly. "Romance, Marginality, Matrilineage: Alice Walker's *The Color Purple* and Zora Neale Hurston's *Their Eyes Were Watching God.*" *Novel* 22, No. 3 (Spring 1989): 257-73.
Argues that "by treating the marginal as central and thereby unsettling the hierarchical relations that structure 'mainstream' genres, Walker and Hurston manage to handle very well the conventions that threaten to enslave them in a system or representation not of their own making."

Howard, Lillie P. *Zora Neale Hurston.* Boston: Twayne Publishers, 1980, 192 p.
Critical study of Hurston's career and literary works.

Johnson, Barbara, "Metaphor, Metonymy, and Voice in *Their Eyes Were Watching God.*" In her *A World of Difference,* pp. 155-83. Baltimore: The Johns Hopkins University Press, 1987.
Deconstructionist analysis of *Their Eyes Were Watching God.* Johnson describes the novel as a "brilliant and subtle transition from the seduction of a universal language through a progressive de-universalization that ends in the exclusion of the very protagonist herself."

Jordan, Jennifer. "Feminist Fantasies: Zora Neal Hurston's *Their Eyes Were Watching God.*" *Tulsa Studies in Women's Literature* 7, No. 1 (Spring 1988): 105-17.
Assesses the strengths and weaknesses of *Their Eyes Were Watching God* in terms of its commitment to feminism.

Plant, Deborah G. "The Folk Preacher and Folk Sermon Form in Zora Neale Hurston's *Dust Tracks on a Road.*" *Folklore Forum* 21, No. 1 (1988): 3-19.
Examines how Hurston's autobiography is informed by her spiritual convictions.

Walker, Alice. "In Search of Zora Neale Hurston." *Ms.* III, No. 9 (March 1975): 74-9, 85-9.
Personal account of Walker's trip to Eatonville, Florida, where she sought information about Hurston from those who knew her and provided a headstone for Hurston's previously unmarked grave.

Willis, Susan. "Wandering: Zora Neale Hurston's Search for Self and Method." In her *Specifying: Black Women Writing/The American Experience,* pp. 26-52. Madison: University of Wisconsin Press, 1987.
Maintains that Hurston's novels "develop a literary mode of discourse out of a folk tradition whose basic component is name calling."

Charles Johnson

1948-

(Full name Charles Richard Johnson) American novelist, short story writer, essayist, and cartoonist.

Johnson, whose balance of philosophy and folklore has been praised since the publication of his first novel in 1974, gained prominence when his novel *Middle Passage* (1990) won the National Book Award in 1990. Like his other works of fiction, *Middle Passage* embodies Johnson's controversial vision of black literature, defined in his *Being and Race: Black Writing since 1970* (1988) as "a fiction of increasing artistic and intellectual growth, one that enables us as a people—as a culture—to move from narrow complaint to broad celebration."

Born in Evanston, Illinois, Johnson began his career as a cartoonist. Under the tutelage of cartoonist Lawrence Lariar, he saw his work published by the time he was seventeen years old. His two collections of cartoons were acclaimed for their subtle but pointed satire of race relations, and their success led to "Charlie's Pad," a 1971 series on public television that Johnson created, coproduced, and hosted. As an undergraduate at Southern Illinois University, Johnson studied with novelist and literary theorist John Gardner, whose conception of "moral fiction"—demanding from the author a near-fanatical commitment to technique, imagination, and ethics—deeply impressed Johnson. Johnson's first novel, *Faith and the Good Thing,* was published in 1974 when the author was studying for his Ph.D. in phenomenology and literary aesthetics at the State University of New York at Stonybrook. *Faith and the Good Thing* is an intricate, often humorous, philosophical work that depicts a Southern black girl's journey to Chicago in search of the "Good Thing": the true meaning of life. During her odyssey, Faith, the story's Candide-like protagonist, suffers physical degradation but nonetheless attains spiritual resurrection. In his next novel, *Oxherding Tale* (1982), Johnson again employed humor and philosophy to trace the development of his hero from innocence to experience. The plot of this work is modeled on the slave narratives of nineteenth-century author Frederick Douglass. Using a combination of realism and allegory and mixing modern slang with mid-nineteenth-century vernacular, Johnson follows a slave's escape to freedom and quest for knowledge. Critics generally agreed that Johnson handled characterization and philosophical digression more adeptly in *Oxherding Tale* than he did in *Faith and the Good Thing*. Stanley Crouch observed: "[The protagonist's] growth is thrilling because Johnson skillfully avoids melodramatic platitudes while creating suspense and comedy, pathos and nostalgia. In the process, he invents a fresh set of variations on questions about race, sex, and freedom."

Johnson's collection of short stories, *The Sorcerer's Apprentice* (1986), also exhibits his interest in moral

tales. The pieces in this volume examine the cultural alienation of black Americans through a blend of formal language and street argot. Fred Pfeil commented: "[In *The Sorcerer's Apprentice*], Johnson demonstrates more clearly than ever his Melvillean ambition to use narrative to fuse concept and event, politics, philosophy and drama, and to make ideas dance."

Set in 1830, Johnson's most recent novel, *Middle Passage,* chronicles the misadventures of twenty-two-year-old Rutherford Calhoun, a well-educated, mischievous freed slave from southern Illinois. Rutherford is released in New Orleans by his master—a clergyman who provided him with a broad education—and revels in the city's sordid underworld. Intending to escape his creditors and an impending marriage to a priggish schoolteacher that would free him of his debts, Rutherford boards the first available boat, which, to his horror, is a slave clipper bound for Africa. On the dangerous round-trip voyage, recounted in the form of a ship's log, Rutherford becomes divided in his allegiance to his white American crewmates and his sympathy for the ship's woeful cargo, a group of suffering Allmuseri tribesmen. Rutherford ultimately sides with the captives when they mutiny and, through his traumatic experience with his oppressed shipmates, gains new knowledge about slavery, race relations, and himself. Although Johnson was criticized for interspersing modern idioms with nineteenth-century maritime jargon and naturalistic prose in *Middle Passage,* many commentators lauded his blending of such genres as the picaresque tale, historical romance, sea yarn, slave narrative, and the philosophical novel. Arend Flick observed: "[*Middle Passage* is] informed by a remarkably generous thesis: that racism in general, and the institution of slavery in particular, might best be seen as having arisen not from political or sociological or economic causes, not (God help us) from pigment envy, but from a deep fissure that characterizes Western thought in general, our tendency to split the world into competing categories."

Johnson's outspoken views on the direction of black literature have been harshly criticized as being unfair to such heralded writers as Alice Walker and Toni Morrison, whose works offer more direct challenges to racism than do Johnson's. The issues he raises, however, as well as his elevated expectations for the philosophical content of black literature, remain key issues in an ongoing debate in the literary community. Johnson commented: "As a writer I am committed to the development of what one might call a genuinely systematic philosophical black American literature, a body of work that explores classical problems and metaphysical questions against the background of black American life. Specifically, my philosophical style is phenomenology, the discipline of Edmund Husserl, but I also have a deep personal interest in the entire continuum of Asian philosophy from the Vedas to Zen, and this perspective inevitably colors my fiction to some degree. I have been a martial artist since the age of nineteen and a practicing Buddhist since about 1980. So one might also say that in fiction I attempt to interface Eastern and Western philosophical traditions, always with the hope that some new perception of experience—especially 'black experience'—will emerge from these meditations."

(For further information about Johnson's life and works, see *Black Writers; Contemporary Authors,* Vol. 116; *Contemporary Literary Criticism,* Vols. 7, 51, 65; and *Dictionary of Literary Biography,* Vol. 33: *Afro-American Fiction Writers after 1955.*)

PRINCIPAL WORKS

Black Humor (cartoons) 1970
Half-Past Nation-Time (cartoons) 1972
Faith and the Good Thing (novel) 1974
Oxherding Tale (novel) 1982
The Sorcerer's Apprentice (short stories) 1986
Being and Race: Black Writing since 1970 (essays) 1988
Middle Passage (novel) 1990

Annie Gottlieb (essay date 1975)

[*In the following excerpt, Gottlieb praises the philosophical energy and ambition of* Faith and the Good Thing.]

[*Faith and the Good Thing*] is a strange and often wonderful hybrid—an ebullient philosophical novel in the form of a folktale-cum-black girl's odyssey. It is a book bubbling like a conjure woman's kettle with African lore, preserved intact in the half-magical, half-demeaning world of Hatten County, Georgia. There are beautiful tall tales, thunder-rolling sermons, folk exaggerations ("They say it was so dark that raindrops knocked on people's doors, begging for candles just to see how to strike the ground"); there are scenes of lower-depths Chicago as the Seventh Circle of Hell; and—hold on—of Plato's Cave; there's the Buddhist view of the world as a fiery wheel of illusion and Sartre's understanding of the battle of subjects to render each other object (well translated back into the terms of the heroine Faith's experience, when to survive she becomes a whore for a time), and dozens of other virtuosic philosophical references I am too ignorant to identify....

[There] are times when the mix of [Johnson's] novel is too thick with academic in-jokes and erudite references; that's when the magic falls flat, although in principle I like the audacity of having the hideous old Swamp Woman of Hatten County, Georgia, rattle on about Plato's Symposium. It's a back-handed way of saying that *all* the world's wisdom rests in beings like her. But I did grit my teeth at sentences like, "In their corner of the bar, Faith tried to make her peace with the problems of change, permanence, and the free-will-destroying tyranny of history."

Fortunately, such moments are overwhelmed by the poetry and wisdom of the book. It's a *Pilgrim's Progress* fable—Faith's journey in search of the Good Thing that makes life on earth worthwhile....

This is a flawed yet still fabulous book, at its best a many-splendored and ennobling weaving-together of thought, suffering, humor and magic.

> *Annie Gottlieb, in a review of "Faith and the Good Thing," in* The New York Times Book Review, *January 12, 1975, p. 6.*

Elizabeth A. Schultz (essay date 1978)

[*In the following excerpt, Schultz evaluates* Faith and the Good Thing *as a response to Ralph Ellison's novel* Invisible Man.]

Perhaps closest to Ellison's [*Invisible Man*] in overall mythic design is Charles Johnson's *Faith and the Good Thing* (1974). Faith, cautioned by her dying mother to get herself a "Good Thing," begins a Platonic search in the cave of life for Truth, an Arthurian quest for the Grail, or, like the African Kujichagulia, a climb toward the peak of Mount Kilimanjaro and the source of knowledge. Traveling from rural Georgia to urban Chicago, she embraces numerous roles and ideologies—her mother's fundamentalist Christianity, middle-class materialism and opportunism, a street-walker's self-sacrifice, an artist's solipsism. As she passes from one ideology to another—ever hopeful—she also finds herself involved with a variety of people, most of whom exploit her for their own ends, few of whom see her according to her own needs and complexity. Burned by an apocalyptic fire at the novel's conclusion, she becomes a wraith: seen and not seen, a visual symbol of her former existence and an obvious analogy to Ellison's Invisible Man. Faith's invisibility differs, however, from that of Ellison's protagonist, for throughout her travels she has been in touch with the unseen world—not the unseen world of Plato's perfect forms, Kujichagulia's absolute answers, or the nightmares of Ellison's protagonist, which are no alternative to his waking world; she is in touch with memories, or more accurately, the spiritual presences of three human beings who persist in haunting her; they keep alive the faith in her, the faith which gives her her name and identity, the faith that believes that the search itself is its own end. These familiar presences are "the living dead," and only when Faith stops searching, momentarily convinced she has found the "Good Thing" in a materialistic middle-class life, and joins "the dead living," do they cease to appear before her. Following the fire and a hospital internment—events which also force Ellison's protagonist to new perspectives on himself—they are restored to her, however, as she herself becomes one of them.

Indeed, as Faith, the wraith, returns to the swamp from which she had started her journey, she is reincarnated as the Swamp Woman. In his cellar Ellison's hero gains perspective on his personal agonies by reviewing in a dream sequence the ambiguities of his own life and of black Americans from the days of slavery; similarly, Faith's sufferings seem to give her access to the werewitch's esoteric and folk wisdom, her knowledge of Western and African philosophical and cabalistic systems as well as her consciousness of the terrible history of oppression. Like Ellison's protagonist's, Faith's journey has also been cyclical, returning her to her own past—the swamp and the Briar Patch of her own mind—as well as to the historical past, represented by the conflation of her experiences with the Swamp Woman's lore. By Faith's return to the swamp as well as by the old crone's marvelous subsequent assumption of Faith's guise and her return to the world to continue Faith's search, Johnson demonstrates his commitment, however, to myth rather than history, for he seeks to guarantee its truth by suggesting its endless repetition. Finally, Faith, like Ellison's protagonist, contemplates the possibilities of the mind to conceive a pattern for living; she, living in a state of faith rather than of paralysis, imagines both progress and responsibility beyond the control of history:

> When she'd traveled the existing paths, she would create a new, untrodden one. That was progress. If she discovered X number of paths and traveled them all, then she, before she died, would leave X-plus-1. That was responsibility: factoring the possible number of paths to the Good Thing, but not becoming fixed, or held to those paths in her history, or the history of the race.

Finally, then, unlike Ellison's protagonist, she envisions a way to reconcile the many with the one.

In the conclusion of his novel, Johnson informs us that Faith's way will not be a solitary one. Not only do we learn that she is preparing to relate Aristotle's Illusion and "Stagolee's great battle with Lucifer in West Hell" to two children who seek her out in the swamp as she herself had once sought the werewitch, but we are also reminded that we ourselves have been children throughout the novel, listening to Johnson relate Faith's own tale. Ellison, too, somewhat perfunctorily, reminds us in the last sentence of his novel that we have also been an audience for his protagonist's story when he queries, "Who knows but that, on the lower frequencies, I speak for you?" Johnson's repeated imperative reference to his readers as "Children" and Faith's preparations for her young visitors suggest, however, a more than rhetorical involvement with others; the "Good Thing" is not only the search itself but also the fact that the search is everyone's, and that we are on it together. (pp. 106-08)

Elizabeth A. Schultz, "The Heirs of Ralph Ellison: Patterns of Individualism in the Contemporary Afro-American Novel," in CLA Journal, *Vol. XXII, No. 2, December, 1978, pp. 101-22.*

Stanley Crouch (essay date 1983)

[*In the following excerpt, Crouch views* Oxherding Tale *as a humorous and intelligent exploration of the meaning of freedom.*]

Since most contemporary novels involving race are scandals of contrivance, unwheeled wagons hitched to cardboard horses, it's a particular pleasure to read Charles Johnson's *Oxherding Tale.* This is his second novel and, being a long ball past his first, *Faith and the Good Thing* (1974), it separates him even further from conventional sensibilities. In *Faith,* Johnson told the tall tale of a black girl's search for meaning—What is the good life? What is good?—and soaked it through with skills he had developed as a cartoonist, television writer, journalist, and student of philosophy. This time out, he has written a novel made important by his artful use of the slave narrative's structure to examine the narrator's developing consciousness, a consciousness that must painfully evaluate both the master and slave cultures.

The primary theme is freedom and the responsibility that comes with it. Given the time of the novel, 1838 to 1860, one would expect such a theme, but Johnson makes it clear in the most human—and often hilarious—terms that the question of freedom in a democratic society is essentially moral, and that social revolution pivots on an expanding redefinition of citizenry and its relationship to law. The adventure of escape only partially prepares Andrew Hawkins, the narrator, for the courage and commitment that come with moral comprehension. Andrew's growth is thrilling because Johnson skillfully avoids melodramatic platitudes while creating suspense and comedy, pathos and nostalgia. In the process, he invents a fresh set of variations on questions about race, sex, and freedom.

Though only 176 pages, **Oxherding Tale** is so rich that Johnson's contrapuntal developments of character and theme gain epic resonance. He expands his tale with adventures of style that span the work of Melville and Ellison, Twain and Bradbury, opting for everything from the facetious philosophical treatise to a variation on *The Illustrated Man*. Like a jazz musician's high-handed use of harmony, Johnson's prose pivots between the language of the novel's time and terms from contemporary slang, regional vernacular, folklore, the blues, academia, and Madison Avenue. The technique recalls American film comedians' pushing the talk and attitudes of the day into period situations, lampooning the conventions of the past and the present. But Johnson is essentially a gallows humorist who manipulates microscopic realism to sober and control the reader's response, just as he takes narrative liberties to create an echoing, circular tension in which characters and dangers rhyme and contrast.

Johnson models his book on the work of Frederick Douglass, especially *Narrative of the Life of Frederick Douglass, An American Slave,* published in 1845. Douglass was an epic hero if there ever was one, and his work spans experience that moves from slavery to partial freedom to escape and eventual celebrity. His greatest importance to Johnson, however, is that he took Hawthorne's assault on New England hypocrisy south. In order to assert his humanity, Douglass questioned the Southern social order and everything that upheld it, from force to compliance, superstition to imposed illiteracy. He continually attacked the amoral sexual practices of the slaveholders and the distortions of American ideals caused by their defense of the chattel system. Douglass's native intelligence allowed for insights that only our finest novelists have been able to extend—the often dangerous nature of personal responsibility, the mutual infantilization of master and slave, the roles of religion and folklore, music and humor, risk and victory. In effect, Douglass is the figure who provides the moral passageway between Hawthorne and Melville and supplies the foundation for *Huckleberry Finn....*

By using Douglass's achievement as a model, Johnson perforates the layers of canvas-thick clichés that block our access to the human realities of American slavery. He also creates a successful metaphor for the 1960s, when black militants and intellectuals (students mostly) rejected Christianity, capitalism, and collided head-on with elements of black culture as basic as food (familial conflicts between emulation of Islam's disdain for pork and the hippie concern with health foods are symbolized by Andrew's embracing vegetarianism in imitation of his first white guru). The metaphor's impact comes from Johnson's sense of the play between history, cultural convention, and the assertion of identity in personal and ethnic terms.

Like Douglass, Andrew Hawkins is a mulatto. Unlike Douglass, he can pass for white, a fact that adds complexity to the moral choices he must make when he becomes a runaway. That fact also places him between what seem only two worlds but are actually many, and it adds the texture of an espionage tale in which "passing" is essential to suspense and victory. To thicken the plot, Johnson introduces a transcendentalist who supplies Andrew with a set of Eastern references and a pursuit of "The Whole"—though all systems of thought the hero encounters are satirized mercilessly. These devices allow Johnson to undercut Andrew's theorizing with concrete summonings of the worlds through which he passes—even inserting, as Melville might, a two-page treatise on the nature of slave narratives!

Johnson's ironic humor resounds at the novel's beginning as he pushes the master's wife into the position of slave woman by proxy.... As the novel opens, a drinking session is in progress. Jonathan Polkinghorne, master of Cripplegate, and his butler, George Hawkins, who is also his favorite slave, are indulging in a distinctly male camaraderie that seems to transcend their races and stations—each catches hell from his spouse when he comes home drunk. Literally inebriated with power, Jonathan proposes that they exchange wives for the evening in order to avoid static in the bedroom. George follows orders after the master makes it clear that he intends for them to be carried out.

Wobbling from the effects of wine and anticipation, George crosses the territory of *Invisible Man* and *The Odyssey*. In Ellison's novel, the narrator is upbraided and expelled from a Southern Negro college for following orders rather than pretending to, for not knowing he should give white people what they *want,* rather than what they ask for. George makes a parallel mistake and proves himself an even bigger fool by revealing his identity. As he makes love to Anna Polkinghorne in the darkness, she yowls with delight, calling him "Jonathan," but George can't resist telling her who's doing the satisfying, just as Odysseus couldn't resist shouting his name to the Cyclops. Like Odysseus, George is humbled by losing almost everything: as Anna swells, pregnant with George's child, his social position diminishes. He falls to the position of field hand—oxherd—outcast and laughing stock of the slave quarters, given his comeuppance for ever having felt secure and superior to his fellow slaves. Though George's wife, Mattie, accepts Andrew as her own after Anna refuses to see him, she is forever fighting with George, a mad battle in which their mutual needs are persistently camouflaged by complaint and derision. (p. 30)

Jonathan is estranged from Anna because of the immoral nature of the order he gave George, and because he is a victim of a system in which immoral power choices can also ricochet. George's problems with Mattie stem from something only he knows—that his action could be explained as the result of many things, including cowardice, but when he felt lust for Anna and rationalized his act as an expression of God's will, he was using the order for his own purposes, embracing the slaveholder's self-justifications, and was culpable. Just as Jonathan and George mirror and provide contrast to each other, so do Anna and Mattie. Anna rejects Andrew because he complicates her identity in a way she finds repulsive, while Mattie, however embittered, saves her outrage for the men responsible and loves the child. While Mattie becomes more contentious, Anna becomes a voluntary spinster whose desexualization by slavery will be echoed by Minty, Andrew's first love and the daughter of a womanizing mulatto slave.... Minty is seen a few years later, after Andrew has escaped and is passing himself off as a white man at a slave auction.

> ... I stood trying to recognize something of the girl in Cripplegate, in whom the world once chose to concretize its possibilities in the casement of her skin.... If you looked, without sentiment, you could see that her dress was too small and crawled up when she moved, flashing work-scorched stretches of skin and a latticework of whipmarks. Her belly pushed forward. From the cholesterol-high, nutritionless diet of the quarters, or a child, I could not tell. She was unlovely, drudgelike, sexless, the farm tool squeezed ... for every ounce of surplus value, then put on sale for whatever price she could bring. She was, like my stepmother, perhaps doubly denied—in both caste and gender—and driven to Christ (she wore a cross) as the only decent man who would have her.

The road to that hideous epiphany is a long one, taking Andrew through continual redefinitions of his identity and the nature of his surroundings. When Anna demands that Andrew be sent away because he symbolizes her humiliation, Jonathan refuses and makes provisions for his education. From Ezekiel William Sykes-Withers, Andrew gets a classical education expanded to include the teachings of the Eastern philosophers and mystics. Andrew embraces the idea of the universe as the Great Mother, becomes an intellectual fop, and makes pompous evaluations of the problems of man. Ezekiel, with his head ever in the clouds, and George, with his pushed into the earth, give Andrew antithetical perspectives experience will allow him to synthesize. George's bitterness at his fall from grace shapes an overview that defines anything connected with white people as bad.... That homemade ethnic nationalism is the spiritual tragedy of Andrew's father, a man who sustains his hurt and sands down the universe to fit his disappointment: "Grief was the grillwork—the emotional grid—through which George Hawkins sifted and sorted events, simplified a world so over-rich in sense it outstripped him ... " George had no knowledge of the threat that education and imagination posed.

Andrew's schooling will later make it possible for him to read and forge documents, to make language work for him, just as the slaves had made Christianity function as religion, self-expression, style, political editorial, and code of revolt. And because of his learning, Andrew, for all his naiveté, comes to realize he must ask for his freedom:

> Consider the fact: Like a man who had fallen or been rudely flung into the world, I owned nothing. My knowledge, my clothes, my language, even, were shamefully second-hand, made by, and perhaps for, other men.... My argument was: Whatever my origin, I would be wholly responsible for the shape I gave myself in the future, for shirting myself handsomely with a new life that called me like a siren to possibilities that were real but forever out of reach.

The oblique references to Caliban and Odysseus are apt: the runaway slave that Andrew will soon become is a man whose knowledge must be used to free him from teachers as he looks for home—except that the home for which slaves felt nostalgia was more the dream of freedom than an actual place. But before Andrew chooses to pursue freedom in concrete geographical terms, he floats along in the philosophical clouds he shares with Ezekiel. Too mystical to trust sensuality, Ezekiel longs for a system that will explain everything and sends Karl Marx the money to visit America. Johnson brilliantly satirizes the relationship between a revolutionary's self-obsession and his theories:

> As of late, political affairs affected Marx physically. When he felt a headcold coming on, a toothache, he looked immediately for its social cause. A new tax law had cost Marx a molar. Nearby at a button factory a strike that failed brought on an attack of asthma. These things were dialectical.

Marx's appearance signals Andrew's first awareness that ideas have human sources or targets. Marx, a jolly family man and sensualist, has as his credo, "Everything I've vritten has been for a voman—is *one* vay to view Socialism, no?" Marx's boredom inspires Andrew to look more closely at the stern Ezekiel:

> Abruptly, I saw my tutor through his eyes: a lonely, unsocial creature unused to visitors, awkward with people as a recluse. Not a Socialist, as he fancied himself. No, his rejection of society, his radicalism, was not, as he thought, due to some rareness of the soul. It was stinginess. Resentment for the richness of things. A smoke screen for his own social shortcomings.

What Andrew had thought the opposite of George's vision was substantially the same—a world view created out of bitterness. Yet Andrew, the pampered mulatto, has still to taste the sourness and terror of slavery, the black world beyond abstraction. His decision to ask for his freedom will bring him cheek to jowl with sexual decadence, drugs, and death.

Andrew's second white mentor is Flo Hatfield, a ruthless voluptuary on whose plantation he expects to earn money that will buy freedom for George, Mattie, and Minty. Middle-aged and beautiful, Flo Hatfield has been infantilized by her power over others, but Johnson makes her as sympathetic as she is repulsive, self-obsessed, and petulant. Good at business and something of a feminist, Hatfield's resentment of male privilege becomes a justification for her appetites. She dresses her lovers, all of whom are slaves, as gigolos; when she tires of them, they're sent to work in her mines, where death is certain. Though she seems sexually free at first, a cosmopolitan upper-class white woman beyond the erotic provincialism of Negro women, she is actually so much a slave to sensation that Andrew's job as sexual servant results in addiction to opium, her favorite aphrodisiac. When Johnson writes that her lovers had "died and gone to Heaven, you might say," he is playing on the black dictum: "A colored man with a white woman is a Negro who has died and gone to heaven," but he is also creating a metaphor for the inevitable fall that follows the spiritual death of decadence.

No more than a tool of Hatfield's narcissism, Andrew falls from her hedonistic heaven when he strikes her in anger after she refuses to allow him to earn his freedom. Andrew is sent to the Yellow Dog Mine, where the landscape echoes Bessie Smith: "Wild country so tough the hootowls all sang bass." With him is Reb, his second father figure. En route, Andrew asserts his white features and they escape, pretending to be master and slave. In the process, they must outwit the Soulcatcher, Horace Bannon, a man who psychologically *becomes* a slave, then goes where slaves would hide. Bannon's technique is close to the one Reb preaches—a slave must learn exactly how masters think so that he can control their relationship as much as possible. Bannon is a psychopath whose "collage of features" suggests mixed ancestry and whose bloodlust is allowed free rein by the constant flight of slaves. Perhaps the greatest condemnation of the chattel system is that it instituted sadistic behavior for the maintenance of injustice. From Reb, Andrew learns what historian Forrest G. Wood meant when he said that what had been endured by the vast majority of Negro slaves exceeded the suffering of even the most oppressed white group. A captured African slave whose name has been changed twice by different masters, Reb is himself a harsh lesson in the stoicism born of tragedy. He no longer dreams of Africa, where Islam was as much an imposition of slavery as Christianity was in America. Reb faces his fate, raising his fists in his own way.

All that Andrew has learned, both intellectual and moral, is put to the test when he decides to marry a white woman—or she decides for him. Once Andrew enters that world, the theme of espionage, of assumed identity that allows for information about the opposition, also allows for a fantastic parody of the liberal wing of the town.... From there, Johnson moves to a climax remarkable for its brutality and humbling tenderness; Andrew must dive into the briar patch of his identity and risk destruction in order to express his humanity.

That a work of such courage and compassion, virtuosity and intelligence, has been published by a university press is further proof that commercial houses have a very circumscribed notion of African-American writing.

But then, any black writer who chooses human nature over platitudes, opportunism, or trends faces probable rejection. Charles Johnson has enriched contemporary American fiction as few young writers can, and it is difficult to imagine that such a talented artist will forever miss the big time that is equal to his gifts. (pp. 30, 32)

Stanley Crouch, "Charles Johnson: Free at Last!" in The Village Voice, *Vol. XXVII, No. 29, July 19, 1983, pp. 30, 32.*

Steven Weisenburger (essay date 1984)

[*In the following review, Weisenburger praises the complexity of the narrative voice in* Oxherding Tale.]

The title of Charles Johnson's strangely delightful novel [*Oxherding Tale*] refers to the "Ten Oxherding Pictures" of Kuoan Shih-yuan, a twelfth century Zen master. In the paintings a young man pursues a wayward animal, a symbol of the self, and the irony is that he never finds the beast. He finds himself always in between loss and recovery, desire and its resolution. To these oppositions Charles Johnson has added black and white. *Oxherding Tale* translates the Zen enigma of in-betweenness to the antebellum South, and to a beautifully voiced narrator named Andrew Hawkins, a mulatto who becomes a master of the in-between.

The novel opens on an autumn night, in 1837, at a South Carolina plantation called "Cripplegate," a locus that is "ruin now, mere parable." This stands as an apt warning. For despite its many gestures toward picaresque, realistic fiction, *Oxherding Tale* is always riskily half-and-half. From its opening "Long ago," to its concluding "This is my tale," Johnson makes equally as many gestures toward realism as he does to the conventions of parable, or, more specifically, allegorical satire. Many of his characters are therefore drawn as grotesque abstracts. They embody an eccentric side of things, and their one-sidedness sets the boundaries within which Andrew's moral odyssey unfolds. At the same time, Johnson gives his eccentrics a roundedness, a power to speak themselves that is rare in comparable satires by an Ishmael Reed or a Flannery O'Connor. As Andrew Hawkins might put it, the novel therefore takes up all the conventions of allegorical satire even as it commences to "worry" them with the needs of historical, realistic fiction.

One immediate result is a stylistic tension that will initially put many readers off stride. Nodding toward realistic conventions, Johnson fills the story with artifacts of nineteenth century culture: beardboxes, coolingboards (for the dead), trollopees, phrenology, Mesmer's "Animal Magnetism," even Karl Marx (who makes a weirdly incongruous visit to Cripplegate). At the same time, Andrew's story is skewed by a more familiar diction, with its "Sensuality 101, Section A" and its "sexual politics," each as obviously anachronistic as the "biology test" Andrew reads, circa 1850. To some extent we can put this aside as an elaborate ruse, saying (with Andrew's father-in-law) that novels are "A tissue of ostrobogulous lies ... with the writer laughing behind each page at the reader's gullibility."

But there is more at stake. With their fullness, Johnson's welter of minor characters cannot simply be read as stick figures in a satirical drama. That temptation is however there from the start, given the low-comedy scene in Chapter One. On an autumn night in 1837 George Hawkins, devoted butler at "the Big House," gets quietly drunk with his master, Jonathan Polkinghorne. When he proposes they swap wives for the night, George, in no position to refuse, gives a reluctant assent. It goes well enough until Anna Polkinghorne groans out her sexual climax in the dark:

> "Oh *gawd,* Jonathan!"

> "No ma'am, it ain't Jonathan."

> "Geo-*o-o-o*rge?" Her voice pulled at the vowel like taffy. She yanked her sheet to her chin. "Is this *George*?"

> "Yo husband's in the quarters." George was on his feet. "He's, uh, with my wife."

Anna screams, then lapses forever into an insane seclusion. Andrew is born a mulatto, banished like the memory of an appendicitis to the quarters, yet raised with the benefit of an extraordinary education—American Transcendentalism, European dialectical philosophy, Eastern mysticism—paid for by his "stepfather," Jonathan. These contrary paternal influences keep pulling at him. George nourishes in Andrew a responsibility for "the world-historical mission of Africa," a sense that everything he does "pushes the Race forward, or pulls us back." His is the philosophy of Inchin' Along. But Andrew objects: "I didn't *want* this obligation." In Part Two of the novel Andrew appears to reject George's advice altogether, when he begins to "pass" in white society. And yet by then the education which was so freely given has begun to weigh on him like an absolute servitude. Ever a bond-servant to the Emersonian ideal of Self-Reliance, Andrew troubles over his isolation, his distance from the family he knew in the quarters.

One answer is to start, however haphazardly, a family of his own. Yet even then Andrew keeps troubling himself over Western definitions of the Self. His Zen training keeps referring the questions back to that wayward, illusory ox. And this is why George, the only actual oxherder in the novel, keeps shadowing Andrew's tale until its end. George is a beautifully drawn comical figure, and something in him arouses a great empathy in us. I think it is the sense that at every fateful moment in his life George, like Andrew, does not act; instead *he is acted*. In between he keeps the fictions going, and this is precisely why he matters.

Other characters have more one-sided roles to fulfill. Ezekiel William Sykes-Withers, Andrew's tutor, is a fine parody of the American Renaissance Intellectual—a cross between Poe the nympholept, the ironist in Melville, and the learnedness of Emerson. When Andrew falls in love with a girl from the quarters, Jonathan Polkinghorne cynically deals his step-son to Flo Hatfield, a cross between Catherine the Great, Mae West, and The White Goddess. After a year of exhausting servility to her sexual appetites at "Leviathan," Andrew is dealt away again, only this time he escapes with a black coffinmaker with the impossible name of "Reb" (remember, this is in 1858). Passing as a white schoolteacher, Reb and Andrew settle in Spartanburg, South Carolina. A doctor railroads Andrew into marrying his spinster daughter, and Reb leaves for Canada. Thus events careen toward certain bleakly unavoidable—that is, realistic—ends. Of course Andrew's black heritage will be discovered; it has been foreshadowed all along.

Yet even as this discovery occurs Johnson brings forward his most allegorical character. Nominally he is Horace Bannon, a murderer who collects bounties on runaway slaves. Allegorically he is "The Soulcatcher," a personification of Death. Andrew listens to his method: "you got to have something dead or static inside you—an image of self—fo' a real slave catcher to latch onto." Give in to that static image of one's self, The Soulcatcher explains, and the hunt is finished: the Slave offers *himself* to the Soulcatcher's knife. This makes for a fine irony with Reb, the master coffin-maker who has "no pockets of death" within him. Reb becomes the only slave ever to elude The Soulcatcher. However, the allegory of Death must also key two of Johnson's biggest risks. It does little to help one through the reappearance of Minty, Andrew's lost love from the quarters who dies a withering death from pellagra, depicted in frighteningly realistic detail. One has somewhat less trouble with the last trick, which is neatly arranged: The Soulcatcher metamorphoses back into Horace Bannon, the simpleminded redneck whose one aim in life is to be happily married. At that moment, the satirical stroke is swift and decisive. But one also has an aftertaste of ashes caused, I think, by the fact that Andrew's marriage to "The White World" of Part 2 is cemented by Minty's death.

The thing I most admire about ***Oxherding Tale*** is the way Charles Johnson wants to unfold such a moment of equilibrium from his shifting terrain. The writing moves in a middle ground between the cultures of the East and the West, between realism and parable. And Johnson sets himself the task of doing it in the first person, though it is exactly the fixture of a Self that his work calls into doubt. In two short, essayistic chapters Johnson steps out of his fictional persona to discuss this paradox. He points to models for his work in Slave Narratives, Puritan narratives of Redemption, and St. Augustine's *The Confessions*. In these, the Self is equally a fiction, a "proposition" in motion between sin and salvation, ignorance and knowledge, slavery and freedom. As "metafictional" interludes such chapters are informative, but I don't think readers need to be reminded how the great works of fiction have "worried" the conventions, hybridized the forms, occupied the in-between.

If anything, these interludes demonstrate how ambitious Charles Johnson is for his writing. *Oxherding Tale* is his second novel. *Faith and the Good Thing* appeared when he was twenty-six, and it was flawed mainly by short lapses into wooden, academic exposition. The metafictional asides of his latest novel are one way of transforming the teaching into performance, but they're still beside the point. Johnson's real gifts are a beautiful sense of voice and a delight in skewing one's formal expectations. (pp. 153-56)

> Steven Weisenburger, "In-Between," in Callaloo, *Vol. 7, No. 1, Winter, 1984, pp. 153-56.*

Michiko Kakutani (essay date 1986)

[*In the following excerpt, Kakutani discusses the integration of philosophical themes and storytelling conventions in* The Sorcerer's Apprentice.]

"Was sorcery a gift given to a few, like poetry?" wonders Allan, the aspiring magician in the title story of Charles Johnson's new collection [*The Sorcerer's Apprentice*] . . . .

In this story, as in the other tales in *The Sorcerer's Apprentice*, Mr. Johnson . . . addresses both the Faustian dilemma of the knowledge-seeker and the more specific condition of the black artist in America, cut off from his cultural roots and suspended between worlds . . . .

It is one of the achievements of these stories that, while concerned at heart with questions of prejudice and cultural assimilation, they are never parochial and only rarely didactic. Rather, Mr. Johnson has used his generous storytelling gifts and his easy familiarity with a variety of literary genres to conjure up eight moral fables that limn the fabulous even as they remain grounded in the language and social idioms of black American communities. The finest ones, in fact, become fables that implicitly mirror the quotation from Herman Melville that Mr. Johnson has chosen as an epigraph for this volume—they "present another world, and yet one to which we feel the tie."

In relating the meeting between a country doctor and the angst-ridden creature from outer space whom he's called upon to treat, **"Popper's Disease"** evolves from a fairly conventional exercise in sci-fi into a Kafkaesque exploration of identity. **"Menagerie, a Child's Fable,"** a parable about racism told from the point of view of a dog, borrows heavily from Orwell's *Animal Farm*—the story tells what happens when the animals in a pet store take over from its absent owner—and **"The Education of Mingo"** invokes Mary Shelley's *Frankenstein* to make its point about the dangers of liberalism and assimilation.

In **"The Education of Mingo,"** a farmer by the name of Moses Green buys a slave named Mingo, whom he attempts to educate. Moses teaches Mingo farming and table etiquette, he teaches him not "to sop cornbread in his coffee; or pick his nose at public market." He teaches him how to think, how to talk and how to behave, and in no time at all, Mingo appears to have become "his own spitting image"—a development that makes Moses feel "now like a father, now like an artist fingering something fine and noble from a rude chump of foreign clay." If Moses' intentions are entirely well-meaning, however, they're also paternalistic and patronizing, and in time they have serious—and violent—consequences that affect both him and Mingo.

With the exception of one direct allusion to *Frankenstein* that feels superfluous and strained, this story attests to Mr. Johnson's narrative finesse—his ability both to rework old legends, and to create a glowing alloy of the colloquial and the mythic, the naturalistic and the surreal. Though its action retains a powerful, symbolic resonance, the tale never gets that sticky, overworked quality that comes from an author trying to force his material into a predetermined mold; in this case, Mr. Johnson simply lets the overall Frankenstein legend gently inform the actions of his characters, without allowing it to dictate their fates or erase their own idiosyncrasies and humor.

Unfortunately, in the weaker stories in this volume, Mr. Johnson's taste for parables—his desire to locate some sort of Aesop-like moral in each tale—tends to overwhelm his delicate conjurations of social detail and vernacular description. **"Exchange Value,"** for instance, entirely robs its characters—two aspiring hoods who end up adopting their would-be victim's peculiar habits—of their individuality, turning them into passive objects doomed to act out their creator's predictable design. And **"Moving Pictures"** moves even further in this unpromising direction—devoid of characters except for a faceless narrator who speaks in the second person, the story is little but a tired one-liner about escapism and the movies. The reader can only conclude that it was included in this otherwise accomplished collection as padding or a silly afterthought.

> Michiko Kakutani, in a review of "The Sorcerer's Apprentice," in The New York Times, *February 5, 1986, p. 24.*

Michael Ventura (essay date 1986)

[*In the following excerpt, Ventura examines major themes in* The Sorcerer's Apprentice.]

Charles Johnson's brief, highly concentrated *Sorcerer's Apprentice* has the feel of a good short novel rather than a collection of stories. These tales—or are they fables?—are realistic without strictly adhering to realism, fantastic without getting lost in fantasy. Mr. Johnson, a professor of English at the University of Washington, writes of truths that intersect and sometimes intercept our everyday trajectories.

Each of the eight fictions not only stands on its own but seems to support and invoke its companions. The opening story, **"The Education of Mingo,"** applies the Frankenstein myth to American Slavery. Mingo is "the youngest son of the reigning king of the Allmuseri, a tribe of wizards," and his mere presence is enough to enslave his American master. In the last tale, **"The Sorcerer's Apprentice,"** the sorcerer is a former slave in South Carolina who was also born an Allmuseri in Africa. He attempts to pass on his knowledge to a boy who was born free and has become, simply and terribly, too American to absorb African magic. The two tales are the opposite poles of a magnetic field within which Mr. Johnson's other stories are held.

They echo one another without straining for effect. As Mingo enslaves his master, so sudden wealth enslaves Mingo's descendants. Loftis and Cooter, the thieves in **"Exchange Value,"** provide a chilling lesson in the witchy powers of money. The reader realizes almost by osmosis that each story in *The Sorcerer's Apprentice* reveals the underside of the last or next.

A structure is just a frame that squeaks if you lean on it—unless the author has a vision of how the world works. Mr. Johnson has been somewhere most people have not. As the narrator of **"Alethia"** says, "I am hardly a man to conjure a fabulation so odd in its transfiguration of things, so strange, so terrifying." Transfigurations are at once Mr. Johnson's subject and vision. He knows how a master becomes a slave, how a postal worker becomes a kung fu knight (**"China"**) and how magic can be gained (**"Alethia"**) and lost (**"The Sorcerer's Apprentice"**). And when Mr. Johnson says magic, he means magic. He's not using the word to invoke a mood. Sometimes it's outright voodoo; sometimes it's something more subtle that gives an otherwise powerless individual the power to transfigure both himself and his world.

According to Mr. Johnson, an exaggerated sense of self is what gets in the way of magic....

Magic, then, requires a surrender of self that terrifies most people. Our terror is Mr. Johnson's meat. Confronting it, his characters take sudden turns, like flowers in a time-lapse film, sometimes surprising, sometimes fascinating, sometimes, like certain unfolding petals, almost repulsive, but always growing, succeeding or failing with their own logic and force.

Mr. Johnson's word magic wears thin only once, with **"Moving Pictures,"** a grouchy diatribe about mass culture that uses the same metaphors for Hollywood that writers intimidated by the movies have used for the better part of a century. But there's no risk in predicting that **"The Education of Mingo," "Exchange Value," "China," "Alethia"** and **"The Sorcerer's Apprentice"** will be anthologized for a very long time. Mr. Johnson's spell of a book comes on with the authority of a classic.

Michael Ventura, "Voodoo and Subtler Powers," in The New York Times Book Review, *March 30, 1986, p. 7.*

Norman Harris (essay date 1989)

[*In the following excerpt, Harris objects to Johnson's phenomenological approach to African-American literature in* Being and Race.]

Charles Johnson's ***Being and Race: Black Writing Since 1970*** is fascinating in its attempt to use phenomenology as a basis to ground African-American literary criticism in experience. He uses Husserl's definition of phenomenology, viewing it as a "philosophy of experience" in which we "set aside all explanatory models for the phenomena we investigate, thereby making possible an intuition of the essence of invariant structures of different forms of experience, specifically in the sciences." For me, Johnson's phenomenology is a false objectivity that has the effect of elevating historical amnesia among critics of African-American literature to a philosophical plane that, quite ironically, relegates the intuited black experience of the author/reader to a position of limited explanatory importance.

In its formulations, rhetoric, and approach, Johnson's book is consistent with varying kinds of formalism (by which I mean critical approaches that mock mimetic modes of criticism in preference for intertextuality and a relentless if casual refutation of the Black Aesthetic) that now enjoy preeminence in African-American literary scholarship. The most striking aspect of Johnson's formulations about the world is that it is somehow possible to be born again. And I choose the phrase "born again" because, to my knowledge, the kind of setting aside of prejudices and stripping away of artifice in order to experience what an artistic product has to offer is not supported by any "science." Indeed, if anything, philosophy and science suggest that being, or reality, is an interminant phenomenon, the meanings of which are contingent on any number of shifting patterns. The epistemology that provides the basis for the experience Johnson wants is simple faith, no more or less profound, or intrinsically preferable to the faith of Black Aesthetic advocates who asserted, among other things, that Black is beautiful.

Johnson's discussion of specific writers is divided by gender, a discussion of men first and women second. Phenomenological differences between African-American women and men writers might be a basis for such a division, but the division is not explained in that way; therefore, discussing men in one chapter and women in another seems more convenient than explanatory. His readings of specific authors are more suggestive than thorough or systematic. When he does go into some detail, as he does with his discussions of Clarence Major and David Bradley, little happens that would help the reader *experience* these writers in a fresh way. Indeed, he seems most intent on illustrating the extent to which these writers stand on the shoulders of their European and Euro-American predecessors.

For African-Americans in general, and African-American artists in particular, preoccupation with form and precedent is generally a prelude to either subtle or overt deracinations of one's own culture. In *Being and Race,* the Black Aesthetic comes in for some heavy body blows. He calls it kitsch, and kitsch is defined this way: "In dread of freedom man pretends that the meanings with which he has endowed the world transcends their creator." African-American political and cultural history is in part based on just such an assumption: the myriad forms that the struggle for self-determination take assume some ultimate right or good (justice) that necessarily transcend the specific form they take at any given point in history. Indeed, this commonplace observation is an accurate aspect of all people's struggle for self-definition and is the epistemological basis or motivator for the works of great women and men.

Although he wrestles with important questions that all people must face, Johnson seems to feel it necessary first to strip himself of his own culture so that he may then see. Maybe he should heed the advice of the heroine in his novel, *Faith and The Good Thing,* and "hook-up" with the Werewitch so that the circle of cultural continuity and development will not be broken. (pp. 307-08)

> *Norman Harris, in a review of "Being and Race: Black Writing Since 1970," in* Modern Fiction Studies, *Vol. 35, No. 2, Summer, 1989, pp. 307-08.*

Thomas Keneally (essay date 1990)

[*In the following excerpt, Keneally contends that the qualities that make* Middle Passage *compelling—its narrative energy and humorous tone—outweigh the novel's tendency towards portentousness.*]

There are problems with Charles Johnson's [*Middle Passage*] that might seem to call forth from a reviewer the old cheap-shot treatment. But the genre switches of *Middle Passage,* from period bodice-ripper to metaphysical drama, are—like every other aspect of this fairly short book—heroic in proportion. There's an endearing and determined recklessness at work here, for Mr. Johnson, who is a professor of English at the University of Washington and the former director of its creative writing program, manages to break with heretic abandon many of the cherished axioms of the writing academies.

Mr. Johnson violates not only the genre-switch rule but Chekhov's "rifle" dictum (that if there's a rifle on the wall, it has to go off before the curtain descends). The assumption that anachronisms are permitted in Elizabethan literature but should be researched out of modern fiction also goes by the board....

All this roughshod riding is achieved with such panache, however, that I wound up wanting to cheer him, even though the scribe in me might disapprove. In fact, I found Mr. Johnson forcing me back to the ultimate question, the one high-toned reviewers are supposed to avoid at any cost: how does the book read? And the answer is: you'll certainly want to go on reading *Middle Passage.*

In the summer of 1830, Rutherford Calhoun, freed slave from Illinois and flamboyantly learned scoundrel, escapes marriage to a cat-loving schoolmarm in New Orleans and hides aboard a slaver called the Republic. Calhoun's former master has given him a humanist education, and his narration of an extraordinary voyage is spiked with 19th-century maritime argot as well as such terms as "velleities," "*haecceitas*" and "*quidditas.*"

The Republic is bound for the Gulf of Guinea to take on African slaves. Rutherford's peculiar position, as a former slave and an American patriot aboard a ship devoted to the enslavement of a fresh set of Africans, provides the lens through which bondage is considered. But Mr. Johnson further enriches this perspective. In the coastal trading post at Bangalang, the tormented dwarf Captain Falcon takes aboard not only a cargo of Allmuseri tribesmen, thought by slavers everywhere to be premium-grade slaves, but also their god. Barely glimpsed and packaged in a crate, the divinity is lowered into the hold. From that point, the Republic seems to the reader to be both massively laden and held together by threads. Mr. Johnson has us by the throat.

Rutherford Calhoun, the manumitted slave, knows how the god unbalances the ship. The Allmuseri are dangerous enough on their own, since they practice an elegant, dancelike form of unarmed combat. And although *they* can be chained and guarded, their many-faced god, packed into an insecure crate, churns in the darkest recesses of the hold like a nuclear reactor on the edge of meltdown.

Middle Passage is a novel in the honorable tradition of *Billy Budd* and *Moby-Dick.* We are often told by the berserk scholar-captain, Falcon, that a ship is "a society, if you get my drift. A commonwealth, Mr. Calhoun." The Republic is therefore also a republic—one with a literal underclass, the Allmuseri, who suck their innate cleverness deeply into themselves in their prison in the bilges. Young Rutherford is torn between loyalty to his white American comrades on deck and his empathy for the pulses of sorrow that emanate from the hold. And this loose federation is likely at any second to be eaten whole, to be reduced to atoms. For the divine force that the mad president of this "commonwealth" has chosen to take aboard is not only vaster than the ship but than the whole damned ocean.

With such a setup, Mr. Johnson's book just about transcends its faults, one of which is a frequent straining for meaning, an unnecessary portentousness. Surely some of the conversations Captain Falcon has with his unwilling confidant, Rutherford, in a cabin booby-trapped in case of mutiny are the fanciest possible ways of expressing the sentiment, "I know slaving's wrong, but it gives me a kick." . . .

The most important device of all, the cosmic rifle that only partly fires, is the Allmuseri deity. When Rutherford Calhoun encounters it, it takes on a form from his past. We are not told that this confrontation with Rutherford slakes the god of his thirst for souls. In fact, it is Rutherford himself who is pretty much extinguished by the meeting. We understand from the aura of threat that Mr. Johnson has managed to build up that the god transcends the elements and is eternal. By contrast, we know from the time we see the slaves being loaded onto the Republic that the ship will ultimately vanish from the tale. And yet, once the Republic does go, the Allmuseri deity is also no longer in the book. In the end, there is a rescue involving a handsome clipper ship, where the tables are glibly turned upon a Creole gangster and slavemonger named Zeringue, whom we first met in the book's opening chapter. But with Zeringue, after being so long in Melville territory, we are back in a neatly whimsical arm of the sea. The cosmic has been supplanted by a variety of nautical sitcom. The question of whether the Allmuseri's enormously powerful god might not come ravening over the gunwales one night is not addressed. The question of how Rutherford can live with himself, having sailed on a slaver and even devoured human meat, seems resolved in the end by an artificial jollity.

Nevertheless, **Middle Passage** is still an engrossing book and—to say it again—one that leaves a reader unsure whether its almost willful failures are not sometimes its very point. This is fiction that hooks into the mind. Above all, it speaks of the legacies and griefs the peculiar institution has brought to the life of the American Republic. (p. 9)

> Thomas Keneally, "Misadventures in the Slave Trade," in The New York Times Book Review, *July 1, 1990, pp. 8-9.*

Joseph Coates (essay date 1990)

[*In the following excerpt, Coates acclaims* Middle Passage *as a highly imaginative work in the tradition of the Great American Novel.*]

Long after we'd stopped believing in the Great American Novel along comes a brief, spellbinding adventure story that may be just that, without being grandiose about it—and from a source where, inexcusably, we seldom look for it: the black experience of America.

Even hearing its author, Charles Johnson, tell how "I've devoted myself to developing a genuinely philosophical black American fiction, which I don't think existed before the work of Jean Toomer, Richard Wright and Ralph Ellison" doesn't quite prepare the reader for what Johnson has accomplished in **Middle Passage** which, he says, "is intended to be serious entertainment, one that

takes black fiction in America into hitherto unexplored regions of our cultural life."

Middle Passage does that, and a lot more. And it's no accident that this tale presents itself as a simple sea-story in its simplest form, " . . . the logbook you [the reader] presently *hold* in your hands," which describes the few months' experience of an Illinois black freedman named Rutherford Calhoun who unwittingly becomes a stowaway aboard the slave clipper Republic.

The first sentence of the first of the log's nine entries (June 14, 1830) should bring the briny scent of another sea story to American noses: "Of all the things that drive men to sea, the most common disaster, I've come to learn, is women." Like Ishmael, Calhoun sees "the watery part of the world" as "the analogue for life," but unlike him he puts polymorphous human sexuality and racism at the center of his story rather than veiling those subjects, as Melville did in *Moby-Dick.*

Middle Passage is both a deliberately brief counter-epic to that oceanic book and a reading of it that shows, among other things, that Ahab's quest for his pale killer whale represents American society's self-destructive obsession with its own dangerous whiteness.

Like Ellison's *Invisible Man,* Johnson's book is less about black experience per se (though it's certainly about that, too) than it is about white blindness to black experience.

Along the way it echoes and partly recapitulates much of the experience of the white Western culture Calhoun so painfully encounters, resonating off everything from Israel's bondage under the Pharaohs (the newly freed Calhoun arrives in New Orleans from southern Illinois—Little Egypt) to the pre-Socratic philosophy of Parmenides to Odysseus' return to Penelope.

Calhoun's Penelope is the prim schoolteacher Isadora Bailey whose "civilizing" intent he went to sea to escape, like Huck Finn fleeing down the big river from Miss Watson. (p. 6)

At the center of the book is Captain Ebenezer Falcon, born in the early hours of the new American nation, "A Faustian man of powerful loves, passions, hatreds: a creature of preposterous, volatile contradictions"—a man of such truly demonic impressiveness that he makes Ahab look like a Rotarian on a Saturday-night fling.

Falcon, a dwarf, is emblematic of the white man's fear that he is the black man's physical inferior; and he assumes that all American blacks he meets are mentally vacant. And in his dealings with Falcon, Calhoun, extensively educated by the guilt-ridden clergyman who inherited him as a slave, shows us how blacks in subordinate positions are forced into feigning the stupidity whites presume they possess.

Falcon's ship is as emblematic as its captain. The Republic "was physically unstable, perpetually flying apart and re-forming during the voyage, falling to pieces beneath us," so that "Falcon's crew spent most of their time literally rebuilding the *Republic* as we crawled along the waves. In a word, she was, from stem to stern, a process."

As for the crew, the "*Republic* was, above all, a ship of men.... [E]veryone felt the pressure, the masculine imperative to prove himself equal to a vague standard of manliness in order to be judged 'regular,'" which led to "a tendency to turn themselves into caricatures of the concept of maleness." ...

Johnson has given us the first real conceptual advance in imagining a true American hero since Saul Bellow's Augie March, who likewise was skeptical of and hostile to other people's definitions of his being.

With Rutherford Calhoun, Johnson transforms Ellison's black victim of white society—who transcends his fate only by an act of will—into a laughing, sensual rogue, fully equipped intellectually, who exults in his difference from white Americans and from the blacks who stereotype themselves in the white image. Calhoun sees the members of both groups as the real slaves—either of bourgeois uptightness or of the rigid code of disreputable maleness that imprisons even those who "light out for the territory" by isolating them from the women who, for Calhoun, make life worth living.

In a marvelous act of the imagination, Johnson has created for us the first really free native American who is not a Native American and who does not have to renounce his citizenship to claim his freedom. (p. 7)

> *Joseph Coates, "Uncharted Waters," in* Chicago Tribune—Books, *July 8, 1990, pp. 6-7.*

George F. Will (essay date 1990)

[*Will is an American educator and columnist whose politically conservative writings are widely syndicated. In the following essay, he argues that* Middle Passage *signals a beneficial change of direction in black fiction and applauds the novel's receipt of the National Book Award.*]

Rutherford Calhoun is one of those rapscallions who have enlivened American literature since Huck Finn decided civilization made him itch and lit out for the territories. Calhoun is a ne'er-do-well who instead of going down a river on a raft, stowed away on a ship to escape the twin horrors of debts and marriage. The ship turned out to be bound for Africa to collect cargo: slaves. And Calhoun is black.

So is his creator, Charles Johnson, who teaches at the University of Washington and has written, without setting out to do so, an emancipation proclamation for black writers. It is his novel *Middle Passage,* winner of the National Book Award. It is an example of triumphant individualism on the part of both Calhoun and Johnson.

Calhoun is a freed slave from southern Illinois whose former master assuaged his guilt by tamping great gobs of learning into Calhoun. Calhoun arrived in New Orleans around 1830 speaking like Spinoza but determined not to be "a credit to his race," a phrase that made him gag. He lived for pleasures, particularly the thrill of theft, until forced to choose either domesticity or punishment by a frightening creditor. Instead, he went to sea, a free black on the crew of a ship bringing slaves to American investors, one of whom was black. Johnson wants you to know that black experiences have been various.

Middle Passage reflects Johnson's years of research in the literature of the sea and the hair-raising facts of slavery. The verisimilitude about the smells, sanitation and diseases aboard ship includes details about the captain, who is a "tight packer" (of slaves; Johnson explains how it was done). When a slave died in transit, the Captain would cut off the ears to verify to the investor that the victim had been aboard.

In opaque remarks opaquely reported, a National Book Award juror suggested that the politics of ideology and ethnic entitlements, a poison in the teaching of literature nowadays, had seeped into the NBA process. But in felicitous remarks made when accepting the award, Johnson made clear what his novel itself makes clear: The "message" of the book is the absence of the sort of "message" that stultifies art.

Johnson noted that he is the first black male to win the award since Ralph Ellison won in 1953 for *Invisible Man.* Ellison's aim, says Johnson, was creation of "a black American personality as complex, as multi-sided and synthetic as the American society that produced it."

A black literature of protest, stressing victimization, appeared about three decades ago. It was, says Johnson, inevitable and important—and limiting. Literature, he says, should be a form of discovery. A writer should not know in advance what, or at least all of what, he is going to say. Literature that is an extension of an ideology, that is didactic to the point of preachiness, lacks the power to change the reader's perceptions as the writer's perceptions change. A serious writer ought to be not only surprising, but himself surprised.

In *Invisible Man* (perhaps the finest American novel since *The Great Gatsby*), Ellison made vivid how blacks are made "invisible" where racial perceptions obliterate perceptions of individuality. That is what white America did to black Americans.

But there is a form of suffocation that blacks can inflict upon themselves. It is to insist on a literature of orthodoxy, a literature of protest which insists on group consciousness. Against this, Ellison was adamant: "Our task is that of making ourselves individuals."

Calhoun learns from his voyage, and especially from his encounter with the dignified but inaccessible (to him) culture of the slaves. He learns that he is a Yankee sailor.

A white crew member tells Calhoun: The slaves, too, are black, but they are not like you. The crew members calls him Illinois, and by the end of the novel Calhoun knows that somewhere in America, perhaps Illinois, is home. The novel is about—quietly about—patriotism.

"If," Calhoun muses, "this weird, upside-down caricature of a country called America, if this land of refugees and former indentured servants, religious heretics and half-breeds, whoresons and fugitives—this cauldron of mongrels from all points of the compass—was all I could rightly call *home,* then aye: I was of it. There, as I lay weakened from bleeding, was where I wanted to be."

Johnson anticipates in the 1990s a black fiction "of increasing intellectual and artistic generosity, one that enables us as a people—as a culture—to move from narrow complaint to broad celebration." I think he means celebration of the possibilities of American individualism. I know that his novel, and the award, are reasons for celebration.

> *George F. Will, "Beyond the Literature of Protest," in* The Washington Post, *December 13, 1990, p. A23.*

Carol Iannone (essay date 1991)

[*In the following excerpt, Iannone criticizes the tone, characterization, and overall structure of* Middle Passage.]

[Charles Johnson] holds the profoundly heterodox belief that black artists should be allowed to write as individuals rather than as "spokesmen for the race." "I find it very difficult to swallow the idea that one individual, black or white, can speak for the experience of 30 million people," he asserts in an interview with the Washington *Post.* "Would anyone ask John Updike to be a spokesman for white America?" Like Ralph Ellison, the first black novelist to win the [National Book Award] (1953), Johnson especially resents the demand that a black writer limit himself to ideological or "protest" novels. He concludes passionately, "All my life, that's what I've fought for, the absolute freedom for the black artist that we extend to the white artist."

The statement is admirable, even courageous, and it is only a pity that *Middle Passage* does not live up to it. Although in some ways a lively and enjoyable book, the novel falls short at least partly *because* it is a deliberate attempt to counter the plight-and-protest school of novel-writing. In place of the numbed, semi-literate, often brutal and inarticulate characters who people such novels, *Middle Passage* is narrated by Rutherford Calhoun, a newly freed slave who is also highly educated and intensely verbal. Upon his arrival in New Orleans, Calhoun falls in with thieves and gamblers and eventually stows away aboard a ship in order to escape from a forced marriage. Once aboard he discovers that the ship, allegorically named the *Republic,* is sailing to Africa to fetch a shipment of slaves, members of the mystical, magical Allmuseri tribe.

Far from being a marginal outsider, Calhoun freely identifies himself with the motley, restless, roaming, exploratory American spirit that the *Republic* embodies; indeed, *Middle Passage* as a whole gleefully embraces the expansive Western tradition, and teems with echoes of Homer, Coleridge, Melville, and Conrad. At the same time, Calhoun must confront the challenge presented by the Allmuseri in their symbolic role as the "Ur-tribe of humanity itself," a people in touch with "the unity of Being everywhere" and thus a countertype to the spirit of Western philosophical dualism.

To describe *Middle Passage* is to begin to suggest some of its shortcomings. As one otherwise admiring reviewer remarked, the characters "sound as if they're all double majors in classics and philosophy." What is more, these characters often seem less important than the ideas or social types they all too obviously express or stand for. It does not take long to surmise, for example, that the reason the captain of the *Republic* is a dwarf is to suggest the stunted humanity implicit in the pure rationalism he represents, the reason he is a homosexual is to suggest its sterility, the reason a pederast to suggest etc., etc. Of course Johnson is hardly the first to deploy physical traits as marks of psychological or spiritual reality, but the reader of *Middle Passage* more often finds himself piecing together an intellectual puzzle than fathoming the depths of human feeling and behavior.

There are other problems, too. Johnson has fashioned a jocular tone for Rutherford Calhoun that is meant to convey his Whitmanesque nature, but the tone works against the tragic revelation that is attempted at the end of the plot. And the book's self-consciously anachronistic quality, which derives from Johnson's deliberate molding of a 19th-century tale to our current social and cultural dilemmas, sometimes produces inadvertently comic effects. Here is the *Republic's* captain denouncing, of all things, affirmative action:

> I believe in *excellence*—an unfashionable thing these days, I know, what with headmasters giving illiterate Negroes degrees because they feel too guilty to fail them, then employers giving that same boy a place in the firm since he's got the degree in hand and saying no will bring a gang of Abolitionists down on their necks.... Eighty percent of the crews on other ships, damn near anywhere in America, are *incompetent,* and all because everyone's ready to lower standards of excellence to make up for slavery, or discrimination, and the problem ... the *problem,* Mr. Calhoun, is, I say, that most of these minorities aren't ready for the titles of quartermaster or first mate precisely because discrimination denied them the training that makes for true excellence.

In short, although much in this novel is engaging, and though Johnson's larger ambitions are noble, it is hard to take his prize-winning book seriously as literature. (pp. 51-2)

Carol Iannone, "Literature by Quota," in Commentary, *Vol. 91, No. 3, March, 1991, pp. 50-3.*

FURTHER READING

Bell, Pearl K. Review of *Faith and the Good Thing,* by Charles Johnson. *The New Leader* LVII, No. 25 (23 December 1974): 11.

Review of *Faith and the Good Thing,* favoring Johnson's conception of black magic over that of author Ishmael Reed. Bell concludes, however, that "Johnson's novel. . . is more often boring than captivating."

Dixon, Melvin. "Mutiny on the Republic." *Book World— The Washington Post* (15 July 1990): 6.

Negative review of *Middle Passage.* Dixon cites Johnson's failure to broaden "our understanding of the elusive past and its presence in contemporary letters the way, say, Toni Morrison's *Beloved* demands a total re-reading of history."

Flick, Arend. "Stowaway on a Ship to Africa." *Los Angeles Times Book Review* (24 June 1990): 1, 7.

Enthusiastically endorses Johnson's fusion of philosophy and art in *Middle Passage.*

Krasny, Michael. "A Black History Tale." *The American Book Review* 6, No. 4 (May-June 1984): 14-15.

Review of *Oxherding Tale.* Krasny finds that Johnson's "mannered prose" obstructs his skills as a storyteller.

McRobbie, Angela. "Hand-Me-Downs." *New Statesman* 106, No. 2751 (9 December 1983): 25-6.

Contends that Johnson's vision of the black experience in *Oxherding Tale* falls short of that of J. M. Coetzee.

Penner, Jonathan. "Magical Mystery Tours." *Book World—The Washington Post* (16 February 1986): 8.

Review of *The Sorcerer's Apprentice.* Penner argues: "Though most of these stories have black protagonists, the author seems interested in black people no more than he is interested in people. Rather, he tends to treat blackness—often ingeniously—as a condition, a state of being, which is already halfway to metaphor."

Phillips, J. J. Review of *The Sorcerer's Apprentice,* by Charles Johnson. *Los Angeles Times Book Review* (30 March 1986): 11.

Describes Johnson's writing in *The Sorcerer's Apprentice* as precise and elegant and offers positive commentary about most of the stories in the collection.

Ross, Michael E. "'Passage' Author Detects New Currents in Modern Black Fiction." *San Francisco Chronicle* (12 August 1990): 1, 12.

Discussion of *Middle Passage,* focusing on Johnson's own prediction for the future of black writing: "I see a greater intellectual and aesthetic generosity. Black writers are getting more and more away from the protest novel."

Skow, John. "Smoky Legend." *Time* 105, No. 1 (6 January 1975): 92.

Mixed review of *Faith and the Good Thing,* finding fault with its philosophical overtones.

Wills, Gary. "The Long Voyage Home." *The New York Review of Books* XXXVIII, Nos. 1 & 2 (17 January 1991): 3.

Review of *Middle Passage.* Wills argues: "It is ironic that Johnson's book won the National Book Award in a panel that was accused, by a judge on it, of choosing ideology over merit. Johnson's merit is as obvious as his opposition to ideological formulas."

Fenton Johnson

1888-1958

American poet, essayist, short story writer, and novelist.

Johnson is recognized as a minor but significant twentieth-century poet and novelist. Writing in the period following the death of fellow black author Paul Laurence Dunbar and before the emergence of black writers Langston Hughes and James Weldon Johnson, Johnson is often overshadowed in critical appraisals of black American literature. Nonetheless, many commentators consider him both a forerunner of the Harlem Renaissance and, as noted by critic Hammett Worthington-Smith, "the foremost Afro-American pioneer of free verse." Although Johnson published three books of poetry—*A Little Dreaming* (1913), *Visions of the Dusk* (1915), and *Songs of the Soil* (1916)—he is best known for only a handful of anthologized poems, most notably "Tired" and "The Scarlet Woman." In these works Johnson portrayed the desolate urban black "trapped inside a dream that is not deferred but dead," according to Shirley Lumpkin. This bitter theme characterizes Johnson's later works and is commonly viewed as the basis for his reputation as a poet.

Johnson's personal life is not well documented. He was born in Chicago in 1888 to Elijah Johnson, a railroad porter, and Jessie Taylor Johnson. The Johnsons owned the building in which they lived and were considered one of the richest black families in Chicago. Johnson attended local schools and later studied at the University of Chicago. According to Arna Bontemps, with whom Johnson maintained a correspondence, he was "a dapper boy who drove his own electric automobile around Chicago." Publishing his first poem, "Absalom's Death," at the age of 12, Johnson went on to publish privately the first of his three volumes of poetry in 1913. For a short time he lived in New York, where he published his second and third books: *Visions of the Dusk* and *Songs of the Soil*. Returning to Chicago in 1916, he edited the *Champion Magazine* and then the *Favorite Magazine,* often contributing his own poems and stories. Around this time he established contact with editor and critic Harriet Monroe and published several poems in *Poetry: A Magazine of Verse* and in the annual anthology *Others.* Unfortunately, Johnson could not keep his magazines afloat, due apparently to a lack of money and the rampant racism existing at the time. After the collapse of his business ventures he moved back to New York and founded the Reconciliation Movement, a group "based on the idea of cooperation among the races," according to Lumpkin. Johnson's radical concept of peaceful coexistence received little welcome, however. Returning to Chicago somewhat dejected, Johnson completed the last of his self-published books, the short story collection *Tales of Darkest America,* in 1920. Although he tried to get a fourth

volume of poetry, *African Nights,* published, he was unsuccessful; some of the poems later appeared in anthologies and have been cited as among his best works. Johnson participated in the Works Progress Administration during the 1930s and produced another collection of poetry, *The Daily Grind: 41 WPA Poems.* The collection remained unpublished at the time of Johnson's death in 1958, but selections from the manuscript later appeared in *American Negro Poetry.*

The poems in Johnson's first published work, *A Little Dreaming,* are written chiefly in a conventional, lyrical style popular during the first decades of the twentieth century. The collection is dominated by romantic motifs but also contains poems about African tradition and common black folk. In the foreword to *A Little Dreaming* Johnson expressed his hope that his "songs" would give readers "sympathy for my people." Accordingly, he included at least three works designed to elicit pathos: "To an Afro-American Maiden," "The Ethiopian's Song," and "Mulatto's Song." Imitating Dunbar, Johnson also wrote poems in Negro dialect: "What Mistah Robin Sais," "Uncle Isham Lies A-Dyin'," "In de Beulahlan'," and "Mah Mammy." Critics regard most of the poems in this volume as negligible, yet two have been given special recognition: "The Vision of Lazarus," written in blank verse, and "The Plaint of the Factory Child." In these poems one glimpses the plaintive style and despairing theme that characterize Johnson's later works.

Encouraged by the reception of *A Little Dreaming,* Johnson published *Visions of the Dusk* in 1915 and *Songs of the Soil* in 1916. In *Visions of the Dusk* Johnson continued to oscillate between what one reviewer, writing in the *Literary World* in 1914, called the "formal cultivated English" and the "corrupted language of the American Negro." He began to favor Negro dialect, however, the more he wrote about black life in America. Two well-recognized dialect poems in this volume are "The Creed of the Slave" and "De Cabin." *Songs of the Soil* was Johnson's last published book of poetry. Johnson considered this volume a departure from his earlier works because here he tossed aside "the English of the Victorians and assume[d] the language of the plantation and levee." Ironically, as Lumpkin noted, at the time Johnson made his decision, "more and more black poets and readers were beginning to consider so-called poetic language restrictive and the dialect representation of blacks degrading." Johnson countered this sentiment by claiming, ". . . unless one gains inspiration from the crudest of his fellows, the greatest of his kind cannot be elevated."

Despite the moderate success of Johnson's books, Johnson himself never gained much recognition until his later poems appeared in anthologies. "Tired," "Children of the Sun," "The New Day," "The Banjo Player," "The Scarlet Woman," and "The Minister"—written sometime between 1917 and the late 1920s—are considered among his best works. These poems, bitter and world-weary, reflect Johnson's own disillusionment with life. In "The Banjo Player," "The Scarlet Woman," and "Tired," Johnson used stark, terse language to describe the urban experiences of blacks. Forsaking the lyrical style of his earlier poems, he frequently wrote in free-verse. According to critic Worthington-Smith, in these poems Johnson explored "the forces in Afro-American life that prevent a human being from realizing his aspirations. . . the social deterrents that thwart the individual's determination to succeed."

Most critics dismiss Johnson's early works as restrictive and traditional. Early commentators—Alice Corbin Henderson, for example—found Johnson's work "commonplace"; a few others, however, notably James Weldon Johnson, praised his use of "formless forms" and his "powerful" portrayal of black urban life. Later critics tended to echo their predecessors. James Hutchinson, writing in 1978, characterized Johnson as "a sentimental lyricist whose poetic output and stylistic contribution were negligible." Most critics agree that Johnson's later "despairing" works are his best. Comparing Johnson's early and late poems, Jean Wagner stated in 1963: "Instantly we pass from the most commonplace traditionalism to the most revolutionary naturalism, from the rhymed, carefully scanned line to free verse, from conventionalized Negro dialect to the brawny language of Sandburg's *Chicago Poems,* and from the confident optimism of Booker T. Washington to disillusionment, bitterness, and cynicism—even to unmitigated despair." While the early works lack the intensity and emotional appeal of his later compositions, Johnson's portrayals of the urban black are considered vivid and startling. Nevertheless, in the minds of most critics Johnson remains a minor poet who responded tardily to the spirit of the times. Thus he spent much of his literary career imitating his contemporaries while just outside his window, burgeoning black voices hammered for his attention.

Johnson's name would have likely disappeared into obscurity had he not written a few memorable poems late in his career. He occupies a modest place in the history of black literature for his portrayals of the black urban experience in the United States. Although he wanted "to impress upon the world that it is not a disgrace to be a Negro, but a privilege," commentators agree that his poems of despair tell another story.

(For further information about Johnson's life and works, see *Black Writers; Contemporary Authors,* Vol. 118; and *Dictionary of Literary Biography,* Vols. 45, 50.)

PRINCIPAL WORKS

A Little Dreaming (poetry) 1913
Visions of the Dusk (poetry) 1915
Songs of the Soil (poetry) 1916
"Tired" (poetry) 1919; published in periodical *Others*
For the Highest Good (essays) 1920
Tales of Darkest America (short stories) 1920
"The Banjo Player" (poetry) 1922; published in *The Book of American Negro Poetry*
"Children of the Sun" (poetry) 1922; published in *The Book of American Negro Poetry*
"The New Day" (poetry) 1922; published in *The Book of American Negro Poetry*
"The Scarlet Woman" (poetry) 1922; published in *The Book of Negro Poetry*
"The Minister" (poetry) 1930; published in *An Anthology of American Poetry: Lyric America, 1630-1930*
"The Daily Grind" (poetry) 1963; published in *American Negro Poetry*
"A Negro Peddler's Song" (poetry) 1963; published in *American Negro Poetry*
"The Old Repair Man" (poetry) 1963; published in *American Negro Poetry*
"The World Is a Mighty Ogre" (poetry) 1963; published in *American Negro Poetry*

Alice Corbin Henderson (essay date 1917)

[An anthologist, critic, and poet, Henderson was also associate editor and cofounder, with Harriet Monroe, of Poetry: A Magazine of Verse. *She regarded folk songs and poems as important sources of inspiration for writers who aimed to create a distinctly American literary tradition. In the following review of* Songs of the Soil, *she analyzes Johnson's use of Negro dialect in his poetry.]*

Although indirectly, the negro has contributed not a little to certain developments of American art, particularly in music, musical shows and folk-stories. But he has himself benefited very little, or been very little concerned individually with the achievements that bear the imprint of his race. The reason is not far to seek. As soon as the negro is educated he begins to think the white man's thoughts, or to try to think them; it is impossible for him to do otherwise. But his emotional reactions, his religious feeling and his imagination are racially different from those of the white man, and if his art is to amount to anything he will have to seek to give expression to what is essentially his. But the negro poet has almost invariably echoed the white man's thought, the white man's vision of the negro. He has projected no new vision of himself. Paul Lawrence Dunbar followed in the foot-steps of Thomas Nelson Page and Joel Chandler Harris, and other white men who used the negro dialect and portrayed the negro character; and succeeding negro poets have followed Dunbar. Usually, when the negro poet discards dialect for plain English, his language is pale and academic, and his thought, again, is not his own but a weak dilution of some already diluted European model. Although this book language is pale and anæmic beside the rich and colored oral expression of the negro race, I do not mean to say that the negro poet should write exclusively in dialect. What I mean to say is that he should discard this prop and invent a new and individual idiom based upon the characteristic speech of his people. And I would also recommend that all negro poets make a study of their folk-songs, collecting all they can, for it is through such songs that they will learn to know their own race.

This little book by Fenton Johnson [*Songs of the Soil*] furnishes substance and text for the foregoing remarks. The poems in dialect are mostly commonplace, but the "Negro Spirituals," written in the spirit of the genuine negro hymns and plantation folksongs (not in dialect), have in them the germ of future development. Here is one of them called "**The Lonely Mother**":

> Oh, my mother's moaning by the river,
> My poor mother's moaning by the river,
> For her son who walks the earth in sorrow.
> Long my mother's moaned beside the river,
> And her tears have filled an angel's pitcher.
> "Lord of Heaven, bring to me my honey,
> Bring to me the darling of my bosom,
> For a lonely mother by the river."
>
> Cease, O mother, moaning by the river,
> Cease, good mother, moaning by the river;

> I have seen the star of Michael shining,
> Michael shining at the Gates of Morning;
> Row, O mighty Angel, down the twilight,
> Row until I find a lonely woman,
> Swaying long beneath a tree of cypress,
> Swaying for her son who walks in sorrow.

Other interesting poems are "**John Crossed the Island on His Knees**"; "**God Be With You**"; "**Shout, My Brother, Shout**"; and "**Lif' Up de Spade**." This last poem would be improved if it were not written in dialect, but in English like the "Spirituals." This is true also of some of the other poems in the book which seem to have a good deal of the folk feeling, but disguised rather than helped by the dialect which has come to be commonplace and banal. (pp 159-60)

> *Alice Corbin Henderson, "Poetry of the American Negro," in* Poetry, *Vol. X, No. 3, June, 1917, pp. 158-60.*

Fenton Johnson (essay date 1920)

[In the following essay, "The Story of Myself," originally published in 1920 in Tales of Darkest America, *Johnson recounts his struggle to be a successful writer.]*

I have gone through the Valley of Despair groping for the light that would aid humanity and caring little for the means of obtaining sustenance. I have borne the taunt of being an idealist but somehow I enjoyed idealism since it was fire and food for humanity.

I struggled through school and through the university, my star the star of the Muse and my hope the opportunity to follow the star of the Muse. When my school days had faded I went South to teach those of the race to which I belong and after a year of abject poverty, not even receiving my meagre salary of forty dollars a month, I returned to Chicago and struggled to obtain a foothold in literature.

It seemed to me like trying to walk the Atlantic ocean to obtain recognition in the literary world and especially when one was attempting to present the life of the race to which I belong. After what seemed to be a hopeless struggle a woman of infinite kindness and sympathy gave my first collection of poetry the material form of a book called *A Little Dreaming,* which brought me recognition from that very good friend of literature, Dr. Albert Shaw, Editor of the American Review of Reviews, and his remarkable literary critic, Jeanne Robert Foster.

I moved to New York and through the kindness of another I attended the Pulitzer School of Journalism at Columbia University and published privately two new volumes of verse, *Visions of the Dusk* and *Songs of the Soil.* Both met with very enthusiastic reviews on the part of the press, and resulted in my return to Chicago and the beginning of my struggle in journalism.

It was during the memorable struggle at Argonne Forest that I founded *The Favorite Magazine.* I had nothing save a meagre allowance from a relative but I was determined to have a magazine and conceived the idea that I could accomplish a large number of reforms and the creation of a new literature through a magazine of my own. I went without meals and postponed paying room rent until I had saved ten dollars and went to a printer whose heart was very large and paid the ten dollars as a deposit on my first issue.

Then I took a dummy and went among my friends and solicited advertisements. At night and during spare moments I wrote the material for the issue and followed that custom until recently. In addition to that I exhausted all the names in the English language for non de plumes to go on the different articles, short stories and poems I wrote for *The Favorite Magazine.*

It was about that time that I met the woman of my dreams and when one meets the woman of his dreams he marries that woman despite the obstacles that might lie in his path. Although I had a magazine that had nothing but determination and imagination to back it and seventy dollars a month to live on, I married. It was not long after that I had nothing but the seventy dollars to support myself and my wife because *The Favorite Magazine* died with everybody recognizing its death but myself and my friend, James H. Moody, who had been with me from the beginning of the struggle.

It seemed to me as if I was about to face the bankruptcy court because I had a nine hundred dollar debt staring me in the face and no means of liquidating it. Everybody including my family turned a deaf ear to my pleas to save *The Favorite Magazine,* although there came appeals from many throughout the country that the magazine should be continued.

An aunt died during those dark days of mine and although her death is one I have mourned a long time I inherited a small sum from her and the name of it saved the magazine and saved me from bankruptcy. Mr. Moody and I renewed our campaign for advertisements and subscriptions and the same kind printer brought out the new *Favorite Magazine.*

I worked as hard as ever and struggled in every way to obtain funds for the purpose of meeting the deficit. One incident I can never forget as long as I live and that is the case of Conkling, Price, Webb & Company, a bonding firm that refused me surety bonds to draw from my aunt's estate so that I could save the magazine from an impending refusal on the part of the poorly paid printer. The only cause given me was "that colored people's estates were too risky."

After that the struggle was more intense than ever. I had no funds to develop a very young proposition and no means of obtaining funds. I was confronted also by the wave of radicalism that was trying to engulf the race to which I belong, but I refused to sell my soul to the agitators of Bolshevism and brought unpopularity to the magazine among a certain class.

When the estate was settled I made a journey to New York and after a speech on "The Co-operation of the Races" I founded The Reconciliation Movement. I used all the money I had in developing this movement which was to me not only the solution of the race problem but also the problem of law and order.

It has been dark days trying to make The Reconciliation Movement successful in a country that until this moment seems to care little for any movement of that sort. No one but myself and James Moody knows the suffering that I have undergone and how near I am to what all of us dread, starvation.

As I write this in the little furnished room that my wife and I call home, I wonder if the Reconciliation Movement is not a grand dream, *The Favorite Magazine* a foolhardy venture and I, myself a failure. I wonder if I was wise in trying to follow the star of the Muse in America or if I should have gone to England or even Paris and cast my lot where I would not have had to climb over the barrier of race.

I know that I am facing ruin and starvation. I know that my dream of a magazine is about to end in the cold gray awakening because of the heavy debt hanging over it and the lack of desire Americans seem to have for the reconciliation of the races. I know that my dream of success in literature is fading because every story I have ever offered a standard magazine has returned to my desk and even in the case of the *Saturday Evening Post,* one story, **"The White Slave,"** returned the day after it was sent.

I have one consolation; and that is that I have lived for the highest good and that I have injured no man, woman or child. All I pray for is that my wife and James Moody will not suffer if this struggle should end in my passing to the other world. (pp. 5-8)

> *Fenton Johnson, "The Story of Myself," in his* Tales of Darkest America, The Favorite Magazine, *1920, pp. 5-8.*

Fenton Johnson (essay date 1927)

[*In the essay below, originally published in Countee Cullen's 1927 collection* Caroling Dusk: An Anthology of Verse by Negro Poets, *Johnson offers a brief autobiography, focusing on the development of his literary career.*]

I came into the world May 7, 1888. No notice was taken of the event save in immediate circles. I presume the world was too busy or preoccupied to note it. It happened in Chicago. I went to school and also college. My scholastic record never attained me any notoriety.

Taught school one year and repented. Having scribbled since the age of nine, had some plays produced on the stage of the old Pekin Theatre, Chicago, at the time I was nineteen. When I was twenty-four my first volume *A Little Dreaming* was published. Since then *Visions of the Dusk* (1915) and *Songs of the Soil* (1916) represent my own collections of my work. Also published a volume of short stories *Tales of Darkest America* and a group of essays on American politics *For the Highest Good.* Work in poetry appears in the following anthologies: *The New Poetry* (Monroe and Henderson), *Victory* (Braithwaite), *Others* (Kreymborg), *The Chicago Anthology* (Blanden), *Anthology of Magazine Verse* (Braithwaite), *Poetry by American Negroes* (White and Jackson), *Negro Poets and their Poetry* (Kerlin), *Poets of America* (Wood), *Book of American Negro Poetry* (J. W. Johnson), *Today's Poetry* (Crawford and O'Neil) and others.

Edited two or three magazines and published one or two of them myself.

My complete autobiography I promise to the world when I am able to realize that I have done something. (pp. 61-2)

> *Fenton Johnson, "Fenton Johnson," in* Caroling Dusk: An Anthology of Verse by Negro Poets, *edited by Countee Cullen, Harper & Row, Publishers, 1927, pp. 61-4.*

James Weldon Johnson (essay date 1931)

[*Johnson was an American poet, novelist, social critic, newspaper editor, lawyer, diplomat, and Broadway songwriter. In the following excerpt from the 1931 revision of his celebrated critical anthology* The Book of American Negro Poetry, *he describes Johnson's poetry as revolutionary in both form and content.*]

[Fenton Johnson] was one of the first Negro revolutionary poets. His earliest work was cast in conventional molds, and with the exception of **"The Vision of Lazarus,"** a poem in blank verse of nearly three hundred lines which closes *A Little Dreaming,* this first volume was without marked distinction. In the same volume a number of the poems were in dialect, but in the war period he broke away from all traditions and ideas of Negro poetry, in both dialect and literary English. Moreover, he disregarded the accepted poetic forms, subjects, and language, adopted free verse, and in that formless form wrote poetry in which he voiced the disillusionment and bitterness of feeling the Negro race was then experiencing. In some of this poetry he went further than protests against wrong or the moral challenges that the wronged can always fling against the wrongdoer; he sounded the note of fatalistic despair. It was his poetry written in this key that brought him recognition. The central idea of this poetry was startling. Doubtless its effect was in some degree due to the fact that it was an idea so foreign to any philosophy of life the Negro in America had ever preached or practiced. Fenton Johnson is the only Negro poet who has ever sounded this precise note. McKay came closer to it than

any of the others in "If We Must Die." There he calls on his brothers to make a last fight, but even so, it is a fight he calls for. W. E. Burghardt Du Bois closes the caustic "A Litany of Atlanta" on a note of faith. After a poem like **"Tired"** there is nothing left to fight or even hope for. Yet, as can be plainly seen, these poems of despair possess tremendous power and do constitute Fenton Johnson's best work.

It is also a fact that Johnson belongs in that group of American poets who in the middle of the second decade of the century threw over the traditions of American poetry and became the makers of the "new" poetry. (pp. 140-41)

> *James Weldon Johnson, "Fenton Johnson," in* The Book of American Negro Poetry, *edited by James Weldon Johnson, revised edition, Harcourt Brace Jovanovich, Inc., 1931, pp. 140-46.*

Robert T. Kerlin (essay date 1935)

[*In the following excerpt from the second (1935) edition of his* Negro Poets and Their Poems, *Kerlin characterizes Johnson as a "prophet" of his people.*]

Dreams and visions—such are the treasures of suffering loyal hearts: dreams, visions, and song. Happy even in their sorrows the people to whom God has given poets to be their spokesmen to the world. Else their hearts should stifle with woe. As the prophet was of old so in these times the poet. As a prophet speaks Fenton Johnson, his heart yearning toward the black folk of our land:

"These Are My People"

These are my people, I have built for them
A castle in the cloister of my heart;
And I shall fight that they may dwell therein.
The God that gave Sojourner tongue of fire
Has made with me a righteous covenant
That these, my brothers of the dusk, shall rise
To Sinai and thence in purple walk
A newer Canaan, vineyards of the West.
The rods that chasten us shall break as straw
And fire consume the godless in the South;
The hand that struck the helpless of my race
Shall wither as a leaf in drear November,
And liberty, the nectar God has blest,
Shall flow as free as wine in Babylon.
O God of Covenants, forget us not!

Fenton Johnson seems to be more deeply rooted in the song-traditions of his people than are most of his fellow-poets. To him the classic Spirituals afford inspiration and pattern. Whoever is familiar with those "canticles of love and woe" will recognize their influence throughout Mr. Johnson's three volumes of song. I shall make no attempt here to illustrate this truth but shall rather select a piece or two that will represent the poet's general qualities. Other poems more typical of him as a melodist could be found but these have special traits that commend them for this place.

"The Plaint Of The Factory Child"

Mother, must I work all day?
All the day? Ay, all the day?
Must my little hands be torn?
And my heart bleed, all forlorn?
I am but a child of five,
And the street is all alive
With the tops and balls and toys,—
Pretty tops and balls and toys.

Day in, day out, I toil—toil!
And all that I know is toil;
Never laugh as others do,
Never cry as others do,
Never see the stars at night,
Nor the golden glow of sunlight,—
And all for but a silver coin,—
Just a worthless silver coin.

Would that death might come to me!
That blessed death might come to me,
And lead me to waters cool,
Lying in a tranquil pool,
Up there where the angels sing,
And the ivy tendrils cling
To the land of play and song,
Fairy land of play and song.

"The Mulatto's Song"

Die, you vain but sweet desires!
Die, you living, burning fires!
I am like a Prince of France,—
Like a prince whose noble sires
Have been robbed of heritage;
I am phantom derelict,
Drifting on a flaming sea.

Everywhere I go, I strive,
Vainly strive for greater things;
Daisies die, and stars are cold,
And canary never sings;
Where I go they mock my name,
Never grant me liberty,
Chance to breathe and chance to do.

"The Vision of Lazarus," contained in *A Little Dreaming,* is a blank-verse poem of about three-hundred lines, original, well-sustained, imaginative, and deeply impressive. (pp. 99-102)

> Robert T. Kerlin, "The Present Renaissance of the Negro," in his Negro Poets and Their Poems, *revised edition, Associated Publishers, Inc., 1935, pp. 51-138.*

Sterling Brown (essay date 1937)

[*Brown was an eminent authority on black literature and an accomplished poet, folklorist, and educator. Noted for his pessimistic realism, he is credited with beginning a new era in black poetry by rejecting the artificial sentimentality of dialect poetry in favor of realistic examples of black folk life and language. In the following excerpt from his 1937 study* Negro Poetry and Drama and the Negro in American Fiction, *he explores underlying themes and motives in Johnson's poetry.*]

Fenton Johnson's works show the two extremes of Negro poetry after 1914. Some of his poems are conventional in form and substance; others, patterned upon his fellow Chicagoan, Sandburg, are striking departures in Negro poetry. With Sandburg's technique and Edgar Lee Masters' outlook, Johnson included in *African Nights* snapshots of bitter experience such as **"Aunt Hanna Jackson"**, **"The Banjo-Player"**, **"The Minister"**, **"The Scarlet Woman"** and **"Tired."** Unfortunately Johnson, like so many of his Negro contemporaries, fell silent shortly after these poems. Perhaps there was little audience for their pessimism, either within a race whose optimism is proverbial, or without, where the Negro's brooding over his lot is generally unwelcome. **"The Scarlet Woman"**, educated for more than a white man's kitchen, is driven by poverty to streetwalking, and gin is her only way of forgetfulness. **"Tired"** indicts civilization:

> I am tired of building up somebody else's civilization . . . . let the old shanty go to rot, the white people's clothes turn to dust, and the Calvary Baptist Church sink to the bottomless pit. . . .
> Throw the children into the river; civilization has given us too many.

Negro "leaders" who direct the race into optimism, condemned this view of life, but it is tonic after such frequent insistence on "a good time coming bye and bye." Like so many modern poets, Fenton Johnson held to the words of Thomas Hardy that

> If way to the better there be, it exacts a full look at the worst.

(pp. 61-2)

> Sterling Brown, "Contemporary Negro Poetry (1914-1936)," in his Negro Poetry and Drama and the Negro in American Fiction, *Atheneum, 1969, pp. 60-81.*

J. Saunders Redding (essay date 1939)

[*Redding was a distinguished American critic, historian, novelist, and autobiographer. His first book,* To Make a Poet Black (1939), *is a scholarly appraisal of black poetry and is considered a landmark in criticism of black writers. In the following excerpt from this work, he briefly compares Johnson's poetry to works by Langston Hughes and James Weldon Johnson.*]

The years from 1903 to 1917 mark a gap in the continuity of creative drive and purpose in the works of those Negro writers whose talents earned them the hearing of the general public. This can be accounted for in only one way: during the intense struggle between liberal and conservative the Negro was taking stock, weighing opinions, and awaiting with bated breath the collapse of the gates through which he could pass into his creative freedom. In general the Negro felt that the larger public of white America was not ready for the new ideas, was not prepared to accept the new Negro he felt he had become. Here and there attempts were made to hasten the day of enlightenment, but they were as forewarning sparks of a general conflagration. Three volumes *A Little Dreaming, Visions of the Dusk,* and *Songs of the Soil,* by Fenton Johnson are of this nature.

It is probably through Fenton Johnson that the influence of the midwestern poets, Lindsay, Sandburg, and Masters, first touched Negro writers. Johnson himself was born and educated in Chicago. Like the white Chicago group, he contributed to *Others* and to *Poetry, A Magazine of Verse.* Like them, too, he wrote free verse on subjects that were the particular grist of the poets of the Chicago "golden era." He wrote of frustrated hopes, "the easiest way," of streetwalkers, ditchdiggers, saloon roustabouts.

> Once I was good like the Virgin Mary and the
>   minister's wife.
> My father worked for Mr. Pullman and white
>   people's tips;
> But he died two days after his insurance expired.
> I had nothing, so I had to go to work.
> All the stock I had was a white girl's education
>   and a face that enchanted the men of both
>   races.
> Starvation danced with me.
> So when Big Lizzie, who kept a house for white
>   men, came to me with tales of fortune that I
>   could reap from the sale of my virtue I bowed
>   my head to Vice.
> Now I can drink more gin than any man for miles
>   around.
> Gin is better than all the water in Lethe.

The similarity of some of the pieces of Langston Hughes to certain of Johnson's is striking, but the point must not be labored, for in general they differ widely. Essentially, Johnson was a despairing poet, stuffed with the bitterness of Du Bois. The attitude of despair, common among the early "New Negroes," in Johnson's case is ineffectually sustained. The lines,

> Throw the children into the river; civilization has
>   given us too many of them. It is better to die
>   than it is to grow up and find out you're
>   colored,

are supported neither by strong emotion nor apt expression. They are false to the emotion of despair as the Negro feels it, and run counter to an essential quality of spirit. Johnson was more nearly race-expressive when he wrote:

> We are the star-dust folk,
>   Striving folk!
> Sorrow songs have lulled to rest
> Seething passions wrought through wrongs,
> Led us where the moon rays dip
> In the night of dull despair,
> Showed us where the star-gleams shine.

But Fenton Johnson's poetry, like James Weldon Johnson's novel, *The Autobiography of an Ex-Colored Man,* foreran its time. The reception accorded these men as writers of Negro literature of a serious vein was more than cool: it was downright freezing. That their failure to arouse interest was not due to any lack of creative talent is proved by the fact that both of them published pieces of considerable merit in first-rate literary journals of the day, and by the inclusion of some of their early work in recent anthologies. It was theme and spirit with which America would have nothing to do. (pp. 85-8)

> *J. Saunders Redding, "Adjustment," in his*
> To Make a Poet Black, *1939. Reprint by*
> *McGrath Publishing Company, 1968, pp. 49-*
> *92.*

Jean Wagner (essay date 1962)

[*A French author and critic, Wagner is an authority on the works of black and Southern writers of the United States. In the following excerpt from his* Les poètes nègres des États-Unis *(1962;* Black Poets of the United States, *1973), he briefly analyzes Johnson's early and later literary styles.*]

[Among the minor poets] Fenton Johnson is assuredly the most interesting.... [He wrote] familiar, sentimental pieces in Dunbar's manner, with no lack of backward glances, expressed in dialect, at the wonderful old-time plantation. His first book, *A Little Dreaming* (1913), contains the customary Scottish poem and Irish poem, even a Yiddish poem, thus making abundantly clear the sources of his inspiration. But in *Visions of the Dusk* (1915) and *Songs of the Soil* (1916), certain attempts, such as his spirituals, show that he has already reached an awareness of the cultural past of his race. "The Negro has a history," he declares, "and is something more than a peasant." This feeling for history manifests itself most distinctly in **"Ethiopia,"** which celebrates the past grandeur of African civilizations and gives vent to his impatient longing that the time of their resurrection may come:

> Thy hour! Thy hour! Oh when shall come thy
>   hour?

His reputation today depends not on his first three volumes, however, but on the fragments of his later work that have been published. These place Fenton Johnson among the poets who, toward the middle of the twentieth century's second decade, participated in the making of America's New Poetry. The poems that made known Fenton Johnson's new manner appeared in *Poetry* and subsequently in the anthologies *Others* (1916, 1917, 1920), compiled by Alfred Kreymborg, with whom Johnson was friendly, and later in *The Liberator.* Instantly we pass from the most commonplace traditionalism to the most revolutionary naturalism, from the rhymed, carefully scanned line to free verse, from conventionalized Negro dialect to the brawny language of Sandburg's *Chicago Poems,* and from the confident optimism of Booker T. Washington to disillusionment, bitterness, and cynicism—even to unmitigated despair. **"The Scarlet Woman"** pillories society and its injustices, which it holds to be responsible for the degradation of a girl who had been "good like the Virgin Mary and the Minister's wife":

> My father worked for Mr. Pullman and white
>   people's tips; but he died two days after his
>   insurance expired.
> I had nothing, so I had to go to work.
> All the stock I had was a white girl's education
>   and a face that enchanted the men of both
>   races.

She ends up as a prostitute, seeking forgetfulness in gin. Obliquely, this poem reaches out beyond the protests of a Du Bois. It tends to show how barren the hope is that education might one day contribute to the advancement of the race. The truth, as Fenton Johnson sees it, is that America has no place for a young black girl who has finished her schooling. Her education does not enable her to escape the fate of her less privileged sisters; she must choose between two forms of slavery, the lot of the proletarian or that of the prostitute. No less doomed are the hopes placed in the education of Negro ministers, for the churches are aiming not at the spiritual elevation of the masses but at monetary returns. This is the message of **"The Minister,"** a poem in which Johnson voices the same criticism as his compatriot Sandburg who, in "To a Contemporary Bunkshooter," was denouncing at almost the same time religion's profiteers:

> I mastered pastoral theology, the Greek of the
>   Apostles, and all the difficult subjects in a
>   minister's curriculum.
> I was as learned as any in this country when the
>   Bishop ordained me.
> And I went to preside over Mount Moriah, largest
>   flock in the Conference.
> I preached the Word as I felt it, I visited the sick
>   and dying and comforted the afflicted in spirit.
> I loved my work because I loved my God.
> But I have lost my charge to Sam Jenkins, who
>   has not been to school four years in his life.
> I lost my charge because I could not make my
>   congregation shout. And my dollar money was
>   small, very small.
> Sam Jenkins can tear a Bible to tatters and the
>   congregation destroys the pews with their
>   shouting and stamping.
> Sam Jenkins leads in the gift of raising dollar
>   money.
> Such is religion.

It seems possible to detect, in these poems on the pointlessness of education, an echo of Fenton Johnson's own disappointment, for his financial well-being was never so uncertain as after his period of study at the University of Chicago. He had paid for the publication of his first three volumes of poems but was unable to bring out the next, which was to have been called *African Nights.* It would have included those poems which establish him as a notable figure in the Negro literary movement of the time. This judgment is confirmed by the unpublished poem **"Others,"** written at a

later date, when he was enjoying the support of the Federal Writers' Project:

> We are Others, the great Forgotten, the scoffed at,
>   the scum of the publishing houses;
>   . . . .
> We have never known royalties and we will never
>   know royalties; but empty pockets
> Will haunt us as the raven and tobacco cheer us as
>   wine does a Wall Street royalist.
> We are not respectable . . . .

Fenton Johnson must remain, ultimately, the poet of utter despair, the despair that engulfs one when every value has crumbled and all struggle has become useless. It is expressed to perfection in **"Tired,"** his most frequently cited poem:

> I am tired of work; I am tired of building up
>   somebody else's civilization.
> Let us take a rest, M'lissy Jane.
> I will go down to the Last Chance Saloon, drink a
>   gallon or two of gin, shoot a game or two of
>   dice and sleep the rest of the night on one of
>   Mike's barrels.
> You will let the old shanty go to rot, the white
>   people's clothes turn to dust, and the Calvary
>   Baptist Church sink to the bottomless pit.
> You will spend your days forgetting you married
>   me and your nights hunting the warm gin Mike
>   serves the ladies in the rear of the Last Chance
>   Saloon.
> Throw the children into the river; civilization has
>   given us too many. It is better to die than it is
>   to grow up and find out that you are colored.
> Pluck the stars out of the heavens. The stars mark
>   our destiny. The stars marked my destiny.
> I am tired of civilization.

This cry of despair, uttered by Fenton Johnson at a time when the Negro Renaissance had not yet begun, is unique in the whole body of black poetry. Its depths will not be plumbed again, even in the most dreadful days of the 1929 Depression. (pp. 179-83)

> *Jean Wagner, "The Negro Renaissance," in his* Black Poets of the United States: From Paul Laurence Dunbar to Langston Hughes, *translated by Kenneth Douglas, University of Illinois Press, 1973, pp. 149-94.*

James P. Hutchinson (essay date 1976)

[*In the following essay, Hutchinson offers a negative assessment of Johnson's poetic canon.*]

Fenton Johnson is remembered, if at all, for the no more than fifteen poems which are repeatedly anthologized in collections of Negro verse. These poems, mostly vignettes of Negro urban life, are products of his later work and are not characteristic of his highly stylized and sentimental early verse. An overview of his poetry and a glance at the volume of his short stories should reveal that themes in the later poems are the exception rather than the rule in Johnson's poetry.

Johnson's output was not prodigious. All of his writing was completed by the 1930's even though he lived until 1958. The publications are: *A Little Dreaming,* 1913; *Visions of the Dusk,* 1915; *Songs of the Soil,* 1916; *The Daily Grind: 41 WPA Poems,* 1963 (posthumous); *Tales of Darkest America,* 1920 (short stories); and, *For the Highest Good,* 1920 (essays). As can be seen from the dates of publication, Johnson exhausted his well-spring of inspiration quite early (he was born in 1888). Judging from the paucity of critical comment on the few poems worth considering there must not have been too much of significance in that well-spring at all.

Four reputable commentators on Johnson's poetry give the fundamental critical climate in which his verse is presently found. Robert T. Kerlin, in *Negro Poets and Their Poems,* 1935, sees Johnson's poetry as "deeply rooted in the song-traditions of his people" [see excerpt dated 1935]. James Weldon Johnson, in the 'Preface' to his *The Book of American Negro Poetry,* 1931, devotes one sentence to Johnson and asserts that he is an "ultra-modern" who promises more than he has yet produced. In *To Make a Poet Black,* 1939, J. Saunders Redding views Johnson as a poet of despair and as the earliest recorder of the Negro in the city [see excerpt dated 1939]. Finally, Robert Hayden, in the 1967 anthology *Kaleidoscope: Poems by American Negro Poets,* labels Johnson's early poems as "downright amateurish." There is, obviously, little critical substance treating Fenton Johnson's poetry. This fact surely results from the large amount of negligible poetry in the body of Johnson's work.

From the first volume of poetry *(A Little Dreaming)* to the later poems of urban Negro life, Johnson was a lyricist. Most of the poems in *A Little Dreaming* (fifty-nine poems) drip with saccharine artificiality. Johnson evidently began writing imitatively, shackling himself to the banal style and emotional content of the worst English poets of the sixteenth and seventeenth centuries. Nowhere in this collection is a unique and singular poem to be found. The language is archaically and traditionally that of the stylized, sentimental lyric. In only one poem, **"The Plaint of the Factory Child,"** is Johnson's urban background (his rearing and education in Chicago) portrayed. Three dialect poems freshen the stale, abstract atmosphere of the volume: **"What Mistah Robin Sais," "Uncle Isham Lies A-Dyin'," and "In de Beulahlan'."** Johnson is convincing but ridiculously 'White' in the two poems in Scottish dialect, **"Kathleen"** and **"When I Speak of Jamie."** It is evident, then, that in *A Little Dreaming* Johnson sacrifices his own experience and tradition for that line of disembodied, sentimental and lyric verse written in a style which deservedly became outmoded by the end of the third quarter of the nineteenth century.

In the second volume of verse, *Visions of the Dusk,* which contains sixty-two poems, Johnson exchanges the lyric tradition for the Negro dialect tradition. None of the poems in this collection has, to the best of my knowledge, been anthologized. However, *Visions of the Dusk* is much better poetry than that in the first volume of verse. The poetry is still sentimental in tone but the subject matter is largely the portrayal of Negro life in America. In **"Prelude,"** the opening poem, Johnson observes that "The native strain alone is poetry." He then asks that the reader "come with me" and "hear the mother-croon of far-away,/ The dying note of Georgia lullaby." This "mother-croon" is sounded in such successful dialect poems as **"De Cabin," "De Ol' Home," "Long de Cool O'Night," "Fiddlah Ike," "De Chu'ch," "De Mule,"** and **"Washin' Day."** In general, the poems of this volume are stylistically imitative of the hymns and spirituals of the Negro. The rhythm is very melodic and most lines are tetrameter, thus recalling the structure of Protestant hymns upon which many of Emily Dickinson's poems are patterned. The longest poem in the collection, **"Ethiopia,"** is a free verse treatment of the tradition of bondage which the dark-skinned races have experienced. At the end of this poem Johnson indicates:

> And thus I sing the song of Ethiop
> Though I am dwelling in a stranger's land,
> A lonely minstrel, born to serve and love
> Throughout the world his fellows of the dusk.

Although he had published two volumes of poetry by 1916, Fenton Johnson had not sounded a noteworthy or unique note in either the theme or the style of his work.

Johnson's innovative theme of the Negro in the city began to appear in his 1920 collection of six short stories, *Tales of Darkest America.* There is nothing very memorable, however, in the volume except the presence of the urban settings. The stories are, like nearly all the poems, in simple language. There is almost no external concrete description; rather, Johnson focuses upon individuals in one specific situation. The most memorable sketch, **"A Woman of Good Cheer,"** succeeds because it treats the discrepancy between the uncomplicated life of the rural Negro and the destruction apparent in the urban experience of Blacks. This latter theme is, fortunately, the subject of most of Johnson's poems written after the publication of *A Little Dreaming* and *Visions of the Dusk.*

If fifteen poems by Johnson had to be chosen as memorable, I would list these, twelve of which are his later poems: **"The Creed of the Slave," "Ethiopia," "De Cabin," "Tired," "The Minister," "The Banjo Player," "The Scarlet Woman," "The Daily Grind," "The World is a Mighty Ogre," "A Negro Peddler's Song," "The Old Repair Man," "Rulers," "Aunt Jane Allen," "The New Day,"** and **"Children of the Sun."** The first three poems are from *Visions of the Dusk,* and, with the exception of the extended **"Ethiopia,"** are short dialect poems. **"The Minister," "The Banjo Player,"** and **"The Old Repair Man"** are the later products of a more sophisticated poet, although the subject matter is still concerned with the rural Negro and his viewpoint. **"The World is a Mighty Ogre"** is reminiscent of the Johnson in *Visions of the Dusk;* also revealing this very similarity are **"The New Day"** and **"Children of the Sun." "A Negro**

Peddler's Song" continues Johnson's interest in melodic verse. **"The Daily Grind," "Rulers,"** and **"Aunt Jane Allen"** transfer Johnson's treatment of Negro life to the city, and in **"Tired"** and **"The Scarlet Woman"** Johnson nihilistically portrays the destructive impact of this urban experience upon the Negro.

Johnson is presently characterized by and primarily remembered for **"Tired"** and **"The Scarlet Woman."** However, these two poems are, as has been seen, not typical of Johnson's body of poetry. The reason for their critical popularity seems to be both their divergence from the body of Johnson's insipid poetry and their true ring of emotion and theme. Had Johnson continued to publish poetry after the 1930's he probably would have written more of this bitter type of poetry. Although these latter poems were beginning to deal with the urban Negro's life they cannot be viewed as typical of Fenton Johnson's poetry. To do so is to engage in critical distortion. In general, Johnson must be characterized as a sentimental lyricist whose poetic output and stylistic contribution were negligible. Until a search through Johnson's unpublished material at Fisk University reveals more poetry in the vein of **"Tired"** and **"The Scarlet Woman,"** this view of his poetic voice must prevail. Fenton Johnson seems to be fated to the portrayal of himself in **"When April Comes"** from *Visions of the Dusk:*

> Oh, heavy is this life of mine,
> And I, a broken reed 'mongst men.
> I lived a plaintive melody,
> Unsung, unloved, unknown, unwept.

At present the critical world can only advance the opinion that Fenton Johnson was a poet who could have been noteworthy; instead, he failed in his poetry to harvest fully that significant crop of the earliest Negro experience in the migration to America's cities. (pp. 14-15)

> *James P. Hutchinson, "Fenton Johnson: Pilgrim of the Dusk," in* Studies in Black Literature, *Vol. 7, No. 3, Autumn, 1976, pp. 14-15.*

Eugene B. Redmond (essay date 1976)

[*A poet, critic, journalist, playwright, and educator, Redmond was instrumental in helping shape the Black Arts Movement of the late 1960s. His poems are particularly notable for their allusions to Negro spirituals, blues, jazz, and soul music. In the following excerpt from his 1976 study* Drumvoices: The Mission of Afro-American Poetry, *he surveys Johnson's literary career, characterizing Johnson as "the poet of the blues."*]

[Fenton Johnson] had several of his plays performed in Chicago's Pekin Theatre when he was nineteen and is generally seen as one of the most creative links between the poets of Dunbar's era and the Harlem Renaissance. Born in Chicago in an economically sound family, he

attended the city's namesake university and taught school for a year in the South. He privately published three volumes of poetry, one (*A Little Dreaming,* 1917) in Chicago, and two (*Visions of the Dusk,* 1915; and *Songs of the Soil,* 1916) in New York, where he lived for a short time. Harriet Monroe and "The New Poetry" group had established *Poetry* (1912) in his home town, and Johnson made contact with her. In 1920, he published *Tales of Darkest America*—short stories. A participant in the "poetry revival" in America, Johnson had his work accepted for *Poetry* and the anthologies *Others* (1916, 1917, 1920), *The New Poetry* and *An Anthology of American Poetry: Lyric America, 1630-1930.*

In saying Fenton Johnson was ultimately the poet of "despair" and that he was the only poet writing in such a vein (as Brown, Redding, Johnson, Wagner, and others have done), critics presented only part of the man. He did borrow from Masters, Lindsay and Sandburg; this allowed him to voice something *relatively* new in black poetry while he provided an avenue of experimental exchange between his black and white contemporaries. But in poems such as **"Tired," "The Banjo Player," "The Scarlet Woman"** and **"Rulers"** he displays much more than "despair." Reflecting, as Brown noted, the "two extremes of Negro poetry after 1914" [see excerpt dated 1937], Johnson can deal with either the brawling urban blues or the down-home, "we shall overcome" motifs. Because his work does not contain a consistent spirit of hope, James Weldon Johnson said his message mirrored ideas "foreign to any philosophy of life the Negro in America had ever preached or practiced" [see excerpt dated 1931]. Johnson thought this was "startling" despite the "birth," about the same time as Fenton Johnson's work, of the blues era—and the work of W. C. Handy (1873-1958), who is sometimes called its "father." Fenton Johnson is **"Tired"** of a civilization that has given him "too many" children and no chance for them to share in the American dream. He proposes to his wife that they

> Throw the children into the river:

and observes that

> . . . It is better to die than it is to grow up and find
> out that you are colored.

Johnson writes about roustabouts, prostitutes, vagrants, laborers, and strong will, and is, as Jay Wright said (during the late 1960s) of Henry Dumas, "the poet of the dispossessed." He is also the poet of the blues. In breaking away from traditional black poetic diction and form, Johnson not only received influence from the white experimenters of free verse but he borrowed heavily from the blues and, at this level, must share some of the accolades usually reserved almost solely for Hughes. (pp. 166-67)

> *Eugene B. Redmond, "A Long Ways from Home (1910-1960)," in his* Drumvoices: The

Mission of Afro-American Poetry, A Critical History, *Anchor Press, 1976, pp. 139-293.*

FURTHER READING

Brawley, Benjamin. "The New Realists: The Forerunners." In his *The Negro Genius: A New Appraisal of the Achievement of the American Negro in Literature and the Fine Arts,* pp. 236-410. New York: Dodd, Mead & Co., 1937.
Contends that "few poets have struck a more passionate note" than did Johnson.

Review of *A Little Dreaming,* by Fenton Johnson. *The Crisis* 7, No. 6 (April 1914): 301.
Brief unsigned review of *A Little Dreaming.* According to the critic, the poems in the collection "are very uneven in value, but here and there are bits of real singing and hint of an unusual message, as in the 'Ethiopian's Song'."

Review of *Visions of the Dusk,* by Fenton Johnson. *The Crisis* 12, No. 2 (June 1916): 69-78.

Reviews contemporary works by and about blacks, noting that Johnson's *Visions of the Dusk* has "bits of beauty here and there."

Firkins, O. F. Review of *Visions in the Dusk,* by Fenton Johnson. *The Nation* 101, No. 2631 (2 December 1915): 654.
Brief review of *Visions in the Dusk.* Firkins writes: "The negro whom Mr. Fenton Johnson has depicted in his not unreadable dialect idyls is unmistakably the white man's negro. The borrowers of an alien culture are doomed to borrow eventually even their conception of themselves. It is curious that the one poem of documental significance in Mr. Johnson's volume, 'De Mule,' should express a psychology that antedates his culture."

Gloster, Hugh M. "Fiction of the Negro Renascence: Early Postwar Fiction." In his *Negro Voices in American Fiction,* pp. 118-27. New York: Russell & Russell, 1965.
Overview of post-World War I fiction by black authors, containing a summary appraisal of *Tales of Darkest America.*

White, Newman Ivey, and Jackson, Walter Clinton. "Fenton Johnson." In their *An Anthology of Verse by American Negroes,* pp. 160-63. 1924. Reprint. Folcroft, Pa.: Folcroft Press, 1969.
Concise overview of Johnson's career, with selections from *A Little Dreaming.*

James Weldon Johnson

1871-1938

American novelist, poet, autobiographer, historian, and critic.

Johnson distinguished himself equally as a man of letters and as a civil rights leader in the early decades of the twentieth century. A talented poet and novelist, he is credited with bringing a new standard of artistry and realism to black literature in such works as *The Autobiography of an Ex-Colored Man* (1912) and *God's Trombone: Seven Negro Sermons in Verse* (1927). His pioneering studies of black poetry, music and theater also helped introduce many white Americans to the genuine African creative spirit, hitherto known chiefly through the distortions of the minstrel show and dialect poetry. Meanwhile, as head of the National Association for the Advancement of Colored People (NAACP) during the 1920s, Johnson led determined civil rights campaigns in an effort to remove the legal, political, and social obstacles hindering black achievement. Johnson's multifaceted career, which also included stints as a diplomat in Latin America and a successful Tin Pan Alley songwriter, testified to his intellectual breadth, self-confidence, and deep-rooted belief that the future held unlimited opportunities for black Americans.

Johnson was born in Jacksonville, Florida, where his father worked as headwaiter at a luxury resort hotel and his mother taught grammar school. Throughout his life Johnson was influenced by his family's adoption of American middle-class ideals as a means to racial equality. Considered a good student at Jacksonville's Stanton Grammar School, he showed early virtuosity in both music and literature, but because secondary education was not available to black students, he was sent to a preparatory school at Atlanta University in Georgia. He remained at the university as an undergraduate, and during this period he composed lampoons of teachers and fellow students as well as what he himself called "rather ardent love poems." Johnson graduated in 1894 and received a scholarship to Harvard University medical school; he chose, however, to return to Stanton as its principal. His work at Stanton resulted in an enlarged curriculum that included the teaching of Spanish and, by adding a grade level each year, accreditation through the secondary level. Although he continued to teach for several years, Johnson simultaneously pursued other careers: as a lawyer with a private practice; as founder of the *Daily American,* one of the first black daily newspapers in the country; and as lyricist for Cole and Johnson Brothers songwriters. With his younger brother Rosamond and his song-and-dance partner Bob Cole, Johnson wrote successful popular songs and later acted as road manager of the group when it toured the United States and Europe. In 1906 Rosamond Johnson and Cole decided to produce their own musical, but John-

son, apprehensive about prospects for the group's future, abandoned show business to accept a position in the U.S. Consular Service, which he was offered in recognition of his work with the Colored Republican Club during Theodore Roosevelt's successful presidential campaign. He began service at a small post in Venezuela, using his free time to write most of *The Autobiography of an Ex-Colored Man,* which he had begun in New York. Later he was advanced to a post in Nicaragua, where he completed the novel. In 1913, when a new Democratic administration refused to send him to a more desirable location, Johnson resigned his post and spent the next year traveling between New York, where he hoped to find work, and Jacksonville, where he was settling the estate of his late father. When "Fifty Years," a poem commemorating the Emancipation Proclamation, appeared in the *New York Times* in January 1913, Johnson's literary reputation soared. The work's popularity influenced publishers of the *New York Age* to hire him as an editorial writer in 1914. His popular column in this newspaper was conciliatory toward the opposing political factions aligned with either Booker T. Washington—who emphasized industrial education and repudiated political agitation for Black Americans—and W. E. B. Du Bois, whose militant leadership challenged and eventually ursuped that of Washington. Johnson also candidly stated his belief that the black press should serve as an instrument of propaganda and used his column to attack Jim Crow laws at home and American policies abroad in such occupied lands as Haiti. In 1916 he joined the NAACP and served as the organization's executive secretary from 1920 to 1930, during a time when the NAACP gained enormous influence among blacks and wielded power on Capitol Hill. During these years Johnson published the poetry collections *Fifty Years and Other Poems* (1917) and *God's Trombones.* He also wrote the historical study *Black Manhattan* (1930) and edited the works of lesser-known black poets in an anthology titled *The Book of American Negro Poetry* (1922). In 1931 he returned to teaching as professor of creative literature at Fisk University in Nashville, Tennessee, a position that was created for him. Johnson died tragically in June 1938 after a train struck the car he was riding in at an unguarded rail crossing in Wiscasset, Maine. The poet and civil rights leader was widely eulogized, and more than two thousand mourners attended his funeral in Harlem.

Despite Johnson's contemporary celebrity as a diplomat and political activist, he is best known today as an important forerunner of the revival in black literature known as the Harlem Renaissance. Johnson's first work, *The Autobiography of an Ex-Colored Man,* was published anonymously in 1912. While Johnson's anonymity served the practical purpose of dissociating him from a potentially controversial work, this strategy also lent verisimilitude to the fictional narrator, who claimed a secret identity was essential to his survival. Most critics accepted the novel as an authentic autobiography but an inartistic one, finding interest primarily in the work's detailed delineation of class stratification and other aspects of black American culture—a subject that would be sensationalized in Harlem Renaissance literature. Edmund Wilson, for example, argued that the literary value of *The Autobiography* did not equal its value as a "human and sociological document." Modern critical reassessments recognize the novel as a complex work in which understanding the narrator is central to understanding the work as a whole. The narrator, whose father was white, is "legally" a black man who has successfully passed as a white businessman and who considers his impersonation a practical joke on white America. Since early childhood, the narrator had invariably fled confrontation with the social consequences of his racial identity, often turning the "joke" upon himself. For example, after years of taunting the "niggers" in school, he is told abruptly by a teacher that he is black. While throughout the major part of the novel the narrator speaks abstractly about his racial pride and the work he intends to do on the behalf of other black people, his squeamish reaction to the squalid life of rural black America, and his condemnation of the

behavior he found there as offensively unrefined, reveal his essentially middle-class white sensibility. Because the story is plotless, the picaresque "hero" is free to comment upon what he observes in the American North and South. However, critics have questioned the reliability of his perceptions of his environment and reactions to it. His over-sensitivity to pain and fear, Marvin P. Garrett and Nicholas Canaday have argued, is a result of insecurities that will not allow the narrator to face his identity. Similarly, Ladell Payne has compared the narrator to the ten-dollar gold piece in which his father had drilled a hole in order to place it around his son's neck, a memento "which proclaims its value yet is absolutely worthless because much of its substance is gone." Maurice O'Sullivan posited that Johnson's preoccupation with the contradictions in his narrator are rooted in the "double consciousness" theory of Du Bois and Alain Locke, which recognizes the psychological tension in persons who have no clear identification as either black or white; thus, according to O'Sullivan, the novel ultimately offers no resolution, but only the possibilities for both tragedy and pathos.

God's Trombones is considered Johnson's most artistically successful work. Locke contended that it achieves epic proportions. Locke, like Richard A. Long, noted the assertion of black pride throughout the work and the rejection of American and European standards and perspectives. Familiar biblical imagery of old-time Southern preachers is echoed rhythmically through repetition, alliteration, and other devices designed to induce "hypnotic grandeur." *God's Trombones* sustains the rhythm as well as the speech patterns of black preachers without using limiting conventional dialect, an accomplishment Payne regarded as "one of [Johnson's] greatest skills as an artist." Later critics, however, have considered the collection "tame" and less potent than the sermons it imitates, mirroring Harriet Monroe's early assertion that in poems like "The Creation," Johnson "should have let himself go more rashly" in his interpretations. Nevertheless, *God's Trombones* remains an impressive poetic achievement for its translation of the rhythms and metaphors of black preachers into literary language rather than the minstrel show dialect often used by poets of the time.

Johnson's relatively small literary production greatly influenced later generations of writers. *The Autobiography of an Ex-Colored Man* helped move the black novel beyond simplistic autobiography and sentimental apology for the "tragic mulatto," and Johnson's poetry emphasized the black American's contributions to folk literature. According to biographer Eugene Levy, "Johnson took what he considered the raw material of folk art and transformed it into an artistic form to which readers of the era could favorably respond."

(For further information about Johnson's life and works, see *Black Writers; Concise Dictionary of American Literary Biography, 1917-1929; Contemporary Authors,* Vols. 104, 125; *Dictionary of Literary Biography,* Vol. 51: *Afro-American Writers from the Harlem Renais-*

sance to 1940; Something about the Author, Vol. 31; and Twentieth-Century Literary Criticism, Vols. 2, 19.)

PRINCIPAL WORKS

*The Autobiography of an Ex-Colored Man (novel) 1912; also published as *The Autobiography of an Ex-Coloured Man,* 1927
"Fifty Years" (poetry) 1913; published in periodical *The New York Times*
Fifty Years and Other Poems (poetry) 1917
The Book of American Negro Poetry [editor] (poetry anthology) 1922; enlarged edition, 1931
The Book of American Negro Spirituals [editor] (song collection) 1925
The Second Book of American Negro Spirituals [editor] (song collection) 1926
God's Trombones: Seven Negro Sermons in Verse (poetry) 1927
Black Manhattan (history) 1930
St. Peter Relates an Incident of the Resurrection Day (poetry) 1930
Along This Way: The Autobiography of James Weldon Johnson (autobiography) (1933)
Negro Americans, What Now? (essay) 1934
Saint Peter Relates an Incident: Selected Poems (poetry) 1935
Selected Poems (poetry) 1936

*The 1912 edition of this work was published anonymously.

––––––––––

Brander Matthews (essay date 1917)

[*In the following excerpt from his introduction to* Fifty Years and Other Poems, *Matthews praises Johnson as a master poet.*]

In poetry, especially in the lyric, wherein the soul is free to find full expression for its innerlost emotions, [the American Negroes'] attempts have been, for the most part, divisible into two classes. In the first of these may be grouped the verses in which the lyrist put forth sentiments common to all mankind and in no wise specifically those of his own race.... Whatever their merits might be, these verses cast little or no light upon the deeper racial sentiments of the people to whom the poets themselves belonged. But in the lyrics to be grouped in the second of these classes there was a racial quality. This contained the dialect verses in which there was an avowed purpose of recapturing the color, the flavor, the movement of life in "the quarters," in the cotton field and in the canebrake. (pp. xii-xiii)

In [*Fifty Years and Others Poems*] Mr. James Weldon Johnson conforms to both of these traditions. He gathers together a group of lyrics, delicate in workmanship, fragrant with sentiment, and phrased in pure and unexceptionable English. Then he has another group of dialect verses, racy of the soil, pungent in flavor, swinging in rhythm and adroit in rhyme. But where he shows himself a pioneer is the half-dozen larger and bolder poems, of a loftier strain, in which he has been nobly successful in expressing the higher aspirations of his own people. It is in uttering this cry for recognition, for sympathy, for understanding, and above all, for justice, that Mr. Johnson is most original and most powerful. In the superb and soaring stanzas of **"Fifty Years"** (published exactly half-a-century after the signing of the Emancipation Proclamation) he has given us one of the noblest commemorative poems yet written by any American,—a poem sonorous in its diction, vigorous in its workmanship, elevated in its imagination and sincere in its emotion. In it speaks the voice of his race; and the race is fortunate in its spokesman. In it a fine theme has been finely treated. (pp. xiii-xiv)

> *Brander Matthews, in an introduction to* Fifty Years & Other Poems *by James Weldon Johnson, The Cornhill Company, 1917, pp. xi-xiv.*

Alain Locke (essay date 1927)

[*Locke, an American essayist and critic, edited* The New Negro: An Interpretation *(1925), a key book on Harlem Renaissance writers. Because of the high merit of the works in this anthology, critics were forced to take black writing much more seriously than they had before.* The New Negro *also served as a unifying link for struggling black authors who had thought they were alone in their literary endeavors. In the following excerpt, Locke discusses the literary and cultural significance of the folk sermons in* God's Trombones: Seven Negro Sermons in Verse.]

The subject matter of [*God's Trombones: Seven Negro Sermons in Verse*]—the bardic role of the ante-bellum Negro preacher, clothed even in his literacy with the inspiration of faith and swaying his audiences with epic power and conviction, conjures up a background that would dwarf any but a major poet's voice and stature. In a flash of inspiration several years ago Mr. Johnson gave us what still remains perhaps the best of these folk-pictures in **"The Creation,"** which now in beautiful and elaborate format, is given to us with six companion poems and an essay on the originating genius, the old-time Negro shorter. The essay has the advantage of the commentator, and at this perspective Mr. Johnson offers us a vivid view of these "shepherds of the people." They and their flock will some day be the epic background and tradition of the Negro poet if ever Negro poetry becomes what it can become—a spiritual world and sun instead of remaining just a satellite of American verse in general.

What Mr. Johnson felt by instinct in **"The Creation,"** he now puts explicitly before the reader, and his fellow artists, the inspiring thought that there is an epic background here in the humble past of the Negro which, if treated with dignity and reverence, will be a rich and fair new province of poetry. It is not too much to say, in spite of the actual accomplishment of one of the most distructive of the year's volumes in verse, the real and final significance of Mr. Johnson's work will be this prophetic vision and influence pointing to what is yet to come.

The problem of the actual writing of these folk sermons is admittedly difficult: complete identification with the themes and idioms of a by-gone generation, a thoroughly incandescent revitalizing of its mood and faith, are perhaps impossible. At this late distance rhetoric must come to the rescue of a lapsing diction and poetic fictions re-kindle the primitive imagination. It is a question of Ossian all over again. The comparison with genuine folk-poetry is constantly in mind and the poet judged by the hard epic standard of objectivity, impersonality and the extent to which he approximates the primitive originals or reproduces their authentic quality. That Mr. Johnson succeeds as often as he does in passages of really fervid and simple folk poetry is great credit to his artistry. At least three of these poems in my judgment have this quality and are really great. **"The Creation," "Judgment Day,"** and in the main **"Go, Down Death."** To proclaim too enthusiastically the perfection of poems like the last-mentioned is to forget, in an age of personalism, the touch and tang of epic poetry. These are folk-things, and the epic standard must apply.

But especially after one has heard these poems read aloud or almost chanted in keeping with the rhapsodic fervor of the originals, one's ear does learn to discriminate and appreciate the true epic quality. (pp. 473-74)

> *Alain Locke, "The Negro Poet and His Tradition," in* Survey, *Vol. LVIII, No. 9, August 1, 1927, pp. 473-74.*

Countee Cullen (essay date 1927)

[*Cullen has been called the most representative voice of the Harlem Renaissance. He knew Johnson personally, and Johnson himself admired Cullen's decision not to recognize in his literary works "any limitations to 'racial' themes and forms." In Cullen's wish not to be "a negro poet," Johnson insisted, the writer was "not only within his right; he is right." In the following excerpt, Cullen reviews* God's Trombones: Seven Negro Sermons in Verse, *noting that the seven sermon-poems are like "the seven blasts blown by Joshua at Jericho."*]

James Weldon Johnson has blown the true spirit and the pentecostal trumpeting of the dark Joshuas of the race in **God's Trombones,** composed of seven sermon-poems and a prayer. The seven sermons are like the seven blasts blown by Joshua at Jericho.

An experiment and an intention lie behind these poems. It will be remembered that in **The Book of American Negro Poetry** Mr. Johnson spoke of the limitations of dialect, which he compared to an organ having but two stops, one of humor and one of pathos. He felt that the Negro poet needed to discover some medium of expression with a latitude capable of embracing the Negro experience. These poems were written with that purpose in view, as well as to guarantee a measure of permanence in man's most forgetful mind to that highly romantic and fast disappearing character, the old time Negro preacher.

The poet here has admirably risen to his intentions and his needs; entombed in this bright mausoleum the Negro preacher of an older day can never pass entirely deathward. Dialect could never have been synthesized into the rich mortar necessary for these sturdy unrhymed exhortations. Mr. Johnson has captured that peculiar flavor of speech by which the black sons of Zebedee, lacking academic education, but grounded through their religious intensity in the purest marshalling of the English language (the King James' version of the Bible) must have astounded men more obviously letter-trained....

There is a universality of appeal and appreciation in these poems that raises them, despite the fact that they are labeled "Seven Negro Sermons in Verse"...far above a relegation to any particular group or people. (p. 221)

In considering these poems one must pay unlimited respect to the voice Mr. Johnson has recorded, and to the pliable and agony-racked audience to whom those great black trombones blared their apocalyptic revelations, and their terrible condemnation of the world, the flesh, and the devil. Theirs was a poetic idiom saved, by sincerity and the heritage of a colorful imagination, from triteness. (pp. 221-22)

[Certain] technical crudities and dissonances can be explained away. The interpolation here and there of a definitely rhymed couplet among the lines of this vigorous free and easy poetry will not jar, when one reflects that if poetry is the language of inspiration, then these black trumpeters...could well be expected to fly now and then beyond their own language barriers into the realms of poetic refinements of which they knew nothing, save by intuitive inspiration. And if on occasion the preacher ascended from *you* and *your* to *thee* and *thou,* this too is in keeping with his character. (p. 222)

> *Countee Cullen, "And The Walls Came Tumblin' Down," in* The Bookman, *New York, Vol. LXVI, No. 2, October, 1927, pp. 221-22.*

James Weldon Johnson (essay date 1927)

[*In the following excerpt from his introduction to* God's Trombones: Seven Negro Sermons in Verse, *Johnson discusses the poetic style he used in this collection.*]

A good deal has been written on the folk creations of the American Negro: his music, sacred and secular; his plantation tales, and his dances; but that there are folk sermons, as well, is a fact that has passed unnoticed. I remember hearing in my boyhood sermons that were current, sermons that passed with only slight modifications from preacher to preacher and from locality to locality. Such sermons were, "The Valley of Dry Bones," which was based on the vision of the prophet in the 37th chapter of Ezekiel; the "Train Sermon," in which both God and the devil were pictured as running trains, one loaded with saints, that pulled up in heaven, and the other with sinners, that dumped its load in hell; the "Heavenly March," which gave in detail the journey of the faithful from earth, on up through the pearly gates to the great white throne. Then there was a stereotyped sermon which had no definite subject, and which was quite generally preached; it began with the Creation, went on to the fall of man, rambled through the trials and tribulations of the Hebrew Children, came down to the redemption by Christ, and ended with the Judgment Day and a warning and an exhortation to sinners. (pp. 1-2)

The old-time Negro preacher has not yet been given the niche in which he properly belongs. He has been portrayed only as a semi-comic figure. He had, it is true, his comic aspects, but on the whole he was an important figure, and at bottom a vital factor. It was through him that the people of diverse languages and customs who were brought here from diverse parts of Africa and thrown into slavery were given their first sense of unity and solidarity. He was the first shepherd of this bewildered flock. His power for good or ill was very great. It was the old-time preacher who for generations was the mainspring of hope and inspiration for the Negro in America. (pp. 2-3)

The old-time preacher was generally a man far above the average in intelligence; he was, not infrequently, a man of positive genius. The earliest of these preachers must have virtually committed many parts of the Bible to memory through hearing the scriptures read or preached from in the white churches which the slaves attended. They were the first of the slaves to learn to read, and their reading was confined to the Bible, and specifically to the more dramatic passages of the Old Testament. A text served mainly as a starting point and often had no relation to the development of the sermon. (p. 4)

The old-time Negro preacher of parts was above all an orator, and in good measure an actor. He knew the secret of oratory, that at bottom it is a progression of rhythmic words more than it is anything else. Indeed, I have witnessed congregations moved to ecstasy by the rhythmic intoning of sheer incoherencies. He was a master of all the modes of eloquence. He often possessed a voice that was a marvelous instrument, a voice he could modulate from a sepulchral whisper to a crashing thunder clap. His discourse was generally kept at a high pitch of fervency, but occasionally he dropped into colloquialisms and, less often, into humor. He preached a personal and anthropomorphic God, a sure-enough heaven and a red-hot hell. His imagination was bold and unfettered. He had the power to sweep his hearers before him; and so himself was often swept away. At such times his language was not prose but poetry. (p. 5)

At first thought, Negro dialect would appear to be the precise medium for these old-time sermons; however, . . . the poems [in *God's Trombones*] are not written in dialect. My reason for not using the dialect is double. First, although the dialect is the exact instrument for voicing certain traditional phases of Negro life, it is, and perhaps by that very exactness, a quite limited instrument. Indeed, it is an instrument with but two complete stops, pathos and humor. This limitation is not due to any defect of the dialect as dialect, but to the mould of convention in which Negro dialect in the United States has been set, to the fixing effects of its long association with the Negro only as a happy-go-lucky or a forlorn figure. The Aframerican poet might in time be able to break this mould of convention and write poetry in dialect without feeling that his first line will put the reader in a frame of mind which demands that the poem be either funny or sad, but I doubt that he will make the effort to do it; he does not consider it worth the while. . . . The passing of dialect as a medium for Negro poetry will be an actual loss, for in it many beautiful things can be done, and done best; however, in my opinion, *traditional* Negro dialect as a form for Aframerican poets is absolutely dead. The Negro poet in the United States, for poetry which he wishes to give a distinctively racial tone and color, needs now an instrument of greater range than dialect; that is, if he is to do more than sound the small notes of sentimentality. I said something on this point in *The Book of American Negro Poetry,* and because I cannot say it better, I quote: "What the colored poet in the United States needs to do is something like what Synge did for the Irish; he needs to find a form that will express the racial spirit by symbols from within rather than by symbols from without—such as the mere mutilation of English spelling and pronounciation. He needs a form that is freer and larger that dialect, but which will still hold the racial flavor." . . . (pp. 7-8)

The second part of my reason for not writing these poems in dialect is the weightier. The old-time Negro preachers, though they actually used dialect in their ordinary intercourse, stepped out from its narrow confines when they preached. They were all saturated with the sublime phraseology of the Hebrew prophets and steeped in the idioms of King James English, so when they preached and warmed to their work they spoke another language, a language far removed from traditional Negro dialect. It was really fusion of Negro idioms with Bible English; and in this there may have been, after all, some kinship with the innate grandiloquence of their old African tongues. To place in the mouths of the talented old-time Negro preachers a language that is a literary imitation of Mississippi cotton-field dialect is sheer burlesque.

Gross exaggeration of the use of big words by these preachers, in fact by Negroes in general, has been commonly made; the laugh being at the exhibition of ignorance involved. What is the basis of this fondness for big words? Is the predilection due, as is supposed, to ignorance desiring to parade itself as knowledge? Not at all. The old-time Negro preacher loved the sonorous, mouth-filling, ear-filling phrase because it gratified a highly developed sense of sound and rhythm in himself and his hearers.

I claim no more for these poems than that I have written them after the manner of the primitive sermons. (pp. 9-10)

> *James Weldon Johnson, in a preface to his* God's Trombones: Seven Negro Sermons in Verse, *1927. Reprint by The Viking Press, 1969, pp. 1-11.*

Jean Wagner (essay date 1962)

[*A French author and critic, Wagner is an expert on the works of black and Southern writers of the United States and an authority on American slang and dialects. In the following excerpt from his* Les poètes nègres des États-Unis (*1962; *Black Poets of the Unites States, *1973), he examines a selection of Johnson's best-known poems.*]

[Johnson's poems] suffer from a major blemish, their impersonal character.... Only rarely did he show himself capable of the limitless abandon without which there can be no real poetic emotion. His verses reveal nothing or almost nothing of his own intimate depths, and may even seek to hide them from us. Johnson can hardly be classed as a lyric poet, since he is too often satisfied with a borrowed or purely conventional lyricism. Compared with [Claude] McKay's earliest American poems, those making up Johnson's first collection, which came out that same year, resemble less the work of a forerunner than of a man trailing behind his time.

His chief contribution to the poetic harvest of the Renaissance was *God's Trombones,* Negro sermons in verse in which, availing himself of the example of his contemporary John Millington Synge, he tried to carry over, into a more respectable idiom than the rough Negro dialect, the essentials of the naïve, clumsy religious lyricism of the oldtime Negro preacher. (pp. 351-52)

Under the collective title of "Jingles and Croons," the dialect poems make up one-third of [*Fifty Years and Other Poems*], some of them previously having been popular hits.... [They] are all basically commercial pieces, put together with every necessary precaution to ensure monetary success. (p. 356)

In most of these poems Johnson rather unimaginatively follows [Paul Laurence] Dunbar's themes and manner; he does not always even bother to change the title of the imitated poems or the names of the characters. Here to

be found once again are all the types of song that had been in circulation twenty-five years earlier: the naïve, sugary love song, the cradle song with which the black mammy lulls her picaninny to sleep, the story of the rival rural swains, the fable that pays homage to Brer Rabbit, and even, on occasion, a discreet hymning of the good old days and of good oldtime Georgia. Johnson's portrait of the Negro, in its main lines, still adheres to the minstrel tradition. He is carefree and optimistic, plays the banjo, eats watermelon and 'possum, and steals chickens and turkeys—all traits necessary to arouse an easy sense of superiority in the white public. (p. 357)

In the domain of dialect poetry, it was hard to do better than, or even as well as, Dunbar, and in "Jingles and Croons" Johnson never attains the spontaneity of expression, the vivacious rhythm, or the melodiousness of his distinguished forerunner. (p. 358)

[Johnson] does not seem to have thought that the hostility dividing black and whites disproved the fact that they were destined to be brothers—quarreling brothers, perhaps, but brothers all the same. How else could he have given the title **"Brothers"** to a poem on lynching which, according to Sterling Brown, is "the most vigorous poem of protest from any Negro poet up to his time"? How else could he have put these last words in the mouth of the Negro, as he dies at the hands of his lynchers:

> Brothers in spirit, brothers in deed are we?

To behold the poet thus unflinchingly manifesting his faith in racial brotherhood leaves one divided between admiration for his idealism and awareness of a certain incoherence in the sequence of episodes that make up this "American drama." The most authentic and gripping part of the poem is the forceful, realistic description of the lynching—which is the first of its kind in American poetry. With greater audacity than Dunbar in "The Haunted Oak," Johnson piles up the macabre details, depicts the flesh of the victim blistering in the flames and falling away in strips, and stresses the sadism of the killers who, when it threatens to end all too rapidly, throw water on the fire to slow it down, so that they may still revel in this ghastly spectacle. We may also admire the poet's notion of having the victim's last words arouse anguish in the minds of the lynchers. He does not, however, anticipate Cullen by suggesting to us that there is a parallel between this burning and the death of Christ on the cross, though he does eloquently suggest the victim's spiritual triumph and the moral defeat or triumphant brute force.

But how clumsily this powerful scene is introduced! It follows immediately, without the least psychological motivation, upon a no less implausible dialogue between the mob and the Negro they have seized. Doubtless it was Johnson's intention to demonstrate by concrete example that many lynchings had not a shadow of justification, and three lines before the end there is some mention of a "fiendish crime" the victim is said to have committed. But this does not eliminate the incoherence, which actually is double—for the lynching scene, to which is grafted the idea of brotherhood heralded by the title, has no organic connection with the first forty lines or so, which could have been utilized in a separate poem. (pp. 367-68)

Johnson presents [the theme of brotherhood] much more satisfactorily in another poem, **"The Black Mammy."** Frankly departing from the sentimentality the plantation tradition had attached to every mention of this figure, who often received a somewhat hypocritical veneration in the great families of the South, the poet is interested in and illuminates only the tragic aspect of the black nurse's situation. She must lavish the same generosity on her own child and on the other, who may one day crush him.... (p. 369)

If Johnson rang so many changes on the theme of the hostile brothers, the reason is that this concept's internal contradiction, with its elements suggesting both fraternal love and the opposite, no doubt provided him with a fitting symbol for that other contradiction falsifying relations between blacks and whites who, though the children of the same fatherland and proclaiming the same ideal of liberty, nevertheless are divided by history and by descent.

Johnson hits upon the same contradiction once more, in different form, when he takes up the theme of interracial love in **"The White Witch."** This is probably the best poem in the volume, as it assuredly is the most "modern."

Yet, at first glance, the symbolism here may seem bewildering. (pp. 369-70)

The white witch stands, in the first place, for the eternal feminine. As early as the second stanza the poet forthrightly declares that this is no old, toothless creature who terrifies little children; quite the contrary, she is adorned with all the charms of youth. Yet she is as old as the world. Thus, her bewitching nature is principally that of love.

This portrait is rendered more complex by the racial context into which it is introduced, for the white witch is also the incarnation of the Aryan racial type with blue eyes, fair hair, and lily-white skin. At the same time she symbolizes the white purity which racist America is intent on defending against any admixture of black blood. Such, at all events, is the official doctrine, for in reality the attraction she possesses for the Negro is equaled only by the attraction she feels for him. Since she sees the Negro as closer to the state of nature than the white man, because he is still in close contact with the earth from which, like Antaeus, he derives his strength, the white woman rightly or wrongly attributes to him a greater sexual potency, and initially she expects him to reveal carnal delights hitherto unknown....

Yet the witch of the poem is not only a passionate lover; she has also [an] undeniably maleficent character.... (p. 370)

It would still be necessary to specify the danger against which Johnson warns his racial brothers. This is the very point at which the poem moves to the symbolic level. There is no question of the traditional punishment meted out to the Negro whose love for a white woman has become known. The danger is bound up, rather, with another feature in the portrait of the white witch. The poet, who tells us that he has already yielded to her charms, has learned that beneath the fascinating exterior of the woman passionately in love she hides her vampire-like nature, and that in the sexual embrace she seeks to rob of his substance the prey who lets himself be entrapped by her wiles....

Thus the poem's meaning reaches far beyond the theme of interracial love on which it is based, and in the last resort the white witch stands for the whole world of the white man. The reciprocal attraction between the two races is not only of the flesh; it is also felt throughout the many forms of civilization and culture, and in this lies, for the Negro, the chief risk of emasculation. By giving in to the powerful attraction the majority culture exerts on him, the Negro runs the risk of losing his own personality, together with his weapons of defense against the basic hostility of the white world. That is why Johnson advises him to seek safety only in flight. (p. 371)

At any level, consequently, at the heart of this poem—as was true also for the theme of the hostile **"Brothers"**—is the association of those two opposites, love and enmity.... Johnson does not more than state the terms of the antithesis. It will remain for others to raise the level of the debate and to strive for a synthesis. But the fact remains that Johnson broke truly fresh ground by endeavoring to elucidate, via this symbol, the extent of the basic contradiction keeping the races apart. Especially if one bears in mind the inadequacy of the few poems he published in [his later collection, *St. Peter Relates an Incident*], it is no exaggeration to assert that his genuinely creative poetic effort is contained in its entirety in [*Fifty Years and Other Poems*]. (pp. 371-72)

In Johnson's poem ["**St. Peter Relates an Incident of the Resurrection Day**"], which sets out to be humorous, Saint Peter tells the angels, long after time has ended, how on Resurrection Day all the American patriotic groups came in a body to witness the resurrection of the unknown soldier, and to escort him into paradise. But when the tombstone was raised the unknown soldier, amid universal consternation, turned out to be a Negro.... While this was an original idea, it was frittered away in this poorly structured poem. There is a shocking imbalance between the central theme, which extends over 56 lines of the fourth part, and the far too long introductory section of 68 lines, often uninteresting and in dubious taste.... But the poem fails above all because Johnson is simply not a humorist. (p. 372)

[Johnson's] intent in writing *God's Trombones* is succinctly expressed in these two sentences from the preface: "The old-time Negro preacher is rapidly passing. I have here tried sincerely to fix something of him."...

The conventionality of these eight poems is already apparent from the fact that they are monologues, whereas in reality a part of the sermon, at least, would have consisted of a dialogue between preacher and congregation. Here the presence of the latter is not even suggested, as it might have been by appropriate monologue technique—for example, by using the repeated question, as [others] had done. Nor is the monologue able to reproduce the oratorical gestures, always so important for the Negro preacher, who is equally actor and orator. (p. 378)

In principle, the language of *God's Trombones* is normal English, not Negro dialect, but here and there it is possible to note a few minor deviations from the norm. True, the dialect or familiar forms that creep in are for the most part American rather than specifically Negro. They include, for example, the intermittent usage of the double negation and of the gerundive preceded by the preposition "a"—except, however, in these two lines of **"Noah Built the Ark,"** in which "a-going" is not just typically Negro but directly borrowed from the first line of a spiritual.... But such forms are exceptional, no more than two or three dozen of them are to be noted in the more than 900 lines of *God's Trombones,* and their contribution to the effect Johnson was aiming at is but subsidiary.

Much more effective in giving these sermons their Negro character are the countless, more or less extensive echoes of actual spirituals with which they are studded. Sometimes a mere word or expression that has long been familiar crops up in the sermon and by its own power suddenly evokes in the reader's mind the whole naïve imagery that makes up the religious context of the spirituals, to which the preacher untiringly returns to find subject matter for his sermon. There are the pearly gates and golden streets of the New Jerusalem, mentioned in Revelation; the custom of calling Jesus "Mary's Baby," and the warning words to sinners and backsliders that they should repent before it is too late. (pp. 378-80)

Johnson gives a correct idea of the preacher's technique, designed to move rather than convince his audience, alternately raising the congregation's hopes and filling them with terror, and arousing their pity by presenting scenes from Holy Writ as though these were taking place before their eyes. (p. 381)

The most personal aspect of the preacher's art is what he creates out of his own fantasy with the aim of stirring the imaginations of his hearers. A ready fabulist, he constantly interpolates in order to supplement the bareness of the biblical narrative. Thus the creation of the world is unfolded before the eyes of the astounded congregation as though it were a fairy tale or a child's

game.... His preaching ever relies on the concrete, with an anthropomorphism that brings down to the human level the Eternal Father, who is addressed as one would speak to a friendly neighbor.... Naïve, homely, and extravagant in turn, but always direct and forceful, these images have no compunction about blending in with those of the Bible so unexpectedly at times as to be almost grotesque.... (pp. 381-82)

If allowance is made for his borrowings from the Bible, from the spirituals, and from the Negro sermons he had heard, what then is the poet's share in *God's Trombones*? Johnson was certainly not the creator of these sermons but, as Synge remarked of his own indebtedness to the Irish people, every work of art results from a collaboration. In *God's Trombones,* the artist is clearly present on every page, and he gives even while he receives. The simplicity and clarity, so striking in these poems, are the fruits of his efforts. His musical sense is manifested in the choice of sonorities for the free-verse line which, in his hands, becomes docile and supple, and adjusts to the preacher's rhythm as well as to the rise and fall of his voice. Taking what were, after all, the heterogeneous elements of his raw materials, the poet has marked them

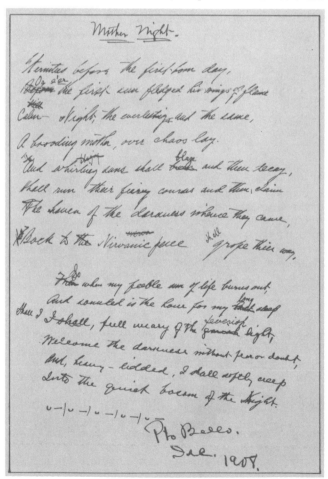

Holograph copy of Johnson's poem "Mother Night."

with the unity and the stamp of his own genius, so that these sermons, as they come from his hands, have undeniably become his own to some degree.

If he deserves any reproach, it might be for his excessive zeal in idealizing and refining—or, in other words, for having thought it necessary to impose too much respectability on essentially popular material whose crudity is one of its charms, as it is also a voucher for its authenticity. His sermons are still folklore, perhaps, but stylized folklore. (p. 383)

> Jean Wagner, "James Weldon Johnson," in his Black Poets of the United States: From Paul Laurence Dunbar to Langston Hughes, translated by Kenneth Douglas, University of Illinois Press, 1973, pp. 351-84.

Robert A. Bone (essay date 1965)

[In the following excerpt from the 1965 revision of his 1958 study The Negro Novel in America, Bone explores the artistry of The Autobiography of an Ex-Colored Man.]

Johnson is the only true artist among the early Negro novelists. His superior craftsmanship is undoubtedly due to his early training in the musical comedy field.... Johnson's seven years as a "conscious artist" in musical comedy proved to be an invaluable apprenticeship. He acquired a skill with words in this exacting medium, and entered a sophisticated world which helped him to attain a cosmopolitan outlook.

The Autobiography of an Ex-Colored Man, simply by virtue of its form, demanded a discipline and restraint hitherto unknown in the Negro novel. It is written in the first person, and as the title indicates it purports to be an autobiography. Johnson, let it be noted, deliberately fostered this illusion by publishing the book anonymously. So well did he succeed in his deception that most of the early reviewers accepted the book at face value. Even after Johnson revealed his identity, he was so beset by readers who thought it was the story of his life that he was forced to write a real autobiography in self-defense.

The narrative structure of the novel consists of a series of episodes which runs the gamut of Negro life in America. (p. 46)

The theme that runs persistently through this narrative is the moral cowardice of the protagonist. A dramatic tension develops between his boyhood resolve "to be a great colored man" and the tragic flaw which prevents him from realizing this ambition. At every crisis in his life he takes the line of least resistance, allowing circumstances to determine his fate.

In spite of his ironical success as a white businessman, the protagonist is a failure on his own terms. Overpowered by life, he becomes a symbol of man's universal failure to fulfill his highest destiny.... (p. 47)

Much of the novel's meaning is conveyed by its tone, which is a subtle blend of tragedy and irony. This tone flows naturally from the life of the protagonist, which has both tragic and ironic aspects.... He avoids self-pity, however, through an attitude of ironic detachment. (p. 48)

Because of his sympathetic portrayal of Bohemian life, Johnson has been widely regarded as a precursor of the Harlem School. It is certainly true that he is the first Negro novelist to show overt sympathy for this aspect of racial life. He champions ragtime music and the cakewalk, for example, as accomplishments of which the race should be proud rather than ashamed. Nevertheless, in terms of the structure of the novel, the Bohemian episode is presented as an evasion of the protagonist's higher responsibility. A transitional figure, Johnson is no Claude McKay; the low-life milieu of the Harlem School is hardly his natural habitat.

Johnson indisputably anticipates the Harlem School by subordinating racial protest to artistic considerations. For the most part, the racial overtones as of the novel form an organic part of its aesthetic structure. While in one sense the racial identity of the protagonist is the central fact of his existence, in another, it is almost irrelevant. The protagonist faces a series of situations from which he flees; his flight into the white race is merely the crowning instance of his cowardice. To be sure, his tragedy is heightened because there are good objective reasons for his final flight, but these reasons in no sense constitute a justification. The focus of the novel is not on the objective situation but on the subjective human tragedy.

Compared to the typical propaganda tract of the period, The Autobiography of an Ex-Colored Man is a model of artistic detachment. Yet even Johnson cannot wholly repress a desire to educate the white folks. Artificially contrived discussions of the race problem mar the novel, and at times the author is needlessly defensive. But despite an occasional lapse, he retains a basic respect for his function as an artist. (pp. 48-9)

> Robert Bone, "Novels of the Talented Tenth: James Weldon Johnson," in his The Negro Novel in America, revised edition, Yale University Press, 1965, pp. 45-9.

David Littlejohn (essay date 1966)

[In the following excerpt from his Black on White: A Critical Survey of Writing by American Negroes, Littlejohn, an American novelist and critic, discusses the strengths and shortcomings he sees in Johnson's poetry and his novel The Autobiography of an Ex-Colored Man.]

Negroes in America have been writing and publishing as long as white masters, slave owners and publishers, have allowed them to do so.... From Phillis Wheatley to the Harlem Renaissance of the 1920's, few colored Americans had the training or the leisure to write, and their scattered efforts were at best mediocre. These efforts took the form, most often, of either Old Black Joe dialect or poorer imitations of poor white models: genteel fictions, village librarian's verse. (p. 22)

Two poets of the pre-Renaissance period stand slightly apart—Paul Dunbar and James Weldon Johnson—if only for their celebrity. (p. 23)

James Weldon Johnson..., a contemporary of Dunbar's outlived him to become one of the most distinguished Negro Americans of his time: a lyricist for Broadway shows, U.S. Consul in Venezuela and Nicaragua, a teacher, attorney, novelist, poet, editor, professor, and executive secretary of the NAACP. His autobiography, *Along This Way,* is one of the more dependable and readable of Negro leaders' autobiographies. His noteworthy "serious" poems are black propaganda pieces in nineteenth-century rhetoric, on the "This Land Is Our Land" theme; they include, in **"Brothers,"** ... what may be the first outspoken dramatization of a lynching in verse.

His claim to a degree of poetic celebrity, however, rests on *God's Trombones* and **"St. Peter Relates an Incident,"** both written well after the end of the period in question, though still obviously the work of an older writer. The former, a collection of seven imitations of Negro sermons, once appeared striking and original; but so many examples of the colored preacher's sermon have appeared since (Faulkner's, Ellison's, Baldwin's, Ossie Davis', etc.), examples more compulsive, more stirring and effective, that Johnson's versions may read today like tame, overcivilized outlines, without the real spirit, the crescendo rhythms, the extraordinary imagery one associates with the genre. Although **"The Creation"** is the best known, **"Judgment Day"** strikes me as the best, the most rhapsodic and rolling. Certain sequences of others are effective—the Flood in **"Noah Built an Ark,"** Pharoah's Army in **"Let My People Go,"** the nailing on the cross in **"The Crucifixion"**—

> Jesus, my lamb-like Jesus,
> Shivering as the nails go through his hands;
> Jesus, my lamb-like Jesus,
> Shivering as the nails go through his feet.
> Jesus, my darling Jesus,
> Groaning as the Roman spear plunged in his side;
> Jesus, my darling Jesus,
> Groaning as the blood came spurting from his
>   wound.
> Oh, look how they done my Jesus.

But the collection as a whole still seems slightly anthropological-condescending, a book of imitations far less potent than their originals.... (pp. 24-5)

J. W. Johnson's *The Autobiography of an Ex-Colored Man* ... is more a social phenomenon than a novel, and its notoriety—some of which has endured—is the combined product of its once-daring title, its anonymous publication (which led readers to presume it factual for fifteen years), and the novelty of its "outspo-

ken" message to 1912 America. It reveals itself today as an utterly artless, unstructured, unselective sequence of Negro-life episodes, written in a style as flat and directionless as the floor of an enormous room. The climactic episodes, moreover—the hero's high life in Bohemian New York as a ragtime pianist, his European tour with a millionaire patron—betray only adolescent fantasies beneath the dull surface of prose. More interesting is what Johnson reveals, of America and himself, between the lines of plot. His essayette digressions, for example, offer a fair view of the antediluvian race relations in America during this period, albeit a view peculiarly fogged by his own prejudices: W. E. B. DuBois is a far more dependable authority. The prejudices themselves, though, the self-revelation, may have for some white readers still a strangely pathetic appeal. He—the "hero," if not Johnson—is a pure example of the self-styled "better class of Negroes," a member of DuBois' "Talented Tenth," who hoped in these distant, deluded years to effect a liaison with "the better class of whites," and to detach himself utterly from the despised lower Negro classes. (p. 26)

Along with this class consciousness goes a dilettantish championing of the popular Negro arts, reminiscent of the detached folklorist's interest one feels in *God's Trombones.* His hero lists, in fact, the Uncle Remus stories, the Jubilee songs, ragtime, and the cake-walk as the four great cultural contributions of the American Negro, and paragraphs of his prose are devoted to the latter two. *The Autobiography* is anything but a "good" book; but, for all the naïvete, the snobbery, the fantasy, and the flatness, it does afford a unique and perhaps useful portrait of a period and a type. (p. 27)

> *David Littlejohn, "Before 'Native Son': The Dark Ages," in his* Black on White: A Critical Survey of Writing by American Negroes, *the Viking Press, 1966, pp. 21-38.*

Allan H. Spear (essay date 1968)

[*In the following excerpt from his introduction to a 1968 edition of* Black Manhattan, *Spear labels Johnson a "transitional figure" in the history of black culture.*]

Black Manhattan is a document of the 1920's—a celebration, with reservations, of both the artistic renaissance of the era and the dream of a black metropolis. Although set in a broader context, it is not, as its author tells us, "in any strict sense a history," ... Nevertheless, much of *Black Manhattan* remains of lasting value. The heart of the book is an impressionistic evocation of the Harlem of the 1920's by an astute and knowledgeable observer. Its most important contribution is its informed and frequently perceptive analysis of the changing role of Negro artists in music, literature and, especially, the theater. (p. viii)

Johnson was a transitional figure in the history of Negro culture. The product of a late-nineteenth-century upbringing, he came of age at a time when the general tradition still held a firm grip on both white and black creative artists. But although his world view was always anchored in the Victorian values of the black bourgeoisie, he himself was part of the movement to create a positive and vital culture rooted in the folk experience of the Negro people. His Broadway career made him deeply aware of the dilemma of the black artist. In the nineteenth century, the only commercially successful Negro songwriters and performers had been those who tailored their work to the demands of white stereotypes. They had operated within the minstrel tradition, playing the role of the irresponsible but lovable "darky" that white audiences expected of them. By the turn of the century, however, the best of the black vaudevillians began to rebel against such blatant pandering to white tastes and attempted to create a more three-dimensional portrait of Negro life.... In *Black Manhattan,* Johnson writes with feeling and perception about this "middle period of the development of the Negro in the American theater." (pp. ix-x)

[Johnson's creative writing] stands midway between the genteel literary works of the early Negro novelists and poets and the celebration of Negro "low life" that characterized the Harlem renaissance of the 1920's. (p. x)

In *Black Manhattan,* Johnson views the Harlem renaissance as a close observer and sympathetic supporter— but as a man who is himself too much the Victorian gentleman to wholeheartedly participate. He is impressed by the powerful poetry of Claude McKay, Countee Cullen and Langston Hughes, the music of the great jazz figures of the 1920's, and the joyous song and dance of the black revues and variety shows. But he occasionally feels obliged to apologize for their primitiveness, to praise works for their vitality *despite* their concern with the "low life." He clearly retains the Victorian notion that "serious"—i.e., respectable—literature stands at the apex of cultural achievement.

If as a cultural critic Johnson emerges as a *haut-bourgeois* making a valiant, if not quite successful, attempt to understand the *avant garde,* so too as a social thinker he stands midway between conservatives and radicals. (p. xi)

Johnson's vision of Harlem was more a dream than a reality. Before World War I, Harlem had been, to be sure, a community of great promise, the finest neighborhood that Negroes had ever occupied in an American city. By 1930, however, conditions had badly deteriorated.... Rather than a black metropolis, Harlem was a black ghetto. (pp. xiii-xiv)

Johnson's failure to see the realities of ghetto life was the result of his own world view and of the racial ideology to which he subscribed.... A proper Victorian gentleman, he was frequently blind to the unpleasant aspects of life. He shared his optimisms with many Negro leaders of the 1920's who found in the artistic ferment of the decade, in the new interest of white

intellectuals in Negro creative activities, and in the dream of a black metropolis, sources of hope for a better future. Ironically, Johnson completed *Black Manhattan* on the very eve of the Great Depression. Within months after the publication of the book, the tragedy of Harlem would lie exposed, visible even through the rosiest lenses. For with economic collapse, black Manhattan's tinsely façade was punctured. (p. xiv)

Black Manhattan is in many ways a period piece. Dated almost as soon as it was written, its sanguine tone seems naïve today. Yet it does evoke an era in Negro life and thought, an era in which a new and better life for black Americans seemed just beyond the horizon. It reveals a great deal about the mind of a man who made a major contribution to both Negro literature and Negro organizational activities. It provides us with an intimate account of the black theatrical and musical world of which Johnson had been a part. And it raises searching questions about the black man's struggle to find his identity. Johnson's formulations may seem out of date, but the central problem with which he grapples is not. (p. xv)

> *Allan H. Spear, in a preface to* Black Manhattan *by James Weldon Johnson, Atheneum, 1968, pp. v-xv.*

Robert E. Fleming (essay date 1971)

[*In the following excerpt, Fleming comments on irony and characterization in* The Autobiography of an Ex-Colored Man.]

[*The Autobiography of an Ex-Coloured Man*] has frequently been lauded for its objective presentation of Negro manners in various parts of the country, from rural Georgia to New York City. While this recognition of the novel's sociological importance is merited, it has tended to draw attention from the artistic elements of the work; those critics who admire the novel often do so for the wrong reasons.... *The Autobiography* is not so much a panoramic novel presenting race relations throughout America as it is a deeply ironic character study of a marginal man who narrates the story of his own life without fully realizing the significance of what he tells his readers.

It is the irony of *The Autobiography* which sets it apart from a number of novels which deal with a similar theme, for it belongs to a class of novels which was by no means new in 1912. The general theme of the tragic mulatto who fits into neither culture had been employed by [many others].... *The Autobiography*...features a protagonist-narrator born after the emancipation of slaves and so light that he may choose the race to which he will belong. External difficulties such as the fear of discovery are almost nonexistent; rather, emotional conflicts become the major concern of the novelist. Johnson's ironic technique is well-suited to such material. (pp. 83-4)

The narrator's first paragraph gives the reader the impression of a self-assured man with a rather objective, analytical approach to what promises to be a searching and honest account of his life. However, the second and last paragraphs alert the reader to the fact that the narrator-protagonist is in reality disturbed, torn by doubt; therefore, his statements should be examined carefully to determine the psychological facts concealed by superficial meanings. The unreliable nature of the narrator is thus suggested, and the reader who keep this in mind will appreciate *The Autobiography* as a novel rather than as a guidebook to Negro life, as an account of emotional and psychological responses rather than as a mere history of the protagonist's social and financial rise in the world.

The main character's relationship with his father and mother, treated mainly in chapters 1 through 3, illustrates Johnson's ironic use of the unreliable narrator. An examination of what the narrator tells us suggests that he harbors an unrealized resentment toward each of his parents. The father, in particular, is treated harshly, although he is not overtly criticized for his treatment of the narrator and his mother. The narrator's earliest memories of his father center not on traits of character or physique but on the material objects associated with him . . . . When the father is about to send his mistress and son north so that his white fincée will not learn about them, he drills a hole in a gold piece and ties it around his son's neck. . . . This flawed gold piece serves as a fitting symbol for most gifts the white man has given the black as well as for the white man's materialistic values, values which the protagonist later adopts as his own. The father's action evokes suggestions of slavery, and his choice of a going-away present is another example of his substitution of material gifts for overt recognition. Another suggestion of a master-slave relationship occurs later when the father comes to visit: he addresses his son as "boy" and the son responds, "yes, sir." . . . Thus the reader is prepared to recognize the irony in the mother's statement to her son that his father is "a great man, a fine gentleman" who loves them both very much . . . ; moreover, there is a sort of double-edged irony in her assertion that "the best blood of the South" is in her son. . . . The relationship between father and son is epitomized in one incident: the father sends his son a new upright piano; however, the boy wonders why the gift was not a grand piano. Clearly, although the narrator tells of his father's kindness and his own emotional indifference in purely objective terms, the suggestiveness of the illustrative details and the psychologically revealing nature of apparently casual remarks make the reader aware of the protagonist's true feelings—resentment toward the father and his strictly materialistic expressions of affection. (pp. 85-6)

Johnson's most notable irony is reserved for the narrator's comments about himself. It is significant that passages which deal with his reactions and feelings are characterized by a neoromantic style, by sentimental and rather inflated diction. The narrator views himself in romantic terms, as a tragic hero whose flaw is the black blood he has inherited from his beloved mother. Yet the reader, responding to the irony which undercuts the romantic pose, is more likely to view him as an antiheroic or pathetic character, frequently indulging in self-pity and unable to accept his total identity and assume his position in a race for which he feels little sympathy or admiration. (p. 87)

From time to time throughout the novel, the narrator interrupts the movement of the story to generalize about Negro life and experience, and the reader can hardly help being struck by the objective tone of his observations. . . . Although the protagonist has apparently accepted his membership in the face he is describing, his attitude toward black people is curiously aloof. In the next section of the novel, chapters 4 through 10, the main character's experiences provide him with opportunities to observe many facets of Negro life, but he consistently views that life as an outsider might and constantly reverts to white values, attitudes, and responses. The fact that the narrator's observations of black life in America have been so highly praised by readers and critics adds an element of irony that Johnson may not have foreseen. (p. 89)

[There are many instances of his sociological observations. Once, for example,] adopting that clinical tone so characteristic of his comments on the black race, he analyzes the socioeconomic classes of black people in the South and points out the curious relationships between the three classes and the white Southerner. . . . Objective analyses like this one . . . have encouraged readers and critics to consider *The Autobiography* a sociological guidebook with only a suggestion of plot; but such disgressions tell us something about the narrator as well. He is able to view "his" race in detached sociological terms because he never feels a part of it. He never succeeds in his attempts to find his identity within the race to which the country's laws and customs consign him, the race which he embraced because it was his mother's. This ability to step outside the race is a reminder of the ironic gap between his true character and the flattering self-portrait the narrator draws of a man earnestly attempting to do what he knows is right. However, beneath his air of detachment, the reader is allowed to glimpse an individual whose racial identity changes because he bases his life on unstable principles. The protagonist's vacillating principles as well as his changing "color" were emphasized by Johnson's alternate title for the novel, *The Chameleon*. (pp. 90-1)

The incident to which the main character attributes his decision to pass for white is indeed traumatic. After a successful trip through the rural South, during which he collects lyrics and music and observes the spontaneous reactions of Negroes at camp meetings, the narrator witnesses a burning. Unable to help or to leave the scene, he watches as the whites chain their victim to a stake, pile wood around him, and ignite the fuel with coal oil. The narrator's reaction is notable for two reasons: he seems to feel no pity for the victim, yet for himself he feels humiliation and shame.... Thus he decides to take the step toward which he has unconsciously been moving from the beginning, but there is bitter irony in the fact that the narrator chooses to ally himself with the persecutors rather than the persecuted, to be one of those who can, without shame or remorse, treat other human beings as animals. (pp. 94-5)

For a time he enjoys the sensation of playing a practical joke on white society and thinks how surprised his new acquaintances would be if he revealed his true identity. However, the joke recoils on him when he falls in love [with a white girl and reveals his secret to her].... She bursts into tears, and the narrator sums up his own feelings by confessing, "This was the only time in my life that I ever felt absolute regret at being coloured, that I cursed the drops of African blood in my veins and wished that I were really white." ... This statement, as the reader has had ample opportunity to see, is false. From the time he was first called "nigger" by his schoolmates, the main character has fought against being classified as a Negro. It is only at this point, however, that he permits himself to recognize the revulsion against his black blood, his inheritance from his beloved mother.

Eventually the girl accepts the protagonist as he is (something he has never been able to do himself) and marries him.... However, the happiness of being a successful white man now seems insufficient recompense for his unfulfilled dreams of contributing to Negro musical achievement. Self-realization has come at last, if only reluctantly and tentatively, and the ex-colored man fears that he has been the real victim of the practical joke he has played on society. The low keyed ending of the novel is much more effective and realistic than the melodramatic conclusions so typical of earlier black novels on the "tragic mulatto" theme.

Although Johnson wrote no other novels, his achievement in *The Autobiography of an Ex-Coloured Man* deserves recognition. The book has a significant place in black literature because it overthrows the stereotyped black character, employed even by early black writers, in favor of one that is complex and many-sided. Johnson gains depth and subtlety by using the first-person point of view rather than the third-person favored by his contemporaries. Moreover, his skill in using an unreliable narrator who reveals more than he intends—indeed, more than he knows—adds important psychological dimensions to the main character and his story. Finally, Johnson's skill in conveying his vision of black life in America through irony rather than by means of the heavy-handed propagandistic techniques of his predecessors marks a new, more artistic direction for the black novelist. (pp. 95-6)

> *Robert E. Fleming, "Irony as a Key to Johnson's 'The Autobiography of an Ex-Coloured Man'," in* American Literature, *Vol. 43, No. 1, March, 1971, pp. 83-96.*

Nicholas Canaday (essay date 1980)

[*In the following excerpt, Canaday discusses autobiographical method in* The Autobiography of an Ex-Colored Man.]

To place James Weldon Johnson's *The Autobiography of an Ex-Coloured Man* within the context of the black autobiography is to reinforce the ironic interpretation of that work, for Johnson's novel is an ironic black autobiography. As a student of black literature, historian, and compiler of anthologies, Johnson was very much aware of the tradition of black prose in the nineteenth century. It begins, of course, with the slave narratives and proceeds through the autobiographies of the long years before the turn of the century. (p. 76)

While choosing the title of the novel, Johnson no doubt realized that his work would be thought of, at least by some readers, within the framework established by the black autobiographies of the past. When first published anonymously in 1912, the book was in fact received as an autobiography, but of course at face value as that of a Negro passing for white who was unwilling to reveal his name. Since the "colored" man has abandoned his race, as even the title announces, for some readers the title reverberates ironically with the well known attitudes of all the proud black autobiographical accounts that tell of growth into a new identity.

Anonymity, in fact, is a strategy that emerges as a function of the character of Johnson's narrator. Besides the fact that he refuses to reveal his own name, he will not mention the name of the Georgia town in which he was born, nor any names, places, or dates by which he or those who are part of his story may be identified. He is not seeking recognition; he is fleeing from it. In the traditional black autobiography people are identified because the author seeks to give them credit for aiding or inspiring him and because they will take pride in reading about his achievements. Because of fear and shame—not confidence and pride—anonymity is a major motif in Johnson's novel.

The tone reflects these elements. In the context of the black autobiography this tone is unique: it speaks in the beginning of "a vague feeling of unsatisfaction, of regret, of almost remorse, from which I am seeking relief...." This pervasive mood of sadness is in contrast to the usual tone in black autobiography of determination and confidence, sometimes even triumph. Such books were written primarily to leave a record of success and a story of a life to be emulated. Johnson's ironic narrative is an object lesson, too, but a sad one, a lesson in failure.

The fact is that Johnson's narrator—and here the author's deliberate irony is apparent—was never really a "colored" man as Johnson used the term. This black autobiography goes from white to white with a very superficial playing of the role of colored in between. His "faint recollection" ... of the place of his birth, Georgia, seems a dim racial memory. His roots are not in the black world at all: "I have only a faint recollection of the place of my birth. At times I can close my eyes and call up in a dreamlike way things that seem to have happened ages ago in some other world." ... Conscious memory in fact begins for the narrator in his boyhood in Connecticut, and his life there as a child is very untypical of the black experience. It is as though he were middle class and white: his house, his schooling, a financial support from an absent father. These conditions are the basis for the traumatic shock that occurs when his teacher in school reveals that he is considered a Negro, and on that day, in his words, he made a "transition from one world into another." ... The best description of that new world is DuBois' concept of "twoness"—a condition that haunts him for the rest of his life and affects every decision he makes.... The ambivalence of being both American and black is, of course, never resolved by the narrator until at the end when he repudiates his black heritage altogether. Thus during the main action of the novel he is condemned to be neither white nor black, and at the end he sees this in tragic recognition: "Sometimes it seems to me that I have never really been a Negro, that I have been only a privileged spectator of their inner life." ... More accurately, what he has in fact seen has been his own version of the inner life of black folk.

The unknown white father in the tradition of the black autobiography is a figure typically referred to as a member of an oppressing and exploiting caste, who rather casually takes a black woman and then discards her. Either he completely lacks concern for his progeny, or he punishes them for reminding him of his guilt. Johnson's novel presents the reader with what are in effect two white fathers of the narrator. The biological father, despite the mother's pathetic devotion to him, gives him only a ten dollar gold piece that cannot be spent because it has a hole in it and, on the last occasion they meet, a piano. The father, according to the sentimental mother, was supposed to have used his influence to have helped the narrator get started in the world, but that prospect is inevitably betrayed. The narrator's surrogate father, his millionaire patron, develops in him a fine appreciation for comfortable living—it turns into a love of luxury—and encourages the nervous sensuality he has learned from his mother. Just as his mother had been ashamed of their Negro heritage, so the patron urges him to give up his race. The patron strongly insists that the narrator has no responsibility to anyone but himself.... In the end the resigned cynicism of his white patron combines with an overwhelming sense of reserve taught him by his mother to produce the narrator's final decision to become white forever.

Yet neither of these white fathers was really a sufficient, strong model. As the narrator moves through the early part of his life—spoiled, rather indolent, accustomed to pleasant surroundings—it becomes clear that what he lacks is a firm principle in his life. Neither parent has evidenced any such conviction, and without the ballast of any settled values his actions spring only from nervous impetuousness, fear, and shame. Not only is he impressed with the shallow and selfish arguments of his white patron, but he even admires such an ignorant and biased person as the Texan whom he hears on the train mouthing standard racist arguments about Negroes: As a matter of fact, the narrator judges the Texan's opponent in the debate, the college professor from Ohio, as a "pitiable character" ..., even though the professor has shown courage as well as intelligence in his statements. The only plausible explanation for the narrator's admiration for the Texan is that the narrator is unduly impressed with the force and conviction of the man, however wrong-headed his cause.

Force and conviction are typically absent in the narrator of this novel; fear and shame are present. In the tradition of the black autobiography shame is expressed for one reason: failure to meet one's obligations to the black community. Such shameful behavior can take the form of exploitation of other blacks or even betrayal. More often it simply is a failure to cooperate in some mutual endeavor. In Johnson's *The Autobiography of an Ex-Coloured Man* the narrator feels shame for the wrong reasons. A sense of it is expressed when he sees "those lazy, loafing, good-for-nothing darkies" ..., as his physician friend calls them, on the streets of Washington. This view reflects basically a white sensibility and the narrator's own class bias. More serious is his shame when he views the lynching that finally drives him out of the South permanently. He expresses horror rather than terror because he has no fear for himself as a victim, and shame rather than anger because of what he takes to be his own disgrace.... His fear is that he will be revealed as a Negro and his shame made public. Thus he adds at the moment he makes his decision to leave his race that "it was not discouragement or fear or search for a larger field of action and opportunity that was driving me out of the Negro race," but that "it was shame, unbearable shame." ... (pp. 76-9)

Once the traditional narrator is free and ready to begin a new life it is usual for him to take a new name.... A new name is the requisite label for a new identity, and taking a new name in self-baptism is an act of will that symbolizes dedication and determination. In Johnson's novel, on the contrary, the taking of a new name at the end of the story represents surrender. It is a name that the narrator will not even mention, certainly not a proud proclamation of a new identity. (p. 80)

Nicholas Canaday, "'The Autobiography of an Ex-Coloured Man' and the Tradition of Black Autobiography," in Obsidian: Black Literature in Review, *Vol. 6, Nos. 1 and 2, Spring and Summer, 1980, pp. 76-81.*

Howard Faulkner (essay date 1985)

[*In the following excerpt, Faulkner argues that* The Autobiography of an Ex-Colored Man *is "the first fully realized black American novel.... The ex-coloured man is the first protagonist in black fiction to be destroyed from within. In his striving to free himself from limitation, he is perfectly successful in effacing himself, in reducing himself and his life to invisibility."*]

[*The Autobiography of an Ex-Coloured Man*] is the first black novel to be totally of a piece; a small masterpiece of control. What critics have faulted is not truly digression or artlessness. Rather, the insipid style and the apparent lack of purposeful selectivity are a direct expression of the narrator's character and of his inability to feel deeply what is happening to him and to put those events in perspective; similarly, the discussion and analysis of black life and people are not adventitious nor are they intrusions of Johnson's own beliefs, but further revelations of character. Our reaction is more problematic than it would be were the irony less subtle, for the narrator is an educated, articulate, and sensitive hero, or anti-hero, and we are thus likely to begin by giving his ideas credence. But we must never mistake the persona for Johnson or think that Johnson lets the ironic tone drop: He does not, in his life story of a man who finally realizes that he has had no life to report.

It is a novel to set beside such other small works of "the unlived life" as Henry James' "The Beast in the Jungle," F. Scott Fitzgerald's "The Rich Boy," and Saul Bellow's *Seize the Day*. In each of these novellas, as in *The Autobiography,* a protagonist of sufficient intelligence, means, and sophistication has a chance to make of his life something significant. Each work is structured around a series of events which involves a protagonist who fails to act or whose action may more accurately be defined as a withdrawal. Each story thus risks boredom; the "fallacy of imitative form" seems for each author a real peril: how to portray boredom without becoming wearisome. The protagonists have chance after chance to act, to learn, to be, but fail over and over again, and the story must present this slow, willful, and consistent failure in order for us to understand the texture of their lives. Because the focus is consistently on one character and because that character's lack of perception is the tonal key, the narrative style must have about it a certain flatness. Finally, each story ends with the protagonist's epiphany, his understanding that though he remains literally alive, his chance to live meaningfully is behind him; ironically, though, the habits of their lifetime make the protagonists unable even to feel completely the horror of that understanding. In each of the works, that epiphany follows immediately the death of another character: James' protagonist learns after the death of May Bartram, the woman who has loved him; Fitzgerald's learns after the death of his first love, Paula Legendre. For Bellow's protagonist the funeral he stumbles into is of a man he has not known, and yet his sorrow rises like waves, engulfing him; and in *The Autobiography,* the protagonist has just realized what he calls the second great sorrow of his life, the death of his wife.

The Autobiography of an Ex-Coloured Man also resembles that great work of black fiction *Invisible Man*. Each is framed by a passage in the present time, providing one explanation of, and justification for, the telling of the story. Both begin with the word *I*, for both are first-person narratives with protagonists who fathom slowly the meanings of the world, nameless narrators seeking to define themselves. And both are structured episodically, with movement through space providing a series of encounters, events, and characters from which the narrators carry away experience, if not knowledge. There is, however, one crucial difference. In Ellison's work, the movement is toward visibility: At the novel's conclusion, the narrator is finally about to undertake the task of making himself a visible individual, a free man. Conversely, Johnson's protagonist spends the novel making himself invisible, promoting a continuing self-effacement, as if, by blotting himself out, he can make of himself a success. He defines himself, then, not by what he has done or is or might be, but by what he once was, but is no longer: an ex-coloured man.

The narrative structure is supplied by a series of episodes: the narrator's childhood, culminating in his discovery that he is black, not white; the abandonment of the family by the white father, a man whom the mother continues to love but about whom the son has no feelings; the death of the mother; the narrator's wanderings in young adulthood—education, travel, a carefree life in New York and Europe; a return to the South; love and marriage. The episodes themselves are often sparsely narrated, presented in various degrees of detail. What we are interested in is the narrator's reaction to them—or, more accurately, his failure to react.

The prologue, two paragraphs before the flashback begins, suggests the author's motives: The book, he writes, is the revelation of a secret, and the first paragraph couches it in rather dramatic terms. The narrator compares himself to a criminal confessing his crimes, with his undoing the probable result of his honesty, but at the end we know that there are no consequences to flow from what the narrator tells us here. He is "playing with fire" out of a "savage and diabolical desire to gather up all the little tragedies of [his] life," but we will learn that the important word here is *little,* not *tragedies.* The second paragraph is more revealing than the first, for it is brief and flat; undoing the tension of the first, it makes plain the narrators real motive: "A vague feeling of unsatisfaction," even the last word an oblique evasion of the stronger *dissatisfaction.* Thus, from the beginning, we get contrasting views of the narrator: his perception of his life as a tragedy against our developing understanding that the chief tragedy of his life has been its lack of tragedy.

Early in the first chapter, the narrator describes his having, as a young boy, often walked up to a cow which grazes in a small enclosure. He offers her a piece of his bread and molasses, but if the cow makes any motion to accept the offer, the narrator quickly jerks his hand back. That pattern, tentative offering and hurried retreat, is the basic pattern of the narrator's life. A few pages later, he thinks back to an evening at home with his mother at the piano, to his listening to her play and falling asleep as he lays his head against her face. He says of that memory that it has more than once kept him "from straying too far from the place of purity and safety in which her arms held" him. *Purity* and *safety* are important words for the narrator, and because the world is neither pure nor safe, it is a place he encounters only tentatively, pulling himself back, withdrawing the offer whenever he meets impurity or danger.

What Johnson does early in the book is to suggest a character for the narrator that the reader thinks is a familiar literary stereotype—the dreamy, sensitive youth as image of the author, a portrait of the artist as a young man—; he then slowly reveals the inaccuracy of the expectations this stereotype sets up. The narrator plays the piano so well that he gives benefit recitals—himself the recipient of the benefits—, and he assures us that his greatest musical gift is that he plays with feeling. Although he later receives training, he first plays by ear, scorning to learn the names of notes. He is not a "child prodigy," for he does not play like a child. And he is intelligent as well, a mama's boy, a pretty boy, a little aristocrat. Throughout the book the narrator defines himself as an artist and his views as those of an artist, and yet while he continues to play the piano, primarily for the amusement of a rich white patron who takes him to Europe, he creates nothing.

The book becomes, then, a series of contrasts between his self-image, a view unqualified by authorial analysis, and the continuing revelations of his moral cowardice and retreat. There are three climactic moments when, confronted with experience, the narrator enthusiastically resolves to do great things. Having been stirred at graduation by the speech of his black friend "Shiny," the narrator begins "to form wild dreams of bringing glory and honour to the Negro face." Later, having heard another musician play ragtime as if it were classical music, he thinks," . . . It can be done, why can't I do it? From that moment on my mind was made up. I clearly saw the way of carrying out the ambition I had formed when a boy." And even near the end of the novel, he still thinks, "I was in that frame of mind which, in the artistic temperament, amounts to inspiration. I was now ready and anxious to get to some place where I might settle down to work, and give expression to the ideas which were teeming in my head . . . ." But these moments result from enthusiasm, and the narrator's excitement passes before he ever acts. He says of himself early in the book, in a brief flash of self-understanding, "I dwelt in a world of imagination, of dreams and air castles—the kind of atmosphere that sometimes nourishes a genius, more often men unfitted for the practical struggles of life."

That he is "unfitted for the practical struggles of life" is revealed in his series of confrontations. After his mother's death, he is on his own, having saved enough money to go to college. On his way to Atlanta, he is befriended by a porter, and for a night they share a room at a boarding house, but while the narrator is visiting the university, reveling in its homelike atmosphere—the matron is motherly, the president fatherly, the environment unsullied—, the porter steals his money. When he attempts to return to the university to tell his new friends of the theft, he cannot face them; characteristically, he turns and retreats.

Befriended once again, he rides to Jacksonville, Florida, on a train, hidden in a closet, that confinement an apt image of the limitations he is placing on himself. Sometime later he meets the porter who has stolen the money and notices that the man is wearing a tie he has also purloined. The narrator is as much interested in the tie as the cash, but instead of taking action about either, he feels only astonishment and "ironical humour" and so does nothing.

The narrator informs us frequently that humor is a good self-defense. On the opening page of the novel he justifies his work as a practical joke on those who have played tragedies on him. Later, revolted by lower-class blacks, noticing only the "shambling, slouching gait and loud talk and laughter of *these people*" (italics mine), he thinks that the ability to laugh heartily is a part of their salvation. He counsels, after suggesting that " . . . the majority of intelligent coloured people are, in some degree, too much in earnest about the race question," that "a slight exercise of the sense of humour would save much anxiety of soul." This advocacy of irony and laughter becomes a leitmotif of the narration, yet what is clear is that the narrator has no sense of humor at all. The book's tone is never leavened by any wit or mirth on the narrator's part—and for good reason: His own "anxiety of soul" is well-founded. There is one source of humor, of course: the irony that arises from our understanding of just how inadequate the narrator's views and responses are, the horrible discrepancy between the true tragedy of the life around him, the life of the poor, which disgusts the narrator, and the pathos of his inability to understand them or himself. How critics could mistake the narrator's analysis for an attempt by narrator to educate his readers is quite a puzzle.

The narrator is more successful financially in the North than he has been in the South. Much of the action of the middle of the book is centered on a New York gaming house known as the "Club." From his first time shooting craps—when he is, ironically, admired by all for his "nerve"—until he leaves, the narrator lives comfortably. Socially, too, he does well; it is here that he meets the white patron, who, impressed by his piano playing, will take him to live in Europe for over a year of dreamlike happiness, a fantasy year in which the only pull of reality will be the inconvenience of his patron's demands that he play the piano. But the narrator remains as ignorant about himself and the world as ever. There is at the club, for example, a man who was once a promising physician, much as the narrator is an artist of promise. He has had two years at Harvard Medical School, but now he is enhanced by the conviviality of life in New York and spends his time and energy gambling. He is known affectionately as "the doctor,"

Johnson (center) with vaudeville partners Bob Cole (left) and Rosamond Johnson.

but the title is a sham and does not disguise the triviality and waste of his life. As the narrator says, "... his will and moral sense [were] so enervated and deadened that it was impossible for him to break away. I do not doubt that the same thing is going on now, but I have sympathy rather than censure for these victims..."—as well he should, for he is of their number. Soon, though the narrator does not make the connection, he, living the same empty life, has also acquired a title, "the professor," one equally unearned. A rich white woman, who has a black lover, becomes interested in the narrator. Though he knows that he is being used only to make the other man jealous, he allows himself to participate briefly in the triangle. The women is shot, the narrator flees—foolish offer and fast retreat, the pattern of his life.

His limitations are most striking in the narrator's treatment of those moments in his life that ought to be the most meaningful, his loves and their loss. The pattern is evident and established in his first adolescent crush. He is an accompanist for a violinist, a girl older than himself, with whom he is infatuated. Yet he is as much taken by the atmosphere, the "half-dim church" and the romantic music, as by the girl. In looking back he things, "... I am subconscious of a faint but distinct fragrance which, like some old memory-awakening perfume, rises and suffuses my whole imagination, inducing a state of reverie so airy as just to evade the powers of expression." The test of his loves similarly affect him: not as deeply-felt experiences but as half-remembered reveries. As suggested by his unusual use of *subconscious* and his justification for the fact that the losses of his life cannot be expressed, love never seems fully to touch the narrator. He says again of the girl that he built her "air castles," and he likes his first love perhaps most of all, for it is secret, shadowy, mystical; it is, in other words, "unsullied"—pure and safe.

For his father, too, he lacks feeling. When his father has made secret visits to the narrator's mother in Georgia, the narrator has not understood who this white man is; later, the father visits them in the North, where he has set them up, but again the narrator feels nothing, except, perhaps, admiration for his father's shiny shoes. He encounters his father one last time at the Paris Opera, during a performance of *Faust,* but he does not speak or act constructively, merely flees. When his mother dies, the narrator calls her death the first great tragedy of his life, yet he had not realized she was growing ill (though she was too weak to get out of bed), and when she dies, he says, "I will not rake over this...." Most tellingly, though he says he is unutterably sorrowful, he goes directly on with his life.

He meets what he calls his next love when he is living and working in Jacksonville. She is relegated to one sentence at the end of a long paragraph about his life there, a life he finds agreeable, "comfortable and pleasant," for he discovers "a number of educated and well-to-do coloured people." He supplies neither background nor explanation about this love, only the fact that he begins to dream about matrimonial bliss; his dream ends when " . . . another turn in the course of my life brought these dreams to an end." The protagonist seems here almost absent from the action, as if his life acts upon him with a volition of its own, leaving him a passive, vicarious observer.

Love and sorrow are not the only powerful emotions that elude the narrator. When he is living in Europe, he is questioned about racial injustice in the United States, specifically whether blacks are ever burned here. He says that he cannot remember his reply, but the question foreshadows an encounter the narrator soon will have. Near the end of the novel, he is once again living among blacks in the South. A mob gathers in preparation for a lynching, and the narrator, knowing that he can pass for white, out of curiosity joins the onlookers. There he watches the burning of a black man, describing the event in vivid and violent detail to the reader; for the first time in the book, the narrator does not reason abstractly as he has so often done before about racial matters, but rather spends several pages describing his personal reaction as a black man: "My heart turned bitter within me," he says, and the ensuing paragraphs continue his description. And yet, as much as the reader wants the narrator to preserve this bitterness, he seems unable to. His first reaction has, after all, been shame—not shame at the white behavior, but a self-hating "shame that I belong to a race that could be so dealt with." He has scoffed at those Southerners who, when describing the Atlanta riots, felt the need to preface their criticism with a tribute to whites in general. But how does the narrator continue? "The Southern whites are in many respects a great people. Looked at from a certain point of view, they are picturesque." The inappropriateness of this point of view, the discrepancy between how the narrator now feels and the feelings which would be appropriate to what he has just witnessed belie the true bitterness of the book, an emotion located not within the narrator, but in Johnson's profoundly ironic portrait of him. It is immediately after this experience that the narrator abandons his race altogether, deciding to pass for white.

The narrator's retreat from his race, like his retreat from life, is one that his careful and persistent analyses fail to understand or account for. Again, it is vital to read these discursive passages not as a reflection of Johnson's views, but as revelations of the protagonist's mind. What makes the reader's task difficult—perhaps more difficult than the case I have been making would indicate—is that, while we are likely to divorce ourselves from the narrator's lack of commitment, we are much slower to withdraw our approval from his thoughts because he assures us so often that he is an artist and because he is so articulate. Moreover, he is not stupid, and the carefully balanced tone would be destroyed if we saw through the narrator immediately: The narrator's analysis *is* occasionally interesting or suggestive. Early, for example, he discusses life in terms of the black and white struggle, and he concludes that the effect on blacks is that they must live a double life. Since they must always see events first from the perspective of a black—not as a man or an American, but always initially as a black—, they see things doubly, and they must act out their identity, then, from this dual perspective. After, however, this promising beginning, the narrator's didacticism veers quickly off course.

A first characteristic of the explanations that follow is that the narrator has a penchant for classifying, for making distinctions not among individuals, but among groups. For example, the very first scene of the novel is a spelldown at his school; each student must spell the word that corresponds to his station in the line: first, second, third. From that point on, the narrator continues the practice of ranking. There are, he tells us, three classes of blacks, dividing them according to an economic criterion: those completely severed from society, the poor, and the independent. Not only are the three classes conventional, but each is described stereotypically. Here, for instance, is his analysis of the middle group: "These may be generally characterized as simple, kind-hearted, and faithful . . . ." Later in the book, while enjoying the easy life of a New York City gambler, he classifies the losers; there are three kinds of them as well. He lists four important contributions of blacks to American life (Uncle Remus is among them) and is compulsive in his analysis of Europeans: how the French are different from the British, both groups distinguished from the Germans. Throughout the book, then, the narrator is a crude appraiser of groups, not a keen observer of individuals.

Having made these distinctions, he is an insufferable snob. Wherever he goes, he strikes up friendships, but they are always with the "better class" of blacks. When he returns to the South for the first time, he is disappointed by the impurity of the surroundings and horrified by the large numbers of poor blacks. He has early called himself a little aristocrat, and his snobbery continues unabated throughout his life. He is particularly a linguistic snob, priding himself on his ability to learn languages and finding virtually the only interest in lower-class blacks to be their dialect. It is, after all, hardly accidental that *coloured* in the title of the book and *humour* and *honour* throughout are spelled in this patently affected way. His snobbery about class is revealed during a trip he takes through the impoverished South. He is uncomfortable, because of the poor food and housing, and wishes himself back with his millionaire patron in Europe. He agrees to spare us the unpleasantness of a description of "'darkies'" (his word), for they "are perhaps better known in American literature than any other single picture of our national life." Yet when he does comment on them, his picture does not differ from those stereotypes he has just cited approvingly: They are "dull, simple people . . . hard working, in their relations with the whites submissive, faithful, and often affectionate." His choice of *Uncle Tom's Cabin,* the book that gave him his "first perspective of the life [he] was entering," is hardly surprising. Though he spends a paragraph enumerating its faults, he concludes, "I do not think it is claiming too much to say that *Uncle Tom's Cabin* was a fair and truthful panorama of slavery . . . ."

What is the narrator's emotional response to the conditions he observes? He realizes that the difficulties of being black, especially for the "advanced element of the coloured race," among whom, of course, he counts himself, are often "very trying." Later, musing upon the situation created when whites sometimes discover he is black after he has passed for white, he writes, "At times this led even to embarrassment." In general, however, the narrator remains immune even to such pale emotions. Confronted at the point of his departure from Europe with two radically opposite views of the world as well as of the possibilities for black progress—the first from his white patron, who argues that one must act totally from self-interest since the condition of the whole will never improve; the second from a black with a "distinguished air" who argues that all is inevitably progressing, that even an increase in black crime is a part of progress—, the narrator not only makes no attempt to resolve the contradiction but does not seem even to notice it.

Riding into the South, he is passing for white in a railway smoker, listening to a conversation about race that degenerates into an argument between an ex-Union soldier and an ignorant Texan. The narrator seems unaffected by the substance of the argument, preferring rather to analyze the Southern propensity for friendly conversation. Among the listeners is a Jew, who remains uncommitted; the narrator concludes, "in the discussion of the race question the diplomacy of the Jew was something to be admired; he had the faculty of agreeing with everybody without losing his allegiance to any side." Irritatingly, then, the narrator ultimately most admires the prejudiced Texan for his stubborn defense of his indefensible ideas and vices.

The narrator's character undergoes one last test during the novel's climactic pages. Having decided that "to forsake one's race to better one's condition was no less worthy an action than to foresake one's country for the same purpose," the latter presumably being acceptable behavior, the narrator is passing for white in the North, doing well financially, and living the secure and comfortable life he has so desired. Then he falls in love once more. He is now faced with the question of whether to tell the women he loves of his race. Before he has decided, they are standing on the street when they accidentally meet "Shiny" his black friend from childhood. The three talk briefly, without disclosure that the narrator is also black; "Shiny" seems to understand

what is to remain unsaid. Yet later, after professing his love, the narrator makes the one moral and brave choice of his life: Much out of character, he does tell the woman that he is black. She leaves him, but by chance they meet again, and she says that she still loves him. They marry and have two children, but during the birth of the second, she dies. The details of the marriage, like those of his wife's death, are omitted, although he assures us that her death is the second great tragedy of his life. Nevertheless, we cannot believe that his life has changed, for though " . . . no cloud ever came to mar [their] life together . . . ," he also writes that their marriage was haunted by his new dread of something spoiling it, "a constant fear that she would discover in me some shortcoming which she would unconsciously attribute to my blood rather than to a failing of human nature."

The last three paragraphs of the novel are the dejected close, a brief admission of how few of his dreams of glory and purpose and artistry he has accomplished. He realizes that he has never really been a black man, but only "a privileged spectator," that he has, like Esau, sold his birthright "for a mess of pottage," having only yellowing manuscripts to remind him of "a vanished dream, a dead ambition, a sacrificed talent." Yet even these realizations do not seem to touch him deeply, his reaction more melancholy than reflection of true sorrow.

The Autobiography of an Ex-Coloured Man is the first fully realized black American novel, a beautiful story of the fear of never living, of being only a detached observer of life. Johnson gives it the peculiar twist that the birthright sold, the beast in the jungle that never springs, the day that is never seized—all depend on the acceptance of blackness, of manhood, of life with all its dangers and impurities. The ex-coloured man is the first protagonist in black fiction to be destroyed from within. In his striving to free himself from limitation, he is perfectly successful in effacing himself, in reducing himself and his life to invisibility. (pp. 148-51)

> *Howard Faulkner, "James Weldon Johnson's Portrait of the Artist as Invisible Man,"* in Black American Literature Forum, *Vol. 19, No. 4, Winter, 1985, pp. 147-51.*

Robert E. Fleming (essay date 1987)

[*In the following essay, Fleming examines manuscript drafts of Johnson's "Fifty Years," commenting on the thematic evolution of the poem.*]

James Weldon Johnson (1871-1938) has frequently been recognized as the sort of black writer and leader who achieved a great deal by working within the American legal and political system. Educated at Atlanta University, Johnson taught in an all-black rural elementary school and a black high school and college, practiced law in Florida, wrote for black newspapers and magazines, and worked for his race as secretary of the National

Association for the Advancement of Colored People. Always a political realist, he campaigned among black voters for the election of Theodore Roosevelt, and after Roosevelt's election he gladly accepted diplomatic appointments as U.S. consul in Venezuela and later in Nicaragua. Through all these careers, Johnson also found time to write prose, poetry, and song lyrics. His first major poem to find a large audience was the occasional poem "Fifty Years," a work that still represents Johnson in many anthologies of Afro-American literature.

"Fifty Years" serves as an example of the side of Johnson to which many modern readers object. Written to commemorate the fiftieth anniversary of the Emancipation Proclamation, "Fifth Years" traces the history of the black race from slavery to freedom, noting its accomplishments in clearing and settling the new nation and in defending its principles from the Revolutionary War on. Implicit in the poem is the idea that the black population should be content to be assimilated into American culture and to wait patiently for full citizenship to be granted. In only three of the twenty-six stanzas of the poem does Johnson suggest that black Americans are still held down by law and custom:

> And yet, my brothers, well I know
>   The tethered feet, the pinioned wings,
> The spirit bowed beneath the blow,
>   The heart grown faint from wounds and stings;
>
> The staggering force of brutish might,
>   That strikes and leaves us stunned and dazed;
> The long, vain waiting through the night
>   To hear some voice for justice raised.
>
> Full well I know the hour when hope
>   Sinks dead, and 'round us everywhere
> Hangs stifling darkness, and we grope
>   With hands uplifted in despair.
>
> (11. 77-88)

More typical of the tone of the poem are lines that stress the gradual nature of the process of assimilation and the necessity for black people to grow into the new roles to which they aspire:

> Far, far the way that we have trod,
>   From heathen kraals and jungle dens,
> To freedmen, freemen, sons of God,
>   Americans and Citizens.
>
> (11. 13-16)
>
> With open hearts ask from above
>   New zeal, new courage and new pow'rs,
> That we may grow more worthy of
>   This country and this land of ours.
>
> (11. 33-36)

Especially during the years of the "black is beautiful" movement, such sentiments, like those expressed in Phillis Wheatley's "On Being Brought from Africa to America," seemed to accept a second-class citizenship for the black race and thus alienated the black reader.

Reading the poem as it was published, first in the *New York Times* of 1 January, 1913, and later in Johnson's

first collection of poetry, *Fifty Years and Other Poems* (1917), it is hard to disagree with Johnson's biographer Eugene Levy, who says that the poem is "much closer in spirit to *Up from Slavery* than to *The Souls of Black Folk*." Yet Johnson had to overcome deep feelings of bitterness before he was able to produce a poem full of so much sweet reasonableness. A study of the manuscript drafts of "Fifty Years" in the Beinecke Rare Book Room and Manuscript Library, Yale University, shows that Johnson's first efforts to write the poem resulted in a diatribe against racial bigotry and would probably have shocked his white readers and created a mood of despair among his black readers. Four drafts and a number of fragments exist in the collection of autograph manuscripts of "Fifty Years," but the entire first draft of nine stanzas was scrapped by Johnson and never found its way into the published poem because, as Johnson reflected some twenty years later, the omitted portion would have "nullified the theme, purpose, and effect of the poem as a whole."

Nevertheless, an examination of Johnson's first draft helps to clarify not only Johnson's mental attitude, but the state of black morale in the first years of the twentieth century. Johnson wrote "Fifty Years" in the American consulate in Nicaragua, where he was enjoying his reward for his political efforts on behalf of the Republican Party. If he was tempted to despair while assessing the racial progress since the Emancipation, what must have been the attitude of black people who were less fortunate than he?

Draft one begins not at the beginning of the poem as published, but at the end. The first lines that came to Johnson were the stanzas with which he would close the poem, to bring "into view the other side of the shield, and [end] on a note of bitterness and despair." Having planned to recount the history of the fifty years just past, Johnson asks if the strides that have been made will truly lead to the goal the race has been stiving for:

> But, Oh, my brothers, if the tears
>   You've shed, the fight that you have fought,
> The grueling struggle of the years,—
>   If none of these should count for ought,
>
> If what you've built in faith and hope,
>   To make you worthy of this Land,
> Is sneered at by the misanthrope,
>   And struck down by the bigot's hand
>
>   . . . . .
>
> If on the ladder you would climb,
>   They force you downward rung by rung,
> Into the quagmire and the slime,
>   Back down into the dirt and dung,
>
> Then loose your hold, your grip let free,
>   No longer strain, no longer try,
> Slip back where they would have you be
>   And wallow where you're forced to lie.
>
> (11. 1-8, 13-20)

These lines refer not only to the losses suffered by former slaves following their first successes after the

Civil War, but to some particularly disturbing developments shortly before Johnson wrote the poem: Thomas Dixon's *The Leopard's Spots: A Romance of the White Man's Burden, 1965-1900* had appeared in 1902, and was soon followed by Dixon's *The Clansman* (1905). Both books enjoyed widespread popularity. Johnson saw in the attitudes which Dixon's books epitomized an American tendency to turn away from the former slaves, or as he put it, to "refuse your need of help and love,/ And balk each effort made to rise" (11. 11-12).

In an apparent allusion to Paul Laurence Dunbar's famous poem "We Wear the Mask" (1896), Johnson ironically urges his black readers to

> Drop off the shamming mask of man,
> Go backward, downward, grovelling,
> Till you are more than they would plan,
> A vile, polluted, dying thing.
>
> (11. 25-28)

At the end of the century, the prevailing strategy of Booker T. Washington, like that of Johnson's alma mater, Atlanta University, was to put on the best possible face for the white race; a strategy which Johnson had personally adopted in making his way through careers in education, law, musical comedy, and politics. Here, however, he found himself suggesting, though rhetorically, that black people deliberately display to whites the negative side of human nature, to show to what depths humanity can fall if it is forced to respond always to the most adverse conditions.

The final lines of Johnson's first draft reveal how this degradation of the black race will affect the rest of the nation.

> Then one more struggle—Leap the length
> Of one last goal before your eyes,
> And with your all remaining strength
> Up to your trembling feet arise.
>
> Stretch out your hands, leprous and lean,
> One curse, one last despairing cry!
> Touch them, and leaving them unclean,
> Sink back, and die!
>
> (11. 29-36)

Far from ending in a positive, conciliatory way, **"Fifty Years"** would have anticipated Claude McKay's lines in "If We Must Die":

> What though before us lies the open grave?
> Like men we'll face the murderous, cowardly
>   pack,
> Pressed to the wall, dying, but fighting back!
>
> (11. 12-14)

But Johnson, even though he needed to purge these bitter feelings from his system, was not ready to abandon his moderate approach. As he later stated in his autobiography, **Along This Way,** "I saw that I had written two poems in one," and his "artistic taste and best judgment" caused him to cut the bitter stanzas from the poem. He set aside the section of the poem that

he had excised, intending to use it as the basis for another poem someday, but he never wrote a poem using those exact lines. Their main idea, however, appears in the poem directly following **"Fifty Years"** in Johnson's first collection. In **"To America,"** first published in *The Crisis* in 1917, Johnson rhetorically asks his country:

> How would you have us, as we are?
> Or sinking 'neath the load we bear?
> Our eyes fixed forward on a star?
> Or gazing empty at despair?
>
> Rising or falling? Men or things?
> With dragging pace or footsteps fleet?
> Strong, willing sinews in your wings?
> Or tightening chains about your feet?

It is a sign of the times in which Johnson lived that even this cool literary spokesman of black America should have been haunted by racism to the extent that he was. Like his contemporary, Paul Laurence Dunbar, Johnson learned to stifle his anger so that he might produce art acceptable to a broad audience and affirm the positive side of life in America. But the lost stanzas of **"Fifty Years"** show that Johnson's placid exterior concealed a raging awareness of the wrongs committed against his race. (pp. 51-5)

> *Robert E. Fleming, "The Composition of James Weldon Johnson's 'Fifty Years',"* in American Poetry, *Vol. 4, No. 2, Winter, 1987, pp. 51-6.*

FURTHER READING

Adelman, Lynn. "A Study of James Weldon Johnson." *The Journal of Negro History* LII, No. 2 (April 1967): 128-45.
  Biographical sketch tracing Johnson's early life and various careers.

Amann, Clarence A. "Three Negro Classics: An Estimate." *Negro American Literature Forum* 4, No. 4 (Winter 1970): 113-19.
  Faults the structure, form, plot, and theme of *The Autobiography of an Ex-Colored Man.* Amann writes of the work: "Suffice it to say that in Johnson, in this specimen at least, the genuine initiation process loses its thrust and emotional force in the distraction of inept form."

Aptheker, Herbert. "Du Bois on James Weldon Johnson." *Journal of Negro History* LII, No. 3 (July 1967): 224-27
  Details Johnson's accomplishments in all fields but literature.

Baker, Houston A., Jr. "A Forgotten Prototype: *The Autobiography of an Ex-Coloured Man* and *Invisible Man.*" *The Virginia Quarterly Review* 49, No. 3 (Summer 1973): 433-49.

Compares *The Autobiography of an Ex-Colored Man* with Ralph Ellison's novel *Invisible Man,* arguing that Johnson was Ellison's forerunner in many aspects of theme and technique.

Bontemps, Arna. Introduction to *The Autobiography of an Ex-Coloured Man,* by James Weldon Johnson, pp. v-ix. New York: Hill and Wang, 1960.
Brief biography of Johnson, with a survey of the high points of the Harlem Renaissance.

Braithwaite, William S. "The Poems of James Weldon Johnson." *Boston Evening Transcript* (12 December 1917): Part 2, p. 9.
Praises Johnson's verse as intellectually superior to Paul Laurence Dunbar's and free of the latter poet's sensuality.

Brawley, Benjamin. "James Weldon Johnson." In his *The Negro in Literature and Art in the United States,* pp. 97-104. New York: Duffield and Co., 1930.
Biographical sketch of Johnson.

Bronz, Stephen H. "James Weldon Johnson." In his *Roots of Negro Racial Consciousness: The 1920's, Three Harlem Renaissance Authors,* pp. 18-46. New York: Libra Publishers, 1964.
Biographical and critical discussion, viewing Johnson as the "one-man symbol of the New Negro."

Carroll, Richard A. "Black Racial Spirit: An Analysis of James Weldon Johnson's Critical Perspective." *Phylon* XXXII, No. 4 (Winter 1971): 344-64.
Assesses Johnson as a literary critic.

Collier, Eugenia W. "James Weldon Johnson: Mirror of Change." *Phylon* XXI, No. 4 (December 1960): 351-59.
Overview of Johnson's literary career. Collier concludes: "Johnson reflected the change from stilted poetics to the more natural poetry of living, a change which was taking place in Negro poetry as well as in American poetry in general."

Du Bois, W. E. B. "Whither Bound, Negroes?" *New York Herald Tribune Books* (18 November 1934): 4.
Reviews Johnson's *Negro Americans, What Now?* Du Bois rebuts what he regards as Johnson's superficial handling of economic and racial solutions to problems faced by blacks in America.

Gale, Zona. "An Autobiography of Distinction." *The World Tomorrow* XVII, No. 1 (4 January 1934): 20-1.
Favorable review of Johnson's autobiography *Along This Way.*

Garrett, Marvin P. "Early Recollections and Structural Irony in *The Autobiography of an Ex-Coloured Man.*" *Critique* XIII, No. 2 (December 1971): 5-14.
Analyzes the apparent self-serving posturings of the narrator in *The Autobiography of an Ex-Colored Man,* maintaining that the novel is a study of a weak individual rather than a study of a subjugated race.

Gibbs, William E. "James Weldon Johnson: A Black Perspective on 'Big Stick' Diplomacy." *Diplomatic History* 8, No. 4 (Fall 1984): 329-47.

Examines Johnson's tenure as U. S. consul in Venezuela and Nicaragua.

Gloster, Hugh M. "Negro Fiction to World War I." In his *Negro Voices in American Fiction,* pp. 23-100. Chapel Hill: University of North Carolina Press, 1948.
Praises *The Autobiography of an Ex-Colored Man* for "its restraint, its adumbration of the Negro Renascence of the 1920's. At a time when most Negro fictionists were giving blow for blow and painting extravagantly favorable pictures of members of the race, Johnson set out neither to glorify Negroes nor to malign whites but to interpret men and conditions as he knew them...."

Greene, J. Lee. "The Pain and the Beauty: The South, the Black Writer, the Conventions of the Picaresque." In *The American South: Portrait of a Culture,* edited by Louis D. Rubin, Jr., pp. 264-88. Baton Rouge: Louisiana State University Press, 1980.
Compares four major works of Southern black literature: *The Autobiography of an Ex-Colored Man;* Jean Toomer's *Cane;* Ralph Ellison's *Invisible Man;* and Ernest Gaines's *The Autobiography of Miss Jane Pittman.*

Huggins, Nathan Irvin. *Harlem Renaissance,* pp. 5ff. New York: Oxford University Press, 1971.
Includes numerous references to Johnson's political and literary activities during the Harlem Renaissance.

Koprince, Susan J. "Femininity and the Harlem Experience: A Note on James Weldon Johnson." *CLA Journal* XXIX, No. 1 (September 1985): 52-6.
Explores Johnson's images of women in *God's Trombones: Seven Negro Sermons in Verse.*

Kostelanetz, Richard. "The Politics of Passing: The Fiction of James Weldon Johnson." *Negro American Literature Forum* 3, No. 1 (Spring 1969): 22-4, 29.
Discusses the theme of racial "passing" in *The Autobiography of an Ex-Colored Man.*

Levy, Eugene. "Ragtime and Race Pride: The Career of James Weldon Johnson." *Journal of Popular Culture* 1, No. 4 (Spring 1968): 357-70.
Documents Johnson's work as a composer of ragtime and show songs.

———. *James Weldon Johnson: Black Leader, Black Voice.* Chicago: University of Chicago Press, 1973, 380 p.
Full-length biography of Johnson.

Long, Richard A. "A Weapon of My Song: The Poetry of James Weldon Johnson." *Phylon* XXXII, No. 4 (Winter 1971): 374-82.
General overview of Johnson's poetry, focusing on stylistics and thematics.

Mackethan, Lucinda H. "*Black Boy* and *Ex-Coloured Man:* Version and Inversion of the Slave Narrator's Quest for Voice." *CLA Journal* XXXII, No. 2 (December 1988): 123-37.
Studies the narrative voice in *The Autobiography of an Ex-Colored Man,* emphasizing links with American slave narratives.

Margolies, Edward. "The First Forty Years: 1990-1940." In his *Native Sons: A Critical Study of Twentieth-Century Negro American Authors,* pp. 21-46. Philadelphia and New York: J. B. Lippincott, Co., 1968.

Labels *The Autobiography of an Ex-Colored Man* "by far the best novel produced by a Negro prior to the 1920's."

Mencken, H. L. "Si Mutare Potest Aethiops Pellum Suam . . . ." *The Smart Set* LIII, No. 1 (September 1917): 138-44.

Contains a brief overview of racial issues in *The Autobiography of an Ex-Colored Man.*

Monroe, Harriet. "Negro Sermons." *Poetry* XXX, No. V (August 1927): 291-93.

Review of *God's Trombones: Seven Negro Sermons in Verse,* praising Johnson's capturing of the "spirit and rhythm" of his model sermons.

O'Sullivan, Maurice J., Jr. "Of Souls and Pottage: James Weldon Johnson's *The Autobiography of an Ex-Coloured Man.*" *CLA Journal* XXIII, No. 1 (September 1979): 60-70.

Contends that the narrator's internal conflicts and contradictions result in a wavering between pathos and tragedy in *The Autobiography of an Ex-Coloured Man,* leaving the novel unresolved.

Payne, Ladell. "Themes and Cadences: James Weldon Johnson's Novel." *The Southern Literary Journal* XI, No. 2 (Spring 1979): 43-55.

Compares the themes and techniques of *The Autobiography of an Ex-Colored Man* to earlier, contemporary, and later works of Southern literature.

Redding, J. Saunders. "Emergence of the New Negro." In his *To Make a Poet Black,* pp. 93-126. Chapel Hill: University of North Carolina Press, 1939.

Contains a highly favorable overview of *God's Trombones: Seven Negro Sermons in Verse.* Redding states: "God's Trombones [is] a brilliant example of the maturing of [Johnson's] thoughts on folk material and dialect. Aside from the beauty of the poems, the essay which prefaces them is of the first importance for it definitely hails back from the urban and sophisticated to the earthy exuberance of the Negro's kinship with the earth, the fields, the suns and rains of the South."

Rosenberg, Harold. "Truth and the Academic Style." *Poetry* XLIX, No. 1 (October 1936): 49-51.

Praises Johnson's motives in "Saint Peter Relates an Incident" but faults the literary quality of the poem itself. Rosenberg claims: "Whatever part it may play in the social and political progress of the people it aims to represent, the official gesture is irreconcilable with good poetry."

Rosenblatt, Roger. "The Hero Vanishes." In his *Black Fiction,* pp. 159-200. Cambridge, Mass.: Harvard University Press, 1974.

Examines *The Autobiography of an Ex-Colored Man* as part of the "tragic mulatto" tradition.

Ross, Stephen M. "Audience and Irony in Johnson's *The Autobiography of an Ex-Coloured Man.*" *CLA Journal* XVIII, No. 2 (December 1974): 198-210.

Explores three key elements in *The Autobiography of an Ex-Colored Man:* 1) irony; 2) "the general tradition's tale of class"; and 3) love story conventions.

Skerrett, Joseph R., Jr. "Irony and Symbolic Action in James Weldon Johnson's *The Autobiography of an Ex-Colored Man.*" *American Quarterly* 32, No. 5 (Winter 1980): 540-58.

Examines critical controversy surrounding the reliability of the protagonist of *The Autobiography of an Ex-Colored Man.*

Stepto, Robert B. "Lost in a Quest: James Weldon Johnson's *The The Autobiography of an Ex-Coloured Man.*" In his *From Behind the Veil: A Study of Afro-American Narrative,* pp. 95-127. Urbana: University of Illinois Press, 1979.

Places *The Autobiography of an Ex-Colored Man* in the historical context of slave narratives and early black autobiographies, particularly Booker T. Washington's *Up From Slavery* and W. E. B. Du Bois's *The Souls of Black Folk.* Stepto calls *The Autobiography* the single work that ushered in the modern black American novel.

Tolbert-Rouchaleau, Jane. *James Weldon Johnson.* Black Americans of Achievement, edited by Nathan Irvin Huggins. New York: Chelsea House, 1988, 110 p.

Biography of Johnson for young readers.

White, Walter F. "Negro Poets." *The Nation* CXIV, No. 2970 (7 June 1922): 694-95.

Laudatory review of Johnson's anthology *The Book of American Negro Poetry.*

Wilson, Edmund. "An Ex-Colored Man." *The New Republic* 53, No. 687 (1 February 1928): 303-04.

Mixed review of *The Autobiography of an Ex-Colored Man,* noting: "Mr. Johnson lacks the power to convince one emotionally of the stark, hard truth of the scenes which he presents. He fumbles his climaxes, even when the material offers him superb opportunities. Moreover, he does not distinguish with sufficient clearness between the trivial and the supremely relevant."

Gayl Jones

1949-

American novelist, short story writer, and poet.

A provocative American writer, Jones is best known for the novels *Corregidora* (1975) and *Eva's Man* (1976). Both works feature a female protagonist who is victimized by sexual and racial exploitation. Jones wrote these brutal, highly sexual accounts in the first person, causing several critics to compare the novels to slave narratives. Jones has remarked that she writes in the first person in an effort to evoke oral history and the tradition of storytelling. "I think of myself principally as a storyteller," she said in a 1979 interview. "[Many of the fictional works] I write that seem to work have been those in which I am concerned with the storyteller, not only the author as storyteller but also the characters."

Jones grew up in Lexington, Kentucky, where her mother entertained Jones and her siblings by writing stories and reading them aloud. "So I first knew stories as things that were heard," Jones remarked in a 1975 interview. "That you listened to. That someone spoke." The Lexington schools—which were segregated until Jones was in the tenth grade—provided Jones with little education in writing and English, however. She eventually attended Connecticut College and Brown University, where William Meredith and Michael S. Harper guided her graduate studies. While still at Brown, Jones wrote and published *Corregidora* with the help of her editor, Toni Morrison.

Corregidora explores the psychological effects of slavery and sexual abuse on a modern black woman. Ursa Corregidora, a blues singer from Kentucky, descends from a line of women who are the progeny of a Portuguese slaveholder named Corregidora; he is the father of both Ursa's mother and grandmother. "All of the women, including the great-granddaughter Ursa, keep the name Corregidora as a reminder of the depredations of the slave system and of the rapacious natures of men," explained Keith E. Byerman. "The story is passed from generation to generation of women, along with the admonition to 'produce generations' to keep alive the tale of evil." Partly as a result of this history, Ursa becomes involved in abusive relationships with men. The narrative itself arises from an incident of violence. After being thrown down a flight of stairs by her first husband and rendered unable to bear children, Ursa "discharges her obligation to the memory of Corregidora by speaking [the] book," noted John Updike. *Corregidora* was acclaimed as a novel of unusual power and impact. "No black American novel since Richard Wright's *Native Son* (1940)," wrote Ivan Webster, "has so skillfully traced psychic wounds to a sexual source." Critics praised Jones's treatment of sexual detail and its illumination of the central character. "One of the book's merits," according to Updike, "is the ease

with which it assumes the writer's right to sexual specifics, and its willingness to explore exactly how our sexual and emotional behavior is warped within the matrix of family and race."

With her second novel, *Eva's Man,* Jones continued to explore the psychological effects of brutality, but here she presented a character who suffers more extreme persecution. Eva Medina Canada, incarcerated for the murder and dental castration of a male acquaintance, narrates a personal history that depicts the damaging influences of a sexually aggressive and hostile society. Updike described the exploitative world that shaped the mentally deranged Eva: "Evil permeates the erotic education of Eva Canada, as it progresses from Popsicle-stick violations to the witnessing of her mother's adultery and a growing awareness of the whores and 'queen bees' in the slum world around her, and on to her own reluctant initiation through encounters in buses and in bars, where a man with no thumb monotonously propositions her. The evil that emanates from men becomes hers." In a narrative that is fragmented and disjointed, Eva gives no concrete motive for the crime committed; furthermore, she neither shows remorse nor any signs of rehabilitation. *Eva's Man* was praised for its emotional impact, yet some reviewers found the character of Eva extreme or inaccessible. June Jordan called *Eva's Man* "the blues that lost control. This is the rhythmic, monotone lamentation of one woman, Eva Medina, who is nobody I have ever known." Jordan explained: "Miss Jones delivers her story in a strictly controlled, circular form that is wrapped, around and around, with ambivalence. Unerringly, her writing creates the tension of a problem unresolved." Jordan concluded that the fragmented details of Eva's story "do not mesh into illumination." On the other hand, some reviewers regarded the gaps in *Eva's Man* as appropriate and integral to its meaning. Darryl Pinckney called the novel "a tale of madness; one exacerbated if not caused by frustration, accumulated grievances" and commented on aspects that contribute to this effect: "Structurally unsettled, more scattered than *Corregidora*, *Eva's Man* is extremely remote, more troubling in its hallucinations.... The personal exploitation that causes Eva's desperation is hard to appreciate. Her rage seems never to find its proper object, except, possibly, in her last extreme act."

In 1977 Jones published a collection of short stories, *White Rat*, which received mixed reviews. While a number of critics noted the presence of Jones's characteristic themes, they sensed that her shorter fiction did not allow enough room for character development. Diane Johnson commented that the stories in *White Rat* "were written in some cases earlier than her novels, so they confirm one's sense of her direction and preoccupations: sex is violation, and violence is the principal dynamic of human relationships." Mel Watkins also found fault in Jones's short fiction. "The focus throughout is on desolate, forsaken characters struggling to exact some snippet of gratification from their lives.... Although her prose here is as starkly arresting and indelible as in her novels, except for the longer stories such as 'Jeveta' and 'The Women,' these tales are simply doleful vignettes—slices of life so beveled that they seem distorted." Jones has also written several collections of poetry, including *Song for Anninho* (1981). Almeyda narrates her love for her husband Anninho in this work; both are residents of Palmares, a settlement of fugitive slaves in Brazil.

Although Jones's writing often emphasizes a tormented side of life, it also raises the possibility for more positive interactions between men and women. Jones pointed out that "there seems to be a growing understanding—working itself out especially in *Corregidora*,—of what is required in order to be genuinely tender. Perhaps brutality enables one to recognize what tenderness is." Melvin Dixon concluded that what "Jones is after is the words and deeds that finally break the sexual bondage men and women impose upon each other."

(For further information about Jones's life and works, see *Black Writers; Contemporary Authors*, Vols. 77-80; *Contemporary Authors New Revision Series*, Vol. 27; *Contemporary Literary Criticism*, Vols. 6, 9; *Dictionary of Literary Biography*, Vol. 33: *Afro-American Fiction Writers After 1955;* and *Major 20th-Century Writers.*)

PRINCIPAL WORKS

Chile Woman (drama) 1974
Corregidora (novel) 1975
Eva's Man (novel) 1976
White Rat (short stories) 1977
Song for Anninho (poetry) 1981
The Hermit-Woman (poetry) 1983
Xarque and Other Poems (poetry) 1985

Gayl Jones with Michael S. Harper (interview date 1975)

[*Harper is a noted African-American poet. He was Jones's mentor at Brown University, and she considers him a major influence on her work. Harper spoke with Jones at Brown in 1975, just after the publication of her first novel. In the following excerpt from this interview, Jones discusses the influence of oral history on her work.*]

[Harper]: *Do you have any models for artistic conception, literary, historical, or autobiographical?*

[Jones]: I used to say that I learned to write by listening to people talk. I still feel that the best of my writing comes from having *heard* rather than having read. This isn't to say that reading doesn't enrich or that reading isn't important, but I'm talking about foundations. I think my language/word foundations were oral rather than written. But I was also learning how to read and write at the same time I was listening to people talk. In the beginning, *all* of the richness came from people rather than books because in those days you were reading some really unfortunate kinds of books in school. I'm talking about the books children learned to read out of when I was coming up. But my first stories were heard stories—from grown-up people talking. I think it's important that we—my brother and I—were never sent out of the room when grown-up people were talking. So we heard their stories. So I've always heard stories of people generations older than me. I think that's important. I think that's the important thing.

Also, my mother would write stories for us and read them to us. She would read other stories too, but my favorite ones were the ones she wrote herself and read to us. My favorite one of those was a story called "Esapher and the Wizard." So I first knew stories as things that were heard. That you listened to. That someone spoke. The stories we had to read in school—I didn't really make connections with them as stories. I just remember us sitting around in the circle and different people being called on to read a sentence. But my mother's reading the stories—I connected with that. And I connected with the stories people were telling about things that happened back before I was born.

When I was in the fifth grade, I had a teacher who would have us listen to music and then write stories. We had to write the stories that came to us while we were listening and then we would have to read the stories aloud to the whole class. I had started writing stories when I was in the second or third grade, when I was seven or eight, but didn't show them to anybody until her. Of course, my mother knew I was writing. Of course, I showed things to her. But my fifth-grade teacher was the first teacher I showed any work to. Her name was Mrs. Hodges. I remember I used to make stories and put the names of people in the class in them so that everybody would laugh. So then there was the music and the heard stories. It was an all-black school. I went to an all-black school until the tenth grade when there was integration. I say that because I think it's important. I think it's important about the music and the words, too.

A lot of connections I made with tradition—with historical and literary things—I started making later. I was writing stories in first-person before I made connections with the slave narrative tradition or the tradition of black autobiography, before "oral storytelling" became something you talked about. At first, I just felt that the first-person narrative was the most authentic way of telling a story, and I felt that I was using my own voice—telling a story the way I would talk it. I liked the way the words came out better than the way they came out in third-person. And I liked writing dialogue in stories, because I was "hearing" people talk. But I hadn't made any of the kinds of connections you make with your traditions other than the connections you make in living them and being a part of them. I didn't really begin to make the other kinds of connections till graduate school. I still don't like to stand away from the traditions, talking about them. You ought to be able to talk about them standing right inside of them.

In storytelling, you can do that—that's why I like storytelling. When you tell a story, you automatically talk about traditions, but they're never separate from the people, the human implications. You're talking about language, you're talking about politics and morality and economics and culture, and you never have to come out and say you're talking about these things—you don't have to isolate them and therefore freeze them— but you're still talking about them. You're talking about all your connections as a human being. You're talking about many dimensions instead of just one. You don't start with the answers. Someone asked me what answers did I have for such and such a thing. I said that I didn't have any answers. She said that when she read my book she could see answers. She could see I had answers. But you don't start with the answers, I don't start with the

answers, I start with the telling, and sometimes the answers come out of the telling.

Can you distinguish between oral and literary or written influences?

Yes. When I'm working even. I know I can reconnect them if I read over something. There are a lot of sounds, though. A lot of times, literary (written) things also become oral influences for me, because of the way I read. I have to hear the words in my head—almost in my ears, too—all the sounds have to be there when I read—and when I'm writing too. I don't necessarily have to re-read things out loud because I hear the words while I'm writing them. In the process of writing them I have to hear them. My mouth isn't moving, but the vocal connections are being made, the sound connections—the same kind of speech energy is being used. When I write I can also hear other people talking. A lot of times if I'm having a person say something, other connections are being made with people I've already heard. Of course, sometimes I'll have people say things that I've heard said in another context. But other times, I'll just remember the patterns of the way things were said. The people will be saying entirely different things, but they'll be saying it with the patterns, the rhythms, that I've heard before. So a lot of times one's own speech rhythms and the speech rhythms of other people go into making a story. All the "heard" things go there.

I have a tendency to trust a lot of my oral influences more than my literary ones, with some exceptions. Those have to do with personal contacts and trusting the people's writing whose "voice" I can trust and who I feel can "hear." I usually trust writers who I feel I can hear. A lot of European and Euro-American writers—because of the way their traditions work—have lost the ability to hear. Now Joyce could hear and Chaucer could hear. A lot of Southern American writers can hear. Chaucer had to hear because he was writing in the "vernacular" at a time when "writers" wrote in Latin. The ballads were in the vernacular but they were oral. The "people" made them, not "writers." So Chaucer had to hear. Joyce had to hear because of the whole historical-linguistic situation in Ireland—the Irish spoke a different kind of "English," and of course they were forced to speak English by the invaders, and of course language has its obvious political implications. But *Finnegans Wake* is an oral book. You can't sight-read *Finnegans Wake* with any kind of truth. And they say only a Dubliner can really understand the book, can really "hear" it.

Of course, black writers—it goes without saying why we've always had to hear. And Native American writers, and Latin American writers. It's all tied in with linguistic relationships, and with the whole socio-psychological-political-historical manifestations of these linguistic relationships. I could keep giving reasons why different people have to hear and others don't. If you don't have to hear, if your humanity isn't somehow involved in hearing, you don't. Hearing has to be essential. You have to be able to hear other people's voices and you have to be able to hear your own voice. You say, in one of your poems, a man is another man's face. Maybe a man is another man's voice too. Most of my influences are essentially oral because even the written ones have to be "translated" into the oral before I can understand them. "Understand" really isn't the word, because "understand" is one-dimensional and it's a multi-dimensional thing. Maybe I should say: "I have to bring the written things into the oral *mode* before I can *deal with* them."

I guess language as heard fascinates me more than language as written—but I like to see words, too. I really do. I guess I wouldn't write if I didn't also like to see them. To hear them and to see them while I'm hearing them. But I don't always have to see them while I'm hearing them. But I always have to hear them while I'm seeing them. So many things in writing, though, are simultaneous. It's a simultaneous process. Many things occupy the same space and time. (pp. 352-55)

> *Gayl Jones and Michael S. Harper, in an interview in* Chant of Saints: A Gathering of Afro-American Literature, Art, and Scholarship, *edited by Michael S. Harper and Robert B. Stepto, University of Illinois Press, 1979, pp. 352-75.*

Keith Byerman (essay date 1980)

[*In the following excerpt, Byerman analyzes* Eva's Man *as a gothic novel.*]

Gothic literature has long been a vehicle for the expression of the repressed, violent, terrifying, erotic, and obsessive aspects of human experience that could not be adequately articulated elsewhere. Although best known as a popular form, its place in serious writing has been increasingly noticed by critics. In modern American literature, this recognition has principally come in discussions of such southern writers as Faulkner, O'Connor, and Capote. However, what has thus far not been realized is that the nature of Gothic has made it an effective mode for other literary groups as well. As a means of treating themes of violence, sexuality, obsession, and power, its patterns and techniques have been found useful by both women and black writers. An especially powerful rendering of the Gothic is found in the novel, *Eva's Man* (1976), written by the contemporary black author, Gayl Jones.

Implicit in this novel is the Gothic monomyth, which, as G. R. Thompson defines it, "is the embodiment of demonic-quest romance, in which a lonely self-divided hero embarks on insane pursuit of the Absolute. This self-destructive quest is metaphysical, mythic, and religious, defining the hero's dark or equivocal relationship to the universe." For the purposes of this essay, the principal interest of *Eva's Man* is the structural means for expressing this "insane pursuit."

The structural metaphor for the Gothic quest is, according to J. Douglas Perry, the downward, ever-tightening, ever-faster spiral of the whirlpool. He sees this image in three interrelated structural principles: concentricity, predetermined sequence, and character repetition. (p. 93)

Eva's Man, though not specifically designed as a Gothic novel, follows this structural pattern very closely. The central character, Eva, describes for us her movement through ever more intense experiences that the reader can see are more and more destructive of her sanity. Repeated images, scenes, and words reflect the increasing restriction of her range of response. Finally, obsessed with an object that she believes to hold the secret of power and truth, she takes violent possession of that object. Specifically, she responds to her victimization in a male-dominated society by literally excising the root of that evil: she bites off the penis of her lover after poisoning him. This violence is taken as the evidence of her insanity, and her quest ends in the still center of a hospital for the criminally insane. She is last seen speaking to and uncertainly enjoying sexual favors from a mirror-image character, Elvira. Her journey has been through a Gothic whirlpool.

The structure of *Eva's Man* is very clearly defined, perhaps reflecting Jones's stated interest in abnormal psychology. In an interview, she commented on the narrative significance of psychotic characters:

> The person who is psychotic might spend a great deal of time on selected items, so there might be a reversal in the relative importance of the trivial and what's generally thought of as significant. In Eva's mind, time and people become fluid. Time has little chronological sequence, and the characters seem to coalesce into one personality.

The story is consistently told from such a point of view. The narrative voice is Eva's throughout. Judgments about characters and events are conditioned by the fact that the supplier of the information becomes less reliable as the narrative continues. Thus, the structure of the tale embodies not only the increasing intensity of events but also the increasing madness of the narrator.

The fluidity and coalescence mentioned above, which are necessary to the creation of this mad teller and her mad tale, are achieved in a variety of ways in the text. Within the chapters, scenes that are initially easily distinguishable in time and place become increasingly interwoven and confused; the associative markers that make it possible to comprehend the connections within and between scenes gradually become so private and obscure that following the narrative is nearly impossible. Dialogue is not attributed, identical phrases and images are used in widely divergent contexts, and pronouns have ambiguous referents. The chapters themselves become shorter and more condensed as the narrative progresses, with the shortest chapters immediately preceding the most violent scene. All these devices serve to reinforce the confusing, intensifying, descending structure of the narration.

The major narrative elements, however, are the ever more extreme versions of very similar scenes and characters. The earliest scene chronologically, though innocent enough in itself perhaps, is a precursor and even model of the violence that occurs later. In that initial scene, Freddy, a prepubescent boy, is fascinated by the sexual differences between himself and the girl-child Eva. Too young for actual physical intercourse, he substitutes a dirty popsicle stick and uses it to explore Eva's genital arca. Although Eva co-operates in this experience, she has no desire to repeat it, despite Freddy's persistent demands:

> "You let me do it once."
> "I ain't gon let you do it no more."
> "When you gon let me fuck you again, Eva?"
> "You didn't fuck me before."

This demand-rejection pattern continues until Freddy moves away. Just before he leaves, he gives Eva a gift, a pocket knife, symbol of the dangerous potency of the male. The entire sequence of events seen as threatening by Eva, is consistently laughed at and applauded by other members of the community.

All the other major scenes replicate this initial one. In each, a male attempts to dominate a woman through some forceful act. The woman responds with a combination of passivity and resistance. Both the man and the community assume that the woman is helplessly attracted to men and sex; resistance is a sign of perverseness. In each case, she receives what is considered her just deserts, either reward for cooperation, or punishment for her rejection of a particular man; and in each case, the society reinforces the actions of the man. The sequence is considered to be both inevitable and desirable.

The scene with Freddy also indicates the character of the narrator. Eva reveals an obsession with sexuality and, more specifically, with what she perceives as the brutal nature of men. She finds both sexuality and men simultaneously enthralling and repulsive; she is inexplicably drawn to them even though her encounters are consistently painful and unattractive. This aspect of her character lends an air of inevitability to her experiences. They are both inescapable and damning. Each encounter builds on and reflects earlier ones and makes the involvement and the repulsion more intense. While the scene with Freddy has a certain playfulness and innocence that limit its impact on Eva, she finds in it the potential arrogance and violence of men.

That arrogance and violence are more distinct in another scene from her childhood. This scene, though it only indirectly involves Eva, offers her a demonstration of actual violence that the encounter with Freddy did not. The conflict, between her father and her mother, is based on the assumption of a love affair between the mother and another man, Tyrone. Although Eva, a witness to many of the meetings of the "lovers," claims never to have seen any sexual contact, the father presumes that the only explanation for male-female relationship is sexual intercourse. In this case the woman is punished rather than rewarded for her sexuality. Although Eva only hears what happens from the next room, she describes it with precision:

> Then it was like I could hear her clothes ripping. I don't know if the gentleness had been for me, or if it had been the kind of hurt gentleness one gets before they let go. But now he was tearing that blouse off and those underthings. I didn't hear nothing from her the whole time. I didn't hear a thing from her.
> "Act like a whore, I'm gonna fuck you like a whore. You act like a whore, I'm gonna fuck you like a whore."
> He kept saying that over and over. I was so scared. I kept feeling that after he tore all her clothes off, and there wasn't anymore to tear, he'd start tearing her flesh.

This scene is the inverse of the one with Freddy. The nature of woman, according to these males, is to want sex unceasingly. But this belief means that she cannot be trusted to limit herself to one particular man. Though promiscuity is a necessary aspect of her character, she must be punished for it if male dominance is to be maintained. By inflicting that punishment with the organic equivalent of Freddy's dirty stick, the father forces upon his wife the knowledge that the instrument of pleasure is also the instrument of control. By entrapping Eva in a room where she must hear the conflict, he teaches her the violent and inevitable consequences of her womanhood.

This indirect experience becomes direct when Eva marries a man of the age and attitude of her father. Though she is told by others and sees for herself the neurotic character of James's personality, she adapts herself to him rather than challenge or avoid him. When they move to a new house in a new town, he refuses to allow a telephone to be installed because, he repeatedly says, he doesn't want her lovers to call. When a fellow student from the university visits her to discuss an assignment, James takes this as evidence of her infidelity and replicates her father's behavior:

> He didn't say anything else. He was just sitting there, real hard, and then he just reached over and grabbed my shoulder, got up and started slapping me.
> "You think you a whore, I'll treat you like a whore. You think you a whore, I'll treat you like a whore."
> Naw, he didn't slap me, he pulled up my dress and got between my legs.
> "Think I can't do nothing. Fuck you like a damn whore."
> Naw, I'm not lying. He said, "Act like a whore, I'll fuck you like a whore."
> Naw, I'm not lying.

The virtual identity of this scene with the previous one illustrates three important points about the narrator of this novel. First, the exactness of duplication raises doubts about the reliability of Eva's story-telling: is she describing a discrete event, or is she simply changing the names in the original version? The former possibility indicates a coherent, reasonable narrator urging her listeners to accept an implausible coincidence. The alternative suggestion, that she is repeating herself, implies a narrative mind that is a hall of mirrors in which the reality of events is lost in distorted reflections. This reading, which is more consistent with the evidence of the text, is reinforced throughout the book, as identical bits of dialogue and narrative are associated with widely divergent characters and times. Eva's mind seems very much a sealed, mirrored enclosure in which facts and memory form illogical and often grotesque patterns.

The second point to be made about Eva's character is that her experiences are moving in an ever faster and tighter downward spiral. The conflict with James involves her directly, and it occurs much more rapidly than the parental one. Her father waited patiently, accumulating evidence of repeated rendezvous between his wife and Tyrone; he only became violent when he actually saw them together. In contrast, James, in his prohibition of a telephone, presumes guilt from the beginning and metes out punishment at the first sign of Eva's contact with another man. If this scene is a duplication of the earlier one, Eva has endowed it with much greater intensity.

The passivity of the female participant is the final point to be made about the conflict between Eva and James. The line which follows "Naw, I'm not lying," reads: "I squeezed my legs around his neck." Eva and the other women she describes not only accept but seem to approve the punishment they receive. Throughout the novel, female characters do not resist what they consider to be their destinies. An excellent example of this is the Queen Bee, a character that Eva identifies herself with late in the story. The Queen Bee is a sentimental woman who had the misfortune of falling in love with men who died shortly thereafter. Convinced that she is responsible for the deaths, she commits suicide after becoming infatuated once again. This fatalistic attitude is adopted in various degrees by most of the women of the book. This perception of themselves as objects caught helplessly in the flow of events and circumstance obviously strengthens the whirlpool structure of the novel.

Eva's next and climactic encounter would seem to contradict the idea of her passivity. During it she poisons and then mutilates the body of her lover. However, as shall be seen, this aggressiveness itself is an aspect of fate and does not bring relief but instead greater imprisonment. The sequence begins when Eva accepts the invitation of Davis to his apartment. Despite his clear intentions and insistence, she will not engage in sexual activity because she is having her period. He tolerates this delay but insists that she must remain until menstruation is over. He then locks her in the apartment whenever he leaves and refuses to allow her to go out for any reason. The various entrapments that she experienced with Freddy, her father, and James have now become a literal prison. The physical quality of her incarceration is reinforced by the imagery. The bodily functions of menstruation, sexuality, flatulence, urination, and defecation, all of which the tone indicates

are to be considered unpleasant, are accompanied by foods that can be construed as parallel to these functions: sausage covered with mustard, beer, hard-boiled eggs, cabbage. Eva's existence has been reduced to the most basic level; all of the rationalizations and social amenities have been stripped away and what remains is a woman reduced to the dehumanized object of a man's unquenchable sexual desire. She is not even permitted to comb her hair, since such an attempt at attractiveness is irrelevant at the level at which Davis uses her.

She offers little resistance to this treatment and cooperates even when he takes her while she is still menstruating. Her only complaint about the constant pattern of eating, sleeping, and copulating is that Davis has no interest in her sexual satisfaction. She does not express hatred or even dislike for him or what he is doing to her. Nevertheless, after several days, she puts rat poison in his food. This act, which she makes no effort to explain, seems to come from some deep, unexplored compulsion. The actions which follow his death certainly suggest this:

> I opened his trousers and played with his penis. My mouth, my teeth, my tongue went inside his trousers. I raised blood, slime from cabbage, blood sausage. Blood from an apple. I slid my hands around his back and dug my fingers up his ass, then I knelt down on the wooden floor, bruising my knees. I got back on the bed and squeezed his dick in my teeth. I bit down hard. My teeth in an apple. A swollen plum in my mouth. . . . A red swollen plum in my mouth. A milkweed full of blood. What would you do if you bit down and your teeth raised blood from an apple? Flesh from an apple? What would you do? How would you feel? . . . I got the silk handkerchief he used to wipe me after we made love, and wrapped his penis in it. I laid it back in his trousers, zipped him up. I kissed his cheeks, his neck. I got naked and sat on the bed again. I spread my legs across his thighs and put his hand on my crotch, stuffed his fingers up in me. I put my whole body over him. I farted.

Eva has eaten of the fruit of this perverse, imprisoning Eden and in doing so has found revenge, relief, and pleasure. In the most intense, most exploitive of her encounters with men, she responds to her treatment by literally removing the source of their obsessive behavior. She demonstrates that she has gained knowledge, though her education is the inverse of the one intended by Freddy, her father, James, and Davis. Her solution to the cycle of sexual obsession is not her mother's silent acceptance, or the Queen Bee's suicide, or her own escape from James; rather it is the truly radical choice of excising the root of the problem. Ironically, she sees this as an act of love, in that it relieves Davis of the stress of his compulsive behavior. Her sexual enjoyment of his corpse suggests that she is not repulsed by him but only released from the burden of his domination. In wrapping his organ in silk and returning it to him, she indicates a respect for his manhood that is separate from her attack on his compulsiveness. In death and dismemberment, he becomes the ideal man she has been searching for.

The end of her search, however, does not mean the end of the whirlpool pattern. Eva does not liberate herself from the predetermined sequence, but rather is actively complicitous in the final turn of the spiral. She accepts the consequences of her act by calling the police and then returning to the scene of the crime. She in effect chooses her final prison at the still center of the whirlpool. Her cell in the women's wing of a hospital for the criminally insane locks her in, but it also locks out the madly whirling world she has experienced. She is left along with Elvira, another man-killing woman, who repeatedly offers to give Eva sexual satisfaction. Eva resists, but the patience and understanding of her alter ego finally win out. In the last scene, she finds the peace she has been seeking: "'Tell me when it feels sweet, Eva. Tell me when it feels sweet, honey.' I leaned back, squeezing her face between my legs, and told her, 'Now.'" Elvira's concern for Eva's satisfaction makes possible the only pleasurable sexual intercourse in the novel. In the most physical of her prisons, at the bottom of the whirlpool, Eva finds a quiet freedom. That the whirlpool still exists is evidenced by the intrusions throughout the last part of the book by police officials and psychiatrists who insist that she endlessly repeat her story. This mental violation by men can only be escaped by an inward turning, by holding the face of her double, Elvira, between her legs. The concentric, spiraling structure of the book comes to its inmost circle in the image of Eva deriving sexual satisfaction in the contemplation of herself.

That Eva is insane, is obsessed with sexuality in the telling of her story, is unreliable as a narrator, and is quite properly imprisoned for murder offer some counterpoint to her final satisfaction. Her act does not free her from her own or the world's obsessiveness, but only forces her into the self-imprisonment of narcissism. The constant duplication and circularity of her narration suggests a character who has escaped nothing, explained nothing. Though she tells her most private experiences, she does not thereby make herself comprehensible.

Thus, to argue implicitly, as John Updike and Addison Gayle have done, that *Eva's Man* is a feminist attack on men, or more specifically, on black men compelled to prove their manhood, is to read the book much too narrowly. On the one hand, the novel *is* a powerful ideological statement. Eva draws the reader into the whirlpool of her desire, frustration, and hatred; she has the narrative skill to make believable her anger at the mistreatment she and other women have endured. Her ability to find patterns and duplications give validity to the implicit ideology. The Gothic structure embodies Eva's dark vision in which all people are trapped by the irrational forces that are an inevitable part of their lives. For the purposes of her tale, the most basic of those forces is sexuality. This force is by no means attractive; Eva's sense of sweetness at the end is only an aspect of her latest mental disorder, narcissism.

However, it is exactly at this point that the distinction between author and character must be made. The dark vision, the ideology, the madness are Eva's, not Gayl Jones's. To confuse their values and purposes is to oversimplify the novel. Jones has dramatized an attitude toward, and a perspective on, life through the creation of Eva and her story. She has carefully complicated any ideological interpretation by making the narrator a forceful, articulate, but clearly insane character. The degree to which Eva's ideology is taken seriously is a measure of Jones's accomplishment as a storyteller and not a measure of her own polemical intent. The Gothic structure has the double purpose of drawing us into the tale and demonstrating at the same time its artfulness. The final turn of the whirlpool is the willingness of the reader to be drawn into Eva's story through Jones's art. (pp. 94-100)

> *Keith Byerman, "Black Vortex: The Gothic Structure of 'Eva's Man'," in* MELUS, *Vol. 7, No. 4, Winter, 1980, pp. 93-101.*

Melvin Dixon (essay date 1984)

[*In the following excerpt, Dixon examines the importance of African-American language in* Corregidora.]

Since the publication of her first novel, *Corregidora* (1975), Gayl Jones has figured among the best of contemporary Afro-American writers who have used Black speech as a major aesthetic device in their works. Jones also holds a prominent place among women writers who have tried to rescue the Black female personality from the devastation and neglect it has suffered in a racist and sexist society. Like Alice Walker, Toni Morrison, Sherley Williams, Toni Cade Bambara, and such male writers as Ernest Gaines and Ishmael Reed, Jones uses the rhythm and structure of spoken language to develop authentic characters and to establish new possibilities for dramatic conflict within the text and between readers and the text itself. (p. 236)

Jones's fictional landscape is the relationship between men and women, a field her characters mine with dishonesty, manipulation, mutual abuse. The battleground is sex, and Jones uses the right sexual vocabulary to strategize the warfare. Results vary; it can be the ambiguous yet healing reconciliation of a blues stanza shared between Mutt and Ursa in *Corregidora* or a lonely woman's solo cry at orgasm in *Eva's Man.* What Jones is after is the words and deeds that finally break the sexual bondage men and women impose upon each other. When language is drawn from the musical and sexual idiom and shared with the reader like a song or an incantation, there is a chance that painful wounds may be healed. Such reconciliation is possible through an evidence of words spoken, sung, communicated. Acts of language can be regenerative: predatory characters can recover their briefly lost selves by reconnecting to the textures of love and identity articulated in the Black American speech community. (p. 237)

• • • • •

Corregidore, in Portuguese, means "judicial magistrate." By changing the gender designation, Jones makes Ursa Corregido*ra* a female judge charged by the women in her family to "correct" (from the Portuguese verb *corrigir*) the historical invisibility they have suffered, "to give evidence" of their abuse, and "to make generations" as a defense against their further annihilation. Ursa's name also comes from the man responsible for much of this pain, the Brazilian coffee planter and whoremaster Corregidora. Ursa must bring justice to bear upon his past exploitation of Blacks as slaves and women as whores and upon his present haunting contamination of her life.

Corregidora opens with an act of violence: Mutt Thomas in a jealous rage knocks Ursa, his newly pregnant wife and blues singer, down a flight of stairs. Hospitalized, Ursa loses her child and womb and can never fulfill the pledge made by the women in her family "to make generations." The novel details Ursa's attempt to free herself from guilt imposed by her physical limitation and from resentment against her now-estranged husband. Mutt, however, is not the only culprit. Ursa learns

Dust jacket of Jones's second novel, Eva's Man.

that she comes from generations of abused women and women abusers. Great-Gram was the slave and concubine of Corregidora. Their child became his mistress and bore another woman, Ursa's mother. When "papers" were burned to deny that slavery ever existed, that these women may not have ever existed, their sole defense is to make generations to preserve the family. As Ursa has been admonished to do from the time she was five: "They didn't want to leave no evidence of what they done—so it couldn't be held against them. And I'm leaving evidence too. And you got to leave evidence . . . we got to have evidence to hold up. That's why they burned all the papers, so there wouldn't be no evidence to hold up against them." This oral pledge must accomplish what the written record no longer can do.

The pledge not only binds Ursa to procreation, it also revives in her mind the specter of cruel Corregidora himself. When Ursa is abused by Mutt and forced to come to new terms with her femininity, the images of Corregidora and Mutt merge and she feels abused by both simultaneously. Paradoxically, however, Mutt attacked Ursa without knowing she was pregnant. He made it impossible for her to "give evidence" through making generations and she must find another way. Indirectly, Mutt has made it possible for Ursa to free herself from the pattern of *mutual* abuse implicit in the pledge itself. Ursa, haunted by the relationship between Great-Gram and Corregidora, learns that she was about to continue the oppressive matrilineage that held men and women captive to the need for generations in the manner preordained by her foremothers:

> I realized for the first time I had what those women had. I'd always thought I was different. *Their* daughter, but somehow different. Maybe less Corregidora. I don't know. But when I saw that picture, I knew I had it. What my mother and my mother's mother before her had. The mulatto women. Great-Gram was the coffee-bean woman, but the rest of us . . . But I am different now, I was thinking, I have everything they had, except generations. I can't make generations. And even if I still had my womb, even if the first baby had come—what would I have done then? Would I have kept it up? Would I have been like *her,* or *them?*

Mutt's deed forces Ursa to come to new terms, new language, about her personal and generational identity. The different way Ursa comes to offer evidence is by singing the blues in what she suspects is a "new voice" following her convalescence. She is then prepared to confront her past and transcend it as best she can.

At the end of the novel and after a separation of twenty-two years—the narrative's only strain on credibility—Ursa reunites with Mutt. She is no longer a passive victim of abuse nor is she a solo blues singer. When Ursa performs fellatio on Mutt, she retains control over herself and Mutt. Ursa thus exchanges her role as a blues singer whose mouth contains "a hard voice," a voice that "hurts you and makes you still want to listen," into an instrument of direct sexual power: "What is it a woman can do to a man that make him hate her so bad he wont to kill her one minute and keep thinking about her and can't get her out of his mind the next?" The rhetorical question is meant to bridge historical time, to unite Ursa's present coupling with Mutt to the act between Great-Gram and Corregidora. "It had to be sexual," Ursa thinks. "It had to be something sexual that Great-Gram did to Corregidora.... In a split second I knew what it was, in a split second of hate and love I knew what it was.... A moment of pleasure and excruciating pain at the same time...a moment that stops before it breaks the skin: 'I could kill you.'" Mutt and Ursa are in the same Drake Hotel where they spent the early days of their marriage. "It wasn't the same room, but the same place. The same feel of the place. I knew what he wanted. I wanted it too. We didn't speak. We got out of our clothes. I got between his knees." The return to their own past simultaneously returns them to the past of the initial tension and conflict between Ursa's ancestors: "It was like I didn't know how much was me and Mutt and how much was Great-Gram and Corregidora." And it is this metaphorical return that allows Ursa to go forward; her reconciliation with Mutt is achieved through sex and a ritualized dialogue that assumes the rhythm, structure, and tone of a blues stanza:

> "I don't want a kind of woman that hurt you," he said.
> "Then you don't want me."
> "I don't want a kind of woman that hurt you."
> "Then you don't want me."
> "I don't want a kind of woman that hurt you."
> "Then you don't want me."

The blues language is evidence for the *re*generation Ursa and Mutt experience: "He shook me till I fell against him crying. 'I don't want a kind of man that'll hurt me neither,' I said. He held me tight."

Furthermore, the six-line call-response pattern above reflects the blues structure of the entire novel and the pattern of Ursa's developing consciousness. The narrative is shaped by the three-part incremental repetition of story line from Great-Gram to Gram, Gram to Mama, Mama to Ursa: "My great-grandmama told my grandmama the part she lived through that my grandmama didn't live through and my grandmama told my mama what they both lived through and my mama told me what they all lived through and we suppose to pass it down like that from generation to generation so we'd never forget. Even though they'd burned everything to play like it didn't never happen." Ursa, however, sings a different song. And like the last line in most blues stanzas, her new words resolve the song's narrative only after she reunites with Mutt.

Corregidora, immortalized by the oral history, is the lover and husband of all the women, including Mama, who, although she married Martin and later separated from him, kept her maiden name. Corregidora also threatens to possess Ursa until Mutt's jealous rage frees her from the grip of those generations. During the years of her estrangement from Mutt, Ursa grows aware of mutual abuse and the danger of her potential acquiescence, "like Mama when she started talking like Great-Gram." The knowledge Ursa gains that leads her from blues solo to the blues duet above concerns the arbitrary exchange of power and the mutual consent which produces authority: "But was what Corregidora had done to *her,* to *them,* any worse than what Mutt had done to me, than what we had done to each other, than what Mama had done to Daddy, or what he had done to her in return, making her walk down the street looking like a whore?" The justice Ursa finally wields comes from the fundamental ambivalence of the blues condition, what Ralph Ellison once defined as an "autobiographical chronicle of personal *catastrophe* expressed *lyrically*" (emphasis mine); from language comes control, a form to contain and transmit experience.

Mutt, although inarticulate about his deepest feelings and love for Ursa, understands her dilemma. His jealousy is understandable on the one hand because he views Corregidora as a rival for Ursa's attention, indeed *love,* and on the other because he feels caught in the abusive stereotype of a male breeder, a role that Martin rejected as soon as he realized the conspiracy of the elder Corregidora women. Mutt was drawn to Ursa by the bewitching power of her songs. Ursa's voice, like that of a Black siren, lures men to a potentially tragic fate. But Ursa is also trapped in the act of luring men. In this regard she bears strong resemblance to Lula in Baraka's *Dutchman,* who never finds her way *out* of the underground subway. Ursa is similarly ensnared by history; she finds release only by learning the truth behind her mother's marriage and by reuniting with Mutt.

Feeling that he knows Ursa "from way back," Mutt is both her opponent and her friend largely because of what he intuits from the evidence of her songs.

> When I first saw Mutt I was singing a song about a train tunnel. About this train going in the tunnel, but it didn't seem like they was no end to the tunnel, and nobody knew when the train would get out, and then all of a sudden the tunnel tightened around the train like a fist. Then I sang about this bird woman, whose eyes were deep wells. How she would take a man on a long journey, but never return him.

Ursa's attraction to Mutt makes him an audience of one: "he got to be the man I was singing to. I would look at him when I began a song and somehow I would be looking at him when I ended it." Mistaking him for all men, Ursa is slow to appreciate Mutt's individuality or his ability to help her escape the oppressive hold of Corregidora. Ursa is also guilty of trying to make Mutt play Corregidora's role:

> When I'd flared back at him with his own kind of words, he'd say, "You never used to talk like that. How'd you get to talk like that?"
> I answered, "I guess you taught me. Corregidora taught Great-Gram to talk the way she did."
> "Don't give me hell, Ursa," he said. "You know this is hell. Don't you feel anything? Don't you want

me?"
   "Yes," I said.
   "I want to help you, but I can't help you unless you help me."

Mutt tries to tell Ursa that she isn't the hard woman she thinks she must be. But she persists in wearing the mask. When he refuses Ursa sex, it is his way of reacting to her use and abuse of him. Mutt's last act of aggression, knocking Ursa accidentally down a flight of stairs, breaks their dual tie to Corregidora—Ursa's womb.

The loss of her womb precipitates Ursa's journey back into the past to recover a female identity that was lost along with her inability to make generations, the main source of identity for her foremothers. Ursa rejects the lesbian advances of Cat Lawson and Jeffey, and has a brief marriage with Tadpole, a bar owner who also tries to help Ursa feel like a woman again. But the only people who can help are her mother and Mutt, who lead Ursa right back to a new kind of struggle with Corregidora.

When Ursa takes the initiative to visit her mother and urges her to talk, she learns how Mama was virtually made into a whore, not by Martin but by Great-Gram and Gram, who needed generations to pursue their rage against Corregidora more than they needed men as stable family partners. "They be telling me," Mama says, "about making generations, but I wasn't looking for no man. I never was looking for no man. I kept thinking back on it, though, and it was like I had to go there, had to go there and sit there and have him watch me like that . . . you know how mens watch you when they wont something." And this is the same look Mutt accuses Ursa of giving other men: "If you wasn't one of them you wouldn't like them mens watching after you." But by the time she met Martin Ursa's mother was already trapped. "Like my body or something knew what it wanted even if I didn't want no man. Cause I knew I wasn't looking for none. But it was like it knew it wanted you, and knew it would have you, and knew you'd be a girl. It was like my whole body knew you'd be a girl." The unnamed force is Corregidora.

Martin's discovery that he was simply a surrogate breeder for Corregidora causes the breakup of the marriage. Martin tells Mama:

> Money's not how I helped you. I helped you that night didn't I . . . I lived in that house long enough to know I helped you. How long was it? Almost two years, wasn't it? That's long enough for any man to know if he's helped. How could I have missed. I mean, the first time. The other times were all miss, weren't they, baby? They were all miss, weren't they?

Martin then retaliates by making Mama walk through the town looking like a whore, which is what the other women were, Corregidora's whores. Following Ursa's birth and her divorce, Mama returns to the celibacy she has always preferred. She has fulfilled her pledge and she retains her maiden name, which suggests that Mama is symbolically married to Corregidora not to Martin.

Ursa also tries to keep her name in what we must now see ironically as a sign not of independence but of dependence: "That's my name not my husband's." If Ursa is indeed about to repeat her mother's act, then Mutt's harsh reaction appears more perceptive than irrational: "Ain't even took my name. You Corregidora's ain't you. Ain't even took my name. You ain't my woman." Mutt re-creates Martin's rage. Martin was not totally defeated by Corregidora or the women because he poses the one question that diminishes the moral superiority these women claimed, for themselves as victims, a question which even Mama was afraid to ask: "How much was hate for Corregidora and how much was love?" Martin, not Mama, had the courage to stand up against the women and demand that they acknowledge their true feelings, that they admit to the ambivalence which governed their lives. Ursa's discovery of this ambivalence both frees her from the past and allows her to return to Mutt.

Like Martin, Mutt unmasks Ursa's hardness, ambivalence, enslavement to Corregidora's history, as well as her lack of identity (although Ursa is on the way to recovering her identity after the visit to Mama). "Forget what they went through," Mutt pleads with Ursa, who answers, "I can't forget. The space between my thighs. A well that never bleeds," and, "I never told you how it was. Always their memories, but never my own." Ursa earns her own memory and identity once she hears Mama's story and learns the painful truth that her blues singing, meant to give evidence and witness ("They stuffed Corregidora in me and I sang back in return"), only served to bind her closer to the past. What she must now articulate is not language itself but the rhythm *between* people talking, the emotions communicated in speech, not merely the words: "If you understood me, Mama, you'd see I was trying to explain it, in blues without words, the explanation somewhere behind the words." Ursa tries to replace the ambiguity of language and the pain of violence with a direct exchange of feeling between two parties. That exchange happens in the multiple levels of communication in the altered, ritualized speech between Mutt and Ursa at the novel's close. Ursa has brought memory with her but it is *her* memory, less oppressive and debilitating for the lines are sung by them both:

> "I don't want a kind of woman that hurt you."
> "Then you don't want me."

Ursa's main task has been to find justice for herself *first,* then the others. Ursa served as nemesis for the women and for Corregidora, as Mutt has been for her. Mutt is also what Albert Murray has called an "antagonistic co-operator"; he helps Ursa break the stranglehold of the past. "Whichever way you look at it," he tells her. "We ain't them." And Mutt rejects the ambivalence cultivated by the women as the family's legacy for Ursa. In a brief tale about his own great-grandfather, who tried to control his anger and bitterness after the sudden loss of his wife by consuming contradictory kinds of food, Mutt offers an alternative: "He wouldn't eat nothing but onions and peppermint. Eat the onions so people wouldn't come around him, and then eat the peppermint so they could. I tried it but it didn't do nothing but make me sick." Mutt's lesson to Ursa is that justice is not a blues solo of ambivalence or alienation but a healing communication between reconciled opposites. The voice Ursa gains is the triptych narrative itself, for it returns to Ursa a quality and range of evidence she can sing about and a healthier emotion behind the words she can communicate. (pp. 239-45)

> *Melvin Dixon, "Singing a Deep Song: Language as Evidence in the Novels of Gayl Jones," in* Black Women Writers (1950-1980): A Critical Evaluation, *edited by Mari Evans, Anchor Press/Doubleday, 1984, pp. 236-48.*

FURTHER READING

Bell, Roseann Pope. "Gayl Jones: A Voice in the Whirlwind." *Studia Africana* 1, No. 1 (Spring 1977): 99-107.
> Examines Jones's poetry, concluding that the author "may be viewed as an iconoclastic seed, germinating with a cadre of new writers who are determined to explode myths and stereotypes shrouding the efforts of Black women writers."

————. "Gayl Jones Takes a Look at 'Corregidora'—An Interview." In *Sturdy Black Bridges: Visions of Black Women in Literature,* edited by Roseann P. Bell, Bettye J. Parker, and Beverly Guy-Sheftall, pp. 282-87. Garden City, N.Y.: Anchor Press/Doubleday, 1979.
> Interview in which Jones discusses the influences of Brazilian history, oral history, and folklore on *Corregidora.*

Byerman, Keith E. "Intense Behaviors: The Use of the Grotesque in *The Bluest Eye* and *Eva's Man.*" *CLA Journal* XXV, No. 4 (June 1982): 447-57.
> Examines the grotesque and gothic aspects of *Eva's Man* and Toni Morrison's *The Bluest Eye.*

Johnson, Diane. "The Oppressor in the Next Room." *The New York Review of Books* XXIV, No. 18 (10 November 1977): 6, 8.
> Review of Jones's *White Rat,* Toni Morrison's *Song of Solomon,* and James Alan McPherson's *Elbow Room.* Johnson determines that the stories in *White Rat* "confirm one's sense of [Jones's] direction and preoccupation: sex is violation, and violation is the principal dynamic of human relationships."

Lee, Valerie Gray. "The Use of Folktale in Novels by Black Women Writers." *CLA Journal* XXIII, No. 3 (March 1980): 266-72.
> Contends that "the folktalk that goes on among mothers and daughters in novels by modern black women writers all centers on the menfolk," using Zora Neale Hurston's *Their Eyes Were Watching God,* Toni Morrison's *Sula,* and *Corregidora* as examples.

Mano, D. Keith. "How to Write Two First Novels with Your Knuckles." *Esquire* 86, No. 6 (December 1976): 62, 66.
> A critical attack accusing Jones of writing two "first" novels, using as evidence identical dialogue in *Corregidora* and *Eva's Man.* Mano asserts: "The practical truth is, if *Corregidora* had been written, say, by some white first novelist it'd still be in manuscript."

Tate, Claudia C. "*Corregidora:* Ursa's Blues Medley." *Black American Literature Forum* 13, No. 4 (Winter 1979): 139-41.
> Contends that the structure of *Corregidora,* though seemingly simple, is intricate.

————. "Gayl Jones." In her *Black Women Writers at Work,* pp. 89-99. New York: Continuum, 1983.
> Interview with Jones, who talks about her method of writing, her influences, and criticism of her works.

Weixlmann, Joe. "A Gayl Jones Bibliography." *Callaloo* 7, No. 1 (Winter 1984): 119-31.
> Primary and secondary bibliography of Jones.

Adrienne Kennedy

1931-

(Full name Adrienne Lita Kennedy) American dramatist and memoirist.

Kennedy, a contemporary American dramatist, is known for her controversial, often violent plays. Although some audiences have expressed discomfort with the dark, brutal nature of these works, critics have praised their lyricism and expressionistic structure and frequently compared the plays to poetry. Commentators have also noted the multiple or uncertain identities of many of Kennedy's African-American characters, interpreting this aspect of Kennedy's dramas as a reflection of the struggle for self-knowledge in a white-dominated society. Kennedy has acknowledged an autobiographical side to her work: "I see my writing as being an outlet for inner psychological confusion and questions stemming from childhood . . . . It's really figuring out the 'why' of things—that is, if that is even possible."

Kennedy grew up in a multi-ethnic neighborhood in Cleveland, Ohio, where her father was an executive at the local YMCA and her mother was a teacher. A gifted child, she learned to read at the age of three. Kennedy credits her mother as an early literary influence: "I really owe writing to her in a sense, because my mother is a terrific storyteller and I feel that all my writing basically has the same tone as the stories she told about her childhood. She used to tell funny stories, but they always had this terror in them, a blackness." Kennedy's memoir, *People Who Led to My Plays* (1987), documents Kennedy's creative development; it includes discussion of her early fascination with glamorous film stars and her reverence for the work of Tennessee Williams, whose play *The Glass Menagerie* first attracted her to the theatre. She did not begin writing, however, until she enrolled in a course on twentieth-century literature at Ohio State University: "That course fired something in me. I suddenly found myself writing short stories instead of studying." Soon after graduating with a degree in social work, Kennedy married, had her first child, and began writing plays while staying up late with the baby. She received encouragement from editors and writing instructors, but her work was consistently rejected by publishers. At the age of twenty-nine Kennedy traveled to West Africa—an event that led to a turning point in her writing: "I couldn't cling to what I had been writing—it changed me so . . . . I think the main thing was that I discovered a strength in being a black person and a connection to West Africa." During this time she also traveled to Rome; the contrast between her African and European experiences provided the background for her first play, *Funnyhouse of a Negro* (1962). When Kennedy returned to the United States she submitted the drama to a workshop taught by playwright Edward Albee. Soon

afterward, the play enjoyed a successful off-Broadway run, and it won an Obie Award in 1964.

Funnyhouse of a Negro focuses on a young girl named Sarah whose confused identity is linked with her ambiguous feelings about her white mother and black father. Simultaneously obsessed with and alienated from European culture, she is tormented by visions involving her light-skinned mother, Queen Victoria, the Duchess of Habsburg, and Jesus. The play was praised as an innovative depiction of characters with multiple personas. Reviewers also commented on Kennedy's use of historical figures to represent various aspects of Sarah's identity, and several critics noted the author's own fascination with European royalty. Discussing the work, Kennedy revealed: "I struggled for a long time to write plays—as typified by *Funnyhouse*—in which the person is in conflict with their inner forces, with the conflicting sides to their personality, which I found to be my own particular, greatest conflict . . . . I finally came up with this one character, Sarah, who, rather than talk to her father or mother, talked with these people she created about her problems."

Like *Funnyhouse of a Negro,* Kennedy's next work, the one-act play *The Owl Answers* (1963), is about a black woman's quest for identity in a world dominated by whites. The main character, named She, is the illegitimate daughter of a wealthy white man and his black cook, who is also "the town whore." Rejected by both parents, She is consumed by feelings of estrangement, and her psyche is fragmented into several identities: Clara, the Virgin Mary, the Bastard, and the Owl. Throughout the play, She's black, white, and mythical personalities transform and merge in a dream-like manner until she finally appears as a lonely teacher who, after threatening her lover with a butcher knife, becomes an owl. Critics emphasized the recurring owl symbolism in the work, stressing associations with death, trees, ill fortune, anti-Christian nuances, quests for love, and feminine mythology. Another drama of the period, *A Beast Story* (1966), presents stark, monolithic characters who engage in a pattern of destructive family relationships. At the opening of the play, Beast Girl describes her father performing an ominous ceremony in which she and Dead Human are wed: "My father preached our wedding service and a black sun floated over the altar. A crow flew through an open window while my mother played the organ and the black sun floated . . . ." Throughout the play, Beast Girl is victimized by her family; she is stalked by her lustful father, Beast Man, and then raped by Dead Human when she refuses his advances. Later, her parents force her to kill her child, and in an apocalyptic fit of rage and despair, she murders her husband as well. Kimberly W. Benston observed: "[*A Beast Story*] deals with the impossibility of maintaining a dream untarnished—specifically, the dream of identity achieved through love—amid the corruption which is life. The play is unrelentingly melancholy—we have sublimations and deaths, tiredness and disillusion, frustration and disenchantment."

Also among Kennedy's critically acclaimed works of the 1960s are the lesser-known *A Rat's Mass* (1966) and *Lesson in a Dead Language* (1968), which portray worlds of surrealistically distorted religion and focus on the loss of childhood innocence through sexual initiation rites. *Sun: A Poem for Malcolm X Inspired by His Murder* (1970), a short play about creation, is one of Kennedy's few dramas dominated by a male voice.

In 1971 Kennedy joined five other women playwrights to found the Women's Theatre Council, a cooperative devoted to producing the works of women playwrights and providing opportunities for women in other aspects of the theatre, such as directing and acting. Mel Gussow of the *New York Times* noted that the council's "founding sisters all come from Off Off Broadway, are exceedingly prolific, have had their plays staged throughout the United States and in many foreign countries and feel neglected by the New York commercial theater. Each has a distinctive voice, but their work is related in being largely non-realistic and experimental. The women feel unified as innovators and by their artistic consciousness."

Kennedy branched out into theatre for children in 1980 after being commissioned by the Empire State Youth Theatre Institute. *A Lancashire Lad* (1980), her first play for children, is a fictionalized version of Charles Chaplin's childhood. Narrated by the hero, the play traces young Charles's life growing up in Dickensian England and the beginning of his career as a performer in British music halls. Although an entertaining musical, the show confronts the poverty and pain of Chaplin's youth. Praising Kennedy's language for achieving "powerful emotional effects with the sparest of means," *New York Times* reviewer Frank Rich concluded: "The difference between *The Lancashire Lad* and an adult play is, perhaps, the intellectual simplicity of its ambitions. Yet that simplicity can also be theater magic in its purest and most eloquent form."

(For further information about Kennedy's life and works, see *Black Writers; Contemporary Authors,* Vol. 103; *Contemporary Authors Bibliographical Series,* Vol. 3; *Contemporary Authors New Revision Series,* Vol 26; and *Dictionary of Literary Biography,* Vol. 38: *Afro-American Writers after 1955, Dramatists and Prose Writers.*)

PRINCIPAL WORKS

Funnyhouse of a Negro (drama) 1962
The Owl Answers (drama) 1963
A Beast Story (drama) 1966
A Rat's Mass (drama) 1966
A Lesson in a Dead Language (drama) 1968
Boats (drama) 1969
*Cities in Bezique (dramas) 1969
Sun: A Poem for Malcolm X Inspired by His Murder (drama) 1970
An Evening with Dead Essex (drama) 1973
A Movie Star Has to Star in Black and White (drama) 1976
Black Children's Day (drama) 1980
A Lancashire Lad (drama) 1980
Orestes and Electra (drama) 1980
People Who Led to My Plays (memoir) 1987
In One Act (dramas) 1989

*This work contains the one-act plays *The Owl Answers* and *A Beast Story.*

Robert L. Tener (essay date 1975)

[*In the following excerpt, Tener examines symbolism in Kennedy's* The Owl Answers.]

One of the most provocative and least studied black American dramatists to emerge in the sixties is Adrienne Kennedy. Set in the surrealistic theatre of the mind, her dramas are rich collages of ambiguities, metaphors, poetic insights, literary references, and mythic associations, all of which provide a dramatic form unique to Miss Kennedy. Having the power of myths, her dramas suggest an awareness of reality contingent upon the images that man is conditioned to expect in his culture. Moreover, they draw upon that peculiar quality of myths which enables man to externalize his deepest feelings about his own nature, identity, and relationship with the sacred. In *The Owl Answers,* one of Miss Kennedy's most compact plays, this effect of myths is achieved through extending the metaphoric values of the owl. While on one level of literary meaning the owl stands for evil omens and darkness, in association with the fig tree it is the controlling metaphor in the play anchoring the heroine's problem of identity with the worlds of her white and black parents and her many self-images.

The Owl Answers, a one act play, takes place in a New York Harlem subway which changes at times into the Tower of London, St. Peter's Chapel, or a Harlem hotel room. As the action moves from the present time on the subway to the past time of memories and dreams, the setting becomes variously one of the other three areas. There are three major actions blurring and blending with each other so that setting as well as identity become fragmented and swirl through time and memory as in a dream. Characters pass from one role to another with the removal of an item of clothing or a change in hair. The heroine is named She, the bastard daughter of a black cook and a white man.

The first major action, created partly from memory and fantasy, takes place largely in London. According to She's fantasy, she and her white father, William Mattheson, visit London on a literary pilgrimage. There he dies of a heart attack, and she is locked in the Tower to prevent her attending his funeral. Her guards are Chaucer and Shakespeare, their names suggesting the white literary heritage she had studied. Another historical character appears, Anne Boleyn, who apparently reflects attitudes toward love as expressed in Western literature and political history. She turns to Anne and asks for her help.

Blending with the events in London and in the Tower, the second major action takes place in the past and, representing expository reality, communicates religious and social attitudes. In his home town in Georgia, the white father who had conceived She on his black cook calls his daughter a bastard and apparently rejects her. She is adopted and brought up by the Reverend Passmore and his wife, both of whom are black, who call her Clara. Occasionally, however, they refer to her as an owl and lock her in a fig tree. When her white father died, she wanted to attend his funeral and was told not to. She also wants to make a literary pilgrimage to Europe. Sometime in the past she had been married once and has become a school teacher in Savannah, Georgia. Her adopted parents, the Passmores, like She, are associated with specific attitudes. Seeing herself as God's bride, the Virgin Mary, the wife refuses to allow her husband to touch her. Her bed she turns into an altar by means of owl feathers and there she commits suicide with a butcher knife. As for her husband, Reverend Passmore believes in the white man's Christian religion and has as his symbol the white bird of the church which flies into a canary cage.

The blurring together of both actions develops when the Reverend Passmore's wife becomes successively She's real black mother and then Anne Boleyn. She's white father is presented just as ambiguously. In the events located in London and in the Tower, he is apparently emotionally close to his daughter; in those placed in the real past, he has obviously ignored her. As for his daughter, she appears at times as Clara; in other instances she is the Bastard, or the Virgin Mary, or the Owl. The consequent merging of the two actions emphasizes She's feeling of love and estrangement.

The third major action develops in the present time on a subway in New York. Here Clara sits, a thirty-four-year-old lonely school teacher who searches for love and spends her summers hunting men in New York to take to her hotel room. As Clara brings to life in her memory the events and actions of the first two plots, her latest pick-up, a black man watches her. Eventually she calls him God and asks him to take her so that she can go to St. Paul's chapel. When he tries to undress her, the setting shifts to the hotel room and the bed transforms into an altar. Now she wants him to call her Mary and shows him her letters written daily to her dead father on her trip to Europe (it is not clear if she has really taken the trip or if it was made only in her fantasy). Then she takes a bloody butcher knife from the letters and attacks him. Frightened, he runs away. Now alone, she kneels at the bed-altar which catches on fire, and in its light gradually she begins to look more and more like an owl.

The play suggests no simple answers to its complexities. It would appear that She is confused by her multiple identities or their sources, none of which seems to be really her, yet all of which help determine her inner relationships. Some of them, like Bastard and daughter, come from the black world; others like Virgin Mary come from the white man's religious world; but one, the Owl, comes from the world of myth and legend. She is on a quest for her identity, and her identity cannot be separated from love for which she also searches. Nor can her need for identity and love be divorced from her desire for a father. Her multiple father images are her blood father (a white man), her adopted father (a black man), and her religious father (God); the love which she searches for is love for a father image: love for a real father whom she can be close to, love for a man whom she hunts for in the subways, and religious love which she identifies with God. Her sense of personal identity is equally fragmented as it is confused by her fractured living as a black person in a white world filled with white images and concepts, none of which is directly related to herself as a black woman.

The play focuses on the problems of identity as conceived in She's mind on two different levels of complexity. In a sense her least complicated roles are that she is a woman, she is a black, and she is a bastard. Her other roles are, however, culturally more complex. She has been educated in college in the white man's literary and political heritage; she has been brought up in the white man's Christian religion none of whose symbols have the mythic power of uniting man with the sacred for the black person; and she has been forced to live in two worlds, one black and one white, because she is a mulatto.

The major thematic content of the play then is the problem of how She's fragmented identities relate to her quest for a stable and unified self-image. The problem is an internal one for She, and Adrienne Kennedy has externalized it by joining the metaphor of the owl with the mythic qualities of the fig tree. (pp. 1-2)

It is clearly more than merely a bird of ill omen. In the more common mythologies of the world, the owl is, among many things, a symbol for non-believers in God who dwell in darkness; a messenger of witches or the bird transformation of a witch; another name for a harlot who works the night; one of the epiphanies of Athene, the Greek goddess of wisdom and the female domestic arts; or the metamorphosis of the baker's daughter who begrudged Christ her father's bread. Its hooting cry is the call of death; at night its voice is the spirit of a women who has died in childbirth and is crying for her dead child; its presence in a tree near a home presages ill fortune to the inhabitants. Its legendary associations with death, trees, ill fortune, anti-Christian nuances, quest for love, and a female principle thus make it a richly ambiguous metaphor suitable for Kennedy's intentions.

In the play the owl is She, the mulatto daughter of a rich white man. Her identity has historical roots both in the English literary, political, religious world of her white blood father and in the white-black world of her mother, the town's black whore. In addition her identity has an anchorage in the mythical world of folklore and legend from which Kennedy draws her controlling metaphors. If in the white world the owl has one set of governing associations, in the world of myths it has another.

The structure for Adrienne Kennedy's use of the owl and fig tree is one of association with different events, situations, attitudes, and persons. First, as a bird, the owl balances the white bird identified in the play with Christianity and the Reverend Passmore. Like a canary, the white bird prefers to fly into a cage. On the other hand, while the white bird is not related to She, the owl is. The obvious inference is that Christianity as a religion of white men is not psychologically and historically suited to She.

Second, in the play the owl is associated with a fig tree. As the bastard daughter of William Mattheson and the black whore (or as the adopted daughter of the Passmore's, the point of view not being clear on this matter), she is "locked" in a fig tree. The metaphoric term "locked" relates this action with her being locked in the Tower of London. Both situations suggest that what is important is not what happened but how she responds to or feels about the events. Thus as an owl, She sits in the fig tree.

Third, the bird is associated with the dead. In She's memory it occurs in relation to her white father, now dead, who had called her an owl, and somewhat like her white father, she is similar to a dead thing. She feels sterile, barren, loveless.

Fourth, the owl is presented in the context of the beginning of things and in relation to sacred notions. When her mother tells her that "the Owl was your beginning," she says that she belongs to "God and the owls." Her bastard birth is thus anchored by the owl. In addition the owl extends some of its meaning to her black mother who uses owl feathers to construct an altar. Exploring her responses to the owl, She says that she calls "God and the Owl answers." Later she exclaims that

> it haunts my Tower calling, its feathers are blowing against the cell wall, speckled in the garden on the fig tree, it comes feathered great hollowed-eyed with yellow skin and yellow eyes, the flying bastard. From my Tower I keep calling and the only answer is the Owl God. . . . I am only yearning for our kingdom God.

Fifth, the owl is presented against a background of personal and religious ritual which suggests the frustra-tions of the three black women who dominate the play in their tripartite roles as the biological mother, the religious mother, and the maiden. The black whore mother sits like an owl and pecks at red rice on the floor. She becomes more owl-like as owl feathers appear on her and as she drags in a "great dark bed." At this point the real mother's identity fuses with those of Mrs. Passmore and of the owl. She acquires more owl feathers and her hair becomes black and long and straight like that of the Reverend's wife. In this transformation she turns her bed into a high altar with owl feathers and candles. There she sits. And now as all three concepts (mother, adopted mother, and owl), with a white dress and "wild kinky hair," and partly covered with owl feathers, the figure calls to She, the "Owl in the fig tree," and says that "there is a way from owldom." That way, however, is to St. Paul's Chapel. As both figures kneel in prayer, a green light suffuses the tableau, and the mother image kills herself with a butcher knife.

Sixth, the owl is always associated with She, as can be seen in the many references already suggested. But especially is the association stressed in the final scene of the play. When the black man tries to undress She on the altar-bed, she "screams like an owl," struggles, and begs to be allowed to go to St. Paul's Chapel to see her white father. Suddenly from her notebooks, she draws the butcher knife, bloody and covered with feathers and attacks him. As he runs away frightened, she falls onto the bed which begins to burn. In the background up in the dome, as though suggestive of the Chapel, the white bird laughs. She is transformed almost magically into an owl-like figure and can only say "Ow . . . oww."

Quite clearly the owl is intended by Adrienne Kennedy to be black woman lost intellectually and emotionally in a white world. Confused about her black identity and its related basic values of love, father, and religion, She becomes at times a harlot. As the owl who answers, she is the nonbeliever, the harlot, the woman anguished by the lack of love, the spirit of the dead. But being black she feels related to the night; she cries of the woe to come. (pp. 2-3)

In the play She is the composite overlay of her father's cultural heritage and her mother's racial background. Her identity is fragmented because half of her physical roots are black but almost all of her intellectual heritage is white. The consequence is that she feels alienated from her many selves and cannot integrate them. She asks herself on her literary pilgrimage to London if this is her past. And she says that she is never going back there. When her white father died, he returned to the home of his ancestors, but she cannot.

Within the context of the play then, She is the owl for whom instead of solace Christianity offers only the vision of the white virgin Mary equated with a black Christian step-mother who had called her a child of darkness. She is a harlot who hunts for love at night time, a prophetess of death. Especially is she a barren woman crying for the love and children which she does not have. But the owl is also her alter ego, her bird sister, her epiphany. She sits in the fig tree and her presence reflects the death of her father and of Mrs. Passmore and of all those like them. The two metaphors suggest that her anguish is profound and timeless, growing from her basic sense of self. Sitting like an owl in the tree of knowledge about good and evil, she has learned about the white man's literature, but she has also acquired a sense of her personal loss.

Specifically, Adrienne Kennedy in *The Owl Answers* appears to focus on the concept that the black in America has no historical or literary heroes to identify with and to achieve personal unity through, a unity necessary to prevent the self from being alienated from the continuity of life. This is a theme that Amiri Baraka has developed many times also. But Kennedy has restricted the idea by treating it from a woman's point of view. In this way the owl and the fig tree become uniquely appropriate images because they are historically associated with the female principle and reflect the rootless aspects of She's nature. They strongly emphasize her mythic qualities as well as her need for a spiritual or sacred relationship with her dead. In addition they provide metaphorical comments on her problems as a woman in finding a love and a religion which can be meaningful for her within the framework of her two disparate worlds.

If she accepts herself as a Christian (Christianity being a religion which reflects white culture), then she can identify with the virgin Mary and become symbolically the wife of God. In this way her bed becomes an altar on which she surrenders to God, and every man whom she picks up is transformed by her into God. On the other hand if she accepts herself as an owl, her bed is the place of a sacred and non-Christian marriage that she has with both a real man and her ancestral spirit; it remains barren despite her yearning for life. This polarized ambivalence overlaps with her submergence at times in the identity of Mrs. Passmore who commits suicide to become God's bride, finding Christianity and release from the pains of the flesh in death. Here the owl metaphor suggests the confusion of the woman's role in sex, in love, and in religion when it is conceived in the frame of Christianity set against the awareness of its non-Christian associations. Uniquely She becomes a collage of many roles and in one of them must be the bride of God (an alien spirit in her owl transformation), literally and repetitively sacrificing herself (that is, her physical self). That belief forces her to repulse the real man before he can become her lover. In the end her search for love becomes hopelessly involved with religion, sex, and self. Perhaps then, her essence, her soul or her spirit, is the only positive thing that she has. But her essence also has to be owl-like because when she kneels at the altar confused by what she is, she looks more and more like an owl.

Adrienne Kennedy uses in the play the images of historical and religious figures and those of birds and the fig tree to make a bitter and satirical comment on the American black female trapped by the conflict of cultures and sexual roles in twentieth-century America. As a mulatto, an educated school teacher, the daughter of a white man, and an intellectual inheritor of his English historical and literary past. She can find no meaning or solace in that past, nothing to reassure the continuity of her own life. She finds kinship only with man's mythic assertions about his nature and its identification with the non-human forms of life.

In this view the setting of *The Owl Answers* is the mind of She and reveals through metaphors her internal responses to external events. Thus past and present and different places become one in a dramatic montage.

It is no wonder then that with her confused dream of love, She becomes lost in the insistence of the dream of the virgin Mary and can not find satisfaction with men. She calls God, but only the owl, the ambivalent fusion of non-Christian forces and of her alter ego, answers. Living in owldom, the land of ambivalence, the vague featureless past of darkness, she feels as though she is locked in a prison from which there is no escape. Because her mother in the role of Mrs. Passmore had denied life by approaching God through suicide, every embrace with a man becomes for She a perpetual religious sacrifice. Trapped in the mystery of the sacred, she sits alone in the fig tree and remains barren. For the Christian the dove as a symbol bridges the gap between the transitory nature of physical identity and the more permanent transcendental spiritual identity which extends like some power from the past into the future as a unifying element. But for the half-white, half-black, part-Christian, part-pagan, the owl and the fig tree emphasize the gulf between the physical self and the spiritual center. (pp. 3-4)

> *Robert L. Tener, "Theater of Identity," in* Studies in Black Literature, *Vol. 6, No. 2, Summer, 1975, pp. 1-5.*

Kimberly W. Benston (essay date 1976)

[*In the excerpt below, Benston discusses the themes and expressionistic form of Kennedy's* Cities in Bezique.]

Afro-American drama has, until recently, been rooted in the mimetic tradition of modern Euro-American realism. Yet contemporary black playwrights have come to reject increasingly the formal limitations of the theatrical mainstream to which they are heirs. For the naturalism of which Hansberry's, Baldwin's, Bullins's, and Imamu Baraka's early works are exemplary seems to be satisfied, more or less, with the forms it finds in life: prose; non-figurative language; an illusion of non-selected events; a "natural" sense of emphasis; and a non-musical (not necessarily cacophonous) sound. The most distinctive attribute of this form is its guiding sociological and materialistic conception of man. Naturalism takes man to be a part and function of his environment and depicts him as a being who, instead of controlling concrete reality, is himself controlled and absorbed by it. The milieu takes a preponderant part in shaping human destiny; all actions, decisions, and feelings contain an element of the extraneous, something that does not originate in the subject and that makes man seem the unalterable product of a mindless and soulless reality. So long as Afro-American drama maintained naturalism as its dominant mode, then, it could do little more than express the "plight" of black people. Its heroes might declare the madness of reality but reality inevitably triumphed over them. (p. 235)

For the Black Arts Movement, Baraka's *Four Black Revolutionary Plays* showed the way to putting new life into sterile forms, and even though the salient feature of these works is their platitudinous satire, stirrings of a more profound insight were evident. Yet more quietly, less influentially, the strange, surrealistic plays of Adrienne Kennedy had already taken the first steps toward a complete departure from naturalism. The overall effect of her *oeuvre,* from *Funnyhouse of a Negro* (1962) to *Sun* (1970), is one of mystery, mythic fantasy, and poetic ambiguity. The growing interest in and appreciation of her work among Afro-American artists and critics attest to their increased acceptance of expressionistic, or "subjective" explorations of the black psyche.

Cities in Bezique—a dramatic distich composed of *The Owl Answers* and *A Beast Story*—is one of Kennedy's most complex and lyrically beautiful pieces. Though written at different times, these plays are quite clearly complementary investigations of black identity organized around a specific cluster of themes (sexuality, family/tribal structure, death) and symbols (animals, light/dark motifs, musical accompaniments, and innumerable objects of all kinds). Together they provide an excellent model of Kennedy's dramaturgy and vision.

Cities in Bezique is enacted in scenes of strange power, achieved by Kennedy's departures in method: the breakdown of autonomous "characters"; the elaboration of a pattern of verbal themes; and rejection of the representational stage for a kaleidoscope of imaged expressionistic scenes. Kennedy's settings, for example, are a mixture of real and surreal which reinforces the plays' thematic ambiguities: *The Owl Answers* takes place in a subway that is simultaneously St. Peter's, the Tower of London, and a Southern black preacher's den; the set of *A Beast Story* is the "gloomy house of a minister in a drab section of a midwestern city" that is transformed into a bleak landscape of monsters, apparitions, and nightmares. Kennedy includes with her text a "costume plot" and set design, thereby emphasizing the importance of visual elements in the total meaning of her work. Most crucial is the way in which an economy of symbols and motifs, usually concretized by objects such as the ax in *A Beast Story* or by symbolic figures such as *The Owl Answers*'s Negro Man, join with spectacular and supernatural effects to create an aura of lyric other-worldliness and a conciseness of dramatic statement.

The result of such an assembling and ordering of symbols is to add a function to action itself. Instead of treating a plot that explores human relations in their moral aspect, Kennedy makes action into another signature of emotion. It is not an end in itself, flowing from and dependent on what we naturalistically call "character," but invokes instead the intimacies, ecstasies, and anguish of the Afro-American's soul-life. In her plays, relations between men matter less than the struggle of a soul with an all-enveloping spiritual mystery. The coherent action-sequence that illustrates the moral nature of black life (*vide* Hansberry's *A Raisin in the Sun* or Bullins's *The Corner*) gives place to a complex pattern communicating a spiritual insight. In this pattern action is sometimes, it is true, an element of the life of human relations; more often it is an element of the unseen life of the soul and of spiritual powers, presented in poetry through anthropomorphic images.

In the mingling of these elements of seen and unseen, of natural and fantastic, of human and divine, "action" comes to have the force of symbol, and conversely symbol assumes sometimes the character of action. Kennedy opened the way for black writers to become poetic dramatists rather than simply dramatic poets. Her plays allow the spectator to close the gap between himself and the spectacle only by an act of interpretation. Thus, a typical Kennedy drama invades the spectator's mind, putting him in intimate contact with the inner visions he and the playwright share. Ultimately, the characters' struggles become the audience's empathic concern.

The Owl Answers is what Paul Carter Harrison would call a *Hantu* form; that is, its structure turns upon a fluid time/space relationship which eschews linear presentation of images in favor of a more interpretive and poetic design. Thus the multiple personalities of the characters and their various environments change rapidly, often obscurely, and together form an intricate matrix of associations which alone defines the totality of their world. The main figure is "She Who Is Clara Passmore who is The Virgin Mary who is The Bastard who is the Owl"; she has come from Georgia to London to mourn her Dead White Father who was once "Goddam Father who is the richest White Man in the Town" and who is also her stepfather, the black Reverend Passmore. She Who Is is held prisoner in the Tower of London by a chorus composed of Shakespeare, Chaucer, William the Conqueror, and Anne Boleyn (who is also both the Bastard's Black Mother—once a cook for Goddam Father—and the Reverend's wife). SHE's attempt to assume the white, English patrimony of the Dead Father by visiting his bier, which lies in St. Paul's, is the play's central action. SHE's claim is to the lineage of her blood ancestors, a claim made poignant by the juxtaposition of her love for English culture and her brutal rejection by the chorus of exemplary Anglo-Saxon heroes:

SHE.   My father loved you William . . .

THEY.   (*Interrupting.*) If you are his ancestor why are you a Negro?...

SHE.   Let me into the chapel. He is my blood father. I am almost white, am I not?...I am his daughter.

For SHE, as Robert L. Tener has observed, the search for the father and the quest for identity become one [see excerpt dated 1975]. While the individual roles of the father and mother are unique beings, each representative of a distinct and partially valid aspect of SHE's ancestry, SHE's roles are fragments of a single personality, either designated imperialistically by others or personally embraced in her desperate pursuit of selfhood. THEY are cold, abstract, aloof; she moves among their apparitions desiring love in a lifeless world:

DEAD FATHER (*Rises, goes to her, then dies again. Great clang.*)

BASTARD'S BLACK MOTHER (*Shakes a rattle at* SHE.)

SHE (*Screams at the* DEAD FATHER *and the* MOTHER.)

SHE.   You must know how it is to be filled with yearning.

THEY.   (*Laugh.*)

Finally, a dark Negro Man, whom SHE calls "God," tries to supplant her vision of love with the sordid sexuality of a Harlem hotel:

NEGRO MAN.   What is it? What is it? What is wrong? (*He tries to undress her. Underneath her body is black. He throws off the crown* SHE *has placed on him.*)...Are you sick?

SHE.   (*Smiles*) No, God. (SHE *is in a trance.*) No, I am not sick. I only have a dream of love. A dream.

Her dream-world bursts into flame as she and the Negro Man grapple in a space that is suddenly transformed from hotel room to High Altar. SHE's once-calm demands upon the past give way to a final hysteria in which she strips through each available identity—Clara, the Negro child of Reverend Passmore; Mary, the martyred Virgin; Bastard, the Mulatto daughter of Dead White Father—until, enflamed and dripping in her suicidal mother's blood, she at last becomes the mysterious Owl. The owl, solitary, wise, dispassionate, cries out the question embedded within the name "SHE WHO IS"—*Whooo?* Denied the complex legacy of her blood ancestors, surrounded by deception and death, SHE nearly answers by asserting an identity with the nocturnal creature. Yet this concluding statement is only a muted, seemingly painful, and ultimately enigmatic moan: "Ow...ow."

One of the most notable features of this play is the addition to naturalistic psychological torment of symbolic overtones that actually alter the character's psyche as they resonate at climactic moments, so that, as the play progresses, character becomes symbol and the work moves into another dimension entirely. Kennedy's plays require of their audiences a sensitivity to these shifts in aesthetic key—some slight, some abrupt, some daring—and especially to those moments of symbolic expansion when the characters lunge forward, thrusting their significance at the beholder. The feeling of dislocation that the audience experiences as the plays move back and forth between the realistic psychological mode and the symbolic one involves it in a constant, conscious process of readjustment to the fictional world. It also accounts, in considerable part, for the sense of menace that pervades Kennedy's work. But it is the threat of meaning, of horrible or blinding revelation, rather than the threat of violence that lies at the root of this menace. It is the fear that what lurks in the inner self and the collective past will emerge still-born, grotesque, or useless. The result is that when the audience begins to hear the play's symbolic resonances it also begins to feel the special frightening unease characteristic of them. For that sense of menace is intimately related to a paradoxical phenomenon: the further the plays move into the symbolic realm, the nearer they come to the world of the audience itself.

In a work like *The Owl Answers,* Kennedy is pioneering for black theatre a subjective-critical mode which is a deeply innovative dramatic response to the visionary aspect of the Black Arts Movement. The conventional nature of her drama should be clear; borrowing from both the folk-tale and the Strindbergean dream-play, it crashes the barriers of realism by establishing a lyric metaphysical emphasis. *A Beast Story* is essentially an extension of *The Owl Answers* in theme and technique. Yet in the later play pretensions to realism are shed even more while the symbolic investigations of identity, sexuality, and death are rendered with greater clarity. In addition, *A Beast Story* adds to *The Owl Answers* an interest in the confused relation between Nature and the self—the animal and the social being inscribed into and enacted out of a single consciousness.

The multi-dimensional personalities of *The Owl Answers* are reduced in *A Beast Story* to stark, monolithic figures whose only role-fragmentation is evinced in their dual nature of "beast" and Negro. The four characters—Beast Woman, Beast Man, their daughter Beast Girl, and Beast Girl's husband Dead Human—form a "black family" locked in a timeless struggle of wills, desires, and antipathies. *The Owl Answers*'s study of ancestral connection is here supplanted by a concern with the poisonous inheritances possible within a given family structure. Beast Man, a minister, has performed the marriage rite for his daughter and her now dead lover. This event was shrouded in uncertainty and accompanied by evil portents. Yet for Beast Girl it seemed a moment of perfection in which the truth of selfhood was found:

Beast Girl.   My father preached our wedding service and a black sun floated over the altar. A crow flew through an open window while my mother played the organ and the black sun floated.... He had to stop singing, he had to stop singing, the room was silent.... It was morning when I awakened, a red sunrise morning, the first day of my marriage. At last I knew who I was...no shadow of myself, I was revealed...to myself.

The darkened sky, ominous bird, and interrupted ceremony are merely outward signs of the horror that awaits the young couple. Beast Girl, stalked by her enigmatically lustful father and frightened of her sexuality by her mother's passionate denial ("I cut the throat of a pigeon poult to keep myself untouched"), shuns her husband's advances. They struggle and he wins. Their child seems to her a reward of sin; her parents force her to kill it and, with a countenance of ravaged innocence, she slays her husband also.

Beast Girl's acts of murder are to be seen in two terms: the religious outrage of life's denial and the chaotic sensuality of passion in which death, too, plays its part. Beast Girl is forced into a criminal position which is repulsive to her. She accepts her acts as final and yet her obligation remains to herself, a conscience which will not allow her an artificial martyrdom. It is plain that in the background of elemental, sexual struggle between father and mother—initiated by Black Man and Black Woman and tragically repeated by Beast Girl and Dead Human—is the issue of the emergence of woman as an individual. She comes to recognize the destructive cycle of suppressed desire, bestiality, and death which her forebears—"southern Negroes who came to the city"—have traversed:

> *Beast Girl.* My father built a crib. (*Staring at her father.*) How he loved me, saw me in the crib, circled by the golden aureole. My mother. Black shadows were etched under those pale eyes, for she hardly slept at night and suffered endless wakeful fits. . . . Above the bed hung a doleful picture of the Virgin and Child. . . . Now the moon is out. A bird perches on my bedpost, a great toad runs through the house. I killed his baby with quinine and whiskey.

Beast Girl seems to divine, as the play progresses through moments of accusation and insight, that the antidote to her parents' sublimation of inherited burdens is violent repudiation. Killing her husband and child, however, is useless and cowardly—their ever-present forms and the wild beasts (jackal, toad, crow) who are "glad" at their passing attest to her continued weakness. Haunted by the "nightmares and visions" of her mysterious father (Beast Girl: "My father comes toward me, saying something I do not comprehend and the sky turns black"), Beast Girl is finally driven to an apocalyptic destructiveness. As her parents look on with satisfaction, she hacks away at the monsters and loved ones of her life, ending in utter despair:

> *(A blue crow behind her, she turns and instantly kills it with the ax. A giant toad hops to the room, Croaking. She sees it and wildly axes it to pieces. Beast noises. She swings the ax, wildly screaming. Noises louder. She drops the ax, falls down weeping.)*

> *(Silence.)*

> *Beast Man* and *Beast Woman.* Now the sky above our house is blue, three robins with red chests appear on the horizon. All is warm and sunlit.

> *(Silence. Strange bright sunlight, then darkness.)*

I have traced the narrative of *A Beast Story* in a summary way, omitting a mass of detail, because it is necessary to assert that the play is a controlled formulation of a specific theme. The play's inquiry, when its pattern is accepted, can be seen, not as obscure, but as a powerfully original projection of deeply considered experience. It deals with the impossibility of maintaining a dream untarnished—specifically, the dream of identity achieved through love—amid the corruption which is life. The play is unrelentingly melancholy—we have sublimations and deaths, tiredness and disillusion, frustration and disenchantment. The cultural institutions it probes, from the family to the "Old Spirituality" represented by Beast Woman's insidious prayers and vanity-table altars, are depicted as vapid and ruinous. As the sun turns black at Beast Girl's wedding, so her world grows dark until only the "strange" light of her failure illumines it again.

Nevertheless, the final impression left by *Cities In Bezique* is painfully complex. Though Kennedy's heroines are caught in webs of congenital horrors, products of both the history of race and the human condition, they still pass through crisis to epiphany, shattering though this process may be. Moreover, a more concrete, positive apologue is discernible in both plays: neither SHE nor Beast Girl fully embrace the realities of her past, her sexuality, or her blackness. The menacing quality of their unfulfilled quests is perhaps less a reflection of the author's nihilism than a warning to those who look on. Kennedy furnishes her plays with a reality of motives and inclinations but her world is like a beachhead on the edge of a darkness teeming with a host of spirits, generally inimical to man. Her plays leave an impression of restlessness and an unresolved longing to believe. They have helped infuse an overriding and overt spiritual impulse into black theatre. Thus far, it has been left to others to evolve in this spiritual mode from search to celebration. (pp. 236-44)

> *Kimberly W. Benston, "Cities in Bezique: Adrienne Kennedy's Expressionistic Vision," in* CLA Journal, *Vol. XX, No. 2, December, 1976, pp. 235-44.*

Adrienne Kennedy (essay date 1977)

[*In the following essay, Kennedy discusses the personal experiences and perceptions that have influenced her writing.*]

Autobiographical work is the only thing that interests me, apparently because that is what I do best. I write about my family. In many ways I would like to break out of that, but I don't know how to break out of it. In fact I would really like to write more about the people who were before my own immediate family, like my grandparents and their family. I have two children, but I've never been able to write about them.

I feel overwhelmed by family problems and family realities. I see my writing as being an outlet for inner, psychological confusion and questions stemming from childhood. I don't know any other way. It's really figuring out the "why" of things—that is, if that is even possible. I'm not sure you can figure out the "why" of anything anymore.

You try to struggle with the material that is lodged in your unconscious, and try to bring it to the conscious level. You try to remain as honest about that as possible, without fear. I don't believe you intentionally set out to write the things you write. For instance, I would like to write mystery stories like Agatha Christie, or much lighter things which are far less torturous, but I feel you must be honest by letting the material come to the surface. And just accept it.

It's not necessarily that easy, because I think your intellect is always working against you to censor. You must just let the material come out and not be frightened about it and not censor it. Just trust yourself and do not have an opinion of your previous work. One must always fight against that imitation of oneself.

My writing, therefore, really requires a certain amount of time-lapse between the event and the written product. I do keep a journal and have always kept some type of written diary, but I have never been happy with that. Diaries and journals always seem so time-consuming.

You can only spend so many hours a day writing about yourself or your world. I trust those periods when I'm not writing constantly. I believe in long periods of resting, not working against yourself by forcing yourself to write when you don't want to. I believe in being relaxed but not in letting things lie dormant for a long time or in between times.

Work does, however, play a very big part in my life. I do write and then go back and work on it some more. Most important, it's really a lot of hard work.

I think about things for many years and keep loads of notebooks, with images, dreams, ideas I've jotted down. I see my writing as a growth of images. I think all my plays come out of dreams I had two or three years before; I played around with the images for a long period of time to try to get to the most powerful dreams.

As an example, *A Rat's Mass* was based on a dream I had once when I was on a train. I was very frightened, doing something I had never done before. I was on a train going from Paris to Rome, and I was going to try to live in Rome for a few months. I was with my seven-year-old son. It was very difficult thing for me to do because I'm not really that adventurous. I had never tried to do something like this. In a way, I just wanted to turn around and go back. I had this dream in which I was being pursued by red, bloodied rats. It was very powerful dream, and when I woke up the train had stopped in the Alps. It was at night. I had never felt that way. It was a crucial night in my life. So, I was just haunted by that image for years, about being pursued by these big, red rats.

Then I try to take these images and try to find what the source for them are. All this is unconscious, all this takes a long time. I'm not in that much control of it. In the case of *A Rat's Mass*, there was a connection to my brother. At that time my brother was in an automobile accident, from which he subsequently died. This evoked an almost unreal memory of when we were children we used to play in the attic and there used to be a closet in the floor of the attic. I didn't like to go up there by myself because I would imagine that there would be something in that closet.

In *Cities in Bezique*, the character of Clara Passmore was a composite of my aunt and my mother and, of course, myself. Clara was very much my aunt's life. She was this girl who grew up in a small Georgia town. She was quite brilliant. Her father was white. She came to live with us when I was in high school. They wanted her to go to school in Cleveland because they figured she was so smart. This was many, many years ago—more than twenty-five years ago she got her Masters at Teacher's College at Columbia. She teaches English somewhere in the South now. I used to listen to her talk a lot. She was very hysterical. I haven't seen her for many years now, but what struck me as a child—as a young person, not necessarily as a child—was how she used to talk, how she didn't belong anywhere. She's very much a basis to that girl in *The Owl Answers*, and my mother also, in a different way, talks about things like that.

Yes, those two people did have a very big influence on me; they both are very articulate and, in different ways, both are very pretty. Somehow, it always struck me, unconsciously, what a tragedy that these very pretty women seemed so tormented. So of course I used them as a model.

I was always interested in English literature and I've traveled in England. There's always been a fascination with Queen Victoria. It always seemed to amaze me that one person could have a whole era named after them. I find the obsession with royalty fascinating. Not only Queen Victoria, but other great historical literary figures such as Patrice Lamumba and, it's obvious, Jesus Christ. Well, I took these people, which became a pattern in *The Owl Answers*, and then used them to represent different points of view—metaphors really.

Obviously there was always great confusion in my own mind of where I belonged, if anywhere. It's not such a preoccupation now, since I see myself as a writer I don't worry about the rest of it anymore.

I first had my plays done in the early sixties and, as a result, I'm really a product of that time of when *Zoo Story* and *American Dream* were the models of success. I studied with Edward Albee at one point, just after I had written *Funny House of a Negro.* I would never have even gone for the one-act, except for the fact that everyone was going to see *Zoo Story* and because I was not happy with any of the three-acts I had written up to that point. I couldn't seem to sustain the power and still can't seem to write really long, huge works.

I admire Tennessee Williams and Garcia Lorca, and I struggled for a long time to write plays—as typified by *Funny House*—in which the person is in conflict with their inner forces, with the conflicting sides to their personality, which I found to be my own particular, greatest conflict. I am a relatively quiet person who just mulls over all these things and, in a sense, it was an attempt to articulate that—your inner conflicts. I had worked for a long time before I did *Funny House* on having people in a room with conflicts. I was very much in awe of Tennessee Williams at the time and so I imitated him. Somehow it just didn't work. It didn't have any power. I just didn't believe it when I read it. Starting with *Funny House,* I finally came up with this one character, Sarah, who, rather than talk to her father or mother, talked with these people she created about her problems. It's very easy for me to fall into fantasy.

Most people seem to feel that *Funny House of a Negro* is still my most powerful play. Of course I find that depressing, seeing that I wrote that over sixteen years ago. But *Funny House* was a build-up of an idea I had been working on for over five years. Finally that idea just suddenly exploded. The subsequent plays were ideas that I had been trying to work on in my twenties, but then they just suddenly came at the same time, because all those plays were written quite close together. They all came out eleven months to a year from the time *Funny House* came out. All those plays are a product of ideas I've been working on from the time I was twenty-five to thirty. I was struggling with those ideas for a long time. Once I found a way to express them in *Funny House,* I think that was when I found a technique. I employed that technique for the rest. (pp. 41-8)

> *Adrienne Kennedy, "A Growth of Images," in an interview with Lisa Lehman, in* The Drama Review, *Vol. 21, No. 4, December, 1977, pp. 41-8.*

Adrienne Kennedy with Kathleen Betsko and Rachel Koenig (interview date 1987)

[*In the interview excerpted below, Kennedy illuminates the experiences that have shaped her writing and chronicles the highlights of her career.*]

[Betsko and Koenig]: *When did you begin writing?*

[Kennedy]: I really started to write when I was a senior at Ohio State University. The year I was a junior, I took a course which was very inspirational; we studied Faulkner, Fitzgerald, D. H. Lawrence, T. S. Eliot. That course fired something in me. I suddenly found myself writing short stories instead of studying.

You once said that you were disappointed with college.

It was an ordeal. There were twenty-seven thousand students attending Ohio State, and southern Ohio was almost like the deep South in those days, much more bigoted than northern Ohio where I'd grown up. I majored in education. I expected to be a teacher like my mother. Then I majored in social work for a while. All the women—black women, especially—I knew majored in education and a few wanted to be social workers. I was a poor college student, I found college extremely boring, something to just get through. But there were these few English courses; when I was a senior, I had a couple of credits left over and took a survey course in twentieth-century drama. I did better in that than I did in any course the whole time I was at Ohio State. Looking back, it was important.

Did you pursue a profession in social work?

I managed to graduate and got married a month later. From then on, I wrote. My husband went to Korea, and while he was away I gave birth. I lived with my parents and when I wasn't taking care of the baby, I wrote. After my husband returned, we came to New York. I remember the exact date, January 4, 1955. We drove in the snow from Cleveland. Joe worked while he was in graduate school, and I had a certain kind of energy; I would stay up all night and write. You have to do that when you have a baby! I wrote parts of plays . . . then I started taking courses, which I did for ten years, at various places such as Columbia University and the American Theatre Wing. I was always in a writing course. I wrote my first play about a year after I came to New York.

Did you write as a child?

I always kept diaries on people in my family. My mother used to sneak into my room and read them. I really owe writing to her in a sense, because my mother is a terrific storyteller and I feel that all my writing basically has the same tone as the stories she told about her childhood. She used to tell funny stories, but they always had this terror in them, a blackness. I was the only daughter, and we were very close. I feel that my writing is an extension of my relationship with my mother, of talking with her.

How does she feel about your writing?

It makes her edgy. My writing has a lot of violence in it. As a mother myself, I would find it disturbing if my sons were writing that kind of violence and darkness.

What attracted you to dramatic writing?

Like most people at that age, I was always writing poetry and short stories. But I really admired Tennessee Williams because he was the leading playwright then, and I'd seen *The Glass Menagerie* when I was sixteen, and I'd read his plays at Ohio State. I saw a lot of theater in New York. I worked two years on my first play in my spare time and it was very imitative of Williams, of *The Glass Menagerie.* I still have it. I was twenty-three then, and I sent the play to Audrey Wood [Williams's agent], who wrote me a long letter which said she couldn't take me as a client, but that she thought I was very talented. That was a great encouragement to me. I had written the play in a course at the New School taught by Mildred Kuner. She said I wrote the best play in the class, and entered it in a play contest in Chapel Hill, North Carolina, which also meant a lot to me. Well, I didn't win. And that was a pattern I had for a long, long time. People would respond very enthusiastically to my writing, then it would fall through.

How did you maintain the stamina to continue writing plays?

I became discouraged from playwriting and went back to writing stories and a novel. I went to the General Studies Program at Columbia University where I met John Shelby, the former editor of Rinehart, who played a very big part in my life. I had written some short stories and part of a novel which Shelby read. I remember one cold winter afternoon, I went to his office and he said: "I don't know if you will ever have a big success, but I think you are touched with genius." He took the novel and sent it around. He felt the novel would definitely get published. It never did, though he sent it everywhere. Then he moved to San Francisco, but before he left he put me in touch with another editor who'd done some work for *The New Yorker*. I worked with him on my stories off and on for two years. We sent the stories around and an agent at MCA, Richard Gilston, decided to represent me. By this time, I was twenty-seven and had been writing for six years. Gilston sent the stories around, but he could never get them published. One well-known editor tried to get me to write a novel based on a character in one of the short stories. I was unable to do that, although I worked on it for nine months. It is hard for me to take another person's idea and write about it. I was very frustrated by this time. I used to get despondent, and I must confess my former husband was extremely encouraging. He had his doctorate by this time and was teaching at Hunter College. I became discouraged; it bothered me that I'd begun at twenty-one and by twenty-eight, nothing had happened. I stopped writing for a year or so, and then Joe got a grant from the Africa Research Foundation to do a study in Africa. We went to Europe first, then Ghana, Nigeria...we traveled for over a year and it totally changed my writing.

In what way?

In the fourteen months I spent out of this country, my writing became sharper, more focused and powerful, and less imitative. It was a tremendous turning point. I was exactly twenty-nine when I wrote *Funnyhouse of a Negro* (1964), which many people still consider to be my best play. The masks in the play were very specific. I would say almost every image in *Funnyhouse* took form while I was in West Africa where I became aware of masks. I lived in Ghana at a most fortunate time. Ghana had just won its freedom. It was wonderful to see that liberation. And I thought the landscape of Africa was so beautiful, and the people were beautiful—it gave me a sense of power and strength. We lived in a huge house. I went into the bush and visited many villages. My husband went into the bush every day, and my son, who was five, went to school; I had a lot of time to write.

More time probably than I'd ever had in my entire life. I tend to be restless in hot weather, so I'd wake up very early and could not sleep until very late. That combination produced some of the most powerful images I'd ever had. And we'd been to London, Paris, Madrid, Casablanca—it was a total regeneration. I couldn't cling to what I'd been writing—it changed me so. I didn't realize it was going to have this big impact on me. I think the main thing was that I discovered a strength in being a black person and a connection to West Africa.

Did it bother you to be constantly referred to as a "new writer"' in the **Funnyhouse of a Negro** *reviews, even though you had already been writing for ten years?*

No. Finally being recognized as a writer was tremendously gratifying. But *Funnyhouse of a Negro* presented some other problems; it is such an intense play, and so very revealing of my psyche—if not me, personally... It was very dramatic. People who know me think of me as quiet, and to suddenly have this play staged which, again, is quite violent, put a lot of tension in my relationships. Also, to read about yourself in the newspaper is very anxiety producing. I found *Funnyhouse* created tremendous anxiety for me for at least two years.

Was this anxiety solely connected to being in the public eye, or were there other factors which contributed to it?

Well, it was also going through the production which, as you know, is always full of tension and hatreds and personality problems. To this day, I have fear when a production is started. I wonder how I will get along with the director, and how I will relate to the actors. Even though I had a great director, Michael Kahn, and was thrilled to be working with the people in Edward Albee's workshop, *Funnyhouse of a Negro* wasn't what I would call a good experience simply because I am a writer who is happier at the typewriter than in the arena. (pp. 246-49)

It seems your work is either highly praised or harshly criticized.

That's right. My reviews are always split. It was clear early on that many people hated my writing. The initial shock came at the Edward Albee workshop production of *Funnyhouse of a Negro* at Circle in the Square. Nothing has ever been as shocking to me as that particular night...many people hated my writing. Then, when it went on to a production at Actor's Studio [1964] and people said things like, "It's really nothing—you've just written the same lines over and over again..." Rumors went around that people were saying, "She's psychopathic." So you see, I got it all at once, and from the very beginning. Other people felt the play was very lyrical, et cetera. But I realized then that many people disliked my writing. When I said it took two years to recover from *Funnyhouse,* that was part of it. Even now, there is that fear—that's why I want to leave town on opening night. You never know when the critics will attack you.

Was the darkness and violence evident in your early writing, the stories, the novel?

Yes, but it was tempered. I censored my writing more.

Because you felt your work might shock people?

Oh, I don't think it had anything to do with what other people might think. I wasn't that sophisticated. When I would read my work over and write a second draft, I would censor things which I, personally—sitting there at the typewriter—found uncomfortable. I had a certain image—even my friends thought of me as quiet and shy, and because I am small, I was labeled "sweet" from the time I was a kid. My writing, quite naturally, turned out to be just the opposite. It was a surprise for me when I would write stories which were so dark. I was censoring my work all the time. In that sense, I owe a lot to Edward Albee. I joined his workshop at Circle in the Square several months after I returned to the United States with my husband. I had written *Funnyhouse of a Negro* in Rome and handed it in to Albee's workshop. There was a lot of suspense about which sixteen people Albee would select for his workshop. After they accepted me, I went through *Funnyhouse* and edited it, very carefully. When they were ready to do my workshop production, I gave Michael Kahn, who was then Albee's assistant, my edited-out version. I'll never forget sitting in Michael's office; he said, "Isn't there something different about this play?" I said, "This is the version I want done in the workshop." He said okay, but mentioned it to Albee. After class, Albee said, "I hear you've given Michael another version of your play." I said, "I don't want that original version done in the workshop, that would be too upsetting. I used the word *nigger* throughout and I'm worried about what I said about my parents, even though it's fictionalized. I don't want it performed." That was a very big moment. We were standing at the back of the stage, and he said, "I really think you should try—I know it's hard—but maybe we should try to put the first version on." Then he said, "If a playwright has a play on, it should be his guts on that stage . . . . If you really think you can't, it's okay. But you should try." I was in tears. But I made the effort. I was the only black person in the workshop. I became very worried.

Did you ever get strong, negative response when your writing was more censored?

People always liked my writing in those early workshops. It was softened, and highly imitative of Tennessee Williams and García Lorca.

In an earlier interview, you said that during this imitative phase, you realized that Williams's style would not work for you. Why?

The structure wouldn't work. I couldn't sustain a three-act play. It was a huge breakthrough for me when my main characters began to have other personas—it was in fact my biggest breakthrough as a writer, something I really sweated over, pondered. It was very clear to me that my plays and novels lacked something. I read my work over and over, and found there was a stilted quality. I kept intensive diaries. I can remember the room I was sitting in when I said to myself, "You are very drawn to all these historical people, they are very powerful in your imagination, yet you are not interested in writing about them historically." That's when I decided to use historical people as an extension of the main character, and also to give up the idea that I had to write a full-length play. I would say those were my two big realizations, and to me, they were *really* worth the ten years.

Returning to the **Funnyhouse of a Negro** *productions, we read that the play almost closed after twenty-two performances and then was extended by private funds.*

Isabel and Fredrick Eberstadt came to the last performance and decided they would like to contribute money to extend the run. It's hard to explain, but those in the theater really loved that play, and other people were alienated from it and felt that it was bad or offensive—which I still find amazing. It was catastrophic when it was a failure . . . .

A box-office failure?

Yes. When it closed, I thought it was the end of the world. But other things came out of it, like Rockefeller grants and a Guggenheim. And it gave me a feeling of affinity for people in the theater which has lasted to this day. I still consider writers my best friends. I trust writers.

Were you surprised, then, at winning an Obie?

Yes. Yes. It was a very strange period. I was barely able to handle the extremes. The play closed. I was very upset—almost suicidal—then it won an Obie. It was utterly confusing. (pp. 250-52)

How did the black arts community react to **Funnyhouse of a Negro***?*

A lot of blacks hated this particular play and said it was pretentious and imitative. It was upsetting. People wanted me to be part of the movement, but, frankly, I was always at home with my children. So apart from my temperament, the hours didn't exist.

You were not outspoken in your politics?

That's right. I remember there was an article written in the sixties that attacked my writing specifically and said that I was an irrelevant black writer. That sort of criticism was pretty pervasive at the time, so I built up a little resistance to it. I was criticized because there were heroines in my plays who were mixed up, confused. But I knew what my alliances were. My father was a social worker and went to Morehouse College, where Martin Luther King studied. He even had the same cadence in his voice, and was always giving speeches. I grew up in a house where people wrote and we were members of the

NAACP and the United Negro College Fund. I knew my alliances.

Would you discuss your symbolism, the repeated motifs such as blood, birds... (p. 252)

I've always been drawn to the written word and have found solace in symbolism, even as far back as when I was eleven years old and read *Jane Eyre*. I have an affinity for symbolism as a way of surviving. What always impressed me, whether it was Brontë or Fitzgerald, T. S. Eliot or Lorca, was the way that writers took anguish and turned it into symbolism.

Do you have a strong religious background?

I was expected to go to Sunday School and church. I think all those stories at Sunday School played a big part in my imagination. And I am overlooking the influence of my grandparents, whom my brother and I went to visit every summer. They lived in Georgia, in a town of about five hundred people. I remember the red clay of Georgia, the white churches, going to prayer meetings with my grandmother on Thursday night and to church on Sunday morning. All of that was so powerful. Everybody in my family is very dramatic. I look exactly like my grandmother and express myself like her. The whole family is emotional; people tend to cry a lot....

Are you conscious of the religious imagery in your work?

Oh, sure. I'm drawn to religious symbols. They are very powerful. Yet I did not have parents who were constantly preaching to me and I did not go to church more that the average person. I did grow up in a neighborhood which was at least sixty percent Italian. I did see people going to catechism in their white dresses (an image from *A Rat's Mass*, 1967). So that and those summers in Georgia played a huge role.

What is the source of the imagery in your work? How do you get in touch with it?

When I was in my twenties, I studied the symbolism of other writers such as Ibsen, Lorca, Chekhov. And my dreams were very strong. I used to write them down in a few sentences: "Last night I dreamed I was running through white walls..." It appeared to me that those sentences had a certain power. I began to feel that my diaries had much more life than my work. I began to examine them. I started using the symbolism in my journals that came from dreams. Realizing that my dreams had a vitality that my other writing did not was another breakthrough.

How did you begin to incorporate the dream imagery into your work?

I had many recurrent dreams, so I started to write tiny stories based on them, never thinking that they could be a "work," and not really seeing how I could turn them into a short story. I started to let the images accumulate by themselves. When I made the breakthrough where I discovered that the character could have other personas,

the images then seemed more indigenous. Another source of imagery which I am overlooking is the fact that my father used to read to me every night when I was growing up. Sometimes just two or three lines of poetry from Langston Hughes, Paul Laurence Dunbar, James Weldon Johnson. That, too, must have played a role in my development. There is obviously a lot of pleasure in having someone read poetry to you.

Do you agree with critic Rosemary K. Curb's analysis of the menstrual blood in **Lesson in a Dead Language** *(1964): "A sign, almost the antisacrament of the inherited guilt of womanhood"?*

(Laughter) Let me tell you something, I get very upset when I read people's analysis of my work. I try not to read it. It makes me uncomfortable.

More uncomfortable than reviews?

Yes. Yes... to have people sort of dissect my psyche... I think I fear that it will inhibit me in my future work. I find it disturbing. Reading a review compels me because it concerns whether or not the play is going to run.

Would you tell us about **Lesson in a Dead Language** *in your own words? How did the play begin in your mind?*

Apparently—because it is hindsight—I just have this thing about blood. I had always wanted to write something about menstruation. To me, menstrual periods, no matter how long you've been having them, are traumatic—simply the fact that you bleed once a month. I wanted to write about the fear... the fear that you will get blood on your clothes.... I tend to forget that play, but I like it very much. That play has almost been lost because it was published so long ago. Gaby Rogers did an exquisite production of it at Theatre Genesis (1970). She captured it.

You have dealt with many "taboo" subjects in your work—rape, incest, domestic violence. How did you find the courage to reveal such volatile truths?

I wouldn't use the word *courage*. I got the *impetus* from **Funnyhouse of a Negro.** In the decade after, I wrote many one-act plays in rapid succession. It was a confident period... I felt confident because I knew I had revealed my obsessions in **Funnyhouse.** Many people like Ellen Stewart at La Mama and Joe Papp [New York Shakespeare Festival] were very responsive and receptive to my work. I'm not sure I could write those plays now. I was riding an emotional crest. After all those years of rejection slips, people suddenly wanted to do my plays. I got letters from Paris, London, Germany... it made me very productive. Then, maybe twenty years later (I was about forty), I realized that although I had many first-class productions, apart from grants my plays did not seem to generate an income. That produced another set of conflicts. I had been living on grants, and hadn't quite realized that. (pp. 252-55)

Were you affected by the women's movement?

No. First of all, I hate groups. Secondly, I'd been through all of those struggles... alone. I'd been through that decade from age twenty to thirty, 1955 to 1965, trying to write with babies, trying to be a wife, and then experiencing divorce.

You once described your divorce as "a choice for writing...." Would you elaborate?

I don't know whether I ever said that. There were so many tensions and writing was a comfort. It was much more complicated. I think my husband and I had a typical marriage of that time. He was very busy and on his way "up" and tensions built between us.

Because you were a two-career family?

I didn't have a career. I was a housewife. I wrote on the side at night and my husband was constantly busy. Each year was a step and the tensions built. Looking back, I think that people put those words in my mouth, because the divorce was not that clear-cut. One paradox I've never quite recovered from is that I feel my former husband encouraged me to write more than anybody has since then. And he supported me financially, and wanted to, and enjoyed doing it.

How did he feel about your success?

I don't know. By that time there was a lot of sadness that we weren't together. I had known him since I was nineteen. We were married thirteen years. So it wasn't that clear-cut. I am not a heroine who chose writing over marriage. It's not like that at all. I think divorce is futile. I would never divorce again, not with children.

What inspired **Evening With Dead Essex** *(1973), which dealt with the Mark Essex snipings? [Mark Essex, a troubled black ex-Navy man left six persons dead and fifteen wounded after sniping from the tower of a seventeen-story New Orleans Howard Johnson's Motor Lodge in January, 1972].*

When I go through periods when I can't write, I'm glued to the television news. I was following the Munich Olympics, and the Mark Essex snipings happened around the same time.

How did you come up with the multimedia dramatic form—headlines are read, slides are shown...

I was trying to capture how you feel when you hear all that on television. Isn't that funny? I've almost forgotten that play.

Evening With Dead Essex *was the first play by a woman to be produced at the Yale Repertory Theater. Were there subsequent productions of the play?*

It was done at The American Place Theatre first, in a small space, directed by Gaby Rogers, who is brilliant. It did not work well on the main stage at Yale; the actors got lost. Then it was done by a theater company in Louisiana; but nothing ever happened to that play.

Apparently, my plays are sometimes expensive and hard to put on. They seem to be taught more than they are produced.

How did your unusual and imaginative use of stage space evolve?

Martha Graham was very popular in the fifties. I was in my own way attempting to imitate her. I also had a fixation for Picasso. I read everything Picasso had written about his work. Then, in Cleveland, there was one foreign movie house where in my teens I saw all of the French surrealist films, by people like Cocteau, Buñuel... my writing is definitely influenced by French film, Martha Graham and Picasso.

What, specifically, were you drawn to in Martha Graham's staging?

There were always many things happening simultaneously. And everything seemed to come out of darkness. People played many parts, she used a lot of black and white—there was a fluidity and a deemphasis on the narrative. The narrative was being presented to you in another way. I want to say that I wasn't yet capturing this in my short stories or in my plays, though there is no doubt that from 1955, it was on my mind. I'm sure I was also influenced by O'Neill's long monologues about people's torments—by the use of interior monologue.

Do you believe there is a female aesthetic in drama?

Yes, I think we can make a special contribution to theater.

Virginia Woolf said that however much we may go to the work of male artists for pleasure, it is difficult to go to them for help in finding a voice....

That is a fascinating statement. I remember reading the stories of Colette when I was young. We carry that around with us. Women writers do affect me differently than male writers. That is probably the female aesthetic at its height. You see, *Jane Eyre* is my favorite novel. I'm glad that Charlotte Brontë was a woman. I think if you can bring your woman's experience to something, it is really great. It's important not to censor or inhibit that experience. Alice Childress has also been a great inspiration to me.

Do you teach the work of women writers in your courses?

That is a problem. I taught an American drama course at UC (University of California at) Davis and used O'Neill, Sam Shepard, Lorraine Hansberry... many writers. The girls complained that there weren't enough women in the course and they complained about the female characters in the plays. I'm not sure what the answer is for that particular period. Not many women playwrights have had recognition. And they are not in the textbooks.

How do you feel about being called a "Woman Playwright," or a "Black Woman Playwright?"

Ten years ago, it might have bothered me because I would have felt that people were saying I was lesser than say, Norman Mailer. [Laughs] I am a woman writer and a black writer and that doesn't disturb me anymore.

Playwright Wendy Wasserstein says that our cultural idea of a playwright is a white male—anything else is some kind of subset.

In some ways I have made peace with that. But when I say I have made peace, it is crystal clear to me what is really the issue: as a black woman, or as a woman writer, or as a black writer, I don't stand in line for the income and the rewards, and that bothers me a lot. The white male writer can take steps. He's Off Broadway and the next thing you know, he's writing screenplays for Sidney Lumet. He does stand eighty percent more chance of getting his writing career to pay off. It's that simple. (pp. 255-58)

> *Adrienne Kennedy with Kathleen Betsko and Rachel Koenig in an interview in* Interviews with Contemporary Women Playwrights *by Kathleen Betsko and Rachel Koenig, Beech Tree Books, 1987, pp. 246-58.*

FURTHER READING

Barnes, Clive. "*Cities in Bezique* Arrives at the Public." *The New York Times* (13 January 1969): 26.
> Favorable review of *Cities in Bezique,* emphasizing poetic aspects of the work.

Binder, Wolfgang. "A *MELUS* Interview: Adrienne Kennedy." *MELUS* 12, No. 3 (Fall 1985): 99-108.
> Kennedy discusses the events leading to the production of *Funnyhouse of a Negro.*

Diamond, Elin. "An Interview with Adrienne Kennedy." *Studies in American Drama* 4 (1989): 143-57.
> Focuses on personal experiences that have influenced Kennedy's writing.

Forte, Jeanie. "Realism, Narrative, and the Feminist Playwright—A Problem of Reception." *Modern Drama* XXXII, No. 1 (March 1989): 115-27.
> Feminist critical analysis of *The Owl Answers.*

Kolin, Philip C. Review of *In One Act,* by Adrienne Kennedy. *World Literature Today* 63, No. 1 (Winter 1989): 101-02.
> Positive review of *In One Act,* briefly summarizing works included in the collection.

Solomon, Alisa. "Stardust Memories: Adrienne Kennedy Shows and Tells." *The Village Voice* XXXII, No. 44 (3 November 1987): 61, 65.
> Positive review of *People Who Led to My Plays,* highlighting excerpts from the memoir.

Jamaica Kincaid

1949-

(Born Elaine Potter Richardson) West Indian-born American short story writer, novelist, and essayist.

Kincaid is recognized as a major new voice in contemporary American literature. She draws on her childhood and her native land, the Caribbean island of Antigua, for the subjects of much of her work. Her strongly autobiographical fiction—*At the Bottom of the River* (1983), *Annie John* (1985), and *Lucy* (1990)—often concerns the intense emotional bonds between mothers and daughters, while the book-length essay *A Small Place* (1988) examines post-colonial Antigua. Critics have responded favorably to these four works, almost universally praising Kincaid's writing style and technique. According to Jacqueline Austin, Kincaid's language fuses "folk tale with novel, poetry with fiction, West Indian locutions and rhythms with 'European' ones."

Kincaid was born Elaine Potter Richardson in St. John's, Antigua, in the British West Indies. In a 1987 interview she described herself as a precocious child. "I started school when I was about three and a half years old," she explained, "and the reason my mother sent me to school was that I gave her so much trouble at home!" Kincaid found it impossible to uphold the image expected of her—"well-behaved child" and loyal subject of the British Empire—so at sixteen she left the island for the United States to become an *au pair* girl. Although she initially planned to pursue a career in nursing, she instead studied photography at the New York School for Social Research and spent time at Franconia College in New Hampshire. After working briefly as a free-lance writer, she obtained a job at the *New Yorker*. Of this position she commented: "I don't think anyone really thought I could do it—I mean, I know I didn't think so." Kincaid's new profession gave her the opportunity to change her name. She noted: "I had always hated my name and wanted to change it, but it was only when I started to write and actually started to sign my name to things that I decided I just couldn't do this. Since my family disapproved of my writing, it was easy for me to change names." She took the name Jamaica Kincaid—not a very "meaningful" name, she insisted, but one that was symbolic of the region from which she came.

Kincaid's first work, *At the Bottom of the River,* is a collection of ten short stories; critics occasionally call them "prose poems." In "Girl," a work composed chiefly of a string of commands from a mother, the woman tells her daughter to "wash the white clothes on Monday and . . . wash the color clothes on Tuesday" and warns her to walk "like a lady, and not like the slut you are so bent on becoming." Many commentators remarked on the lyrical quality of Kincaid's language in

these stories. Anne Tyler, for example, praised the "care for language, joy in the sheer sound of words, and evocative power" of Kincaid's writing, but she echoed the reactions of other critics by calling the collection "almost insultingly obscure." Kincaid's next work, *Annie John,* was originally published as a series of short stories in the *New Yorker*. Yet many critics regard this book as a novel because it focuses on the life of the precocious title character, who struggles to assert her individuality and escape the influence of her domineering and possessive mother. As Annie John's mother gradually becomes unresponsive to her needs, a fierce love-hate relationship develops. Annie's confusion about her changing life is reflected in her surreal and often grotesque flights of imagination—for instance, when a hunchbacked girl dies, Annie muses, "On hearing that she was dead, I wished I had tapped the hump to see if it was hollow." Annie eventually leaves Antigua and her mother to pursue a nursing career in the United States. Critics recognized *Annie John* as an expansion and refinement of the ideas originally presented in *At the Bottom of the River.*

Kincaid followed *Annie John* with *A Small Place,* an essay initially addressed to an "incredibly unattractive, fat and pastry-like fleshed" tourist from "North America (or, worse, Europe)" traveling in Antigua. In this work, Kincaid described the aftermath of colonialism on her native island, particularly the destructive effects of greed and vice in the government of the impoverished society. Critical reaction to *A Small Place* was mixed. Many commentators praised Kincaid's intention but contended that the work suffers from misdirected rage. Kincaid's most recent publication is the novel *Lucy,* which, like *Annie John,* first appeared in the *New Yorker. Lucy* is about a young woman from Antigua who comes to New York to work as an *au pair* girl. Lucy lives with and works for a disintegrating family. She is alone in America, yet she refuses to open mail from her mother, one of the people she sought to escape by leaving Antigua. Of *Lucy*'s highly autobiographical narrative, Kincaid commented: "I've never really written about anyone except myself and my mother."

Although Kincaid's writing reflects her own life, her work is often praised as "universal." According to scholar Henry Louis Gates, Jr., Kincaid "never feels the necessity of claiming the existence of a black world or a female sensibility. She assumes them both." He continued: "I think that more and more black American writers will assume their world the way that she does. So that we can get beyond the large theme of racism and get to the deeper themes of how black people love and cry and live and die. Which, after all, is what art is all about."

(For further information about Kincaid's life and works, see *Black Writers; Contemporary Authors,* Vol. 125; and *Contemporary Literary Criticism,* Vol. 43.)

PRINCIPAL WORKS

At the Bottom of the River (short stories) 1983
Annie John (novel) 1985
A Small Place (essay) 1988
Lucy (novel) 1990

Jamaica Kincaid with Selwyn R. Cudjoe (interview date 1987)

[*Cudjoe is the author of* Resistance and Caribbean Literature *(1980), a source Kincaid consulted often when writing* A Small Place. *Cudjoe has stated that the following interview, conducted in 1987 in North Bennington, Vermont, is a "valuable companion piece" to* A Small Place *and* Annie John. *Here, Kincaid discusses her childhood and works.*]

[Cudjoe]: *Tell me about your early education.*

[Kincaid]: I started in school when I was about three and a half years old, and the reason my mother sent me to school was that I gave her so much trouble at home! At that time, however, she had already taught me to read. You know, simple things . . . I knew how to spell *cat* and words like that. So she enrolled me in this school—it was a Moravian school—and she said, "Now remember, if anyone asks you, say you're five." You see, I was very tall.

Since I was five, school lasted only half a day. I was supposed to come home and take a nap in the afternoons, but I'd come home and make so much trouble that when I was three and a half she finally had to let me go to school for the entire day.

From there I went to school in Antigua. I went to all the regular government schools. Then I went to one school, the name of which I absolutely hate. It was called, "The Princess Margaret School."

You developed a great dislike for colonialism?

Yes. When I was nine, I refused to stand up at the refrain of "God Save Our King." I hated "Rule, Brittania"; and I used to say that we weren't Britons, we were slaves. I never had any idea why. I just thought that there was no sense to it—"Rule Brittania, Brittania rule the waves, Britons never ever shall be slaves." I thought that we weren't Britons and that we were slaves.

No one ever told you this—it was just instinctive?

No, no one ever told me that. In those days—well, my mother used to be an Anglophile, but I realize now that it was just a phase of my mother's life. She was really a stylish person; it must just have been a phase in her development.

Anyway, I went to Princess Margaret School. I got a scholarship to go there, and my mother now tells me that I came in second on the island of Antigua to go to that school. I now realize that I left without taking the "O levels" of the General Certificate of Education. I came to America without taking them.

Did you come to America intending to be a writer?

No, not at all. You see, the educational system in Antigua. Well, Antigua has this incredible history. It went from colonialism to the modern world—that is, from about 1890 to 1980—in five years. When I was growing up, we still celebrated Queen Victoria's birthday on May 24, and for us England (and I think this was true for V. S. Naipaul, too) and its glory was at its most theatrical, its most oppressive. Everything seemed divine and good only if it was English.

So my education, which was very "Empire," only involved civilization up to the British Empire—which would include writing—so I never read anything past

Kipling. Kipling wasn't even considered a serious writer.

Who were the serious writers?

Well, the Brontes, Hardy, Shakespeare, Milton, Keats.... We were taught to read from Shakespeare and Milton when I was five. They were read to us while we sat under a tree.

What induced you to write?

Well, as I was going to say, I didn't know that people were still writing. I somehow thought that writing had been this great "thing" and that it had stopped. I thought that all the great writing had been done before 1900. Contemporary writers just didn't exist. I mean, I read Enid Blighton and so on, but that wasn't really writing... it was something to entertain me. But I never wanted to be a writer because I didn't know that any such thing existed.

Let us go on to your name. Why the name "Jamaica"?

That's not the name my mother gave me. The name my mother gave me was Elaine Potter Richardson, which was her family's name. I had always hated my name and then it turned out that my mother had named me after someone whom I particularly came to loath—a Lebanese woman, one of these people who come through the West Indies to get something from it but they don't actually inhabit it. I know this sounds awfully racist, but I just can't stand those people.

At any rate, I had always hated my name and wanted to change it, but it was only when I started to write and actually started to sign my name to things that I decided I just couldn't do this. Since my family disapproved of my writing, it was easy for me to change names.

What kind of family did you come from?

Well, we were poor, ordinary people. My mother's family comes from Dominica; they were land peasants. They had a lot of land, which they lost through my aunt making a bad marriage and my mother falling out with her family. My mother says that my real father can't even read, but he made a lot of money.

This is your real father, as opposed to your stepfather?

Yes, but the man I speak of as my father [in my works] is really my step-father. I grew up thinking he was my father.

So you don't know your real father?

Well, actually I do, now. I know a sort of person who is my father. We see each other, but I can't get myself to call him "father." He's sort of typical West Indian men: I mean, they have children, but they never seem to connect themselves with these children.

About my name, though: my mother disapproved of my writing, and all of my friends who had come to America had gotten respectable jobs and were building something for their families. They were sending something back home, but I just wouldn't hear of it. I lived in my own sort of poverty, and I thought I might come to something; but I didn't know, really.

At one point I thought I would never see Antigua or my parents again because I didn't like what they thought of me. At the time I didn't know I was thinking this, but now I realize that the convention of being this "well-behaved child"... I just couldn't do it.

Are there echoes of that in **Annie John?**

Yes. It's very interesting for me to think about that. When I was writing that [**Annie John**], I was sort of giving voice to something which—well, I just didn't have any words for it. But if I had not been successful at anything I'd done, I probably wouldn't have seen my parents. First of all, they would have laughed at me.

I remember that when I was at Franconia College, it was much colder than I had ever thought possible. In one of my weak moments I had written to my mother telling her how cold it was—a pleading letter, I guess. At any rate, she wrote back very harshly, telling me that I was always trying to be something I wasn't. I thought, "Well, that's the last time I tell her anything about me."

When I read **Annie John,** *I sense that tremendous dislike for your mother.*

Well, I hope it's an adolescent dislike, because now we get along very well. It's possible that as human beings we don't like each other at all but that as a mother and daughter we love each other. I think that if I were to meet my mother in a certain context, I wouldn't like her. She's an extraordinary person, there's no question about that.

But you've never forgiven her for that letter that said you're always trying to be something you're not?

Well, yes, I think that I have forgiven her—but I shall never forget that, because what is so odd about that is that the way I am is solely owing to her. I was always being told I should be something, and then my whole upbringing was something I was not: it was English. It was sort of a middle-class English upbringing—I mean, I had the best table manners you ever saw.

In your book there is a sense of revolt against these values.

Oh, yes. I never knew we were poor: we ate well; my mother was always grand in every gesture; I was very well brought up. I could never speak bad English in her presence.

A kind of middle-class respectability that, as you look back, may seem repulsive, but which—for people trying to make something of themselves—is a saving grace, as it were.... But why did you choose the name Jamaica Kincaid?

It wasn't really anything meaningful. By the time I decided to change my name, that part of the world had become very remote to me. It was a kind of invention: I wouldn't go home to visit that part of the world, so I decided to recreate it. "Jamaica" was symbolic of that place. I didn't come from Jamaica. I changed my name before Jamaica became fashionable—at least, before I was aware of it. If I had been aware, I would probably have changed my name to "Scandinavia" or something like that, because I hate being popular.

And "Kincaid"?

Well, it just seemed to go with it.

What West Indian writers did you read before you came to America?

I didn't know anything about West Indian literature before I came to this country. I loved to read, which was something my mother encouraged. Later it grew to be a bone of contention between us because I liked to do nothing but read and would neglect my household duties. She could see that it gave me ideas, that it took me away from her influence.

What kinds of things did you read?

I used to read novels, biographies. I would just READ.

So is **Annie John** *autobiographical?*

The feelings in it are autobiographical, yes. I didn't want to say it was autobiographical because I felt that that would be somehow admitting something about myself, but it is, and so that's that.

At what point did you begin to read West Indian writers?

Well, I've read very little. Years ago someone gave me *A Bend in the River* so I've read that, but really I've read very little West Indian writing. When you say you're having this conference on West Indian women writers I think, "God—I didn't know there were more!" That's wonderful.

So you have no sense of a tradition in West Indian literature?

No. I just started to write. I never thought anyone would read it. Since I wrote for the *New Yorker,* I assumed that only white people in the suburbs would be reading it.

I don't know how many black people read your work, but when you read your work at Boston University recently, most of your audience was white; so I know that you do have a strong white following.

It's a strange thing to get letters from white women saying, "Oh, that sounds just like my relationship with my mother." In a way, I'd like to think that I could write in the universal, that if I say the oppression by the English was such-and-such, that I say it in such a way that any human being will say, "Yes, that was wrong."

My father was this sort of person—someone who anyone could understand.

You say that you would like to see your work as being universal. How do you see your works fitting into the contemporary emphasis on feminist writings?

I don't really see it, but that's only because I don't really see myself in any school. I mean, there has turned out to be a rise in West Indian literature, but I wouldn't know how I fit in. I am very glad that there is such a thing, but on the other hand, belonging to a group of anything, an "army" of anything, is deeply disturbing to me. I think I owe a lot of success, or whatever, to this idea of feminism, but I don't really want to be placed in that category. I don't mind if people put me in it, but I don't claim to be in it. But that's just me as an individual. I mean, I always see myself as alone. I can't bear to be in a group of any kind, or in the school of anything. I think I started to write a certain way because I just didn't like certain stories that were being written. I didn't like the way young white Americans wrote—a deadpan way— and the way they always mentioned products and songs and supermarkets. They don't really write, they just mention things. They suppose that the reader is just like them, so he understands if you just use some brand name. I found that horrid—I mean, it was sort of like pop songs. If I wanted to have universal references, I'd listen to rock and roll for "universal teenage references." So I said I'd never write like that.

Of course, I now see that my writing had nothing to do with my not wanting to write like a young white American—I can't write like a white American. I'm not a white American, and I don't have the same experience. I don't have the luxury of longing to be a displaced person, that is, a person who doesn't fit into his parent's life, or a person who doesn't fit into the town he grew up in. I don't have the luxury of wanting that: it actually did happen to me. That I couldn't fit in was a real pain for me. It wasn't an act, so I couldn't write like that.

But to a certain extent your writing is against that ability not to fit in?

To me, when I read the writings of young white Americans, it's an invented pain. I would grant that the agony is real, that they really feel that way, but it's completely an invention. So I thought, I'm going to write this other way, but of course the way I wrote really had nothing to do with a reaction. It's just the way I wrote.

My point in asking you whether you would fit into the mold of feminine discourse, whether you consciously intended it or not, is that the nature of feminist discourse is intensely personal, a very interior kind of writing, and your writing does seem to fit into that mold.

Yes, perhaps so. You could place my writings there, but I could not. I wrote that way because that was the way I could write, so it does not feel to me that this is the way women write. My second book, **Annie John,** is about a girl's relationship with her mother because the fertile soil of my creative life is my mother. When I write, in some things I use my mother's voice, because I like my mother's voice. I like the way she sees things. In that way, I suppose that if you wanted to say it was feminist, it can only be true. I feel I would have no creative life or no real interest in art without my mother. It's really my "fertile soil." (pp. 397-402)

It might be a good time to talk about your first story, **"Antigua Crossings."** *There was one character, the grandmother, who was a Carib Indian. There was a real sense of dignity and of fierceness. There's one part in particular which I think is so wonderful, I'd like to read it and get your response to it:*

> We live on an island, Antigua, and on one side runs the Atlantic Ocean and on the other side is the Caribbean Sea. The Atlantic Ocean does not matter much to us. It comes from too far away and it shares itself with too many other people who are too different from us. The Caribbean Sea is ours and we share it with people who live on islands like us, islands that are sometimes made out of coral, sometimes made out of dead volcanoes. All these islands surround the Caribbean Sea like a ring around the rosy pocket full of posey games, preventing it from spilling out into the larger world of seawater. I know there are other seas which seem more important and more special, but they exist for me only in books.

I'm sure you haven't read it in a long time . . . what's your response to that?

I'm amazed. I mean, I actually like it. It was my first real attempt at writing a piece of fiction and completing it. In some ways I'm amazed at . . . oh, I don't know how to say this without sounding too . . . well, I think it's very beautiful, and very true—the idea that the Caribbean Sea embraces the West Indies in this way. I'm amazed at that because I'm very stupid, and I always think that I don't get smarter from any time by my present. Also, the gentleness of it, and the generosity, surprises me, because I was much harsher then.

The entire work seems gentle to me, and lyrical. But it's written from the point of view of a young girl of twelve years, so I think it captures how she sees the island. That vision, I think, is what created its beauty.

Well, I'm amazed at that. You see, I spent all the time I had been away from the West Indies and from my mother building some kind of "literary monument" to it [the island of Antigua], and it was interesting that when I got back it had changed so radically. I was shocked that it had changed for the worse. All the things I had thought made it a bad place were gone—but it was worse, and it's not that things would be better should they go back in time.

When I look at what you just read, written in that naive way, and I look at the West Indies now, if I were to write that, I think I would have to say that I had been betrayed, and in fact the Caribbean Sea, which used to include us, which used to be only for us—well, we've rather assaulted [it].

In Antigua, the average Antiguan no longer owns the beach—it's all owned by foreigners. There's no seaside property in Antigua; only the foreigners can afford it, and so it's very rare that an Antiguan sees the Caribbean Sea. But it turns out that we're not interested in the Caribbean Sea—we're interested in New York. The Caribbean Sea is no longer ours; it cannot be observed in that way. It can't be observed as being so big and so blue and so beautiful anymore. It's now so much money.

But it's probably also part of our innocence when we're young. That's all we have and all we know.

But it turns out that coincident with the loss of innocence on my part, the description of the loss of the sea is true. Basically, it's owned by travel agents—you only have to look in the magazines—and it's not so big and so beautiful anymore. It accommodates millions of people who make much money so they can go on their holiday.

When you speak of your grandmother—who was a Carib Indian, very tall and very dark—you say that she accepted Christianity but then went back to her own native religion. Were you trying to juxtapose the two worlds?

Well, I don't think I was trying to compare them, but if I were a person who did compare these things, I would obviously choose my grandmother's original religion because, to be quite frank, my grandmother's religion committed no crime against humanity.

She was pagan; her deep belief was not Christian, and then she married a man who, as it turned out, lived a really wild life. He was a policeman, but then he became rather pious. He owned some land and was a lay preacher. So she accommodated his beliefs while, I think, always keeping her own beliefs. Then there was the tragedy of my uncle dying. She felt her beliefs would have saved him, and he [her husband] felt that his beliefs—his beliefs being faith in God and Western medicine—would have saved him. Well, it turns out that his illness was of a type that my grandmother's beliefs would have cured.

What was the illness?

Well, he was possessed, and something was set on him.

That's where the obeah *just keeps coming up.*

Yes, my family practiced, and now my mother is in this high state of excitement—what is it called? She's one of those Christians—they sing and clap—"the charismatics." She's a charismatic, and she embraces it the way she embraces everything that she's embracing at the moment. It's all for her, but before this stage in her life, she was really quite devoted—well, somewhat devoted, and, I think, more devoted than I was really conscious of—to *obeah* things. Every Friday she'd go and have her cards read, and it also has to be said that she felt she lived in a state of war with the other woman my father had loved—or not loved but just had a child with—so she was always consulting people, with the memory of her brother in mind, I think.

Her brother died? He was sick at home, during the rains.

Her brother John had died when she was a child, from *obeah* things. He had a worm crawl out of his leg. Now, this sounds odd, but it did happen.

When I came to America, among the many things I was glad to be in America for, one of them was to not be afraid of God anymore, of any God—to be so unafraid of God that I wouldn't even have to go to church, which is to say that I wouldn't have to admit the existence of such a thing as God. I had felt the overbearingness of God from every direction, top to bottom.

So I think that in this particular piece [that is, literary work] I wasn't making a comparison [between Christianity and *obeah*]. In any case, I don't think I had the skill to make a comparison: I didn't have the knowledge.

But your grandmother, the Carib Indian, was she an obeah *woman?*

Well, yes. She was an *obeah* woman, perhaps not on the Haitian scale—they are very different—but she did believe in spirits. (pp. 404-06)

Let's talk a bit about **Annie John.** *Annie seems to be very hardhearted at the end of the text. Is there any reason for that?*

Well, it's a mask—she's not really hardhearted. She really wants to break down and be taken back in, but there's a parting place. She says she remembers that she's been told, "Once you start to do something, you have to see it through," and so she's got to see this thing through. But it's a hardness that has no substance, really, and if I were to continue to write this character—which I won't—you would see how the hardness is easily broken. She becomes enough of a woman to start imposing hardnesses on other people, but it's not a real hardness, and I think that the very last line shows that. It goes, "It's as if a vessel of liquid had been placed on its side and now was finally emptying out."

This is one of those hard-won victories that you have, I think, when you're an adolescent or when you're not quite an adult. You have all these little victories that you've won, and only you know how deep they go. The roots of them are just this big, and can be washed away. Any slightly powerful force can uproot it; it doesn't really set, and for her to leave these people, she has to harden herself against them.

It's a very fragile "hard," and if they would just say, "Oh, don't go, we love you, stay here," she would be undone by it, even if she decided, "Well, no, I must." Though actually, looking at the chemistry of these things, if they had said, "Oh, do stay," she would have said, "No, I must go." The roots of her rebellion . . . well, it gets a little deeper. The more you can sustain your convictions or whatever, the better they are—I mean, the stronger they are. But it's not a real hardness, I don't think. And it couldn't be conciliatory.

No, not at that point. If you had kept on writing about her long enough, there might have been a reconciliation.

Perhaps, twenty years later. But I think that one of the things you detect about this character when you read is that if you met her you would expect an interesting person, and you expect that it would work out. Some students from the West Indies with whom I've spoken have said they felt there should have been a reconciliation right then and there, before Annie left.

Well, they want to impose their own romanticism on it. My wife says she wouldn't like to be a teenager anymore because it's such a very different period for a young woman. What the daughters do with their mothers is try to carve out their own turf—their own sense of independence—and it seems to be necessary in many cases.

But you know how unusual it is in the West Indies, the idea of carving out one's own territory. I don't really notice it being done; one lives very much the life of one's parents.

What is the role of obeah *in your work?*

Well, until you mentioned it, I never thought that it had any particular role. I was very interested in it—it was such an everyday part of my life, you see. I wore things, a little black sachet filled with things, in my undershirt. I was always having special baths. It was a complete part of my life for a very long time.

At night I would collect my urine in my little potty, and in the morning my mother would wash my feet in it. Then she'd put mine in with theirs in their pot—it's called a china-pot but it's not china—and then, after bathing her feet in it, she'd go and dribble it down the steps and around the house. Sure enough, sometimes there would be fresh dirt dug up around the house, and there would be a bottle with things in it. So this was a part of my actual life, and it's lodged not only in my memory, but in my own unconscious. So the role *obeah* plays in my work is the role it played in my life. I suppose it was just there.

I'll give you an example from my life. My mother used to tell the story of this couple who fought and fought with each other from the first day of their marriage. They could never get along. One night in a dream, the wife was told to go and look below the front steps of her house—it was the kind of house that was built slightly above the ground—and she would see a pin cushion with a ball of pins inside stuck all together. She was to take it, unravel it, and everything would be all right. The next morning she did just that and, as my mother told the story, all was well with the couple after that. There is no question that she believed that story.

One way to explain my mother's belief in that story is to postulate that there is another reality over which we, in our modernity, have no control—and certainly of which we know very little, because we're too scientific.

Oh, yes, absolutely. Once I knew of a woman who wanted a man, but he would never look at her—and the next thing you know, they were married. They would say, "Oh, she tied him," and somehow it involved having him to dinner and all sorts of body fluids being used, but she was successful. Or somehow when he was asleep, she would rub something on his head and she would get the man. These stories were accepted; this was a part of my reality.

My mother would go to a woman every Friday who could tell if things were being done to us and if these women were having successes with my father. I'm pretty sure he was faithful, but that's only because he was old. But there were always these consultations, and really it was a sort of psychiatrist, someone keeping the unconscious all oiled up.

Each society has its own means of coming to terms with that other part of its world. Call it what you may, one has to come to terms with it if one wishes to lead a healthy life. Each society constructs its own mechanisms: we tend to privilege the Western and call it "good" and "proper" and call ours "bad," "pagan," and everything else, but I guess it's how one looks at it. Many of these ideas come through in your work, more particularly in your first book At the Bottom of the River. *What about the function of dreams in your books? They seem to recur in both books.*

Well, again, to be honest I don't really think I make these distinctions between dreaming and waking. This, again, goes back to my childhood, because there is little difference between dreaming and waking. Dreams could tell you things about your waking life—which turns out to be quite accepted in Western psychiatry. Your dream could tell you things about your waking life; it illuminates your waking life.

I used to be quite afraid [of dreams] because they would tell me things I didn't want to know, and I really believed all my dreams and took them very seriously. I still do, in quite the same way. So when I write about dreams, it's not really a dream, it's something that happens, but in this way.

And, as I say, this had to do with the strange perception about reality where I grew up. Reality was not to be trusted; the thing you saw before you was not really quite to be trusted, because it might represent something else. And the thing you didn't see might be right there—I mean, there were so many stories about people who were followed home by a dead person, and the dead person eventually led them into a pond. People would say, "Oh, the *Jablesse* are out tonight."

My mother had this experience, and I've written about that—I think it's in **"Antigua Crossing."** If I haven't, I will have to write about it. They were going to school,

and saw a beautiful woman bathing in the river—Dominica has so many rivers. In those days they didn't have many bridges, so they had to cross this river—which was particularly full because it had rained a lot. At the mouth of this river they saw a woman, a beautiful woman, surrounded by these mangoes, wonderful mangoes. In fact, my mother has shown me the mango trees and the place where this happened. Well, they were about to swim to her, but some people realized that this was not real—it was too beautiful, the mangoes were too beautiful. One boy swam to her, and he drowned. His body was never found. He vanished; everything vanished. My mother didn't tell me that as a folk-tale; that was an illustration to me of not believing what I saw, of really not being deceived by appearances, of really being able to tell that it was really a woman and not someone who would drown you.

If you wouldn't call it folklore, how would you call it?

I would say it was my mother's experience with life.

Which, to her, was real.

Yes…it's not more folkloric than if, say, a child was walking to school here in America and was kidnapped and never found. In that case you would say to your child, "Don't stop for anybody to pick you up." I thought that all of these things were a way of making me understand that the world was not what it seemed—which is true.

In light of this view of the other world, how do you explain the symbol of light in one of your books? It appears quite often. Perhaps you're not conscious of it…but what are these lights?

That I can see…I think I have an explanation for that. It must be the obsession with these "things," because they all seemed to happen in the dark, and to be part of darkness. (Apart from the fact that I grew up in this extraordinary light, this blinding, thick light of the sun, that seems to give off a light that makes things transparent.) But the sun is almost hellish, really. Sometimes it would turn from something wonderful, the light of the sun, into a kind of hell.

I think that at some point I became obsessed with things being not that unclear, that things could not just vanish, that there could be some light that would show the reality of a thing, that this was false and this was right. I think it was my obsession. I think I really get obsessed sometimes with the idea that there could be just ONE undeniable truth, something that is so true, not for any purpose—it's just true: "This is true, and you can't deny it…." It's very childish. That section on the river, I understood when I was doing it that it was very naive, that only a child, really, would ask, "Well, can't you just give me one answer, and that's that, and it stays there and it doesn't move, and it doesn't do anything except…what it does, and it's just itself. And it's not two-sided, and it's not full of this-and-that." I think the image for light—I know it always comes up in my writing—is just my hope that there will be just one true thing.

And isn't that the charm of your work?

Well, I don't know....

It's certainly uncomplicated at one level.

Yes, that's the "one true thing." I hope for that. I want for there to be just one true thing that doesn't come and go, and I think that's how the light functions. I think that some parts of *At the Bottom of the River* are really very simple. I had sort of gone through a lot—not in terms of anything personal—I had hoped to write something, and that part of it was a sort of yearning for something.

There's a part of it where I write about the green color of the grass. In that piece, I suppose I just want things to stay still, just something that won't perish or won't go away; that it would remain just sort of paradisical. Not eternal...but just the possibility of...well, maybe three minutes of the day one could enter that sort of place. Just absolute peace, not happiness. I decided that happiness is too much activity, too busy. I don't really yearn for happiness; I yearn for an absence of anxiety. I don't yearn to be happy, because I don't know what it is, really. I don't really understand the phenomenon.... (pp. 407-11)

Jamaica Kincaid and Selwyn R. Cudjoe, in an interview in Callaloo, *Vol. 12, No. 2, Spring, 1989, pp. 396-411.*

Isabel Fonseca (essay date 1989)

[*In the following essay, Fonseca offers a generally unfavorable review of* A Small Place.]

In a short book whose style owes more to the manifesto than the essay, Jamaica Kincaid condemns her native Antigua's tragic development, from its colonial past to the new tourism which has replaced it and which she sees, alarmingly, as identical.

Christopher Columbus discovered Antigua in 1493, and shortly thereafter the nine-by-twelve-mile island was settled in the usual ghoulish manner "by human rubbish from Europe." [In *A Small Place*] Kincaid asks us to question "why it is that all people like me seem to have learned from you is how to imprison and murder each other, how to govern badly, and how to take the wealth of our country and place it in Swiss bank accounts?" Unfortunately, she does not offer any explanation except to say that it is "mostly your fault". And now, in a perverse homage to the former power, the ruling élite has invited in a new species of "imperialist", the tourist—"an ugly human being from America (or worse, Europe)".

Kincaid's (laudable) purpose is to make the readers of this grisly tale as uncomfortable as possible. Her shrill,

radically subjective method, however, serves only to alienate. She buries Antigua's sad and familiar story in a graveyard of clichés (for "only a cliché can explain you") and the result is a deadened and dogmatic prose which tells all but reveals little. Antigua is presented as a generic outpost of colonial memory. It is true that Antigua, like all of the Caribbean islands, has for centuries always been fought over and owned by foreign powers. What Kincaid does not say is that for more than twenty-five years Antigua, along with its own dependencies, Redonda and Barbuda, has had full internal self-government and the right to opt for full independence at any time without reference to—permission from—the British Government. Nor does she discuss what is probably a greater source of misery to the Antiguan people than a colonial past or a dependency on tourism: the fact that Antigua, unlike the other Leeward Islands, has no rivers. Rainfall is slight and the island suffers from severe droughts and, in turn, severe deforestation.

No one would question the gist of the story as Kincaid tells it. Who could doubt her when she says—or her

Cover of Kincaid's 1983 short story collection At the Bottom of the River.

propriety in saying—that "nothing can erase my rage—not an apology, not a large sum of money, not the death of a criminal—for this wrong can never be made right". More dubious, perhaps, is her characterization of all visitors to Antigua as stingy, incurious and contemptuous (not to mention "incredibly unattractive, fat and pastry-like fleshed"). Her idea of contemporary Britain is of a nation of retired officers, lamenting the lost empire: "the English have become such a pitiful lot these days, with hardly any idea what to do with themselves now that they no longer have one quarter of the earth's population bowing and scraping before them. They . . . should, at least, be wearing sackcloth in token penance for wrongs committed . . . ." The force of her argument is further undercut by a curiously wilful scrappiness about such things, for example, the food an overfed tourist might eat, which is supposed to convey the pervasive corruption of the island in a single bite: "A good guess is that it came from a place like Antigua first, where it was grown dirt cheap, went to Miami, and came back. There is a world of something in this, but I can't go into it right now." Her savage tone is also diffused by the shapelessness of the essay: she shifts from an attack on the Swiss (which they earn partly for being so clean and partly for harbouring blood-money), to rambling reminiscences of her childhood, notably of happy days spent stealing from the now destroyed public library ("once I had read a book I couldn't bear to part with it"). The book is full of inconsequential anecdote and *non sequitur*. It is hard, for example, to grasp why the library, which she remembers as the place where "you distorted and erased my history and glorified your own", should, more than any other place, come to symbolize her beloved "old Antigua".

Kincaid's disregard for both her reader and her subjects suggest that her central purpose in *A Small Place* is not illumination, but something more personal. She is trying, from her adopted home in the place most unlike Antigua except in size (the cold New England state of Vermont), to "work through her rage". However satisfying it may be for the writer, rage seems an ill-chosen idiom for the expression of anything one really wants to make understood—like the letters that one writes but should never send.

> *Isabel Fonseca, "Their Island Story," in* The Times Literary Supplement, *No. 4476, January 13-19, 1989, p. 30.*

Wendy Dutton (essay date 1989)

[*In the following essay, Dutton argues that* At the Bottom of the River *and* Annie John *form one cohesive story.*]

"Now I am a girl, but one day I will marry a woman—a red-skin woman with black bramblebush hair and brown eyes, who wears skirts that are so big I can easily bury my head in them. I would like to marry this woman and live with her in a mud hut near the sea." The magic of *At the Bottom of the River* (1983) comes from its language. It is as rhythmic and riddlesome as poetry. Lovely though the words are, they often read like a coded message or a foreign language. Throughout *At the Bottom of the River* the reader is left wondering how to decipher this writing. The decoder comes in the form of Jamaica Kincaid's novel *Annie John. Annie John* was published in 1985, two years after *At the Bottom of the River.* Its chapters had all appeared as individual stories in the *New Yorker. Annie John* tells the same story as *At the Bottom of the River,* that of a girl coming of age in Antigua, but uses straightforward novel talk and presents few comprehension barriers to the reader. *Annie John* is a kind of personification of *At the Bottom of the River.* It fleshes out the fantasy and the philosophy of *At the Bottom of the River*'s poetry, and between the two books there exists a dialogue of questions and answers. They ultimately read as companion pieces or sister texts.

The similarities between *Annie John* and *At the Bottom of the River* are striking. The two books share the girl narrator's anxiety about growing bigger. In *At the Bottom of the River* someone asks the girl what she has been doing lately. She wants to reply, "I have been praying not to grow any taller." In *Annie John* we read: "I thought of begging my mother to ask my father if he could build for me a set of clamps into which I could screw myself at night before I went to sleep and which would surely cut back on my growing." Even the "redskin girl" whom she wants to marry in **"In the Night"** shows up in *Annie John,* in a chapter called **"The Red Girl."** The Red Girl is Annie John's girlfriend, whose "face was big and round and red, like a moon—a red moon," and her hair is bramblebush-wild. Not surprisingly, *At the Bottom of the River* offers a more cosmic view. By its final story, the girl narrator turns into the very same red girl whom she loves. She says, "I saw my skin, and it was red." A sort of self-acceptance is obtained, and Kincaid illustrates this by referring back to an earlier image and bringing it full circle.

This technique of bringing her images and themes full circle is especially prevalent in *At the Bottom of the River.* **"What I Have Been Doing Lately,"** for example, opens into a dream sequence that rolls over and repeats itself in the end with only slight changes. Regarding this story, the critic Edith Milton claims, "The development of choral repetitions is used as a sort of anchor to hold down the increasingly surreal fantasy." This cyclical pattern is followed in the collection as a whole, making it read like a complete piece rather than ten separate stories. **"Blackness,"** for example, echoes **"In the Night,"** sharing its theme of darkness. **"Holidays"** and **"The Letter Home"** operate as companion pieces about a girl's vacation. **"In the Night"** and **"At Last"** can also be read as companion pieces. **"In the Night"** ends with a girl's wish to hear her mother tell stories about life before the girl's birth (such stories also appear in *Annie John*). **"At Last"** reads like one of these "before you were born" stories, especially since it slips into the mother's narrative rather than the girl's. The mother says, "They weren't here yet, the children. I could hear their hearts beating; but they weren't here yet." These sister stories, quite beautifully, hold mirrors up to each other, but this is to say nothing of the more internal echoes that weave a strong thread connecting the stories. In fact, echoes pervade the book, for Kincaid's writing is composed almost entirely of echoes. The most prominent echo of all, however, exists between the two books themselves.

Since *Annie John* tells the same story as *At the Bottom of the River,* it is instrumental in illuminating the difficult text of the latter. It fills in the spaces. It replaces the fuzziness of *At the Bottom of the River* with facts. For example, Annie is an exceptional student and at fifteen is accelerated to a class with girls who are two or three years older than herself. Once this specialness is clearly defined in *Annie John,* the intense imagination and inventiveness of *At the Bottom of the River* is easier to understand. Then a strange thing happens, however. Annie, at fifteen, has a nervous breakdown. The same breakdown occurs in *At the Bottom of the River* in the story **"Blackness,"** but the language in **"Blackness"** is so clouded and intentionally sparse that the point is almost completely missed. The story reads as a mere mood piece, with passages like, "In the blackness, then, I have been erased. I can no longer say my own name. I can no longer point to myself and say 'I'."

The moody, evocative world in *At the Bottom of the River,* with its fine line between truth and images, helps justify the hypersensitive emotion that must have fed into the breakdown. Nonetheless, the reader is not well prepared for that occurrence. Annie is shown as different and exceptional, but these traits are not stressed enough to necessitate a breakdown. Moreover, Annie's childhood has not been rough; rather, it was a childhood filled with passion, adoration, and adventure.

Annie John does use much more concrete imagery to illustrate Annie's sickness. Annie says, "It must have come on me like a mist"; "My happiness was something deep inside me, and when I closed my eyes I could see it .... It took the shape of a small black ball, all wrapped up in cobwebs." Her symptoms too are related with a vivid clarity that eludes the ethereal quality of *At the Bottom of the River.* For example, Annie is struck by some photos on her bedside table. She takes them into the bathroom and washes them: "When I finished, I dried them thoroughly, dusted them with talcum powder, and then laid them down in a corner covered with a blanket, so that they would be warm while they slept." In her book *On Photography* Susan Sontag makes the point that "photographs have become one of the principal devices for experiencing something, for giving an appearance of participation." Photographs allow people to avoid experience, avoid going below the surface. Annie wants to put a stop to this. She treats the photographs as human and thereby expresses a desire to experience life to the fullest, to go below the surface, as she does in *At the Bottom of the River.*

Compared to *At the Bottom of the River, Annie John* reads like a photo album. Though it is immensely helpful in translating *At the Bottom of the River, Annie John* looks at the surface of things and lacks rationale, explanation, motivation. *At the Bottom of the River* acts as the cerebral text for the pictures in *Annie John.* Together the two books allow the reader to develop one cohesive story.

● ● ● ● ●

At the Bottom of the River has been billed as "Caribbean fiction" portraying "a childhood in the Caribbean" that is "partly remembered, partly divined," but the most obvious alternative reading of Kincaid's collection of stories interprets it as being not so much about growing up on the islands as about growing up female. Every sentence of Kincaid's writing breathes this feminine sensibility. The first story, **"Girl,"** reads like a list: "Don't walk barehead in the hot sun; cook pumpkin fritters in a very hot sweet oil; soak your little cloths right after you take them off," and so on. The reader gets the impression that the story is about a girl who is in training. She is in training to be a woman, and these household chores—on the surface anyway—are what a woman does. The womanly duties in **"Girl"** are carried over in *Annie John,* "each chore being a small rehearsal for that faraway day, thank God, when I would be mistress of my own house."

By the end of **"Girl"** a more complex female view unfolds, as the mother warns the daughter not to become "the kind of woman who the baker won't let near the bread." In *Annie John* too the mother accuses the daughter of trying to grow into a slut. It is an intriguing progression in **"Girl,"** considering the entire story is just one sentence. *At the Bottom of the River* as a whole also blossoms into a much more cosmic view of womanhood by the end of the collection. Growing up is not seen as something that is inevitable, something that will happen anyway. For the girl, the process is intrinsically connected to her mother. Both books revolve around the mother and are indeed mother-obsessed, much as the girl character herself is. In **"My Mother"** the narrator states, "I had grown big, but my mother was bigger, and that would always be so." She adds, "Sometimes I cannot see from her breasts on up, so lost is she in the atmosphere."

The all-consuming mother-daughter relationship is more metaphorical in *At the Bottom of the River.* The intensity of it is difficult to reckon with. As with the breakdown in *Annie John,* the reader is not given enough groundwork to comprehend fully the relationship in *At the Bottom of the River. Annie John,* however, makes the maternal conflict a universal one, the natural rebellion of a fifteen-year-old girl against her mother. Therefore *Annie John* fills in some of the missing pieces in the groundwork for this conflict. For example, Annie speaks of her mother's "betrayal": "Why, I wonder, didn't I see the hypocrite in my mother when, over the years, she said that she loved me and could hardly live without me, while at the same time proposing and arranging separation after separation." Then there is the breadfruit incident. The seeds of the story were sown in **"At the Bottom of the River,"** when "my mother made up elaborate tales of the origins of food, just so that I would eat it." Since Annie hates breadfruit, her mother disguises it as Belgian rice. After Annie eats it, her mother tells her the truth and laughs. It is at this point that the relationship with the mother turns hostile: "When she laughed, her mouth opened to show off her big, shiny, sharp white teeth. It was as if my mother had suddenly turned into a crocodile."

Another time Annie walks in on her parents as they are having sex. The scene matches the powerful man-woman encounter that the girl witnesses in **"Wingless,"** where the man's erection is described as follows: "Then he put wind in his cheeks and blew himself up until in the bright sun he looked like a boil." The version in *At the Bottom of the River* reads like a meeting of monsters: the woman "smiled—a red, red smile—and like a fly he dropped dead."

The father's absence is keenly felt in *At the Bottom of the River.* He mainly appears in a five-page male perspective in **"At the Bottom of the River"** that offsets the mother's perspective in **"Blackness."** The father in **"At the Bottom of the River"** "cannot conceive of the union of opposites, or, for that matter, their very existence." He cannot conceive of anything, because he is a man outside the woman's world. The reader is left wondering where the father is, and indeed who the father is.

The father's perspective comes after the breakdown. **"At the Bottom of the River"** is a story of recovery, of the girl's coming to terms with her place in the universe. To do this, she too needs to reconcile with "the union of opposites," the father part of her as well as the mother part. In *Annie John* the father is as much a part of her growing-up anxiety as the mother. She says: "For most of my life, when the three of us went anywhere together I stood between the two of them or sat between the two of them. But then I got too big, and there I was, shoulder to shoulder with them more or less, and it became not very comfortable to walk down the street together."

Annie's father is thirty-five years older than her mother. This adds to the sense of Annie and her mother living in a separate world, since they are both children compared to the father. On one occasion Annie and her mother were walking down the street when they were attacked by another woman. Annie concludes: "I knew that it was one of the women that my father had loved and with whom he had had a child or children, and who never forgave him for marrying my mother and having me." Annie and her mother are the chosen ones, the adored ones. This shines light on Annie's specialness. She is an only child, doted upon; but are special dynamics with her parents enough to bring on an adolescent nervous breakdown? Illuminating though *Annie John* is in bringing out these dynamics, the breakdown still remains a mystery.

● ● ● ● ●

Annie John offers another explanation for the breakdown, which plays a potent but undeveloped part in both books: voodoo, or "obeah" in patois. In *At the Bottom of the River* the mother mentions a "jablesse," explaining, "It's a person who can turn into anything.... Take good care when you see a beautiful woman. A jablesse always tries to look like a beautiful woman." In the same story a woman removes her skin, an act associated with voodoo priestesses. Kincaid writes: "The night-soil man can see a bird walking in the trees. It isn't a bird. It is a woman who has removed her skin and is on her way to drink the blood of her enemies. It is woman who has left her skin in the corner of a house." *At the Bottom of the River* is rife with conjure references such as this, though the world of conjure is treated more literally in *Annie John.*

The mother believes Annie's breakdown has been brought on by a hex and that one of her husband's former mistresses administered the hex. In addition to the British physician Dr. Stephens, she also consults an obeah woman named Ma Jolie. Annie describes the encounter:

> When my father came in to see me, he looked at all my medicines—Dr. Stephens's and Ma Jolie's—lined up side by side and screwed up his face, the way he did when he didn't like what he saw. He must have said something to my mother, for she arranged the shelf in a new way, with Dr. Stephens's prescriptions in the front and Ma Jolie's prescriptions in the back.

Voodoo has always been a religion in which power is associated with women. Here is a voodoo ceremony recounted by Zora Neale Hurston, one of the first blacks to do formal research on the subject:

> She [the voodoo priestess] replies by throwing back her veil and revealing her sex organs. The ceremony means that this is the infinite, the ultimate truth.... It is considered the greatest honor for all males participating to kiss her organ of creation for Damballa, the god of gods has permitted them to come face to face with truth.

The Caribbean became the originating source of voodoo when Catholicism mixed with the tribal religions. Voodoo is seen as a legitimate religion for many islanders, and it is not surprising that it carries over into Kincaid's work.

When Annie continues to be sick despite Ma Jolie's and Dr. Stephen's efforts, Annie's grandmother Ma Chess appears, herself a formidable obeah woman. The reader learns that conjure is like a family trade: "Whatever Ma Jolie knew, my grandmother knew at least ten times more. How she regretted that my mother did not show more of an interest in obeah things." Though her mother rejected voodoo, Annie's exceptionalness suggests she is clicking into her power. Then Ma Chess disappears as mysteriously as she appeared, and Annie is cured after three-and-a-half months. Ma Chess is never given credit for Annie's cure, however. It is Annie who cures herself. Through the long internal and spiritual rigmarole outlined best in **"At the Bottom of the River,"** she reasons her way back to sanity and finds a place for herself in civilization.

Annie has her own private power, and delicately she steps into it. Take, for example, the idea of a voodoo woman removing her skin. As *At the Bottom of the River* progresses, the girl narrator is also seen removing her skin. In **"The Letter Home"** she says, "My hair went limp, my waist grew folds, I shed my skin," and in **"My Mother"** she states, "My skin had just blackened and cracked and fallen away and my new impregnable carapace had taken hold." This is the same thing that happened with the red-skin girl. The narrator starts out marveling at the red-skin girl, then turns into her. Similarly, the narrator starts out describing a skinless woman, then turns into one. Like shedding, the girl loses her skin as she grows, but by a more literal translation, she is also identifying herself with conjure. In this case, growing into a woman is the same as growing into power.

The idea of a skinless woman calls to mind someone who· is exposed, raw, a painful receptacle for the experiences that touch her. This takes the reader one step closer to reckoning with the curious nature of an adolescent breakdown. It also suggests an alternative reading for both *At the Bottom of the River* and *Annie John.* The standard reading asks the reader to believe the breakdown was caused by severe growing pains, a theory that is difficult to accept despite the fact that Kincaid takes great care to set Annie apart from regular girls. It is easier to believe that Annie has inherited her grandmother's mystic powers. In addition to being a "skinless woman," Annie (and the girl in *At the Bottom of the River*) demonstrates considerable storytelling powers. This kind of creative power is greatly akin to conjure. Creative women have long been called conjurers. The sheer act of creation classified women writers as witches of sorts. By taking up the previously male task of writing, they were seen not purely as creators but as warped creators, "as if the very process of writing had itself liberated a madwoman, a crazy woman and an angry woman." This madwoman is not only the author, but often the female character which she creates.

The idea of voodoo running in her family sets Annie up for a unique kind of matrilineage. As just mentioned, however, this matrilineage is not for the protagonist alone; the author shares in it as well. The history of women's writing moves in fits and starts and often centers on the quest for literary foremothers. Foremothers act as a sort of launching pad for contemporary women writers, and they also give the woman writer a history of her own, a tradition. Until recently, literary foremothers were difficult to find. Often the creative precursors of women writers had to be found in the traditional domestic world. They were the quiltmakers, the fine cooks, the women with "green thumbs." Similarly, the conjure woman serves as a creative foremoth-er, especially for the black woman writer. This was the case for Zora Neale Hurston, who admired voodoo priestesses such as Marie Leveau and Kitty Brown. Hurston herself then became a literary foremother for Alice Walker. Walker discovered Hurston when writing "The Revenge of Hannah Kemhuff," a story about voodoo. This is the sort of matrilineage that carries down to Kincaid. Just as Annie learns from Ma Chess, Kincaid too allows conjure to inform her work. It has been said of Hurston and could also be said of Kincaid that she "used the power of the written text itself as a form of magic."

● ● ● ● ●

Annie's breakdown can also be read as a breakdown with the past, with tradition, with our mothers. Both *Annie John* and *At the Bottom of the River* portray a longing for connection with the past. This does not encompass just the immediate past or even a past that includes literary foremothers. Instead, Kincaid reaches back through the history of humankind. Prehistoric allusions run like an undercurrent or a subtheme through the book. The girl declares, "I am primitive and wingless." She watches her mother turn into a reptile, then does the same: "Silently, she had instructed me to follow her example, and now I too travelled along on my white underbelly, my tongue darting and flickering in the hot air." Before long, mother and daughter "merge and separate; merge and separate; soon we shall enter the final stage of our evolution." In this passage the girl aligns herself with the universe, not just with her personal world. This is a crucial connection that aids in her recovery.

The preoccupation with pits and caves in *At the Bottom of the River* also reflects this need for prehistory. Here is just one of that book's pit scenes: "A deep hole had opened up before me . . . . On purpose I fell in. I fell and I fell, over and over, as if I were an old suitcase. On the sides of the deep hole I could see things written, but perhaps it was a foreign language because I couldn't read them. Still I fell, for I don't know how long." Annie tells a twin version of this story in *Annie John*: "A huge black space then opened up in front of me and I fell inside it. I couldn't see what was in front of me and I couldn't hear anything around me. I couldn't think of anything except that my mother was no longer near me. Things went on in this way for I don't know how long." This cave or pit is the prehistoric woman's place, a crude home, much in the same way that the girl in *At the Bottom of the River* always seems to be "playing house." Building these makeshift dwellings seems like part of the girl's training for womanhood.

While the Platonic imagery of the cave cannot be ignored, a quite different cave offers an alternative, feminist interpretation of Kincaid: "Although Plato does not seem to have thought much about this point, a cave is—as Freud pointed out—a female place, a womb-shaped enclosure, a house of earth, secret and often sacred." Mary Shelley invented such a cave in her novel

The Last Man (1826). Shelley's account was fictional but has developed into a myth about women's writing. She recounts the time when she and her husband Percy Bysshe Shelley got lost and discovered a cave that belonged to an ancient woman called the Sibyl. The Sibyl was said to sit on a boulder in her cave writing voraciously on the only tools available to her: leaves and pieces of bark and cornhusks. She wrote "in various languages."

The Sibyl's cave can only be reached through a maze of underground tunnels. It is near the sea and has no ceiling, opening up like a window to heaven through which the Sibyl receives her "divine intuitions." Her cave resembles "the mud hut near the sea" where the girl in *At the Bottom of the River* wants to live with the red-skin woman. It seems when the girl falls into the deep dark hole, she is somehow falling into the Sibyl's primitive cave, where "on the sides of the deep hole I could see things written, but perhaps it was a foreign language." Though Kincaid most likely did not intend to draw the analogy, these hieroglyphics past which the girl tumbles resemble the Sibyl's scribblings.

The Sibyl's cave relates to the tradition of women's writing on this level: if the Sibyl's leaves were not discovered and translated, they would be lost forever. As it is, they can only be translated by the man, who has received formal education: "The whole meaning of the sibylline leaves can only be re-membered through painstaking labor: translation, transcription, and stitchery, revision and re-creation" (the hyphens are the authors' own). Kincaid too seems to be caught up in this act of "re-vision and re-creation." Using the sibylline interpretation, it can be said that she does not rely on the resource of her personal life alone; she goes back to the first woman writer, her cosmic originatory source.

It is also a journey that Annie makes to bring herself back from sickness. She must revise and recreate herself. Her problem as proposed in **"Blackness"** is not only one of being erased, but one of silence, long the enemy of women. She is "living in the silent voice." The problem is solved in the apocalyptic **"At the Bottom of the River"** when, in the last paragraph, she gets her voice back. The first thing she then says is her name.

> And so, emerging from my pit, . . . I see things in the light of the lamp, all perishable and transient, how bound up I know I am to all that is human endeavor, to all that is past and all that shall be, to all that shall be lost and leave no trace. I claim these things then—mine—and now feel myself grow solid and complete, my name filling up my mouth.

This is echoed in the last chapter of *Annie John,* which begins, "'My name is Annie John.' These were the first words that came into my mind as I woke up on the morning of the last day I spent in Antigua." Annie adds, "My name was the last thing I saw the night before, just as I was falling asleep; it was written in big, black letters all over my trunk."

It is as if Kincaid herself were "emerging from this pit," as if she were emerging from the Sibyl's cave, leaves of writing in her hand. Kincaid has taken her burgeoning bag of echoes to the primeval cave of the original conjure woman. Upon returning, she looks about and paints a still life in her mind of the civilized room around her. She says, "I see a chair, I see a table, I see a pen; I see a bowl of fruit." Surfacing from her writer's trance, she feels "bound up" with the tradition of women's writing. In fact, *At the Bottom of the River* is so strange and new that it often reads like not only a foreign language, but an entirely new kind of writing that could specifically be called a woman's writing. The name filling up her mouth is not only "Annie John" and not only "Jamaica Kincaid." The name is also "woman." (pp. 406-10)

> *Wendy Dutton, "Merge and Separate: Jamaica Kincaid's Fiction," in* World Literature Today, *Vol. 63, No. 3, Summer, 1989, pp. 406-10.*

Thulani Davis (essay date 1990)

[*In the following review, Davis examines theme, motive, and style in* Lucy.]

Jamaica Kincaid's new novel, *Lucy,* the first-person narrative of a young woman coming to America, runs like a quiet brook, rising and falling over rocks and gullies, brushing past places it has run before but never resting, never latching onto anything in its path. Lucy herself is like this, absorbing only small details of her new home (where she will work as an *au pair*), never trying to take in the place as a whole, not looking beyond what is at hand. On her first day in America she reacts only to a few new experiences: the lights of the unnamed city, the dingy ordinariness of the landscape, her first elevator ride, food from a refrigerator. "I slept soundly that night, but it wasn't because I was happy and comfortable—quite the opposite; it was because I didn't want to take in anything else."

Lucy has come to get away from her home in Antigua and all its familiarity. Her story is not about the shock of emigrating from one culture to another; it dwells in the psychological space between leaving and arriving. In sparse prose punctuated with the most economical yet precise description, Ms. Kincaid's Lucy makes an accounting of her first year abroad—a year in which she never quite arrives where she expected to be, or even unpacks her trunk of documents that purport to show who she is and what she will be doing. By some arrangement she has come directly to the maid's room of a spacious apartment, to take care of the four children of Mariah and Lewis and to become ensconced in the couple's cozy but eroding family life.

She seems to have used her nursing studies as an excuse to get away from home, but she never mentions time spent at school and soon gives it up. After her first winter Lucy reflects: "It was my past, so to speak, my first real past—a past that was my own and over which I had the final word. I had just lived through a bleak and cold time, and it is not to the weather outside that I refer." Lucy's real preoccupation is her own unhappy state of mind and the sad discovery that, as the old folks used to say, every goodbye ain't gone.

Lucy finds no home in her warm but distant relationship with the unfaithful Lewis, tolerant Mariah and their children; in her casual, unremarkable liaisons with men; or in her friendship with Peggy, an Irish working woman who offers easy company if not genuine compatibility. It is as if in choosing to leave home to loosen her connection to people, the young woman finds she can no longer make any connections at all.

And there is the problem of those memories Lucy confronts at odd moments. Seeing a man's tongue lick a woman's ear, Lucy recalls a boy back home. She remembers her father the philanderer trying to count up how many children he had—perhaps 30—without ever being sure. And more and more she stumbles upon reminders of the advice and habits of her mother, whose letters she refuses to open.

Ms. Kincaid is a marvelous writer whose descriptions are richly detailed; her sentences turn and surprise even in the bare context she has created, in which there are few colors, sights or smells and the moments of intimacy and confrontation take place in the wings, or just after the door closes. Lucy moves affectlessly through the unnamed places, among the new people, reacting with almost insensitive frankness to their desires and disappointments. Lucy is a delicate, careful observer, but her rage prevents her from reveling in the deliciousness of a moment. At her happiest, she simply says, "Life isn't so bad after all." Lucy in America is a much-disappointed girl, despairing over unfulfilled expectations. Of course one knows what demons expectations are, but it is never clear what Lucy's particular expectations have been. Lucy in Antigua was a fiery girl who had bitter fights with her idol-mother and felt driven to leave home forever once she sensed she could no longer worship this perfect, self-sacrificing woman; Lucy in America is lost without an object for such passion.

But I am very puzzled by *Lucy.* If I had not read Jamaica Kincaid's other fiction, I might have been left with the feeling of wanting to know more about this young woman, who is not at home in her skin, and about the unresolved relationships left behind in Antigua. One gets only small tastes of those parts of life that filled and consumed Lucy earlier. While the book would seem to tell a story of the floating life of one of the nameless brown faces we see strolling with blond-haired tots along city streets, it also provides a new rendering of material explored in Ms. Kincaid's two very different, previous works of fiction. The manner of telling varies, but the seminal events and the narrow, internal focus are the same in all three books. With the passage of time her first book, *At the Bottom of the River* (1983), a collection of gorgeous, incantatory stories of young life in Antigua,

can now be viewed as the sketchbook from which was drawn her more conventional coming-of-age novel, *Annie John* (1985). Whereas the images in the first book are luminous and disjointed, as if refracted through a pool of water, they return as singular, sparkling pictures in the more orderly, representational narrative of *Annie John.* In *Lucy,* they recur as slightly misshapen by memory and distance.

At the Bottom of the River opens with a mother's voice reciting years' worth of warnings, how-tos and little gems like "This is how to behave in the presence of men who don't know you very well, and this way they won't recognize immediately the slut I have warned you against becoming." This mother in *Annie John* is a never-sits-still kind of woman—washing the clothes and drying them on rocks, fetching fish from the two fishermen who share their catch with her. And it is this same woman, with her wash, advice and all, from whom Lucy has run so hard. She is the loving, frightening mother-goddess looming in all three books, creating a blissful, verdant paradise in *At the Bottom of the River* that some might call an idealized "woman-space," a place of unending nurture, where a voice always closes the night with a story that begins, "Before you were born."

Lucy could be construed as a kind of sequel to *Annie John,* but I am not convinced there was any such intent. The two books are like night and day in style and structure: one lush and descriptive, moving chronologically and underscoring its major themes with imagery and metaphor; the other narrative sparse and seemingly scattered, meandering in and out of situations rather than resolving or coming to conclusions, perhaps more like life. And I found it difficult to recognize the lively, curious and engaged child Annie in the angry but disengaged Lucy. Unfairly, perhaps, I found myself drawing from the other books to complete the picture— assuming, for instance, that this young Lucy (also called Little Miss in all the books), who hates Wordsworth, loves the Brontës and has no plans to continue her education, *could* be the gifted scholar and irreverent class prefect Annie. When Lucy berates her mother for ignoring her intelligence, it comes late and as a surprise that this is a matter of rage for her. When Lucy wonders—rather oddly, it would seem—who made her father's coffin, I knew she might be asking that question because Annie John's father made everyone's coffin at home. I remain puzzled, wondering still who exactly is telling this story, who is accounting for herself here and there by saying, "It must have been my age." Surely it was more than that.

Thulani Davis, "Girl-Child in a Foreign Land," in The New York Times Book Review, *October 28, 1990, p. 11.*

FURTHER READING

Ellsberg, Peggy. "Rage Laced with Lyricism." *Commonweal* CXV, No. 19 (4 November 1988): 602-04.

> Praises *A Small Place,* noting that Kincaid "bursts into a different voice—no longer just sassy, but now really angry—and Antigua becomes the main character."

Garis, Leslie. "Through West Indian Eyes." *The New York Times Magazine* (7 October 1990): 42-44, 70, 78, 80, 91.

> Profile of Kincaid's life amidst the publication of *Lucy,* focusing on her reputation and nature as a writer.

Hill, Alison Friesinger. Review of *A Small Place,* by Jamaica Kincaid. *The New York Times Book Review* XCIII, No. 28 (10 July 1988): 19.

> Mixed review of *A Small Place,* lamenting, "the writing is distorted by [Kincaid's] anger, which backs the reader into a corner...."

Ismond, Patricia. "Jamaica Kincaid: 'First They Must Be Children.'" *World Literature Written in English* 28, No. 2 (Autumn 1988): 336-41.

> Explores Kincaid's place among other Caribbean writers and examines the portrayal of childhood in her fiction.

Murdoch, H. Adlai. "Severing the (M)other Connection: The Representation of Cultural Identity in Jamaica Kincaid's *Annie John.*" *Callaloo* 13, No. 2 (Spring 1990): 325-40.

> Investigates the separation of mother and daughter in *Annie John,* drawing on psychoanalytical concepts and Caribbean social structures to explain Annie's developing hatred for her mother.

Martin Luther King, Jr.

1929-1968

American civil rights leader, orator, and essayist.

King is recognized as the driving force of the civil rights movement in the United States during the 1960s. An eloquent orator, he delivered at the height of his fame an average of 450 speeches a year throughout the country, calling for racial equality. He passionately embraced nonviolence as a method for social reform and encouraged others to fight social injustice, not with anger or hate but with Christian love. *Letter from Birmingham City Jail* (1963) and "I Have a Dream" (1963), two of his most famous works, have come to symbolize the civil rights struggle. Scholars rank these documents with Abraham Lincoln's Gettysburg Address, Emile Zola's Dreyfus Letter, and John F. Kennedy's Inaugural Address as equals in power and eloquence. Filled with biblical imagery and resounding emotion, they cry out for justice, equality, and freedom. Today they are considered documents of universal ownership and serve as reminders of the man who proclaimed: "From every mountainside, let freedom ring.... When we allow freedom to ring, when we let it ring from every village and every hamlet, from every state and every city, we will be able to speed up that day when all God's children, black men and white men, Jews and Gentiles, Protestants and Catholics, will be able to join hands and sing in the words of the old Negro spiritual: 'Free at last. Free at last. Thank God Almighty, we are free at last'."

King was a gifted and precocious child. He was born in Atlanta, Georgia, and grew up listening to his father, Rev. Martin Luther King, Sr., preach. Young King was astonished, according to biographical accounts, that by forming words and flinging them out "in a crescendo of sound," his father could make people cry, shout, and respond. "You just wait and see," King told his mother at age six, "I'm going to get me some big words." He later told Lawrence D. Reddick, his friend and biographer, that his "greatest talent, strongest tradition, and most constant interest [is] the eloquent statement of ideas." King's parents and grandmother encouraged young Martin's public speaking, and he often sang and recited biblical passages for church audiences. Sundays were strictly reserved for church activities, but on weekdays, King played basketball—or, in the summer, baseball—with his brother and sister. His childhood was relatively comfortable; unlike most of the black families in the neighborhood, the Kings were solidly middle-class. King, Sr., once proudly admitted, "We've never lived in a rented house and never ridden too long in a car on which payment was due." Before bed and prayers, the Kings spent the evening hours reciting Bible verses and discussing the day's events.

King's childhood was far from idyllic, however. Growing up in the South, one of the first phrases King learned

to read was "Whites Only." At age six he learned that there was a "white" school and a "colored" school. At age eight he discovered that whites came first; they sat in the front of the bus and were served first in restaurants and in stores. He and his friends were called "black sons of bitches" by hostile whites. When he was fourteen, he was called a "nigger" for refusing to give up his bus seat to a white person. He and a teacher were returning home after participating in an oratorical contest when, "at a small town along the way," King recalled, "some white passengers boarded the bus, and the white driver ordered us to get up and give the whites our seats. We didn't move quickly enough to suit him, so he began cursing us.... I intended to stay right in that seat, but Mrs. Bradley finally urged me up, saying we had to obey the law. And so we stood up in the aisle for the 90 miles to Atlanta.... It was the angriest I have ever been in my life." So enraged was King by this and other similar encounters that he resolved "to hate every white person." On the surface, however, he appeared a well-mannered young man and a model student when he entered Morehouse College at the age of fifteen.

Although King grew up in a family of preachers, he declared himself agnostic, partly because he was nagged by the question: "If God is as all-powerful and as good as everyone says, why is there so much evil on the face of the earth?" He was also repelled by the religious emotionalism he found in black churches. Persuaded by Morehouse teachers—particularly Benjamin E. Mays, the college president—that religion was more than hand-clapping and shouting "hallelujahs," King enrolled at Crozer Theological Seminary in Pennsylvania. "There for the first time," David Halberstam wrote in *Harper's Magazine,* "he entered the white world." One of six black students in a predominantly white school, "he was terribly aware of their whiteness and his blackness and the stereotypes they had of Negroes. Negroes were always late for things, Martin King was always first in a classroom. Negroes were lazy and indifferent, Martin King worked hard and studied endlessly. Negroes were dirty, Martin King was always clean, always properly, perhaps too properly, dressed. Negroes were always laughing, Martin King was deadly serious. If there was a school picnic, Martin King did not eat watermelon." King was an excellent student, graduating at the top of his class in 1951. At Crozer he formed strong friendships with a number of white students, who found King a bit too serious but fun and enjoyable nonetheless. They also envied his rich baritone voice, which commanded attention wherever they went. For the first time in his life, King realized that whites could be his allies. Most importantly, however, at the seminary he was exposed to the works of two men who would shape him as a minister and as a civil rights leader: Walter Rauschenbusch and Mahatma Gandhi.

During his senior year, King read Rauschenbusch's *Christianity and the Social Crisis,* a book that "left an indelible imprint on my thinking," he said. Rauschenbusch contended that the church must work to undo social injustices; the Gospel message *must* be a social message. At about the same time King was also exposed to Gandhi's philosophy of nonviolence. Gandhi advocated *satyagraha,* which he translated as "the vindication of truth not by infliction of suffering on the opponent but on one's self." Furthermore, he encouraged his followers to denounce violence and to repay evil with good instead. In the midst of the civil rights battle, King would later remind his own followers: "Rivers of blood may have to flow before we gain our freedom, but it must be our blood." Thus, when King was graduated from Crozer, he was armed with a rudimentary plan for eradicating segregation in the South.

In the fall of 1951 King enrolled at Boston University to pursue a doctorate in theology. Two years later he married Coretta Scott, a student at Boston's New England Conservatory of Music. Completing his doctoral thesis, "A Comparison of the Conceptions of God in the Thinking of Paul Tillich and Henry Nelson Wie-

man," he received his Ph.D. in systematic theology in 1955. The same year he was elected president of the Montgomery Improvement Association (M.I.A.) in Alabama, a group formed to protest the arrest of Rosa Parks, a black woman who refused to give up her bus seat to a white man. Planning to end the humiliating treatment of blacks on city bus lines, King organized a bus boycott that was to last more than a year. Despite receiving numerous threatening phone calls, being arrested, and having his home bombed, King and the boycott prevailed. The U.S. Supreme Court eventually declared Montgomery's bus segregation laws illegal, and, in December 1956, King rode on Montgomery's first integrated bus. "Montgomery was the soil," wrote King's widow in her autobiography, *My Life with Martin Luther King, Jr.,* "in which the seed of a new theory of social action took root. Black people found in nonviolent, direct action a militant method that avoided violence but achieved dramatic confrontation which electrified and educated the whole nation."

King was soon made president of an organization of much wider scope than the M.I.A., the Southern Christian Leadership Conference (S.C.L.C.). The group's goal was to increase black voter registration and eventually eliminate segregation in the South. A few years later, in 1959, two important events took place. First, King and his wife spent a month in India, visiting the sites of Gandhi's struggle against the British and meeting people who had known the Indian leader. Second, upon returning home, King resigned as pastor of Dexter Avenue Baptist Church in Montgomery so he could devote more of his time to the civil rights effort. The trip to India greatly inspired King. As Stephen B. Oates observed: "He came home with a deeper understanding of nonviolence and a deep commitment as well. For him, nonviolence was no longer just a philosophy and a technique of social change; it was now a whole way of life."

Despite his adherence to the nonviolent philosophy, King was unable to avoid the bloodshed that was to follow. Near the end of 1962 he decided to focus his energies on the desegregation of Birmingham, Alabama. Alabama's capital was at that time what King called in his book *Why We Can't Wait* (1964) "the most segregated city in America"—which was precisely why he had chosen it as his target. In this work King detailed the advance planning that went into the Birmingham campaign. Most important was the training in nonviolent techniques given those who volunteered to participate in the demonstrations. "The focus of these training sessions," King noted, "was the socio-dramas designed to prepare the demonstrators for some of the challenges they could expect to face. The harsh language and physical abuse of the police and self-appointed guardians of the law were frankly presented, along with the non-violent creed in action: to resist without bitterness; to be cursed and not reply; to be beaten and not hit back."

One of the unusual aspects of the Birmingham campaign was King's decision to use children in the demonstrations. When the protests came to a head on May 3, 1963, it was after the arrests of nearly 1,000 young people the previous day. As another wave of protestors, mostly children and teenagers, took to the streets, they were suddenly hit with jets of water from powerful fire hoses. Police dogs were also released on the demonstrators. The photographs circulated by the media of children being attacked brought cries of outrage from throughout the country and the world. President Kennedy sent a Justice Department representative to Birmingham to work for a peaceful solution to the problem. Within a week negotiators produced an agreement that met King's major demands, including desegregation of lunch counters, restrooms, fitting rooms, and drinking fountains in the city and hiring of blacks in positions previously closed to them.

Although the Birmingham campaign ended in triumph for King, at the outset he was criticized for his efforts. Imprisoned at the beginning of the protest for disobeying a court injunction forbidding him to lead any demonstrations in Birmingham, King spent some of his time in jail composing an open letter to his critics. This document, the celebrated *Letter from Birmingham City Jail,* is described by Oates as "a classic in protest literature, the most elegant and learned expression of the goals and philosophy of the nonviolent movement ever written." In the letter King addressed eight clergymen who claimed that as an "outsider" he had no business in Birmingham. King responded: "I am in Birmingham because injustice is here.... I cannot sit idly by in Atlanta and not be concerned about what happens in Birmingham. Injustice anywhere is a threat to justice everywhere. We are caught in an inescapable network of mutuality, tied in a single garment of destiny."

Another important event of 1963 was a massive march on Washington, D.C., which King planned together with leaders of other civil rights organizations. An estimated 250,000 people were on hand to hear King and other dignitaries speak at the march's end point, the Lincoln Memorial. While King's biographers have noted that the young minister struggled all night writing words to inspire the marchers, he subsequently deviated from his prepared text and gave the most eloquent and powerful speech of his career. In the speech, which contained the rhythmic repetition of the phrase "I have a dream," King painted a vision of a "promised land" of racial equality and justice for all. He proclaimed: "I have a dream that one day this nation will rise up and live out the true meaning of its creed, 'We hold these truths to be self-evident, that all men are created equal.' I have a dream that one day on the red hills of Georgia, sons of former slaves and the sons of former slave owners will be able to sit down together at the table of brotherhood.... I have a dream that my four little children will one day live in a nation where they will not be judged by the color of their skin, but by the content of their character. I HAVE A DREAM TODAY!"

On January 3, 1964, King was proclaimed "Man of the Year" by *Time* magazine, the first black to be so honored. Later that year he received the Nobel Peace Prize, becoming the twelfth American, the third black, and the youngest—he was thirty-five—person ever to receive the award. He donated the $54,600 prize to the S.C.L.C. and other civil rights groups. The Nobel Prize gave King even wider recognition as a world leader. "Overnight," commented Flip Shulke and Penelope O. McPhee in *King Remembered,* "King became... a symbol of world peace. He knew that if the Nobel Prize was to mean anything, he must commit himself more than ever to attaining the goals of the black movement through peace."

The next two years were marked by both triumph and despair. First came King's campaign for voting rights, concentrating on a registration drive in Selma, Alabama. Selma would be, according to Oates, "King's finest hour." In March 1965, nearly 500 school children were arrested and charged with juvenile delinquency after they cut classes to show their support for King. In another incident, over one hundred adults were arrested when they picketed the county courthouse. On March 7, state troopers beat nonviolent demonstrators who were trying to march from Selma to Montgomery to present their demands to Governor George Wallace. Angered by such confrontations, King sent telegrams to religious leaders throughout the nation calling for them to meet in Selma for a "ministers' march" to Montgomery. Although some 1500 marchers assembled, they were again turned back by a line of state troopers, but this time violence was avoided.

King was elated by the show of support he received from religious leaders around the country, but his joy soon turned to sorrow when he learned that several of the white ministers who had marched with him had been beaten by club-wielding whites. One of them died two days later. The brutal murder of the clergyman again focused the nation's attention on Selma. Within a few days, President Lyndon Johnson made a televised appearance before a joint session of Congress in which he demanded passage of a voting rights bill. Later that year President Johnson signed the 1965 Voting Rights Act into law, with King looking on. The act made voter literacy test requirements illegal, gave the Attorney General the power to supervise federal elections, and urged the Attorney General to challenge the legality of poll taxes in state and local elections.

By this time King was ready to embark on his next project: moving his nonviolent campaign to the black ghettoes of the North. Chicago was chosen as the first target, but the campaign did not go the way King had planned. Rioting broke out in the city just two days after King initiated his program. Discord was beginning to be felt within the civil rights movement as well. King was afraid that advocates of "black power" would doom his dream of a nonviolent black revolution. In his book *Where Do We Go from Here: Chaos or Community?* (1967), King described the black power movement as "negative, even nihilistic in its direction," "rooted in hopelessness and pessimism" and "committed to racial—and ethical—separatism."

Where Do We Go from Here also touched on several issues that became King's major concerns during the last two years of his life. He wanted to continue nonviolent demonstrations in the North, to stop the war in Vietnam, and to join underprivileged persons of all races in a coalition against poverty. His first wish never materialized. Instead of nonviolent protest, riots broke out in Boston, Detroit, Milwaukee and more than thirty other U.S. cities. King also vehemently attacked the Vietnam War, even though some of his followers begged him not to participate in anti-war activities, fearful that King's actions would antagonize the Johnson administration. In a radio address posthumously published in *The Trumpet of Conscience* (1968), King explained why speaking out on Vietnam was so important to him. He stated: "I cannot forget that the Nobel Prize for Peace was also a commission—a commission to work harder than I ever worked before for the 'brotherhood of man.' This is a calling which takes me beyond national allegiances." In 1967 King formed the Poor People's Campaign, hoping to pressure the government into enacting anti-poverty legislation. A year later—on April 4, 1968—King was assassinated while standing on the balcony of the Lorraine Motel in Memphis, Tennessee. James Earl Ray, a white man whom King had never met, was later convicted of the crime.

During his lifetime, King was a man of controversy, hated by whites who opposed racial equality and by militant blacks who considered his philosophy of nonviolence "self-deceiving." Eldridge Cleaver, for example, supported Malcolm X, who called for "black liberation by any means necessary." Two days after the assassination of King, Cleaver announced: "[It] becomes clear that the only way for black people in this country to get the things that they want—and the things that they have a right to and that they deserve—is to meet fire with fire.... America has said 'no' to the black man's demand for liberation, and this 'no' is unacceptable to black people. They are going to strike back, they are going to reply to the escalation of this racist government, this racist society... now there is the gun and the bomb, dynamite and the knife, and they will be used liberally in America. America will bleed. America will suffer." Prophetically, on hearing of King's death, angry blacks rioted in 125 cities across the nation. As a result, thirty people died, hundreds suffered injuries, and more than $30 million worth of property damage was incurred.

Controversy still surrounds King nearly twenty-five years after his death. Recent works—particularly Rev. Ralph Abernathy's *And the Walls Came Tumbling Down* and David Garrow's Pulitzer Prize-winning *Bearing the Cross*—allege that King had extramarital sexual relations. Most recently, Clayborne Carson, engaged by Coretta Scott King to compile a collection of King's writings, announced that King may have plagiarized parts of his doctoral dissertation and other writings. These disclosures prompted scores of newspaper editorials and other responses arguing that the allegations had no bearing on King's contributions to the civil rights struggle. "[King's] achievement glows unchallenged through the present shadow," stated a 1990 editorial in the *New York Times.* "Martin Luther King's courage was not copied; and there was no plagiarism in his power."

"There are few men of whom it can be said their lives changed the world," wrote Shulke and McPhee. Indeed, chiefly because of King, social, political, and economic equality for blacks has been a major concern in America for the last three decades. Despite his monumental accomplishments, in a sermon preached at Ebenezer Baptist Church on February 4, 1968—exactly two months before his assassination—King humbly asked: "If any of you are around when I have to meet my day, I don't want a long funeral. And if you get somebody to deliver the eulogy, tell them not to talk too long. Every now and then I wonder what I want them to say... if you want to say that I was a drum major, say that I was a drum major for justice; say that I was a drum major for peace; I was a drum major for righteousness. And all of the other shallow things will not matter. I won't have any money to leave behind. I won't have the fine and luxurious things of life to leave behind. But I just want to leave a committed life behind."

(For further information about King's life and works, see *Black Writers; Contemporary Authors,* Vols. 25-28; *Contemporary Authors New Revision Series,* Vol. 27; and *Something about the Author,* Vol. 14.)

PRINCIPAL WORKS

"A Comparison of the Conceptions of God in the Thinking of Paul Tillich and Henry Nelson Wieman" (dissertation) 1955

"The Montgomery Story" (speech) 1956

"Give Us the Ballot—We Will Transform the South" (speech) 1957

"The Method of Non-Violence" (essay) 1957

Stride toward Freedom: The Montgomery Story (nonfiction) 1958

The Measure of a Man (meditations and essays) 1959

"The American Dream" (speech) 1961

"America's Greatest Crisis" (speech) 1961

"Love, Law and Civil Disobedience" (speech) 1961

"I Have a Dream" (speech) 1963

Letter from Birmingham City Jail (letter) 1963; also published as *Letter from Birmingham Jail,* 1968

Strength to Love (sermons) 1963

"Unwise and Untimely?" (letters) 1963

A Martin Luther King Treasury (sermons, speeches, and essays) 1964

"Nobel Lecture" (speech) 1964

"Why We Can't Wait" (letter and essays) 1964

"Address at Valedictory Service" (speech) 1965

"The Ware Lecture" (speech) 1966

"Beyond Vietnam" (speech) 1967

"A Declaration of Independence from the War in Vietnam" (speech) 1967

"A Time to Break Silence" (speech) 1967

Where Do We Go from Here: Chaos or Community? (nonfiction) 1967

"A Drum Major for Justice" (speech) 1968

"I Have a Dream": The Quotations of Martin Luther King, Jr. (speech excerpts) 1968

*"I See the Promised Land" (speech) 1968

The Trumpet of Conscience (broadcasts) 1968

We Shall Live in Peace: The Teachings of Martin Luther King, Jr. (juvenilia and speech excerpts) 1968

The Wisdom of Martin Luther King in His Own Words (meditations and sermons) 1968

A Martin Luther King Reader (speeches and essays) 1969

Speeches about Vietnam (speeches) 1969

Words and Wisdom of Martin Luther King (meditations and speech excerpts) 1970

Speeches of Martin Luther King, Jr. (speeches) 1972

Loving Your Enemies, Letter from Birmingham Jail, Declaration of Independence from the War in Vietnam (letter and speeches) 1981

The Words of Martin Luther King, Jr. (meditations and speeches) 1983

A Testament of Hope: The Essential Writings of Martin Luther King, Jr. (essays, speeches, sermons, and interviews) 1986

*This was King's last speech, delivered on April 3, 1968—the day before his assassination.

August Meier (essay date 1965)

[*In the following excerpt from an essay that originally appeared in* New Politics *in 1965, Meier, an authority on twentieth-century black American history, argues that King is "more a symbol than a power in the civil rights movement." Evaluating King's appeal among black and white audiences, the critic states that "by uttering moral clichés, the Christian pieties, in a magnificent display of oratory, King becomes enormously effective."*]

The phenomenon that is Martin Luther King consists of a number of striking paradoxes. The Nobel Prize winner is accepted by the outside world as *the* leader of nonviolent direct action movement, but he is criticized by many activists within the movement. He is criticized for what appears, at times, as indecisiveness, and more often denounced for a tendency to accept compromise. Yet, in the eyes of most Americans, both black and white, he remains the symbol of militant direct action. So potent is this symbol of King as direct actionist, that a new myth is arising about his historic role. The real credit for developing and projecting the techniques and philosophy of nonviolent direct action in the civil rights arena must be given to the Congress of Racial Equality

which was founded in 1942, more than a dozen years before the Montgomery bus boycott projected King into international fame. And the idea of mass action by Negroes themselves to secure redress of their grievances must, in large part, be ascribed to the vision of A. Philip Randolph, architect of the March on Washington Movement during World War II. Yet, as we were told in Montgomery on March 25, 1965, King and his followers now assert, apparently without serious contradiction, that a new type of civil rights strategy was born at Montgomery in 1955 under King's auspices.

In a movement in which respect is accorded in direct proportion to the number of times one has been arrested, King appears to keep the number of times he goes to jail to a minimum. In a movement in which successful leaders are those who share in the hardships of their followers, in the risks they take, in the beatings they receive, in the length of time they spend in jail, King tends to leave prison for other important engagements, rather than remaining there and suffering with his followers. In a movement in which leadership ordinarily devolves upon persons who mix democratically with their followers, King remains isolated and aloof. In a movement which prides itself on militancy and "no compromise" with racial discrimination or with the white "power structure," King maintains close relationships with, and appears to be influenced by, Democratic presidents and their emissaries, seems amenable to compromises considered by some half a load or less, and often appears willing to postpone or avoid a direct confrontation in the streets.

King's career has been characterized by failures that, in the larger sense, must be accounted triumphs. The buses in Montgomery were desegregated only after lengthy judicial proceedings conducted by the NAACP Legal Defense Fund secured a favorable decision from the U. S. Supreme Court. Nevertheless, the events in Montgomery were a triumph for direct action, and gave this tactic a popularity unknown when identified solely with CORE (Congress of Racial Equality]. King's subsequent major campaigns—in Albany, Georgia; in Danville, Virginia; in Birmingham, Alabama; and in St. Augustine, Florida—ended as failures or with only token accomplishments in those cities. But each of them, chiefly because of his presence, dramatically focused national and international attention on the plight of the Southern Negro, thereby facilitating overall progress. In Birmingham, in particular, demonstrations which fell short of their local goals were directly responsible for a major Federal Civil Rights Act. Essentially, this pattern of local failure and national victory was recently enacted at Selma, Alabama.

King is ideologically committed to disobeying unjust laws and court orders, in the Gandhian tradition, but generally he follows a policy of not disobeying Federal Court orders. In his recent Montgomery speech, he expressed a crude, neo-Marxist interpretation of history romanticizing the Populist movement as a genuine union of black and white common people, ascribing race prejudice to capitalists playing white workers against black. Yet, in practice, he is amenable to compromise with the white bourgeois political and economic Establishment. More important, King enunciates a superficial and eclectic philosophy and by virtue of it he has profoundly awakened the moral conscience of America.

In short, King can be described as a "Conservative Militant."

In this combination of militancy with conservatism and caution, of righteousness with respectability, lies the secret of King's enormous success.

Certain important civil rights leaders have dismissed King's position as the product of publicity generated by the mass communications media. But this can be said of the successes of the civil rights nonviolent action movement generally. Without publicity it is hard to conceive that much progress would have been made. In fact, contrary to the official nonviolent direct action philosophy, demonstrations have secured their results not by changing the hearts of the oppressors through a display of nonviolent love, but through the national and international pressures generated by the publicity arising from mass arrests and incidents of violence. And no one has employed this strategy of securing publicity through mass arrests and precipitating violence from white hoodlums and law enforcement officers more than King himself. King abhors violence; as at Selma, for example, he constantly retreats from situations that might result in the deaths of his followers. But he is precisely most successful when, contrary to his deepest wishes, his demonstrations precipitate violence from Southern whites against Negro and white demonstrators. We need only cite Birmingham and Selma to illustrate this point.

Publicity alone does not explain the durability of King's image, or why he remains for the rank and file of whites and blacks alike, the symbol of the direct action movement, the nearest thing to a charismatic leader that the civil rights movement has ever had. At the heart of King's continuing influence and popularity are two facts. First, better than anyone else, he articulates the aspirations of Negroes who respond to the cadence of his addresses, his religious phraseology and manner of speaking, and the vision of his dream for them and for America. King has intuitively adopted the style of the old fashioned Negro Baptist preacher and transformed it into a new art form; he has, indeed, restored oratory to its place among the arts. Second, he communicates Negro aspirations to white America more effectively than anyone else. His religious terminology and manipulation of the Christian symbols of love and nonresistance are partly responsible for his appeal among whites. To talk in terms of Christianity, love, nonviolence is reassuring to the mentality of white America. At the same time, the very superficialities of his philosophy—that rich and eclectic amalgam of Jesus, Hegel, Gandhi and others as outlined in his *Stride Toward Freedom*—makes him appear intellectually profound to the superfi-

cially educated middle class white American. Actually, if he were a truly profound religious thinker, like Tillich or Niebuhr, his influence would of necessity be limited to a select audience. But by uttering moral clichés, the Christian pieties, in a magnificent display of oratory, King becomes enormously effective.

If his success with Negroes is largely due to the style of his utterance, his success with whites is a much more complicated matter. For one thing, he unerringly knows how to exploit to maximum effectiveness their growing feeling of guilt. King, of course, is not unique in attaining fame and popularity among whites through playing upon their guilt feelings. James Baldwin is the most conspicuous example of a man who has achieved success with this formula. The incredible fascination which the Black Muslims have for white people, and the posthumous near-sanctification of Malcolm X by many naive whites (in addition to many Negroes whose motivations are, of course, very different), must in large part be attributed to the same source. But King goes beyond this. With intuitive, but extraordinary skill, he not only castigates whites for their sins but, in contrast to angry young writers like Baldwin, he explicitly states his belief in their salvation. Not only will direct action bring fulfillment of the "American Dream" to Negroes but the Negroes' use of direct action will help whites to live up to their Christian and democratic values; it will purify, cleanse and heal the sickness in white society. Whites will benefit as well as Negroes. He has faith that the white man will redeem himself. Negroes must not hate whites, but love them. In this manner, King first arouses the guilt feelings of whites, and then relieves them—though always leaving the lingering feelings in his white listeners that they should support his nonviolent crusade. Like a Greek tragedy, King's performance provides an extraordinary catharsis for the white listener.

King thus gives white men the feeling that he is their good friend, that he poses no threat to them. It is interesting to note that this was the same feeling white men received from Booker T. Washington, the noted early 20th Century accommodator. Both men stressed their faith in the white man; both expressed the belief that the white man could be brought to accord Negroes their rights. Both stressed the importance of whites recognizing the rights of Negroes for the moral health and well-being of white society. Like King, Washington had an extraordinary following among whites. Like King, Washington symbolized for most whites the whole program of Negro advancement. While there are important similarities in the functioning of both men vis-à-vis the community, needless to say, in most respects, their philosophies are in disagreement.

It is not surprising, therefore, to find that King is the recipient of contributions from organizations and individuals who fail to eradicate evidence of prejudice in their own backyards. For example, certain liberal trade union leaders who are philosophically committed to full racial equality, who feel the need to identify their organizations with the cause of militant civil rights, although they are unable to defeat racist elements in their unions, contribute hundreds of thousands of dollars to King's Southern Christian Leadership Conference (SCLC). One might attribute this phenomenon to the fact that SCLC works in the South rather than the North, but this is true also for SNCC [Student Nonviolent Coordinating Committee] which does not benefit similarly from union treasuries. And the fact is that ever since the college students started their sit-ins in 1960, it is SNCC which has been the real spearhead of direct action in most of the South, and has performed the lion's share of work in local communities, while SCLC has received most of the publicity and most of the money. However, while King provides a verbal catharsis for whites, leaving them feeling purified and comfortable, SNCC's uncompromising militancy makes whites feel less comfortable and less beneficent.

(The above is not to suggest that SNCC and SCLC are responsible for all, or nearly all, the direct action in the South. The NAACP has actively engaged in direct action, especially in Savannah under the leadership of W. W. Law, in South Carolina under I. DeQuincy Newman, and in Clarksdale, Mississippi, under Aaron Henry. The work of CORE—including most of the direct action in Louisiana, much of the nonviolent work in Florida and Mississippi, the famous Freedom Ride of 1961—has been most important. In addition, one should note the work of SCLC affiliates, such as those in Lynchburg, Virginia, led by Reverend Virgil Wood; in Birmingham led by Reverend Fred Shuttlesworth, and in Savannah, by Hosea Williams.

(There are other reasons for SNCC's lesser popularity with whites than King's. These are connected with the great changes that have occurred in SNCC since it was founded in 1960, changes reflected in the half-jocular epigram circulating in SNCC circles that the student Nonviolent Coordinating Committee has now become the "Non-Student Violent Non-Coordinating Committee." The point is, however, that even when SNCC thrilled the nation in 1960-1961 with the student sit-ins that swept the South, it did not enjoy the popularity and financial support accorded to King.)

King's very tendencies toward compromise and caution, his willingness to negotiate and bargain with White House emissaries, his hesitancy to risk the precipitation of mass violence upon demonstrators, further endear him to whites. He appears to them a "responsible" and "moderate" man. To militant activists, King's failure to march past the State Police on that famous Tuesday morning outside Selma indicated either a lack of courage, or a desire to advance himself by currying Presidential favor. But King's shrinking from a possible bloodbath, his accession to the entreaties of the political Establishment, his acceptance of face-saving compromise in this, as in other instances, are fundamental to the particular role he is playing, and essential for achieving and sustaining his image as a leader of heroic moral stature in the eyes of white men. His caution and

compromise keep open the channels of communication between the activists and the majority of the white community. In brief: King makes the nonviolent direct action movement respectable.

Of course, many, if not most, activists reject the notion that the movement should be made respectable. Yet, American history shows that for any reform movement to succeed, it must attain respectability. It must attract moderates, even conservatives, to its ranks. The March on Washington made direct action respectable; Selma made it fashionable. More than any other force, it is Martin Luther King who impressed the civil rights revolution on the American conscience and is attracting that great middle body of American public opinion to its support. It is this revolution of conscience that will undoubtedly lead fairly soon to the elimination of all violations of Negroes' constitutional rights, thereby creating the conditions for the economic and social changes that are necessary if we are to achieve full racial equality. This is not to deny the dangers to the civil rights movement in becoming respectable. Respectability, for example, encourages the attempts of political machines to capture civil rights organizations. Respectability can also become an end in itself, thereby dulling the cutting edge of its protest activities. Indeed, the history of the labor movement reveals how attaining respectability can produce loss of original purpose and character. These perils, however, do not contradict the importance of achieving respectability—even a degree of modishness—if racial equality is ever to be realized.

There is another side to the picture: King would be neither respected nor respectable if there were not more militant activists on his left, engaged in more radical forms of direct action. Without CORE and, especially, SNCC, King would appear "radical" and "irresponsible" rather than "moderate" and "respectable."

King occupies a position of strategic importance as the "vital center" within the civil rights movement. Though he has lieutenants who are far more militant and "radical" than he is, SCLC acts, in effect, as the most cautious, deliberate and "conservative" of the direct action groups because of King's leadership. This permits King and the SCLC to function—almost certainly unintentionally—not only as an organ of communication with the Establishment and majority white public opinion, but as something of a bridge between the activist and more traditionalist or "conservative" civil rights groups, as well. For example, it appears unlikely that the Urban League and NAACP, which supplied most of the funds, would have participated in the 1963 March on Washington if King had not done so. Because King agreed to go along with SNCC and CORE, the NAACP found it mandatory to join if it was to maintain its image as a protest organization. King's identification with the March was also essential for securing the support of large numbers of white clergymen and their moderate followers. The March was the brainchild of the civil rights movement's ablest strategist and tactician, Bayard Rustin, and the call was issued by A. Philip

Young King (seated, far right) with his parents and beloved grandmother. Next to him are his brother A.D. and sister Christine, with whom he played basketball and baseball.

Randolph. But it would have been a minor episode in the history of the civil rights movement without King's support.

Yet curiously enough, despite his charisma and international reputation, King thus far has been more a symbol than a power in the civil rights movement. Indeed his strength in the movement has derived less from an organizational base than from his symbolic role. Seven or eight years ago, one might have expected King to achieve an organizationally dominant position in the civil rights movement, at least in its direct action wing. The fact is that in the period after the Montgomery bus boycott, King developed no program and, it is generally agreed, revealed himself as an ineffective administrator who failed to capitalize upon his popularity among Negroes. In 1957, he founded SCLC to coordinate the work of direct action groups that had sprung up in Southern cities. Composed of autonomous units, usually led by Baptist ministers, SCLC does not appear to have developed an overall sense of direction or a program of real breadth and scope. Although the leaders of SCLC affiliates became the race leaders in their communities—displacing the established local conservative leadership of teachers, old-line ministers, businessmen—it is hard for an observer (who admittedly has not been close to SCLC) to perceive exactly what SCLC did before the 1960's except to advance the image and personality of King. King appeared not to direct but to float with the tide of militant direct action. For example, King did not supply the initiative for the bus boycott in Montgomery, but was pushed into the leadership by others, as he himself records in *Stride Toward Freedom.* Similarly, in

the late Fifties and early Sixties, he appeared to let events shape his course. In the last two years, this has changed, but until the Birmingham demonstrations of 1963, King epitomized conservative militancy.

SCLC under King's leadership called the Raleigh Conference of April 1960 which gave birth to SNCC. Incredibly, within a year, the SNCC youth had lost their faith in the man they now satirically call "De Lawd," and had struck out on their own independent path. By that time, the Spring of 1961, King's power in the Southern direct action movement had been further curtailed by CORE's stunning Freedom Ride to Alabama and Mississippi.

The limited extent of King's actual power in the civil rights movement was illustrated by the efforts made to invest King with the qualities of a Messiah during the recent ceremonies at the state capital in Montgomery. Reverend Abernathy's constant iteration of the theme that King is "our Leader," the Moses of the race, chosen by God, and King's claim that he originated the nonviolent direct action movement at Montgomery a decade ago, are all assertions that would have been superfluous if King's power in the movement was very substantial.

It is, of course, no easier today than it has been in the past few years to predict the course of the Negro protest movement, and it is always possible that the current state of affairs may change quite abruptly. It is conceivable that the ambitious program that SCLC is now projecting—both in Southern voter registration and in Northern urban direct action programs—may give it a position of commanding importance in civil rights. As a result of the recent demonstrations in Selma and Montgomery, King's prestige is now higher than ever. At the same time, the nature of CORE and NAACP direct action activities at the moment has created a programmatic vacuum which SCLC may be able to exploit. Given this convergence of circumstances, SCLC leaders may be able to establish an organizational base upon which to build a power commensurate with the symbolic position of their president.

It is indeed fortunate that King has not obtained a predominance of power in the movement commensurate with his prestige. For today, as in the past, a diversity of approaches is necessary. Needed in the movement are those who view the struggle chiefly as a conflict situation, in which the power of demonstrations, the power of Negroes, will force recognition of the race's humanity and citizenship rights, and the achievement of equality. Equally needed are those who see the movement's strategy to be chiefly one of capitalizing on the basic consensus of values in American society by awakening the conscience of the white man to the contradiction between his professions and the facts of discrimination. And just as necessary to the movement as both of these are those who operate skillfully, recognizing and yet exploiting the deeply held American belief that compromise among competing interest groups is the best *modus operandi* in public life.

King is unique in that he maintains a delicate balance among all three of these basic strategy assumptions. The traditional approaches of the Urban League (conciliation of the white businessmen) and of the NAACP (most pre-eminently appeals to the courts and appeals to the sense of fair play in the American public), basically attempted to exploit the consensus in American values. It would of course be a gross oversimplification to say that the Urban League and NAACP strategies are based simply on attempting to capitalize on the consensus of values, while SNCC and CORE act simply as if the situation were purely a conflict situation. Implicit in the actions of all civil rights organizations are both sets of assumptions—even where people are not conscious of the theoretical assumptions under which, in effect, they operate. The NAACP especially encompasses a broad spectrum of strategies and types of activities, ranging from time-tested court procedures to militant direct action. Sophisticated CORE activists know very well when a judicious compromise is necessary or valuable. But I hold that King is in the middle, acting in effect as if he were basing his strategy upon all three assumptions described above. He maintains a delicate balance between a purely moral appeal and a militant display of power. He talks of the power of the bodies of Negro demonstrators in the streets, but unlike CORE and SNCC activists, he accepts compromises at times that consist of token improvements, and calls them impressive victories. More than any of the other groups, King and SCLC can, up to this point at least, be described as exploiting all three tactical assumptions to an approximately equal degree. King's continued success, I suspect, will depend to a considerable degree upon the difficult feat of maintaining his position at the "vital center" of the civil rights movement.

Viewed from another angle King's failure to achieve a position of power on a level with his prestige is fortunate because rivalries between personalities and organizations remain an essential ingredient of the dynamics of the movement and a precondition for its success as each current tries to outdo the others in effectiveness and in maintaining a good public image. Without this competitive stimulus, the civil rights revolution would slow down.

I have already noted that one of King's functions is to serve as a bridge between the militant and conservative wings of the movement. In addition, by gathering support for SCLC, he generates wider support for CORE and SNCC, as well. The most striking example is the recent series of demonstrations in Selma where SNCC had been operating for nearly two years with only moderate amounts of publicity before King chose that city as his own target. As usual, it was King's presence that focused world attention on Selma. In the course of subsequent events, the rift between King and SNCC assumed the proportions of a serious conflict. Yet people who otherwise would have been hesitant to support SNCC's efforts, even people who had become disillusioned with certain aspects of SNCC's policies during the Mississippi Summer Project of 1964, were drawn to demonstrate in Selma and Montgomery. Moreover, although King received the major share of credit for the demonstrations, it seems likely that in the controversy between King and SNCC, the latter emerged with more power and influence in the civil rights movement than ever before. It is now possible that the Administration will, in the future, regard SNCC as more of a force to be reckoned with than it has heretofore.

Major dailies like the *New York Times* and the *Washington Post,* basically sympathetic to civil rights and racial equality, though more gradualist than the activist organizations, have congratulated the nation upon its good fortune in having a "responsible and moderate" leader like King at the head of the nonviolent action movement (though they overestimate his power and underestimate the symbolic nature of his role). It would be more appropriate to congratulate the civil rights movement for *its* good fortune in having as its symbolic leader a man like King. The fact that he has more prestige than power; the fact that he not only criticizes whites but explicitly believes in their redemption; his ability to arouse creative tension combined with his inclination to shrink from carrying demonstrations to the point where major bloodshed might result; the intellectual simplicity of his philosophy; his tendency to compromise and exert caution, even his seeming indecisiveness on some occasions; the sparing use he makes of going to or staying in jail himself; his friendship with the man in the White House—all are essential to the role he plays, and invaluable for the success of the movement. It is well, of course, that not all civil rights leaders are cut of the same cloth—that King is unique among them. Like Randolph, who functions very differently, King is really an institution. His most important function, I believe, is that of effectively communicating Negro aspirations to white people, of making nonviolent direct action respectable in the eyes of the white majority. In addition, he functions within the movement by occupying a vital center position between its "conservative" and "radical" wings, by symbolizing direct action and attracting people to participate in it without dominating either the civil rights movement or its activist wing. Viewed in this context, traits that many activists criticize in King actually function not as sources of weakness, but as the foundations of his strength. (pp. 442-54)

> *August Meier, "On the Role of Martin Luther King," in* Black History: A Reappraisal, *edited by Melvin Drimmer, Doubleday and Company, Inc., 1968, pp. 442-54.*

Eldridge Cleaver (essay date 1968)

[*A contemporary of King, Cleaver is best known for the part he played in the black protest movement of the 1960s. He was a member of the Black Panthers and traveled across the country advocating "black libera-*

tion from white America." In the following essay, dictated two days after the assassination of King, he recounts King's philosophy of nonviolence. Claiming that the period of nonviolence is now over, he writes: "[The] war has begun. The violent phase of the black liberation struggle is here, and it will spread.... America will be painted red." Cleaver's essay ends abruptly; the editor of Violence in America *(1969), in which Cleaver's essay appeared, explained: "[Cleaver] was interrupted in midsentence by a phone call. Cleaver immediately left to cross San Francisco Bay and go to Oakland where, as an official of the Black Panthers party, he was helping to keep things cool while other cities in America were burning. Within a few more hours, Cleaver himself was in jail.']*

The murder of Dr. Martin Luther King came as a surprise—and surprisingly it also came as a shock. Many people, particularly those in the black community who long ago abandoned nonviolence and opted to implement the slogan of Malcolm X—"black liberation by any means necessary"—have been expecting to hear of Dr. King's death for a long time. Many even became tired of waiting. But that Dr. King would have to die was a certainty. For here was a man who refused to abandon the philosophy and the principle of nonviolence in face of a hostile and racist nation which has made it indisputably clear that it has no intention and no desire to grant a redress of the grievances of the black colonial subjects who are held in bondage.

To black militants, Dr. King represented a stubborn and persistent stumbling block in the path of the methods that had to be implemented to bring about a revolution in the present situation. And so, therefore, much hatred, much venom and much criticism was focused upon Dr. King by the black militants. And the contradiction in which he was caught up cast him in the role of one who was hated and held in contempt, both by the whites in America who did not want to free black people, and by black people who recognized the attitude of white America and who wanted to be rid of the self-deceiving doctrine of nonviolence. Still, black militants were willing to sit back and watch, and allow Dr. King to play out his role. And his role has now been played out.

The assassin's bullet not only killed Dr. King, it killed a period of history. It killed a hope, and it killed a dream.

That white America could produce the assassin of Dr. Martin Luther King is looked upon by black people— and not just those identified as black militants—as a final repudiation by white America of any hope of reconciliation, of any hope of change by peaceful and nonviolent means. So that it becomes clear that the only way for black people in this country to get the things that they want—and the things that they have a right to and that they deserve—is to meet fire with fire.

In the last few months, while Dr. King was trying to build support for his projected poor people's march on Washington, he already resembled something of a dead man. Of a dead symbol, one might say more correctly.

Hated on both sides, denounced on both sides—yet he persisted. And now his blood has been spilled. The death of Dr. King signals the end of an era and the beginning of a terrible and bloody chapter that may remain unwritten, because there may be no scribe left to capture on paper the holocaust to come.

That there is a holocaust coming I have no doubt at all. I have been talking to people around the country by telephone—people intimately involved in the black liberation struggle—and their reaction to Dr. King's murder has been unanimous: the war has begun. The violent phase of the black liberation struggle is here, and it will spread. From that shot, from that blood, America will be painted red. Dead bodies will litter the streets and the scenes will be reminiscent of the disgusting, terrifying, nightmarish news reports coming out of Algeria during the height of the general violence right before the final breakdown of the French colonial regime.

America has said "no" to the black man's demand for liberation, and this "no" is unacceptable to black people. They are going to strike back, they are going to reply to the escalation of this racist government, this racist society. They are going to escalate their retaliation. And the responsibility for all this blood, for all this death, for all this suffering... well, it's beyond the stage of assigning blame. Black people are no longer interested in adjudicating the situation, in negotiating the situation, in arbitrating the situation. Their only interest now is in being able to summon up whatever it will take to wreak the havoc upon Babylon that will force Babylon to let the black people go. For all other avenues have been closed.

The assassin's bullet which struck down Dr. King closed a door that to the majority of black people seemed closed long ago. To many of us it was clear that that door was never open. But we were willing to allow those who wanted to bank upon that door for entry, we were willing to sit back and let them do this. Indeed, we had no other choice. But now all black people in America have become Black Panthers in spirit. There will, of course, be those who stand up before the masses and echo the eloquent pleas of Dr. King for a continuation of the nonviolent tactic. They will be listened to by many, but from another perspective. They will look back upon Dr. King and upon his successors with somewhat the emotions one feels when one looks upon the corpse of a loved one. But it is all dead now. It's all dead now. Now there is the gun and the bomb, dynamite and the knife, and they will be used liberally in America. America will bleed. America will suffer.

And it is strange to see how, with each significant shot that is fired, time is speeded up. How the dreadful days that we all somehow knew were coming seem to cascade down upon us immediately, and the dreadful hours that we thought were years away are immediately upon us, immediately before us. And all eternity is gone, blown away, washed away in the blood of martyrs.

Is the death of Dr. King a sad day for America? No. It is a day consistent with what America demands by its actions. The death of Dr. King was not a tragedy for America. America should be happy that Dr. King is dead, because America worked so hard to bring it about. And now all the hypocritical, vicious madmen who pollute the government of this country and who befoul the police agencies of this country, all of the hypocritical public announcements following the death of Dr. King are being repudiated and held in contempt, not only by black people but by millions of white people who know that had these same treacherous political gangsters made the moves that clearly lay within their power to make, Dr. King would not be dead, nonviolence would prevail and the terror would not be upon us. These people, the police departments, the legislatures, the government, the Democratic party, the Republican party, those commonly referred to as the establishment or the power structure, they can be looked upon as immediate targets and symbols of blame.

But it has been said that a people or a country gets the leaders and the government that it deserves. And here we have at the death of Dr. King a President by the name of Lyndon Baines Johnson who has the audacity to stand before this nation and mourn Dr. King and to praise his leadership and the nonviolence he espoused, while he has the blood of hundreds of thousands of people and the slaughtered conscience of America upon his hands. If any one man could be singled out as bearing responsibility for bringing about the bloodshed and violence to come, it would be Lyndon Baines Johnson. But not just Lyndon Baines Johnson. All of the greedy, profit-seeking businessmen in America, all of the unspeakable bootlickers, the big businessmen of the civil rights movement and the average man on the street who feels hatred instilled in his heart by this vicious and disgusting system—the blame is everywhere and no-where.

Washington, D.C., is burning. My only thought at that is I hope Stokely Carmichael survives Washington. Chicago is burning, Detroit is burning and there is fire and the sound of guns from one end of Babylon to the other.

Last night I heard Lyndon Baines Johnson admonishing his people, admonishing black people to turn away from vicious and disgusting system—the blame is everywhere and of all the corn pone that he spouted forth one thing struck me and I felt insulted by it. He was ringing changes on a famous statement made by Malcolm X in his speech, "The Ballot or the Bullet." Malcolm X had prophesied that if the ballot did not prevail in gaining black people their liberation, then the bullet would be made to prevail. And Lyndon Johnson said last night that he was going to prove to the nation and to the American people that the ballot and not the bullet would prevail. Coming from him, it was pure insult.

Those of us in the Black Panther party who have been reading events and looking to the future have said that this will be the Year of the Panther, that this will be the

Year of the Black Panther. And now everything that I can see leaves no doubt of that. And now there is Stokely Carmichael, Rap Brown, and above all there is Huey P. Newton. Malcolm X prophesied the coming of the gun, and Huey Newton picked up the gun, and now there is gun against gun. Malcolm X gunned down. Martin Luther King gunned down.

I am trying to put a few words on tape because I was asked to do so by the editor of this magazine, to try to give my thoughts on what the assassination of Dr. King means for the future, what is likely to follow and who is likely to emerge as a new or a prevailing leader of black people. It is hard to put words on this tape because words are no longer relevant. Action is all that counts now. And maybe America will understand that. I doubt it. I think that America is incapable of understanding *anything* relevant to human rights. I think that America has already committed suicide and we who now thrash within its dead body are also dead in part and parcel of the corpse. America is truly a disgusting burden upon this planet. A burden upon all humanity. And if we here in America... (pp. 235-39)

> *Eldridge Cleaver, "Requiem for Nonvio-lence," in* Violence in America: A Historical and Contemporary Reader, *edited by Thomas Rose, Random House, 1969, pp. 235-39.*

Wesley T. Mott (essay date 1975)

[*In the following excerpt, Mott examines* Letter from Birmingham Jail *as an emotion-charged sermon in the tradition of "old-time Negro preaching."*]

[Martin Luther King, Jr.'s, *Letter from Birmingham Jail*] is one of the most frequently collected items in college English anthologies and has proved the most popular reading among black and white students in basic literature courses for several years. The success of the *Letter* can be attributed, I think, to the remarkable confluence of three distinct rhetorical traits: King's heritage of the highly emotional Negro preaching tradition; his shrewd sense of political timing and polemical skill; and his conscious literary ability.

In view of King's rich legacy of sermons and speeches, it may seem inappropriate to emphasize the oral tradition behind *Letter from Birmingham Jail.* But the *Letter* has proved to be one of King's most eloquent utterances; and much of its power (and a few of its defects) arises from the same rhetorical elements that he employed in his oral addresses. His written style is only a slightly more formalized version of his platform style. In the *Letter* King retains the emotional power that is the trademark of the Negro sermon while he overcomes the flaws that hinder the utility of the sermon in the political and literary spheres.

The traditional Negro sermon derives largely from the preaching of such evangelists as Whitefield. It aims to arouse the hearer's emotions to the point where he is persuaded to turn to God or to experience God's presence. Although loosely based on a Biblical theme, this kind of preaching emphasizes emotional arousal to such a degree that "the theme itself is relatively unimportant" [Bruce A. Rosenberg in *The Art of the American Folk Preacher,* 1970]. Furthermore, because the preacher claims that inspiration for the sermon comes directly from God, he is not concerned with "logical organization." Rhythm and cadence almost unaided achieve the desired effect. One scholar [Rosenberg] notes that "the preacher relies upon stock phrases and passages to fill out the skel[e]ton of the sermon, and develops the message through repetition." The sermon is based, then, on a formulaic method that employs such devices as repetitive refrains, recurrent rhetorical questions, and formalized dialogue and narrative. The rhythm thus established is all-important: "The rhythm is the message; congregations have been moved to ecstasy by the rhythmic chanting of incoherencies" [Rosenberg]. The sermons of Martin Luther King, Jr., are unmistakably part of the tradition of "old-time Negro preaching." His *Letter from Birmingham Jail* draws power from this genre while avoiding its main weakness: a self-contained emotionalism that historically has encouraged the aloofness of blacks from social reform.

"Old-time preaching" is characterized by its lack of concern for logic. [William H. Pipes in *Say Amen, Brother! Old-Time Negro Preaching: A Study in American Frustration,* 1951], nevertheless, identifies a recurrent structural pattern in the sermons: (1) an introduction "to establish a common ground of religious feeling" among the audience or to establish rapport between speaker and audience; (2) a "statement of the text," which, of course, is almost always drawn from the Bible; (3) the "body of the sermon," which consists of repeated emotional climaxes; and (4) the conclusion, which resolves the emotional tension aroused by the sermon by drawing the sinners to God. Pipes's framework shows that the traditional Negro sermon, however much it derives its strength from formulaic repetition, is not mere unartistic incoherencey. It justifies our treating the sermons—and, by inference, *Letter from Birmingham Jail*—as an art form.

The *Letter* is essentially a written sermon that both answers charges and exhorts to action. It is a measure of the artistic control that King exerts over the *Letter* that he creates a vivid persona aimed at arousing the sympathy of the audience. The ideal "old-time preacher" is a majestic, imposing figure; but King's projection of the image of a meek, suffering prisoner effectively strikes an appropriate rapport with his "audience." He immediately introduces himself, "confined here in the Birmingham city jail." And yet, despite adversity, he is capable of benevolence and generosity toward those eight clergymen, those "men of genuine good will" who have criticized his protest activities; he hopes his answer "will be [in] patient and reasonable terms." He is patient with the slowness the clergymen show in coming

to terms with his arguments: "I hope you are able to see the distinction I am trying to point out"; "I must honestly reiterate that I have been disappointed with the church"; "I had hoped that each of you would understand. But again I have been disappointed."

It quickly becomes clear, however, that this understatement is not the sign of an Uncle Tom cringing before his oppressors: it is a calculated rhetorical stance. The *Letter* is, of course, more than a letter to eight Birmingham clergymen: it is an open letter. King's conciliatory tone—while apparently conceding ground in its humility—is intended to reveal the inhumanity of the clergymen's position and to hold it up to the scorn of those of us who are reading over their shoulders. Against the outrages King so powerfully exposes, the recalcitrance of the eight clergymen reveals them as the true felons for their toleration of evil. *Letter from Birmingham Jail* transcends the problem of social evil in its very real Christian vision of love and brotherhood. But King's tone here is a rhetorical strategy. Its "inoffensiveness" allows an audience which might not fully sympathize with his program to participate, at least, in his argument—and perhaps unwittingly to share his lofty disdain for the kind of short-sighted criticism of which the audience itself might normally be guilty. King's stance does not hide his rage. By suppressing his personal anger and frustration, and by resisting the human impulse to bombast and diatribe, he has given structure to individual misfortune and achieved a compelling piece of polemic.

The narrator confined in the Birmingham city jail, then, is not simply the activist minister who languishes in solitary confinement, irritated by isolation from comrades, family, and the wife who had just given birth to their fourth child. The narrator is also a construction of polemical expediency and literary imagination. He is further defined in the "second stage" of the exposition of the sermon/letter, the "statement of the text." Like the traditional Negro sermon, King's *Letter* has a broad thematic unity; and like the sermon, the *Letter* draws its "text" from the Bible. King is pressed to defend his nonviolent direct action, his "meddling"; his defense is based largely upon Biblical precedent, that God commands Christians to spread the gospel and to aid their brethren regardless of where they live: "Just as the prophets of the eighth century B. C. left their villages and carried their 'thus saith the Lord' far beyond the boundaries of their home towns, and just as the Apostle Paul left his village of Tarsus and carried the gospel of Jesus Christ to the far corners of the Greco-Roman world, so am I compelled to carry the gospel of freedom beyond my own home town. Like Paul, I must constantly respond to the Macedonian call for aid." The *Letter* is both a social manifesto and a religious testament. King is arguing for a religious life that translates vision into practice and that finds the spiritual life enriched by communal efforts for justice. Although the details of King's program remain open to challenge from reactionary and radical points of view, the vision itself is virtually above criticism in the context of the letter.

Having established his text, with its justification of the active Christian life, King's persona subtly exposes the timid inaction of the eight clergymen as an ungodly denial of the necessary fruits of the religious life. To the religious man, "injustice anywhere is a threat to justice everywhere.... Never again can we afford to live with the narrow, provincial 'outside agitator' idea."

As we have seen in Pipes's scheme, the "third stage" of the sermon, the "body," with its repeated emotional climaxes, essentially is the sermon. Much of the raw emotional power of King's *Letter* arises simply from the increasing tempo and from the relentless force of repetition and parallelism. The first few paragraphs, which establish the speaker's personality and the text, contain relatively short sentences presented matter-of-factly; but as it proceeds, the *Letter* accelerates a strong rhythm, the sentences become longer in key emotional passages. Bruce Rosenberg has observed that many oral preachers "were unaware of creating" the moving passages of parallelism that characterize such preaching; but he suspects that "in the case of Dr. King and other preachers of comparable learning who preach spontaneously, it is hard to believe that they were not aware of the effect on the audience." King is certainly in full control of the effects produced by parallelism and repetition in the *Letter.* A few of the weaknesses of King's written style arise from the attempt to translate oral rhetoric onto paper: it is occasionally grating to hear philosophical definitions artificially confined in a paragraph structured on rigid parallelism; and repeated neat antitheses ("dark clouds of racial prejudice/radiant stars of love") are often predictable and trite. When one recalls King's ability on the platform to make clichés sound fresh and exciting, however, one is aware that these are weaknesses of adapting the message to a different medium. Even in the *Letter* he achieves great power from parallelism and repetition.

The measure of this power cannot be appreciated fully, however, by examining emotional effects apart from other rhetorical elements. Pipes notes that the Negro sermon has always contained implicitly various kinds of deductive and inductive logic, that ethics accompany emotional arousal as a secondary concern, that sources outside the Bible are sometimes cited, and that argument from authority often complements simple formulaic progression. King effectively exploits this potential in *Letter from Birmingham Jail.*

King begins his defense of the Birmingham campaign by listing the "four basic steps" of "any nonviolent campaign." One is finally less interested in the logic of his analysis than with the opportunities the "four basic steps" afford for his powerful denunciations of injustice and exhortation to action. It is the nature of men caught up in emotionally charged debate to be unimpressed by rational discourse and logical argument; certainly no one will be convinced by the logical force of King's "four basic steps" who is not already sympathetic to his nonviolent philosophy. It is not to deny the logic of King's argument, then, to say that his logical scheme is effective on a largely verbal level. Yet his logic throughout the *Letter* is unanswerable. In a brilliant paragraph he answers the charge that his actions "precipitate violence": he challenges the logic of the clergymen and in a series of increasingly dramatic, grammatically parallel rhetorical questions, he reveals that those who make direct action necessary are guilty of precipitating violence: "Isn't this like condemning a robbed man because his possession of money precipitated the evil act of robbery? Isn't this like condemning Socrates because his unswerving commitment to truth and his philosophical inquiries precipitated the act by the misguided populace in which they made him drink hemlock? Isn't this like condemning Jesus because his unique God-consciousness and never-ceasing devotion to God's will precipitated the evil act of crucifixion?" He concludes in an eloquent understatement that resolves the tension created by the rhetorical questions: "Society must protect the robbed and punish the robber." King's devastating logic, then, exploits an untapped root of the traditional Negro minister's resources. It lends authority and dignity to his argument. It permits a sharp analysis that reveals unexpected and stunning truth which our comfortable commonplaces too often prevent us from seeing; it reminds us that the eight clergymen deny, in effect, the very truths their offices were created to perpetuate. But the great impact of *Letter from Birmingham Jail* does not arise from King's being a clinical logician. It is his ability to discover fundamental moral flaws in his opponents' charges that makes his argument so unanswerable. And it is his conscious literary skill with parallelism and understatement that makes his argument so emotionally convincing.

King's theme of the social and ethical implications of Christianity is reinforced by another strategy uncharacteristic of the traditional Negro sermon: reference to sources and authorities outside the Bible. The *Letter* remains, I think, an essentially Christian statement; but it gains force from King's eagerness to cite contemporary events and people and to muster authorities from Moses to Buber and Tillich, from Socrates to Jefferson and Lincoln. The references to Aquinas, Buber, and Tillich have special relevance, of course, to King's immediate audience, the clergymen. But the general effectiveness of citing authorities again lies in its impressive verbal impact. (He is not concerned here with such complex historical problems as Jefferson's keeping of slaves, or Lincoln's playing politics with the Emancipation Proclamation.) The very weight of his authorities assuages a reluctant audience's fear that his actions are frighteningly without precedent.

Herein lies King's greatest strength as a rhetorician: his ability to gently answer charges that he is impatient, radical, an "outside agitator"; to surprise the reader into an unexpected awareness of what the charges really imply; and to transform the very charges leveled against him into an occasion for exhortation and encouragement for his own camp. King has an uncanny ability to translate familiar terms into new and challenging concepts; but at the same time he convinces us that his seemingly revolutionary techniques belong to tested and revered traditions. To the assertion that negotiation would be better than the forms of direct action which produce "tension" in the community, King replies that "tension" is a necessary ingredient of any "creative" process; without continual challenge to existing conditions, opportunities for constructive change will never appear. When King says "I therefore concur with you in your call for negotiation," he has not given any ground to his accusers; on the contrary, he has usurped their ground by showing that the "negotiations" they prefer can be achieved only by his method of forcing a recalcitrant South to welcome the "tension" necessary for creative change—by nonviolent direct action. He has thus redefined a term that commonly connotes unpleasant friction into a concept that evokes promise and vitality. The dense antitheses in this paragraph depend upon rather trite metaphors ("from the bondage of myths and half-truths to the unfettered realms of creative analysis and objective appraisal"; "from the dark depths of prejudice and racism to the majestic heights of understanding and brotherhood"). But the cumulative force of King's interchangeable, formulaic metaphors carries the weight of his argument in a flight of noble emotion. Profound but elemental truth can find expression often only in language that borders on triteness.

To the charge that his actions are "illegal," King replies that "legality' and "justice" are not always compatible. Through rhetorical antitheses he demonstrates that to serve justice one must sometimes break the law: "An unjust law is a code that a numerical or power majority group compels a minority group to obey but does not make binding on itself. This is a *difference* made legal. By the same token a just law is a code that a majority compels a minority to follow and that it is willing to follow itself. This is *sameness* made legal"; "Sometimes a law is just on its face and unjust in its application"; "We should never forget that everything Adolf Hitler did in Germany was 'legal' and everything the Hungarian freedom fighters did in Hungary was 'illegal.'"

By carefully establishing precedents for his nonviolent direct action, King convinces us that his program is a means of restoring what rightfully belongs to the blacks. He assures us that "there is nothing new about this kind of civil disobedience" and cites Biblical figures, Socrates, and American patriots as his predecessors. Blacks seek nothing extraordinary or alien to "the American dream." On the contrary, "our destiny is tied up with America's destiny. Before the pilgrims landed at Plymouth, we were here. Before the pen of Jefferson etched the majestic words of the Declaration of Independence across the pages of history, we were here." The very act of protest against repression, then, is not an act of arrogance but an attempt to restore and fulfill the ideals on which our nation was founded: "One day the South will know that when these disinherited children of God sat down at lunch counters, they were in reality standing up for what is best in the American dream and for the most sacred values in our Judaeo-Christian heritage."

King is not simply lending "respectability" to his philosophy by citing revered precedents; he is employing sound methods of persuasive rhetoric by arguing within the frame of reference familiar to a broad audience. Again he swallows the natural impulse to assault the sacred cows of the opposition; in so doing, he has produced prose that is both inspiring and polemically effective.

King thus gives historical and philosophical justification to his movement. He proceeds to handle deftly more specific and gnawing criticism from both the clergymen and black nationalists. In one of his most brilliant passages of "redefinition," King rejects the clergymen's charge that his action is "extreme." He warns them that his "extremism" has been the last stop-gap between responsible protest and violence; for white Birmingham to ignore his movement is to invite "a frightening racial nightmare." Essentially, then, King redefines himself as a "moderate" trying to "stand in the middle of two opposing forces in the Negro community": "complacency" and black nationalism. Not to remain a sitting duck for Muslim critics, King launches into an impassioned account of the results of repression and frustration; he concludes that his philosophy of nonviolent direct action has been a "creative outlet" for these forces. That this action had been termed "extremist" King admits "initially disappointed" him. But, in another of those marvellous paragraphs that combine sophisticated technique and emotional preaching power, King decides that the charge of extremism is cause for satisfaction; for if fidelity to noble principles of love, faith, and conscience be "extreme," then extremist he admits he is. He cites towering authorities: Jesus, Amos, Paul, Luther, Bunyan, Lincoln, Jefferson—all "extremists" in the cause of truth. The relentless parallelism with which he alternates rhetorical questions with quotations from his authorities gives an air of inevitability to his self-defense.

King has here resolved attacks from white racists, white moderates, Uncle Toms, and Black Muslims. On one level, he has simply and eloquently rediscovered the kind of extremism that is always latent in social action against sharp and painful criticism from divergent groups. Surely King was especially hurt by the hostility of other blacks who felt that he had begun to drag his feet, had become ineffectual; for the moment, at least, King transcends such conflict in a vision of Christian perfection.

With authorities firmly established and the cry for freedom for blacks clearly rooted in sacred American institutions, King truly can turn the accusations of the clergymen upon their own heads. Authentic Christianity never shirks the truth. The original "God-intoxicated" Christians so faithfully followed the inner light regardless of persecution that "they brought an end to such ancient evils as infanticide and gladiatorial contests." It is the most telling blow against the clergymen that they stand accused of hypocrisy and of defending a dead institution: "Things are different now. So often the contemporary church is a weak, ineffectual voice with an uncertain sound.... If today's church does not recapture the sacrificial spirit of the early church, it will lose its authenticity, forfeit the loyalty of millions, and be dismissed as an irrelevant social club with no meaning for the twentieth century." King is no longer on the defensive, a man charged with "extremism"; he is now the discoverer and champion of old, cherished, and sacred values. Like the Birmingham that denies the promises of the Founding Fathers and the American dream, the eight clergymen represent a sterile convention that mocks the body of sacred truth from which it was born.

Probably the most memorable passage in *Letter from Birmingham Jail* is that in which King explores the familiar injunction to "Wait!" for civil rights rather than to provoke turmoil. Here King's greatest rhetorical assets operate simultaneously. He curtly states that "This 'Wait' has almost always meant 'Never.'" His definition is not that of a skilled grammarian: it provides an adverb as a synonym for a verb. But the meaning rings clear. In a painful, powerful paragraph, King presents the numerous abuses that black people have endured for generations. But he does more than enumerate complaints: in the merging of content and style, he also achieves great artistry. An agonizingly long series of dependent clauses establishes intellectually and sensuously the conditions that make "waiting" no longer possible ("when you have seen vicious mobs lynch your mothers and fathers at will and drown your sisters and brothers at whim; when ... ; when ... "). The very process of reading the series of abuses becomes so physically wearying, the cumulative impact of the grammatically parallel dependent clauses so enervating, that the long-awaited independent clause that resolves all the conditional statements deflates our expectation of a thundering protest with its eloquent understatement: "then you will understand why we find it difficult to wait." King continues: "There comes a time when the cup of endurance runs over." What better metaphor than this, not only for a recapitulation of theme, but also for what King has achieved stylistically! The torrent of adverbial clauses capturing the agony of "waiting" literally pours over the simple little cup of the main clause, moving us emotionally while convincing us intellectually that "waiting" can no longer be expected. King concludes the paragraph with another masterly stroke of understatement: "I hope, sirs, you can understand our legitimate and unavoidable impatience." Controlled irony is infinitely more devastating than self-indulgent vitriol.

Pipes notes that the "fourth stage" of the Negro sermon, the conclusion, attempts to resolve the emotional intensity aroused throughout the sermon and to call the sinners to God. King releases us from the repeated emotional climaxes of *Letter from Birmingham Jail* in the final three paragraphs, a kind of apology (in the sense of "justification") for the *Letter* and a benediction urging Christian brotherhood. The next to last paragraph is an eloquent reminder that, however concilia-

tory and brotherly his tone has been, he has in no way conceded merit to the charges of the clergymen: "If I have said anything in this letter that overstates the truth and indicates an unreasonable impatience, I beg you to forgive me. If I have said anything that understates the truth and indicates my having a patience that allows me to settle for anything less than brotherhood, I beg God to forgive me." Most of King's rhetorical trademarks are here: the antithesis, the parallelism, the logic cloaked in strong rhythm, the understatement that cuts more deeply than overstatement. By grammatically paralleling the clergymen ("you") with God, he underlines their failure to measure their complaints against simple standards of morality; he shows that unswerving commitment to truth too often belongs to the man of God "alone in a narrow jail cell." There is release here only from the driving rhythm that marks the *Letter;* there is no escape from the quiet but profound irony of King's conclusion—only the temporary esthetic satisfaction of having comprehended anger and frustration. *Letter from Birmingham Jail* is finally more than a self-defense; it is a challenge to recognize real justice, real truth, and ultimately a challenge to act.

I have not tried to claim that King's final significance is literary rather than social and political; his lasting achievement is that he made civil rights protest a viable tactic for social change. Nor do I mean to suggest that

King in Birmingham jail in 1963. While imprisoned here, he wrote his famous Letter from Birmingham Jail.

King's vision of the struggle of blacks is more valid than that of any other faction that succeeded him; only history can determine that. What I have tried to show is that King was capable of the kind of sustained eloquence that has made Malcolm X's *Autobiography* and Eldridge Cleaver's *Soul on Ice* acknowledged masterpieces of the black experience. It is a measure of King's achievement that he pushed the traditional Negro sermon beyond its historical limitations. His *Letter* borrows the most prominent traits of this genre and successfully translates them to previously unexplored fields of polemic.

From its inception in the South in the eighteenth century, the "old-time" style of preaching was an effective tool of repression. White slavemasters actually encouraged the presence of itinerant preachers on their plantations because "they usually taught a religion of consolation rather than of revolt against their white masters" [Rosenberg]. Emotional release through religion did much "to encourage the slave along the road of mental escape from his conditions" [Pipes]. Pipes respects the "old-time" sermon as a folk-art form. But he argues that its survival continues to be an index of repression of Negroes. As Negroes have access to "new opportunities of normal expression," and educational and economic advancement, their "degree of frustration is . . . lowered." It is easy to see, then, why a new brand of black activists would be tempted to dismiss completely the politics—and indeed the style—of Martin Luther King, Jr., as outdated, irrelevant to the continuing black revolution.

Apart from its unfortunate historical connotations, the "old-time" Negro sermon has recently attained a large measure of respect for its unique artistic achievement. Bruce Rosenberg praises the old oral tradition because it "frees the minds of the audience from concern with what language, music, or story element is to come next, and so they are freer to involve themselves with the rhythm and the music and the emotion of the performance." King's achievement—as preacher, public leader, and writer—is that he harnessed the profound emotional power of the old Negro sermon for purposes of social action, thus overcoming the historical limitations of the tradition. Whether or not he had become irrelevant to the protest movement, as Cleaver has charged, King's service in transforming the Negro sermon was crucially important. He did not abandon the genre for the sake of social engagement: he used the emotional power of the tradition to serve the protest movement. *Letter from Birmingham Jail* is convincing largely because it has an appealing emotional depth rare in argumentative writing. History will decide whether Martin Luther King, Jr. died at the peak of his effectiveness as a reform leader. *Letter from Birmingham Jail* has a timeless eloquence that finally transcends such concerns. (pp. 412-21)

> *Wesley T. Mott, "The Rhetoric of Martin Luther King, Jr.: 'Letter From Birmingham Jail',"* in PHYLON: The Atlanta University Review of Race and Culture, *Vol. XXXVI, No. 4, December, 1975, pp. 411-21.*

Malinda Snow (essay date 1985)

[*In the following excerpt, Snow discusses the influence of St. Paul's writings on King's* Letter from Birmingham Jail. *The critic observes: "[In] Paul, King discovered a model or type for himself . . . King assumed both a Pauline role and a Pauline literary form in the* Letter From Birmingham Jail.*"*]

Martin Luther King's **"Letter from Birmingham Jail"** was published in 1963. Since then, it has been widely read, admired, and reprinted as an eloquent expression of the philosophy of the American civil rights movement of the fifties and sixties. Yet it has generated surprisingly little critical discussion. Only three essays examine the **"Letter"** as a literary document. The earliest, by Haig A. Bosmajian, was written while King was still alive and a figure of controversy. Bosmajian's chief goal was to set King outside the crowd of polemicists and demagogues who raised their voices at the time, and also to set him, as a master rhetorician, above the other well-meaning civil-rights activists who spoke or wrote for the cause. Comparing King to such public letter writers as Thomas Mann and Emile Zola, Bosmajian analyzed the **"Letter"** paragraph by paragraph, commenting on its logical structure, rhetorical appeals, and style. Richard P. Fulkerson, while noting the similarity between Zola's Dreyfus letter and King's **"Letter,"** focused on a rhetorical analysis of King's argumentative techniques, particularly refutation. He also considered King's effective use of references to theological writers, his choice of similes, and his management of tone. Fulkerson discussed King's appeal to his complex audience: the eight clergymen named in the salutation and the members of the general public who read the published letter. Mia Klein concentrated on the emotional appeals in the **"Letter,"** particularly rhythm in sentence structure.

These essays analyze King's work in classical, Aristotelian-Ciceronian terms. While such analyses are worthwhile, they do not consider principles or models outside classical rhetoric. Although both Bosmajian and Fulkerson describe King's **"Letter"** as a public letter, neither mentions St. Paul's letters and their possible influence upon King. Bosmajian, Fulkerson, and Klein praise King's diction and figurative language but do not consider how the diction and imagery of the English Bible affected his style.

Similarities between the **"Letter"** and Paul's writings have not gone entirely unnoticed, however. Soon after its publication, a reader wrote to the *Christian Century* to point out that King's work should be seen "in the best tradition of Pauline prison letters." No scholar, however, has pursued the relationships between King's **"Letter"** and Paul's letters or biblical literature generally.

My purpose is to show the ways in which biblical literature informs King's **"Letter."** I will argue that, in Paul, King discovered a model or *type* for himself and that from the English Bible he garnered images that contributed notably to its rhetorical success. My argument has three major propositions: first that, following the homiletic traditions of black American Protestantism, King assumed both a Pauline role and a Pauline literary form in the **"Letter from Birmingham Jail"**; second, that this role was only the most prominent of many scriptural allusions that King used; and, third, that the **"Letter,"** like many of Paul's epistles, was not merely a letter but also sermon. Like Paul, King was separated from those to whom he would have spoken. Like Paul, he shrewdly used his prison cell as an ironic pulpit and the letter as a means to reach his audience. Like Paul, King meant his letter not only for those named in the salutation but also for a larger, more general group. Finally, like Paul, King declared his own apostleship so that he might present himself as one possessed of religious truth and able to define moral action in light of that truth.

TYPE AND ANTITYPE IN RELIGIOUS DISCOURSE

A preacher sets out to discover in biblical texts symbolic lessons applicable to human experience. Similarly, in traditional biblical exegesis, one searches for (or discovers) *types:* people or events in sacred history, usually in the Old Testament, that anticipate or foreshadow people or events, usually in the New Testament. For example, Moses may be seen as a type of Christ, the tree of Eden as a type of the "tree" of Calvary, and so on (the second item in these and similar pairs is the *antitype*). Both the homiletic scriptural example and the type depend upon a correspondence between a biblical occurrence or person and something to be explained—whether an event in one's life or another biblical circumstance.

Before the reformation, Christian typology usually concentrated upon the prefigurative relationship of the Old Testament to the New. With the reformation came "the new Protestant emphasis upon the application of Scripture to the self, that is, the discovery of scriptural paradigms and of the workings of Divine Providence, in one's own life" [Barbara Lewalski, "Typological Symbolism and the 'Progress of the Soul' in Seventeenth-Century Literature," in *Literary Uses of Typology from the Late Middle Ages to the Present,* 1977, edited by Earl Miner]. This change meant that biblical situations became types of, not merely examples for, modern life. English Puritans, particularly the Puritan settlers of New England, who saw themselves as Israel, the Chosen People, offer striking examples of Protestant typology.

The general Protestant inclination to discover contemporary antitypes for biblical types influenced black American Protestantism. When the slaves embraced Christianity, they found in biblical narratives a way to express their own experience profoundly and metaphorically. Biblical stories of suffering prefigured their suffering; biblical stories of victory over impossible odds prefigured their hopes. In the story of the Children of Israel in Egypt, they discovered the central type of their experience, which prefigured their own deliverance from slavery. They merged biblical and contemporary time. As Henry H. Mitchell observed, a black preacher tends to speak of a biblical character "as one who might have known him." The singer who asks, "Were you there?" is presuming at least the possibility of "Yes" as an answer. The merging of biblical and contemporary time still marks black Protestant theology and homiletics: the slaves' descendants often still treat biblical narrative as current event.

As a theologian, King understood the applications of typology and spoke of types and antitypes in his sermons. And, following the tradition of the black church, he found biblical types for modern antitypes. For instance, in one sermon he treated Mahatma Gandhi as an antitype of Moses and the British leaders as antitypes of the Pharaohs. In another sermon he used St. Paul as a type for those who do not reach all their goals; he told his hearers: "One of the most agonizing problems within our human experience is that few, if any, of us live to see our fondest hopes fulfilled." The biblical analogue is Paul's unrealized hope—described in the Letter to the Romans—to visit Spain.

On another occasion, Paul became King's type and persona. The sermon entitled **"Paul's Letter to American Christians"** is in the form of a Pauline letter, which King pretended to have received. In it King imitated the New Testament letter form and style, speaking as "Paul" against racial segregation in the American church. By identifying with Paul and adopting the form of the Pauline letter, King not only made vivid reference to the apostle's teaching and made ancient texts pertinent to modern affairs, he also lent authority and force to his own argument against racial prejudice.

In the **"Letter from Birmingham Jail"** written seven years after **"Paul's Letter to American Christians,"** King did not imitate the Pauline epistle as explicitly as in his earlier sermon. In the **"Letter,"** he wrote as himself and closed with his own name. Nevertheless, the **"Letter"** exploits the form and scope of the Pauline letter, and it is worth noting that King did not hesitate to compare himself to Paul. Early in it he argued:

> I am in Birmingham because injustice is here....
> Just as the Apostle Paul left his village of Tarsus and carried the gospel of Jesus Christ to the far corners of the Greco-Roman world, so I am compelled to carry the gospel of freedom beyond my own home town. Like Paul, I must constantly respond to the Macedonian call for aid.

A crucial word here is *apostle.* Paul opened many letters with a formula; the opening of the Epistle to the Romans serves as an example: "Paul, a servant of Jesus Christ, called to be an apostle, separated unto the gospel of God (which he had promised afore by his prophets in the holy scriptures)..." (Romans 1:1-2). The word...*apostolos,* "one who is sent," becomes a rhetorical device through which Paul asserted that he belonged, that he had authority and was not an outsider. King not only compared himself to Paul but he also insisted upon his own position as apostle, one *sent* to Birmingham, not an outsider there. The "Macedonian call for aid" refers to a message that Paul received in a vision while at Troas: "There stood a man of Macedonia, and prayed him, saying, 'Come over into Macedonia and help us'" (Acts 16:9). This incident became for later missionaries a type of their own call and an affirmation that no one called to preach the gospel in a distant place is an intruder or outsider.

Paul's position as apostle, as a stranger but not an outsider, exemplifies the irony manifested in his career. Paul was an enemy of Christians turned Christian, a persecutor persecuted, an imprisoned preacher using his cell as a platform. He was quite aware of the irony of his own situation and, indeed, the irony of the Christian gospel: "But hath God chosen the foolish things of the world to confound the wise; and hath God chosen the weak things of the world to confound the things which are mighty" (I Corinthians 1:27). The **"Letter from Birmingham Jail"** is a masterly work whose author recognized both the irony of the gospel and the parallels between his own life and Paul's that could be rhetorically exploited.

King's life also manifested its ironies and, like Paul, King capitalized on them. The **"Letter"** depends upon a series of ironies: the prisoner boldly writes of freedom, the lawbreaker confidently defines justice, the white community's attempt to shut away and ignore the black leader enhances that leader's public recognition and humiliates his opponents.

To examine King's **"Letter"** as a Pauline epistle and sermon, it is helpful to recall the occasion that prompted it. With other marchers, King was arrested in Birmingham in April 1963 after violating an injunction forbidding further demonstrations. Jailed on Friday, April 12, he found in the Saturday Birmingham *Post Herald* a statement by eight clergymen who called the demonstrations "unwise" and "untimely." Because that statement is not readily accessible and may be unfamiliar to King's readers, I quote it in full:

> We the undersigned clergymen are among those who, in January, issued "An Appeal for Law and Order and Common Sense," in dealing with racial problems in Alabama. We expressed understanding that honest convictions in racial matters could properly be pursued in the courts, but urged that decisions of those courts should in the meantime be peacefully obeyed.
>
> Since that time there had been some evidence of increased forbearance and a willingness to face facts. Responsible citizens have undertaken to work on various problems which cause racial friction and unrest. In Birmingham, recent public events have given indication that we all have opportunity for a new constructive and realistic approach to racial problems.
>
> However, we are now confronted by a series of demonstrations by some of our Negro citizens, directed and led in part by outsiders. We recognize the natural impatience of people who feel that their hopes are slow in being realized. But we are convinced that these demonstrations are unwise and untimely.
>
> We agree with certain local Negro leadership which has called for honest and open negotiations of racial issues in our area. And we believe this kind of facing of issues can best be accomplished by citizens of our town metropolitan area, white and Negro, meeting with their knowledge and experience of the local situation. All of us need to face that responsibility and find proper channels for its accomplishment.
>
> Just as we formerly pointed out that "hatred and violence have no sanction in our religious and political traditions," we also point out that such actions as incite to hatred and violence, however technically peaceful actions may be, have not contributed to the resolution of our local problems. We do not believe that these days of new hope are days when extreme measures are justified in Birmingham.
>
> We commend the community as a whole, and the local news media and law enforcement officials in particular, on the calm manner in which these demonstrations have been handled. We urge the public to continue to show restraint should the demonstrations continue, and the law enforcement officials to remain calm and continue to protect our city from violence.
>
> We further strongly urge our own Negro community to withdraw support from these demonstrations, and to unite locally in working peacefully for a better Birmingham. When rights are consistently denied, a cause should be pressed in the courts and in negotiations among local leaders, and not in the streets. We appeal to both our white and Negro citizenry to observe the principles of law and order and common sense. (Birmingham *Post Herald,* April 13, 1963, p. 10)

Writing first on the margins of his newspaper, then on paper brought top him, King composed the **"Letter"** in answer to this statement.

When he responded to the statement, King made four rhetorically astute choices: to respond at all; to respond at length to each proposition in the statement; to adopt a tone of patience and goodwill; and to cast his message in the form of a Pauline letter. The second and third choices have been discussed at length by Bosmajian, Fulkerson, and Klein. I shall concentrate on the first and fourth choices.

RHETORICAL STRATEGIES

As civil-rights leader and as rhetor, King, like Paul, knew how to seize an opportunity. Plainly, the clergymen expected no answer to their statements. By answering, however, King achieved for himself the legitimacy that the eight had denied him by failing to name him in their statement and suggesting that mere "outsiders" came to cause trouble. The salutation, "My Dear Fellow Clergymen," makes King a colleague, an equal. If King is a colleague or "brother," his response is not only appropriate but also obligatory—one's brothers deserve an answer. The conclusion of the **"Letter"** tells us that King meant to maintain the position of brother and equal: "I also hope that circumstances will soon make it possible for me to meet each of you, not as an integrationist or a civil-rights leader, but as a fellow clergyman and a Christian brother." This sentence resembles the "greeting" that often came at the close of Pauline and other Greek letters. "The greeting was a distinct literary form which was intended to establish a bond of friendship. It was essentially one of those gestures which has emotional expression as its main purpose" [Terence Y. Mullins, "Greeting as a New Testament Form," in *Journal of Biblical Literature* (1968)]. In King's case, the expressed hope of a meeting was both irreproachably natural, on the one hand, and notably audacious, on the other.

King achieved authority and power by using the apostolic letter form along with biblically grounded imagery and syntax. Although the eight clergymen used their positions as religious leaders to gain a hearing, they employed virtually no religious references (except for the statement that "hatred and violence have no sanction in our religious and political traditions"). Rather than avoiding religious forms, allusions, and diction King embraced them and used them extensively. The churchmen, on the other hand, simply signed their names, as if to invest their statement with religious authority by implication. This, of course, they could not do. As Kenneth Burke has said, "If you want to operate, like a theologian, with a terminology that includes 'God' as its key term, the only sure way to do it is to put in the term, and that's that." King used the key term and transformed the discussion into a religious dialogue.

When King chose the Pauline model, he took on not the Hellenized Jew of the Greek texts but the Paul of the English translators, notably the 1611 translators. The **"Letter"** contains many significant passages where King's style clearly echoes the Pauline epistles of the Authorized Version. Furthermore, additional images and syntactic patterns in the **"Letter"** may be traced to other biblical books. Like Paul's epistles themselves, King's **"Letter"** is a complex allusive structure, reflecting the author's grasp of scriptural literature.

The **"Letter"** contains a number of straightforward references to St. Paul's letters. Most obvious is the quotation in King's response to the charge of extremism: "Was not Paul an extremist for the Christian gospel: 'I bear in my body the marks of the Lord Jesus'" (p. 92; the reference is to Galatians 6:17). Discussing the middle way between complacency and black nationalism, King observed, "there is the more excellent way of love and nonviolent protest." Paul wrote to the Corinthians, "and yet shew I unto you a more excellent way. Though I speak with the tongues of men and of angels, and have not charity, I am become as sounding brass..." (I Corinthians 12:31-13:1). Through the phrase "a more excellent way," King associated his *love,* for which nonviolent action is a medium, and the love ("charity") of St. Paul's famous meditation. After having brought Paul's meditation into his reader's mind, King recalled the passage again a few pages later, as he confessed disappointment with the church. "There can be no disappointment where there is not deep love.

Yes, I love the church." St. Paul asserted that despite spiritual gifts, one was nothing without love (I Corinthians 13:1-3). In his **"Letter,"** King broadened the power of love, arguing that it is a necessary condition for disappointment and thus for the nonviolent protest that arises from disappointment. Like Paul, he placed love at the foundation of constructive action.

King alluded to Paul's characterization of the church as the body of Christ: "Yes, I see the church as the body of Christ. But, oh! How we have blemished and scarred that body...." The point made by Paul and developed by King is that the church is a whole: "For as the body is one, and hath many members, and all the members of that one body, being many, are one body: so also is Christ" (I Corinthians 12:12). If the church is a whole, then segregation and other racist practices unnaturally divide that whole.

Among the exponents of divisive behavior, King cited as the worst "not the White Citizen's Counciler or the Ku Klux Klanner, but the white moderate, who is more devoted to 'order' than to justice...." He is "the Negro's great stumbling block in his stride toward freedom...." St. Paul warned the Romans, "Let us not therefore judge one another any more: but judge this rather, that no man put a stumbling block or an occasion to fall in his brother's way" (Romans 14:13). To those at Corinth, Paul wrote: 'But take heed lest by any means this liberty of yours become a stumbling block to them that are weak" (I Corinthians 8:9). In both these uses, the apostle urged a sense of responsibility upon his audience. More particularly, the passages are interesting because Paul argued for a consideration of one's fellows over a narrow concern for what is "legal." These Pauline allusions highlight two thematically important ideas in the **"Letter"**: first, King's love for the church and reliance on that love to provide integrity to his protest, and, second, his disappointment with the white moderate churchman.

During the course of his letters, Paul often addressed his audience directly. A few examples will illustrate the style: "Nevertheless, brethren, I have written the more boldly unto you..." (Romans 15:15). "Now concerning spiritual gifts, brethren, I would not have you ignorant" (I Corinthians 12:1). "I marvel that ye are so soon removed from him that called you into the grace of Christ..." (Galatians 1:6). King used a similar technique. Examples are not so much allusions to particular statements by Paul as evidence that King was using the same epistolarly technique. "I must make two honest confessions to you, my Christian and Jewish brothers." "I commend you, Reverend Stallings, for your Christian stand on this past Sunday...." These and similar passages maintain a dialectic rhythm in the **"Letter,"** giving it the immediacy and vigor of a dialogue—the same immediacy and vigor one senses in Paul's letters.

The last paragraph of King's **"Letter"** expresses a wish: "I hope this letter finds you strong in the faith." To his converts Paul also spoke of such strength. For example, he praised Abraham, who "staggered not at the promise of God through unbelief, but was strong in faith, giving glory to God" (Romans 4:20). In closing his first letter to Corinth, he admonished: "Watch ye, stand fast in the faith, quit you like men, be strong" (I Corinthians 16:13). King did not admonish; he merely expressed a hope. Nevertheless, that expression reminds us that he, like Paul, although more subtly, offered spiritual advice to his audience. Through a gently expressed hope, King exhorted them to be strong in faith. His strategy was to appeal to his audience as a traditional theologian and preacher, not as a rabble-rouser or as a dangerous outsider. His Pauline allusions, like his more obvious—indeed deliberately obvious—references to Augustine, Aquinas, Tillich, Buber, Jefferson, Eliot, Socrates, and others, help cast him in this role of the theologian, advisor, and preacher. Like Paul, King used the scriptures as a quarry for proofs, examples, and phraseology.

A stylistic habit that strengthens the link between the **"Letter"** and the English Bible is King's use of a prepositional phrase to express a metaphor, in which the headword of the phrase is a concrete noun, and the object of the preposition is an abstract noun. Examples include "garment of destiny," "darts of segregation," and "cup of endurance." In such phrases the headword establishes a lexical connection to a metaphor in the Bible. King was not simply quoting, however. He modified his use of the headword either by changing the object of the preposition or adding a prepositional phrase. For instance, Isaiah wrote of exchanging "the garment of praise for the spirit of heaviness" (61:3). King wrote, "We are caught in an inescapable network of mutuality, tied in a single garment of destiny."

In a significant phrase, King's headword is *cup*. The word appears metaphorically several times in the Bible, as in the image of Psalm 23, "my cup runneth over." The Psalmist wrote, "I will take the cup of salvation, and call upon the name of the Lord" (116:13). Paul, perhaps recalling the Psalmist's usage, wrote of the eucharist: "The cup of blessing which we bless, is it not the communion of which we speak?" (I Corinthians 10:16). In the gospels the word *cup* takes on a somber

At the Lincoln Memorial in Washington, D.C., King greets the 250,000 marchers who gathered to "demonstrate for freedom." Here he delivered his "I Have a Dream" speech, the most powerful and eloquent speech of his career.

meaning. Jesus asked James and John, "Are ye able to drink of the cup that I shall drink of...?" (Matthew 20:22). In Gethsemane just before his arrest, he prayed, "Take away this cup from me" (Mark 14:36; see also Luke 22:42). King's usage carries the dark connotation of the gospels, with an ironic recollection of the cheerful image of Psalm 23. King wrote: "There comes a time when the cup of endurance runs over, and men are no longer willing to be plunged into the abyss of despair." In the rhetoric of Christian literature, *cup* signifies the redemptive suffering of the innocent. King's reference to the suffering of America's black population recalls biblical uses and ties the black Americans to previous innocent sufferers.

In fact, King used the prepositional phrase with the biblically significant headword several times when he described the victims of racial prejudice. As examples, consider the headwords *shadow, dart,* and *chain.*

The headword *shadow* appears in the image of the broken promises and failed negotiations in Birmingham. "As in so many past experiences," King said, "our hopes had been blasted, and the shadow of deep disappointment settled upon us." "Shadow of disappointment" calls to mind the image of Psalm 23, "the valley of the shadow of death." Actually "the shadow of death," a proverbial phrase used to describe death and despair, also appeared in Psalm 44:19, "covered us with the shadow of death," and in Job 3:5 and 10:21-22. King's usage rhetorically joins the suffering of contemporary black Americans to that of biblical speakers who are both faithful and (at least in Job's case) plainly innocent.

Like *shadow, dart* appears in a description of suffering. To the charge that his march was "untimely," King responded with a diatribe against those who would cry, "Wait!" "For years now I have heard the word 'Wait!' It rings in the ear of every Negro with piercing familiarity." The word *piercing* echoes uncomfortably as the reader proceeds several sentences further: "Perhaps," wrote King, "it is easy for those who have never felt the stinging darts of segregation to say, 'Wait'." In the Bible, *dart* may refer to a literal weapon: "The sword of him that layeth at him cannot hold: the spear, the dart, nor the habergeon" (Job 41:26). Likewise in Proverbs: "Till a dart strike through his liver..." (7:23). But a dart may also be a metaphoric danger. Paul used it thus in his famous passage on "the whole armor of God": "Above all, taking the shield of faith, wherewith ye shall be able to quench all the fiery darts of the wicked" (Ephesians 6:16).

Just as King used *dart* to represent an inward pain, he used *chains* to describe inward restraints. As he despaired of the church, he wrote, "But again I am thankful to God that some noble souls from the ranks of organized religion have broken loose from the paralyzing chains of conformity and joined us...." Biblical writers spoke of chains, both literal and figurative. The author of II Peter described fallen angels, who were "delivered into chains of darkness" (2:4). The Psalmist wrote of those whose "pride compasseth them about as a chain" (73:6). Presumably they, like the fallen angels, deserved their suffering, but in the following use from Lamentations one cannot know whether the sufferer is guilty. The author spoke as one afflicted by an enemy: "He hath hedged me about, that I cannot get out: he hath made my chain heavy" (3:7). Chains are metaphors of punishment and despair. None of the writers suggested that such chains can be broken. On one occasion, however, a literal chain was broken. Peter, imprisoned by Herod, was miraculously set free: "And his chains fell off from his hands" (Acts 12:7). In King's usage, "the chains of conformity" would appear to have been forged, like the Psalmist's chain of pride, by the wearers themselves. But King suggested even those chains can be broken, like Peter's.

As he used *cup, shadow, dart,* and *chain* to summon up biblical accounts of suffering, King used the metaphors of *rock* and *quicksand* to recall biblical characterizations of stability and instability. Arguing that his audience must cease waiting and act, King urged: "Now is the time to lift our national policy from the quicksand of racial injustice to the solid rock of human dignity." Old Testament people frequently used *rock* as an image for God. For example, in Deuteronomy: "He is the Rock his work is perfect" (32:4). Hannah declared: "neither is there any rock like our God" (I Samuel 2:2). A rock may also symbolize any heroic figure; Isaiah retold the coming of a king who would be "as the shadow of a great rock in a weary land" (32:2). Jesus, punning on Peter's name, announced, "Thou art Peter, and upon this rock I will build my church" (Matthew 16:18). Quicksands are a variation on the sand foundation in the parable of the men who built houses: "The wise man, which built his house upon a rock..." and the "foolish man, which built his house upon the sand: and the rain descended, and the floods came, and the winds blew, and beat upon that house; and it fell: and great was the fall of it" (Matthew 7:24-27). King may also have had in mind a couplet from a popular hymn:

> On Christ the solid rock I stand,
> All other ground is sinking sand.

Treacherous, sinking quicksand typifies racial injustice. The rock, an image of righteousness, stability, and dignity, resonates with its Old Testament associations with God and the godly.

These and similar images in the **"Letter"** exist on at least two figurative levels. At the first level is simple metaphor, making the abstract not merely concrete but felt. One feels the weight of the garment, the sinking into the quicksand, the coldness of the shadow, the piercing of the darts, and the impediment of the chains. King made his audience literally feel the burden of racial bigotry. At the second level, each headword—*shadow, dart,* and so on—brings with it its biblical associations. King's image of the shadow or the dart stimulates the reader to recall other shadows or darts, much as one infers a meaning for a painting in which iconographically significant objects appear. These images become the keys to a meaning that the reader works out, usually subconsciously.

It is easy to see how nouns can function in this iconographic manner, but verbs may also have iconographic significance. The **"Letter from Birmingham Jail"** includes some biblical images contained not in prepositional phrases but in verbs or verbal constructions. Consider two examples: *root out* and *walk.* Discussing the need for "creative extremists" to take action where white moderates had failed, King observed, "Few members of the oppressor race can understand the yearnings of the oppressed, and still fewer have the vision to see that injustice must be rooted out by strong, persistent, and determined action." Whatever must be rooted out is, naturally, *rooted* and well established. It must be dug up, with no fragment left to take root again. The Deuteronomist characterized the treatment of those who worshipped false gods: "And the Lord rooted them out of their land in anger . . ." (29:28). Bildad, Job's "comforter," promised that the wicked man's "confidence shall be rooted out of his tabernacle" (Job 18:14). The Psalmist addressed a similar threat to boastful deceivers: "God shall likewise destroy thee for ever, he shall take thee away, and pluck thee out of thy dwelling place, and root thee out of the land of the living" (52:5). The biblical use of *root out* appears either in statements of what has occurred or in promises (threats) of what will occur. And furthermore, it is often a person or persons who will be rooted out. By contrast, King's usage, applied to an abstraction (injustice) seems mild. King is only observing what *should* be done. Yet even in the **"Letter,"** *root out* retains some of the violence of the biblical usage: the thing to be rooted out will be manhandled and tossed aside as worthless and malignant. *Rooting out* is an "extreme" action, and King bound his usage to biblical images of the same sort of extreme conduct.

At first glance, the verb *to walk* seems entirely free of biblical associations and not likely to operate as a biblical image. Yet, King praised the few whites who have broken from convention and joined in his cause: "They have left their secure congregations and walked the streets of Albany, Georgia, with us." In fact, in the English Bible one may find *walk* as a metonymy standing for a series of actions that might be conveyed in the phrases "to conduct oneself," "to pass through life," "to live one's life," or more simply "to live" or "to exist." Biblical writers often modified *walk,* so as to mean "the righteous person's safe passage through life." There are exceptions: danger may also walk, as in the Psalmist's description of "the pestilence that walketh in darkness" (91:6); but in the majority of cases, one who walks is both righteous and protected. The biblical examples are so numerous that a few selections must suffice:

> But as for me, I will walk in mine integrity: redeem me, and be merciful unto me. (Psalm 26:11)

> Better is the poor that walketh in his uprightness, than he that is perverse in his ways, though he be rich. (Proverbs 28:6)

> . . . as ye have received of us how ye ought to walk and to please God, so ye would abound more and more. (I Thessalonians 4:1)

For King, to walk was as morally significant an action as to go to jail. His career saw him do both often and lead others in them. He used the phrase "stride toward freedom" as a book title. Those who walked with him in Albany and in America performed an action of magnitude and moral significance. To walk was an act expressing personal courage, a faith in the rightness of one's action, and a trust of those walking along with oneself. All these meanings have their source in the biblical image *to walk.* In his marches, King took the biblical metaphor of "walking uprightly" and made it literal. In the **"Letter"** his use of the verb *to walk* summons up a biblical context for the civil-rights marches.

THE "LETTER" AS SERMON

The **"Letter from Birmingham Jail"** is both an epistle in the Pauline style and also a sermon. Among modern students of Paul, it is not unusual to find the contention that the Pauline epistles themselves are sermons. Despite the private queries, messages, and asides appearing here and there, Paul's letters were essentially public documents, composed and delivered orally. Beda Rigaux argued that Paul's letters "are official acts in his capacity of being an Apostle." He added, "In many instances, the letters seem to be nothing more than a literary prolongation of a previous sermon text which had been delivered orally." Bo Reicke explains that "Most New Testament epistles are not literary substitutes for conversation, like private letters, but ways of speaking publicly to congregations that could not be addressed in person." Furthermore, following the practice of the day, Paul dictated to an amanuensis, usually writing only a sentence or two of greeting in his own hand (see, for instance, I Corinthians 16:21 and Colossians 4:18). He spoke the text of the letter aloud and in doing so might easily have used specific passages from sermons previously delivered.

Like Paul, King had well established habits of delivery that characterized his sermons and marked his writing. King's habits of composition were those of the extempore preacher. Despite the fact that some of his sermons were written down and later published, he grew up in a tradition where the preacher was expected to compose as he delivered the sermon. Much of what he said the preacher drew from a mental storehouse stocked from the Bible. For the extempore preacher, the Bible became a resource similar to the stock of phrases and images retained by the Homeric rhapsode. Thus, like Homeric epic, the "extempore" sermon may be less spontaneous and more conventional than would first appear. King successfully used the methods of extempore preaching as he composed the **"Letter"**; he had read widely and his mental storehouse was well stocked. He took advantage of his uncommon skill and knowledge, avoiding the pitfalls (e.g., redundancy, shapelessness, illogicalness) that people of less skill might have stumbled into.

A good deal of the beauty of the **"Letter"** comes from King's skillful use of the extempore preacher's techniques. His references and allusions, for example, sound natural rather than bookish because they did not come directly from books. In jail without notes or books, King had only his memory to consult. He could recall the gist of Martin Buber's "I and Thou" relationship and summarize it easily. The reader is not obliged to plow through lengthy quotations from Tillich or Aquinas, but in these and other cases King has given us the kernel of their thought.

Memory is developed and honed by the extempore preacher. He is able to remember short passages and to use key phrases to summarize longer passages. King quoted Amos from memory, not quite accurately, but upon revision he left the sentence as he recalled it, because pedantic correctness of detail was not his stylistic goal. The imagery and diction that we have traced to biblical usages came into the **"Letter"** through King's memory, not simply a lexical memory but a capacity to remember rhythm, tone, and context as well.

Parallel structure, effectively managed throughout the **"Letter,"** frequently marks King's sermons and speeches. Speakers within many traditions, of course, use parallel structure, but the elaborate repetition King used to build to a climax is particularly popular in the tradition of black pulpit oratory. In the **"Letter"** the best example of such a device is the remarkable sentence—more than a page long—composed of "when" clauses in parallel, building to a conclusion. The sentence comes when King dismissed the urging of white Americans that blacks wait to let justice be done rather than seek to bring it about by direct action:

> But when you have seen vicious mobs...;
> when you have seen hate-filled policemen...;
> when you see the vast majority...;
> when you suddenly find your tongue twisted...;
>   and see tears welling up...;
>   and see ominous clouds of inferiority...;
>   and see her beginning to distort...;
> when you have to concoct an answer...;
> when you take a cross-country drive...;
> when you are humiliated day in and day out...;
> when your first name becomes "nigger"...;
> when you are harried by day and haunted by night...;
> when you are forever fighting...;
> then you will understand why we find it difficult to wait.

The effect of such passages is to transform King's readers into auditors.

To grant that King's oral style influenced the **"Letter"** is not to grant that the **"Letter"** is itself a sermon, however. Modern readers, accustomed to thinking of sermons as discourses occurring only in fixed services of worship, might object that to be a sermon, a message must be *spoken* from a pulpit to a congregation. These readers would certainly point out that King had no pulpit, did not speak, and had no congregation.

All these objections are accurate. King did not deliver the **"Letter from Birmingham Jail"** from a pulpit or even a church; he did not address a body of listeners seated before him. And yet in the **"Letter"** he performed one of a preacher's major tasks—that of prophecy. The Hebrew word for preaching is related to that for prophecy. The prophets, proclaiming the message of God, were preachers, not writers. Walter Russell Bowie reminded his modern-day readers of the preacher's role: preaching "must be prophetic." He went on to explain the prophet's task: "The prophet first of all will be helping his people remember the everlasting reality of God, the moral accountability of man, the sacredness of personality, and the seriousness of life." Here Bowie described in general terms the task and the topics King set for himself in the **"Letter."**

Defending himself against the implied charge of being an outsider, King compared himself not only to Paul but also to the prophets: "Just as the prophets of the eighth century B.C. left their villages and carried their 'thus saith the Lord' far beyond the boundaries of their home towns... so I am compelled to carry the gospel of freedom...." Later, calling Amos an "extremist for justice," King quoted him: "Let justice roll like waters and righteousness like an ever-flowing stream" (the reference is to Amos 5:24). The biblical prophets did not call for justice or righteousness in the abstract; they spoke of particular contemporary injustices and transgressions. They wept at the wrongdoing and suffering around them. Isaiah lamented: "Look away from me; I will weep bitterly, labor not to comfort me..." (22:4). Likewise Jeremiah said: "Oh, that my head were waters, and mine eyes a fountain of tears..." (9:11). The author of Nehemiah confessed: "I sat down and wept..." (1:4). King admitted: "I have wept over the laxity of the church." "But the judgment of God is upon the church as never before." Like the biblical prophets, King saw wrongdoing and was moved to tears; he was also spurred to denounce the injustice he saw.

King's **"Letter,"** then, is by no means a sermon in any limited, modern sense. On the other hand, in it King performed the preacher's traditional role as prophet, as one who sees clearly and speaks the truth plainly. Moreover, when one recalls what truth King spoke and why he was separated from a potential congregation, one comes closer to understanding how the **"Letter from Birmingham Jail"** can be seen as a sermon.

One of the major themes of the **"Letter"** is the failure of the white church to promote racial justice. King accused white churchmen of not doing what they should have done and of not seeing what they should have seen:

> Some have been outright opponents, refusing to understand the freedom movement and misrepresenting its leaders; all too many others

have...remained silent behind the anesthetizing security of stained-glass windows.

White American churchgoers, blinded by the religious clichés and prejudices that the stained-glass windows symbolize in King's text, are the major audience of the **"Letter."** They are the congregation: to them King is really speaking, despite his ostensible address to the eight clergymen. Thus the fact that the **"Letter"** was not delivered in a church before a congregation should not be seen as proof that it is not a sermon.

CONCLUSION

At the outset of this essay, I introduced three propositions: that Martin Luther King, in the **"Letter from Birmingham Jail,"** used the Apostle Paul as a type for himself and the Pauline epistle as a model for the **"Letter"**; that he took from the English Bible not just a literary form but also a series of iconographically significant words and images; and that he shaped his material into a text that, like Paul's letters, should be seen as a sermon. It is appropriate to examine a few of the implications of this argument.

One clear implication is that for King the Bible was heuristic. In the constrained circumstances under which the **"Letter"** was composed, his heuristic devices consisted largely of the clergymen's statement and the biblical images, word-clusters, literary forms, and *personae* that he carried in his memory. Using these devices, he constructed his text. For the reader, the Bible may also be heuristic. When we see his allusions and recall their biblical contexts, we find King's text more accessible, more readable. In recognizing his allusions, we are in a sense inventing the text for ourselves rather than reading something invented according to a system we do not understand. An extensive discussion of the relationships between memory and invention, on the one hand, and memory and readability, on the other, is far beyond the scope of my essay, but one cannot investigate biblical allusion in the **"Letter"** without recognizing those relationships.

Clearly, King identified with Paul. A reader might well ask, "Why Paul?" King's career, like Paul's, developed in such a way that his ministry extended beyond the traditional institutions of the day. Having left the conservative Jewish community, Paul moved on the fringes of Roman society, never again settling down as one rooted in a particular place. Of the various congregations he founded or visited, none was his special home. King, although officially pastor of several churches, did not limit himself to ministering only to those congregations. Like Paul, he spoke not *for* one church or *to* one church. More and more, he moved impatiently beyond the bounds set by institutional religion.

Of all biblical personages, Paul perhaps best stands for the destruction of barriers. Had King chosen an Old Testament type or model, as many seventeenth-century New England Puritan preachers did, he might have created various implications of a Chosen People, of insiders and outsiders. This is precisely what he could not do. His message was against division or separation and all the social institutions, including jails and segregated churches, that can be used to promote division or segregation.

More important than any historical similarities between King and Paul, however, is the rhetorical opportunity that King seized when he borrowed Paul's literary form. The epistle as written by Paul has not been widely used outside the New Testament. He and his contemporaries invented it; it flourished for several generations but died away in the second century. By reviving this ancient form, King was able to take advantage of its particular rhetorical conventions: its dialectic rhythm of statement and response, its use of scriptural texts and imagery, and—perhaps most important for King at the moment of writing—its author-audience relationship. The very composing of an epistle (as a proxy sermon) defines one's audience as people who are to be advised, guided, and convinced, but who, more significantly, are to be persuaded of certain conclusions not merely because they are logical or appealing but because they are in accord with the audience's own beliefs. Paul did not try to convert his audience with his letters. Presumably he and his fellow missionaries accomplished conversions through more direct and intimate means. Paul's letters aimed to strengthen the belief of the converted, to show them how to conduct themselves in light of their belief, and to teach them the implications of their belief.

Like Paul, King assumed the common ground of belief between himself and his audience. The rhetorical prominence of the Bible in the **"Letter"** is one sign of this assumption. King's overall rhetorical strategy in the **"Letter"** was the strategy of Pauline epistle. He said, in effect, "If you believe in these truths, then you must act in a certain way." The eight clergymen could not deny their beliefs, nor can the white moderate public whom King sought to reach in his larger audience. King used the beliefs of his audience urging them that civil order and routine must, according to those beliefs, be subordinate to the freedom and welfare of their fellow human beings.

"All real living is meeting," wrote Martin Buber. In the **"Letter from Birmingham Jail"** King closes, as we have seen, with a wish to meet the eight clergymen. Paul also wished to be with those to whom he wrote. As Amos Wilder has observed, "Paul writes always as one thwarted by absence and eagerly anticipating meeting or reunion." Early in his letter to the Romans, for example, he confessed that he prayed, "making request, if by any means now at length I might have a prosperous journey by the will of God to come unto you" (1:10). Paul's letters are the written substitutes for a face-to-face meeting.

The New Testament scholar Robert W. Funk has argued that such a passage in a Pauline letter should be called the "apostolic *parousia*," after the Greek word for "presence." In these sections Paul expresses his hopes to visit the recipients. For Paul, writing was not the best means of reaching his audience and manifesting his authority as an apostle: "Since Paul gives precedence to the oral word, the written word will not function as a primary medium of his own apostleship." Nevertheless Paul used all his literary abilities to make his letters effective. Like Paul, King used a language that encouraged a meeting of people. The success of his biblically founded language may be seen immediately when one compares his **"Letter"** to the clergymen's statement: their dry, secular prose conveys only self-satisfaction and the demand that others fit their preconceptions. No meeting with their readers is sought. Their language is civil rather than pastoral; it expresses little human concern. King's language, on the other hand, is pastoral in that the writer shows genuine care for a well-defined audience whom he sought to guide and teach.

The rhetoric of Paul's letters (and of much biblical literature) is not the rhetoric of the classical oration. Argument was not Paul's major goal, nor is it King's no matter how effectively each man could argue specific issues. Paul's and King's rhetoric is closer to that of liturgy than to that of argument. It is a commonplace of rhetorical instruction that argument begins not with disagreement but with doubt. One might say that liturgy begins with faith: It is the acting out of the premises one accepts as truths. All the components of liturgy, including its language, are intended to move an audience to become participants. Liturgy, that is to say, facilitates *meeting,* in the sense that Buber used the term. Liturgy may be written but it cannot be read in the way that an argument can be read, alone and silently. To exist, liturgy depends upon the presence and participation of a group, or at least of "two or three."

Like liturgy, King's activities in Birmingham were belief acted out. Those who marched with him joined his action as believers join in a liturgy. In traditional Christianity, liturgy recreates the events in Jesus's life taken as central to the faith—notably, the Last Supper, as recreated in the Eucharist. In the typology of black American Protestantism, biblical events have a significance that may be expressed liturgically. King's going to jail and composing the epistle/sermon in jail recreated Paul's action, in the manner of liturgical re-creation. The **"Letter"** seeks to reach its audience (both the eight clergymen and the moderate white public) and to unite them in action with King. Speaking in 1962 to the National Press Club, King explained his methods (as practiced most recently in Albany): "I feel that this way of nonviolence is vital because it is the only way to reestablish the broken community." His activities in Birmingham the next year had the same goal.

With its Pauline form and its extensive biblical imagery, the **"Letter from Birmingham Jail"** appeals to an audience familiar with Judeo-Christian literature and who accept the ethical teachings of the Bible. Using the resources of the preacher, King urged his audience to enter into a liturgical acting out of their belief, as in all

liturgy, with the goal of meeting; for without the brotherhood and respect generated through meeting, no true justice can be done. King's apostolic mission in Birmingham was to bring about union and seek justice. His arrest was planned to act out the separation and injustice he opposed. The longer-than-planned stay in jail and the clergymen's statement provided opportunity to create unity and bring about justice. It is through the active, liturgical rhetoric of the Pauline letter that he accomplished his mission. (pp. 318-32)

> *Malinda Snow, "Martin Luther King's 'Letter from Birmingham Jail' as Pauline Epistle," in* The Quarterly Journal of Speech, *Vol. LXXI, No. 3, August, 1985, pp. 318-34.*

Keith Miller (essay date 1989)

[*In the following excerpt, Miller examines King's "I Have a Dream" speech, asserting that the work derives its power and persuasiveness from elements of the "black folk pulpit."*]

"I Have a Dream" is a profoundly paradoxical speech. Martin Luther King, Jr. invokes a national past of Jefferson and Lincoln and embraces Old Testament prophets and Christianity as he presents an entire inventory of patriotic themes and images typical of Fourth of July oratory. Yet King devotes the first half of his address not to celebrating a dream but to cataloguing a nightmare, not to hailing the bounty of the present but to damning the horror of a status quo that demeans all black Americans. No other liberal or radical in this century has approached King's success in defining the stock motifs of nationalism and Biblical religion as demands for massive social change. How do we explain this success?

King scholars interpret King's ideas and persuasiveness mainly as reflections of what King's biographer Stephen Oates calls "theological erudition" gained in a white seminary and in his Ph.D. program at Boston University School of Theology. For example, historian Harvard Sitkoff maintains, "[King's] training in systematic theology had left him with an appetite for transcendent ideas, for theoretical constructs"; according to Sitkoff, this training also exerted considerable force in shaping the civil rights revolution. At least two entire books, one by Kenneth Smith and Ira Zepp, another by John Ansbro, examine King's graduate studies course by course in an attempt to comprehend the development of King's politics, theology, and discourse. Claiming that King's doctoral curriculum allowed his mind to flourish far beyond the constraints and limitations imposed in his hometown of Atlanta, Donald Smith seems to speak for a number of King scholars in declaring, "Atlanta is a thousand miles from Boston, but for Martin Luther King the distance was measurable in intellectual light years." Even that most painstaking scholar, David Garrow, whose richly detailed biography of King earned a Pulitzer Prize in 1986, implicitly accounts for King's rhetorical and political achievements in large measure as a function of his reading of Hegel, Marx, Thoreau, Paul Tillich, Reinhold Niebuhr and other white thinkers. And even King's friend, the distinguished black preacher and scholar Henry Mitchell, implies that, while King's delivery embodied the cadences of the black pulpit, the lion's share of his intellectual training derived from white academe.

This essay tacks in another direction. I maintain that King's persuasiveness stems not from ideas expounded at Boston University but from the typological epistemology of the black folk pulpit and from the methods of voice merging and self making that proceed from that epistemology. Instead of viewing King's thought and rhetoric as an outgrowth of Hegel's dialectic, Thoreau's dissent and Niebuhr's social analysis, I propose treating **"I Have a Dream"** as an updated expression of the Weltanschauung of American slaves. Marshalling this argument necessitates a consideration of the persistent themes and typology of the slaves, the practice of voice merging and self making in black folk preaching, King's general relationship to the folk pulpit, and voice merging and self making in **"I Have a Dream."**

EPISTEMOLOGY OF SLAVE RELIGION

Noting the vividness and immediacy of a black sermon, one scholar [William Pipes] remarks the preacher's ability to talk "to his congregation about Moses and Daniel at mid-day as though he had eaten breakfast with them." This immediacy is also apparent in the spiritual that asks: "Didn't the Lord deliver Daniel?/Why can't He deliver me?" Lawrence Levine explains this quality of identification as an expression of what Mircea Eliade terms sacred time:

> ...for [slaves and other] peoples in traditional societies religion is a means of extending the world spatially upward so that communication with the other world becomes ritually possible and extending it temporally backward so that the paradigmatic acts of the gods and mythical ancestors can be continually re-enacted and indefinitely recoverable. [Slaves] extended the boundaries of the restrictive universe until it fused with the world of the Old Testament and upward until it became one with the world beyond.

According to Frederick Douglass and many subsequent observers, slaves affirmed the inseparability of the sacred and the secular through the double meaning of spirituals, which pointed both to salvation in heaven and to freedom on earth. Slaves strongly identified with the Hebrews suffering from bondage in Egypt and embraced what Eugene Genovese terms "a pervasive theme of deliverance," confident that the God who liberated the Hebrews would eventually unlock their own shackles. As Genovese explains, slaves often blended Moses and Jesus "into the image of a single deliverer, at once thisworldly and otherworldly" and "associated Moses with all great historical events, including the most recent."

King addressing a crowd at Chicago's Soldier Field. King delivered hundreds of speeches throughout the country, and his fiery oratorical style never failed to move his audience. After his "I Have a Dream" speech, thousands of people cheered and wept.

This telescoping manifests what can only be termed a typological view of history, typology constituting, in Linda Peterson's words, "a system of interpretation in which characters, events, and sacred rituals of the Old Testament are treated as prefigurations of Christ, but in popular practice the types were also applied to the lives of individual Christians." In George Landau's view, the advantage of this system is that it organizes all of history and provides access to the central meaning of human experience; furthermore, one may employ typology to place an audience in what Landau describes as a "completely ordered world."

VOICE MERGING AND SELF MAKING IN BLACK FOLK PREACHING

In the black folk pulpit ministers often create their own identities not through original language but through identifying themselves with a hallowed tradition. In his MLA award-winning study, *The Art of The American Folk Preacher,* Bruce Rosenberg declares that experienced pastors borrow homiletic material from many sources, including the sermons of their predecessors and peers. Some sermons are ubiquitous and long-lived: one began at least as early as 1868 and was still preached during the 1960s and 1970s; another has been recorded by at least four different preachers; and a third by at least seven different speakers, not to mention the occasions these floating homilies appealed to ministers who lacked recording studios. Pastors profit from their audiences' familiarity with sermons, for familiarity enables churchgoers to participate more freely through speaking, clapping, gesturing or dancing.

Preachers also engage in voice merging at the end of their sermons. Like their slave predecessors, contemporary black preachers often conclude their sermons by chanting and then singing. (Such a finale is appropriate because a hymn of invitation to join the church customarily follows the sermonizing, the ritual of invitation serving as the climax of the worship experience.) For example, I once heard a black Baptist minister finish his presentation by stating:

> Some people sing because they're in the shower.
> Some people sing because they're a movie star.
> Some sing because they've got a record contract.
> But not me.
>
> I sing because I'm happy.
> I sing because I'm free.

Then he chanted:

> If His eye is on the sparrow,
> Then I know he watches me.

At that point the congregation joined him in singing the lines of his chant, which constitute the words of a beloved hymn. Consider this question: When the preacher declares, "I sing because I'm happy," who is the "I" of the sentence? The "I" is obviously the homilist himself, the person who has delivered God's Word. But the "I" is also the narrative voice of the hymn. In addition the "I" is each person in the pew who identifies with the sentiments of the lyrics and who vocalizes the lyrics. The "I" is also the voice of each churchgoer who sang the hymn in years and decades gone by, including those who are now dead. The "I" of the pastor merges with the narrative voice of the hymn and with past and present Christians who sing or have sung it. The minister creates a self as his identity converges with those of others. A typological epistemology makes this convergence possible by affirming that knowable and repeatable types of human experience recur from generation to generation. Using the lyrics of spirituals, gospel songs and hymns, a black Baptist clergyman creates a self as his identity converges with those of others.

KING AND THE FOLK PULPIT

King's maternal grandfather, Rev. A. D. Williams, was a whooping and moaning folk preacher who doubled as a political activist. He organized a boycott that put a racist newspaper out of business, defeated a city bond proposal that ignored black schools and served as the chief NAACP fundraiser in Atlanta. Establishing himself in the folk pulpit, Martin Luther King, Sr. began his homiletic career when he could scarcely read and write; like his father-in-law, he agitated for social change, leading a 1935 voting rights march to Atlanta's city hall and supporting the demands of black teachers for salaries comparable to those of white teachers. Preaching in the church King co-pastored with his father the last eight years of his life, both Williams and King, Sr. worked to save souls for heaven and to achieve racial equality on earth.

King's initiation in the folk pulpit occurred when he attended church every Sunday as a child until becoming an ordained minister before leaving home for seminary. Although King scholars frequently portray his mind as a virtual *tabula rasa* before his matriculation at white graduate schools, King's rhetoric and leadership do not comport with such an interpretation.

Rather, his political crusades, ability to revive the Hebrew/Pharoah typology, delivery, style and voice merging all reflect the black folk pulpit. Devoting his life to the struggle against segregation begun by his father and grandfather, he updates the identification of slaves with the Hebrew people by habitually labelling his segregation opponents as Pharoahs; by repeatedly preaching "Death of Evil on the Seashore," a sermon that celebrates the Israelites' escape from Egypt and the drowning of Pharoah's army; by being called a "black Moses" by many (including white journalists); and, in his final speech, **"I See the Promised Land,"** by explicitly identifying himself with Moses in his opportunity to gaze upon the Promised Land but not to enter it. In his many sermons and speeches (including **"I Have a Dream"**), his delivery consistently features two time-honored trademarks of black sermonizing: first, a calm-to-storm manner that begins in measured, professorial phrases and swings gradually to a powerfully emotional climax; and second, call-and-response interaction with listeners that sends and returns an electrical charge back and forth between pulpit and pew. His use of a cornucopia of schemes and tropes manifests a common practice in the folk pulpit, where schemes and tropes often help both preachers and churchgoers to remember the content of sermons. King also concluded not only sermons but virtually every major speech and many other addresses by merging his voice with the lyrics of hymns. And, as I explain elsewhere, he often borrowed sermons from other preachers.

VOICE MERGING AND SELF-MAKING IN "I HAVE A DREAM"

According to Chaim Perelman and L. Olbrechts-Tyteca, "A stereotyped metaphorical expression can come to life again in the mouth of certain speakers because it is presumed that, when they use it, it cannot have its usual banal meaning." I claim that voice merging, self making, and the typological epistemology underlying those practices enabled King to reanimate stereotyped expressions in **"I Have a Dream"**—the same expressions that other liberals and radicals have failed to reawaken, in part because their speeches lacked typological resonance and did not evoke any Eliadean sense of sacred time. I will examine three instances of voice merging in King's oration, the first involving Amos, the second Isaiah, and the third, "My country tis of thee."

Amos

Consider the first instance:

> There are those who are asking the devotees of civil rights, "When will you be satisfied?" We can never be satisfied as long as the Negro is the victim of the unspeakable horrors of police brutality.
> We cannot be satisfied as long as our bodies . . . cannot find lodging in the motels of the highways and the hotels of the cities . . .
> We cannot be satisfied as long as the Negro in Mississippi cannot vote . . . .
> No . . . we will not be satisfied until justice rolls down like waters and righteousness like a mighty stream.

Who are the "we" of this anaphora? The devotees of civil rights—the muted group of disenfranchised blacks whom King represents. In this speech more than any other, King succeeds in articulating the needs and demands of an oppressed people and by doing so makes visible those who are invisible and renders powerful those who are powerless. The national audience understands King's voice as the voice of millions of black people.

But who constitutes the "we" of the last sentence? Again, the devotees of civil rights because this "we" concludes the series of lines beginning with "We can never be satisfied . . . ." But this line harnesses the most famous exclamation of the Old Testament prophets—Amos's cry, "Let justice roll down like waters and righteousness like a mighty stream!" So Amos is also speaking here as King merges Amos's persona with his own. This union reflects back to the preceeding sentences of the anaphora: The "we" who cannot be satisfied until justice reigns are the same "we" who seek lodging in the motels of the highways and the hotels of the cities. The typologically identical voices of King and Amos call for justice to roll down like waters and for Congress to build irrigation ditches by mandating desegregation in all motels and hotels. King lends an unimpeachably authoritative tone to the aspirations of a muted group by enlisting Amos as a spokesman for their hopes.

But isn't King merely employing a looser comparison, some version of analogy? No. If Christians treated the Bible as a source of analogy, the Christian worldview would never have proven persuasive; for, as Perelman and Olbrechts-Tyteca explain, analogy functions as "an unstable form of argument" and refutation of an analogy by extension is "nearly always possible." Why? In the case of analogy, either set of terms is susceptible to challenge; by contrast, in the case of typology, the first set of terms may not be challenged because it is Biblical and Biblical truth serves as its own warrant and proof. Furthermore, believers view Biblical truth as applying necessarily to the present. The task of the Christian—in this context King—is simply to discern the proper correspondence between Biblical and contemporary circumstance. This divinely ordained form of truth-seeking is much harder to refute than the straightforward use of analogy.

Isaiah

The second instance of voice merging occurs in the most famous passage of King's oratory:

> I have a dream that one day this nation will rise up and live out the true meaning of its creed, "We hold these truths to be self-evident, that all men are created equal." I have a dream that my four little children will one day . . . not be judged by the color of their skin but by the content of their character. I have a dream today! I have a dream that one day every valley shall be exalted and every hill and mountain shall be made low, the rough places will be made plain, and the crooked places will be made straight, and the glory of the Lord shall be revealed, and all flesh shall see it together.

Who is the "I" of this anaphora? The "I" is surely King, a man with four young children who is delivering a speech. But who is the "I" of the last sentence? This dream is not simply King's dream. Isaiah initially sketched the eschatological scene of valleys exalted, mountains laid low and rough places made plain. Jesus reaffirmed this prophet's powerfully imaginative conception by quoting this example of Isaiah's visionary language. Then Handel enshrined Isaiah's imagery in the words of *The Messiah*. Uniting his persona with those of Amos, Isaiah, Jesus and the narrative voice of *The Messiah*, King constructs an identity by fitting himself into a set of prearranged, overlapping forms. Underlying this process of selfmaking is the typological epistemology of the folk pulpit, specifically the assumption that personality reasserts itself in readily understandable and invariable patterns that govern all human history, patterns exemplified in scripture, music, liturgy, prayers and sermons.

And joining King's choir of the prophets, Jesus, the narrative voice of *The Messiah,* and the muted group is the most distinguished of all possible members, God Almighty. King orchestrates the divine voice into his ensemble through several methods. First, his status as a Baptist minister helps to generate such a voice. (Six years earlier King literally donned his pulpit robe to speak to a crowd of twenty-five thousand people gathered at the same spot on the Washington mall in a Prayer Pilgrimage for Freedom organized to demand the right to vote.) Second, his reiteration of Biblical revelation expresses God's Word because Jews and Christians insist that God speaks directly through the mouths of the prophets and, in the case of Christians, through the pronouncements of Jesus Christ, who is God incarnate.

Third, King's use of the vocal dynamics and anaphoric style of the black pulpit reinforces and heightens the religious overtones of the address. Significantly, King begins his oration by invoking patriotic authority, the Declaration of Independence, the Constitution and the Emancipation Proclamation. Religion does not enter the speech overtly until Amos speaks at the halfway point. Engaging in the customary practice of folk preachers, King begins to accentuate rhythm and vocal contrasts halfway through his presentation. When the words of Amos emerge, so do the cadences of the black pulpit. At the same point King begins to pack series of anaphoras against each other, seven series in all. King's chockablock use of this scheme recalls the abundant schemes of the highly oral (and therefore somewhat formulaic) tradition of black folk homiletics.

Through his catalogue of an American nightmare in the first half of the oration, King maintains that the finest secular presences, including Jefferson and Lincoln, have failed miserably. The "architects of our republic," he declares, offered a "promissory note" to all Americans, guaranteeing the rights of life, liberty and the pursuit of happiness; but for black people the note proved "a bad check," a check "marked insufficient funds." By replacing secular authority with divine authority in the second half of **"I Have a Dream,"** King suggests that God Almighty, whose patience has finally expired, will now overrule secular forces and install justice without delay. If God ordains justice to roll down like waters, the flood must eventually cross the Mason-Dixon line. Why? Because goodness inevitably asserts itself, even in the secular world, for in the end the sacred and secular worlds are inseparable.

Such a conception of good and evil revives and reiterates the holistic vision of slaves, not the principle of synthesis valorized by Hegel, the complexities of love dissected by Anders Nygren, the theological abstractions beloved by Tillich, the ambiguities embraced by Niebuhr or other notions and precepts of white philosophers and theologians repeatedly alleged to have empowered King to direct a civil rights revolution.

"My Country, Tis of Thee"

The final examples of voice merging and self making happen, not surprisingly, at the end of **"I Have a Dream."** The civil rights leader apparently develops his conclusion by adjusting and honing a passage from Archibald Carey. Consider the final portion of Carey's 1952 address to the Republican National Convention:

> We, Negro Americans, sing with all loyal Americans:
> My country, tis of thee,
> Sweet land of liberty,
> Of thee I sing.
> Land where my fathers died,
> Land of the Pilgrims' pride,
> From every mountain side
> Let freedom ring!
> That's exactly what we mean—from every mountain side, let freedom ring. Not only from the Green Mountains and the White Mountains of Vermont and New Hampshire; not only from the Catskills of New York; but from the Ozarks in Arkansas, from the Stone Mountain in Georgia, from the Blue Ridge Mountains of Virginia—let it ring not only for the minorities of the United States, but for . . . the disinherited of all the earth—may the Republican Party, under God, from every mountain side, LET FREEDOM RING!

Through voice merging Carey harnesses "America the Beautiful" as an agent not for self-satisfaction but for radical political change, uniting his identity with the patriotic narrative voice of our unofficial national anthem. Largely preoccupied with King's training in white graduate schools, King scholars ignore Carey. Yet King's peroration adapts and refines Carey's visionary proclamation:

> This will be the day when all of God's children will
> be able to sing with new meaning:
> My country, tis of thee,
> Sweet land of liberty,
> Of thee I sing.
> Land where my fathers died,
> Land of the Pilgrims' pride,
> From every mountain side
> Let freedom ring!
> So let freedom ring from the prodigious hilltops of New Hampshire.
> Let freedom ring from the mighty mountains of New York.
> Let freedom ring from the heightening Alleghenies of Pennsylvania . . . .
> Let freedom ring from Stone Mountain of Georgia.
> Let freedom ring from Lookout Mountain of Tennessee.
> Let freedom ring from every hill and molehill in Mississippi.
> From every mountain side, let freedom ring.

Note that the "Let freedom ring" sequence seems to continue "America the Beautiful." This extension is both stylistic and metaphorical. King employs the last three words he (and Carey) quoted from the song to establish his concluding anaphora, "Let freedom ring." The extension is metaphorical as well, for both "America the Beautiful" and King's oration compare freedom to a mighty bell whose peal echoes across every mountain in the country. The effect of King's stylistic and metaphorical repetition is to add another verse to the anthem as he merges his voice with that of "America the Beautiful": The "my" of "My Country, Tis of Thee" refers to King as well as to the narrative voice of the song.

But that's not all. Hailing Carey's utopian future, King envisions a day when Americans will dismantle social barriers and merge voices and identities by singing "America the Beautiful." King simultaneously engages in voice merging with the lyrics of the anthem and reflects on the possibility of massive voice merging that would collapse all racial distinctions.

In his final sentence King reinforces this entire rhetorical process by quoting yet another source:

> ... when we allow freedom to ring ... from every village and every hamlet, from ever state and every city, we will be able to speed up that day when all of God's children—Black men and white men, Jews and gentiles, Protestants and Catholic, will be able to join hands and sing in the words of the old Negro spiritual:
>
> Free at last! Free at last! Thank God Almighty, we are free at last!

Again King projects a future when brotherhood triumphs over racial and religious separation; where identities converge; and where the typological epistemology of the black folk pulpit reigns, enabling every American to merge voices and thereby to create a self and a nation. (pp. 23-9)

> *Keith Miller, "Voice Merging and Self-Making: The Epistemology of 'I Have a Dream',"* in Rhetoric Society Quarterly, *Vol. 19, No. 1, Winter, 1989, pp. 23-31.*

New York Times (essay date 1990)

[*The following 1990* New York Times *editorial was written in response to then-surfacing allegations that King plagiarized part of his doctoral dissertation. Here, the editors assert that King's achievements as a civil rights activist are not diminished by his apparently poor scholarship: "Martin Luther King's courage was not copied; and there was no plagiarism in his power."*]

To millions of admirers around the world, the disclosures about Dr. Martin Luther King Jr. and his doctoral dissertation cast a shadow on his memory; a shadow should not, however, be confused with a cloud.

Scholarship rests on truth and trust, which is why scholars are right to denounce plagiarism mercilessly; that's why it is so dismaying to learn that Dr. King's doctoral thesis contained an extraordinary amount of material borrowed or copied, unattributed, from the work of others.

But however just it may be to denounce his scholarship, that should not be confused with his leadership. Whether or not, as a student, he wrote what he wrote, Dr. King did what he did.

One way to describe his achievement is with other words of his, from his famous **"Letter from Birmingham City Jail."** Some say he solicited the assistance of others for that famous essay, but even if so, that's no more to be faulted than John Kennedy turning to Theodore Sorensen, or George Bush to Peggy Noonan. What counts is the conviction he expressed, speaking for millions seeking racial justice, in response to eight Alabama clergymen who declared his direct, nonviolent protests to be "unwise and untimely."

He wrote: "We know through painful experience that freedom is never voluntarily given by the oppressor; it must be demanded by the oppressed. Frankly, I have never yet engaged in a direct action movement that was 'well-timed,' according to the timetable of those who have not suffered unduly from the disease of segregation. For years now I have heard the words 'Wait!' It rings in the ear of every Negro with a piercing familiarity. This 'Wait' has almost always meant 'Never.'"

Even now, even after the civil rights revolution, the truth of such words is evident to a new generation of Americans who have never heard the name Emmett Till and have no recollection of Selma. That truth makes the disclosures of plagiarism even more lamentable now, so soon after Arizona voters refused to establish a holiday on Dr. King's January birthday. News of the distant academic lapse may be taken, carelessly, to explain or perhaps excuse the voters' rejection.

What the world honors when it honors Dr. King is his tenacity on behalf of racial justice—tenacity equally against gradualism and against violence. He and many with him pushed Americans down the long road to racial justice. That achievement glows unchallenged through the present shadow. Martin Luther King's courage was not copied; and there was no plagiarism in his power.

> *"What Dr. King Wrote and What He Did,"* in The New York Times, *November 13, 1990, p. A30.*

FURTHER READING

Baldwin, James. "The Dangerous Road before Martin Luther King." *Harper's Magazine* 222, No. 1329 (February 1961): 33-42.
    Personal account of Baldwin's meeting with King. The critic writes: "Martin Luther King, Jr., by the power of his personality and the force of his beliefs, has injected a new dimension into our ferocious struggle. He has succeeded, in a way no Negro before him has managed

to do, to carry the battle into the individual heart and make its resolution the province of individual will."

Baldwin, Lewis V. *There Is a Balm in Gilead: The Cultural Roots of Martin Luther King, Jr.* Minneapolis: Fortress Press, 1991, 348 p.

Explores King's "roots in black folk culture, particularly that of the South."

Bennett, Lerone, Jr. *What Manner of Man: A Biography of Martin Luther King, Jr.* Chicago: Johnson Publishing Company, 1964, 245 p.

Biography of King. Bennett—a former schoolmate and friend of King—recalls King's early years and schooling at Morehouse College and at Crozer Theological Seminary.

Bosmajian, Haig A. "The Rhetoric of Martin Luther King's *'Letter from the Birmingham Jail'*." *The Midwest Quarterly* XXI, No. 1 (Autumn 1979): 46-62.

Discusses structure, rhetoric, and style in *Letter from Birmingham Jail.*

Cone, James H. *Martin and Malcolm and America: A Dream or a Nightmare.* Maryknoll, N. Y.: Orbis Books, 1991, 358 p.

Challenges popular caricatures of King as an American hero and Malcolm X as "a black demagogue," arguing instead that King and Malcolm X were two men "whose complementary visions were converging at the time of their deaths."

Duberman, Martin. Review of *Where Do We Go from Here: Chaos or Community?,* by Martin Luther King, Jr. In his *The Uncompleted Past,* pp. 181-87. New York: Random House, 1969.

Review of *Where Do We Go from Here: Chaos or Community?* The critic notes: "King's new book... is his attempt to summarize the recent conflicts within the civil rights movement, to consider the larger context, both national and international, which helps to account for these conflicts, and finally, to suggest possible lines for action. King is far more successful... in dealing with the first two of these considerations than with the third...."

"The Living King." *Ebony* XLI, No. 3 (January 1986).

Special issue devoted to King, celebrating the instatement of his birthday as a national holiday. Includes speech excerpts, photographs, brief book reviews, and articles by Coretta Scott King and Christine King Farris. Also contains tributes by Rev. Ralph Aberna-

thy, Evelyn Ashford, Howard Baker, Rev. Jesse Jackson, and Edward Kennedy.

Fulkerson, Richard P. "The Public Letter as a Rhetorical Form: Structure, Logic, and Style in King's *'Letter from Birmingham Jail'*." *The Quarterly Journal of Speech* 65, No. 2 (April 1979): 121-36.

Analysis of King's argumentative techniques in *Letter from Birmingham Jail.*

Garrow, David J. *Bearing the Cross: Martin Luther King, Jr., and the Southern Christian Leadership Conference.* New York: William Morrow and Company, 1986, 800 p.

Comprehensive biography of King. This book, winner of the 1987 Pulitzer Prize, is based on more than 700 interviews with King's friends and associates. "The central, unifying theme of the book," the dust jacket states, "is King's growing awareness of the symbolic meaning of the cross... and the awareness of how this calling would shape his life."

Gasnick, Roy M. Review of *Strength to Love,* by Martin Luther King, Jr. *America* 109, No. 7 (17 August 1963): 173-74.

Favorably reviews *Strength to Love,* concluding: "As the civil rights crisis becomes more dangerous,... we all need to be reminded that it *does* take strength to love. Martin Luther King, in these sermons, has pointed out the source of that strength."

Halberstam, David. "The Second Coming of Martin Luther King." *Harper's Magazine* 235, No. 1407 (August 1967): 39-51.

Personal observations about King made while traveling with him throughout the United States. Halberstam writes: "Being with [King] is a little like being with a Presidential candidate after a long campaign.... He has finally come to believe his myth, just as the people in the Pentagon believe theirs and the man in the White House believes his...."

Klein, Mia. "The Other Beauty of Martin Luther King, Jr.'s *'Letter from Birmingham Jail'*." *College Composition and Communication* XXXII, No. 1 (February 1981): 30-7.

Examines the emotional appeal of *Letter from Birmingham Jail,* focusing on sentence structure.

Rohler, Janet. "The Life and Death of Martin Luther King." *Christianity Today* XII, No. 15 (26 April 1968): 37-40.

Tribute to King, summarizing his life, his philosophy of nonviolence, and his role as a civil rights leader.

Etheridge Knight

1931-1991

American poet, essayist, editor, and short story writer.

Knight was one of the most popular poets of the Black Arts Movement, a period during the 1960s of literary and cultural revival for black writers and artists. Sometimes called "the prison poet," he began writing poetry when he was an inmate at the Indiana State Prison. In many of his poems he expressed a desire for freedom and protested the oppression of blacks and the underprivileged in "the bigger prison of society." He strove for a balance between "the poet, the poem, and the people," deliberately using direct language, slang, and simple poetic techniques to make his work accessible to the greatest possible number of readers. "I see the art of poetry as [a] trinity," he explained. "You can't have one without the other. The poet-person, the poem and the audience. And they're equally important, and I never assume that an audience does not have feelings and sense just like I do."

Born in Corinth, Mississippi, in 1931, Knight had a rough childhood. He dropped out of school after the eighth grade and began frequenting bars and poolrooms. He spent hours on street corners reciting "toasts." Toasts, Shirley Lumpkin explained, are long, memorized narrative poems in which "sexual exploits, drug activities, and violent aggressive conflicts involving a cast of familiar folk . . . are related . . . using street slang, drug and other specialized argot, and often obscenities." At the age of sixteen Knight joined the United States Army; he served in Korea as a medical technician. To dull what he called the "psyche" pain of the war and of his physical wounds, he turned to using drugs. By the time he was discharged in 1957 he had become a serious drug addict and was committing crimes to support his habit. In 1960 he was found guilty of armed robbery and sentenced to ten to twenty-five years in prison.

Again, to cope with the harsh environment in which he found himself, Knight looked for an outlet and now found it in poetry: "I died in Korea from a shrapnel wound and narcotics resurrected me. I died in 1960 from a prison sentence and poetry brought me back to life." While an inmate he published his first volume of poetry, *Poems from Prison* (1968). This collection of verse, which reflects the brutality of prison life, was praised by critics and readers alike. Such noted figures as Gwendolyn Brooks, Sonia Sanchez, and Dudley Randall corresponded with the young poet and encouraged him to keep writing. His next work, *Belly Song and Other Poems* (1973)—nominated for both the Pulitzer Prize and the National Book Award—consists of poetry written after Knight's release from prison (he was paroled in 1968). It was with the publication of *Born of a Woman: New and Selected Poems* (1980), however, that Knight enjoyed his greatest success among critics.

Born of a Woman is divided into three sections: "Inside-Out," "Outside-In," and "All About—And Back Again." The poems in the first section convey different aspects of prison life: "For Freckle-Faced Gerald" concerns a young boy who is raped and brutalized by older convicts—an act that also symbolically represents society's oppression of the innocent and defenseless; "Hard Rock" depicts a strong and rebellious hero who defies the system's attempts to break his spirit until brain surgery forcibly changes his character; and "The Idea of Ancestry" reveals the loneliness and isolation of a prisoner who reflects upon his crime, his family, and his heritage while looking at photographs of his relatives on his cell wall. The second section contains poems about love, and the final section includes Knight's most recent poetry and develops a greater scope of themes and subjects. In a review of *Born of a Woman*, Craig Werner commented: "A polished craftsman, capable of exploiting both traditional Euro-American and experimental Afro-American (frequently musical) terms, Knight has emerged as a major voice in the tradition of

Langston Hughes and Gwendolyn Brooks." Some critics, however, found Knight's work "objectionable" and "unpoetic." A few also thought his "black power rhetoric" outdated. Nonetheless, as Lumpkin pointed out: "Those with reservations and those who admire [Knight's] work all agree ... upon his vital language and the range of his subject matter. They all agree that he brings a needed freshness to poetry, particularly in his extraordinary ability to move an audience.... A number of poets ... consider him a major Afro-American poet because of his human subject matter, his combination of traditional techniques with an expertise in using rhythmic and oral speech patterns, and his ability to feel and to project his feelings into a poetic structure that moves others."

When Knight died in 1991 at the age of fifty-nine from lung cancer, he left only a handful of books, all of which remain popular with black and white audiences alike. His "For Black Poets Who Think of Suicide" seems a fitting eulogy to a man who wanted to be remembered as "a trumpet": "For Black Poets belong to Black People. Are / The Flutes of black Lovers. Are / The Organs of Black Sorrows. Are / The Trumpets of Black Warriors / Let all Black Poets die as trumpets / And be buried in the dust of marching feet."

(For further information about Knight's life and works, see *Black Writers; Contemporary Authors*, Vols. 21-24; *Contemporary Authors New Revision Series*, Vol. 23; *Contemporary Literary Criticism*, Vol. 40; and *Dictionary of Literary Biography*, Vol. 41: *Afro-American Poets since 1955.*)

PRINCIPAL WORKS

Poems from Prison (poetry) 1968
A Poem for Brother/Man (after His Recovery from an O. D.) (poetry) 1972
Belly Song and Other Poems (poetry) 1973
Born of a Woman: New and Selected Poems (poetry) 1980
The Essential Etheridge Knight (poetry) 1986

Patricia Liggins Hill (essay date 1980)

[*In the excerpt below, Hill maintains that Knight's works of poetry—particularly his prison poems—function as a liberating force for readers.*]

Unless the Black artist establishes a "Black aesthetic" he will have no future at all.... The Black artist must create new forms and new values, sing new songs (or purify old ones) ... must create a new history, new symbols, myths and legends ... , [and] in creating his own aesthetic, must be held accountable for it only to the Black people....

Etheridge Knight's statement on poetics echoes the controversial new Black aesthetic. The credo of the aesthetic, that the primary objective of all Black artistic expression is to achieve social change and moral and political revolution has been developed by LeRoi Jones (Amiri Baraka), Clarence Major, Don L. Lee (Haki Madhubuti), and Etheridge Knight himself. According to Theodore Hudson in *From LeRoi Jones to Amiri Baraka*, the credo of the aesthetic became firmly implanted when Baraka announced in his mid-Sixties poem "Black Art" that Black poetry must function as fists, daggers, and guns to clean up the sordid black experience as well as to "clean out the world for virtue and love." ... [The] society in which Blacks are involved tends to be bound by a vision of reality formulated by whites. The function of the Black artist, therefore, is to break through the boundaries of that vision in order to express the Blackness of his or her people.

The credo of the new aesthetic has been resisted by traditional literary critics.... But these objections have been answered by the new Black poets.... Etheridge Knight vehemently disagrees with the white aesthetic principle that would cover up the Black man's continued enslavement by suggesting that all men have the same problems. In his poem **"On Universalism,"** Knight proclaims: "I see no single thread / That binds me one to all / No universal laws / Of human misery / Create a common cause / Or common history / That ease black people's pains / Nor break black people's chains."

Thus, the new Black poets insist that Black art must stand for the collective consciousness and subconsciousness of Black people in particular. (p. 115)

The poetry of Etheridge Knight does function as a liberating force. Since slavery has been a crucial reality in Black history, much of Knight's poetry focuses on a modern kind of enslavement, imprisonment, and searches for and discovers ways in which a person can be free while incarcerated. While he shares with Baraka, Madhubuti, Major, and the other new Black poets the bond of Black cultural identity (the bond of the oppressed, the bond formed by Black art, etc.), he unlike them, has emerged, after serving an eight-year prison term (1960-1968) for robbery, from a second consciousness of community—a community of criminals, a community which Frantz Fanon calls "the lumpenproletariat," "the wretched of the earth."

Ironically, Knight's major contribution to the new aesthetic derives from this second sense of consciousness, which favorably reinforces his strong collective mentality and identification as a *Black* artist.... [It] is logical that Knight would bring his prison consciousness, in which the individual is institutionally destroyed and the self becomes merely one number among many, to the verbal structure of his transcribed oral verse.

Specifically, what Knight relies on for his prison poetry are various temporal/spatial elements which allow him to merge his personal consciousness with the consciousness of Black people. His reason for using temporal/spatial modalities is obvious: A prison consciousness is preoccupied with the concepts of "time" and "space." In prison, "time" comes to mean "restriction," and "space" implies "confinement." When Knight was in prison, he remembers, for instance, that everyone talked in terms of "time": "How much time are you in for?" or "I have so much time left to do." Furthermore, the idea of space becomes all important to the convict. As Knight recalls, "When I was in prison, my major form of exercise was running. That sense of space, freedom, wide open space, probably comes out in some unconscious way." As a result, in his prison poems, Knight is concerned with freeing "time" and "space" from inertia. In particular, he fuses various elements and definitions of "time" and "space" not only to denote his own imprisonment, but also to connote the present social conditions of Black people in general. In his prison poems Blacks are seen as existing in a void (or what I prefer to term "the violent space," which is also the title of one of his poems), a "space" that must be filled with freedom if the race is to have a future.

In Knight's **"The Violent Space (or when your sister sleeps around for money)"** (*Poems from Prison* . . .), one of his major poetic achievements, both the poet and his sister are depicted as existing in a void. The first three stanzas embody painful reminiscences of a long ago time, in childhood, when the need for freedom was not fully recognized . . . . The poet's sister, as the subtitle of the poem implies, is caught in "the violent space." The refrain of the poem, "(Run sister run—the Bugga man comes!)," calls to mind childhood space, childhood fear and fantasy, from which the poet warns his sister to run. The childhood space is enlarged in the second stanza as the poet reminds her of a previous incident in which she was [stung by a red wasp]. As the third stanza returns in time to the present of the first, the remembrance of the wasp brings the concept of the demon to the poet's mind. He begins to ponder how to lift the wasp/demon's sting from his sister's brow and starts to ask her a series of questions till, out of sustained frustration, he finally asks, "Shall I chant a spell to drive the demon away?"

In the fourth stanza, leaving the reader with the sense of magical time he has established in the previous stanza, the poet changes the time and space of the poem's consciousness:

> In the beginning you were the Virgin Mary,
> And you are the Virgin Mary now.
> But somewhere between Nazareth and Bethlehem
> You lost your name in the nameless void.

The traveling of the pregnant Virgin from Nazareth to Bethlehem, where she delivered her child, becomes a parallel to the situation of the sister in the poem, whom the poet still sees as virginal despite her intercourse and possible pregnancy. Deliberately, Knight has involved the Virgin Mary myth to connote the suffering and oppression of the Black woman. His sister seems to be suffering physically from the hostile environment's sting (Knight's play on the term "WASP"), which has been

unsuccessful in touching her soul . . . . [The] poet goes on to promise his sister the freedom that they both desire . . . . He foresees a time when Black people can do what they wish without worrying about what the "white eyes" are seeing or the white minds are thinking. Yet he feels unable to effect the needed freedom.

His sense of frustration is carried further in the final stanza . . . . "And what do I do"—the opening line of this stanza may or may not be a question (there is no question mark). The lines "I boil my tears in a twisted spoon / And dance like an angel on the point of a needle" suggest the ongoing anguish of a prisoner/addict, yet there is hope even though he "can not yet take hold of the demon." His determination to do so is implied. But, for the present time, the poet must be content: "So I grab the air and sing my song./(But the air can not stand my singing long.)" Songs dissipate in the air of "the violent space," a space on the level which separates and entraps the sister and the brother. But if we understand the opening line of the stanza to be a question, we see that, even though the poet now grabs the air to sing his song, he seems to know that the need for freedom will reach such a crisis point in the future that an explosion will occur. The time will come when actions must replace the words of his song. A person cannot live without freedom, for by doing so, that individual is living in a void, a nothingness, a "violent space."

By defining the poem through space (most notably the progression from the sister's relative space to his own), the poet removes the poem from linear time. Divergent historical times (from that of the Virgin Mary traveling between Nazareth and Bethlehem to the childhood of his sister to her condition at the age of seventeen), mythic and fantasy time (communicated through constant references to the Bugga man, angels, and demons)—these various elements work through space in order to de-emphasize the sense of historical time in regard to the enslavement of Black people. All elements of time are fused into one—the past and present conditions of Black people in "the violent space."

In the poem **"The Idea of Ancestry"** (*Poems from Prison* . . .), which Paul Mariah has hailed as "the best poem of Black cultural history," Knight himself becomes "the violent space." In the first section of the poem, which flows in a Whitmanesque style, the poet is spatially defined in his prison cell:

> Taped to the wall of my cell are 47 pictures: 47
>   black
> faces: my father, mother, grandmothers (1 dead),
>   grand
> fathers (both dead), brothers, sisters, uncles,
>   aunts,
> cousins (1st & 2nd), nieces, and nephews. They
>   stare
> across the space at me sprawling on my bunk. I
>   know
> their dark eyes, they know mine. I know their
>   style,

they know mine. I am all of them, they are all of
   me;
they are farmers, I am a thief, I am me, they are
   thee . . . .

The poet is conscious of the fact that all of his ancestors, except for his smiling, seven-year-old niece, stare at him across the space. He shares the same name as one grandfather, three cousins, three nephews, and one uncle. The uncle is an empty space in the family, just as the poet is. And yet in spite of the poet's being an empty space, he takes a Whitmanesque stance in the poem: He stands at the center of his universe, his ancestry, and sings, "I am all of them, they are all of me." But he realizes his separation from his ancestry as well: "they are farmers, I am a thief, I am me, they are thee."

The prosaic quality of the first section of the poem is striking. For the most part, it takes on the narrative qualities of an autobiography and flows with long, rolling, sonorous lines controlled by the breath of the poet; declarative statements; story-like details; and specific references to people, places, and actions. The soothing, sweet-flowing rhythms in Part I reflect the poet's reminiscences about his relationships with his relatives—memories that are filled with warmth, gentleness, regret, and nostalgia.

In Part II, the pace quickens. The thoughts recollected by examining the pictures of his relatives on his cell wall (in Part I) lead the poet gradually to a retelling of his personal ritual of suffering . . . . "Each Fall," the poet enacts the ritual of return to the home of his ancestry. From this mythic sense of time, the poet switches to direct references and specific definitions of time: "Last yr . . . That night . . . ." The experience is relived, but with qualification: " . . . I had almost caught up with me." The rhythms in Part II explode with violence. Separations are made: "That night I looked at my grandmother / and split / my guts were screaming for junk ; . . ." The slashes, which are absent in Part I of the poem, crowd several activities into one sentence: "I walked barefooted in my grandmother's backyard / I smelled the old / land and woods / I sipped corn-whiskey from fruit jars with the men / I flirted with the women / I had a ball till the caps ran out / and my habit came down." Words collide at the slashes to build up the tension evident in the countercurrents of the poet's life: "birthstream / I hitchhiked," "backyard / I smelled," "woods / I sipped cornwhiskey," "men / I flirted with the women," "junk / but I was almost / contented." The crackling sounds explode with meaning: The poet uses such terms as "croaker" (doctor) and "crib" (house) for their harsh alliterative impact.

In the last lines of the final stanza, the quickened pace exhausted, the drama rests:

> This yr there is a grave stone wall damming my
>   stream, and when
> the falling leaves stir my genes, I pace my cell or
>   flop on my bunk
> and stare at 47 black faces across the space. I am
>   all of them,

they are all of me, I am me, they are thee, and I
   have no sons
to float in the space between.

"Time" and "space" have traveled full circle in the poem—back to the present condition of the poet in his cell. But whereas the space between the poet and the pictures described in the first stanza is chiefly the distance between his bunk and the wall where the pictures hang, the last notation of space in the poem involves the galvanization of the poet's genes—his sense of ancestry. He has no sons to hold his ritualistic space within the family. No sons of his are marked in the family Bible. This is a quiet time of despair for the poet: "they are farmers, I am a thief." Now, *he* is "the violent space," an entity separate from his ancestry. He is different: At this moment in the time and space of the poem, he has no physical linkage to his history, his family. And, unfortunately, because he is imprisoned, he can do nothing at present about the situation. The spatial/temporal movement of the poem is carried along by the tide of his music: from the very concrete reality of a prison cell, to a ritual revitalization of a sense of ancestry through a returning home, to this year when there will be no re-enactment of the ritual and no one to move for him: "I have no sons / to float in the space between." With this line the poem reaches an abrupt halt. The reader then becomes aware of the vastness of space, "the violent space," which follows the line.

The form of the poem as well as the idea of ancestry in the poem also represents the problem of ancestral lineage for the Black race as a whole. Many Blacks, such as Knight himself, can only trace their ancestral lineage back two or three generations because of the conditions of Black slavery which were imposed on them. (pp. 115-18)

In **"Cell Song"** . . . , Knight explores the possibilities of the freedom of mind and spirit while in "the violent space" of imprisonment . . . . In the poem, Knight is awakened by the "Slanted Light" which "strike[s] the cave / of sleep." The light which is slanted appears to be apocalyptic in nature, since it penetrates the cave of sleep—perhaps, the subconscious mind. He begins to "tread the red circle" and twist the empty, violent space of his existence with speech. The slanted light apparently reveals to him a poetic vision. It instructs him to ritualize his words, to use his words to promote action, perhaps social change: "take / your words and scrape / the sky, shake rain / on the desert, sprinkle / salt on the tail / of a girl." Apparently, by the end of the poem, Knight has answered his own question: "can there anything / good come out of / prison." There is no question mark. The answer is obviously yes. The poet's words can penetrate through the prison walls and fill the void of "the violent space." (p. 118)

Etheridge Knight's prison poetry, by means of its temporal/spatial references and movements, liberates the minds and spirits of his readers, and of his people as a whole. At times, the poet leads the reader from a concrete definition of space into a space that refuses definition. And he controls time with the same fluidity. Space can be a movement which is defined through time, as in **"The Idea of Ancestry"**; and time can be, as the poem **"He Sees through Stone"** demonstrates, a movement defined through space. In **"The Violent Space,"** these patterns regularly reverse, yet the reader is never lost inside the structure of Knight's poems because, at one point or another, the poet offers a concrete reference grounded in either time or space. In **"The Violent Space,"** for example, the poet says, in the third stanza, "You are all of seventeen and as alone now / In your pain as you were . . . "; in **"He Sees through Stone,"** the reader knows where the old man is sitting; and, in **"The Idea of Ancestry,"** the poet stares at his prison cell wall. The poet's constant use of such references and time/space movements serve an important function: They allow him to merge his consciousness with the consciousness of his people. As a result, his personal prison experiences become a microcosm of the collective experiences of Black people.

That Knight means for his prison experiences to serve as a microcosm of the freedomless void that his people are experiencing is made clear in the "Preface" to his anthology *Black Voices from Prison:*

> From the time the first of our fathers were bound and shackled and herded into the dark hold of a "Christian" slaveship—right on up to the present day, the whole experience of the black man in America can be summed up in one word: prison . . . and it is all too clear that there is a direct relationship between men behind prison walls and men behind myriad walls that permeate society . . . .

While Knight was "inside" prison, he was constantly aware that other Blacks resided in the "larger prison outside" . . . . The "inside" and "outside" prison experiences become interchangeable within the structure of Knight's poems by means of his concrete references and temporal/spatial movements. These references and movements allow the poet to lead his reader, via the heightened experience of good poetry, to a mythic consciousness in which all space is "the violent space" and all time is eternal. Knight imparts this consciousness, its time and its space, to his people as a unifying force. The human being's particular way of experiencing time and space is his only way of knowing life itself. It *is* life for him, it *is* vital. If this conception of time and space is held in common by a people, they achieve a group identity.

Knight brings this conception of group identification to the new Black aesthetic. Yet, ironically, it is this conception that sets him apart from the other new Black poets. While Baraka, Madhubuti, and Major see themselves as poets/priests—as leaders, teachers, and/or spokesmen of the Black revolutionary movement of the 1960s and '70s—, Knight sees himself as being one with Black people. Whereas Major, Madhubuti, and Baraka seem to share W. E. B. Du Bois's vision of the social structure of the Black community—that a "talented tenth," a Black intelligentsia, must lead and uplift the masses of Black people—, Knight identifies closely with

the folk . . . . He is one with the only participants, his race as a whole. Knight's reliance on various time/space elements for group identification is successful: His poetry functions as a vital, liberating force for the new rites. As Gwendolyn Brooks has said of Knight's poetry in her preface to his *Poems from Prison,* the writing embodies "a Blackness that is at once inclusive, possessed and given, freed and terrible and beautiful." . . . This is the particular way of living Blackness that Etheridge Knight expresses. (pp. 119-20)

> *Patricia Liggins Hill, "'The Violent Space': The Function of the New Black Aesthetic in Etheridge Knight's Prison Poetry," in* Black American Literature Forum, *Vol. 14, No. 3, Fall, 1980, pp. 115-21.*

Darryl Pinckney (essay date 1981)

[*In the following excerpt, Pinckney offers a generally negative review of* Born of a Woman, *noting that the new poems in the work "do not indicate much artistic growth."*]

A critic who is young and not confident in his scholarship should not write about poetry, particularly if he—or she—dislikes the work under consideration. It does not help the young critic to go about knocking poets who take themselves seriously. It does not help poetry—not that poetry needs help from anyone. If, however, a critic has chosen a subject—Afro-American literature, for example—perhaps he might discover something in thinking about the works of Jay Wright and Etheridge Knight, two American poets who are also black men. (p. 306)

The poems brought together in *Born of a Woman* are, for the most part, simple to the point of being facile, even crude. . . . Knight's subjects include the loneliness of prison cells, women leaving, trying to kick drugs, black musicians, family feeling, Malcolm X, politics—a wide range of experience and admirable concerns. That is not the problem. Anything can be the occasion for a poem. But not just anything on the page makes for a poem. Etheridge Knight writes in a loose, funky style associated with the Sixties and black militancy, a period that was loud and noisy with talk against the tyranny of so-called white poetics. (p. 310)

The history of literature is a quest for new forms. But many, since the Sixties, seemed to use the call for a new aesthetic as an apologia for the unrendered. Discussions of the oral tradition became popular, as if the oral, in black culture, acquitted the black poet of his—or her—responsibility to the language. Anyone who has heard Robert Hayden's "Runagate Runagate" or Sterling Brown's "The Strong Men" knows that the written and the spoken abide by the same unnameable rules. Those who feel that poetry, in essence, is a performance art ought to join a circus.

The world Knight portrays in his poems is often harsh and brutal. He aspires to a language that will remain true to these experiences, words that will not give any falsifying distance. It makes for a very vigorous and immediate style that is often successful.... Far too often, however, the poems evince that uninteresting tendency to feel that a *rap* is all that need be offered. **"A Poem for 3rd World Brothers"**:

> or they will send their lackeys to kill for them.
> and if those negroes fail
> white/ america will whip out her boss okie doke:
> make miss ann lift the hem of her mystic skirt
> and flash white thighs in your eye to blind
> you....

A rap is not enough, however true, politically, the message is taken. Raps that are trying to pass for poems have a strange redundant quality: we feel we know all this already and not much is going on in the poem to make us see or feel this in a new way. The ordinariness of the imagery makes the poems degenerate into sentimentality, which is a disservice to Knight's capacity for tender expression. "Our love is a rock against the wind, / Not soft like silk or lace." Another danger of the rap is that it dates quickly. There are some poems in which Knight is embarrassingly on the wrong side, such as **"Love Song to Idi Amin."**... (pp. 310-12)

Knight seems to have a fondness for the haiku, which is an acquired taste even when written well.... He is also given to a not very sophisticated use of internal rhyme.... There are moments of painful formal constraint: **"Apology for Apostasy?"**:

> Soft songs, like birds, die in poison air
> So my song cannot now be candy.
> Anger rots the oak and elm; roses are rare,
> Seldom seen through blind despair.

Clumsily deployed rhymes or metrics do not enhance the playfulness or irony of his poems and are disastrous when he is reaching toward the poignant. Knight is best in the more open, rapid, darting poems, such as **"A Conversation with Myself."**... (pp. 312-13)

Knight's **Poems from Prison** brought him recognition when it appeared in 1968, and it is easy to understand why his radical message and comfortable style were so well received. Though Knight has not renounced his interest in investigating the consequences of racism, it is disappointing that the new poems do not indicate much artistic growth. (p. 313)

What can the young critic discover? Only what has always been true and so general that it can hardly count as an insight: the black experience, however real, does not by itself make poetry; it must be turned into art, like everything else. Erudition or mere feeling will not make poetry; African myth or familiarity with prison is, weirdly, not enough. It does not matter that a poet is black. The tradition and demands of the language—in this case, English—matter. A work of art can only be correct in the political sense when it is first correct in the

literary sense, Walter Benjamin wrote. Black poets must be judged by the same standards as for any other poets. Any other considerations are racist. There is no need for a minority admissions program into the canon of literature. Vision and mastery of form are the bootstraps that lift. (p. 314)

> *Darryl Pinckney, "You're in the Army Now,"*
> in Parnassus: Poetry in Review, *Vol. 9, No.
> 1, 1981, pp. 306-14.*

Howard Nelson (essay date 1981)

[*In the following excerpt, Nelson identifies a recurring theme in Knight's poetry: the celebration of human relationships.*]

What keeps us alive? In or out of prison, one answer is other people. "We must love one another or die," as Auden put it. Knight has always been sure to acknowledge this. In the preface to the *Black Voices from Prison* anthology, he acknowledged "Gwendolyn Brooks, Sonia Sanchez, Dudley Randall, and Don L. Lee: black poets whose love and words cracked these walls." In **Born of a Woman,** he gives a list that has grown to over forty people he feels indebted to.

In a way, Knight's poetry itself is another form of acknowledgement. People, relationships between and among people, are his compelling theme; it is present in nearly all his work in one form or another. I want to follow this thread in talking about Knight's poetry.

In **Belly Song** Knight had a nice existential individualist blues fragment, dated 8/72, called **"Evolutionary Poem No. 1"**:

> I ain't got nobody
> that i can depend on
> 'cept myself

In **Born of a Woman** he has followed this piece immediately with **"Evolutionary Poem No. 2,"** in which a switch to the plural pronoun points in a different direction:

> We ain't got nobody
> that we can depend on
> 'cept ourselves.

"No. 2" is dated September 1979, the same date as that of the book's preface, nine months before its publication. Very likely Knight noticed, as he was rereading and reorganizing his work for the new collection, that his earlier statement, though in large ways true for himself and everyone, was counter to the fundamental current running through his poems: the impulse to celebrate nourishing human relationships, to lament their various breakdowns, to protest their betrayals.

On the broadest scale, this impulse appears in a sense of racial solidarity, as in **"Poem for 3rd World Brothers"** and **"For Black Poets Who Think of Suicide,"** both exhortations to blacks to give themselves deeply to the energies and causes of their people. Elsewhere on the spectrum, the same basic theme emerges out of such a small, unexpected incident as the one in **"A WASP Woman Visits a Black Junkie in Prison."** At first outraged by the absurdity of this unasked-for visit from a "prim blue and proper-blooded" stranger, he soon recognizes that it is a situation of one loneliness reaching out toward another, and ultimately he finds himself strangely moved and quieted by the simple exchange they manage to construct.

The theme often appears in the form of celebrations of "heroes" of various kinds. There are poems honoring artists—Langston Hughes, Max Roach, Otis Redding—, and three strong elegies to Malcolm X. There are also other sorts of heroic characters, from Pooky Dee, whose "great 'two 'n' a half' gainer" from a railroad trestle one summer afternoon long ago ended with the sickening "sound of his capped / Skull as it struck the block," and left a permanent scar in his watchers' memories; to Shine, the black stoker on the Titanic in Knight's marvelous version of the folk poem, who rejected the pleas and bribes of various white establishment figures who couldn't stay afloat by themselves, and "swam on"; to Hard Rock, a black convict who refuses to cooperate in his own imprisonment and performs exploits of resistance which end in his lobotomy but also confront the other inmates with an unsettling example of courage and integrity. Each of these people, real or legendary (often both), from Langston Hughes to Hard Rock, has in some form or other given a gift, left a mark, that turns mere existence into reality.

In the last three poems mentioned, there is a blend of vivid lyric and narrative impulses which is typical of Knight. **"Hard Rock,"** for example, is a character sketch and an elegy, a compressed short story and a meditation on moments of intense feeling and realization. Another poem that contains the matter of a story and the music and intensity of a lyric is **"For Freckle-Faced Gerald."** While most of Knight's poems are in one way or another expressions of admiration or gratitude or love—are in one way or another affirmations—in the case of Gerald the most the poet can do is offer grief and outrage in the form of clear-eyed description of his subject's hopeless situation. Truly written and felt, this turns out to be an expression of a kind of love too.

The poem deals with a sixteen-year-old boy who has been sent to prison. In addition to his youth and inexperience, Gerald has going against him his inability even to strike a pose of self-assurance and toughness. Instead, he has "precise speech and an innocent grin." For him, being put in prison amounts, as the poem tersely puts it, to being "thrown in as 'pigmeat' / for the buzzards to eat." The buzzards in prison are the men who exploit Gerald sexually and otherwise. But they are only part of a much larger scenario of exploitation and dehumanization . . . . Knight is as aware of the violations human beings commit against one another, on all levels, in endless forms, as he is of the bonds that help to sustain us. (pp. 3-4)

Another strong character sketch is **"He Sees Through Stone."** It is a portrait of an old black convict, apparently long imprisoned, who has taken on a wisdom that gives him a kind of mythic significance. "Pressed by the sun / against the western wall / his pipe between purple gums," the old man is surrounded by young inmates. Possibly they gather around him to hear stories he has to tell, but the poem does not tell us this. Instead, it describes a more subtle attraction. The poet says, "I have known him / in a time gone by," and goes on to describe a sense in the old man's presence of a timeless guide or initiator who has somehow been with him through all the rites of passage of his life . . . . Apparently the other younger men sense this in him also. It is this recognition that sets up the old man's ability to "see through stone."

In the work of most poets there are certain words or images that recur regularly, in some cases obsessively. Not surprisingly in a poet who spent years in prison, one of Knight's persistent images is stone. It represents not just physical walls and imprisonment, of course; more importantly it stands for emotional barriers, insensitivity, the dead weight in the spirit that needs to be pushed away or penetrated or transformed in order for caring energies to flow again.

There are two kinds of stone in the poem: the stone walls of the prison, and the stone wall each person sets up himself. Knight picks up the slang metaphor "cats" and elaborates its suggestions: the "black cats" "circle," "flash white teeth," "snarl," have "shining muscles." But all this fierceness is a pose, a mask, ultimately another kind of stone wall erected in the name of defense. The old man leaning in the sun against actual stone is not impressed by the posturing. He understands and penetrates it: "he smiles / he knows"—knows the vulnerability that lives behind it. And somehow, the poem suggests, he is consequently a reassuring force, an outer presence who is also an inner presence, a kind of steady witness and companion to the hidden life the self lives within walls within walls.

In a broad sense, about ninety per cent of Knight's work could be called love poetry. And naturally, poems that fit that term in the conventional sense make up an important part of his book. My personal favorites in this category are **"As You Leave Me,"** which creates haunting currents of emotion through imagery of great precision and dramatic effect, and **"Feeling Fucked Up,"** marvelous in its use of sound, a profane litany, a down-to-earth lament, written wonderfully at gut level all the way through to its culminating repetitions . . . . (pp. 5-6)

Another strong group is the poems that deal with family. Some of these take a sort of ritual form—words spoken for important events, such as a birth (**"On the Birth of a Black/Baby/Boy"**) or an escape from death (**"Another Poem for Me—after Recovering from an O.D."**). There are straight-forward elegies, such as **"The Bones of My Father,"** and anecdotes, as in the warm, low-key **"Talking in the Woods with Karl Amorelli."** Also within this group are two poems which, rightfully, have usually been among those representing Knight in anthologies: **"The Idea of Ancestry"** and **"The Violent Space."** (p. 6)

I want to...[discuss a] key element in Knight's work...: sound. [**Born of a Woman**] is laced together by Knight's unabashed sense of verbal music, right down to the titles of its three sections: "Inside-Out," "Outside-In," "All About—And Back Again." But I want to talk about sound not just in terms of poetic devices within poems, but also in terms of the actual spoken voice, the whole question of how we read and appreciate poetry.

I know that many people don't consider it quite legitimate to talk in criticism about poetry as a spoken, performed thing. There are various reasons for this. In America, most people who read poetry have been conditioned to think that the poem on the page is what really matters. (It is—but not exclusively.) Contributing to this is a training that leads us to think of poetry as a set of ideas and techniques rather than as an experience that includes them, the notion that there is an equation between greatness in poetry and how much explication it will sustain, and a condescension toward poetry whose strength lies in direct oral communication of emotion. We're suspicious of poetry which doesn't seem to have the impact on the page that it did when we heard it read well aloud. This is sometimes valid, but one needs to be careful here. Just as the poem must do its work well, so must the reader. I have often seen poems undervalued or misunderstood because of failures of aural (i.e., oral) imagination on the part of readers.

Ironically, the proliferation of poetry readings in recent years has also fed the prejudice against poetry in its oral incarnation. I certainly wouldn't deny that poetry readings can be creepy and tedious occasions, or that some poets are such poor readers that they do their audience and poetry a disservice when they give a reading. On the other hand, there is a cranky, reactionary attitude that is blind to the fact that it is fundamentally proper and healthy that poetry is being read aloud to audiences across the country....

In the years since his release from prison Etheridge Knight has earned his living principally by giving poetry readings. He is an excellent reader. His deep, resonant voice is a gift. He is sensitive to the rhythms and inflections of poetry and "ordinary" speech, and he is sensitive to his audiences and knows how to reach them. As a black poet he stands in a living tradition of toast-tellers, rhymers, and singers. He believes that poetry is most fully itself when it is spoken aloud to other people; and as I've said, his poems have an immediacy and music that lend themselves to that kind of presentation. So I suppose he has all the qualifications to be called an oral poet. (p. 9)

My point is simply that reading poetry aloud is fundamental to the art, and that oral presentation draws forces out of the words which otherwise lie in them to some degree lost or wasted. Some poems lose more than others in a reading that doesn't do justice to their oral

aspects, but whether one is reading *The Waste Land* or "After Apple-Picking" or "The Windhover" or "The Sea Elephant" or "The Navajo Night Chant," one needs really to hear the sounds, the tones, the voices, to truly receive the poem. Poetry readings—good ones, such as Etheridge Knight or Allen Ginsberg or Donald Hall or Gwendolyn Brooks or Galway Kinnell or William Heyen, for example, are capable of giving—become therefore not only heartening public performances but lessons we might learn in trying to become better readers ourselves—of all poetry, not just that of the poets we've heard reading.

In relation to these ideas, consider Knight's **"Ilu, the Talking Drum."** The best way to learn to read this poem is to hear Knight's extraordinary rendering of it, but this is not essential. While it's true that probably no one else could speak the poem as well as he does, it has its power within its words and will have still a hundred years from now.

The theme is again a human relationship, and in this case the poem describes how sound and rhythm themselves can create a bond among people. The poet is with a group of fifteen Nigerians. The setting is somewhat ambiguous, except for the fact that it is alien. A mood of torpor and restlessness hangs over them, and is communicated largely through the sounds of the words. We begin in a chafing silence: "The stillness was skinny and brittle and wrinkled." Those stingy, shallow i sounds are soon picked up again, joined by sharp p's, t's, and s's and bald long a's: "We twisted, turned, shifted positions, picked our noses, / stared at our bare toes, hissed air through our teeth..." The stifling tedium is also conveyed through a series of monosyllabic phrases using doubled, very ordinary adjectives: "wide green lawn," "wide white porch," "big white house."

A breakthrough occurs, however, when one of the Nigerians rises and begins to play a rhythm on "Ilu, the talking drum." The emotional change is announced before it begins to happen, through sound—the entrance of long, open o's and u's: "Then Tunji, green robes flowing, as he rose, strapped on Ilu, the talking drum." It is in what follows that the poem becomes either boring or marvelous, depending on how we read. The drum speaks, and Knight lets us hear it:

> kah doom/kah doom-doom/kah doom/kah doom-
>   doom-doom
> kah doom/kah doom-doom/kah doom/kah doom-
>   doom-doom
> kah doom/kah doom-doom/kah doom/kah doom-
>   doom-doom
> kah doom/kah doom-doom/kah doom/kah doom-
>   doom-doom

If one follows habits learned from reading newspapers and most other prose, and skims over this as if it were so much filler, the point of the poem is missed. But if one reads the words carefully, actually sensing the reverberations, one is pulled inside a rhythmic flow that stands for life itself. In the next stanza Knight does in fact

Dust jacket of Knight's 1980 book of poems, which takes its title from the book of Job: "Man that is born of a woman is of few days and full of trouble."

identify the drum beat with the heart beat. Much repetition; generous sound; a profound theme . . . . (p. 10)

At the end of the poem Knight suggests the great human distances that can be spanned within such sound, the freshened consciousness and sense of liberation it can create. Then he closes with the drum beat. When the poem ends there is an amazing silence, in which we seem to hear the echoes of the drum, or possibly it is the buried sound of our own blood beating—a very different silence from that which the opening of the poem described. **"Ilu, the Talking Drum"** is a marvelous poem, with rich veins of music and meaning and feeling. But it needs to be read truly.

There are other chant-like poems in **Born of a Woman,** such as **"We Free Singers Be"** and, especially, **"Belly Song."** But the book as a whole, from the incantatory effects of **"Ilu"** and **"Belly Song,"** to the fine unsolemn repetitions of **"Feeling Fucked Up"** and **"Welcome Back, Mr. Knight: Love of My Life,"** to the simple refrains of **"It Was a Funky Deal"** and **"I and Your Eyes,"** to the small, tight rhymes of **"A Shakespearean Sonnet: To a Woman Liberationist,"** to notations like **"Cop-Out Session,"** where the music is just the live

music of black speech itself (working everywhere in Knight's poems): the whole book is wound around sound—vigorous, invigorating sound . . . .

Born of a Woman contains a harsh, generous, beautiful poetry. It is breath of life. (p. 11)

> *Howard Nelson, "Belly Songs: The Poetry of Etheridge Knight," in* The Hollins Critic, *Vol. XVIII, No. 5, December, 1981, pp. 1-11.*

Etheridge Knight with Steven C. Tracy (interview date 1985)

[*In the following 1985 interview, Knight and Tracy discuss writing by black poets, by black women novelists, and by the author himself. In the preface to the interview, Tracy states: "I picked Knight up at his hotel at 8:00 a.m. the day after his reading [at the University of Cincinnati]. After he paid his bill, we stopped by a United Dairy Farmers store to pick up a six-pack of Stroh's beer before arriving at my apartment, where the interview took place. Because Knight is currently doing some work with Afro-American toasts, I played him recordings of 'Signifyin' Monkey' and 'Hey Shine' by Snatch and the Poontangs and*

Will Shade's version of 'The Dirty Dozens' while I set up the equipment for the interview. Finally, with echoes of 'clock on the mantel piece goin' tick, tick, tick' coming from the Shade recording, we settled down to the interview before he left at 12:00 noon for his flight.']

[Tracy]: *I'd like to go back to Mississippi for awhile—judging from "A Poem for Myself" you won't mind. It seems that a lot of Black writers who are Southern born and raised are heavily influenced by their Southern background: its folkways, customs, traditions, etc. Richard Wright, John O. Killens, Margaret Walker, and others have been shaped artistically by their background. What impact has Mississippi had on the shaping of your art?*

[Knight]: I think a great deal. In the first place it's where I learned the American language. The stories and the music. Growing up in the South, especially in the country, the main forms of—not entertainment is not the right word—*recreating*, was done mainly through music, songs, and story-telling. Poems and things. So my view of the world was shaped by the people that I came in contact with who—guitar players, and played the harmonica, and the storytellers. And I think this is generally true of any writer, Black or white, whether they grew up in the South or North. I think that's generally true. But growing up in the South, the two main influences, naturally, were the blues and country and western. I mean those are the two musics that you hear all the time. It fills the airways. You turn on the radio and you're gonna hear the Grand Ole Opry, you know what I mean, and we listened to the Grand Ole Opry just about as much as anybody else did. And I think the guitars probably, and the harmonica, because those are talking instruments. And almost every place there would be storytellers, so the stories and the songs were generally about the economy, about country peoples' lives. You know, their loves, their fights, their hates, their hardships. And so that's how my consciousness was developed. It's the only way... and as I say I think that's true of any artist. That frame of reference is what I grew up with.

Do you think that predisposed you to being a poet? I think you said last night that you had written poetry before you were in prison, but you didn't think any of it was any good. What kind of poems were you writing before you were in prison?

Oh, I'd make up poems that... about the dozens for me. And then stories about who's messing with whose old lady. Sometimes there'd be a big fight or catastrophies. Any event, I'd tell about them and I'd tell about them in rhyme, mainly.

You said you were a great dozens player: could you whip off a dozens right now? Can you go with that?

Well...

> I saw your mama laying on the railroad track.

> Fucking all the engineers and she like it like that.

You know. You're always talking, you're always... usually it's about the person's mother and—I've forgotten a lot of them. You would say like,

> Somebody told me that your mama was a whore
> And your sister started turning tricks on the cabin
>   floor,
> And your brother's a punk and he likes it even
>   more.

You know, you just talking about things like that. And in school. It's a pretty cruel thing. The ability to talk is a power. I learned that very young, that the people who could rap and write, you didn't have to fight as much. You know, it was my weapon.

I'd like to talk about your use of blues and jazz figures and motifs in your poetry. You've written poems about blues people, or using blues people in them, and also your own blues songs. You have several of those. Some folklorists and blues researchers have argued that the blues have no place on the printed page. Paul Oliver writes that,

> *Blues is for singing. It is not a form of folk song that stands up particularly well when written down... The beauty of the blues resides so often in the relationship of the vocal and the words expressed to the music that it is a part of. As folk art in its origins and popular art today, it is remarkable, but to date, it has not been a convincing source for an ethnic literature.*

Do you think that the blues belongs on the printed page, that it can stand up on the page?

I think the blues can stand up on the page just about as much as a poem can or a story can. You know, where he's off base is that it's *all* oral. You know, the short story, the novel is an extension of the storyteller; a poem on the page is an extension of the bard. *Any* song does not stand up well on the page as it is—nothing stands as well on the page as it is out loud. So I mean that whole shit, that's bullshit. You know blues stands up on the page just about as well as a poem does. In fact, that's what a blues song is: a poem, a lyrical poem. So I think his separation is off base. The spoken word, and since it's all, it's primarily, oral, none of it stands up on the page as well as it does out loud.

How do the blues that you write differ from "traditional" blues lyrics?

I think if there's any difference at all, the subject matter is more contemporary. See, a lot of these fucking blues scholars and folklorists place their authority for lore as something in the past. I'm a toast-teller—lore goes on right now. Lore exists right now. People are telling stories and are saying toasts in the jails and prisons right now. Lore is not something just happened back in the thirties or twenties—lore is going on right now. Blues are going on now. So that whole... sure, there's an authority that stems from the past, you know. "Old John Lee Hooker," the song back in 1920. Well, hell, there's better blues singers singing right now. I mean, to me, art is always right now. It is contemporary. So that's a lie that lore has to be something past. Lore exists right now. I mean, the term itself, "lore." You know folk*lore* is something that people talk about at the time: Folklore, the stories people told in the past are, to me, not as good as lore that is going on now. Because they didn't have as much information. And the songs and the poems and the stories that they made up were dealing with their times. They were not concerned somebody in 1983 heard it; they were concerned somebody in 1933 heard it. And that's the way I am. (pp. 7-10)

As far as Black writing is concerned now, it seems that current appeal leans more toward Black women novelists. You were talking about writing for Black male audiences. Toni Morrison, Toni Cade Bambara, Paule Marshall, Alice Walker seem to have captured more attention than other Black writers. What do you think accounts for the interest of the Black female audience and what do you think about works like The Color Purple *or* The Song of Solomon *for example?*

What I think accounts for it is that a lot of the Black male writers have grown fat, you know, they may have positions at universities, and they still mainly trying to break into the literary world, and Black women, the sociology of this country, the politics of this country, they feel a double edge being a woman and being Black. Lots of Black male writers who were speaking during the 60's and you don't hear them anymore because they aren't being kicked in the ass as hard. Black women are getting kicked in the ass harder; therefore, their creative impulse is greater... their voices are clearer. That's the main reason... Black women, ... you hear more about them because of that. They're Black and they're women. Generally speaking, in poetry, in my opinion, to me, the best poetry that is being sung around this country now is being sung by women, white and Black.

Such as?

Such as Denise Levertov, Gwendolyn Brooks, Elizabeth McKim, Anne Waldman, Audre Lorde, Adrienne Rich, Marge Piercy, Margaret Atwood, Sonia Sanchez, Nikki Giovanni, you know, across the board. To me, they ain't bullshitting. They know the language; they're masters of the language. The things that they are addressing are relevant and, not only Black male writers, but white male writers also fool around with irrelevant shit. That's why they ain't getting published and women are: because women are honed in on what's very relevant.

So you consider yourself a secondary audience to a woman writer? You were talking about primary and secondary audiences.

Yeah... of course some work that I feel that if we have to start labeling work "protest work," I feel that the direct address of some women writers are to a male audience to try to maybe educate and sensitize or complain. But I think their best work is when they are addressing their primary audience, and it's pretty clear.

If I talk clearly about my loneliness to an audience, if I'm saying a poem about loneliness in jail or fear in prison and there are some people in the audience that have been in prison or in jail, the evocativeness is easier and it's not the same as when I'm talking clear enough about my own loneliness or pain, that other people cannot relate to it. The nuances are images, and the images personally come out; language and art come out of the lives of groups of people. We live in an ethnic world. We way away from universal. We're not even provincial yet and the language and the references come out of our economics, our politics, our life situations. You know, a guy who has spent his life mainly in, say, in the Northwest, where lumber, cutting down trees and stuff, the metaphors are gonna be made up...the language is a living...it's actually a living organism. And language comes into being basically out of our economy. We develop metaphors and similes that relate directly to our life situation, mainly our economy. You know, that's what we'll start likening things to. So...Heather McHugh has a poem entitled "Housewife." I like the poem, you know. I read it a lot. And I read it, I can see in it audience, I can watch the audience, and I can see it affects women in the audience differently than it affects men. That's what I mean.

Nathan Scott has written in the Howard Guide to Contemporary American Writing *that Richard Wright is the presiding genius of the new Black urban poetry. What do you think about that?*

That Richard Wright is...

... is the presiding genius of the new Black urban poetry.

Uh-huh. If I had to name any one person it'd be Amiri Baraka. I don't think so. I don't see Richard Wright as a poet at all.

I think he was speaking about the tone of anger in his work, and as that being something traceable to Wright.

The militant tone? No, I still wouldn't say so. If I understand what you're saying that Richard Wright.... There was anger and protest in his poetry, but Richard Wright's audience was mainly white people. And Richard Wright was constantly writing protest and constantly moving. One could never get a sense of place in his work, as you can say in Killens or Baraka, I mean, or Faulkner. And it has to do with power. Take, for instance, two Mississippi writers: Faulkner and Wright. Faulkner, being a white man, had such a sense of power that he literally created a whole county. Everywhere you walked was in that. In good art, good poetry or prose, there's a definite sense of time and place. And Wright, you remember his novels, was constantly moving. You remember now, the one, you know the guy gets killed in a subway accident and takes another identity and goes. And Wright's life was like that, you know. From Mississippi to Memphis to Chicago to New York to Paris; he had no sense of place. So it was not the kind of militancy that I see in the novels of, say now of John Williams, you know. I mean, he brought to light a lot of social injustices everybody else knew, but he kept moving, you know. Not to... I think he's one of the greatest writers around. But, no, I don't think he... I think Baraka was, in answer to that question.

Back in the late 60's, and early 70's when Randall's Broadside Press introduced many of your works and those of Sonia Sanchez, Nikki Giovanni and Haki Madhubuti, the four of you were recognized as a group of young Black poets who had a very positive influence on Black Americans, especially the youth. In what specific ways do you feel your poetry positively influenced Black youth?

Generally, in the same way that any poetry positively influences anybody who hears it. As far as Black youths are concerned—art requires a relationship between the artist and one's audience, and that relationship has to be freedom. It has to be free. And, I mean, you cannot force art on anybody, you know what I mean; they have to be open to it. And what you address is that part of the person, what freedom is. And essentially I think that poetry... we all human beings know on some level that we are good. No matter how many of the outer authorities—our parents, the law, the judges, the segregation laws—say otherwise, the historians say otherwise. We all human beings know on some level that we are good. And we ought to be free. So, when Black poets start singing to Black youths that they are good and they deserve to be free and that they are oppressed they instantly say, "Well, hey." You know, that's that thing of... Robert Bly talks about the "Ah!" in poetry. Sometimes, you know, you be reading a poem and you listen to music and you say, "Ah!" It's that "Ah!" that happens. I think feeling like that to hear an outer authority affirm what they already felt, that's all art does. That's all art does really. You know.

Some critics have distinguished your poetry from some of your contemporaries, specifically some of the early Broadside poets, by pointing to the personal reflection and perhaps introspection in some of your poems that was absent in some of the other poets. In other words, some of your poems probe inner conflicts and turmoils of the individual, while many of the other poets spoke for the collective. But you've also suggested that the Black artist must "perceive and conceptualize the collective aspirations, the collective vision of Black people, and through his art form give back to the people the truth he has gotten from them." Do you agree with what the critics have said about you in deference to your other contemporary poets? And how do you reconcile the individual with the collective aspirations—the exploration of the inner conflicts with presenting the collective aspirations of Black people?

Well, you listen. You pay attention to what's going on outside of you and what's going on inside of you, and if you pretty much tell the truth, express in such a way that your audience recognizes it's valid and recognizes those same feelings. Again, the poetry is evocative, and then you know that you're generally speaking the truth. You

know, we might react differently but if a three-headed bird flew in this window, I'm going to get scared, you know you might keep a cool face, you know. I might jump up and say "aah." If I know myself pretty well, I know you scared too. I operate from that point. I believe that one has to move from the "I," subjective, through the verb, to the "we." If I verbalize, see, I am a Black male in this country and if I, through my own self-examination, expressed that, I bet you I'm pretty much going to be hitting what most other Black males feel. A poet should speak only for himself; the "I." That's what always gets me when I hear some of these critics talking about "I've read this book objectively." There ain't no such thing. As soon as I hear this word "objectively" I throw it away because I know they're bullshitting. There is no way you can approach art objectively. Art is not an objective thing, you know, but in our language now when one says I'm being objective, that's as if to say I'm being truthful. That's a lie. The truth is more in subjectivity than objectivity.

Back in the late 60's and early 70's Black writers shared a common purpose, a common objective: to use their art as a vehicle toward social, political, moral revolution. Many seem to have spoken as a collective, but now there are many voices addressing many and varied issues. What do you feel accounts for the changes that have occurred among Black writers over the last decade and a half; or do you think it has changed?

I think it's changed somewhat and one of the reasons is America's ability to co-opt. Some Black poets, like any other poets, were simply protesting. And all that you have to do when someone is protesting is to satisfy what it is they are protesting. Poetry in the world, all art, is essentially revolutionary because it essentially appeals to freedom. And art cannot exist in an oppressive society and the more oppressive the society, the louder the artist will work, you know, whether it's a poet or painter or what. Sometimes they will escape. It happened in America especially among a lot of the whites, they expatriated. Take Pound and Eliot; rather than become revolutionary they retreated into the past, into Europe, history, and their vision became narrow. They had no vision of a bright future. Some of them jump off bridges, some find some kind of retreat into the past— Hemingway, for instance. All of that whole time of expatriating of American artists was because of the oppressiveness. We were a country who was concerned more with the material than the immaterial. This country is very culturally deprived. I often laugh when they say minority children are being culturally deprived. Bullshit! You know, when their lives are filled with art, with music, song and dance and sight. Somebody made a statement about critics and their evaluation of art and how they always seem to "be objective" in a vacuum, and art does not exist in a vacuum. Art exists within a context, a political, economic, and social context and the only real critics of any artist is that artist's audience. You know what I mean. Really.

You began speaking of Eliot and Pound, people like that. When we think of the haiku *we generally connect that with Pound—as having brought it into the language, along with people like Hulme and Stevens also employing it. What motivated you to use* haiku *as a form? Where'd you get it from?*

From Gwendolyn Brooks. Yeah, she's the first one turned me on to *haiku.* She used to come visit me when I was in prison. And this is in the Sixties, remember, this is long before they had poets in the prison programs and poets in schools. I mean, she just came on her own; she wasn't getting paid for it or anything. And she brought me some books and Japanese *haiku.* Years later I asked her how come and she said, "it was because you were too wordy in your poems." And I like *haiku.* I try to use it, I try to follow the general form. I try to bring my own American consciousness to it. You know. I try to do with the *haiku* just about what Ray Charles does with country and western. You know what I'm saying? I like them because you gotta deal with the noun and the verb. You ain't got too much time to fool around with some abstractions, you know, a lot of adverbs and adjectives and stuff. But I like them.

That's a good teacher, though, to see what you're doing wrong in your poetry and then just bring you in things to read. Instead of saying "You're too wordy," or, you know, "just start cutting out words." Just bring stuff in to read to you.

Yeah. Yeah, she's my favorite. I watch her. Her, Dudley Randall, Robert Bly, Galway Kinnell, Sonia—I watch her. I listen to Nikki Giovanni a lot, too. I trust her instincts. I haven't seen her in a long time, ain't talked to her in a long time, but essentially I figure when I hear her, you know I've seen her read—I figure she pretty much knows what she's doing. You know. A lot of poets, a few Black poets, kind of like turned a little negative. That's something else that I found that does not happen as much among Black poets as among white poets is competition. Because I personally don't feel that competition has any place in art—one cannot be creative competing. You know, it's not a question of who's the best poet or who's the worst poet. If you wind up doing that shit you won't be addressing honestly your own audience, you'll be screwing around competing with other poets. And I take poetry seriously. I think poetry is a serious form of communication. It's essential for me. I think I can pretty much say that poetry has kept me sane.

And when you read your poems there's quite a lot of humor and quite a lot of interaction. I know last night as you read your poems there was quite a lot of laughter in response to the poems that you read. So it's a serious business but you do treat those aspects of experience that evoke that kind of response in people.

Yeah, I don't think that poets should confuse themselves with preachers. At times, sure. At times the audience feels like it, especially if the audience feels like being slapped on the wrist. But I think a good poet understands the direct relationship between the poet, the poem, and the people. I see the art of poetry as this trinity. You can't have one without the other. The poet-person, the poem and the audience. And they're *equally* important, and I never assume that an audience does not have feelings and sense just like I do. You know what I mean? To me, good art both entertains and enlightens. OK. Too much entertainment and you get bullshit. You know what I mean, it's a jackoff. People laugh, and then they go away not feeling any differently about things and not looking at things any differently. But too much, just enlightenment, too much preaching and no entertainment. You know, take some comedians. Dick Gregory, for instance. He teaches and have you laughing at the same time, you know. Learning and laughing. You know. Well, that's a good way. But I definitely believe that poetry should entertain and enlighten at the same time. (pp. 13-19)

We've been kind of talking about this all along, but just as a kind of summarizing statement—what do you feel is your primary mission as a Black artist?

Hmm. The word "mission" bothers me.

Why?

It makes it sound a little theological, a little . . . I think my primary thrust or mission is to tell as clearly as possible what it is that I feel and think about my world and my relationship with my world—other people and myself and nature and with gods, as I see them. As Baraka say, "The duty of a poet is to say as exactly as possible what it is he or she means." Because what you're dealing with is so intangible. It's why we have to speak in similes and parables and metaphors. You can't speak in the language of the technocrat. And I think my primary duty is to stay in touch with myself and be as true as I possibly can in examining myself, and to communicate that to other people and to let them know that I am essentially a good human being and that they are too. And that's what communication is. I've had some readings that—and you can tell when a good reading go down, because people start talking to each other, they'll start touching. *That's* the art. *That's* when the art happens. The art happens when the poet and the poem and the people are in communion. It's communication happening. Art doesn't happen in a book. Or a picture hanging on that wall. You know, it takes people. You know what I mean? It ain't no such thing as a masterpiece—you could paint, hang a Picasso in a school for the blind, and it's never looked at, it ain't no masterpiece. It takes people there to see it. A poem is the same way. People have to hear it, or read it. There ain't no masterpieces in the library. They ain't being read, you know what I mean? So that's what I think my main mission is—is to speak and sing as exactly as possible what it is that I feel and think, and a few things that I know about me and my relationship with the world. (p. 23)

Etheridge Knight and Steven C. Tracy, in an interview in MELUS, *Vol. 12, No. 2, Summer, 1985, pp. 7-23.*

FURTHER READING

Crowder, Ashby Bland. "Etheridge Knight: Two Fields of Combat." *Concerning Poetry* 16, No. 2 (Fall 1983): 23-25.
  Discusses Knight's "2 Poems for Black Relocation Centers" as a work about black men who are victimized by "white racist America."

Hill, Patricia Liggins. "'Blues for a Mississippi Black Boy': Etheridge Knight's Craft in the Black Oral Tradition." *Mississippi Quarterly* XXXVI, No. 1 (Winter 1982-83): 21-33.
  Explores the influence of the black oral tradition on Knight's work. The critic writes: "By extending the literary/artistic dimensions of the blues, toasts and African musical/art forms and idioms without losing their authenticity, [Knight] functions as the traditional/communal blues singer for his contemporary era: he delivers the call for his race to return to its elemental self—its African spirituality and its Southern ancestral roots."

Pinsker, Sanford. "A Conversation with Etchridge Knight." *Black American Literature Forum* 18, No. 1 (Spring 1984): 11-14.
  Interview with the poet. Pinsker and Knight discuss the concepts of black aesthetics and "poeting."

Vendler, Helen. "Good Black Poems One by One." *The New York Times Book Review* (29 September 1974): 3, 10, 14, 16.
  Examines works by Dudley Randall, Haki R. Madhubuti, Sonia Sanchez, Audre Lorde, and Etheridge Knight.

George Lamming

1927-

(Full name George William Lamming) Barbadian novelist, poet, and essayist.

Lamming, a Barbadian novelist, is known for works that explore the colonial experience of the West Indies. In novels commended for their nationalism and poetic prose style, he has depicted the enduring effects of European colonization on the West Indies and portrayed the West Indian search for a distinct political, economic, and cultural identity free from the influence of early colonial rule.

Born in Barbados in 1927, Lamming has witnessed and participated in much of the social and political upheaval that has taken place in the West Indies during his lifetime. Throughout the 1930s, rapid population growth, widespread economic depression, and the shift from a primarily agrarian to an industrial economy inexorably and profoundly altered traditional Barbadian village life. Trade unions became an increasingly effective political force, with organized labor leading the drive for political reform that ultimately resulted in the Barbadian independence movement. These and related historical factors and events had an impact on Lamming's life and are reflected in his fiction. In 1946 Lamming went to Trinidad, where he worked as a teacher and met a number of Trinidadian writers, including Clifford Sealy and Cecil Herbert. During this time he published poems in literary magazines. In 1950 he moved to England, where he worked for the British Broadcasting Corporation and as a journalist while pursuing his own literary career. His first novel, *In the Castle of My Skin,* was published in 1953; three other novels and a book of essays, *The Pleasures of Exile* (1960), appeared over the next seven years. In 1955 Lamming visited the United States on a Guggenheim Fellowship, serving as writer-in-residence at the University of Texas. He returned to the Caribbean a year later and became involved with various political causes, including the movement for Barbadian independence, which was realized in 1966. He published two further novels, *Natives of My Person* and *Water with Berries,* in 1972. Lamming remains associated with the educational and cultural projects of the Barbados Workers' Union and the Barbados Labour College, and he divides his time among England, the West Indies, and the United States.

Regarded as a national classic of West Indian literature, *In the Castle of My Skin* is a semiautobiographical story of childhood and adolescence. Set on the fictional island of San Cristobal in the 1930s and 1940s, the novel follows a male protagonist identified only as G. from age nine to eighteen; the story concludes with G.'s preparations to leave the island to pursue his education. This work has been commended for its poetic narrative,

close observation and faithful depiction of village life, accurate portrayal of the social changes of the period, and meticulous recreation of Barbadian speech. The author also garnered praise for employing local color with dignity and restraint, avoiding exoticism and idealization. Michael Gilkes called *In the Castle of My Skin* "one of the earliest novels of any substance to convey, with real assurance, the life of ordinary village folk within a genuinely realized, native landscape: a 'peasant novel' . . . written with deep insight and considerable technical skill."

In the Castle of My Skin is the first of four novels that outline the cycle of expatriation and return undergone by many West Indians of Lamming's generation. His next novel, *The Emigrants* (1954), follows a diverse group of people from the West Indies and the Caribbean who move to England, a country that they have been taught to believe is culturally superior to their native islands. There they find little happiness, and they long for home. The next two novels, *Of Age and Innocence*

(1958) and *Season of Adventure* (1960), feature expatriate protagonists who return to San Cristobal in an effort to rediscover their native heritage. A prominent theme in these works is the futility of attempting social and political progress without a full understanding of the past.

Natives of My Person and *Water with Berries,* published almost simultaneously, continue Lamming's exploration of West Indian history, chronicling the profound impact of colonialism on the present circumstances of the region. Commentators have called these novels only partially successful, with many contending that Lamming's combination of fantasy, allegory, and symbolism with social realism results in dense, complex prose that is difficult to understand. All of Lamming's novels published after *In the Castle of My Skin* have met with mixed critical response: only his first novel is generally regarded as an unqualified success, and most critics agree that Lamming is most successful with autobiographical themes.

The nationalist sympathies evident in Lamming's fiction also inform *The Pleasures of Exile.* This essay collection addresses the role of the artist, maintaining that it is incumbent upon the West Indian writer to challenge the values and beliefs that colonizers have imposed on native populations. For his repudiation of the assumption that the culture of the European colonizers is superior to indigenous culture, and for his affirmation of a distinctly West Indian national identity, Lamming remains a central figure in West Indian literature. Wrote critic George Davis of Lamming: "I can think of very few writers who make better use of the fictional moments of their stories to explore the souls of any of us—West Indian or not."

(For further information about Lamming's life and works, see *Black Writers; Contemporary Authors,* Vols. 85-88; *Contemporary Authors New Revision Series,* Vol. 26; and *Contemporary Literary Criticism,* Vols. 2, 4, 66.)

PRINCIPAL WORKS

In the Castle of My Skin (novel) 1953
The Emigrants (novel) 1954
Of Age and Innocence (novel) 1958
The Pleasures of Exile (essays) 1960
Season of Adventure (novel) 1960
Natives of My Person (novel) 1972
Water with Berries (novel) 1972

Richard Wright (essay date 1953)

[*One of the most influential authors of the twentieth century, Wright was among the first African-American literary figures to attain international prominence. In* the novel Native Son *(1940) and his autobiography* Black Boy: A Record of Childhood and Youth *(1945), he presented racial issues in a visceral, realistic manner. In the following essay, he commends Lamming's portrayal of Barbadian life in* In the Castle of My Skin.]

Accounting for one of the aspects of the complex social and political drama in which most of the subject people of our time are caught, I once wrote: " . . . to a greater or less degree, almost all of human life on earth today *can* be described as moving away from traditional, agrarian, simple handicraft ways of living toward modern industrialization."

These words deal with vast, cold, impersonal social forces which are somewhat difficult to grasp unless one has had the dubious fortune of having had one's own life shaped by the reality of those forces. The act of ripping the sensitive human personality from one culture and the planting of that personality in another culture is a tortured, convoluted process that must, before it can appeal to peoples' hearts, be projected either in terms of vivid drama or highly sensual poetry.

It has been through the medium of the latter—a charged and poetic prose—that George Lamming, a young West Indian Negro of Barbados, has presented his autobiographical summation of a tropical island childhood that, though steeped in the luminous images of sea, earth, sky, and wind, drifts slowly toward the edge of the realms of political and industrial strife. Notwithstanding the fact that Lamming's story, as such, is his own, it is, at the same time, a symbolic repetition of the story of millions of simple folk who, sprawled over half of the world's surface and involving more than half of the human race, are today being catapulted out of their peaceful, indigenously earthy lives and into the turbulence and anxiety of the twentieth century.

I, too, have been long crying these stern tidings; and, when I catch the echo of yet another voice declaiming in alien accents a description of this same reality, I react with pride and excitement, and I want to urge others to listen to that voice. One feels not so much alone when, from a distant witness, supporting evidence comes to buttress one's own testimony. And the voice that I now bid you hear is sounding in Lamming's ***In the Castle of My Skin.*** What, then, is this story that Lamming tells?

Without adequate preparation, the Negro of the Western world lives, in *one* life, *many* lifetimes. Most whites' lives are couched in norms more or less traditional: born of stable family groups, a white boy emerges from adolescence, enters high school, finishes college, studies a profession, marries, builds a home, raises children, etc. The Negro, though born in the Western world, is not quite of it; due to policies of racial exclusion, his is the story of *two* cultures: the dying culture in which he happens to be born, and the culture into which he is trying to enter—a culture which has, for him, not quite yet come into being; and it is up the shaky ladder of all the intervening stages between these two cultures that

Negro life must climb. Such a story is, above all, a record of shifting, troubled feelings groping their way toward a future that frightens as much as it beckons.

Lamming's quietly melodious prose is faithful not only to social detail, but renders with fidelity the myth-content of folk minds; paints lovingly the personalities of boyhood friends; sketches authentically the characters of schoolmasters and village merchants; and depicts the moods of an adolescent boy in an adolescent society.... Lamming rehearses the rituals of matriarchal families so common to people upon whom the strident blessings of an industrial world are falling—families whose men have been either killed, carted off to war, or hired to work in distant lands, leaving behind nervous mothers to rule with anxious hysteria over a brood of children who grow up restless, rebellious, and disdainful of authority.

Lamming recounts, in terms of anecdote, the sex mores of his people, their religious attitudes, their drinking habits, their brawls in the sunlit marketplaces, the fear of the little people for the overseers, and the fear of the overseers for the big white boss in the faraway house on the hill. (Unlike the population ratio in the United States, the English in these tiny islands comprise a minority surrounded by a majority of blacks; hence, that chronic, grinding, racial hatred and fear, which have so long been the hallmark of both white and black attitudes in our own Southland, are largely absent from these pages.)

Lamming objectifies the conscience of his village in those superbly drawn character portraits of Pa and Ma, those folk Negroes of yesteryear whose personalities, bearing the contours of Old Testament, Biblical heroes, have left their stamp upon so many young Lammings of the Western world. I feel that Lamming, in accounting for himself and his generation, was particularly fortunate in creating this device of a symbolic Pa and Ma whose lineaments evoke in our minds images of simple, peasant parents musing uncomprehendingly upon the social changes that disrupt their lives and threaten the destinies of their children....

The clash of this dying culture with the emerging new world is not without its humor, both ribald and pathetic: the impact of the concept of marriage upon the naïve, paganlike minds is amusingly related by Lamming in his story of Bots, Bambi, and Bambina. The superstitions of his boyhood friends are laid engagingly before us. And there's a kind of poetry suggested even in the outlandish names of his boyhood playmates: Trumper, Boy Blue, Big Bam, Cutsie, Botsie, Knucker Hand, Po King, Puss-in-Boots, and Suck Me Toe....

Just as young Lamming is ready to leave Barbados Island for Trinidad, Trumper, who has gone to America and has been influenced by mass racial and political agitation, returns and, in a garbled manner, tells of the frenzied gospel of racial self-assertion—that strange soul-food of the rootless outsiders of the twentieth century. The magnetic symbol of Paul Robeson (shown here purely in racial and *not* political terms!) attracts as much as disturbs young Lamming as he hears Robeson sing over a tiny recording device: *Let My People Go!*

Even before Lamming leaves his island home, that home is already dying in his heart; and what happens to Lamming after that is something that we all know, for we have but to lift our eyes and look into the streets and we see countless young, dark-skinned Lammings of the soil marching in picket lines, attending political rallies, impulsively, frantically seeking a new identity....

Filtered through a poetic temperament like Lamming's, this story of change from folk life to the borders of the industrial world adds a new and poignant dimension to a reality that is already global in its meaning.

Lamming's is a true gift; as an artist, he possesses a quiet and stubborn courage; and in him a new writer takes his place in the literary world. (pp. ix-xii)

> *Richard Wright, in an introduction to* In the Castle of My Skin *by George Lamming, McGraw-Hill Book Company, Inc., 1953, pp. ix-xii.*

Wilson Harris (lecture date 1964)

[*Harris is a Guyanese novelist and critic. In the following excerpt from a lecture delivered to the London West Indian Students' Union in 1964, he examines reasons for the perceived failure of Lamming's novel* Of Age and Innocence.]

One of the most interesting novelists out of the West Indies is George Lamming. Lamming was—and still is—regarded as a writer of considerable promise. What is the nature of his promise? Let us look at his novel *Of Age and Innocence.* This is a novel which somehow fails, I feel, but its failure tells us a great deal. The novel would have been remarkable if a certain tendency—a genuine tendency—for a tragic feeling of dispossession in reality had been achieved. This tendency is frustrated by a diffusion of energies within the entire work. The book seems to speak with a public voice, the voice of a peculiar orator, and the compulsions which inform the work appear to spring from a verbal sophistication rather than a visual, plastic and conceptual imagery. Lamming's verbal sophistication is conversational, highly wrought and spirited sometimes: at other times it lapses into merely clever utterance, rhetorical, as when he says of one of his characters: 'He had been made Governor of an important colony which was then at peace with England.' It takes some effort—not the effort of imaginative concentration which is always worthwhile but an effort to combat the author's self-indulgence. And this would not arise if the work could be kept true to its inherent design. There is no necessary difficulty or complexity in Lamming's novels—the necessary difficulty or complexity belonging to strange symbolisms—and I feel if the author concentrated on the sheer essentials of his experience a tragic disposition of feeling would gain a true ascendancy. This concentration is essential if the work is not to succumb to a uniform tone which gives each individual character the same public-speaking resonance of voice. I would like to stress a certain distinction .... In the epic and revolutionary novel of associations the characters are related within a personal capacity which works in a poetic and serial way so that a strange jigsaw is set in motion like a mysterious unity of animal and other substitutes within the person. Something which is quite different to the over-elaboration of individual character within the conventional novel. And this over-elaboration is one danger which confronts Lamming. For in terms of the ruling framework he accepts, the individuality of character, the distinctions of status and privilege which mark one individual from another, must be maintained. This is the kind of realism, the realism of classes and classifications—however limited it may be in terms of a profound, poetic and scientific scale of values—the novel, in its orthodox mould, demands. Lamming may be restless within this framework (there are signs and shadows of this in his work) but mere extravagance of pattern and an inclination to frequent intellectual raids beyond his territory are not a genuine breakthrough and will only weaken the position of the central character of his work. He must school himself at this stage, I believe, to work for the continuous development of a main individual character in order to free himself somewhat from the restrictive consolidation he brings about which unfortunately, I find, blocks one's view of essential conflict. This becomes a necessity in terms of the very style and tone of his work. He cannot afford to crowd his canvas when the instinctive threat of one-sidedness is likely to overwhelm all his people and in fact when this one-sidedness may be transformed into a source of tremendous strength in a singleness of drive and purpose which cannot then fail to discipline every tangential field and exercise. The glaring case is Shephard whom you may recall in *Of Age and Innocence*. Here was an opportunity which was not so much lost—as lost sight of—to declare and develop the tragic premises of individual personality by concentrating on the one man (Shephard) in order to bring home a dilemma which lay in his coming to terms with the people around him by acting—even when he was playing the role of the great rebel—in the way everyone else appeared to see him rather than in the way he innocently may have seen himself.

It is illuminating...to compare V.S. Naipaul's *A House for Mr Biswas* with George Lamming's *Of Age and Innocence*. Naipaul never loses sight of his Mr Biswas throughout a very long chronicle in the way Lamming disposes of Shephard again and again. Naipaul's style is like Lamming's in one respect: it is basically conversational though without the rhetoric and considerable power Lamming displays and it follows a flat and almost banal everyday tone. On this flat conversational level the novel has been carefully and scrupulously written. The possibility for tragedy which lay in *Of Age and Innocence,* the vein of longing for a lost innocence associated with Shephard's world is nowhere apparent in *A House for Mr Biswas.* Mr Biswas is essentially comic—a mixture of comedy and pathos—where Shephard may have been stark and tragic. Naipaul's triumph with Mr Biswas is one which—in the very nature of the novel—is more easily achieved, I feel, than a triumph with Shephard for Lamming would have been. To achieve the nuclear proportions of tragedy in Shephard, Lamming needed a remarkable and intense personal centre of depth; this he never held, overlooking the concrete challenge which stems from such a presence in his novel whose status is obscure. (pp. 37-9)

Wilson Harris, "Tradition and The West Indian Novel," in his Tradition, the Writer and Society: Critical Essays, *New Beacon Publications, 1967, pp. 28-47.*

Mervyn Morris (essay date 1968)

[*In the following excerpt, Morris surveys Lamming's novels.*]

It has become commonplace, yet it is perhaps still useful, to describe George Lamming as a poet, though all his books are in prose. The description may usefully direct us to certain qualities of Lamming's prose, particularly in the earlier books. For him there is a constant need to use the resources of language as fully as possible; before he took to writing novels, prose had struck him 'as an inferior way for any serious writer to use words'. Sometimes, too, the description 'poet' is used to indicate not the eloquent nobility of Lamming's concern for what language may do but, rather, to suggest limitations in his work as a novelist. When one admires each page and yet finds the novel difficult to get through, what better conveys reluctant admiration than to call its author 'poet'? In West Indian literature there is surely no finer work than *In the Castle of My Skin* (1953) which keen, if not dutiful, readers have put down and forgotten ever again to take up; the crab-like movement of parts of this book and the slowness of the first part of *The Emigrants* (1954) have discouraged many from 'bothering with Lamming'. It is a pity they have been discouraged. For *Of Age and Innocence* (1958) and *Season of Adventure* (1960) are nowhere dull, and both offer a good deal more than simple narrative interest. (p. 73)

[Lamming] is an author some of whose fiction has been, unwarily, described as autobiographical or—meaningless term—'semi-autobiographical'. Lamming himself seems to give some warrant for regarding *In the Castle of My Skin* as quite closely related to the facts of his boyhood. In the last pages of *The Pleasures of Exile,* he speaks of 'the shattering experience of seeing old Papa Grandison, my godfather, forced to move his small house from the site which generations of children had learnt to speak of as "the corner where Papa who keeps goats does live"'.' And, Lamming writes, 'the meaning of Papa's departure is the story of *In the Castle of My Skin*'. He quotes the last paragraphs of *Castle* and says he would have liked to read back Papa his own dialogue.

But from Lamming's own account this is not, in any simple sense, Papa's dialogue at all: essentially, maybe it is, but the narrator's cadences contribute as much to the moving quality as the words which Papa is made to say. Nor are the details of what happened to Lamming's godfather the same as what happened to Papa in the novel: in real life, according to Lamming, Papa was moved to a new village; in the novel he is to go to an Alms House. Clearly, this is done to deepen our sorrow for the old man. The facts, whatever they were, are only the raw material of the novelist's art.

In the Castle of My Skin is about a Barbadian village, about colonialism, poverty, class, colour, nature and the world of the senses. The central event is growth, change. The main narrative thread, such as it is, is the growing-up of a group of small boys, Bob, Trumper, Boy Blue and G (who is narrator). As the boys grow older their paths diverge. Winning a scholarship to a secondary school, G grows away from his roots. When he finally departs for Trinidad he knows he is saying goodbye to his peasant origins. 'The earth where I walked was a marvel of blackness and I knew in a sense more deep than simple departure I had said farewell, to the land.' The book is a compassionate evocation of that world which is the village: its school, its religion, its gossip, family relationships, quarrels, love, hatreds and its daily life. Some of the long peasant anecdotes are very funny and often there is an underlying seriousness in them. The speech of some of the characters has been well described by V. S. Pritchett as 'something between garrulous realism and popular poetry'. The dialogue of Ma and Pa often has great dignity and beauty.

> So far so good, but I'll say this much an' no more, I'm a old woman with little or no sense, but sometimes it seem a sort of understandin' walk straight into my head. I look out over yonder in front o' me an' I see how the pigeon put out his wing an' fly better than any airplane in the big blue sky. An' that poor pigeon ain't got no engine, no oil nor no pilot to put him from here to there, yet he move wondrous in the air, too wondrous for my words or yours, or any of these who study big big books, an' I says to myself the works o' the Lord is really wondrous. 'Tis beyond the wisdom o' the wise, an' if the Almighty God can put His hand out to help a poor pigeon who ain't mean more to Him than your soul an' mine, I says to myself there ain't no reason why He won't deliver us in His own good time. I pray the grace of God go with Mr Slime in all what he do or don't do, but bank or no bank, the riches o' this life is as naught in the sight of my Saviour. 'Cause this world's evil, Pa, 'tis very evil. That's all I got to say.

Throughout the book experience is, appropriately, related to the creatures and objects of the villagers' surroundings: crabs, frogs, cats, jackasses, the sea, sand and pebbles. Many things or incidents described have symbolic overtones: a fowl messes in a white man's face; when, forced to leave the village after thirty years there, the shoemaker is having his house moved, it collapses; when G is to go away, a pebble he placed carefully under a grape leaf has vanished. Slow change in the village is symbolized in the movement of crabs: 'with each

movement their bodies were pushed up another inch or two along the shore'. The symbolism is not often insisted on; the crabs are crabs observed by a small boy, whatever else they may signify.

The horizons of the village are measured against the happenings and attitudes from outside the village. A riot in the town causes villagers great fear and in a tense scene some rioters wait in the village to ambush a white landlord. The village is alarmed, but nobody does anything except the (later treacherous) ex-schoolmaster Mr Slime. When Trumper returns from the United States he brings with him another way of seeing.

There are faults in this warm and moving book, and some should be mentioned. When the boys steal into the landlord's grounds at night they come upon cats copulating and frogs copulating, and we are left in no doubt that the humans will be at it next. And so they are. But Lamming is betrayed into falseness by his apparent desire to make the visiting British sailor ridiculous; he and the girl are not credible.

> 'How do you know nothing will happen?' the girl said. She was anxious.
> 'England expects every man to know his duty,' the male voice said. 'Come close.'

Similarly, when the waterfront workers are involved in a riot they humiliate their overlords and do some damage; but so keen is the author to present the workers favourably that there is absolutely no looting.

Unconvincing behaviour, which is an occasional blemish in *Castle,* is the ruin of *The Emigrants.* In this book it is Lamming's attempt to give his plot a certain neatness that has fathered the worst absurdities. Miss Bis, a fair-skinned Trinidadian, left Trinidad because a calypso had made her notorious as a jilted woman. She has a rough time in England, where she changes her name to Una. Finally she is to marry Frederick, who is none other than the man who left her wearing his ring in Trinidad. Like her, he is greatly altered in appearance. We are to believe that neither recognizes the other. It is difficult, also, to accept the deft murder of Queenie by Una/Miss Bis, especially as the landlord conveniently gets rid of the body while Una is away and we never learn what he did with it. Governor, having left his unfaithful wife in Trinidad, tries unsuccessfully to help a stowaway get through immigration on arrival in England. (He is actually a stowaway himself.) At the end of the book the stowaway has finally made it, but he brings with him his woman: who is, of course, Governor's unfaithful wife.

The Emigrants follows the fortunes of a number of emigrants, with most of whom we travel the entire voyage from the West Indies to England. It is a long voyage and it takes a very long time to get started. Pages and pages of 'we were waiting for something to happen', 'we waited to see what would happen', and similar variations, seem to suggest that we need to share this interminable waiting if we are to believe in its existence.

We are introduced to several characters but because so little that is memorable happens on the voyage, some readers will find that when, later in the book, we become more interested in the people, we cannot remember which character adopted which attitude in those elaborate discussions on the boat, those debates on the meaning of West Indianism, personal independence and so on.

Although this is not at all a good novel, there are fine things in it, even in Part One: that prose poem, for example, an impressionistic patterning of fragments of speech, thought, feeling and incident on the train; one of the passages which offer persuasive evidence of Lamming's gifts. In England, Africans and English people help to focus elements of West Indian attitudes and experience, and the writing is sometimes adroit, as in the visit of Collis to the Pearsons, where the failure to communicate is cleverly observed.

When *The Emigrants* was published, Lamming had been living away from the West Indies for more than three years. It made good sense, therefore, that his third novel, *Of Age and Innocence,* published four years later in 1958, should be set in a fictional West Indian island and not, like *Castle,* in a real one. Lamming's San Cristobal bears many of the social and geographic features and even some of the place names of other West Indian islands. It has a distinct advantage over John Hearne's Cayuna, [the imaginary island setting of many of Hearne's novels]. Cayuna, whatever its author may protest, is taken by most readers to be Jamaica renamed; Hearne invites this by calling his capital Queenshaven and by other close echoes in place names or similarities in topography. So the reader tends to judge a novel set in Cayuna partly by the standard of what he himself thinks Jamaica is really like. Lamming avoids this sort of annoyance. His San Cristobal is firmly an imaginary island, even if we think we recognize Dr Eric Williams on it. On Lamming's island we can have steel band and the Haitian ceremony of souls. It nevertheless makes possible a subtle, realistic and intelligent analysis of West Indian society.

The beginning of *Of Age and Innocence* suggests that Lamming has learnt that to compel attention early is not necessarily to compromise one's artistic integrity. Some of the major characters are introduced on an aeroplane: a writer, Mark Kennedy, and his mistress Marcia, their friends Bill Butterfield and his wife Penelope, the little English boy Rowley whose father is San Cristobal's chief of police, and a strange frightening black man who provides some excitement before they touch down. The story is in part the story of that strange man, Shephard, and of his rise to political power and significance in San Cristobal; it also involves the personal lives of the other main characters on the plane and of a few who wait in San Cristobal to be introduced.

Writing on *The Tempest* Lamming comments on 'the distance which separates Age that apprehends, from Innocence which can only see'. Yet, in this novel, Innocence seems in the end to see more accurately than Age. Age is all the adults. Innocence is a small multi-racial group, Bob (Negro), Singh (Indian), Lee (Chinese) and Rowley (European), small boys who form a secret organization they call The Society. Between them there is only the beginning of distrust, and mainly there is fervent loyalty. The adults are not so lucky: Crabbe distrusts the nationalist organization led by Singh, Shephard and Lee; Singh distrusts Shephard briefly because of his association with whites; Baboo, professional double-crosser, distrusts, in his loyalty to his idea of being Indian, everybody except Singh. There is considerable discussion of the need to forgive and the compulsion to revenge. There is some play with the idea of madness. Who really is mad? Is Shephard? Some interest is shown in the various significances, religious and political, of the word Law. San Cristobal is a country preoccupied like many a young country with Tomorrow; there is a good deal of looking forward to Tomorrow. What is the meaning of national, racial, personal identity? Shephard feels the need to break out of the image of himself which others impose on him; Mark's identity is ultimately a mystery; Penelope is shocked by what she discovers is her sexual identity. The plot poses by implication (and in the magnificent fable of 'The Tribe Boys, the Kings and the Warrior Ants') the question: what is heroism?

Of the language of San Cristobal, Penelope observes: 'Their language seemed to give everything the sound of ritual, and there was no end of ritual in San Cristobal.' Any strangeness in the rhythm or diction of the San Cristobal peasant speech is thus explicitly protected; but it is beautiful speech which scarcely needs defence. In this novel language, themes and symbols are so well managed that the final effect is of a statement rich, complex, and yet in its essentials very clear. Here is an extract:

> The night was beginning to slip through the stagnant ridges of mist that surrounded the hills. The sky receded, and the air winced and squirmed from the careless spasms of black wings that fluttered down to the lamps. A street light went on, and the bats dived and circled the hood of glass which now shed yellow over the post. The evening was losing its way behind the houses, the trees were collecting their shadows from the ruined passage of twilight. And somewhere in the cemetery a child's voice emerged from the dark whisper of the crowd. The voice was soft and near as the night, feeling its way through the innocent and unpractised recollection of the words. And the crowd seemed suddenly still, possessed and fixed in their attention as though they had been suddenly freed by a miracle of strength to share in the elements which that voice celebrated. There was a pause as the child struggled to catch breath, and then the voice, innocent of danger, rode calmly through its obvious flaw of breathing with the words which her memory had returned.

> Now the day is over
> Night is drawing nigh,
> Shadows of the evening,
> Steal across the sky.

The silence gradually failed, and Thief's eyes were alerted by the shocking burst of flame which filled the street lamp. Another lamp repeated the signal, and soon the lamps started a hurried procession of light that worked like an invisible relay, leaping from post to post along the street. The bats burst from the trees and swished the air in a furious swoop that pitched them sightless into the light. They grew dizzy in a mad pursuit of shapes, colliding like lines on a map before swinging skyward through the wide, soothing obscurity of the night.

'In the land o' the blind,' said Thief, 'the bat is king.'

That remarkable passage is not just a brilliant description; it pulls together some of the themes of the novel. The child's voice is innocent; the child struggles to catch its breath in a world of adults. The death of a beloved leader, Shephard, invites the political night; without their leader the people are blind, waiting for a bat to lead them. Yet the dead leader who had collided with other leaders was in a sense blind himself. Even the evening is losing its way. The shocking burst of flame recalls the disastrous fire that swept the island, described earlier in the book, the 'invisible relay' of lamps lighting up intimates the cooperation by which the masses had kept oil away from the privileged in the populist movement. The bats are not only blind, they are engaged in a mad pursuit of shapes, recalling the novel's interest in the nature of madness, and suggesting also the indistinctness of what some of the leaders have pursued.

In *Of Age and Innocence* we have a new, and triumphant, combination of the elements of Lamming's talent. In masterly language suited to his varied purposes, he tells efficiently an interesting story, coherent in design yet free of incredible characters and absurd coincidence; a story which implies, and sometimes explicitly argues, a critique of West Indian society.

The beginning of *Season of Adventure* leads us to expect another success. This is, for three-quarters of its length, Lamming's most accomplished work; we get an impression of effortless achievement which distinguishes this from the previous books. We are plunged almost at once into engrossing action. Fola, an intelligent and privileged girl who has recently left school, is taken by her History teacher, an Englishman, to witness a ceremony of souls at the *tonelle*. The girl is shaken by the ceremony. The backward glance into her cultural past has great consequences. In particular, the girl, who is illegitimate, develops an obsessive need to learn who her father is, a fact concealed from her by Agnes, her mother, now married to Piggott, the Commissioner of Police. There are some striking characters: Piggott, and Agnes (beautiful, pretentious, fundamentally common), Chiki (the secondary-educated working-class painter), Therese (the Piggotts' maid). Some scenes are very well done: for example, that in which Fola is confronted by Piggott who is tactfully trying to get her to be kinder to her mother; a scene which turns on Fola's desire to know who her father is and Piggott's wish to be a father. 'And his wish pursues him across the garden, follows

him like a child into the Baby Austin car, cries behind him with the public clock which is now striking twelve.' The subtlety of Lamming's use of language is there, with the ironic reinforcement in 'Baby Austin' and 'cries' of Piggott's desire for children of his own.

Once again there is evidence of skilful design. Several of the characters are linked in their eagerness for, or their fear of, any backward glance into their past. Fola seems, symbolically, to be proto-West Indian in her search for identity: who really is she, who is her father? It is a planted irony, an important part of what Lamming is saying in this novel, that we do not know whether her father is European or African. In this novel there is constant tension between taught knowledge and instinctive experience, between, roughly, our European and our African backgrounds: we see this clearly in Fola, Piggott, and other San Cristobal figures such as Camillon and Mr. Squires. The design of the novel also sets in opposition the law (basically of Europe) and the drums (basically of Africa). 'I don't care who make the country's laws,' says Crim, 'if they let me make the country's music.' In the final scene of the novel the two confront each other. One of the recurring themes is the meaning of freedom, of independence, especially important now that San Cristobal has become a republic. True independence will not put up with patronage; so the visiting Prime Minister arouses Chiki's schoolboy anger:

Take away the past when his country ruled San Cristobal, and there'd be no republic, no college. We all would have been still back in the bush. That's what he was thinking.

Powell seems to feel a similar kind of anger against Fola:

'I only tried to help,' Fola started.
'Exact, exact,' said Powell, 'but what I do I want to do all by myself an' with my kind.'

Charlot, the Englishman, is conceived of in parallel to Chiki, the painter; the sexual fates of Agnes and her daughter, Fola, run parallel. There is some meaningful play with the song

Sometimes I love you
Sometimes I hate you
But when I hate you
It's 'cause I love you,

play which involves relationships between characters and between characters and elements of their past. The illiterate Gort, to whom words are a mystery, who is blind to words, forms a deep friendship with the blind white engineer, Bobby Chalk.

Yet, in spite of excellencies, *Season of Adventure* does not, finally, work. It is in the attempt to make some centrally significant myth out of the music of steel band that the novel does not succeed. One is too much aware of the author laying it on. When Gort's drum is destroyed 'rifle butts puncture the navel of the drum'. 'Gort couldn't answer. He held his head down, staring at the ground like a deaf-mute. His drum had died.' Gort's subsequent behaviour is unconvincing. Other characters too are hard to believe. Even for Fola we do not have a completely satisfactory motivation. Why must she walk the streets, why does the backward glance lay her at the mercy of Powell? Why must we have that cliché prostitute whoring to buy her son's school books? We do not see enough of Powell for the important part he plays towards the end of the novel; and we come upon an 'author's note' between chapters, a great mistake—it is as though the author, recognizing that Powell is not entirely credible, is trying to press us into acceptance of him. 'Believe it or not: Powell was my brother; my half brother by a different mother.' And 'Powell still resides somewhere in my heart, with a dubious love, some strange, nameless shadow of regret; and yet with the deepest, deepest nostalgia.' And after this, at this late stage, we get a good deal of explanation of characters who have already been presented and to whom by now we have firmly reacted. It is too late now to be learning about Powell's reading habits or Agnes's honesty. *Season* fails because of Lamming's preoccupation with themes at the expense of credible life in the characters.

In the novels Lamming has analysed various aspects of West Indian society and, occasionally, as in Collis, Mark and Chiki, has considered the implications of being an artist. In *The Pleasures of Exile,* a collection of essays, his subject 'is the migration of the West Indian writer, as colonial and exile, from his native kingdom once inhabited by Caliban, to the tempestuous island of Prospero's and his language'. *The Pleasures of Exile,* he says, 'is a report on one man's way of seeing'. In spite of all that, the book is a rag-bag collection. Apart from the fact that Lamming wrote them all there is only one thing which links all the chapters: the constant, and finally tiresome, repetition of the words Caliban (meaning, variously, black man, black colonial or black West Indian) and Prospero (white European, normally colonial overlord). This is not good enough: either the essays should be closely related to each other or each must have its intrinsic merit. The account of the visit to Africa is thin and the visit to the U.S.A. not very much better; the summary of C. L. R. James's *Black Jacobins* has outlived its usefulness, as the original is now available in paperback; the discussion of *The Tempest* scarcely illuminates the play, assuming without evidence that Caliban is black, eagerly discussing whether he did try to lay Miranda, and enquiring into the absence of Prospero's wife. What we have left is more or less only what the early announcements promised us: a personal statement, often pungent and sometimes moving, of what it means to be a West Indian writer who feels he must get out of the West Indies if he is to survive as a writer. There is some anecdotal discussion and some sharp analysis of what it means, as a West Indian and as a West Indian writer, to live in Britain. Lamming has quite a reputation as a brilliant talker and a great deal in these essays reads like brilliant talk; but the best essay, **'The Occasion for Speaking'**, is apparently written with formal care. It is the essay which justifies the purchase of the book. Why do West Indian writers leave the West Indies? Lamming describes, painfully, the conditions which makes them want to get out.

We have had to live with a large and self-delighted middle class, who have never understood their function. One cannot accuse an illiterate man of avoiding books, but one wonders what is to be done with people who regard education as something *to have,* but not *to use.*

At present, he reminds us, the West Indian writer must write for foreign readers. The writer's 'only certain knowledge is that this reader is not the West Indian middle-class, taken as a whole'. Why don't the writers return?

There are more reasons than I can state now; but one is fear. They are afraid of returning, in any permanent sense, because they fear that sooner or later they will be ignored in and by a society about which they have been at once articulate and authentic.

What creative artists say about other artists is often most illuminating about themselves. In all Lamming's novels some important characters are peasant, whether placed in peasant surroundings or not; in *Castle, Of Age and Innocence* and *Season of Adventure* Lamming writes deeply and honestly in praise of rooted contact with the soil. So it is not surprising that his critical sympathies are warmest with those writers who seem to him to share his enthusiasm for 'lumps of earth: unrefined, perhaps, but good, warm, fertile earth'. Emphatically, he asserts:

Writers like Selvon and Vic Reid—key novelists for understanding the literary and social situation in the West Indies—are essentially peasant. I don't care what jobs they did before; what kind or grade of education they got in their different islands; they never really left the land that once claimed their ancestors like trees.

Of Hearne he complains: 'His novels suggest the he has a dread of being identified with the land at peasant level.' He over-rates the delightful Selvon, who is, apparently, peasant enough. He observes in Naipaul some embarrassment about the peasant sensibility: 'Naipaul, with the diabolical help of Oxford University, has done a thorough job of wiping this out of his guts'. He then launches against him a very personal and very foolish attack.

This [writes Lamming] may be the dilemma of the West Indian writer abroad: that he hungers for nourishment from a soul which he (as an ordinary citizen) could not at present endure . . . and yet there is always an acre of ground in the New World which keeps growing echoes in my head. I can only hope that these echoes do not die before my work comes to an end.

The books themselves do not suggest that this might happen. Lamming's fictional island of San Cristobal seems strong enough in his imagination to promise us many more words, universal and yet West Indian, from his penetrating, compassionate and very articulate genius. (pp. 74-85)

Mervyn Morris, "The Poet as Novelist: The Novels of George Lamming," in The Islands in Between: Essays on West Indian Litera-

ture, edited by Louis James, Oxford University Press, London, 1968, pp. 73-85.

Jan Carew (essay date 1972)

[*Carew is a Guyanese-born poet, novelist, short story writer, dramatist, and critic. In the following excerpt, he comments on Lamming's career and favorably assesses* Natives of My Person.]

George Lamming is not so much a novelist as a chronicler of secret journeys to the innermost regions of the West Indian psyche. In order to ensure that he is unimpeded by the traditional novelistic conventions, he brings a private vision to bear on time and space, uniting them into an inseparable entity and islanding this entity in his own fertile imagination.

His first novel, *In the Castle of My Skin,* written in prose that was dazzlingly original, described a journey from childhood to adolescence; his second, *The Emigrants,* was the work of a brilliant but detached narrator accompanying a shipload of nomadic West Indians to Britain. *Of Age and Innocence* and *Season of Adventure,* his third and fourth books, almost defeat the reader with the sheer density of their prose, but they were occasionally seeded with ideas and illuminating insights that finally made the labor of reading them worthwhile. They took one back from Britain to the Caribbean, and it was as though Lamming was attempting to rediscover a history of himself by himself. His single nonfiction work, *The Pleasures of Exile,* was a neo-Gothic piece with ideas arching like flying buttresses; along with these ideas were varied and disparate existentialist happenings.

In all of Lamming's previous works he seemed to be balanced in an uneasy equipoise between the white colonizer and the black or brown colonized. But . . . *Natives of My Person,* the glittering product of 10 years of writing and rewriting, has finally released his spirit from its restive thralldom; he sheds the fear and the guilt of the colonized and makes an uninhibited journey to the heart of the colonizer. In order to accomplish this feat he abandons the slave—that ancestral archetype forever looming large in the West Indian psyche—to a limbo on the Guinea Coast. The slave ancestor in *Natives of My Person* is neither native nor person but a gigantic shadow forever lurking in troubled regions of the white imagination. The author gives us deliberately distorted glimpses of the slave coast where master and slave become phantoms moving in and out of primordial silences and where everything that lives is threatened with a sudden death.

The events that unfold in the novel in slow and measured sequences take place somewhere between the 16th and 18th centuries. The doomed venture that the book describes reads like a fictionalized version of a similar one embarked upon by Lope de Aguirre, a Spaniard who had shared in the conquest of Peru with Francisco Pizarro, and who in 1559 was to lead a final and tragic expedition in search of El Dorado . . . .

The main setting of the story is the sea, and as the voyage progresses each of the principal characters (the steward, the pilot, the surgeon, the priest, the cabin boy, the commandant himself) becomes a disinterested narrator of events in his own life—telling no more and no less than the novel requires to complete its gilded baroque structure. Within that structure, however, are deeply felt, austere and classical forms of a voodoo Ceremony of Souls, in which once a year the spirits of the dead are recalled. The fictionalized historical account, which Lamming unfolds is much more a resurrection of dead spirits than a conventional account of blood, lust and adventure. The prose, though far-from-easy-to-read, is evocative and there are somber and unforgettable symbols like the headless white sea hawk floating relentlessly in the wake of the *Reconnaissance.* He also manages with great subtlety to blend the moods of the sea with the dreams of the mariners.

Natives of My Person is undoubtedly George Lamming's finest novel. It succeeds in illuminating new areas of darkness in the colonial past that the colonizer has so far not dealt with, and in this sense it is a profoundly revolutionary and original work. (pp. 4, 30)

> Jan Carew, "Blighted Voyage to Utopia," in The New York Times Book Review, February 27, 1972, pp. 4, 30.

Anthony Boxill (essay date 1973)

[*In the following 1973 review essay, Boxill assesses* Natives of My Person *and* Water with Berries, *arguing that the first novel is successful for its insights into the history of colonialism in the West Indies and contending that the second fails because of the "pretentious complexity" of its symbolic pattern.*]

Admirers of George Lamming's work have had to wait eleven years for a new novel from him. After *Season of Adventure* in 1960, the sixties produced no other novel. Now Lamming has broken his silence with not one but two new novels. At first glance these seem very different: *Water with Berries* is set for the most part in contemporary London and deals with a small group of West Indian artists who live in exile from their native San Cristobal. *Natives of My Person* describes the sixteenth-century voyage that a group of European mariners set out on in an attempt to reach San Cristobal. The voyage ends in murder a day away from its destination and is never completed. Similarly, in *Water with Berries* a murder prevents Teeton, who had planned to give up his artistic career in London to become a political activist in San Cristobal, from returning home. Both novels, then, are about frustrated attempts to return to San Cristobal by men who wish to set it right.

What is it that makes San Cristobal so difficult to return to? Lamming has already written a book about the problems and the pleasures of exile, and in these two novels he explores again and expands the themes of his previous books. In *Water with Berries,* Teeton, a painter; Derek, an actor; and Roger, a musician, are exiled from San Cristobal and bound to London for various personal reasons. Teeton is escaping from a scandal that involved his wife and a foreign diplomat. Roger has to leave because his father's middle-class aspirations threaten to stifle him. By contrast, the rigid morality of the respectable poor proves intolerable to Derek and drives him away. All of the situations and attitudes from which these men flee are in some way connected to the colonial past of San Cristobal. Connecting also the reasons for the exile of these three characters is the fact that each of them is an artist and the suggestion that the society of San Cristobal has little time for art.

For all these interrelated reasons Teeton, Derek, and Roger find themselves living precariously in London. There had been a time when they had been able to combine their creative efforts on a common project: Derek had played Othello at Stratford; Teeton had painted the sets; and Roger had composed the music. At the time when the novel is set, however, Derek can only secure parts as corpses; Roger is forced to live separate from his wife; and Teeton in self-defence has isolated himself from contact with his friends. He has developed

George Lamming.

the knack of keeping other people at their distance. Living in this limbo, Teeton, Derek, and Roger watch helplessly as their lives disintegrate around them. Teeton, by turning to politics and seeking to return to San Cristobal, attempts to arrest this disintegration; but his attempt is too late, and like Roger and Derek, whose rebellion is more pathetic—Roger tries to burn down his hostile world, and Derek rapes a girl—he succumbs to the environment.

To help put across his points about the disintegration of personality, especially in people who are products of a colonial past, Lamming makes elaborate use of a pattern with which by now his readers should be quite familiar. I refer to the Prospero-Miranda-Caliban triangular relationship of Shakespeare's *The Tempest.* Lamming is especially interested in the attitudes of the black man-Caliban toward the white woman-Miranda, and he explores a number of these relationships from various angles. Sometimes his use of this pattern is decidedly ironic. The frequent references in the novel to another of Shakespeare's plays, *Othello,* emphasizes this irony.

However, the *Tempest* pattern which might have been the strength of this novel proves its undoing. Lamming's persistent use of it comes to seem contrived. Even some of the names he has chosen—Myra for his Miranda figure and Fernando for his Ferdinand figure—seem too obvious. In his unrelenting faithfulness to this *Tempest* pattern Lamming loses touch with the characters he is creating; they cease to be credible, and the reader fails to be moved by their final catastrophe. The last impression that this novel leaves, unfortunately, is that the only real thing in it is its reliance on the *Tempest* theme, and that it has been severely overwritten.

By contrast, Lamming's style is admirably suited to the circumstances of his next novel, *Natives of My Person.* Its formality suggests the prose of the sixteenth-century travel account. Its richness, which is frequently Conradian, evokes well the complexity of the relationships between the characters on shipboard. The ship is used here, much as in a Conrad novel, to isolate a group of characters and to suggest a world in microcosm with its own social structure and system of order. Lamming, like Conrad, is aware of the way in which the limitations of space on a ship render more intense human relationships which might have remained dilute in a less constricting environment: "But the ship reduced every movement to an important occasion."

The voyage of the ship *Reconnaissance* is a very important one, for its Commandant is bound for San Cristobal to set up an ideal colony. He forbids the taking of slaves, a custom accepted in his day, severs ties with his European homeland, and hopes in this way to live down in his conscience the violence and bloodshed which had helped raise him to prominence in his native Lime Stone:

> I would plant some portion of the Kingdom in a soil
> that is new and freely chosen, namely the Isles of the
> Black Rock, more recently known as San Cristobal.

For I have seen men of the basest natures erect
themselves into gentlemen of honor the moment . . . .

On this voyage of this symbolic ship Lamming shows
how liable to misdirection human nature makes such
noble excursions. The history of colonialism may be full
of intentions to establish utopias, but none has ever
materialized. Instead, the colonial powers have succeeded mainly in spreading their avarice. Here Lamming's
novel reminds again of Conrad, this time *Heart of
Darkness* with its corrupted colonizer, Kurtz. The
echoes of *Heart of Darkness* are most explicit in the
section of Lamming's novel when the ship lies off the
coast of West Africa and the men are waiting for orders
to begin taking on slaves.

The Commandant's order not to take slaves marks the
beginning of the opening of a rift between him and his
crew, for the men, ignorant of their leader's noble
intentions, are on this voyage to make fortunes; and
slaves represent black gold to them. As the voyage
progresses through its ironic Middle Passage (the ship is
empty of slaves), Lamming gives the reader the opportunity to become intimate with the motivations and
aspirations of the crew, both officers and ordinary
seamen; and these are as diverse as there are men in the
crew.

Until the ship reaches Dolores, the first of the islands, it
is driven and the crew held together by the strength of
the Commandant's will, for he has not divulged to his
crew his real plans for this voyage. As soon as his
intentions waver and he loses his single-mindedness, he
is murdered by his officers and the ship is abandoned by
the crew. Whereas avarice can bind men together and
direct them to a common project, high-minded motives
prove the frailest of bonds, easily susceptible to the
frivolity of human nature. At the end of the novel, the
reader is also left with the question, what right has the
Commandant to choose the destiny of his crew and to
attempt to dictate to them that they should be noble. Is
his project not doomed to disaster because it smacks too
much of the arrogance of the aristocracy in its relation
with the lower classes?

The men on the voyage are motivated negatively as well,
by their weakness and their fear. Lamming uses the
women, the wives of the officers, to suggest this idea.
While the men strive in vain to get to San Cristobal, the
women on another ship arrive without any difficulty
and await the men. The women have acted selflessly for
the good of their men, or at least they think they have:

Surgeon's Wife: It was what I had to do. He was a
piece of my person.

Steward's Wife: It is the same. My husband had
become that too: a native of my person. Whenever
there is a crisis, we must choose against our interests.

Surgeon's Wife: That's how I chose. I didn't think of
a bargain. There was no room for victory in our
future. I simply chose on his behalf. I had to.

The men see this selflessness as a threat to their strength,
and they embark on the voyage to attempt to prove their
dominance to themselves and to their women. By the
end of the book we realize that the men are too weak
and too afraid to colonize the women of whom they are
natives, and consequently have no hope of really
colonizing a new territory. The self-sacrifice of the
women has given them dominance over the men, who
ironically are undone by the very feminine quality
which seeks to help them. Lamming's use of the term
native in this book is also nicely ironic because this time
the emasculated native is a European.

These two novels, different as they are, make the similar
point that founders of utopias, which is what the
Commandant of *Natives of My Person* aspires to be, and
correctors of colonialism, what Teeton aims to become
in *Water with Berries,* require the strength of genuine
selflessness. Both lack this quality and that is why, at
least in part, they fail to reach San Cristobal.

In *Natives of My Person,* Lamming uses a simple
allegorical pattern which is thoroughly convincing. The
ship is almost a complete society; it lacks only the
women. Its members are identified by their occupations—Surgeon, Steward, Priest, Painter, Cook—imply-
ing that they are types; but the characters develop into
very complex individuals. The ship is travelling from a
European country, Lime Stone, which suggests England
with its *white* cliffs, to the Islands of *Black* Rock, which
represent the West Indies. The distance from white to
black is never traversed by the men. Gabriel Tate de
Lysle—an obviously significant name, but not obtru-
sively so this time because it fits appropriately the
directness of the rest of the allegory—represents the
powerful union of commerce and government in Lime
Stone which so thoroughly controls the lives of its
inhabitants.

By contrast to the pretentious complexity of the symbol-
ical pattern of *Water with Berries,* the superficially
simple allegory of *Natives of My Person* provides richly
complex insights into human personality and the history
of colonialism.

Both these novels deserve to be read carefully: *Natives of
My Person* because it is a remarkable success, and *Water
with Berries* because, despite its failure, it is a serious
attempt to follow up on ideas which Lamming has
raised in earlier books. (pp. 111-16)

*Anthony Boxill, "San Cristobal Unreached:
George Lamming's Two Latest Novels," in*
World Literature Written in English, *Vol.
12, No. 1, April, 1973, pp. 111-16.*

Sandra Pouchet Paquet (essay date 1982)

[*Paquet is an American educator and critic. In the
following excerpt, she examines the exploration of the
colonial experience in Lamming's work.*]

The colonial experience is a matter of historical record. What I'm saying is that the colonial experience is a *live* experience in the *consciousness* of these people. And just because the so-called colonial situation is over and its institutions may have been transferred into something else, it is a fallacy to think that the human-lived content of those situations are automatically transferred into something else, too. The experience is a continuing psychic experience that has to be dealt with long after the actual colonial situation formally 'ends' [George Lamming in an interview with George Kent dated 1973].

The colonial experience is the subject matter of all George Lamming's novels to date. In each work he explores aspects of this experience with a comprehensiveness and skill that distinguish him as a major political novelist. His novels characteristically describe the structure and organization of society and the extent to which these shape individual response and action. Private experience is examined in relation to the larger public events at the centre of every novel. There is no separation of the business of politics and private life. Lamming insists always on the 'direct informing influence from the subsoil of life outside', and this emphasis organizes and informs the shape of his fiction. He writes out of an acute social consciousness that is vitally concerned with politics and society, that is, with the function of power in a given society, and its effects on the moral, social, cultural, and even aesthetic values of the people in that society.

Lamming's pursuit of the colonial theme gains authority from the broad range of his concern with this experience. His novels deal specifically with colonization as the political and economic history which informs the quality of life in his home island of Barbados, the Caribbean and Western Europe. Lamming explores the influence of this history on three levels which he distinguishes as the province and responsibility of the writer: the world of the private and hidden self; the world of social relations; and the community of men, to whom the writer is directly responsible in his 'essential need to find meaning for his destiny' [Lamming, **'The Negro Writer and His World,'** *Caribbean Quarterly* 5, No. 2, 1958]. He explains further that the writer's 'responsibility to that other world, his third world, will be judged not only by the authenticity and power with which his own private world is presented, but also by the honesty with which he interprets the world of his social relations. For Lamming, these three worlds influence each other intimately and complexly, so that his concern with the politics of colonialism is a concern with the precise quality of individual experience, as it reflects the weight of history on the total society. As Lamming conceives it, this is the proper function of the novelist and the responsibility of the Caribbean writer in particular.

In his fiction Lamming characteristically examines the present in relation to the past and the future. He returns to this theme continually in references to the Haitian Ceremony of Souls. It is his symbol of a meaningful reconciliation of contemporary post-colonial experience with its historical past, with the artist as pilot in this hopeful venture. The Ceremony of Souls is crucial to an understanding of the politics of Lamming's novels. In **'The West Indian People'** [in *New World Quarterly* 2, No. 2, 1966], Lamming describes the ritual and spells out its significance for him as a writer.

> ... in the republic of Haiti there is a Ceremony of Souls at which all the celebrants are relatives of the dead who return for this occasion to give some report on their previous relations with the living. The dead are supposed to be in a purgatorial state of Water, and it is necessary for them to have this dialogue with the living before they can be released into their final eternity. The living, on the other hand, need to meet the dead again in order to discover if there is any need for forgiveness. This dialogue takes place through the medium of the Priest or *Houngan....* It is not important to believe in the actual details of the ceremony. What is important is its symbolic drama, the drama of redemption, the drama of returning, the drama of cleansing for a commitment towards the future.

These are major concerns in Lamming's fiction. The drama of redemption, of returning, of cleansing for a commitment towards the future; these define the perspective which organizes his fiction and shapes his treatment of the colonial theme.

Lamming locates the determining factor for contemporary Caribbean and European experience in the European colonial experiment which gained momentum in the seventeenth century, and in the subsequent exploitation and enslavement of peoples native to Africa and the Americas. His fiction engages in a comprehensive examination of this past and the present in relation to each other: 'it's very central to me in the sense that the world in which one lives is not just inhabited by the living. It is a world which is also the creation of the dead. And any architecture of the future cannot really take place without that continuing dialogue between the living and the past.' The Ceremony of Souls is Lamming's symbol of this exercise of the creative imagination. But more than this, it articulates his conception of the public role of the artist in the figure of the Priest or *Houngan.*

This conception of the artist's public role is elaborately treated in an early collection of essays, ***The Pleasures of Exile.*** This book, Lamming writes, was 'intended as an introduction to a dialogue', between descendants of the colonizers and the colonized, or as he names them, the descendants of Prospero and Caliban. As an artist whose language is that of the colonizer, and who is nonetheless a descendent of Caliban, he claims singular authority in articulating a perspective that is to create new possibilities for the future:

> For I am a direct descendant of slaves, too near to the actual enterprise to believe that its echoes are over with the reign of emancipation. Moreover, I am a direct descendant of Prospero, worshipping in the same temple of endeavour, using his legacy of language—not to curse our meeting—but to push it further, reminding the descendants of both sides that

what's done is done, and can only be seen as a soil from which other gifts, or the same gift endowed with different meanings, may grow towards a future which is colonized by our acts in this moment, but which must always remain open ['**In the Beginning**', *The Pleasures of Exile*].

Lamming offers an alternative to Caliban's curse. He intends a calculated challenge to the habitual way of seeing that has become a normal part of colonization. He wants to change the inherited values and rationalizations of colonization that stymie both sides, and to offer the descendants of Prospero and Caliban an alternative 'way of seeing'. His artistic purpose is no less than to shape the consciousness and to influence the perspective of both the Caribbean community and the world community at large. He states categorically that the Caribbean writer has a 'public task' beyond the 'creating of so-called works of Art'. He sees the artist as engaged in 'the shaping of national consciousness, giving alternative directions to society'.

While the organization of political movements is not the artist's function, he has social responsibilities similar to the politician's, says Lamming [in an interview with Ian Munro and Reinhard Sander in *Kas-Kas,* 1972]:

> So although I would make a distinction about *functions,* I do not make a distinction about *responsibilities.* I do not think that the responsibility of the professional politician is greater than the responsibility of an artist to his society.

More recently, in a graduation address at the University of the West Indies, Cave Hill, Lamming assigns to the Caribbean writer a variety of specific functions. He is educator, social historian and priest:

> Throughout the literature of the Caribbean, this theme of spiritual dispossession and self-mutilation remains central to the thought and perception of your writers; and it's no wonder that the gradual infiltration of their books into the education of our youth is made a cause of grave concern. But it is the function of the writer to return a society to itself; and in this respect, your writers have been the major historians of the feeling of your people. To separate them by open or hidden forms of censorship from a generation which needs to be provided with a firm sense of historical continuity would be to inflict upon us a second stage of isolation.

According to Lamming, the writer records and interprets the world of social relations; he provides historical continuity; and he liberates a new generation from a cycle of 'spiritual dispossession and self-mutilation'. He emphasizes the revolutionary character of the region's literature. The writer is an arbiter of social change. His art is at once subversive, liberating and restorative.

In the light of such clearly delineated views on the nature of fiction and the social obligations of the artists, Lamming's novels can be termed political not only because the matter they investigate is of a political nature, but because they reflect his commitment to reorganize the imbalance in personal and social relationships engendered by a colonial history. The novels are intended as political acts. In his fiction, Lamming offers no easy solutions and no programme for government. What he offers is a careful evaluation of the social laws and values that perpetuate a colonial mentality, and also an evaluation of those elements in the society that contribute to the making of a new social order.

Lamming's emphasis on colonial history as the appropriate context for exploring the peculiarities of contemporary West Indian experience, and his preoccupation with fiction as an instrument of social transformation, shape the distinctive features of his art. In his novels, individual human experience is always circumscribed by historical and political circumstance. Political events are linked to the development of plot and character. In fact, character and action frequently embody the social and political confrontations around which the plot develops. This allows him to portray the complexities of the total society within the parameters of personal and social relationships among a representative community.

Lamming's fiction typically presents a crowded canvas. His novels are dense and panoramic in scale, at times covering territory that ranges from one end of the Caribbean to the other in the fictive island of San Cristobal, or all of Europe in the Kingdoms of Lime Stone and Antarctica. It is often difficult to focus on a single most important character in the conventional sense of hero or heroine. This is certainly the case in *The Emigrants, Of Age and Innocence, Water with Berries,* and to varying degrees in the other novels, where competing elements in the society, or the society itself, are as important as the unfolding history of any single character. Even in *In the Castle of My Skin,* where autobiography identifies a central character, G. shares the focus of the novel in a complementary way with the village community. In *Season of Adventure,* Fola's predicament individualizes the external drama of a class war and the fall of the second republic; she is interesting because she embodies an important aspect of the upheaval around her. She shares the focus of interest with a variety of other characters. The same is true of the Commandant in *Natives of My Person* even though his enterprise provides the narrative framework of the novel.

Lamming characteristically isolates what is most significant about the structure and development of the society at a particular moment in history, and embodies these trends in characters and confrontations that are representative of social and political forces at work in the society. It is his way of individualizing the general social condition. The motivation for character and action derives from the individual's attachment to the values and images which tie him to a particular class and social function. The complexity of warring elements in the society is reflected in the individual psychology of characters, their relationships with each other, and their choices as private and public crises arise.

As early as *In the Castle of My Skin,* characters and actions have a symbolic resonance that invests the plot with poetic denseness. Lamming relies heavily on what he calls 'collective character'. Such characters are representative of a group or class or value system within the society. Collective characters are often composites fashioned in the way Richard Wright describes in 'How Bigger Was Born'; 'there was not just one Bigger, but many of them, more than I could count and more than you suspect.' Lamming himself describes Powell in *Season of Adventure* as 'a composite member of West Indian society'. Characters such as Ma and Pa in *In the Castle of My Skin* are collective characters in the sense that they express the cumulative experience of the village community. The different responses to social and political change which they articulate reflect a division in the village to which they belong. The dilemma of the village in turn articulates the dilemma of the island, and the frame of reference broadens indefinitely. Lamming says he wanted to make Creighton's village 'applicable to Barbados, to Jamaica, and to all of the other islands. I wanted to give the village that symbolic quality.' With this emphasis in mind it is not surprising to find Lamming moving away from the limitations of a known setting in *In the Castle of My Skin* and *The Emigrants* to the imaginary island of San Cristobal in subsequent novels, and even the fictional European kingdoms of Lime Stone and Antarctica in *Natives of My Person.*

In keeping with Lamming's early reliance on the symbolic representation of experience in *In the Castle of My Skin,* there is a definite movement in his fiction towards what he describes as 'an allegorical interpretation of experience' as opposed to 'a naturalistic rendering of society'. This is especially apparent in his last two novels: *Water with Berries* and *Natives of My Person.* In *Water with Berries,* characters act out their inherited roles as colonizer and colonized in a post-colonial setting with devastating results for all. Plot and characters are loosely derived from Shakespeare's *The Tempest.* This provides a Ceremony of Souls framework for the struggle to be freed from the burden of an inherited colonial relationship to the mother country. When Teeton, the West Indian artist in exile, murders his landlady, Mrs Gore-Brittain, in order to escape the menace of her hospitality and affection turned vindictive, their interests are mutually exclusive and his life and freedom depend on this extreme action. The political comment is abundantly clear as Lamming uses the cloying quality of their relationship and its latent hostilities to describe the destructiveness of a post-colonial attachment to old colonial ties. In *Natives of My Person,* Lamming describes a late-sixteenth century voyage to settle in the New World, with a view to elucidating the dilemma of post-colonial societies, so that the House of Trade and Justice in the Kingdom of Lime Stone functions as a symbol of its modern equivalent:

> I was thinking of the House as a symbol of our contemporary situation, of the post-colonial world like that of San Cristobal. Today, it's the *international corporation.* That is the stupendous body that now rises above what ordinary people and their leaders imagine to be the domestic authority of the land. A

country becomes what is called 'independent', attempts, like the *Reconnaissance* to set out on a journey of very serious *breaking away,* but discovers instead the international corporation—that gigantic arrangement of modern life has the capacity to control or redirect decisions democratically decided by people and their leaders.

The novel is both an analysis of politics and society in the late sixteenth and seventeenth centuries, as well as a political commentary on the lingering influence of that social and political system in post-colonial societies.

Lamming approaches language with the same political awareness that determines the quality of his fiction at large, and his efforts are not always understood. While Stuart Hall remarks that in Lamming's 'hand, the rhythms and idioms of West Indian speech are brought to a condition of sensitivity where language is capable of expressing the deepest reaches of West Indian personality,' Wilson Harris complains about its 'self-indulgence', about 'a verbal sophistication rather than a visual, plastic and conceptual imagery'. What Hall credits with the richness of poetic expression, Harris dismisses as superfluous. More recently, Elizabeth Nunez-Harrell charges that conversational dialect in Lamming's fiction lacks organic spontaneity [see Further Reading]. She is particularly unhappy about the language of the village boys in *In the Castle of My Skin,* as they struggle to verbalize their impressions of the adult world about them. The search for criteria that transcend individual preference is an elusive one.

Lamming argues that the language of Caribbean literature is weighted with 'the cultural and historical associations and discontinuities which the area has experienced'. He identifies three areas of influence at work in Caribbean literature, all of which feature in his novels in a variety of combinations: the British literary tradition, the influence of the King James Bible on the language of the masses in Jamaica and Barbados, and the influence of popular speech. What is important about language in Lamming's Caribbean novels is that, however stylized, it is historically and linguistically based in the experience he describes. Consider the dream vision of Pa, the old man in *In the Castle of My Skin.* In Chapter Ten, the old man struggles to describe a vision of the future that draws on the whole range of memory and accrued experience. His language is a wonderfully creative approximation of Biblical language—the most sophisticated expression of the colonizer's tongue to which Pa has been exposed. The transformation of language which occurs in his attempt to articulate a vision that transcends the mental and physical limitations of slavery and colonization, reflects Lamming's own efforts to free the language from its historical role as a major colonizing agent. The mixture of Biblical rhythms and popular speech are appropriate both to the old man's language experience and to the epic journey of return and discovery he describes.

Lamming contends that once Prospero's language had been accepted by Caliban, 'the future of his development, however independent it was, would always be in some way inextricably tied up with that pioneering aspect of Prospero. Caliban at some stage would have to find a way of breaking that contract, which got sealed by language, in order to reconstruct some alternative reality for himself.' The adoption of a foreign language initiated a spiritual exile from Caliban's native inheritance. The writer's function and responsibility is to alter the pattern of values that came with the colonizer's language. In Lamming's words: 'the language of modern politics is no longer Prospero's exclusive vocabulary. It is Caliban's as well; and since there is no absolute from which a moral prescription may come, Caliban is at liberty to choose the meaning of this moment.' Lamming's fiction is an attempt to realize this liberty in a continuing dialogue concerning various aspects of the colonial experience. He makes no distinction between aesthetics and politics, that is, between his pursuits as an artist and his commitment to change the bias of a colonial inheritance.

Politics becomes a necessary consideration in any critical assessment of Lamming's fiction because it is so much a part of the content and form of the novels. Much in his aesthetic as a political novelist invites comparison with Marxist critical concepts, especially those of totality, typicality and historical overview. But there is a sharp divergence between Lukács' anti-modernism and Lamming's movement towards political allegory. Lukács argues that modern allegory is ahistorical and static, and sacrifices typicality to abstraction. Lamming clearly finds the allegorical rendering of experience perfectly compatible with social criticism and analysis in an historical context. *Water with Berries* is inspired in form and content by his interpretation of Shakespeare's *The Tempest* as political allegory. In this novel, he combines social realism with allegory as a way of linking past history with typical conflicts in the present. Another obvious point of connection with Marxism and literature lies in the Marxist concepts of art as an instrument of social development, and the artist as social enlightener. There is ample evidence of Lamming's commitment to both these principles in both his life and his art.

While he stays clear of propaganda or dogmatism in his fiction, the political bias that shapes Lamming's perspective as a novelist is obviously anti-colonialist and anti-imperialist. But even more basic to the political bias implicit in his fiction, are the peasant and working class sympathies that distinguish the novels in varying degrees. Not only is his fiction nationalistic in its devotion to the concept of a distinct West Indian identity, but it consistently embodies the islands' progression towards independence and nationhood in the motions, aspirations, language and lifestyles of the peasant and working class majority. It becomes increasingly clear in his novels, that Lamming measures the evolution of West Indian society in terms of the peasant struggle against a middle class pursuit of privilege and power. In fact he identifies the peasant orientation of the West Indian novelists, with a few exceptions, as

their distinguishing characteristic. He argues that it was in the West Indian novel that 'the West Indian peasant became other than a cheap source of labour. He became, through the novelist's eye, a living existence, living in silence and joy and fear, involved in riot and carnival. It is the West Indian novel that has restored the West Indian peasant to his true and original status of personality.' Whether Lamming's statement is fair or not, it is certainly true of his own art. For as he says of the West Indian novelist, he was 'the first to relate the West Indian experience from the inside. He was the first to chart the West Indian memory as far back as he could go.' (pp. 1-8)

> *Sandra Pouchet Paquet, in her* The Novels of George Lamming, *Heinemann Educational Books Ltd., 1982, 130 p.*

FURTHER READING

Barthold, Bonnie J. "From Fragmentation to Redemption: Seven Representative Novels—George Lamming, *In the Castle of My Skin.*" In her *Black Time: Fiction of Africa, the Caribbean, and the United States,* pp. 150-57. New Haven: Yale University Press, 1981.
> Close examination of *In the Castle of My Skin,* focusing on Lamming's portrayal of the protagonist's growth and maturation in conjunction with a state of change within Barbadian society.

Birney, Earle. "Meeting George Lamming in Jamaica." *Canadian Literature,* No. 95 (Winter 1982): 16-28.
> Birney, a Canadian poet, reminisces about meeting Lamming while researching Caribbean literature in 1962.

Brown, Carolyn T. "The Myth of the Fall and the Dawning of Consciousness in George Lamming's *In the Castle of My Skin.*" *World Literature Today* 57, No. 1 (Winter 1983): 38-43.
> Analyzes the archetypal theme of a fall from a state of grace in *In the Castle of My Skin.*

Cartey, Wilfred. "Lamming and the Search for Freedom." *New World Quarterly* 3, Nos. 1 and 2 (1966-1967): 121-28.
> Identifies prominent themes in works by Lamming and other expatriate West Indian novelists, including acceptance of the past, anticipation of the future, and establishment of a national identity.

Clarke, Austin C. "Some Speculations as to the Absence of Racialistic Vindictiveness in West Indian Literature." In *The Black Writer in Africa and the Americas,* edited by Lloyd W. Brown, pp. 165-94. Los Angeles: Hennessey & Ingalls, 1973.
> Includes discussion of racial issues in *In the Castle of My Skin* and *The Pleasures of Exile.*

Cudjoe, Selwyn R. "Towards Independence: *Of Age and Innocence, Season of Adventure, Water with Berries.*" In his

Resistance and Caribbean Literature, pp. 179-211. Athens: Ohio University Press, 1980.
Discusses Lamming's literary explorations of colonialism and independence movements in Barbados.

Gilkes, Michael. "Background to Exile." In his *The West Indian Novel,* pp. 86-115. Boston: Twayne Publishers, 1981.
Includes discussion of *In the Castle of My Skin* in an examination of the theme of alienation in West Indian expatriate literature. Scattered references to Lamming elsewhere in the book include an assessment of *In the Castle of My Skin* as a national classic.

Jonas, Joyce E. "Carnival Strategies in Lamming's *In the Castle of My Skin.*" *Callaloo* 11, No. 2 (Spring 1988): 346-60.
Traces the influence of the trickster figure from African folklore on Lamming's first novel.

Larson, Charles R. "Toward a Sense of the Community: George Lamming's *In the Castle of My Skin.*" In his *The Novel in the Third World,* pp. 89-107. Washington, D.C.: Inscape, 1976.
Argues that *In the Castle of My Skin* is an important developmental novel in West Indian literature chiefly because of its combination of autobiographical and fictional elements.

McDonald, Avis G. "'Within the Orbit of Power': Reading Allegory in George Lamming's *Natives of My Person.*" *The Journal of Commonwealth Literature* XXII, No. 1 (1987): 73-86.
Allegorical interpretation of *Natives of My Person.*

Munro, Ian. "George Lamming." In *West Indian Literature,* edited by Bruce King, pp. 126-43. Hamden, Conn.: Archon Books, 1979.
Examines Lamming's novels individually as well as within the larger context of the author's portrayal of Caribbean social, political, and psychological development.

Naipaul, V. S. Review of *Of Age and Innocence,* by George Lamming. *New Statesman* LVI, No. 1447 (6 December 1958): 827.
Contends that *Of Age and Innocence* is unnecessarily complicated by symbol and allegory and maintains that Lamming is most successful with autobiographical themes.

Ngugi wa Thiong'o. "George Lamming's *In the Castle of My Skin*" and "George Lamming and the Colonial Situation." In his *Homecoming: Essays on African and Caribbean Literature, Culture and Politics,* pp. 110-26, 127-44. London: Heinemann, 1972.
Interprets *In the Castle of My Skin* as a study of the forces behind colonial revolt. The second chapter cited discusses exile as a dominant theme in Lamming's novels.

Nunez-Harrell, Elizabeth. "Lamming and Naipaul: Some Criteria for Evaluating the Third-World Novel." *Contemporary Literature* 19, No. 1 (Winter 1978): 26-47.
Examines protest elements in the fiction of Lamming and V. S. Naipaul. The critic characterizes Third-World writers as "descendants of those people of color whose history included colonization and, in some cases, enslavement by peoples of Europe."

Petersen, Kirsten Holst. "Time, Timelessness, and the Journey Metaphor in George Lamming's *In the Castle of My Skin* and *Natives of My Person.*" In *The Commonwealth Writer Overseas: Themes of Exile and Expatriation,* edited by Alastair Niven, pp. 283-88. Brussels, Belgium: Marcel Didier, 1976.
Examines "the theme of the journey" in *In the Castle of My Skin* and *Natives of My Person,* finding that Lamming's purpose "is not to probe the individual mind for its own sake, but rather to give an imaginative insight into the growth of West Indian sensibility and through that to offer an interpretation of West Indian history."

Ramchand, Kenneth. *The West Indian Novel and Its Background.* London: Heinemann, 1983, 310 p.
Includes numerous scattered references to Lamming.

Sunitha, K. T. "The Theme of Childhood in *In the Castle of My Skin* and *Swami and Friends.*" *World Literature Written in English* 27, No. 2 (Autumn 1987): 291-96.
Compares the theme of childhood in novels by Lamming and R. K. Narayan.

West, Anthony. Review of *The Emigrants,* by George Lamming. *The New Yorker* XXXI, No. 15 (28 May 1955): 122, 124.
Charges that Lamming's second novel suffers from disjointed narrative but commends the vivid portrayal of characters and events in individual episodes.

Nella Larsen

1891-1964

American novelist and short story writer.

American novelist Larsen is closely associated with the Harlem Renaissance, an era of unprecedented achievement in African-American art and literature during the 1920s and early 1930s. Although she is less well known than other black writers of this period, she has been highly praised for her two novels *Quicksand* (1928) and *Passing* (1929). In these works Larsen depicted urban middle-class mulatto women, and critics praised her for creating complex female characters constrained by society. Wrote Thadious M. Davis: "[Larsen's] intricate explorations of the consciousness and the psychology of female character form a legacy of the voice of a woman writer struggling to be heard, to convey her special messages, and thereby to free herself from the restrictions imposed upon the female by society."

Although Larsen disclosed very few details about her childhood, scholars have determined that she was the child of a West Indian man and a Danish woman and was born in Chicago. Larsen wrote in a short autobiography for her publisher that her father died when she was two years old and that "shortly afterward her mother married a man of her own race and nationality." Larsen grew up among white family members and apparently felt alienated in this environment. She attended Fisk University in Tennessee for a short time, audited classes at the University of Copenhagen in Denmark, and studied nursing in New York City. While she practiced nursing and worked as a librarian in New York, she and her husband, the physicist Dr. Elmer S. Imes, befriended writers and artists in Harlem. Thadious Davis—Larsen's foremost biographer—wrote that Harlem's activity seemed like a "whirlwind" to her. Larsen described in a 1925 letter to Carl Van Vechten: "It has seemed always to be tea time, as the immortal Alice remarked, with never time to wash the dishes between while." According to Davis, however, Larsen's affiliation with the creativity of Harlem was "controlled by her conscious desire to achieve recognition and [was] perhaps controlled too by her unconscious hope to belong." He added: "While for some the stirrings in Harlem may have been racial and aesthetic, for Larsen they were primarily practical. Her objective was to use art to protract her identity onto a larger social landscape as emphatically as possible."

In 1928 Larsen published her first and best-known novel, *Quicksand.* This semiautobiographical work involves a woman, Helga Crane, who searches in vain for sexual and racial identity. At the beginning of the novel, Helga, the daughter of a West Indian man and a Danish woman, is about to leave her teaching position at a Southern black college. She feels stifled by the environment there, so she journeys to Chicago, New York City,

and then to Copenhagen, where she is regarded as an exotic novelty and entertained in elite social circles. Helga returns to New York City—specifically Harlem—to reaffirm ties with blacks. There she undergoes a religious experience and marries the minister responsible for her awakening, the "jackleg preacher" Reverend Pleasant Green. Helga and the minister move to his home in the Deep South. While the marriage initially fulfills Helga's longing for an uncomplicated existence and for sexual gratification, she realizes her unhappiness as she is bearing her fourth child. *Quicksand* ends with Helga mired in rural poverty and pregnant with her fifth child. W. E. B. Du Bois wrote of the novel: "It is, on the whole, the best piece of fiction that Negro America has produced since the heyday of Chesnutt...." Larsen was praised for using metaphors of drowning and suffocation to depict Helga's foundering psyche, and Arthur P. Davis contended that Helga is "the most intriguing and complex character in Renaissance fiction."

Larsen followed *Quicksand* with *Passing,* the story of a light-skinned mulatto woman, Clare Kendry, who "passes" for white. Clare is attracted to Harlem for its excitement, and she daringly risks revealing her racial heritage to her bigoted white husband and to the society in which she lives. In Harlem Clare renews ties with a childhood friend, Irene Redfield, who could also pass for white. The two friends clash when Clare and Irene's husband begin a relationship. The novel ends in Clare's death—almost certainly at Irene's hand. Critics were divided in their reaction to *Passing,* but most found it inferior to *Quicksand.* Several commentators praised the novel for its depiction of passing; the novel is written from an individual psychological perspective instead of in the more usual broad sociological terms. Robert Bone considered *Passing* "the best treatment of the subject in Negro fiction."

When Larsen was at the height of her popularity in 1930, she was accused of plagiarism in her short story "Sanctuary." Although she was eventually exonerated, she was haunted by the accusation and the scandal. With the publication of *Passing,* Larsen became the first black woman to win a Guggenheim fellowship, but the grant did not help her produce any more fiction. Larsen was also experiencing marital problems at this time, and a crudely sensationalized 1933 divorce from her husband caused her to withdraw from literary circles in Harlem. Larsen spent the last twenty years of her life working as a nurse in Manhattan hospitals; she died in 1964.

Although critics have expressed regret that Larsen's literary career was so brief, they have acknowledged her significance as a portrayer of certain segments of African-American society: urban blacks and mulattos and middle class society—subjects often neglected by other writers. Of Larsen's importance in the development of black writing, Hazel V. Carby concluded: "It is important that Larsen returned her readership to the urban landscape and refused a romantic evocation of the folk, for in this movement she stands as a precursor not only to Richard Wright and Ralph Ellison but to a neglected strand of Afro-American women's fiction."

(For further information about Larsen's life and works, see *Black Writers; Contemporary Authors,* Vol. 125; *Contemporary Literary Criticism,* Vol. 37; and *Dictionary of Literary Biography,* Vol. 51: *Afro-American Writers from the Harlem Renaissance to 1940.* For related criticism, see the topic entry on the Harlem Renaissance in *Twentieth-Century Literary Criticism,* Vol. 26.)

PRINCIPAL WORKS

Quicksand (novel) 1928
Passing (novel) 1929
"Sanctuary" (short story) 1930; published in periodical *Forum*

Addison Gayle, Jr. (essay date 1975)

[*Gayle is an American critic best known as the editor of* The Black Aesthetic *(1971), a collection of essays by prominent black literary figures and artists in which he stated that "the serious black artist of today is at war with American society." In the following excerpt, he surveys Larsen's novels.*]

Quicksand is a novel almost modern in its plot and conflicts. More so than [George Schuyler's] *Black No More,* it seeks to broach the wider question of identity, not the loss of it, but the search for it, and to suggest that this search in a world, race mad, must produce serious psychological problems of the spirit and soul. Helga cannot accept the definition of herself as Black in the terminology of whites or affluent Blacks; therefore, she is forced into a self-destructive encounter with her own fantasies, forced to discover the realities of the world of poverty and desperation. Unlike the black middle class she cannot accept the argument that pigmentation of skin does not indicate a difference in cultural and historical values, cannot believe that the true images of black people do not reside in the "primitive" aspects of lower-class black life.

Thus her romanticism of the "poor suffering Black," in the final analysis, causes her undoing. For her identity cannot be discovered here, any more than it can in the life-style of the middle class or of whites, and the major flaw in the character of Helga is that she knew nothing of her true history and roots. She is incapable, therefore, of maintaining her balance in a world in which conflicting forces demand that she surrender her individuality. Her real conflict is not due to skin color, but to the inability to find self-validation in a world in which all choices are equally reprehensible. That this is the dilemma of Helga Crane does not suggest that it is the dilemma of the author, also.

For though better executed, technically, than *Black No More,* and presenting dimensions of the problem of identity which did not occur to Schuyler, Miss Larsen's novel by implication, at least, suggests, in the fate of the heroine, that the black middle-class values, no matter how imitative, are far superior to those of the white world or to that world of the black poor fantasized in the dreams of Helga Crane. Those who survive the novel, the Anne Greys, the Andersons, and the Vayles, imitative white men and women, though they may be, are conscious of an identity, no matter how flawed, which moves them outside that depicted in the writings of either Van Vechten or Jean Toomer. Theirs is a passive acceptance of the superiority of white images over black, and the ability to accept these minimize psychological difficulties of the kind encountered by Helga Crane.

Thus the middle-class-black reader of the twenties had little difficulty in choosing the fate of Anne Grey, hypocritical and pretentious, over that of Helga Crane, doomed to the quicksand of poverty and want. Anne is, after all, made in the image of James Weldon Johnson's protagonist [in *the Autobiography of an Ex-Coloured Man*]; she is cognizant of the fine distinctions between the black middle class and the black poor as is George Schuyler; unlike her friend, therefore, she engages upon no quest to establish her identity, stays clear of the lifestyle so akin to that of those suggested in the fiction of Jean Toomer. The tragedy of Helga Crane and Nella Larsen, as well, however, is that neither knew of the values of courage and endurance depicted in the lifestyle of Toomer's men and women, and therefore looked upon black life as lived by the poor through the distorted lenses of white sociologists. In their flight from themselves, Blacks have all too often accepted the same images of each other as have whites.

Nella Larsen's second novel, *Passing* (1929), differs fundamentally from the first. In terms of character development, organization, and fidelity to language, the second, divided into three sections—"Encounter," "Re-encounter," and "Finale"—is superior to the first. Though this structure makes for a more well-knit novel, none of her characters possess the stature of a Helga Crane, and Miss Larsen loses both focus and emotional intensity in her attempt to balance Irene Redfield and Clare Kendry against one another.... The experiences of both are juxtaposed in the novel, with the result that Clare's act of passing receives more extensive treatment than Irene's adoption of white-middle-class values. (pp. 111-12)

The dramatic intensity of *Passing* is derived from Miss Larsen's contrast between Irene and Clare.... Passing, as dramatized through the experiences of Clare, entails secrecy, deception, loss of identity, and eventually tragedy. It means to be separated from a life-style, which, for Clare, as for Helga, offers up romantic images of sensation and atavism, to lose something, in the James Weldon Johnson sense, of one's own soul. Even Clare's act of passing is suspect, based more upon expediency and hope of escaping poverty than upon commitment to a belief in the superiority of Euro-American values.... (p. 113)

Irene's life, by comparison, is superior to that of her friend. Though she has more than a casual interest in "passing," having done so in a small way, in department stores, etc., and, to the reader, seeming at times to resent the color of her husband (tea-colored) and of her son (dark), her interest is merely that of a curious woman, one interested in knowing the "...hazardous business of passing, this breaking away from all that was familiar and friendly to take one's chances in another environment...." Possessing the symbolism of the white world, Irene has little reason to completely adopt its images. The wife of a doctor, she has servants, security, and near dictatorial powers over her family. As a black woman, she has more prestige, let alone power, than would be accorded her were she white under similar circumstances. It is this knowledge that induces the paranoia concerning Clare and Brian. For without

Brian, the symbols Irene has acquired disappear. Prestige and standing in the black community amount to nothing in the absence of her doctor husband; her plan to send her children to Europe to study, where they will learn nothing of either sex or race, impossible of bearing fruition were Brian to desert her. Her standing in the white community as a representative of "respectable Blacks" and her role as missionary to the black poor must be forfeited with the loss of her husband. In light of her possessions, it takes no great leap of the imagination to believe that Clare Kendry met her death at the hands of Irene Redfield.

Aspects of Miss Larsen's personal life bear heavily upon both of her novels. Like Helga Crane, she was the product of a mixed marriage, and like both Irene Redfield and Clare Kendry, her own marriage was beset by turmoil. Her conflict between possible marriage to a white man and attempting to make a go of her marriage, all combine to present her as one beset by the problem of psychic dualism—the major theme in *Quicksand* and *Passing*—and accounts of her ambivalence concerning the meaning of blackness. Here she is both analogous to, and different from, Schuyler and Johnson. In the final analysis, her characters, Helga, Anne, Irene, and Clare, must either find their identities in the world of the black middle class, or face disaster. Not as partial to this class as either Johnson, Schuyler, or Jessie Fauset, and privy to its hypocrisies and pretensions, nevertheless, she believes that it is far superior to the lower class, and in some instances, for those like Irene Redfield, offers opportunities that the white world does not. Yet, both novels evidence the fact that she was not altogether happy with this special class, that she was capable of understanding, though not forgiving, their shortcomings. They wished, after all, to be both American and Negro, and yet Negro with limitations, defining the term in ways that moved them outside the sphere of less fortunate Blacks.

Like Miss Larsen herself, and Helga Crane, more specifically, theirs is a romanticism based upon repression or ignorance of the true facts concerning the black poor and their life-style. For Helga, nuances of the problem, occasioned by confusion of images, appear; for the black poor are both symbols of atavism and of the Christ figure, the poor suffering wards of American society.... (pp. 113-14)

Read Miss Larsen's novels and discover the disaster which awaits those who search for identity through fantasy—either by passing into the white world or affectuating too close an association with the poor of the black world. In the final analysis it is better to be Irene Redfield than either Helga Crane or Clare Kendry, though happiness is not, and cannot be, the key to the character of either. For the question is not one of happiness for Miss Larsen, but one of survival. Those characters in her novels, beset by problems of identity, are doomed to destruction; only those who accept the fact that identity is a prerogative of a special class of people are capable of surviving. Theirs is not so much the finding of an identity, but the creation of one out of material bequeathed by both the white and the black worlds. (pp. 114-15)

Addison Gayle, Jr., "The Confusion of Identity," in his The Way of the New World: The Black Novel in America, *Anchor Press, 1975, pp. 97-128.*

Claudia Tate (essay date 1980)

[*In the following excerpt, Tate challenges interpretations of* Passing *as a depiction of a "tragic mulatto."*]

Nella Larsen's **Passing** (1929) has been frequently described as a novel depicting the tragic plight of the mulatto.... Though **Passing** does indeed relate the tragic fate of a mulatto who passes for white, it also centers on jealousy, psychological ambiguity and intrigue. By focusing on the latter elements, **Passing** is transformed from an anachronistic, melodramatic novel into a skillfully executed and enduring work of art. (p. 142)

Ostensibly, **Passing** conforms to the stereotype of the tragic mulatto. However, many factors make such an interpretation inadequate. The conventional tragic mulatto is a character who "passes" and reveals pangs of anguish resulting from forsaking his or her Black identity. Clare reveals no such feelings; in fact, her psychology is inscrutable. Moreover, Clare does not seem to be seeking out Blacks in order to regain a sense of racial pride and solidarity. She is merely looking for excitement, and Irene's active social life provides her with precisely that. An equally important reason for expanding the racial interpretation is that alone it tends to inhibit the appreciation of Larsen's craft. Larsen gave great care to portraying the characters; therefore, the manner of their portrayal must be important and ultimately indispensable to interpreting **Passing**'s meaning. Thus, the "tragic mulatto" interpretation not only is unsuited to the book's factual content, but also disregards the intricately woven narrative.

An understanding of **Passing** must be deduced not merely from its surface content but also from its vivid imagery, subtle metaphors, and carefully balanced psychological ambiguity. For example, although the story has a realistic setting, it is not concerned with the ordinary course of human experience. The story develops from a highly artificial imitation of social relationships which reflect Irene's spiritual adventures. These characteristics are more compatible with the romance than with the tragedy. (pp. 142-43)

The work's central conflict develops from Irene's jealousy of Clare and not from racial issues which are at best peripheral to the story. The only time Irene is aware that race even remotely impinges on her world occurs when the impending exposure of Clare's racial identity threatens to hasten the disruption of Irene's domestic security. Race, therefore, is not the novel's foremost concern, but is merely a mechanism for setting the story in motion, sustaining the suspense, and bringing about the external circumstances for the story's conclusion. The real impetus for the story is Irene's emotional turbulence, which is entirely responsible for the course that the story takes and ultimately accountable for the narrative ambiguity. The problem of interpreting **Passing** can, therefore, be simplified by defining Irene's role in the story and determining the extent to which she is reliable as the sole reporter and interpreter of events. We must determine whether she accurately portrays Clare, or whether her portrait is subject to, and in fact affected by, her own growing jealousy and insecurity. In this regard, it is essential to ascertain precisely who is the tragic heroine—Irene who is on the verge of total mental disintegration or Clare whose desire for excitement brings about her sudden death. (p. 143)

Long before we encounter Clare Kendry, Larsen creates a dense psychological atmosphere for her eventual appearance. In the very first paragraph of the narrative, Larsen describes Clare's letter from Irene's point of view.... Larsen uses ambiguous and emotional terminology to refer to Clare's letter: "alien," "mysterious," "slightly furtive," "sly," "furtive," "peculiar," "extraordinary." Repeated references to the letter's beguiling unobtrusiveness and its enthralling evasiveness heighten the mystery which enshrouds both the almost illegible handwriting and its author. The letter itself is animated with feline cunning—"a thin sly thing." From one perspective the letter is insubstantial; from another, it possesses "extraordinary size." The letter rejects every effort of precise description. Provocative, bewitching, vividly conspicuous and yet elusive, the letter resembles the extraordinary physical appearance of Clare Kendry as she is later described, sitting in Irene's parlor.... (pp. 143-44)

In the next paragraph of the introductory section there are numerous references made to danger which incite a sense of impending disaster. The suspense is associated first with the letter and then with Clare. The letter is, to use T. S. Eliot's term, "an objective correlative," in that it objectifies abstract aspects of Clare's character, and its very presence reflects her daring defiance of unwritten codes of social propriety. Like Clare herself, the letter excites "a little feeling of apprehension,"...which grows in intensity to "a dim premonition of impending disaster,"...and foreshadows the story's tragic ending.

The letter, therefore, is a vivid though subtle narrative device. It foreshadows Clare's actual arrival and characterizes her extraordinary beauty. It also suggests abstract elements of Clare's enigmatic character which evolve into a comprehensive, though ambiguous portrait. Furthermore, it generates the psychological atmosphere which cloaks Clare's character, rendering her indiscernible and mysterious.

Irene is literally obsessed with Clare's beauty, a beauty of such magnitude that she seems alien, impervious, indeed inscrutable.... On one occasion we are told that

"Irene turned an oblique look on Clare and encountered her peculiar eyes fixed on her with an expression so dark and deep and unfathomable that she had for a short moment the sensation of gazing into the eyes of some creature utterly strange and apart."... On another occasion, Irene puzzles "over that look on Clare's incredibly beautiful face.... It was unfathomable, utterly beyond any experience or comprehension of hers."... Irene repeatedly describes Clare in hyperbole—"too vague," "too remote," "so dark and deep and unfathomable," "utterly strange," "incredibly beautiful," "utterly beyond any experience...." These hyperbolic expressions are ambiguous. They create the impression that Clare is definitely, though indescribably, different from and superior to Irene and other ordinary people. (p. 144)

Irene is characterized as keenly intelligent, articulate and clever. In this regard, the social gatherings seem to be more occasions for her to display a gift for witty conversation than actual events. Whether in the midst of a social gathering or alone, Irene often falls prey to self-dramatization, which is half egoism and half ironic undercutting for the evolving story.... Hence, her personal feelings are confined to an outer shell of superficial awareness. Although she is further portrayed as possessing an acute awareness of discernment, she tends to direct this ability entirely toward others and employ hyperbole rather than exact language for its expression. Her perceptions, therefore, initially seem generally accurate enough, until she becomes obsessed with jealousy.

As the story unfolds, Irene becomes more and more impulsive, nervous and insecure, indeed irrational. She tends to jump to conclusions which discredit her credibility as a reliable source of information. For example, on several occasions Irene assumes that Clare questions her racial loyalty.... On another occasion, she assumes that Clare is involved with the man who escorted her to the Drayton Hotel dining room.... And eventually, she concludes that Clare and Brian are having an affair.... Each of her assumptions may indeed be correct, but we observe no tangible evidence of their support; consequently, we cannot know with any certainty whether or not Irene's suspicions are true.

Although we only know the external details of Clare's life, we observe the fatal essence of Irene's psychology. We have also noted that thematic information is seldom communicated directly, but implied through dramatic scenes. Hence, Irene's character, like Clare's, achieves cohesion from the suggestive language Irene employs (especially when describing Clare), the psychological atmosphere permeating her encounters with Clare, and the subtle nuances in characterization. The realistic impact of incidents in and of themselves neither fully characterizes Irene nor conveys the novel's meaning. Meaning in *Passing,* therefore, must be pieced together like a complicated puzzle from allusion and suggestions. Irene gives form to Clare, but we are left with the task of fashioning Irene from her reflections of Clare's extraordinary beauty.

The ambiguous ending of *Passing* is another piece of the puzzle. The circumstances surrounding Clare's death support several interpretations. The most obvious interpretation is that Irene in a moment of temporary insanity pushed Clare out of the window. This interpretation has received widest acceptance, although the manner in which Larsen dramatizes Irene's alleged complicity receives no serious attention at all. Critics take her involvement in Clare's death for granted as merely a detail of the plot. A close examination of the events surrounding Clare's death, however, reveals that the evidence against her, no matter how convincing, is purely circumstantial. No one actually observes Irene push Clare, and Irene never admits whether she is guilty, not even to herself.... [At the] moment Clare falls through the open window,... Irene responds by saying that "she wasn't sorry. (That she) was amazed, incredulous almost."... Larsen provides no clarification for Irene's remark or its emotional underpinning. We do not know whether she is simply glad that Clare is permanently out of her life by means of a quirk of fate, whether she does not regret killing her, or whether she has suffered momentary amnesia and therefore does not know her role in Clare's death. In fact, Larsen seems to have deliberately avoided narrative clarity by weaving ambiguity into Irene's every thought and expression. For example, shortly after Clare's fall, Irene wonders what the other people at the party may be thinking about the circumstances surrounding Clare's death. Her speculations further cloud the narrative with other possible explanations for Clare's death.... A literal interpretation of this passage suggests that Clare may have accidentally fallen through the open window, or that she may have committed suicide. The passage can also be interpreted to mean that Irene hopes that the guests will mistakenly assume her innocence in their effort to arrive at a more agreeable explanation than murder. Of course, the passage may merely reflect Irene's genuine attempt to deduce what the others would necessarily conclude in light of her innocence. A few moments later, Irene fiercely mutters to herself that "it was an accident, a terrible accident."... This expression may be merely her futile effort at denying involvement in murder. Or, it may be her insistence that she is indeed innocent, through she suspects that no one will believe her. Or, she could be uncertain of her involvement and struggling to convince herself that she is innocent. In all cases we must be mindful that there is still no tangible proof to support one interpretation over another. Although we may be inclined to accept the conventional interpretation, we must remember that all evidence is circumstantial, and we cannot determine Irene's guilt beyond a reasonable doubt.

In reference to other explanations for Clare's death..., we note that the possibility of accidental death is the least satisfying interpretation. Consequently, we disregard it, despite its being a plausible assumption as well as the conclusion which the authorities reach.

The last alternative—suicide—tends to be inadvertently neglected altogether, inasmuch as Clare's motives are not discernible. Nothing is left behind, neither note nor explaining discourse, to reveal her motives. However, this interpretation does deserve consideration, since it enhances the ambiguous conclusion and draws heavily on Larsen's narrative techniques of allusion and suggestion.

Early in the text we are given the circumstances surrounding the death of Clare's father. When his body was brought before her, she stood and stared silently for some time. Then after a brief emotional outburst, (s)he glanced quickly about the bare room, taking everyone in, even the two policemen, in a sharp look of flashing scorn. And, in the next instance, she...turned and vanished through the door (never to return)."... the last scene in the story bears a striking resemblance to this, and the motives for Clare's behavior in the early scene suggest a possible motive for her suicide. "Clare stood at the window, as composed as if everyone were not staring at her in curiosity and wonder.... One moment Clare had been there...the next she was gone."... In both instances Clare surveys the fragments of her life, and in both she vanishes, leaving behind a painful situation which she cannot alter. In the latter, she is utterly alone, and suicide is the ultimate escape from the humiliation that awaits her. *Passing*'s conclusion defies simple solution.... What I am certain of, though, is that *Passing* is not the conventional tragic mulatto story at all. It is an intriguing romance in which Irene Redfield is the unreliable center of consciousness, and she and not Clare Kendry is the heroine.

Larsen's focus on a mulatto character, the plagiarism scandal surrounding her short story, **"Sanctuary,"** published in 1930, and aspects of her personal life probably account for the sparsity of serious, critical attention given to her work. Critics, of course, hastily comment on Larsen's skill as they either celebrate other Harlem Renaissance writers or look ahead to the socially conscious writers of the '30s. Few address the psychological dimension of Larsen's work. They see instead a writer who chose to escape the American racial climate in order to depict trite melodramas about egocentric black women passing for white. This critical viewpoint has obscured Larsen's talent and relegated *Passing* to the status of a minor novel of the Harlem Renaissance. But Larsen's craft deserves more attention than this position attracts. *Passing* demands that we recognize its rightful place among important works of literary subtlety and psychological ambiguity. (pp. 144-46)

> *Claudia Tate, "Nella Larsen's 'Passing': A Problem of Interpretation," in* Black American Literature Forum, *Vol. 14, No. 4, Winter, 1980, pp. 142-46.*

Lillie P. Howard (essay date 1987)

[*In the following excerpt, Howard examines* Quicksand *as a portrayal of "the other side of the Harlem Renaissance."*]

That the Harlem Renaissance represents the most phenomenal outpouring of art in all of its forms—music, drama, poetry, fiction, dance, sculpture, painting—by Black Americans since Africans reached these shores in the 1600s, there is no doubt. Much of the art from that period still remains and much of what we find in contemporary Afro-American literature, art, or music is not new but a re-creation of themes, variations of dreams, first posited by black artists during the 1920s. The Harlem Renaissance, then, like no other period before or after it, represents the pinnacle of artistic achievement for Black Americans. It was "the period when the Negro was in vogue." (p. 223)

[But] the many "happenings" in Harlem [during the Harlem Renaissance] were happening for whites rather than for Blacks. And that just as thousands of Southern Blacks had packed up their suitcases and come to Northern cities to look for themselves, so whites were flocking to Harlem, to Greenwich Village, and to Europe, to search for themselves too. In Harlem, the black performers and the white lookers-on were both searching for identity, yet both were mostly unhappy. The jagged irony. Beneath the laughter, then, beneath the loud glitter of the Harlem nightclubs, beneath the heady achievements of the Harlem Renaissance, was an undercurrent of sadness of tragic proportions.

Part of the difficulty for Blacks was the burden of double consciousness as Du Bois describes it in *The Souls of Black Folk:* "The Negro ever feels his twoness; an American, a Negro; two souls, two thoughts, two irreconciled strivings, two warring ideals in one dark body, whose dogged strength alone keeps it from being torn asunder." Part of the problem came from aping whites, no matter what the compelling attractions, to the extent that all identity or the possibility for identity was erased. Nella Larsen's *Passing* is a case in point. The other part of the problem is more elusive, inexplicable, "a lack somewhere"—something missing inside the person who is searching for identity. This is Jean Toomer's story, and this also is the compelling drama of Nella Larsen's *Quicksand* (1929), a novel which, because it explores many of the problems Blacks encountered in their search for identity, may be seen as the Black world distilled, the other side of the Harlem Renaissance—a look beneath the surface at a character who is unable to reconcile the disparate strivings within herself and is thus "torn asunder."

Quicksand depicts a young black woman with all the possibilities for success—which in this case means coming to a knowledge of and acceptance of self in spite of the constraints of the larger world. For reasons she is never able to name, however, Helga Crane is driven to efface herself. What happens to Helga is a fitting comment on the inability of Harlem, New York, or any other city to be more than a gilded six-bits (like Hurston's short story of the same name) to doubly-conscious people who were hankering after whiteness while simultaneously lacking the basic capacity for

Photograph of Larsen, taken by Carl Van Vechten.

knowledge of self, and thus for real identity—what the Harlem Renaissance was all about.

Larsen's **Quicksand** records the picaresque movements of Helga Crane as she seeks a clearer understanding of self and sustained happiness. The novel records this journey toward self which, in spite of her physical movements—from Naxos (in the South) to Chicago to New York to Copenhagen back to New York, then to the Deep South—spins Helga round and round in the same spot until she is virtually bogged down inside of herself. As William Bedford Clark points out, Helga "flees from the imperative of self-knowledge, seeking to allay the dissatisfactions which arise from within her with a change of scene and society. Her refusal to face the reality about herself in turn distorts her perception of the reality around her, finally breeding tragic consequences." By the end of the novel, not even physical movement is possible. The pain the reader is made to feel at the end of the novel is for the death of Helga's search and thus the death of Helga. Crane, who always seemed on the verge of meaningful discovery but who lacked the necessary mettle for real insight and for change, has, by the end of the novel, taken her last feeble stand against herself—

For in some way she was determined to get herself out of this bog into which she had strayed. Or—she would have to die

—and she has lost:

And hardly had she left her bed and become able to walk again without pain, hardly had the children returned from the homes of the neighbors, when she began to have her fifth child.

Helga, whose dilemma is so acute because she cannot reconcile herself to the reality of her race, or her sexuality, is driven toward a materialism which mask the essence of herself, and lacks the basic capacity to accept herself as she is and to move forward from this knowledge. At key points in Helga's life as she quests for happiness, she replaces one obsession with another until having explored and exhausted all obsessions she can name, nothing remains except the nameless. As Mary M. Lay has discovered, each turning point is accompanied by a contemplation scene which rivals that of Isabel Archer in Henry James's *Portrait of a Lady*. For Helga, however, each contemplation is a new exploration of the same question. Family is replaced with materialism, with sexuality, with race. The same question, at least in terms Helga can accept, remains answerless.

When the novel opens, Helga Crane is, by most standards, a success. Young, intelligent, attractive, she is a schoolteacher in a Southern educational institution, "the finest school for Negroes anywhere in the country." She has achieved a certain stature, and though she has no family to speak of, she is nevertheless engaged to a fellow-schoolteacher whose family is of some consequence. Recognizing the need for proper social connections in order to be accepted by the assimilated Black middle class, Helga, who is the offspring of a black father and a Scandinavian mother, has sought legitimacy through her fiancé, James Vayle. She feels that having the proper family connections will still the discontent within her, and give her the necessary entrée to happiness:

No family. That was the crux of the whole matter. For Helga, it accounted for everything, her failure here in Naxos, her former loneliness in Nashville. It even accounted for her engagement to James. Negro society, she had learned, was as complicated and as rigid in its ramifications as the highest strata of white society. If you couldn't prove your ancestry and connections, you were tolerated, but you didn't "belong." You could be queer, or even attractive, or bad, or brilliant or even love beauty and such nonsense if you were a Rankin, or a Leslie, or a Scoville; in other words, if you had a family. But if you were just plain Helga Crane, of whom nobody had ever heard, it was presumptuous of you to be anything but inconspicuous and comfortable.

Even without the proper family connections, however, Helga Crane *has* been anything but "inconspicuous and conformable," and stands apart from her peers for reasons that, at least on the surface, have nothing to do with family. Even her closest friend was "a little afraid of Helga. Nearly everyone was," partly because of "her longing for nice things," partly for what her detractors called "pride" and "vanity"—the beginnings of the trappings of materialism. Seeing the teachings of the school as hypocritical, Helga "had never quite achieved the unmistakable Naxos meld, would never achieve it, in spite of much trying. She could neither conform, nor be happy in her nonconformity... a lack somewhere."

Helga's quest for materialism is inseparable from her quest for the proper family. Both would bring status and security: "Always she had wanted, not money, but the things which money could give, leisure, attention, beautiful surroundings. Things. Things. Things." Most of her teacher salary had gone "into clothes, into books, into the furnishings of the room which held her. All her life Crane had loved and longed for nice things. Indeed it was this craving, this urge for beauty which had helped to bring her into disfavor in Naxos...."

Ironically, though Helga needs money, wants security, she is unable to take the necessary steps to attain either. Marriage to either her colleague at Naxos, James Vayle, or to the artist Axel Olsen in Copenhagen would have given her what she desired. Unlike the characters in Larsen's *Passing,* however, Irene Redfield, who marries a successful black doctor, and Clare Kendry, who marries a successful white businessman—neither for love—Helga marries neither. She admits that "To relinquish James Vayle would most certainly be social suicide, for she had wanted social background"; and when she rejects Olsen's proposal, she feels that "in some way, she would pay for this hour. A quick brief fear ran through her, leaving in its wake a sense of impending calamity. She wondered if for this she would pay all that she'd had."

Helga might even have been able to marry the man she really loves, Dr. Robert Anderson, head of the school in Naxos, later "welfare worker of some big manufacturing concern" in New York. When she might have responded favorably to Anderson's overtures, however, she does so with sarcasm and aloofness, only offering herself to him after he has married her best friend. It is ironic, too, that Helga would love the man who, though attracted to her because of it, refuses to acknowledge her sexuality or his own: "...no matter what the intensity of his feelings or desires might be, he was not the sort of man who would for any reason give up one particle of his own good opinion of himself. Not even for her." Sexuality and "good family" were, after all, contradictory terms. Society said so. And neither Anderson nor Helga was a social rebel, at least not yet, though for Helga, there was the impending "hardiness of insistent desire." And, of course, soon there would be the Reverend Mr. Pleasant Green, "proffering his escort."

That Helga with her aspirations would actually marry the Reverend Green is perhaps the surprise of the novel. But no, she had had enough of simply things. She had had things in Naxos and not been satisfied; things in New York and yet she had fled to Copenhagen; in Copenhagen she had had so many things that she had become one herself, a mannequin dressed by others, a mere exotic decoration that "didn't at all count." "Helga herself felt like nothing so much as some new and strange species of pet dog being proudly exhibited.... And in spite of the mental strain, she had enjoyed her prominence." But as in Naxos, in New York, in Copenhagen, Helga had grown helplessly discontent:

> She desired ardently to combat this wearing down of her satisfaction with her life, with herself. But she didn't know how.... Frankly the question came to this: what was the matter with her? Was there, without her knowing it, some peculiar lack in her? Absurd.... Why couldn't she be happy, content, somewhere? Other people managed, somehow, to be. To put it plainly, didn't she know how? Was she incapable of it?

What Helga has unconsciously resolved, it seems, is to unleash her sexuality, and as Axel accuses her of being capable of doing, selling herself to the highest bidder. Perhaps in that direction she will find the satisfaction, the happiness she seeks. When Anderson will not buy, Helga is so devastated that she becomes ill: "For days, for weeks, voluptuous visions had haunted her. Desire had burned in her flesh with uncontrollable violence. The wish to give herself had been so intense that Dr. Anderson's surprising, trivial apology loomed as a direct refusal of the offering." But then there was the Reverend Mr. Pleasant Green, discovered in a storefront church where the gutterworn, disheveled Helga, taken for a "scarlet 'oman," a "Jezebel," has managed to shelter herself and find religion, a temporary opiate to still her discontent. "And in that moment," says the narrator, Helga "was lost—or saved."

In the "tiny Alabama town" where Green is the "pastor to a scattered and primitive flock," Helga achieves some "relative importance." As with grade school, Naxos, Chicago, New York, and Copenhagen, Helga is at first fascinated by the novelty of the experience. As with each of her prior experiences, she feels that now she would be happy, "compensated for all previous humiliations and disappointments," certain that the feeling of satisfaction would last forever. In each of her prior experiences, she had never been happier longer than a year. In Alabama, however, with the Reverend Green, she was certain that she had found "the intangible thing for which, indefinitely, always she had craved. It had received embodiment." That "the intangible thing" was connected with her sexuality is indisputable:

> And night came at the end of every day. Emotional, palpitating, amorous, all that was living in her, sprang like rank weeds at the tingling thought of night, with a vitality so strong that it devoured all shoots of reason.

Because she has an acceptable outlet for her sexuality, because she is preoccupied with work, her own house, garden, chickens, pig, husband, three children, and God, Helga is able to blot out successfully the reality of her life with Green for twenty months and, with her faith in

God, longer: "Secretly, she was glad that she had not to worry about herself or anything. It was a relief to be able to put the entire responsibility on someone else."

At the beginning of the novel, Helga rejects Naxos because it tried to change the students into what they were not: "Teachers as well as students were subjected to the paring process, for it tolerated no innovations, no individualisms.... Enthusiasm, spontaneity, if not actually suppressed, were at least openly regretted as unladylike or ungentlemanly qualities. The place was smug and fat with self-satisfaction." When she returns to the South several years later, however, Helga approaches her neighbors from the Naxos' advantage:

> Her young joy and zest for the uplifting of her fellow men came back to her. She meant to subdue the cleanly scrubbed ugliness of her own surroundings to soft inoffensive beauty, and to help the other women to do likewise. Too, she would help them with their clothes, tactfully point out that sunbonnets, no matter how gay, and aprons, no matter how frilly, were not quite the proper things for Sunday church wear. There would be a sewing circle. She visualized herself instructing the children ... in ways of gentler deportment.

For reasons the reader finds difficult to understand, Helga now feels smug and self-satisfied. Perhaps having relinquished the responsibility of her own life to another, she now feels free to mold the lives of others.

The pain involved in giving birth to her fourth child, however, proves to be too much for Helga, even with her faith, even with her life in the hands of another. In fact, the pain is so powerful that it becomes a kind of secondary reality, displacing the first reality she has manufactured these many months. By the time she emerges from the clearer darkness of this pain, Helga is ready to admit her love for Anderson, her hatred for Green, the superficiality of her religion. And, of course, as with all contemplation scenes in the past, she has decided to flee: "... for she had no talent for quarrelling—when possible she preferred to flee. That was all." This time, however, she will flee later, after she has regained her strength: "It was so difficult. It was terribly difficult. It was almost hopeless. So for a while—for the immediate present, she told herself—she put aside the making of any plan for her going. I'm still, she reasoned, too weak, too sick. By and by, when I'm really strong—."

Just as Helga's blind quests for materialism, for the proper family, and for an acceptable outlet for her sexuality show fragmentation of self, so her ambiguity about her race shows why she can never be whole, why there will always be a void within her, happiness forever looming. "The end result of the journey from land, from one's roots, from one's ancestral past," says Addison Gayle in a discussion of Toomer's *Cane,* "means to sever all relationships with the race, to become one with the men and women of the novels of Johnson, Fauset, and Nella Larsen. It means, too, this journey from race,

and thus from self, to surrender one's identity, which once lost, is impossible to regain again."

As Gayle describes it, Helga, who comes from mixed parentage, "cannot accept the definition of herself as Black in the terminology of whites or affluent Blacks." She is not comfortable with the middle-of-the-road stance of her middle-class black friend Anne Grey who "hated white people with a deep and burning hatred ... but aped their clothes, their manners, and their gracious ways of living. While proclaiming loudly the undiluted good of all things Negro, she yet disliked the songs, the dances, and the softly blurred speech of the race." Nor is Helga willing to be "yoked to these despised black folk ... self-loathing came upon her. They're my own people, my own people, she kept repeating over and over to herself. It was no good. The feeling would not be routed."

Perhaps to prepare herself for her impending visit to her aunt in Copenhagen, Helga feels its necessary to divorce herself totally from Blacks: "She didn't, in spite of her racial markings, belong to those dark segregated people. She was different. She felt it. It wasn't merely a matter of color. It was something broader, deeper, that made folk kin." On the liner, enroute to Denmark, Helga revels "like a released bird in her returned feeling of happiness and freedom, that blessed sense of belonging to herself alone and not to a race." With Helga determined to disavow her Blackness, it is ironic that it is her color or race that the Danes wish to highlight and do. It is consistent, though again ironic, that Helga would blossom under this accent of her race, see it as right, actually revel in her Blackness, particularly in a country where she is a mere oddity that "did not at all count." Her thinking is decidedly middle class, closer to that of Anne Grey, though Helga never admits that fact.

Helga feels that it is the "acceptable" side of Blackness the Danes are highlighting in her, nothing dark or primitive. When she attends a circus where Black American dancers shamelessly perform, she is "filled with a fierce hatred. She felt ashamed, betrayed, as if these pale pink and white people among whom she lived had suddenly been invited to look upon something in her which she had hidden away and wanted to forget." Later she realizes that what the dancers possess, what the Danes see in her is "a precious thing, a thing to be enhanced, preserved." The portrait Axel Olsen has painted of Helga emphasizes this fact, though Helga disclaims the portrait, contending that it was of "some disgusting sensual creature with her features." When she returns to America, however, her "disgusting" sensuality is in the foreground of her life, central to her relationships with others.

From the beginning of the novel to the end, Helga moves from the black middle class to Naxos to the black middle class in New York to the upper-class whites in Copenhagen to poor "primitive" Blacks in Alabama. At one time or another, she shares allegiances with each group but never squarely shares an allegiance with herself. While she constantly seeks the approval of others, she is incapable of approving herself, of approving her Blackness. Because she can thus never realize an identity which ignores this irrefutable fact of race, Helga Crane is fated to never know who she is.

That society, the world, the irreconcilable fact of being Negro and American are not to blame for Helga's quagmire here, the novel makes clear. The arguments of Hortense Thornton [see Further Reading] to the contrary, there are alternatives all along the way for Helga and the reader to see. James Vayle, who at first is as mortified as Helga at the hypocrisies of Naxos, becomes "naturalized" nevertheless and is able to function well in that environment. When Helga complains to Robert Anderson about the suffocating Naxos environment, he responds with an insight and a prescription for living which Helga might have appropriated for her own use: "Some day you'll learn that lies, injustice, and hypocrisy are a part of every ordinary community. Most people achieve a sort of protective immunity, a kind of callousness, toward them. If they didn't, they couldn't endure." Anne Grey, in spite of her own ambiguities about race, has found a happiness she enjoys; the Danes show Helga the essence of herself, that there is something precious, to be valued, about her Blackness; Robert Anderson shows her that uncontrolled or undisciplined sexuality may hurt more than it helps, may cost more than one can ever pay. Helga admires Miss Denney, a member of the black middle class, who is frequently seen with whites, because Denny "had the assurance, the courage, so placidly to ignore racial barriers and give her attention to people." That her world is filled with alternative ways of being, Helga seems unaware. If she is aware, she is not cognizant of the implications of those lives for her own. Search as one might, one may not find an identity in America or abroad. But characters in the novel point out that one might fashion an identity for one's self, "out of material bequeathed by both the white and the black worlds." A mulatto, then, need not necessarily be tragic. And, in spite of the epigraph to the novel from Langston Hughes's poem, "Cross," one's racial heritage need not automatically be a burden.

That Helga Crane is unable to take advantage of what she has inherited from her black-white past suggests a lack somewhere in her character. That her life, her thwarted dreams, her inability to be reflect realities of the Harlem Renaissance period suggests the impotence of the period for many, while not detracting one whit from the many accomplishments of those who, in spite of or because of their strivings, stood "on top of the mountain free within themselves." (pp. 225-32)

> *Lillie P. Howard, "'A Lack Somewhere': Nella Larsen's 'Quicksand' and the Harlem Renaissance," in* The Harlem Renaissance Re-Examined, *edited by Victor A. Kramer, AMS Press, 1987, pp. 223-33.*

FURTHER READING

Bell, Bernard W. "The Harlem Renaissance and the Search for New Modes of Narrative." In his *The Afro-American Novel and Its Tradition*, pp. 93-149. Amherst: University of Massachusetts Press, 1987.
> Brief sketch of Larsen's life and career, concluding that "contrary to popular opinion," Larsen was "in revolt against the assimilationist assumption that blacks had to deny their color and culture, had to become white in mental outlook if not in personal appearance, in order to become first-class American citizens."

Carby, Hazel V. "The Quicksands of Representation: Rethinking Black Cultural Politics." In her *Reconstructing Womanhood: The Emergence of the Afro-American Woman Novelist*, pp. 163-75. New York: Oxford University Press, 1987.
> Attempts to direct attention to Larsen, noting the author's importance as a portrayer of urban black women.

Cooke, Michael G. "Self-Veiling: James Weldon Johnson, Charles Chesnutt, and Nella Larsen." In his *Afro-American Literature in the Twentieth Century: The Achievement of Intimacy*, pp. 43-70. New Haven: Yale University Press, 1984.
> Maintains that *Passing* "ultimately shows little more than the way the Great Migration had turned the old post-Reconstruction cabin into the Depression ghetto."

Davis, Thadious M. "Nella Larsen's Harlem Aesthetic." In *The Harlem Renaissance: Revaluations,* edited by Amritjit Singh, William S. Shiver, and Stanley Brodwin, pp. 245-56. New York: Garland Publishing, 1989.
> Portrait of Larsen describing her as a writer more interested in attaining fame than in writing. Davis writes: "Larsen 'worked' privately on her writing and publicly on her social standing. She promoted herself on the stage that encouraged her transformation."

Fleming, Robert E. "The Influence of *Main Street* on Nella Larsen's *Quicksand*." *Modern Fiction Studies* 31, No. 3 (Autumn 1985): 547-53.
> Draws parallels between *Quicksand* and *Main Street,* claiming that Larsen was influenced by Sinclair Lewis's work.

Hostetler, Ann E. "The Aesthetics of Race and Gender in Nella Larsen's *Quicksand*." *PMLA* 105, No. 1 (January 1990): 35-46.
> Analyzes *Quicksand* as a "complex representation of the world in which there is no such thing as blackness, whiteness, masculinity, femininity, or art in and of itself."

Stadler, Quandra Prettyman. "Visibility and Difference: Black Women in History and Literature—Pieces of Paper and Some Ruminations." In *The Future of Difference,* edited by Hester Eisenstein and Alice Jardine, pp. 239-46. Boston: G. K. Hall & Co., 1980.
> Determines that Larsen's Helga Crane is similar to a white feminist because she is frustrated, not physically anguished and oppressed.

Thornton, Hortense E. "Sexism as Quagmire: Nella Larsen's *Quicksand.*" *CLA Journal* XVI, No. 3 (March 1973): 285-301.

> Analysis of *Quicksand.* Thornton maintains that previous critics have regarded the novel's heroine as a stereotypical "tragic mulatto"—thus focusing on racism—instead of regarding Helga Crane as a woman persecuted by sexism.

Wall, Cheryl A. "Passing for What? Aspects of Identity in Nella Larsen's Novels." *Black American Literature Forum* 20, Nos. 1-2 (Spring-Summer 1986): 97-111.

> Examines the "tragic mulatto" image in Larsen's works, noting: "In a sense Nella Larsen chose to 'pass' as a novelist; not surprisingly, readers who knew what they were seeing—that is, reading—missed the point."

Youman, Mary Mabel. "Nella Larsen's *Passing:* A Study in Irony." *CLA Journal* XVIII, No. 2 (December 1974): 235-41.

> Contends that Larsen portrayed "passing" ironically in her second novel. Youman argues: "Irene Redfield, the true protagonist, who could (but rarely does) 'pass for white' has more truly lost her heritage than Clare who literally removes herself from Black life and lives as a white among whites.... [It] is Irene who 'passes.'"

Camara Laye

1928-1980

Guinean novelist, autobiographer, and short story writer.

Laye has long been recognized as one of the most important francophone novelists of Africa. Infused with spirituality and the vibrance of traditional African culture, his books confront such modern dilemmas as social and psychological alienation and the search for identity. Laye was exiled from his home country in 1966 because of his opposition to its government and was forced to live in Senegal until his death. As a result, much of his writing chronicles the plight of the exile and the problems of adapting to change and cultural dislocation.

Born in Guinea and raised a Moslem in that nation's countryside, Laye first encountered urban life when he left his tribal village to attend high school in Conakry, the capital of Guinea. In striking contrast to what he had experienced in his birthplace Kourossa, he found Conakry to be frankly modern: twentieth-century technology was everywhere. The vast difference between the two societies startled Laye and made his life in the capital difficult. Upon graduating from high school, Laye accepted a scholarship to study engineering in Paris. He found the contrasts between African and European cultures even more overwhelming. To ease the tension and loneliness of his student life, Laye began to write remembrances of his childhood in the Guinean countryside. These writings became his first book, *L'enfant noir* (1953; *The Dark Child*, 1954). Tracing Laye's emotional and intellectual development—from his tribal childhood, through his schooling in Guinea's capital, to his college life in Paris—*The Dark Child* poses questions about the preservation of traditional ways of life in the face of technological progress.

While some reviewers faulted Laye for ignoring the realities of colonial rule and idealizing the past in *The Dark Child,* others praised his depiction of the beauty and autonomy of African culture. Laye's next book, *Le regard du roi* (1954; *The Radiance of the King*, 1956), is widely considered his finest work. Reversing the conventional idea of a black person in an alien culture, *The Radiance of the King* centers on a white man alone in an African village. The story takes a white European named Clarence into the African countryside, where he is forced to adapt to the traditional culture in order to survive. He has no chance to earn a living unless he can find his way to the king's court and gain a position there. His search for the king forms the basis of the plot. "Clarence's search for the king with whom he hopes to hold an audience," wrote Jeannette Macauley, "becomes an obsession. It's the mirage which lures him on through dark forests with people he doesn't feel anything for, with people who do not understand him."

Critical regard for *The Radiance of the King* has been very favorable, with some commentators placing it among the very best of contemporary African literature. The book's "clever reversals, dreamlike evocations, surreal efforts and implementation in prose of techniques proper to film . . . ," Eric Sellin remarked, "have caused some admirers to deem it the finest African novel." Charles R. Larson called the novel Laye's "masterpiece" and explained that it "has long been hailed as the great African novel."

Laye's third book resulted in his forced exile from his homeland in 1966. *Dramouss* (1966; *A Dream of Africa*, 1968) comments openly on the dictatorial policies of Guinean leader Sekou Toure, who forced Laye into fleeing the country with his family. He was to live in neighboring Senegal, under the protection of Senegal's president Leopold Senghor, for the remainder of his life. *A Dream of Africa* begins with the narrator, Fatoman, returning to Guinea from Paris, where he has been living in exile for six years. Although he is happy to be back in his native land, he soon discovers that his country has serious problems. The independence it will soon be granted by France has brought on political violence and murder. Fatoman warns his people that this will only lead to a new, dictatorial government. "Someone," Fatoman proclaims, "must say that though colonialism... was an evil thing for our country,' the regime you are now introducing will be a catastrophe whose evil consequences will be felt for decades. Some-one must speak out and say that a regime built on spilt blood through the activities of incendiaries of huts and houses is nothing but a regime of anarchy and dictator-ship, a regime based on violence."

In 1970, during a visit back to Guinea to see her ailing mother, Laye's wife was arrested and imprisoned as an enemy of the state. Because he feared for her safety, Laye never again published an overtly political work. His next book did not appear until 1978 when, after teaching in Senegal for many years, he completed *Le maître de la parole: Kuoma Lafolo Kuoma* (1978; *The Guardian of the Word*, 1984). A marked departure from his earlier works, *The Guardian of the Word* is an epic novel set in thirteenth-century West Africa about the life of Soundiata, the legendary leader of the Mali empire. The novel is based on an oral account of the period popular among Guinean storytellers, or griots; Laye first heard the story from Babu Conde, one of the best-known of Guinea's griots. Because the novel focuses in part on the conduct of Mali's first emperor and the standards of behavior he set, it indirectly comments on the proper conduct of all governments, something Laye could not afford to do openly. With *The Guardian of the Word*, Laye drew praise not only for preserving and celebrating a fragment of African culture, but also for bringing to it his own creative force. Martin Tucker observed that "although Laye's last work is filled with surrealistic shades and European psychological insight, it is invigorated by the traditional African vision of the spiritual and historic."

Although he wrote only four books, Laye is considered one of Africa's most skilled francophone novelists. All of his works mirror predominantly European literary modes, yet, in their combination of apparently discor-dant elements, they paradoxically affirm traditional African life and culture. Speaking of *The Radiance of the King* in particular, Neil McEwan explained that "Laye is an artist in whom sources are entirely absorbed and the question whether this novel is French literature or African seems pointless; it is Camara Laye's." Adele King noted that Laye transcended his cultural back-ground, concluding that his work "belongs within the tradition of classic world literature, describing a person-al and cultural dilemma in accents that speak to all mankind."

(For further information about Laye's life and works, see *Black Writers; Contemporary Authors,* Vols. 85-88, 97-100; *Contemporary Authors New Revision Series,* Vol. 25; and *Contemporary Literary Criticism,* Vols. 4, 38.)

PRINCIPAL WORKS

L'enfant noir (autobiography) 1953
   [*The Dark Child,* 1954; also published as *The African Child,* 1959]
Le regard du roi (novel) 1954
   [*The Radiance of the King,* 1956]
Dramouss (novel) 1966
   [*A Dream of Africa,* 1968]
Le maître de la parole: Kuoma Lafolo Kuoma (novel) 1978
   [*The Guardian of the Word,* 1984]

Janheinz Jahn (essay date 1967)

[*In the excerpt below, Jahn praises* The Radiance of the King *as a work that exalts African culture.*]

In *The Dark Child* Camara Laye shows his understand-ing and respect for African traditions, and in *The Radiance of the King* he makes this tradition work on a stranger.

In *The Dark Child* Camara Laye shows the new spirit of French West Africans towards tradition. He did not consider his African childhood as something remote, primitive, something to be ashamed of. On the contrary: looking back on it from a distance, and having learned the technical skills European education had to offer, he discovered these skills had been animated, and had been more closely related to man, in his native civilisa-tion.... (p. 200)

[*The Radiance of the King*] is full of symbolism. It is usually considered as an ingenious allegory about man's search for God. But I think that the book cannot be seen in this sense only; it is ambivalent, even multivalent, as Sénghor says of all African art. Clarence, a European, finds himself without the help and support of his countrymen in an African environment. He is without money, without hope of outside help. He is thrown exactly into that position in which many Africans often find themselves in the European world. He has to conform. And thus he gradually becomes initiated. The whole book can be considered as a lesson in African wisdom.... (p. 201)

Noaga and Nagoa, the two boys who accompany Clar-ence all the time, are neither good nor bad. At any time they take their chance; they steal where there is an opportunity. Clarence is often worried about them, at times he is shocked, at times compelled to admire. They never consider life too seriously. There is no question whether they are to be redeemed by the King or not. "Tomorrow we go with the King," they say. Their redemption is not a question of good or evil, they cannot be rejected by the King, because already they live life as a unity. Clarence on the other hand can only be redeemed after he has learned that his moral problems are not essential. This is one of the strongest arguments against the Christian interpretation of the end of the book . . . . (p. 202)

The end of the novel, often misunderstood, means that even the white man in Africa can be redeemed and accepted when he shows his will to learn and not only to teach. And that Camara Laye in all his lessons does not consider the African way of faith and redemption the only one imaginable and superior. He wants to say that it is the only right way for Africa and that it is of equal value with an other way of mankind. (p. 203)

> *Janheinz Jahn, "Camara Laye: Another Interpretation," in* Introduction to African Literature: An Anthology of Critical Writing from "Black Orpheus," *edited by Ulli Beier, Northwestern University Press, 1967, pp. 200-03.*

Charles R. Larson (essay date 1972)

[*In the following excerpt, Larson surveys Laye's novels, citing* The Radiance of the King *as "the greatest of all African novels."*]

[A] "trapped" portrayal of the African who has been assimilated, and then found it impossible to accept his own traditional culture, has played a part in a number of . . . significant Francophone African works: . . . [including] Camara Laye's autobiography, *L'Enfant noir (The African Child)* (1953) . . . . (p. 170)

[It] is with Laye that the picture of the "assimilated" novelist takes on its most significant twist: the négritude novel. Usually négritude is thought of as a poetic movement, but in the works by Camara Laye, African cultural values have been so thoroughly woven into the novel's form that the result is a kind of assimilated presentation of African values, African traditional life: négritude. The result is a much more unified introduction of anthropological materials into the texture of the novel itself, rather than the inclusion of ethnographical background in isolated passages. The African cultural values have been so deftly handled in the works of Camara Laye that the reader is almost unaware that they are there. It is this use of what I call "assimilated anthropology" that, I believe, is the major distinction between the Francophone African novelist and the Anglophone African novelist, for the Francophone writer has remained much closer to the French classical tradition, changing the novel in fewer ways than his Anglophone counterpart, and, as a result, has produced a more intellectualized concept of African traditions, values, and life . . . .

L'Enfant noir is undoubtedly one of the most significant works by an African writer and certainly the most readable autobiography by a writer from tropical Africa. It is also, I feel, an illustration of Laye's early attempts at unifying cultural materials into a coherent artistic achievement. Anthropological materials are introduced into the narrative, yet, for the most part, they are left unexplained. Laye wants the reader to accept them at face value, and admits that he often has no explanation for the unusual happenings he has recorded . . . . The clear, matter-of-fact tone records incident after incident in the child's growing awareness of the Islamic/animistic world around him. By the end of the narrative, the reader feels an immense sense of personal loss at a way of life which has rapidly come to a halt. *L'Enfant noir* is a beautiful account of traditional African life, as delicately wrought as a Dürer engraving, a detailed tableau of the paradise Laye knew in his youth and later lost. (pp. 171-72)

Dramouss, Laye's third book, published in 1966, is a sequel to *L'Enfant noir,* and the most striking element, that immediately jolts the reader, is the harshness of the book when it is compared to Laye's first work. The softness, the sense of oneness and wholeness expressed in the earlier book is missing in *Dramouss,* which is ostensibly concerned with Laye's life in France and his return to Guinea after living several years in Paris. Laye's interest here is in politics in post-independent Guinea—in the failures of the African regime to live up to the pre-independence promises. As such, this work moves beyond the sense of the personal, which was so vitally important in *L'Enfant noir,* to a concern with problems of nationhood, nationalism, and political charlatanism, resulting in one of the most scathing commentaries on African political institutions written by a Francophone African writer. The publication of *Dramouss* also led to Laye's forced exile from Guinea to Senegal.

Le regard du roi (The Radiance of the King), which was first published in 1954, is, in the view of several critics of African literature, the greatest of all African novels. The novel has won this distinction, it seems, because of Laye's ideal assimilation of African materials into the novel form. As has so frequently been the concern with African novelists, Laye too is outwardly at least concerned with the conflict between African and Western civilization, yet his treatment in *Le regard du roi* is unlike any other we have seen. His main character is not African but European, and instead of recording the conflicts that an African encounters in his exposure to the West, Laye, in this lengthy novel, has reversed the usual pattern and presented a European and his difficulty in coming to grips with Africa. Laye's story goes far beyond this, however, for it is not simply a confrontation which ends in confusion or tragedy, but a story which begins in chaos and ends in understanding, grace, and beauty. The white man may be the protagonist, but Africa is the antagonist. It is the hero's ability to comprehend the magnitude and the complexity of the African experience—to realize that his own culture has little significance at all—which leads us to a basic aspect of what Senghor has seen as the final evolutionary stage of cultural syncretism—"reformed négritude," a kind of world culture which embodies the best of all cultures. Instead of being destroyed in the process, or trapped forever between two cultures like Medza in *Mission terminée,* Laye's hero becomes assimilated into the African culture and through this process achieves salvation.... (pp. 173-74)

[The] final paragraphs of *Le regard du roi* constitute one of the most beautiful passages in all African literature. The reader coming upon this ending for the first time cannot help being deeply affected, deeply startled.... (p. 223)

If Laye spells out his meaning a little too clearly at the end—and I do not believe that he actually does—this, too, as the reader thinks back over the entire novel, may be interpreted as part of a wider fabric textured with ideas of grace and salvation which are present almost from the very beginning of the narrative. There are any number of indications throughout the story that death can be the only fulfillment for Clarence, a final union with the king and Africa. The only major differences I see in Laye's *Le regard du roi* when it is placed next to Anglophone African fiction are an absence of direct transformation of oral literary materials into the text of the story, and a more limited sense of the situational aspect of African fiction. Nevertheless, it can be argued that Camara Laye's *Le regard du roi* is of all African novels that which fits best into the situational category, since Clarence, who is archetypal of Western man in particular, is symbolic of everyman and his difficulties in adjusting not only to a different culture, but to life itself. (p. 226)

> *Charles R. Larson, "Assimilated Négritude: Camara Laye's 'Le regard du roi'," in his* The Emergence of African Fiction, *revised edition, Indiana University Press, 1972, pp. 167-226.*

Abiola Irele (essay date 1980)

[*In the following excerpt, Irele defends Laye's work, arguing that the author's novels are "far from being an endorsement of colonial rule."*]

Shortly after the publication in 1954 of Camara Laye's autobiography, *l'Enfant Noir (The African Child)* [published in the United states as *The Dark Child*], a review signed by a certain Alexandre Biyidi appeared in the journal *Présence Africaine* in which Laye's work was attacked and its author taken to task for turning his attention away from the exactions committed by the French under the colonial system and escaping into a world of African innocence. To Biyidi (none other than Mongo Beti, writing under his real name and at that time, the very beginning of his career, as a novelist of the colonial situation), Laye's book appeared as a futile diversion from the necessary political and social role of the African writer in the historical context of colonialism.

The irony was that, far from being an endorsement of colonial rule, with its specific French justification as a "civilising mission", Laye's book was in fact a form of denial of the assumptions and explicit ideological outgrowth of the French colonial enterprise. For against the idea of a primitive order of life in traditional African society by which the coloniser sought to justify his presence, Laye's autobiography presented an image of a coherence and dignity which went with social arrangements and human intercourse in the self-contained African universe of his childhood. Investing that image with a warmth that gave his book a special appeal as a literary work, Laye also gave it an ideological implication as an ardent defence of his African antecedents against European denigration. For if Laye's book cannot be construed as an explicit anticolonial statement, its whole meaning tended towards the same end, so that its position in the development of a modern Africa expression gives it a historical value of the first importance from both a literary and ideological point of view. (p. 617)

[The] whole bent of Laye's stylistic effort—even with its lapses, understandable in a first work—is specifically the evocation of a particular atmosphere with which his imagination has endowed the life and society he experienced as a child. And it is through this evocation that we are able to participate with our emotions, rather than with our heads, in the quality of life he recreates. Laye's purpose in his autobiography is thus at the opposite pole to that of Maxim Gorky or Ezekiel Mphahlele, for example, whose explicit intention is to present the hard and even sordid conditions under which they did their apprenticeship of life.

It has often been remarked that the dominant feeling in *The African Child* is the pervasive nostalgia determined by its theme, but this element of Laye's autobiography has no real meaning unless taken in its close association with his sense of profound attachment to the world of his African childhood and to its values, a sense which the book evinces so distinctly and with such convincing charm. The human significance of the book resides in its record of the process of development of an individual personality within the living context of a social and cultural environment which defines ultimately a moral and spiritual universe.

It is in this respect that *The African Child* points to the matter and spirit of the two novels that follow. Laye's three imaginative works are in fact organised around his historical personality and express through this organisation his individual understanding of the world as conditioned by his early experience. His preoccupation with the possibilities of a deep spiritual experience which the African world seemed to him to offer constitutes the unifying point of view of all his work, which finds its supreme expression in *Le Regard du Roi (The Radiance of the King).*

As Wilfred Cartey has suggested (in his study, *Whispers from a continent*) Clarence, the white hero of this novel, can be taken as a reversed image of the African Child of the autobiography, the embodiment of Laye himself in his spiritual self at the end of the process it describes.

The adventure of Clarence becomes in this light the return movement of Laye's alienated consciousness towards an original "realm of infancy." ... The wider meaning of Laye's symbolic novel is of course clear— the journey motif immediately calls attention to the archetypal dimension of Clarence's adventure and experience. But if the significance of the novel at this level is large enough not to be missed, it remains clear that its theme is rigorously particularised, related directly to the historical situation in which Laye's imagination is operating. The allegorical reference is thus not to some abstract universal of human consciousness, but rooted in the historical and racial dialectic of the colonial relationship. In other words, the novel prolongs the theme of the autobiography and accomplishes in a symbolic register its implication; for Laye, it is as much a question of projecting a visionary ideal of African spirituality as making a statement upon man's eternal quest for fulfilment and illumination.

The impressive achievement of *The Radiance of the King* has raised two problems which it is necessary to consider for its proper appreciation. The first concerns the extent of Laye's indebtedness to Kafka in the novel. The mazes and labyrinths, the enigmatic characters and the atmosphere of moral oppressiveness that marks the human situations at many points in the novel can certainly be ascribed to the influence of Kafka. But to fasten upon these details is to disregard the important fact that the symbolic scheme of the novel and its very spirit owe nothing to Kafka, but issue directly out of an indigenous African tradition of symbolic narrative. (pp. 617-18)

The other problem concerns the rumour that has been growing in scope and volume and tending to cast doubts on Laye's authorship of the novel, as indeed of *The African Child* .... [The] literary argument is based on the fact of a subsequent disappointing performance which is employed to cast doubts on an earlier achievement. In the case of Laye, the feebleness of *Dramouss (A Dream of Africa)* is taken as an indication of his fundamental incapacity to produce a *tour de force* of the order and quality of *The Radiance of the King.* The weakness of this argument lies in the well-proven fact that even the greatest writers have been known to produce work of indifferent quality in their "nodding moments". It was the same Conrad, for instance, who wrote masterpieces like *Nostromo* and *The Secret Agent* who went on to write the feeble melodrama of *Chance.*

What is more, any sensitive reader ought to be able to discern the remarkable continuity of Laye's style in all his writing ...: a style distinguished by its naive-like pattern of repetitions....

It is true that *A Dream of Africa* must be counted largely a failure, yet it is bound to the earlier works in the sense that it carries forward Laye's preoccupation into the post-colonial situation. Laye's imagination is clearly not a political one, of the order of Ngugi's, for example; in its immediate social and political reference, the last novel does not manifest an intelligence of the realities of contemporary Africa comprehensive enough to sustain a statement as compelling, in its own terms, as that of the preceding novel. Nonetheless, it represents an effort to situate the historical evolution of the continent in the perspective of the spiritual ideal elaborated in *The Radiance of the King.* To that extent, it is the same imagination at work in both novels, an imagination attuned to the spiritual, and bent towards an exploration of the deep recesses of the human mind in its responses to the elemental, to the whole compass of human experience and possibility.

And it is especially in Laye's effort to derive a live sense of this dimension of human life and consciousness from his understanding of and feeling for the spiritual potential of our ancestral culture that, I believe, the value of his achievement will be seen to reside. (p. 618)

Abiola Irele, "Camara Laye: An Imagination Attuned to the Spiritual," in West Africa, *No. 3272, April 7, 1980, pp. 617-18.*

Adele King (essay date 1980)

[*In the following excerpt from her* The Writings of Camara Laye *(1980), King examines theme, narrative technique, and tone in Laye's four novels.*]

L'Enfant noir might be compared to such novels as James Joyce's *Portrait of the Artist as a Young Man,* and Marcel Proust's *A la Recherche du temps perdu,* in which the author's reminiscences have been given an artistic form. In the process the personal becomes universalised and representative of widely shared forms of experience. Thus Joyce's novel is a portrait of *the* artist as a young man, not simply memories of his own youth. Laye's book is about the modern African child. (p. 17)

A major subject of the book is the traditional culture of Laye's childhood and what it means to him. New, European-influenced historical pressures, however, lead him away from his family and society. His life can be said to be representative of many Africans who find it necessary to go to the city and eventually to Europe for further education. To find his place in the modern technological world, the African risks losing contact with his family, village and tribal traditions. African writing in English and French often deals with cultural conflicts or protests against the process of estrangement from traditional life. Unlike many writers, Laye handles this subject with nostalgia; something important has been lost, but the loss is a necessary part of modern life.

Another major theme in the story, not especially African, is the loss of childhood innocence, the necessity of growing up and moving beyond the security of one's family. Related to this theme is a more religious one, the need to follow one's destiny, or maybe the path that God has ordained. Thus the book deals with life in a traditional society, the problems of young Africans at a particular moment of history, and the universal themes of growing up and fulfilling one's destiny. It is in the blend of these various elements that the artistry of *L'Enfant noir* is to be found. (pp. 17-18)

[It] is a carefully controlled story... presented with economy and restraint. The mother is both an individual dramatically portrayed and a symbol of Africa, continent of warmth, mystery and love. The setting is presented vividly, but without strong emphasis.... Effects of contrast are achieved subtly, without explicit statement, through the juxtaposition of events.... [Language] and tone reflect the child's widening awareness of the world. Each chapter is clearly constructed, rising to an emotional climax usually followed by a statement of the narrator's sense of loss. His nostalgic tone, however, is balanced by an awareness of the inevitability of change. The theme of regret for the lost African past is treated not with self-pity or political polemics, but with restraint. A particular moment in Laye's life and in the history of Africa has been transformed into a minor classic, in which the autobiographical form has been raised to the level of art. (pp. 36-7)

[*Le Regard du roi*] is a bizarre, often comic story of a misplaced white man [Clarence] in archetypal Africa, and is narrated from the point of view of this white man. It embodies, however, the same essential themes as *L'Enfant noir:* cultural conflict and the quest for salvation. (p. 38)

Le Regard du roi may be seen as a story about a man's attempt to find meaning in an ambiguous world in which his accepted values have been undermined, in which the behaviour of other people is often incomprehensible and in which perceptions are always fluctuating. (p. 40)

The culture of Aziana [the African village where Clarence lives] is based on closeness to the physical world, on emotion rather than reason, on chance rather than rights. It is a culture opposed to the rationalistic, mechanistic society of modern Europe. Clarence's main aim initially is mere survival.... [Eventually] he changes and his idea of what he is seeking also changes. He loses the need to assert his individuality and his rights; he becomes part of a community and attuned to the physical world surrounding him. His experience might be seen as the correction of European rationality by African sensuality and reliance upon emotions and dreams. The novel suggests that life in such a traditional society may be closer to the fundamental truths of human nature.

Clarence's adaptation to Aziana may therefore be considered as an illustration of some of the themes of the Negritude movement. According to [L.S. Senghor], the black soul is sensitive to 'the apparently imperceptible rhythms of the world'; the black man 'cannot imagine objects as essentially different from man... all of Nature is animated by a human presence'. Black culture is based upon emotion rather than reason. African religion is dominated by love. 'Morality consists in not breaking

the communion of the living, the dead, the spirits and God.' The community is of primary value and the individual develops best within communal organisations: 'the need for fraternal communion is more profoundly human than that of retiring within one's self'. *Le Regard du roi* reflects this view of African culture, a culture which Laye assumes, as does Senghor, to be common to black Africa.

There is a sense, however, in which *Le Regard du roi* can be read as a gentle parody of Negritude. Because the Africa that Clarence discovers doesn't appear to be on the map or in the twentieth century, it seems an ideal for which one might yearn, but not a political or cultural entity to be found in the modern world. Just as in *L'Enfant noir* Laye realizes that the world he is describing is already past..., so in *Le Regard du roi* he paints an ideal for which he might feel nostalgia but which he does not suggest can be recovered. He knows he is not portraying a real Africa and seems to be mocking the concern of the Negritude movement to define an essential African culture as if it did still exist. (pp. 42-3)

As in *L'Enfant noir*, Laye has universalised his story. Beyond being an image of the confrontation of European and African cultures, the novel deals with the theme of any man trying to adjust to a strange society, of every man's homelessness in the world. Clarence is not only a European in a strange land, he is the average man in a world where faults can be committed inadvertently, where nature will often appear cruel, where sensuality will frequently overwhelm common sense. Making this ordinary European a symbol for Everyman is a way of countering 'black racism', a way of showing that the essential human experiences go beyond colour. The story then transcends the realm of human culture to become a tale of man's search for God. Laye has brought to his work his African world view and his personal religious mysticism, but expressed his vision in a work that has universal resonances. (p. 47)

[*Dramouss*] is the story of the development of the African child [introduced in *L'Enfant noir*] (now called Fatoman) when he goes to France, as he learns to blend two cultures—traditional Malinké and French—and tries to find the best of the two worlds to which he is now attached. It is also the story of his disillusionment when he realises that neither of these two cultures has a place in his native land after its independence, and that he cannot find the role for which he thought he had prepared himself. Like the narrator of *L'Enfant noir,* the hero of *Dramouss,* who tells his story in the first-person, is a type, representing the Guinean intellectual of Laye's generation.... (p. 63)

Fatoman as an individual is less important than the community. The story of his life is interwoven with the larger story of the problems of Guinea just before and after its independence, and with reminders of its traditional culture. *Dramouss* is rather a portrait of Guinea than a portrait of a person. Its themes include the demagogy of a developing political system that is moving towards a one-party state, the weakening of the ties with France, and the decline of traditional artistic culture. It is also a portrait of Laye's generation of European-educated Guineans and the problems confronting them as they seek to understand how their homeland has changed.

The story of Fatoman's life since he left Guinea to study in France is told in long chapters, interspersed with other kinds of material; at the centre of the novel there is a folk tale told to Fatoman and his family by a traditional griot. The narrative is episodic: Fatoman's return to pre-independence Guinea after six years in France, and his marriage to Mimie (the Marie of *L'Enfant noir*); a restless night when he thinks back on his life in Paris; a visit to his family home in Kouroussa where he hears the griot's tale, talks to his father in his workshop and attends a political meeting; another restless night during which he has a strange dream, prophetic of his country's future. After a break in the narrative representing a passage of several years, there is an epilogue recounting Fatoman's return to settle in Guinea after independence, when he finds that many of the worst fears expressed by his father or foreseen in his dream have become realities. Essentially, therefore, action in the present is followed by reminiscence or by dreams of the future. Laye deliberately destroys the autobiographical linearity. The broken chronological sequence reflects Fatoman's uncertainty as to how his life is developing. The pattern is present, past, present, future, with an epilogue in which the foreseen future has become the present. (pp. 63-4)

Laye's purpose in *Dramouss* is not to recreate a life story, but to explain, through a mosaic of different situations narrated in varying manners, why the conflict—between his desire to live in his native land and his love of both Malinké and French culture—has arisen. Fatoman is a representative type, embodying a problem that Laye himself was facing: a problem that has little to do with personalities, but rather with fundamental moral and political issues. (p. 74)

Dramouss is addressed to ... the European-educated African who expected that from his own tensions and sufferings would be born a new culture, remaining true to its traditional roots while combining the best of Africa and Europe. The present disillusionment of such hope and the prophecy that the dream of Africa may yet be realised are the basic themes of the novel. Laye sees his role of artist as entailing an analysis of present failings and preserving hope for the future. (p. 80)

The religious theme in *Dramouss,* which goes beyond Fatoman's personal problems and even beyond the dilemma of Guinea, shows Laye's profound conviction that in spite of our tribulations God is watching over us and we must try to follow his way. It is essentially the same quest for salvation as in *Le Regard du roi,* posed here on the level of a people rather than of an individual ....

Dramouss is, however, less successful as a novel than Laye's earlier work .... Characterisation is wooden, dialogue is often rather stilted. Fatoman is primarily a spokesman for the author's opinions and uncertainties concerning the role of the educated elite, the problems of independence and the future of the country; he is not a well-rounded fictional character. (p. 81)

In *L'Enfant noir* Laye found a simple, classic structure, and a way of creating an artistic distance between his experience and the novel through a narrator who looks back on his childhood. In *Dramouss,* Laye changes the names of himself and his wife, simplifies the events in his life—omitting, for instance, any reference to the fact that he had written and published two successful novels while in France—and fragments the chronology of the narrative. Since the emotional wounds he experienced in returning to Guinea were still open, he cannot, however, adopt the detached tone he used in *L'Enfant noir.* (p. 82)

[Nevertheless, the] stylised political allegory, the blending of various kinds of narratives to show the transitional era in which one culture was breaking down when no viable alternative had been established, the evocation of a nightmare tyranny and of an eventual divine salvation, all give *Dramouss* value as an expression of the tensions of Laye and his generation; value which, in the final analysis, outweighs its formal weaknesses as a novel. (p. 83)

[*Le Maître de la parole*] is the story of Soundiata, the thirteenth-century Manding leader who united a number of small kingdoms to form the Empire of Mali, one of the great political dynasties of Africa. It is the history of Camara Laye's own people: Soundiata's capital, Niani, was close to the site of Kouroussa; one of the warrior kings who supported him was Tabon Wanna Fran Camara, from whom Laye claimed descent. The book is a literary transcription of the history of Soundiata told by a Malinké griot, Babou Condé, whom Laye recorded in 1963 in Upper Guinea. Babou Condé, who was at least eighty years old when Laye interviewed him, was a griot of considerable renown. He told Laye the oral tradition he had learned from his own family, which traces its line back to the thirteenth century when an ancestor was the griot of Soundiata's nephew. (p. 86)

Laye speaks of the oral tradition preserved by the griots as essentially artistic; its significance is less as historical document than as aesthetic preservation of the essential values of traditional culture .... (p. 89)

In writing *Le Maître de la parole,* Camara Laye attempts to fulfil the role of the griot in a modern context and for a modern audience. The griot uses traditional material. The basic historical and legendary material of the narrative in *Le Maître de la parole* has been written before, in various renditions in English and French. Laye, however, uses it for his own purposes. By conveying a picture of the essential facts of the moral and social life of his people, he wishes to show the relevance of the legend to modern life and also to amuse his contemporary audience with an entertaining tale. (p. 90)

Before beginning the tale, Laye includes several introductory chapters in which he discusses some of his favourite themes. The material world is not all important; spiritual forces direct our destiny and can be approached by those with mystical insight. Such insight is more readily available to those close to the natural world; thus, in general, to Africans. A knowledge of the past is essential to help modern African countries define themselves.... The problem, as he defines it, is that an assimilationist colonial policy, coupled with a lack of historical documentation on the precolonial era, has left Africans with little knowledge of this past.

Laye's view of traditional Malinké civilisation is that it was only slightly influenced by Islam, that it reached its apex in the fourteenth century in the Mali empire, and that it has since remained static. This means that the history of the Manding people is largely internal; its civilisation rose and fell independent of outside influences; it was already in decline before European colonisation started. Laye has claimed that *Le Maître de la parole* is the most authentically African of his books because it all takes place before the colonial era. He cites, however, among the reasons for the decline of Manding civilisation, the Moroccan invasion and the slave trade. It is the present that will show if this traditional culture can again develop vitality. For Laye such a renaissance means both studying the past and being open to benefits to be gained from other cultures. As usual in his work, respect for tradition goes hand in hand with welcoming the best of foreign culture. (pp. 90-1)

Laye also uses the narrative of Soundiata to attack, rather indirectly, the present regime in Guinea. Soumaoro's dictatorship is based on terror and the destruction of his opponents. The destiny of Soundiata, who came to power with the aid of many rulers oppressed by Soumaoro, was to 'incarnate the collective consciousness of the exasperated peoples of the savannah, to make of it a white-hot fire of revolt against the tyrant.'... *Le Maître de la parole* concludes: 'May the example of Soundiata and his people guide us as we walk on the slow and difficult path of the evolution of Africa,'... thus expressing the hope that a new Soundiata will arise, probably a slight hope to Camara Laye by 1978. (p. 91)

Laye is thus working in a fashion similar to the griot's, stressing moral truths and showing their contemporary relevance. Like the griot he occasionally intervenes in the story (as well as in the notes and introduction) to make observations. He defends, for instance, the role played by women in Malinké society, as he did in *L'Enfant noir.* He speaks of the value of liberty, only recognised when it is lost, and castigates the use of torture—allusions to contemporary Guinea. He makes Soundiata think of how he is different from the Arab traders he meets, defends monotheism, and even com-

ments that the most beautiful woman is always one with whom a man has never spent a night—a curiously modern commentary in a medieval epic. Like the griot, Laye occasionally refers to his own personal experience.

Le Maître de la parole uses techniques common to traditional oral tales. There are praise songs in Malinké (followed by translations into French), and recitations, genealogies and celebrations of heroes, which are undoubtedly close to Babou Condé's own words. There is also a basic story mode, told in the author's words; after the introductory chapters, Laye does not claim that the form of the tale is directly attributable to Babou Condé. Laye aims at simplicity. He called *Le Maître de la parole* an 'exercice de style', an attempt to make an ancient legend seem real to the reader, and comprehensible even to children. If he explains customs for his European reader (divination systems, proof of virginity at marriage rituals, Malinké musical instruments), he is more specifically aiming, as in *Dramouss,* at African readers. The simplified dialogues and action are perhaps explicable in terms of the goal of reaching an audience less sophisticated in the techniques of modern fiction.

The style of *Le Maître de la parole* is appropriate to an epic; it includes frequent repetitions, and more images and metaphors than in Laye's previous work.... While the use of images based on the local environment may in some cases be attributable to Babou Condé, Laye is seeking a style appropriate to the epic story: 'The children nestled in the branches of the trees like clusters of grasshoppers'...; 'the ground into which it sank as if into a ripe papaya.'... Sometimes, however, the comparisons seem modern, anachronistic: 'she became as burning, as feverish as a body attacked by malaria.'...

Laye does, however, make significant changes in the traditional epic, changes influenced by the role of the artist in contemporary Africa and which reflect his own previous work. *Le Maître de la parole* is in many ways a logical continuation of his novels. If it represents a departure from the contemporary world of *L'Enfant noir* and *Dramouss,* it is similar in setting to the feudal African kingdom described in *Le Regard du roi. Le Maître de la parole* also stresses many of the themes of his earlier work: the importance of the sacred, the mystery of the world, best approached by those attuned to nature and able to read its signs; the quest to understand and follow God's will; the need to be part of a community and to be humble in the service of that community; the need to undergo an arduous initiation into adult responsibilities. (pp. 92-3)

Laye has turned the narrative into something closer to the novel form. He often portrays [scenes]... in a realistic fashion; he describes the social organisation of the Niani community, without the idealisation of village life found in *L'Enfant noir.* He builds up longer episodes than those found in other versions of the narrative: the hunters' search for the buffalo, Sogolon's wedding, Soundiata's birth, his first steps at the age of ten, the game of Wori, and Nâna Triban's discovery of Soumaoro's vulnerability. In each of these scenes there is extended dialogue and detailed description of the thoughts of the characters, often presented as a kind of interior monologue. As the story is legendary and filled with miraculous events, the result is a tension between the subject-matter and the method of narration. *Le Maître de la parole* is an interesting, but sometimes disconcerting amalgam of epic events and supernatural occurrences—with no attempt to give them rational explanations—combined with a realistic fictional technique and psychological analysis more common to the European novel. (p. 94)

Le Maître de la parole is less intense in tone than Laye's earlier work. Its aims are perhaps too mixed. Although including historical notes and a word list of Malinké, it is not a scholarly study of Manding culture. As a transcription of a traditional tale, it is perhaps too modern and literary. As a novel within the European tradition, the narrative contains too many long genealogies, secondary characters and interventions in the plot. It is perhaps impossible to combine successfully all the *genres* that Laye was attempting within one work. *Le Maître de la parole,* however, fulfils an essential aim in recalling the relevance of traditional moral values for the present. By writing a story which the contemporary African reader, accustomed to modern fiction, can find entertaining, Laye was continuing, in a new fashion, the work of the griots, and contributing to the search for an African fictional form. (p. 96)

When we look for a psychological unity in Laye's work we may find it in an extreme attachment to his motherland. In *L'Enfant noir,* published six years after he left Guinea, Laye wrote: 'it was a terrible parting! I do not like to think of it. I can still hear my mother wailing. It was as if I was being torn apart.' Although he says that he worked out his anxiety about leaving Upper Guinea by describing his departure, it is probable that this traumatic event has provided the emotional charge behind all his work. (p. 124)

Whether or not *L'Enfant noir* is better than *Le Regard du roi,* the same experience of feeling uprooted from a childhood paradise, of feeling alienated in a foreign culture, directly expressed in *L'Enfant noir,* is transposed in the fiction of *Le Regard du roi,* and explains the emotional trauma of *Dramouss,* written when it was apparent that no return was possible and that exile was inevitable. This trauma is even apparent in *Le Maître de la parole,* Soundiata's exile often suggests a parallel to Laye's own; the triumphal return to Niani, described in other versions of the legend, is omitted.

Laye's life was in many ways an illustration of a moment in cultural history. He was representative of a kind of experience that is unlikely to recur at present. For him the normal problems of growing up were combined with the shock of a radical change in culture, a shock which—in the world of the transistor radio even in the poorest villages of West Africa—can never again be so powerful. Laye gave this experience perhaps its

purest literary expression. In spite of the modesty of his background, in spite of the many obstacles to his desire to write, he managed to produce work of great interest at a moment when West African literature was in its infancy.

African literature in European languages had a remarkable development in the years just before and after independence, a flowering that many critics have predicted will not continue. It was a moment when the tensions of traditional and modern cultures produced a heightened sensibility and when the definition of self seemed also to be the definition of the tribe, the country, or even Africa itself. The poetic and the social functions of literature could be united to a degree seldom possible in modern western civilisation. Camara Laye is one of the seminal figures in this development. If his work never reaches the heights of the masters on whom he modelled himself—Flaubert, Kafka—it belongs within the tradition of classic world literature, describing a personal and cultural dilemma in accents that speak to all mankind. (pp. 124-25)

> *Adele King, in her* The Writings of Camara Laye, *Heinemann Educational Books Ltd., 1980, 144 p.*

FURTHER READING

Balogun, F. Odun. "Mythopoeic Quest for the Racial Bridge: *The Radiance of the King* and *Henderson the Rain King.*" *The Journal of Ethnic Studies* 12, No. 4 (Winter 1985): 19-34.
  Examines Laye's *The Radiance of the King* and Saul Bellow's *Henderson the Rain King,* noting that "both novels create desirable literary myths of racial harmony in order to bridge the racial gap created by undesirable, fallacious racist myths."

Cheuse, Alan. "Empire of the Senses in Africa." *Los Angeles Times Book Review* (2 September 1984): 6.
  Briefly reviews *The Guardian of the Word,* describing it as "one of those books that transmit from one generation to the next elemental visions on which society is founded...."

Scarboro, Ann Armstrong. "The Healing Process: A Paradigm for Self-Renewal in Paule Marshall's *Praisesong for the Widow* and Camara Laye's *Le regard du roi.*" *Modern Language Studies* 19, No. 1 (Winter 1989): 28-36.
  Explores six elements of the paradigm for self-renewal in *The Radiance of the King:* "the decision to depart, psychological disorientation, interaction with a mentor, episodes of purification, psychological reintegration and arrival home."

Sellin, Eric. "Trial by Exile: Camara Laye and Sundiata Keita." *World Literature Today* 54, No. 3 (Summer 1980): 392-95.

Overview of Laye's novels, focusing on *The Guardian of the Word*.

Yoder, Lauren W. "Wall Imagery and Initiation in *Le regard du roi.*" *The French Review* 57, No. 3 (February 1984): 329-35.

Analyzes symbolism in *The Radiance of the King.*

Andrea Lee

1953-

American novelist and nonfiction writer.

Lee has distinguished herself as a noteworthy journalist and novelist. In her nonfiction work, *Russian Journal* (1981), she provided an insightful perspective on contemporary Soviet life, and in her novel, *Sarah Phillips* (1984), she recounted the reckless past of a middle-class black woman. These writings, while embracing different themes, have earned Lee praise as a keen observer and a consummate technician, one whose probing insights are inevitably rendered with concision and grace. As Susan Richards Shreve noted: "Andrea Lee's authority as a writer comes of an unstinting honesty and a style at once simple and yet luminous."

The youngest of a Baptist minister's three children, Lee was born in Philadelphia in 1953. She received an M. A. degree in English literature from Harvard University and has worked as a staff writer for the *New Yorker* magazine. Her first book, *Russian Journal,* derives from a diary she kept in 1978 while in the Soviet Union, where her husband was studying for ten months on a fellowship. Relying on public transportation and a rudimentary grasp of the Russian language, Lee visited a wide variety of places, including public baths, college campuses, farmers' markets, and nightclubs. She met bureaucrats, dissidents, and even contraband sellers; encountered many cynics and youthful materialists; observed a disturbing number of public drunks; and became acquainted with some of the country's more unsettling aspects, notably surveillance. In her journal Lee wrote that, due to their circumstances, she and her husband "got a view of life in Moscow and Leningrad that was very different from that of the diplomats and journalists we knew."

Following the publication of *Russian Journal,* critics cited the book as a refreshing, if narrow, perspective on Soviet life. Susan Jacoby called Lee's book "a subtly crafted reflection of both the bleak and golden shadings of Russian life" and added: "The subject matter of this journal is highly idiosyncratic .... What Miss Lee offers are the people, places and experiences that touched her most deeply." Like Jacoby, Peter Osnos cited the book's worth for "conveying a feeling of place and atmosphere" and declared: "Lee writes very well. There is a warmth and freshness about her style that makes reading [*Russian Journal*] effortless." Osnos was especially impressed with Lee's depiction of the Soviet people, particularly its younger citizens. "What is best about the book—what distinguishes it from other books about the Soviet Union published in recent years—is her accounts of friendships with young people," he contended. Similarly, Walter Clemons praised Lee's "unassuming delicacy and exactness," asserting that "her most winning quality is her capacity for friendship." Michael Irwin

also found Lee an engaging reporter. He praised her "astuteness" and called *Russian Journal* "a considerable exercise in observation, empathy and personal and literary tact."

Lee's refusal to write about being black in the Soviet Union caused a few reservations among critics reviewing *Russian Journal.* Jacoby called this omission "regrettable" and contended that Lee's race "must have affected [her Russian friends'] perceptions (and Miss Lee's) in some say." She added: "Miss Lee's responses would surely have been as interesting as the rest of her observations, and I wish she had included them." Osnos also noted Lee's reluctance to write about race. He described the omission as "slightly awkward" and observed: "Apparently, she feels that her blackness has nothing to do with her time in the Soviet Union. That is her business. But she never even says as much."

As if responding to charges that she avoided racial subjects, Lee followed *Russian Journal* with *Sarah Phillips,* an episodic novel explicitly concerned with a contemporary black woman. The work's title character is introduced as a woman grown disgusted with her boorish, racist acquaintances—and lovers—in Paris, where she has been living in self-exile. At the end of the first chapter Sarah decides to leave Paris, and in the ensuing sections she recalls events—principally from childhood and adolescence—contributing to her present circumstances. Unlike most black characters in American fiction, Sarah is an assimilated elitist whose background is middle class, and her goal is to scandalize her bourgeois parents. She even accepts tokenism when she becomes the first black student at an exclusive girls' school. Her father is a minister involved in the civil rights movement, an involvement that embarrasses her when he is briefly imprisoned for civil disobedience. Bored with America, Sarah leaves the country after her father's death and her graduation from college. She settles in Paris, where she indulges in various interracial sexual shenanigans, including a *ménage-à-quatre*. By novel's end, however, Sarah realizes the emptiness of her assimilation into white society—both European and American—and reaches a greater understanding of herself and her heritage.

With *Sarah Phillips* Lee earned further literary acclaim. Bruce Van Wyngarden described the novel as a "coming-of-age remembrance in which detail and insight are delightfully, and sometimes poignantly, blended." He also deemed it "an engaging and promising" first novel. Likewise, Francis Goskowski called *Sarah Phillips* an "engaging, witty" work and asserted that with it Lee emerged as a "major novelistic talent." Patricia Vigderman was one of several critics who noted the novel's breakthrough perspective on race, particularly the characterization of Sarah as an assimilated black. Vigderman conceded that "this novel does not fit easily into the Afro-American tradition, and may even meet with some disapproval," but she nonetheless considered it "a very gracefully written book about black identity."

With *Russian Journal* and *Sarah Phillips* Lee has gained recognition as a talented writer of immense promise, and her forthcoming works are greatly anticipated. "Without a doubt," stated Goskowski, "Ms. Lee will be heard from again, and she will command our attention."

(For further information about Lee's life and works, see *Black Writers; Contemporary Authors,* Vol. 125; and *Contemporary Literary Criticism,* Vol. 36.)

PRINCIPAL WORKS

Russian Journal (nonfiction) 1981
Sarah Phillips (novel) 1984

Peter Osnos (essay date 1981)

[*In the following excerpt, Osnos praises Lee's insights into Soviet culture in* Russian Journal.]

Lee writes very well. There is a warmth and freshness about her style that makes reading [*Russian Journal*] effortless. She takes us wherever she is, conveying a feeling of place and atmosphere that is the mark of real talent . . . .

In fact, it was probably Lee's innocence that gave her the gall to undertake a work like this in the first place. An aspiring Sovietologist would be daunted by the need to draw conclusions and make judgments. Knowing how much one doesn't know can be debilitating when it comes to taking on a subject as broad as Soviet life today.

Yet, in most respects, Lee succeeds. Her descriptions of what it is like to be Russian are right on technical details and sensitive to cultural patterns. Her visits to the public baths and farmers' markets, her accounts of Sundays spent with friends or of an encounter with Soviet-style hippies strike responsive chords in someone, like me, who has the same memories. Moreover, humanizing the Russian people is especially important in politically tense times such as these.

What is best about the book—what distinguishes it from other books about the Soviet Union published in recent years—is her accounts of friendships with young people . . . . Her insights into the materialism of Russian youth, the conservatism of some, the nihilism of others, tell us a lot about the coming generation of Soviets. This is valuable because the people she met include leaders of the next generation, who are Muscovites, many of them enrolled at Moscow University. A certain selectivity is at work in her sample. Lee's friends are people either authorized to mingle with foreigners or daring enough to do so. Foreigners tend to meet a preponderance of disenchanted or rebellious Soviets; that, evidently, was Lee's experience too.

There is one slightly awkward problem with the book. Andrea Lee, it turns out, is black. The only indication of this comes in a single sentence describing her meeting with an Ethiopian student. "Toward me," she writes, "he showed the absolute lack of interest with which many Africans greet American blacks." Later she quotes the student as saying that the Russian "masses call us black devils and spit at us in the street." There is nothing else in the book about Lee's experiences as a black. She writes in considerable and intimate detail about Russians, but tells us nothing about the part race may have played in her relationships with them.

Lee's husband is white. Interracial couples in the Soviet Union are extremely rare. That this did not lead her into some interesting encounters is hard to believe. Apparently, she feels that her blackness has nothing to do with her time in the Soviet Union. That is her business. But she never even says as much. Discovering that Andrea

Lee is black gave me the feeling that, for all of its candor, **Russian Journal** is holding some things back....

For all its charm, **Russian Journal** is no more than it self-effacingly claims to be: a gifted young writer's impressions of a relatively short time in a new and very different world. That she got as far as she did in that world is a tribute to Andrea Lee.

> Peter Osnos, "Blue Jeans in Red Square: An American in Moscow," in Book World—The Washington Post, *October 25, 1981, p. 10.*

Mary Louise Patterson (essay date 1982)

[*In the following excerpt from a 1982* Freedomways *review, Patterson finds fault with Lee's claim of political objectivity in* Russian Journal.]

[In **Russian Journal,** what Andrea Lee] has written most about are the disaffections of those people whom she apparently spent most of her time seeking out and befriending—dissident Jews and black marketeering Russian youth. Strange. All of these people are deeply alienated from Soviet life and society, seem primarily concerned with acquiring Western friends, clothing, phonograph records and mannerisms (like gum chewing), and dream incessantly of the bygone Russian aristocracy or of escaping to the "free world." The Soviet Union in all of its political and cultural complexity, contradictions, historical richness and profound importance in today's world was not encompassed by Ms. Lee's tunnel vision. Moreover, it is regrettable that the author has placed her excellent and colorful command of the English language in service to the cause of misrepresenting her perceptions as "facts" and then beguiling the reader into accepting them. (p. 116)

Ms. Lee states at the outset that she arrived in the USSR free of political bias, even much endeared to the country based on her fond memories of the many Russian fables she heard during her childhood. Constantly and cleverly, she strains to maintain this fiction of impartiality and political innocence throughout the book. Thus, she is shocked by her dormitory room's "Orwellian" radio, which can only be turned down to an inaudible level and not off—although such radios are frequently found in hotel rooms in the United States, Mexico and Europe. At another point, she mentions that she smuggled letters for Russian dissidents into Moscow, that she and her husband house-sat in Moscow for a vacationing U.S. diplomat, and that she and her husband were State Department approved. Unbiased?

The book lacks any self-questioning or self-examination with respect to the meaning of her Soviet experiences. She doesn't even relate her Afro-American identity to the story. The pretention of honesty is exposed as fraudulent early on when she describes a Friday night dance at the U.S. Embassy, an event into which she and her husband sneaked in a Russian student. She writes:

"When I ... stand in the embassy commissary, with its rows of peanut butter jars and boxes of sugared cereal, or walk among the big shiny Detroit cars in the embassy driveway, or talk to the earnest, affable bureaucrats who work in the offices, I feel as if I'm seeing part of a dream America. The dear, blind, brash, innocent America of television shows and commercials—the kind of vision that we simple souls in exile would naturally long for, and unfailingly recreate." Does Ms. Lee honestly believe that *all* of us *simple* souls would recreate that vision, including us Black folk, if we were abroad? And would we all feel that we were "in exile"?

Andrea Lee's highly subjective views paint a picture of the Soviet Union that has the net effect of reinforcing the fanatical anti-communism, warmongering and bellicosity so much in vogue currently. I don't doubt her experiences or that she met the people she describes. But the journal reminds me of the fabled blindfolded man who, led to the elephant, feels its leg and describes a tree. (pp. 116-17)

> Mary Louise Patterson, "Subjective, Narrow, View," in Freedomways, *Vol. 22, No. 2, second quarter, 1982, pp. 116-17.*

Christopher Booker (essay date 1982)

[*In the following excerpt, Booker praises* Russian Journal *as a "distinguished addition" to Soviet travel literature.*]

Since 1917 there must have been several hundred books by Western visitors describing visits to the Soviet Union—the vast majority falling into one or two clearly defined categories. On the one hand, as landmarks in the history of self-deception, were those stereotyped eulogies of the 1930's and 1940's, extolling the heroic collectivism of an imaginary paradise in the making. On the other, right from the start, has been a very different, much more personal type of book, by authors ranging from H. G. Wells and Malcolm Muggeridge to Laurens van der Post and George Feifer. And despite the enormous variety of their styles and points of view, not the least interesting feature of this second group of books is how often they also have seemed to describe a familiar pattern of experience. (p. 23)

A distinguished addition to this second group of books is **Russian Journal** by Andrea Lee, a black American girl ... who four years ago spent ten months in the Soviet Union.... (pp. 23-4)

She does not attempt any sweeping analysis of Soviet life or 'the Russian character'. She merely observes, with what, if our contemporary novelists wrote so well, one might be tempted to call 'a novelist's eye'—through some 35 almost self-contained vignettes of people and places. We visit scenes familiar and unfamiliar—Moscow student life, a Moscow peasant market, a bathhouse full of giggling Muscovite ladies letting their hair down like children; further afield, Stalin's birthplace in the little Caucasian town of Gori, a Leningrad nightclub (from where they were driven home by a taxi-driver singing Verdi arias at the top of his voice). We join Miss Lee and her husband as they take part, with a 'worker' friend Petya, in the great May Day parade past Lenin's tomb, catching a rare close-up glimpse of Brezhnev and other members of the Politburo....

Some of the longer episodes read like vivid short stories, such as a chilling Christmas Day visit to the luxurious *dacha,* where [journalist] Victor Louis holds court with his upper-middle class English wife Jennifer; or a strange encounter with Tikhon Khrennikov, the unspeakable Chairman of the Union of Soviet Composers, who invites them to a premier of some of his music.... Then there is the moving profile of Ibrahim, a proud, sad Ethiopian, brought to Moscow like so many of his young countrymen to be educated as a loyal Marxist, who has conceived such a passionate hatred of the Soviet Union that he wishes only to return to fight with the anti-Soviet Eritrean nationalists. His brother has already died in this cause, and when Ibrahim requests in a session of table-tapping to speak to his brother's ghost, the answer to his first unspoken question comes back, 'Death'. What did you ask, a girl timidly enquires. 'I asked my brother what I could expect when I get home'.

The dark, oppressive underside of Soviet life is constantly present in the background, but all the more forcefully for being so understated. An old woman sneaks past the guard into the brightly-lit Aladdin's cave of a *beriozka* (hard-currency shop), just to take a look at the forbidden plenty on the shelves before being hustled out. Andrea and her husband go up onto the Lenin Hills with Petya to watch a fireworks display, and are shocked to be brusquely pushed by armed guards into a tiny stockade. Even the loyal Petya is forced to comment 'it embarrasses me to have you see that. Our government is awfully afraid of riots, you see. People gathered together make revolutions, and we can't have another of those'.

In common with so many predecessors, Miss Lee finally records how, when they left Soviet soil, she and her husband were flooded with elation. But they had undoubtedly left behind some part of themselves with the unforgettable people they had met in that poignant land—even with Grigorii, their 'informer', who makes his last appearance taking them out into the woods of the Lenin Hills, in his 'bureaucrat's suit', to hear the nightingales.... What a country! (p. 24)

> Christopher Booker, "Russia Revisited," in The Spectator, *Vol. 248, No. 8031, June 12, 1982, pp. 23-4.*

Michael Irwin (essay date 1982)

[*In the excerpt below, Irwin offers a generally positive review of* Russian Journal.]

The entries [in ***Russian Journal***] are chronologically ordered: there is little theorising and no thesis. Andrea

Lee likens them to 'a set of photographs taken by an amateur who is drawn to his subject by instinct and capricious inclination'. This unpretentiousness is one of the great strengths of her book. She obviously has no interest in selecting or distorting evidence to make out a case.

It is her general good sense which inspires confidence.... [She] is neither complacently nor guiltily American. She recognises that as a Westerner, physically and sartorially, she becomes an automatic focus of attention, an inevitable influence on the scenes in which she takes part: in that sense, what she sees tends to be atypical. It is by no means an irrelevant factor that, in so far as her personality emerges from the notes, she seems friendly but shrewd, always prepared to like people and to enjoy herself but not to the detriment of her alertness. Although she hasn't come looking for bad news, she isn't going to be conned or intimidated. She also wins credit for her refusal to adopt a pose of detachment, to imply that she herself is immune to the pressures she sees as deforming the lives of her acquaintances. When she comes under surveillance as a result of running English classes for a group of Soviet Jews on the verge of emigration, she grows conscious 'of an intense anger forming like a stone in my guts ... a personal anger based on fear'. At first she is put out by the devouring stares of subway passengers fascinated by her clothes, but later, starved of ready visual stimulation in Moscow, she becomes a starer herself whenever she encounters 'a well-cut dress (terribly rare), a handsomely bound book (still rarer), or an attractive face.' She is all the more persuasive an observer for implicating herself in what she observes....

Andrea Lee brings to these vignettes a novelist's talent for conveying moods in very few words. While avoiding grandiose diagnoses she makes many incidental remarks that catch the attention. When describing Yura, a hunchbacked librarian in Leningrad, she reflects that the physically and mentally defective seem far better integrated into the social system than are their American counterparts: 'Deformed by nature or age, they are very often the strictest guardians of social form, many of them, like Yura, deeply patriotic. For him, life does seem good, perhaps the best it could be in any country.' After an evening with some Moscow hippies she comes to the surprising conclusion that their life-style 'isn't as much a rebellious departure from the social norm as it was for hippies in the United States'. Economic pressures and the shortage of housing have made even the most respectable Russians accustomed to pooling resources or dossing down in one another's houses.

Given her astuteness, it is a pity that Andrea Lee isn't prepared to speculate a little more ambitiously. She glances at several issues which she could profitably have explored further. In discussing the deletion of sex-scenes from foreign films she mentions 'the odd mental talents a diet of such films must develop: an ability for elision, for constant suspension of logic'. But comparable deficiencies exist at every level of life in a Communist society. What views can the Soviet citizen hold on housing or agriculture or disarmament if he distrusts the party line but has no alternative source of fact or theory? What profitable occupation can there be for the mortal and intellectual energies that in a democracy are expended on political controversy? The freak diet on which the Russian has to subsist must surely foster not only 'odd mental talents' but odd mental limitations of several kinds. What Andrea Lee remarks in passing she could well investigate at large....

The book suffers from one or two other minor limitations, most of which the author herself would no doubt acknowledge. She describes only a narrow social spectrum. The friends she makes are students, artists, dissidents, professional people, the great mass of those she sees in the streets remaining inscrutable: 'glum workmen in grimy quilted jackets, fantastically fat old women in shawls, girls with exhausted faces under their makeup'. It must be conceded, even of the class she knows best, that the Russian who will consort with a visiting American is likely, by definition, to be unrepresentative.

Her husband, Tom, is said to speak 'near-native' Russian. She herself lays claim to 'a far slighter knowledge of Russian strengthened only by a good ear for language'. It would be reassuring if she admitted to the possibility that she might have misunderstood a conversation or misconstrued its subtext. Arguably she sees too simply, too clearly. She can make participation in the private problems of Russian life sound implausibly unproblematic. She seems to accept her involvement in the crises of her new friends with the amiable unselfconsciousness of a David Copperfield. Some episodes seem too neat, too 'finished'....

This may seem an over-elaborate reaction to a work that is deliberately simple in manner and scope. But the modest truthfulness which Andrea Lee aspires to is most difficult to attain, requiring precariously delicate adjustments of attitude and tone on the author's part. A more theoretical book could stand or fall on the theory: *Russian Journal* must win assent by the authenticity of all its parts. To note the author's few miscalculations is to suggest the difficulty of an ostensibly undemanding enterprise. *Russian Journal* is a considerable exercise in observation, empathy and personal and literary tact.

> Michael Irwin, "Hidden Privilege," in London Review of Books, *Vol. 4, No. 17, September 16 to October 6, 1982, p. 20.*

Susan Richards Shreve (essay date 1984)

[*In the following review, Shreve argues that* Sarah Phillips *reads like "unsentimental autobiography."*]

The central concern of *Sarah Phillips,* Andrea Lee's first novel, is with a young black woman's quest to invent her own history in the long shadow of a powerful inheritance. Sarah is from a serious and prosperous family involved with civil rights and the problems of underprivileged people. She is a smart, clear-eyed, rebellious young woman who has been given the same schooling as any upper-middle-class white girl and wishes at once for her family's absolute disapproval and the comfortable warmth of their society. The book is a series of short pieces, primarily about childhood, some of which have appeared in the New Yorker, as did Miss Lee's first book, *Russian Journal.* The stories read like an unsentimental autobiography in which the narrative thread is the mind's landscape of significant memory.

Sarah Phillips is, of course, more than a single life. Sarah's story is representative of the changing history of blacks in America. For several generations, the leadership of the black people has been primarily vested in preachers providing their congregations—which have extended beyond the church—with a sense of unity and dignity and a future. But their children, like Sarah and Matthew, her brother, have been educated for a new kind of leadership. They are expected to "make it" in the white, middle-class establishment and at the same time to see that world clearly, without romantic illusions. Sarah is not consciously grappling with issues of history in these pieces but it is clear that Miss Lee intended her to be a child of the civil rights movement, representative of a new black woman, educated, sassy, worldly, harshly critical, somewhat self-deprecating and bound for a kind of glory....

The "formal precision" with which Andrea Lee informs us of the fine balance between experience and the development of self is surprising and sharp. One is struck by the sometimes chilling objectivity Sarah has toward her life. The point of view is that of a writer who is at once a part of an experience and an observer of it. *Sarah Phillips* is a work of fiction; nevertheless, the author is certainly examining the relationship between a writer and her life, the "I" and experience. In the chapter in which the Reverend Phillips dies, the event of his death and the emotional detachment implicit in Sarah's recording of it are compelling and disturbing. She is pleased with her dress for the funeral and writes, "When I saw how expensive and beautiful I looked, I was filled with a surge of self-congratulatory excitement, and with the feeling of assuming a glamorous new character with the clothes. Once seated in the gray interior of the big black car, I leaned my head against the window glass in an affected manner, hoping that passers-by in the March night would see and admire me as a tragic heroine."

The difficulty with the narrative is that the book reads like connected short stories instead of a coherent novel; the central character moves through a series of emotional epiphanies that sometimes don't take off. A further problem is that Sarah's intellectual distance, which is part of her character, prevents us from ever catching her off guard. We don't know her well enough to be moved deeply by her insights. We do know her parents, however, and they are quite marvelous, as are many of the minor characters.

Sarah Phillips is finally a pilgrimage through childhood in which a young woman, frightened as we all are of the powerful emotions of the past, discovers in that past the unlimited contours of her life. Andrea Lee's authority as a writer comes of an unstinting honesty and a style at once simple and yet luminous.

Susan Richards Shreve, "Unsentimental Journey," in The New York Times Book Review, *November 18, 1984, p. 13.*

Laura Obolensky (essay date 1984)

[*In the following excerpt, Obolensky offers a mixed review of* Sarah Phillips, *noting that the work "is not the novel it is touted to be, and Lee's forte lies more in the hundred-yard dash of the short story . . . than in the intricately plotted long-distance narrative."*]

"What matters is that something—at last—has happened to me!" remarks a young traveling companion to Sarah Phillips, the eponymous narrator of [*Sarah Phillips*] . . . . It's hardly a startling outburst coming from a recent college graduate long numbed by the tedious business of growing up. And the opening chapter makes it clear that Sarah, taking that remark as her cue, has made something happen to her life. Late out of Harvard, black "but light-skinned . . . with a lively appetite for white boys," she is five months into a European romp which has her bouncing between Paris, the French countryside, and London. She also "plays the queen" in a loose ménage-à-quatre whose other participants are her full-time lover Henri, "an illegitimate child raised outside Paris by his mother and adopted only recently by his rich uncle," and Henri's two childhood cronies—Alain, who comes "from a large and happy petit-bourgeois family," and Roger, a student sprung "From the pettiest of petty nobility" (Sarah isn't coy about her class consciousness)—both of whom she sleeps with occasionally "in a spirit of Brüderschaft." (p. 41)

Indeed, something has happened to Sarah—something light-years removed from her middle-class Philadelphia upbringing, something which would surely raise the eyebrows of her recently deceased, civil rights activist, Baptist minister father, and of her prim, once schoolmarm mother. Which presumably was the whole point of the escapade. But youthful rebellions can be a punishing business, and by the end of the first chapter Sarah clearly senses that her own binge is turning into a bore. When at the end of a bibulous lunch Henri teases that she is the offspring of a mongrel Irish-woman raped "by a jazz musician as big and black as King Kong, with sexual equipment to match," Sarah expediently concludes her Parisian spree has been "nothing more than a slight hysteria," and calls it quits. (Never mind that until then she has delighted in coaxing poor wisecracking Henri into telling her "nigger jokes.")

The balance of the narrative consists of successive flashbacks to Sarah's growing years which, though intended to justify her subsequent Parisian "hysteria,"

fall a bit short of the mark. By her own admission, Sarah and her peers are "the overprotected or horribly spoiled products of a comfortable suburban childhood." . . . In keeping with their middle-class circumstances, the Phillipses seem to have a penchant for conspicuous consumption. Though said to "worship thrift," mother vacations in Europe and shops at Saks, Aunt Emma exudes whiffs of Arpège, and Sunday dinners are invariably "massive" or "extravagant." Brother Matthew goes to summer camp in the Poconos while Sarah heads for Camp Grayfeather in "Wyeth Territory," Delaware; and after the obligatory stints at exclusive private schools, it's Swarthmore for Matthew and Harvard for Sarah. Nothing out of character for any self-respecting affluent suburban family here. Or is there? Well, yes, sort of.

After all, the Phillipses are black, and it's the turbulent early 1960's; though close to being won, the fight for civil rights goes on as does discrimination. Through Reverend Phillips—Lee's strongest characterization apart from that of the narrator herself—we catch glimpses of the Struggle, for this spellbinding preacher, who can throw an occasional member of his mostly female flock "into fits of rapturous shrieks," is also a passionate civil rights activist. When not hectoring from his pulpit, he turns to hectoring the conscience of a refractory America from the airwaves; predictably, he also organizes boycotts and multitudinous marches.

Though she clearly idolizes him, Sarah doesn't quite know what to make of this crusading father. When he lands in an Alabama jail after a more exalted act of civil disobedience, she admits to being "privately embarrassed." . . . And the tokenism that she experiences firsthand when she becomes the first black student to be enrolled at the exclusive Prescott School for Girls leaves her more thrilled than wretched: "It's a little like being in a play," she tells her mother "looking for a laugh"; "everyone's watching me all the time." To her credit, Lee doesn't shy from daubing the Phillipses with the brush of the very racism against which the good Reverend is constantly inveighing. When sitting with her mother in the evenings, Sarah remarks, "Daddy . . . would talk unflatteringly about negroes," and rail against their propensity "for spoiling a community." And when later in the book Matthew brings home his Jewish girlfriend for the parental once-over, it's a reverse case of *Guess Who's Coming to Dinner.*

For all its insight into the little-known world of upper-class blacks, however, *Sarah Phillips* is not the novel it is touted to be, and Lee's forte lies more in the hundred-yard dash of the short story . . . than in the intricately plotted long-distance narrative. (pp. 41-2)

Sarah Phillips makes for a disconcerting read. Despite its talk about rebelling against a childhood during which "civil rights and concern for the under-privileged (were) served up . . . at breakfast, lunch, and dinner," Andrea Lee never really dramatizes the dilemma. And what remain deeply troublesome sociological issues are treated tangentially, or with a tone of detachment often bordering on the sardonic. The moral and emotional conflict that should rend her narrator as she struggles between two worlds, neither of which really claims her allegiance, is never demonstrated. Instead, what Lee proves once more is that affluence is a powerful equalizer—that no matter how adept the irony, and no matter what her ethnicity, a young lady who behaves like an elitist snob and thinks like an elitist snob is an elitist snob. (p. 42)

> *Laura Obolensky, "Scenes from a Girlhood,"*
> *in* The New Republic, *Vol. 191, No. 21,*
> *November 19, 1984, pp. 41-2.*

Patricia Vigderman (essay date 1985)

[*In the following excerpt, Vigderman explores race issues in* Sarah Phillips.]

[The form of] **Sarah Phillips** is deceptive: its twelve chapters at first seem to be merely a dozen neatly crafted short stories...; and because the tale it tells is written in the first person, it has the feel of a memoir. But the formal model for this novel is neither of these. The young heroine of the title grew up on such literary fare as the Melendy family [of Elizabeth Enright's novels] and E. Nesbit's Bastable children, and Lee has given her story a structure very like that of those wonderful children's "novels." Each chapter is a separate adventure, but the book as a whole constructs another world—one that could be your own but is, well, more exciting. Sarah's adventures, like those of the Melendy family, bring to life a clever and well-loved young person who longs to take possession of the wider world. The crucial difference between Sarah and the Melendys, though, is that Sarah's family is black.

What gives Sarah's story is special resonance is the way her race both does and does not define her. Her cultural heritage is as much a matter of the Melendys and Macbeth as it is of anything specifically black or Afro-American. Her family is generations removed from the South; they are professional people "not too dark of complexion" and not given to shouting in church. Sarah is essentially destined for Radcliffe from birth, and the racial component of her identity is extremely subtle.

Born in the North in 1953, Sarah Phillips embodies a dream of color blindness—it's Martin Luther King, Jr.'s dream, to be precise—a dream held for generations before she was born. Like most dreams come true, of course, she is somewhat different from what the dreamers had in mind. Sarah and her older brother Matthew grow up to have a sophistication about being black in America that is far beyond the civil rights ethic or the bitter jokes of her parents' generation. When Sarah is denied the part she deserves in the play at her fancy white prep school and is cast instead as a black maid (it's 1965 in the Philadelphia suburbs), she says, "After that life at Prescott was easier for me. It was simply ... a matter of knowing where you stood." The new

knowledge comes to her as a physical sensation—a giggling fit.... For a daughter of that dream, then, the real moment of puberty is the one on which she sees where she stands in relation to white America—and it's a moment of laughter, not tears or rage.

Only two years earlier, as a child who is still reading *The Melendy Family,* she doesn't yet have that cool understanding. Indeed, when her father takes her with him to Washington, D.C., where he is helping to plan the march that took place in August of 1963, she sees a smile of complicity pass between him and a black taxi driver. "Something began to burn and flutter in my chest: it was as if I had swallowed a pair of fiery wings." Emotionally stirred, she sees the march as a crusade, or maybe the French Revolution. But her parents don't take her with them to the march (too many strangers, too many germs) and she and Matthew watch it on TV. They fight about whether or not it means anything.... (pp. 23-4)

It is not until her senior year at Radcliffe that her confident understanding of where she stands is seriously challenged. The spring before her graduation she is called home to her father's funeral. Her father was a spiritual and social leader, and his death is public property. But she is a kind of arrow shot out of the community that he led, and she is completely unable to respond to the massively attended funeral. Dressed like the heroine of a novel, she sleepwalks through the event, deciding it is easier to "pretend to be a heroine" than to begin dealing with either her grief or the torch that is passed on to her by this death.

This is not a story we read every day. Because Sarah has been set firmly into white America, this novel does not fit easily into the Afro-American tradition, and may even meet with some disapproval. "Until we have put something on (the white man's) streetcorner that is our own," the novelist Zora Neale Hurston wrote in 1934, "we are right back where we were when they filed our iron collar off." Hurston spoke for a distinctly black cultural identity and ridiculed the black intellectuals of her own day who seemed to be imitating white culture. But Sarah is not imitating anything. She is as firmly in possession of the culture we share as (white and middleclass) I am. Like Sarah, as a child I "fell away into a remote dimension when I opened a book"—and we read the same books. Andrea Lee's novel describes one girl's journey from that remote dimension to a story of her own. It's a very gracefully written book about black identity that makes what Sarah and I share seem more important than what we don't. It puts us on the streetcorner together. (p. 24)

> *Patricia Vigderman, in a review of "Sarah Phillips," in* Boston Review, *Vol. X, No. 1, February, 1985, pp. 23-4.*

FURTHER READING

Jacoby, Susan. "One Year in Moscow." *The New York Times Book Review* (25 October 1981): 11, 22.

Generally favorable review of *Russian Journal*. Jacoby states: "[*Russian Journal*] is such a subtly crafted reflection of both the bleak and golden shadings of Russian life that its tones belong more to the realm of poetry than to journalism."

Lee, Andrea, and Rein, Richard K. "An American Student Comes Home from Russia with Love and a Bittersweet Memoir." *People* 16, No. 21 (23 November 1981): 101-02, 105.

Interview in which Lee discusses the time she spent in the Soviet Union preparing *Russian Journal*. She notes: "I went with a blank mind . . . . It always seemed to me that Russia was the country about which Americans have the most stereotypes and know the least."

Van Wyngarden, Bruce. "Pieces of the Past." *Saturday Review* 11, No. 1 (February 1985): 74.

Review of *Sarah Phillips,* noting that the novel is "an engaging and promising start" for Lee.

George Washington Lee

1894-1976

American novelist, short story writer, essayist, and editor.

A successful Memphis, Tennessee, businessman and politician, Lee turned to writing in order to affirm racial pride and promote black-owned businesses during the Great Depression. He immortalized Memphis's Beale Street with his critically acclaimed historical study *Beale Street: Where the Blues Began* (1934), and his novel and collection of short stories attracted a wide audience as well.

Lee, the son of Reverend George and Hattie Lee, was born in Indianola, Mississippi. His father died while Lee was still young, forcing Lee and his mother and siblings to move into a sharecropper's shack. Lee's mother wanted her son to escape the life of a poor farmer and enrolled him in a nearby school. Lee later attended Alcorn Agricultural and Mechanical College in Lorman, Mississippi, where, according to Edward D. Clark, he "demonstrated an insatiable quest for knowledge, and he greatly impressed his professors with his prodigious reading habits." In order to remain in school and support his family, Lee worked as a bellhop in a Memphis hotel from 1912 to 1917. In 1917 he became one of twenty-seven black Tennesseans selected for the new black army officers' training camp in Des Moines, Iowa. Lee fought in France during World War I and, after his discharge in 1919, worked in various occupations—insurance executive, fraternal leader, politician, and writer—in Memphis.

Lee's first work, *Beale Street: Where the Blues Began,* is an informal cultural history of the Memphis avenue that profoundly influenced the lives of innumerable black Tennesseans. *Beale Street* is divided into chapters about various blacks who figured strongly in the history of the neighborhood. These include Robert R. Church, Sr., who after the Civil War built up a multimillion dollar fortune and helped turn Beale Street into a commercial center for the black community; Julia A. Hooks, who started an integrated music school that produced many gifted performers; and composer W. C. Handy, whom Lee credits with "distinguished orchestral work." Lee also described the yellow fever epidemic of 1878, contrasting the many heroic blacks who stayed in Memphis to help save the city with the whites who fled the disease en masse. Although Lee's purpose in *Beale Street* was to instill pride in black accomplishment, he balanced the work by revealing seamier aspects of the community. Pimps, prostitutes, drug dealers, and the destitute who sift through garbage piles for food share pages with Lee's model characters. Some critics complained that in *Beale Street* Lee openly favored financial accomplishments above all others, but Lee's animated descriptions of life on Beale Street have more frequently suggested otherwise. Percy Hutchison commented: "Mr. Lee's tremendously living picture, barbaric in its colors, raucous just as often as it is melodious, was the book's raison d'être and the alluring thing about it."

Lee wrote his novel *River George* (1937) to vindicate himself among black intellectuals and writers who attributed the success of Beale Street to the prominence and notoriety of its subject rather than to the literary qualities of the work itself. *River George* exposes what Lee perceived to be the evils of the Southern sharecropping system. Lee took the title character, Aaron George, from *Beale Street*'s third chapter, then added some of his own personal experiences to the narrative. George goes to Lee's alma mater, Alcorn Agricultural and Mechanical College, and studies to become a lawyer, but his education is interrupted by the death of his father. He returns home and becomes a sharecropper on Beaver Dam Plantation to help support his mother. There he falls in love with Ada Green, who is also involved with the white postmaster, Fred Smith, but George has to flee the plantation after he confronts Smith over the injustices suffered by the tenant farmers—a confrontation that ends in Smith's death by his own gun. Accused of a murder he did not commit, George runs to Memphis for safety and takes up lodgings with a Beale Street madame. Like the author, George enters the U.S. Army and serves as a lieutenant in Europe. When he returns to the United States, he tries to contact his mother and Ada, but he meets trouble in Vicksburg, Mississippi, when he encounters whites who resent his officer's uniform. George becomes a deckhand on the Mississippi River and wins fame for his fighting prowess. He eventually returns to the plantation, however, only to be lynched for the postmaster's murder upon his arrival. While some critics praised Lee's authentic rendering of the tenant farming system in *River George*, others agreed with a reviewer for the *Brooklyn Eagle* who maintained: "[There] are not enough facts to make *River George* good propaganda, and there is not enough artistry to make *River George* a good novel."

With his political career thriving during the late 1930s and early 1940s, Lee became less involved with movements of social protest and black pride. His third and final major work, the short story collection *Beale Street Sundown* (1942), includes accounts of a former prostitute who captivates a minister, a congregation that professes hate instead of love, and a young vocalist torn between careers as a classical singer and a blues stylist. While little national attention was given to *Beale Street Sundown*, a reviewer for the *Memphis Press-Scimitar* commented: "The Boswell of Beale Street has spun the best book of his literary career." Lee also wrote a number of political and fraternal essays, many of which were published in black periodicals and newspapers during the 1950s and 1960s.

Although Lee's works are little known today, they document an important segment of black society—the middle class—and an important site in black history—Beale Street. According to Clark, Lee's works "make him a significant literary figure, for his history and his fiction artistically present and preserve important segments of early and near mid-twentieth century black Americana."

(For further information about Lee's life and works, see *Black Writers; Contemporary Authors,* Vol. 125; *Contemporary Literary Criticism,* Vol. 52; and *Dictionary of Literary Biography,* Vol. 51: *Afro-American Writers from the Harlem Renaissance to 1940.*)

PRINCIPAL WORKS

Beale Street: Where the Blues Began (history) 1934
River George (novel) 1937
Beale Street Sundown (short stories) 1942

Percy Hutchison (essay date 1934)

[*In the following excerpt, Hutchison reviews* Beale Street, *praising the book's "compelling force" but criticizing its weak writing.*]

For many reasons such a book as [*Beale Street: Where the Blues Began*] is neither easy to describe nor to evaluate; the crosscurrents are so many that a reviewer feels as if he had launched into a more than ordinarily choppy sea. To begin with: How is he to begin? Of course, he might start grandiloquently by saying that New York has its Fifth Avenue, Paris its Rue de la Paix, but Memphis has its Beale Street; and all he would have accomplished would be to have got off on the wrong foot.

Again, if he likened Beale Street to Lenox Avenue, the boulevard both of trade and of fashion of New York's Harlem black belt, he would have done no better. Perhaps if he were to imagine Fifth Avenue as skirting the Wailing Wall of Jerusalem he would come nearer, for if Beale Street is, or has been, the dusky thoroughfare of fashion and of trade, it also has been the road of tribulation of a race. And it is such a dramatic contrast which this book by George W. Lee, himself a Memphis Negro—a book often well written, but in part ineptly written—brings out forcibly. Let it be said, however, that the good in the volume so far outweighs the bad as very much to reduce the intrusion of the latter....

The reviewer believes it possible that, purely as a commercial proposition, Mr. Lee's book might have been difficult to place had he not tied it up with the history of the beginnings of syncopation, thereby making possible its subtitle of *Where the Blues Began*. But for this reviewer the chapters devoted to this bit of musical history proved the least interesting. For him, Mr. Lee's tremendously living picture, barbaric in its colors, raucous just as often as it is melodious, was the book's raison d'être and the alluring thing about it. Comedy and tragedy walk hand in hand down George Lee's *Beale Street;* high yellows, light chocolates and coal blacks work, parade the avenue, crowd the dance halls; river roustabouts, where Beale Street meets the Mississippi, heave their bales and roar their songs. And the author has caught something of the rhythm of the Mississippi. "Old Man River" seems to be intoning in his lines....

W. C. Handy, who, incidentally, has written a foreword for the book, is accredited with being the originator of [the Blues] the fundamental of which is, unquestionably, nothing above simple wailing....

It was the political situation of 1909 which put Handy and his new type of music on the map. Three men were running for Mayor of Memphis, of whom one was E. H. Crump. Handy, who had a band and was hired to play for Crump, composed a piece based on the "backward, over-and-over wailing" of his people, to which he had so long listened. (p. 3)

"That tune," writes Lee, "was the vehicle which carried two to victory," Crump and Handy "who rode on it from Beale Street to Broadway." ...

Yet for all of this information, interesting as it is, we still prefer the more objective features of the book. It is an illuminating picture of a civilization within a civilization that George W. Lee has drawn. Far from being a purely dependent growth, parasitically clinging to the white man's culture, the Negro is here displayed as developing a culture of his own, caring for his own needs in medicine, in the law, in religion, education and recreation. One sees Negro life insurance companies proceeding on their useful way; Negro banks operating; burial associations performing their necessary duty. So many of the books on the Negro have dealt with the rural black that not all of us have guessed at the multiple civic life of the urban black. *Beale Street* opens one's eyes.

And because it does, we wish it had no stylistic imperfections to mar its otherwise even flow and compelling force. It is the sort of work which should be carried through objectively from start to finish, and this Mr. Lee seems to have been unable to do. Too often he lapses into mere statistics, becomes solely the recorder. (p. 13)

> Percy Hutchison, "Beale Street, Memphis, Where the Blues Began," in The New York Times Book Review, *July 29, 1934, pp. 3, 13.*

Margaret Larkin (essay date 1934)

[*In the following excerpt, Larkin gives a mixed review of* Beale Street.]

Where the Blues Began is a misleading subtitle for a miscellany of success stories and local legends about the Negro section of Memphis, Tennessee. it is not about music. Two of its twenty chapters deal with Negro bands and orchestras and with the rise to fame of colored entertainers.... Another fifteen pages are devoted to W. C. Handy, who changed the course of American popular music with his "St. Louis Blues" and made a fortune out of it because he had the financial acumen to publish it himself. George W. Lee, a business man on Beale Street, obviously is not equipped to tell Handy's story in any other terms than those of financial success. What he really has written is "Beale Street: Where the Negro Business Man Began." ...

[*Beale Street*] opens with a eulogy of a colored banker and "realtor" who controlled most of the businesses on Beale Street in the late eighties, and ends with a eulogy of his son, a Republican boss there today. It contains biographies and anecdotes of Beale Street's gamblers, dope peddlers, and dark courtesans, whose charms were officially reserved for white men; of colored preachers, bankers, "beauticians," tailors, doctors. It recalls the long, shameful history of lynchings in Memphis and the rumors, lies, and racial slanders that set them off; gives a somewhat technical account of how a few white men were backed by the Ku Klux Klan in seizing control of the Negro insurance companies; gives full details, including speeches and newspaper accounts, of the opening of a park named after a colored philanthropist; solves murders and fixes the blame for the local bank crash. Much of the material of the book is fascinating. But many pages, even chapters, are given over to facts of the kind a census taker might collect, gathered into little biographies that serve to conceal the subjects as effectively as so many obituaries. The valuable portions of the book are drowned in undistinguished matter which obviously did not interest even the author....

The one personality who emerges from the book is Robert R. Church, Tennessee's colored Republican boss. Mr. Lee's admiration for him is naively uncritical; he presents the reader with a full view of his hero's political chicaneries, paternalism, patronage system, trade-ins with the Democrats, and sell-out to the Hoover machine, which he disapproved and which betrayed him. Mr. Church helped to nominate Hoover but threatened to withdraw votes because of the presence of Klan members on the campaign committee. Slight concessions brought him into line. But Hoover did not reward him with handsome patronage as Harding had done; expected Negro appointments were canceled and lily-whites were installed in every important place. Years of careful building to make the Negro a politically important factor in Tennessee politics were swept away.... The next campaign saw him maneuvering to hold his power in the county convention. Futile as it had proved, position in the Republican Party was preferable to political extinction.

The bourgeois Negro is in a peculiarly tragic position in America. By raising himself above the proletarian and farmer Negro he cuts himself off from his own main stream. The whites bar him from further advancement. The correct Babbittry of the middle class is intensified by the incessant need to prove that a Negro banker, doctor, merchant, or civil servant is as good as his white prototype or even better. This is the point of view in *Beale Street*. It accounts for the pedestrian dullness with which Mr. Lee has handled the dramatic and heroic story of a Negro community struggling for economic and political power in the midst of the intolerant South.

> Margaret Larkin, "Success Stories," in The Nation, *New York, Vol. CXXXIX, No. 3609, September 5, 1934, p. 279.*

David M. Tucker (essay date 1971)

[*In the following excerpt from his 1971 study* Lieutenant Lee of Beale Street, *Tucker assesses Lee's literary career, concentrating on* Beale Street *and* River George.]

Since writing offered a medium for promoting the racial pride upon which black business thrived, George Lee took up the pen as a tool for creating profits. His first published articles called for the race to unite against the evils of poverty and discrimination, and his first book celebrated the achievements of Negro Memphians. After the great depression delivered a devastating blow to the black economy of Beale Street, turning the once prosperous street into "one of the longest bread-lines in the life of the city," George Lee felt compelled to begin work on a book that might revive his people's flagging faith in black business.

George Lee had long followed the *Crisis* symposiums on the literary portrayal of Negro characters and naturally hoped that by beating white writers to the Beale Street story he might discourage any local creation of dialect farces such as those with which Octavus Roy Cohen had caricatured Birmingham Negroes. Featuring Hop Sure Peters, a shuffling Pullman porter, who clowned on the Birmingham-to-New York line and was "considerable social pumpkins" in the 18th Street circles, Cohen's blackface caricatures had ignored the very existence of an accomplished middle class, deprived the Negro of human dignity, and exploited the race for the amusement of the whites. It would be tragic, Lee felt, if Beale Street society were ridiculed as Birmingham's 18th Street had been, and so he sought to tell it the way it should be told. Lee wanted to draw a realistic picture which would show Memphis Negroes not as Hop Sures or Hambones but as successful businessmen who, though segregated and deprived, had shown the same potential for self-improvement as the Anglo-Saxon. Nowhere had this potential been realized more dramatically than by the elder Robert R. Church, who gained his freedom in 1862 when the Union Army came to Memphis and went on to build an estate worth more than a million dollars. Since it was Church who had made Beale Street the center of commercial life for Negroes, Lee decided to enclose his picture of the district's life within the frame of Robert Church's success story. George Lee would give his readers close-ups of all the bankers, lawyers, druggists, funeral directors, and insurance men who lived on the street, and who like the beautician, Madame Gorine Morgan Young, had come up from Mississippi and "established themselves solidly in Beale Street's commercial life." (pp. 105-06)

A black Babbitt would have collected only Negro success stories and ignored the sordid and seamy side of life, but George Lee, following the trend of the Negro literary renaissance, also sought a sympathetic portrayal of the lowdown black Negroes, the gamesters who rolled the dice at the Hole in the Wall, dope peddlers such as Ten Dollar Jimmy, and courtesans who ran black and white pleasure palaces. Carl Van Vechten's *Nigger Heaven* had made it current literary fashion to view the Negro as an erotic primitive who was uninhibited by the puritanism that had stifled the spontaneity of the white middle classes. So Lee documented the existence of dissolute blacks alongside the respectable middle class of Beale Street. (pp. 106-07)

[Local] book stores refused to stock *Beale Street: Where the Blues Began* until after Clifton Fadiman had reviewed it in the July *New Yorker*. "I wish to pin a small but distinctive badge (with ribbons) upon the honest colored breast of Lieutenant George Washington Lee," Fadiman wrote. "Mr. Lee's naive Memphis recitals have the authentic color of good crackerbox gossip." After Fadiman's review, the book began selling everywhere, and George Lee's ego swelled as he received the favorable writeups. (p. 111)

Beale Street became popular because it captured so successfully the tempo of the district's life. The street was, George Lee said, "owned largely by Jews, policed by whites, and enjoyed by Negroes." There were hognose sandwiches, chitterling cafes, and an underworld with every vice known to man. The author had told of the bad black roustabout, River George, whose career had carried him through Beale Street like a "bloody comet." No detail had seemed too small for Lee's tableau. The reader learned that gamblers at the Hole In The Wall were normally fined five cents for spitting on the dice, and that while the favors of the bordellos were officially reserved for a white clientele, the alley doors were always opened to the blacks after 3 A.M. This racy, graphic description of Negro Americana made fascinating reading for thousands of whites who lived quiet and routine lives. But the splendor of these descriptions of the colorful activity on Beale was dulled by the uninspired documentary on Negro middle-class achievements. Almost without exception, the critics complained of George Lee's self-imposed mission to catalogue the names and contributions of the street's businessmen, churches, schools, banks, and of course, insurance companies. "Half of it could and should have been junked," said the New York *Sun*. "The rest is pure gold." (p. 113)

Actually, Lee had no further ambitions for writing, until he learned that Negro intellectuals in the East were unimpressed with his literary effort. Bob Church brought back the news from New York that Walter White, secretary of the NAACP, and his Harlem circle of friends felt that Lee himself had no talent as a writer, but that the subject, not its literary treatment, had made *Beale Street* a success. Such reaction made it clear to George Lee that he would have to write another book to show Harlem's pseudosophisticates that the East had no monopoly on talent.

Lee decided to take his third chapter from *Beale Street,* the chapter about River George, a semimythical bad man in the community, and expand it to a full length antisharecrop novel. Ever since George Lee's escape from a Mississippi tenant farm, he had longed to strike a blow at what he called the "damnable sharecrop system"; and now, by telling his story of the half-legendary bad man of Beale Street, he would finally have his chance.

Lee tried to be fair in his work of protest fiction, however, and never denounced all the landlords categorically. His own relationship with [a former employer], Mr. Klingman of Indianola, had been such a happy one that the author put his white benefactor in the novel as Mr. King.... In the novel, this kindly old white man has been the owner of Beaver Dam plantation, a well-run, impressive estate of which he boasted, "I got the best niggers and the best cotton in the whole delta." The old gentleman, however, sells the plantation to the greedy, self-made Mr. Tyler, and under this new owner the potentially vicious system forces the workers into conditions as deplorable as slavery. The exorbitant prices at the plantation store and the shameless dishonesty of the plantation bookkeeper reduces the tenants to virtual peonage; for no matter how many bales of cotton a sharecropper on Beaver Dam produces, he cannot pay off his debt to the plantation.

The central character of the novel, Aaron George, returns home from Alcorn College to his family's sharecrop on Tyler's plantation. Eager to put his education to work by emancipating his people, he promises his dying father he will go to the owner and protest his criminal system. (pp. 114-15)

[Education] has liberated Aaron from his parents' peasant conservatism, and he resolves to improve the condition of the sharecroppers. At the first opportunity, he asks Sam Turner, the plantation agent, to induce Mr. Tyler to make the sharecropper's efforts a bit more profitable when the annual settlements are computed. But only the most naïve of southern Negroes can expect to receive a sympathetic audience from a white overseer. "Ain't no place on Beaver Dam for a nigger that talks like you," Turner snaps. "You better get such damn fool notions out of your head; cause if you try to start anything among these niggers, it's going to be mighty unhealthy for you." (p. 115)

The hero might have moved his mother north and escaped the hopeless Delta, but George Lee has made Aaron an extremely idealistic character, unwilling to run until he has put the system, and himself, to the test ....

Just as he had always done in his own life, George Lee's character, Aaron George, turns to influential white folks for help. Since Mississippi ethics forbid an outsider from intervening in disputes between a planter and his Negroes, Aaron cannot take his complaints about the unjust settlement itself to any white man; yet he can ask his father's former employer to help him find a second job in town. So Aaron goes to Mr. King who is able to place him in a cotton-oil mill in Indianola. There Aaron makes more money in a single month than he had earned in a year on the sharecrop, and other workers begin to follow his example until a score of men are riding their mules into Indianola to work in town rather than spend the short winter months on the plantation in idleness. (p. 116)

George Lee destroyed the unity of his agrarian novel by moving Aaron from the rural South when he was only halfway through the book. The subsequent chapters follow Aaron George to Beale Street, Harlem, and

through the First World War before returning him somewhat unconvincingly to Beaver Dam where he is lynched upon arrival. Artistically, these later chapters detracted from the force of the book, but they gave Lee the chance to include a wider range of autobiographical material and, above all, to retaliate against his Harlem critics. "Listen, big boy," Lee has one eastern Negro say, "we aren't much interested in Harlem in doing anything for the race. The fellows who worry about that usually push their faces into trouble. And who cares? Harlem has a good time." As Lee depicts them, the dissolute Harlemites lack the staunch integrity, the racial concern, and the simple emotional depth of the southern Negro. The spiritual emancipation of the race, Aaron concludes, will never come from Harlem. (pp. 117-18)

[*River George*] was never the success that Lee's first book had been. Although it represented a distinct advance artistically, some reviewers fairly, if ruthlessly, concluded, "there are not enough facts to make *River George* good propaganda, and there is not enough artistry to make *River George* a good novel." At the same time, however, critics generally did appreciate the realistic picture of southern sharecropping with its protest against white violence and bigotry. From Louisville, Kentucky, a reviewer wrote, "Keep writing, books like yours ... will make you more friends than all the articles on racial questions put together. Dickens helped children in old London, *Black Beauty* helped a lot of dumb animals. River George is helping the colored people." So George Lee's second book did draw some degree of applause, at least enough to encourage the author to go on writing. (pp. 118-19)

[George Lee] no longer looked to writing as a medium of social protest, but rather as an outlet for his creative energy. Now he wanted to paint scenes of Beale Street life which were works of art and not merely racial tracts. Lee's stories describe a church congregation filled with hate instead of love, the confidence game which fleeced Beale Streeters out to get rich quick, a Negro girl who was "passing" in a white whore house, and how the Blues created tensions between the brown middleclass and the common black masses. George Lee had his stories published in the *Negro Digest, The World's Digest,* and the *Southern Literary Messenger,* and later published them as **Beale Street Sundown,** a collection which, though attracting little national interest, at least won him the satisfaction of great local praise. "The Boswell of Beale Street," the Memphis *Press-Scimitar* raved, "has spun the best book of his literary career." (p. 119)

David M. Tucker, in his Lieutenant Lee of Beale Street, *Vanderbilt University Press, 1971, 217 p.*

FURTHER READING

Beckwith, E. C. "Sharecroppers." *The New York Times Book Review* (20 June 1937): 16.

Praises *River George*'s "illuminating incidents and sidelights, which graphically amplify the novel's scope and human interest."

Carter, Elmer Anderson. Review of *Beale Street: Where the Blues Began,* by George Washington Lee. *Opportunity* XII, No. 10 (October 1934): 314.

Laudatory review of *Beale Street.* Carter applauds the "gusto and enthusiasm" of the narrative but cites Lee's failure to offer a critical evaluation of Beale Street's importance in black American history.

Simpson, Clinton. Review of *Beale Street,* by George Washington Lee. *Scribner's Magazine* XCVI, No. 3 (September 1934): 14.

Brief review of *Beale Street,* maintaining: "Such a book can scarcely avoid being interesting, and this one is interesting—and valuable, too, since it contains material not printed elsewhere."

Audre Lorde

1934-

(Full name Audre Geraldine Lorde; also wrote under the pseudonym Rey Domini) American poet, essayist, autobiographer, novelist, and nonfiction writer.

American writer Lorde describes herself as "a black lesbian feminist mother lover poet." She has often expressed anger toward racial oppression, urban blight, and personal hardship in her poetry, but she has also cultivated a unique blend of hope and spiritual renewal. Lorde believes that it is the poet's responsibility to reveal truths—no matter how painful. She explained: "I feel I have a duty to speak the truth as I see it and to share not just my triumphs, not just the things that felt good, but the pain, the intense, often unmitigating pain.... But I think what is really necessary is to see how much of this pain I can feel, how much of this truth I can see and still live unblinded."

Lorde grew up in Manhattan and attended Roman Catholic schools. As a young child she was "very inarticulate" and did not speak until the age of five; she noted that she did not "really" speak until she "started reading and writing poetry." "The ability to read poetry ... was an incredible high for me," she commented. "When life just got too difficult for me, I could always retreat into those words." Lorde's parents did not directly encourage her to write poetry, but they influenced her nonetheless. Lorde explained: "Poetry was something I learned from my mother's strangenesses and my father's silences." Lorde published her first poem when she was in high school. Although her English teachers considered her work "much too romantic," Lorde sent it to *Seventeen* magazine and it was accepted. After graduating from high school, Lorde attended Hunter College in New York City from 1951 to 1959. While studying library science, Lorde worked in a number of odd jobs in order to support herself: medical clerk, arts and crafts supervisor, ghost writer, x-ray technician, and factory worker. During this time she also spent a year as a student at the National University of Mexico. "I was nineteen," she noted. "I found in Mexico an affirmation. It was the first time I began to speak in full sentences."

Lorde continued her education at Columbia University, where she earned a master's degree in library science in 1961. During this time she also worked as a librarian and married attorney Edward Ashley Rollins; they divorced in 1970 after having two children, Elizabeth and Jonathan. In 1966 Lorde became head librarian at Town School Library in New York City; library patrons knew her as the "librarian who wrote." In 1968—a year Lorde considers a turning point in her life—she received a National Endowment for the Arts grant, became a poet-in-residence at Tougaloo College in Mississippi, and published her first volume of poetry, *The First*

Cities. This volume was considered innovative and refreshing: critics described its tone as unlike the rhetorical and confrontational tone of much of the black poetry of the time. Calling *The First Cities* a "quiet, introspective book," Dudley Randall asserted that "[Lorde] does not wave a black flag, but her blackness is there, implicit, in the bone." Lorde's second volume, *Cables to Rage* (1970), while addressing such themes as love, betrayal, and the joys of child rearing, was less meditative in tone. This volume is particularly notable for the poem "Martha," in which Lorde revealed her homosexuality for the first time: "yes Martha we have loved each other and yes I hope we still can/ no Martha/ I do not know if we shall ever sleep in each other's arms again."

With the publication of her third book, *From a Land Where Other People Live* (1973), Lorde began to expand the scope of her writing by focusing on racial oppression and worldwide injustice. This volume is considered more universal in conception than the author's previous works and was nominated for the National Book Award for poetry in 1973. Lorde continued to express openly her opinions about social issues in *The New York Head Shop and Museum* (1974), a collection of what is described as her most radical and political poetry. Presenting images of a decaying New York City and the hardships of poverty and urban life, Lorde seemed to advocate extreme political action to heal the ills of modern society: "There is nothing beautiful left in the streets of this city./ I have come to believe in death and renewal by fire." Lorde's next volume of poetry, *Coal* (1976), was the first of Lorde's volumes to be released by a major publisher; it thus exposed her to a broader readership. *Coal,* which focuses on themes similar to those found in *The New York Head Shop and Museum,* demonstrates Lorde's increasing mastery over figurative language. Using coal as the unifying metaphor, Lorde expressed feelings of love and appreciation for her blackness: "I am black because I come from the / earth's insides/ Take my word for jewel in your/ open light." Lorde's next volume, *The Black Unicorn* (1978), is widely considered her most complex and successful work. In this collection Lorde made use of African symbols and mythology to integrate the themes of motherhood, black pride, and spiritual renewal: "Mother I need/ mother I need/ mother I need your blackness now/ as the august earth needs rain." Wrote Adrienne Rich of *The Black Unicorn*: "Refusing to be circumscribed by any simple identity, Audre Lorde writes as a Black woman, a mother, a daughter, a Lesbian, a feminist, a visionary...."

The Cancer Journals (1980), Lorde's first work of nonfiction, chronicles the author's experience with breast cancer. After being diagnosed with cancer, Lorde underwent a partial mastectomy. In *The Cancer Journals* she explored feelings of hopelessness and despair as she confronted the possibility of death. Lorde stated that she wanted "to write a piece of meaning words on cancer as it affects my life and my consciousness as a woman," and she was praised for her honest and revealing account of her illness. While *The Cancer Journals* ultimately presented a life-affirming and hopeful view—in part as a result of her apparent recovery—*A Burst of Light* (1988), which traces the spread of her cancer, is brooding and introspective. Lorde recently discovered that the cancer metastasized to her liver. Instead of undergoing a biopsy, she has chosen a holistic treatment combining homeopathy, meditation, and self-hypnosis. She is currently in remission. As she comes to terms with dying, Lorde parallels her fight for life with black South Africa's struggle for equality and the lesbian community's fight against discrimination. Lorde's continuing focus on global social issues in spite of her serious illness reflects her dedication as a poet. She asserts: "I find I must remember that the pain is not its own reason for being. It is a part of living. And the only kind of pain that is intolerable is pain that is wasteful, pain from which we do not learn."

(For further information about Lorde's life and works, see *Black Writers; Contemporary Authors,* Vols. 25-28; *Contemporary Authors New Revision Series,* Vols. 16, 26; *Contemporary Literary Criticism,* Vol. 18; *Dictionary of Literary Biography,* Vol. 41: *Afro-American Poets Since 1955;* and *Major 20th-Century Writers.*)

PRINCIPAL WORKS

The First Cities (poetry) 1968
Cables to Rage (poetry) 1970
From a Land Where Other People Live (poetry) 1973
The New York Head Shop and Museum (poetry) 1974
Between Our Selves (poetry) 1976
Coal (poetry) 1976
The Black Unicorn (poetry) 1978
The Cancer Journals (nonfiction) 1980
Chosen Poems, Old and New (poetry) 1982
Zami: A New Spelling of My Name (novel) 1982
Sister Outsider: Essays and Speeches (essays) 1984
Our Dead behind Us (poetry) 1986
Burst of Light (essays) 1988

Audre Lorde (essay date 1977)

[*In the following essay entitled "Poems Are Not Luxuries," Lorde underscores the importance of the relationship between poetry and the feminist movement, stating that for women "[poetry] is a vital necessity" because it allows for emotional freedom and active contemplation of ideas in a male-dominated society.*]

The quality of light by which we scrutinize our lives has direct bearing upon the product which we live, and upon the changes which we hope to bring about through those lives. It is within this light that we form those ideas by which we pursue our magic and make it realized. This is poetry as illumination for it is through poetry that we give name to those ideas which are, until the poem, nameless and formless—about to be birthed, but already felt. That distillation of experience from which true poetry springs births thought as dream births concept, as feeling births idea, as knowledge births (precedes) understanding.

As we learn to bear the intimacy of scrutiny, and to flourish within it, as we learn to use the products of that scrutiny for power within our living, those fears which rule our lives and form our silences begin to lose their control over us.

For each of us as women, there is a dark place within where hidden and growing our true spirit rises, "Beautiful and tough as chestnut / Stanchions against our nightmare of weakness" and of impotence. These places of possibility within ourselves are dark because they are ancient and hidden; they have survived and grown strong through darkness. Within these deep places, each one of us holds an incredible reserve of creativity and power, storehouse of unexamined and unrecorded emotion and feeling. The woman's place of power within each of us is neither white nor surface; it is dark, it is ancient, and it is deep.

When we view living, in the european mode, only as a problem to be solved, we rely solely upon our ideas to make us free, for these were what the white fathers told us were precious. But as we become more in touch with our own ancient, black, noneuropean view of living as a situation to be experienced and interacted with, we learn more and more to cherish our feelings, to respect those hidden sources of our power from where true knowledge and therefore lasting action comes. At this point in time, I believe that women carry within ourselves the possibility for fusion of these two approaches as a keystone for survival, and we come closest to this combination in our poetry. I speak here of poetry as the revelation or distillation of experience, not the sterile word play that, too often, the white fathers distorted the word *poetry* to mean—in order to cover their desperate wish for imagination without insight.

For women, then, poetry is not a luxury. It is a vital necessity of our existence. It forms the quality of the light within which we predicate our hopes and dreams toward survival and change, first made into language, then into idea, then into more tangible action. Poetry is the way we help give name to the nameless so it can be thought. The farthest external horizons of our hopes and fears are cobbled by our poems, carved from the rock experiences of our daily lives.

As they become known and accepted to ourselves, our feelings, and the honest exploration of them, become sanctuaries and fortresses and spawning grounds for the most radical and daring of ideas, the house of difference so necessary to change and the conceptualization of any meaningful action. Right now, I could name at least ten ideas I would once have found intolerable or incomprehensible and frightening, except as they came after dreams and poems. This is not idle fantasy, but the true meaning of "It feels right to me." We can train ourselves to respect our feelings and to discipline (transpose) them into a language that catches those feelings so they can be shared. And where that language does not yet exist, it is our poetry which helps to fashion it. Poetry is not only dream or vision, it is the skeleton architecture of our lives.

Possibility is neither forever nor instant. It is also not easy to sustain belief in its efficacy. We can sometimes work long and hard to establish one beachhead of real resistance to the deaths we are expected to live, only to have that beachhead assaulted or threatened by canards we have been socialized to fear, or by the withdrawal of those approvals that we have been warned to seek for safety. We see ourselves diminished or softened by the falsely benign accusations of childishness, of nonuniversality, of self-centeredness, of sensuality. And who asks the question: Am I altering your aura, your ideas, your dreams, or am I merely moving you to temporary and reactive action? (Even the latter is no mean task, but one that must rather be seen within the context of a true alteration of the texture of our lives.)

The white fathers told us, "I think therefore I am," and the black mothers in each of us—the poets—whisper in our dreams, "I feel therefore I can be free." Poetry coins the language to express and charter this revolutionary awareness and demand—the implementation of that freedom. However, experience has taught us that the action in the now is also always necessary. Our children cannot dream unless they live, they cannot live unless they are nourished, and who else will feed them the real food without which their dreams will be no different from ours?

Sometimes we drug ourselves with dreams of new ideas. The head will save us. The brain alone will set us free. But there are no new ideas still waiting in the wings to save us as women, as human. There are only old and forgotten ones, new combinations, extrapolations and recognitions from within ourselves, along with the renewed courage to try them out. And we must constantly encourage ourselves and each other to attempt the heretical actions our dreams imply and some of our old ideas disparage. In the forefront of our move toward change, there is only our poetry to hint at possibility made real. Our poems formulate the implications of ourselves, what we feel within and dare make real (or bring action into accordance with), our fears, our hopes, our most cherished terrors.

For within structures defined by profit, by linear power, by institutional dehumanization, our feelings were not meant to survive. Kept around as unavoidable adjuncts or pleasant pasttimes, feelings were meant to kneel to thought as we were meant to kneel to men. But women have survived. As poets. And there are no new pains. We have felt them all already. We have hidden that fact in the same place where we have our power. They lie in our dreams, and it is our dreams that point the way to freedom. They are made realizable through our poems that give us the strength and courage to see, to feel, to speak, and to dare.

If what we need to dream, to move our spirits most deeply and directly toward and through promise, is a luxury, then we have given up the core—the fountain—of our power, our womanness; we have given up the future of our worlds.

For there are no new ideas. There are only new ways of making them felt, of examining what our ideas really mean (feel like) on Sunday morning at 7 A.M., after brunch, during wild love, making war, giving birth; while we suffer the old longings, battle the old warnings and fears of being silent and impotent and alone, while tasting our new possibilities and strengths. (pp. 282-85)

Audre Lorde, "Poems Are Not Luxuries," in Claims for Poetry, *edited by Donald Hall, The University of Michigan Press, 1982, pp. 282-85.*

R. B. Stepto (essay date 1979)

[*In the following excerpt, Stepto provides a thematic analysis of Lorde's* The Black Unicorn, *a volume he considers to be the apex of the author's poetic and personal vision.*]

Audre Lorde's seventh volume of poems, **The Black Unicorn,** is a big, rich book of some sixty-seven poems.... Perhaps a full dozen—an incredibly high percentage—of these poems are searingly strong and unforgettable. Those readers who recall the clear light and promise of early Lorde poems such as **"The Woman Thing"** and **"Bloodbirth,"** and recall as well the great shape and energy of certain mid-1970s poems including **"To My Daughter the Junkie on a Train," "Cables to Rage,"** and **"Blackstudies,"** will find in **The Black Unicorn** new poems which reconfirm Lorde's talent while reseeding gardens and fields traversed before. There are other poems which do not so much reseed as repeople, and these new persons, names, ghosts, lovers, voices—these new I's, we's, real and imagined kin—give us something fresh, beyond the cycle of Lorde's previously recorded seasons and solstices.

While **The Black Unicorn** is unquestionably a personal triumph for Lorde in terms of the development of her canon, it is also an event in contemporary letters. This is a bold claim but one worth making precisely because, as we see in the first nine poems, Lorde appears to be the only North American poet other than Jay Wright who is sufficiently immersed in West African religion, culture, and art (and blessed with poetic talent!) to reach beyond a kind of middling poem that merely quantifies "blackness" through offhand reference to African gods and traditions. What Lorde and Wright share, beyond their abilities to create a fresh, New World Art out of ancient Old World lore, is a voice or an *idea* of a voice that is essentially African in that it is communal, historiographical, archival, and prophetic *as well as* personal in ways that we commonly associate with the African *griot, dyēli,* and tellers of *nganos* and other oral tales. However, while Wright's voice may be said to embody what is masculine in various West African cultures and cosmologies, Lorde's voice is decidedly and magnificently feminine. The goal of **The Black Unicorn** is then to present this fresh and powerful voice, and to explore the modulations within that voice between feminine and feminist timbres. As the volume unfolds, this exploration charts history and geography as well as voice, and with the confluence of these patterns the volume takes shape and Lorde's particular envisioning of a black transatlantic tradition is accessible.

All this begins, as suggested before, in the first nine poems in which we encounter the legendary women and goddesses—the sisters and especially the mothers—who inaugurate Lorde's genealogy of timbres and visages. In poems such as **"From the House of Yemanjá," "Dahomey,"** and **"125th Street and Abomey,"** mothers including Yemanjá (goddess of oceans, mother of the other *Orisha* or Yoruba goddesses and gods) and Seboulisa ("The goddess of Abomey—'The Mother of us all'")

appears, often in new renderings of the legends that surround them:

> My mother has two faces and a frying pot
> where she cooked up her daughters
> into girls
> before she fixed our dinner.
> My mother has two faces
> and a broken pot
> where she hid out a perfect daughter
> who was not me
> I am the sun and moon and forever hungry
> for her eyes

Much of this would be little more than mere reference of the sort alluded to before were the poems not galvanized and bound by the persona's unrelenting quest for freedom, voice, and women kin. At the beginning of the quest, the persona is a black unicorn, a protean figure who, in one manifestation, is a Dahomean woman with attached phallus dancing the part of Eshu-Elegba (Yemanjá's messenger son of many tongues) in religious ritual. At the end, she is a "severed daughter"—"severed" in that she is in a new but tethered geography (**"125th Street and Abomey"**) and has cut away an imposed ritual tongue—who has found a voice of her own that can utter "Whatever language is needed" (a skill allowed before only to Yemanjá's *son*) and can even laugh.

> Half earth and time splits us apart
> like struck rock,
> A piece lives elegant stories
> too simply put
> while a dream on the edge of summer
> of brown rain in nim trees
> snail shells from the dooryard
> of King Toffah
> bring me where my blood moves
> Seboulisa mother goddess with one breast
> eaten away by worms of sorrow and loss
> see me now
> your severed daughter
> laughing our name into echo
> all the world shall remember.

As we move from the first set of poems about black mothers, daughters, and sisters—women who can "wear flesh like war," conjoin "dying cloth," and "mock Eshu's iron quiver"—to those which come in the remaining three sections, there is a subtle shift in poetic form that appears to signal, in turn, a shift in focus from acquisition of voice to that of art. In the first set, in stanzas such as

> The black unicorn is restless
> the black unicorn is unrelenting
> the black unicorn is not
> free.

and

> Mother I need
> mother I need
> mother I need your blackness now
> as the august earth needs rain.

Lorde makes effective use of the principle of repetition that is at the heart of oral composition in all "pre-literate" cultures, and at the heart as well of such conspicuous Afro-American art forms as the blues. (Indeed, each of the stanzas just presented may be said to be a modified but identifiable blues verse.) In the remaining sections of the volume, repetition and other devices which are, in this context, referents in written art to oral forms, are largely forsaken in favor of the kind of taut free verse Lorde usually employs. What is fascinating about this, as suggested before, is that while the declarative voice forged in the first group of poems remains, that voice speaks less of discovering language and of moving, perhaps, from speech to laughter, and more of poems—of written art readily assuming the posture of a healing force.

This is true even of the poems about social unrest and injustice. In **"Chain,"** for example, a poem prompted by a news item describing two teenage girls who had borne children by their natural fathers, there is the cry,

> Oh write me a poem mother
> here, over my flesh
> get your words upon me
> as he got his child upon me

Similarly, in **"Eulogy for Alvin Frost"** we find,

> I am tired of writing memorials to black men
> whom I was on the brink of knowing
> . . . .
> Dear Danny who does not know me
> I am
> writing to you for your father
> whom I barely knew
> except at meetings where he was
> distinguished
> by his genuine laughter
> and his kind bright words

In the final section, **"Power"** begins with yet another suggested distinction between poetry and speech,

> The difference between poetry and rhetoric
> is being
> ready to kill
> yourself
> instead of your children.

and ends with a very particular statement of confession and self-instruction,

> I have not been able to touch the destruction
>   within me.
> But unless I learn to use
> the difference between poetry and rhetoric
> my power too will run corrupt as poisonous mold
> or lie limp and useless as an unconnected wire.

As the latent sexuality in the final line suggests, the shift in **The Black Unicorn** in poetic concern from acquisition of voice to that of art concerns as well the articulation of a homosexual love that was only barely alluded to before in the many figurations of tongue as women-warriors' sword and speech. Indeed, the pulsing love poems, in

which tongue finally becomes most explicitly an erotic tool and goal—

> I am tempted
> to take you apart
> and reconstruct your orifices
> your tongue your truths your fleshy altars
> into my own forgotten image
>
> **("Fog Report")**

—and in which sex and art most explicitly meet—

> I do not even know
> who looks like you
> of all the sisters who come to me
> at nightfall
> we touch each other in secret places
> draw old signs and stories
> upon each other's back and proofread
> each other's ancient copy.

—consummate the volume in a rich if not altogether unexpected manner.

Whether or not the subject at hand is love, children under assault, people in prison, childhood "wars," or the quest for a certain rare literacy, the poet in **The Black Unicorn** steadily pursues (and defines in that pursuit) a viable heroic posture and voice for womankind. The success of the volume may be seen in the fact that when the poet declares in the final poem,

> I will eat the last signs of my weakness
> remove the scars of old childhood wars
> and dare to enter the forest whistling

we believe her. In this period between renaissance and/or revolutions, Lorde's verse may need promotion in order to sell, but that doesn't mean that the verse is thin or insignificant. **The Black Unicorn** offers contemporary poetry of a high order, and in doing so may be a smoldering renaissance and revolution unto itself. (pp. 315-20)

> *R. B. Stepto, "The Phenomenal Woman and the Severed Daughter," in* Parnassus: Poetry in Review, *Vol. 8, No. 1, 1979, pp. 312-20.*

Audre Lorde with Claudia Tate (interview date 1983)

[*In the following excerpt from an interview published in Tate's* Black Women Writers at Work *(1983), Lorde discusses the meaning and development of her work, her political ideology, and the relationship between feminism and literature.*]

[Tate]: *How does your openness about being a black lesbian feminist direct your work and, more importantly, your life?*

[Lorde]: When you narrow your definition to what is convenient, or what is fashionable, or what is expected, what happens is dishonesty by silence. It is putting all of your eggs into one basket. That's not where all of your energy comes from.

Black writers, of whatever quality, who step outside the pale of what black writers are supposed to write about, or who black·writers are supposed to be, are condemned to silences in black literary circles that are as total and as destructive as any imposed by racism. This is particularly true for black women writers who have refused to be delineated by male-establishment models of femininity, and who have dealt with their sexuality as an accepted part of their identity. For instance, where are the women writers of the Harlem Renaissance being taught? Why did it take so long for Zora Neale Hurston to be reprinted?

Now, when you have a literary community oppressed by silence from the outside, as black writers are in America, and you have this kind of tacit insistence upon some unilateral definition of what "blackness" is, then you are painfully and effectively silencing some of our most dynamic and creative talents, for all change and progress from within require the recognition of differences among ourselves.

When you are a member of an out-group, and you challenge others with whom you share this outsider position to examine some aspect of their lives that distorts differences between you, then there can be a great deal of pain. In other words, when people of a group share an oppression, there are certain strengths that they build together. But there are also certain vulnerabilities. For instance, talking about racism to the women's movement results in "Huh, don't bother us with that. Look, we're all sisters, please don't rock the boat." Talking to the black community about sexism results in pretty much the same thing. You get a "Wait, wait . . . wait a minute: we're all black together. Don't rock the boat." In our work and in our living, we must recognize that difference is a reason for celebration and growth, rather than a reason for destruction.

We should see difference as a dialogue, the same way we deal with symbol and image, in literary study. "Imaging" is the process of developing a dialectic, a tension between opposites that illuminates the differences and similarities between things in apparent opposition. It is the same way with people. We need to use these differences in constructive ways, creative ways, rather than in ways to justify our destroying each other.

With respect to myself specifically, I feel that not to be open about any of the different "people" within my identity, particularly the "mes" who are challenged by a status quo, is to invite myself and other women, by my example, to live a lie. In other words, I would be giving in to a myth of sameness which I think can destroy us.

I'm not into living lies, no matter how comfortable they may be. I really feel that I'm too old for both abstractions and games, and I will not shut off any of my essential sources of power, control, and knowledge. I learned to speak the truth by accepting many parts of myself and making them serve one another. This power fuels my life and my work. (pp. 100-02)

Have your critics attempted to stereotype your work?

Critics have always wanted to cast me in a particular role from the time my first poem was published when I was fifteen years old. My English teachers at Hunter High School said that a particular poem was much too romantic. It was a love poem about my first love affair with a boy, and they didn't want to print it in the school paper, which is why I sent it to *Seventeen* magazine.

It's easier to deal with a poet, certainly with a black woman poet, when you categorize her, narrow her down so that she can fulfill your expectations, so she's socially acceptable and not too disturbing, not too discordant. I cannot be categorized. That has been both my weakness and my strength. It has been my weakness because my independence has cost me a lot of support. But you see, it has also been my strength because it has given me a vantage point and the power to go on. I don't know how I would have lived through the difficulties I have survived and continued to produce, if I had not felt that all of who I am is what fulfills me and fulfills the vision I have of the world, and of the future.

For whom do you write? What is your responsibility to your audience?

I write for myself and my children and for as many people as possible who can read me, who need to hear what I have to say—who need to use what I know. When I say myself, I mean not only the Audre who inhabits my body but all those feisty, incorrigible black women who insist on standing up and saying "*I am* and you cannot wipe me out, no matter how irritating I am, how much you fear what I might represent." I write for these women for whom a voice has not yet existed, or whose voices have been silenced. I don't have the only voice or all of their voices, but they are a part of my voice, and I am a part of theirs.

My responsibility is to speak the truth as I feel it, and to attempt to speak it with as much precision and beauty as possible. I think of my responsibility in terms of women because there are many voices for men. There are very few voices for women and particularly very few voices for black women, speaking from the center of consciousness, from the *I am* out to the *we are* and then out to the *we can*.

My mother used to say: "Island women make good wives; whatever happens they've seen worse." Well, I feel that as black women we have been through all kinds of catastrophe. We've survived, and with style.

I feel I have a duty to speak the truth as I see it and to share not just my triumphs, not just the things that felt good, but the pain, the intense, often unmitigating pain. It is important to share how I know survival is survival and not just a walk through the rain. For example, I have a duty to share what it feels like at three o'clock in the morning when you know "they" could cut you down emotionally in the street and grin in your face. And "they" are your own people. To share what it means to look into another sister's eyes and have her look away and choose someone you know she hates because it's expedient. To know that I, at times, have been a coward, or less than myself, or oppressive to other women, and to know that I can change. All of that anxiety, pain, defeat must be shared. We tend to talk about what feels good. We talk about what we think is settled. We never seem to talk about the ongoing problems. We need to share our mistakes in the same way we share our victories because that's the only way learning occurs. In other words, we have survived the pain, the problems, the failures, so what we need to do is use this suffering and learn from it. We must remember and comfort ourselves with that fact that survival is, in itself, a victory.

I never thought I would live to be forty, and I feel, "Hey, I really did it!" I am stronger for confronting the hard issue of breast cancer, of mortality, dying. It is hard, extremely hard, but very strengthening to remember I could be silent my whole life long and then be dead, flat out, and never have said or done what I wanted to do, what I needed to do because of pain or fear .... If I wait to be assured I'm right before I speak, I would be sending little cryptic messages on the Ouiji board, complaints from the other side.

I really feel if what I have to say is wrong, then there will be some woman who will stand up and say Audre Lorde was in error. But my words will be there, something for her to bounce off of, something to incite thought, activity.

I write not only for my peers but for those who will come after me, to say I was there, and I passed on, and you will pass on, too. But you're here now, so do it. I believe very strongly in survival and teaching. I feel that is my work.

This is so important that it bears repeating. I write for those women who do not speak, for those who do not have a voice because they/we were so terrified, because we are taught to respect fear more than ourselves. We've been taught that silence would save us, but it won't. We *must* learn to respect ourselves and our needs more than the fear of our differences, and we must learn to share ourselves with each other.

Is writing a way of growing, understanding?

Yes. I think writing and teaching, child-rearing, digging rocks (which is one of my favorite pastimes), all of the things I do are very much a part of my work. They flow in and out of each other, help to nourish each other. That's what the whole question of survival and teaching means. That we keep our experience afloat long enough, that we share what we know, so that other people can build upon our experience. There are many ways of doing that in all aspects of our lives. So teaching for me is in many respects identical to writing. Both become ways of exploring what I need for survival. They are survival techniques. Because as I write, as I teach, I am answering those questions that are primary for my own

survival, and I am exploring the response to these questions with other people; this is what teaching is. I think that this is the only way that real learning occurs. Learning does not happen in some detached way of dealing with a text alone, but from becoming so involved in the process that you can see how it might illuminate your life, and then how you can share that illumination.

When did you start to write?

I looked around when I was a young woman and there was no one saying what I wanted and needed to hear. I felt totally alienated, disoriented, crazy. I thought that there's got to be somebody else who feels as I do.

I was very inarticulate as a youngster. I couldn't speak. I didn't speak until I was five, in fact, not really until I started reading and writing poetry. I used to speak in poetry. I would read poems, and I would memorize them. People would say, "Well, what do you think, Audre? What happened to you yesterday?" And I would recite a poem and somewhere in that poem there would be a line or a feeling I was sharing. In other words, I literally communicated through poetry. And when I couldn't find the poems to express the things I was feeling, that's when I started writing poetry. That was when I was twelve or thirteen.

Do black male and female writers dramatize characters and themes in distinctly different ways? Gayl Jones replied to this question by saying she thought one distinction has to do with the kinds of events men and women select to depict in literature. She thinks black women writers tend to select particular and personal events rather than those which are generally considered to be representative.

I think that's true. This reflects a difference between men and women in general. Black men have come to believe to their detriment that you have no validity unless you're "global," as opposed to personal. Yet, our *real power* comes from the personal; our real insights about living come from that deep knowledge within us that arises from our feelings. Our thoughts are shaped by our tutoring. As black people, we have not been tutored for our benefit, but more often than not, for our detriment. We were tutored to function in a structure that already existed but that does not function for our good. Our feelings are our most genuine paths to knowledge. They are chaotic, sometimes painful, sometimes contradictory, but they come from deep within us. And we must key into those feelings and begin to extrapolate from them, examine them for new ways of understanding our experiences. This is how new visions begin, how we begin to posit a future nourished by the past. This is what I mean by matter following energy, and energy following feeling. Our visions begin with our desires.

Men have been taught to deal only with what they understand. This is what they respect. They know that somewhere feeling and knowledge are important, so they keep women around to do their feeling for them, like ants do aphids.

I don't think these differences between men and women are rigidly defined with respect to gender, though the Western input has been to divide these differences into male and female *characteristics*. We all have the ability to feel deeply and to move upon our feelings and see where they lead us. Men in general have suppressed that capacity, so they keep women around to do that for them. Until men begin to develop that capacity within themselves, they will always be at a loss and will always need to victimize women.

The message I have for black men is that it is to their detriment to follow this pattern. Too many black men do precisely that, which results in violence along sexual lines. This violence terrifies me. It is a painful truth which is almost unbearable. As I say in a new poem, it is "a pain almost beyond bearing" because it gives birth to the kind of hostility that will destroy us.

To change the focus, though ever so slightly. Writing by black Americans has traditionally dramatized black people's humanity. Black male writers tend to cry out in rage in order to convince their readers that they too feel, whereas black women writers tend to dramatize the pain, the love. They don't seem to need to intellectualize this capacity to feel, but focus on describing the feeling itself.

It's one thing to talk about feeling. It's another to feel. Yes, love is often pain. But I think what is really necessary is to see how much of this pain I can use, how much of this truth I can see and still live unblinded. That is an essential question that we must all ask ourselves. There is some point at which pain becomes an end in itself, and we must let it go. On the other hand, we must not be afraid of pain, and we must not subject ourselves to pain as an end in itself. We must not celebrate victimization because there are other ways of being black.

There is a very thin but a very definite line between these two responses to pain. And I would like to see this line more carefully drawn in some of the works by black women writers. I am particularly aware of the two responses in my own work. And I find I must remember that the pain is not its own reason for being. It is a part of living. And the only kind of pain that is intolerable is pain that is wasteful, pain from which we do not learn. And I think that we must learn to distinguish between the two.

How do you integrate social protest and art in your work?

I see protest as a genuine means of encouraging someone to feel the inconsistencies, the horror of the lives we are living. Social protest is saying that we do not have to live this way. If we feel deeply, and we encourage ourselves and others to feel deeply, we will find the germ of our answers to bring about change. Because once we recognize what it is we are feeling, once we recognize we can feel deeply, love deeply, can feel joy, then we will

demand that all parts of our lives produce that kind of joy. And when they do not, we will ask, "Why don't they?" And it is the asking that will lead us inevitably toward change.

So the question of social protest and art is inseparable for me. I can't say it is an either-or proposition. Art for art's sake doesn't really exist for me. What I saw was wrong, and I had to speak up. I loved poetry, and I loved words. But what was beautiful had to serve the purpose of changing my life, or I would have died. If I cannot air this pain and alter it, I will surely die of it. That's the beginning of social protest.

How has your work evolved in terms of interest and craft? Let's look at the love poetry, for instance, which dominated your early work [**The First Cities** *and* **New York Head Shop**] *and which appears in* **The Black Unicorn.**

Everyone has a first-love poem that comes out of that first love. Everybody has it, and it's so wonderful and new and great. But when you've been writing love poems after thirty years, the later poems are the ones that really hit the nitty gritty, that meet your boundaries. They witness what you've been through. Those are the real love poems. And I love them because they say, "Hey! We define ourselves as lovers, as people who love each other all over again; we become new again." These poems insist that you can't separate loving from fighting, from dying, from hurting, but love is triumphant. It is powerful and strong, and I feel I grow a great deal in all of my emotions, especially in the capacity to love.

Your love poetry seems not only to celebrate the personal experience of love but also love as a human concept, a theme embracing all of life, a theme which appears more and more emphatically in your later work. Particularly interesting, for instance, are the lesbian love poems ["**Letter for Jan**" *and* "**Walking Our Boundaries**"]. *It didn't seem to make much difference whether the poems depicted a relationship between two women, two men, or a man and a woman . . . . The poems do not celebrate the people but the love.*

When you love, you love. It only depends on how you do it, how committed you are, how many mistakes you make . . . . But I do believe that the love expressed between women is particular and powerful because we have had to love ourselves in order to live; love has been our means of survival. And having been in love with both men and women, I want to resist the temptation to gloss over the differences.

I am frequently jarred by my sometimes unconscious attempt to identify the sex of the person addressed in the poem. Since I associate the speaker's voice with you, and since I'm not always conscious that you are a lesbian, the jarring occurs when I realize the object of affection is likewise a woman. I'm certain this disturbance originates in how society defines love in terms of heterosexuality. So if we are to see love as a "universal" concept, society pressures us to see it as heterosexual.

Yes, we're supposed to see "universal" love as heterosexual. What I insist upon in my work is that there is no such thing as universal love in literature. There is *this* love in *this* poem. The poem happens when I, Audre Lorde, poet, deal with the particular instead of the "UNIVERSAL." My power as a person, as a poet, comes from who I am. I am a particular person. The relationships I have had, in which people kept me alive, helped sustain me, were sustained by me, were particular relationships. They help give me my particular identity, which is the source of my energy. Not to deal with my life in my art is to cut out the fount of my strength.

I love to write love poems. I love loving. And to put it into another framework, that is, other than poetry, I wrote a paper entitled **"The Uses of the Erotic,"** where I examine the whole question of loving as a manifestation, love as a source of tremendous power. Women have been taught to suspect the erotic urge, the place that is uniquely female. So, just as we tend to reject our blackness because it has been termed inferior, as women we tend to reject our capacity for feeling, our ability to love, to touch the erotic, because it has been devalued. But it is within this that lies so much of our power, our ability to posit, our vision. Because once we know how deeply we can feel, we begin to demand from all of our life pursuits that they be in accordance with these feelings. And when they don't we must raise the question why do I feel constantly suicidal, for instance? What's wrong? Is it me, or is it what I am doing? We begin to need to answer such questions. But we cannot when we have no image of joy, no vision of what we are capable of. After the killing is over. When you live without the sunlight, you don't know what it is to relish the bright light or even to have too much of it. Once you have light, then you can measure its intensity. So too with joy. (pp. 103-10)

Would you describe your writing process?

I keep a journal and write in it fairly regularly. I get a lot of my poems out of it. It's like the raw material for my poems. Sometimes I'm blessed with a poem that comes in the form of a poem, but other times I've worked for two years on a poem.

For me, there are two very basic and different processes for revising my poetry. One is recognizing that a poem has not yet become itself. In other words, I mean that the feeling, the truth that the poem is anchored in is somehow not clearly clarified inside of me, and as a result it lacks something. Then it has to be re-felt. Then there's the other process which is easier. The poem is itself, but it has rough edges that need to be refined. That kind of revision involves picking the image that is more potent or tailoring it so that it carries the feeling. That's an easier kind of rewriting and re-feeling.

My journal entries focus on things I feel: feelings that sometimes have no place, no beginning, no end; phrases I hear in passing; something that looks good to me; sometimes just observations of the world.

I went through a period once when I felt like I was dying. I wasn't writing any poetry, and I felt that if I couldn't write I would split. I was recording in my journal, but no poems came. I know now that this period was a transition in my life.

The next year, I went back to my journal, and here were these incredible poems that I could almost lift out of it. Many of them are in *The Black Unicorn.* "Harriet" is one of them; **"Sequelae"** and **"The Litany for Survival"** are others. These poems came right out of the journal. But I didn't see them as poems then.

"Power" was in the journal too. It is a poem written about Clifford Glover, the ten-year-old black boy shot by a cop who was acquitted by a jury on which a black woman sat. In fact, the day I heard on the radio that O'Shea had been acquitted, I was going across town on 88th Street [New York City] and I had to pull over. A kind of fury rose up in me—the sky turned red. I felt so sick. I felt as if I would drive the car into a wall, into the next person I saw. So I pulled over. I took out my journal just to air some of my fury, to get it out of my fingertips. Those expressed feelings are that poem. That was just how **"Power"** was written.

A transition has to occur before you can make poetry out of your journal entries.

There is a gap between the journal and my poetry. I write this stuff in my journal, and sometimes I cannot even read my journals because there is so much pain and rage in them. I'll put it away in a drawer, and six months, a year or so later, I'll pick up the journal, and there will be the seeds of poems. The journal entries somehow have to be assimilated into my living; only then can I deal with what I have written down.

Art is not living. It is the use of living. The artist has the ability to take the living and use it in a certain way and produce art.

Does Afro-American literature possess particular characteristics?

Afro-American literature is certainly part of an African tradition. African tradition deals with life as an experience to be lived. In many respects, it is much like the Eastern philosophies in that we see ourselves as a part of a life force; we are joined, for instance, to the air, to the earth. We are part of the whole-life process. We live in accordance with, in a kind of correspondence with the rest of the world as a whole. And therefore living becomes an experience, rather than a problem, no matter how bad or how painful it may be. Change will rise endemically from the experience fully lived and responded to.

I feel this very much in African writing. And as a consequence, I have learned a great deal from Achebe, Tutuola, Ekwensi, from Flora Nwapa and Ama Ata Aido. Leslie Lacy, a black American who lived temporarily in Ghana, writes about experiencing this transcendence in his book *The Rise and Fall of a Proper Negro.*

It's not a turning away from pain, error, but seeing these things as part of living, and learning from them. This characteristic is particularly African, and it is transposed into the best of Afro-American literature. In addition, we have the legends of our struggle and survival in the New World.

This transcendence appears in Ellison, a little bit in Baldwin. And it is present very much so in Toni Morrison's *Sula,* which is a most wonderful piece of fiction. And I don't care if she won a prize for *The Song of Solomon. Sula* is a totally incredible book. It made me light up inside like a Christmas tree. I particularly identified with the book because of the female-outsider idea. That book is one long poem. Sula is the ultimate black female of our time, trapped in her power and her pain. Alice Walker uses that quality in *The Color Purple,* another wonderful novel of living as power.

The recent writing by many black women seems to explore human concerns somewhat differently than do the men. These women refuse to blame racism alone for every negative aspect of black life. They are examining the nature of what passes between black women and black men—the power principles. Men tend to respond defensively to the writing of black women by labeling them as the "darklings" of the literary establishment. Goodness knows, the critics, especially black male critics, had a field day with Ntozake Shange's For Colored Girls Who Have Considered Suicide When the Rainbow is Enuf. *And they are getting started on Alice Walker's* The Color Purple. *But there are cruel black men, just as there are kind black men. Can't we try to alter that cruelty by focusing on it?*

Let me read an excerpt from a piece in *The Black Scholar* for you, which I wrote a while back:

> As I have said elsewhere, it is not the destiny of black America to repeat white America's mistakes. But we will, if we mistake the trappings of success in a sick society for the signs of a meaningful life. If black men continue to do so, defining "femininity" in its archaic European terms, this augurs ill for our survival as a people, let alone our survival as individuals. Freedom and future for blacks do not mean absorbing the dominant white male disease . . . .
>
> As black people, we cannot begin our dialogue by denying the oppressive nature of male privilege. And if black males choose to assume that privilege, for whatever reason, raping, brutalizing and killing women, then we cannot ignore black male oppression. One oppression does not justify another.

It's infuriating. Misguided black men. And meanwhile they are killing us in the streets. Is that the nature of nationhood?

I find this divisiveness to be oppressive and very persistent. It's been going on for a long time. It didn't start with Ntozake. It's been coming more and more to the forefront now. If you ask any of the black women writers over thirty whom you're interviewing, if she's honest, she will tell you. You know there's as much a black literary mafia in this country as there is a white literary mafia. They control who gets exposure. If you don't toe the line, then you're not published; your works are not distributed. At the same time, as black women, of course, we do not want to be used against black men by a system that means both of us ill.

Do you think that had it not been for the women's movement black women would still be struggling to achieve their voice in the literary establishment?

Without a doubt. Black women writers have been around a long time, and they have suffered consistent inattention. Despite this reality, you hear from various sources that black women really have "it." We're getting jobs; we're getting this and that, supposedly. Yet we still constitute the lowest economic group in America. Meanwhile those of us who do not fit into the "establishment" have not been allowed a voice, and it was only with the advent of the women's movement—even though black women are in disagreement with many

Title page of Lorde's 1978 poetry collection The Black Unicorn.

aspects of the women's movement—that black women began to demand a voice, as women and as blacks. I think any of us who are honest have to say this. As Barbara Smith says, "All the women were white and all the blacks were men, but some of us are still brave." Her book on black women's studies [*Some of Us Are Brave*], which she edited along with Gloria Hull and Patricia Bell Scott, is the first one on the subject.

Are you at a turning point in your career, your life?

I think I have deepened and broadened my understanding of the true difficulty of my work. Twenty years ago when I said we needed to understand each other I had not really perfected a consciousness concerning how important differences are in our lives. But that is a theme which recurs in my life and in my work. I have become more powerful because I have refused to settle for the myth of sorry sameness, that myth of easy sameness. My life's work continues to be survival and teaching. As I said before, teaching is also learning; teach what you need to learn. If we do this deeply, then it is most effective. I have, for example, deepened the questions that I follow, and so I have also deepened the ways I teach and learn.

The work I did on the erotic was very, very important. It opened up for me a whole area of connections in the absence of codified knowledge, or in the absence of some other clear choice. The erotic has been a real guide for me. And learning as a discipline is identical to learning how to reach through feeling the essence of how and where the erotic originates, to posit what it is based upon. This process of feeling and therefore knowing has been very, very constructive for me.

I believe in the erotic and I believe in it as an enlightening force within our lives as women. I have become clearer about the distinctions between the erotic and other apparently similar forces. We tend to think of the erotic as an easy, tantalizing sexual arousal. I speak of the erotic as the deepest life force, a force which moves us toward living in a fundamental way. And when I say living I mean it as that force which moves us toward what will accomplish real positive change.

When I speak of a future that I work for, I speak of a future in which all of us can learn, a future which we want for our children. I posit that future to be led by my visions, my dreams, and my knowledge of life. It is that knowledge which I call the erotic, and I think we must develop it within ourselves. I think so much of our living and our consciousness has been formed by death or by non-living. This is what allows us to tolerate so much of what is vile around us. When I speak of "the good," I speak of living; I speak of the erotic in all forms. They are all one. So in that sense I believe in the erotic as an illuminating principle in our lives.

You've just finished a new work.

Yes. *Zami: A New Spelling of My Name* was just published. It's a biomythography, which is really fiction.

It has the elements of biography and history of myth. In other words, it's fiction built from many sources. This is one way of expanding our vision.

I'm very excited about this book. As you know, it's been a long time coming. Now that it's out, it'll do its work. Whatever its faults, whatever its glories, it's there.

You might call *Zami* a novel. I don't like to call it that. Writing *Zami* was a lifeline through the cancer experience. As I said in *The Cancer Journals,* I couldn't believe that what I was fighting I would fight alone and only for myself. I couldn't believe that there wasn't something there that somebody could use at some other point because I know that I could have used some other woman's words, whatever she had to say. Just to know that someone had been there before me would have been very important, but there was nothing. Writing *The Cancer Journals* gave me the strength and power to examine that experience, to put down into words what I was feeling. It was my belief that if this work were useful to just one woman, it was worth doing.

What can you share with the younger generation of black women writers and writers in general?

Not to be afraid of difference. To be real, tough, loving. And to recognize each other. I can tell them not to be afraid to feel and not to be afraid to write about it. Even if you are afraid, do it anyway because we learn to work when we are tired, so we can learn to work when we are afraid. Silence never brought us anything. Survive and teach; that's what we've got to do and to do it with joy. (p. 111-16)

Audre Lorde and Claudia Tate, in an interview in Black Women Writers at Work, *edited by Claudia Tate, Continuum, 1983, pp. 100-16.*

Jerome Brooks (essay date 1984)

[*An American educator and critic, Brooks is the author of the novels* Uncle Mike's Boy *(1973) and* Make Me a Hero *(1980). In the following excerpt, he analyzes three motifs prevalent throughout Lorde's poetry: her preoccupation with male dominance, her continuing quest for love, and her commitment to moral and intellectual clarity.*]

Audre Lorde has been writing now for more than twenty years, and the turbulent events of the past two decades find eloquent voice in her poetry. What is remarkable, however, as one looks back over her work so far is the powerful personal voice of her own struggles with life. Although she is decidedly political and has enjoyed an extremely engaged and active life, the world is seen in her poetry mainly through the conflicts and confrontation of her coming to terms with herself or with very private pain. Indeed, the words anger and rage come up time and again in her poetry, but the key word is pain. And for her pain is private and intimate. When she writes of her personal suffering, the writing is almost clinically precise, original, and direct.

A central poem in this regard, and one of her finest, is **"Father, Son, and Holy Ghost,"** about the death of her father. It is central also to an understanding of the mind of Audre Lorde. It is appropriately not about his death, but about the young daughter's experience of his absence. The poet cannot bear to visit his grave, so massive and vital a presence was he while alive. His presence was intellectual and moral in nature: "he lived still judgments on familiar things." His physical stature invaded the very details of the house. Although the poet has never seen his grave, there is an imagining of its daily routine, visited each day by a "different woman," and a man "who loved but one" thus being cared for each day by a different woman arouses an unacknowledged jealousy in the bereaved daughter. The jealous grief finds solace in the lively memory that he "died/knowing a January 15 that year me."

This poem of 1960 thus established the three central themes and motifs of Lorde's life and the pattern of her poetry: her preoccupation with the male principle and the issue of power; her profound quest for love; and the commitment to intellectual and moral clarity about "familiar things."

It should be noted that the image of her mother in Lorde's poetry is also a dominant one, but of a different order. The mother, for example, in **"Black Mother Woman,"** is a spirit to be exorcised, for there is nothing gentle and maternal in her memory. The daughter must fend through a thicket of anger and fury to find "the core of love." From her mother, she has acquired a "squadron of conflicting rebellions," elsewhere described as a conflict between racial values. The daughter's identity is achieved through standing apart from, against the mother.

The poetry is, then, a prolonged spiritual effort to reach the father, to be transformed into him, and to be his likeness, more son than daughter. This preoccupation with the male principle and with power is a tribute to the father's legacy. And this concern in turn is at the root of those disconcerting, wild, surrealist images that characterize much of her poetry. One has a feeling often of toughness and determination, of anger, in many of the poems. These are the ghosts of the father.

She speaks of herself as warrior, and she longs for "victories over men, over women, over my selves." In *The Black Unicorn,* the contact with Africa is the contact with the father who is revealed in a wealth of mythological symbols. "It was in Abomey that I felt / the full blood of my father's wars / and where I found my mother Seboulisa." But the poet herself identifies with Eshu, who is both male principle and prankster. The women while working on fabric openly scorn his "iron quiver / standing erect and flamingly familiar / in their dooryard," while the men create the poetry of war into tapestries. The poet is inspired by this warlike company to wear two drums on her head and "to sharpen the knives of my tongue." The fundamental image of the unicorn indicates that the poet is aware that Africa is for her a fatherland, a phallic terrain. It serves this function all the more clearly in that there is an easy passage in this mythic terrain between male and female, between parent and child. This confusion is her favorite trickery. Mawulisa (Mawu and Lisa), for example, is both male and female, or, if you prefer, both parent and son. In a particularly witty passage in **"The Winds of Orisha,"** she reminds us that in Greek legend, Tiresias took five hundred years to become a woman "until nut-like she went to sleep in a bottle." The poet takes heart from this transformation: "Tiresias took 500 years to grow into a woman / so do not despair of your sons."

These symbols are an incantation of the spirit of the father, a quest for his power. Lorde's quest is not for power for its own sake. Nor is it a self-serving quest, but a search for power at the service of a tremendous social anger. Lorde's poetry of anger is perhaps her best-known work and the source of much of her East Coast following, though, in my judgment, it does not always represent her finest work. What I will call her social poetry is sometimes marred by what she herself calls an "avid insistence on detail," or what I would rather term a Whitmanesque democratic litany of events. This litany is redeemed, however, by the internalization of facts through haunting imagery, as in the poem called simply **"Power,"** where the streets of New York become "a desert of raw gunshot wounds" and the poet's dream is disturbed by the "shattered black/face off the edge of my sleep." Her ability to hold event up to her relentlessly clinical analysis often leads to a perception of human character that is, perhaps, the ultimate justification for art. In the same poem, for instance, speaking of the jury that acquitted the policeman who shot down a ten-year-old boy, she singles out for rebuke the "one black woman who said / 'They convinced me' meaning / they had dragged her 4'10" black woman's frame / over the hot coals of four centuries of white male approval / until she let go the first real power she ever had...."

This rage (a favorite word and the title of one of her volumes) is especially apparent in the new poems of her latest book, *Chosen Poems—Old and New* (1982), where, for instance, she reflects on a brief sojourn she spent many years ago in Jackson, Mississippi. The death of Emmett Till in the Pearl River becomes a christening at which the poet becomes his sponsor and he becomes her "son forever." The poet seems to be acknowledging in this poem, **"Afterimages,"** that residence in the South had a deeply transforming effect on her political and poetic awareness. She has a maternal feeling for all outsiders, especially, the young Blacks of New York; I am thinking particularly of the young girl nodding on the subway whom she addresses as her daughter. These are the images by which "A woman measures her life's damage."

In recent years Lorde's militancy has been directed toward sexual oppression, as in the poem **"Need: A Choral of Black Women's Voices."** Arranged as a funeral antiphonal between the ghosts of two Black women and the chorus or congregation of all the living, the most moving part of the poem is the vehement denunciation of Black men whose spurious "need" spells destruction: "Who ever learns to love me / from the mouth of my enemies / walks the edge of my world / like a phantom in a crimson cloak." One may safely question the sweeping nature of this accusation, but the juxtaposition of love and enmity and the vulgarity of the TV phantom are hard to fault.

Lorde's anger is directed not only to popular political issues but to what may be called the slight cruelties and injustices of everyday life. But what is perhaps important to insist on is the relation between the two preoccupying militances of her poetry, namely, sexual and racial oppression. In an essay entitled **"Scratching the Surface"** (*Black Scholar*, 1978), she argues for the inclusion of all Black peoples in the struggle against oppression and for the exclusion of none. She is particularly exercised by the assumption of the larger Black community that those who fight the sexual oppressor are only tepidly devoted to fighting the racial oppressor. These are "kitchen wars," she says, which detract from everyone's genuine self-interest. The root of all social-sexual discrimination, she argues, whether racism, sexism, heterosexism, or homophobia, is the assumption of superiority and the will to power. She seems to be calling for the inclusion of the outsider, or arguing for the outsider as insider in American society. This inclusion is, I think, the meaning of another favorite word, empowering. I need not point out that this, too, is a religious term, and investiture of the daughter with the father's powerful mantle and approval. In **"Who Said It Was Simple,"** she talks about the many roots of anger and the many branches of liberation:

> But I who am bound by my mirror
> as well as my bed
> see causes in colour
> as well as sex
>
> and sit here wondering
> which me will survive
> all these liberations.

For all her militancy, however, there is another side to Audre Lorde and another style in her poetry. She is a woman capable of very deep and quiet love and her poetry here becomes almost traditional in form. It is here above all that her powerful poetic instinct finds fulfillment. Her method here is not the re-creation of event in searing detail and surrealist image. She is at her best in exquisite and economical narrative that is luminous with insight. In these poems the symbolism grows out of, is integral to, the event, and awareness or wisdom is gently released from the form. Here, too, she is freer to be herself and is not limited by political strictures. The subject of her narrative poetry is all-embracing.

"Walking Our Boundaries" is one of her great poems. Elizabeth Janeway, in her chapter on women writers in *The Harvard Guide to Contemporary American Writing*, speaks of Black women writers as survivors, and this is certainly a great poem of survival. It is written after Lorde's bout with cancer and close encounter with death, and the poem catches the sense of wonder at being alive in a small garden that she owns with her friend and at the survival of their love. There is a sureness of tone, a mastery of both sound and symbol, and an infusion of the word pain that takes place in the opening lines:

> This first bright day has broken
> the back of winter
> We rise from war
> To walk across the earth
> around our house
> both stunned that sun can shine so brightly
> after all our pain

The balance of the poem is prefigured by the effortless and natural alliteration of these lines. The ravages of winter reflect last winter's pain. The friends are both "half-afraid there will be no tight buds started / on our ancient apple tree." The symbolism of the scene is illuminated in an excellent line: "it does not pay to cherish symbols / when the substance / lies so close at hand." A light affectionate touch on the shoulder, reaching back to the opening lines of the poem, breaks the back of the spiritual winter of suffering. The sense is clear in spite of the momentary lapse of image in "dead leaves waiting to be burned / to life." The final stanza yields a triumph of the human will over physical decay: "the siding has come loose in spots / our footsteps hold this place together." It is a nearly perfect poem, reminiscent of Robert Frost in its method and mood.

This is her characteristic method in poems of love, beautiful narration, symbolism matched with deep feeling. **"Brother Alvin,"** for instance, tells of a childhood schoolmate who missed a lot of classes between Halloween and Thanksgiving and then just before Christmas disappeared. Their mutual dependence is recalled, and the definitive separation after all these years is symbolic of the final one; the search for him becomes a fascination with the magic that will unlock the mystery of all separations. In **"Eulogy for Alvin Frost,"** the untimely death of someone loved and admired, though not long enough to become friends, is lamented. This Alvin, a cherished acquaintance, evokes the earlier childhood schoolmate of the same name, and stands for all Black men lost too soon, "all the black substance poured into earth / before earth is ready to bear." The poem is in four movements, the narration being the middle movements. A kind of prologue introduces the narrative, which is followed by a simple maternal address by the poet to the survivor's son, Danny, a moving poem in its own right.

Occasionally, as in **"Poem for a Poet,"** an image will trigger the event and become intertwined with it. Sitting in her car in a Greenwich Village street, her mind wanders to North Carolina and the happy memories of Randall Jarrell. The car suddenly becomes his coffin, and she says with childlike affection, "How come being so cool / you weren't also a little bit black." Silent homage is later paid to him in a line from **"Story Books on a Kitchen Table,"** inspired by the opening of "The Death of the Ball Turret Gunner": "Out of her womb of pain my mother spat me."

Invariably the poetry in this mode is a way of reaching out to the memory of the father and capturing his love. These poems have a tone, a unity between event and symbol and feeling, that is very satisfying. They are the most neglected poems of this insufficiently known poet and the works which her vast feminist following is likely to overlook. But they are the most attractive side of a complex woman. She is more like her mother than she knows: powerful and fierce. Yet she much resembles the father: exceedingly thoughtful and kind.

Another kind of narrative poem is a result of the poet's sojourn in West Africa, where she obviously did a great deal of research into Yoruba mythology, particularly as it occurs in Nigeria and Dahomey, present-day Benin. These ancient myths brought a wealth of insight and psychological maturity to the poet. And the work of this period is extremely African in its sense and texture, yet is imbued with the themes and concerns of Audre Lorde. **"Coniagui Women,"** for example, tells the story of how the warrior women wean their sons and force them into becoming men. The last lines are forceful in their directness and economy: "'Let us sleep in your bed' they whisper / 'Let us sleep in your bed' / but she has mothered before them. She closes her door. / They become men." From Africa she learned how to see the symbol residing in the event and to leave it embedded there like a jewel. In a very Wallace Stevens-like short poem entitled **"A Rock Thrown into the Water Does Not Fear the Cold,"** the snails consume a snake at twilight, "Their white extended bodies / gently sucking / take sweetness from the stiffening shape / as darkness overtakes them." The poem has found a surprisingly new image of sexual submission and human development.

A major preoccupation of this poet, indeed, is how really to become her father's daughter, how to acquire the wisdom to find one's way in the world, how to emulate "his judgment on familiar things." Like a great teacher, she is able to sense the confusion in the minds of both young and old, the terror in not being able to do the arithmetic of life. The fourteen-year-old girl in **"Hanging Fire"** worries about her ashy knees and the fact that she has nothing to wear, that her boyfriend secretly sucks his thumb, and that she might die before she grows up. All the while, the person who once held all the secrets of life now hides them and herself: "and momma's in the bedroom / with the door closed." Equally, in **"Litany For Survival,"** those adults who live on the margins of life, "on the constant edges of decision," are filled with another kind of daily fear, "like bread in our children's mouths." These, in a

devastating line, have learned "to be afraid with our mother's milk." The system, "the heavy-footed," did not wish them to survive. And thus they are afraid of life itself:

> And when the sun rises we are afraid
> it might not remain
> when the sun sets we are afraid
> it might not rise in the morning
> when our stomachs are full we are afraid
> of indigestion
> when our stomachs are empty we are afraid
> we may never eat again
> when we are loved we are afraid
> love will vanish
> when we are alone we are afraid
> love will never return
> and when we speak we are afraid
> our words will not be heard
> nor welcomed
> but when we are silent
> we are still afraid.

For such as these the poet offers the comfort that their plight is understood. The real comfort, however, comes from the courage to give a name to the enemy's weapons and purpose: "So it is better to speak / remembering / we were never meant to survive."

This courage is sometimes humorously turned inward, as in **"Chorus,"** where Lorde comes to terms at last with her light-skinned mother while finding herself humming Mozart, who was, she suddenly remembers, "a white dude."

It would be impossible to conclude this aspect of Audre Lorde's writing without mentioning a brave little book called *The Cancer Journals.* It is really a pamphlet based upon a diary that she kept during a very traumatic experience with breast cancer from September 1978 to March 1979, an experience which culminated in radical mastectomy. For a beautiful woman proud of her appearance, it was a profoundly humiliating, sad event. The pamphlet consists of an introduction and three chapters. The introduction contains diary entries, very candid statements of fear for her life and her work, of occasional despair, of the support she found in many women friends. The first chapter is a short address Lorde gave at the annual convention of the Modern Language Association in 1977, at a time when she had just recovered from surgery which discovered a benign tumor of the breast. The theme is "The Transformation of Silence into Language and Action." The second chapter is subtitled "A Black Lesbian Feminist Experience." The subtitle, in my reading, is valid only to identify the author; beyond one discreet episode some twenty-five years earlier that took place in Mexico, it docs not characterize what is in the text. The chapter is a very courageous description of all the emotions lived during and after the operation. Conversations with her friend Frances, with her brother-in-law, Henry, and with her mother are recorded. There is wild grief, as well as humor and love and finally acceptance. As usual, Lorde has done her research into the incidence and treatment of breast cancer, and her remarks are certainly of wider interest than the subtitle would indicate. For this is a problem that arouses vast human sympathy, that has touched many of us, men and women, intimately. The final chapter, in keeping with Lorde's fierce spirit, is on her decision not to wear a prosthesis, a decision, it must be added, that she does not suggest for others, but which she uses to expose some of the hypocrisies of the medical profession as well as the venal practices of an economic system that values profit more than the health and well-being of its people.

Lorde is a poet for whom writing is a serious moral responsibility. She came to poetic and personal awareness in the late fifties and early sixties, but has grown steadily since in both complexity of vision and clarity of purpose. She has worked very hard at her craft and we may expect to see more changes and growth in the years to come. As I have indicated, she has a devoted following in New York and the East Coast generally, but for the gravity of the issues she raises, for her luminous insight, meticulous research and skill, and for the breadth of her interests, she deserves a far wider audience. One can only hope that this valuable voice will survive all its liberations, and in so doing enlarge our own sense of freedom and capacity for life. (pp. 269-76)

> *Jerome Brooks, "In the Name of the Father: The Poetry of Audre Lorde," in* Black Women Writers (1950-1980): A Critical Evaluation, *edited by Mari Evans, Anchor Press/Doubleday, 1984, pp. 269-76.*

FURTHER READING

Annas, Pamela. "A Poetry of Survival: Unnaming and Renaming in the Poetry of Audre Lorde, Pat Parker, Sylvia Plath, and Adrienne Rich." *Colby Library Quarterly* 18, No. 1 (March 1982): 9-25.
>   Examines Lorde's "survival" poetry, asserting that the relationship between poetry and feminism is complex, unique, and necessary because "a poem is a stage in the process of self-definition, a grounding and realizing of self-image."

Avi-ram, Amitai F. *"Apo Koinou* in Audre Lorde and the Moderns: Defining the Differences." *Callaloo* 9, No. 1 (Winter 1986): 192-208.
>   Study of the elements of *Apo Koinou*—"a figure of speech . . . in which a single word or phrase is shared between two distinct, independent syntactic units"—evidenced in Lorde's poetry.

Brown, Joseph A. "We Are Piecing Our Weapons Together." *Callaloo* 9, No. 4 (Fall 1986): 737-39.
>   Review of *Our Dead behind Us,* praising Lorde's use of African images to explore the themes of sisterhood and victimization.

Carruthers, Mary J. "The Re-Vision of the Muse: Adrienne Rich, Audre Lorde, Judy Grahn, Olga Broumas." *The Hudson Review* XXXVI, No. 2 (Summer 1983): 293-322.
>   Comparative analysis of prominent lesbian poets in which Carruthers contends that "for Lorde . . . the most important virtue—imaged by the female bond—is integration."

Daniell, Rosemary. "The Poet Who Found Her Own Way." *The New York Times Book Review* LXXXVII, No. 51 (19 December 1982): 12, 29.
>   Asserts that *Zami: A New Spelling of My Name* is rich with evocative imagery and that *Chosen Poems Old and New* presents a sensitive and intelligent view of contemporary life.

Hammond, Karla. "An Interview with Audre Lorde." *The American Poetry Review* 9, No. 2 (March/April 1980): 18-21.
>   Interview with Lorde in which she discusses her personal life, political ideology, and the repercussions of racism.

———. "Audre Lorde: Interview." *Denver Quarterly* 16, No. 1 (Spring 1981): 10-27.
>   In-depth interview in which Lorde discusses trends in African-American literature and the development of her writing.

Hull, Gloria T. "Living on the Line: Audre Lorde and *Our Dead behind Us."* In *Changing Our Own Words: Essays on Criticism, Theory, and Writing by Black Women,* edited by Cheryl A. Wall, pp. 150-72. New Brunswick, N.J.: Rutgers University Press, 1989.
>   Analyzes *Our Dead behind Us,* asserting that the theme of displacement in this volume of poetry is prevalent throughout all of Lorde's work.

Joaquim Maria Machado de Assis

1839-1908

Brazilian novelist, short story writer, poet, critic, dramatist, essayist, and journalist.

Machado is considered "the greatest and most complete man of letters in Brazil," according to Afrânio Coutinho, and he is widely known as one of the most important writers of Latin America. He is particularly noted for the novels *Memórias póstumas de Bras Cubas* (1881; *Epitaph of a Small Winner,* 1952) and *Dom Casmurro* (1899; *Dom Casmurro,* 1953). His fiction has been called bitterly pessimistic and sardonic. Machado often used satire to illuminate trivial human vanities and selfishness, particularly among the white Brazilian upper middle class; he rarely addressed his own mulatto culture. Although his works have not found a large audience, Machado was, according to David T. Haberly, "the most original novelist to appear in the Western Hemisphere in the nineteenth century."

Machado was born in Rio de Janeiro, the son of a black house painter and Portuguese mother. After the early death of his mother, he was raised by his mulatto stepmother, Maria Inês, who is credited with introducing the youth to literature. At seventeen Machado was apprenticed to a printer and became a proofreader and typesetter. In the course of his work he met many important literary figures, some of whom later helped him get his first works published. After his printing apprenticeship he joined the civil service and spent most of his life as a middle-level bureaucrat. Popular with readers and critics alike—he was already acclaimed in his native country by the time he was twenty-five—Machado was made president for life of the newly founded Brazilian Academy of Letters in 1897. He continued to write until his death in 1908.

Machado began his literary career by writing dramas and poetry. Most of these works went unpublished or unproduced, but his poetry collection *Occidentais,* which appeared in 1901 in *Poesias completas,* was well received. Critics have noted that while these poems are often stylistically mundane, they nevertheless faithfully reflect Machado's belief that life is essentially meaningless. They also convey the author's characteristic attitude of ironic resignation. These beliefs and attitudes are displayed more extensively and with greater artistic success in Machado's early novels. His first four—*Ressurreição* (1872), *A mão e a luva* (1874; *The Hand and the Glove,* 1970), *Helena* (1876; *Helena,* 1984), and *Iaiá Garcia* (1878; *Yayá Garcia,* 1976)—are products of the Romantic movement in Brazilian literature and are considered inferior to his later fiction. Like other works of this movement, Machado's novels, which center on thwarted love or ambition, are often criticized for their unrealistic situations and lack of character motivation. In these works Machado presented detailed

portraits of female characters, meticulously examining the moral and social implications of the marriage of convenience. In his later works he abandoned both female protagonists and his concern with the delineation of class and social distinctions.

Epitaph of a Small Winner is the autobiography of a dead writer—"I am a deceased writer not in the sense of one who has written and is now deceased," writes the narrator, Bras Cubas, "but in the sense of one who has died and is now writing." This often humorous novel features an unreliable narrator and has been likened to Laurence Sterne's *The Life and Opinions of Tristram Shandy.* In *Epitaph of a Small Winner* Machado explored the effects of egotism, focusing on the extremes of self-love and on the absurdity of life and inevitability of death. Machado viewed human nature as fundamentally irrational and found self-love to be the only consistent motivating force in human behavior. While characterizing this worldview as pessimistic, critics have also noted that Machado's fiction conveys amusement rather than bitterness toward the folly of selfish, passion-driven humanity. Throughout his novels, and particularly in *Epitaph of a Small Winner,* Machado mockingly challenged the accepted beliefs of society. Richard J. Callan noted that "at the heart of [Machado's] criticism of mankind lies the hope that he can move his readers to a reform of manners." Similarly, William L. Grossman argued that *Epitaph of a Small Winner* affirms important human values by destroying many false gods and illusions.

Like *Epitaph of a Small Winner, Dom Casmurro* is told by an unreliable narrator. This novel, which is considered Machado's masterpiece, is full of deception and ambiguity. The narrator's self-destructive conviction that his wife and best friend cuckolded him, and that his son is in fact theirs, was long accepted as a central fact of the novel. But critics have recently questioned whether the narrator's conclusion was perhaps based merely on suspicion, circumstantial evidence, and unfounded jealousy—all prevalent themes in Machado's novels. Most later commentators agree that the narrator seems to be pleading his case before a jury of readers in an attempt to let them decide for themselves, and for him, if his cruelty toward those closest to him may be justified.

Machado's last two novels, *Esaú e Jacó* (1904; *Esaú and Jacob,* 1965) and *Memorial de Aires* (1908; *Counselor Ayres' Memorial,* 1972), are considered extended allegorical interpretations of turn-of-the-century Brazilian social conflicts. The warring twins of *Esaú and Jacob,* for example, have been interpreted as symbols of the emancipation period in Rio de Janeiro; they represent conflicts between liberal and conservative factions, between tradition and modern values, and between colonial life and the birth of an independent Brazil. In *Counselor Ayres' Memorial,* Machado again metaphorically evoked Brazil, but this time he expressed hope for his country, provided Brazilians learn to be guided by selfless love—the force that rejuvenates the jaded ambassador Ayres in the novel. Machado's affirmations of life and love in *Counselor Ayres' Memorial* are regarded as foils for the total pessimism he expressed in his earlier works.

Machado is also considered a master of the short story. Although he dealt with many of the same issues he treated in his novels—hidden or unconscious motives as well as human egotism and inadequacy—his range as a short story writer was much broader. This is especially evident in Machado's experimental use of styles and forms and the diversity of his subjects and techniques.

Critics have found Machado's racial heritage problematic in analyzing his works. Raymond S. Sayers commented: "One of the strange paradoxes of literature is that the greatest Brazilian novelist, Joaquim Maria Machado de Assis..., was a mulatto who wrote very little about his fellow Negroes and their lives but instead drew most of his material for his novels from the lives of the upper classes of Carioca society, which were predominantly white." Because blacks and mulattoes rarely have more than minor roles in Machado's works, some critics have accused the author of denying that he was a *mestizo*—a person of mixed race—and condemned him for not decrying slavery in Brazil. Yet Machado was at least partially black and certainly encountered discrimination in his life. David T. Haberly noted that of the "catalogue of social and physical handicaps that late nineteenth-century Brazilians would have defined as *taras,* or hereditary defects," Machado had not only weak health and epilepsy but, most importantly, he "was not white." Haberly argued that Machado consequently tried to hide his race. The process of becoming "white" is therefore a major facet of Machado's works, which, he added, "can be seen as a highly evasive and ambiguous journal of his passage from nonwhiteness to whiteness." Sayers, however, has maintained that Machado was interested in satirizing Brazilian society, not in rejecting his race. Thus blacks and mulattoes could not reasonably be targets for Machado. Sayers explained: "The Negro could not serve as a subject for the irony of Machado, for the Negro could never determine his own conduct or fix his own position in society; he was not a free agent, and therefore he could not be made a subject for satire."

Most commentators agree that Machado is one of the greatest, if critically neglected, writers of Latin America. "I am astonished," wrote Susan Sontag, "that a writer of such greatness does not yet occupy the place he deserves." Machado's reputation as a writer has grown in recent years, but his works remain ambiguous to critics. As Waldo Frank noted: "Within the quiet, courses a complex fugue: innocence cruelly punished and revealed as guilt; pleasure pleasurably crushed; the 'good' and the 'beautiful' on the wrack and dissolving into their contraries. The blood, indeed the core, of the fictive world of Machado de Assis is ambiguity—ambiguity raised to a principle and a substance."

(For further information about Machado's life and works, see *Contemporary Authors,* Vol. 107 and *Twentieth-Century Literary Criticism,* Vol. 10.)

PRINCIPAL WORKS

Desencantos [first publication] (drama) 1861
Teatro (dramas) 1863
Crisálidas (poetry) 1864
*Quase ministro (drama) 1864
Os deuses de casaca (drama) 1866
Contos fluminenses (short stories) 1870
Falenas (poetry) 1870
Ressurreição (novel) 1872
Histórias de meia-noite (short stories) 1873
A mão e a luva (novel) 1874
  [*The Hand and the Glove,* 1970]
Americanas (poetry) 1875
Helena (novel) 1876
  [*Helena,* 1984]
Iaiá Garcia (novel) 1878
  [*Yayá Garcia,* 1976; also published as *Iaiá Garcia,* 1977]

Memórias póstumas de Bras Cubas (novel) 1881
  [*Epitaph of a Small Winner*, 1952; also published as
    Posthumous Reminiscences of Braz Cubas, 1955]
Tu, só tu, puro amor (drama) 1881
  [*You, Love, and Love Alone*, 1972]
Papéis avulsos (short stories) 1882
Histórias sem data (short stories) 1884
Quincas Borba (novel) 1891
  [*Philosopher or Dog?*, 1954; also published as *The
    Heritage of Quincas Borba*, 1954]
Várias histórias (short stories) 1896
Dom Casmurro (novel) 1899
  [*Dom Casmurro*, 1953]
Páginas recolhidas (short stories) 1899
Poesias completas (poetry) 1901
Esaú e Jacó (novel) 1904
  [*Esaú and Jacob*, 1965]
Relíquias de casa velha (short stories) 1906
Memorial de Aires (novel) 1908
  [*Counselor Ayres' Memorial*, 1972]
Crítica (essays) 1910
The Psychiatrist, and Other Stories (short stories) 1963
What Went on at the Baroness': A Tale with a Point
  (short story) 1963
The Devil's Church, and Other Stories (short stories)
  1977

*The publication date of this work is uncertain.

William L. Grossman (essay date 1952)

[Epitaph of a Small Winner, *Grossman's 1952 translation of* Memórias póstumas de Bras Cubas, *marked
the first appearance of a novel by Machado in English.
In the following excerpt from his introduction to this
work, Grossman discusses Machado's pessimism.*]

For all his restraint and good humor, Machado de Assis
hurls at his readers a fierce challenge, unrecognized by
many, offensive to some, a joy to those who are strong
enough to accept it. The challenge lies in Machado's vast
iconoclasm, which is likely to involve destruction of the
reader's own icons. In his best work, Machado is
perhaps the most completely disenchanted writer in
occidental literature. Skeptics generally destroy certain
illusions in order to cling to others. Machado rejects
everything mundane. (p. 11)

[**Epitaph of a Small Winner**] sets forth Machado's
pessimism with a fastidious minuteness that leaves the
reader only two alternatives: to reject Machado or, with
Machado, to reject the world. The latter alternative still
permits affirmation of certain supramundane values
which Machado does not touch. Many religious persons
regard agnostic Machado as a great writer—perhaps
because, by destroying so many false gods, he leaves
room for none but the true.

Braz Cubas, the protagonist of this novel, is spiritually
and psychologically a very ordinary man. Machado
endows him with wealth, good looks, and health,
doubtless to avoid dwelling upon the frustration occasioned by the lack of these characteristics. For Machado
has more esoteric game in mind than the sources of
unhappiness that everyone recognizes as such. Braz's
pursuits embrace sex, politics, philosophy, even "doing
good." Yet in the final chapter, when he comes to
calculate the net profit in his life, he finds it to be zero—
until he remembers that, having had no children, he has
handed on to no one the misery of human existence.
And so, he concludes, he is a little ahead of the game, a
small winner.

The abject and ironic pessimism of the book is based on
nature's indifference and man's egoism. Indeed, virtually all of Braz's interests can be reduced to one: the
affirmation of Braz. In the other two of Machado's three
great novels—**Quincas Borba**... and **Dom Casmurro**..., Machado emphasizes a third factor, which is
perhaps implicit in egoism: the indifference of the
human environment to the individual's welfare. Braz
Cubas betrays himself; the chief character in **Dom
Casmurro** is betrayed by the indifference (to him) of his
wife and of his friend. A commonplace triangle becomes, in Machado's hands, a tragedy of the frustration
of a sensitive man's love by the ruthless but natural lust
of two stronger persons. In a sense, the human environment takes on much of the aspect of the physical
environment, leaving the individual without recourse.
(pp. 11-12)

[Machado's] poor health may have been in part responsible for the Machadian irony, but it cannot account
for—rather it makes all the more unaccountable—his
rejection of the superman; there are surely Nietzschean
elements in Quincas Borba's philosophy, which Machado ridicules in the latter part of this book. As for the
source of Machado's classic taste, implicit in his rejection of false models and explicit in some of his critical
writings, we are even more at sea and can hardly avoid
reliance upon undiscovered, possibly undiscoverable,
subject factors. (pp. 13-14)

Without denying the tragic power of **Dom Casmurro,** the
present translator chose **Epitaph of a Small Winner**
because the creative release of Machado's inhibited (by
compliance with romantic conventions) sentiments
makes it the liveliest and most inventive of his novels
and because, as a cogent and nearly complete statement
of Machado's attitude, it provides a suitable introduction to his work. (p. 14)

> *William L. Grossman, in an introduction to*
> Epitaph of a Small Winner *by Joaquim
> Maria Machado de Assis, translated by Wil-
> liam L. Grossman, Noonday Press, 1952, pp.
> 11-14.*

Raymond S. Sayers (essay date 1956)

[In the following excerpt, Sayers defends Machado against charges that he failed to use his works to further the cause of black liberation in Brazil.]

One of the strange paradoxes of literature is that the greatest Brazilian novelist, Joaquim Maria Machado de Assis (1839-1908), was a mulatto who wrote very little about his fellow Negroes and their lives but instead drew most of his material for his novels from the lives of the upper classes of Carioca society, which were predominantly white. Yet in his formative years he must have been surrounded almost exclusively by other Negroes or mulattoes. (p. 201)

During his first twenty years ... Machado de Assis owed almost all the affection he received, almost all the opportunities he was given, to people of his own race, to other mulattoes. It might be expected that in return he would strive to lend his talents to the cause of the Negro, to the struggle against slavery .... Or he might at least develop the theme of Salomé Queiroga and Bernardo Guimarães, that the genuine Brazilian type is the Negro mestizo, and write novels with mulatto protagonists. That he did not do so is common knowledge. His Negro personages are slaves or servants, and in only one of his novels and four of his short stories are there Negro characters of more than secondary importance. (pp. 201-02)

Machado de Assis was not indifferent to the plight of the slaves or to the injustice of slavery. There is enough in his writings to show that he sympathized with the Negroes and hated all injustice. However, his sympathy for the Negroes did not cause him to take any part in the struggle against slavery. Why he did not do so is a moot question .... Was it because of his rise in the Brazilian bureaucracy, which in time brought him an excellent salary and an important official position? Perhaps it was because of his growing literary fame, which led to his being the first President of the *Academia Brasileira de Letras*. It may have been his epilepsy, which caused him to shrink from conflict and, for that matter, from any activity that would attract the attention of others to his person. (pp. 202-03)

Or it may be that his failure to take an emphatic stand on the question of abolition is to be explained on other grounds. His life seems to have been guided by the philosophy of enlightened egotism which is the predominant characteristic of so many of his creatures, an egotism which may have caused him to feel that he would be justified in making any sort of sacrifice to attain the goals that he had set for himself .... He was not an upstart who was dazzled by luxury or by the friendship of bankers, ministers and the diplomatic set that gathered around the intellectual D. Pedro II. His novels demonstrate, on the contrary, a constant skepticism about all the qualities for which that society has been praised: the integrity of the bankers, the intelligence of the statemen, the selfishness of the diplomats, the virtue of the women. It is not that he believes that these people or their world could have been improved; indeed, he seems to believe that people are a rather sorry lot and they are unlikely to change. His satire does not envisage a finer race or a happier world, but at its mildest, in his last book, *Memorial de Ayres,* suggests the need for a resigned acceptance of the banalities that constitute our existence. (p. 203)

His goal was not an important position in his world but perfection in his art. He took for his own the urban novel about the upper middle classes, a very small segment of the Brazilian human comedy, it is true, which Macedo and Alencar had developed, and he distorted, twisted, polished and refined it until he had made it the vehicle of his pessimistic view of life. Influenced by his wide reading in English literature, ... in which he probably preferred Thackeray to Dickens, he chose Rio de Janeiro's Vanity Fair for his subject. His reason for this choice was not the superficial one that English manners and ideas were the mode, for the more democratic, proletarian French influence was also strong, as is evident in the writings of the *condor* poets, but rather that, in writing about the upper classes, with their money and their assured position in the world, he was able to deal with the group of people who were least subject to economic pressures and who should therefore have been best able to live independently and to emerge from the mean dimensions that form the world of most men—and who failed to do so.

From two points of view, then, it is hardly to be expected that he would choose the slave or even the free Negro as a subject. In the first place his models, if one may use the word for writers like Alencar and Macedo, or even Thackeray, do not deal with the proletariat in their novels of urban life, and in the second place even the free Negro was not able to move unhampered through life as Machado de Assis wanted his characters to do. The question is not one, here, of Brazilian prejudice or lack of prejudice toward people of colored blood. There is no doubt as to the great part played in Brazilian history and the arts by Negroes and mulattoes. On the other hand, the Negro, even if he was a wealthy intellectual, was always in an ambiguous position in the society of the latter days of the Empire .... The Negro could not serve as a subject for the irony of Machado, for the Negro could never determine his own conduct or fix his own position in society; he was not a free agent, and therefore he could not be made a subject for satire.

Nevertheless Machado de Assis has more Negro characters than any other writer of the urban school, and to the gallery of Negro types found in Brazilian literature he adds some studies that are more complete and satisfying than any previous ones. Furthermore, he almost always treats the Negroes and their problems with sympathy .... In 1876 he satirized a man who sighed for the good old days when slaves were whipped, and in 1877 he ridiculed one who had emancipated a sixty-five year old slave and then had written to the papers about his meritorious act .... In these chronicles, which are often in a light or humorous vein, he is always serious or satirical in his references to slavery. In 1887 he wrote a satirical poem in Negro dialect criticizing the Parliamentary debates about the subject; in it a Negro says that all the talking does not improve his position.... (pp. 203-05)

In four stories and two novels Negro characters have a rather important role. In **"O Caso da Vara"** ... he shows his pessimism about human nature.... There is no other story in pre-Abolition Brazilian literature that gives so revealing a glimpse as this of the life of the urban slave child. Nor is there any more affecting tale of the fugitive slave than the one that Machado de Assis published in his **Reliquias de Casa Velha**..., eighteen years after the passage of the *Lei Aurea*. (p. 205)

There are significant references to slavery and its pernicious effects upon slave and master in Machado's first great novel, **Memorias Posthumas de Braz Cubas**.... (p. 206)

Machado's only full length portrait of a Negro is found in his novel **Yayá Garcia**.... Raymundo is the Faithful Slave whose loyalty continues after he has been granted his freedom. In **"Encher Tempo,"** a short story published in his posthumous **Historias Romanticas,** Machado has a sketch of the faithful freedwoman.... But since she is a secondary character in a short story, the author cannot develop her personality as he does that of Raymundo in **Yayá Garcia.** This African might be considered as Machado's tribute to the Negro and as the most complete study that he could make of a member of that race, within the limits that he had set for his subject matter, the upper classes of Rio de Janeiro. He is the contrary of the Machadean hero—the ingenuous Dom Casmurro, the insane Rubião, the egotistic Braz Cubas—for he represents a healthy if instinctive acceptance of life, with it necessary requisites of honesty, integrity and good sense in human relations. At the beginning of the book the author describes him as an African type, of medium size, strong in spite of his fifty years.... Unlike the romantic conception of the Faithful Slave, he is not a melancholy being, fond of singing sad songs about his native land. On the contrary, when he plays the marimba at night in the garden, he sings happy, warlike songs, and when he has an opportunity, he plays merrily with the young heroine of the story. He is quite sure of his place in the family, and he does not hesitate to act as he thinks best to protect the people he loves.... If Machado did not depict another character like Raymundo, it is probably because as an artist he did not want to repeat himself, for except for the servant, there was no Negro type that could be logically introduced into a novel about the upper classes of Rio.

Machado de Assis disapproved of slavery and felt that its effects upon Brazilian society and the Brazilian character were harmful. Yet although he praised anti-slavery novels and plays in his literary criticism, he himself did not attempt to produce works of propaganda, for the type of novel in which he could best express himself could hardly be twisted to the needs of the anti-

slavery campaign. He did not write much about Negroes, just as in general he did not write about the lower classes of Rio, because he could only illustrate his theme of man's essential puniness by using as his personages members of the upper classes, people who did not have enough imagination to use their privileged economic position as a means of obtaining spiritual freedom. (pp. 207-08)

> *Raymond S. Sayers, "The Negro in the Novels of Machado de Assis and the Naturalists," in his* The Negro in Brazilian Literature, *Hispanic Institute in the United States, 1956, pp. 201-22.*

Helen Caldwell (essay date 1970)

[*Caldwell is Machado's most important English-language critic as well as a translator of several of his works. In the following excerpt from her* Machado de Assis: The Brazilian Master and His Novels *(1970), she argues that the* Posthumous Memoirs of Braz Cubas *is not a pessimistic novel and analyzes* Dom Casmurro *as the culmination of Machado's work.*]

With his fifth novel, **Posthumous Memoirs of Braz Cubas**..., Machado de Assis returned both to the simple theme sounded in his first novel, **Resurrection,** and to the comic genre of his second, **Hand and Glove.** After tracing the intricacies of the feminine psyche..., he abandoned the female protagonist for good and all and resumed his exploration of the male heart and the basic problem of love and self-love, life and death, good and evil. In **Posthumous Memoirs of Braz Cubas** he gave self-love a thorough going-over. Consequently death enters its every page; even life takes on the role of death at times; and death, of life. There is no gentle Raymundo in this narrative—practically nothing in the way of unadulterated love, or of unadulterated good or evil or life or death, although self-love does hold the scene, assuming many masks, as greed, vanity, envy, ambition, and so on.

For all its concern with dead and half-dead souls, **Posthumous Memoirs of Braz Cubas** is cast in the form of a comedy, with comic personages and comic action arising out of their comic natures. It is a little strange, therefore, that it has generally been regarded as a work of profound pessimism.

It was probably the hero-narrator himself, Braz Cubas, who put ideas of pessimism into the critics' heads in the first place, with his prefatory note, "To the Reader."

> If I have adopted the free form of a Sterne or of a Xavier de Maistre, I am not sure but what I have also inserted a certain cantankerous pessimism of my own.

And, finally, there is his remark on the last page of the novel, the remark that no critic neglects to quote, the remark from which William Grossman coined the title for his translation, **Epitaph of a Small Winner.** When he balanced his life's accounts, says Braz, the good against the evil, he discovered he had a small amount on the credit side: he had never had a child, had transmitted to no living being the legacy of our human wretchedness. True, there seems to be a bitter taste here, but if we have followed the narration closely, this remark will invite an amusing as well as a pessimistic interpretation. (pp. 73-4)

As Sterne in *Tristram Shandy* borrowed from, and at the same time burlesqued and parodied, the epics, romances, comic epics, and picaresque tales of his predecessors, Machado de Assis in this novel did the same for Sterne. Sterne, in order to satirize the long romance that begins with the birth or childhood of the hero and gradually takes him up to maturity, or beyond into middle age, began his *Life and Opinions of Tristram Shandy* before his hero's birth, with his begetting. It took the first three of the novel's nine volumes to get him born, almost another volume to get him through the first day of his life, another half-volume or so to get him into breeches, and, so far as the narrative goes, it is difficult to determine whether he ever did come of age.

Machado de Assis, in his turn, parodied the older romances, and *Tristram Shandy* into the bargain. Only, he went about it from the opposite direction. *His* hero-author, Braz Cubas, begins his story with his own death notice.... (pp. 75-6)

Braz Cubas's method is a refinement on Shandy's. It too progresses through digressions, and even through retrogressions, that are economical and dramatic. (p. 76)

[The] title's second half perhaps bears a trace of that picaresque novel par excellence, *Gil Blas de Santillane* by Le Sage. The name Braz is the Portuguese form of the Spanish *Blas,* and Assis, who frequently mentions Le Sage's hero in his writings, always refers to him as Gil Braz. Conversely, the Spanish translations of **Posthumous Memoirs** have been titled **Memorias Póstumas de Blas Cubas.** (p. 77)

Braz could say at the end of his memoirs that as a hero of romance and even as a picaresque hero he was something of a failure. He listed his defeats: no page with blood on it; he suffered no remorse; with Don Quixote he did not win fame, although, like him, he had tried to win it—through his medicinal plaster to cure melancholy, the disease of which Don Quixote was thought to have died. He never became "caliph" or "minister," never knew marriage, had no children—not even the two-child minimum, the boy and girl of a Gil Blas or Tom Jones. Finally he adds in a tone between regret and perhaps genuine relief the phrase that has been taken ever so seriously and applied to Machado de Assis as well as, or even more than, to his creature Braz Cubas—the remark about leaving no legacy of our human misery to a child of his.

In spirit, however, Braz was a Gil Blas, though an unsuccessful one. Wide-awake, witty, handsome, reckless, light-minded, of an easy virtue and adaptable morals, accepting all situations and turning most of them to his own advantage, tolerant of vice in himself and in others, yet not completely vicious—he gradually learned something as he made his "circuit of life"; but, unlike the more conventional, the true picaro, he never got around to reforming or having any regrets. Yet his story contains traces of pessimism, he says: he warns of it in his prefatory note, "To the Reader," and frequently reminds us in the course of the narrative that his is a lugubrious tale, that it reeks of death; and he will drive home a point by saying, "I assure you of this from the depths of my tomb." Although he thus insists on his pessimism, his manner is far from pessimistic. He is about as carefree a corpse as one is likely to come across. Even the worm of his dedication, that is, death (perhaps his critics also), is patted on the back, so to speak, with a certain camaraderie, and one suspects that Braz's tomb was a snug affair with hot and cold running water and a good library.

Life, as well as death, is given the comic treatment. The butt of the comedy is in all cases the same—human vanity. All the characters suffer from it, some more than others, none more than Braz, except, perhaps, his father. The elder Cubas is the incarnation of vanity—a simple, unaffected, undisguised, harmless, and inoffensive vanity.... (pp. 84-5)

Vanity is the backbone, the very viscera, not only of silly and of vicious acts on the part of the characters, but of their good and generous actions as well. Take charity for example: nothing could have induced Cotrim to make donations to charity except to get his generosity written up in the newspaper or to have his portrait painted in oils and hung on the wall of a benevolent society.

Vanity begets ambition, which in Braz's world is what stokes the engine of human progress. Ambition, he shows us, promotes science (exemplified in his invention), politics and letters (to cite himself, Neves, and Luiz Dutra), and snobbery, or social distinction if you prefer, like Bento Cubas's.

Vanity is the very essence of sexual love and fidelity: it was in great measure responsible not only for Braz's love of Virgilia but also for his faithfulness to her over so many years. (pp. 86-7)

Vanity is responsible for honesty; and it is honesty, we are told, that gives rise to dishonesty....

When vanity is stifled, it is replaced by some less amusing form of self-love.... (p. 87)

It is not often that Braz's vanity fails him. He is such a thoroughgoing egoist, so sure in his superior wisdom, so indulgent toward his own imperfections, that it is no wonder he can view with Olympian calm the slips and errors of the less than perfect mortals that bask in the sun of his presence. The villain of the piece is not any of the personages. It is human nature, life itself. (pp. 87-8)

Humanitism, the philosophy invented by the mad Quincas Borba, is a kind of exuberant development of Pandora—a thoroughgoing egoism. According to Quincas Borba's explanation, humanitas, the principle of all things, is Man shared by and summed up in every man. Each man is not merely humanitas's vehicle; he is at one and the same time vehicle, driver, and passenger.

Quincas Borba's Humanitism has been interpreted variously by various critics—as a satire on Leibnitz, Nietzsche, evolution, and so on. Probably there are shafts at these and some other philosophies in it; but there is little doubt that superficially Assis was poking fun at Auguste Comte and Positivism with its professed aim of securing the victory of altruism over egoism.... Machado de Assis delivered many a body blow to Positivism in the columns of his journalism, and in other writings also. (p. 89)

Humanitism has the all-embracing quality of Positivism: it covers metaphysics, ethics, science, literature, economics, and has a religious dogma with liturgies. Quincas spent a great deal of thought and perspiration over his liturgies for the Church of Humanitism. Humanitism, he explained to Braz, was to be the church of the future, the only true religion; Christianity was all right for women and beggars, and other religions in his opinion were no better. (p. 90)

All these resemblances, however, are more apparent than real. Assis is poking fun not only at Positivism but at all other illusory *isms,* and particularly at materialistic ones. In addition, I believe, he is poking fun at himself, as though to say, "The opinions Braz Cubas spouts and this Pandora I inserted into his delirium are the same as Quincas Borba's philosophy; they are as crazy as Positivism. I am as crazy as Quincas Borba, that is, I am as crazy as Auguste Comte." Perhaps it is worth noting that Quincas is the nickname for Joaquim, which was Assis's first name as well as Borba's. (pp. 90-1)

Finally, the determinism to be found both in Positivism and in Quincas's Humanitism is also a part of the Cubas philosophy, and as such is turned to artistic purpose: it becomes a dramatic device in the novel. Quincas Borba constantly maintains that since humanitas is in all men, and vice versa all men are a part of humanitas, every man has a stake in every other man's life, thought, and actions. (p. 91)

Braz's determinism is much less complex than Quincas's. He calls it his "theory of rolling balls." ... Braz likens himself and others to rolling balls: the ball Marcella rolled against the ball Braz; it, set in motion, rolled against Virgilia. Thus one may say Marcella changed the course of Virgilia's life, and even of Lobo Neves's without coming into contact with either of them.... In the same way, the purpose of Dona Placida's birth and existence, and of the unlovely coupling of her parents, was to foster an illicit love affair between Braz and Virgilia. The witty Braz remarks that

the principle of the rolling balls is responsible for the "solidarity of human boredom."

Although Braz laughs and blames everything on Nature, the projection of his rolling-balls theory into the novel's action does inject a moral tone—a suggestion of human responsibility. Thus a combination, or interlocking, of human will and chance seems to close round the characters with the vicelike grip of inescapable Fate, and is perhaps one more reason for critics calling this novel "pessimistic." The individual cannot escape his own past and that of his parents and ancestors, nor even from acts—present and past—of strangers. (pp. 92-3)

Like Tristram Shandy, Braz gives minute analyses not only of his own thoughts, but smells out the secret opinions, feelings, and ambitions of all the other characters as well. It is through these opinions and sentiments, rather than through their actions, that Assis's personages, like Sterne's, come alive, grow on our affections, and move our pity or laughter. More often than not it is our laughter, for that, after all, is Braz's purpose. (p. 96)

In the novel itself [Assis] leaves Braz to shift for himself and make what impression he will with his memoirs. This is a far cry from **Resurrection,** into which the author frequently entered without ceremony to explain the faults, virtues, and doubts of his characters.... Although the least personages of Braz's **Memoirs** vibrate with a life of their own, still we must never forget that we see them in the mirrors of Braz's mind.

Another point of difference between Braz and his creator is this matter of Humanitism. Although Braz seems to subscribe to Quincas Borba's mad philosophy, there is no reason to believe that Assis did. There is some reason to believe he did not.... Positivism's literary outgrowth, Naturalism, on the whole, [Assis] loathed. He particularly condemned a writer's use of shocking physical details with little or no motivation, and implied that Zola sometimes followed such practices with a view to increasing his income. (pp. 112-13)

His criticism of the Naturalist novel was that it aimed at representing superficial appearance—content to be an "inventory of events and fortuitous" actions unmotivated by human passion and, in its most extreme form, a photographic and slavish reproduction of the low and ignoble—sordid details related for the purpose of politico-social propaganda or with nothing more than a view to arousing momentary physical sensation in the reader, and with no meaning beyond. (p. 117)

Assis's seventh novel, **Dom Casmurro,** is the culmination of the six that preceded it. Not only does it surpass the others as an artistic work, but elements of the first six novels appear here in more perfect form: composition of characters, narrative structures, theme developments—the whole novelist's art. In particular, Assis's ever-increasing strands of symbolism send subtle threads all through these other elements and weave a wonderful thing. (p. 142)

Dom Casmurro's hero, Bento Santiago, . . . has two men within him, but his is a . . . sinister combination: Othello and Iago. In addition to superior passion, Santiago was possessed of attributes essential to a tragic hero . . . namely, those of high degree. . . . Santiago was born to wealth and position; he was handsome, well educated, and by no means stupid. Since he narrates his own story, he not only manages to convey the impression that he is the aristocratic descendant of a long line of great plantation owners with countless slaves, he also contrives to envelop himself in an aura of superstitiously religious, almost divine, eminence. This he does by dwelling on a special relationship between his mother and God and by insinuating that his very birth was a miracle, and so regarded by the family priest. He informs us that his story was Othello's—except that his Desdemona was guilty. But soon, however, we discover the hidden Iago. With a criminal's urge to talk, he discloses, in carefully guarded metaphor, that his jealousy was rooted in aboriginal evil, that it antedated its object, groped until it found an object, then pursued and clung to it with obdurate blindness. (p. 143)

The titles of Assis's novels are in every instance an important element of the whole. Each is what he called in his preface to *Esau and Jacob* a resumé of the *matter*. . . . In *Dom Casmurro* he went so far as to permit his hero-narrator to deliberately mislead us.

Santiago tells how the nickname Dom Casmurro had been given him by an irate neighbor, and explains that *casmurro,* as applied to him means a morose, tight-lipped man withdrawn within himself, a definition not to be found in dictionaries. Since those days, however, Portuguese dictionaries have expanded their definition to include the meaning Santiago gives. In Assis's day, they defined casmurro as "obstinate, stubborn, wrong-headed." And this, perhaps, is the more important definition for the understanding of the novel. Santiago did become casmurro by *his* definition, but he also had in his nature that "resistance to persuasion" found in Sophocles' tragic heroes.

The dom, Santiago informs us, was intended to make fun of his aristocratic airs, for this word is a titular prefix to the name of a member of the higher nobility. (pp. 144-45)

The superficial story Santiago would tell us is of his betrayal by Capitu with his friend, Escobar. Through the language of metaphor, however, he tells a different story. . . . *Dom Casmurro*'s tragedy takes place within Santiago's own psyche, the war of passions, the exercise of moral freedom. It is he who makes the choice between good and evil, and, although time hardens his cold heart, he cannot rid himself of twinges of guilt. That is why he tells his story. The interplay of natures is within him—his generous, loving nature fighting against and finally overcome by the strong powers of evil. Although these latter are within himself, he projects them upon others—especially upon Capitu; but, as he himself tells us, he carried "death on his own retina."

Good in this novel is equated with love, and love with life; evil with self-love and death. Santiago's struggle with his destiny resembles that of Felix, the hero of *Resurrection,* who tried to revive his dead heart. "I appear to be alive but am not," Santiago tells us. I am a corpse painted and made up to look like life, but the "inner structure will not take dye." He repeats this theme louder and more clearly: "I tried to connect the two ends of my life—restore adolescence (love) in old age (lack-love), but the middle, myself (the essential part, love, life), is missing." He tore down the old house (his heart) and had the original duplicated in another part of town. He tried to bring ghosts to life. He could not fill in the sonnet "battle of life," between the first and last line, because love failed him. . . . All these symbols tell the same story: living death, death in life. Although he lived on, his soul, like Dante's traitorous Alberigo's, was in the icy depths of hell . . . . (pp. 146-47)

Evil assumes a . . . terrifying aspect in *Dom Casmurro.* The death of Santiago's heart is enveloped in an atmosphere of mystery and ominous suggestion: ghosts, revenge, guilt, torture, broken vows, Faust and Macbeth—both of whom were in league with the powers of darkness; the libretto of his life's "opera" was written by God, music by Satan—and Santiago danced to that music. These innuendos give one a feeling that unholy murder has been done. Santiago insinuates that it was his wife Capitu and his friend Escobar who murdered his heart with their cruel betrayal. But his own words give him the lie: his metaphors tell the more forthright tale. He himself murdered the loving Bento and projected that murder upon Capitu and Escobar. Many readers, convinced by Santiago's cunning, believe implicitly the plain Portuguese of his clever insinuations. But even if Capitu were guilty of adultery with Escobar, the tragedy of Dom Casmurro would remain: it is *in him.* Santiago's "heart" had been killed long before the supposed betrayal—his jealous cruelty manifested itself before Capitu ever saw Escobar. If Capitu deceived him, it was not the loving Bento she deceived: it was Dom Casmurro. The title of the book is *Dom Casmurro,* not *Capitu*; the tragedy is his—the terror of a life without love, and Santiago was formed for love. Yet his life, like Macbeth's, became "a tale told by an idiot." When we finally recognize the fate that has closed in upon him we are struck with awe and horror; and, as in great tragedies, we have a feeling that there has been a "change in the face of the universe." Our sadness over the sacrifice of Capitu's love and beauty is not unmixed with a kind of joy. She won life's battle: her self-love, her original vanities and jealousies, were driven out; only love remained in her life. This victory of hers was mirrored in the soul's battles of the other characters—José Dias, Dona Gloria, Cousin Justina, and the rest.

But all these personages, and even the portraits on the wall, who seem to speak with their mute eyes and gesture, are melded into the life of the principal character, Santiago, into his very brain, so to speak. It is he who tells us of them; they are, or become in the telling, aspects of his personality. It is he who dominates the story, dominates the mystery-charged atmosphere, dominates our emotions—on which he leaves a mark that never completely fades away. He stands at the center of the whole structure; everything—plot, symbolism, characters, theme—all converge in him, making this Assis's most emotionally powerful work. (pp. 148-49)

Helen Caldwell, in her Machado de Assis: The Brazilian Master and His Novels, *University of California Press, 1970, 270 p.*

David T. Haberly (essay date 1983)

[*Haberly is a noted scholar of Brazilian literature. In the following excerpt, he attempts to reconcile Machado's life as a mulatto with the ideas the novelist presented in his works.*]

It is difficult indeed to summarize and characterize the life and works of Joaquim Maria Machado de Assis (1839-1908), Brazil's greatest writer and the most original novelist to appear in the Western Hemisphere in the nineteenth century; such are the ironies and ambiguities of Machado's ideas about life and about literature, and the self-deprecating, reader-mocking subtleties of his style. Critics have inevitably tended to focus upon the search for constants and certainties in a literary career that lasted for more than half a century. But Machado never claimed to be consistent; the unreliability of the narrative voice—in his first-person novels and, even more remarkably, in the third-person *Quincas Borba*—is one of the hallmarks of his fiction. His works, in fact, make clear his extreme distrust of all unitary explanations of human character and behavior.

One fundamental problem, with which all of Machado's critics and biographers have wrestled, is the relationship between Machado the man and Machado the author. Some scholars have respected the novelist's public insistence that his works were entirely independent of his life; other critics, frustrated and fascinated by the enormous lacunae in our knowledge of Machado's personal life, have viewed all of his works as detailed autobiographies. I believe that it is possible to strike some sort of balance between these two critical traditions—to recognize the universality of the basic human problems that Machado treated in his fiction, while seeking to understand how his life and his society helped form Machado's consciousness of those problems.

It is symptomatic of the uncertainty and controversy that surround Machado that even the most basic of facts, his racial identity, remains the subject of an often heated debate. Our concrete knowledge of Machado's ancestry can be briefly summarized: Both his paternal great-grandmothers appear to have been black slaves; at least one paternal great-grandfather was white, possibly a priest. Machado's paternal grandparents were legally defined as free and brown-skinned (*pardos*), but one effect of the social component of racial identity in Brazil was the classification of slaves as black (*prêtos*) and

freedmen as *pardos,* independent of their ancestry or somatology. His father was a free artisan attached to a wealthy white family whose lands covered much of Livramento Hill, overlooking Rio de Janeiro's harbor. Machado's mother was a white woman born in the Azores and, most probably, brought to Brazil as a child. She was at least minimally literate, and worked for the same noble family; it appears likely that she served as a lady's maid and companion. Machado's mother died of tuberculosis in 1849, and his father married a mulatto woman, Maria Inês, in 1854. (pp. 70-2)

How black was Machado de Assis? The only honest answer is that we really do not know, since racial identity in Brazil is so variable, so much a function of nongenetic, nonsomatic elements. The early photographs of the novelist show a very dark young man, with traits that surely would have been perceived as clear evidence of African ancestry: lightly-kinked hair, a thick lower lip, and a broad and flat nose. The social component of the racial continuum, however, allowed Machado de Assis—refined, well-dressed, surrounded and protected by influential friends—to be perceived as light-skinned. It even enabled many of his contemporaries to ignore the somatic evidence altogether and to accept him as entirely white and European. Writing after Machado's death, José Veríssimo described him as a "mulatto, [who] was in reality a Greek of the greatest [*i.e.,* classical] period." One of the novelist's friends, the distinguished statesman Joaquim Nabuco, wrote Veríssimo to complain:

> I would not have called Machado a *mulatto,* and I believe that nothing would hurt him more than this classification ... Machado was white to me, and I think he thought of himself in the same say: whatever alien blood there might have been [in his veins], it in no way affected his purely Caucasian character. I, at least, saw in him only the Greek.

The most reasonable approach to the question of Machado's race, I believe, is simply to accept the impossibility of any single classification. As a boy and as a young man, it seems highly unlikely that Machado was unaware of his African ancestry and its social implications; he was, after all, only a bit more than two generations away from the slave quarters. He learned, while still very young, that certain behavior patterns could counteract or at least attenuate the prejudice his appearance might awaken. So he struggled to improve himself—to dress well; to know the right people; to speak and write correctly; to learn more foreign languages than his white friends, and to know them better. He was determined to appear immensely learned in both classical and modern literature, to shun confession and controversy at all cost, and to avoid personal slurs by gently poking fun at himself first.

It is clear that Machado's refinement, the product of this struggle, led many of his friends and associates to perceive him as at or very near the white end of the racial continuum; it is probable that their support and acceptance allowed Machado to think of himself as white, perhaps much of the time. It is also true, however, that this whiteness was situational rather than intrinsic, and it is illogical to suggest that Machado did not occasionally find himself in situations in which his somatology was more visible than his culture, in which he was treated, even if only momentarily, as a nonwhite.

Though it is important to avoid falling into the autobiographical trap, pursuing one-on-one correlations between life and work, Machado's isolated and fundamentally vulnerable existence on the other side of the mulatto escape hatch inevitably influenced his ideas and his writing. His works can be seen as a highly evasive and ambiguous journal of his passage from nonwhiteness to whiteness, a journal that focuses upon three central problems: the nature of identity, the nature of time, and the character and meaning of the transformations in identity that occur as an individual moves through time and through society.

Machado de Assis wrote that he was suckled, as a young man, on "pure Romantic milk," and the general themes of Brazilian Romanticism can be found throughout his superficially anti-Romantic work. The emphasis upon antithesis, deeply embedded in the lives and verses of Castro Alves and his generation, appears in Machado's works as well—not only in his early poetry, but also in his mature fiction. Although his view of the essential bifurcation of life was both more complex and more psychological than that of the Romantics, Machado similarly defined every individual as a binomial, and explored the symbiotic relationship between these two distinct identities.

The first of these, the internal identity, is the essence of the being at birth, its original natural (that is, physical) and social condition. It was inevitable that Machado, born socially dependent, physically frail, and nonwhite, should have meditated at length upon the meaning of the vast disparities that exist in nature's creations. Braz Cubas, in his *Posthumous Memoirs (Memórias Póstumas de Braz Cubas),* ponders a few of the many examples of such disparities that exist in Machado's fiction: Eugênia, born beautiful but crippled; Prudência, doomed to a miserable and utterly meaningless existence; the black butterfly Braz kills, but would have spared had it been blue. Despite all his efforts to use fictional characters and situations as a means of clarifying and rationalizing these disparities in origin, Machado finds no solution; our beginnings, the internal identities that we retain forever, are the result of pure chance (the lottery in *Dom Casmurro*) or of the equally aleatory egotism and occasional bad taste of Nature-Pandora as she appears to Braz Cubas.

If the internal identity is both incomprehensible and beyond our control, like Machado's ancestry and his physical defects, the external identity—our image in the mirror the world holds up to us; not what we are but what we are perceived to be—would seem to be social rather than natural, learned rather than genetic. To Machado, however, the social imperatives of the exter-

nal identity—to be respected and loved, to rise to the limits of ambition, to feel superior to all those around us—appeared as irrational and as inescapable as the laws or whims of nature.

Ideally, the external identity should conform exactly to the contours of the internal self in a balanced symbiosis, defining it and protecting it—like a uniform, in "**The Mirror**" ("**O Espelho**"), Machado's most complete exposition of the two selves and their relationship; like a well-fitted glove; like Braz Cubas' medicinal plaster for the soul. Such balance and conformity, however, is almost always as illusory as Braz Cubas' miraculous medical discovery, and the few cases Machado does present create other problems—for his characters as well as for us, the readers. In "**The Secret Cause**" ("**A Causa Secreta**"), Fortunato is the truly happy man; he has managed to structure his external self—his career as a nurse, his many good deeds and his consequent fame as a humanitarian, even his choice of a wife and of a best friend and partner—so that it perfectly conforms to his internal identity. The most fundamental characteristic of that internal identity, however, is a terrifying sadism that feeds hungrily on the suffering of others.

In general, however, Machado's characters are not as congruent as Fortunato; the external identity contradicts or dwarfs the internal self, creating a destructive, antipathetic symbiosis. The effects of such imbalance are sometimes hilarious, sometimes tragic, but always ironic. In the most extreme cases of discontinuity, moreover, individuals whose own identities fail to satisfy their needs form fragile and mutually parasitic relationships with others, relationships that lead inevitably to exploitation and betrayal.

The complex and problematic symbiosis of the double self, however, is not static, but moves through time. Machado's use of fictive time is astonishingly modern. It is quite distinct from chronological time, and its perceived velocity—the duration of events within the text—depends upon the importance of those events, how much they alter characters or situations. More fundamental than the velocity of time and of the changes it brings is its direction, a problem Machado raises again and again. Is time cyclical, repetitive, and therefore susceptible of some rational organization; or is it linear and infinite and irrational? Can it be described as a circle—for Ezequiel Maya the first and most basic of human abstractions? Or is time a series of unconnected words, each written down, erased, and then replaced by another? If time is cyclical, the changes that it measures can be arranged, understood, perhaps even predicted. If time is linear and particulate, then even the most fundamental events in an individual's life are disconnected, irrational, and ultimately meaningless.

Machado's most coherent yet pessimistic response to these problems appears in Braz Cubas' delirium. The existence of individuals and of humanity itself, as Pandora presents it to Braz, fuses both possible visions of time and of change: There are real or apparent cycles—birth and death, the rise and fall of people and of nations—but the whole sweep of past, present, and future is terrifying in its immensity and maddening in its utter meaninglessness. The best revenge is not to live well, but to deny Pandora the pleasure of creating and destroying yet another plaything—to follow Braz Cubas' example: "I had no children; I did not pass on to any other being the legacy of our human misery."

This vision, while the most extreme, is not Machado's only approach to the problem of metaempirical change. In his fiction, the passage of time brings with it two orders of transformations, natural and social. There are, first, the changes that affect the internal identity: A child is born, grows up, ages, and dies. These transformations of the inner, physical self as it moves through time may be difficult to face, but they are at least regular, predictable, and universal. The second set of changes transforms the external self and is far more difficult for the individual to come to terms with and to understand.

As an individual moves through society, the inescapable dictates of ambition require a series of metamorphoses of the external self; such transformations are contingent upon hard choices between the imperatives of the external identity and the basic morality—often described by Machado in nonmoral terms as simple pride—of the inner self. In Machado's works, the needs of the mirror-self almost invariably triumph, destroying the ideal balance of the two symbiotic identities. What we call society, in fact, is for Machado no more than the sum of an infinite number of immoral or amoral interactions. Every external self strives endlessly to assert, improve, or protect itself at the expense of others, a process Machado describes in terms of rolling balls that clack into one another, transferring their kinetic energy in a series of random reactions. The inner self demands an accounting, however, and the two identities can only be reintegrated if the external self can order and justify its actions and its metamorphoses as both rational and inevitable.

Machado, it is true, was not the first writer to recognize the gap between what we are and what we appear to be, between self and image; it seems equally true, however, that his obsession with the double self was firmly rooted in his awareness of his own situation as a nonwhite who had managed to move his perceived identity to the white extreme of the racial continuum, but who could not escape the remnants of his past. Similarly, although the conflict between morality and ambition is a universal theme, that conflict must have often been acute as Machado himself passed through the escape hatch. He simply could not have moved so successfully along the continuum had he not sacrificed conscience to ambition in several fundamental areas: He separated himself from his family; he turned his back on other nonwhite intellectuals; and he refused to use his prestige, at least publicly, to advance the abolitionist cause. (pp.73-8)

> *David T. Haberly, "A Journey through the Escape Hatch: Joaquim Maria Machado de Assis, in his* Three Sad Races: Racial Identi-

ty and National Consciousness in Brazilian Literature, *Cambridge University Press, 1983, pp. 70-98.*

Susan Sontag (essay date 1990)

[*Sontag is a contemporary American novelist and literary critic. In the following analysis of* Epitaph of a Small Winner, *she describes her astonishment at the lack of critical attention accorded to Machado. This essay was specially revised by Sontag for inclusion in* Black Literature Criticism.]

Imagine a writer who in the course of a moderately long life, in which he never travelled farther than seventy-five miles from the capital city where he was born, created a huge body of work— A nineteenth-century writer, you will interrupt, and you will be right: author of a profusion of novels, novellas, stories, plays, essays, poetry, reviews, political chronicles, as well as reporter, magazine editor, government bureaucrat, candidate for public office, and founding president of his country's Academy of Letters; a prodigy of accomplishment, of the transcending of social and physical infirmity (he was a mulatto in a country where slavery was not abolished until he was almost fifty; he was epileptic), who, during this vividly prolific, exuberantly national career, managed to write a sizable number of novels and stories deserving of a permanent place in world literature, and whose masterpieces, outside his native country, which honors him as its greatest writer, are little known, rarely mentioned.

Imagine such a writer, who did exist, and his most original books, which continue to be discovered, more than eighty years after his death. Normally, the filter of time is just, discarding the merely successful, rescuing the forgotten, promoting the underestimated. It is in the afterlife of a great writer when the mysterious questions of value and permanence are resolved. Perhaps it is fitting that this writer, whose afterlife has not brought his work the recognition that it merits, should himself have had so acute, so ironic, so endearing a sense of the posthumous.

What is true of a reputation is true—should be true—of a life. Since it is only a completed life that reveals its shape and whatever meaning a life can have, a biography that means to be definitive must wait until after the death of its subject. Unfortunately, autobiographies can't be composed under these ideal circumstances. And virtually all the notable fictional autobiographies have respected the limitation of real ones while conjuring up a next-best equivalent of the illuminations of death. Fictional autobiographies, even more often than real ones, tend to be autumnal undertakings: an elderly (or, at least, loss-seasoned) narrator, having retired from life, now writes. But, close as old age may bring the fictive autobiographer to the ideal vantage point, he or she is still writing on the wrong side of the frontier beyond which a life, a life story, finally makes sense.

I know only one example of that enthralling genre the imaginary autobiography which grants the project of autobiography its ideal—as it turns out, comical—fulfillment, and that is the masterpiece called *Memórias Póstumas de Brás Cubas* (1880), by the Brazilian writer Machado de Assis, and known in English by the rather interfering title *Epitaph of a Small Winner.* In the first paragraph of Chapter 1, "The Death of the Author," Brás Cubas announces gaily, "I am a deceased writer not in the sense of one who has written and is now deceased, but in the sense of one who has died and is now writing." Here is the novel's first, framing joke, and it is about the writer's freedom. The reader is invited to play the game of considering that the book in hand is an unprecedented literary feat: posthumous reminiscences written in the first person.

Of course, not even a single day, much less a life, can ever be recounted in its entirety. A life is not a plot. And quite different ideas of decorum apply to a narrative constructed in the first person and to one in the third person. To slow down, to speed up, to skip whole stretches; to comment at length, to withhold comment—to do these as an "I" gives them another weight, another feel, than to say them about or on behalf of someone else. Much of what is affecting or pardonable or insufferable in the first person would seem the opposite if uttered in the third person, and vice versa: an observation easily confirmed by reading aloud any page from this book first as it is and a second time with "he" for "I." (To sample the fierce difference *within* the codes governing the third person, then try substituting "she" for "he.") There are registers of feeling, such as anxiety, that only a first-person voice can accommodate. And aspects of narrative performance as well: digressiveness, for instance, seems natural in a text written in the first person but amateurish in an impersonal, third-person voice. Thus any piece of writing that features an awareness of its own means and methods should be understood as in the first person, whether or not the main pronoun is "I."

To write about oneself, to tell the true—that is, the private—story, used to be felt to be presumptuous, and to need justifying. Montaigne's *Essays,* Rousseau's *Confessions,* Thoreau's *Walden,* and most of the other spiritually ambitious classics of autobiography have a prologue in which the author directly addresses the reader, acknowledging the temerity of the enterprise, evoking scruples or inhibitions (modesty, anxiety) that had to be overcome, laying claim to an exemplary artlessness or candor, alleging the usefulness to others of all this self-absorption. Like real autobiographies, most fictional autobiographies of any stylishness or depth also start with an explanation, defensive or defiant, of the decision to write the book the reader has just begun—or, at least, a flourish of self-deprecation, suggesting an attractive sensitivity to the charge of egotism. This is no mere throat-clearing, some polite sentences to give the reader time to be seated. It is the opening shot in a campaign of seduction, in which the autobiographer tacitly agrees that there is something unseemly, brazen, in *volunteering* to write at length about oneself—in exposing oneself to unknown others without the justification of a great career or a great crime, or without some documentary ruse, such as pretending that the book merely transcribes existing private papers, like a journal or letters, indiscretions originally destined for the smallest, friendliest readership. With a life story offered straight out, in the first person, to as many readers as possible (a "public"), it seems only minimal prudence as well as courtesy for the autobiographer to seek permission to begin. The splendid conceit of Machado de Assis's book, that these are memoirs written by someone who is dead, just puts an additional spin on this regulatory caring about what the reader thinks. The autobiographer can profess not to care.

But writing from beyond the grave has in fact not relieved this narrator from showing an ostentatious amount of concern about the reception of his work. His mock anxiety is embodied in the very form and the distinctive velocity of the book. It is in the way the narrative is cut and mounted, in stop-and-start rhythms: a hundred and sixty chapters, several as brief as two sentences, few longer than two pages. It is in the playful directions, usually at the beginning or end of chapters, for making the best use of the text: "This chapter is to be inserted between the first two sentences of Chapter 129"; "Please note that this chapter is not intended to be profound"; "But let us not become involved in psychology"; et cetera. It is in the pulse of ironic attention to the book's means and methods, the repeated disavowal of large claims on the reader's emotions: "I like jolly chapters." Asking the reader to indulge the narrator's penchant for frivolity is as much a seducer's ploy as promising the reader strong emotions and new knowledge. The autobiographer's suave fussing over the accuracy of his narrative procedures parodies the intensity of his self-absorption.

Digression is the main technique for controlling the emotional flow of this book. The narrator, whose head is full of literature, shows himself adept at expert descriptions—of the kind flattered with the name of realism—that chronicle how poignant feelings persist, change, evolve, devolve. He also shows himself understandably beyond such concerns by the dimensions of the telling: the cutting into short episodes; the ironic, didactic overviews. This oddly fierce, avowedly disenchanted voice (but then what else should we expect the voice of a narrator who is dead to be?) never relates an event without drawing some lesson from it. Chapter 133 opens, "The episode serves to illustrate and perhaps amend Helvetius' theory that . . . " Begging the reader's indulgence, worrying about the reader's attentiveness (Does the reader get it? Is the reader amused? Is the reader becoming bored?), the autobiographer continually breaks out of his story to invoke a theory it illustrates, to formulate an opinion about it—as if such devices were needed to make the story more interesting. Brás Cubas's socially privileged, self-important existence is, as such lives often are, starkly uneventful; the main events are those which did not happen or were judged disappointing. The rich production of witty opinions exposes the emotional poverty of the life, by exhibiting the narrator as seeming to sidestep conclusions he might otherwise be drawing. The digressive method also generates much of the book's humor, starting with the very disparity between the life described (modest in events, subtly articulated) and the theories (portentous, blunt) invoked.

The Life and Opinions of Tristram Shandy is, of course, the principal model for these savory procedures of reader awareness. The method of tiny chapters, and also some of the typographical stunts, as in Chapter 55 ("The Venerable Dialogue of Adam and Eve") and Chapter 139 ("How I Did Not Become a Minister of State"), recall the whimsical narrative rhythms and pictographic witticisms of *Tristram Shandy.* That Brás Cubas begins his story after his death, as Tristram Shandy famously begins the story of his consciousness before he is born (at the moment of his conception)—that, too, seems an homage to Sterne by Machado de Assis. The authority that *Tristram Shandy,* published in installments between 1759 and 1767, exerted on a writer born in Brazil in the nineteenth century should not surprise us. While Sterne's books, so celebrated in his lifetime and shortly afterward, were being reassessed in England as too peculiar, occasionally indecent, and finally boring, they continued to be enormously admired on the Continent. In the English-speaking world, where in this century Sterne has again been thought very highly of, he still figures as an ultra-eccentric, marginal genius (like Blake), who is most notable for being uncannily, and prematurely, "modern." When looked at from the perspective of world literature, however, he may be the English-language writer who, after Shakespeare and Dickens, has had the greatest influence; for Nietzsche to have said that his favorite novel was *Tristram Shandy* is not quite as original a judgment as it may seem. Sterne has been an especially potent presence in the literatures of the Slavic languages, as is reflected in the centrality of the example of *Tristram Shandy* in the theories of Shklovsky and other Russian formalists, from the nineteen-twenties forward. Perhaps the reason so much commanding prose literature has been issuing for decades from Central and Eastern Europe as well as from Latin America is not only that writers there have been suffering under monstrous tyrannies and therefore have had importance, seriousness, subjects, relevant irony bestowed on them (as many writers in Western Europe and the United States have half-enviously concluded) but also that these are the parts of the world where for over a century the author of *Tristram Shandy* has been the most admired.

Machado de Assis's novel belongs in that tradition of narrative buffoonery—the talkative first-person voice attempting to ingratiate itself with readers—which runs from Sterne through, in our own century, Natsume Sōseki's *I Am a Cat,* the short fiction of Robert Walser, Svevo's *Confessions of Zeno* and *As a Man Grows Older,* Hrabal's *Too Loud a Solitude,* much of Beckett. We meet again and again, in different guises, the chatty, meandering, compulsively speculative, eccentric narrator: reclusive (by choice or by vocation); prone to futile obsessions and fanciful theories and comically designed efforts of the will; often an autodidact; not quite a crank; though sometimes driven by lust, and at least one time by love, unable to mate; usually elderly; invariably male. (No woman is likely to get even the conditional sympathy these ragingly self-absorbed narrators claim from us, because of expectations that women will be more sympathetic, and sympathizing, than men; a woman with the same degree of mental acuity and emotional separateness would be regarded as simply a monster.) Machado de Assis's valetudinarian Brás Cubas is considerably less exuberant than Sterne's madcap, effusively garrulous Tristram Shandy. It is only a few steps from the incisiveness of Machado's narrator, with his rueful superiority to the story of his own life, to the plot malaise that characterizes most recent fiction in the form of autobiography. But storylessness may be intrinsic to the genre—the novel as autobiographical monologue—as is the isolation of the narrating voice. In this respect the post-Sternean antihero like Brás Cubas parodies the protagonist of the great spiritual autobiographies, who is always profoundly, not just by circumstances, unmarried. It is almost a measure of an autobiographical narrative's ambition: the narrator must be, or be recast as, alone, a solitary, certainly without a spouse, even when there is one; the life must be unpeopled at the center. (Thus such recent achievements of spiritual autobiography in the guise of a novel as Elizabeth Hardwick's *Sleepless Nights* and V. S. Naipaul's *The Enigma of Arrival* leave out the spouses who were actually there.) Just as Brás Cubas's solitariness is a parody of a chosen or an emblematic solitude, his release through self-understanding is, for all its self-confidence and wit, a parody of that sort of triumph.

The seductions of such a narrative are complex. The narrator professes to be worrying about the reader—whether the reader gets it. Meanwhile, the reader can be wondering about the narrator—whether the narrator understands all the implications of what is being told. A display of mental agility and inventiveness which is designed to amuse the reader and which purportedly reflects the liveliness of the narrator's mind mostly measures how emotionally isolated and forlorn the narrator is. Ostensibly, Machado's novel is the book of a life. Yet, despite the narrator's gift for social and psychological portraiture, it remains a tour of the inside of someone's head. Another of Machado's models was a marvellous book by Xavier de Maistre, a French expatriate aristocrat (he lived most of his long life in Russia), who invented the literary micro-journey with his *Journey Around My Room,* which was written in 1794, when he was in prison for duelling, and which recounts his diagonal and zigzag visits to such diverting sites as the armchair, the desk, and the bed. A confinement, mental or physical, that is not acknowledged as such can make a very funny story as well as one charged with pathos.

At the beginning, in a flourish of authorial self-knowingness that graciously includes the reader, Machado de

Assis has his autobiographer name the eighteenth-century literary models of his narrative with the following sombre warning:

> It is, in truth, a diffuse work, in which I, Brás Cubas, if indeed I have adopted the free form of a Sterne or of a Xavier de Maistre, have possibly added a certain peevish pessimism of my own. Quite possibly. The work of a man already dead. I wrote it with the pen of Mirth and the ink of Melancholy, and one can readily foresee what may come of such a union.

However modulated by whimsy, a vein of true misanthropy runs through the book. If Brás Cubas is not just another of those repressed, desiccated, pointlessly self-aware bachelor narrators who exist only to be seen through by the full-blooded reader, it is because of his anger—which by the end of the book is full out, painful, bitter, upsetting.

The Sternean playfulness is lighthearted. It is a comic, albeit extremely nervous, form of friendliness with the reader. In the nineteenth century, this digressiveness, this chattiness, this love of the little theory, this pirouetting from one narrative mode to another, takes on darker hues. It becomes identified with hypochondria, with erotic disillusionment, with the discontents of the self (Dostoyevski's pathologically voluble Underground Man), with acute mental distress (the hysterical narrator, deranged by injustice, of Multatuli's *Max Havelaar*). To natter on obsessively, repetitively, used to be invariably a resource of comedy. (Think of Shakespeare's plebeian grumblers, like the porter in *Macbeth*; think of Mr. Pickwick, among other inventions of Dickens'.) That comic use of garrulousness does not disappear. Joyce used garrulousness in a Rabelaisian spirit, as a vehicle of comic hyperbole, and Gertrude Stein, champion of verbose writing, turned the tics of egotism and sententiousness into a good-natured comic voice of great originality. But most of the verbose first-person narrators in the ambitious literature of this century have been radically misanthropic. Garrulousness is identified with the baleful, aggrieved repetitiveness of senility (Beckett's prose monologues that call themselves novels) and with paranoia and unslakable rage (the novels and plays of Thomas Bernhard). Who does not sense the despair behind the loquacious, sprightly musings of Robert Walser and the quirkily erudite, bantering voices in the stories of Donald Barthelme?

Beckett's narrators are usually trying, not altogether successfully, to imagine themselves as dead. Brás Cubas has no such problem. But then Machado de Assis was trying to be, and is, funny. There is nothing morbid about the consciousness of his posthumous narrator; on the contrary, the perspective of maximum consciousness—which is what, wittily, a posthumous narrator can claim—is a comic perspective. What Brás Cubas is writing from is not a true afterlife (it has no geography) but only another go at the idea of authorial detachment. The neo-Sternean narrative high jinks of these memoirs of a disappointed man do not issue from

Sternean exuberance, or even from Sternean nervousness. They are a kind of antidote, a counter-force, to the narrator's despondency: a way of mastering dejection considerably more specialized than the "great cure, an anti-melancholy plaster, designed to relieve the despondency of mankind" which the narrator fantasizes about inventing. Life administers its hard lessons. But one can write as one pleases—a form of liberty.

Machado de Assis was only forty-one when he published these reminiscences of a man who has died at sixty-four, as we learn at the opening of the book. (Machado was born in 1839; he makes his creation Brás Cubas, the posthumous autobiographer, a full generation older, born in 1805). The novel as an exercise in anticipating old age is a venture to which writers of a melancholy temperament continue to be drawn. I was in my late twenties when I wrote my first novel, *The Benefactor,* which purports to be the reminiscences of a man then in his early sixties, a rentier, dilettante, and fantasist, who announces at the beginning of the book that he has reached a harbor of serenity where, all experience finished, he can look back on his life. The few conscious literary references in my head were mostly French— above all, *Candide* and Descartes's *Meditations.* I thought I was writing a satire on optimism and on certain cherished (by me) ideas of the inner life and of a religiously nourished inwardness. (What was going on unconsciously is, as I think about it now, another story.) When I had the good fortune to have *The Benefactor* accepted by the first publisher to whom I submitted it— Farrar, Straus—I had the further good luck of having assigned to me as my editor Cecil Hemley, who in 1952, in his previous incarnation as the head of Noonday Press... had brought out the translation (by William L. Grossman) of Machado's novel that really launched the book's career in English. At our first meeting, Hemley said to me, not implausibly, "I can see you have been influenced by **Epitaph of a Small Winner.**" Epitaph of a what? "By, you know, Machado de Assis." Who? He lent me his copy, and several days later I declared myself retroactively influenced.

Although I have since read a good deal of Machado in translation, this book—the first of his five last novels (he lived twenty-eight years after writing it), generally thought the summit of his genius—remains my favorite. It is, I am told, the one that non-Brazilians often prefer, although critics usually pick **Dom Casmurro** (1899). I am astonished that a writer of such greatness does not yet occupy the place he deserves. Up to a point, the relative neglect of Machado outside Brazil may be no more mysterious than the neglect of another prolific writer of genius whom Eurocentric notions of world literature have marginalized: Natsume Sōseki. Surely Machado would be better known if he hadn't been Brazilian and hadn't spent his whole life in Rio de Janeiro—if he were, say, Italian or Russian, or even Portuguese. But the impediment is not simply that Machado was not a European writer. Even more remarkable than his absence from the stage of world literature is that he has been very little known and read in the rest of Latin

America—as if it were still hard to digest the fact that the greatest author ever produced in Latin America wrote in the Portuguese, rather than the Spanish, language. Brazil may be the continent's biggest country (and, in the nineteenth century, Rio its largest city), but it has always been the outsider country, regarded by the rest of South America—Hispanophone South America—with a good deal of condescension and even racism. A writer from one of those countries is far likelier to know any of the European literatures or literature in English than to know the literature of Brazil, whereas Brazilian writers are acutely aware of Spanish-American literature. Borges, the second-greatest writer produced on that continent, seems never to have read Machado de Assis. Indeed, Machado is even less well known to Spanish-language readers than to those who read him in English. *Epitaph of a Small Winner* was translated into Spanish only in the nineteen-sixties, some eighty years after it was written and a decade after it was translated (twice) into English.

With enough time, enough afterlife, a great book does find its rightful place. And perhaps some books need to be rediscovered again and again. **Epitaph of a Small Winner** is probably one of those thrillingly original, radically skeptical books which will always impress readers with the force of a private discovery. It doesn't seem much of a compliment to say that this novel, written more than a century ago, is—well, modern. Isn't every work that speaks to us with an originality and lucidity we're capable of acknowledging something we then want to conscript into what we understand as modernity? Our standards of modernity are a system of flattering illusions, which permit us to selectively colonize the past, as are our ideas of what is provincial, which permit certain parts of the world to condescend to all the rest. Being dead may stand for a point of view that cannot be accused of being provincial. Surely **Epitaph of a Small Winner** is one of the most entertainingly unprovincial books ever written. And to love this book is to become a little less provincial about literature, about literature's possibilities, oneself. (pp. 102-08)

> Susan Sontag, "Afterlives: The Case of Machado de Assis," in The New Yorker, *Vol. LXVI, No. 12, May 7, 1990, pp. 102-08.*

FURTHER READING

Caldwell, Helen. *The Brazilian Othello of Machado de Assis: A Study of 'Dom Casmurro'.* Berkeley and Los Angeles: University of California Press, 1960, 194 p.
  The first comprehensive analysis of Machado's *Dom Casmurro.* Caldwell debates the question of the heroine Capitu's guilt, comments on ambiguity in the work, and explores the author's allusions to Shakespeare.

Coutinho, Afrânio. "Joachim Maria Machado de Assis." In *Latin American Writers,* edited by Carlos A. Solé, pp. 253-68. New York: Charles Scribner's Sons, 1989.
  Comprehensive overview of Machado's career, focusing on realism, symbolism, nationalism, pessimism, and humor in his works. Includes primary and secondary bibliographies.

Gledson, John. "Machado de Assis between Romance and Satire: A Parasita Azul." In *What's Past Is Prologue: A Collection of Essays in Honour of L. J. Woodward,* edited by Salvador Bacarisse, Bernard Bentley, Mercedes Clarasó, and Douglas Gifford, pp. 57-69. Edinburgh: Scottish Academic Press, 1984.
  Close study of the short story "A Parasita Azul"—"a surprising work which does not merit the almost complete critical neglect which has been its lot."

Loos, Dorothy Scott. *The Naturalistic Novel of Brazil.* New York: Hispanic Institute of the United States, 1963, 163 p.
  Traces historical roots of the Naturalistic movement in Brazilian literature, referring to Machado as a predecessor of the movement.

MacAdam, Alfred J. "Rereading *Ressurreição." Luso-Brazilian Review* IX, No. 2 (December 1972): 47-57.
  Contends that Machado's *Ressurreição* has been inappropriately labeled a novel. MacAdam reexamines *Ressurreição* as a masterpiece of satire that exhibits different aims and formal characteristics from those usually attributed to the novel form.

Nunes, Maria Luisa. "An Artist's Identity versus the Social Role of the Writer: The Case for Joaquim Maria Machado de Assis." *CLA Journal* XXVII, No. 1 (September 1983): 187-96.
  Attempts to refute Machado's image as "the epileptic product of syphilitic blacks and mulattoes" and "an ugly street urchin who stuttered and spent his childhood in abject poverty." Nunes also disagrees that Machado was a "self-centered and social-climbing snob" who "repudiated his mulatto stepmother, who had made inordinate sacrifices to educate him" and betrayed "other men of color in Brazil" as well as "the cause of abolition."

Param, Charles. "Machado de Assis and Dostoyevski." *Hispania* XLIX, No. 1 (March 1966): 81-7.
  Examines similarities in the works of Machado and Dostoyevski.

———. "The Case for *Quincas Borba* As Confession." *Hispania* L, No. 3 (September 1967): 430-41.
  Discusses the dog in *Quincas Borba* as a symbol of his master Rubiao's various moral compromises. Param sees the psychological makeup of Rubiao as analogous to that of Machado.

———. "Jealousy in the Novels of Machado de Assis." *Hispania* LIII, No. 2 (May 1970): 198-206.
  Discusses the theme of jealousy in Machado's works.

Pritchett, V. S. "A Brazilian." In his *A Man of Letters: Selected Essays,* pp. 259-63. London: Chatto & Windus, 1985.

Brief overview of several of Machado's major works. Pritchett contends: "[Machado's] aim, in all his books, seems to be to rescue a precise moment just before it sinks into the past or reaches into its future. He is a mixture of comedian, lyrical poet, psychological realist and utterly pessimistic philosopher."

Verissimo, Erico. "Yes, But Snakes and Slaves Too." In his *Brazilian Literature: An Outline,* pp. 55-73. New York: Macmillan, 1945.

Examination of style and theme in Machado's first three novels.

Haki R. Madhubuti

1942-

(Born Don L. Lee; changed name in 1973 to Haki R. Madhubuti) American poet, critic, and essayist.

An influential critic of black literature, Madhubuti is also a leading contemporary American poet. His collections of verse have alternately been called "explosive works of power" and "a kind of literary or artistic crime." In 1969 David Llorens prophetically observed: "At once [Madhubuti] will be hailed and damned for the same reason: because he refuses to write a single line in forgetfulness of his blackness." "For Madhubuti," Catherine Daniels Hurst added, "blackness (Africanness) is the source from which all of his other themes originate and radiate. Consequently, he writes about all facets of black life: black pride, black identity, black beauty, black women, black heroes, black education, black love, as well as black revolution."

Madhubuti was born Don L. Lee in Little Rock, Arkansas, and raised in Detroit, Michigan. His father abandoned the family when Madhubuti was a young boy, thereby forcing Madhubuti to take care of his alcoholic mother. "Taking her to hospitals and seeing the terrible way she was treated opened my eyes to racism," he recalled in the *Washington Post*. When he was sixteen, his mother died. He went to live with his aunt in Chicago, where he earned money by delivering newspapers and cleaning a nearby bar. He attended Dunbar Vocational High School and, soon after graduation, joined the U.S. Army. "This was the first time in my life I didn't have to worry about where I was going to be the next day, or what I was going to eat," he related. "The Army was an education for me. I read a lot and mingled with whites for the first time." Upon his discharge in 1963 he returned to Chicago and enrolled at Crane Junior College (now Malcolm X College), eventually earning a master's degree in Fine Arts from the University of Iowa.

Madhubuti began writing poetry in the early 1960s while working odd jobs in the Chicago area. Encouraged by the favorable reception of his first two books, *Think Black!* (1967) and *Black Pride* (1968), he decided to pursue a full-time career in writing. In 1968 he became a writer-in-residence at Cornell University, and in the following years he published several more books of poetry. Denouncing all things white—white values, white art, white influences—he rejected his "slave name" in 1973 and began writing as Haki R. Madhubuti, meaning "Justice, Awakening, Strong" in Swahili. He devoted the next years to publishing political essays and to critiquing black literature. In 1990 he published *Black Men: Obsolete, Single, Dangerous? (The Afrikan American Family in Transition),* a collection of essays that examines black family relationships. He is currently a professor of English at Chicago State University and

editor of Third World Press, a publishing company he founded in 1967 to promote black writers.

Madhubuti's development from a "rather quiet accommodationist" to a "revolutionary Black poet," according to Marlene Mosher, is reflected in the several stages of the author's literary career. Madhubuti's early verses, written during the poet's "awakening" phase, are sometimes called his "Anti-White" works because they attack Western culture. In contrast, *Don't Cry, Scream* (1969) and *We Walk the Way of the New World* (1970) reflect Madhubuti's "Pro-Black" period. "[In these] two volumes of poetry...Lee's voice became progressively 'louder, but softer'," Mosher observed. "Rather than violently attack White evil, he chose to accentuate the positive virtues and abilities of Black people...." Madhubuti's more recent works, *Directionscore: Selected and New Poems* (1971), *Book of Life* (1973), and *Killing Memory, Seeking Ancestors* (1987), also praise blacks and black culture. Writing for the "average black person who reads, speaks, and understands black vernacular," Jerry B. McAninch noted, Madhubuti deliberately forsook standard English for "hip street talk" and short, staccato phrases. He distinguished between "niggers" and blacks and called for "niggers" to "react / NOW niggers / & you won't have to / act / false-actions / at your children's graves." In *Don't Cry, Scream* Madhubuti warned: "know the realenemy, the world's enemy. / know them know them know them the / realenemy change your enemy change your change... / change change your change change change. / your / mind nigger." While urging black men to create a "new world," Madhubuti also addressed black women in *We Walk the Way of the New World*. In this book he exalted the "natural" black woman and attacked middle-class "negro sisters in two hundred dollar wigs & suits"; in the poem "On Seeing Diana go Maddddddddd," Madhubuti derided entertainer Diana Ross for denying her blackness to embrace "whi-te" values.

Critical reaction to Madhubuti's work has been mixed. Llorens called Madhubuti "a lion of a poet who splits syllables, invents phrases, makes letters work as words, and gives rhythmic quality to verse that is never savage but often vicious and always reflecting a revolutionary black consciousness." As a result, his "lines rumble like a street gang on the page," observed critic Liz Gant. Likewise, Hurst added: "Madhubuti's style is kinetic: quick, explosive, full of movement and high energy. His startling metaphors, variations of refrain, unexpected turns-of-phrase, wordplay, and staccato repetitions combine to produce an impact that keeps audiences spellbound." Not all reviewers were so impressed with the poet's work, however. Jascha Kessler wrote: "I've not seen poetry in Don L. Lee. Anger, bombast, raw hatred, strident, aggrieved, perhaps charismatically crude religious and political canting, propaganda and racist nonsense, yes; and utterly unoriginal in form and style; humorless; cruel laughter bordering on the insane.... But poetry? Lee is deluded in thinking he has it." Similarly, others have labeled his poems an "all-out ranting," "ugly, jarring work," and "outdated." Gwendolyn Brooks, in the 1969 introduction to *Don't Cry, Scream*, disagreed: "Don Lee knows that nothing human is elegant. He is not interested in modes of writing that aspire to elegance.... He speaks to blacks hungry for what they themselves refer to as '*real* poetry.' These blacks find themselves and the stuff of their existence in his healthy, lithe, lusty reaches of free verse. The last thing these people crave is elegance."

Madhubuti's work remains controversial even today. Nonetheless, as Stephen Henderson has observed, Madhubuti is "more widely imitated than any other Black poet with the exception of Imamu Baraka (LeRoi Jones). His unique delivery has given him a popular appeal which is tantamount to stardom. His influence is enormous and is still growing." While Madhubuti's style and tone have changed slightly with each new book, his goal has remained the same: to incite blacks to action. "Blackpoetry is excellence & truth and will continue to seek such," Madhubuti wrote in the 1969 preface to *Don't Cry, Scream*. "Blackpoetry will move to expose & wipe-out that which is not necessary for our existence as a people.... Blackpoetry is like a razor; it's sharp & will cut deep, not out to wound but to kill the inactive blackmind. Like, my oldman used to pickup numbers and he seldom got caught & I'm faster than him; this is a fight with well defined borders & I know the side I'm ON...."

(For further information about Madhubuti's life and works, see *Black Writers*; *Contemporary Authors*, Vols. 73-76; *Contemporary Authors New Revision Series*, Vol. 24; *Contemporary Literary Criticism*, Vols. 2, 6; *Dictionary of Literary Biography*, Vols. 5, 41; and *Dictionary of Literary Biography Documentary Series*, Vol. 8: *The Black Aesthetic Movement*.)

*PRINCIPAL WORKS

Think Black! (poetry) 1967
Black Pride (poetry) 1968
For Black People (and Negroes Too) (poetry) 1968
Don't Cry, Scream (poetry) 1969
We Walk the Way of the New World (poetry) 1970
Directionscore: Selected and New Poems (poetry) 1971
Dynamite Voices I: Black Poets of the 1960's (essays) 1971
Kwanzaa (poetry) 1972
Book of Life (poetry) 1973
From Plan to Planet: Life Studies, The Need for Afrikan Minds and Institutions (essays) 1973
Enemies: The Clash of Races (essays) 1978
Earthquakes and Sun Rise Missions: Poetry and Essays of Black Renewal, 1973-1983 (poetry) 1984
Killing Memory, Seeking Ancestors (poetry) 1987
Say that the River Turns: The Impact of Gwendolyn Brooks (poetry and prose) 1987
Black Men: Obsolete, Single, Dangerous? (The Afrikan American Family in Transition) (essays) 1990

*Works before 1973 were published under the name Don L. Lee.

Gwendolyn Brooks (essay date 1969)

[*A major contemporary poet and the first black American writer to win a Pulitzer Prize, Brooks is best known for her sensitive portraits of ordinary urban blacks. In the following excerpt from her 1969 introduction to* Don't Cry, Scream, *she evaluates Madhubuti as a poet.*]

At the hub of the new wordway is Don Lee.

Around a black audience he puts warm healing arms.

He knows that the black man today must ride full face into the whirlwind—with small regard for "correctness," with limited concern for the possibilities of "error." He knows that there are briefs even for the Big

Mistake. The Big Mistake is at least a violent Change—and in the center of a violent Change are the seeds of creation.

Don Lee knows that nothing human is elegant. He is not interested in modes of writing that aspire to elegance. He is well-acquainted with "elegant" literature (what hasn't he read?) but, while certainly respecting the advantages and influence of good workmanship, he is **not** interested in supplying the needs of the English Departments at Harvard and Oxford nor the editors of *Partisan Review*, although he could mightily serve as factory for these. He speaks to blacks hungry for what they themselves refer to as "**real** poetry." These blacks find themselves and the stuff of their existence in his healthy, lithe, lusty reaches of free verse. The last thing these people crave is elegance. It is very hard to enchant, with elegant song, the ears of a fellow whose stomach is growling. He can't hear you. The more interesting noise is too loud.

Don Lee has no patience with black writers who do not direct their blackness toward black audiences. (p. 9)

"The black writer learns from his people," says Don L. Lee. "...Black artists are culture stabilizers, bringing back old values, and introducing new ones."

Poetry should—"allatonce"—distil, interpret, and extend. Don Lee's poetry does.

Black poets are the authentic poets of today. Recently, one of The Critics [Jascha Kessler] opined (of white poets): "...it's hardly surprising to find a deep longing for death as the terrible sign of their self-respect and indeed the means by which they continue to live—if not as men, at least as poets." And on: "Although death may not be the resolution of everyone's problems, it is nevertheless the one poets wait and pray for...."

Can you imagine Don Lee subscribing to any of this? Black poets do not subscribe to death. When choice is possible, they choose to die only in defense of life, in defense and in honor of life.

White poetry! Never has white technique-in-general been as scintillant and various. Never has less been said. Modern corruption and precise limpness, modern narcissism, nonsense, dry winter and chains have a grotesque but granular grip on the white verse of today.

Sometimes there is a quarrel. "Can poetry be 'black'? Isn't all poetry just POETRY?" The fact that a poet is black means that his life, his history and the histories of his ancestors have been different from the histories of Chinese and Japanese poets, Eskimo poets, Indian poets, Irish poets. The juice from tomatoes is not called merely **juice.** It is always called TOMATO juice. If you go into a restaurant desiring tomato juice you do not order the waiter to bring you "juice": you request, distinctly, TOMATO juice. The juice from cranberries is called cranberry juice. The juice from oranges is called orange juice. The poetry from black poets is black

poetry. Inside it are different nuances AND outright-nesses.

This is part of the decision of Don Lee—who is a further pioneer and a positive prophet, a prophet not afraid to be positive even though aware of a daily evolving, of his own sober and firm churning. He is a toughness. He is not a superficial toughness. He is the kind of toughness that doesn't just sass its mammy but goes right through to the bone. (pp. 12-13)

> *Gwendolyn Brooks, in an introduction to*
> Don't Cry, Scream *by Don L. Lee, Broadside*
> *Press, 1969, pp. 9-14.*

Don L. Lee (essay date 1969)

[*In the following 1969 introduction to a revision of his 1967 work* Think Black!, *Madhubuti identifies himself as a black first and a poet second.*]

I was born into slavery in Feb. of 1942. In the spring of that same year 110,000 persons of Japanese descent were placed in protective custody by the white people of the United States. Two out of every three of these were American citizens by birth; the other third were aliens forbidden by law to be citizens. No charges had been filed against these people nor had any hearing been held. The removal of these people was on racial or ancestral grounds only. World War II, the war against racism; yet no Germans or other enemy agents were placed in protective custody. There should have been Japanese writers directing their writings toward Japanese audiences.

Black. Poet. Black poet am I. This should leave little doubt in the minds of anyone as to which is first. Black art is created from black forces that live within the body. These forces can be lost at any time as in the case of Louis Lomax, Frank Yerby and Ralph Ellison. Direct and meaningful contact with black people will act as energizers for the black forces. Black art will elevate and enlighten our people and lead them toward an awareness of self, i.e., their blackness. It will show them mirrors. Beautiful symbols. And will aid in the destruction of anything nasty and detrimental to our advancement as a people. Black art is a reciprocal art. The black writer learns from his people and because of his insight and "know how" he is able to give back his knowledge to the people in a manner in which they can identify, learn and gain some type of mental satisfaction, e.g., rage of happiness. We must destroy Faulkner, dick, jane and other perpetuators of evil. It's time for Du Bois, Nat Turner and Kwame Nkruma. As Frantz Fanon points out: destroy the culture and you destroy the people. This must not happen. Black artists are culture stabilizers; bringing back old values, and introducing new ones. Black art will talk to the people and with the will of the people stop the impending "protective custody."

America calling.
negroes.

can you dance?
play foot/baseball?
nanny?
cook?
needed now. negroes
who can entertain
ONLY.
others not
wanted.
(& are considered extremely dangerous.)

d. l. l.

Don L. Lee, in his Think Black!, *third
edition, Broadside Press, 1969, 24 p.*

Helen Vendler (essay date 1974)

[*In the following excerpt from an essay first published
in* The New York Times Book Review *in 1974,
Vendler examines a selection of Madhubuti's poems,
noting: "[Madhubuti] does not sell comfortable sentimentality. He sells on nerve, stamina, and satire."*]

Lee's poems, written in a rapid, jerky, intense speech-
rhythm in almost Morse shorthand, have sold over
100,000 copies without any large-scale advertising or
mass distribution, a phenomenon which (like the success of Ginsberg's *Howl*) means that something is
happening. Lee is not Rod McKuen or Lois Wyse; he
does not sell comfortable sentimentality. He sells on
nerve, stamina, and satire. In him the sardonic and
savage turn-of-phrase long present in black speech as a
survival tactic finds its best poet; here it is in his elegy
for Coltrane ("**Don't Cry, Scream**"):

the ofays heard you &
were wiped out spaced.
one clown asked me during,
my favorite things, if
you were practicing.
I fired on the motherfucker & said.
"i'm practicing."

These clean cool acid vignettes run side by side with the
staccato rhythms of Lee's long poems, most of them too
long to quote, depending as they do on quick sharp
changes of focus in devastating snapshots—like the
much-anthologized "**But He Was Cool or: he even
stopped for green lights**":

super-cool
ultrablack
a tan/purple
had a beautiful shade

he had a double-natural
that wd put the sisters to shame.
his dashikis were tailor made
& his beads were imported sea shells
(from some blk/country I never heard of)
he was triple-hip.

The downfall of the super-cool is one of Lee's themes,
and he pursues it smartly; but there is likely to be some
change from satire to sympathy—not a bad turn—in his

current alignment with the Pan-Africanists. Lee can do,
besides long poems, tiny epigrams:

in 1959
my mom
was dead at the
age of
35
& nobody thought it
unusual; not even
me

He catches, before they vanish, words of conversation,
undeniably exact; "**Big Momma**" (his grandmother?)
speaks to him:

...the way niggers cut each other up round
here every weekend that whiteman don't haveta
worry bout no revolution...anyhow all he's
gotta do is drop a truck load
of dope out there
on 43rd st. & all the niggers & yr revolutionaries
be too busy getten high and then they'll turn
round
and fight each other over who got the mostest.

Because Lee's impartial accuracy catches survival as
well as succumbing, his poems dispense faith along with
satire. As he leaves "**Big Momma**" he sees a derelict
bearing out her gloom; but last and best he sees her own
resilience:

touching the snow lightly i headed for 43rd st.
at the corner i saw a brother crying while
trying to hold up a lamp post,
thru his watery eyes i cd see big momma's words.

at sixty-eight
she moves freely, is often right
and when there is food
eats joyously with her own
real teeth.

The whole of "**Big Momma**" is even more touching and
funny than its parts, and there are many more poems
like it in Lee's six collections. The sales of Lee's books
will continue as long as his spurts of anger, of derisive
force, of bitter warning, and of undeniable hope continue to find a mirror in the black readers who wait for
each new collection, but it is time for a wider public to
hear his voice. (pp. 315-17)

*Helen Vendler, "Broadsides: Good Black
Poems, One by One," in her* Part of Nature,
Part of Us: Modern American Poets, *Cambridge, Mass.: Harvard University Press,
1980, pp. 313-22.*

Marlene Mosher (essay date 1975)

[*In the following excerpt from her* New Directions
from Don L. Lee *(1975), Mosher chronicles Madhubuti's development as a poet, focusing on* Think
Black!, Don't Cry, Scream, *and* We Walk the Way of
the New World.]

A careful study of Don Lee's poetry will reveal that Lee has developed fairly steadily throughout his poetic career, in terms both of perfecting his technical skill and of solidifying the ideological content of his verse. Lee's organic, progressive development follows the general "pattern" for revolutionary development that was earlier described by Frantz Fanon in *Wretched of the Earth,* and this steady movement has taken him to the opposite extreme from what was, before he began to write poetry, essentially an inarticulate, accommodationist position on the controversial subject of White racism. In his "early escape/period," Lee secretly wanted and even "tr[ied] to be white." By the time that he was writing his first two volumes of poetry, however, he was already passing through a strongly reactionary—and harshly, violently, elementarily verbal—period. During this second stage of his development, Lee moved to reject all Whiteness—White people, a White value system, the White aesthetic, and what he and other present-day Black Nationalists call a "European frame of reference." In fact, motivated by his strong hatred of Whiteness, Lee moved, during this reactionary phase, to reject the entire Western tradition—even including those "negroes" who still subscribed to what Lee then considered an essentially decadent Western tradition. As a result of Lee's anti-White, anti-Western bias, his first volumes of poetry, *Think Black!* and *Black Pride,* were extremely negative works.

Shifting his focus from "anti-" (White) to "pro-" (Black), Lee soon began to draw from both his own inner strength and the combined strength of other struggling Black poets. Consequently, in his next two volumes of poetry, *Don't Cry, Scream* and *We Walk the Way of the New World,* Lee's voice became progressively "louder, but softer." Rather than violently attack White evil, he chose to accentuate the positive virtues and abilities of Black people—while still hoping to eliminate the lingering negative White influence on his people. Accordingly, his early vociferous condemnation of Whites was largely absent from his next two volumes— although there still were a number of attacks on "negroes" (particularly in *Don't Cry, Scream*). Developing steadily as he wrote these second two volumes, Lee emerged, in *We Walk the Way of the New World,* as what Gwendolyn Brooks has since called "a new Black [man.] . . . a tall-walker. Almost firm." He had become a Black man who could, with quiet confidence, work with other young Black poet-prophets to give positive "identity, purpose, and direction" to Black people. With this very positive goal in mind, Lee gathered together, in 1971, a collection of his poems called *Directionscore: Selected and New Poems.* The appearance of this fifth volume brought Lee full circle; from being an insecure denier of his Black self, Lee had become a mature, confident, and fluent revolutionary spokesman for Black people throughout the United States.

In the beginning, in what I have called his "accommodationist" period, Lee did not publish poetry. Such silence is fairly typical of Blacks who have allowed themselves to be absorbed within the essentially racist Establishment of the United States. The accommodationist who *does* write, however, strives in his writings to give

> proof that he has assimilated the culture of the occupying power. His writings correspond point by point with those of his opposite numbers in the mother country. His inspiration is European . . . .

and his poetry usually rhymes. The so-called Afro-American writer, then, who has been in effect "colonized" within his native land (the United States), writes according to the predominant White aesthetic of the United States. Just as the earlier actual slave, Phillis Wheatley, laboriously imitated the heroic couplets of the leading English poet of her day, Alexander Pope, so a later, and more subtly colonized, poet like Gwendolyn Brooks would consciously set out to imitate the poetics of Ezra Pound and T. S. Eliot, who were the European-American poetic pacesetters during her "apprenticeship" period. But Don Lee himself, as noted above, published no early accommodationist, or "conventional," poetry.

That Lee did, however, experience an "accommodationist" period is revealed in some of the highly autobiographical, "confessional" poems that he wrote later. Hence, in **"Understanding but not Forgetting"** Lee honestly discusses his "early escape/period, trying to be white." And again in **"The Self-Hatred of Don L. Lee,"** Lee admits that,

> i,
> at one time,
> loved
> my
> color—
> it
> opened sMall
> doors of
> tokenism
> &
> acceptance.

In the same poem, however, Lee condemns this former attitude as revealing his "blindness" at that time. That Lee clearly does *not* hold the same accommodationist attitude at the time he writes this poem is indicated in the concluding stanza of the poem, where Lee asserts:

> i
> began
> to love
> only a
> part of
> me—
> my inner
> self which
> is all
> black—
> &
> developed a
> vehement
> hatred of
> my light
> brown
> outer.

This change in Lee occurred, he tells us in **"Blood-smiles,"** on "9/15/63 the day I left this society." Again he condemns his former attitude, seeing it as reflecting his own considerable "ignorance." Several examples of just how Lee's "ignorance" affected his early responses to events that touched him appear in his poetry; for instance, in the ninth of his **"Black Sketches,"** Lee states rather bluntly:

> in 1959
> my mom
> was dead at the
> age of
> 35
> & nobody thought it unusual;
> not even
> me.

Since Lee was born in 1942, he would have been seventeen years old at this time; and this rather callous manner of adjusting to his "colonized" status presumably remained with Lee until he was twenty-one. Then,

> in 1963
> i
> became black
> & everyone thought it unusual;
> even me.

With his new-found Blackness came the desire to know more about the Afrikan culture which had helped to shape him, and Don Lee began to read voraciously. He

> . . . painfully
> struggl[ed]
> through Du Bois,
> Rogers, Locke,
> Wright & others,

he says: and finally

> my blindness
> was vanquished
> by pitchblack
> paragraphs of
> "us, we, me, i"
> awareness.

Increased racial awareness led to Black pride, and a newly proud Don Lee discovered his ability to articulate, in poetry, just exactly what it meant to be a Black man in White America. In 1967 Lee, in a violent, invective-filled burst of creativity, began to flood Broadside Press in Detroit with a steady flow of poetry. As this stream broadened, it became less violent—but even more effective—for, in Frantz Fanon's terms, Don Lee began to replace "muscular action" with "concepts." Lee matured from being, essentially, a cacaphonous voice crying out in anger against the cruelties of White America to become a confident, steady teacher of Black cultural values, a significant voice in the Black Nationalist Movement.

That Frantz Fanon was in fact one of those anonymous "others" whose works Lee referred to (in **"The Self-Hatred of Don L. Lee"**) as having read became apparent with the appearance of Lee's first book of poetry, *Think Black!* In his remarks on national culture, Fanon had argued that colonized Afrikan intellectuals, whatever their current "nation of dispersal," must first unite, psychologically, with other Blacks throughout the world, by reaffirming both the existence of and the value of an Afrikan culture that predated the advent of the European colonialists. According to Fanon, even the modern Afrikan who has grown up in America should seek to reassert an *Afrikan* culture and to affirm his own hereditary bond with that Afrikan culture. In this way, he would at once escape the "mind-forged manacles" of a *European* frame of reference and begin to operate from a more positive *Afrikan* frame of reference. Such a move is of vital importance to Black people worldwide, for the widespread European (White-biased) frame of reference is essentially anti-Black in all important aspects; for instance, there are no positive self-images, no—or few—successful role-models for Blacks operating from within such an alien frame of reference. Consequently, European cultural values must be discarded by Blacks and an age-old Black (Afrikan) value system must be revised and refitted to the needs of modern, and widely dispersed, Afrikans.

Don Lee acknowledges his debt to Fanon in the "Introduction" to this first small collection of poems, and here he also depicts himself as having been "born into slavery in Feb. of 1942." By seeing himself in this light, Lee becomes at one with other colonized Black intellectuals throughout the world. His own conscious attempt to reject the European frame of reference that the American Establishment has foisted upon him and to establish a more positive (for him, a Black man) Afrikan frame of reference is reflected in the very title *Think Black!* This attempt to establish an Afrikan frame of reference is also apparent from his introductory remarks, where Lee asserts that "Black art will elevate and enlighten our people and lead them toward an awareness of self, i.e., their blackness. It will show them mirrors. Beautiful symbols." To underscore his own interest in promulgating Black awareness, Lee asserts that he himself is "Black" foremost; only secondarily is he a "poet." His true role as a Black artist, Lee argues, is to be a "culture stabilizer"; that is, he must "[bring] back old values, and [introduce] new ones."

The very first poem in this collection, **"Back Again, Home,"** mirrors Lee's own earlier rejection of the White value system by which he had been entrapped. To escape the "insecurity" and the "ostracism" that are attendant upon Blacks who attempt to function within the alien culture of White America, the "ex-executive" in the poem—after having denied and constricted his Black "self" for years, in an attempt to succeed within the White Establishment—finally "resigns" his important position, reverts to his former "unprogrammed" (and unemployed) way of life, rejoins his former (Black) friends, and comes "home"—"home" to his Blackness. Only by accepting his essential Blackness, his "otherness" from the predominantly White world that surrounds him, can the Black protagonist of this poem relieve his tension and begin to grow into full personhood. And it is this ex-executive's new position at the end of this poem, a position shared by the younger protagonist of **"Education,"** which seems to have been precisely the position of Don Lee when he wrote *Think Black!* Lee, almost surely the prototype for these Black heroes—as he is for the "meditator" in **"Understanding but not Forgetting"**—is painfully aware that of "positive images as a child" he had "NONE," that his "negative images as a child [were]—all black," and that the value system of the predominantly White United States is essentially "mind-crippling" for Blacks: judged by White America's standards, "niggers" always emerge as "the 'Culturally Deprived'"; they are repeatedly "proven" to be "inferior/with technical terms and pretty diagrams." It is Lee's job, then, as an aware Black poet, to reverse this trend—to write a poetry that extolls Blackness while denying, even denigrating, White standards and values.

Such a position on the part of the Black artist corresponds with what Fanon had earlier described as the "phase of consciousness which is in the process of being liberated," and the style of such a writer reflects the intellectual struggle that is going on within him: It "is a harsh style, full of images," says Fanon. "It is a vigorous style, alive with rhythms, struck through and through with bursting life; it is full of color, too, bronzed, sunbaked, and violent." And just such is the vigorous, often violent, style of Don Lee in *Think Black!* For example, in *"Wake-Up Niggers"* Lee depicts the Lone Ranger (here emblematic of both the White American individualistic hero and the entire Western tradition) as being burned at the stake while Tonto, a non-White, finally asserts his own selfhood and flees to safety, rather than placing his self-interest in a secondary position to that of the Lone Ranger and so destroying himself by remaining. Just as the "third-class" Indian finally left the Lone Ranger, so, Lee argues, Blacks ("second-class" citizens in White America) must stop "following" the White man; they must be "hip" like Tonto was (at least this once) and abandon White values (i.e., the Lone Ranger), returning "home" to their own Black selves and adopting a Black value system.

Just as he rejects White social values, so Lee also chooses to operate outside the bounds of the White aesthetic in *Think Black!* Here the drumbeat repetition of "re-act" in Lee's poem **"Re-Act for Action"** parallels what Fanon earlier called "the poetic tom-tom's rhythms." It also looks forward to Lee's even greater stylistic experimentation in his next two volumes of poetry, *Black Pride* and *Don't Cry, Scream.* In this poem, Lee plays with the words "re-act," "act," and "actions," attempting to incite his Black audience to

> re-act to whi-te actions:
>   with real acts of blk/action.
>   BAM   BAM   BAM
>   . . . .
>   re-act
>   NOW niggers

> & you won't have to
> act
> false-actions
> at
> your/children's graves.

The immediate urgency of the need for Blacks to react against White oppression is reflected in the short lines, the abbreviations, the staccato rhythm, the use of the slash (/), the capitalization of "BAM BAM BAM" and "NOW." A similar sense of the need for urgent reaction against

> . . . society—white anglo-saxon,
>   standard setting,
>   example setting,

appears in **"'They Are Not Ready,'"** as a Black man, having "PREPARE[D] MYSELF," asserts that he will "continue/to fight dirty [against White America]."

The inability of Blacks to assimilate successfully into the "Mainstream of [American] Society" (see Lee's poem by that name) is one of the main recurring themes in *Think Black!* Blacks should acknowledge this inability, asserts Lee, and, instead of striving to do the impossible (successfully assimilate into an alien culture while retaining some positive sense of selfhood), they should reorient themselves, "THINK BLACK," and adopt both a Black value system and a Black aesthetic. Lee himself has done this; thus, he uses mostly cacaphonous free verse and Black "ghettoese" in this volume, abandoning standardized verse patterns and language. This action is completely in accord with what both Fanon (in *Wretched*) and Imamu Amiri Baraka (writing in 1966, as LeRoi Jones) had earlier asserted was absolutely essential for a Black writer functioning in a "colonized" situation: he has dissociated himself from the mainstream of White American literature, by asserting his Blackness first and his status as a poet second; and he has assumed his responsibility as being a positive-image maker for his fellow Black people.

Think Black! is, however, as pointed out earlier, more a volume of "reaction" than a volume of "action"; as such it concerns itself more with the destruction of established White values than it does with the construction of new Black values. And the same preoccupation is apparent, in part at least, in Lee's next volume of poetry, *Black Pride.* The latter volume does, however, reflect both some growth toward intellectual positivism on Lee's part and a sharpening of Lee's poetic techniques.

The now-familiar attack on White values recurs again and again in *Black Pride,* but here it has broadened to include attacks on the entire "Western" tradition—on European values *wherever* they are found. Middle-class Blacks ("negroes," as opposed to true Blacks) repeatedly come under violent attack in this volume. They, with their "raped . . . minds," function as "toms," as spies (for the White man) in the Black community. Having completely accepted the dominant White value system of America, these "negroes" need to be "watch[ed, for they are] . . . enemies of black people." They have had

"their minds [blown] literally with whi/te thoughts &
images of western whi/te woman." They have accepted
both the images and the values of White America and,
as a result, these "negroes" live meaningless lives;
they—the "negro" women, in particular—confine their
thoughts to

> ... hair styles,
>   clothes
>   face care and
>   television

They are taught, says Lee ironically:

> Instructive things, such as, to talk on the phone
> for hours, without saying something, to view
> TV, listen to radio & sleep at the same time,
> how to wish the dishes washed, how to be the
> best dressed, brokest employee at work ...

Such people as these are "wasted" people, according to
Lee, and their only "hope" is to

> .... see.
> ... to come back
>   to us.
> ain't you glad you is/black?
>   me too

That it is completely impossible for successful, meaningful integration of the various races—particularly Whites
and Blacks—to occur in America is a note that Lee
strikes again and again in *Black Pride:*

> first. the color black/naturally
> beautiful canNot be mixed, with whi
>   teness .... must not
>   it's
> mine, ours ...
>   ... me. we. living. they existing

Blacks are inherently superior to Whites, argues Lee, as
he repeatedly turns the tables against the White racist
system of America. Hence, Whites are depicted in
revolting, degrading (and usually sexual) images: they
are

> ... maggot colored,
> gaunt creatures from europe
> who came here/put on pants, stopped eating
>   with their hands
> stole land, massacred indians,
> hid from the sun, enslaved blacks &
> thought that they were substitutes
> for gods.

They are "faggots," "sissies," "honkies," and "stupid
muthafuckas." Lee's images here immediately call to
mind the "White devil" stereotype that had earlier been
popularized in America by the "Black Muslims" (particularly by Malcolm X, whom Lee compares to Christ in
"The Black Christ"). In fact, much of Lee's separatist
doctrine, in this second volume, quite closely parallels
the tenets advanced by Elijah Muhammad's Chicago-
headquartered Nation of Islam.

Blacks, Lee argues, possess all the virtues that correspond to the various vices of the Whites. Hence, the
Black youth in Lee's highly autobiographical **"The
Death Dance"** is repeatedly told by his mother, "son you
is a man, a black man." As his self-confidence and pride
in his Blackness grows, the youth begins

> ... to dance dangerous steps,
> warrior's steps.
> my steps took on a cadence with other blk/
>   brothers.

He can already "tapdanc[e] on ... / [the] balls" of the
White man, and, he warns, when he dances again, "it
will be the /Death Dance." Lee's emphasis here on the
violent physical separation of Blacks from White (and
White-minded) oppressors and on political Third-
Worldism (as opposed to the political isolation of Blacks
in America from other Third World peoples) also
appears in **"Message to a Black Soldier,"** where a dying
Viet Cong cries out to the Black soldier who has just
shot him: "We are both niggers ...." Implicit in this
statement is the idea that the Viet Cong and the Black
soldier should unite and together throw off their
White/European oppressors.

Lee completely rejects the mode of "nonviolent resistance" in **Black Pride** and either hints (as in **"Message to
a Black Soldier"**) or openly states that physical violence
is the only adequate/workable response to White oppression. Hence, in **"No More Marching"** he points out that
the "marchen/& singen" of the nonviolent resisters have
affected nothing; Black protesters are still

> gettin hit and
> looken dumb/ &
> smilen

He foresees "world war 3" as pitting the forces of the

> ussr, england, france and u ass
>   vs.
> third world
> 30 million niggers ...

This belief in violent physical revolution against the
White forces of oppression was, however, one that Lee
would largely abandon in his next volumes of poetry.
The time was not ripe, in the late 1960s, for physical
revolution by Blacks in America, as Don Lee himself
soon realized—particularly after carefully considering
the deaths of Malcolm X, countless Black Panthers, and
even Martin Luther King, Jr.—all of whom were
wantonly gunned down by the established powers they
were struggling against. Lee would soon turn away from
belief in a physical revolution as being the "answer" to
the Black man's problems in America and would place
his faith, first, in an ideological "revolution." Such an
ideological "revolutionary course leads," as Addison
Gayle, Jr., has since confirmed in *The Politics of
Revolution,* "through the destruction of the images,
metaphors, and symbols created by American mirror
makers and forced upon Black people."

This "destruction of . . . [White] images" that Gayle refers to is, of course, largely what Lee has been working towards in his poetry from the outset. In *Black Pride* Lee subtly reinforces his contention that White/Western/European values and institutions are crumbling by having his very language "disintegrate" when he is speaking of such institutions (and people). Hence, the term *White* is never capitalized and is always printed in two parts (*whi te*); similarly, *Western* is fairly consistently *west ern* , and *Catholic* becomes *cat holic*. In a like manner, Black "toms" are consistently referred to as "negroes" (uncapitalized). That Lee is consciously manipulating his language to reflect, to reinforce his ideas is clear, for he becomes more consistently "irregular" with respect to capitalization, punctuation, and "standard" speech patterns in his next volume of poetry.

There are more "positive" (Black) images in *Black Pride* than there were in *Think Black!* and in this respect Lee comes closer in *Black Pride* to achieving his goal of being a "culture stabilizer" than he did in his earlier volume. Such Black heroes as Malcolm X and Langston Hughes—both of whom "told the truth" about the Black experience in America—are extolled by Lee (the former in **"The Black Christ;"** the latter in **"Only a Few Left"**), and the many Black men and women who appear on "the wall" in Chicago are also meant to serve as positive role-models for readers of Lee's poetry. Hence:

> black artists paint,
>   du bois/ garvey/ gwen brooks
>   stokley/ rap/ james brown
>   trane/ miracles/ ray charles
>   baldwin/ killens/ muhammad ali
>   alcindor/ blackness/ revolution
> our heroes, we pick them, for the wall
> the mighty black wall/ about our business,
>   blackness
>
> > can you dig?

Although *Black Pride* does contain a considerable number of reactionary (and, consequently, primarily "negative") poems, it also contains several works which are far more "positive" than "negative." Lee is, however, still struggling consciously "to be as near as possible to the people." He is not yet unconsciously at one with them—hence, the "distress and difficulty . . . and disgust" that are evident throughout *Black Pride.*

Don Lee's stance as a poet seems to become somewhat solidified after *Black Pride,* for his next volume, *Don't Cry, Scream,* differs significantly from the earlier two volumes. In his earlier, heavily reactionary (and highly autobiographical) volumes, he was, in fact, often crying out against his White oppressors; in effect, he was begging them—and their "negro" imitators—to see their "sickness" and to change—hence, the large number of "negative" poems in those volumes. Rather typical of these earlier volumes is Lee's concluding query in **"Understanding but not Forgetting,"** where he, pondering "About the American System," wonders:

> . . . will it change
> before it's too late—AND BEFORE I AND
> OTHERS STOP GIVING A [DAMN]

In his third volume, however, Lee moves into action. The title, *Don't Cry, Scream,* is significant, for in these poems Lee asserts himself more positively and makes *demands,* not *requests.* And he directs these new demands almost exclusively at Blacks and at "Euro-Blacks," ignoring Whites almost completely. Here Lee concerns himself at once with pointing out and condemning the evils and with praising the many "goods" that are to be found within the Black community—both in America and in Afrika. He challenges his Black readers to act in accordance with these goods and to act to rid themselves of these evils. Lee also very deliberately and carefully replaces the mind-destroying (for Blacks) White aesthetic with his own developing Black aesthetic—the latter of which he outlines in the preface to *Don't Cry, Scream.*

Clearly, several positive forces have been at work on Don Lee since he began writing poetry, and in this third volume two influences seem particularly obvious. The first is the *ujamaa*–based system of Afrikan socialism, which was widely publicized, both in Afrika and in the United States, by Julius K. Nyerere in the 1960s. The second is the doctrine of *Kawaida,* as espoused by Maulana Ron Karenga in his Los Angeles-based United States Organization at approximately the same time.

In *Don't Cry, Scream* Lee, for the first time, chooses his subject matter almost exclusively from the Black world of Afrika and the United States; in fact, in only one short poem—the bullet-riddled, bomb-shattered **"communication in whi te"**—does he deal exclusively with Whites. However, his poetry in this volume is no less incisive than the earlier poetry was; for as Lee probes and cuts through the various social strata of the Black community, he exposes various "diseased members" within the Black community itself. Middle-class "negroes," Lee's popular butt in the earlier volumes, are several times held up for exposure and ridicule. Black politicians, for example, are attacked in the person of "ed brooke" [sic] who, according to Lee,

> sat at his
> desk
> crying and slashing
> his wrist
> because somebody
> called him
> black

Such a politician as Brooke is clearly far removed from "the Black Christ," Malcolm X, who was lauded in Lee's second volume. Brooke is even deemed "less" than the nonviolent (but still martyred) Martin Luther King, Jr. All too often, however, as Lee pointed out earlier in both *Think Black!* and *Black Pride* and as he reiterates in *Don't Cry, Scream,* Black political "leaders" *are* corrupted by the White Establishment through what Lee will later come to call "the European-American Corruptibles": "money, power, sex." Moreover, that such corruptible politicians are not confined solely to the United State's political arena is made uncompromisingly clear by Lee in his **"Nigerian Unity/or little niggers killing little niggers,"** as he exposes various "Euro-Afrikans" on the mother continent (Afrika).

Money, power, and sex can also corrupt potential Black Nationalists, and Don Lee is extremely conscious of this fact. Thus, he repeatedly exposes those Black "hipster" radicals who dress the part of radicals but remain essentially uninvolved in the real struggles of Black people. In **"But He Was Cool"** Lee effectively "dissects" just such a "super-cool/ultrablack" radical who, for all his "double-natural," his "dashikis [that] were tailor made/...his beads," and "his tikis [that] were hand carved," is out of touch with the actual needs of Black people. For all of his surface radicalness, the "hipster" is essentially "ill tel li gent" (or sick, misguided), says Lee. Such "super-cool" radicals as these are again attacked by Lee in **"Malcolm Spoke/who listened?"** for merely

> wear[ing] yr/blackness in
> outer garments
> & blk/slogans fr/the top 10.
> ....
> u are playing that
> high-yellow game in blackface
> minus the straighthair.

At once mouthing Black slogans in the daytime and sleeping "with undercover whi/te girls" at night, these radicals, like their fellow Black "revolutionist[s]" who "often talked/ of the third world...." while making

> ...bonds
> with the
> 3rd world
> thru
> chinese women,

really contribute nothing positive to the revolutionary cause, asserts Lee.

Some Black leaders—in all fields—however, do remain steadfastly incorruptible. Among this number in the field of literature is Gwendolyn Brooks who, like Langston Hughes before her, always tells the truth about the Black experience. As a truth-teller, she is diametrically opposed to those Black literary "whores" who accept the White aesthetic and in doing so contribute to the

> mental genocide of blackpeople
> while
> he/she switches down the
> street with
> his/her ass wide-open bleeding
> whi-te blood

Lee's violent hatred of these Euro-Black "literary prostitutes" clearly reflected in this violent, purposely shocking image, is reiterated in his appeal to Black writers to "discover" and be guided by "black aesthetic stars that will damage the whiteminded," which appeal appears in

the final poem in this volume, **"A Message All Black-people Can Dig."**

Black musicians, like their fellow artists, Black writers, very frequently "sell out" to the White Establishment; thus, Lee laments that he is

> real sorry about
> the supremes
> being dead,

as he places the Supremes among the class of "realpeople" who are "becoming unpeople," due to their having begun

> singin
> rodgers & hart
> & some country & western

On the other hand, one of the musical heroes of the entire Black Nationalist Movement, John Coltrane, is given his due by Lee in the title-poem for this volume, **"Don't Cry, Scream,"** as Lee tries to capture, in the screaming beat of the poem itself, the characteristic wail of Coltrane's horn. Coltrane's greatness was that he "gave...truth"—and true images—to Black Americans, says Lee:

> he left man images
> he was a life-style of
> man-makers & annihilator
> of attaché case carriers

Coltrane, with his manly scream of self-assertion, is contrasted to Billie Holiday, one of the great ladies of the blues, by Lee, as he asserts; "(all the blues did was/make me cry)," whereas Coltrane, by replacing Billie's "illusions of manhood" with true "man images," made him "ascen[d] into: /scream-eeeeeeeeeeeeeee-ing." Lee's dismissal, here, of the blues as a nonviable form of Black (mental) protest (one much akin to nonviolent physical protest) almost parallels that made by his sister Black Nationalist, Sonia Sanchez, in her "liberation/ poem," when she asserts:

> when i hear billie's soft
> soul/ful/sighs
>   of "am I blue"
>   i say
> no. sweet/billie.
>   no mo.
> ....
> no. i'm blk/
>   & ready.

Once again the suggestion that violent actions are a necessary response to White aggression is fairly clear.

The significant role that the Black artist must play in the struggle for Black survival is emphasized again and again by Lee in **Don't Cry, Scream,** as he argues that one important end of "blackpoetry is...to negate the negative influences of the mass media." It is only as a result of the "anti-self" lessons which are daily perpetrated by the media upon Blacks that Black soldiers can be induced to kill other Third World peoples, argues Lee, for such unconscionable actions are really a part of a worldwide White genocide scheme; hence, in **"Hero"**

> little willie
> a hero in
> the american tradition,

after being traduced by White imperialists into killing Vietnamese "niggers," was finally killed by them; consequently,

> he
> received his medals
> p
> o
> s
> t
> h
> u
> m
> o
> u
> s
> l
> y
> .
> .
> .

Similarly in **"Nigerian Unity..."** "little niggers" fall right into the schemes of Whites by "killing [other] little niggers." On a more insidious level, unthinking non-Whites, worldwide, willfully "join the deathbringers club" (bringing death to future Third World peoples) when they subscribe to White-inspired "family-planning" schemes and decide that they "don't want more than two children." Such repeated cries of "genocide" (both "mental" and "physical") were characteristic of the Black nationalistic poetry of the late 1960s, and they served as grim precursors of Sam Yette's searching—and well-documented—exposé of what he considers a worldwide White Genocide scheme for doing away with "obsolete" Third World peoples.

The role of the Black poet in halting this worldwide genocide of non-Whites is rather clearly outlined by Lee in **Don't Cry, Scream,** where most of his aesthetic and social ideas seem to fully crystallize for the first time. The Black poet, according to Lee, has a twofold role in the worldwide struggle between what he terms "the unpeople" (White mind-distorters and body-annihilators of non-White peoples) and "the realpeople" (Blacks and other Third World peoples): (1) He must replace the mind-boggling (for Blacks) White aesthetic with a Black aesthetic. He must move away from an "arty" poetry like that advocated by Archibald MacLeish in "Ars Poetica"—a poetry that does not *mean* but merely *bes*—to a poetry whose "most significant factor... is the *idea.*" In fact, Lee argues, "most, if not all, blackpoetry will be *political*"; it "will continue to define what *is* and what *isn't.* Will tell what is *to be* and how to *be* it." Moreover, it will tell these things in "black language or Afro-american language in contrast to standard english, & c." (2) He must also (as Lee pointed out earlier in

Think Black!) function as a "culture stabilizer," and Lee does this more successfully than ever before in this third volume of poetry, as he repeatedly points out the pre-colonial qualities of Afrikan life which should serve as models for widely dispersed Afrikans today. Lee has, in fact, been doing both of these things, in his poetry, from the beginning. The real significance of his stated poetic credo in **Don't Cry, Scream** is, then, not that it points a new direction for Lee, but that it reveals a new confidence on Lee's part that the course he has been following all along really *is* the "right" course for the modern Black poet to take.

Lee describes, in the final poem in this volume, what he *hopes* will be the future way of life for Black people: "we'll move together," he says,

> hands on weapons & families
> blending into the sun,
> into each/other.
> we'll love,
> we've always loved.
> just be cool & help one/another.
> go ahead

Lee's emphasis, here, on unity of purpose, on collective work and responsibility, and on mutual faith is quite similar to Karenga's emphasis on those same qualities in his *Kawaida* doctrine. Moreover, such a way of life as this clearly looks back to the traditional *ujamaa*-village lifestyle of pre-colonial Afrika where, according to Nyerere, there were three basic "principles of life": (1) mutual love, or respect, between all people, (2) shared wealth, or goods, and (3) shared work.

Both **"Black love"** (which Lee's sister Black Nationalist Nikki Giovanni refers to in "Nikki-Rosa" as "Black wealth") and the Black woman assume highly significant positions in this third volume of Lee's poetry. Black love is a unifying force among Black people, and the Black woman, unlike the Black man, has seldom "sold out" to the White Establishment, argues Lee again and again in most of the poems towards the end of this volume. As she watches her Black man stumbling, confusedly, through a White-controlled world, the Black woman waits, lovingly, for the "blackman [to return and] take her." Such "uncorrupted" (by White values and images) Black women are "the real blackgold," argues Lee, and only when their full value is both known to and asserted by Black men can Blacks resume their former position of leadership in the world; only then can

> blackpeople
> ...[move] to return
> this earth into the hands of
> human beings.

By the end of **Don't Cry, Scream,** then, Lee has assumed the stance of a poet/prophet for his people; he relentlessly urges them, through his repeated poetic "screams," through his repetitive, almost incantatory, demands, to CHANGE. For this reason, if any one poem in the volume might be seen as a kind of epitome of the entire volume, it would surely be **"a poem to complement other** poems." Lee appeals here to all "niggers"—hippies, liberals, and conservatives alike—to "change nigger. / . . . change. i say change into a realblack righteous aim." Each "nigger" *must* "change, into a necessary black-self," for only by "chang[ing],/[by] know[ing] the realenemy," can "niggers" survive in an essentially European-controlled world. Moreover, Lee asserts, as "nigger[s] change. / . . . be[coming] the realpeople. / . . . . black-poems / will change," too.

The truth of this last statement is seen in the poetry of Lee himself. Lee is, indeed, by the time he writes *Don't Cry, Scream,* what Gwendolyn Brooks calls him in her introduction to that volume: "a positive prophet, a prophet not afraid to be positive even though aware of a daily evolving, of his own sober and firm churning." Seen in terms of Fanon's three "stages" of revolutionary writing, Lee has achieved the final, or "revolutionary," plateau in *Don't Cry, Scream:* he is intent on "shak[ing] the people" in this volume; he has "turn[ed] himself into an awakener of the people; hence comes a fighting literature, a revolutionary literature, and a national literature."

Lee's new assurance is even more clearly reflected in his fourth volume of poetry, *We Walk the Way of the New World,* which differs primarily from his third volume not in *content* (i.e., ideas) but in *form* (i.e., the way in which the ideas are put together). There are, in fact, essentially no "new" *ideas* in this volume. Lee is still functioning as a poet/prophet who advocates CHANGE. He is still pursuing his own multi-faceted role as establisher, and entrencher, of both a Black aesthetic and an Afrikan frame of reference. He also continues to reassert the contemporary validity/functionality of certain pre-colonial (Afrikan) cultural values. Moreover, the final "goal" towards which Lee aims the poems in this fourth volume is still the making of the earth into a *people*-centered place. And all of these ideas had surfaced earlier in Lee's poetry—at least by the time of *Don't Cry, Scream.* The essential difference between Lee's third and fourth volumes, then, is not one of *kind;* rather, it is a difference of *degree.* *Don't Cry, Scream* might almost be seen as a kind of *improvisational* volume, in which Lee presents his various themes (many by now quite familiar)—and even plays variations on these themes—in a somewhat haphazard manner. That is, there is little structural unity in *Don't Cry, Scream.*

Dust jacket of Madhubuti's 1968 collection of poetry.

Lee is following no particular "program" in his arrangement of the poems in that third volume.

Just the opposite is true, however, of Lee's fourth volume; here the poems—at least the larger groupings of poems—are very carefully arranged, for Lee has his final goal firmly in mind from the outset. Accordingly, in the introduction Lee briefly discusses the book's tripartite structure: "The new book is in three parts," he says:

> *Black Woman Poems, African Poems,* and *New World Poems.* Each part is a part of the other: Blackwoman is African and Africa is Blackwoman and they both represent the *New World.*

Moreover, Lee asserts that "the whole book is based upon the direction I feel blackman should be traveling." In this last statement lies what seems to be the real key to the tight structural unity of *We Walk the Way of the New World;* for this entire fourth volume may be considered as a kind of symphonic poem (or perhaps "fugue" would be a more appropriate term), in which the introduction functions as a prelude to the three main movements. There are, in fact, a great many similarities between this fourth volume by Don Lee and the much shorter (and much more clearly orchestrated) "Dark Symphony" by Melvin B. Tolson.

In the single poem that appears in the introductory section of *We Walk the Way of the New World,* **"Blackman/ an unfinished history,"** Lee introduces "blackman," who is, essentially, the main character in the ensuing world drama. In this introductory poem, Lee summarizes, in brief, the history of the Black man in the United States. Black men were already losing touch with their Afrikan heritage, argues Lee, even when they (most of them) were still in the South. After they took "the trip north / or up south ... [and] entered the cities," however, their alienation from their essential Afrikanness became even greater; they became

> ...a part of the pot that was supposed to melt it
> did and we burned
> and we burned into something different & un-
>   known we acquired a new ethic a new morality
>   a new history and we lost
> we lost much we lost that that was
> we became americans ...
> ....
> our minds wouldn't *function.*
> ....
> we took on the language, manners, mores, dress &
>   religion
> of the people with the unusual color

By attempting to assimilate into an alien culture, Black men became essentially "anti-self," argues Lee here (as he has so often before). Worse yet, because Black men accepted the European frame of reference advanced by the dominant Whites, their standards of beauty were affected: no longer was the "natural" Black woman an object for admiration; rather,

> we wished her something else,

> & she became that wish.
> she developed into what we wanted,
> she not only reflected *her,* but reflected us,
> was a mirror of our death-desires

Black *man,* then, is the real reason for Black woman's Black-self-denial, argues Lee (a point that he had only *suggested* in **Don't Cry, Scream**). Moreover, this self-denial by both Black men and Black women is the underlying cause of the fragmentary state of the Black community (and, by extension, the cause of the nonexistence of a real, functioning Pan-Afrikan community).

The remainder of this introductory poem outlines the "program" which blackman must follow if he is, indeed, to create a "New World" for future generations: first, he must assert, and take pride in, his own Blackness; second, he must instill in his Black woman and his daughters this same self-pride; third, he must focus his attention, his interest, and his desires within his own Black community, where he must strive to introduce, and to live by, a Black value system; hence, he must

> design yr own neighborhoods, Zoom it can be,
> teach yr own children, Zoom Zoom it can be,
> build yr own loop, Zoom Zoom it can be,
> feed yr own people, Zoom Zoom it can be,
>   ....
> protect yr own communities, Zoom Zoom it can
>   be;

fourth, he must finally expand his interest, moving from just the local community to include the world scene. If blackman does these things, Lee argues,

> ... world greatness is coming, click click.
>   ....
> Go head, *universe,*
> Zoommmmmmmm. Zooommmmmmmm
> Zoooommmmmmmmmmmm click click.
> be it,
> blackman

And blackman, filled with new confidence, presumably moves off—charging, zooming toward future greatness. In the next three parts of this volume (or, movements of the larger symphonic poem), Lee shows his readers just what blackman experiences as he attempts to "walk the way of the new world," where he first encounters Black woman, then tries to reassemble an essentially Afrikan value system, and finally works to create a new, clean, people-oriented world.

In the first movement, "Blackwoman Poems," Lee presents a rather complex Black woman who is at once "soft," "hard," "warm," and "sure." In the several love poems that appear in this section, Lee emphasizes the softness, the warmth, and the beauty of the "natural" Black woman, whose love is so sure that she remains true even "After her Man had left her / for the Sixth time that year." These usually young Black women/lovers are complemented by older Black women, who are both hard (i.e., "durable," or "tough") and wise—like **"Big Momma."** Thus, blackman encounters several Black women who, like the Black heroines of **Don't Cry,**

Scream, are already on the "right track"; in fact, in **"Blackgirl Learning,"** "Blackgirl," who writes (people-concerned) love verse that is reminiscent of "gwendolyn brooks & margaret walker," asserts that, although her Black man

> worshiped her,
> he wasn't there.
> . . . he had other things to do:
> learning to walk straight

Presumably, she already can.

Not all Black women are "positive" role-models, however, and Lee contrasts his healthy, "natural" Black women with unnatural, self-denying, middle-class "negro" "sisters in two hundred dollar wigs and suits." Similarly, in **"On Seeing Diana go Maddddddddd,"** Lee examines Diana Ross, a "negro" entertainer who has succumbed to what Lee sees as the essentially White "personal success syndrome." Diana does "the monkey" (a dance) "with authority," says Lee ironically; then he goes on to depict how she imitates Whites both by denying her physical self—by wearing false eyelashes and a wig—and by completely dissociating herself from the Black community—by caring for *dogs* more than she does for people and by considering her own "bent ego" above all else. Through her total acceptance of the alien European frame of reference, Diana Ross has, Lee argues, "become the symbol of a new aberration, / . . . . [she has] become one of the real animals of this earth." That Don Lee laments the loss of such previously Black, but now "negro," women as Diana Ross is made clear through his use of the refrain from one of Diana Ross's popular songs; Lee (and, presumably, his world-travelling blackman) would draw such wanderers as Diana Ross back to their Blackness "in the name of love"—for, upon the base of Black love rests the foundation of the developing Black community.

Lee's blackman moves on to Afrika, to better consider just what functional pre-colonial Black values ought to be reintroduced into the modern Black community, in the second (and quite brief) movement of Lee's symphony, "African Poems." Here again, Lee (like both Sékou Touré in Guinea and Julius Nyerere in Tanzania) asserts the importance of rural Afrika's maintaining her essentially communal way of life and not allowing herself to fall victim to Western industrialization. Speaking directly to "Africa" in **"Change is Not Always Progress,"** Lee says:

> don't let them
> steal
> your face.

That is, don't allow your essential (rural) nature to be distorted, thus making you into an industrialized, steel giant who

> arrogantly
> scrape[s]
> the

sky

This message, if heeded by blackman (whose present habitat is the United States), could have considerable importance for the relatively "undeveloped" states of the United States.

A further attack on the causers of environmental ills like those that are presently afflicting the United States occurs in **"A Poem for a Poet."** Here Whites, motivated by egotism, hypocrisy, and self-interest, consume great portions of the world's natural resources; and, Lee warns, "the waste from their greed/ will darken your sun and hide your moon, will dirty your grass and mis-use your water." Life in an *ujamaa*-community would, of course, be far more free of environmental "blight" than industrialized areas are; so, Lee further asserts that:

> you must eat yr/ own food
> and that which is left,
> continue to share in earnest

Self-interest and egotism do not, however, affect only Whites, and blackman, in his brief Afrikan travels, meets a fellow Black from America, Ted Joans, who seems to be a victim of these same "aberrations." Joans, who considers himself "a worldman./ a man of his world" (in **"Knocking Donkey Fleas off a Poet from the Southside of Chi"**), wanders through Afrika "looking for a piece" (a "piece of tail," or a homeland, or a sense of identity—or all three?), asserting that "blacks must colonize europe," and making egotistical boasts of "I did, I was, I am." Joans, here an example of a continent-jumping "super-cool" radical (much like those domestic "hipsters" that were attacked so vehemently by Lee in **Don't Cry, Scream**), will only "find" his "piece" (that is, his "peace"), says Lee, somewhat ironically:

> . . . (in the only place he hasn't been)
>
> among the stars,   that star.
> the one that's missing [i.e., his essential
> Blackness].

For all his "hipness," Ted Joans is really too caught up with "the rest of the world" to make a meaningful contribution to Pan-Afrikanism. Blackman should beware of him, suggests Lee, for the egotistical Joans seems to be far too much like Diana Ross; that is, he functions from a European—not an Afrikan—frame of reference; he is essentially "unBlack."

Having left the geographical limits of Afrika behind him and, presumably, both accompanied by Black woman and armed with a functional Black value system, blackman, in the final movement of *We Walk the Way of the New World,* moves to create, first within the physical boundaries of the United States, that new people-centered community which Lee directed him towards in "Blackman/an unfinished history." This final section reemphasizes the importance of CHANGE—but only that change which is in the right direction, not change just for the sake of change. The importance of the Black community as a social, cultural force is again emphasized, and in **"One Sided Shoot-out,"** Lee reiterates the idea that revolutionary *words* are useless; only united (i.e., community-wide) revolutionary *actions* will finally prevail over the unpeople and give meaning to Black people's lives.

Although there is a "negative" voice in this final movement (as there has been in each of the others), most of the poems here are extremely "positive." In fact, the two most significant poems in this final section—**"For Black People"** and the title-poem, **"We Walk the Way of the New World"**—echo the same movement that blackman has been taking in the course of the entire volume. In each of these poems, however, blackman has been replaced, as hero, by Black men (and Black women and Black children). That is, the entire Black race is depicted, in each of these poems, as moving from a state of inactivity (accommodation within, or acceptance of, a White-controlled [and essentially "unclean"] world), through a period of reaction, or protest against that world, and finally into a period of positive action, of self-assertion.

Consequently, **"For Black People"** is divided by Lee into three distinct sections: "In the Beginning," "Transition and Middle Passage," and "The End Is the Real World." In "In the Beginning," Black people are forced into ghettoes within the United States, and they are effectively kept positive-imageless by the White Establishment's various stratagems: "catholic churches," "bars, taverns and houses/of prostitution," and "up-ward bound programs." Black women are being forced to prostitute themselves to Jewish landlords in order to buy groceries, and Black men couldn't care less—for their minds have been confused with images of White women. Mis-educated "negroes" (who have been educated by European teachers and textbooks) are operating completely according to a White value system; as a result, they know mainly "how to be negroes and homosexuals." This is a blighted, polluted world, and the condition of Black people here is the condition that blackman was in at the beginning of Lee's volume; it is also the condition that Fanon described, earlier, as "the period of unqualified assimilation" into the alien culture. Moreover, this condition was, as demonstrated earlier, precisely the "inarticulate" condition that Don Lee himself was apparently in before he wrote *Think Black!*

In "Transition and Middle Passage," Black people begin to react to the situation in which they find themselves. They begin to reject White values and images and "to believe in themselves"; hence, they replace White heroes with Black ones and read Black writers instead of White ones. Many "negroes" become Black again, and Blacks move to take control of their own communities. Acting together, the Black community moves to drive out (or kill) pimps, dope pushers, and other "undesirables." At this stage, "Amiri Baraka wrote the words to the blk/national anthem & pharoah sanders composed the music. tauhid became our war song." This period of reaction, in which the awakening of Black people occurs,

corresponds at once to blackman's similar awakening, to Fanon's second phase of revolutionary action, and to Lee's own psychological position at the time he wrote *Think Black!* and *Black Pride.*

In "The End Is the Real World," Black people have begun *acting* (positively), not just *reacting* (negatively). They have chosen to follow Allah (the Muslim Supreme Being) rather than Jesus Christ. They read works that are written in accordance with a Black (not a White) aesthetic, and they themselves operate from an Afrikan (not a European) frame of reference. A socialistic economy based on mutual love and respect prevails, and people share both goods and work responsibility. The world has become a clean, peaceful place for people of all colors (although the "few whi-te communities . . . were closely watched"). This (rather idyllic) world is the world that blackman is trying to structure at the end of *We Walk the Way of the New World.* It is also the world that Don Lee (having attained Fanon's "revolutionary phase" as a writer) himself has been trying to bring into reality through the revolutionary volumes *Don't Cry, Scream* and *We Walk the Way of the New World.*

The program of action that Lee has been advocating throughout *We Walk the Way of the New World*—in fact, throughout his career as a poet—is, then, quite clearly operative in **"For Black People."** This program of action just as clearly provides the framework for the title-poem in this volume, **"We Walk the Way of the New World,"** where Black people move from accommodation or inaction ("run[ning] the dangercourse") through reaction (having "[run] the dangercourse") and finally into action in "the New World." Both of these poems, in addition to the final **"Move Un-noticed to be Noticed: A Nationhood Poem,"** have a scope, a sweep, an air of victory about them that is reminiscent of the final (and much briefer) section of Tolson's "Dark Symphony." The tone of these poems in particular, and of the whole "New World Poems" section in general, is one that would best be rendered, musically, in *tempo di marcia.* For *We Walk the Way of the New World* emerges as a "victorious" volume: here Lee presents the message he has been preaching all along, but he preaches it more coherently and effectively than ever before.

This fourth volume of poetry marks, then, the culmination of Lee's poetic career: he early set himself a goal, and he has reached it here by effectively using "the past . . . [in order to open] the future, as an invitation to action and a basis for hope." Not content merely to leave "the sometimes seemingly disjointed fragments of the black experience strewn carelessly about," Lee "makes them wholes, integrating them into some kind of meaning, into a historical and cultural context" [Paula Giddings; see Further Reading]. With this volume, Lee has become a "revolutionary" Black poet in the fullest sense of that term:

> He is an African in America, knowledgeable of his history and culture, who loves his people and who is determined to fight for their survival as a nation. He

is outside of American morality, history, and culture and, in so being, he is one who . . . "walks the way of the new world," and charts a righteous path for Black people who follow him. [Addison Gayle, Jr. in *The Politics of Revolution,* 1972].

Through the program advanced in this fourth volume, Lee has truly become what Hoyt W. Fuller, in the "Dedication" to *Journey to Africa,* calls him: "One of the shapers of the Black Tomorrow."

Apparently fully conscious of his important position as **"A Strong New Voice Pointing the Way"** to a **"New World,"** Lee collected most of the poems from these first four volumes, added five new poems, and in 1971 came out with *Directionscore: Selected and New Poems,* a volume intended, as its title suggests, to provide positive *direction* for Black people throughout the diaspora. Lee's intent in this volume is praiseworthy: he would direct Black people to better life by providing them with a kind of poetic score which shows the various roles to be filled by Black world-shapers.

Because Lee's intention in *Directionscore* was to provide *positive* direction, he carefully culled most of the negative poems that had appeared in his first two volumes. Thus, seven poems were deleted from the *Think Black!* section, and another seven were culled from *Black Pride. Don't Cry, Scream* lost only one poem, however; and *We Walk the Way of the New World* was presented intact. Instead of taking the time to reorder these early poems into some new "pattern," Lee merely arranged this fifth volume chronologically—a schema which not only saved him time in assembling the volume but also provided his readers with some key to Lee's own growth and development from 1966 to 1971.

Lee takes no new stance in the few poems that appear for the first time here. **"Positives: for Sterling Plumpp"** reemphasizes the importance of positive "visions of yr self" (or Black people) and stresses that Black poets must "run the mirror of ugliness into its inventors." A direct attack on hypocritical, brutal Whites appears in **"With All Deliberate Speed,"** and the need for Black unity and cooperation is stressed in both **"To Be Quicker"** and **"Mwilu/or Poem for the Living."** Gwendolyn Brooks, who has long been Lee's primary poetess-heroine, is lauded in **"An Afterword: for Gwen Brooks."**

The title of this fifth volume is, then, a little misleading; although there was some "selection" done in assembling the volume, there are only five "new" works included. And these "new" works do not break new ground. *Directionscore* makes it seem that unless Lee were to significantly alter his socio-politico-aesthetic principles, about all he could do—as a poet—would be to keep writing analogous versions of the same program. And repetition has, all along, been one of Lee's major weaknesses. In fact, the frequent repetitiveness of Lee's poetry (and of Black revolutionary poetry in general) has led critic Arthur P. Davis, a rather conservative professor of Black literature at Howard University, to complain that "too much of this hate poetry is repeti-

tive, mouthing over and over again the same revolutionary slogans and themes." Even Dudley Randall, the more radical editor of Broadside Press, has questioned the value of the endless repetition that one finds in Black revolutionary poetry: "One word or phrase chanted over and over with different voices and different intonations may sound exciting when heard, but is it poetry?"

The charge of repetitiveness in Lee's poetry can easily be substantiated (as this essay makes clear), but at least *some* of Lee's repetitiveness may become more "acceptable" when the reader remembers that: (1) Lee's poetry is, above all else, exhortative, and (2) people can better be moved to virtuous action if they hear reiterated just exactly *what* "virtuous action(s)" they are to perform. But it seems that even Lee himself sensed that he was falling into redundancy by the time he had completed *We Walk the Way of the New World;* hence, after that volume, he turned his attention largely away from the writing of poetry and towards both the criticism of other modern Black poetry and the writing of social essays. (pp. 9-42)

> *Marlene Mosher, in her* New Directions from Don L. Lee, *Exposition Press, 1975, 148 p.*

Paula Giddings (essay date 1990)

[*In the following essay, Giddings briefly introduces Madhubuti's most recent work,* Black Men: Obsolete, Single, Dangerous? (The Afrikan American Family in Transition).]

"What does a Black man do when he can't support his family?" asked Haki R. Madhubuti, the Chicago-based writer who is the director of the Institute of Positive Education and publisher and editor of Third World Press.

For Haki, who is married and a father of three sons and three daughters, the question was not rhetorical. After publishing *Enemies: The Clash of Races* in 1978—a penetrating analysis of racism on the part of the white left as well as the right—Madhubuti was "whitelisted," and avenues of income were effectively shut off.

"It was necessary to create my own options," he recalled, and that experience made him think about writing a book of essays with analyses, solutions and guidance about family relationships and responsibilities. The result is the recently published *Black Men: Obsolete, Single, Dangerous? (The Afrikan American Family in Transition)* (Third World Press). The essays range from **"Black Manhood: Toward a Definition"** and **"AIDS: The Purposeful Destruction of the Black World"** to **"The Five Most Often Used Excuses Black Men Give Black Women"** and **"What's a Daddy? Fathering and Marriage."**

The book's first printing of 7,500 sold out within four weeks. "There hasn't been such a strong reaction to any of my books since **Don't Cry, Scream** [1969]," Madhubuti says. "The truth of the matter is that the brothers don't listen to sisters about these things," he observes. "But since my teachers were always women, I talk to men as women have talked to me."

The 48-year-old activist, a professor of English at Chicago State University, talks urgently about the need to "deal with ideas, analyze our situation and get rid of false definitions of what men and women are supposed to do." Most poignant, however, is his urging us to confront the fact that Black men often act in certain ways because "we're scared, and don't control anything."

But, he adds, "fear shouldn't stop us from reaching our vision or our dreams. Our relationships have got to get better. Racism cannot be an excuse for walking away from them."

Paula Giddings, "Haki Madhubuti: A Guide for Black Men," in Essence, *Vol. 21, No. 2, June, 1990, p. 44.*

FURTHER READING

Giddings, Paula. "From a Black Perspective: The Poetry of Don L. Lee." In *Amistad 2,* edited by John A. Williams and Charles F. Harris, pp. 297-316. New York: Random House, 1971.
    Discusses Madhubuti's growth as a poet.

Llorens, David. "Don Lee." *Ebony* XXIV, No. 5 (March 1969): 72-8, 80.
    Critically examines Madhubuti's life and works, noting: "With monk-like singlemindedness and extraordinary passion Don L. Lee casts an unsparing eye on the events of our times.... Don Lee has no energy for crying in appeal to the conscience of the white world. He is a screaming, urgent appeal to the reason of dark victims everywhere."

Melhem, D. H. "Interview with Haki R. Madhubuti." In his *Heroism in the New Black Poetry,* pp. 101-30. Lexington: The University Press of Kentucky, 1990.
    Interview with Madhubuti. Melhem and Madhubuti discuss black poetry and the author's most recent works: *Book of Life* and *Earthquakes and Sun Rise Missions.*

Miller, Eugene E. "Some Black Thoughts on Don L. Lee's *Think Black!* Thunk by a Frustrated White Academic Thinker." *College English* 34, No. 8 (May 1973): 1094-1102.
    Negative assessment of *Think Black!* The critic wonders: "What does one say critically about a collection of Don Lee's poems? Or how does one teach it?... If the teacher and the class are black, perhaps they need not discuss the poem at all.... But what if only the teacher, or the class, or neither, is black?"

Palmer, Roderick R. "The Poetry of Three Revolutionists: Don L. Lee, Sonia Sanchez, Nikki Giovanni." *CLA Journal* XV, No. 1 (September 1971): 25-36.
    Thematic discussion of *Don't Cry, Scream.*

Redding, Saunders. "The Black Arts Movement in Negro Poetry." *American Scholar* 42, No. 2 (Spring 1973): 32, 34, 36.
    Examines poets of the Black Arts Movement, briefly mentioning Madhubuti as "the shrillest of the new black poets."

Shands, Annette Oliver. "The Relevancy of Don L. Lee as a Contemporary Black Poet." *Black World* XXI, No. 8 (June 1972): 35-48.
    Reviews *We Walk the Way of the New World,* focusing on theme, imagery, and symbolism. The critic writes: "[Lee] demands that the Black poet, in a mutual alliance with Black people, interchange, formulate, communicate, possess, and strengthen values *apart from* and completely *unrelated to* the white American society."

West, Hollie I. "The Black Bard of Revolution." *Washington Post* 26 (December 1971): F1, F6-7.
    Assesses Madhubuti's impact on the black community.

Clarence Major

1936-

American novelist, poet, critic, editor, essayist, and short story writer.

A leading figure in contemporary black literature, Major is considered a pioneer in the field of American experimental fiction. His works—characterized by self-reflexive narratives and authorial intrusions—focus on the nature of fiction and reality. Using vivid imagery and disjointed assemblages of fiction, commentary, and allusions to popular culture, he explores the relationship between author, reader, and text. He is best known for *All-Night Visitors* (1969), *No* (1973), *Reflex and Bone Structure* (1975), and *Emergency Exit* (1979), novels about young black men who struggle for self-definition in a hostile society. In these works Major blurred the line between the fictive world of the story and the "real" world; in *Emergency Exit,* for example, the author wrote, "My favorite character in this whole book [Deborah Ingram] has become my lover." Major's innovative style prompted Joe Weixlmann to declare: "[Major] has pioneered a new direction for black American fiction, expressing his psychological, racial, and social concerns within a metafictional framework that leads his readers to explore, with him, the very nature of fictive discourse."

Major was born in 1936 in Atlanta, Georgia, and raised in Chicago, Illinois. Although his mother and father divorced when he was a boy, he maintained a warm and close relationship with both of his parents, sometimes spending the summer months with his father in the South. Major's desire to become a writer began while he was still in grade school. In "Necessary Distance: Afterthoughts on Becoming a Writer," an essay published in *Black American Literature Forum,* Major explained: "I think I was in the fifth grade when a girl who sat behind me snuck a copy of Raymond Radiguet's *Devil in the Flesh* to me. This was *adult fiction!* And judging from the cover, the book was going to have some *good* parts. But as it turned out the *single* good part was *the writing itself.* I was reading that book one day at home, and about halfway through, I stood up and went crazy with an important discovery: *Writing had a life of its own!* And I soon fell in love with the *life* of writing...." Shortly after this "discovery," Major read avidly, diving into the works of Richard Wright, Chester Himes, Ernest Hemingway, and William Faulkner. At the age of eighteen he published his first collection of poetry, *The Fires That Burn in Heaven* (1954), a book he now describes as "very, very bad poetry." Major joined the United States Air Force in 1955 and continued writing poetry and short stories. After a two-year military service he accepted a scholarship to study painting at the Art Institute of Chicago. "I think my experience with painting, the way that I learned to see

the physical world of lines, color, and composition," Major recalled, "definitely influenced my writing." In the mid-1960s, however, he decided to focus on his writing career and moved to New York City, where he wrote more poetry and several novels. His poetry has been collected in *Love Poems of a Black Man* (1965), *The Syncopated Cakewalk* (1974), and *Inside Diameter: The France Poems* (1985). Major's numerous nonfiction works include *Dictionary of Afro-American Slang* (1970) and *The Dark and Feeling: Black American Writers and Their Work* (1974), a collection of essays on black literature. His most recent publications are the book-length poem *Some Observations of a Stranger at Zuni in the Latter Part of the Century* (1989) and a volume of short stories, *Fun and Games* (1989). Major is currently at work on another novel and teaches at the University of Colorado.

While critics praise Major's poetry, short stories, and nonfiction work, his reputation as a writer rests solidly on his novels. His most popular novels focus on the interaction between language, fiction, and reality. *All-Night Visitors* is the story of Eli Bolton, a "sexual voyager," according to one critic, who searches for self-identity and a sense of manhood through his relationships with women. *No,* Major's next work, "moves beyond the first novel in insisting that the self is a phenomenon of language and the imagination rather than of actual experience, time, and place," noted John O'Brien. In *No* Moses Westby's chaotic search for self is reflected in the structure of the novel: past and present merge, fantasy and reality intermingle, points of view shift, and identities blur (Moses is alternately called Boy, Junebug, and Nat Turnips). In addition, "the printed page is manipulated through such devices as the use of indentation, irregular spacing within and between lines, italics, capitalization, a variety of type fonts, and hand-drawn words and emblems," Weixlmann observed.

Most critics consider Major's next two novels, *Reflex and Bone Structure* and *Emergency Exit,* the author's most accomplished works of fiction. In the former Major deliberately subverted the conventions of the detective novel by refusing to reveal the killer's identity. Nevertheless, readers realize at the book's end that Cora and her lover were killed by the narrator. Weixlmann explained: "...the narrator 'killed' them, [but] he did so only in his role as narrator, as the controller of the book's events: 'Dale gives Cora a hand. At the edge of the desert they step into a city. They step into a house. It explodes. It is a [literary] device. I am responsible. I set the device'." Klinkowitz added: "Major slips deliberately surreal images into otherwise realistic scenes (a rubber plant dries the dishes, the TV slushes back and forth), reminding the reader that for all the comfortable associations with reality this is still an artificially constructed work." Major himself maintained that fiction creates its own reality; instead of trying to mirror life, his work urges readers to question conceived notions of truth and "real-ness." His next novel, *Emergency Exit,* further blurs the line between fiction and reality; at one point in the story, the author even asks, "Well, dear reader, how do you feel about it?" Interweaving a traditional love-triangle story with surreal episodes consisting of fantasy, anecdotes, dreams, and poems, *Emergency Exit* also includes real incidents from Major's life and actual news reports. "As in *Reflex,*" a critic noted, "images are culled from American popular culture—movies, records, and folk mores....A mood emerges from them quite independently of the narrative story line, and as a result that story line becomes less important to the reader. Attention has been focused on the writing and the words."

With *All-Night Visitors, No, Reflex and Bone Structure,* and *Emergency Exit,* Major is credited with charting a new course in American fiction. "Major's innovations have made a fully nonrepresentational fiction possible," Klinkowitz concluded in *The Practice of Fiction in America.* "Such a radical aesthetic makes for an entirely new kind of fiction...." More importantly, this type of fiction liberates its readers, according to Doug Bolling:

"[Major's] way and that of other postmodern writers can help us realize all over again that the activity of 'reading' is a highly conditioned one, too often a matter of the learned response rather than an engagement of the free and open mind. Thus, time spent with the fictions can be both a trip into the richness and surprise of words and their relationships and a way of redefining the self...the reader of Major's fiction finds that he must himself take part in the creation of the work and that in doing so he experiences a pleasurable liberation...."

(For further information about Major's life and works, see *Black Writers; Contemporary Authors,* Vols. 21-24; *Contemporary Authors Autobiography Series,* Vol. 6; *Contemporary Authors New Revision Series,* Vols. 13, 25; *Contemporary Literary Criticism,* Vols. 3, 19, 48; and *Dictionary of Literary Biography,* Vol. 33: *Afro-American Fiction Writers after 1955.*)

PRINCIPAL WORKS

The Fires That Burn in Heaven (poetry) 1954
Love Poems of a Black Man (poetry) 1965
Human Juices (poetry) 1966
Man Is Like a Child: An Anthology of Creative Writing by Students [editor] (anthology) 1968
All-Night Visitors (novel) 1969
The New Black Poetry [editor] (anthology) 1969
Dictionary of Afro-American Slang (nonfiction) 1970; also published as *Black Slang: A Dictionary of Afro-American Talk,* 1971
Swallow the Lake (poetry) 1970
Private Line (poetry) 1971
Symptoms and Madness (poetry) 1971
The Cotton Club: New Poems (poetry) 1972
No (novel) 1973
The Dark and Feeling: Black American Writers and Their Work (essays) 1974
The Syncopated Cakewalk (poetry) 1974
Reflex and Bone Structure (novel) 1975
Emergency Exit (novel) 1979
The Other Side of the Wall (poetry) 1982
Inside Diameter: The France Poems (poetry) 1985
My Amputations: A Novel (novel) 1986
Such Was the Season: A Novel (novel) 1987
Painted Turtle: Woman with Guitar (novel) 1988
Surfaces and Masks (poetry) 1988
Fun and Games (short stories) 1989
Some Observations of a Stranger at Zuni in the Latter Part of the Century (poetry) 1989

Eugene B. Redmond (essay date 1975)

[*In the following excerpt, Redmond reviews* The Cotton Club, *describing it as an "economic [work] almost to the point of emaciation."*]

[Clarence Major] has been in the forefront of experimental poetry and prose. In prose he fits "loosely" into a category with William Melvin Kelley and Ishmael Reed. But his influences and antecedents in poetry are not so easy to identify. He is usually very competent as a writer, and he has written better poetry than *The Cotton Club* (see *Swallow the Lake* and *Symptoms and Madness*), which is economic almost to the point of emaciation. His subject matter is "vital," as Gwendolyn Brooks might put it . . . . [Major] is aware of the need to preserve and present a Black past . . . . [In *The Cotton Club*] Major conducts narrative tours of Harlem and urban Black America, primarily during the first two or three decades of the Twentieth Century . . . . [There] is a tapestry-of-a-poem (one of the best in the book: **"Madman of the Uncharmed Debris of the South Side"**) in which Major employs obscure references, a suggestion of the supernatural, tidbits of history, and other erudite meanderings. The poem contains a Gwendolyn Brooks-like economy which is where any resemblance between these two poets stops. (pp. 162-63)

Many of the themes that recur in the literature and conversation about these times (the mulatto, violence against Blacks, the creation and development of jazz and blues, etc.) occupy space here . . . . The language in these poems is direct, sometimes almost unpoetic—reminiscent of the "listings" of Michael S. Harper—and maybe there is a move afoot to dispense with metaphor and simply be sparse. Too, one has some trouble identifying the personae. The speaker seems, alternately, to be an unlettered street denizen or itinerant observer. At other times he appears to be the poet himself, divided between two or more people in a dialogue. Major keeps it unclear until near the end of the book when he breaks through nicely with "importers" . . . . Last, the fine but unsettling poem that closes out the book (**"Personal and Sexual Freedom"**) would certainly not be taken with coffee at the offices of *Ms* or *Encore*. After an undecorated look at the pros and cons of Women's liberation, he tells the women to remember that in " . . . sailing/keep your helm up." We want to replace "helm" with "hem" or "hymn" or even "him"—to make the double *entendre* work. Major has written well in the past and, being young, will write well again. His history work is important but he has not worked out the most effective way to present his ideas. We await *The Syncopated Cakewalk*. (pp. 163-64)

> Eugene B. Redmond, "Five Black Poets: History, Consciousness, Love, and Harshness," in Parnassus: Poetry in Review, Vol. 3, No. 2, 1975, pp. 153-72.

Doug Bolling (essay date 1979)

[*In the following excerpt, Bolling praises Major's short fiction, arguing that it is "valuable in its own right" and deserves wide readership.*]

Although to date the greatest strength of Clarence Major's achievement seems to lie in the novel—especially in *Reflex and Bone Structure*—, his short fiction is valuable in its own right and deserves wide reading and critical discussion. The stories complement the longer fictions in their range and interests, their explorations of new subject matter, forms, and implications, and their suggestion of a writer deeply involved both with his craft and the age. As with the novels so with the stories: There is an unevenness which lets the critic say that some of the pieces are stronger than others. Such a judgment is no doubt inevitable for any writer, but in Major's case it reflects more than anything else his commitment to innovation and experimentation in each of the short fictions. With such writers as Raymond Federman, Steve Katz, James Purdy, Ronald Sukenick, and others, Major stands clearly on the fictive frontier. And with all of these he pays a price for his engagement of the new and untried. No more than readers and literary critics can he tell us where he is going and what new discoveries he will make—that is the health and beauty of the kind of journey he is on. My guess is that, interesting and significant as the completed writings are, his best work lies ahead. In the meantime his fiction challenges us to articulate a criticism adequate to its special force and sense of presence rather than attempt to retreat behind traditional strictures and expectations. (p. 51)

For Major and a number of other writers now on the scene, traditional fiction fails to become its own reality because it is so largely a creature of a literalist mimetic on the one hand and the more or less uncritical voice of philosophical and cultural "meanings," values, and tropisms on the other. Both pressures must be resisted if the "deconstruction" process of the new fiction (and of other art forms) is to generate the kind of authenticity and autonomy under discussion . . . . Within the story itself we typically find that Major defies, breaks apart, or ignores the aesthetic of teleology, in which all "parts" point toward, imply, or subsist in an Aristotelian end or "whole." Rather than a concern for the "form" courted so strenuously by modernist writers and critics, we see that this fictionist works with "process," with open forms, with the inconclusive, and with the interplay of formal and nonformal tensions.

When he is at his best Major helps us to see that fiction created within an aesthetic of fluidity and denial of "closure" and verbal freedom can generate an excitement and awareness of great value; that the rigidities of plot, characterization, and illusioned depth can be softened and, finally, dropped in favor of new and valid rhythms. Spaces and times need no longer conform to the abstract demands either of plot or symbolic urgency, for example, but can be free to float in their own energies. Similarly what the textbooks sometimes still call "authorial intrusion" need not be construed as a felony or even a misdemeanor but rather as another manifestation of verbal energy and in fact as no "intrusion" at all. If some of the stories seem difficult or even incoherent to readers, it is because they are attempting to read by means of categories applicable to older fictional contexts but inadequate to the highly elliptical and at times improvisational way of Major's fiction. His way and that of other postmodern writers can help us realize all over again that the activity of "reading" is a highly conditioned one, too often a matter of the learned response rather than an engagement of the free and open mind. Thus, time spent with the fictions can be both a trip into the richness and surprise of words and their relationships and a way of redefining the self. In place of the hermetic quality with its correlative webbing of internally sustained ironies and symbols that one associates with modernist writing, the reader of Major's fiction finds that he must himself take part in the creation of the work and that in doing so he experiences a pleasurable liberation quite removed from the kind of response elicited by older fiction. In place of the glimpse into archetypal profundities often claimed—and justly so—for the latter, the reader of the new fiction experiences the relatively "informal" release of the creative and perhaps a sense of collaboration—communion even—with the writer. Because these are affirming and positive responses they may suggest, at least to whatever remains of the New Critical rear guard, that Major's work is shallow and lacking in seriousness. Such a view deserves no reply.... (pp. 51-2)

[Major's stories] reveal a writer of range, depth, and flexibility.... Clarence Major shows us how fiction may bring its strengths to bear on the confusions and compromises of American culture while at the same time preserving its integrity as an art form and its right to break through the conventions of the academy in order to create new and potent rhythms, shapes, and perceptions. The stories are "experimental" in two important senses of the term: In the first place they demonstrate how fragile and provincial many of our sacrosanct aesthetic norms were/are; in the second place they move beyond parody and "deconstruction" to create new modes and new fictional life. Importantly also the stories reveal a writer who is as sensitive to the claims of his craft as he is willing to try new forms on new subject matters. In the stronger stories, especially, we find a subtle concern for the right phrase and a sensitivity for spaces and silences which only a craftsman can have. Finally, it should be said that the sheer energy and range of the stories point again to the healthy and growing nature of prose fiction. Each story is unique; each is itself; each is a challenge to both the old and the new. (p. 56)

> *Doug Bolling, "A Reading of Clarence Major's Fiction," in* Black American Literature Forum, *Vol. 13, No. 2, Summer, 1979, pp. 51-6.*

Fanny Howe (essay date 1979)

[*In the following excerpt, Howe admires Major as a poet.*]

An intricate dance step, which becomes true style, is achieved in [**The Syncopated Cakewalk**].... Not only the style but also the content of these recent poems is different from those before. The timing is slower, history closer; the poems sound wonderful aloud.... A tone of sadness and a renunciation of a harsher view pervade this collection....

Major's early work, by a leap of the imagination, can be seen geometrically as a star, or asterisk. The center is hot, the edges are myriad and take off into many directions. In the more recent work, the geometrical vision is that of a cross—vertical and horizontal and austere. He views other people as a series of details (horizontal); their history, or the cakewalk, is horizontal too. But all these figures must pass through a central point, himself, the poet; and so a moral viewpoint which is vertical emerges. The presence of the writer is here, as witness. Morality is one symptom of sanity. The narrator, as witness, serves justice by seeing all sides of a matter....

[Major] has created a kind of code [by the way in which he uses language]. What is not stated is what the poem is about. But that's a secret. It is said that a poem should not seem, but be. The modern poem does not so much "be" as imply, by the use of sound and tone. Major's poetry has tone....

In the main, Major's poetry is never free of the tone of pain. Never sentimental, nor empty of humor, the poetry is still singed, burning.... And it is way down there, at that level of tone and mood, that the individual poet's voice remains linked to his history. While it is true that good art bests class, race, and economics, the effects of those three are still the tools used in the construction of good art. The absence of a historical memory is what accounts for the vacuity of much contemporary work. Without historical memory, questions of good and evil, guilt, and responsibility are meaningless.

Major, with his facility for poetic language, and his personal history, could have exploited both by fusing them into a slick and popular expression. What is honorable about his work is the unusual task it assumes, of welding a complex modern diction to a constant historical consciousness. There are not many writers, black or white, engaged in this struggle.... (p. 69)

> *Fanny Howe, "Clarence Major: Poet & Language Man," in* Black American Literature Forum, *Vol. 13, No. 2, Summer, 1979, pp. 68-9.*

Jerome Klinkowitz (essay date 1984)

[*In the following excerpt, Klinkowitz characterizes Major as a leading stylist whose novels "push fiction beyond a mechanical self-reflexiveness into true literary self-apparency."*]

Major is a leading stylist and innovator in the second wave of American experimentation. His first novel, **All-Night Visitors** (1969), challenged the emerging black culture of the earlier 1960s which had yet to merge its own aesthetics with the revolution going on within the mainstream culture's fiction. Major's second novel *No* (1973), likewise shows more of his own developing interests (especially in the lyricism of Jean Toomer and Gertrude Stein, innovators of a half-century earlier) than evidence of racial politics. His works of the mid- and late Seventies, *Reflex and Bone Structure* and *Emergency Exit,* employ a wide range of experimental techniques to push fiction beyond a mechanical self-reflexiveness into true literary self-apparency.

Reflex and Bone Structure reveals its own compositional process on every page, yet it still manages to tell a story replete with human fascination. As Tzvetan Todorov has remarked, of all fictive sub-genres it is the detective novel which "tends toward a purely geometric architecture," and it is that form which Major chose for his first experiment with self-apparency. In detective fiction, the subject matter of the plot has been concluded before the novel begins: The crime is an established fact, and now the author and reader must concentrate on its solution. In other words, the novel must compose itself not around the unfolding of a represented story but rather with the more epistemological business of sorting things out—mediating, as it were, between the a priori fact and the reader's appreciation of it. The text, therefore, assumes a reality of its own, as the reader's relationship to the author takes on the deeply realistic qualities of the detective's posture toward the crime. Narrative action is not something reported or even reflected; it is the existence of the book itself.

Yet *Reflex and Bone Structure* is more than a conventional detective novel, for every element of its composition—character, theme, action, and event—expresses the self-apparent nature of its making. Characterization is done through metaphors, emphasizing artifice to the point of allegory. Even events take on this supra-real quality....

Every element within Major's narrative is animated, sometimes by the characters and other times by the narrator himself.... Anthropologically speaking, there is no simple reality in this novel, only a plethora of cultural descriptions all competing for persuasive presence. An actress on TV is never just that; there is the role she's playing, the physical conditions of the production within which she works, plus the equally real life she may be living at that very moment in her apartment across town. Television, music, fantasies, and history— all conspire to create a larger reality which Major's writings dutifully embrace.... (pp. 203-04)

Within the narrative of the crime's detection (Cora has been murdered), Major treats us to the characters' own projective fantasies.... The narrator is prone to these same fantasies as well; indeed, the characters' fiction making is simply a microcosmic example of his own activity in creating this novel. Therefore he marshals these emotions to help construct *Reflex and Bone Structure.* His own feelings for Cora are ravaged by the jealousy he feels when pairing her with the other two males, Canada and Dale. His imagination sometimes runs to violence, picturing his characters in airplane crashes or explosions—as well he might, for he is after all writing the novel and enjoys a God-like power over his creations. Most importantly, he has his own voice in this fiction, convincing to the reader because it reveals his fully human plight in dealing with the emotions at hand.... On a more specific level, the narrator identifies problems he is having with his characters. Cora comes easily, for she is his obsession. Canada he respects, partly because this figure can wield the violent impulses which the narrator can only express in writing. But Dale, the necessary third point of this triangle, presents a problem. Throughout... this brief novel there are no less than seven references to this dilemma. "I have almost no sense of Dale except I know I don't like him," we are told, and soon the narrator sends him out to North Dakota so he can have some creative rest. "The fact that Dale really has little or no character doesn't help matters," he complains. "I cannot help him if he refuses to focus." There is even a bit of jealousy here, for "whatever it was about him that attracted Cora shall always remain a mystery to me." There is a temptation to punish this character, to run him through a series of embarrassing episodes, but in the end the narrator admits the key to the problem: "Dale was never meant to make it. He was that side of myself that should be rewritten. Dale was an argument I had with the past." Here once more a temptation of the life-seeking reader—that characters are projections of different facets of the author's own personality—is turned around to become a self-apparent component in the work itself.

Cora is indeed the narrator's obsession, and the male figures—Canada and Dale—have been the respectively positive and negative aspects of his own mania which blossom forth into fiction. The only unconventional aspect of all this has been Major's willingness to let the reader see behind the scenes and to incorporate this perspective into the making of his novel. There are many ways to approach Cora. "Canada tries too hard some times," we're told at the beginning. "He tries to crack into Cora. Burst into Cora. Open Cora with his sledge-hammer. But I weave *around* the stern cathedrals in her holy city, her very pure spirit." A world war can erupt over a person as a sex object, Major recalls, alluding to Troy and subsequent human disasters: *Reflex and Bone Structure* is an attempt to locate this energy within one narrator and show how it can create a novel just as well.

Throughout the novel Major makes integral references to the work at hand.... Major's travails as author are much like the fictive-making agonies of his characters within their various jealousies, fantasies, and paranoid reactions; because he establishes the identities among these acts and the correlative reality between his feelings and his characters', *Reflex* becomes a meaningful text for the reader—both as an adventure of its characters and of its author. Having alerted his readers to what's happening, Major can move his perception from character to character as the mood demands, so that "... I'm never alone. It is either Canada or Cora and sometimes Dale." At times they can become fictionists as well, as Canada "invents and reinvents the world as he wishes it to be." What is real for a character is just as real for the author, and vice versa; the text of **Reflex and Bone Structure** is essentially one thing, added to the world, rather than a representation of any one part.

At the heart of it all is the narrator's obsession with Cora.... The novel becomes his infatuation, his seduction, his recreation of her.... Once vitalized, Major can do what Beckett requested of Joyce, that his fictions not be about something but rather be something themselves.... Above all, as in a detective novel, the final truth is less important than the process of getting to it in its full implications. (pp. 204-07)

Emergency Exit [Major's next novel] is an even fuller work, just as any novel per se eclipses the effect of a subgenre in effect. In it Major focuses on every componential level of writing as a thing in itself, creating a virtual catalogue of self-apparent effects in fiction. Superintending the whole is an anthropological device around which the novel's action is based: the institution of a "threshold law" which requires all the women of a modern American town to be carried across doorways, a symbolic act based upon ancient tribal taboos regarding menstruation. "Stop: The doorway of life," Major's novel begins, and then immediately takes "this cliché" and revitalizes the dead metaphor with meaning. As Wittgenstein would suggest, it is all a problem with language, here expressed as a "male attitude toward the female" which because of fundamental confusions between signifier and signified leads to a misconstrued symbology:

> Because women are eternally guilty of sin they had to be lifted and carried across the threshold and they could not *touch* the doorway. Yet they, the givers of life itself, were the *source* of the symbolism and the ritual. They were the doorway of life.

A threshold law, then, is an originally transparent signifier which because of faulty syntax has become an opaque sign, a thing in itself, signifying nothing but its own dead language.

Major parallels his own act of writing with *Emergency Exit*'s theme, using each component in fiction, right down to the very words themselves, as opaque objects before incorporating them in the novel's larger syntax. In this manner words, sentences, paragraphs, vignettes, short stories, and the plot line itself are established as things in themselves before taking on their larger referential duties—and even then the reader's attention will be directed not off the page but back to it, where each word was first introduced as an artifact. (pp. 208-09)

"... in a novel, the only thing you really have is words," Major emphasized in his interview with John O'Brien. "You begin with words and you end with words. The content exists in our minds. I don't think that it has to

be a reflection of anything. It is a reality that has been created inside of a book." Therefore his strategy in *Emergency Exit* is to emphasize that every device of human interest (which critics of conventional fiction demand) is first of all a problem in language. His elementary notion of "threshold" is explored by studying every dictionary meaning of the word, from Webster's to dictionaries of symbols and indices of folklore. We are also given other documents reporting the word's effect on the community: the phone book, card files in the library, and arrests on the police blotter for its violation. As for the novel's action, it is established to be fist of all linguistic. Individual sentences are written on the page, apparently leading nowhere, so that the reader's attention is to their writerly art. (p. 210)

The plot itself is emphasized as artifice at every turn. As in **Reflex and Bone Structure,** Major makes frequent reference to his act of writing, even "employing gimmicks," and near the end begins an affair with a character whose liaisons have formed an interesting part of the story (and who has certainly been seducing the reader). Characters themselves are described in surreal terms, so that there is little chance to get lost in their verisimilitude.... (p. 211)

To forestall any attempt to receive Major's characters as real, yet to place his inventions within an even more sociologically precise category, he mixes in the self-apparent inventiveness of cartoon figures with the more ordinary actions of his plot.... (pp. 211-12)

On at least a dozen occasions Major refers to some ensuing action as "like a soap opera" or to a person as behaving "like a character in naturalistic fiction." Here again the effect is double, using a type of literary-historical shorthand which contributes to plot and characterization while at the same time noting that it is all arbitrary convention. At times Major can be a theorist as well, such as when his narrator remarks, "He could hear her going and coming. The process of her movements was like Gertrude Stein's fiction. She was in the continuous present"—an indication that aesthetics is just as much about life as it is of art. When someone is introduced as "a very realistic person," theory and practice coalesce, reminding us that choices in fictional theory are finally indices of personal value.... As all self-apparent fiction ultimately must do, *Emergency Exit* summons the full range of the reader's experience to complete the work, conventions being important not only for what they capsulize in fiction but also for the attitudes they bring from real life. It is all artifice, and knowing that yields a fuller reading. (pp. 212-13)

Emergency Exit, therefore, demonstrates how the familiar materials of novel-making can be used as things in themselves while still providing all the human interest readers demand. Indeed, self-apparent fiction compliments the reader by providing more to do. Major's novel summarizes in form the history of the last half-century of American art, from the building blocks of abstract expressionism through a certain pop iconography (once again, things from real life as themselves) to the experimental techniques of the superrealists. A regard for the material integrity of art's own making has been at the center of these developments, and with *Emergency Exit* Major shows us how they can be natural for fiction as well. In the face of such work, even realism becomes different, self-apparent in a way that it never was before, just as the radically new superrealism in painting grew from the principles of abstract expressionism. In this way the techniques of Major's fiction enrich the mainstream, creating a style of "experimental realism" in which the simple act of vision becomes not just an integral work of art but an interpretation of our cultural act of seeing as well. (pp. 213-14)

> *Jerome Klinkowitz, "The Self-Apparent Word: Clarence Major's Innovative Fiction," in* Studies in Black American Literature: Black American Prose Theory, Vol. 1, *edited by Joe Weixlmann and Chester J. Fontenot, The Penkevill Publishing Company, 1984, pp. 199-214.*

Richard Perry (essay date 1986)

[*In the excerpt below, Perry favorably reviews* My Amputations, *noting that the novel is "distinguished by a rich and imaginative prose poetry of evocative power."*]

My Amputations is a dense and complex work, as readers familiar with Clarence Major's four previous novels . . . might expect. A book in which the question of identity throbs, like an infected tooth. *My Amputations* is a picaresque novel that comes wailing out of the blues tradition: it is ironic, irreverent, sexy, on a first-name basis with the human condition, and defined in part by exaggeration and laughter.

Mason Ellis, the protagonist, is an endearing character who's gone through periods when, were it not for bad luck, he'd have had no luck at all. He is a writer whose muse has deserted him. His first marriage results in five children, for whom he and his wife have difficulty providing. Told by a welfare worker that the father's absence would mean larger checks for the family, the parents agree to split up . . . .

Early in the novel, Mason is in a Kafkaesque predicament. Serving a sentence in Attica for a crime he didn't commit, one day he sees on television an award ceremony during which a writer he is convinced is passing for him—but using an assumed name—accepts a prize meant for Mason.

Upon his release, Mason goes searching for the impostor, accompanied by acquaintances who include a pornographic film actress, an American Indian and a man named Jesus. He finds the impostor, kidnaps him and subjects him to tortures designed to extract a confession. But the man, Clarence McKay, won't break, and Mason, his certainty shaken, is suspended in a frustrating twilight zone—holding a man who he believes has stolen his identity and who won't (or can't) give it back. In a caper worthy of good adventure novels, Mason disposes of the impostor and creates an identity by appropriating the latter's assumed name (and cash award). He also complicates what by now has become his consuming question: who am I, really?

Is Mason suffering from delusions? Is he just another recidivist ex-con? These legitimate questions fade in the face of his obsession with who he is; all that matters for readers, as for him, is *his* question.

Possessing money and acclaim, but tormented by fear that he'll be exposed, Mason goes looking for an answer. His quest, like that of more than one American writer before him, takes him to Europe, where he encounters underworld thugs, neo-Nazis, literary groupies and several Greek citizens fond of antebellum Southern costume parties. Ultimately, Mason arrives in Africa, where he meets a Liberian tribesman who holds an envelope in which, apparently, the secret of Mason's true identity is enclosed.

Mr. Major has said that one of his objectives in writing is to "attempt to break down the artificial distinctions between poetry and fiction." *My Amputations* is distinguished by a rich and imaginative prose poetry of evocative power. Sometimes the effect is spectacular, like the eruption of fireworks against a dark, featureless sky . . . . At other times the language is a distraction that calls attention to itself and delays the unfolding of a story I want very much to continue reading.

One of the most provocative aspects of *My Amputations* is Mr. Major's third-person narrator. Street-smart, versed in the blues, jazz, literature, art, European classical music and philosophy, this narrator is familiar with the cultural signposts of Western civilization. Not only is he hip and learned, he is brash, often injecting himself into the novel by commenting on the action or blurring what small distinctions exist between reality and dream. He strikes me as a voice who knows who he is, an ironic and sometimes disconcerting counterpoint to the tale of a man whose thirst for identity literally threatens his life.

The narrator doesn't reveal the source of his identity, at least not directly, and for good reason. Were we able to isolate him outside the novel, he would probably smile and say that the question of identity is extremely personal and not easily deciphered. Perhaps, sometimes, it is not decipherable at all. But Mr. Major has demonstrated in *My Amputations* that the attempt to do so can prove the stuff of an imaginative and compelling tale.

> *Richard Perry, "Hunting the Thief of Identity," in* The New York Times Book Review, *September 28, 1986, p. 30.*

Bernard W. Bell (essay date 1987)

[*In the following excerpt from his* The Afro-American Novel and Its Tradition, *Bell examines theme and structure in four novels by Major: 1)* All-Night Visitors, *2)* No, *3)* Reflex and Bone Structure, *and 4)* Emergency Exit.]

Major's thematic and structural movement beyond racial and political consciousness to a preoccupation with exploring the boundaries of language and imaginative consciousness can be traced in his four novels. Each is told by a first-person, unreliable, dramatized narrator-protagonist; each is more fragmented and discontinuous in structure than its predecessor; and each engages in linguistic play that blurs the line between the worlds of fantasy and social reality. *All-Night Visitors,* divided into two essentially surreal parts called "The Early Warning System" and "The Intricacy of Ruined Landscapes," is the episodic journey of Eli Bolton, a black, neurotic, twenty-eight-year-old Vietnam veteran. Driven to despair and alienation because of his loveless childhood in an orphanage and by witnessing the brutal rape and murder of children and women in Vietnam, Eli seeks to reconstruct his fragmented self and reconcile himself to the bizarre, equally violent reality of life in Chicago and New York. However, Major's impressionistic, occasionally lyrical celebration of sex, especially fellatio, as the primal expression of the narrator-protagonist's selfhood is predictably chauvinistic and provocative. The emphasis on sexual orgasm is less effective as an iconoclastic assault on puritan morality and the inhumanity of the Vietnam war than as a metaphorical expression of the link between sex and death. As a graphic, phenomenological description of sexual exploits with a series of all-night partners it also gives a problematic, existential meaning to Eli Bolton's quest for an integrated, responsible self, culminating in his loving and losing a young white VISTA worker. This climactic episode sets the stage for the symbolic resolution of the novel in which a dispossessed, pregnant Puerto Rican mother and her seven small children awaken Eli's will to translate human compassion into socially responsible action. Whether we believe this transformation, marked by a thunderstorm and Eli's declaration that he "had become firmly a man," depends on the degree to which, first, we interpret his experiences as surreal or real and to which, second, we accept the definition of contemporary black manhood that these experiences and the author imply.

No, as critic [John] O'Brien states, "moves beyond the first novel in insisting that the self is a phenomenon of language and the imagination rather than of actual experience, time, and place." Divided into three parts whose titles—"influence of the moon," "the witchburning," and "the mount meru"—suggest the surreal landscape of the novel, it is the retrospective narrative of the narrator-protagonist's growing awareness of his multifaceted, fluid identity, from his first sexual experiences as a child on a farm in Chickamauga, Mississippi, to his full self-awareness as an adult confronting a bull in a bullring in a Latin American country. "I didn't realize," the adult narrator-protagonist states in the opening expository paragraph of the novel, "that I was really trying to crash out of a sort of penal system in which I was born and grew up. Looking back though, I do realize that the activity of my life indicates merely the position of various political, social, and moral incidents." Called such names as Moses Westby, the Boy, Junebug, and Nat Turnips, the protagonist, whom the reader has difficulty distinguishing from the father, Moses Westby, the guard, is not conscious of being on the road to self-determination until after he and other members of the family are shot in a suicidal rage by his father, and after he consummates his marriage to Oni Dunn. Constantly and abruptly shifting nominal, temporal, spatial, and cultural references create a confusing, uninhibited linguistic world that contrasts with the protagonist's personal and social sense of living in a prison.

Liberation comes only in the bullring, where touching the bull's head invested life with essence: "In other words I had to give meaning to it," he reflects; "and it had to contain courage. And at the same time I argued with the shallowness of it. With myself—with being." That this crucial event, including the protagonist's subsequent goring by the bull, actually occurred is called into question by the narrator-protagonist's anticlimactic statement: "When I woke up it was a full hour before I began to put the pieces of myself together again. Whether the Hemingwayesque bullring episode of manly courage and grace in the face of danger and death is an actual or imagined experience is less important to the implied author and narrator-protagonist than the shaping influence it has on the ever-changing sense of self. Thus, in the closing line of the novel the narrator-protagonist is flying back to the United States toward what he ambiguously "believed to be a new beginning." For Major, then, as O'Brien notes, "the self is created by and emerges as the product of an imagination that can give it meaning and direction through language."

Unquestionably, the most radically experimental and aesthetically challenging of Major's four novels are *Reflex and Bone Structure* and *Emergency Exit.* A composite of everything from a catalog of names from a telephone directory and police report to informational graphics and reproductions of abstract paintings, including a picture of the author in a cow pasture, *Emergency Exit* is a dazzling experiment in collage or montage writing. Major introduces us to the black Ingraham family and their largely white liberal neighbors in Inlet, Connecticut, through an elaborately extended metaphor—the juxtaposing and rapid succession of disparate fragments and images whose principal recurring motif is a doorway—which stresses, as the narrator states, that the ultimate *thingness* of our lives operate as a sort of *extended* metaphor.

Less self-indulgent and more satisfying to the average reader's search for a sense of order is *Reflex and Bone Structure.* Divided into two melodramatically titled parts, "A Bad Connection" and "Body Heat," it is a metafictional mystery novel in what two critics call the antidetective tradition. Major's narrator-protagonist is a fiction writer who discusses the process of constructing a mystery novel while he is simultaneously involved as suspect and detective in a murder mystery. "I want this book to be anything it wants to be," the narrator-protagonist tells us near the end of the first part of the novel, suggesting a close relationship between his aesthetic ideas and those of the author. "I want the mystery of the book to be an absolute mystery." Earlier, Cora Hull, a black Greenwich Village actress who is involved in a love quadrangle that results in her murder, tells the nameless narrator-protagonist, "This book you're writing isn't nearly as strange as reality. The only way you're going to make any sense is to stick with the impossible. Any resemblance to the past or present should be purely accidental." From the opening page of the murder mystery, when scattered pieces of bodies are found, to its resolution on the final page when the narrator-protagonist identifies the bodies and himself as the murderer in a burst of short, staccato statements, we are witnesses to and participants in the creative energy of Major's fabulation and linguistic collage.

As the characters are developed in fragments, we are constantly reminded by the narrator-protagonist that he is the self-conscious creator of this murder mystery and that he is "extending reality, not retelling it." In addition to the elusive, promiscuous Cora, who "needs variety, still a child at heart, still dreaming of the prince who won't ever come," and the narrator-protagonist, who is not only a writer and a suspect in the murder but also a detective paradoxically "trying to solve a murder. No, not a murder. It's a life," the other characters involved in the love quadrangle are Canada Jackson and Dale. Canada collects guns, seeks to improve the world, and "invents and reinvents the world as he wishes it to be." Because he "sometimes . . . can even handle Canada from the inside out," the narrator-protagonist feels emotionally and psychologically close to him. However, he hates Dale, whom he only vaguely delineates and jealously blows to bits with Cora:

> The fact that Dale really has little or no character doesn't help matters. I cannot help him if he refuses to focus. How can I be blamed for his lack of seriousness. And it isn't that he doesn't talk to me. He talks too much to me, really, and he plots too much, has too many secrets, leaves nothing in the open. Whatever it was about him that attracted Cora shall always remain a mystery to me.

Like the protagonist, we are challenged to either solve the mystery of the novel or accept it.

Unlike the structure of traditional detective novels, however, in which the solution of the murder is gradually achieved through the discovery of clues and the construction of a logical, lucid case against a single suspect, *Reflex and Bone Structure* is self-consciously fragmented, bizarre, and ambiguous. Parodying the traditional form of the detective novel and extending its possibilities, Major, like his narrator, is primarily con-

cerned with comparing and contrasting the difficult task of the contemporary novelist and the detective in constructing a meaningful sense of self and others, both private and public, out of fragments. As critics [Larry] McCaffrey and [Nancy] Gregory state, "the detective and the antidetective . . . seek different answers which suggest the differing epistemological assumptions of the ages in which they were produced: One looks to eliminate the temporary description of an ordered universe, the other for an arbitrary fictional pattern that will not explain away mystery but will enable him to live with it." The aesthetic bond between Major and his narrator-protagonist is apparent in the experimental style and form of the narrative as well as in the explicit internal references to the title of his novel and to the protgagonists of Major's first two novels.

In *Reflex and Bone Structure* Major breaks away from the black detective tradition of Rudolph Fisher and Chester Himes, and in each of his novels he does something new with language and form. Although Ralph Ellison's influence can be seen in the depiction of Moses Westby in *No* and the nameless narrator-protagonist in *Reflex and Bone Structure,* Major, like Demby in *The Catacombs,* is more clearly influenced by the Euro-American post-modernist approach to writing than other contemporary black American novelists. Rejecting social realism and "militant fictionists," he states, with more disdain and dogmatism than understanding and tolerance, that "the deliberate effort, propaganda, has never helped anyone toward a larger sense of self. It has always been the novel or poem that begins from and spreads all across the entire human experience that ends liberating minds." In defense of his own novels, he argues in **"Formula or Freedom"** [in *The Dark and Feeling: Black American Writers and Their Work,* 1974] that

> the novel *not* deliberately aimed at bringing about human freedom for black people has liberated as many minds as has the propaganda tract, if not more. This does not mean that a wholly human novel by a black writer necessarily becomes assimilable for just anybody. It does mean, though, that a work that takes long root in its author's experience—race being a part of that experience—not only makes sense anywhere in any language but also is likely either to raise hell or to lower heaven.

In other words, Major correctly perceives that he and other black novelists who are committed to modernism and postmodernism can at least depend for support on a small, select readership. This readership does not, however, include many blacks, for whom neither the self nor life can be meaningfully or satisfactorily reduced to the blissful, liberating linguistic constructs of structuralist and poststructuralist theory that is advanced in books like Roland Barthes's *Pleasure of the Text.* Many white readers, as Frank Kermode suggests in *The Sense of an Ending,* also "find that there is an irreducible minimum of geometry—of humanly needed shape or structure—which finally limits our ability to accept the mimesis of pure contingency." Nevertheless, judged on their own terms, all four of Major's novels extend the experimental tradition of the Afro-American novel by their subordination of race to a phenomenological exploration of sex and language as a ritualistic rebirth and affirmation of self. Their attempt to resolve Afro-American double-consciousness by the subordination of social truth and power for blacks to the expressionistic truth and freedom of the artist also extends this tradition. (pp. 316-20)

> *Bernard W. Bell, "The Contemporary Afro-American Novel, 2: Modernism and Postmodernism," in his* The Afro-American Novel and Its Tradition, *The University of Massachusetts Press, 1987, pp. 281-338.*

Clarence Major (essay date 1989)

[*In the following excerpt from an essay published in* Black American Literature Forum *in 1989, Major explains his reasons for becoming a writer and comments on how his passion for painting influenced his writing. In the preface to the essay, the editor of the magazine states: "Had I not come to trust Clarence Major's judgment, I'd have thought it odd, at the very least, that he would propose to introduce the fiction of his contemporaries with the tale of his becoming a writer. Pushing back skepticism, I began to read, turned skeptical for a time (forgive me, Clarence), then discovered the aptness of the writerly gesture. So step freely across this less than self-apparent threshold, reader, into the fiction of life and the life of contemporary black American fiction."*]

People have a tendency to ask a writer, *Why* did you become a writer? *How* did you become a writer? Every writer hears such questions over and over. You ever hear anybody ask a butcher a question like that?

So, what's so special about being a writer? Maybe we are simply fascinated by people who are brave (or foolish) enough to go against—and lucky enough to beat—the odds.

We seem fascinated in the same way by the lives of people in show business, and probably for the same reasons the lives of writers interest us.

It is also always amazing to see someone making a living doing something he or she actually enjoys.

I never seriously tried to deal with the questions till I was asked to write my life story. If my autobiography were going to make sense, I thought I'd better try my best to answer both questions.

So, my speaking on the page to you is—in a way—an effort to answer those questions—for myself and possibly for others. I don't expect to succeed—but here goes.

It seems to me that the impulse to write, the *need* to write, is inseparable from one's educational process—which begins at the beginning and never ends.

In some sort of nonobjective way, I can remember being an infant and some of the things I thought about and touched. I had a sister, but my sister didn't have a brother. I had no self because I was *all* self. Gradually, like any developing kid, I shed my self-centered view of the world: saw myself reflected in my mother's eyes, began to perceive the idea of a self. In a way it was at this point that my *research* as a writer, and as a painter, began. (For me, the two impulses were always inseparable.) The world was a place of magic, and everything I touched was excruciatingly *new.* Without knowing it, my career had begun.

In his meditation on the art of fiction, *Being and Race,* novelist Charles Johnson says: "All art points to others with whom the writer argues about what is . . . . He must have models with which to agree . . . or outright oppose . . . for Nature seems to remain silent . . . ." Reading this passage reminded me of Sherwood Anderson's short story "Death in the Woods," in which the narrator retells the story (we are reading) because his brother, who had told it first, hadn't told it the way it was supposed to be told. In a similar way, that early self of mine, then, had already started its long battle with the history of literature and art.

In the early stages of that battle, some very primary things were going on. By this, I mean to say that a writer is usually a person who has to learn how to keep his ego—like his virginity—and lose it at the same time. In other words, he becomes a kind of twin of himself. He remains that self-centered infant while transcending him to become the observer of his own experience and, by extension, the observer of a wide range of experience within his cultural domain.

Without any rational self-consciousness at all, early on, my imagination was fed by the need to invent things. My older cousins taught me how to make my own toys—trucks, cars, houses, whole cities. We used old skate wheels for tires. Our parents couldn't afford such luxuries as toys—we were lucky if we got new clothes. Watching physical things like the toys we made take shape, I think, showed me some possibilities. (William Carlos Williams said a poem is like a machine. If I understand what he meant, I can see a connection between what I was making at age seven and poems and stories I tried to write later on.)

Plus the *newness* of everything—trees, plants, the sky—and the *need* to define everything, on my own terms, was a given. At my grandparents' farm, my cousins and I climbed trees and named the trees we climbed. Painfully, I watched my uncle slaughter hogs and learned about death. I watched my grandmother gather eggs from the chicken nests and learned about birth. I watched her make lye soap and the clothes we wore. But I didn't fully trust the world I was watching. It seemed too full of *danger,* even while I dared to explore it and attempt to imprint the evidence of my presence upon it—by making things such as toys or drawing pictures in the sand.

Daydreaming—as a necessity in the early disposition of a writer—is not a new idea. Whether or not it was necessary in my case, I was a guilty practitioner. I say this because I had an almost *mystical* attachment to nature. If looked at from my parents' point of view, it was not a good sign. I could examine a leaf for hours or spend hours on my knees watching the way ants lived. Behaving like a lazy kid, I followed the flights and landings of birds with spiritual devotion. The frame of mind that put me through those motions was, later, the same frame of mind from which I tried to write a poem or a story: daydreaming, letting it happen, connecting two or three previously unrelated things, making them mean something—together—entirely new. I was hopeless.

And dreams—in dreams I discovered a self going about its business with a mind of its own. I began to watch and to wonder. I was amazed by some of the things I had the nerve to dream about. Sex, for example. Or some *wonderful,* delicious food! One guilty pleasure after another! This other self often invented these wonderful ways for me to actually get something—*even* a horse once—that I *knew* I wanted, something no one *seriously* wanted to give me.

At times, waking up was the hard part. Dream activity was all invention—maybe even the rootbeds of all the conscious, willful invention I wanted to take charge of in the hard indifference of daylight. Unlike the daydreams I spent so much time giving myself to, *these* dreams were not under my control. Later, I started trying to write them down, but I discovered that it was impossible to capture their specific texture. They had to stay where they were. But I tried to imitate them, to make up stories that *sounded* like them. The pattern of these dreams became a model for the imaginative leaps I wanted to make (and couldn't—for a long time!) in my poetry and fiction.

My first novel, written at the age of twelve, was twenty pages long. It was the story of a wild, free-spirited horse, leading a herd. Influenced by movies, I thought it would make a terrific movie, so I sent it to Hollywood. A man named William Self read it and sent it back with a letter of encouragement. I never forgot his kindness. It was the beginning of a long, long process of learning to live with rejection—not just rejection slips. And that experience too was necessary as a correlation to the writing process, necessary because one of the most *important* things I was going to have to learn was *how* to detect my own failures and be the first to reject them.

Was there, then, a particular point when I said: *Hey! I'm going to become a writer!* I think there *was,* but it now seems irrelevant because I must have been evolving toward that conscious moment long, long before I had any idea what was going on. (I was going to have to find my way—with more imperfection than not—through *many* disciplines—such as painting, music, anthropology, history, philosophy, psychology, sociology—before such a consciousness would begin to emerge.)

I think I was in the fifth grade when a girl who sat behind me snuck a copy of Raymond Radiguet's *Devil in the Flesh* to me. This was *adult fiction!* And judging from the cover, the book was going to have some *good* parts. But as it turned out the *single* good part was *the writing itself.* I was reading that book one day at home, and about halfway through, I stood up and went crazy with an important discovery: *Writing had a life of its own!* And I soon fell in love with the *life* of writing, by way of this book—Kay Boyle's translation of Radiguet.

From that moment on, up to about the age of twenty, I set out to discover other books that might change my perception—forever. Hawthorne's *The Scarlet Letter* showed me how *gracefully* a story could be told and how *terrifying* human affairs—and self-deception within those affairs—can be. Conrad's *Heart of Darkness* caught me in an aesthetic network of *magic* so powerful I never untangled myself. I then went on to read other nineteenth-century—and even earlier—works by Melville, Baudelaire, Emerson, Dostoyevsky, and the like.

But I always hung on—with more comfort—to the twentieth century. I read J. D. Salinger's *The Catcher in the Rye* early enough for it to have spoken profoundly

Major at age twenty-one.

and directly to me about what I was *feeling* and *thinking* about the adult world at the time that its agony affirmed my faith in life. Richard Wright's *Native Son* was an overwhelming experience, and so was Rimbaud's poetry. But the important thing about these discoveries is that each of them led to Cocteau and other French writers, going back to the nineteenth century; Salinger led me to a discovery of modern and contemporary American fiction—Hemingway, Faulkner, Sherwood Anderson, and on and on. Wright led to Dos Passos, to James T. Farrell, to Jean Toomer, to Chester Himes, to William Gardner Smith, to Ann Petry, to Nella Larsen and other Afro-American writers; and Rimbaud led to the discovery of *American poetry*—which was not so much of a leap as it sounds—to Williams, to Marianne Moore, to Eliot, to cummings. This activity began roughly during the last year of grade school and took on full, focused direction in high school. Now, none of these writers was being taught in school. I was reading them on *my own*. In school we had to read O'Henry and Joyce Kilmer.

But during all this time, it was hard to find books that came *alive*. I had to go through *hundreds* before hitting on the special ones, the ones with the power to shape or reshape perception, to deepen vision, to give *me* the means to understand *myself* and other things, to drive away fears and doubts. I found the possibilities of wedding the social and political self and the artistic self in the essays of James Baldwin. Autobiographies such as Billie Holiday's *Lady Sings the Blues* and Mezz Mezzrow's *Really the Blues* were *profound* reading experiences: These books, and books like them, taught me that even life, with more pain than one individual had any right to, was still worth spending some time trying to get *through*—and, like Billie's and Mezz's, with dignity and inventiveness.

Although I was learning to appreciate good writing, I had no command of the language myself. I had the *need* to write well, but that was about all. Only the most sensitive teacher—and there were two or three along the way—was able to detect some talent and imagination in my efforts. Every time I gathered enough courage to dream of writing seriously, the notion ended in frustration or, sometimes, despair. Not only did I not have command of the language, I didn't have the *necessary distance* on experience to have anything important to say about even the things I knew something about.

I daydreamed about a solution to these problems: I could *learn* to write and I could go out and *live it up* in order to have experience. But this solution would take time. I was not willing to *wait* for time. In my sense of urgency, I didn't have that much time.

Meanwhile, there were a few adults I ventured to show my efforts to. One teacher told me I couldn't *possibly* have written the story I showed her. It was *too good*— which meant that it was a hell of lot better than I had thought. But rather than gaining more self-confidence, the experience became grounds for the loss of respect for

her intelligence. Among the other adults who saw my early efforts were my mother—who encouraged me as much as her understanding permitted—and a young college-educated man who was a friend of the family's. He told me I was pretty good.

I was growing up in Chicago, and my life therefore had a particular social shape. The realities I was discovering in books didn't—at first—seem to correspond to the reality around me. At the time, I didn't have enough distance to see the connections.

The fact is, the writerly disposition that was then evolving was *shaped* by my life in Chicago—in the classroom and on the playground—as well as it was being shaped during the times I spent alone, with books, and anywhere else, for that matter. Which is only one way of saying that a writer doesn't make most of his or her own decisions about personal vision or outlook.

Jean Paul Sartre, in *What is Literature?*, makes the observation that Richard Wright's destiny as a writer was chosen *for* him by the circumstances of birth and social history. One can go even further and say that it's as difficult to draw the line between *where* a sensibility is influenced by the world around it and where it is asserting its own presence in that world, as it is to say whether or not essence precedes existence.

To put it *another* way, the educational process against which my *would-be* writerly disposition was taking formation was *political*. Political because I quickly had to learn how to survive—for example, on the playground. It was not easy since I had instinctive dislike for violence. But the playground was a place where the *dramas* of life were acted out. Radiguet's book (and Jean Paul Rossi's *Awakening,* too) had—to some extent— dealt with the same territory. As a microcosm of life, it was no doubt one of the *first* social locations in which I was forced to observe some of the ways people relate— or don't relate—to each other. Among a *number* of things, I learned how to survive the *pecking-order* rituals—with my wits rather than my fists. This was an area where books and art could not save me. But later on, I was going to see how what I *had* to learn—in self-defense—carried over to the creative effort.

The classroom, too, was *not* a place where one wanted to let one's guard down for too long. To be liked and singled out by a teacher often meant getting smashed in the mouth or kicked in the stomach on the playground. If one demonstrated intelligence in school, one could most certainly expect to hear about it later, on the way home. It was simply not cool for *boys* to be smart in class. A smart boy was a sissy and deserved to get his butt kicked.

I had to be very quiet about my plans to become a writer. I couldn't talk with friends about what I read. I mean—why wasn't I out playing basketball?

All of this, in terms of education—or plans to become a writer—, meant that, if you wanted to learn anything (or try to write something, for example), you had to do it without *flaunting* what you were doing. Naturally, some smart but less willful kids gave in, in the interest of survival; they learned how to *fail* in order to live in the safety zone of the majority. And for those of us who didn't *want* to give in, it was hard to keep how well we were doing a *secret* because the teacher would tell the class who got the best grades.

I was also facing another crisis. If, for example, I wanted to write, eventually I had to face an even larger problem—publication. I thought that, if I were ever lucky enough to get anything published (say, in a school magazine or newspaper), that would be a success I would have to keep quiet about among most of my friends and certainly around those out to put me in my place. And God forbid that my first published work should be a poem. Only sissies wrote poetry.

But I couldn't go on like that. I remember once breaking down and saying to hell with it. I walked around the school building with a notebook, writing down *everything* I saw, trying to translate the life around me, minute by minute, into words. I must have filled twenty pages with very boring descriptions. A girl I liked, but didn't have the nerve to talk to, saw me. She thought I was doing homework. When I told her what I was up to, she gave me this strange, big-eyed look, then quickly disappeared—*forever*—from my life.

I now realize that I must have been a *difficult* student for teachers to understand. At times I was sort of smart, at other times I left a *lot* to be desired. One teacher thought I might be retarded, another called me a genius. Not knowing what else to do with me, the administrators— in frustration—appointed me art director of the whole school of 8,000 students, during my last year.

Why art director? Actually, as I implied, my first passion was for painted pictures rather than the realities I discovered in books. Before my first clear memories, I was drawing and painting, while the writing started at a time within memory. So, I think it is important (in the context of "how" and "why," where the writing is concerned) to try to understand what this visual experience has meant for me.

At about the age of twelve, I started taking private art lessons from a South Side painter, Gus Nall. I even won a few prizes. So, confidence in an ability to express myself *visually* came first. But what I learned from painting, I think, carried over into the writing from the beginning.

My first articulate passion was for the works of Vincent van Gogh. This passion started with a big show of his work the Art Institute of Chicago hung in the early fifties. There were about a hundred and fifty pieces.

I pushed my way through the crowded galleries— stunned every step of the way. I kept going back. I was not sophisticated enough to know how to articulate for myself what these things were doing to me, but I knew I was *profoundly* moved. So—on some level—I no doubt did sense the *power of the painterliness* of those pictures of winding country paths, working peasants, flower gardens, rooftops, the stillness of a summer day. They really got to me.

Something in me went out to the energy of Vincent's *Sunflowers,* for example. I saw him as one who broke the rules and transcended. Where I came from, no socially well-behaved person, for example, ever went out and gathered *sunflowers* for a vase in the home. No self-respecting *grown* man spent ten years painting pictures he couldn't sell. On the South Side of Chicago everything of value had a price tag.

Vincent, then, was at least one important model for my rebellion. The world I grew up in told me that the only proper goal was to make money and get an education and become a productive member of society and go to church and have a family—pretty much in that order. But I had found my alternative models, and it was too late for my world to get its hooks in me. I wasn't planning to do anything less than the greatest thing I could think of. I wanted to be like van Gogh, like Richard Wright, like Jean Toomer, like Rimbaud, like Bud Powell.

In the meantime, I went home from the van Gogh exhibition and tried to create the same effects from the life around me: I drew my stepfather soaking his feet in a pan of water, my older sister braiding my younger sister's hair, the bleak view of rooftops from my bedroom window, my mother in bed sick, anything that struck me as compositionally viable. In this rather haphazard way, I was learning to *see.* I suspect there was a certain music and innocence in Vincent's lines and colors that gave me a foundation for my own attempts at representing—first, through drawing and painting, and very soon after, in poetry I was writing. The poems I first tried to write were strongly imagistic in the Symbolist tradition.

I made thousands of sketches of this sort of everyday thing. I was responding to the things of *my* world. And I had already lived in two or three different worlds: in a Southern city, Atlanta; in a rural country setting; and now in Chicago, an urban, brutal, stark setting. We moved a lot—so much so that my sense of place was always changing. Home was where we happened to be. Given this situation, I think the fact that Vincent felt like an alien in his own land (and was actually an alien in France, and that this sense of being estranged carried over emotionally into his work) found a strong correlating response in me.

If there were disadvantages in being out of step, there were just as many advantages. I was beginning to engage myself passionately in painting and writing, and this passion would carry me through a lot of difficulties and disappointments—simply because I *had* it. I saw many people with no passionate interest in *anything.* Too many of them perished for lack of a passionate dream long before I thought possible.

At fourteen, this passionate need to create (and apparently the need to *share* it, too) caused me to try to go public—despite the fact that I knew I was doing something eccentric. One of my uncles ran a printing shop. I gathered enough confidence in my poetry to pay him ten dollars to print fifty copies of a little booklet of my own poetry. The poems reflect the influence of Rimbaud, van Gogh, and Impressionism generally—I *even* used French words I didn't understand.

Once I had the books in hand, I realized that I didn't know more than *three* people who might be interested in seeing a copy. I gave one to one of my English teachers. I gave my mother three copies. I gave my best poet friend a copy. I may have also given my art teacher, Mr. Fouche, a copy. And the rest of the edition was stored in a closet. They stayed there till, by chance, a year or two later, I discovered how bad the poems were and destroyed the remaining copies.

Shortly after the van Gogh exhibition, the Institute sponsored a large showing of the works of Paul Cézanne, whose work I knew a bit from the few pieces in the permanent collection. I went to the exhibition not so much because I was *attracted* to Cézanne but because it was *there*—and I felt that I *should* appreciate Cézanne. At fifteen that was not easy. And the reasons I found it difficult to appreciate Cézanne as much as I thought I should had to do with (I later learned) my inability to understand, at a gut level, *what* he was about, what his *intentions* were. Cézanne's figures looked stiff and ill-proportioned. His landscapes, like his still lifes, seemed made of stone or wood or metal. Everything in Cézanne was unbending, lifeless.

I looked at the apples and the oranges on the table and understood their *weight* and how important the *sense* of that weight was in understanding Cézanne's intentions. I wanted to say, yes, it's a great accomplishment. But why couldn't I *like* it? I was not yet sophisticated enough to realize that all great art—to the unsophisticated viewer—, at first, appears *ugly*—even repulsive. And I had yet to discover Gertrude Stein in any serious way, to discover her attempts to do with words what Cézanne was doing with lines and color.

It took many years to acquire an appreciation for Cézanne—but doing so, in its way, was as important to my development as a writer as was my passion for van Gogh. But the appreciation started, in its troubled way, with that big show. When I finally saw the working out of the *sculpturing* of a created reality (to paraphrase James Joyce), I experienced a breakthrough. Cézanne appealed to my *rational* side. I began going to Cézanne for a knowledge of the inner, mechanical foundation of art, and for an example of an self-conscious exploration of composition. All of this effort slowly taught me how to *see* the significant aspects of writing and how they correspond to those in painting. Discovering *how* perspective corresponded to point of view, for example, was a real high point.

These two painters, van Gogh and Cézanne, were catalysts for me, but there were other painters important for similar reasons: Toulouse-Lautrec, Degas, Bonnard, Cassatt, Munch—for intensely scrutinized private and public moments—; Edward Hopper for his ability to invest a view of a house or the interior of a room with a profound sense of mortality; Matisse—for his play, his rhythm, his design. I was attracted by the intimacy of subject matter in their work.

I also had *very* strong responses to Gauguin. He excited and worried me at the same time. At first, I was suspicious of a European seeking *purity* among dark people. (And I placed D. H. Lawrence in the same category.) Later, I realized Gauguin's story was more *complex* than that (as was Lawrence's). But more important to me was the fact of Gaugin's work: paintings with flat, blunt areas of vivid colors. Their sumptuousness drew a profoundly romantic response in me. Not only did I try to paint *that way* for a period, I also thought I saw the possibility of creating simple, flat images with simple sentences or lines.

For a while I was especially attracted to painters who used paint thickly. Turner's seascapes were incredible. Up close they looked abstract. Utrillo's scenes of Paris, Rouault's bumpy people, Albert Ryder's horrible dreams, Kokoschka's profusion of layered effects—these rekindled feelings that had started with van Gogh. (Years later, I came to appreciate Beckman and Schiele for similar reasons.) To paint that way—expressively, and apparently fast—had a certain appeal. It was just a theory but worth playing with: In correlation, it might be possible to make words move with that kind of self-apparent urgency, that kind of reflexive brilliance. The expressionistic writers—Lawrence, Mansfield, Joyce, and others—had done it.

I kept moving from one fascination to another. Later, the *opposite* approach attracted me. The lightness of Picasso's touch was as remarkable as a pelican in flight. If I could make a painting or poem *move* like that—like the naturalness of walking or sleeping—, I would be lucky.

I was easily seduced. I got lost in the dreams of Chagall, in the summer laziness of Monet, in the waves of Winslow Homer, in the blood and passion of Orozco, in the bright, simple designs of Rivera, in the fury of Jackson Pollock, in the struggle of de Kooning, in the selflessness of Vermeer, in the light and shadow of Rembrandt, in the plushness of Rubens, in the fantastic mystery of Bosch, in the power of Michelangelo and Tintoretto, in the incredible sensitivity and intelligence of Leonardo da Vinci, in the earthly dramas of Daumier and Millet. (Later on, when I discovered Afro-American art, I got equally caught up in the works of Jacob Lawrence, Archibald Motley, Henry Tanner, Edward Bannister, and others. I was troubled from the beginning at the absence of Afro-American painters, novelists, poets, generally, I might turn to as models. I was seventeen before—on my own—I discovered the *reason* they were absent: The system had hidden them. It was that simple. They had existed since the beginning but were, for well-known reasons, made officially nonexistent.)

Although this learning process was a slow and very long one, and I wasn't always conscious of even the things I successfully managed to transfer into my own painting and writing, I can now look back and realize that I must always have been more fascinated by technique—in painting and in writing—than I was by subject matter. The subject of a novel or a painting seemed irrelevant: a nude, a beach scene, a stand of trees, a story of an army officer and a seventeen-year-old girl in a foreign country, a lyrical view of a horrible accident. It didn't matter! What did matter was *how* the painter or storyteller or poet had seduced me into the story, into the picture, into the poem.

I guess I also felt the need to submerge myself in the intellectual excitement of an artistic community—but I couldn't find one. Just about every writer I'd ever heard of seemed to have had such nourishment: Hemingway in Paris among the other expatriates.... But I was not in touch with any sort of *exciting* literary or artistic life (outside of visits to the Institute) on the South Side. True, I had met a couple of writers—Willard Motley and Frank London Brown—and a few painters—Gus Nall, Archibald Motley, and a couple of others—; but I felt pretty isolated. Plus these people were a lot older and didn't seem to have much time to spare. So, I had clumsily started my own little magazine—a thing called *Coercion Review*. It became my substitute for an artistic community and, as such, a means of connecting (across the country and even across the ocean) with a larger, cultural world—especially with other writers and poets.

I published the works of writers I corresponded with, and they published mine; and in a way this became our way of *workshopping*—as my students say—our manuscripts. When we found something acceptable, it meant—or so we thought—that the particular piece had succeeded. We were wrong more often than not. It was an expensive way to learn what *not* to publish (and how to live with what couldn't be unpublished).

Seeing my work in print increased my awareness of the many problems I still faced in my writing at, say, the age of eighteen. I wrote to William Carlos Williams for help. I wrote to Langston Hughes. They were generous. (In fact, Williams not only criticized the poetry but told me of his feelings of despair as a poet.)

Rushing into print was teaching me that I not only needed distance on approach (the selection of point of view, for example) and subject matter *before* starting a work, but I needed also to slow down, to let a manuscript wait, to see if it could stand up under my own developing ability to edit during future readings, when my head would be clear of manuscript birth fumes. As a result, my awareness of what I was doing—of its aesthetic value—increased. I became more selective about what I sent out.

During all this time, I was also listening to music. Critics of Afro-American writing often find reason to compare black writing to black music. Each of my novels, at one time or another, has been compared to either Blues songs or jazz compositions. I've never doubted that critics had a right to do this. But what was *I* to make of the fact that I had *also* grown up with Tin Pan Alley, Bluegrass, and European classical music? I loved Chopin and Beethoven.

Something was wrong. It seemed to me that Jack Kerouac, for example, had gotten as many jazz motifs into his work as had, say, James Baldwin. At a certain point, when I noticed that critics were beginning to see rhythms of music as a basis for my lines or sentences—to say nothing of content—I backed up and took a closer look. I had to argue—at least with myself—that *all* of the music I'd loved while growing up found its aesthetic way into my writing—or *none* of it did.

True, I had been overwhelmingly caught up in the Bebop music of Bud Powell when I was a kid—I loved "Un Poco Loco," thought it was the most inventive piece of music I had ever heard, loved all of his original compositions ("Hallucinations," "I Remember Clifford," "Oblivion," "Glass Enclosure," and on and on—and as I said before, I swore by the example of his devotion to his art).

But I soon moved on out, in a natural way, from Powell into an appreciation of the progressive music of other innovators—such as Thelonius Monk, Lester Young, Sonny Stitt, John Coltrane, Clifford Brown, Miles Davis, Dizzy Gillespie, Charlie Parker, Dexter Gordon, and Ornette Coleman—, and, at the same time, I was discovering Jimmy Rushing, Bessie Smith, Billie Holiday, Joe Turner, Dinah Washington—singers of my father's generation and before.

My feeling, on this score, is that Afro-American music generally (along with other types of music I grew up hearing) had a pervasive cultural importance for me. I think I need to take this assumption into consideration in trying to trace in myself the shape of what I hope has become some sort of sensitivity not only to music but also to poetry, fiction, painting, and the other arts—film, photography, dance.

I've already mentioned the importance of other disciplines—anthropology, history, philosophy, psychology, sociology—in an attempt to lay some sort of intellectual foundation from which to write. Without going through the long, hopelessly confusing tangle of my own confusion and profoundly troubled questing, I think I can sum up what I came away with (as it relates to themes I chose or the themes that *chose me*) in pretty simple terms.

I remember my excitement when I began to understand cultural patterns. Understanding the nature of kinship—family, clan, tribe—gave me insight into relationships in the context of my own family, community, country. I was also fascinated to discover, while reading about tribal people, something called a caste system. I immediately realized that I had grown up in communities, both in the South and the North, where one kind of caste system or another was practiced. For one to be *extremely* dark or *extremely* light often meant that one was penalized by the community, for example.

Totem practices also fascinated me because I was able to turn from the books and see examples in everyday life: There were people who wore good-luck charms and fetishes such as rabbits' feet on keychains. I became aware, in deeper ways, of the significance of ritual and ceremony—and how to recognize examples when I saw them. It was a breakthrough for me to begin to understand *how* cultures—my own included—rationalized their own behavior.

The formation of myths—stories designed to explain why things were as they were—was of deep interest to me. Myths, I discovered, governed the behavior and customs I saw every day—customs concerning matters of birth, death, parents, grandparents, marriage, grief, luck, dances, husband-and-wife relationships, siblings, revenge, joking, adopting, sexual relations, murder, fights, food, toilet training, game playing. You name it.

Reading Freud (and other specialists of the mind) I thought would help me understand better how to make characters more convincing. At the same time I hoped to get a better insight into myself—which in the long run would also improve my writing. I read Freud's little study of Leonardo da Vinci. I was interested also in gaining a better understanding of the nature of creativity itself.

But even more than that, I was interested in the religious experience psychologists wrote about. I consciously sought ways to understand religious frenzy and faith in rational terms. I was beginning to think how, as too much nationalism tends to lead to fascism, too much blind religion could be bad for one's mental health. To me, the human mind and the human heart began to look like very, very dangerously nebulous things. But at the same time, I kept on trying to accept the world and its institutions at face value, to understand them on their own terms. After all, who was I to come along and seriously question *everything?* The degree to which I *did* question was more from innocence than from arrogance.

I was actually optimistic because I thought *Knowledge* might lead me somewhere refreshing, might relieve the burden of ignorance. If I could only understand schizophrenia or hysteria, mass brainwashing and charisma, paganism, asceticism, brotherly love . . . ? Why did some individuals feel called to preach and others feel overwhelmed with galloping demons? What was the function of dreaming? I skimmed the Kinsey reports and considered monastic life. I read Alan Watts and was a Buddhist for exactly one week.

I liked the gentle way Reich criticized Freud and, in the process, chiseled out his own psychoanalytical principles. If I ever thought psychoanalysis could help me

personally, I was not mad enough to think we could afford it. I did notice, though, how writers of fiction and poets too, from around the turn of the century on, were using the principles of psychoanalysis as a tool for exploring behavior in fiction and poetry. So I gave it a shot. But the real challenge, I soon learned, was to find a way to absorb some of this stuff and at the same time to keep the *evidence* of it out of my own writing.

Yet I kept hoping for some better—more suitable—approach to human experience. If a better one existed, I had no idea. But there wasn't much to hold on to in psychoanalysis or psychology, and even less in sociology—where I soon discovered that statistics could be made to prove anything the researcher wanted to prove. If the *very presence* of the researcher were itself a contamination, what hope was there for this thing everybody called objectivity?

While I was able to make these connections between theory and reality, I was still seeking answers to questions I had asked since the beginning—*Who and what am I?* Questions we discover later in life are not so important. Everywhere I turned—to philosophy, to psychology—I was turned back upon myself and left with *more* questions than I had had at the start.

Growing up in America when I did, while aiming to be a writer, was a disturbing experience. (Every generation is sure it is more disturbed than the previous one and less lucky than the forthcoming one.) This troublesome feeling was real, though; it wasn't just growing pains. There was something else, and I knew it. And I finally found part of the explanation. My *sense* of myself was hampered by my country's sense of *itself.* My country held an idealistic image of itself that was, in many aspects of its life, vastly different from its actual, unvarnished self. Examples: There was severe poverty, ignorance, disease, corruption, racism, sexism, and there was war—*all* too often undeclared.

But I, as a writer, could not afford the luxury of vision of my own experience as sentimental as the one suggested by my country (of itself, of me). As I grew up, I was trying to learn *how* to *see* through the *superficial* and to touch, in my writing, the essence of experience—in all of its possible wonderment, agony, or glory.

Despite the impossibility of complete success, I continue.

I want to be as forthright as possible with these afterthoughts—because I know that afterthoughts can never *truly* recapture the moments they try to touch back upon. Each moment, it seems to me, in which a thought occurs has more to do with *that moment itself* than with anything in the past. This, to my way of thinking, turns out to be more positive than negative, because it supports the *continuous* nature of life—and that of *art,* too. The creative memory, given expression, is no enemy of the past, nor does its self-focus diminish its authority. (pp. 197-212)

Clarence Major, "Necessary Distance: Afterthoughts on Becoming a Writer," in Black American Literature Forum, *Vol. 23, No. 2, Summer, 1989, pp. 197-212.*

FURTHER READING

Aldan, Daisy. Review of *Surfaces and Masks,* by Clarence Major. *Library Journal* 114, No. 1 (January 1989): 89.
Briefly reviews Major's poetry collection *Surfaces and Masks,* concluding: "This is a work to read once with nostalgia and enjoyment, but only once."

Bradfield, Larry D. "Beyond Mimetic Exhaustion: *The Reflex and Bone Structure* Experiment." *Black American Literature Forum* 17, No. 3 (Fall 1983): 120-23.
Examines the "non-mimetic aesthetic" nature of Major's *Reflex and Bone Structure.* The critic writes: "Generating... fiction not from the world *outside* his imagination but from the world *of* his imagination, Major presents *Reflex and Bone Structure* as an account of an author's sustained imaginative interaction with a set of characters and a story."

Klinkowitz, Jerome. "Art as Life." *The American Book Review* 8, No. 5 (September-October 1986): 12.
Praises *My Amputations* as a "triumph," describing the novel as a "negative autobiography of life that didn't happen."

Quartermain, Peter. "Trusting the Reader." *Chicago Review* 32, No. 2 (Autumn 1980): 65-74.
Structural and thematic discussion of *Emergency Exit.*

Werner, C. Review of *Surfaces and Masks,* by Clarence Major. *Choice* 27, No. 1 (September 1989): 126.
Favorable review of *Surfaces and Masks,* noting of the work: "Focusing on a lengthy visit to Venice, Major considers fundamental questions concerning national, racial, and personal identity."

Young, Al. "God Never Drove Those Cadillacs." *The New York Times Book Review* (13 December 1987): 19.
Describes *Such Was the Season* as "an old-fashioned, straight-ahead narrative crammed with action, a dramatic storyline and meaty characterization."

Malcolm X

1925-1965

(Born Malcolm Little; changed name to Malcolm X; also known by adopted religious name El-Hajj Malik El-Shabazz) American autobiographer and orator.

A dynamic and influential twentieth-century African-American leader, Malcolm X rose to prominence in the mid-1950s as the outspoken national minister of the Nation of Islam under Elijah Muhammad. He opposed the mainstream civil rights movement, publicly calling for black separatism and rejecting non-violence and integration as effective means of combatting racism. Malcolm repudiated Muhammad and the Nation of Islam in the 1960s, however, and embraced conventional Islam. He documented this change and his various identities throughout his life in *The Autobiography of Malcolm X* (1965), a work prepared with the help of American writer Alex Haley. Published after his assassination, Malcolm X's autobiography has been called "a compelling and irreplaceable book" about "a great American life."

Born Malcolm Little in Omaha, Nebraska, Malcolm was exposed to white supremacists and the black separatist movement at an early age. His father, Earl Little, was a Baptist minister and a follower of Jamaican-born black nationalist Marcus Garvey. When the Littles lived in Nebraska, the Ku Klux Klan tried to prevent Reverend Little from inciting the "good" blacks with Garvey's teachings. The Littles consequently left, eventually settling in Mason, Michigan, where they found the racial climate to be no better. In 1929 members of the Black Legion, a white supremacist group, burned down the Littles' home. The group later murdered Malcolm's father by throwing him under a trolley car. His death was labeled suicide, and Louise Little was left to care for their children. The strain was too much for Malcolm's mother, however; she was placed in a mental institution, and the children were separated and sent to foster homes. Despite the traumas of his early youth, Malcolm was perhaps the best student in his class. He was also popular—his white classmates elected him president of their seventh-grade class. Yet when he told an English teacher that he wanted to become a lawyer, the teacher suggested carpentry instead, urging Malcolm "to be realistic about being a nigger."

Shattered by his teacher's suggestion, Malcolm went to live with his half sister in Boston. He quit school after the eighth grade and held several menial jobs. Although he initially looked like a "hick" in his new environment, he soon got a "conk," or treated his hair with corrosive chemicals to straighten it, and donned a zoot suit. As "Detroit Red" (a name his fair complexion and red hair earned him), he acquired a formidable reputation as a hustler, pimp, and drug dealer. Malcolm was arrested in early 1946 and charged with robbery. Not yet twenty-

one, he was sentenced to ten years in prison; the exceptionally long term is thought to reflect the judge's revulsion at Malcolm's liaisons with white women. Malcolm was rebellious in prison. "I would pace for hours like a caged leopard, viciously cursing aloud to myself," he noted. "Eventually the men in the cellblock had a name for me: 'Satan.'" Another convict, Bimbi, introduced him to the prison's extensive library, and Malcolm began his education anew. When his siblings revealed to him that they had become followers of Elijah Muhammad, Malcolm poured over Muhammad's teachings. He read voraciously in an effort to make his daily letters to Muhammad worthy of the "Messenger of Allah." Upon his release from prison in 1952, Malcolm became a follower of Muhammad. He took the name "Malcolm X" to signify the loss of his true African name and reject the "slave name" of Little.

Elijah Muhammad preached a doctrine of black pride based on the contention that whites are devils. Converts to the Nation of Islam—popularly called Black Muslims—believe in the teachings of W. D. Fard, Muhammad's teacher. Fard held that a black scientist, Yacub, genetically produced the white race out of the original black race in order to test the strength of the latter. Although the whites will rule for six millennia, the Muslims believe, the end of that reign is quickly approaching. I. F. Stone commented on Muhammad's teachings: "The tendency is to dismiss Elijah Muhammad's weird doctrine as another example of the superstitions, old and new, that thrive in the Negro ghetto. It is not really any more absurd than the Virgin Birth or the Sacrifice of Isaac. The rational absurdity does not detract from the psychic therapy." In 1953 Malcolm was appointed assistant minister of Detroit's Temple Number One of the Nation of Islam. He believed that a black person would gravitate to Muhammad's teachings, for "when he thinks about his own life, he is going to see where, to him personally, the white man sure has acted like a devil." Malcolm rose swiftly in the ranks of the Black Muslims, becoming Muhammad's national representative and, in 1954, the head of a major mosque in Harlem. There he achieved an impressive status as an articulate, mercurial spokesperson for the radical black perspective. Peter Goldman recalled: "Offstage and off-camera, he was a man of enormous charm, priestly in his bearing and his private life, warm and witty in company, gallant toward white people even in the days when he considered them universally and irremediably evil. But given a platform and a microphone, he became a pitiless scold." In addition to denouncing integration, nonviolence, and Martin Luther King, Jr., Malcolm "identified whites as the enemy of blacks and cheered at tornadoes, hurricanes, earthquakes, airplane crashes, even the Kennedy assassination—anything that might cause them anguish or pain." Malcolm termed the killing of John F. Kennedy a case of "chickens coming home to roost"—a statement that severely damaged Malcolm's career. He later explained that he meant only that "the hate in white men ... finally had struck down the President," but he was immediately censured by Muhammad. "That was a very bad statement," Muhammad told Malcolm. "The country loved this man." Muhammad ordered him to refrain from public comment for ninety days, and Malcolm complied.

Malcolm's remark about the Kennedy assassination gave Muhammad an opportunity to expel his national minister from the religion's hierarchy, for Malcolm had been in conflict with the leader of the Nation of Islam for some time. Malcolm had condemned Muhammad's materialism—his expensive cars and business suits and lavishly furnished estate—and was shocked by allegations that Muhammad had seduced several women and sired their children. Feeling estranged from Muhammad, Malcolm canceled the original dedication to his autobiography-in-progress—he had written that Muhammad "found me here in the muck and mire of the filthiest civilization and society on this earth ... and made me the man that I am today." Only at the urging of Alex Haley did Malcolm agree not to make his autobiography into a polemic against his former mentor. Malcolm proceeded to break officially with the Nation of Islam, and he made a pilgrimage to Mecca, taking the religious name El-Hajj Malik El-Shabazz. In Mecca he underwent a transformation in his beliefs. He explained in his autobiography: "Since I learned the *truth* in Mecca, my dearest friends have come to include *all* kinds—some Christians, Jews, Buddhists, Hindus, agnostics, and even atheists! I have friends who are called capitalists, Socialists, and Communists! Some of my friends are moderates, conservatives, extremists—some are even Uncle Toms! My friends today are black, brown, red, yellow, and *white!*" On a diplomatic trip to Africa, Malcolm began work in uniting blacks across the world, and he later established the Organization of Afro-American Unity in the United States. Yet Malcolm now believed that the Nation of Islam saw him as a threat. "Now I'm out," he once said. "And there's the fear [that] if my image isn't shattered, the Muslims in the movement will leave." Elijah Muhammad wrote in his periodical *Muhammad Speaks* that Malcolm was "worthy of death," and Malcolm soon discovered that members of the Nation of Islam were plotting to kill him. On February 21, 1965, he was assassinated while addressing an audience of four hundred in the Audubon Ballroom in Harlem. Three men—Talmadge Thayer, Norman 3X Butler, and Thomas 15X Johnson—were apprehended and eventually convicted of the crime.

The Autobiography of Malcolm X was published after Malcolm's death to much critical acclaim. Although some critics questioned Haley's influence in the work's production, commentators generally agreed that the story is Malcolm's own. Of the work's importance, Charles H. Nichols asserted in 1985: "*The Autobiography of Malcolm X* is probably the most influential book read by this generation of Afro-Americans. For not only is the account of Malcolm Little an absorbing and heart-shattering encounter with the realities of poverty, crime and racism. It is a fantastic success story. Paradoxically, the book, designed to be an indictment of American and European bigotry and exploitation, is a triumphant affirmation of the possibilities of the human spirit." Several of Malcolm's speeches have also been published, but his autobiography remains by far his greatest contribution to literature. As Malcolm X has increasingly been recognized as a leading figure in the African-American struggle for recognition and equality, *The Autobiography of Malcolm X* has grown in stature. Truman Nelson concluded: "Viewed in its complete historical context, this is indeed a great book. Its dead-level honesty, its passion, its exalted purpose, even its manifold unsolved ambiguities will make it stand as a monument to the most painful of truths: that this country, this people, this Western world has practiced unspeakable cruelty against a race, an individual, who might have made its fraudulent humanism a reality."

(For further information about Malcolm X's life and works, see *Black Writers* and *Contemporary Authors*, Vols. 111, 125.)

PRINCIPAL WORKS

The Autobiography of Malcolm X [with Alex Haley]
    (autobiography) 1965
Malcolm X Speaks: Selected Speeches and Statements
    (speeches) 1965
Malcolm X on Afro-American History (speeches) 1967
The Speeches of Malcolm X at Harvard (speeches) 1968
*Malcolm X and the Negro Revolution: The Speeches of
    Malcolm X* (speeches) 1969
Malcolm X Talks to Young People (speeches) 1969
Two Speeches by Malcolm X (speeches) 1969
*By Any Means Necessary: Speeches, Interviews, and a
    Letter by Malcolm X* (speeches, interviews, and
    letter) 1970
The End of White World Supremacy: Four Speeches
    (speeches) 1971

Bayard Rustin (essay date 1965)

[*As head of the War Resisters' League and special
assistant to Dr. Martin Luther King, Jr., Rustin had a
long and distinguished career as a civil rights activist.
His resistance to black political violence estranged
him from more radical elements of the civil rights
movement, however. In the following review of* The
Autobiography of Malcolm X, *he surveys Malcolm
X's life and analyzes his role as a leader in the black
community.*]

This odyssey of an American Negro in search of his
identity and place in society [*The Autobiography of
Malcolm X*] really begins before his birth 40 years ago in
Omaha, Neb. He was born Malcolm Little, the son of an
educated mulatto West Indian mother and a father who
was a Baptist minister on Sundays and dedicated
organizer for Marcus Garvey's back-to-Africa movement the rest of the week.

The first incident Malcolm recounts, as if it were his
welcome to white America, occurred just before he was
born. A party of Ku Klux Klanners galloped up to his
house, threatened his mother and left a warning for his
father "to stop spreading trouble among the good"
Negroes and get out of town. They galloped into the
night after smashing all the windows. A few years later
the Klan was to make good on its threat by burning
down the Littles' Lansing, Mich., home because Malcolm's father refused to become an Uncle Tom. These
were the first in a series of incidents of racial violence,
characteristic of that period, that were to haunt the
nights of Malcolm and his family and hang like a pall
over the lives of Negroes in the North and South. Five
of Reverend Little's six brothers died by violence—four
at the hands of white men, one by lynching, and one
shot down by Northern police officers. When Malcolm
was six, his father was found cut in two by a trolley car
with his head bashed in. Malcolm's father had committed "suicide," the authorities said. Early in his life

Malcolm concluded "that I too would die by violence.... I do not expect to live long enough to read
this book."

Malcolm's early life in the Midwest was not wholly
defined by race. Until he went to Boston when he was
14, after his mother suffered a mental breakdown from
bringing up eight children alone, his friends were often
white; there were few Negroes in the small Midwestern
towns where he grew up. He recounts with pride how he
was elected president of his eighth-grade class in an
almost totally white school.

But the race problem was always there, although Malcolm, who was light-skinned, tried for a time to think of
himself as white or just like anyone else. Even in his
family life, color led to conflict that interfered with
normal relationships. The Reverend Little was a fierce
disciplinarian, but he never laid a hand on his light-
skinned son because, unconsciously, according to Malcolm, he had developed respect for white skin. On the
other hand, Malcolm's mother, whose father was a white
man, was ashamed of this and favored Malcolm's darker
brothers and sisters. Malcolm wrote that he spent his life
trying to purge this tainted white blood of a rapist from
his veins.

Race also set the limits on his youthful ambitions during
what he describes as his "mascot years" in a detention
home run by whites with mixed feelings of affection and
superiority towards him. One of the top students in his
school and a member of the debating club, Malcolm
went to an English teacher he admired and told him of
his ambition to become a lawyer. "Mr. Ostrowsky
looked surprised and said, 'Malcolm, one of life's first
needs is for us to be realistic...a lawyer, that's no
realistic goal for a nigger...you're good with your
hands...why don't you plan on carpentry?'" How
many times has this scene been repeated in various
forms in schoolrooms across the country? It was at this
point, Malcolm writes, "that I began to change—inside.
I drew away from white people."

Too many people want to believe that Malcolm "the
angry black man sprang full grown from the bowels of
the Harlem ghetto." These chapters on his childhood are
essential reading for anyone who wants to understand
the plight of American Negroes.

Malcolm Little was 14 when he took the Greyhound to
Boston to live with his half-sister, Ella, who had fought
her way into the Boston "black bourgeoisie." The
"400," as they were called, lived on "the Hill," only one
step removed socially, economically and geographically
from the ghetto ("the Town"). Malcolm writes that "a
big percentage of the Hill dwellers were in Ella's
category—Southern strivers and scramblers and West
Indian Negroes, whom both the New Englanders and
Southerners called 'Black Jews.'" Ella owned some real
estate and her own home, and like the first Jews who
arrived in the New World, she was determined to
shepherd new immigrants and teach them the strange
ways of city life. There were deep bonds between Ella

and her younger brother, and she tried to help him live a respectable life on the Hill.

But for Malcolm the 400 were only "a big-city version of those 'successful' Negro bootblacks and janitors back in Lansing...8 out of 10 of the Hill Negroes of Roxbury...actually worked as menials and servants.... I don't know how many 40- and 50-year-old errand boys went down the Hill dressed as ambassadors in black suits and white collars to downtown jobs 'in government,' 'in finance,' or 'in law.'" Malcolm instead chose "the Town," where for the first time he felt he was part of a people.

Unlike the thousands of Negro migrants who poured into the Northern ghettos, Malcolm had a choice. But from the moment he made it, the options narrowed. He got a job at the Roseland Ballroom, where all the jazz greats played. His title was shoeshine boy but his real job was to hustle whiskey, prophylactics and women to Negroes and whites. He got his first conk and zoot suit and a new identity, "Red," and his secondary education began before he was 15. "I was...schooled well, by experts in such hustles as the numbers, pimping, con games of many kinds, peddling dope, and thievery of all sorts, including armed robbery."

It is significant that it was Malcolm's good qualities—his intelligence, integrity, and distaste for hypocrisy—as well as his sickness that made him choose crime rather than what passed in the Negro community for a respectable bourgeois life. Later he moved on to bigger things in Harlem, became "Detroit Red," went on dope and at one time carried three guns.

His description of the cutthroat competition between the hustlers and their fraternity is both frightening and moving. "As in the case of any jungle," he writes, "the hustler's every waking hour is lived with both the practical and the subconscious knowledge that if he ever relaxes, if he ever slows down, the other hungry, restless foxes, ferrets, wolves, and vultures out there with him won't hesitate to make him their prey." He summed up his morality at the time: "The only thing I considered wrong was what I got caught doing wrong...and everything I did was done by instinct to survive." As a "steerer" of uptown rich whites to Harlem "sex specialties," he recounts perversions with racial overtones, of white men begging to be beaten by black women or paying large amounts to witness interracial sex that make Genet's "The Balcony" seem inhibited by comparison.

"Detroit Red" was a limited success in his trade for four years. But even in this business, success was limited by race. The big operators, the successful, respectable, and safe executives of policy, dope, and prostitution rackets, were white and lived outside the ghetto.

Malcolm left Harlem to return to Boston, and a few months later was caught as the head of a burglary gang. In February, 1946, not quite 21, he was sentenced to 10 years in prison, though the average sentence for burglary was about two years—the price for his being caught with his white girl friend and her sister.

Most of the first year in prison, Malcolm writes, he spent in solitary confinement, cursing: "My favorite targets were the Bible and God." Malcolm got a new name from the other prisoners—"Satan"—and plenty of time to think. He went through what he described as a great spiritual crisis, and, as a result, he, the man who cursed God, bowed down and prayed to Allah. It will be difficult for those readers who have never been in prison to understand the psychological torment that prisoners experience, their feelings of isolation, their need to totally commit their minds to something outside of themselves. Men without any of the external economic symbols of status seek security in a religion, philosophy or ideology. Malcolm particularly, with his great feelings of rebelliousness, hatred and internal conflict, turned to books and ideas for relief. When his brothers and sisters wrote to him that they had become followers of Elijah Muhammad and sent him Elijah's teachings, Malcolm seized on the tracts. Stimulated, he read other books on religion and philosophy voraciously. In his spiritual and psychological crisis he underwent religious conversion.

He took on a new identity and became Malcolm X, a follower of Elijah Muhammad. Now he had a God to love and obey and a white devil responsible for his plight. Many Negro prisoners accepted the "Messenger," Elijah Muhammad, for similar reasons. Excluded from American society, they are drawn to another one, the Nation of Islam. (This analysis of why Malcolm joined the Muslims is mine, for although Malcolm writes about Muslim ideas, nowhere does he discuss the reasons for his conversion beyond a surface level.)

Out of prison, Malcolm, while remaining religious, arrived at a balanced view of the more fantastic elements of Elijah's teachings and a deeper understanding of one of the driving forces: "So many of the survivors whom I knew as tough hyenas and wolves of the streets in the old days now were so pitiful. They had known all the angles, but beneath that surface they were poor ignorant, untrained men; life had eased up on them and hyped them.... I was thankful to Allah that I had become a Muslim and escaped their fate."

Alex Haley, who assisted Malcolm with the book, rightly commends him for deciding not to rewrite the first parts of the book and make it a polemic against his old leader, although in the interim they had broken and now were in competition with each other. As a result, the book interestingly shows changes in Malcolm's thinking.

After seven years in prison, Detroit Red emerged as Malcolm X and was soon to be the brightest star of the Nation of Islam. But as in every conversion, the man himself was not entirely reborn. Malcolm brought with him his traits of the past—the shrewd and competitive instincts learned on the ghetto streets, combined now with the language and thoughts of the great philosophers of Western culture he applied from reading Hegel, Kant, and Nietzsche, and great Negro intellectuals like Du

Bois. Remaining, too, with his burning ambition to succeed, was the rebellious anger of his youth for being denied a place in society commensurate with his abilities. But on the other side of the coin was a desire for fraternity, family and respectability.

Because of his ability, he was sent to New York, where he struck a responsive chord with a great many Harlem Negroes. The Nationalist sects provided an arena of struggle for power and status denied lower-class Negroes in the outside world.

But the same qualities that made him a successful ghetto organizer soon brought him into conflict with other Muslim leaders, especially Elijah's children and prospective heirs. They saw Malcolm as a threat to their domain and apparently were able to convince Elijah that there was a threat to himself as well. For although Malcolm always gave corollary credit to Elijah—and the limits put upon him by Elijah's demands made many underestimate the exceptional nature of his mind—he could not totally constrain his brilliance, pride or ambition. "Only by being two people could I have worked harder in the service of the Nation of Islam. I had every gratification that I wanted. I had helped bring about the progress and additional impact such that none could call us liars when we called Mr. Muhammad the most powerful black man in America."

As Malcolm's star rose higher in the western sky, Mr. Muhammad saw his eastern star setting and grew jealous. The conflict grew, although Malcolm made efforts toward conciliation. Finally, there was a total break that can be fatal to the erring Muslim who is cast away. Malcolm was aware of the dangers. "I hadn't hustled in the streets for nothing. I knew I was being set up ... As any official in the Nation of Islam would instantly have known, any death-talk for me could have been approved of—if not actually initiated—by only one man." Later, just before his death, Malcolm said the attempt to murder him would come from a much greater source than the Muslims: he never revealed about whom he was talking.

Under a death sentence and without money or any substantial organization, Malcolm opted for action, although it was unclear whether he was running away from or toward something as he began another phase of his odyssey—a pilgrimage to Mecca where he became El-Hajj Malik El-Shabazz. Throughout his many conversions and transformations, he never was more American than during his trip to Mecca. Because his ankles were not flexible enough, he was unable to sit properly cross-legged on the traditional Muslim rug with the others, and at first he shrank from reaching into the common food pot. Like many American tourists, he projected desires for hospitality and fraternity, frustrated at home, on the Muslims he met, most of whom he could not communicate with because of the language barrier. Back in America, he acknowledged that it would be a long time before the Negro was ready to make common struggle with the Africans and Arabs.

In Mecca, Malcolm also dramatically announced that he had changed his view on integration, because he had seen true brotherhood there between black and white Muslims. In reality he had begun changing his attitude on integration and the civil rights movement many months before as the divisions between him and Elijah Muhammad widened. Part-way through the book his attacks on the movement became muted, and in the epilogue Haley concludes that Malcolm "had a reluctant admiration for Dr. Martin Luther King."

The roots of Malcolm's ambivalence were much more profound than personal opportunism. In a touching confession of dilemma he told Haley, "'the so-called moderate' civil rights organizations avoided him as 'too militant' and the 'so-called militants' avoided him as 'too moderate.' 'They won't let me turn the corner!' he once exclaimed. 'I'm caught in a trap!'" Malcolm was moving toward the mainstream of the civil rights movement when his life was cut short, but he still had quite a way to go. His anti-Semitic comments are a symptom of this malaise.

Had he been able to "turn the corner," he would have made an enormous contribution to the struggle for equal rights. As it was, his contribution was substantial. He brought hope and a measure of dignity to thousands of despairing ghetto Negroes. His "extremism" made the "mainstream" civil rights groups more respectable by comparison and helped them wrest substantial concessions from the power structure. Malcolm himself clearly understood the complicated role he played. At a Selma rally, while Dr. King was in jail, Malcolm said, "Whites better be glad Martin Luther King is rallying the people because other forces are waiting to take over if he fails." Of course, he never frightened the racists and the reactionaries as much as he made liberals feel uncomfortable, and moderates used his extremism as an excuse for inaction.

Behind the grim visage on television that upset so many white Americans there was a compassionate and often gentle man with a sense of humor. A testament to his personal honesty was that he died broke and money had to be raised for his funeral and family.

Upset by the comments in the African and Asian press criticizing the United States government for Malcolm's fate, Carl T. Rowan, Director of the United States Information Agency, held up some foreign papers and told a Washington audience, according to Alex Haley, "... All this about an ex-convict, ex-dope peddler, who became a racial fanatic." Yes, all this and more, before we can understand. Malcolm's autobiography, revealing little-known aspects of his life and character, makes that tortured journey more understandable.

One of the book's shortcomings is that M. S. Handler and Haley, in their sensitive and insightful supplementary comments, make no comprehensive estimate of Malcolm X as a political leader. His often conflicting roles in the civil rights movement are described rather than analyzed. Perhaps this couldn't be helped, for

Haley writes that Malcolm wanted a chronicler, not an interpreter. Obviously, Malcolm was not ready to make a synthesis of his ideas and an evaluation of his political role.

Shortly after Malcolm's death Tom Kahn and I wrote in New America and Dissent: "Now that he is dead, we must resist the temptation to idealize Malcolm X, to elevate charisma to greatness. History's judgment of him will surely be ambiguous. His voice and words were cathartic, channeling into militant verbiage emotions that otherwise might have run a violently destructive course. But having described the evil, he had no program for attacking it. With rare skill and feeling he articulated angry subterranean moods more widespread than any of us like to admit. But having blown the trumpet, he could summon, even at the very end, only a handful of followers."

Of course we cannot judge political effectiveness by numbers alone, but we cannot ignore his inability to build a movement. As a spokesman for Negro anger and frustration, he left his mark on history, but as a militant political leader he failed—and the Negro community needed both. Till the end, his program was a maze of contradictions. He was a brilliant psychologist when it came to articulating the emotions and thoughts of ghetto Negroes, but he knew virtually nothing about economics, and more important, his program had no relevance to the needs of lower-class Negroes. His conception of the economic roots of the problem is reflected in such remarks as "it is because black men do not own and control their community retail establishments that they cannot stabilize their own communities." And he advocates, as a solution, that Negroes who buy so many cars and so much expensive whiskey should own automobile franchises and distilleries. Malcolm was urging Negroes to pool their resources into small business establishments at a time when small businesses were declining under the pressure of big business and when an unplanned technological revolution is creating massive unemployment for unskilled Negroes. Malcolm's solutions were in fact almost a mirror image of many proposals made by white economic moderates; those advocates of "self-help" without a massive program for jobs remind me of no one so much as those black nationalist sects and their "build it yourself" black economy without capital. In short, Malcolm's economic program was not radical. It was, in fact, petty bourgeois.

Malcolm got a wide hearing in the ghetto because large sections of the Negro working class were being driven into the "underclass" and made part of the rootless mass by the vicissitudes of the economy. He articulated the frustration and anger of these masses, and they admired his outspoken attack on the racists and white hypocrites. But while thousands came to his funeral (I was there, too, to pay my respects), few joined his organization. Nor should it be surprising that the Negro masses did not support his proposed alliance of black Americans, Africans, and Arabs, including such leaders as Prince Faisal. For what did a Harlem Negro, let alone

an Arab Bedouin, have in common with a feudal prince like Faisal? And at home Malcolm maintained an uneasy coexistence with the Harlem political machine. Today, Malcolm's organization, the OAAU, hardly exists. In addition, he never clearly understood that as progress was made toward social integration, the problem for America's Negroes would become just as much one of class as of race.

Malcolm was with the Negro masses, but he was not of them. His experience and ambitions separated him from working-class Negroes. But to say this is not enough. In a sense Malcolm's life was tragic on a heroic scale. He had choices but never took the easy or comfortable ones. If he had, he might today be, as he says, a successful lawyer, sipping cocktails with other members of the black bourgeoisie. He chose instead to join the Negro masses who never had this freedom of choice. And, before his death he was working toward a more creative approach to the problems of the ghetto. Perhaps he might have been successful in "turning this corner."

After reflecting on the old days at Mosque 7, shortly before he was killed, Malcolm told Haley, "That was a bad scene, brother. The sickness and madness of those days—I'm glad to be free of them. It's a time for martyrs now. And if I'm to be one, it will be in the cause of brotherhood."

Our journey through the madness of racism continues, and there is much we can learn about both the sickness and the cure from Malcolm X. (pp. 1, 8, 10, 12, 16-17)

> *Bayard Rustin, "Making His Mark: A Strong Diagnosis of America's Racial Sickness in One Negro's Odyssey," in* Book Week—New York Herald Tribune, *November 14, 1965, pp. 1, 8, 10, 12, 16-17.*

Robert Penn Warren (essay date 1966)

[*Author of the novel* All the King's Men *(1946), Warren is recognized as one of the most distinguished men of letters in twentieth-century America. In the following essay, he profiles Malcolm X and speculates about what his future would have been had he lived.*]

James Farmer, lately the National Director of the Committee of Racial Equality, has called Malcolm X a "very simple man." Elijah Poole, better known to the Black Muslims as Muhammad and, indeed, as Allah, called him a "star gone astray." An editorial writer of the *Saturday Evening Post* put it: "If Malcolm X were not a Negro, his autobiography would be little more than a journal of abnormal psychology, the story of a burglar, dope pusher, addict and jailbird—with a family history of insanity—who acquires messianic delusions and sets forth to preach an upside-down religion of 'brotherly' hatred." Carl Rowan, a Negro, lately the director of the United States Information Service, substantially agreed with that editorial writer when he said, in an interview after Malcolm's assassination, that he was "an ex-convict, ex-dope peddler who became a racial fanatic." Another editorial writer, that of the *Daily Times* of Lagos, Nigeria, called him a martyr.

Malcolm X may have been, in varying perspectives, all these things. But he was also something else. He was a latter-day example of an old-fashioned type of American celebrated in grammar school readers, commencement addresses, and speeches at Rotary Club lunches—the man who "makes it," the man who, from humble origins and with meager education, converts, by will, intelligence, and sterling character, his liabilities into assets. Malcolm X was of that breed of Americans, autodidacts and homemade successes, that has included Benjamin Franklin, Abraham Lincoln, P. T. Barnum, Thomas A. Edison, Booker T. Washington, Mark Twain, Henry Ford, and the Wright brothers. Malcolm X would look back on his beginnings and, in innocent joy, marvel at the distance he had come.

But in Malcolm X the old Horatio Alger story is crossed, as has often been the case, with another typical American story. America has been prodigally fruitful of hot-gospellers and prophets—from Dr. Graham and his bread, Amelia Bloomer and her bloomers, Emerson and the Oversoul, and Brigham Young, on to F.D.R. and the current Graham, Billy. Furthermore, to round out his American story and insure his fame, Malcolm X, like John Brown, Abraham Lincoln, Joseph Smith (the founder of Mormonism), and John Fitzgerald Kennedy, along with a host of lesser prophets, crowned his mission with martyrdom. Malcolm X fulfills, it would seem, all the requirements—success against odds, the role of prophet, and martyrdom—for inclusion in the American pantheon.

Malcolm Little, who was to become Malcolm X and El-Hajj Malik El-Shabazz, was born in Omaha, Nebraska, on May 19, 1925. All omens were right, and all his background. He was the seventh child of his father. One night during the pregnancy of his mother, hooded Ku Klux Klansmen, mounted and brandishing rifles and shotguns, surrounded the house, calling for the father to come out; the mother faced them down and persuaded them of the fact that her husband was not at home. The mother, a West Indian who looked white, was ashamed, not proud, of the white blood. The father, a Baptist preacher, was a militant follower of Marcus Garvey, and this was to lead to another attack on the Little home, in 1929, in Lansing, Michigan, this time by the Black

Malcolm X and Elijah Muhammad.

Legion, which except for black robes was indistinguishable from the Klan; the house burned to the ground, while white police and firemen looked on. The memory of that night stayed with Malcolm from childhood—that and the pictures his father showed him of Marcus Garvey "riding in a fine car, a big black man dressed in a dazzling uniform with gold braid on it, and he was wearing a thrilling hat with tall plumes," and the Garveyite meetings at which his father presided and which always ended with the exhortation, "Up, you mighty race, you can accomplish what you will!" The people would chant these words after Malcolm's father.

To complete the picture of the preparation of the hero for his mission, his father, who had seen two brothers killed by white men and a third lynched, was found, one night, on a streetcar track, with skull crushed and body cut almost across. Negroes in Lansing—and the son all his life—believed that he had been attacked by white men, and then laid on the track. Malcolm always believed that he, too, would meet a violent death. When he first became aware of the long stalk, which was to end in gunfire in the Audubon Ballroom, Malcolm might accept it, then, as a fulfillment of old omens and intuitions.

In spite of the powerful image of the father, the pictures of Garvey in uniform, and the tales of black kings, Malcolm's early notion of Africa was still one "of naked savages, cannibals, monkeys and tigers and steaming jungles." He says that he never understood why. But that statement must be an example, in a form more bland than usual, of his irony, for a large part of his autobiography (*The Autobiography of Malcolm X*) is devoted to explaining *why*—that is, by the white man's "brain-washing"; and then explaining *how,* step by step, he came to the vision of another Africa, and of another self, different from the hustler, pimp, dope-addict, dope-pusher, burglar, and, by his own account, generally degraded and vice-ridden creature known as "Satan," who, in 1948, in Concord Prison, in Massachusetts, heard, in a letter from his brother Philbert, of the "natural religion for the black man." The religion was called the "Nation of Islam."

This autobiography is "told" to Alex Haley, a Negro, a retired twenty-year man of the Coast Guard turned journalist. From 1963 up to the assassination, Haley saw Malcolm for almost daily sessions when Malcolm was in New York, and sometimes accompanied him on his trips. Haley's account of this period, of how he slowly gained Malcolm's confidence and how Malcolm himself discovered the need to tell his story, is extremely interesting and, though presented as an Epilogue, is an integral part of the book; but the main narrative has the advantage of Malcolm's tone, his characteristic movement of mind, and his wit, for Haley has succeeded admirably in capturing these qualities, as can be checked by the recollection of Malcolm's TV appearances and conversation and by his taped speeches (*Malcolm X Speaks: Selected Speeches and Statements*).

The *Autobiography* and the speeches are an extraordinary record of an extraordinary man. They are, among other things, a record that may show a white man (or some Negroes, for Malcolm would say that many Negroes do not know the nature of their own experience) what it means to be a Negro in America, in this century, or at least what it so dramatically meant to one man of unusual intelligence and powerful personality. Being a Negro meant being "black"—even if black was no more than a metaphor for Malcolm, who was himself "marigny," a dull yellowish skin, pale enough to freckle, pale eyes, hair reddish-coppery. He had been "Detroit Red" in his hustling days.

To be black, metaphorically or literally, meant, according to Malcolm, to wear a badge of shame which was so mystically and deeply accepted that all the practical injustices the white world might visit upon the black would seem only a kind of inverted justice, necessary in the very nature of things, the working out of a curse. The black man had no history, no country, no identity; he was alienated in time and place; he lived in "self-hate," and being unable to accept "self," he therefore was willing to accept, supine or with random violence, his fate. This was the diagnosis of his own plight, as Malcolm learned it from the "Nation of Islam."

As for the cure, what he found was the doctrine of the Black Muslims. This involved a history of creation and a metaphysic which made the black man central and dominant, and a secular history of kingly achievement in Africa. The divine and secular histories provided a justification for the acceptance of the black "self." In addition, the doctrine provided an understanding of the iniquity of the white man which would account for the black man's present lot and would, at the same time, mobilize an unquenchable hate against him. Total withdrawal from the white man and all his works was the path to virtue, until the day of Armageddon when he would be destroyed. Meanwhile, until the Chosen People had been relieved of the white man's presence, the black man was presented with a practical program of life: thrift, education, cleanliness, diet (no pork, for example, pork being a "nigger" food), abstemiousness (no alcohol or tobacco), manners and courtesy, puritanical morality and reverence for the home and Muslim womanhood—a general program of "wake up, clean up, and stand up." In fact, on the practical side, in spite of the hatred of the white man and contempt for his culture, the Black Muslim doctrine smuggled into the life of the Negro slum the very virtues which had made white middle-class America what it was—i.e., successful.

After Malcolm's death Dr. Kenneth B. Clark, the Negro psychologist and the author of an important book called *Dark Ghetto,* said that he had been "cut down at the point when he seemed on the verge of achieving the position of respectability he sought." In the midst of the gospel of violence and the repudiation of the white world, even in the Black Muslim phase, there appears now and then the note of yearning. In the *Autobiography* we find, for instance, this passage: "I was the invited speaker at the Harvard Law School Forum. I happened to glance through a window. Abruptly, I realized that I was looking in the direction of the apartment house that was my old burglary group's hideout.... And there I stood, the invited speaker, at Harvard."

Malcolm, still in prison, gave up pork and tobacco, and undertook a program of reading in the good library there available. He read in Plato, Aristotle, Schopenhauer, Kant, Nietzsche, and the "Oriental philosophers." He read and reread the Bible, and could match quotations with a Harvard Seminary student who conducted a class for prisoners. He studied *The Loom of Language,* by Frederick Bodmer, and memorized Grimm's Law. He read Durant's *Story of Civilization,* H. G. Wells' *Outline of History,* Herodotus, Fannie Kimball, *Uncle Tom's Cabin,* Gandhi, Gregor Mendel, pamphlets of the "Abolitionist Anti-Slavery Society of New England," and J. A. Rogers' *Sex and Race.* He was trying to find the black man's place—and his own—in history, trying, in other words, to document the doctrine of the Black Muslims. He wrote regularly to Muhammad to tell what he had found. While he was still in prison Malcolm also had a vision. He had written an appeal to Muhammad to reinstate his brother Reginald, suspended as a Muslim for "improper relations" with the secretary of the New York Temple. That night he spent in desperate prayer. The next night he woke up and saw a man sitting, there in the cell, in a chair by him. "He had on a dark suit, I remember. I could see him as plainly as I see anyone I look at. He wasn't black, and he wasn't white. He was light-brown-skinned, an Asiatic cast of countenance, and he had oily black hair.... I had no idea whatsoever who he was. He just sat there. Then suddenly as he had come, he was gone." The color of the man in the vision is an interesting fact. So is his immobility and silence.

When Malcolm Little came out of prison, he was Malcolm X, the "X," according to the practice of the Black Muslims, standing for the true name lost long ago in Africa to take the place of the false white name that had been forced on him. He had been reborn, and he now entered upon his mission. Soon he was an accredited minister of Muhammad, the official defender of the faith and the intellectual spokesman of the movement. His success, and especially the fact that he was invited to colleges, where Muhammad would never be invited, led to jealousy and, as Malcolm reports, contributed to his "silencing" as soon as a good justification appeared.

Malcolm X was not the only man drawn from the lower depths to be reborn in the Nation of Islam. It is generally admitted that the record of rehabilitation by the Black Muslims of dope-addicts, alcoholics, prostitutes, and criminals makes any other method seem a waste of time. They have, it would seem, found the nerve center that, once touched, can radically change both the values and the way of life for a number of Negroes in America; and it is important here to use the phrase "Negroes in America" with special emphasis,

and no other locution, for those redeemed by the Black Muslims are those who have been only *in,* but not *of,* America, those without country, history, or identity. The Black Muslims have found, then, a principle that, if not of universal validity (or, in one perspective, isn't it? for white as well as for black?), at least involves a truth of considerable psychological importance. That truth is, indeed, shrouded in metaphysical mumbo-jumbo, political and economic absurdity, and some murderous delusions, but even these elements have a noteworthy symbolic relation to the central truth. It is reported that Martin Luther King, after seeing Malcolm X on TV, remarked: "When he starts talking about all that's been done to us, I get a twinge of hate, of identification with him. But hate is not the only effect." A man as intelligent, as cultivated, and as experienced as James Farmer has testified in his recent book *Freedom When?* that the Black Muslims and Malcolm X have had a very important impact on his own thinking and in helping to change his basic views of the Negro Revolution, especially on the question of "blackness" and on the nature of integration and the Negro's role in an open society.

If this is the case, then the story of Malcolm X assumes an added dimension. It shows the reader the world in which that truth can operate; that is, it shows the kind of alienation to which this truth is applicable. It shows, also, the human quality of the operation, a man in the process of trying to understand his plight, and to find salvation, by that truth. But there is another aspect to the *Autobiography.* Malcolm X was a man in motion, he was a seeker, and that motion led, in the end, away from orthodox Black Muslim doctrine. The doctrine had been, he said, a straitjacket. He was now in the process of stripping away, perhaps unconsciously, the mumbo-jumbo, the absurdities, and the murderous delusions. He was trying, as it were, to locate the truth that had saved him, and divest it of the irrelevancies. In the end, he might have come to regard the religion that, after his break with the Black Muslims, he had found in Mecca as an irrelevancy, too. Certainly, just before his death he could say that his "philosophy" was still changing. Perhaps what Mecca gave him, for the time being at least, was the respectability, the authority, of the established thing. But he might have finally found that authority in himself, for he could speak as a man whose very existence was witness to what he said. Something of that purely personal authority comes through in these books.

Malcolm X had, in his last phase, lost the mystique of blackness so important to the Black Muslims; he had seen the blue-eyed and fair-haired pilgrims in Mecca. He was no longer a separatist in the absolute sense of the Black Muslims. He had become enough of an integrationist to say: "I believe in recognizing every human being as a human being...and when you are dealing with humanity as a family, there's no question of integration or intermarriage. It's just one human being marrying another human being or one human being living around with another human being." And just before his death he had made a down-payment on a house, in Long Island, in a largely Jewish neighborhood. He no longer saw the white man as the "white devil"—metaphysically evil; and he was ready, grudgingly, not optimistically, and with a note of threat, to grant that there was in America a chance, a last chance, for a "bloodless revolution." He was ready to work with other Negro organizations, even those which he had most derided, to try to find common ground and solutions at a practical level.

Certain ideas were, however, carried over from the Black Muslim days. The question of "identity" remained, and the question of race pride and personal self-respect divested of chauvinism, and with this the notion of "wake up, clean up, and stand up," the notion of self-reliance, self-improvement, self-discipline. If he could say such things, which smacked of the discredited philosophy of Booker T. Washington, and which few other Civil Rights leaders would dare to utter, it was because he did so in the context of his intransigence vis-à-vis the white world and his radical indictment of white society. Even in the last phase, even if he believed in "recognizing every human being as a human being," and no longer took the white man to be metaphysically evil, his indictment of white society was still radical; unless that society could really be regenerated, the chance for the "bloodless revolution" was gone.

This radical indictment leads to what may be the greatest significance of Malcolm X, his symbolic role. He was the black man who looked the white man in the eye and forgave nothing. If the white man had turned away, in shame or indifference, from the awful "forgiveness" of a Martin Luther King, he still had to face the unforgivingness, with its shattering effect on his accustomed view of himself and with the terrifying discovery, as Malcolm's rage brought his own rage forth, of the ultimate of which he himself would, under pressure, be capable. To put it another way, Malcolm X let the white man see what, from a certain perspective, he, his history, and his culture looked like. It was possible to say that that perspective was not the only one, that it did not give the whole truth about the white man, his history, and his culture, but it was not possible to say that the perspective did not carry a truth, a truth that was not less, but more, true for being seen from the angle of "Small's Paradise" in Harlem or of the bedroom to which "Detroit Red," the "steerer," brought the "Ivy League fathers" to be ministered to by the big black girl, whose body had been greased to make it look "shinier and blacker" and whose Amazonian hand held a small plaited whip.

On the afternoon of Sunday, February 21, 1965, at a meeting of his struggling new Organization of Afro-American Unity, in the Audubon Ballroom, on West 166th Street, in Harlem, Malcolm X rose to speak and uttered the ritual greeting, "Asalaikum, brothers and sisters!" He was immediately cut down by shotgun and revolver fire from assassins waiting in the front of the audience. At 3:30 at the Columbia-Presbyterian Hospital, he was pronounced dead. Three men—Talmadge

Thayer, Norman 3X (Brown), and Thomas 15X (Johnson)—were arrested in the case and tried for first-degree murder. Thayer denied Black Muslim connections, but Thomas 15X was identified as a member and Norman 3X as a lieutenant in the "Fruit of Islam"—the bodyguards of Elijah Muhammad. After deliberating for twenty hours a jury found them guilty, and all three were given life sentences.

What would have been Malcolm's role had he lived? Perhaps, as some Negro leaders said shortly before his death, he had no real organization, and did not have the talent to create one. Perhaps his being in motion was only, as some held, a result of confusion of mind, a groping that could not be trusted to bring results. Perhaps, as James Farmer had put it, Malcolm, for all his talk, was not an activist; he had managed all along to be out of harm's way whenever harm was brewing, and he was afraid of the time when he "would have to chirp or get off the perch."

But perhaps the new phase of the Negro Revolution, with the violence of the great city slums, might have given him his great chance. He might have, at last, found himself in action. He might have found himself committed to blind violence, but on the other hand he might have had the power to control and canalize action and do something to reduce the danger of the Revolution's degenerating into random revolt. For, in spite of all the gospel of intransigence, Malcolm had always had a governing idea of a constructive role for the Negro, some notion of a society. After all, he had personal force, as no one who ever spent as little as ten minutes with him would have doubted: charisma, to use the fashionable word, and that to a degree possessed by no other leader except Martin Luther King. And he had one great asset which Martin Luther King does not have: he was from the lower depths and possessed the authority of one who had both suffered and conquered the depths.

Whatever the future might have held for him had he lived, his actual role was an important one, and in one sense the importance lay in his *being* rather than his *doing*. He was a man of passion, depth, and scale—and his personal story is a moving one. There is the long struggle. There is the sense of desperation and tightening entrapment as, in the last days, Malcolm recognized the dilemma developing in his situation. The "so-called moderate" Civil Rights leaders, he said, dodged him as "too militant," and the "so-called militants" dodged him as "too moderate." Haley reports that he once exclaimed "They won't let me turn the corner! I'm caught in a trap!" For there is a trap in the story, a real and lethal one. There is the gang of Black Muslims covering his every move in the Statler Hilton at Los Angeles, the mysterious Negro men who tried to get his room number at the Hilton in New York City, and the sinister telephone call to his room in the hotel the morning of his death. There is the bombing of his house, and his despairing anger when the event was widely taken as a publicity stunt. There is his remark to Haley, as he asked to read the manuscript of his book for a last, unnecessary time: "I just want to read it one more time, because I don't expect to read it in finished form"—wanting, as it were, to get a last sense of the shape of his own life as he felt the trap closing. There is, as with a final accent of pathos, the letter by his six-year-old daughter Attilah (named for the Scourge of God), written just after his death: "Dear Daddy, I love you so. O dear, O dear, I wish you wasn't dead." But entrapment and pathos was not all. He had been bred to danger. When he stepped on the platform that Sunday afternoon, in the face of odds which he had more shrewdly estimated than anybody else, he had nerve, confidence, style. He made his last gesture.

As one reads the ***Autobiography,*** one feels that, whatever the historical importance of Malcolm Little, his story has permanence, that it has something of tragic intensity and meaning. One feels that it is an American story bound to be remembered, to lurk in the background of popular consciousness, to reappear some day in a novel, on the stage, or on the screen. No—the right medium might be the ballad. Malcolm was a figure out of the anonymous depth of the folk, and even now, in a slum bedroom or in the shadowy corner of some bar, fingers may be tentatively picking the box, and lips fumbling to frame the words that will mean, long after our present problems are resolved and forgotten, the final fame, and the final significance. (pp. 161-71)

> *Robert Penn Warren, "Malcolm X: Mission and Meaning," in* The Yale Review, *Vol. LVI, No. 2, December, 1966, pp. 161-71.*

Warner Berthoff (essay date 1971)

[*In the following excerpt, Berthoff analyzes* The Autobiography of Malcolm X *as a "contemporary classic."*]

No one can read very much of Malcolm's writing, more precisely listen to the voice transcribed in the autobiography (dictated to the journalist Alex Haley) or the printed versions of his public speeches, without forming the sense of an extraordinary human being: fiercely intelligent, shrewdly and humanely responsive to the life around him despite every reason in the world to have gone blind with suspicion and hate, a rarely gifted leader and inspirer of other men. The form of autobiographical narration adds something further; he comes through to us as the forceful agent of a life-history that was heroic in the event and has the shape of the heroic in the telling, a protagonist who (in Francis R. Hart's fine description) has himself created and now recreates "human value and vitality in each new world or underworld he has entered."

The power of Malcolm's book is that it speaks directly out of the totality of that life-history *and* the ingratiating openness of his own mind and recollection to it. It seems to me a book that...does not require any softening or suspension of critical judgment. In the first place it is written, or spoken, in a quick, pungent, concrete style, again the plain style of popular idiom, improved and made efficient by the same sort of natural sharpness and concentration of attention that gives life and color to the best of Mark Twain's recollective writing, or Franklin's, or Bunyan's. In the run of the narrative the liveliness of observation and recollection, the "histrionic exuberance" (Professor Hart again), are continuously persuasive—and incidentally confirm as elements of a true style Alex Haley's assurance that the book is indeed Malcolm's own and not a clever piece of mimicry or pastiche. The casually vivid rendering of other persons is worth remarking, a test some quite competent novelists would have trouble passing. People who were especially important to Malcolm—his strong-minded half-sister Ella; the motherly white woman who ran the detention home he was sent to at 13, who was always kind to him and would call his people "niggers" to his face without a flicker of uneasiness; Shorty from Boston, who set him up in business; West Indian Archie, who "called him out"; or the tough convict Bimbi in Charlestown prison, strange little man of unexpected thoughts and arguments, who broke through the wall of rage and hate Malcolm was closing around himself—all these figures are precisely defined, according to their place in the story. The grasp of the narrative extends in fact to whole sociologies of behavior. The Harlem chapters in general, with their explanation of hustling in all its major forms—numbers, drugs, prostitution, protection, petty in-ghetto thievery—offer one of the best accounts in our literature of the cultural underside of the American business system, and of the bitter psychology that binds its victims to it; Malcolm came to see very clearly how the habituations bred by ghetto poverty operate to destroy individual efforts to break out of it, and he could use that insight with force and point in his preaching. Most generally it is just this blending of his own life-story with the full collective history of his milieu and the laws of behavior controlling it that gives Malcolm's testimony its strength and large authority—and sets it apart, I think, from the many more or less skillfully designed essays in autobiography we have had recently from writers like Frank Conroy, Claude Brown, Norman Podhoretz, Willie Morris, Paul Cowan, David McReynolds, to mention only a few; sets it apart also from the great run of novels about contemporary city life.

But it is Malcolm himself, and his own active consciousness of the myth of his life's progress, that most fills and quickens the book, making it something more than simply a valuable document. His past life is vividly present to him as he speaks; he gives it the form, in recollection, of a dramatic adventure in which he himself is felt as the precipitating agent and moving force. It is not unreasonable that he should see himself as someone who has a special power to make things happen, to work changes on the world around him (and to change within himself); and thus finally as one whose rise to authority is in some sense in the natural order of things, the working out of some deep structure of fortune. That is my way of putting it; Malcolm himself, as a Muslim, of course uses other words.

Malcolm X and students at Atlanta University in 1964.

The force of this continuously active process of self-conception and self-projection is fundamental to the book's power of truth. It gives vitality and momentum to the early parts of the story, the picture of Malcolm's salad days as a Roxbury and Harlem sharpie, with conked hair and "knob-toed, orange-colored 'kick-up' shoes," the wildest Lindy-hopper and quickest hustler of all, delighting always in his impact on others—as in the interlude of his first trip back to Lansing, Michigan, to wow the yokels with his Harlem flashiness—finding satisfaction, too, in the names, the folk-identities, that attach to him at each new stage: "Homeboy," "Harlem Rcd" or "Detroit Red," "Satan" in the storming defiance of his first imprisonment. Most decisively, this force of self-conception is what brings alive the drama of his conversion, and his re-emergence within the Nation of Islam as a leader and teacher of his people. For Malcolm's autobiography is consciously shaped as the story of an "education," and in so describing it I am not merely making the appropriate allusion to Henry Adams or the *Bildungsroman* tradition; "education" is Malcolm's own word for what is taking place.

Above all, the book is the story of a conversion and its consequences. We can identify in it various classic features of conversion-narrative. A full detailing of the crimes and follies of his early life makes more astonishing the change of changes that follows ("The very enormity of my previous life's guilt prepared me to accept the truth"). In the central light of this new truth, particular events take on symbolic dimensions; they stand as the exemplary trials and challenges which the redeemed soul must pass through and by which it knows the meaning, feels the reality, of its experience. That meaning and reality, to repeat, are not merely personal. The outlines of grander historical patterns are invoked and give their backing to the story—the whole long history and tragedy of the black race in America; then, at the crisis, the radically clarifying mythology of the Black Muslim movement (a mythology which, to any one willing to consider it objectively, has the character of a full-blown poetic mythology; a source, once you place yourself inside it, of comprehensive and intrinsically rational explanations for the life-experience it refers to, that of the mass of black people in a historically racist society).

And always there is Malcolm's own fascination with what has happened to him, and what objectively it means. As if establishing a leitmotif, the climaxes of his story repeatedly focus on this extraordinary power to change and be changed that he has grown conscious of within himself and that presents itself to him as the distinctive rule of his life. Malcolm speaks with a just pride of his quickness to learn, to "pick up" how things are done in the world; of his readiness, even when it humiliates him, to accept schooling from those in possession of some special competence or wisdom; of a "personal chemistry" of openmindedness and quick realism that requires him to find out the full vital truth of his own experience and that keeps it available to consciousness from that time forward. His curiosity about life is unquenchable ("You can hardly mention anything I'm not curious about"). He has a driving need to understand everything that happens to him or around him and to gain a measure of intelligent control over it; it is a passion with him to get his own purchase on reality.

It thus makes *narrative* sense, of a kind only the best of novelists are in command of, that he should discover his calling in life as a teacher and converter. Malcolm has his own theories for nearly everything that interests him—theories of language and etymology (he has an autodidact's sense of word-magic, dating from the time in prison when studying a dictionary, page by page, in a folklorish fury of self-improvement, began quite literally to give him an extravagant new intuition of power and freedom, as of one suddenly finding a key to his enemy's most treasured secrets); theories about how Socrates' wisdom came from initiation into the mysteries of black Egypt and about the persecuted black philosopher Spinoza and the black poet Homer (cognate with Omar and Moor) and about who really wrote Shakespeare and translated the English Bible and why. Of course we can laugh at a lot of this from the pewboxes of a more orderly education, but I find myself impressed even in these odd instances with the unfailing rationality of the uses to which Malcolm put his thought, the intelligence even here of what really matters to him—which is the meaning of his life as a black man in the United States and the enormous responsibilities of a position of authority and leadership in which he can count on no help from the official, institutionalized culture but what he wrenches out for himself.

But it is, again, the prodigy of his own conversion that gives him the most direct confirmation of his beliefs; the awareness of himself as a man capable of these transforming changes that gives him confidence in his testimony's importance, that lets him say, "Anything I do today, I regard as urgent." *The Autobiography* was written to serve at once a religious and a political cause, the cause of the religion of Islam and the cause of black freedom, and it is filled with the letter of Malcolm's teaching. In the later chapters especially, more and more of the text is portioned out to explanations of essential doctrine and to social and political commentary and analysis. But here, too, it is a personal authority that

comes through to us and makes the difference. I should like to try to characterize this authority a little further. I first read Malcolm's autobiography when I happened also to be reading through the Pauline epistles in the New Testament; the chance result was a sharp consciousness of fundamental resemblances. Resemblances, I mean, to the voice and manner of the Paul who not only is teaching his people the law of the new faith (to which he himself is a late comer, and by hard ways) but who suffuses his teaching with all the turbulence of his own history and masterful personality. Two recent students of Paul's letters, Charles Buck and Greer Taylor, have commented on the singularity of this element in Paul: "a presumption of personal authority on the part of the writer which is quite unlike that of any other New Testament author." Malcolm, too, writes as the leader of a new, precariously established faith, which he is concerned to stabilize against destructive inner dissensions yet without losing any of the priceless communal fervor and dedication that have been released by it. So at every point he brings to bear the full weight of his own reputation and active experience, including his earlier follies and excesses—precisely as Paul does in, for example, the astonishing final chapters of Second Corinthians, full as they are of the liveliest and most immediate self-reference. The tangible genius of both Paul and Malcolm as writers is to bring the authority of living personality, and of self-mastery, into the arena of what is understood to be an argument of the utmost consequence; a matter of life and death for those who commit themselves to it.

Malcolm's concerns are of course civil and political as well as sectarian. In his last years he had become, and knew it, a national leader as important as Dr. King; a leader moreover who, as the atmosphere of the Washington March of August 1963 gave way to the ghetto riots of the next summer, was trusted inside Harlem and its counterparts as the established black leadership no longer was. And the last academic point I want to make about the literary character of Malcolm's book is that in this regard, too, as a political statement, its form is recognizably "classic." The model it quite naturally conforms to is that of the Political Testament, the work in which some ruler or statesman sets down for the particular benefit of his people a summary of his own experience and wisdom and indicates the principles which are to guide those who succeed him. The historian Felix Gilbert has called attention to this rather special literary tradition in his study of the background of Washington's Farewell Address. It is necessarily, in the number of its members, a limited tradition; besides Washington's address Professor Gilbert mentions examples attributed to Richelieu, Colbert, the Dutch republican Jan de Witt, Robert Walpole, Peter the Great, and Frederick the Great, who wrote at least two of them. My argument is not that Malcolm was in any way guided by this grand precedent, merely that in serving all his book's purposes he substantially recreated it—which is of course what the work of literature we call "classic" does within the occasion it answers to. (pp. 316-21)

Warner Berthoff, "Witness and Testament: Two Contemporary Classics," in New Literary History, *Vol. II, No. 2, Winter, 1971, pp. 311-27.*

Barrett John Mandel (essay date 1972)

[*In the following essay, Mandel examines* The Autobiography of Malcolm X *as a didactic account of a conversion experience.*]

The Autobiography of Malcolm X is a richly didactic work—didactic in the best sense of the word. As a man who spent the greater part of his life in learning how to be a *human* being, always working toward the goal of humanizing those around him, Malcolm X has written his autobiography in the hagiographical spirit of one who has found hope and even peace and now wishes to help others find them.

Malcolm's recollections carry him from his birth as Malcolm Little on 19 May 1925 to 1965 just before his death as El-Hajj Malik El-Shabazz. Between those two dates, he traces his history. It begins with a nightmarish account of the Ku Klux Klan galloping out of the Omaha night to threaten his father, a Marcus Garvey enthusiast. Malcolm tells of his unhappy boyhood in Michigan where his family was victimized by a racist society's contempt and where on parole from a detention home, he made a success of himself in school by adopting the white man's standards and customs. The autobiography traces Malcolm's descent into the dizzying life of the black underworld of Boston and New York. As "Detroit Red" Malcolm experienced the desperate criminal existence of Harlem, involving himself in narcotics, hustling, and robbery. At last caught by the police and sentenced more for consorting with white women than for burglary, Malcolm is sent to prison. While in jail, he converts to Elijah Muhammad's Nation of Islam, introduced to it and guided by his brother Reginald. From the moment of conversion, Malcolm's life is directed toward personal, spiritual growth, and dedication in his mission to the black world. The Muslim faith could lead all Negroes to a new position of self-respect and dignity. Malcolm traces his ascent in the Nation of Islam ministry until his charismatic power makes him a threat to Elijah Muhammad. Malcolm is forced out of the Muslim Community and so he makes his fateful trip to Mecca and embraces the "true" Muslim faith. He ends his account in the aftermath of his trip to Asia and Africa. Back in New York, he tries, in vain, to fend off the fatal blow which he fears is about to strike him down. At first Malcolm suspects the Black Muslims of wishing his death, but toward the end he has begun to assume that such a plot to cut off his life must be a larger, more sinister affair than that of which the Black Muslims would be capable.

Like St. Augustine, John Bunyan, Jonathan Edwards, and Vavasor Powell, Malcolm has written a spiritual conversion autobiography. The *Autobiography* is that of a sinner who becomes a saint, and the saint, like his Christian parallels, is a preacher. One notices the parallels especially to John Bunyan, who as he became a "saint"—the word was commonly used for puritan bretheren in the seventeenth century and was still used by the Plymouth Bretheren in the nineteenth century—became increasingly repugnant to the established authorities, who went to great lengths to stop his preaching.

Malcolm, trapped in a Manichean world of Evil and Good, is pulled from pole to pole in his slow ascent to self-knowledge. And there are many other parallels to familiar conversion literature. The treatment of sex can serve as an important example. Malcolm tells of his youth spent among pimps and whores. Like the young St. Augustine, Malcolm at first found the good life to be one of fleshly pursuits; his narrative skill goes a long way toward recreating the attractiveness of the early temptations. It is only as the rhythm of his life starts to carry him toward self-regeneration in Islam that he recognizes the need of self-imposed abstinence: "I had always been very careful to stay completely clear of any personal closeness with any of the Muslim sisters. My total commitment to Islam demanded having no other interests, especially, I felt, no women." In *The Autobiography of Malcolm X,* St. Augustine's *Confessions,* Bunyan's *Grace Abounding,* one finds lusty men repressing their physical desires and channeling their energy into their social and spiritual obligations. Sex is vitally, but negatively, important in most spiritual autobiographies; the author's life is to some degree molded by his self-conscious avoidance of sexual intercourse. One's life becomes the phallus.

In an autobiography whose rhetorical end is to reach out and serve as a pattern of moral regeneration, it becomes acceptable, paradoxically, for an author to leave the actual facts and fictionalize when such verbal manipulation can serve the larger moral ends of the work. Malcolm embroiders the facts when he feels that art can create a higher kind of truth than that to which mere "reality" can aspire.

> Talking to them [his criminal accomplices] laying down the plans, I had deliberately sat on a bed away from them. All of a sudden, I pulled out my gun, shook out all five bullets, and then let them see me put back only one bullet. I twirled the cylinder, and put the muzzle to my head.
> "Now, I'm going to see how much guts all of you have," I said.
> I grinned at them. All of their mouths had flapped open. I pulled the trigger—we all heard it *click.*
> "I'm going to do it again, now."
> They begged me to stop. I could see in Shorty's and Rudy's eyes some idea of rushing me.
> We all heard the hammer *click* on another empty cylinder.
> The women were in hysterics. Rudy and Shorty were begging, *"Man . . . Red . . . cut it out, man! . . . Freeze!"* I pulled the trigger once more.
> "I'm doing this, showing you I'm not afraid to die," I told them. "Never cross a man not afraid to die . . . now, let's get to work!"

The importance of this episode in Malcolm's life is that it helps to create the character—the aesthetic illusion—of the man who later will be capable of suffering for his beliefs and worthy of leadership in a trying period.

Anyone who has read the **Autobiography** knows the impact of this episode in context. But the event narrated so convincingly in Chapter Nine is only partially true to the facts of Malcolm's life. Malcolm has left out relevant, crucial details, and has produced, therefore, a fiction—the same sort of distortion of data common in *exempla* and medieval hagiography. In the Epilogue to the book, Alex Haley, the writer to whom the "autobiography" was dictated, reports Malcolm's attitude toward this dramatic episode upon reading it several months after he had dictated it. Haley's whole paragraph is important:

> The manuscript copy which Malcolm X was given to review was in better shape now, and he pored through page by page intently, and now and then his head would raise with some comment. "You know," he said once, "why I have been able to have some effect is because I make a study of the weaknesses of this country and because the more the white man yelps, the more I know I have struck a nerve." Another time, he put down upon the bed the manuscript he was reading, and he got up from his chair and walked back and forth, stroking his chin, then he looked at me. "You know this place here in this chapter where I told you how I put the pistol up to my head and kept pulling the trigger and scared them so when I was starting the burglary ring—well," he paused, "I don't know if I ought to tell you this or not, but I want to tell the truth." He eyed me, speculatively. "I palmed the bullet." We laughed together. I said, "Okay, give that page here, I'll fix it." Then he considered, "No, leave it that way. Too many people would be so quick to say that's what I'm doing today, bluffing."

There are two especially interesting words in this passage: "bluff" and "effect." Malcolm's actual life was not a bluff; the bullets which killed him were no bluff. But in some significant ways, his autobiography is a bluff. His comment to Haley and the episode in Chapter Nine allow us to catch a glimpse of Malcolm at his literary task. He is caught fashioning a character or a "type" which does not mirror the whole truth of his real life, but which generates its own kind of convincing, fictional truth. The reason for Malcolm's "creative" rendering of the facts is that he wishes to have a particular *effect* on his readers—both black and white—and to do this, he sensed that he would have to create a particular illusion. As a writer who knew that he had to capture not the daily habits and chronological routines of his life, but its essence or meaning, Malcolm X has entered the ranks of the great artist-autobiographers—Gibbon, Wordsworth, Gosse. Like all great autobiographers, Malcolm X knew that one's memories take on importance as they are shaped by one's perspective on them and by one's *Weltanschauung* in general.

In real life Malcolm was one emerging Negro leader among several. The book reviewer of *Newsweek* put Malcolm into perspective by speaking of his wasted gifts. (What, one wonders, should Malcolm have done with his "gifts" in order not to have wasted them.) Indeed, during his lifetime, as Haley points out, Malcolm had considerably less appeal for the majority of Negroes than either Roy Wilkins or Martin Luther King (whose death Malcolm predicted). Whites feared and hated him as a peripheral maniac, acrimonious and aggressive.

But Malcolm designed his autobiography in order to *effect* his readers. Malcolm's artistic task is to convert his reader from the fiction of him as a threat to society, operating on the fringes of the black world, to the fiction (or suggestion) of him as a central figure of major stature and integrity. The book's artistry reduces the significance of the other black leaders by placing Malcolm's own ego at the center of the literary action. The world one discovers in his pages is not the world of *Newsweek* or CBS Television ("fictions" in their own right) in which Malcolm appeared as a bitter fanatic, but a world which *needs* the dynamic, not to say the titanic, moral honesty, modesty, and dedication of this man, a one-time hustler turned puritan turned culture-hero. Because Malcolm's sensibility is at the center of the work, the reader sees and understands the world through Malcolm's eyes. Instead of a perspective on Malcolm characterized by the vulgar gaping of a frightened white world, the perspective is Malcolm's, as he scrutinizes, judges, and, finally opens his arms to the black and white world. The reader is inevitably caught up—effected—by the rhetoric of inclusion.

> Since I learned the *truth* in Mecca, my dearest friends have come to include *all* kinds—some Christians, Jews, Buddhists, Hindus, agnostics, and even atheists! I have friends who are called capitalists, Socialists, and Communists! Some of my friends are moderates, conservatives, extremists—some are even Uncle Toms! My friends today are black, brown, red, yellow, and *white*!

We do not see the unexplained data of a life. What we see is the special perspective which is the result of the narrator's continual sifting. He tells us what to see and how to see it. Regardless of how one has been accustomed to judging Malcolm in real life, the book's brilliant rhetoric creates the illusion of a man who suffers, learns, and loves. This is a man whose language is hard and uneuphemistic: "To come right down to it, if I take the kind of things in which I believe, then add to that the kind of temperament that I have, plus the one hundred per cent dedication I have to whatever I believe in—these are ingredients which make it just about impossible for me to die of old age." This kind of language, more striking and unsettling, even, than the brilliant descriptions of his hustling days, is written to do a job, to have an effect. The job Malcolm feels his autobiography must do necessitates that he project himself in the role of "hero" or "natural leader."

Malcolm's seemingly immodest presentation of himself as a culture-hero and his departure from verifiable fact, are justified by the work's didacticism—a word which should be understood in its fullest sense. Malcolm is not depicting a human life for the sake of the portrayal itself; he is trying to be of use or service in the community. It was not enough that he actually had a following in Harlem and elsewhere. He needed to extend his appeal to a larger more suspicious audience of middle-class blacks and whites. The aim of his autobiography is to galvanize all sorts of people into action. One must put the book down chastened, subdued, ennobled, and converted. The book is a modern saint's life and wants to make saints of its readers. Malcolm's drive is to convert his reader—the black man to self-respect, the white man to human decency. This consuming moral drive finds the sculpture in the marble. As author, Malcolm creates a narrator, whose task it is to tell the story of a huge man singled out for a huge task by God himself. The narrator is a preacher—and where he does not convert, he, at least, confronts his reader:

> Where the really sincere white people have got to do their "proving" of themselves is not among the black *victims,* but out on the battle lines of where America's racism really *is*—and that's in their own home communities; America's racism is among their own fellow whites. That's where the sincere whites who really mean to accomplish something have got to work.

Because the book is an allegedly true story of a real man and the issues pressingly contemporary, the reader is steadily made to feel that he is part of the author-preacher's congregation. Malcolm may not have every reader's sympathy, but he does have every man's attention.

Malcolm's conversion is essentially true to the familiar regeneration pattern. Life before the moment of transcendent illumination is bestial. "When you become an animal," he says of his own pre-conversion days, "a vulture, in the ghetto, as I had become, you enter a world of animals and vultures. It becomes truly the survival of only the fittest." You think you are living by a code, and you think that life is hanging together tolerably. Only in retrospect does the sinner know that he has been "going through the hardest thing," struggling toward an ability "to accept that which is already within you, and around you." ("But what good was all this to me," St. Augustine cries in *The Confessions,* "holding, as I did, that you, Lord God and Truth, were a vast luminous body and that I was a sort of piece broken off from this body? What an extraordinary perversity I showed! Yet this was what I was then.")

Malcolm undergoes a false conversion—also typical of spiritual autobiographers. How does one tell the difference between the true God and beguiling, cunning Satan? Through his false conversion to the Muslim faith of Elijah Muhammad ("I found Allah and the religion of Islam and it completely transformed my life"), he made possible his final illumination at Mecca in 1964 and also his ultimate martyrdom. Malcolm's worst sin was not knowing the true God soon enough. This mistake started the train of events which destroyed him.

Malcolm's hajj to Mecca was a pilgrim's progress. Saudi Arabia treated him regally. "Never would I have even thought of dreaming that I would ever be a recipient of such honors—honors that in America would be bestowed upon a king—not a Negro. All praise is due to Allah, the Lord of all the Worlds." To the rest of society, this second, real conversion seemed like instability and immature emotionalism. *Newsweek* found in Malcolm's renunciation of Elijah Muhammad and in his affirmation of True Islam a "maze of contradictory words." When Malcolm could be simplistically characterized as a Black Muslim (an expression he rejected), he could be dealt with by the white world, but as he grew in complexity and depth, he became less accessible to reductive minds and, consequently, a target for their resentful attacks. To Malcolm this painful reappraisal of his life and views was a great awakening; it was a sudden expansion of his intellect, conscience, and social sensibility. He was now in possession of what he felt to be the full truth and able to accommodate whatever spiritual value there had been in the creed of Mr. Muhammad, while rejecting the narrow, hate-producing mythology.

The autobiography does not end in the moment of spiritual illumination at Mecca, a fitting end for a novel, but not for a conversion autobiography. No Rex Warner has written *The Converts* on the theme of Malcolm X yet, ending the book, as Warner does his on Augustine in the moment of religious intensity which transforms the subject's life. Anxiety characterizes the last pages of most conversion autobiographies. William Cowper's *Memoir* traces his sincere religious regeneration but ends the account by the record of fears of "back-sliding" and "many a lifeless and unhallowed hour" since the conversion. The last pages of Malcolm's autobiography are characterized by the ambivalent tension generated by the devotee's desire to keep his faith pure and intense in the face of terrible earthly catastrophes and temptations. It is Malcolm, after all, who has been converted, not society. To be alive in New York and to be El-Hajj Malik El-Shabazz is to experience unendurable assaults on one's fledgling convictions. The struggle of spirituality is never over, the struggle is Now.

There are two Malcolm X's in this book: the protagonist (the young man who struggles from darkness to light, from cynicism and despair to hope and integrity) and the older, wiser man—the narrator—who tells the story. The autobiography is greatly enriched by the fact that the narrator is engaged in his *own* struggle, though it is no longer the same kind of struggle that characterized his past. Not only does he have the struggle to fight off bitterness and "backsliding." He also has the artist's struggle inherent in attempting to preach the truth which is upon him, responding with modesty to a call which demands that he immodestly present himself and his life as a model worthy of emulation. If Malcolm as narrator (soon in reality to be engulfed by the very destructive power described with such gothic fear in the last pages of the book) creates a protagonist somewhat too fictionally heroic and invincible, it is because he is responding to the call of a Force larger than himself.

This Force magnifies Malcolm by singling him out to preach but, of course, the same call to the foot of Allah's throne humbles the spokesman. "What," cries John Bunyan, "shall I be proud because I am a sounding Brass? is it so much to be a Fiddle"? Malcolm ends his book: "And if I can die having brought any light, having exposed any meaningful truth that will help destroy the racist cancer . . . then, all of the credit is due to Allah. Only the mistakes have been mine." The narrator continually interjects the modest tone of the true believer: "I believe, today, that it was written, it was meant for Reginald [his brother] to be used for one purpose only: as a bait, as a minnow to reach into the ocean of blackness where I was, to save me." Malcolm is the chief of sinners to whom grace has been abounding: in a fallen world this paradox produces a modest culture-hero.

To the degree that Malcolm's spiritual growth and commitment seem enviable (that is, worth imitating), the autobiography is an important twentieth-century document. It clearly has lasting value for sociologists, cultural historians, psychologists, theologians, and literary critics. Besides revealing the emotional structure of one of the most compelling radicals of the century, the book will continue to be read for its brilliant depiction of the struggle up from the back alleys and brothels of the black ghetto by one of the major directors of the social revolution currently under way.

Principally, however, *The Autobiography of Malcolm X* is a great work of didactic literature with a wide audience which its narrative and emotional appeal are doing their share to mold and direct. The impact of the work on most readers is intense, immediate, and enduring.

The character portrayal at each stage is compellingly vivid. Malcolm's ability to capture the scene and sound of the city and its lingo is that of the novelist. But just as we are caught up in the rhythms of his dissipation, he reminds us, however indirectly, of his slow and painful self-mastery.

> Shorty would take me to groovy, frantic, scenes in different chicks' and cats' pads, where with the lights and juke down mellow, everybody blew gage and juiced back and jumped. I met chicks who were fine as May wine, and cats who were hip to all happenings.

> That paragraph is deliberate, of course; it's just to display a bit more of the slang that was used by everyone I respected as "hip" in those days. And in no time at all, I was talking the slang like a lifelong hipster.

The gap in time, space, and sensibility suggested by the differences between these two paragraphs is that yawning abyss which only the agonizing process of real education can fill.

Malcolm's autobiography exists as a personal testimony to the fact that it is yet possible, even in the face of very great social and psychological opposition, for a man to

learn how to be human. Malcolm's literary aim is to put that seemingly easy goal within the reach of many people. Conversion is possible: the message is loud and clear. (pp. 269-74)

> *Barrett John Mandel, "The Didactic Achievement of Malcolm X's Autobiography," in* Afro-American Studies, *Vol. 2, No. 4, March, 1972, pp. 269-74.*

Paul John Eakin (essay date 1976)

[*In the following essay, Eakin argues that Malcolm X's memoirs challenge traditional definitions of the word autobiography.*]

When a complex and controversial figure writes a book that has achieved the distinction and popularity of *The Autobiography of Malcolm X,* it is inevitable that efforts will be made to place him and his work in the perspective of a literary tradition. Barrett John Mandel, for example, has identified in Malcolm X's story the paradigm of the traditional conversion narrative. His reading of Malcolm X's autobiography, and it is a characteristic one, assumes that the narrative expresses a completed self [see excerpt dated 1972]. Further, Ross Miller has suggested that such an assumption is central to the expectations we bring to the reading of any autobiography: "The pose of the autobiographer as an experienced man is particularly effective because we expect to hear from someone who has a completed sense of his own life and is therefore in a position to tell what he has discovered" [see Further Reading]. Even Warner Berthoff, who has admirably defined Malcolm X's "extraordinary power to change and be changed" as "the distinctive rule of his life," seems to have been drawn to this sense of the completed self when he attempts to locate the *Autobiography* in a special and limited literary tradition, that of the political testament in which "some ruler or statesman sets down for the particular benefit of his people a summary of his own experience and wisdom" [see excerpt dated 1971]. The rhetorical posture of Malcolm X in the last chapter would seem to confirm Berthoff's reading and to fulfill Miller's autobiographical expectations, for it is indeed that of the elder statesman summing up a completed life, a life that has, as it were, already ended:

> Anyway, now, each day I live as if I am already dead, and I tell you what I would like for you to do. When I *am* dead—I say it that way because from the things I *know,* I do not expect to live long enough to read this book in its finished form—I want you to just watch and see if I'm not right in what I say: that the white man, in his press, is going to identify me with "hate."

If Malcolm X's anticipation of his imminent death confers on this final phase of autobiographical retrospection a posthumous authority, it is nevertheless an authority that he exercises here to defend himself against the fiction of the completed self that his interpreters—both black and white, in the event—were to use against him. Each of his identities turned out to be provisional, and even this voice from the grave was the utterance not of an ultimate identity but merely of the last one in the series of roles that Malcolm X had variously assumed, lived out, and discarded.

Alex Haley's "Epilogue" to the *Autobiography* reveals the fictive nature of this final testamentary stance which Berthoff regards as definitive. Here Haley, Malcolm X's collaborator in the *Autobiography,* reports that the apparent uncertainty and confusion of Malcolm X's views were widely discussed in Harlem during the last months of Malcolm X's life, while Malcolm X himself, four days before his death, said in an interview, "I'm man enough to tell you that I can't put my finger on exactly what my philosophy is now, but I'm flexible." Moreover, the account of the composition of the *Autobiography* given by Haley in the "Epilogue" makes it clear that the fiction of the autobiographer as a man with "a completed sense of his own life" is especially misleading in the case of Malcolm X, for even Haley and the book that was taking shape in his hands were out of phase with the reality of Malcolm X's life and identity. Thus Haley acknowledges that he "never dreamed" of Malcolm X's break with Elijah Muhammad "until the actual rift became public," although the break overturned the design that had guided Malcolm X's dictations of his life story to Haley up to that point. The disparity between the traditional autobiographical fiction of the completed self and the biographical fact of Malcolm X's ceaselessly evolving identity may lead us, as it did Malcolm X himself, to enlarge our understanding of the limits and the possibilities of autobiography.

• • • • •

The original dedication of the *Autobiography,* which Malcolm X gave to Haley before the dictations had even begun, places the work squarely in one of the most ancient traditions of the genre, that of the exemplary life:

> This book I dedicate to the Honorable Elijah Muhammad, who found me here in America in the muck and mire of the filthiest civilization and society on this earth, and pulled me out, cleaned me up, and stood me on my feet, and made me the man that I am today.

This dedication (later cancelled) motivates more than half of the *Autobiography* in its final version. This book would be the story of a conversion, and Malcolm X's statement recapitulates in capsule form the essential pattern of such narratives: in the moment of conversion a new identity is discovered; further, this turning point sharply defines a two-part, before-after time scheme for the narrative; the movement of the self from "lost" to "found" constitutes the plot; and, finally, the very nature of the experience supplies an evangelical motive for autobiography.

What concerns us here, however, is not the much-studied features of conversion and the ease with which they may be translated into the formal elements of autobiographical narrative, but rather the natural and

seemingly inevitable inference that the individual first discovers the shape of his life and then writes the life on the basis of this discovery. Some version of this temporal fiction, of course, lies behind most autobiography, and I would emphasize it as a corollary to Miller's definition of the completed self: the notion that living one's life precedes writing about it, that the life is in some sense complete and that the autobiographical process takes place afterward, somehow outside the realm of lapsing time in which the life proper necessarily unfolds. The evangelical bias of conversion narrative is especially interesting in this regard, for it supplies a predisposition for such an autobiographer to accept this supporting fiction as fact, since he believes that conversion works a definitive transition from shifting false beliefs to a fixed vision of the one truth. It is, accordingly, when a new discovery about the shape of one's life takes place during the writing of one's story that an autobiographer may be forced to recognize the presence and nature of the fictions on which his narrative is based. The experience of Malcolm X in his final period did foster such a recognition, and this knowledge and its consequences for autobiographical narrative may instruct us in the complex relation that necessarily obtains between living a life and writing about it. However, before we consider the *Autobiography* from the vantage point of the man who was becoming "El-Hajj Malik El-Shabazz" (Chapter 18), let us look at the *Autobiography* as it was originally conceived by the man whose first conversion in prison had transformed him from "Satan" (Chapter 10) to "Minister Malcolm X" (Chapter 13). This is, of course, the way we do look at the *Autobiography* when we begin to read it for the first time, especially if we are relatively unfamiliar with the life of Malcolm X.

The Malcolm X of these years was firmly in command of the shape of his life, tracing his sense of this shape to the pivotal and structuring illumination of conversion itself. At this point his understanding of the design of his experience, especially his baffled fascination with the radical discontinuity between the old Adam and the new, closely parallels the state of St. Augustine, Jonathan Edwards, and many another sinner touched by gracious affections, so much so that the student of spiritual autobiography is likely to feel himself at home on familiar ground:

> For evil to bend its knees, admitting its guilt, to implore the forgiveness of God, is the hardest thing in the world . . . . When finally I was able to make myself stay down—I didn't know what to say to Allah . . . . I still marvel at how swiftly my previous life's thinking pattern slid away from me, like snow off a roof. It is as though someone else I knew of had lived by hustling and crime. I would be startled to catch myself thinking in a remote way of my earlier self as another person.

If we consider Malcolm X's account of his life up to the time of his break with Elijah Muhammad (in Chapter 16, appropriately entitled "Out"), what we have in fact is a story that falls rather neatly into two sections

Malcolm X poses with his family—wife Betty Shabazz and daughters Attilah, Qubilah, and Ilyasah—and heavyweight boxing champion Muhammad Ali.

roughly equal in length, devoted respectively to his former life as a sinner (Chapters 3-9) and to his present life as one of Elijah Muhammad's ministers (Chapters 10-15). This two-part structure is punctuated by two decisive experiences: his repudiation of the white world of his youth in Mason, Michigan, and his conversion to Islam in prison at Norfolk, Massachusetts.

Malcolm X describes the "first major turning point of my life" at the end of the second chapter, his realization that in white society he was not free "to become whatever *I* wanted to be." The shock to the eighth-grade boy was profound, for despite his traumatic childhood memories of the destruction of his family by white society, Malcolm X had embraced the white success ethic by the time he was in junior high school: "I was trying so hard . . . to be white." What follows, in Chapters 3 through 9, is Malcolm X's account of his life as a ghetto hustler, his first "career," just as his role as a Black Muslim minister was to be his second. If Allah preserved him from the fate of an Alger hero or a Booker T. Washington, from a career as a "successful" shoeshine boy or a self-serving member of the "black bourgeoisie," he was nevertheless destined to enact a

kind of inverse parody of the white man's rise to success as he sank deeper and deeper into a life of crime. This is the portion of the ***Autobiography*** that has been singled out for its vividness by the commentators, with the result that the conversion experience and its aftermath in Chapters 10 through 15 have been somewhat eclipsed. It would be possible, of course, to see in the popularity of this section nothing more than the universal appeal of any evocation of low life and evil ways. In addition, this preference may reflect an instinctive attraction to a more personal mode of autobiography with plenty of concrete self-revelation instead of the more formal testimony of an exemplary life. Certainly Alex Haley responded strongly to this narrative, and so did Malcolm X, though he tried to restrain himself:

> Then it was during recalling the early Harlem days that Malcolm X really got carried away. One night, suddenly, wildly, he jumped up from his chair and, incredibly, the fearsome black demagogue was scat-singing and popping his fingers, "re-bop-de-bop-blap-blam-" and then grabbing a vertical pipe with one hand (as the girl partner) he went jubilantly lindy-hopping around, his coattail and the long legs and the big feet flying as they had in those Harlem days. And

then almost as suddenly, Malcolm X caught himself and sat back down, and for the rest of that session he was decidedly grumpy.

Haley captures here the characteristic drama of the autobiographical act that the juxtaposition of the self as it is and as it was inevitably generates. Malcolm X's commitment to his public role as "the fearsome black demagogue" conflicts with his evident pleasure in recapturing an earlier and distinctly personal identity, the historical conked and zooted lindy champ of the Roseland Ballroom in Roxbury, the hustling hipster of Small's Paradise in Harlem.

If the *Autobiography* had ended with the fourteenth or fifteenth chapter, what we would have, I suggest, is a narrative which could be defined as an extremely conventional example of autobiographical form distinguished chiefly by the immediacy and power of its imaginative recreation of the past. It is true that this much of the *Autobiography* would usefully illustrate the survival of the classic pattern of conversion narrative in the contemporary literature of spiritual autobiography, but this interest would necessarily be a limited one given Malcolm X's reticence about the drama of the experience of conversion itself. For Malcolm X the fact of conversion is decisive, life-shaping, identity-altering, but unlike the most celebrated spiritual autobiographers of the past he chooses not to dramatize the experience itself or to explore its psychological dynamics.

● ● ● ● ●

It seems probable that when Malcolm X began his dictations to Haley in 1963 he anticipated that his narrative would end with an account of his transformation into the national spokesman of Elijah Muhammad's Nation of Islam (the material covered in Chapters 14 and 15 of Haley's text). This was not destined to be the end of the story, however, for the pace of Malcolm X's history, always lively, became tumultuous in 1963 and steadily accelerated until his assassination in 1965. In this last period Malcolm X was to experience two events that destroyed the very premises of the autobiography he had set out to write. The most well-known convert to the Black Muslim religion was first to break with Elijah Muhammad (Chapter 16, "Out") and then to make a pilgrimage to Mecca (Chapter 17), where he underwent a second conversion to what he now regarded as the true religion of Islam. The revelation that Elijah Muhammad was a false prophet shattered the world of Malcolm X and the shape of the life he had been living for twelve years:

> I was like someone who for twelve years had had an inseparable, beautiful marriage—and then suddenly one morning at breakfast the marriage partner had thrust across the table some divorce papers.

> I felt as though something in *nature* had failed, like the sun or the stars. It was that incredible a phenomenon to me—something too stupendous to conceive.

The autobiographical fiction of the completed self was exploded for good, although Malcolm X, with a remark-

able fidelity to the truth of his past, was to preserve the fragments in the earlier chapters of the *Autobiography,* as we have seen.

The illumination at Mecca made Malcolm X feel "like a complete human being" for the first time "in my thirty-nine years on this earth," and he assumed a new name to symbolize this new sense of identity, El-Hajj Malik El-Shabazz. In the final chapters of the book (18 and 19) we see Malcolm X in the process of discarding the "old 'hate' and 'violence' image" of the militant preacher of Elijah Muhammad's Nation of Islam, but before he created a design for the life of this new self he was brutally gunned down on February 21, 1965. In fact, it is not at all certain that Malcolm X would have arrived at any single, definitive formulation for the shape of his life even if he had continued to live. In the final pages of the last chapter he observes:

> No man is given but so much time to accomplish whatever is his life's work. My life in particular never has stayed fixed in one position for very long. You have seen how throughout my life, I have often known unexpected drastic changes.

With these words Malcolm X articulates a truth already latent but ungrasped in the autobiographical narrative he originally set out to write in his evangelical zeal: his life was not now and never had been a life of the simpler pattern of the traditional conversion story.

Because this complex vision of his existence is clearly not that of the early sections of the *Autobiography,* Alex Haley and Malcolm X were forced to confront the consequences of this discontinuity in perspective for the narrative, already a year old. It was Haley who raised the issue when he learned, belatedly, of the rift between Malcolm X and Elijah Muhammad, for he had become worried that an embittered Malcolm X might want to rewrite the book from his new perspective, and this at a time when Haley regarded their collaboration as virtually complete ("by now I had the bulk of the needed life story material in hand"). Malcolm X's initial response settled the matter temporarily: "I want the book to be the way it was." Haley's concern, however, was justified, for a few months later, following Malcolm X's journey to Mecca, Haley was "appalled" to find that Malcolm X had "red-inked" many of the places in the manuscript "where he had told of his almost father-and-son relationship with Elijah Muhammad." Haley describes this crisis of the autobiographical act as follows:

> Telephoning Malcolm X, I reminded him of his previous decision, and I stressed that if those chapters contained such telegraphing to readers of what would lie ahead, then the book would automatically be robbed of some of its building suspense and drama. Malcolm X said gruffly, "Whose book is this?" I told him "yours, of course," and that I only made the objection in my position as a writer. He said that he would have to think about it. I was heartsick at the prospect that he might want to re-edit the entire book into a polemic against Elijah Muhammad. But late that night, Malcolm X telephoned. "I'm sorry. You're right. I was upset about some-

thing. Forget what I wanted changed, let what you already had stand." I never again gave him chapters to review unless I was with him. Several times I would covertly watch him frown and wince as he read, but he never again asked for any change in what he had originally said.

Malcolm X's refusal to change the narrative reflects, finally, his acceptance of change as the fundamental law of existence, and yet, curiously, by the very fidelity of this refusal he secures for the remembered past, and for the acts of memory devoted to it, such measure of permanence as the forms of art afford.

The exchange between the two men poses the perplexing issue of perspective in autobiography with an instructive clarity: to which of an autobiographer's selves should he or even can he be true? What are the strategies by which he may maintain a dual or plural allegiance without compromise to his present vision of the truth? In fact, the restraint of the "telegraphing" does leave the climax intact, and yet Malcolm X's decision not to revise the preceding narrative does not produce the kind of obvious discontinuity in authorial perspective that we might expect as a result. Haley's part in this is considerable, for his contribution to the ultimate shape of the *Autobiography* was more extensive and fundamental than his narrowly literary concerns here with foreshadowing and suspense might seem to suggest. Despite his tactful protest that he was only a "writer," Haley himself had been instrumental in the playing out of the autobiographical drama between one Malcolm X, whose faith in Elijah Muhammad had supplied him with his initial rationale for an autobiography, and another, whose repudiation of Elijah Muhammad made the *Autobiography* the extraordinary human document it eventually became. If the outcome of this drama was formalized in Malcolm X's expulsion from the Nation of Islam, it was already in the wind by the time the dictations began in earnest in 1963. Alex Haley was one to read between the lines.

Haley recalls in the "Epilogue" that at the very outset of the project he had been in fundamental disagreement with Malcolm X about the narrative he would help him write. He reports that Malcolm X wanted the focus to be on Elijah Muhammad and the Nation of Islam: "He would bristle when I tried to urge him that the proposed book was *his* life." At this early stage of the collaboration Haley portrays two Malcolms: a loyal public Malcolm X describing a religious movement in which he casts himself in a distinctly subordinate and self-effacing role, and a subversive private Malcolm X scribbling a trenchant counter-commentary in telegraphic red-ink ball point on any available scrap of paper. Determined to feature this second Malcolm X in the autobiography, Haley lured this suppressed identity out into the open by leaving white paper napkins next to Malcolm X's coffee cup to tap his closed communications with himself. Haley carefully retrieved this autobiographical fall-out, and taking his cue from one of these napkin revelations, interestingly about women, Haley "cast a bait" with a question about Malcolm X's mother. Haley

reports that with this textbook display of Freudian savvy he was able to land the narrative he was seeking:

> From this stream-of-consciousness reminiscing I finally got out of him the foundation for this book's beginning chapters, "Nightmare" and "Mascot." After that night, he never again hesitated to tell me even the most intimate details of his personal life, over the next two years. His talking about his mother triggered something.

From the very earliest phase of the dictations, then, the autobiography began to take on a much more personal and private coloration than Malcolm X originally intended. What Elijah Muhammad accomplished, autobiographically speaking, when he "silenced" Malcolm X, was to legitimatize the private utterance of the napkins which had already found its way into the mainstream of a narrative initially conceived as an orthodox work of evangelical piety. After his separation from the Nation of Islam, Malcolm X comments that he began "to think for myself," "after twelve years of never thinking for as much as five minutes about myself." Haley reports two napkin messages of this period that signal the consequences of Malcolm X's new sense of himself and his power for the nearly-completed *Autobiography*:

> He scribbled one night, "You have not converted a man because you have silenced him. John Viscount Morley." And the same night, almost illegibly, "I was going downhill until he picked me up, but the more I think of it, we picked each other up."

Not only was Malcolm X rejecting the simple clarity of the original conversion narrative he had set out to tell, but he was no longer disposed to sacrifice to the greater glory of Elijah Muhammad his own agency in the working out of his life story.

● ● ● ● ●

In the final chapters of the *Autobiography* and in the "Epilogue," as Malcolm X moves toward a new view of his story as a life of changes, he expresses an impressive, highly self-conscious awareness of the problems of autobiographical narrative, and specifically of the complex relationship between living a life and writing an autobiography. All of his experience in the last packed months, weeks, and days of his life worked to destroy his earlier confident belief in the completed self, the completed life, and hence in the complete life story. Thus he writes to Haley in what is possibly his final statement about the *Autobiography*: "I just want to read it one more time because I don't expect to read it in finished form." As Malcolm X saw it at the last, all autobiographies are by nature incomplete and they can not, accordingly, have a definite shape. As a life changes, so any sense of the shape of a life must change; the autobiographical process evolves because it is part of the life, and the identity of the autobiographical "I" changes and shifts. Pursuing the logic of such speculations, Malcolm X even wonders whether any autobiography can keep abreast of the unfolding of personal history: "How is it possible to write one's autobiography in a world so fast-changing as this?" And so he observes to Haley, "I hope the book is proceeding rapidly, for events concerning my life happen so swiftly, much of what has already been written can easily be outdated from month to month. In life, nothing is permanent; not even life itself."

At the end, then, Malcolm X came to reject the traditional autobiographical fiction that the life comes first, and then the writing of the life; that the life is in some sense complete and that the autobiographical process simply records the final achieved shape. This fiction is based upon a suspension of time, as though the "life," the subject, could sit still long enough for the autobiographical "I," the photographer, to snap its picture. In fact, as Malcolm X was to learn, the "life" itself will not hold still; it changes, shifts position. And as for the autobiographical act, it requires much more than an instant of time to take the picture, to write the story. As the act of composition extends in time, so it enters the life-stream, and the fictive separation between life and life story, which is so convenient—even necessary—to the writing of autobiography, dissolves.

Malcolm X's final knowledge of the incompleteness of the self is what gives the last pages of the *Autobiography* together with the "Epilogue" their remarkable power: a vision of a man whose swiftly unfolding career has outstripped the possibilities of the traditional autobiography he had meant to write. It is not in the least surprising that Malcolm X's sobering insights into the limitations of autobiography are accompanied by an increasingly insistent desire to disengage himself from the ambitions of the autobiographical process. Thus he speaks of the *Autobiography* to Haley time and again as though, having disabused himself of any illusion that the narrative could keep pace with his life, he had consigned the book to its fate, casting it adrift as hopelessly obsolete. Paradoxically, nowhere does the book succeed, persuade, more than in its confession of failure as autobiography. This is the fascination of *The Education of Henry Adams,* and Malcolm X, like Adams, leaves behind him the husks of played-out autobiographical paradigms. The indomitable reality of the self transcends and exhausts the received shapes for a life that are transmitted by the culture, and yet the very process of discarding in itself works to structure an apparently shapeless experience. Despite—or because of—the intractability of life to form, the fiction of the completed self, which lies at the core of the autobiographical enterprise, cannot be readily dispatched. From its ashes, phoenix-like, it reconstitutes itself in a new guise. Malcolm X's work, and Adams' as well, generate a sense that the uncompromising commitment to the truth of one's own nature, which requires the elimination of false identities and careers one by one, will yield at the last the pure ore of a final and irreducible selfhood. This is the ultimate autobiographical dream. (pp. 230-42)

> *Paul John Eakin, "Malcolm X and the Limits of Autobiography," in* Criticism, *Vol. XVIII, No. 3, Summer, 1976, pp. 230-42.*

FURTHER READING

Abbott, II. Porter. "Organic Form in the Autobiography of a Convert: The Example of Malcolm X." *CLA Journal* XXIII, No. 2 (December 1979): 125-46.
> Compares the lives of Malcolm X and St. Augustine in terms of their mothers, their religious conversions, and the structure of their autobiographies.

Abbott, Philip. "Hustling: Benjamin Franklin, Malcolm X, Abbie Hoffman." In his *States of Perfect Freedom: Autobiography and American Political Thought,* pp. 27-57. Amherst: University of Massachusetts Press, 1987.
> Examines autobiographies of three political figures—Benjamin Franklin, Abbie Hoffman, and Malcolm X—and explores their images as "hustlers."

Benson, Thomas W. "Rhetoric and Autobiography: The Case of Malcolm X." *The Quarterly Journal of Speech* 60, No. 1 (February 1974): 1-13.
> Argues that *The Autobiography of Malcolm X* "achieves a unique synthesis of selfhood and rhetorical instrumentality."

Boulware, Marcus H. "Minister Malcolm: Orator Profundo." *Negro History Bulletin* 30, No. 7 (November 1967): 12-14.
> Profile of Malcolm X, focusing on his skills as an orator.

Couser, G. Thomas. "Three Contemporaries: Malcolm X, Norman Mailer, and Robert Pirsig." In his *American Autobiography: The Prophetic Mode,* pp. 164-96. Amherst: University of Massachusetts Press, 1979.
> Analyzes *The Autobiography of Malcolm X,* placing it within a tradition of American narratives.

Davis, Lenwood G. *Malcolm X: A Selected Bibliography.* Westport, Conn.: Greenwood Press, 1984, 146 p.
> First book-length bibliography of works about Malcolm X.

Demarest, David P., Jr. *"The Autobiography of Malcolm X: Beyond Didacticism."* *CLA Journal* XVI, No. 2 (December 1972): 179-87.
> Explores the literary significance of Malcolm X's autobiography, arguing that it is an effective work for white readers as well as black because it transcends didacticism.

Groppe, John D. "From Chaos to Cosmos: The Role of Trust in *The Autobiography of Malcolm X.*" *Soundings* LXVI, No. 4 (Winter 1983): 437-49.
> Argues that Malcolm X's autobiography is "the story of the loss, and then the regaining, of the capacity to trust," adding that Malcolm's ability to trust brings about "his pilgrimage from self to cosmos."

Hoyt, Charles Alva. "The Five Faces of Malcolm X." *Negro American Literature Forum* 4, No. 4 (Winter 1970): 107-12.
> Divides Malcolm X's life into five stages and five identities: Malcolm Little, Detroit Red, Satan, Malcolm X, and El-Hajj Malik El-Shabazz. Concludes that Malcolm had "*earned* his way to the top; not inherited it, or bought it or fallen into it, as almost every other

American political leader seems to have done, but earned it by the pain of his own experience, his growth from mascot to hustler to criminal to controversialist to philosopher.... "

Johnson, Timothy V. *Malcolm X: A Comprehensive Annotated Bibliography.* New York: Garland Publishing, Inc., 1986, 192 p.

Bibliography of works by and about Malcolm X; seeks to improve on Davis's bibliography (see above) by including a subject index, citations from African newspapers, and citations from Malcolm's own writings and speeches.

Miller, Ross. "Autobiography as Fact and Fiction: Franklin, Adams, Malcolm X." *The Centennial Review* XVI, No. 3 (Summer 1972): 221-32.

Reconstructs a "coherent American literary tradition" from autobiographies by Benjamin Franklin, Henry Adams, and Malcolm X, showing the mixture of fact and fiction in their works.

Nelson, Truman. "Delinquent's Progress." *The Nation* 201, No. 15 (8 November 1965): 336-38.

Laudatory review of *The Autobiography of Malcolm X.* Nelson concludes: "Viewed in its complete historical context, this is indeed a great book."

Nichols, Charles H. "The Slave Narrators and the Picaresque Mode: Archetypes for Modern Black Personae." In *The Slave's Narrative,* edited by Charles T. Davis and Henry Louis Gates, Jr., pp. 283-98. New York: Oxford University Press, 1985.

Analyzes the influence of slave narratives on modern black autobiographies, including *The Autobiography of Malcolm X.*

Ohmann, Carol. *"The Autobiography of Malcolm X:* A Revolutionary Use of the Franklin Tradition." *American Quarterly* XXII, No. 2 (Summer 1970): 131-49.

Compares *The Autobiography of Malcolm X* and Benjamin Franklin's *Autobiography,* arguing that both "testify to certain strengths and certain weaknesses in our national ethos, strengths and weaknesses that have characterized us very nearly from, if not from, the beginning."

Perry, Bruce. *Malcolm: The Life of a Man Who Changed Black America.* Barrytown, N.Y.: Station Hill Press, 1991, 568 p.

Comprehensive biography of Malcolm X, focusing on the more personal aspects of the leader's life. In the work Perry examines the psychological factors that influenced Malcolm X: his poverty-stricken childhood, his anger towards his parents, his troubled adolescence, his self-hatred, and his prison experience.

Rose, Shirley K. "Metaphors and Myths of Cross-Cultural Literacy: Autobiographical Narratives by Maxine Hong Kingston, Richard Rodriguez, and Malcolm X." *MELUS* 14, No. 1 (Spring 1987); 3-15.

Finds a "complementary relationship between the literacy myths of autonomy and participation" in autobiographies and investigates this relationship in the memoirs of Maxine Hong Kingston, Richard Rodriguez, and Malcolm X.

Stone, Albert E. "Collaboration in Contemporary American Autobiography." *Revue Française d'Études Américaines,* No. 14 (May 1982): 151-65.

Briefly explores the collaboration between Alex Haley and Malcolm X on *The Autobiography of Malcolm X.*

Stone, I. F. "The Pilgrimage of Malcolm X." *The New York Review of Books* 5, No. 7 (11 November 1965): 3-5.

Praises Malcolm X's autobiography and *Malcolm X Speaks,* concluding: "These two books will have permanent place in the literature of the Afro-America struggle."

Taylor, Gordon O. "Voices from the Veil: Black Amer Autobiography." *The Georgia Review* XXXV, No. 2 (S mer 1981): 341-61.

Examines autobiographies by African-American cluding Malcolm X. Taylor maintains: "Quest human individuality, identifying the personal v race's general condition, believing that wh condition persists it will be America's nationa tion as well, claiming a representative role not only relation to American blacks but also in relation to the idea of America—on each level, for these self-narrators, the human predicament and the compositional problem are essentially one."

Terry, Eugene. "Black Autobiography: Discernible Forms." *Okike* 19 (September 1981): 6-10.

Investigates a trend in autobiographies by Malcolm X, W. E. B. Du Bois, and Frederick Douglass in which the subject "is first unaware of his life as it differs from the lives of others," then becomes aware and despairs, and ultimately experiences a conversion of some sort. After "growing," the subject writes of himself and of his race; finally, "these autobiographies...claim the authors' humanity through an ultimate insistence on brotherhood with the humanity of others...."